牛津初阶
英汉双解词典

OXFORD ELEMENTARY LEARNER'S ENGLISH-CHINESE DICTIONARY

第二版

Second edition

英语原版编辑：**Angela Crawley**

英汉版编译：李北达

商务印书馆

The Commercial Press

OXFORD

UNIVERSITY PRESS

牛津大学出版社

OXFORD
UNIVERSITY PRESS

牛津大学出版社隶属牛津大学，出版业务遍布全球，致力弘扬牛津大学推动优质研究、学术和教育的宗旨。

牛津　纽约
雅典　奥克兰　曼谷　波哥大　布宜诺斯艾利斯　加尔各答
开普敦　马德拉斯　达累斯萨拉姆　德里　弗罗伦萨　香港
伊斯坦布尔　卡拉奇　吉隆坡　马德里　墨尔本　墨西哥城　孟买
奈罗比　巴黎　圣保罗　新加坡　台北　东京　多伦多　华沙

联营公司：柏林　伊巴丹

OXFORD 为牛津大学出版社之注册商标
牛津初阶英汉双解词典（第二版）

第一次印刷 1999
印次（即最小之数字） 20　19　18　17　16

ISBN 7-100-02863-9/H·735 （简体字本）

出版：商务印书馆
北京王府井大街 36 号
（邮政编码 100710）
牛津大学出版社（中国）有限公司
香港鲗鱼涌英皇道 979 号太古坊和域大厦东翼十八楼
印刷：中国
国内总发行：商务印书馆
国外以及香港、澳门、台湾地区总发行：牛津大学出版社（中国）有限公司

牛津初阶英汉双解词典（第二版）
（简化汉字本）

出版说明

本词典英语原文版名为 Oxford Elementary Learner’s Dictionary (Second edition)，其英汉双解版由牛津大学出版社（中国）有限公司于 1997 年在香港推出。该书特别适合初级英语学习者的需要，它的词义解释通俗易懂，例句浅显生动而又能显示词义的典型用法，英美读音并注，收录的单词、短语和词义切合初学者水平，汉语译文流畅传神，英汉双解的编排方式有助于读者准确理解英语原义，此外还配有多幅精美的彩色插图，因此一经问世便受到香港学界的热烈欢迎。现经牛津大学出版社惠允，我馆在内地出版发行该词典英汉双解版的简化汉字本。出版前，我们对原书作了些微文字上的技术处理，使其更适合内地读者的习惯。我们相信，本书一定会像它的繁体汉字版畅销于香港一样，也会受到内地读者的广泛欢迎。

商务印书馆编辑部

1999 年 4 月

出版说明

《牛津初阶英汉双解词典》第二版是根据 Oxford Elementary Learner's Dictionary, Second edition 翻译而成。英语原版在编纂过程中参考了很多教师与学生的意见。英汉双解版特别适合以汉语为母语的初阶英语学习者的需要。全书选收一万五千多个词语、词组、习语等，其中有很多新词语。

第二版的特色简述如下：

（一）释义准确

本书以浅显的语言解释词目。为便于使用者清楚理解英语的含义，部分容易混淆的词附有插图或注释。

（二）相关用语

本词典详列动词的不同形式及名词的复数形式，部分词条更提供不同的词类（如动词、名词、形容词等）、有关语法的注解及相关用语等。

（三）英美读音

原英语版标音只有英式英语标音，英汉版增加美式英语的标音，使用范围更广。

（四）示例实用

本书数千示例清楚阐释词目的含义和实际用法，有助学习者理解与应用。

（五）彩图精美

本版有32页彩色插图，内容丰富；一方面是表明正确用法，如词语搭配、书信写法、电话对话、介词使用等；另一方面是介绍日常生活用词，如衣物、交通工具、动植物、乐器等，一目了然。

我们期望本词典能帮助使用者准确理解和运用英语，还可进一步培养学习英语的兴趣。

牛津大学出版社（中国）有限公司

一九九七年初

编译者序

《牛津初阶英汉双解词典》第二版是初学英语的人需要的第一本实用英汉词典。编译本词典的目的是帮助初学者打好扎实的基础，正确地理解和使用英语。本词典精选英语基本词语15 000个，提供正确拼写方法、读音、意义、词类、搭配方式、用法举例等重要项目，详见编辑体例说明。有几点值得一提的独特之处，各举一例说明如下（为节省篇幅有些只列出译文部分）：

1. 词义更新，如 actor 演员（现指男女演员均可，以前只作“男演员”）
2. 注释准确，如 house 注释中说明“不止一层”，故示例中译作“小楼”
3. 有些注释后列出相关词语，如 elephant 象（象的鼻子叫做 trunk）
4. 示例多为短句，既便于记忆也有助于理解词义，如 school 词条中：He left school when he was 16. 他16岁时中学毕业。（不是“离开学校”）
5. 汉语译文规范，如 gear（汽车的）排挡（多误译作“排档”，“挡”字与“档”字音、形、义均不同）

本词典原版定义多为描述式，如 adventurous 的定义是 An adventurous person likes to do exciting, dangerous things. 原文把需定义的 adventurous 使用于句中，而实际上并无定义。用这种方式编纂的词典难以按传统方法翻译，且尚无前例可援，只好试行连编带译，如上例定义作“爱做有刺激性的、危险的事情的；爱冒险的”。在编译过程中多从中文角度考虑译文的准确，如 headmistress 若译作“女校长”，初学者或可能误解为大学校长，或可能写出这样可笑的翻译句子：“我母亲是女校长。”本词典译作“（中小学的）（女）校长”。又如 times 这一名词，既可表示增加的量也可表示减少的量，所以原版只有“Edinburgh is five times bigger than Oxford,”一个示例。但是在汉语中表示增加或减少的量要用两种完全不同的表达方式，所以我又将该示例反过来说“Oxford is five times smaller than Edinburgh,” 增加一个示例，以免初学者可能受英文影响而写出“小几倍”这样的错误汉语词组。

参加本词典部分翻译工作的还有李竹小姐，将全部词条输入电脑并协助我校订中文的是李沙沙女士，谨在此一并表示衷心的感谢。牛津大学出版社英汉词典组的各位编辑长期认真校对原稿、细心查证，在此深表谢忱。本词典译文中的错误或不妥之处，均由我个人负责，切望得到广大读者和专家学者的批评指正。

李北达
香港大学

Contents 目 录

Acknowledgements 鸣 谢

We would like to thank the following for permission to reproduce photographs and illustrations:
图片承蒙下列机构及人士提供，谨此致谢。

Aerospatiale; Australian Tourist Commission; Cathay Pacific; Citybus Limited; Consulate General of The Republic of Indonesia; Corel Corporation; Crocodile Garments Limited; Crown Motors Ltd.; G2000 (Apparel) Limited; Gazelle Technologies, Inc.; Hong Kong Philharmonic Society Ltd.; Hong Kong Trade Development Council; Images © 1996 PhotoDisc, Inc.; Kowloon-Canton Railway Corporation; Marks and Spencer (Hong Kong) Limited; National Aeronautics and Space Administration (NASA); NYK Line (H.K.) Ltd.; Ocean Park Corporation; Shun Hing Electronic Trading Co., Ltd.; Shun Tak Group; Tom Lee Music Co., Ltd.; Wharf Transport Investments Limited; World Wide Fund For Nature Hong Kong; Yamaha Motor China Ltd.; Mr. Rocky Chang Woon Pang; Mr. Pun Ka Bun

THE INFORMATION IN THE DICTIONARY 编辑体例说明

Finding words and phrases 查找词和词组

Words with the **same spelling** have different numbers.
拼法相同的首词，以不同号码列出。

Related words are given below the main word.
在首词下面列出的是相关的词。

> **mould¹** /məʊld; mold/ *noun* 名词 (no plural 无复数)
> soft green, grey or blue stuff that grows on food that is too old 霉；霉菌
> **mouldy** *adjective* 形容词
> covered with mould 发霉的：*mouldy cheese* 发霉的乳酪
> **mould²** /məʊld; mold/ *verb* 动词 (**moulds, moulding, moulded**)

different meanings of a word
一个首词的不同义项

idioms and **phrasal verbs** (which have a special meaning)
习语和短语动词（有特殊含义）

> **diet** /'daɪət; 'daɪət/ *noun* 名词
> **1** the food that you usually eat 经常吃的食物；日常的饮食：*It is important to have a healthy diet.* 经常吃有益于健康的食物十分重要。
> **2** special foods that you eat when you are ill or when you want to get thinner（生病时的或为减轻体重时的）规定饮食
> **be** or 或 **go on a diet** eat only special foods because you want to get thinner（为减轻体重）节食

Grammar 语法

the **part of speech** (for example *noun*, *verb* or *adjective*)
词类（如名词、动词或形容词）

the **forms of a verb.** 动词形式。
We show the *he/she* form, the *-ing* form, the *past tense* (and the *past participle* at irregular verbs). 标示出与 he [she] 连用的形式、-ing 形式、过去时态（不规则动词均列出其过去分词）。

> **catch** /kætʃ; kætʃ/ *verb* 动词 (**catches, catching, caught** /kɔːt; kɔt/, **has caught**)
> **1** take and hold something that is moving 抓住或接住移动中的东西：

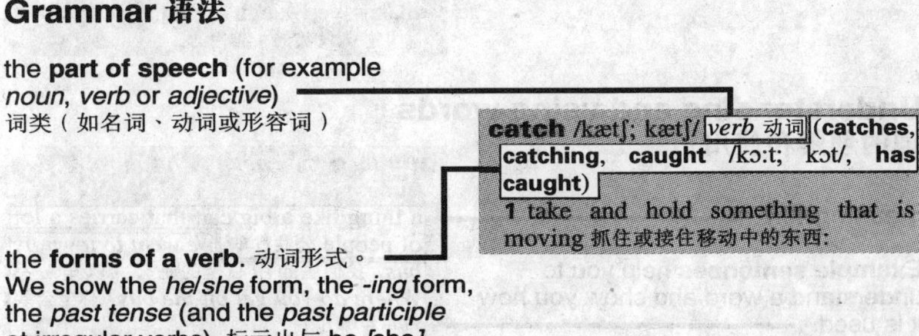

To make the plural of most nouns, you add -s (for example girl girl**s**). 大多数名词在词尾加 -s 可构成复数形式（如 girl girl**s**）。For all other nouns, we give you full information 其余的名词均有详细标示:

Some nouns have a completely different **plural form**, or there is a change to the spelling. 有些名词复数形式完全不同，或拼法有所改变。

knife /naɪf; naɪf/ *noun* 名词 (*plural* 复数作 **knives** /naɪvz; naɪvz/) a sharp metal thing with a handle, that you use to cut things or to fight 刀

Some nouns are always **plural**. 有些名词只用作复数。

clothes /kləʊðz; kloz/ *noun* 名词 (plural 复数) things like trousers, shirts and coats that you wear to cover your body 衣服；衣物

Sometimes a noun has **no plural** form and it cannot be used with *a* or *an*. 有时某个名词没有复数，不能与 a 或 an 连用。

advice /əd'vaɪs; əd'vaɪs/ *noun* 名词 (no plural 无复数) words that you say to help somebody decide what to do 帮助某人做决定的言语；建议；劝告

a note giving information about **grammar** 语法注释

✪ Be careful! You cannot say 'an advice'. You can say 'some advice' or 'a piece of advice' 注意！不要说 an advice，可以说 some advice 或 a piece of advice: *I need some advice.* 我需要有人给我出主意。◇ *Let me give you a piece of advice.* 我来给你提个建议吧。

Comparative and **superlative** forms are given, unless they are formed with *more* and *most*. 比较级和最高级形式分别列出，但与 more 和 most 构成的比较级和最高级不标示。

funny /'fʌni; 'fʌnɪ/ *adjective* 形容词 (**funnier, funniest**)
1 A person or thing that is funny makes you laugh or smile（指人或事物）使人发笑的；有趣的

Understanding and using words 词的理解和使用

meaning 词义

Example sentences help you to understand a word and show you how it is used. 示例既有助于理解词义也用于示范使用方法。

pronunciation and **stress** 读音和重音

bus /bʌs; bʌs/ *noun* 名词 (*plural* 复数作 **buses**)
a thing like a big car, that carries a lot of people 公共汽车: *We went to town by bus.* 我们去市中心坐的是公共汽车。◇ *Where do you get off the bus?* 你坐公共汽车在哪儿下？

bus-stop /'bʌs stɒp; 'bʌs,stɑp/ *noun* 名词
a place where buses stop and people get on and off 公共汽车站

elephant /ˈelɪfənt; ˈɛləfənt/ *noun* 名词
a very big wild animal from Africa or Asia, with a long nose (called a **trunk**) that hangs down 象（象的鼻子叫做 **trunk**）

related words 相关的词

short /ʃɔːt; ʃɔrt/ *adjective* 形容词 (**shorter, shortest**)
1 very little from one end to the other 短的: *Her hair is very short.* 她的头发很短。◇ *We live a short distance from the beach.* 我们住的地方离海滩很近。✪ opposite 反义词: **long**

The **opposites** of many words are given.
很多首词下面均列出反义词。

lion /ˈlaɪən; ˈlaɪən/ *noun* 名词
a wild animal like a big cat with yellow fur. Lions live in Africa and parts of Asia. 狮子（产于非洲和南亚）
✪ A female lion is called a **lioness** and a young lion is called a **cub**. 母狮子叫做 **lioness**，幼小的狮子叫做 **cub**。

vocabulary notes giving related words
词汇注释列出相关词语

purchase /ˈpɜːtʃəs; ˈpɝtʃəs/ *verb* 动词 (**purchases, purchasing, purchased** /ˈpɜːtʃəst; ˈpɝtʃəst/)
buy something 购买: *The company has purchased three new shops.* 这家公司收购了三个新商店。✪ **Buy** is the word that we usually use. ＊ **buy** 是常用词。

Some words are used only in special situations and there may be a word that is used more often, especially in speech.
有些词只用于某种场合；而在一般情况下，尤其是在口语中可能有较常用的词。

☞ tells you about a note or picture on a different page, or about a related word that you should look at. 这个符号表示参看某页的注释或插图，或应参看的另一个相关的词。

DICTIONARY QUIZ 词典知识测验

This quiz shows how the **Oxford Elementary Learner's English-Chinese Dictionary** can help you. 这个小测验可以表达出**《牛津初阶英汉双解词典》**能够在哪些方面帮助使用本词典的人。You will find the answers to all these questions in the dictionary. 下列问题的答案均可在本书中找到。

---

1 On which part of your body do you wear **wellingtons**? **wellingtons** 是用于身体哪个部位的衣物？

2 When is **Boxing Day**? **Boxing Day** 是在哪一天？

Meanings 词义

The dictionary explains the meanings of words in simple language. 本词典使用浅显的语言解释词义。 The example sentences also help you to understand words and use them correctly. 示例既有助于理解词义，也用于示范正确的使用方法。For more about this, look at page C28. 此点在第C28页有进一步解释。

---

3 What is a young **goat** called? 幼小的 **goat** 叫做甚么？

4 What is the opposite of **wide**? **wide** 的反义词是甚么？

5 *I bought this book in the* ***library***.
In this sentence, the word **library** is wrong. What is the right word? 上述句中 **library** 这个词用错了。用哪个词正确呢？

6 What is the name of the thick part of a **tree**, that grows up from the ground? 树木的主体部分叫甚么？

7 What is the name of this shape? 这种形状的名称是甚么？

Vocabulary 词汇

There are many notes (shown by ✪) that give useful extra vocabulary or show the differences between words. 本词典有很多注释（用✪标示），借以扩展常用的词汇范围或说明词语的区别。

The dictionary has a lot of pictures that help you understand words and that give extra vocabulary. 另有很多插图，有助于理解词义，也可借以扩大词汇量。As well as the pictures in the main part of the dictionary, there are special pages (with blue edges) that have pictures showing things like The Human Body and Shapes and Sizes. 除正文各处附插图外，还有些图解专页（有蓝色页边），解说诸如人体部位和形状与大小等各类事物。

8 Is the word **lung** a noun, a verb or an adjective? **lung** 这个词是名词、动词还是形容词？

Grammar 语法

You can check if a new word is a noun, a verb, an adjective, etc by looking in the dictionary. 使用本词典可以查检生词的词类，是名词、动词或形容词等。

9 Is it correct to say 下面的说法对不对：Can you give me some **information**s?

The dictionary tells you about nouns. 对于名词有进一步说明。For example, it gives irregular and difficult noun plurals and tells you if a word cannot be used in the plural. 例如列出不规则的和难记住的复数形式，也注明某词不可用作复数。

10 What is the past tense of the verb **break**? 动词 **break** 的过去时态是怎样的？

The important verb forms are listed for each verb, and there is a list of irregular verbs with their past tenses and past participles on page 580. 每个动词均标示出重要词形，第580页另附不规则动词表列出过去时态及过去分词。

---

11 What is the *-ing* form of the verb **hit**? 动词 **hit** 的 -ing 形式是怎样的？

12 How do you spell the plural of **party**? **party** 这个词的复数是怎样拼写的？

Spelling 拼写

You can use the dictionary to check how to spell a word, and it also shows small changes in the spelling of other forms of the word, for example the plurals of nouns and the *-ing* forms of verbs. 本词典可用以查检字的拼写方法，也可以查出词形的细微变化，例如名词的复数或动词的 -ing 形式。

---

13 Do the words **peace** and **piece** have the same sound? **peace** 和 **piece** 的读音一样吗？

Pronunciation 读音

The dictionary gives the pronunciation of words, and on page 588 you will find help with reading the symbols. 本词典标示字词的读音，第588页列有读音符号便于使用参考。

---

14 How do you say this **date** 下列 **date** 怎样读出：4 July 2010?

Extra information 额外资料

The special pages (with blue edges) also give useful information on topics like Dates, Numbers and Time. 分类专页（有蓝色页边的）还列有常用的专项资料，例如日期、数目和时间等。

15 What is the word for a person who comes from **Germany**? 用哪个词来表示 **Germany** 这个国家的人？

At the back of the dictionary there is a list of geographical names. 本词典后面附有地名表。

Answers 答案

1 your feet **2** 26 December **3** a kid **4** narrow **5** bookshop **6** the trunk
7 a cylinder **8** a noun **9** No. (The word 'information' does not have a plural form.)
10 broke **11** hitting **12** parties **13** yes **14** the fourth of July (or July the fourth), two thousand and ten **15** a German

Grammar 语法

You can check if a word is a noun, a verb, an adjective, etc by looking in the dictionary. [illegible]

The dictionary tells you about nouns. [illegible] For example, it gives irregular and difficult noun plurals and tells you if a word cannot be used in the plural. [illegible]

The important verb forms are listed for each verb and there is a list of irregular verbs with their past tenses and past participles on page 380. [illegible]

Spelling 拼写

You can use the dictionary to check how to spell a word, and it also shows small changes in the spelling of other forms of the word, for example the plurals of nouns and the -ing forms of verbs. [illegible]

Pronunciation 读音

The dictionary gives the pronunciation of words, and on page 388 you will find help with reading the symbols. [illegible]

Extra information 额外资料

The special pages (with blue edges) also give useful information on topics like Dates, Numbers and Time. [illegible]

At the back of the dictionary there is a list of geographical names. [illegible]

Aa

a /ə, eɪ; ə, e/ *article* 冠词

1 one or any 一个；任何一个: *Would you like a drink?* 您想喝点儿东西吗？◇ *A dog has four legs.* 狗有四条腿。◇ *He's a teacher.* 他是教师。

2 each, or for each 每一个；对每一个来说: *She phones her mother three times a week.* 她每星期给母亲打三次电话。◇ *This wine costs £4 a bottle.* 这种葡萄酒4英镑一瓶。

> **a** or **an**? 用 **a** 还是用 **an**？
>
> Before a word that starts with the sound of a, e, i, o or u, you use **an**, not **a**. 在读音以 a、e、i、o 或 u 开始的字之前，用 **an**，不用 **a**。Be careful! It is the sound that is important, not the spelling 要留心！重要的是发音，不是拼写的字母:
>
> ***a** box* 一个盒子
> ***a** singer* 一个歌唱者
> ***a** university* 一所大学
>
> ***an** apple* 一个苹果
> ***an** hour* 一个小时
> ***an** MP* 一位议员

abandon /əˈbændən; əˈbændən/ *verb* 动词 (**abandons**, **abandoning**, **abandoned** /əˈbændənd; əˈbændənd/)

1 leave somebody or something completely 彻底离开某人或某事物；遗弃；抛弃；离弃: *He abandoned his car in the snow.* 他抛弃了陷在大雪中的汽车。

2 stop doing something before it is finished 某事物尚未完成而不再继续做下去；放弃: *When the rain started, we abandoned our game.* 下起雨来了，我们不继续做游戏了。

abbey /ˈæbi; ˈæbɪ/ *noun* 名词 (*plural* 复数作 **abbeys**)

a building where religious men or women (called **monks** and **nuns**) live or lived 男女神职人员（修士叫做 **monk**，修女叫做 **nun**）居住的或居住过的建筑物；修道院

abbreviate /əˈbri:vieɪt; əˈbrivɪˌet/ *verb* 动词 (**abbreviates**, **abbreviating**, **abbreviated**)

make a word shorter by not saying or writing some of the letters 省略某些字母而说出或写出某词；简称；缩写: *The word 'telephone' is often abbreviated to 'phone'.* ✳ telephone 这个字常缩略为 phone。

abbreviation /əˈbri:viˈeɪʃn; əˌbrivɪˈeʃən/ *noun* 名词

a short form of a word 缩写词；略语: *TV is an abbreviation for 'television'.* ✳ TV 是 television 的缩略式。

ability /əˈbɪləti; əˈbɪlətɪ/ *noun* 名词 (*plural* 复数作 **abilities**)

the power and knowledge to do something 做某事物的力量或知识；能力: *She has the ability to pass the exam, but she must work harder.* 她能够考及格，但是得用功才行。

able /ˈeɪbl; ˈebl̩/ *adjective* 形容词

be able to have the power and knowledge to do something 有做某事物的力量或知识；能够: *Will you be able to come to the party?* 你能来参加聚会吗？◇ *Is Simon able to swim?* 西蒙会游泳吗？☞ Look at **can**. 见 **can**。

aboard /əˈbɔ:d; əˈbɔrd/ *adverb, preposition* 副词，介词

on or onto a ship, train, bus or an aeroplane 在船上、火车上、公共汽车上或飞机上；向船上、火车上、公共汽车上或飞机上: *Are all the passengers aboard the ship?* 所有乘客都上船了吗？◇ *We went aboard the plane.* 我们上了飞机。

abolish /əˈbɒlɪʃ; əˈbɑlɪʃ/ *verb* 动词 (**abolishes**, **abolishing**, **abolished** /əˈbɒlɪʃt; əˈbɑlɪʃt/)

stop or end something by law 依法停止或结束某事物；废除；废止: *The Americans abolished slavery in 1863.* 美国在1863年废除了奴隶制度。

abolition /ˌæbəˈlɪʃn; ˌæbəˈlɪʃən/ *noun* 名词 (*no plural* 无复数)

the abolition of hunting 废除狩猎活动

about /əˈbaʊt; əˈbaʊt/ *preposition, adverb* 介词，副词

1 a little more or less than; a little before or after 比…稍多或稍少；在…稍前或稍后；或多或少；大约；左右: *She's about 50 years old.* 她50岁上下。◇ *I arrived at*

about two o'clock. 我是在两点钟前后到达的。

2 of; on the subject of 关于；对于；有关: *a book about cats* 关于猫的书 ◇ *We talked about the problem.* 我们谈过这个问题。◇ *What are you thinking about?* 你想什么呢？

3 in or to different places or in different directions 在各处；向各处；朝各方向: *The children were running about in the garden.* 孩子们在花园里四处跑。◇ *There were books lying about on the floor.* 地上到处都是书。

4 almost 将近；差不多: *Dinner is about ready.* 就要开饭了。

5 in a place; here 在某处；在这里: *Is your mother about? I want to speak to her.* 你母亲在吗？我想和她谈谈。

be about to be going to do something very soon 即将做某事物: *The film is about to start.* 电影就要开演了。

above /ə'bʌv; ə'bʌv/ *preposition, adverb* 介词，副词

1 in or to a higher place; higher than somebody or something 在上面；到上面；比某人或某物高: *I looked up at the sky above.* 我抬头看着上面的天空。◇ *My bedroom is above the kitchen.* 我的卧室在厨房的上面。◇ *There is a picture on the wall above the fireplace.* 壁炉上面的墙上有幅画。☞ picture on page C1 见第C1页图

2 more than a number or price（指数目或价钱）大于: *children aged ten and above* 年龄在十岁或十岁以上的儿童

above all more than any other thing; what is most important 比其他事物尤甚；最为重要: *He's handsome and intelligent and, above all, he's kind!* 他又漂亮又聪明，尤其可贵的是他很和蔼！

abroad /ə'brɔ:d; ə'brɔd/ *adverb* 副词

in or to another country 在另一国；向另一国；在国外；到国外: *Are you going abroad this summer?* 你今年夏天到外国去吗？◇ *She lives abroad now.* 她住在国外。

absence /'æbsəns; 'æbsn̩s/ *noun* 名词 (no plural 无复数)

a time when a person or thing is not there 某人或某物不在某处的时候；缺席: *I am doing Julie's job in her absence.* 朱莉不在，我正在做她的工作。

absent /'æbsənt; 'æbsn̩t/ *adjective* 形容词

not there; away 不在该处的；离开的: *He was absent from work yesterday because he was ill.* 他昨天病了，没上班。

absolute /'æbsəlu:t; 'æbsə,lut/ *adjective* 形容词

complete 绝对的；完全的: *I've never played chess before. I'm an absolute beginner.* 我以前没下过国际象棋，完全是个生手。

absolutely *adverb* 副词

completely 绝对；完全: *You're absolutely right.* 你完全正确。

absorb /əb'sɔ:b; əb'sɔrb/ *verb* 动词 (**absorbs**, **absorbing**, **absorbed** /əb'sɔ:bd; əb'sɔrbd/)

take in something like liquid or heat, and hold it 吸收或吸进（液体或热量）: *The dry ground absorbed all the rain.* 地面很干，把雨水都吸收了。

abstract /'æbstrækt; 'æbstrækt/ *adjective* 形容词

1 about an idea, not a real thing 关于意念的（非实物的）；抽象的: *abstract thought* 抽象的思维

2 not like a real thing 不像实物的；抽象式的: *an abstract painting* 抽象画

absurd /əb'sɜ:d; əb'sɝd/ *adjective* 形容词

so silly that it makes you laugh 愚蠢得可笑的；荒谬的；荒唐的: *You look absurd in that hat!* 你戴着那顶帽子，看起来怪模怪样的！◇ *Don't be absurd! Of course I can't learn Japanese in three days!* 别那么荒唐了！我当然不能在三天之内学会日语了！

abuse /ə'bju:z; ə'bjuz/ *verb* 动词 (**abuses**, **abusing**, **abused** /ə'bju:zd; ə'bjuzd/)

1 use something in a wrong or bad way 错误地或胡乱地使用某事物；滥用: *The manager often abuses her power.* 那个（女）经理常常滥用职权。

2 be cruel or unkind to somebody 残暴地或狠毒地对待某人；虐待: *The children were abused by their father.* 这些孩子受到父亲的虐待。

3 say rude things to somebody 对某人说粗野的话；辱骂

abuse /ə'bju:s; ə'bjus/ *noun* 名词 (no plural 无复数)

1 using something in a wrong or bad way 对某事物错误的或胡乱的使用；滥用: *drug abuse* 滥用麻醉药品

2 being cruel or unkind to somebody 残暴的或狠毒的对待；虐待: *child abuse* 虐待儿童

3 rude words 粗野的话；粗话；脏话: *The lorry driver shouted abuse at the cyclist.* 那个卡车司机破口大骂那个骑自行车的人。

accent /'æksent; 'æksɛnt/ *noun* 名词

1 the way a person from a certain place or country speaks a language 某地或某国的人说话的方式；口音；方言；方音: *She speaks English with an American accent.* 她说英语带有美国口音。

2 saying one word or part of a word more strongly than another 把一个词或一个词里的某部分读得重些；重读；重音: *In the word 'because', the accent is on the second part of the word.* ✳ because 这个词里，第二部分重读。

accept /ək'sept; ək'sɛpt/ *verb* 动词 (**accepts**, **accepting**, **accepted**)

1 say 'yes' when somebody asks you to have or do something 同意；认可；接受: *I accepted the invitation to his party.* 我接受了他的邀请去参加聚会。◇ *Please accept this present.* 请收下这个礼物。

2 believe that something is true 认为某事物属实；相信某事物: *She can't accept that her son is dead.* 她无法相信儿子已经死了。

acceptable /ək'septəbl; ək'sɛptəbḷ/ *adjective* 形容词

allowed by most people; good enough 多数人认可的；够好的: *It's not acceptable to make so many mistakes.* 出现这么多错误是不行的。

access /'ækses; 'æksɛs/ *noun* 名词 (no plural 无复数)

a way to go into a place or to use something（进入某地的）通路；（使用某事物的）方法: *We don't have access to the garden from our flat.* 从我们的公寓到花园没有通路。◇ *Do you have access to a computer at home?* 你在家里有机会使用计算机吗？

accident /'æksɪdənt; 'æksədənt/ *noun* 名词

something, often bad, that happens by chance 偶然发生的事（常为坏事）；事故；故障；意外: *I had an accident when I was driving to work—my car hit a tree.* 我开车上班时出了事故——我的汽车撞在树上了。◇ *I'm sorry I broke your watch—it was an accident.* 对不起，我把你的手表弄坏了——不是成心的。

by accident by chance; not because you have planned it 偶然；意外地；并非特意地: *I took Jenny's book by accident. I thought it was mine.* 我无意中拿了珍妮的书。我还以为是我的呢。

accidental /ˌæksɪ'dentl; ˌæksə'dɛntḷ/ *adjective* 形容词

If something is accidental, it happens by chance 偶然发生的；意外造成的；并非特意安排的: *accidental death* 意外死亡

accidentally /ˌæksɪ'dentəli; ˌæksə-'dɛntḷɪ/ *adverb* 副词

He accidentally broke the window. 他无意间把窗户打破了。

accommodation /əˌkɒmə'deɪʃn; əˌkɑmə'deʃən/ *noun* 名词 (no plural 无复数)

a place to stay or live 住宿或居住的地方: *It's difficult to find cheap accommodation in London.* 在伦敦很难找到便宜的住处。

accompany /ə'kʌmpəni; ə'kʌmpənɪ/ *verb* 动词 (**accompanies**, **accompanying**, **accompanied** /ə'kʌmpənid; ə'kʌmpənɪd/)

1 go with somebody to a place 陪某人去某处；伴随: *Four teachers accompanied the class on their skiing holiday.* 有四个教师陪同全班同学滑雪度假。

2 happen at the same time as something else 与某事物同时发生或出现: *Thunder is usually accompanied by lightning.* 打雷时通常也打闪。

3 play music while somebody sings or plays another instrument（有人演唱或演奏时）用器乐配合；伴奏: *You sing and I'll accompany you on the guitar.* 你来唱，我用吉他给你伴奏。

accord /ə'kɔːd; ə'kɔrd/ *noun* 名词 (no plural 无复数)

of your own accord because you want to, not because somebody has asked you 自愿地；主动地: *She left the job of her own accord.* 是她自愿辞去那份工作的。

according to /ə'kɔːdɪŋ tə; ə'kɔrdɪŋ tə/ *preposition* 介词

as somebody or something says 根据某人或某事物所说: *According to Mike, this film is really good.* 据迈克说，这部电影

A

真好。◇ *The church was built in 1395, according to this book.* 按照这本书的说法，这座教堂建筑于1395年。

account /ə'kaʊnt; ə'kaunt/ *noun* 名词

1 words that somebody says or writes about something that happened 某人对所发生的事说的话或写的文字；陈述；描写；报道: *He gave the police an account of the car accident.* 他向警方叙述了汽车出事的情况。

2 an amount of money that you keep in a bank 存在银行里的钱；账户: *I paid the money into my bank account.* 我把钱存进我的银行账户里了。

3 accounts (plural 复数) lists of all the money that a person or business receives and pays 个人或公司收支的项目；账目: *Who keeps* (= does) *the accounts for your business?* 你们公司谁管账？

on no account, not on any account not for any reason 不管什么原因或理由；决不可以: *On no account must you open this door.* 这个门绝对不要开。

take account of something, take something into account remember something when you are thinking about other things 考虑某事物时想到另一件事；把某事物考虑在内: *John is always last, but you must take his age into account—he is much younger than the other children.* 约翰总是最后，但是要考虑到他的年纪——他比别的孩子小得多。

accountant /ə'kaʊntənt; ə'kauntənt/ *noun* 名词

a person whose job is to make lists of all the money that people or businesses receive and pay 为大家或公司登记收支账目的人；会计: *Kitty is an accountant.* 基蒂是会计。

accurate /'ækjərət; 'ækjərɪt/ *adjective* 形容词

exactly right; with no mistakes 正确无误的；准确的；精确的: *He gave an accurate description of the thief.* 他把那个贼描述得很准确。✪ opposite 反义词: **inaccurate**

accurately *adverb* 副词

The map was accurately drawn. 这张地图画得很精确。

accuse /ə'kju:z; ə'kjuz/ *verb* 动词 (**accuses, accusing, accused** /ə'kju:zd; ə'kjuzd/)

say that somebody has done something wrong 说出某人做错了事；指责；指控: *The police accused the woman of stealing.* 警方指控那个女子偷了东西。◇ *He was accused of murder.* 他被控告犯有谋杀罪。

accusation /ˌækju'zeɪʃn; ˌækjə'zeʃən/ *noun* 名词

The accusations were not true. 这些指责都不属实。

ace /eɪs; es/ *noun* 名词

a playing-card which has only one shape on it 只有一个点的纸牌；幺点的纸牌: *the ace of hearts* 红桃幺

ache /eɪk; ek/ *verb* 动词 (**aches, aching, ached** /eɪkt; ekt/)

give you pain 引起疼痛: *My legs ached after the long walk.* 我走了长路以后两腿发疼。

ache *noun* 名词

a pain that lasts for a long time（长时间的）疼痛: *I've got a headache.* 我头疼。◇ *She's got toothache.* 她牙疼。◇ *stomach-ache* 胃疼 ◇ *earache* 耳朵疼

achieve /ə'tʃi:v; ə'tʃiv/ *verb* 动词 (**achieves, achieving, achieved** /ə'tʃi:vd; ə'tʃivd/)

do or finish something well after trying hard 经过努力而做好或做成某事物；达到；实现: *He worked hard and achieved his aim of becoming a doctor.* 他很用功，达到了当医生的目的。

achievement /ə'tʃi:vmənt; ə'tʃivmənt/ *noun* 名词

something that somebody has done after trying hard 经过努力而做成的事物；成就；成绩: *Climbing Mount Everest was his greatest achievement.* 登上了埃佛勒斯峰（即珠穆朗玛峰）是他最大的成就。

acid /'æsɪd; 'æsɪd/ *noun* 名词

a liquid that can burn things（能腐蚀东西的）酸

acid rain /ˌæsɪd 'reɪn; ˌæsɪd 'ren/ *noun* 名词 (no plural 无复数)

rain that has chemicals in it from factories, for example. It can damage trees, rivers and buildings. 酸雨（含有化学物质的雨，例如含有由工厂排出的物质的雨。这种雨能损害树木、河流、建筑物。）

acknowledge /ək'nɒlɪdʒ; ək'nɑlɪdʒ/ *verb* 动词 (**acknowledges, acknowledging, acknowledged** /ək'nɒlɪdʒd; ək'nɑlɪdʒd/)

1 agree that something is true 承认某事物

属实：*He acknowledged that he had made a mistake.* 他承认犯了错误。

2 say or write that you have received something 说出或写出自己知道了或收到了某事物：*She never acknowledged my letter.* 她从来没说收到过我的信。

acorn /'eɪkɔ:n; 'eˌkɔrn/ *noun* 名词

a small nut that is the fruit of an oak tree 橡实（栎树的果实）

acquaintance /ə'kweɪntəns; ə'kwentəns/ *noun* 名词

a person that you know a little 认识（但不很熟）的人

acquire /ə'kwaɪə(r); ə'kwaɪr/ *verb* 动词 (**acquires**, **acquiring**, **acquired** /ə'kwaɪəd; ə'kwaɪrd/)

get or buy something 获得或购买某事物：*He acquired some English from listening to pop songs.* 他听流行歌曲学到了些英语。

acre /'eɪkə(r); 'ekɚ/ *noun* 名词

a measure of land (= 0.405 of a hectare) 英亩（= 0.405公顷）：*a farm of 40 acres* 一个有40英亩的农场

acrobat /'ækrəbæt; 'ækrəˌbæt/ *noun* 名词

a person who does difficult movements of the body, for example in a **circus** 杂技演员（例如马戏团里的，马戏团叫做 **circus**）

across /ə'krɒs; ə'krɔs/ *adverb*, *preposition* 副词，介词

1 from one side to the other side of something 从某物的一边到另一边；横过（某物）：*We walked across the field.* 我们走过这片地。☞ picture on page C4 见第C4页图

2 on the other side of something 在（某物）的另一边；在（某物）的对面：*There is a bank across the road.* 这条路对面有个银行。

3 from side to side 从一边到另一边：*The river is two kilometres across.* 这条河宽两公里。

act[1] /ækt; ækt/ *verb* 动词 (**acts**, **acting**, **acted**)

1 do something, or behave in a certain way 做某事；做某动作：*Doctors acted quickly to save the boy's life after the accident.* 出事后医生们迅速行动抢救那个男孩儿的生命。◇ *Stop acting like a child!* 别像个孩子那样！

2 pretend to be somebody else in a play, film or television programme（在戏剧、电影或电视节目中）扮演某人

act as something do the job of another person, usually for a short time 代某人做事（通常指短期的）：*He acted as manager while his boss was ill.* 他们老板生病时，他代行经理职务。

act[2] /ækt; ækt/ *noun* 名词

1 something that you do 做的事；行动：*an act of kindness* 善意的举动

2 one part of a play（戏剧的）一幕：*This play has five acts.* 这出话剧共有五幕。

3 a law that a government makes（政府制定的）法案；法令

in the act of while doing something wrong 在做坏事时；当场：*I caught him in the act of stealing the money.* 我看见他当时正在偷钱。

acting /'æktɪŋ; 'æktɪŋ/ *noun* 名词 (no plural 无复数)

being in plays or films（在戏剧或电影中）演出：*Have you ever done any acting?* 你参加过演出吗？

action /'ækʃn; 'ækʃən/ *noun* 名词

1 (no plural 无复数) doing things 做事；动作：*Now is the time for action!* 现在该做事了！◇ *I like films with a lot of action in them.* 我爱看动作片。

2 (*plural* 复数作 **actions**) something that you do 所做的事：*The little girl copied her mother's actions.* 这个小女孩儿模仿着做她母亲做的事。

in action doing something; working 做某事物；工作：*We watched the machine in action.* 我们看到机器在运转。

active /'æktɪv; 'æktɪv/ *adjective* 形容词

If you are active, you are always busy and able to do a lot of things 总是很忙；能做很多事；活跃：*My grandmother is 75 but she's still very active.* 我祖母75岁了，可是仍然闲不住。

in the active where the person or thing doing the action is the subject of a sentence or verb 主动语态（发出动作或行为的人或事物是句子的主语或动词的主体）：*In the sentence 'A girl broke the window', the verb is in the active.* 在 A girl broke the window 这句话里，用的是主动语态的动词。

✪ opposite 反义词：**passive**

activity /æk'tɪvəti; æk'tɪvətɪ/ *noun* 名词

1 (no plural 无复数) a lot of things happening and people doing things 出现

A

很多事；活动: *On the day of the festival there was a lot of activity in the streets.* 过节那天街上很热闹。

2 (*plural* 复数作 **activities**) something that you do 做的事；活动: *Watching TV is one of his favourite activities.* 看电视是他一大爱好。

actor /'æktə(r); 'æktɚ/ *noun* 名词
a person who acts in plays, films or television programmes 参加戏剧、电影或电视表演的人；演员

actress /'æktrəs; 'æktrɪs/ *noun* 名词 (*plural* 复数作 **actresses**)
a woman who acts in plays, films or television programmes 女演员

actual /'æktʃuəl; 'æktʃuəl/ *adjective* 形容词
that really happened; real 实际的；真实的；确实的: *He said the price of the holiday would be £300, but the actual cost was more.* 他说度假费用定价是300英镑，可是实际花费比这个数多。

actually /'æktʃuəli; 'æktʃuəlɪ/ *adverb* 副词
1 really; in fact 实际地；实在地: *We thought it was going to rain, but actually it was sunny all day.* 我们原以为要下雨呢，可是实际上整天都是晴天。
2 a word that you use to disagree politely or when you say something new 表示不同意的礼貌用语或引起新话题的用语: *'Let's go by bus.' 'Actually, I think it would be quicker to go by train.'* "咱们坐公共汽车去吧。" "说实在的，我看还是坐火车快。" ◇ *I don't agree. I thought the film was very good, actually.* 我不同意。我认为这部电影很好，说老实话。

ad /æd; æd/ *short for* **advertisement** ＊**advertisement** 的缩略式

AD /ˌeɪ 'di:; ˌe 'di/
'AD' in a date shows that it was after Christ was born ＊AD表示所指的是耶稣出生后的日期；公元: *AD 1066* 公元1066年 ☞ Look at **BC**. 见 **BC**。

adapt /ə'dæpt; ə'dæpt/ *verb* 动词 (**adapts**, **adapting**, **adapted**)
1 change the way that you do things because you are in a new situation 在新情况下改变做事的方法；适应: *He has adapted very well to being at a new school.* 他到了新学校很能适应。
2 change something so that you can use it in a different way 改变某事物另作他用: *The car was adapted for use as a taxi.* 这辆汽车已经改装作计程车用了。

add /æd; æd/ *verb* 动词 (**adds**, **adding**, **added**)
1 put something with something else 加上；添上: *Mix the flour with the milk and then add the eggs.* 把面粉和奶搅拌好再加上鸡蛋。◇ *Add your name to the list.* 把你的名字加进名单里。
2 put numbers together 把数目合在一起；加: *If you add 2 and 5 together, you get 7.* ＊5加2等于7。✪ opposite 反义词: **subtract**
3 say something more 又说；补充说: *'Go away—and don't come back again,' she added.* "走开——再也别回来了，" 她又加上一句。

addict /'ædɪkt; 'ædɪkt/ *noun* 名词
a person who cannot stop wanting something that is very bad for him/her 忍不住想要某种对自己有害的东西的人；有瘾的人: *a drug addict* 吸毒的人

addicted /ə'dɪktɪd; ə'dɪktɪd/ *adjective* 形容词
not able to stop wanting something that is bad for you 忍不住想要某种对自己有害的东西的；有瘾的: *He is addicted to heroin.* 他有海洛因毒瘾。

addition /ə'dɪʃn; ə'dɪʃən/ *noun* 名词
1 (no plural 无复数) putting numbers together 加；加法: *We learnt addition and subtraction at primary school.* 我们上小学的时候，学过加减法。
2 (*plural* 复数作 **additions**) a thing or person that you add to other things or people 加进其他东西或人群里的东西或人；增加的人或事物: *They have a new addition to their family* (= a new baby). 他们家又添了一口人（＝新生儿）。
in addition also 还有；还；也: *She plays the guitar, and in addition she writes her own songs.* 她弹吉他，还自己创作歌曲。
in addition to something as well as 除某事物以外；…还…: *He speaks five languages in addition to English.* 除英语外，他还会说五种外语。

address /ə'dres; 'ædrɛs/ *noun* 名词 (*plural* 复数作 **addresses**)
the number of the house and the name of the street and town where somebody

lives or works 居住或工作处所的城镇、街道的名称和门牌号数；地址: *My address is 18 Wilton Street, London NW10.* 我的地址是伦敦NW10，威尔顿街18号。◇ *Are you still living at that address?* 你还是住在那个住处吗？☞ picture on page C31 见第C31页图

address /ə'dres; ə'drɛs/ *verb* 动词 (**addresses, addressing, addressed** /ə'drest; ə'drɛst/)
write on a letter or parcel the name and address of the person you are sending it to（在信件或包裹上）写收件人的姓名和地址: *The letter was addressed to James Philips.* 这封信写的收信人是詹姆斯·菲利普斯。

adequate /'ædɪkwət; 'ædəkwɪt/ *adjective* 形容词
enough for what you need 足够的；充足的: *They are very poor and do not have adequate food or clothing.* 他们很穷，食物和衣服都不够。✪ opposite 反义词: **inadequate**

adjective /'ædʒɪktɪv; 'ædʒɪktɪv/ *noun* 名词
a word that you use with a noun, that tells you more about it 形容名词的词；形容词: *In the sentence 'This soup is hot', 'hot' is an adjective.* 在 This soup is hot 这句话里，hot是形容词。

adjust /ə'dʒʌst; ə'dʒʌst/ *verb* 动词 (**adjusts, adjusting, adjusted**)
make a small change to something, to make it better 把某物稍加改动，使之更好；调整: *You can adjust the height of this chair.* 你可以调整一下这把椅子的高度。

administration /əd͵mɪnɪ'streɪʃn; əd͵mɪnə'streʃən/ *noun* 名词 (no plural 无复数)
controlling or managing something, for example a business, an office or a school 对某事物的控制或管理（如对公司、办事处或学校的管理）；行政

admiral /'ædmərəl; 'ædmərəl/ *noun* 名词
a very important officer in the navy 海军将官

admire /əd'maɪə(r); əd'maɪr/ *verb* 动词 (**admires, admiring, admired** /əd'maɪəd; əd'maɪrd/)
think or say that somebody or something is very good 认为或说出某人或某事物非常好；称赞；赞赏: *I really admire you for doing such a difficult job.* 我真佩服你能做这么困难的工作。◇ *They were admiring the view from the top of the tower.* 他们在塔顶上赞叹那里的景色。

admiration /͵ædmə'reɪʃn; ͵ædmə'reʃən/ *noun* 名词 (no plural 无复数)
I have great admiration for her work. 我十分钦佩她的工作。

admission /əd'mɪʃn; əd'mɪʃən/ *noun* 名词 (no plural 无复数)
1 letting somebody go into a place 允许某人进入某处: *There is no admission to the park after 8 pm.* 晚上8时以后不准进入这个公园。
2 the money that you pay to go into a place 进入某处须付的钱；入场费；门票钱: *Admission to the zoo is £4.* 这个动物园的门票是4英镑。

admit /əd'mɪt; əd'mɪt/ *verb* 动词 (**admits, admitting, admitted**)
1 say that you have done something wrong 说出自己做错了事；承认: *He admitted stealing the money.* 他承认偷了钱。◇ *I admit that I made a mistake.* 我承认犯了错误。✪ opposite 反义词: **deny**
2 let somebody or something go into a place 允许某人或某物进入某处: *This ticket admits one person to the museum.* 这张票准予一人进入博物馆。

adopt /ə'dɒpt; ə'dɑpt/ *verb* 动词 (**adopts, adopting, adopted**)
take the child of another person into your family to become your own child 把别人的孩子领入自己的家当做自己的孩子；收养: *They adopted Stephen after his parents died.* 他们在斯蒂芬父母死后收养了他。

adore /ə'dɔ:(r); ə'dɔr/ *verb* 动词 (**adores, adoring, adored** /ə'dɔ:d; ə'dɔrd/)
love somebody or something very much 非常喜爱某人或某事物: *She adores her grandchildren.* 她非常疼爱孙子、孙女。

adult /'ædʌlt; 'ædʌlt/ *noun* 名词
a person or an animal that has grown to the full size; not a child 成年的人或动物: *Adults as well as children will enjoy this film.* 成人和儿童都会喜欢这部电影。
adult *adjective* 形容词
an adult ticket 成人票

advance /əd'vɑ:ns; əd'væns/ *noun* 名词 (no plural 无复数)

in advance before something happens 在某事物发生以前；预先；事前；事先: *We paid for the tickets in advance.* 我们预先付了票钱。

advanced /əd'vɑ:nst; əd'vænst/ *adjective* 形容词
of or for somebody who is already good at something; difficult 在某方面已经很好的人的；为某方面已经很好的人的；程度高的；水平高的；高深的: *an advanced English class* 英语高班

advantage /əd'vɑ:ntɪdʒ; əd'væntɪdʒ/ *noun* 名词
something that helps you or that is useful 有帮助的或有用处的事物；益处；好处；优势: *When you're travelling in South America, it's a great advantage if you speak Spanish.* 到南美洲去，要是会说西班牙语很有用处。◇ *One advantage of camping is that it's cheap.* 露营活动的一大优点是花钱少。✪ opposite 反义词: **disadvantage**
take advantage of something use something to help yourself 利用某事物从中获得好处: *Buy now and take advantage of these special prices!* 立即购买，特价优惠！

adventure /əd'ventʃə(r); əd'vɛntʃɚ/ *noun* 名词
something exciting that you do or that happens to you 惊险的事；奇遇: *She wrote a book about her adventures in Africa.* 她写了一部关于她在非洲冒险经历的书。

adventurous /əd'ventʃərəs; əd'vɛntʃərəs/ *adjective* 形容词
An adventurous person likes to do exciting, dangerous things. 爱做有刺激性的、危险的事情的；爱冒险的

adverb /'ædvɜ:b; 'ædvɝb/ *noun* 名词
a word that tells you how, when or where something happens 说明某事物怎么样、什么时候或在哪里的词；副词: *In the sentence 'Please speak slowly', 'slowly' is an adverb.* 在Please speak slowly 这句话里，slowly 是副词。

advertise /'ædvətaɪz; 'ædvɚˌtaɪz/ *verb* 动词 (**advertises, advertising, advertised** /'ædvətaɪzd; 'ædvɚˌtaɪzd/)
give people information on posters, in newspapers or on television about jobs, things to buy or events to go to 刊登或广播广告: *I saw those trainers advertised on TV.* 我在电视广告里看到过那种运动鞋。◇ *We sold our car by advertising it in the newspaper.* 我们在报纸上登广告把汽车卖了。

advertisement /əd'vɜ:tɪsmənt;ˌædvɚ'taɪzmənt/ *noun* 名词
information on a poster, in a newspaper or on television that tells you about a job, something to buy or an event to go to 在招贴中的、报纸上的或电视里的关于要找的工作、要买的东西或要参加的活动等的消息；广告: *I saw an advertisement on TV for a new kind of chocolate bar.* 我在电视里看到一个新出的巧克力糖广告。✪ The short form is **advert** /'ædvɜ:t; æd'vɝt/ or **ad**. 缩约式是 **advert** /'ædvɜ:t; æd'vɝt/ 或 **ad**。

advertising /'ædvətaɪzɪŋ; 'ædvɚˌtaɪzɪŋ/ *noun* 名词 (no plural 无复数)
telling people about things to buy 广告宣传；登广告: *He works in advertising.* 他从事广告业。◇ *The magazine gets a lot of money from advertising.* 这份杂志从刊登的广告中赚到很多钱。

advice /əd'vaɪs; əd'vaɪs/ *noun* 名词 (no plural 无复数)
words that you say to help somebody decide what to do 帮助某人做决定的言语；建议；劝告: *He will give you advice about where to go.* 他会给你出主意让你到哪儿去的。
take somebody's advice do what somebody says you should do 采纳某人的建议；接受某人的劝告: *I took the doctor's advice and stayed in bed.* 我听医生的话，躺在床上。
✪ Be careful! You cannot say 'an advice'. You can say 'some advice' or 'a piece of advice' 注意！不要说 an advice，可以说 some advice 或 a piece of advice: *I need some advice.* 我需要有人给我出主意。◇ *Let me give you a piece of advice.* 我来给你提个建议吧。

advise /əd'vaɪz; əd'vaɪz/ *verb* 动词 (**advises, advising, advised** /əd'vaɪzd; əd'vaɪzd/)
tell somebody what you think they should do 告诉某人你认为他应该怎样做；建议；劝告: *The doctor advised him to stop smoking.* 医生叫他别再抽烟了。

aerial /'eəriəl; 'ɛrɪəl/ *noun* 名词
a wire that receives radio or television signals 天线

aerials 天线

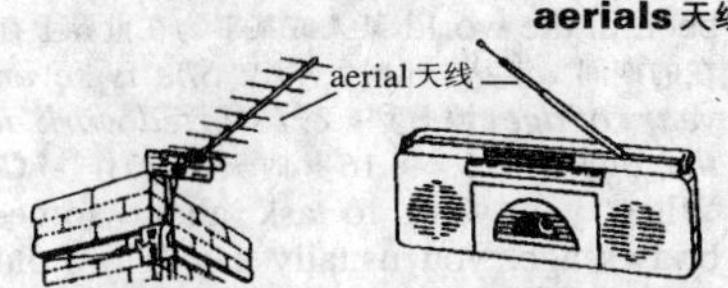

aeroplane /'eərəpleɪn; 'ɛrəˌplen/ *noun* 名词
a machine that has wings and can fly 飞机

✪ An aeroplane (or **plane**) **lands** and **takes off** at an **airport**. 飞机（或称 **plane**）在飞机场（**airport**）降落（**land**）或起飞（**take off**）。

aeroplane 飞机

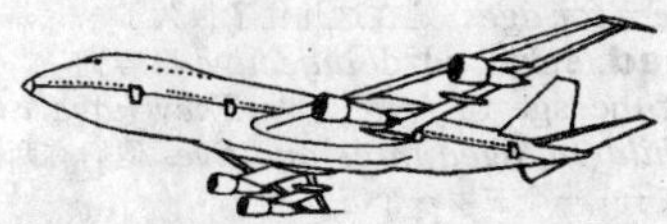

aerosol /'eərəsɒl; 'ɛrəˌsɔl/ *noun* 名词
a can with liquid in it. You press a button to make the liquid come out in a lot of very small drops. 喷雾器（盛有液体的罐子，一按钮就能喷出很多小水点儿来）

affair /ə'feə(r); ə'fɛr/ *noun* 名词
1 something that happens; an event 发生的事情；大事；事件: *The wedding was a very quiet affair.* 那个婚礼办得静悄悄的。
2 something that you need to do or think about; business 需要做的或需要思考的事情；事务: *Don't worry about that—it's not your affair.* 别操心了——那不是你的事。◇ *foreign affairs* 外交事务

affect /ə'fekt; ə'fɛkt/ *verb* 动词 (**affects, affecting, affected**)
make something different 使某事物起变化；影响: *Smoking can affect your health.* 吸烟影响健康。

affection /ə'fekʃn; ə'fɛkʃən/ *noun* 名词 (no plural 无复数)
the feeling of loving or liking somebody 疼爱或喜欢某人的这种感情；喜爱: *She has great affection for her aunt.* 她很爱她的姑姑。

affectionate /ə'fekʃənət; ə'fɛkʃənət/ *adjective* 形容词
that feels or shows love 感觉到或表现出喜爱的: *She gave him an affectionate kiss.* 她满怀爱意吻了他一下。

affectionately *adverb* 副词
He smiled at his son affectionately. 他怀着疼爱的心情对着儿子微笑。

afford /ə'fɔ:d; ə'fɔrd/ *verb* 动词 (**affords, affording, afforded**)
can afford something If you can afford something, you have enough money to pay for it 有付某事物的钱；买得起: *I can't afford a holiday this year.* 我今年没钱度假。

afraid /ə'freɪd; ə'fred/ *adjective* 形容词
If you are afraid of something, it makes you feel fear 怕；害怕: *Some people are afraid of snakes.* 有的人怕蛇。◇ *I was afraid to open the door.* 我不敢去开门。
I'm afraid ... a polite way of saying that you are sorry 表示遗憾的礼貌用语: *I'm afraid I've broken your calculator.* 对不起，我把你的计算器弄坏了。◇ *I'm afraid that I can't come to your party.* 很抱歉，我不能参加你的聚会。

after[1] /'ɑ:ftə(r); 'æftɚ/ *preposition* 介词
1 later than somebody or something 比某人或某事物晚；在…之后: *Jenny arrived after dinner.* 珍妮是在饭后来的。◇ *After doing my homework, I went out.* 我做完功课就出去了。
2 behind or following somebody or something 在某人或某事物的后面；跟在某人或某事物之后；在…后面: *Ten comes after nine.* 十在九的后边。◇ *Close the door after you.* 随手关门。
3 trying to get or catch somebody or something 尽力赶上或抓到某人或某事物: *The police officer ran after her.* 警察追她。
after all 1 when you thought something different would happen 以为会出现另一种情况；毕竟；归根结底: *I was worried about the exam, but it wasn't difficult after all.* 我很担心这次考试，却原来并不困难。 **2** do not forget 不要忘记: *She doesn't understand. After all, she's only two.* 她不明白。别忘了，她才两岁。

after[2] /'ɑ:ftə(r); 'æftɚ/ *conjunction, adverb* 连词，副词
at a time later than somebody or something 比某人或某事物晚: *We arrived after the film had started.* 我们在电影开演以后才到。◇ *Jenny left at ten o'clock and I*

left soon after. 珍妮是十点钟离开的，过了一会儿我也走了。

afternoon /ˌɑːftəˈnuːn; ˌæftɚˈnun/ *noun* 名词
the part of a day between midday and the evening 从中午到晚上的这段时间；下午: *We had lunch and in the afternoon we went for a walk.* 我们吃了午饭，下午出去散了散步。◇ *I saw Jenny this afternoon.* 我今天下午看见珍妮了。◇ *Yesterday afternoon I went shopping.* 昨天下午我去买东西了。◇ *I'll see you on Monday afternoon.* 我星期一下午见你吧。

afterwards /ˈɑːftəwədz; ˈæftɚwɚdz/ *adverb* 副词
later 后来；然后；以后: *We had dinner and went to see a film afterwards.* 我们吃完饭以后去看了场电影。

again /əˈgen; əˈgɛn/ *adverb* 副词
1 one more time; once more 再一次；又一次；再；又: *Could you say that again, please?* 请再说一遍行吗？◇ *I will never see him again.* 我再也不见他了。
2 in the way that somebody or something was before 像某人或某事物以前的样子: *You'll soon feel well again.* 你很快就又会心情舒畅了。
again and again many times 很多次；一次又一次；再三: *I've told you again and again not to do that!* 我一再告诉你不要做那件事！

against /əˈgenst; əˈgɛnst/ *preposition* 介词
1 on the other side in a game, fight, etc 在游戏、争斗等的另一方；对着: *They played against a football team from another village.* 他们跟另一村的足球队比赛。
2 If you are against something, you do not like it 不喜欢；反对: *Many people are against the plan.* 很多人都反对这个计划。
3 next to and touching somebody or something 紧接着或接触某人或某事物: *Put the cupboard against the wall.* 把这个橱柜放在靠墙的地方。☞ picture on page C1 见第C1页图
4 to stop something 止住某事物；防止；预防: *Have you had an injection against the disease?* 你注射过这种疾病的预防针了吗？

age /eɪdʒ; edʒ/ *noun* 名词
1 (*plural* 复数作 **ages**) the amount of time that somebody or something has been in the world 某人或某事物在世界上存在的期间；年岁；年龄；年纪: *She is seven years of age.* 她七岁。◇ *I started work at the age of 16.* 我16岁时开始工作。✪ When you want to ask about somebody's age, you usually say 'How old are you?' 问人年纪时，通常说 How old are you?
2 (no plural 无复数) being old 老年；晚年: *Her hair was grey with age.* 她因为年老，头发已经花白了。
3 (*plural* 复数作 **ages**) a certain time in history 历史上的时期；年代: *the Stone Age* (= when people used stone tools) 石器时代（＝人类使用石头制造工具的时期）
4 ages (plural 复数) a very long time 很长的时间: *We waited ages for a bus.* 我们等公共汽车等了很长时间。◇ *She's lived here for ages.* 她在这儿住了很久了。

aged /eɪdʒd; edʒd/ *adjective* 形容词
at the age of 年龄…岁: *They have two children, aged three and five.* 他们有两个孩子，一个三岁一个五岁。

agency /ˈeɪdʒənsi; ˈedʒənsɪ/ *noun* 名词 (*plural* 复数作 **agencies**)
the work or office of somebody who does business for others 为别人做事的工作或处所；代理；代理处: *A travel agency plans holidays for people.* 旅行社专门给人安排度假活动。

agent /ˈeɪdʒənt; ˈedʒənt/ *noun* 名词
a person who does business for another person or for a company 为别人或别的公司做事的人；代理人；经理人: *An actor's agent tries to find work for actors and actresses.* 演员的经理人总是尽力为演员寻找工作。◇ *a travel agent* 旅行社经理人

aggressive /əˈgresɪv; əˈgrɛsɪv/ *adjective* 形容词
If you are aggressive, you are ready to argue or fight 好争吵或争斗的；侵略的: *He often gets aggressive after drinking alcohol.* 他喝过酒以后常常爱生事。

ago /əˈgəʊ; əˈgo/ *adverb* 副词
before now; in the past 以前；过去: *His wife died five years ago.* 他妻子在五年前死了。◇ *I learned to drive a long time ago.* 我很久以前就学会开车了。
long ago a very long time in the past 很久以前: *Long ago there were no cars or aeroplanes.* 很久以前没有汽车也没有飞机。

A

agony /ˈæɡəni; ˈæɡənɪ/ *noun* 名词 (*plural* 复数作 **agonies**)
very great pain 极大的痛苦: *He screamed in agony.* 他痛苦得尖声喊叫起来。

agree /əˈɡriː; əˈɡri/ *verb* 动词 (**agrees, agreeing, agreed** /əˈɡriːd; əˈɡrid/)
1 have the same idea as another person about something 在某事物上与某人持相同的意见: *Martin thinks we should go by train but I don't agree.* 马丁认为我们应该坐火车去，可是我不同意。◇ *I agree with you.* 我同意你的意见。✪ opposite 反义词: **disagree**
2 say 'yes' when somebody asks you to do something 赞成；同意: *Amy agreed to give me the money.* 埃米同意付给我钱。
3 decide something with another person 与别人约定某事物；商定: *We agreed to meet on March 3rd.* 我们约好3月3日见。◇ *Liz and I agreed on a plan.* 利兹和我商定好了一个计划。

agreement /əˈɡriːmənt; əˈɡrimənt/ *noun* 名词
1 (*plural* 复数作 **agreements**) a plan or decision that two or more people or countries have made together 人与人或国家与国家共同作出的计划或决定；协定；协议；合约: *There is a trade agreement between the two countries* (= they have agreed to buy things from and sell things to each other). 这两国之间有个贸易协定（= 他们同意彼此买卖东西）。
2 (no plural 无复数) having the same ideas as somebody or something 与某人或某事物有相同的意见；一致: *We talked about which film we wanted to see, but there was not much agreement.* 我们商量要看哪部电影，但是没有什么相同的想法。
✪ opposite 反义词: **disagreement**

agriculture /ˈæɡrɪkʌltʃə(r); ˈæɡrɪˌkʌltʃɚ/ *noun* 名词 (no plural 无复数)
keeping animals and growing plants for food; farming 养动物或种植物用作食物；农业
agricultural /ˌæɡrɪˈkʌltʃərəl; ˌæɡrɪˈkʌltʃərəl/ *adjective* 形容词
agricultural workers 农业工作者

ahead /əˈhed; əˈhɛd/ *adverb* 副词
1 in front of somebody or something 在某人或某事物的前面: *We could see a light ahead of us.* 我们看见前面有光。
2 into the future 到将来: *We must look ahead and make a plan.* 我们得向前看来制定计划。
3 doing better than other people 比别人做得好: *Fiona is ahead of the other students in her class.* 菲奥纳比班上其他同学功课好。
go ahead do something that you want to do; start to do something 做想做的事；开始做某事: *'Can I borrow your bicycle?' 'Yes, go ahead.'* "我借你的自行车用用，行吗？""行，用吧。"

aid /eɪd; ed/ *noun* 名词 (no plural 无复数)
help, or something that gives help 帮助；援助；有帮助的事物: *He walks with the aid of a stick.* 他借助拐杖走路。◇ *The government sent aid to the children of Ethiopia.* 政府给埃塞俄比亚儿童送去了援助物资。◇ *a hearing aid* (= a small thing that you put in your ear so you can hear better) 助听器
in aid of somebody or 或 **something** to get money for somebody or something 为某人或某事物收集钱: *There was a concert in aid of the new hospital.* 为这所新医院筹款举办了音乐会。

AIDS /eɪdz; edz/ *noun* 名词 (no plural 无复数)
a serious illness that stops the body protecting itself against diseases 艾滋病；爱滋病

aim[1] /eɪm; em/ *verb* 动词 (**aims, aiming, aimed** /eɪmd; emd/)
1 point something, for example a gun, at somebody or something that you want to hit 把某物（例如枪）对准要打的人或东西；瞄准: *The farmer aimed his gun at the rabbit and fired.* 那农民把枪对准了那只兔子，然后发射。
2 want or plan to do something 想要或计划做某事: *He's aiming to leave at nine o'clock.* 他打算九点钟离开。
3 plan something for a certain person or group 为某人或某部分人计划某事物: *This book is aimed at teenagers.* 这本书是为十几岁的青少年编写的。
aim *noun* 名词
something that you want and plan to do 想要的并且打算做的事物；目标；目的: *Kate's aim is to find a good job.* 凯特的目标是要找一份好工作。

air /eə(r); ɛr/ *noun* 名词 (no plural 无复数)
1 what you take in through your nose

A

and mouth when you breathe 空气
2 the space around and above things 空中；天空: *He threw the ball up in the air.* 他把球向空中扔去。
by air in an aircraft 坐飞机: *It's more expensive to travel by air than by train.* 坐飞机比坐火车贵。
on the air on the radio or on television（电台或电视）广播: *The programme will go on the air next month.* 这个节目将于下个月播出。

air-conditioning /ˈeə kənˌdɪʃnɪŋ; ˈɛr-kənˌdɪʃənɪŋ/ *noun* 名词 (no plural 无复数)
a way of keeping the air in a building dry and not too hot 空气调节（保持建筑物的空气干燥又不太热而使用的办法）
air-conditioned /ˈeə kənˌdɪʃnd; ˈɛr-kənˌdɪʃənd/ *adjective* 形容词
with air-conditioning 有空气调节的: *an air-conditioned office* 有空气调节的办公室

aircraft /ˈeəkrɑːft; ˈɛrˌkræft/ *noun* 名词 (*plural* 复数作 **aircraft**)
a machine that can fly, for example an aeroplane or a helicopter 飞行器（能够飞行的工具，例如普通飞机或直升飞机）

air force /ˈeə fɔːs; ˈɛr ˌfɔrs/ *noun* 名词
the aircraft that a country uses for fighting, and the people who fly them 空军（国家用于战斗的飞机和开飞机的人）

air-hostess /ˈeə həʊstəs; ˈɛrˌhostɪs/ *noun* 名词 (*plural* 复数作 **air-hostesses**)
a woman whose job is to look after people on an aeroplane 空中小姐；（客机上的）女乘务员: *Alison is an air-hostess.* 艾莉森是空中小姐。

airline /ˈeəlaɪn; ˈɛrˌlaɪn/ *noun* 名词
a company with aeroplanes that carry people or goods 航空公司（用飞机运送人或货物的公司）: *Lufthansa is a German airline.* ✻ Lufthansa 是德国的航空公司。

airmail /ˈeəmeɪl; ˈɛrˌmel/ *noun* 名词 (no plural 无复数)
a way of sending letters and parcels by aeroplane 空邮（用飞机运送信件和包裹的方法）: *an airmail letter* 航空信

airplane /ˈeərpleɪn; ˈɛrˌplen/ *American English for* **aeroplane** 美式英语，即 **aeroplane**

airport /ˈeəpɔːt; ˈɛrˌpɔrt/ *noun* 名词
a place where people get on and off aeroplanes, with buildings where passengers can wait 飞机场（上下飞机的地方，设有供乘客等候飞机的建筑物）: *I'll meet you at the airport.* 我在机场见你吧。

aisle /aɪl; aɪl/ *noun* 名词
a way between lines of seats, for example in a church or theatre（成排座位之间的）走道（例如教堂或戏院中的）

alarm[1] /əˈlɑːm; əˈlɑrm/ *noun* 名词
1 (no plural 无复数) a sudden feeling of fear 突然害怕的感觉；惊慌: *He heard a noise, and jumped out of bed in alarm.* 他听见声响，慌忙从床上下来。
2 (*plural* 复数作 **alarms**) something that tells you about danger, for example by making a loud noise 能发出有危险信号的器具（例如发出大的声音）；警报: *Does your car have an alarm?* 你的汽车有警报器吗？
3 an alarm clock 闹钟

alarm[2] /əˈlɑːm; əˈlɑrm/ *verb* 动词 (**alarms**, **alarming**, **alarmed** /əˈlɑːmd; əˈlɑrmd/)
make somebody or something suddenly feel afraid or worried 使某人或某事物突然感到害怕或担心；惊吓: *The noise alarmed the bird and it flew away.* 那个声音把鸟吓飞了。◇ *She was alarmed to hear that Peter was ill.* 她听说彼得病了，大吃一惊。

alarm clock /əˈlɑːm klɒk; əˈlɑrm klɑk/ *noun* 名词
a clock that makes a noise to wake you up 闹钟（能发出声响把人吵醒的钟）

alarm clock 闹钟

album /ˈælbəm; ˈælbəm/ *noun* 名词
1 a cassette, compact disc or record with about 50 minutes of music on it 有约50分钟音乐的盒式带、激光唱片或普通唱片: *Have you heard this album?* 你听过这张唱片吗？☞ Look at **single.** 见 **single**。
2 a book with empty pages where you can put photographs or stamps, for example（用以存放照片或邮票之类的）空白本子: *a photograph album* 相册

alcohol /ˈælkəhɒl; ˈælkəˌhɔl/ *noun* 名词 (no plural 无复数)
1 the liquid in drinks, for example wine, beer or whisky, that can make people feel drunk 能使人醉的饮料（例如葡萄酒、啤酒或威士忌）中的某种液体；酒精
2 drinks like wine, beer or whisky 酒（葡萄酒、啤酒或威士忌之类的饮料）

alcoholic /ˌælkəˈhɒlɪk; ˌælkəˈhɔlɪk/ *adjective* 形容词
an alcoholic drink 酒类饮料

ale /eɪl; el/ *noun* 名词 (no plural 无复数)
beer 啤酒 ✪ **Beer** is the more usual word. ✻ **beer** 是常用字。

alert[1] /əˈlɜːt; əˈlɝt/ *adjective* 形容词
awake and ready to do things 清醒而随时准备行动的；警觉的；机警的: *A good driver is always alert.* 好的司机时刻都很机警。

alert[2] /əˈlɜːt; əˈlɝt/ *noun* 名词
a warning of danger 警报（将有危险到来的警告）: *There was a bomb alert at the station.* 车站有个炸弹要爆炸的警报。

A level /ˈeɪ levl; ˈe lɛvḷ/ *noun* 名词
an examination in one subject that children at schools in England, Wales and Northern Ireland take when they are 18（英国普通教育文凭的）高级证书考试（英格兰、威尔士和北爱尔兰学校里18岁的学生参加的考试） ✪ 'A level' is short for **Advanced level**. ✻ A level 是 **Advanced level** 的缩略式。

alien /ˈeɪliən; ˈelɪən/ *noun* 名词
a person or an animal that comes from another planet in space 从别的星球上来的人或动物；外星人

alight /əˈlaɪt; əˈlaɪt/ *adjective* 形容词
on fire; burning 烧着的；燃烧的: *A fire started in the kitchen and soon the whole house was alight.* 厨房里先着了火，很快整座房子都烧了起来。
set something alight make something start to burn 使某物开始燃烧；点燃某物: *The petrol was set alight by a cigarette.* 汽油被香烟点着了。

alike /əˈlaɪk; əˈlaɪk/ *adjective* 形容词
almost the same; not different 差不多相同的；一样的；相似的: *The two sisters are very alike.* 这对姐妹长得很像。
alike *adverb* 副词
in the same way 同样地: *The twins always dress alike* (= wear the same clothes). 这对双胞胎总是穿一样的（= 穿戴同样的衣物）。

alive /əˈlaɪv; əˈlaɪv/ *adjective* 形容词
living; not dead 活着的；没死的: *Are your grandparents alive?* 你的祖父母还健在吗？

all[1] /ɔːl; ɔl/ *adjective, pronoun* 形容词，代词
1 every one of a group 一群中的每一个；所有的；全体: *All cats are animals but not all animals are cats.* 所有的猫都是动物，但是并非所有的动物都是猫。◇ *I invited thirty people to the party, but not all of them came.* 我邀请了三十人参加聚会，可是并不是所有的人都来了。◇ *Are you all listening?* 你们大家都注意听着呢吗？
2 every part of something; the whole of something 某事物的每一部分；全部；整体: *She's eaten all the bread.* 她把面包都吃了。◇ *It rained all day.* 雨下了一整天。

all[2] /ɔːl; ɔl/ *adverb* 副词
completely 完全；一切: *She lives all alone.* 她完全是独自生活。◇ *He was dressed all in black.* 他穿着一身黑衣服。
all along from the beginning 从开始起就: *I knew all along that she was lying.* 我从一开始就知道她在撒谎。

alley /ˈæli; ˈælɪ/ *noun* 名词 (*plural* 复数作 **alleys**)
a narrow path between two buildings 两座建筑物之间的狭窄通道；胡同；小巷

alliance /əˈlaɪəns; əˈlaɪəns/ *noun* 名词
an agreement between countries or people to work together and help each other 国与国或人与人之间一道工作、互相帮助的协定；联盟；同盟

alligator /ˈælɪgeɪtə(r); ˈæləˌgetɚ/ *noun* 名词
a big long animal with sharp teeth. Alligators live in and near rivers in hot parts of the world. 鳄鱼；短吻鳄

allow /əˈlaʊ; əˈlaʊ/ *verb* 动词 (**allows, allowing, allowed** /əˈlaʊd; əˈlaʊd/)
say that somebody can have or do something 说出某人可以有某事物或做某事物；允许；许可；准许: *My parents allow me to stay out late at weekends.* 我父母允许我周末晚点儿回家。◇ *Smoking is not allowed in most cinemas.* 大部分电影院里都不准吸烟。◇ *You're not allowed to park your car here.* 不准在这儿停放汽车。

all right /ˌɔːl ˈraɪt; ˌɔl ˈraɪt/ *adjective* 形容词
1 good or good enough 好的；还好的: *Is everything all right?* 一切都好吗？
2 well; not hurt 健康的: *I was ill, but I'm all right now.* 我生了病，可是现在病好了。
3 yes, I agree 行；我同意: *'Let's go home now.' 'All right.'* "咱们回家吧。""好吧。"

ally /ˈælaɪ; ˈælaɪ/ *noun* 名词 (*plural* 复数作 **allies**)
a person or country that agrees to help

another person or country, for example in a war 同意帮助另一人或另一国这样的人或国家（例如在战争中）；同盟者；同盟国

almond /'ɑ:mənd; 'ɑmənd/ *noun* 名词
a nut that you can eat 杏仁

almost /'ɔ:lməʊst; 'ɔlˌmost/ *adverb* 副词
nearly; not quite 差不多；差一点儿: *It's almost three o'clock.* 差不多三点钟了。◇ *I almost fell into the river!* 我差一点儿掉进河里！

alone /ə'ləʊn; ə'lon/ *adverb* 副词
1 without any other person 没有别的人；独自；单独: *I don't like being alone in the house.* 我不喜欢一个人呆在房子里。◇ *My grandmother lives alone.* 我的祖母独自生活。
2 only 只有: *You alone can help me.* 只有你才能帮助我。

along[1] /ə'lɒŋ; ə'lɔŋ/ *preposition* 介词
1 from one end of something towards the other end 从某物的一头到另一头；沿着；顺着: *We walked along the road.* 我们沿着那条路走。☞ picture on page C4 见第C4页图
2 in a line next to something long 在靠近某物的长边的线上: *There are trees along the river bank.* 河的沿岸长着树。

along[2] /ə'lɒŋ; ə'lɔŋ/ *adverb* 副词
1 forward 向前: *He drove along very slowly.* 他慢慢向前开着车。
2 with me, you, etc 同某人（我、你等）一起: *We're going to the cinema. Why don't you come along too?* 我们要去看电影。你也和我们一起去吗？

alongside /ə'lɒŋsaɪd; ə'lɔŋ'saɪd/ *preposition* 介词
next to something 紧挨着某物；靠着: *Put your bike alongside mine.* 把你的自行车放在我的自行车旁边儿吧。

aloud /ə'laʊd; ə'laʊd/ *adverb* 副词
speaking so that other people can hear 说话能让别人听见；出声地: *I read the story aloud to my sister.* 我给妹妹读这个故事听。

alphabet /'ælfəbet; 'ælfəˌbɛt/ *noun* 名词
all the letters of a language 一种语言的所有的字母；字母表: *The English alphabet starts with A and ends with Z.* 英语字母从A开始到Z结束。

alphabetical /ˌælfə'betɪkl; ˌælfə'bɛtɪkḷ/ *adjective* 形容词
in the order of the alphabet 按字母顺序的: *Put these words in alphabetical order* (= with words beginning with A first, then B, then C, etc). 把这些字按字母顺序排列起来（= 开头是A的字、然后是B的字、然后是C的字等）。

already /ɔ:l'redi; ɔl'rɛdɪ/ *adverb* 副词
before now or before then 以前；那时以前；已经: *'Would you like something to eat.' 'No, thank you—I've already eaten.'* "你想吃点儿东西吗？""不想吃，谢谢你——我已经吃过了。" ◇ *We ran to the station but the train had already left.* 我们跑到车站，可是火车已经开走了。

> **already** and **yet** ＊ **already** 和 **yet** 的用法
>
> **Yet** means the same as **already**, but you only use it in negative sentences and in questions ＊ **yet** 的意思和 **already** 一样，但是只用于否定句和疑问句中:
>
> *I have finished this book* ***already***. 我已经看完这本书了。
>
> *I haven't finished this book* ***yet***. 我还没看完这本书呢。
>
> *Have you finished this book* ***yet***? 你看完这本书了吗？

alright /ˌɔ:l'raɪt; ɔl'raɪt/ = **all right**

also /'ɔ:lsəʊ; 'ɔlso/ *adverb* 副词
as well; too 也；还: *She speaks French and she is also learning Spanish.* 她会说法语，她还学着西班牙语呢。

alter /'ɔ:ltə(r); 'ɔltɚ/ *verb* 动词 (**alters, altering, altered** /'ɔ:ltəd; 'ɔltɚd/)
1 become different; change 改变；变化
2 make something different; change something 更改或修改某事物；改动: *These trousers are too long—I'm going to alter them* (= make them shorter by sewing). 这条裤子太长——我要改一改（= 缝短些）。

alteration /ˌɔ:ltə'reɪʃn; ˌɔltə'reʃən/ *noun* 名词
a small change 小的改变、更改、修改或改动

alternate /ɔ:l'tɜ:nət; 'ɔltɚnɪt/ *adjective* 形容词
first one and then the other 先是一个，然后是另一个；倒换的；交替的: *At school we have English and German lessons on alternate days* (= English on Mondays, German on Tuesdays, English again on

Wednesdays, etc). 我们上学的时候，隔日交替上英语和德语课（= 星期一英语、星期二德语、星期三又是英语，以此类推）。

alternative[1] /ɔ:l'tɜ:nətɪv; ɔl'tɝnətɪv/ *adjective* 形容词
different; other 别的；其他的: *We have no theatre tickets for the first of June — can you choose an alternative date?* 剧院没有六月一日的票——您另选一天行吗？

alternative[2] /ɔ:l'tɜ:nətɪv; ɔl'tɝnətɪv/ *noun* 名词
a thing that you can choose instead of another thing 可替换另一事物的事物: *We could go by train — the alternative is to take the car.* 我们可以坐火车去——另一个方法是坐汽车去。

although /ɔ:l'ðəʊ; ɔl'ðo/ *conjunction* 连词
1 in spite of something; though 虽然；尽管；即使: *Although she was ill, she went to work.* 她虽然病了，但是还是上班去了。◇ *I bought the shoes although they were expensive.* 尽管这双鞋很贵，我还是买了。
2 but 但是；可是；不过: *I think he's from Sweden, although I'm not sure.* 我认为他是瑞典人，可是我并没有把握。

altogether /ˌɔ:ltə'geðə(r); ˌɔltə'gɛðɚ/ *adverb* 副词
1 counting everything or everybody 把每个事物或每个人都计算在内；总共；一共: *Chris gave me £3 and Simon gave me £4, so I've got £7 altogether.* 克里斯给我3英镑，西蒙给我4英镑，我一共得到7英镑。
2 completely 完全；全部: *I don't altogether agree with you.* 我并不完全同意你的意见。

aluminium /ˌæljə'mɪnɪəm; ˌæljə'mɪnɪəm/ *noun* 名词 (no plural 无复数)
a light metal 铝

aluminum /ə'lu:mɪnəm; ə'lumɪnəm/ *American English for* **aluminium** 美式英语，即 **aluminium**

always /'ɔ:lweɪz; 'ɔlwez/ *adverb* 副词
1 at all times; every time 总是；一直；每次: *I have always lived in London.* 我一直都住在伦敦。◇ *The train is always late.* 这列火车总晚点。
2 for ever 永远: *I will always remember that day.* 我永远记住那一天。
3 again and again 一次又一次；次次: *My sister is always borrowing my clothes!* 我妹妹老是借我的衣服穿！

am *form of* **be** ✳ **be** 的不同形式

a.m. /ˌeɪ 'em; 'e 'ɛm/
You use 'a.m.' after a time to show that it is between midnight and midday 用于时间词之后，表示从半夜到中午的时间；午前；上午: *I start work at 9 a.m.* 我早晨9点钟上班。✪ We use **p.m.** for times between midday and midnight. 用 **p.m.** 表示从中午到半夜的时间。

amateur /'æmətə(r); 'æməˌtɝ/ *noun* 名词
a person who does something because he/she enjoys it, but does not get money for it 出于爱好而做某事（并不从中得到钱）的人；业余爱好者
amateur *adjective* 形容词
an amateur photographer 业余摄影爱好者
☞ Look at **professional**. 见 **professional**。

amaze /ə'meɪz; ə'mez/ *verb* 动词 (**amazes**, **amazing**, **amazed** /ə'meɪzd; ə'mezd/)
make somebody very surprised 使某人非常惊奇: *Matthew amazed me by remembering my birthday.* 马修记得我的生日，真叫我惊讶。
amazed *adjective* 形容词
If you are amazed, you are very surprised 非常吃惊的: *I was amazed to see John — I thought he was in Canada.* 我看见约翰而大吃一惊——我还以为他在加拿大呢。
amazement /ə'meɪzmənt; ə'mezmənt/ *noun* 名词 (no plural 无复数)
great surprise 非常惊奇: *She looked at me in amazement.* 她十分惊奇地看着我。
amazing *adjective* 形容词
If something is amazing, it surprises you very much 令人惊奇的: *She told us an amazing story.* 她给我们讲了一个很离奇的故事。
amazingly *adverb* 副词
Jo plays the violin amazingly well. 乔拉小提琴拉得好极了。

ambassador /æm'bæsədə(r); æm'bæsədɚ/ *noun* 名词
an important person who goes to another country and works there for the government of his/her own country 大使（代表国家到另一国工作的重要人物）: *the British Ambassador to Germany* 英国驻德国大使 ✪ An ambassador works in an **embassy**. 大使馆叫做 **embassy**。

A

ambition /æmˈbɪʃn; æmˈbɪʃən/ *noun* 名词
1 (no plural 无复数) a very strong wish to do well 要好好干的强烈愿望；雄心；志气；野心: *Louise is intelligent, but she has no ambition.* 路易丝很聪明，可是她胸无大志。
2 something that you want to do 想要做的事；抱负: *My ambition is to become a doctor.* 我的志向是要当医生。

ambitious /æmˈbɪʃəs; æmˈbɪʃəs/ *adjective* 形容词
A person who is ambitious wants to do well. 有雄心的；有志气的；有抱负的；有野心的

ambulance /ˈæmbjələns; ˈæmbjələns/ *noun* 名词
a special van that takes people who are ill or hurt to hospital 救护车（把伤病人员运送到医院去的专用汽车）

ammunition /ˌæmjəˈnɪʃn; ˌæmjəˈnɪʃən/ *noun* 名词 (no plural 无复数)
things that you throw or fire from a gun to hurt or damage people or things 弹药（从枪炮中射出的或用手扔出的用以伤害人或破坏物体的东西）: *The plane was carrying ammunition to the soldiers.* 那架飞机装载着给士兵运送的弹药。

among /əˈmʌŋ; əˈmʌŋ/, **amongst** /əˈmʌŋst; əˈmʌŋst/ *preposition* 介词
1 in the middle of 在…的中间: *The house stands among the trees.* 那所房子在那些树的中间。☞ picture on page C1 见第C1页图
2 for or by more than two things or people 对两个以上的东西或人；由两个以上的东西或人: *He divided the money amongst his six children.* 他把钱分给了六个子女。

> **among** or **between**? 用 **among** 还是用 **between**？
>
> We use **among** and **amongst** when we are talking about more than two people or things. 谈到不止两个人或两个事物时用 **among** 和 **amongst**。If there are only two people or things, we use **between** 要是只有两个人或两个事物就要用 **between**:
>
> *Sarah and I divided the cake between us.* 我和萨拉把那块糕点分了。
>
> *I was standing between Alice and Kathy.* 我站在艾丽斯和凯西中间。

amount[1] /əˈmaʊnt; əˈmaunt/ *noun* 名词
how much there is of something 数量: *He spent a large amount of money.* 他花了很多钱。

amount[2] /əˈmaʊnt; əˈmaunt/ *verb* 动词 (**amounts**, **amounting**, **amounted**)
amount to something make a certain amount when you put everything together 把所有的都放在一起的数量；总数；总和: *The cost of the repairs amounted to £500.* 修理费共计500英镑。

amp /æmp; æmp/ *noun* 名词
a measure of electricity 安培（电流的计量单位）

amplifier /ˈæmplɪfaɪə(r); ˈæmpləˌfaɪɚ/ *noun* 名词
an electrical machine that makes sounds louder 扩音器（能把声音扩大的电器）

amuse /əˈmju:z; əˈmjuz/ *verb* 动词 (**amuses**, **amusing**, **amused** /əˈmju:zd; əˈmjuzd/)
1 make somebody smile or laugh 使某人发笑；逗某人笑: *Rick's joke did not amuse his mother.* 里克讲的笑话并没把他母亲逗乐。
2 keep somebody happy and busy 使某人一直愉快而不闲着: *We played games to amuse ourselves on the long journey.* 我们在长途行程中做游戏玩儿。

amusement /əˈmju:zmənt; əˈmjuzmənt/ *noun* 名词 (no plural 无复数)
the feeling that you have when you think something is funny 认为某事物可笑的这种感觉；快乐: *We watched in amusement as the dog chased its tail.* 我们快活地看着那条狗追着自己的尾巴。

amusing /əˈmju:zɪŋ; əˈmjuzɪŋ/ *adjective* 形容词
Something that is amusing makes you smile or laugh 使人欢笑的；逗乐的: *Jenny told me an amusing story.* 珍妮给我讲了一个可笑的故事。

an /ən, æn; ən, æn/ *article* 冠词
1 one or any 一个或任何一个: *I ate an apple.* 我吃了一个苹果。
2 each, or for each 每一个；对每一个: *It costs £2 an hour to park your car here.* 在这里停放汽车每小时2英镑。
☞ Note at **a** 见 **a** 词条注释

anaesthetic /ˌænəsˈθetɪk; ˌænəsˈθɛtɪk/ *noun* 名词
something that a doctor gives you so that you will not feel pain in an

operation 麻醉剂（手术叫做 **operation**）

ancestor /ˈænsestə(r); ˈænsɛstɚ/ *noun* 名词
Your ancestors are the people in your family who lived a long time before you 祖宗；祖先（家族很久以前的上辈）：*My ancestors came from Norway.* 我的祖先是挪威人。

anchor /ˈæŋkə(r); ˈæŋkɚ/ *noun* 名词
a heavy metal thing that you drop into the water from a boat to stop the boat moving away 锚（沉重的铁器，可以从船上放进水中让船停住不动）

ancient /ˈeɪnʃənt; ˈenʃənt/ *adjective* 形容词
very old; from a time long ago 很老的；很久以前的；古代的：*ancient buildings* 古代的建筑物

and /ənd, ænd; ənd, ænd/ *conjunction* 连词
a word that joins words or parts of sentences together（连接两个词、词组或句子的词）和；跟；与；而且；但是：*fish and chips* 鱼和炸土豆条儿 ◇ *They sang and danced all evening.* 他们整个晚上又唱歌又跳舞。◇ *The cat was black and white.* 那只猫是黑白花猫。

anesthetic *American English for* **anaesthetic** 美式英语，即 **anaesthetic**

angel /ˈeɪndʒl; ˈendʒəl/ *noun* 名词
a messenger that comes from God. In pictures, angels usually have wings. 天使（上帝的使者，在图画中的天使一般有翅膀）。

anger /ˈæŋɡə(r); ˈæŋɡɚ/ *noun* 名词 (no plural 无复数)
the strong feeling that you have when you are not pleased about something 怒气（对某事物不愉快时的强烈感情）：*He was filled with anger when he saw the boy trying to steal his car.* 他看见有个男孩子正在偷他的汽车，十分气愤。

angle /ˈæŋɡl; ˈæŋɡl̩/ *noun* 名词
the space between two lines that meet 角（两条线相交形成的空间）：*an angle of 40°* ＊40°的角 ☞ picture on page C5 见第C5页图

angry /ˈæŋɡri; ˈæŋɡrɪ/ *adjective* 形容词 (**angrier, angriest**)
If you are angry, you feel or show anger 生气的；愤怒的：*My father was angry with me when I got home late.* 我回家很晚，父亲对我十分生气。

angrily /ˈæŋɡrəli; ˈæŋɡrəlɪ/ *adverb* 副词
'Somebody has taken my book!' she shouted angrily. “有人把我的书拿走了！”她生气地喊道。

animal /ˈænɪml; ˈænəml̩/ *noun* 名词
1 any living thing that is not a plant 动物（除去植物以外的一切生物）
2 any living thing that is not a bird, fish, insect, reptile or human 四足动物；兽；牲畜（除去植物、鸟、鱼、虫、爬行动物或人以外的一切生物）：*Cats, horses and rats are animals.* 猫、马、老鼠都属于兽类。

ankle /ˈæŋkl; ˈæŋkl̩/ *noun* 名词
the part of your leg where it joins your foot 脚腕子（小腿和脚接连的部分）☞ picture on page C2 见第C2页图

anniversary /ˌænɪˈvɜːsəri; ˌænəˈvɝsərɪ/ *noun* 名词 (*plural* 复数作 **anniversaries**)
a day when you remember something special that happened on the same day in another year 周年纪念日（纪念某年同一天发生的特殊事情的日子）：*Today is their 25th wedding anniversary.* 今天是他们结婚25年纪念日。

announce /əˈnaʊns; əˈnaʊns/ *verb* 动词 (**announces, announcing, announced** /əˈnaʊnst; əˈnaʊnst/)
tell a lot of people about something important 把重要的事情告诉大家；宣布；宣告：*The teacher announced the winner of the competition.* 老师宣布了谁是竞赛的优胜者。◇ *She announced that she was going to have a baby.* 她告诉大家她快生孩子了。

announcement /əˈnaʊnsmənt; əˈnaʊnsmənt/ *noun* 名词
telling people about something 宣布；宣告；通告：*I have an important announcement to make.* 我要宣布一项重要事情。

announcer /əˈnaʊnsə(r); əˈnaʊnsɚ/ *noun* 名词
a person whose job is to tell us about programmes on radio or television（电台或电视广播的）广播员；播音员

annoy /əˈnɔɪ; əˈnɔɪ/ *verb* 动词 (**annoys, annoying, annoyed** /əˈnɔɪd; əˈnɔɪd/)
make somebody a little angry 使某人有些生气；惹恼：*My brother annoys me when he leaves his clothes all over the floor.* 我弟弟真气人，他把他的衣服扔得满地都是。

A

annoyance /ə'nɔɪəns; ə'nɔɪəns/ *noun* 名词 (no plural 无复数)
the feeling of being a little angry 有些生气的感觉；烦恼: *She could not hide her annoyance when I arrived late.* 我来晚了，她流露出不高兴的样子。

annoyed *adjective* 形容词
a little angry 有些生气的；不高兴的: *I was annoyed when he forgot to phone me.* 他忘了给我打电话了，我很不痛快。◇ *My dad is annoyed with me.* 我爸爸生我的气了。

annoying *adjective* 形容词
If a person or thing is annoying, he/she/it makes you a little angry 惹人生气的；让人烦恼的: *It's annoying when people don't listen to you.* 你说话大家不注意听，真叫人生气。

annual /'ænjuəl; 'ænjʊəl/ *adjective* 形容词
1 that happens or comes once every year 每年发生或来到一次的；一年一次的: *There is an annual meeting in June.* 六月份有个年度会议。
2 for one year 一年的: *What is your annual income?* (= How much money do you get for one year's work?) 你一年的收入是多少？（= 你工作一年得到多少钱？）

annually /'ænjuəli; 'ænjʊəlɪ/ *adverb* 副词
The company makes 50 000 cars annually. 这个公司每年制造50 000辆汽车。

anonymous /ə'nɒnɪməs; ə'nɑnəməs/ *adjective* 形容词
1 If a person is anonymous, other people do not know his/her name 不知道姓名的: *An anonymous caller told the police about the robbery.* 有个未透露姓名的人把抢劫的事打电话告诉警方了。
2 If something is anonymous, you do not know who did, gave or made it 不知道是谁干的、给的或做的: *She received an anonymous letter.* 她收到了一封匿名信。

anorak /'ænəræk; 'ænəˌræk/ *noun* 名词
a short coat with a part (called a **hood**) that covers your head 带有风帽（叫做 **hood**）的短外套

another /ə'nʌðə(r); ə'nʌðɚ/ *adjective, pronoun* 形容词，代词
1 one more thing or person 再有一个事物或人；又一；再一: *Would you like another drink?* 你要再来一杯吗？◇ *I like these cakes — can I have another one?* 我很喜欢这种糕点，能再来一块吗？
2 a different thing or person 不是同一个的事物或人；另一: *I can't see you tomorrow — can we meet another day?* 我明天不能见你——改天行吗？◇ *I've read this book. Do you have another?* 我看过这本书了。你还有别的吗？

answer[1] /'ɑ:nsə(r); 'ænsɚ/ *verb* 动词 (**answers**, **answering**, **answered** /'ɑ:nsəd; 'ænsɚd/)
1 say or write something when somebody has asked a question 回答；答复；作答: *I asked him if he was hungry but he didn't answer.* 我问他饿不饿，他没回答。◇ *I couldn't answer all the exam questions.* 考试题我不完全会答。
2 write a letter to somebody who has written to you 回信: *She didn't answer my letter.* 她没有给我回信。

answer the door open the door when somebody knocks or rings（有人敲门或按门铃时）开门；应门: *Can you answer the door, please?* 请你去开门看谁来了，行吗？

answer the telephone pick up the telephone when it rings, and speak 接电话: *His job is to type letters and answer the telephone.* 他负责打字和接电话的工作。

answer[2] /'ɑ:nsə(r); 'ænsɚ/ *noun* 名词
1 something that you say or write when you answer somebody（说出的或写出的）回答；答复；答案；回信: *I asked Lucy a question but she didn't give me an answer.* 我问露西一个问题，可是她没回答。◇ *Have you had an answer to your letter?* 你收到回信了吗？
2 a way of stopping a problem 解决问题的办法: *If you are tired, the answer is to go to bed early!* 要是累了，有个办法是早点儿睡觉！

answerphone /'ɑ:nsəfəʊn; 'ænsɚˌfon/, **answering machine** /'ɑ:nsərɪŋ məʃi:n; 'ænsərɪŋ mə'ʃin/ *noun* 名词
a machine that answers the telephone for you and keeps messages so that you can listen to them later 电话录音机: *He wasn't at home, so I left a message on his answerphone.* 他没在家，我在他的电话录音机里给他留了个话儿。

ant /ænt; ænt/ *noun* 名词
a very small insect that lives in big groups 蚂蚁

A

antelope /ˈæntɪləʊp; ˈæntḷop/ *noun* 名词
a wild animal with horns and long thin legs, that can run fast 羚羊

anti /ˈænti; ˈæntɪ/ *prefix* 前缀
anti- at the beginning of a word often means 'against' ＊ **anti-** 位于一个字的开头，意思常为"反"：
an anti-smoking campaign 反吸烟运动

anticipate /ænˈtɪsɪpeɪt; ænˈtɪsəˌpet/ *verb* 动词 (**anticipates**, **anticipating**, **anticipated**)
think that something will happen and be ready for it 认为某事要发生而做好准备: *We didn't anticipate so many problems.* 我们没预料到有这么多问题而没有准备。

anticlockwise /ˌæntiˈklɒkwaɪz; ˌæntɪˈklɑkwaɪz/ *adjective, adverb* 形容词，副词
When something moves anticlockwise, it moves in the opposite direction to the hands of a clock. 与时针运转方向相反(的)；反时针(的)

antique /ænˈtiːk; ænˈtik/ *noun* 名词
an old thing that is worth a lot of money 古董；古玩: *These chairs are antiques.* 这些椅子是古董。
antique *adjective* 形容词
an antique vase 古董花瓶

anxiety /æŋˈzaɪəti; æŋˈzaɪətɪ/ *noun* 名词 (*plural* 复数作 **anxieties**)
a feeling of worry and fear 忧虑；担心；焦虑

anxious /ˈæŋkʃəs; ˈæŋkʃəs/ *adjective* 形容词
1 worried and afraid 忧虑的；担心的；焦虑的: *She's anxious because her daughter hasn't arrived yet.* 她女儿还没有到，她很担心。
2 If you are anxious to do something, you want to do it very much 急切想做某事物: *My family are anxious to meet you.* 我家里的人都非常想见你。
anxiously *adverb* 副词
We waited anxiously. 我们担心地等着。

any /ˈeni; ˈɛnɪ/ *adjective, pronoun* 形容词，代词
1 a word that you use in questions and after 'not' and 'if'; some 用于疑问句中或用于 not 和 if 之后；任何: *Have you got any money?* 你有钱吗？◇ *I don't speak any Spanish.* 我不会说西班牙语。◇ *She asked if I had any milk.* 她问我有牛奶没有。◇ *I want some chocolate but there isn't any.* 我想要些巧克力，可是没有。
2 no special one 非特指的一个；无论哪个: *Come any day next week.* 下星期随便哪一天来吧。◇ *Take any book you want.* 你想拿哪本书就拿哪本书。
any *adverb* 副词
a little 一点儿: *I can't walk any faster.* 我无法走得再快点儿了。

anybody /ˈenibɒdi; ˈɛnɪˌbɑdɪ/, **anyone** /ˈeniwʌn; ˈɛnɪˌwʌn/ *pronoun* 代词
1 any person 任何人: *There wasn't anybody there.* 那儿什么人都没有。◇ *Did you see anyone you know?* 你看见你认识的人了吗？
2 no special person 非特指的人；无论谁: *Anybody* (= all people) *can play this game.* 谁（= 大家）都可以做这个游戏。

anything /ˈeniθɪŋ; ˈɛnɪˌθɪŋ/ *pronoun* 代词
1 a thing of any kind 任何事物: *Is there anything in that box?* 那个箱子里有东西吗？◇ *I can't see anything.* 我什么都看不见。
2 no special thing 非特指的事物；无论什么事物: *'What would you like to drink?' 'Oh, anything. I don't mind.'* "你想喝什么？""噢，什么都行，无所谓。"
anything else something more 其他的: *'Would you like anything else?' asked the waitress.* "你还想要什么？"女服务员问道。
anything like the same as somebody or something in any way 有些像某人或某事物: *She isn't anything like her sister.* 她一点儿都不像她姐姐。

anyway /ˈeniweɪ; ˈɛnɪˌwe/, **anyhow** /ˈenihaʊ; ˈɛnɪˌhaʊ/ *adverb* 副词
1 a word that you use when you give a second reason for something 对某事物提出第二点理由时用的词；再说；况且: *I don't want to see the film and anyhow I haven't got any money.* 我不想看那部电影，再说我也没钱。
2 no matter what is true; however 即使如此；无论如何；反正: *It was very expensive but she bought it anyway.* 那个东西很贵，可是她还是买了。

3 a word that you use when you start to talk about something different 转变话题用的词: *That's what John said to me. Anyway, how are you?* 这是约翰说的。对了，你现在怎么样？

anywhere /'eniweə(r); 'ɛnɪˌhwɛr/ *adverb* 副词

1 at, in or to any place 在任何地方；到任何地方；无论哪里: *Are you going anywhere this summer?* 你今年夏天要到哪儿去吗？◇ *I can't find my pen anywhere.* 我哪儿也找不着我的钢笔了。

2 no special place 非特指的地方: *'Where shall I sit?' 'Oh, anywhere—it doesn't matter.'* "我坐在哪儿呢？""噢，哪儿都行——无所谓。"

apart /ə'pɑ:t; ə'pɑrt/ *adverb* 副词

1 away from the others; away from each other 与其他的相离；互相分开: *The two houses are 500 metres apart.* 这两所房子相隔500米。◇ *My mother and father live apart now.* 我母亲和我父亲分开生活。

2 into parts 成为各部分: *He took my radio apart to repair it.* 他把我的收音机拆开来修理。

apart from somebody or 或 **something** if you do not count somebody or something 不把某人或某事物计算在内: *There were ten people in the room, apart from me.* 屋子里有十个人，不算我。◇ *I like all vegetables apart from carrots.* 除了胡萝卜以外，我什么蔬菜都爱吃。

apartment /ə'pɑ:tmənt; ə'pɑrtmənt/ *American English for* **flat**[1] 美式英语，即 **flat**[1]

ape /eɪp; ep/ *noun* 名词

an animal like a big monkey with no tail 猿；猩猩: *Gorillas and chimpanzees are apes.* 大猩猩和黑猩猩都是猿。

apologize /ə'pɒlədʒaɪz; ə'pɑləˌdʒaɪz/ *verb* 动词 (**apologizes**, **apologizing**, **apologized** /ə'pɒlədʒaɪzd; ə'pɑləˌdʒaɪzd/)

say that you are sorry about something that you have done 道歉；赔不是: *I apologized to John for losing his book.* 我把约翰的书给丢了，向他道了歉。

apology /ə'pɒlədʒi; ə'pɑlədʒɪ/ *noun* 名词 (*plural* 复数作 **apologies**)

words that you say or write to show that you are sorry about something you have done 道歉；认错: *Please accept my apologies.* 我向你道歉。

apostrophe /ə'pɒstrəfi; ə'pɑstrəfɪ/ *noun* 名词

the sign (') that you use in writing. （书写时用的）撇号（'）。You use it to show that you have left a letter out of a word, for example in 'I'm' (I am). 用以表示一字中省略了一个字母，如 I'm (I am)。You also use it to show that something belongs to somebody or something, for example in 'the boy's room'. 还用以表示某事物属于某人或某事物，如 the boy's room（那个男孩儿的房间）。

appalling /ə'pɔ:lɪŋ; ə'pɔlɪŋ/ *adjective* 形容词

very bad; terrible 极坏的；糟糕的: *appalling cruelty* 极其残忍

apparent /ə'pærənt; ə'pærənt/ *adjective* 形容词

easy to see or understand; clear 容易看见或理解的；清楚的: *It was apparent that she didn't like him.* 很明显，她不喜欢他。

apparently *adverb* 副词

1 You use 'apparently' to talk about what another person said, when you do not know if it is true 用 apparently 表示别人说的话你不知道是否属实: *Apparently, she has a big house and three cars.* 据说，她有一所大房子和三辆汽车。

2 it seems 看来；似乎: *He went to school today, so he's apparently feeling better.* 他今天上学去了，看来身体已经好些了。

appeal[1] /ə'pi:l; ə'pil/ *verb* 动词 (**appeals**, **appealing**, **appealed** /ə'pi:ld; ə'pild/)

ask in a serious way for something that you want very much 恳求；呼吁: *They appealed for food and clothing.* 他们恳求给他们食物和衣物。

appeal to somebody please or interest somebody 使某人愉快或感兴趣: *Living in a big city doesn't appeal to me.* 我对住在大城市里并不感兴趣。

appeal[2] /ə'pi:l; ə'pil/ *noun* 名词

asking for something in a serious way 恳求；呼吁: *They made an appeal for help.* 他们恳求帮助。

appear /ə'pɪə(r); ə'pɪr/ *verb* 动词 (**appears**, **appearing**, **appeared** /ə'pɪəd; ə'pɪrd/)

1 come and be seen 出现；显现: *The sun suddenly appeared from behind a cloud.* 太阳突然从云彩后面露出来了。◇ *We waited* *for an hour but he didn't appear.* 我们等了一个小时，但是他并没有露面。

2 seem 显得；似乎: *She's only twelve but she appears to be older.* 她只有十二岁，但看来比实际年龄大。◇ *It appears that I was wrong.* 看来是我错了。

appearance /əˈpɪərəns; əˈpɪrəns/ *noun* 名词

1 the coming of somebody or something; when somebody or something is seen（某人或某事物的）到来；出现；被看见: *Jenny's appearance at the party surprised everybody.* 珍妮来参加聚会，大家都很惊奇。◇ *Is this your first appearance on television?* 这是你第一次上电视吗？

2 what somebody or something looks like（某人或某事物的）样子；外表；外貌: *Her new glasses change her appearance.* 她戴上新眼镜，样子变了。

appetite /ˈæpɪtaɪt; ˈæpəˌtaɪt/ *noun* 名词

the feeling that you want to eat 想吃东西的感觉；胃口；食欲: *Swimming always gives me an appetite* (= makes me hungry). 我一游泳就容易饿。

applaud /əˈplɔːd; əˈplɔd/ *verb* 动词 (**applauds, applauding, applauded**)

make a noise by hitting your hands together to show that you like something 拍手；鼓掌（表示喜欢某事物）: *We all applauded loudly at the end of the song.* 那支歌唱完后我们都热烈地鼓起掌来。

applause /əˈplɔːz; əˈplɔz/ *noun* 名词 (no plural 无复数)

when a lot of people hit their hands together to show that they like something（大家的）掌声（表示喜欢某事物）: *loud applause* 响亮的掌声

apple /ˈæpl; ˈæpl̩/ *noun* 名词

a hard round fruit 苹果

apple 苹果

appliance /əˈplaɪəns; əˈplaɪəns/ *noun* 名词

a useful machine for doing something in the house 家用器械: *Washing-machines and irons are electrical appliances.* 洗衣机和熨斗是家用电器。

applicant /ˈæplɪkənt; ˈæpləkənt/ *noun* 名词

a person who asks for a job or a place at a university, for example 申请人（求职或上大学等的）: *There were six applicants for the job.* 有六个人申请这份工作。

application /ˌæplɪˈkeɪʃn; ˌæpləˈkeʃən/ *noun* 名词

writing to ask for something, for example a job（要求某事物，如求职的）申请

application form /ˌæplɪˈkeɪʃn fɔːm; ˌæpləˈkeʃən fɔrm/ *noun* 名词

a special piece of paper that you write on when you are trying to get something, for example a job 申请表；申请书

apply /əˈplaɪ; əˈplaɪ/ *verb* 动词 (**applies, applying, applied** /əˈplaɪd; əˈplaɪd/)

1 write to ask for something（用书面形式）申请: *Simon has applied for a place at university.* 西蒙填写了报考大学的申请书。

2 be about or be important to somebody or something 对某人或某事物有关或关系重大；适用: *This notice applies to all children over the age of twelve.* 此通知适用于十二岁以上的所有儿童。

appoint /əˈpɔɪnt; əˈpɔɪnt/ *verb* 动词 (**appoints, appointing, appointed**)

choose somebody for a job 挑选某人做某工作；任命；委派: *The bank has appointed a new manager.* 这家银行委任了一位新经理。

appointment /əˈpɔɪntmənt; əˈpɔɪntmənt/ *noun* 名词

1 a time that you have fixed to meet somebody 约会；预约: *I've got an appointment with the doctor at ten o'clock.* 我和医生十点钟有个预约。◇ *You can telephone to make an appointment.* 你可以打电话预约。

2 a job 一份工作 ✪ **Job** is the word that we usually use. ＊ **job** 是常用词。

appreciate /əˈpriːʃieɪt; əˈpriʃɪˌet/ *verb* 动词 (**appreciates, appreciating, appreciated**)

1 understand and enjoy something 理解并欣赏某事物；赏识: *Van Gogh's paintings were only appreciated after his death.* 凡·高的画儿在他死后才受到赏识。

2 understand something 理解某事物: *I appreciate your problem, but I can't help you.* 我理解你的困难，但是没法帮助你。

3 be pleased about something that somebody has done for you 对某人为你做的事感到高兴；感激；感谢: *Thank you for your help. I appreciate it.* 谢谢你的帮助，我十分感激。

A

appreciation /əˌpri:ʃi'eɪʃn; əˌpriʃɪ-'eʃən/ *noun* 名词 (no plural 无复数)
We gave her some flowers to show our appreciation for her hard work. 我们向她献花，表示感谢她工作努力。

apprentice /ə'prentɪs; ə'prɛntɪs/ *noun* 名词
a young person who is learning to do a job 学着做某工作的年轻人；学徒工；徒弟

approach[1] /ə'prəʊtʃ; ə'protʃ/ *verb* 动词 (**approaches**, **approaching**, **approached** /ə'prəʊtʃt; ə'protʃt/)
come near or nearer to somebody or something 接近某人或某事物；靠近；临近: *When you approach the village, you will see a big house on your right.* 快到那个村子的地方，能看到右边有一所大房子。◇ *I was approached by an old lady.* 有个老太太向我走来。◇ *The exams were approaching.* 快要考试了。

approach[2] /ə'prəʊtʃ; ə'protʃ/ *noun* 名词
1 (no plural 无复数) coming near or nearer to somebody or something（向某人或某事物的）接近；靠近；临近: *the approach of winter* 冬天的来临
2 (*plural* 复数作 **approaches**) a way of doing something 做某事物的方法: *This is a new approach to learning languages.* 这是学习语言的新方法。

appropriate /ə'prəʊpriət; ə'proprɪɪt/ *adjective* 形容词
right for that time or place; suitable（对某时或某地）适合的；合适的: *Jeans and T-shirts aren't appropriate for an interview.* 牛仔裤和短袖汗衫不适于面试的时候穿用。✪ opposite 反义词: **inappropriate**

approval /ə'pru:vl; ə'pruvl̩/ *noun* 名词 (no plural 无复数)
showing or saying that somebody or something is good or right 表示某人或某事物好或正确；赞成；满意；认可；同意: *Tania's parents gave the marriage their approval.* 坦尼亚的父母同意他们结婚。

approve /ə'pru:v; ə'pruv/ *verb* 动词 (**approves**, **approving**, **approved** /ə'pru:vd; ə'pruvd/)
think or say that something or somebody is good or right 认为或说出某事物或某人好或正确；赞成；满意；认可；同意: *My parents don't approve of my friends.* 我父母不满意我结交的朋友。◇ *She doesn't approve of smoking.* 她不赞成吸烟。
✪ opposite 反义词: **disapprove**

approximate /ə'prɒksɪmət; ə'prɑksəmɪt/ *adjective* 形容词
almost correct but not exact 接近正确但不完全准确的: *The approximate time of arrival is three o'clock.* 到达的大约时间是三点钟。

approximately *adverb* 副词
about; not exactly 大约；不很精确: *I live approximately two kilometres from the station.* 我住的地方离车站有两公里左右。

apricot /'eɪprɪkɒt; 'eprɪˌkɑt/ *noun* 名词
a small soft yellow fruit 杏

April /'eɪprəl; 'eprəl/ *noun* 名词
the fourth month of the year 四月

apron /'eɪprən; 'eprən/ *noun* 名词
a thing that you wear over the front of your clothes to keep them clean, for example when you are cooking 围裙（如烹饪时用的）

arch /ɑ:tʃ; ɑrtʃ/ *noun* 名词 (*plural* 复数作 **arches**)
a part of a bridge, building or wall that is in the shape of a half circle 拱（桥梁，房屋或墙壁的半圆形部分）

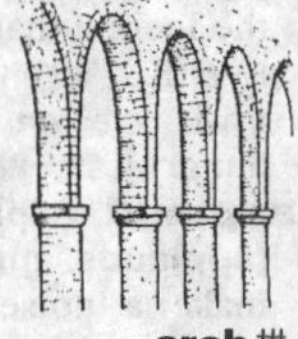
arch 拱

archaeology /ˌɑ:ki'ɒlədʒi; ˌɑrkɪ-'ɑlədʒɪ/ *noun* 名词 (no plural 无复数)
the study of very old things like buildings and objects that are found in the ground 考古学（研究古代建筑物和出土文物的科学）

archaeologist /ˌɑ:ki'ɒlədʒɪst; ˌɑrkɪ-'ɑlədʒɪst/ *noun* 名词
a person who studies or knows a lot about archaeology 考古学研究者；考古学家

archbishop /ˌɑ:tʃ'bɪʃəp; 'ɑrtʃ'bɪʃəp/ *noun* 名词
a very important priest in the Christian church 大主教: *the Archbishop of Canterbury* 坎特伯雷大主教

archeologist, archeology *American English for* **archaeologist, archaeology** 美式英语，即 **archaeologist**、**archaeology**

architect /'ɑ:kɪtekt; 'ɑrkəˌtɛkt/ *noun* 名词
a person whose job is to plan buildings 建筑师（做设计建筑物工作的人）

A

architecture /ˈɑːkɪtektʃə(r); ˈɑrkəˌtɛktʃɚ/ *noun* 名词 (no plural 无复数)

1 planning and making buildings 建筑物的设计和制造

2 the shape of buildings 建筑物的形式；建筑风格: *Do you like modern architecture?* 你喜欢现代建筑风格吗？

are *form of* **be** ＊ **be** 的不同形式

area /ˈeəriə; ˈɛrɪə/ *noun* 名词

1 a part of a town, country or the world 城镇、国家或世界的一部分；地域；地区；地带: *Do you live in this area?* 你住在这一带吗？◇ *the desert areas of North Africa* 北非的沙漠地带

2 the size of a flat place. If a room is three metres wide and four metres long, it has an area of twelve square metres. 平面地方的大小；面积（要是一个房间三米宽四米长，那么它的面积就是十二平方米。）

3 a space that you use for something special 作某种用途的地方: *The restaurant has a non-smoking area* (= a part where you must not smoke). 这家饭馆有个禁止吸烟区（= 不准吸烟的范围）。

arena /əˈriːnə; əˈrinə/ *noun* 名词 (*plural* 复数作 **arenas**)

a place with seats around it where you can watch things like sports matches and concerts 周围有看台座位可以欣赏运动比赛和音乐会的地方

aren't /ɑːnt; ɑrnt/ = **are not**

argue /ˈɑːgjuː; ˈɑrgju/ *verb* 动词 (**argues**, **arguing**, **argued** /ˈɑːgjuːd; ˈɑrgjud/)

1 talk angrily with somebody because you do not agree（因为持有不同的意见）与某人气愤地说话；争吵；争论: *My parents argue a lot.* 我父母常吵架。◇ *I often argue with my brother about music.* 我常和哥哥争论音乐问题。

2 say why you think something is right or wrong 说出你认为某事物正确或错误的理由: *Helen argued that we shouldn't eat meat.* 海伦提出不应该吃肉的道理。

argument /ˈɑːgjəmənt; ˈɑrgjəmənt/ *noun* 名词

an angry talk between people with different ideas 意见不一致的人之间气愤的谈话；争吵；争辩: *They had an argument about where to go on holiday.* 他们为到哪儿去度假争吵了起来。◇ *I had an argument with my father.* 我和父亲吵了一顿。

arithmetic /əˈrɪθmətɪk; əˈrɪθməˌtɪk/ *noun* 名词 (no plural 无复数)

working with numbers to find an answer 计算；算术

arm /ɑːm; ɑrm/ *noun* 名词

the part of your body from your shoulder to your hand 手臂；上肢（从肩到手的部分）: *Put your arms in the air.* 把胳膊举起来。◇ *He was carrying a book under his arm.* 他胳膊下夹着一本书。☞ picture on page C2 见第C2页图

arm in arm with your arm holding another person's arm 臂挽着臂；两人（挎着胳膊）: *The two friends walked arm in arm.* 这两个朋友挽着胳膊走。

armchair /ˈɑːmtʃeə(r); ˈɑrmˌtʃɛr/ *noun* 名词

a soft chair with parts where you can put your arms 单座沙发: *She was asleep in an armchair.* 她坐在单座沙发上睡着了。

armchair 单座沙发

armed /ɑːmd; ɑrmd/ *adjective* 形容词

with a weapon, for example a gun 带着武器的（例如枪）；武装的: *an armed robber* 带着武器的劫匪 ◇ *Are the police armed in your country?* 你们国家的警察带枪吗？

the armed forces /ði ˌɑːmd ˈfɔːsɪz; ðɪ ˌɑrmd ˈfɔrsɪz/ *noun* 名词

the army, air force and navy 武装力量（陆军、空军、海军）

armor *American English for* **armour** 美式英语，即 **armour**

armour /ˈɑːmə(r); ˈɑrmɚ/ *noun* 名词 (no plural 无复数)

metal clothes that men wore long ago to cover their bodies when they were fighting（古时的）盔甲；甲胄: *a suit of armour* 一套盔甲

arms /ɑːmz; ɑrmz/ *noun* 名词 (plural 复数)

guns, bombs and other weapons for fighting 枪炮、炸弹和其他作战武器

army /ˈɑːmi; ˈɑrmɪ/ *noun* 名词 (*plural* 复数作 **armies**)

a large group of soldiers who fight on land in a war 陆军: *He joined the army when he was 17.* 他17岁的时候加入了陆军。◇ *the Swiss Army* 瑞士陆军

A

around /ə'raʊnd; ə'raund/ *preposition, adverb* 介词，副词

1 in or to different places or in different directions 在各处；向各处；朝各方向: *We walked around for an hour looking for a restaurant.* 我们为找饭馆四处走了一个小时。◇ *The children were running around the house.* 孩子们在房子里各处跑。◇ *Her clothes were lying around the room.* 屋子里到处都是她的衣服。

2 on or to all sides of something, often in a circle 在某事物的各边；向某事物的各边（常指周围）: *We sat around the table.* 我们围着桌子坐着。◇ *He ran around the track.* 他围着跑道跑。◇ *There is a wall around the garden.* 这个花园有围墙。

3 in the opposite direction or in another direction 朝相反的方向；朝另一个方向: *Turn around and go back the way you came.* 向后转，沿着你来的路走回去。

4 a little more or less than; a little before or after 比…稍多或稍少；稍前或稍后: *We met at around seven o'clock.* 我们七点钟左右见的面。

5 in a place; near here 在某处；在这儿附近: *Is there a bank around here?* 这儿附近有银行吗？◇ *Is Helen around? I want to speak to her.* 海伦在这儿吗？我想跟她说话。

arrange /ə'reɪndʒ; ə'rendʒ/ *verb* 动词 (**arranges**, **arranging**, **arranged** /ə'reɪndʒd; ə'rendʒd/)

1 make a plan for the future 为将来订计划；安排: *I have arranged to meet Tim at six o'clock.* 我安排好了六点钟和蒂姆见面。◇ *We arranged a big party for Debbie's birthday.* 我们为戴比的生日准备了一个大型聚会。

2 put things in a certain order or place 把事物排好顺序或位置；排列；布置；整理: *Arrange the chairs in a circle.* 把椅子摆成一圈儿。

arrangement /ə'reɪndʒmənt; ə'rendʒmənt/ *noun* 名词

1 something that you plan or agree for the future 为将来做的计划或商定的事: *They are making the arrangements for their wedding.* 他们正在为婚礼做准备。

2 a group of things put together so that they look nice 摆放得好看的一些东西: *a flower arrangement* 插花

arrest /ə'rest; ə'rɛst/ *verb* 动词 (**arrests**, **arresting**, **arrested**)

When the police arrest somebody, they make that person a prisoner because they think that he/she has done something wrong 逮捕: *The thief was arrested yesterday.* 这个窃贼昨天已遭逮捕。

arrest *noun* 名词

arresting somebody 逮捕: *The police made five arrests.* 警方逮捕了五个人。

be under arrest be a prisoner of the police 遭警方逮捕

arrival /ə'raɪvl; ə'raɪvl̩/ *noun* 名词

coming to a place 到达；抵达: *My brother met me at the airport on my arrival.* 我到达的时候，我哥哥正在机场接我。◇ *We are sorry for the late arrival of this train.* 这班火车晚点了，我们非常抱歉。☞ Look at **departure**. 见 **departure**。

arrive /ə'raɪv; ə'raɪv/ *verb* 动词 (**arrives**, **arriving**, **arrived** /ə'raɪvd; ə'raɪvd/)

1 come to a place 到达；抵达: *What time does the train arrive in Paris?* 这列火车什么时候到巴黎？◇ *Has my letter arrived?* 我的信到了吗？

2 come or happen 来；发生: *Summer has arrived!* 夏天到了！◇ *Her baby arrived* (= was born) *yesterday.* 她的小孩儿是昨天出生的。

arrogant /'ærəgənt; 'ærəgənt/ *adjective* 形容词

A person who is arrogant thinks that he/she is better or more important than other people. 高傲的；自大的

arrows 箭和箭号

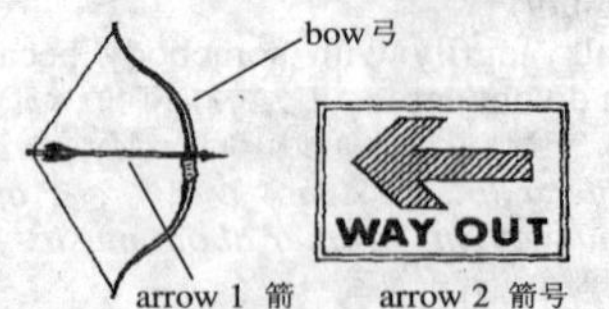

arrow 1 箭　arrow 2 箭号

arrow /'ærəʊ; 'æro/ *noun* 名词

1 a long thin piece of wood or metal with a point at one end. You shoot an arrow from a **bow**. 箭（用弓射箭，弓叫做 **bow**）

2 a sign in the shape of an arrow, that shows where something is or where you should go 箭号（指示某物的位置或应去之处）

art /ɑ:t; ɑrt/ *noun* 名词

1 (no plural 无复数) making beautiful things, like paintings and drawings 绘画:

He's studying art at college. 他正在大学学习绘画。

2 (no plural 无复数) beautiful things like paintings and drawings that somebody has made 美术: *modern art* 现代美术

3 the arts (plural 复数) things like films, plays and literature 艺术（如电影、戏剧、文学）: *How much money does the government spend on the arts?* 政府在艺术方面花费多少钱？

article /'ɑ:tɪkl; 'ɑrtɪkl̩/ *noun* 名词

1 a piece of writing in a newspaper or magazine 报刊上的文章: *Did you read the article about Spain in yesterday's newspaper?* 你看没看昨天报纸上关于西班牙的那篇文章？

2 a thing 东西；物件；物品: *Many of the articles in the shop are half-price.* 这个商店很多东西现在都半价。◇ *articles of clothing* (= things like skirts, coats and trousers) 衣物（= 裙子、大衣、裤子之类的物品）

3 The words 'a', 'an' and 'the' are called articles. 冠词（a、an、the 这三个词叫做冠词）

artificial /ˌɑ:tɪ'fɪʃl; ˌɑrtə'fɪʃəl/ *adjective* 形容词

made by people; not natural 人造的；人工的；非自然的: *artificial flowers* 人造的花

artist /'ɑ:tɪst; 'ɑrtɪst/ *noun* 名词

a person who paints or draws pictures 画画儿的人；画家: *Monet was a famous French artist.* 莫奈是著名的法国画家。

artistic /ɑ:'tɪstɪk; ɑr'tɪstɪk/ *adjective* 形容词

good at painting, drawing or making beautiful things 善于绘画或制造艺术品的: *He's very artistic.* 他很有艺术才能。

as /əz, æz; əz, æz/ *conjunction, preposition* 连词，介词

1 while; at the same time that something is happening 当…的时候；在某事发生的同时: *As I was going out, the telephone rang.* 我正要出去的时候，电话铃响了。

2 because 因为；由于: *She didn't go to school as she was ill.* 她因病没去上学。

3 in the same way; like 像…一样；像…那样: *Please do as I tell you!* 请按照我告诉你的那样去做！

4 in the job of 做…工作: *She works as a secretary for a big company.* 她给一家大公司当秘书。

as ... as words that you use to compare people or things; the same amount（用以比较人或事物的词组）相同的量或程度: *Paul is as tall as his father.* 保罗跟他父亲一样高。◇ *I haven't got as many clothes as you have.* 我没有你的衣服多。

ash /æʃ; æʃ/ *noun* 名词 (*plural* 复数作 **ash** or 或 **ashes**)

the grey stuff that you see after something has burned 灰末；灰: *cigarette ash* 香烟灰

ashamed /ə'ʃeɪmd; ə'ʃemd/ *adjective* 形容词

sorry and unhappy about something that you have done, or unhappy because you are not as good as other people in some way 感到羞耻的；感到惭愧的: *I was ashamed about lying to my parents.* 我向父母撒了谎，觉得羞愧。◇ *She was ashamed of her old clothes.* 她对自己的旧衣服感到惭愧。

ashore /ə'ʃɔ:(r); ə'ʃɔr/ *adverb* 副词

onto the land 上陆地；上岸: *We left the boat and went ashore.* 我们下了船，上了岸。

ashtray /'æʃtreɪ; 'æʃtre/ *noun* 名词

a small dish for cigarette ash and the ends of cigarettes 烟灰缸

aside /ə'saɪd; ə'saɪd/ *adverb* 副词

on or to one side; away 在一边；向一边；离开: *He put the letter aside while he did his homework.* 他做功课的时候，把信放在一边了。

ask /ɑ:sk; æsk/ *verb* 动词 (**asks, asking, asked** /ɑ:skt; æskt/)

1 try to get an answer by using a question 问: *I asked him what the time was.* 我问他什么时间了。◇ *'What's your name?' she asked.* "你叫什么名字？" 她问道。◇ *Liz asked the teacher a question.* 利兹问老师一个问题。◇ *I asked if I could go home early.* 我问能不能早点儿回家。

2 say that you would like somebody to do something for you 要求: *I asked Sara to drive me to the station.* 我让萨拉开车送我到车站去。

3 invite somebody 邀请某人: *Mark has asked me to a party on Saturday.* 马克请我星期六参加聚会。

ask for somebody say that you want to speak to somebody 要求和某人说话: *Phone this number and ask for*

Mrs Green. 打这个电话号码，就说跟格林夫人通话。

ask for something say that you want somebody to give you something 要求某人给你某事物: *He asked his parents for a computer.* 他向父母要个计算机。

asleep /ə'sli:p; ə'slip/ *adjective* 形容词
sleeping 睡着: *The baby is asleep in the bedroom.* 小孩儿在卧室里睡觉呢。✪ opposite 反义词: **awake**
fall asleep start sleeping 睡起觉来: *He fell asleep in front of the fire.* 他在火炉前睡着了。

aspect /'æspekt; 'æspɛkt/ *noun* 名词
one part of a problem, idea, etc 问题、意见等的一部分；方面: *Spelling is one of the most difficult aspects of learning English.* 词语拼写是学习英语最困难的一个方面。

aspirin /'æsprɪn; 'æspərɪn/ *noun* 名词
a medicine that stops pain 阿司匹林（止痛药）: *I took two aspirins* (= two tablets of aspirin) *for my headache.* 我头疼，吃了两片阿司匹林。

assassinate /ə'sæsɪneɪt; ə'sæsn̩ˌet/ *verb* 动词 (**assassinates**, **assassinating**, **assassinated**)
kill an important or famous person 暗杀；行刺（要人或名人）: *John F Kennedy was assassinated in 1963.* 约翰·肯尼迪在1963年遭暗杀。
assassination /əˌsæsɪ'neɪʃn; əˌsæsn̩'eʃən/ *noun* 名词
killing an important or famous person（对要人或名人的）暗杀；行刺

assault /ə'sɔ:lt; ə'sɔlt/ *verb* 动词 (**assaults**, **assaulting**, **assaulted**)
suddenly start fighting or hurting somebody 突然攻击某人；暴力伤害: *He assaulted a policeman.* 他殴打了一个警察。
assault *noun* 名词
an assault on an old lady 对一个老太太的暴力伤害

assembly /ə'sembli; ə'sɛmblɪ/ *noun* 名词 (*plural* 复数作 **assemblies**)
a meeting of a big group of people for a special reason 集会: *Our school assembly* (= a meeting of all the students and teachers in the school) *is at 9.30 in the morning.* 我们全校大会（全体师生的集会）在上午9时30分举行。

assist /ə'sɪst; ə'sɪst/ *verb* 动词 (**assists**, **assisting**, **assisted**)
help somebody 帮助某人；援助: *The driver assisted her with her suitcases.* 司机帮助她搬手提箱。
assistance /ə'sɪstəns; ə'sɪstəns/ *noun* 名词 (no plural 无复数)
help 帮助；援助: *I can't move this piano without your assistance.* 没有你帮忙，我可挪不动这架钢琴。
✪ **Assist** and **assistance** are more formal than **help**. ＊ **help** 较 **assist** 及 **assistance** 常用。

assistant /ə'sɪstənt; ə'sɪstənt/ *noun* 名词
a person who helps 助手；助理: *Ms Dixon is not here today. Would you like to speak to her assistant?* 狄克逊女士今天不在，你愿意和她的助手谈谈吗？
☞ Look also at **shop assistant**. 另见 **shop assistant**。

associate /ə'səʊʃieɪt; ə'soʃɪˌet/ *verb* 动词 (**associates**, **associating**, **associated**)
put two ideas together in your mind 联想: *We usually associate Austria with snow and skiing.* 我们一想到奥地利，就往往联想到雪和滑雪活动。

association /əˌsəʊsi'eɪʃn; əˌsosɪ'eʃən/ *noun* 名词
a group of people who join or work together for a special reason 联合；联盟；合伙: *the Football Association* 足球协会

assume /ə'sju:m; ə'sum/ *verb* 动词 (**assumes**, **assuming**, **assumed** /ə'sju:md; ə'sumd/)
think that something is true when you are not completely sure（无十分把握时）认为某事属实；假定；假设: *Jo is not here today, so I assume that she is ill.* 乔今天不在，我看她是病了。

assure /ə'ʃʊə(r); ə'ʃʊr/ *verb* 动词 (**assures**, **assuring**, **assured** /ə'ʃʊəd; ə'ʃʊrd/)
tell somebody what is true or certain so that they feel less worried 告诉某人真相或实情使之放心；保证: *I assure you that the dog isn't dangerous.* 我保证这条狗不咬人。

astonish /ə'stɒnɪʃ; ə'stɑnɪʃ/ *verb* 动词 (**astonishes**, **astonishing**, **astonished** /ə'stɒnɪʃt; ə'stɑnɪʃt/)
surprise somebody very much 使某人吃惊: *The news astonished everyone.*

这个消息大家都感到很惊讶。

astonished *adjective* 形容词
If you are astonished, you are very surprised 吃惊；惊讶: *I was astonished when I heard that Louise was getting married.* 听说路易丝要结婚了，我大吃一惊。

astonishing *adjective* 形容词
If something is astonishing, it surprises you very much 使人吃惊的；惊人的: *astonishing news* 使人惊讶的消息

astonishment /ə'stɒnɪʃmənt; ə'stɑnɪʃmənt/ *noun* 名词 (no plural 无复数)
great surprise 惊讶；惊奇: *He looked at me in astonishment when I told him the news.* 我告诉他那个消息的时候，他吃惊地看着我。

astronaut /'æstrənɔ:t; 'æstrəˌnɔt/ *noun* 名词
a person who travels in a spaceship 宇航员；航天员；太空人

astronomy /ə'strɒnəmi; ə'strɑnəmɪ/ *noun* 名词 (no plural 无复数)
the study of the sun, moon, planets and stars 天文学（研究太阳、月亮、星星的学科）

astronomer /ə'strɒnəmə(r); ə'strɑnəmə˞/ *noun* 名词
a person who studies or knows a lot about astronomy 天文学研究者；天文学家

at /ət, æt; ət, æt/ *preposition* 介词
1 a word that shows where（表示处所）在: *They are at school.* 他们在学校呢。◇ *Jenny is at home.* 珍妮在家呢。◇ *The answer is at the back of the book.* 答案在书的后面。
2 a word that shows when（表示时间）在: *I go to bed at eleven o'clock.* 我十一点钟睡觉。◇ *At night you can see the stars.* 夜晚能看见星星。☞ picture on page C29 见第C29页图
3 towards somebody or something 向；朝；对（某人或某事物）: *Look at the picture.* 看看这张画儿。◇ *I smiled at her.* 我对她微笑。◇ *Somebody threw an egg at the President.* 有人向总统扔鸡蛋。
4 a word that shows what somebody is doing or what is happening 正在: *The two countries are at war.* 这两国正在打仗。
5 a word that shows how much, how fast, etc 表示多少、多快等的词: *I bought two lemons at 20 pence each.* 我买了两个柠檬，每个20便士。
6 a word that shows how well somebody or something does something 表示某事做得好坏的词: *I'm not very good at maths.* 我的数学不怎么样。
7 because of something 因为；由于: *We laughed at his jokes.* 我们听了他说的笑话都大笑起来。

ate *form of* **eat** ∗ **eat** 的不同形式

athlete /'æθli:t; 'æθlit/ *noun* 名词
a person who is good at sports like running, jumping or throwing 运动员: *Athletes from all over the world go to the Olympic Games.* 来自世界各地的运动员参加奥林匹克运动会。

athletics /æθ'letɪks; æθ'lɛtɪks/ *noun* 名词 (plural 复数)
sports like running, jumping or throwing 体育运动

atlas /'ætləs; 'ætləs/ *noun* 名词 (*plural* 复数作 **atlases**)
a book of maps 地图集；地图册: *an atlas of the world* 世界地图集

atmosphere /'ætməsfɪə(r); 'ætməsˌfɪr/ *noun* 名词
1 (no plural 无复数) all the gases around the earth 大气；大气层（地球周围的所有气体）
2 (no plural 无复数) the air in a place 某一地方的空气: *a warm atmosphere* 暖空气
3 (*plural* 复数作 **atmospheres**) the feeling that places or people give you 气氛: *The atmosphere in the office was very friendly.* 那个办公室里的气氛很好。

atom /'ætəm; 'ætəm/ *noun* 名词
one of the very small things that everything is made of 原子: *Water is made of atoms of hydrogen and oxygen.* 水是由氢原子和氧原子构成的。

atomic /ə'tɒmɪk; ə'tɑmɪk/ *adjective* 形容词
1 of or about atoms 原子的；关于原子的: *atomic physics* 原子物理学
2 using the great power that is made by breaking atoms 利用原子分裂的巨大能量的；原子能的: *an atomic bomb* 原子弹 ◇ *atomic energy* 原子能

attach /ə'tætʃ; ə'tætʃ/ *verb* 动词 (**attaches**, **attaching**, **attached** /ə'tætʃt; ə'tætʃt/)
join or fix one thing to another thing 把一物加入另一物里；把一物固定在另一物上:

I attached the photo to the letter. 我把照片附在信里了。

be attached to somebody or 或 **something** like somebody or something very much 极喜爱某人或某事物: *He's very attached to you.* 他非常喜欢你。

attack /ə'tæk; ə'tæk/ *verb* 动词 (**attacks, attacking, attacked** /ə'tækt; ə'tækt/) start fighting or hurting somebody or something 攻击或伤害某人或某事物: *The army attacked the town.* 军队攻打那个城镇。◇ *The old man was attacked and his money was stolen.* 那个老先生遭到殴打，钱也让人偷走了。

attack *noun* 名词

1 trying to hurt somebody or something 对某人或某事物欲加伤害: *There was an attack on the President.* 有人要伤害总统。

2 a time when you are ill（疾病的）侵袭，发作: *an attack of flu* 染上流感

attempt /ə'tempt; ə'tɛmpt/ *verb* 动词 (**attempts, attempting, attempted**) try to do something 想要做某事；尝试；试图；企图: *He attempted to swim from England to France.* 他打算从英国游到法国去。✪ **Try** is the word that we usually use. ✳ **try** 是常用词。

attempt *noun* 名词

She made no attempt to help me. 她不想帮助我。

attend /ə'tend; ə'tɛnd/ *verb* 动词 (**attends, attending, attended**) go to or be at a place where something is happening 参加；出席: *Did you attend the meeting?* 你参加那次会议了吗？

attention /ə'tenʃn; ə'tɛnʃən/ *noun* 名词 (no plural 无复数) looking or listening carefully and with interest 专心地看或听: *Can I have your attention, please?* (= please listen to me) 请注意一下儿，行吗？（= 请听我说）

pay attention look or listen carefully 留心看或注意听: *Please pay attention to what I'm saying.* 请注意听我说。

attic /'ætɪk; 'ætɪk/ *noun* 名词 the room or space under the roof of a house（房子的）顶楼；阁楼: *My old clothes are in a box in the attic.* 我的旧衣服都在阁楼的箱子里。

attitude /'ætɪtju:d; 'ætəˌtud/ *noun* 名词 the way you think or feel about something 想法；看法；态度: *What's your attitude to marriage?* 你对婚姻有什么看法？

attorney /ə'tɜ:ni; ə'tɝnɪ/ *American English for* **lawyer** 美式英语，即 **lawyer**

attract /ə'trækt; ə'trækt/ *verb* 动词 (**attracts, attracting, attracted**)

1 make somebody or something come nearer 使某人或某事物靠近；吸引: *Magnets attract metal.* 磁石能吸铁。◇ *The birds were attracted by the smell of fish.* 鱼的气味把鸟引来了。

2 make somebody like somebody or something 使某人喜欢某人或某事物；吸引: *He was attracted to her.* 他很喜欢她。

attraction /ə'trækʃn; ə'trækʃən/ *noun* 名词

1 (*plural* 复数作 **attractions**) something that people like and feel interested in 喜爱的或感兴趣的事物；吸引: *London has a lot of tourist attractions, like Big Ben and Buckingham Palace.* 伦敦有很多吸引游客的去处，例如大本钟和白金汉宫。

2 (no plural 无复数) liking somebody or something very much; being liked very much 极喜爱某人或某事物；很受喜爱: *I can't understand his attraction to her.* 我不明白他怎么看上她了。

attractive /ə'træktɪv; ə'træktɪv/ *adjective* 形容词

1 A person who is attractive is nice to look at（指人）好看的，漂亮的: *He's very attractive.* 他很招人喜欢。

2 Something that is attractive pleases you or interests you（指事物）使人愉快的，使人感兴趣的: *That's an attractive idea.* 这倒是个好主意。

✪ opposite 反义词: **unattractive**

auction /'ɔ:kʃn; 'ɔkʃən/ *noun* 名词 a sale where each thing is sold to the person who will give the most money for it 拍卖

auction *verb* 动词 (**auctions, auctioning, auctioned** /'ɔ:kʃnd; 'ɔkʃənd/) sell something at an auction 拍卖

audience /'ɔ:diəns; 'ɔdɪəns/ *noun* 名词 all the people who are watching or listening to a film, play, concert or the television, for example 欣赏电影、戏剧、音乐会或电视的所有的人；听众；观众

August /'ɔ:gəst; 'ɔgəst/ *noun* 名词 the eighth month of the year 八月

aunt /ɑːnt; ænt/ *noun* 名词
the sister of your mother or father, or the wife of your uncle 母亲的或父亲的姐妹；伯父的或叔父的或舅父的妻子；姑母；姨母；伯母；婶母；舅母: *Aunt Mary* 玛丽舅母
☞ picture on page C3 见第C3页图

auntie /ˈɑːnti; ˈæntɪ/ *noun* 名词
aunt 姑母；姨母；伯母；婶母；舅母

au pair /ˌəʊ ˈpeə(r); oˈpɛr/ *noun* 名词
a young person from another country who stays with a family for a short time to learn a language. An au pair helps in the house and looks after the children. 换工（为学习语言暂住在某家的年轻的外国人，同时帮助做家务事和照看孩子）

authentic /ɔːˈθentɪk; ɔˈθɛntɪk/ *adjective* 形容词
real and true 真实的；真正的: *That's not an authentic Van Gogh painting — it's just a copy.* 那张画儿不是凡·高的真迹——只不过是个复制品。

author /ˈɔːθə(r); ˈɔθɚ/ *noun* 名词
a person who writes books or stories 写书或写小说的人；著者；作家: *Who is your favourite author?* 你最喜欢哪个作家？

authority /ɔːˈθɒrəti; ɔˈθɑrətɪ/ *noun* 名词
1 (no plural 无复数) the power to tell people what they must do 权力；权威: *The police have the authority to stop cars.* 警察有权让汽车停住。
2 (*plural* 复数作 **authorities**) a group of people that tell other people what they must do 向大家发号施令的团体；当局；官方: *the city authorities* 市政当局

autobiography /ˌɔːtəbaɪˈɒgrəfi; ˌɔtəbaɪˈɑgrəfɪ/ *noun* 名词 (*plural* 复数作 **autobiographies**)
a book that a person has written about his/her life 自传（叙述自己生平经历的书）

autograph /ˈɔːtəgrɑːf; ˈɔtəˌgræf/ *noun* 名词
a famous person's name, that he/she has written（名人的）亲笔签名: *He asked Madonna for her autograph.* 他请求麦当娜给他签名。

automatic /ˌɔːtəˈmætɪk; ˌɔtəˈmætɪk/ *adjective* 形容词
1 If a machine is automatic, it can work by itself, without people controlling it（指机器）自动的: *an automatic washing-machine* 自动洗衣机
2 that you do without thinking 未加思索而做出的；无意识的: *Breathing is automatic.* 呼吸是无意识的动作。

automatically /ˌɔːtəˈmætɪkli; ˌɔtəˈmætɪklɪ/ *adverb* 副词
This light comes on automatically at five o'clock. 这个灯一到五点钟就自动亮了。

automobile /ˈɔːtəməbiːl; ˈɔtəməˌbil/ *American English for* **car** 美式英语，即 **car**

autumn /ˈɔːtəm; ˈɔtəm/ *noun* 名词
the part of the year between summer and winter 秋季；秋天: *In autumn, the leaves begin to fall from the trees.* 秋天，树叶开始落下。✪ The four seasons are **spring**, **summer**, **autumn** and **winter**. 一年的四季为春 **(spring)**、夏 **(summer)**、秋 **(autumn)**、冬 **(winter)**。

available /əˈveɪləbl; əˈveləbḷ/ *adjective* 形容词
ready for you to use, have or see 可随时使用、得到或看到的: *I phoned the hotel to ask if there were any rooms available.* 我给旅馆打了电话，问问有没有空着的房间。◇ *I'm sorry — the doctor is not available this afternoon.* 很抱歉——大夫今天下午没有空儿。

avenue /ˈævənjuː; ˈævəˌnu/ *noun* 名词
a wide road or street 大的马路或街道: *I live in Connaught Avenue.* 我住在康诺特道。✪ The short way of writing 'Avenue' in addresses is **Ave** 写地址时，Avenue 可缩写作 **Ave**: *Burnham Ave* 伯恩翰道

average /ˈævərɪdʒ; ˈævərɪdʒ/ *noun* 名词
1 (*plural* 复数作 **averages**) a word that you use when you work with numbers 平均数: *The average of 2, 3 and 7 is 4* (2 + 3 + 7 = 12, and 12 ÷ 3 = 4). ＊2、3、7 的平均数目是 4 (2 + 3 + 7 = 12, 12 ÷ 3 = 4)。
2 (no plural 无复数) what is ordinary or usual 普通的；一般的；平常的: *Tom's work at school is above average* (= better than the average). 汤姆的功课高于一般水平（比一般的好）。

average *adjective* 形容词
The average age of the students is 19. 这些学生的平均年龄是19岁。

avoid /əˈvɔɪd; əˈvɔɪd/ *verb* 动词 (**avoids**, **avoiding**, **avoided**)
1 stay away or go away from somebody or something 避开或躲避某人或某事物: *We*

crossed the road to avoid our teacher. 我们穿过马路为的是躲着老师。

2 stop something from happening; try not to do something 不使某事发生；防止发生某事；尽量不做某事: *You should avoid eating too much chocolate.* 你应该尽量少吃巧克力。

awake /ə'weɪk; ə'wek/ *adjective* 形容词
not sleeping 醒着的: *The children are still awake.* 孩子还都没睡着。✪ opposite 反义词: **asleep**

award /ə'wɔ:d; ə'wɔrd/ *noun* 名词
a prize or money that you give to somebody who has done something very well 奖品；奖状；奖金: *She won the award for best actress.* 她赢得最佳女演员奖。

award *verb* 动词 (**awards**, **awarding**, **awarded**)
give a prize or money to somebody 向某人颁发奖品、奖状或奖金: *He was awarded first prize in the writing competition.* 他获得写作比赛一等奖。

aware /ə'weə(r); ə'wɛr/ *adjective* 形容词
If you are aware of something, you know about it 知道的；了解的: *I was aware that somebody was watching me.* 我知道有人正在注视着我。◇ *He's not aware of the problem.* 他没意识到有困难。
✪ opposite 反义词: **unaware**

away /ə'weɪ; ə'we/ *adverb* 副词
1 to or in another place 向另一处；在另一处: *She ran away.* 她跑了。◇ *He put his books away.* 他把书放在一边。

2 from a place 从一处: *The sea is two kilometres away.* 大海离这儿有两公里。

3 not here 不在这里: *Tom is away from school today because he is ill.* 蒂姆今天因病没上学。

4 in the future 在将来: *Our holiday is only three weeks away.* 我们的假期离现在只有三个星期了。

awful /'ɔ:fl; 'ɔfl̩/ *adjective* 形容词
very bad 极坏的；糟糕的: *The pain was awful.* 疼得很厉害。◇ *What awful weather!* 多坏的天气！

awfully /'ɔ:fli; 'ɔfl̩ɪ/ *adverb* 副词
very 极；非常: *It was awfully hot.* 热极了。◇ *I'm awfully sorry!* 我万分抱歉！

awkward /'ɔ:kwəd; 'ɔkwəd/ *adjective* 形容词
1 difficult to do or use, for example 难做的或难用的: *This big box will be awkward to carry.* 这个大箱子很难携带。

2 not comfortable 不舒服的；不自在的: *I felt awkward at the party because I didn't know anybody.* 我在聚会中感到很不自在，因为我谁都不认识。

3 difficult to please 不容易高兴的: *My daughter is very awkward. She never likes the food I give her.* 我女儿真别扭，我给她什么东西她都不喜欢吃。

4 not able to move your body in an easy way 身体不灵活的；动作笨拙的: *He's very awkward when he dances.* 他跳舞跳得很笨。

ax *American English for* **axe** 美式英语，即 **axe**

axe /æks; æks/ *noun* 名词
a tool for cutting wood 斧子: *He chopped down the tree with an axe.* 他用斧子把树砍倒了。

B

Bb

baby /'beɪbi; 'bebɪ/ *noun* 名词 (*plural* 复数作 **babies**)
a very young child 非常小的孩子；幼儿；婴儿: *She's going to have a baby.* 她快生孩子了。

baby 幼儿

babysit /'beɪbisɪt; 'bebɪsɪt/ *verb* 动词 (**babysits, babysitting, babysat** /'beɪbisæt; 'bebɪsæt/, **has babysat**)
look after a child for a short time when the parents are not there 代人临时照看孩子；当临时保姆

babysitter *noun* 名词
a person who babysits 代人临时照看孩子的人；临时保姆

bachelor /'bætʃələ(r); 'bætʃələ˞/ *noun* 名词
1 a man who has never married 没结过婚的男子；单身汉
2 a person who has finished studying at a university or college and who has a first **degree** 获得学士学位的人（学位叫做 **degree**）: *a Bachelor of Science* 理学士

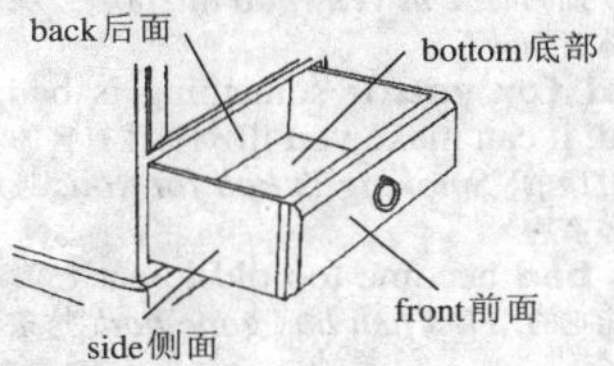

back[1] /bæk; bæk/ *noun* 名词
1 the part that is behind or farthest from the front 后部；后面；背面；反面: *The answers are at the back of the book.* 答案在书的后面。◇ *Write your address on the back of the cheque.* 把你的地址写在支票的背面。◇ *We sat in the back of the car.* 我们坐在汽车的后排座位上。
2 the part of a person or an animal between the neck and the bottom（人或动物的）后背: *He lay on his back and looked up at the sky.* 他仰卧着看着天空。☞ picture on page C2 见第C2页图

back to front 前后穿反

back to front with the back part in front 前后颠倒
behind somebody's back when somebody is not there, so that he/she does not know about it 某人不在场因而不知情；背着某人: *Don't talk about Kate behind her back.* 别在背后议论凯特。

back[2] /bæk; bæk/ *adjective* 形容词
away from the front 在后部的；在后面的；在背面的；在反面的: *the back door* 后门

back[3] /bæk; bæk/ *adverb* 副词
1 away from the front 在后部；在后面；在背面；在反面: *I looked back to see if she was coming.* 我向后瞧了瞧，看她来了没有。
2 in or to the place where somebody or something was before 在原处；向原处: *I'll be back* (= I will return) *at six o'clock.* 我六点钟回来。◇ *Give the book back to me when you've read it.* 你看完这本书就把它还给我。◇ *We walked to the shops and back.* 我们走着去商店，走着回来。
3 as a way of returning or answering something 作为回答: *He paid me the money back.* 他把钱还给我了。◇ *I wrote her a letter, but she didn't write back.* 我给她写了封信，可是她没有回信。◇ *I was out when she phoned, so I phoned her back.* 她来电话的时候我出去了，所以我给她回了个电话。
back and forth first one way and then the other, many times 来回地；往复地: *She travels back and forth between London and Glasgow.* 她来往于伦敦和格拉斯哥两地。

back[4] /bæk; bæk/ *verb* 动词 (**backs, backing, backed** /bækt; bækt/)
1 move backwards or make something move backwards 向后退；使某物向后移动: *She backed the car out of the garage.* 她把汽车从车房里倒退出来。
2 say that you think that somebody or something is right or the best 说出某人或某事物正确或最好；拥护；支持: *They're backing their school team.* 他们拥护他们的校队。
back away move away backwards 向后退以躲避；退避: *Sally backed away from the big dog.* 萨莉看见那条大狗就往后退。

back out not do something that you promised or agreed to do 不做曾经承诺要做的或同意要做的事；不履行: *Paul backed out of the game, so we only had ten players.* 保罗退出比赛，所以我们只有十个运动员了。

B

backbone /'bækbəʊn; 'bæk'bon/ *noun* 名词
the line of bones down the back of your body 脊柱；脊椎

background /'bækgraʊnd; 'bæk,graʊnd/ *noun* 名词
the things at the back in a picture（画儿、图片等的）背景，后景: *This is a photo of my house with the mountains in the background.* 这是我的房子的照片，背景是山。✪ opposite 反义词: **foreground**

backpack /'bækpæk; 'bækpæk/ *noun* 名词
a bag that you carry on your back, for example when you are walking or climbing 背包

backstroke /'bækstrəʊk; 'bæk,strok/ *noun* 名词 (no plural 无复数)
a way of swimming on your back 仰泳

backward /'bækwəd; 'bækwɚd/ *adjective* 形容词
1 towards the back 向后的: *a backward step* 倒退的一步
2 slow to learn or change 学习或变化慢的；落后的: *They live in a backward part of the country, where there is no electricity.* 他们住在该国的落后地区，没有电。

backwards /'bækwədz; 'bækwɚdz/, **backward** /'bækwəd; 'bækwɚd/ *adverb* 副词
1 away from the front; towards the back 在后；向后: *He fell backwards and hit the back of his head.* 他向后倒下，碰到了头的后部。
2 with the back or the end first 由后向前；倒着: *If you say the alphabet backwards, you start with 'Z'.* 要是倒着念字母表，就由Z开始。
backwards and forwards first one way and then the other way, many times 来回地: *The dog ran backwards and forwards.* 那条狗跑来跑去。

bacon /'beɪkən; 'bekən/ *noun* 名词 (no plural 无复数)
thin pieces of meat from a pig, that is prepared using salt or smoke 腌的或熏的猪肉片: *We had bacon and eggs for breakfast.* 我们早饭吃的是腌猪肉片和鸡蛋。☞ Note at **pig** 见 **pig** 词条注释

bacteria /bæk'tɪəriə; bæk'tɪrɪə/ *noun* 名词 (plural 复数)
very small things that live in air, water, earth, plants and animals. Some bacteria can make us ill. 细菌

bad /bæd; bæd/ *adjective* 形容词 (**worse**, **worst**)
1 not good or nice 坏的；不好的: *The weather was very bad.* 天气太坏了。◇ *He's had some bad news—his uncle has died.* 他得到了个坏消息——他叔叔死了。◇ *a bad smell* 坏的气味
2 serious 严重的: *She had a bad accident.* 她出了严重意外。
3 not done or made well 干得或做得坏的: *bad driving* 车开得不好
4 not able to work or do something well 能力差的；不胜任的: *My eyesight is bad.* 我的视力很差。◇ *He's a bad teacher.* 他是个差劲的教师。
5 too old to eat; not fresh 腐坏而不能吃的；不新鲜的: *bad eggs* 腐坏的蛋
bad at something If you are bad at something, you cannot do it well 不擅长的；拙劣的: *I'm very bad at sports.* 我不擅长体育运动。
bad for you If something is bad for you, it can make you ill 对身体有害的；不利健康的: *Smoking is bad for you.* 吸烟于身体有害。
go bad become too old to eat 已腐坏而不能吃的: *This fish has gone bad.* 这条鱼腐烂了。
not bad quite good 很好；不错: *'What was the film like?' 'Not bad.'* "这部影片怎么样？""不错。"
too bad words that you use to say that you cannot change something（用以表示某事物无法改变）没办法；没辙: *'I want to go out.' 'Too bad—you can't!'* "我想出去。""不行——你不能出去！"

badge /bædʒ; bædʒ/ *noun* 名词
a small thing made of metal, plastic or cloth that you wear on your clothes. A badge can show that you belong to a school or club, for example, or it can have words or a picture on it 徽章: *His jacket had a school badge on the pocket.* 他的短上衣口袋上有个校徽。

badly /'bædli; 'bædlɪ/ *adverb* 副词 (**worse, worst**)
1 in a bad way; not well 坏；糟糕: *She played badly.* 她表现得很差。◇ *These clothes are badly made.* 这些衣服做得真次。
2 very much 非常: *He was badly hurt in the accident.* 他在事故中受伤很重。◇ *I badly need a holiday.* 我真需要休假了。

badminton /'bædmɪntən; 'bædmɪntən/ *noun* 名词 (no plural 无复数)
a game for two or four players who try to hit a kind of light ball with feathers on it (called a **shuttlecock**) over a high net, using **rackets** 羽毛球运动（羽毛球叫做 **shuttlecock**，球拍叫做 **racket**）: *Do you want to play badminton?* 你想打羽毛球吗？

bad-tempered /ˌbæd 'tempəd; 'bæd 'tɛmpɚd/ *adjective* 形容词
often angry 脾气坏的；常发怒的: *He's bad-tempered in the mornings.* 他早晨爱发脾气。

bag /bæg; bæg/ *noun* 名词
a thing made of cloth, paper, leather, etc, for holding and carrying things 袋；包；提包: *He put the apples in a paper bag.* 他把苹果放在纸袋里了。◇ *a plastic shopping bag* 购物用的塑料袋 ☞ Look also at **carrier bag** and **handbag** and at the picture at **container**. 另见 **carrier bag** 和 **handbag** 及 **container** 词条插图。

baggage /'bægɪdʒ; 'bægɪdʒ/ *noun* 名词 (no plural 无复数)
bags and suitcases that you take with you when you travel 行李: *We put all our baggage in the car.* 我们把行李都放在汽车里了。

baggy /'bægi; 'bægɪ/ *adjective* 形容词
If clothes are baggy, they are big and loose（指衣服）肥大的，宽松的: *He was wearing baggy trousers.* 他穿的裤子又肥又大。

bagpipes /'bægpaɪps; 'bægˌpaɪps/ *noun* 名词 (plural 复数)
a musical instrument that is often played in Scotland 苏格兰风笛

bake /beɪk; bek/ *verb* 动词 (**bakes, baking, baked** /beɪkt; bekt/)
cook food in an oven 用烤箱烘烤食物: *My brother baked a cake for my birthday.* 我哥哥为我过生日烤了个蛋糕。◇ *baked potatoes* 烤的土豆儿

baked beans /ˌbeɪkt 'bi:nz; ˌbekt 'binz/ *noun* 名词 (plural 复数)
beans cooked in tomato sauce, that you buy in a tin 烘豆（用番茄汁烹调的罐头菜豆）

baker /'beɪkə(r); 'bekɚ/ *noun* 名词
a person who makes and sells bread and cakes 烘制并出售面包和蛋糕的人；面包师傅
✪ A shop that sells bread and cakes is called a **baker's** or a **bakery**. 面包和糕点店叫做 **baker's** 或 **bakery**。

balance¹ /'bæləns; 'bæləns/ *verb* 动词 (**balances, balancing, balanced** /'bælənst; 'bælənst/)
make yourself or something stay without falling to one side or the other 使平衡: *He balanced the bag on his head.* 他用头顶着袋子使之平衡。◇ *She balanced on one leg.* 她用一条腿站着保持平衡。

balance² /'bæləns; 'bæləns/ *noun* 名词
1 (no plural 无复数) when two sides are the same, so that something will not fall 平衡
2 (no plural 无复数) when two things are the same, so that one is not bigger or more important, for example 均衡；均势: *You need a balance between work and play.* 应该劳逸结合。✪ opposite 反义词: **imbalance**
3 (*plural* 复数作 **balances**) how much money you have or must pay after you have spent or paid some（花钱或付部分款项后）剩下的或该付的钱；结余；差额: *The jacket costs £100. You can pay £10 now and the balance* (= £90) *next week.* 这件短上衣100英镑。你可以先付10英镑，下星期再付清（= 90英镑）。
keep your balance stay steady without falling 保持身体平衡: *He tried to keep his balance on the ice.* 他在冰上竭力保持身体平衡。
lose your balance become unsteady; fall 失去平衡；摔倒: *She lost her balance and fell off her bike.* 她失去了平衡，从自行车上摔了下来。

balcony /'bælkəni; 'bælkənɪ/ *noun* 名词 (*plural* 复数作 **balconies**)
a small place on the outside wall of a building, above the ground, where you can stand or sit 阳台

balcony 阳台

B

bald /bɔːld; bɔld/ *adjective* 形容词
with no hair or not much hair 秃顶的；无头发或头发少的: *My dad is going* (= becoming) *bald.* 我爸爸都快秃顶了。☞ picture at **hair** 见 **hair** 词条插图

ball /bɔːl; bɔl/ *noun* 名词
1 a round thing that you use in games and sports 球: *Throw the ball to me.* 把球扔给我。◇ *a football* 足球 ◇ *a tennis-ball* 网球
2 any round thing 球形物: *a ball of string* 一团绳子 ◇ *a snowball* 雪球 ☞ picture on page C25 见第C25 页图
3 a big formal party where people dance（正式举办的）大型舞会

ballerina /ˌbæləˈriːnə; ˌbæləˈrinə/ *noun* 名词
a woman who dances in ballets 芭蕾舞女演员

ballet /ˈbæleɪ; ˈbæle/ *noun* 名词
a kind of dancing that tells a story with music but no words 芭蕾舞: *I went to see a ballet.* 我去看芭蕾舞了。◇ *Do you like ballet?* 你喜欢芭蕾舞吗？
ballet dancer /ˈbæleɪ dɑːnsə(r); ˈbæle ˈdænsɚ/ *noun* 名词
a person who dances in ballets 芭蕾舞演员

balloon /bəˈluːn; bəˈlun/ *noun* 名词
1 a small thing like a bag made of coloured rubber. You fill it with air or gas to make it big and round（彩色橡胶制的）气球: *We are going to hang balloons around the room for the party.* 我们要在聚会的屋里挂起气球。
2 a very big bag that you fill with gas or air so that it can fly. People ride in a basket under it（悬有吊篮可载人的）热气气球: *I would like to go up in a balloon.* 我真想坐坐热气气球升空。

ballot /ˈbælət; ˈbælət/ *noun* 名词
when people choose somebody or something by writing secretly on a piece of paper 无记名投票: *We held a ballot to choose a new president.* 我们举行无记名投票来选举新会长。

ball-point /ˈbɔːl pɔɪnt; ˈbɔl pɔɪnt/ *noun* 名词
a pen that has a very small ball at the end 圆珠笔

ban /bæn; bæn/ *verb* 动词 (**bans, banning, banned** /bænd; bænd/)
say that something must stop or must not happen 禁止: *The film was banned* (= people were not allowed to see it). 这部影片已遭禁映（= 不准大家看）。
ban *noun* 名词
There is a ban on smoking in petrol stations. 在加油站禁止吸烟。

banana /bəˈnɑːnə; bəˈnænə/ *noun* 名词
a long yellow fruit 香蕉

banana 香蕉

band /bænd; bænd/ *noun* 名词
1 a group of people who play music together 乐队: *a rock band* 摇滚乐队 ◇ *a jazz band* 爵士乐队
2 a thin flat piece of material that you put around something 带子；箍: *I put a rubber band round the letters to keep them together.* 我用橡皮筋把信捆在一起。◇ *The hat had a red band round it.* 那顶帽子上有个红箍。

bandage /ˈbændɪdʒ; ˈbændɪdʒ/ *noun* 名词
a long piece of white cloth that you put around a part of the body that is hurt 绷带
bandage *verb* 动词 (**bandages, bandaging, bandaged** /ˈbændɪdʒd; ˈbændɪdʒd/)
put a bandage around a part of the body 用绷带包扎身体某部: *The doctor bandaged my foot.* 医生用绷带把我的脚包上了。

bandit /ˈbændɪt; ˈbændɪt/ *noun* 名词
a person who attacks and robs people who are travelling 拦路抢劫的人；土匪；强盗: *They were killed by bandits in the mountains.* 他们遭山里土匪杀害。

bang[1] /bæŋ; bæŋ/ *noun* 名词
1 a sudden very loud noise 突然发出的巨响: *He shut the door with a bang.* 他砰的一声把门关上了。
2 hitting somebody or something hard; being hit hard 猛击某人或某物；遭猛击: *He fell and got a bang on the head.* 他跌倒了，脑袋磕得很厉害。
3 *American English for* **fringe 1** 美式英语，即 **fringe 1**

bang[2] /bæŋ; bæŋ/ *verb* 动词 (**bangs, banging, banged** /bæŋd; bæŋd/)
make a loud noise by hitting something hard or by closing something（猛击某物或关闭某物）发出巨响: *He banged his head*

on the ceiling. 他脑袋砰的一声撞在天花板上了。◇ *Don't bang the door!* 不要砰砰地关门！

banisters /'bænɪstəz; 'bænɪstɚz/ *noun* 名词 (plural 复数)
a thing like a fence at the side of stairs that you hold on to when you go up or down 楼梯的扶手

bank /bæŋk; bæŋk/ *noun* 名词
1 a place that keeps money safe for people 银行: *I've got £300 in the bank.* 我在银行里有300英镑。

✪ If you have a bank **account**, you can **save** money, **pay** money **in** (or **deposit** it), or **draw** it **out** (or **withdraw** it). 如果有银行账户(**account**)，就可以把钱储蓄(**save**)起来，或存钱 (**pay** money **in**，或称 **deposit** it)，或取钱 (**draw** it **out**，或称 **withdraw** it)。At a bank, you can also **exchange** the money of one country for the money of another. 在银行还可以兑换(**exchange**)外币。If you want to **borrow** money, a bank may **lend** it to you. 要是想借 (**borrow**)钱的话，银行可以借(**lend**)给你。

2 the land along the side of a river 河岸: *I climbed out of the boat onto the bank.* 我好不容易从船上出来，登上了岸。

bank holiday /ˌbæŋk 'hɒlədeɪ; ˌbæŋk 'hɑləˌde/ *noun* 名词
a day when the banks are closed and everybody in Britain has a holiday 银行假日(银行停止营业的日子，在英国大家都放假)

banknote /'bæŋknəʊt; 'bæŋknot/ *noun* 名词
a piece of paper money 纸币；钞票: *These are German banknotes.* 这是德国钞票。

bankrupt /'bæŋkrʌpt; 'bæŋkrʌpt/ *adjective* 形容词
not able to pay the money that you should pay to people 无力偿付应付的款项的；破产的: *His business went* (= became) *bankrupt.* 他的公司破产了。

banner /'bænə(r); 'bænɚ/ *noun* 名词
a long piece of cloth with words on it. People carry banners to show what they think (有标语或口号的) 横幅: *The banner said 'Stop the war'.* 横幅上写着："停止战争"。

baptize /bæp'taɪz; bæp'taɪz/ *verb* 动词 (**baptizes**, **baptizing**, **baptized** /bæp'taɪzd; bæp'taɪzd/)
put water on somebody or put somebody in water, and give them a name, to show that they belong to the Christian Church 为某人施行圣洗让其加入基督的教会；施洗；授洗

baptism /'bæptɪzm; 'bæptɪzəm/ *noun* 名词
a special time when somebody is baptized 洗礼；圣洗

bar[1] /bɑ:(r); bɑr/ *noun* 名词
1 a place where people can buy and have drinks and sometimes food 可以买到饮料有时也可买到食物的处所；酒吧；小卖部: *There's a bar in the hotel.* 这个旅馆有个酒吧。◇ *a coffee bar* 咖啡饮品部
2 a long table where you buy drinks in a bar or pub 酒吧或酒馆里出售饮料的长桌子或柜台: *We stood at the bar.* 我们站在酒吧柜台处。
3 a long piece of metal 长条金属: *an iron bar* 一根铁棒
4 a piece of something hard 条形硬物: *a bar of soap* 一条肥皂 ◇ *a bar of chocolate* 一条巧克力 ☞ picture on page C25 见第C25页图

bar[2] /bɑ:(r); bɑr/ *verb* 动词 (**bars**, **barring**, **barred** /bɑ:d; bɑrd/)
put something across a place so that people cannot pass 在某处设置某物使人不能通过: *A line of police barred the road.* 警察在路上排成人墙禁止通行。

barbecue /'bɑ:bɪkju:; 'bɑrbɪˌkju/ *noun* 名词
a party where you cook food on a fire outside 户外烧烤餐会；烧烤野餐: *We had a barbecue on the beach.* 我们在海滩举行了个野餐烧烤会。

barbed wire /ˌbɑ:bd 'waɪə(r); 'bɑrbd 'waɪr/ *noun* 名词 (no plural 无复数)
wire with a lot of sharp points on it. Some fences are made of barbed wire. 刺钢丝；铁丝网

barber /'bɑ:bə(r); 'bɑrbɚ/ *noun* 名词
a person whose job is to cut men's hair (给男子剪发的) 理发师: *I went to the barber's* (= the barber's shop) *to have my hair cut.* 我去理发馆理发去了。

bare /beə(r); bɛr/ *adjective* 形容词
1 with no clothes or anything else

B

covering it 无衣物或其他东西遮盖的；裸露的：*He had bare feet* (= he wasn't wearing shoes or socks). 他光着脚（= 没穿鞋袜）。◇ *The walls were bare* (= with no pictures on them). 墙上光秃秃的（= 没有画儿）。

2 empty 空的: *The garden always looks very bare in winter.* 这个花园冬天看上去总是空荡荡的。

barefoot /ˈbeəfʊt; ˈbɛrˌfʊt/ *adjective, adverb* 形容词，副词
with no shoes or socks on your feet 光脚的；赤脚的（不穿鞋袜的）: *The children ran barefoot along the beach.* 孩子们在沙滩上光着脚跑。

barely /ˈbeəli; ˈbɛrlɪ/ *adverb* 副词
almost not; only just 几乎没有；仅够: *She barely ate anything.* 她简直没吃东西。

bargain[1] /ˈbɑ:gən; ˈbɑrgɪn/ *noun* 名词
something that is cheaper than usual 廉价的东西: *This dress was a bargain—it only cost £10.* 这件连衣裙是廉价品——仅仅10英镑。

bargain[2] /ˈbɑ:gən; ˈbɑrgɪn/ *verb* 动词 (**bargains, bargaining, bargained** /ˈbɑ:gənd; ˈbɑrgɪnd/)
talk with somebody about the right price for something 讨价还价: *I think she'll sell the car for less if you bargain with her.* 我看你要是跟她讲讲价儿，她那辆汽车能卖便宜点儿。

barge /bɑ:dʒ; bɑrdʒ/ *noun* 名词
a long boat with a flat bottom for carrying things or people on rivers or canals 驳船

bark[1] /bɑ:k; bɑrk/ *noun* 名词 (no plural 无复数)
the stuff that covers the outside of a tree 树皮

bark[2] /bɑ:k; bɑrk/ *noun* 名词
the short loud noise that a dog makes 狗的叫声

bark *verb* 动词 (**barks, barking, barked** /bɑ:kt; bɑrkt/)
make this noise（狗）叫；吠: *The dog always barks at people it doesn't know.* 这条狗总是冲着生人叫。

barley /ˈbɑ:li; ˈbɑrlɪ/ *noun* 名词 (no plural 无复数)
a plant that we use for food and for making beer and some other drinks 大麦

barmaid /ˈbɑ:meɪd; ˈbɑrˌmed/ *noun* 名词
a woman who sells drinks in a bar or pub 酒吧或酒馆的女服务员

barman /ˈbɑ:mən; ˈbɑrmən/ *noun* 名词 (*plural* 复数作 **barmen** /ˈbɑ:mən; ˈbɑrmən/)
a man who sells drinks in a bar or pub 酒吧或酒馆的男服务员

barn /bɑ:n; bɑrn/ *noun* 名词
a large building on a farm where you keep crops or animals 农场的仓房或家畜、家禽的棚舍

barometer /bəˈrɒmɪtə(r); bəˈrɑmətə/ *noun* 名词
an instrument that helps us to know what the weather will be 气压计；晴雨表

barracks /ˈbærəks; ˈbærəks/ *noun* 名词 (plural 复数)
a building or group of buildings where soldiers live 兵营；营房: *an army barracks* 陆军营房

barrel /ˈbærəl; ˈbærəl/ *noun* 名词
1 a big container for liquids, with round sides and flat ends 桶；琵琶桶: *a beer barrel* 啤酒桶 ◇ *a barrel of oil* 一桶石油
2 the long metal part of a gun that a bullet goes through 枪管

barricade /ˌbærɪˈkeɪd; ˌbærəˈked/ *noun* 名词
a wall of things that people build quickly to stop other people going somewhere 匆匆设置的壁垒；路障: *There was a barricade of lorries across the road.* 路上横着一辆辆卡车挡住了路。

barricade *verb* 动词 (**barricades, barricading, barricaded**)
stop people going somewhere by building a barricade 设壁垒或路障: *He barricaded the door to keep the police out.* 他封住了门不让警察进来。

barrier /ˈbæriə(r); ˈbærɪə/ *noun* 名词
a fence or gate that stops you going somewhere 栅栏；屏障；关卡: *You must show your ticket at the barrier before you get on the train.* 必须在检票处出示车票，才能上火车。

barrow /ˈbærəʊ; ˈbæro/ *noun* 名词
a small cart that you can push or pull 手推车

base[1] /beɪs; bes/ *noun* 名词
1 the bottom part of something; the part

that something stands on 底部；底座；基底: *The lamp has a flat base.* 这个灯底座是平的。

2 the place that you start from and go back to 基地；根据地: *She travels all over the world but London is her base* (= the place where she lives). 她周游世界而伦敦是她居住的地方。◇ *an army base* 陆军基地

base[2] /beɪs; bes/ *verb* 动词 (**bases, basing, based** /beɪst; best/)

base something on something make something, using another thing as an important part 以某事物为另一事物的根据、证据等: *The film is based on a true story.* 这部影片是根据事实拍摄的。

baseball /ˈbeɪsbɔːl; ˈbesˌbɔl/ *noun* 名词

1 (no plural 无复数) an American game for two teams of nine players who try to hit a ball with a **bat** on a large field 棒球运动（球棒叫做 **bat**）: *We played baseball in the park.* 我们在公园里打棒球。

2 (*plural* 复数作 **baseballs**) a ball for playing this game 棒球

basement /ˈbeɪsmənt; ˈbesmənt/ *noun* 名词

the part of a building that is under the ground 地下室

bases *plural of* **basis** ✳ **basis** 的复数形式

bash /bæʃ; bæʃ/ *verb* 动词 (**bashes, bashing, bashed** /bæʃt; bæʃt/)

hit somebody or something very hard 猛击或猛撞某人或某物: *I fell and bashed my knee.* 我摔倒了，把膝盖磕了。

basic /ˈbeɪsɪk; ˈbesɪk/ *adjective* 形容词

most important and necessary; simple 最重要的和最必要的；基本的；根本的；基础的: *A person's basic needs are food, clothes and a place to live.* 人最基本的需要就是食物、衣服、住处。

basically /ˈbeɪsɪkli; ˈbesɪklɪ/ *adverb* 副词

mostly; mainly 最重要地；主要地；基本上；根本上: *Basically I like her, but I don't always agree with what she says.* 我基本上很喜欢她，可是她说的话我并不是每次都同意。

basin /ˈbeɪsn; ˈbesn̩/ *noun* 名词

a round bowl for cooking or mixing food（烹饪或搅拌食物用的）盆 ☞ Look also at **wash-basin**. 另见 **wash-basin**。

basis /ˈbeɪsɪs; ˈbesɪs/ *noun* 名词 (*plural* 复数作 **bases** /ˈbeɪsiːz; ˈbesiz/)

the most important part or idea, from which something grows 最重要的部分或意见（借以引发某事物）；基础: *Her notes formed the basis of a book.* 她的笔记构成了一部书的基础。

basket /ˈbɑːskɪt; ˈbæskɪt/ *noun* 名词

a container made of thin sticks or thin pieces of plastic or metal, that you use for holding or carrying things 篮子；篓子；筐子: *a shopping basket* 购物篮子 ◇ *a bread basket* 面包筐 ☞ Look also at **waste-paper basket**. 另见 **waste-paper basket**。

basket 篮子

basketball 篮球运动

basketball /ˈbɑːskɪtbɔːl; ˈbæskɪtˌbɔl/ *noun* 名词

1 (no plural 无复数) a game for two teams of five players who try to throw a ball into a high net 篮球运动

2 (*plural* 复数作 **basketballs**) a ball for playing this game 篮球

bass /beɪs; bes/ *adjective* 形容词

with a deep sound 低音的: *She plays the bass guitar.* 她演奏低音吉他。◇ *a bass drum* 低音鼓

bat /bæt; bæt/ *noun* 名词

1 an animal like a mouse with wings. Bats come out and fly at night. 蝙蝠

2 a piece of wood for hitting the ball in a game like cricket or table tennis（板球或乒乓球等的）球板；球棒；球拍: *a baseball bat* 棒球的球棒

batch /bætʃ; bætʃ/ *noun* 名词 (*plural* 复数作 **batches**)

a group of things 一批: *She made a batch of cakes.* 她做了一批糕点。

bath /bɑ:θ; bæθ/ *noun* 名词 (*plural* 复数作 **baths** /bɑ:ðz; bæðz/)
1 a large thing that you fill with water and sit in to wash your body 澡盆；浴缸
2 washing your body in a bath 洗澡：*I had a bath this morning.* 我今天早晨洗澡了。

bathe /beɪð; beð/ *verb* 动词 (**bathes**, **bathing**, **bathed** /beɪðd; beðd/)
1 wash a part of your body carefully 仔细清洗身体某部：*He bathed the cut on his finger.* 他仔细清洗手指上的伤口。
2 swim in the sea or in a lake or river（在海里、湖里或河里）游泳：*On hot days we often bathe in the lake.* 天热的时候，我们常在湖里游泳。✪ It is more usual to say **go swimming**. 通常说 **go swimming**。

bathroom /'bɑ:θru:m; 'bæθˌrum/ *noun* 名词
a room where you can wash and have a bath or shower 浴室 ✪ In American English, a **bathroom** is also a room with a toilet in it. 在美式英语中，**bathroom** 还指有抽水马桶的厕所。

battery /'bætri; 'bætərɪ/ *noun* 名词 (*plural* 复数作 **batteries**)
a thing that gives electricity. You put batteries inside things like torches and radios to make them work 电池：*The car needs a new battery.* 这辆汽车需要换新电池了。

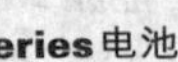
batteries 电池

battle /'bætl; 'bætḷ/ *noun* 名词
1 a fight between armies in a war 战斗；战役；交战：*Who won the battle?* 这场战役谁打胜了？
2 trying very hard to do something difficult 奋斗；斗争：*a battle against the illness* 对抗这种疾病的斗争
battled *verb* 动词 (**battles**, **battling**, **battled** /'bætld; 'bætḷd/)
try very hard to do something difficult 奋斗；斗争：*The doctors battled to save her life.* 医生们奋力抢救她。

bay /beɪ; be/ *noun* 名词 (*plural* 复数作 **bays**)
a place where the land goes inwards and the sea fills the space 海湾：*There was a ship in the bay.* 海湾里有一艘船。◇ *the Bay of Biscay* 比斯开湾

bazaar /bə'zɑ:(r); bə'zɑr/ *noun* 名词
a market in Asia or Africa 亚洲的或非洲的集市

BC /ˌbi: 'si:; 'bi 'si/
'BC' in a date shows it was before Christ was born ✳ BC 表示所指的是耶稣出生前的日期；公元前：*Julius Caesar died in 44 BC.* 凯撒死于公元前44年。☞ Look at **AD**. 见 **AD**。

be /bi, bi:; bɪ, 'bi/ *verb* 动词
1 a word that you use when you name or describe somebody or something 指称某人或某事物的用词：*I'm* (= I am) *Ben.* 我的名字叫本。◇ *Grass is green.* 草是绿色的。◇ *Are you hot?* 你热吗？◇ *Lucy is a doctor.* 露西是医生。◇ *Where were you*

be

present tense 现在时态		*short forms* 缩略式	*negative short forms* 否定缩略式
I	**am** /æm; æm/	I**'m**	I**'m not**
you	**are** /ɑ:(r); ɑr/	you**'re**	you **aren't**
he/she/it	**is** /ɪz; ɪz/	he**'s**/she**'s**/it**'s**	he/she/it **isn't**
we	**are**	we**'re**	we **aren't**
you	**are**	you**'re**	you **aren't**
they	**are**	they**'re**	they **aren't**

past tense 过去时态		
I	**was** /wɒz; wʌz/	*present participle* 现在分词 **being**
you	**were** /wɜ:(r); wɝ/	*past participle* 过去分词 **been**
he/she/it	**was**	
we	**were**	
you	**were**	
they	**were**	

yesterday? 你昨天在哪儿呢？◇ *It is six o'clock.* 现在六点钟了。

2 happen 发生: *Her birthday was in May.* 她的生日在五月份。

3 a word that you use with another verb 与另一动词连用的词: *'What are you doing?' 'I am reading.'* "你干什么呢？" "我看书呢。"

4 a word that you use with part of another verb to show that something happens to somebody or something 与另一动词的某种形式连用，表示某人或某事物发生某事: *This cheese is made in France.* 这种乳酪是法国做的。◇ *The house was built in 1910.* 这所房子是1910年建的。

5 a word that shows that something must or will happen 表示某事物一定发生或将要发生的词: *You are to go to bed immediately!* 你得马上睡觉去！

beach /bi:tʃ; bitʃ/ *noun* 名词 (*plural* 复数作 **beaches**)
a piece of land next to the sea that is covered with sand or stones 海滩: *a sandy beach* 沙滩 ◇ *We lay on the beach in the sun.* 我们躺在海滩上晒太阳。

bead /bi:d; bid/ *noun* 名词
a small ball of wood, glass or plastic with a hole in the middle. Beads are put on a string to make a necklace.（木制的、玻璃的或塑料的）珠子（中间有孔可穿线绳）

beak /bi:k; bik/ *noun* 名词
the hard pointed part of a bird's mouth（鸟的）嘴 ☞ picture at **bird** 见 **bird** 词条插图

beam /bi:m; bim/ *noun* 名词
1 a long heavy piece of wood that holds up a roof or ceiling（房屋的）梁

2 a line of light 一道光；光束: *sunbeams* 阳光束

bean /bi:n; bin/ *noun* 名词
the long thin part of some plants, or the seeds inside it, that we use as food 豆子；豆荚: *green beans* 豆角 ◇ *coffee beans* 咖啡豆

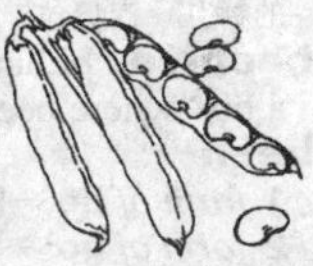
bean 豆子

bear¹ /beə(r); bɛr/ *noun* 名词
a big wild animal with thick fur 熊 ☞ Look also at **teddy bear**. 另见 **teddy bear**。

bear² /beə(r); bɛr/ *verb* 动词 (**bears, bearing, bore** /bɔ:(r); bɔr/, **has borne** /bɔ:n; bɔrn/)
1 have pain or problems without complaining 有痛苦或困难而不吭声；忍耐；忍受: *The pain was difficult to bear.* 痛苦难忍。

2 hold somebody or something up so that they do not fall 承载或支撑某人或某事物: *The ice is too thin to bear your weight.* 这块冰很薄，禁不住你。

can't bear something hate something 讨厌某事物: *I can't bear this music.* 我很讨厌这种音乐。◇ *He can't bear having nothing to do.* 什么事都不干，他可受不了。

beard /bɪəd; bɪrd/ *noun* 名词
the hair on a man's chin and cheeks 胡须；络腮胡子: *He has got a beard.* 他留着大胡子。

bearded *adjective* 形容词
with a beard 有胡须的；留着络腮胡子的: *a bearded man* 长着大胡子的男子

beard 胡须

beast /bi:st; bist/ *noun* 名词
1 a big animal 大的动物；走兽 ✪ **Animal** is the word that we usually use. ＊ **animal** 是常用词。

2 an unkind or cruel person 恶人；野蛮的人

beat¹ /bi:t; bit/ *noun* 名词
a sound that comes again and again 反复出现的声音: *We heard the beat of the drums.* 我们听到了鼓声。◇ *Can you feel her heartbeat?* 你感觉到她心跳吗？

beat² /bi:t; bit/ *verb* 动词 (**beats, beating, beat, has beaten** /'bi:tn; 'bitn̩/)
1 win a fight or game against a person or group of people（打斗或比赛）打败或战胜某人或对方: *Daniel always beats me at tennis.* 丹尼尔跟我打网球，他总是赢我。◇ *Our team was beaten.* 我们队输了。

2 hit somebody or something very hard many times 连续猛击某人或某物: *She beats her dog with a stick.* 她用棍子打她的狗。◇ *The rain was beating on the roof.* 雨点敲打着屋顶。

3 make the same sound or movement

many times 连续发出同一声音或做出同一动作: *His heart was beating fast.* 他的心脏跳动得很快。

4 mix food quickly with a fork, for example 很快地搅拌食物（例如用叉子）: *Beat the eggs and sugar together.* 把鸡蛋和糖搅拌一起。

beautiful /'bju:təfl; 'bjutəfəl/ *adjective* 形容词

very nice to see, hear or smell; lovely 非常好看、好听或好闻的；漂亮的；可爱的；美丽的: *Those flowers are beautiful.* 那些花儿真漂亮。◇ *What a beautiful song!* 多好听的歌儿啊！◇ *a beautiful woman* 美女

> ✪ When we talk about people, we usually use **beautiful** and **pretty** for women and girls, and **handsome** and **good-looking** for men and boys. 形容人时，指女的一般用 **beautiful** 和 **pretty**，指男的用 **handsome** 和 **good-looking**。

beautifully /'bju:təfli; 'bjutəfəlɪ/ *adverb* 副词

Louis sang beautifully. 路易斯唱得好听极了。

beauty /'bju:ti; 'bjutɪ/ *noun* 名词 (no plural 无复数)

being beautiful 美: *She was a woman of great beauty.* 她是个大美人。◇ *the beauty of the mountains* 山景之美

because /bɪ'kɒz; bɪ'kɔz/ *conjunction* 连词

for the reason that 因为: *He was angry because I was late.* 因为我迟到了，他很生气。

because of something as a result of something 由于某事物: *We stayed at home because of the rain.* 我们因雨而呆在家里。

become /bɪ'kʌm; bɪ'kʌm/ *verb* 动词 (**becomes**, **becoming**, **became** /bɪ'keɪm; bɪ'kem/, **has become**)

grow or change and begin to be something 变成；成为: *She became a doctor in 1982.* 她在1982年成了医生。◇ *The weather is becoming colder.* 天气渐渐冷了。

become of somebody or 或 **something** happen to somebody or something 某人或某事物的情况: *What became of David? I haven't seen him for years.* 戴维怎么了？我好些日子没看见他了。

bed /bed; bɛd/ *noun* 名词

1 a thing that you sleep on 床: *I was tired, so I went to bed.* 我当时很累，就上床睡觉了。◇ *The children are in bed.* 孩子都在床上呢。

2 the bottom of a river or the sea 河床；海床

bed and breakfast a small hotel or a house where you can sleep and have breakfast 可住宿并有次日早餐的小旅馆或房子: *I stayed in a bed and breakfast.* 我住在一家管早饭的小旅馆里。

make the bed put the covers on a bed so that it is tidy and ready for somebody to sleep in it 铺床

bedclothes /'bedkləʊðz; 'bɛdˌkloz/ *noun* 名词 (plural 复数)

all the covers (for example **sheets**, **blankets** or **duvets**) that you put on a bed 床上用品（床单叫做 **sheet**、毯子叫做 **blanket**、羽绒被叫做 **duvet**）

bedroom /'bedru:m; 'bɛdˌrum/ *noun* 名词

a room where you sleep 卧室

bedsit /'bedsɪt; 'bɛdsɪt/, **bedsitter** /ˌbed'sɪtə(r); ˌbɛd'sɪtɚ/ *noun* 名词

one room that you live and sleep in 卧室兼起居室

bee /bi:; bi/ *noun* 名词

a small insect that flies and makes honey 蜜蜂

beef /bi:f; bif/ *noun* 名词 (no plural 无复数)

meat from a cow 牛肉: *roast beef* 烤牛肉

☞ Note at **cow** 见 **cow** 词条注释

beefburger /'bi:fbɜ:gə(r); 'bifˌbɝgɚ/ *noun* 名词

beef cut into very small pieces and made into a flat round shape 用碎牛肉做的饼儿；汉堡包

beehive /'bi:haɪv; 'biˌhaɪv/ *noun* 名词

a box where bees live 蜂房

been

1 *form of* **be** ✱ **be** 的不同形式

2 *form of* **go**[1] ✱ **go**[1] 的不同形式

have been to have gone to a place and come back 到某处后返回: *Have you ever been to Scotland?* 你去过苏格兰吗？

☞ Note at **go** 见 **go** 词条注释

beer /bɪə(r); bɪr/ *noun* 名词

1 (no plural 无复数) an alcoholic drink made from grain 啤酒: *a pint of beer* 一品脱啤酒

2 (*plural* 复数作 **beers**) a glass, bottle or can of beer 一杯、一瓶或一罐啤酒: *Three beers, please.* 请来三杯啤酒。

beetle /ˈbiːtl; ˈbitl̩/ *noun* 名词
an insect with hard wings and a shiny body 甲虫

beetroot /ˈbiːtruːt; ˈbitˌrut/ *noun* 名词
a round dark-red vegetable that you cook before you eat it 甜菜根

before[1] /bɪˈfɔː(r); bɪˈfɔr/ *preposition* 介词
1 earlier than somebody or something 比某人或某事物早；在某人或某事物以前: *He arrived before me.* 他比我到得早。◇ *I lived in America before coming to England.* 我来英国以前住在美国。
2 in front of somebody or something 在某人或某事物的前面: *B comes before C in the alphabet.* 在字母表里，B在C的前边。

before[2] /bɪˈfɔː(r); bɪˈfɔr/ *adverb* 副词
at an earlier time; in the past 以前；过去: *I've never met them before.* 我从来没见过他们。◇ *I've seen this film before.* 我以前看过这部电影。

before[3] /bɪˈfɔː(r); bɪˈfɔr/ *conjunction* 连词
earlier than the time that 在…以前: *I said goodbye before I left.* 我临走前说了声再见。

beforehand /bɪˈfɔːhænd; bɪˈfɔrˌhænd/ *adverb* 副词
at an earlier time than something 较早时；预先: *Tell me beforehand if you are going to be late.* 要是你得晚来就事先告诉我一声。

beg /beg; bɛg/ *verb* 动词 (**begs, begging, begged** /begd; bɛgd/)
1 ask for money or food because you are very poor 乞求钱或食物；行乞: *There are a lot of people begging in the streets.* 街上有很多人要饭。
2 ask somebody for something in a very strong way 恳求；请求；央求: *She begged me to stay with her.* 她央求我跟她在一起。◇ *He begged for help.* 他求人帮忙。
I beg your pardon **1** I am sorry 对不起；请原谅: *'You've taken my seat.' 'Oh, I beg your pardon.'* "您占了我的座位了。""噢，真对不起。" **2** What did you say? 您说什么？

beggar /ˈbegə(r); ˈbɛgɚ/ *noun* 名词
a person who asks other people for money or food 乞丐；叫花子

begin /bɪˈgɪn; bɪˈgɪn/ *verb* 动词 (**begins, beginning, began** /bɪˈgæn; bɪˈgæn/, **has begun** /bɪˈgʌn; bɪˈgʌn/)
start to do something or start to happen 开始: *The film begins at 7.30.* 电影7点30分开演。◇ *The baby began crying.* 孩子哭起来了。◇ *I'm beginning to feel cold.* 我渐渐感觉到冷了。◇ *The name John begins with a 'J'.* 约翰这个名字开头的字母是J。
to begin with at first; at the beginning 首先；起初: *To begin with he was afraid of the water, but he soon learned to swim.* 他起初怕水，可是不久就学会了游泳。

beginner /bɪˈgɪnə(r); bɪˈgɪnɚ/ *noun* 名词
a person who is starting to do or learn something 新手；初学者

beginning /bɪˈgɪnɪŋ; bɪˈgɪnɪŋ/ *noun* 名词
the time or place where something starts; the first part of something 开始的时间或地方；开始的部分: *I didn't see the beginning of the film.* 我没看到这部影片的开头。

begun *form of* **begin** ＊ **begin** 的不同形式

behalf /bɪˈhɑːf; bɪˈhæf/ *noun* 名词
on behalf of somebody, on somebody's behalf for somebody; in the place of somebody 为某人；代表某人: *Mr Smith is away, so I am writing to you on his behalf.* 史密斯先生不在，我代表他给你写信。

behave /bɪˈheɪv; bɪˈhev/ *verb* 动词 (**behaves, behaving, behaved** /bɪˈheɪvd; bɪˈhevd/)
do and say things in a certain way when you are with other people（与他人相处时）做事或说话的方式；表现；为人: *They behaved very kindly towards me.* 他们对我非常和蔼。◇ *The children behaved badly all day.* 孩子们整天都表现得很差。
behave yourself be good; do and say the right things 规矩些；乖乖地: *Did the children behave themselves?* 孩子们乖不乖？

behavior *American English for* **behaviour** 美式英语，即 **behaviour**

B

behaviour /bɪˈheɪvjə(r); bɪˈhevjɚ/ *noun* 名词 (no plural 无复数)
the way you are; the way that you do and say things when you are with other people 举止；行为；表现；为人: *The teacher was pleased with the children's good behaviour.* 那位老师很满意学生的良好表现。

behind /bɪˈhaɪnd; bɪˈhaɪnd/ *preposition, adverb* 介词，副词
1 at or to the back of somebody or something 在某人或某物的后面；向某人或某物的后面: *I hid behind the wall.* 我藏在墙的后面。◇ *I went in front and Jim followed behind.* 我在前边走，吉姆在后边跟着。☞ picture on page C1 见第C1页图
2 slower or less good than somebody or something; slower or less good than you should be 比某人或某物慢或差；比自己正常情况慢或差: *She is behind with her work because she is often ill.* 她因病把工作落下了。
3 in the place where you were before 在原来的地方: *I got off the train and left my suitcase behind* (= on the train). 我下了火车把手提箱落下了（= 落在火车上了）。

being¹ *form of* **be** ✳ **be** 的不同形式

being² /ˈbiːɪŋ; ˈbiɪŋ/ *noun* 名词
a person or living thing 人；生物: *a being from another planet* 从另一星球来的生物

belief /bɪˈliːf; bɪˈlif/ *noun* 名词
a sure feeling that something is true or real 相信；信仰: *his belief in God* 他对上帝的信仰

believe /bɪˈliːv; bɪˈliv/ *verb* 动词 (**believes**, **believing**, **believed** /bɪˈliːvd; bɪˈlivd/)
feel sure that something is true or right; feel sure that what somebody says is true 认为某事物属实或正确；相信某人说的话: *She says she didn't take the money. Do you believe her?* 她说她没拿那笔钱。你相信吗？◇ *Long ago, people believed that the earth was flat.* 很久以前，大家认为地球是扁平的。
believe in somebody or 或 **something** feel sure that somebody or something is real 相信某人或某事物存在: *Do you believe in ghosts?* 你相信有鬼吗？

bell /bel; bɛl/ *noun* 名词
a metal thing that makes a sound when something hits or touches it 钟；铃: *The church bells were ringing.* 教堂的钟声响着。◇ *I rang the bell and he answered the door.* 我按了按铃以后他来开门。

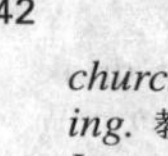
bell 铃

belly /ˈbeli; ˈbɛlɪ/ *noun* 名词 (*plural* 复数作 **bellies**)
the part of your body between your chest and your legs; your stomach 肚子；胃

belong /bɪˈlɒŋ; bəˈlɔŋ/ *verb* 动词 (**belongs**, **belonging**, **belonged** /bɪˈlɒŋd; bəˈlɔŋd/)
have its right or usual place 在应在之处；在原处: *That chair belongs in my room.* 那把椅子是我屋的。
belong to somebody be somebody's 属于某人: *'Who does this pen belong to?' 'It belongs to me.'* "这枝钢笔是谁的？" "是我的。"
belong to something be in a group, club, etc 从属于某组织、俱乐部等: *She belongs to the tennis club.* 她是网球俱乐部的。

belongings /bɪˈlɒŋɪŋz; bəˈlɔŋɪŋz/ *noun* 名词 (plural 复数)
the things that you own 个人的所有物；财物: *They lost all their belongings in the fire.* 这场火灾过后他们失去了一切财物。

below /bɪˈləʊ; bəˈlo/ *preposition, adverb* 介词，副词
1 in or to a lower place than somebody or something 在某人或某事物的下面；在下方；往下: *From the plane we could see the mountains below.* 我们从飞机上能看到下面的山。◇ *Your mouth is below your nose.* 嘴长在鼻子下面。◇ *Do not write below this line.* 不要在这条线之下写字。
2 less than a number or price 低于某一数目或价格: *The temperature was below zero.* 气温在零度以下。☞ picture on page C1 见第C1页图

belt /belt; bɛlt/ *noun* 名词
a long piece of cloth or leather that you wear around the middle of your body 腰带 ☞ picture at **suit**. 见 **suit** 词条插图。Look also at **safety-belt** and **seat-belt**. 另见 **safety-belt** 和 **seat-belt**。

bench /bentʃ; bɛntʃ/ *noun* 名词 (*plural* 复数作 **benches**)
1 a long seat made of wood or metal,

bench 长椅

usually outside 长椅，长凳（通常指户外用的）: *They sat on a park bench.* 他们坐在公园的长椅上。

2 a long table where somebody, for example a carpenter, works（长形的）工作台（例如木工用的）

bend[1] /bend; bɛnd/ *verb* 动词 (**bends**, **bending**, **bent** /bent; bɛnt/, **has bent**)
become curved; make something that was straight into a curved shape 弯；把直的弄弯: *Bend your legs!* 曲腿！◇ *She couldn't bend the metal bar.* 她弄不弯那条金属棒。

bend down, bend over move your body forward and down 弯腰；弯身: *She bent down to put on her shoes.* 她弯下身来穿鞋。

He is **bending** down.
他弯下身来。

bend[2] /bend; bɛnd/ *noun* 名词
a part of a road or river that is not straight（道路或河流的）转弯处: *Drive slowly—there's a bend in the road.* 慢驶——路上有个弯。

beneath /bɪ'ni:θ; bɪ'niθ/ *preposition*, *adverb* 介词，副词
in or to a lower place than somebody or something 在某人或某事物的下面；在下方；往下: *From the tower, they looked down on the city beneath.* 他们从塔顶俯视下面的城市。✪ **Under** and **below** are the words that we usually use. ✳ **under** 和 **below** 是常用词。

benefit /'benɪfɪt; 'bɛnəfɪt/ *verb* 动词 (**benefits**, **benefiting**, **benefited**)
be good or helpful in some way 有益于；有助于: *The new law will benefit families with children.* 新法规可使有孩子的家庭获益。

benefit from something get something good or useful from something 从某事物中获益: *She will benefit from a holiday.* 她度假对她能有好处。

benefit *noun* 名词
something that is good or helpful 好处；益处；助益: *What are the benefits of having a computer?* 有个计算机有什么好处？◇ *I did it for your benefit* (= to help you). 我那样做是为你好（= 为帮助你）。

bent *form of* **bend**[1] ✳ **bend**[1] 的不同形式

berry /'beri; 'bɛrɪ/ *noun* 名词 (*plural* 复数作 **berries**)
a small soft fruit with seeds in it 浆果；聚合果: *a strawberry* 草莓 ◇ *a blackberry* 黑莓 ◇ *raspberries* 悬钩子

beside /bɪ'saɪd; bɪ'saɪd/ *preposition* 介词
at the side of somebody or something; next to somebody or something 在某人或某物的旁边；紧挨着某人或某物: *Come and sit beside me.* 过来坐在我旁边。☞ picture on page C1 见第C1页图

besides[1] /bɪ'saɪdz; bɪ'saɪdz/ *preposition* 介词
as well as somebody or something; if you do not count somebody or something 除某人或某事物之外（还有）；要是不把某人或某事物计算在内: *There were four people in the room, besides me and Jim.* 房间里有四个人，不算我和吉姆。

besides[2] /bɪ'saɪdz; bɪ'saɪdz/ *adverb* 副词
also 而且；还有: *I don't like this shirt. Besides, it's too expensive.* 我不喜欢这件衬衫。再说，也太贵了。

best[1] /best; bɛst/ *adjective* 形容词 (**good**, **better**, **best**)
most good 最好的: *This is the best ice-cream I have ever eaten!* 这是我吃过的最好的冰激凌！◇ *Tom is my best friend.* 汤姆是我最好的朋友。

best[2] /best; bɛst/ *adverb* 副词
1 most well 最好地: *I work best in the morning.* 我早晨工作效果最好。
2 more than all others; most 最为；最: *Which picture do you like best?* 你最喜欢哪张画儿？

best[3] /best; bɛst/ *noun* 名词 (no plural 无复数)
the most good person or thing 最好的人或事物: *Mike and Ian are good at tennis but Paul is the best.* 迈克和伊恩网球打得好，可是保罗打得最好。

all the best words that you use when you say goodbye to somebody, to wish them success（告别时的祝愿用语）一切顺利

do your best do all that you can 竭尽全力: *I don't know if I can finish the work today, but I'll do my best.* 我不知道今天能不能把工作做完，但是我一定尽力而为。

best man /ˌbest ˈmæn; ˌbɛst ˈmæn/ *noun* 名词
a man at a wedding who helps the man who is getting married 男傧相；伴郎

B

bet /bet; bɛt/ *verb* 动词 (**bets**, **betting**, **bet** or 或 **betted**, **has bet** or 或 **has betted**)
say what you think will happen. If you are right, you win money, but if you are wrong, you lose money 打赌: *I bet you £5 that our team will win.* 我和你打5英镑的赌，我们队一定赢。
I bet I am sure 我敢肯定: *I bet it will rain tomorrow.* 我管保明天下雨。◇ *I bet you can't climb that tree.* 我肯定你爬不上那棵树去。
bet *noun* 名词
I lost the bet. 我赌输了。

betray /bɪˈtreɪ; bɪˈtre/ *verb* 动词 (**betrays**, **betraying**, **betrayed** /bɪˈtreɪd; bɪˈtred/)
do something that harms somebody who was your friend 背叛: *The guards betrayed the King and let the enemy into the castle.* 卫兵背叛了国王，把敌人放进了城堡。

better /ˈbetə(r); ˈbɛtɚ/ *adjective* 形容词 (**good**, **better**, **best**)
1 more good 更好的: *This book is better than that one.* 这本书比那本好。
2 less ill 病好一些: *I was ill yesterday, but I feel better now.* 我昨天病了，但是现在好些了。
better *adverb* 副词
more well 更好: *You speak French better than I do.* 你法语说得比我好。
better off happier, richer, etc 情况更好: *You look ill—you would be better off in bed.* 你气色不好——卧床会好一些。◇ *I'm better off now that I've got a new job.* 我有了新工作，情况好了。
had better ought to; should 应该；得；最好: *You'd better go now if you want to catch the train.* 你要想赶上火车，最好现在就走。

between /bɪˈtwiːn; bəˈtwin/ *preposition* 介词
1 in the space in the middle of two things or people 在两事物或两人之间: *The letter B comes between A and C.* ✱ B这个字母在A与C之间。◇ *I sat between Sylvie and Bruno.* 我坐在西尔维和布鲁诺的中间。☞ picture on page C1 见第C1页图
2 to and from two places 往返于两地之间: *The boat sails between Dover and Calais.* 这条船来往于多佛尔和加来之间。
3 more than one thing but less than another thing 比一数量多而比另一数量少；介于两数目之间: *The meal will cost between £10 and £15.* 这顿饭要用10英镑到15英镑。
4 after one time and before the next time 在一时间之后而在另一时间之前；介于两时间之间: *I'll meet you between 4 and 4.30.* 我在4点至4点30分之间见你。
5 for or by two or more people or things 为至少两个人或事物；由至少两个人或事物: *We shared the cake between us* (= each of us had some cake). 我们把蛋糕分了（= 我们每人吃了一些）。
6 a word that you use when you compare two people or things 比较两人或两事物的用词: *What is the difference between the two hotels?* 这两个旅馆有什么区别？
☞ Note at **among** 见 **among** 词条注释
in between in the middle of two things, people, times, etc 在两事物、人、时间…之间: *I found my shoe in between two rocks.* 我发现我的一只鞋在两块石头之间。

beware /bɪˈweə(r); bɪˈwɛr/ *verb* 动词
beware of somebody or 或 **something** be careful because somebody or something is dangerous（因某人或某事物很危险）要留心；要提防: *Beware of the dog!* (words written on a sign) 小心有狗！（招贴用语）

bewildered /bɪˈwɪldəd; bɪˈwɪldɚd/ *adjective* 形容词
If you are bewildered, you do not understand something or you do not know what to do 困惑；不知所措: *He was bewildered by all the noises of the big city.* 大城市的各种声音把他弄得晕头转向。

beyond /bɪˈjɒnd; bɪˈjɑnd/ *preposition*, *adverb* 介词，副词
on the other side of something; further than something 在某事物的另一方；比某事物远: *The road continues beyond Birmingham.* 这条路经过伯明翰向前延伸。◇ *We could see the lake and the mountains beyond.* 我们看见湖和对面的山。

bib /bɪb; bɪb/ *noun* 名词
a piece of cloth or plastic that a baby

wears under its chin when it is eating (幼儿用的) 围嘴儿

Bible /'baɪbl; 'baɪbl̩/ *noun* 名词
the holy book of the Christian and Jewish religions 圣经

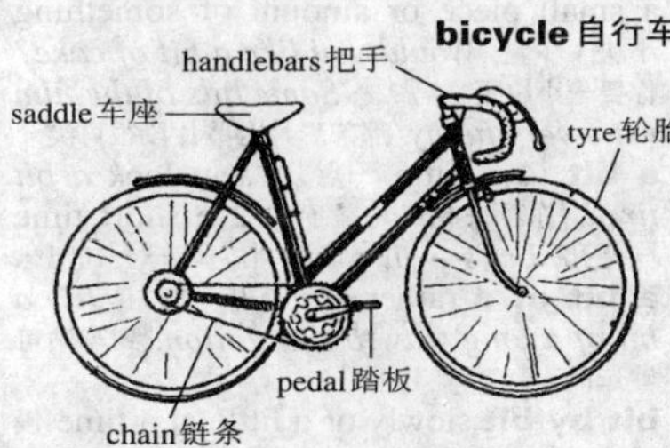

bicycle /'baɪsɪk(ə)l; 'baɪˌsɪkl̩/ *noun* 名词
a machine with two wheels. You sit on a bicycle and move your legs to make the wheels turn 自行车；脚踏车: *Can you ride a bicycle?* 你会骑自行车吗？✪ The short form of 'bicycle' is **bike**. ✱ bicycle 的缩略式为 **bike**。**Cycle** means to travel by bicycle. ✱ **cycle** 意为骑自行车。

bid /bɪd; bɪd/ *verb* 动词 (**bids**, **bidding**, **bid**, **has bid**)
offer some money because you want to buy something (为购买某物) 出价: *He bid £10 000 for the painting.* 他出价10 000英镑买那幅画儿。

bid *noun* 名词
an offer of money for something that you want to buy (为购买某物的) 出价: *She made a bid of £250 for the vase.* 她出价250英镑购买那个花瓶。

big /bɪg; bɪg/ *adjective* 形容词 (**bigger**, **biggest**)
1 not small; large 大的: *Milan is a big city.* 米兰是个大城市。◇ *This shirt is too big for me.* 这件衬衫我穿着太大。◇ *How big is your flat?* 你们的公寓有多大？☞ picture on page C26 见第C26页图
2 great or important 巨大的或重要的: *a big problem* 一个大难题
3 older 年纪更大: *Amy is my big sister.* 埃米是我姐姐。

bike /baɪk; baɪk/ *noun* 名词
a bicycle or a motorcycle 自行车；摩托车

bill /bɪl; bɪl/ *noun* 名词
1 a piece of paper that shows how much money you must pay for something 账单: *Can I have the bill, please?* (in a restaurant) 请给我结账行吗？(在饭馆里)
2 *American English for* **note¹ 3** 美式英语，即 **note¹ 3**: *a ten-dollar bill* 一张十美元的钞票

billion /'bɪliən; 'bɪljən/ *number* 数词
1 000 000 000; one thousand million 千兆；十亿: *five billion pounds* 五十亿英镑 ◇ *There are billions of people in the world.* 全世界有几十亿人。

bin /bɪn; bɪn/ *noun* 名词
1 a thing that you put rubbish in 垃圾箱: *I threw the empty bag in the bin.* 我把空袋子扔进垃圾箱里了。☞ Look also at **dustbin**. 另见 **dustbin**。
2 a thing with a lid that you keep things in 有盖儿的容器: *a bread bin* 面包箱

bind /baɪnd; baɪnd/ *verb* 动词 (**binds**, **binding**, **bound** /baʊnd; baʊnd/, **has bound**)
tie string or rope round something to hold it firmly 捆；绑: *They bound the prisoner's arms and legs together.* 他们把那个囚犯的胳膊和腿都捆上了。

bingo /'bɪŋgəʊ; 'bɪŋgo/ *noun* 名词 (no plural 无复数)
a game where each player has a card with numbers on it. When the person who controls the game says all the numbers on your card, you win the game. 宾戈 (一种游戏，参加者的卡上的数字与主持人报出的数字相同者赢)

binoculars /bɪ'nɒkjələz; bɪ'nɑkjələ˞z/ *noun* 名词 (plural 复数)
special glasses that you use to see things that are far away 双筒望远镜

biography /baɪ'ɒgrəfi; baɪ'ɑgrəfɪ/ *noun* 名词 (*plural* 复数作 **biographies**)
the story of a person's life, that another person writes (由其他人撰写的) 传记: *Have you read the biography of Nelson Mandela?* 你看过纳尔逊·曼德拉的传记吗？

biology /baɪ'ɒlədʒi; baɪ'ɑlədʒɪ/ *noun* 名词 (no plural 无复数)
the study of the life of animals and plants 生物学: *Biology is my favourite subject at school.* 我上学最喜欢的是生物科。

biologist /baɪ'ɒlədʒɪst; baɪ'ɑlədʒɪst/ *noun* 名词
a person who studies or knows a lot about biology 生物学研究者；生物学家

bird 鸟

bird /bɜ:d; bɝd/ *noun* 名词
an animal with feathers and wings 鸟: *Gulls and sparrows are birds.* 鸥和麻雀都是鸟。

✪ Most birds can **fly** and **sing**. 鸟大都会飞 (**fly**) 也会叫 (**sing**)。They build **nests** and **lay eggs**. 鸟会筑巢 (**nest**)，也会下蛋 (**lay eggs**)。

bird of prey /ˌbɜ:d əv ˈpreɪ; ˌbɝd əv ˈpre/ *noun* 名词
a bird that catches and eats small birds and animals 猛禽（吃其他鸟类和小动物的鸟）: *Eagles are birds of prey.* 雕是猛禽。

Biro /ˈbaɪərəʊ; ˈbaɪro/ *noun* 名词 (*plural* 复数作 **Biros**)
a pen that has a very small ball at the end 圆珠笔 ✪ **Biro** is a trade mark. ✳ **Biro** 是商标。

birth /bɜ:θ; bɝθ/ *noun* 名词
the time when a baby comes out of its mother; being born 出生；诞生: *the birth of a baby* 一个婴儿的出生 ◇ *What's your date of birth?* (= the date when you were born) 你是哪天出生的？
give birth have a baby 生孩子；分娩: *My sister gave birth to her second child last week.* 我姐姐上星期生了第二个孩子。

birthday /ˈbɜ:θdeɪ; ˈbɝθˌde/ *noun* 名词 (*plural* 复数作 **birthdays**)
the day each year that is the same as the date when you were born 生日: *My birthday is on May 2nd.* 我的生日是5月2日。◇ *a birthday present* 一份生日礼物
✪ When it is a person's birthday, we say **Happy Birthday!** or **Many happy returns!** 庆祝别人过生日时，要说 **Happy Birthday!** 或 **Many happy returns!**

biscuit /ˈbɪskɪt; ˈbɪskɪt/ *noun* 名词
a kind of small thin dry cake 饼干: *a packet of biscuits* 一盒饼干 ◇ *a chocolate biscuit* 巧克力饼干

biscuits 饼干

bishop /ˈbɪʃəp; ˈbɪʃəp/ *noun* 名词
an important priest in the Christian church, who looks after all the churches in a large area（基督教的）主教

bit /bɪt; bɪt/ *noun* 名词
a small piece or amount of something 小块；少量: *Would you like a bit of cake?* 你要一小块蛋糕吗？◇ *Some bits of the film were very funny.* 那部影片有些片段很可笑。
a bit 1 a little 一点儿: *You look a bit tired.* 你看来有点儿累了。**2** a short time 一会儿: *Let's wait a bit.* 咱们等一会儿吧。
a bit of a rather a 有点儿；颇为: *It's a bit of a long way to the station.* 到车站可够远的。
bit by bit slowly or a little at a time 慢慢地；一点儿一点儿地: *Bit by bit, I started to feel better.* 我一点儿一点儿觉得好起来了。
come to bits, fall to bits break into small pieces 破碎: *The cake fell to bits when I tried to cut it.* 这块蛋糕我一切就碎了。

bite[1] /baɪt; baɪt/ *verb* 动词 (**bites, biting, bit** /bɪt; bɪt/, **has bitten** /ˈbɪtn; ˈbɪtn̩/)
1 cut something with your teeth 咬: *That dog bit my leg!* 那条狗把我的腿咬了！
2 If an insect or snake bites you, it hurts you by pushing a small sharp part into your skin（指昆虫）咬；叮；蜇；（指蛇）咬: *I've been bitten by mosquitoes.* 我让蚊子给叮了。

bite[2] /baɪt; baɪt/ *noun* 名词
1 a piece of food that you can put in your mouth（可放入口中的）一块食物: *He took a bite of his sandwich.* 他咬了一口三明治。
2 a painful place on your skin made by an insect or dog, for example（由虫子或狗等咬伤的）皮肤上的痛处: *a snake bite* 蛇咬的伤口

bitter[1] /ˈbɪtə(r); ˈbɪtɚ/ *adjective* 形容词
1 with a sharp unpleasant taste, like very strong coffee; not sweet 苦的
2 angry and sad about something that has happened 气愤的；难过的: *He felt very bitter about losing his job.* 他失去了工作感到很难受。
3 very cold 极冷的: *a bitter wind* 刺骨的寒风

bitter[2] /ˈbɪtə(r); ˈbɪtɚ/ *noun* 名词 (no plural 无复数)

a dark beer 苦啤酒: *A pint of bitter, please.* 请来一品脱苦啤酒。

black /blæk; blæk/ *adjective* 形容词 (**blacker**, **blackest**)

1 with the colour of the sky at night 黑色的: *a black dog* 一条黑狗

2 with dark skin 黑皮肤的;黑人的: *Martin Luther King was a famous black leader.* 马丁·路德·金是著名的黑人领袖。

3 without milk 不加奶的: *black coffee* 不加奶的咖啡

black *noun* 名词

1 the colour of the sky at night 黑色: *She was dressed in black.* 她穿着黑衣服。

2 a person with dark skin 黑人

black and white with the colours black, white and grey only 黑白的(仅有黑、白、灰三色的): *We watched a black and white film on TV.* 我们看了电视播放的黑白影片。

blackberry /ˈblækbəri; ˈblækˌbɛrɪ/ *noun* 名词 (*plural* 复数作 **blackberries**)

a small soft black fruit that grows on a bush 黑莓

blackbird /ˈblækbɜ:d; ˈblækˌbɝd/ *noun* 名词

a bird with black feathers 黑鹂

blackboard /ˈblækbɔ:d; ˈblækˌbord/ *noun* 名词

a dark board that a teacher writes on with chalk 黑板: *Look at the blackboard.* 看看黑板。

blackcurrant /ˌblækˈkʌrənt; ˌblækˈkɝənt/ *noun* 名词

a small round black fruit that grows on a bush 黑醋栗

blackmail /ˈblækmeɪl; ˈblækˌmel/ *noun* 名词 (no plural 无复数)

saying that you will tell something bad about somebody if they do not give you money or do something for you 勒索;敲诈

blade /bleɪd; bled/ *noun* 名词

1 the flat sharp part of a knife, sword or another thing that cuts (刀、剑等的)刃

2 a long thin leaf of grass or wheat (草或小麦的)长叶片: *a blade of grass* 一片草叶

blame /bleɪm; blem/ *verb* 动词 (**blames**, **blaming**, **blamed** /bleɪmd; blemd/)

say that a certain person or thing made something bad happen 责备;责怪;指责;埋怨: *The other driver blamed me for the accident.* 那个司机指责说事故责任在我。

blame *noun* 名词 (no plural 无复数)

take the blame say that you are the person who did something wrong 承担责任: *Eve took the blame for the mistake.* 伊夫承担这个错误的责任。

blank /blæŋk; blæŋk/ *adjective* 形容词

1 with no writing, pictures or anything else on it 空白的(没有字、图等的): *a blank piece of paper* 一张空白的纸

2 If your face is blank, it shows no feelings or understanding 没表情的(没感情的或不理解的): *I asked her a question, but she just gave me a blank look.* 我问她一个问题,她给我来个木头木脑。

blanket /ˈblæŋkɪt; ˈblæŋkɪt/ *noun* 名词

a thick cover that you put on a bed 毯子

blast[1] /blɑ:st; blæst/ *noun* 名词

1 when a bomb explodes 爆炸: *Two people were killed in the blast.* 这次爆炸死了两个人。

2 a sudden movement of air 一股气流: *a blast of cold air* 一股冷空气

3 a loud sound made by a musical instrument like a trumpet (由喇叭等乐器发出的)响亮的声音

blast-off /ˈblɑ:st ɒf; ˈblæst ɔf/ *noun* 名词

the time when a spacecraft leaves the ground (宇宙飞船的)发射;升空(时间)

blast[2] /blɑ:st; blæst/ *verb* 动词 (**blasts**, **blasting**, **blasted**)

make a hole in something with an explosion 炸开: *They blasted through the mountain to make a tunnel.* 他们把山炸穿,修建隧道。

blaze /bleɪz; blez/ *noun* 名词

a large strong fire 火焰;火光: *The firemen put out the blaze.* 消防队员把火扑灭了。

blaze *verb* 动词 (**blazes**, **blazing**, **blazed** /bleɪzd; blezd/)

burn strongly and brightly 猛烈地燃烧并发光: *a blazing fire* 熊熊大火

blazer /ˈbleɪzə(r); ˈblezɚ/ *noun* 名词

a jacket. Blazers sometimes show which school or club you belong to. 短外套(有时用做校服或俱乐部制服)

bleak /bli:k; blik/ *adjective* 形容词 (**bleaker**, **bleakest**)

cold and grey 寒冷而阴沉的: *It was a*

B

bleak winter's day. 那是冬天寒冷而阴沉的一天。

bleed /bli:d; blid/ *verb* 动词 (**bleeds, bleeding, bled** /bled; blɛd/, **has bled**)
lose blood 流血: *I have cut my hand and it's bleeding.* 我把手弄破了，直流血。

blend /blend; blɛnd/ *verb* 动词 (**blends, blending, blended**)
1 mix 混合: *Blend the sugar and the butter together.* 把糖和黄油混在一起。
2 look or sound good together（合在一起时，看起来或听起来）协调；和谐: *These colours blend very well.* 这些颜色相配很协调。
blend *noun* 名词
a mixture of things 混合物: *This is a blend of two different kinds of coffee.* 这是两种混在一起的咖啡。

bless /bles; blɛs/ *verb* 动词 (**blesses, blessing, blessed** /blest; blɛst/)
ask for God's help for somebody or something 祈求上帝保佑某人或某事物；祝福: *The priest blessed the young couple.* 司铎为这对年轻夫妇祝祷。
Bless you! words that you say to somebody when they sneeze 向打喷嚏的人说的祝福语

blew *form of* **blow**[1] ✳ **blow**[1] 的不同形式

blind[1] /blaɪnd; blaɪnd/ *adjective* 形容词
not able to see 瞎的: *The blind man had a dog to help him.* 那个盲人有条狗来帮助他。◇ *My cat is going* (= becoming) *blind.* 我的猫快瞎了。
the blind *noun* 名词 (plural 复数)
people who are blind 盲人；瞎子
blindness /'blaɪndnəs; 'blaɪndnɪs/ *noun* 名词 (no plural 无复数)
being blind 瞎

blind[2] /blaɪnd; blaɪnd/ *noun* 名词
a piece of cloth or other material that you pull down to cover a window（下拉式的）窗帘

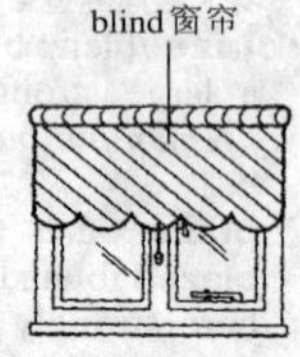

blindfold /'blaɪndfəʊld; 'blaɪnd,fold/ *noun* 名词
a piece of cloth that you put over somebody's eyes so that they cannot see 蒙住人的眼睛的布条
blindfold *verb* 动词 (**blindfolds, blindfolding, blindfolded**)
put a piece of cloth over somebody's eyes so that they cannot see 用布条蒙住某人的眼睛

blink /blɪŋk; blɪŋk/ *verb* 动词 (**blinks, blinking, blinked** /blɪŋkt; blɪŋkt/)
shut and open your eyes very quickly 眨眼

blister /'blɪstə(r); 'blɪstɚ/ *noun* 名词
a small painful place on your skin, that is full of liquid. Rubbing or burning can cause blisters（皮肤上的）水疱（可因摩擦或烧伤产生）: *My new shoes gave me blisters.* 我的新鞋把脚磨出水疱来了。

blizzard /'blɪzəd; 'blɪzɚd/ *noun* 名词
a very bad storm with snow and strong winds 暴风雪

blob /blɒb; blɑb/ *noun* 名词
a small piece of a thick liquid 一小块黏稠的液体: *There are blobs of paint on the floor.* 地板上有一块块的油漆。

block[1] /blɒk; blɑk/ *noun* 名词
1 a big heavy piece of something, with flat sides 一大块重物（各面是平的）: *a block of wood* 一块木头 ◇ *The bridge is made of concrete blocks.* 这座桥是混凝土块砌成的。
2 a big building with a lot of offices or flats inside 办公楼；公寓大厦: *an office block* 一座办公楼 ◇ *a block of flats* 一座公寓大厦
3 a group of buildings with streets all round it（四面临街的）建筑群: *We drove round the block looking for the hotel.* 我们开着车环绕这片房子找旅馆。
4 a thing that stops somebody or something from moving forward 阻止某人或某物之物；障碍物: *The police have put road blocks around the town.* 警方在全城周围都设置了路障。

block[2] /blɒk; blɑk/ *verb* 动词 (**blocks, blocking, blocked** /blɒkt; blɑkt/)
stop somebody or something from moving forward 阻挡某人或某物: *A fallen tree blocked the road.* 有棵树倒下堵住了这条路。

blond /blɒnd; blɑnd/ *adjective* 形容词
with light-coloured hair 头发浅色的: *He's got blond hair.* 他头发浅色。✪ The spelling **blonde** is used for women 用于指女子时拼写为 **blonde**: *She is tall and blonde.* 她个子高，发色金黄。
blonde *noun* 名词

a woman who has blond hair 头发为浅色的女子

blood /blʌd; blʌd/ *noun* 名词 (no plural 无复数)

the red liquid inside your body 血；血液

bloody[1] /'blʌdi; 'blʌdɪ/ *adjective* 形容词 (**bloodier**, **bloodiest**)

1 covered with blood 带血的: *a bloody nose* 带血的鼻子

2 with a lot of killing 有很多伤亡的: *It was a bloody war.* 那场战争伤亡惨重。

bloody[2] /'blʌdi; 'blʌdɪ/ *adjective, adverb* 形容词，副词

a rude word that you use to make what you say stronger, often because you are angry 为加强语气用的粗俗字眼（常常因发怒而用）: *The bloody train was late again!* 这列倒霉的火车又晚点了！

bloom /blu:m; blum/ *verb* 动词 (**blooms**, **blooming**, **bloomed** /blu:md; blumd/)

have flowers 开花: *Roses bloom in the summer.* 玫瑰在夏天开花。

blossom /'blɒsəm; 'blɑsəm/ *noun* 名词 (no plural 无复数)

the flowers on a tree or bush 树木上的花: *The apple trees are covered in blossom.* 苹果树都开花了。

blossom *verb* 动词 (**blossoms**, **blossoming**, **blossomed** /'blɒsəmd; 'blɑsəmd/)

have flowers 开花: *The cherry trees are blossoming.* 樱桃树开花了。

blouse /blaʊz; blaʊs/ *noun* 名词

a piece of clothing like a shirt that a woman or girl wears on the top part of her body 女衬衫

blow[1] /bləʊ; blo/ *verb* 动词 (**blows**, **blowing**, **blew** /blu:; blu/, **has blown** /bləʊn; blon/)

1 When air or wind blows, it moves（空气或风）流动: *The wind was blowing from the sea.* 那阵风是从海上刮来的。

2 move something through the air 通过空气移动某物: *The wind blew my hat off.* 风把我帽子刮掉了。

3 send air out from your mouth 吹气；呼气

4 send air out from your mouth into a musical instrument, for example, to make a noise 吹响（例如乐器）；吹奏: *The referee blew his whistle.* 裁判吹过了哨子。

blow up 1 explode; make something explode, for example with a bomb 爆炸；使某物爆炸（例如用炸弹）: *The plane blew up.* 那架飞机爆炸了。◇ *They blew up the station.* 他们把车站炸了。**2** fill something with air 给某物充气: *We blew up some balloons for the party.* 我们筹备这次聚会，给一些气球充气。

blow[2] /bləʊ; blo/ *noun* 名词

1 hitting somebody or something hard; being hit hard 猛击某人或某物；遭猛击: *He felt a blow on the back of his head and he fell.* 他感到头部后面遭到猛击而倒下。

2 something that happens suddenly and that makes you very unhappy 突然发生的使人难过的事: *Her father's death was a terrible blow to her.* 她父亲去世对她是个极大的打击。

blue /blu:; blu/ *adjective* 形容词 (**bluer**, **bluest**)

with the colour of a clear sky on a sunny day 蓝色的: *He wore a blue shirt.* 他穿着蓝衬衫。◇ *dark-blue* 深蓝色的 ◇ *Her eyes are bright blue.* 她的眼睛是浅蓝色的。

blue *noun* 名词

She was dressed in blue. 她穿着蓝衣服。

blunt /blʌnt; blʌnt/ *adjective* 形容词

1 with an edge or point that is not sharp 不锋利的；不尖的；钝的: *This pencil is blunt.* 这枝铅笔秃了。

2 If you are blunt, you say what you think in a way that is not polite 嘴直而不客气的: *She was very blunt and told me that she didn't like my plan.* 她直截了当告诉我她不喜欢我的计划。

blur /blɜ:(r); blɝ/ *verb* 动词 (**blurs**, **blurring**, **blurred** /blɜ:d; blɝd/)

make something less clear 使某事物模糊不清: *If you move while you are taking the photo, it will be blurred.* 要是照相的时候移动，照片就模糊不清了。

blush /blʌʃ; blʌʃ/ *verb* 动词 (**blushes**, **blushing**, **blushed** /blʌʃt; blʌʃt/)

If you blush, your face suddenly becomes red because you are shy, for example 脸红（例如因害羞引起）: *She blushed when he looked at her.* 他看她的时候，她脸红了。

boar /bɔ:(r); bɔr/ *noun* 名词

1 a male pig 公猪

2 a wild pig 野猪

board[1] /bɔ:d; bɔrd/ *noun* 名词

1 a long thin flat piece of wood 长木板: *I nailed a board across the broken window.* 我在破碎的窗户上钉上了一条木板。◇ *floorboards* 地板板条

B

2 a flat piece of wood, for example, that you use for a special purpose (作某用途的) 板子: *There is a list of names on the notice-board.* 在布告板上有个名单。◇ *a chessboard* 棋盘 ◇ *an ironing-board* 熨衣板 ☞ Look also at **blackboard**. 另见 **blackboard**。

3 a group of people who have a special job, for example controlling a company 委员会;董事会: *the board of directors* 董事会

on board on a ship or an aeroplane 在轮船或飞机上: *How many passengers are on board?* 飞机上有多少乘客?

board[2] /bɔ:d; bɔrd/ *verb* 动词 (**boards**, **boarding**, **boarded**)

get on a ship, bus, train or an aeroplane 登上轮船、公共汽车、火车或飞机: *We boarded the plane at Gatwick.* 我们在盖特威克机场登机。◇ *Flight BA 193 to Paris is now boarding* (= is ready for passengers to get on). 英航193号飞往巴黎的班机现在可以登机。

boarding card /'bɔ:dɪŋ kɑ:d; 'bɔrdɪŋ kɑrd/ *noun* 名词

a card that you must show when you get on an aeroplane or a ship 登机证;登船证

boarding-school /'bɔ:dɪŋ sku:l; 'bɔrdɪŋ skul/ *noun* 名词

a school where the pupils live 寄宿学校

boast /bəʊst; bost/ *verb* 动词 (**boasts**, **boasting**, **boasted**)

talk in a way that shows you are too proud of something that you have or something that you can do 自夸;自吹自擂: *He boasted that he was the fastest runner in the school.* 他自我吹嘘说是学校里跑得最快的。

boats 船

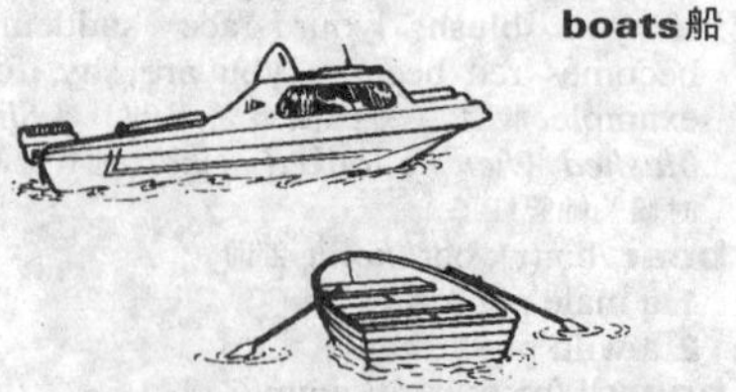

boat /bəʊt; bot/ *noun* 名词

a small ship for travelling on water 小船: *a fishing boat* 渔船 ◇ *We travelled by boat.* 我们坐的是小船。

body /'bɒdi; 'bɑdɪ/ *noun* 名词 (*plural* 复数作 **bodies**)

1 all of a person or an animal, but not the mind 身体;身躯: *Arms, legs, hands and feet are all parts of the body.* 胳膊、腿、手、脚都是身体的部分。◇ *the human body* 人的身体

2 all of a person or animal, but not the legs, arms or head 躯干

3 a dead person 死尸;尸体: *The police found a body in the river.* 警方在河里发现一具尸体。

bodyguard /'bɒdigɑ:d; 'bɑdɪˌgɑrd/ *noun* 名词

a person or group of people whose job is to keep an important person safe (重要人物的) 侍卫;卫队;保镖: *The President's bodyguards all carry guns.* 总统的侍卫都佩带着枪。

boil /bɔɪl; bɔɪl/ *verb* 动词 (**boils**, **boiling**, **boiled** /bɔɪld; bɔɪld/)

1 When a liquid boils, it becomes very hot and makes steam and bubbles 沸腾: *Water boils at 100°C.* 水在100°C时沸腾。

2 heat a liquid until it boils 将液体加热至沸腾: *I boiled some water for the noodles.* 我把水坐开了煮面条。

3 cook something in very hot water 用热水煮某物: *Boil the rice in a pan.* 把米放在锅里煮。◇ *a boiled egg* 煮鸡蛋

boil over boil and flow over the sides of a pan 沸腾溢出;潽: *Don't let the milk boil over.* 别把奶煮潽了。

boiler /'bɔɪlə(r); 'bɔɪlɚ/ *noun* 名词

a big metal container that heats water for a building 锅炉;热水器

boiling /'bɔɪlɪŋ; 'bɔɪlɪŋ/ *adjective* 形容词

very hot 极热的: *Open the window—I'm boiling.* 开开窗户吧——我热极了。

bold /bəʊld; bold/ *adjective* 形容词 (**bolder**, **boldest**)

brave and not afraid 勇敢的;大胆的;无畏的: *It was very bold of you to ask for more money.* 你要求再增加些钱,胆子可真大。

boldly *adverb* 副词

He boldly said that he disagreed. 他大着胆子说他不同意。

bolt /bəʊlt; bolt/ *noun* 名词
1 a piece of metal that you move across to lock a door 门闩；插销
2 a thick metal pin that you use with another piece of metal (called a **nut**) to fix things together 螺栓（螺母叫做 **nut**）
bolt *verb* 动词 (**bolts**, **bolting**, **bolted**)
lock a door by putting a bolt across it 用闩把门闩上；用插销把门插上

bomb /bɒm; bɑm/ *noun* 名词
a thing that explodes and hurts or damages people or things 炸弹：*Aircraft dropped bombs on the city.* 飞机向这个城市投下了炸弹。◇ *A bomb went off* (= exploded) *at the station.* 有颗炸弹在车站爆炸了。
bomb *verb* 动词 (**bombs**, **bombing**, **bombed** /bɒmd; bɑmd/)
attack people or a place with bombs 用炸弹炸人或物：*The city was bombed in the war.* 那座城市在战争中遭到轰炸。

bone /bəʊn; bon/ *noun* 名词
one of the hard white parts inside the body of a person or an animal 骨头：*She broke a bone in her foot.* 她脚骨骨折。◇ *This fish has a lot of bones in it.* 这种鱼有很多刺。

bonfire /ˈbɒnfaɪə(r); ˈbɑnˌfaɪr/ *noun* 名词
a big fire that you make outside 篝火
Bonfire Night /ˈbɒnfaɪə naɪt; ˈbɑnˌfaɪr naɪt/ *another word for* **Guy Fawkes Night** 即 **Guy Fawkes Night** ☞ Note at **guy** 见 **guy** 词条注释

bonnet /ˈbɒnɪt; ˈbɑnɪt/ *noun* 名词
1 the front part of a car that covers the engine（汽车的）发动机罩盖 ☞ picture at **car** 见 **car** 词条插图
2 a soft hat that you tie under your chin 在颏下系带的软帽

book[1] /bʊk; bʊk/ *noun* 名词
a thing that you read or write in, that has a lot of pieces of paper joined together inside a cover 书；本子：*I'm reading a book by George Orwell.* 我正在看乔治·奥威尔的书。◇ *an exercise book* 练习本

book[2] /bʊk; bʊk/ *verb* 动词 (**books**, **booking**, **booked** /bʊkt; bʊkt/)
ask somebody to keep something for you so that you can use it later 预订：*We booked a table for six at the restaurant.* 我们在饭馆预订了六个人一桌的位子。◇ *The hotel is fully booked* (= all the rooms are full). 这家旅馆的房间都预订出去了。
book in tell the person at the desk in a hotel that you have arrived 在旅馆登记住宿

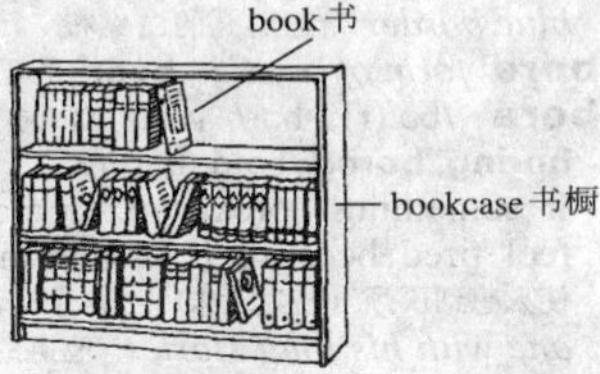

bookcase /ˈbʊk keɪs; ˈbʊkˌkes/ *noun* 名词
a piece of furniture that you put books in 书橱；书柜

booking /ˈbʊkɪŋ; ˈbʊkɪŋ/ *noun* 名词
asking somebody to keep something for you so that you can use it later 预订：*When did you make your booking?* 你什么时候预订的？
booking-office /ˈbʊkɪŋ ɒfɪs; ˈbʊkɪŋ ˌɔfɪs/ *noun* 名词
a place where you buy tickets 售票处

booklet /ˈbʊklət; ˈbʊklɪt/ *noun* 名词
a small thin book 小册子

bookshop /ˈbʊkʃɒp; ˈbʊkˌʃɑp/ *noun* 名词
a shop that sells books 书店

boom /buːm; bum/ *verb* 动词 (**booms**, **booming**, **boomed** /buːmd; bumd/)
make a loud deep sound 发出深沉的声音：*We heard the guns booming in the distance.* 我们听到远处的炮声。

boots 靴子

boot /buːt; but/ *noun* 名词
1 a shoe that covers your foot and ankle and sometimes part of your leg 靴子
2 the part of a car where you can put bags and boxes, usually at the back（汽车的）行李箱（通常在后部） ☞ picture at **car** 见 **car** 词条插图

border /'bɔ:də(r); 'bɔrdɚ/ *noun* 名词

1 a line between two countries 两国的边境线: *You need a passport to cross the border.* 通过边境要有护照。

2 a line along the edge of something 物体的边线: *a white tablecloth with a blue border* 带蓝边儿的白桌布

B

bore[1] *form of* **bear**[2] ＊ **bear**[2] 的不同形式

bore[2] /bɔ:(r); bɔr/ *verb* 动词 (**bores, boring, bored** /bɔ:d; bɔrd/)

If something bores you, it makes you feel tired because it is not interesting 使人感到厌烦（因为乏味）: *He bores everyone with his long stories.* 他讲的长故事谁都厌烦。

bored *adjective* 形容词

not interested; unhappy because you have nothing interesting to do 不感兴趣；感到厌烦或无聊: *I'm bored with this book.* 我觉得这本书真没劲。◇ *I'm bored. What can I do?* 我觉得很无聊。我能干点儿什么呢？

boredom /'bɔ:dəm; 'bɔrdəm/ *noun* 名词 (no plural 无复数)

being bored 厌烦；厌倦

boring *adjective* 形容词

not interesting 无趣的；乏味的: *That lesson was boring!* 那堂课真没意思！

bore[3] /bɔ:(r); bɔr/ *verb* 动词 (**bores, boring, bored** /bɔ:d; bɔrd/)

make a thin round hole in something 在某物上弄个小圆洞: *These insects bore holes in wood.* 这些虫子能在木头上掏洞。

born /bɔ:n; bɔrn/ *adjective* 形容词

be born start your life 出生: *I was born in 1980.* 我生于1980年。◇ *Where were you born?* 你是在哪儿出生的？

borne *form of* **bear**[2] ＊ **bear**[2] 的不同形式

borrow or **lend?**
用**borrow**还是用**lend?**

She is **lending** her son some money.
她借给儿子一些钱。

He is **borrowing** some money from his mother.
他向母亲借了一些钱。

borrow /'bɒrəʊ; 'bɑro/ *verb* 动词 (**borrows, borrowing, borrowed** /'bɒrəʊd; 'bɑrod/)

take and use something that you will give back after a short time 借来: *I borrowed some books from the library.* 我从图书馆借了一些书。◇ *He borrowed £10 from his father.* 他向父亲借了10英镑。

boss /bɒs; bɑs/ *noun* 名词 (*plural* 复数作 **bosses**)

a person who controls a place where people work and tells people what they must do 老板；上司；负责人: *I asked my boss for a holiday.* 我向负责人申请度假。

bossy /'bɒsi; 'bɑsɪ/ *adjective* 形容词 (**bossier, bossiest**)

A bossy person likes to tell other people what to do 爱发号施令的；爱指使人的: *My sister is very bossy.* 我姐姐很爱指使人。

both /bəʊθ; boθ/ *adjective*, *pronoun* 形容词，代词

the two; not only one but also the other 两；二者；两者都: *Hold it in both hands.* 用双手拿着。◇ *Both her brothers are doctors.* 她两个哥哥都是医生。◇ *Both of us like skiing.* 我们俩都爱滑雪。◇ *We both like skiing.* 我们俩都爱滑雪。

both *adverb* 副词

both... and not only… but also 不但…而且…；既…又…；又…又…: *She is both rich and intelligent.* 她不但很阔而且很聪明。

bother /'bɒðə(r); 'bɑðɚ/ *verb* 动词 (**bothers, bothering, bothered** /'bɒðəd; 'bɑðɚd/)

1 do something that gives you extra work or that takes extra time 做额外的工作或用额外时间做事；添麻烦；费工夫: *Don't bother to do the washing-up—I'll do it later.* 别麻烦你去洗碗了——我呆一会儿洗。

2 worry somebody; stop somebody from doing something, for example thinking, working or sleeping 烦扰某人；打扰某人: *Don't bother me now—I'm busy!* 现在别打扰我——我正忙着呢！◇ *Is this music bothering you?* 这个音乐影响你吗？◇ *I'm sorry to bother you, but could you tell me the way to the station?* 对不起，打扰您一下，请问到车站怎么走？

bother *noun* 名词 (no plural 无复数)

trouble or difficulty 麻烦；困难: *'Thanks for your help!' 'It was no bother.'* "感谢您的帮助！""不算什么。"

bothered *adjective* 形容词
worried 忧虑的；担心的
can't be bothered If you can't be bothered to do something, you do not want to do it because it is too much work 嫌麻烦而不想做某事：*I can't be bothered to do my homework now.* 我现在懒得做功课。

bottle /'bɒtl; 'bɑtḷ/ *noun* 名词
a tall round glass or plastic container for liquids, with a thin part at the top 瓶子：*a beer bottle* 啤酒瓶 ◇ *They drank two bottles of water.* 他们喝了两瓶水。

bottle 瓶子

bottom /'bɒtəm; 'bɑtəm/ *noun* 名词
1 the lowest part of something 底部；底：*They live at the bottom of the hill.* 他们住在山脚下。◇ *The book was at the bottom of my bag.* 那本书在我的袋子里最下边儿。◇ *Look at the picture at the bottom of the page.* 看看这一页下边的图。✪ opposite 反义词：**top** ☞ picture at **back** 见 **back** 词条插图
2 the last part of something; the end 最后的部分；末端：*The bank is at the bottom of the road.* 银行是在这条路的尽头。✪ opposite 反义词：**top**
3 the part of your body that you sit on 臀部；屁股：*She fell on her bottom.* 她摔倒时屁股着地。☞ picture on page C2 见第C2页图
bottom *adjective* 形容词
lowest 最低的；最底下的：*Put the book on the bottom shelf.* 把书放在最下面那层架子上。✪ opposite 反义词：**top**

bought *form of* **buy** ✳ **buy** 的不同形式

boulder /'bəʊldə(r); 'boldɚ/ *noun* 名词
a very big rock 巨石

bounce 弹起

bounce /baʊns; bauns/ *verb* 动词 (**bounces**, **bouncing**, **bounced** /'baʊnst; baunst/)
1 When a ball bounces, it moves away quickly after it hits something hard（指球碰到硬物）弹开：*The ball bounced off the wall.* 那个球碰到墙后弹开了。
2 make a ball do this 使球碰到硬物弹开：*The boy was bouncing a basketball.* 那个男孩儿拍着篮球。
3 jump up and down a lot 蹦蹦跳跳：*The children were bouncing on their beds.* 孩子们在床上又蹦又跳。

bound¹ *form of* **bind** ✳ **bind** 的不同形式

bound² /baʊnd; baund/ *adjective* 形容词
bound to certain to do something 一定做某事：*She works very hard, so she is bound to pass the exam.* 她很用功，一定能考及格。

bound³ /baʊnd; baund/ *adjective* 形容词
bound for going to a place 准备去某处：*This ship is bound for New York.* 这艘轮船是开往纽约的。

bound⁴ /baʊnd; baund/ *verb* 动词 (**bounds**, **bounding**, **bounded**)
jump, or run with small jumps 跳；蹦着跑：*The dog bounded up the steps.* 那条狗连蹦带跳地跑上台阶。

boundary /'baʊndri; 'baundrɪ/ *noun* 名词 (*plural* 复数作 **boundaries**)
a line between two places 两地之间的分界线：*This fence is the boundary between the two gardens.* 这个篱笆是这两个花园的分界线。

bouquet /bu'keɪ; bu'ke/ *noun* 名词
a group of flowers that you give or get as a present（做为礼物的）一束花：*She gave me a bouquet of roses.* 她送给我一束玫瑰花。

bow¹ /baʊ; bau/ *verb* 动词 (**bows**, **bowing**, **bowed** /baʊd; baud/)
bend your head or body forward to show respect（为表示尊敬）点头，低头；鞠躬：*The actors bowed at the end of the play.* 演员们在话剧结束时鞠躬谢幕。
bow *noun* 名词
He gave a bow and left the room. 他鞠了个躬就离开了房间。

bow² /bəʊ; bo/ *noun* 名词
a kind of knot with two round parts, that you use when you are tying shoes, ribbons, etc 蝴蝶结

bow 蝴蝶结

bow³ /bəʊ; bo/ *noun* 名词
1 a curved piece of wood with a string

B

between the two ends. You use a bow to send **arrows** through the air. 弓（箭叫做 **arrow**）☞ picture at **arrow** 见 **arrow** 词条插图

2 a long thin piece of wood with strong strings along it. You use it to play a **violin** or another musical instrument that has strings. 琴弓（用以拉小提琴之类的弦乐器，小提琴叫做 **violin**）☞ picture at **violin** 见 **violin** 词条插图

bowl[1] /bəʊl; bol/ *noun* 名词

a deep round dish or container 碗；钵：*a sugar bowl* 糖钵 ◇ *a bowl of soup* 一碗汤

bowl 碗

bowl[2] /bəʊl; bol/ *verb* 动词 (**bowls**, **bowling**, **bowled** /bəʊld; bold/)

throw a ball so that somebody can hit it in a game of cricket（板球运动中）投球（以便对方击球）

box[1] /bɒks; bɑks/ *noun* 名词 (*plural* 复数作 **boxes**)

a container with straight sides. A box often has a lid 箱子；盒子: *Put the books in a cardboard box.* 把书放在纸箱子里。◇ *a box of chocolates* 一盒巧克力 ◇ *a box of matches* 一盒火柴 ☞ picture at **container** 见 **container** 词条插图

box[2] /bɒks; bɑks/ *verb* 动词 (**boxes**, **boxing**, **boxed** /bɒkst; bɑkst/)

fight with your hands, wearing thick gloves, as a sport 拳击

boxer *noun* 名词

a person who boxes as a sport 拳击手: *Muhammad Ali was a famous boxer.* 穆罕默德·阿里是著名的拳击手。

boxing *noun* 名词 (no plural 无复数)

the sport of fighting with your hands, wearing thick gloves 拳击运动

Boxing Day /ˈbɒksɪŋ deɪ; ˈbɑksɪŋ ˌde/ *noun* 名词

the day after Christmas Day; 26 December 节礼日（圣诞节的次日；12月26日）✪ In England and Wales, Boxing Day is a holiday. 在英格兰和威尔士，节礼日放假一天。

box office /ˈbɒks ɒfɪs; ˈbɑks ˌɔfɪs/ *noun* 名词

a place where you buy tickets in a theatre or cinema（影剧院的）售票处

boy /bɔɪ; bɔɪ/ *noun* 名词 (*plural* 复数作 **boys**)

a male child; a young man 男孩儿；年轻男子

boyfriend /ˈbɔɪfrend; ˈbɔɪˌfrɛnd/ *noun* 名词

a boy or man who is somebody's special friend 男朋友: *She has had a lot of boyfriends.* 她有过很多男朋友。

Boy Scout /ˌbɔɪ ˈskaʊt; ˈbɔɪ ˌskaʊt/ *noun* 名词

a member of a special club for boys 男童子军队员

bra /brɑ:; brɑ/ *noun* 名词 (*plural* 复数作 **bras**)

a thing that a woman wears under her other clothes to cover and support her breasts 乳罩

bracelet 手镯

bracelet /ˈbreɪslət; ˈbreslɪt/ *noun* 名词

a pretty piece of metal, wood or plastic that you wear around your arm 手镯

brackets /ˈbrækɪts; ˈbrækɪts/ *noun* 名词 (plural 复数)

marks like these ( ) that you use in writing 括号，如（ ）: *(This sentence is written in brackets.)*（本句子就是在括号中。）

braid /breɪd; bred/ *American English for* **plait** 美式英语，即 **plait**

brain /breɪn; bren/ *noun* 名词

the part inside the head of a person or an animal that thinks and feels 脑；脑子: *The brain controls the rest of the body.* 脑子控制整个身体。

brake /breɪk; brek/ *noun* 名词

a thing that you move to make a car, bicycle, etc go slower or stop 制动器；闸；刹车: *I put my foot on the brake.* 我踩了刹车。

brake *verb* 动词 (**brakes**, **braking**, **braked** /breɪkt; brekt/)

use a brake 用制动器；刹（车）: *A child ran into the road and the driver braked suddenly.* 有个孩子跑到了路上，司机立即刹住了车。

branch /brɑ:ntʃ; bræntʃ/ *noun* 名词 (*plural* 复数作 **branches**)

1 one of the parts of a tree that grow out from the **trunk** 树枝（树干叫做 **trunk**）☞ picture at **tree** 见 **tree** 词条插图
2 an office or a shop that is part of a big company（大公司的）分公司；分店；分部: *This bank has branches all over the country.* 这家银行在全国各地都有分行。

brand /brænd; brænd/ *noun* 名词
the name of a thing you buy that a certain company makes 商品的牌子: *'Nescafé' is a famous brand of coffee.* “雀巢”是名牌咖啡。

brand-new /ˌbrænd 'nju:; 'brænd'nju/ *adjective* 形容词
completely new 全新的；崭新的 *a brand-new car* 一辆崭新的汽车

brandy /'brændi; 'brændɪ/ *noun* 名词
1 (no plural 无复数) a strong alcoholic drink 白兰地（一种烈酒）
2 (*plural* 复数作 **brandies**) a glass of brandy 一杯白兰地

brass /brɑ:s; bræs/ *noun* 名词 (no plural 无复数)
a yellow metal 黄铜

brave /breɪv; brev/ *adjective* 形容词 (**braver, bravest**)
ready to do dangerous or difficult things without fear 勇敢的；无畏的: *It was brave of her to go into the burning building.* 她进入了燃烧着的大楼，真勇敢。
bravely *adverb* 副词
He fought bravely in the war. 他作战十分勇敢。
bravery /'breɪvəri; 'brevərɪ/ *noun* 名词 (no plural 无复数)
being brave 勇气；胆量

bread 面包

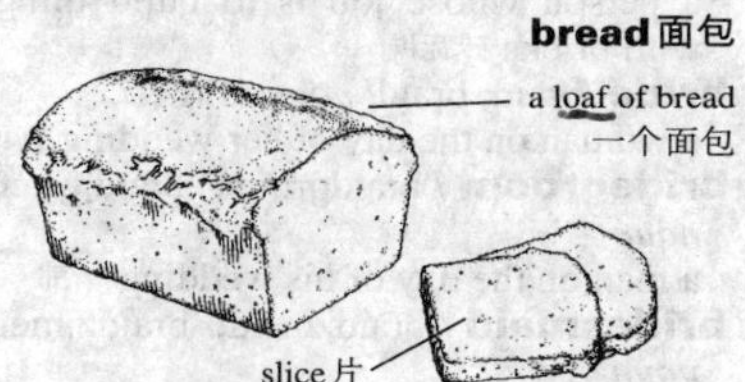

bread /bred; brɛd/ *noun* 名词 (no plural 无复数)
food made from flour and baked in an oven 面包: *I bought a loaf of bread.* 我买了一块面包。◇ *a slice of bread and butter* 一片面包夹黄油

breadth /bredθ; brɛdθ/ *noun* 名词
how far it is from one side of something to the other 宽度 ✪ The adjective is **broad**. 形容词为 **broad**。

break[1] /breɪk; brek/ *verb* 动词 (**breaks, breaking, broke** /brəʊk; brok/, **has broken** /'brəʊkən; 'brokən/)
1 make something go into smaller pieces by dropping it or hitting it, for example 使某物破、碎或断（例如掉下或撞击）: *He broke the window.* 他把窗户打破了。◇ *She has broken her arm.* 她把胳膊弄断了。
2 go into smaller pieces by falling or hitting, for example 破、碎或断（例如掉下或撞击）: *I dropped the cup and it broke.* 我把杯子摔碎了。
3 stop working; damage a machine so that it stops working 损坏: *The TV is broken.* 电视机坏了。◇ *You've broken my watch.* 你把我的手表弄坏了。
break down **1** If a machine or car breaks down, it stops working（指机器）停止运转；（指汽车）抛锚: *We were late because our car broke down.* 我们来晚了，因为我们的汽车抛锚了。 **2** If a person breaks down, he/she starts to cry（指人）哭起来: *He broke down when he heard the bad news.* 他一听到这个坏消息就哭起来了。
break in, break into something go into a place by breaking a door or window so that you can steal something 破门而入或破窗而入进行盗窃: *Thieves broke into the house. They broke in through a window.* 有贼进入了那所房子。他们是撬开窗户进去的。
break off take away a piece of something by breaking it 折断某物以取部分: *He broke off a piece of chocolate for me.* 他掰下一块巧克力给我。
break out **1** start suddenly 突然开始: *A fire broke out last night.* 昨天夜里突然失火了。 **2** get free from a place like a prison 从（如监狱处）逃出: *Four prisoners broke out of the jail last night.* 昨天夜里有四个囚犯越狱了。
break up start the school holidays 学校开始放假: *We break up at the end of July.* 我们从七月底放假。
break up with somebody stop being with somebody, for example a

B

husband or wife, boyfriend or girlfriend 与某人分离（例如夫妻或男女朋友）: *Susy broke up with her boyfriend last week.* 苏吉上星期和她男朋友分手了。

B

break[2] /breɪk; brek/ *noun* 名词

1 a short time when you stop doing something（在做某事时）暂时停止: *We worked all day without a break.* 我们一口气干了一整天。

2 a place where something opens or has broken 某物打开之处或破裂之处: *The sun shone through a break in the clouds.* 太阳从云隙中露了出来。

breakdown /'breɪkdaʊn; 'brek,daʊn/ *noun* 名词

a time when a machine, car, etc stops working（机器、汽车等的）故障: *We* (= our car) *had a breakdown on the motorway.* 我们（= 我们的汽车）在高速公路上抛了锚了。

breakfast /'brekfəst; 'brɛkfəst/ *noun* 名词

the first meal of the day 早饭；早餐: *I had breakfast at seven o'clock.* 我七点钟吃的早饭。

breast /brest; brɛst/ *noun* 名词

1 one of the two soft round parts of a woman's body that can give milk（女子的）乳房

2 the front part of a bird's body（鸟的）胸脯

breast-stroke /'brest strəʊk; 'brɛst-,strok/ *noun* 名词 (no plural 无复数)

a way of swimming on your front 蛙泳

breath /breθ; brɛθ/ *noun* 名词

taking in or letting out air through your nose and mouth（呼吸的）吸或呼: *Take a deep breath.* 深吸一口气。

hold your breath stop breathing for a short time 暂时屏住呼吸

out of breath breathing very quickly 呼吸急促: *She was out of breath after climbing the stairs.* 她爬上了台阶，已经上气不接下气了。

breathe /bri:ð; brið/ *verb* 动词 (**breathes**, **breathing**, **breathed** /bri:ðd; briðd/)

take in and let out air through your nose and mouth 呼吸: *The doctor told me to breathe in and then breathe out again slowly.* 医生让我吸一口气然后再慢慢呼出。

breathless /'breθləs; 'brɛθlɪs/ *adjective* 形容词

If you are breathless, you are breathing quickly or with difficulty. 呼吸急促或困难的

breed[1] /bri:d; brid/ *verb* 动词 (**breeds**, **breeding**, **bred** /bred; brɛd/, **has bred**)

1 make young animals（指动物）生育；繁殖: *Birds breed in the spring.* 鸟类在春天繁殖。

2 keep animals to make young ones 饲养动物使能繁殖: *They breed horses on their farm.* 他们在农场上养马。

breed[2] /bri:d; brid/ *noun* 名词

a kind of animal（动物的）品种: *There are many different breeds of dog.* 狗有很多种。

breeze /bri:z; briz/ *noun* 名词

a light wind 微风

brewery /'bru:əri; 'bruərɪ/ *noun* 名词 (*plural* 复数作 **breweries**)

a place where beer is made 啤酒厂

bribe /braɪb; braɪb/ *noun* 名词

money or a present that you give to somebody to make them do something 贿赂

bribe *verb* 动词 (**bribes**, **bribing**, **bribed** /braɪbd; braɪbd/)

give a bribe to somebody 行贿；贿赂: *The prisoner bribed the guard to let him go free.* 囚犯买通了看守，让他逃走。

brick /brɪk; brɪk/ *noun* 名词

a small block made of hard clay, with two long sides and two short sides. Bricks are used for building 砖；土坯: *a brick wall* 砖墙

bricklayer /'brɪkleɪə(r); 'brɪk,leɚ/ *noun* 名词

a person whose job is to build things with bricks 砖瓦匠

bride /braɪd; braɪd/ *noun* 名词

a woman on the day of her wedding 新娘

bridegroom /'braɪdgru:m; 'braɪd,grum/ *noun* 名词

a man on the day of his wedding 新郎

bridesmaid /'braɪdzmeɪd; 'braɪdz,med/ *noun* 名词

a girl or woman who helps a bride at her wedding 女傧相；伴娘

bridge /brɪdʒ; brɪdʒ/ *noun* 名词

a thing that is built over a road, railway or river so that people, trains or cars can cross it 桥梁: *We walked over the bridge.* 我们走过了桥。

brief /bri:f; brif/ *adjective* 形容词 (**briefer, briefest**)
short or quick 时间短的或快的: *a brief telephone call* 简短的通话
in brief in a few words 简言之；简断截说: *Here is the news in brief.* (words said on a radio or television programme) 现在是新闻简报。(电台或电视广播节目用语)
briefly *adverb* 副词
We stopped work briefly for a drink. 我们暂时放下工作喝点儿东西。

briefcase /'bri:fkeɪs; 'brif͵kes/ *noun* 名词
a flat case for carrying papers in 公事包
bright /braɪt; braɪt/ *adjective* 形容词 (**brighter, brightest**)
1 with a lot of light 明亮的: *It was a bright sunny day.* 天气晴朗、日光充足的一天。◇ *That lamp is very bright.* 这灯很亮。
2 with a strong colour 鲜艳的: *a bright-yellow shirt* 鲜明的黄衬衫
3 clever 聪明的: *She is the brightest child in the class.* 她是班上最聪明的孩子。
brightly *adverb* 副词
brightly coloured clothes 色彩鲜艳的衣服
brightness /'braɪtnəs; 'braɪtnɪs/ *noun* 名词 (no plural 无复数)
the brightness of the sun 阳光的明亮
brighten /'braɪtn; 'braɪtn̩/, **brighten up** *verb* 动词 (**brightens, brightening, brightened** /'braɪtnd; 'braɪtn̩d/)
become brighter or happier; make something brighter 变得明亮、鲜艳、聪明或愉快；使某事物明亮或鲜艳: *These flowers will brighten the room up.* 这些花能使满室生辉。◇ *Her face brightened when she heard the good news.* 她听到这个好消息时喜形于色。
brilliant /'brɪliənt; 'brɪljənt/ *adjective* 形容词
1 with a lot of light; very bright 光辉的；极明亮的: *brilliant sunshine* 灿烂的阳光
2 very intelligent 极聪明的: *a brilliant student* 有才华的学生
3 very good; excellent 极好的；优秀的: *The film was brilliant!* 那部影片好极了！
brilliance /'brɪliəns; 'brɪljəns/ *noun* 名词 (no plural 无复数)
the brilliance of the light 光辉灿烂
brilliantly *adverb* 副词
She played brilliantly. 她表现得好极了。
brim /brɪm; brɪm/ *noun* 名词
1 the edge around the top of something like a cup, bowl or glass（杯口、碗口等的）边；边缘
2 the wide part around the bottom of a hat 帽檐
bring /brɪŋ; brɪŋ/ *verb* 动词 (**brings, bringing, brought** /brɔ:t; brɔt/, **has brought**)
1 come to a place with somebody or something 带着某人或某物来: *Can you bring me a glass of water?* 你给我拿杯水来行吗？◇ *Can I bring a friend to the party?* 我带个朋友参加聚会行吗？☞ picture on page 58 见第58页图
2 make something happen 使某事发生: *Money doesn't always bring happiness.* 金钱未必准能带来幸福。
bring back **1** return something 归还某物: *I have brought back the book you lent me.* 我把你借给我的书带来还给你。 **2** make you remember something 使回忆起某事物: *These old photographs bring back a lot of happy memories.* 这些旧照片引起许多愉快的回忆。
bring somebody up look after a child until he/she is grown up 把孩子养育成人: *He was brought up by his aunt after his parents died.* 他父母死后，他姑母把他养大成人。
bring something up **1** be sick, so that food comes up from your stomach and out of your mouth 呕吐某物 **2** start to talk about something 开始谈论某事物: *Can you bring up this problem at the next meeting?* 你能不能在下次会议上提出这个问题？

bring, fetch or **take?** 用**bring**、**fetch**还是用**take?**

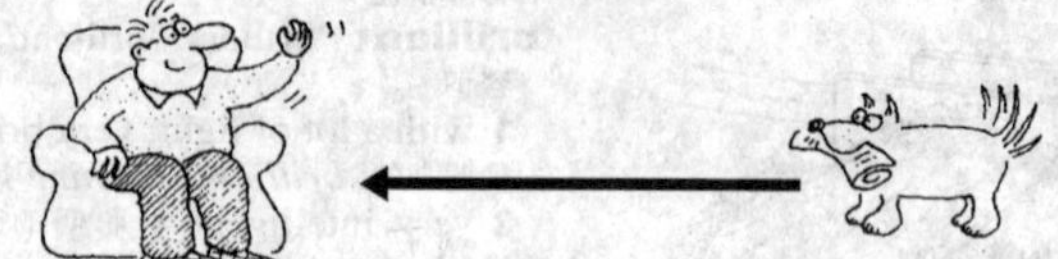

Bring the newspaper. 把报纸拿来。

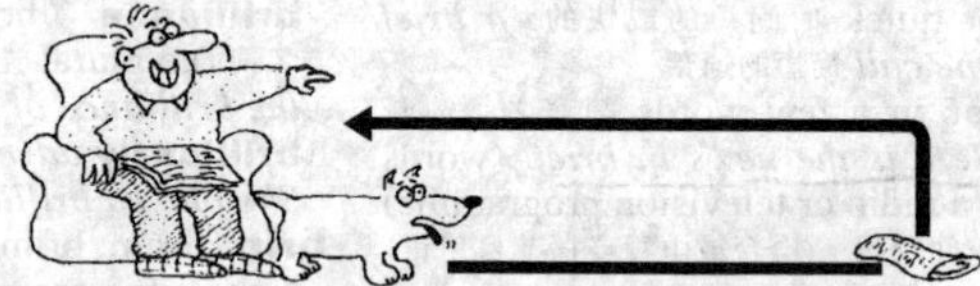

Fetch the newspaper. 去把报纸拿来。

Take the newspapers. 把报纸拿走。

brisk /brɪsk; brɪsk/ *adjective* 形容词 (**brisker, briskest**)
quick and using a lot of energy 迅速而耗费精力的: *We went for a brisk walk.* 我们轻快地散了散步。

bristle /'brɪsl; 'brɪsḷ/ *noun* 名词
a short thick hair like the hair on a brush 短而硬的毛发（像刷子似的）

brittle /'brɪtl; 'brɪtḷ/ *adjective* 形容词
Something that is brittle is hard but breaks easily 硬而易碎的；脆弱的: *This glass is very brittle.* 这个玻璃杯很容易碎。

broad /brɔ:d; brɔd/ *adjective* 形容词 (**broader, broadest**)
large from one side to the other; wide 宽的；宽阔的: *a broad river* 宽阔的河 ✪ The noun is **breadth**. 名词是 **breadth**。
✪ opposite 反义词: **narrow**

broadcast /'brɔ:dkɑ:st; 'brɔdˌkæst/ *verb* 动词 (**broadcasts, broadcasting, broadcast, has broadcast**)
send out sound or pictures by radio or television（广播电台或电视台）广播；播送: *The BBC broadcasts the news at 9 p.m.* 英国广播公司晚上9点钟播送新闻。

broadcast *noun* 名词
something that is sent out by radio or television（广播电台或电视台的）广播: *a news broadcast* 新闻广播

broadcaster *noun* 名词
a person whose job is to talk on radio or television 广播员

brochure /'brəʊʃə(r); bro'ʃʊr/ *noun* 名词
a thin book with pictures of things you can buy or places you can go on holiday（宣传购物或度假的）小册子: *a travel brochure* 旅游指南

broke, broken *forms of* **break**[1] ＊ **break**[1] 的不同形式

broken /'brəʊkən; 'brokən/ *adjective* 形容词
in pieces or not working 破碎的；损坏的: *a broken window* 破碎的窗户 ◇ *'What's the time?' 'I don't know –my watch is broken.'* “几点钟了？”“不知道——我的手表坏了。”

bronze /brɒnz; brɑnz/ *noun* 名词 (no plural 无复数)
a brown metal made from copper and tin 青铜: *a bronze medal* 铜牌

brooch /brəʊtʃ; brotʃ/ *noun* 名词 (*plural* 复数作 **brooches**)
a pretty thing with a pin at the back that you wear on your clothes 胸针

broom /bru:m; brum/ *noun* 名词
a brush with a long handle that you use for sweeping 扫帚

brother /'brʌðə(r); 'brʌðɚ/ *noun* 名词
Your brother is a man or boy who has the same parents as you 哥哥；弟弟: *My younger brother is called Tim.* 我弟弟叫蒂姆。◇ *Gavin and Nick are brothers.* 加文和尼克是哥俩。☞ picture on page C3 见第C3页图

brother-in-law /'brʌðər ɪn lɔ:;'brʌðər-ɪn,lɔ/ *noun* 名词 (*plural* 复数作 **brothers-in-law**)
1 the brother of your wife or husband 妻子或丈夫的哥哥或弟弟；内兄；内弟；大伯子；小叔子
2 the husband of your sister 姐姐或妹妹的丈夫；姐夫；妹夫
☞ picture on page C3 见第C3页图

brought *form of* **bring** ✳ **bring** 的不同形式

brow /braʊ; braʊ/ *noun* 名词
the part of your face above your eyes 前额

brown /braʊn; braʊn/ *adjective* 形容词 (**browner**, **brownest**)
with the colour of coffee 褐色的；棕色的: *brown eyes* 棕色的眼睛 ◇ *She is brown* (= she has brown skin) *because she has been in the sun.* 她晒过太阳，所以皮肤是褐色的。

brown *noun* 名词
the colour of coffee 褐色；棕色

bruise /bru:z; bruz/ *noun* 名词
a dark mark on your skin that comes after something hits it 挫伤

bruise *verb* 动词 (**bruises**, **bruising**, **bruised** /bru:zd; bruzd/)
He fell and bruised his leg. 他跌倒以后腿部受了挫伤。

brush /brʌʃ; brʌʃ/ *noun* 名词 (*plural* 复数作 **brushes**)
a thing that you use for sweeping, cleaning, painting or making your hair tidy 刷子；画笔；毛笔: *She swept the snow off the path with a brush.* 她用刷子把路上的雪清除掉。
☞ Look also at **hairbrush**, **paintbrush** and **toothbrush**. 另见 **hairbrush**、**paintbrush** 及 **toothbrush**。

brushes 刷子

brush *verb* 动词 (**brushes**, **brushing**, **brushed** /brʌʃt; brʌʃt/)
use a brush to do something（用刷子、画笔或毛笔）刷、画或写: *I brush my teeth twice a day.* 我每天刷两次牙。◇ *Brush your hair!* 用发刷梳梳头发！

Brussels sprout /ˌbrʌslz 'spraʊt; 'brʌsl̩z 'spraʊt/ *noun* 名词
a round green vegetable like a very small cabbage 汤菜（状似极小的洋白菜）

brutal /'bru:tl; 'brutl̩/ *adjective* 形容词
very cruel 残忍的；野蛮的: *a brutal murder* 残忍的谋杀

brutally /'bru:təli; 'brutl̩ɪ/ *adverb* 副词
She was brutally attacked. 她遭到残忍的暴力伤害。

bubble /'bʌbl; 'bʌbl̩/ *noun* 名词
a small ball of air or gas inside a liquid（液体中的）小气泡: *You can see bubbles in a glass of champagne.* 香槟酒杯里能看见有小气泡。

bubble *verb* 动词 (**bubbles**, **bubbling**, **bubbled** /'bʌbld; 'bʌbl̩d/)
make a lot of bubbles 冒出很多小气泡: *When water boils, it bubbles.* 水开了就冒泡。

bucket /'bʌkɪt; 'bʌkɪt/ *noun* 名词
a round metal or plastic container with a handle. You use a bucket for carrying water, for example（带提梁的）圆桶；提桶

bucket 桶

buckle /'bʌkl; 'bʌkl̩/ *noun* 名词
a metal or plastic thing on the end of a belt or strap that you use for joining it to the other end（皮带等的）锁扣；扣环

bud /bʌd; bʌd/ *noun* 名词
a leaf or flower before it opens 芽；花蕾: *There are buds on the trees in spring.* 春天树都发芽了。☞ picture at **plant** 见 **plant** 词条插图

Buddhist /'bʊdɪst; 'bʊdɪst/ *noun* 名词
a person who follows the religion of **Buddhism**, started in India by Buddha 佛教徒（佛教叫做 **Buddhism**）

B

Buddhist *adjective* 形容词
a Buddhist temple 佛教的寺院
budge /bʌdʒ; bʌdʒ/ *verb* 动词 (**budges, budging, budged** /bʌdʒd; bʌdʒd/)
move a little or make something move a little（使某物）稍微移动: *I'm trying to move this rock but it won't budge.* 我使劲挪这块石头，可是一点儿都挪不动。
budgerigar /ˈbʌdʒərɪɡɑː(r); ˈbʌdʒərɪ,ɡɑr/, **budgie** /ˈbʌdʒi; ˈbʌdʒɪ/ *noun* 名词
a small blue or green bird that people often keep as a pet 虎皮鹦鹉
budget /ˈbʌdʒɪt; ˈbʌdʒɪt/ *noun* 名词
a plan of how much money you will have and how you will spend it 预算: *We have a weekly budget for food.* 我们每星期都有购买食物的预算。
budget *verb* 动词 (**budgets, budgeting, budgeted**)
plan how much money you will have and how you will spend it 做预算: *I am budgeting very carefully because I want to buy a new car.* 我现在精打细算想买辆新汽车。
buffet /ˈbʊfeɪ; bʊˈfe/ *noun* 名词
1 a place on a train or at a station where you can buy food and drinks（火车里的或车站上的）饮食柜台
2 a meal when all the food is on a big table and you take what you want 自助餐
bug /bʌɡ; bʌɡ/ *noun* 名词
1 a small insect 昆虫；臭虫
2 an illness that is not serious（不太重的）病: *I've caught a bug.* 我得了病了。
build /bɪld; bɪld/ *verb* 动词 (**builds, building, built** /bɪlt; bɪlt/, **has built**)
make something by putting parts together 建造；建筑: *He built a wall in front of the house.* 他在房前修了一道墙。◇ *The bridge is built of stone.* 这座桥是石头的。
builder /ˈbɪldə(r); ˈbɪldɚ/ *noun* 名词
a person whose job is to make buildings 建造者；建筑者
building /ˈbɪldɪŋ; ˈbɪldɪŋ/ *noun* 名词
a thing with a roof and walls. Houses, schools, churches and shops are all buildings.（有屋顶和墙的）建筑物（房子、学校、教堂、商店都是建筑物。）
building society /ˈbɪldɪŋ səsaɪəti; ˈbɪldɪŋ səˈsaɪətɪ/ *noun* 名词 (*plural* 复数作 **building societies**)
a kind of bank that lends you money when you want to buy a house or flat 房屋建筑互助会（类似银行贷款助人买房的机构）
built *form of* **build** ✳ **build** 的不同形式
bulb /bʌlb; bʌlb/ *noun* 名词
1 the glass part of an electric lamp that gives light 电灯泡
2 a round thing that some plants grow from 鳞茎: *a tulip bulb* 郁金香鳞茎
bulge /bʌldʒ; bʌldʒ/ *verb* 动词 (**bulges, bulging, bulged** /bʌldʒd; bʌldʒd/)
become bigger than usual; go out in a round shape from something that is usually flat 鼓起；凸起；膨胀: *My stomach is bulging—I have eaten too much.* 我肚子都鼓起来了——吃得太多了。
bulge *noun* 名词
a round part that goes out from something that is usually flat 鼓起；突出: *a bulge in the wall* 墙上的一个鼓包
bulky /ˈbʌlki; ˈbʌlkɪ/ *adjective* 形容词 (**bulkier, bulkiest**)
big, heavy and difficult to carry 巨大、笨重而难以搬动的
bull /bʊl; bʊl/ *noun* 名词
the male of the cow and of some other animals 公牛；某些雄性动物 ☞ Note and picture at **cow** 见 **cow** 词条注释和插图
bulldozer /ˈbʊldəʊzə(r); ˈbʊl,dozɚ/ *noun* 名词
a big heavy machine that moves earth and makes land flat 推土机
bullet /ˈbʊlɪt; ˈbʊlɪt/ *noun* 名词
a small piece of metal that shoots out of a gun 子弹: *The bullet hit him in the leg.* 子弹打中了他的腿。
bulletin-board /ˈbʊlətɪn bɔːd; ˈbʊlətɪn-bɔrd/ *American English for* **notice-board** 美式英语，即 **notice-board**
bully /ˈbʊli; ˈbʊlɪ/ *noun* 名词 (*plural* 复数作 **bullies**)
a person who hurts or frightens a weaker person 恃强凌弱的人
bully *verb* 动词 (**bullies, bullying, bullied** /ˈbʊlid; ˈbʊlɪd/)
hurt or frighten a weaker person 恃强凌弱；威吓；欺负；伤害（弱者）: *She was bullied by the older girls at school.* 她在学校里受到年岁大的女学生的欺负。
bum /bʌm; bʌm/ *noun* 名词
the part of your body that you sit on 屁股 ✪ Be careful! Some people think

this word is quite rude. 注意！有的人认为这个字很粗俗。**Bottom** is the more usual word. ✳ **bottom** 是较常用的字。

bump[1] /bʌmp; bʌmp/ *verb* 动词 (**bumps, bumping, bumped** /bʌmpt; bʌmpt/)

1 hit somebody or something when you are moving 运动时碰撞到某人或某物: *She bumped into a chair.* 她碰到了椅子了。

2 hit a part of your body against something hard 身体某部碰撞到硬物: *I bumped my head on the ceiling.* 我的头撞到天花板了。

bump into somebody meet somebody by chance 遇见某人: *I bumped into David today.* 我今天碰见戴维了。

bump[2] /bʌmp; bʌmp/ *noun* 名词

1 when something hits another thing; the sound that this makes 碰撞；碰撞声: *He fell and hit the ground with a bump.* 他砰的一声跌倒在地上了。

2 a small round fat place on your body where you have hit it（因碰撞引起的）小包，疙瘩，肿块: *I've got a bump on my head.* 我头上起了个疙瘩。

3 a small part on something flat that is higher than the rest 隆起处；隆起物: *The car hit a bump in the road.* 汽车碰着了路上的隆起处。

bumper /ˈbʌmpə(r); ˈbʌmpɚ/ *noun* 名词

a bar on the front and back of a car, lorry, etc. It helps to protect the car if it hits something.（汽车前后的）保险杠

bumpy /ˈbʌmpi; ˈbʌmpɪ/ *adjective* 形容词 (**bumpier, bumpiest**)

1 with a lot of bumps 多隆起处或隆起物的: *a bumpy road* 有很多隆起处的路

2 that shakes you 颠簸的: *We had a very bumpy journey in an old bus.* 我们坐的旧公共汽车非常颠。

bun /bʌn; bʌn/ *noun* 名词

a small round cake or piece of bread 小而圆的蛋糕或面包

bunch /bʌntʃ; bʌntʃ/ *noun* 名词 (*plural* 复数作 **bunches**)

a group of things that grow together or that you tie or hold together 长在一起的东西；捆住或握住的一些东西: *a bunch of grapes* 一串葡萄 ◇ *a bunch of flowers* 一束花 ☞ picture on page C25 见第C25页图

bundle /ˈbʌndl; ˈbʌndl̩/ *noun* 名词

a group of things that you tie or wrap together 捆或包在一起的东西: *a bundle of old newspapers* 一捆旧报纸 ☞ picture on page C25 见第C25页图

bungalow /ˈbʌŋgələʊ; ˈbʌŋgəˌlo/ *noun* 名词

a house that has only one floor, with no upstairs rooms 平房

bunk /bʌŋk; bʌŋk/ *noun* 名词

a narrow bed that is fixed to a wall, on a ship or train, for example（架设于壁上的）狭窄铺位（如在轮船或火车上的）卧铺

bunny /ˈbʌni; ˈbʌnɪ/ *noun* 名词 (*plural* 复数作 **bunnies**)

a child's word for **rabbit**（儿语）兔子；兔兔

buoy /bɔɪ; bɔɪ/ *noun* 名词 (*plural* 复数作 **buoys**)

a thing that floats in the sea to show ships where there are dangerous places 浮标

burger /ˈbɜːgə(r); ˈbɝgɚ/ *noun* 名词

meat cut into very small pieces and made into a flat round shape, that you eat between two pieces of bread（夹在两片面包之间的）用肉末做的饼儿；汉堡包: *a beefburger* 牛肉末饼儿

burglar /ˈbɜːglə(r); ˈbɝglɚ/ *noun* 名词

a person who goes into a building to steal things（进入建筑物内偷东西的）窃贼

burglary /ˈbɜːgləri; ˈbɝglərɪ/ *noun* 名词 (*plural* 复数作 **burglaries**)

going into a house to steal things 入户行窃: *There were two burglaries in this street last week.* 上星期这条街上有两起入户盗窃案。

burgle /ˈbɜːgl; ˈbɝgl̩/ *verb* 动词 (**burgles, burgling, burgled** /ˈbɜːgld; ˈbɝgl̩d/)

go into a building to steal things 入户行窃: *Our house was burgled.* 我们家进贼了。

burial /ˈberiəl; ˈbɛrɪəl/ *noun* 名词

the time when a dead body is put in the ground 埋葬 ✪ The verb is **bury**. 动词是 **bury**。

buried, buries *forms of* **bury** ✳ **bury** 的不同形式

burn[1] /bɜːn; bɝn/ *verb* 动词 (**burns, burning, burnt** /bɜːnt; bɝnt/ or 或 **burned** /bɜːnd; bɝnd/, **has burnt** or 或 **has burned**)

1 make flames and heat; be on fire 燃烧；着火: *Paper burns easily.* 纸很容易

B

烧着。◇ *She escaped from the burning building.* 她从失火的大楼中逃了出来。

2 harm or destroy somebody or something with fire or heat 用火或高温伤害或毁坏某人或某物；烧伤；烫伤；烧毁: *I burnt my fingers on a match.* 我手指让火柴烫伤了。◇ *We burned the wood on the fire.* 我们烧木头。

burn down burn, or make a building burn, until there is nothing left 将建筑物焚为平地；烧塌: *Their house burnt down.* 他们的房子烧塌了。

burn² /bɜːn; bɝn/ *noun* 名词

a place on your body where fire or heat has hurt it（身上的）烧伤或烫伤之处: *I've got a burn on my arm from the cooker.* 我胳膊让炉具给烫伤了一块。

burp /bɜːp; bɝp/ *verb* 动词 (**burps, burping, burped** /bɜːpt; bɝpt/)

make a noise from your mouth when air suddenly comes up from your stomach 打嗝儿: *He burped loudly.* 他打嗝声音很大。

burp *noun* 名词

I heard a loud burp. 我听到很大的打嗝声。

burrow /ˈbʌrəʊ; ˈbʌro/ *noun* 名词

a hole in the ground where some animals, for example rabbits, live（某些动物挖的，例如兔子挖的）地洞

burst¹ /bɜːst; bɝst/ *verb* 动词 (**bursts, bursting, burst, has burst**)

1 break open suddenly because there is too much inside; make something break open suddenly 胀破；使某物突然破裂: *The bag was so full that it burst.* 这个袋子撑破了。◇ *The balloon burst.* 气球爆了。

2 go or come suddenly 突然去或来；闯入: *Steve burst into the room.* 史蒂夫闯进了房间。

burst into something start doing something suddenly 突然做某事: *He read the letter and burst into tears* (= started to cry). 他看着信就哭了起来。◇ *The car burst into flames* (= started to burn). 汽车突然着火了。

burst out laughing suddenly start to laugh 突然笑起来: *When she saw my hat, she burst out laughing.* 她一看到我的帽子就大笑起来。

burst² /bɜːst; bɝst/ *noun* 名词

something that happens suddenly and quickly 突然或迅速发生的事物: *a burst of laughter* 一阵大笑

bury /ˈberi; ˈbɛrɪ/ *verb* 动词 (**buries, burying, buried** /ˈberid; ˈbɛrɪd/, **has buried**)

1 put a dead body in the ground 埋葬尸体 ✪ The noun is **burial**. 名词是 **burial**。

2 put something in the ground or under something 埋在地下或放在某物之下: *The dog buried a bone in the garden.* 狗把骨头埋在花园里了。

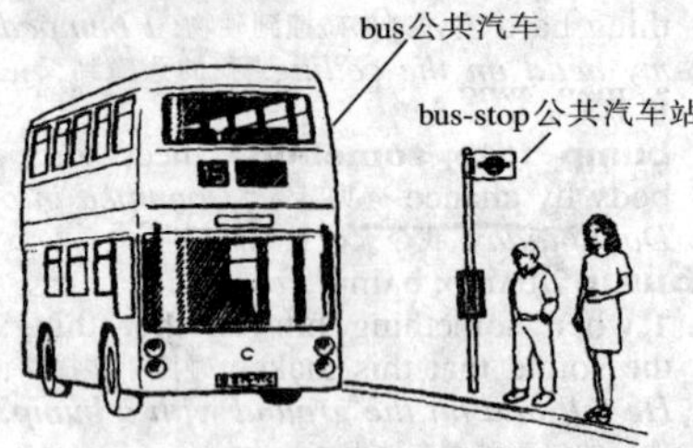

bus /bʌs; bʌs/ *noun* 名词 (*plural* 复数作 **buses**)

a thing like a big car, that carries a lot of people 公共汽车: *We went to town by bus.* 我们去市中心坐的是公共汽车。◇ *Where do you get off the bus?* 你坐公共汽车在哪儿下？

bus-stop /ˈbʌs stɒp; ˈbʌsˌstɑp/ *noun* 名词

a place where buses stop and people get on and off 公共汽车站

bush /bʊʃ; bʊʃ/ *noun* 名词

1 (*plural* 复数作 **bushes**) a plant like a small tree with a lot of branches 灌木: *a rose bush* 一株玫瑰

2 the bush (no plural 无复数) wild country with a lot of small trees in Africa or Australia 非洲或澳洲有矮树丛的荒野

business /ˈbɪznəs; ˈbɪznɪs/ *noun* 名词

1 (no plural 无复数) buying and selling things 买卖；生意；商业: *I want to go into business when I leave school.* 我打算中学毕业以后做买卖。◇ *Business is not very good this year.* 今年生意不太好。

2 (*plural* 复数作 **businesses**) a place where people sell or make things, for example a shop or factory 出售或制造物品的处所，（例如）公司；商店；企业；工厂

it's none of your business, mind your own business words that you use when you do not want to tell somebody about something that is private（不愿把私事告诉别人时说的话）与你无关；少管闲事: *'Where are you going?' 'Mind your own business!'* "你上哪儿去？""你管不着！"

on business because of your work 为公事: *John is in Germany on business.* 约翰现在出差在德国呢。

businessman /'bɪznəsmən; 'bɪznɪsˌmæn/ *noun* 名词 (*plural* 复数作 **businessmen**)
a man who works in an office and whose job is about buying and selling things（男的）商人

businesswoman /'bɪznəswʊmən; 'bɪznɪsˌwʊmən/ *noun* 名词 (*plural* 复数作 **businesswomen**)
a woman who works in an office and whose job is about buying and selling things（女的）商人

busy /'bɪzi; 'bɪzɪ/ *adjective* 形容词 (**busier**, **busiest**)
1 with a lot of things that you must do; working or not free 忙；忙碌；不得空: *Mr Jones can't see you now—he's busy.* 琼斯先生现在不能见你——他很忙。
2 with a lot of things happening 事情多的: *I had a busy morning.* 我早晨做了很多事。◇ *The shops are always busy at Christmas.* 商店在圣诞节总是很热闹。

busily /'bɪzɪli; 'bɪzḷɪ/ *adverb* 副词
He was busily writing a letter. 他正忙着写信。

but[1] /bət, bʌt; bʌt/ *conjunction* 连词
a word that you use to show something different 但是；可是: *My sister speaks French but I don't.* 我姐姐会说法语，我可不会。◇ *He worked hard but he didn't pass the exam.* 他很用功，但是没考及格。◇ *The weather was sunny but cold.* 天气晴，可是很冷。

but[2] /bət, bʌt; bʌt/ *preposition* 介词
except 除了（表示所说的不计算在内）: *She eats nothing but chocolate.* 她除了巧克力什么都不吃。

butcher /'bʊtʃə(r); 'bʊtʃɚ/ *noun* 名词
a person who cuts and sells meat 切割和出售肉的人；屠工；肉商 ✪ A shop that sells meat is called a **butcher's**. 肉铺叫做 **butcher's**。

butter /'bʌtə(r); 'bʌtɚ/ *noun* 名词 (no plural 无复数)
soft yellow food that is made from milk. You put it on bread or use it in cooking 黄油: *She spread butter on the bread.* 她把黄油涂在面包上了。

butter *verb* 动词 (**butters**, **buttering**, **buttered** /'bʌtəd; 'bʌtɚd/)
put butter on bread 把黄油涂在面包上: *I buttered the toast.* 我把黄油涂在烤面包片上了。

butterfly /'bʌtəflaɪ; 'bʌtɚˌflaɪ/ *noun* 名词 (*plural* 复数作 **butterflies**)
an insect with big coloured wings 蝴蝶

butterfly 蝴蝶

button /'bʌtn; 'bʌtn̩/ *noun* 名词
1 a small round thing on clothes. You push it through a small hole (a **buttonhole**) to hold clothes together. 钮扣；扣子（钮扣孔或扣眼叫做 **buttonhole**）
2 a small thing on a machine, that you push（机器的）按钮: *Press this button to ring the bell.* 按这个钮，电铃就响了。☞ picture on page C32 见第C32页图

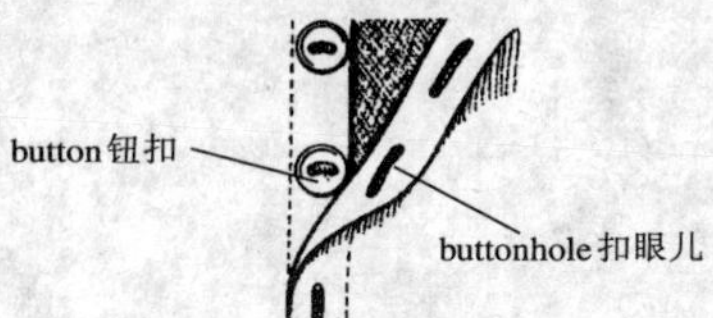

buy /baɪ; baɪ/ *verb* 动词 (**buys**, **buying**, **bought**/ bɔ:t; bɔt/, **has bought**)
give money to get something 买；购买: *I bought a new watch.* 我买了块新手表。◇ *He bought the car from a friend.* 他从朋友手中买的这辆汽车。☞ Look at **sell**. 见 **sell**。

buzz /bʌz; bʌz/ *verb* 动词 (**buzzes**, **buzzing**, **buzzed** /bʌzd; bʌzd/)
make a sound like bees 发出（似蜜蜂的）嗡嗡声

buzz *noun* 名词 (*plural* 复数作 **buzzes**)
the buzz of insects 昆虫的嗡嗡声

by[1] /baɪ; baɪ/ *preposition* 介词
1 very near 靠近: *The telephone is by the door.* 电话在门的附近。◇ *They live by the sea.* 他们住在海边。
2 from one side of somebody or something to the other; past 从某人或某

物的一边到另一边；经过: *He walked by me without speaking.* 他从我身旁经过，没说话。

3 not later than 不迟于: *I must finish this work by six o'clock.* 我六点钟以前得把工作做完。

4 a word that shows who or what did something 由；被: *a painting by Matisse* 由马蒂斯画的画儿 ◇ *She was caught by the police.* 她被警方捉住了。

5 using something 使用某事物: *I go to work by train.* 我坐火车去上班。◇ *He paid by cheque.* 他用支票付款。

6 a word that shows how 表示方法或手段用的词: *You turn the computer on by pressing this button.* 按这个钮就可以开动计算机。

7 a word that shows how you measure something（表示量度用的词）: *We buy material by the metre.* 我们买材料论米计算。

8 a word that shows which part（表示某部分用的词）: *She took me by the hand.* 她拉住我的手。

by² /baɪ; baɪ/ *adverb* 副词
past 经过: *She drove by without stopping.* 她开车经过时，没停车。

bye /baɪ; baɪ/, **bye-bye** /ˌbaɪˈbaɪ; ˈbaɪˌbaɪ/
goodbye 再见

Cc

C *short way of writing* **Celsius, centigrade** ✳ **Celsius**、**centigrade** 的缩写形式

cab /kæb; kæb/ *noun* 名词
1 *another word for* **taxi** ✳ **taxi** 的另一种说法
2 the part of a lorry, train or bus where the driver sits（卡车、火车或公共汽车的）驾驶室，司机室

cabbage /'kæbɪdʒ; 'kæbɪdʒ/ *noun* 名词
a large round vegetable with thick green leaves 洋白菜；卷心菜

cabin /'kæbɪn; 'kæbɪn/ *noun* 名词
1 a small bedroom on a ship（轮船的）舱室
2 a part of an aircraft（飞机的）机舱: *the passengers in the first-class cabin* 飞机上的头等舱的乘客
3 a small simple house made of wood 简陋的小木屋: *a log cabin at the edge of the lake* 湖边用圆木建的小房子

cabinet /'kæbɪnət; 'kæbənɪt/ *noun* 名词
1 (*plural* 复数作 **cabinets**) a piece of furniture that you can keep things in 储藏柜: *a bathroom cabinet* 浴室柜橱 ◇ *a filing cabinet* (= one that you use in an office to keep files in) 文件柜
2 the Cabinet (no plural 无复数) a group of the most important people in the government 内阁

cable /'keɪbl; 'kebl̩/ *noun* 名词
1 a wire that carries electricity or messages 电缆
2 a very strong thick rope or wire 缆；绳索

cable television /ˌkeɪbl 'telɪvɪʒn; ˌkebl̩ 'tɛləˌvɪʒən/ *noun* 名词 (no plural 无复数)
a way of sending pictures and sound along wires 缆线电视；有线电视

cactus /'kæktəs; 'kæktəs/ *noun* 名词 (*plural* 复数作 **cactuses** or 或 **cacti** /'kæktaɪ; 'kæktaɪ/)
a plant with a lot of sharp points that grows in hot dry places 仙人掌

café /'kæfeɪ; kæ'fe/ *noun* 名词
a place where you can have a drink and something to eat 小餐馆

cage /keɪdʒ; kedʒ/ *noun* 名词
a place with bars round it where animals or birds are kept so that they cannot escape 兽槛；鸟笼

cage 笼子

cake /keɪk; kek/ *noun* 名词
sweet food that you make from flour, eggs, sugar and butter and bake in the oven 蛋糕: *a chocolate cake* 巧克力蛋糕 ◇ *Would you like a piece of cake?* 你要蛋糕吗？

calculate /'kælkjuleɪt; 'kælkjəˌlet/ *verb* 动词 (**calculates, calculating, calculated**)
find the answer by using mathematics 计算: *Can you calculate how much the holiday will cost?* 你能不能算一下这次度假得用多少钱？

calculator /'kælkjuleɪtə(r); 'kælkjəˌletɚ/ *noun* 名词
an electronic instrument that adds, subtracts, multiplies and divides 电子计算器

calendar /'kæləndə(r); 'kæləndɚ/ *noun* 名词
a list of the days, weeks and months of one year 日历: *Look at the calendar and tell me what day of the week December 2nd is this year.* 看看日历，告诉我今年12月2日是星期几？

calf[1] /kɑ:f; kæf/ *noun* 名词 (*plural* 复数作 **calves** /kɑ:vz; kævz/)
a young cow 小牛；犊 ☞ Note and picture at **cow** 见 **cow** 词条注释及插图

calf[2] /kɑ:f; kæf/ *noun* 名词 (*plural* 复数作 **calves** /kɑ:vz; kævz/)
the back of your leg, below your knee 腿肚子；腓（小腿后部）☞ picture on page C2 见第C2页图

call[1] /kɔ:l; kɔl/ *noun* 名词
1 a loud cry or shout 呼喊；喊叫: *a call for help* 大声呼救
2 using the telephone 电话；通话: *I had a call from James.* 詹姆斯给我来了个电话。◇ *I haven't got time to talk now—I'll give you a call later.* 我现在没空儿说话——我呆一会儿给你打电话。
3 a short visit to somebody 访问某人: *We paid a call on Katie.* 我们拜访了凯蒂。

call² /kɔ:l; kɔl/ *verb* 动词 (**calls, calling, called** /kɔ:ld; kɔld/)

1 speak loudly and clearly so that somebody who is far away can hear you 大声而清楚地说（好让远处的人听见）；喊；嚷：*'Breakfast is ready,' she called.* "吃早饭了，"她喊了一声。◇ *She called out the names of the winners.* 她大声宣布了获胜者的名字。

2 ask somebody to come 要求某人来: *He was so ill that we had to call the doctor.* 他病得很重，我们只好把大夫请来了。

3 give a name to somebody or something 给某人或某事物取名；把某人或某事物叫做: *They called the baby Sophie.* 他们给孩子起名叫索菲。

4 telephone somebody 给某人打电话: *I'll call you later.* 我呆会儿给你打电话。◇ *Who's calling, please?* 请问，您是哪位？

be called have as a name 名字叫做: *'What is your teacher called?' 'She's called Mrs Gray.'* "你们老师怎么称呼？""我们管她叫格雷夫人。"

call somebody back telephone somebody again 给某人回电话: *I can't talk now—I'll call you back later.* 我现在说话不方便——呆会儿再给您回电话吧。

call collect *American English for* **reverse the charges** 美式英语，即 **reverse the charges**

call for somebody go to somebody's house on your way to a place so that they can come with you 顺路到某人家约之同行: *Rosie usually calls for me in the morning and we walk to school together.* 罗齐经常早晨找我一起走着去上学。

call in make a short visit 访问；拜访: *I'll call in to see you this evening.* 我今天晚上去探望您。

call off say that something that you have planned will not happen 取消或放弃原计划的事: *We called off the race because it was raining.* 因为下雨，我们取消了这场赛事。

call-box /'kɔ:l bɒks; 'kɔl,bɑks/ *noun* 名词 (*plural* 复数作 **call-boxes**)

a kind of small building in the street or in a public place that has a telephone in it 电话亭

calm¹ /kɑ:m; kɑm/ *adjective* 形容词 (**calmer, calmest**)

1 quiet, and not excited or afraid 安静的；沉着的；冷静的: *Try to keep calm—there's no danger.* 要镇静些——没有危险。

2 without much wind 无大风的: *calm weather* 无风的天气

3 without big waves 无大浪的: *calm sea* 无浪的海面

calmly *adverb* 副词

He spoke calmly about the accident. 他泰然自若地讲述那次事故。

calm² /kɑ:m; kɑm/ *verb* 动词 (**calms, calming, calmed** /kɑ:md; kɑmd/)

calm down become less afraid or excited; make somebody less afraid or excited（使某人）镇定下来: *Calm down and tell me what happened.* 镇定一下，告诉我怎么回事。

calorie /'kæləri; 'kælərɪ/ *noun* 名词

Food that has a lot of calories in it can make you fat. 卡路里

calves *plural of* **calf** ✳ **calf** 的复数形式

came *form of* **come** ✳ **come** 的不同形式

camel /'kæml; 'kæml̩/ *noun* 名词

a large animal with one or two round parts (called **humps**) on its back. Camels carry people and things in the desert. 骆驼（驼峰叫做 **hump**）

camera /'kæmərə; 'kæmərə/ *noun* 名词

a thing that you use for taking photographs or moving pictures 照相机；摄影机: *I need a new film for my camera.* 我的照相机得装个新胶卷了。

camp /kæmp; kæmp/ *noun* 名词

a place where people live in tents for a short time 营地

camp *verb* 动词 (**camps, camping, camped** /kæmpt; kæmpt/)

live in a tent for a short time 露营: *Ask the farmer if we can camp in his field.* 问问那个农民，我们能不能在他的地里露营。

✪ It is more usual to say **go camping** when you mean that you are living in a tent on holiday 以露营方式度假，一般说 **go camping**: *We went camping last summer.* 我们去年夏天去露营了。

camping *noun* 名词 (no plural 无复数)

living in a tent for a short time 露营: *Camping isn't much fun when it rains.* 露营要碰上下雨就没什么意思了。

camp-site /'kæmp saɪt; 'kæmp,saɪt/ *noun* 名词

a place where you can camp 露营区

campaign /kæm'peɪn; kæm'pen/ *noun* 名词
a plan to get a special result（为获得某种结果而制定的）计划运动: *a campaign to stop people smoking* 戒烟运动

can¹ /kən, kæn; kən, kæn/ *modal verb* 情态动词
1 be able to; be strong enough, clever enough, etc 能；会: *She can speak three languages.* 她能说三种语言。◇ *Can you ski?* 你会滑雪吗？
2 be allowed to 可以: *You can go now.* 你现在可以走了。◇ *Can I have some more soup, please?* 请你再给我来点儿汤行吗？◇ *The doctor says she can't go back to school yet.* 大夫说她还不能回校上课。
3 a word that you use when you ask somebody to do something 要求某人做某事用的词: *Can you tell me the time, please?* 请问，现在几点钟了？
4 be possible or likely 有可能: *It can be very cold in the mountains in winter.* 冬天山里有可能非常冷。
5 a word that you use with verbs like *'see', 'hear', 'smell' and 'taste'* 与 see、hear、smell、taste 等动词连用的词: *I can smell something burning.* 我闻出有东西烧着了的味儿。◇ *'What's that noise?' 'I can't hear anything.'* "这是什么声音？" "我什么也没听到。"

> ✪ The negative form of 'can' is **cannot** /'kænɒt; 'kænɑt/ or the short form **can't** /kɑːnt; kænt/ ＊ can 的否定形式是 **cannot** /'kænɒt; 'kænɑt/，缩略式是 **can't** /kɑːnt; kænt/:
>
> *She can't swim.* 她不会游泳。
>
> The past tense of 'can' is **could**. You use **be able to**, not **can**, to make the future and perfect tenses ＊ can 的过去式是 **could**，将来式或完成式要用 **be able to**，不要用 **can**:
>
> *I **can** see it.* 我看得见。
>
> *You **will be able** to see it if you stand on this chair.* 你站在这把椅子上就看得见了。
>
> ☞ Look at the Note on page 314 to find out more about **modal verbs**. 见第 314 页对 **modal verbs** 的进一步解释。

can² /kæn; kæn/ *noun* 名词
a metal container for food or drink that keeps it fresh（金属罐装的）食物或饮料: *a can of lemonade* 一罐汽水 ☞ picture at **container** 见 **container** 词条插图

canal /kə'næl; kə'næl/ *noun* 名词
a path that is made through the land and filled with water so that boats can travel on it 运河: *the Suez Canal* 苏伊士运河

canary /kə'neəri; kə'nɛrɪ/ *noun* 名词 (*plural* 复数作 **canaries**)
a small yellow bird that people often keep as a pet 金丝雀；加那利雀

cancel /'kænsl; 'kænsḷ/ *verb* 动词 (**cancels**, **cancelling**, **cancelled** /'kænsld; 'kænsḷd/)
say that something that you have planned will not happen 取消: *The singer was ill, so the concert was cancelled.* 歌手病了，所以音乐会取消了。✪ In American English the spellings are **canceling** and **canceled**. 美式英语拼写作 **canceling** 和 **canceled**。

cancellation /ˌkænsə'leɪʃn; ˌkænsḷ'eʃən/ *noun* 名词
the cancellation of the President's visit 总统访问的取消

cancer /'kænsə(r); 'kænsɚ/ *noun* 名词
a very dangerous illness that makes some **cells** (very small parts in the body) grow too fast 癌（细胞叫做 **cell**）: *Smoking can cause cancer.* 吸烟可以致癌。

candidate /'kændɪdət; 'kændəˌdet/ *noun* 名词
1 a person who wants to be chosen for something 候选人；申请人: *When the director leaves, there will be a lot of candidates for her job.* 董事长离职时，将有很多人申请这一职位。
2 a person who takes an examination 参加考试的人

candle /'kændl; 'kændḷ/ *noun* 名词
a long round piece of wax with a string in the middle that burns to give light 蜡烛

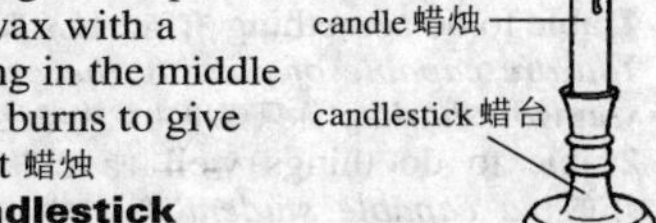

candlestick /'kændlstɪk; 'kændḷˌstɪk/ *noun* 名词
a thing that holds a candle 蜡台；烛台

candy /'kændi; 'kændɪ/ *American English for* **sweet**[2] **1** 美式英语，即 **sweet**[2] **1**

cane /keɪn; ken/ *noun* 名词
the hollow stem of some plants 某些植物的中空的茎: *sugar cane* 甘蔗

canned /kænd; kænd/ *adjective* 形容词
in a can（食品或饮料）金属罐装的: *canned drinks* 罐装饮料

C

cannibal /'kænɪbl; 'kænəbḷ/ *noun* 名词
a person who eats other people 吃人肉的人

cannot /'kænɒt; 'kænɑt/ = **can not**

canoe /kə'nu:; kə'nu/ *noun* 名词
a light narrow boat that you use on rivers. You move it through the water with a piece of wood (called a **paddle**). 狭窄的轻舟；独木舟（桨叫做 **paddle**）✪ When you talk about using a canoe, you often say **go canoeing** 划独木舟，常说 **go canoeing**: *We went canoeing on the river.* 我们到河里划独木舟去了。

can't /kɑ:nt; kænt/ = **can not**

canteen /kæn'ti:n; kæn'tin/ *noun* 名词
the place where people eat when they are at school or work（学校或工作处的）食堂

canvas /'kænvəs; 'kænvəs/ *noun* 名词 (no plural 无复数)
strong heavy cloth. Tents and sails are often made of canvas, and it is also used for painting pictures on. 帆布（用来做帐篷和船帆，还可用做油画布）

cap /kæp; kæp/ *noun* 名词
1 a soft hat 软帽；便帽；制服帽子: *a baseball cap* 棒球帽
2 a thing that covers the top of a bottle or tube（瓶子、牙膏管等的）盖儿: *Put the cap back on the bottle.* 瓶子用后要把盖儿盖好。

cap 帽子

capable /'keɪpəbl; 'kepəbḷ/ *adjective* 形容词
1 able to do something 有能力做某事物的: *You are capable of passing the exam if you work harder.* 你只要用功就能考及格。
2 able to do things well 能把事情做好的: *a capable student* 有才能的学生
✪ opposite 反义词: **incapable**

capacity /kə'pæsəti; kə'pæsətɪ/ *noun* 名词 (*plural* 复数作 **capacities**)
how much a container can hold 容积；容量: *a tank with a capacity of 1 000 litres* 能盛1 000升的容器

cape /keɪp; kep/ *noun* 名词
1 a piece of clothing like a coat without sleeves 披肩；斗篷
2 a high part of the land that goes out into the sea 海角；岬: *Cape Horn* 合恩角

capital /'kæpɪtl; 'kæpətḷ/ *noun* 名词
1 the most important city in a country, where the government is 首都: *Rome is the capital of Italy.* 罗马是意大利的首都。
2 (*also* 亦作 **capital letter**) a big letter of the alphabet 大写字母: *A, B and C are capitals, a, b and c are not.* ＊A、B、C是大写字母，a、b、c不是大写字母。◇ *Names of people and places begin with a capital letter.* 人名和地名的开头用大写字母。

capsize /kæp'saɪz; kæp'saɪz/ *verb* 动词 (**capsizes**, **capsizing**, **capsized** /kæp'saɪzd; kæp'saɪzd/)
turn over in the water 在水中翻转；翻船: *During the storm, the boat capsized.* 船在暴风雨中翻了。

captain /'kæptɪn; 'kæptɪn/ *noun* 名词
1 the person who is in charge of a ship or an aircraft 船长；舰长；机长: *The captain sent a message by radio for help.* 船长用无线电发出了求救信号。
2 the leader of a group of people 队长: *He's the captain of the school football team.* 他是学校足球队的队长。

caption /'kæpʃn; 'kæpʃən/ *noun* 名词
the words above or below a picture in a book or newspaper, that tell you about it（书报的图片上的）说明文字

captive /'kæptɪv; 'kæptɪv/ *noun* 名词
a person who is not free; a prisoner 无自由的人；囚犯

captivity /kæp'tɪvəti; kæp'tɪvətɪ/ *noun* 名词 (no plural 无复数)
in captivity kept in a place that you cannot leave 被束缚或囚禁于某处: *Wild animals are often unhappy in captivity* (= in a zoo, for example). 关着的野生动物往往不愉快（= 例如在动物园里）。

capture /'kæptʃə(r); 'kæptʃɚ/ *verb* 动词 (**captures**, **capturing**, **captured** /'kæptʃəd; 'kæptʃɚd/)
catch somebody and keep them somewhere so that they cannot leave 捉住某人

car 汽车

并囚禁起来；逮捕；捕获：*The police captured the robbers.* 警方捉住了劫匪。

capture *noun* 名词 (no plural 无复数)
the capture of the escaped prisoners 捉住逃犯

car /kɑ:(r); kɑr/ *noun* 名词
1 a vehicle with four wheels, usually with enough space for four or five people（有四个轮子的，通常可坐四五人的）汽车；轿车：*She travels to work by car.* 她乘坐小轿车上班。
2 *American English for* **carriage** 美式英语，即 **carriage**

car park /ˈkɑ: pɑ:k; ˈkɑr pɑrk/ *noun* 名词
a piece of land or a building where you can put your car for a time 汽车停车场

caravan /ˈkærəvæn; ˈkærəˌvæn/ *noun* 名词
a small house on wheels, that a car or a horse can pull（用汽车或马拉的，可居住的）拖车；篷车

carbon /ˈkɑ:bən; ˈkɑrbən/ *noun* 名词 (no plural 无复数)
the chemical that coal and diamonds are made of and that is in all living things 碳

card /kɑ:d; kɑrd/ *noun* 名词
1 a piece of thick stiff paper with writing or pictures on it（有文字或图画的）卡片：*We send Christmas cards, birthday cards and postcards to our friends.* 我们给朋友寄圣诞卡、生日贺卡和明信片。☞ Look also at **credit card** and **phonecard**. 另见 **credit card** 和 **phonecard**。
2 a playing-card; one of a set of 52 cards called a **pack of cards** that you use to play games. A pack has four groups of thirteen cards: **hearts**, **clubs**, **diamonds** and **spades** 一张纸牌；一张扑克牌（一副共52张，叫做 **pack of cards**。一副有四种花色，各13张：红桃叫做 **hearts**、梅花叫做 **clubs**、方块叫做 **diamonds**、黑桃叫做 **spades**）：*Let's have a game of cards.* 咱们打扑克吧。◇ *They often play cards in the evening.* 他们晚上常打扑克。

cardboard /ˈkɑ:dbɔ:d; ˈkɑrdˌbɔrd/ *noun* 名词 (no plural 无复数)
very thick paper that is used for making boxes, etc（用以制纸盒、纸箱等的）硬纸板

cardigan /ˈkɑ:dɪgən; ˈkɑrdɪgən/ *noun* 名词
a knitted woollen jacket（对襟的）毛衣

cardinal /ˈkɑ:dɪnl; ˈkɑrdn̩əl/ *noun* 名词
an important priest in the Roman Catholic church 红衣主教；枢机主教

care[1] /keə(r); kɛr/ *noun* 名词 (no plural 无复数)
thinking about what you are doing so that you do not make a mistake or break something 小心；谨慎：*Wash these glasses with care!* 洗这些玻璃杯要加小心！

care of somebody ☞ Look at **c/o**. 见 **c/o**。

take care be careful 当心；留心；小心：*Take care when you cross the road.* 过马路要当心。

take care of somebody or 或 **something** look after somebody or something; do what is necessary 照顾某人或某事物；照看；照料：*Alison is taking care of her sister's baby today.* 艾莉森今天给她姐姐看孩子。◇ *I'll take care of the shopping if you do the cleaning.* 你要是做扫除我就去买东西。

care[2] /keə(r); kɛr/ *verb* 动词 (**cares**, **caring**, **cared** /keəd; kɛrd/)
think that it is important 关心：*The only thing he cares about is money.* 他关心的就是钱。◇ *I don't care who wins — I'm not interested in football.* 我不管谁赢——我对足球不感兴趣。✪ You use expressions like **I don't care, who cares?** and **I couldn't care less** when you feel a little angry and want to be rude. 用 **I don't care, who cares?** 和 **I couldn't care less** 表示有些生气而出言不逊。

care for somebody or 或 **something** 1 do the things for somebody that they need 照顾某人: *After the accident, her parents cared for her until she was better.* 她出了事故以后，她父母照看她，直到她身体好些。 **2** like somebody or something 喜爱某人或某事物: *Would you care for a cup of tea?* 你想来杯茶吗？

C

career /kə'rɪə(r); kə'rɪr/ *noun* 名词
a job that you learn to do and then do for many years 职业；事业: *a career in teaching* 教学工作

careful /'keəfl; 'kɛrfəl/ *adjective* 形容词
If you are careful, you think about what you are doing so that you do not make a mistake or have an accident 小心；当心；留心: *Careful! The plate is very hot.* 小心！这个盘子很烫。◇ *Be careful with those glasses.* 当心那些玻璃杯。

carefully /'keəfəli; 'kɛrfəlɪ/ *adverb* 副词
Please listen carefully. 请留心听。

careless /'keələs; 'kɛrlɪs/ *adjective* 形容词
If you are careless, you do not think enough about what you are doing, so that you make mistakes 不小心的；粗心的: *Careless drivers can cause accidents.* 粗心大意的司机就可能出事故。

carelessly *adverb* 副词
She carelessly threw her coat on the floor. 她满不在乎地把大衣扔到地上。

carelessness /'keələsnəs; 'kɛrlɪsnɪs/ *noun* 名词 (no plural 无复数)
being careless 不小心；粗心

caretaker /'keəteɪkə(r); 'kɛrˌtekɚ/ *noun* 名词
a person whose job is to look after a large building like a school or a block of flats（照管大型建筑物如学校或公寓大楼等的）管理员；看门人

cargo /'kɑ:gəʊ; 'kɑrgo/ *noun* 名词 (*plural* 复数作 **cargoes**)
the things that a ship or an aeroplane carries（轮船或飞机运送的）货物: *a cargo of wheat* 一船小麦

carnation /kɑ:'neɪʃn; kɑr'neʃən/ *noun* 名词
a pink, white or red flower with a nice smell 康乃馨（麝香石竹花，呈粉色、白色或红色，有香味）

carol /'kærəl; 'kærəl/ *noun* 名词
a religious song that people sing at Christmas 圣诞颂歌

carpenter /'kɑ:pəntə(r); 'kɑrpəntɚ/ *noun* 名词
a person who makes things from wood 木匠；木工

carpentry /'kɑ:pəntri; 'kɑrpəntrɪ/ *noun* 名词 (no plural 无复数)
making things from wood 木工工艺；木作

carpet /'kɑ:pɪt; 'kɑrpɪt/ *noun* 名词
a soft covering for a floor that is often made of wool and is usually the same size as the floor 地毯

carriage /'kærɪdʒ; 'kærɪdʒ/ *noun* 名词
1 one of the parts of a train where people sit（火车的）客车厢: *The carriages at the back of the train were empty.* 这列火车后面的客车厢都是空的。
2 a vehicle that is pulled by horses and is used at special times 马车: *The Queen rode in a carriage through the streets of the city.* 女王坐着马车穿过市区街道。

carried *form of* **carry** ＊ **carry** 的不同形式

carrier bag /'kæriə bæg; 'kærɪɚ bæg/, **carrier** *noun* 名词
a large bag made from plastic or paper that you use for carrying shopping（塑料的或纸的）购物袋

carrot /'kærət; 'kærət/ *noun* 名词
a long thin orange vegetable 胡萝卜

carrot 胡萝卜

carry /'kæri; 'kærɪ/ *verb* 动词 (**carries, carrying, carried** /'kærid; 'kærɪd/, **has carried**)
1 hold something and take it to another place or keep it with you 携带某物到另一处；随身携带: *He carried the suit to my room.* 他把手提箱送到我的房间里了。◇ *I can't carry this box—it's too heavy.* 我拿不动这个箱子——太重了。◇ *Do the police carry guns in your country?* 你们国家警察带枪吗？✪ Be careful! You use **wear**, not **carry**, to talk about having clothes on your body 注意！穿衣物的"穿"字要用 **wear**，不用 **carry**: *She is wearing a red dress and carrying a black bag.* 她穿着红色的连衣裙，拿着黑色的手提包。
2 move people or things 运送人或物: *Special fast trains carry people to the city centre.* 特快列车可载乘客至市中心。

C

carry on continue doing something 继续做某事: *Carry on with your work.* 继续做你的工作。◇ *If you carry on to the end of this road, you'll see the post office on the right.* 沿着这条路走到头，就能看到右边的那个邮局。

carry out do or finish what you have planned 实行或完成计划: *The swimming-pool was closed while they carried out the repairs.* 那个游泳池维修期间停止开放。

cart /kɑ:t; kɑrt/ *noun* 名词
a wooden vehicle with two or four wheels that a horse usually pulls (木制的) 大车 (通常为马拉的，有两轮或四轮)

carton /'kɑ:tn; 'kɑrtn̩/ *noun* 名词
a container made of cardboard or plastic (纸板的或塑料的) 箱子或盒子: *a carton of milk* 一纸盒奶 ☞ picture at **container** 见 **container** 词条插图

cartoon /kɑ:'tu:n; kɑr'tun/ *noun* 名词
1 a funny drawing, for example in a newspaper 漫画 (例如报纸上的)
2 a television or cinema film made with drawings, not pictures of real people and places 动画片；卡通片: *a Mickey Mouse cartoon* 米老鼠卡通片

carve /kɑ:v; kɑrv/ *verb* 动词 (**carves, carving, carved** /kɑ:vd; kɑrvd/)
1 cut wood or stone to make a picture or shape 雕刻: *Her father carved a little horse for her out of wood.* 她父亲用木头给她刻了一匹小马。
2 cut meat into thin pieces after you have cooked it 把熟肉切成薄片

case /keɪs; kes/ *noun* 名词
1 a container like a box for keeping something in (类似箱子、盒子等的) 容器: *Put the camera back in its case.* 把照相机放回套里。☞ Look also at **briefcase** and **suitcase**. 另见 **briefcase** 和 **suitcase**。
2 an example of something 事例: *There were four cases of this disease in the school last month.* 上个月学校里有四个人得了这种病。
3 something that happens or something that is true 情形；实情: *'There's no coffee.' 'Well, in that case we'll have tea.'* "没有咖啡。" "那么我们喝茶吧。"
4 a question that people in a court of law must decide about (法院审理的) 案件；诉讼案: *a divorce case* 离婚案
5 a problem that the police must find an answer to (警方调查的) 案件: *a murder case* 谋杀案

in any case words that you use when you give a second reason for something (提出另一理由时的用语) 再说；反正；无论如何: *I don't want to see the film, and in any case I'm too busy.* 我不想看这部电影，再说我也太忙了。

in case because something might happen 因为可能发生某事；以防万一；万一: *Take an umbrella in case it rains.* 带着把伞吧，以防下雨。

cash[1] /kæʃ; kæʃ/ *noun* 名词 (no plural 无复数)
money in coins and notes 现款；现金: *How would you like to pay: cash or cheque?* 您愿意怎样付款，付现金还是付支票？

cash desk /'kæʃ desk; 'kæʃ dɛsk/ *noun* 名词
the place in a shop where you pay (商店中的) 付款处

cash[2] /kæʃ; kæʃ/ *verb* 动词 (**cashes, cashing, cashed** /kæʃt; kæʃt/)
give a cheque and get money for it 把支票兑换成现金: *I'd like to cash some traveller's cheques, please.* 请给我把旅行支票兑换成现金。

cashier /kæ'ʃɪə(r); kæ'ʃɪr/ *noun* 名词
the person who gives or takes money in a bank (银行的) 出纳员

cassette /kə'set; kə'sɛt/ *noun* 名词
a plastic box with special tape inside for storing and playing sound, music or moving pictures (盒式的) 录音带；录像带: *a video cassette* 录像带 ◇ *Put on* (= play) *your new cassette.* 放一放你那盘新带子。

cassette player /kə'set pleɪə(r); kə'sɛt 'pleɚ/, **cassette recorder** /kə'set rɪˌkɔ:də(r); kə'sɛt rɪ'kɔrdɚ/ *noun* 名词
a machine that can put (**record**) sound or music on tape and play it again later 录音机 (录音叫做 **record**)

castle /'kɑ:sl; 'kæsl̩/ *noun* 名词
a large old building that was built to keep people safe from their enemies 城堡；古城堡: *Windsor Castle* 温莎宫

casual /'kæʒuəl; 'kæʒʊəl/ *adjective* 形容词
1 showing that you are not worried about something; relaxed 不担忧的；不在乎的: *She gave us a casual wave as she*

passed. 她从我们旁边经过，向我们漫不经心地摆了摆手。

2 not for serious or important times 不为在庄重的或重要的场合用的；随便的: *I wear casual clothes like jeans and T-shirts when I'm not at work.* 我不上班的时候就穿随便点儿的衣服，像牛仔裤和短袖汗衫什么的。

C

casually /'kæʒuəli; 'kæʒʊəlɪ/ *adverb* 副词

He was dressed too casually for the interview. 他面试的时候穿得太随便了。

casualty /'kæʒuəlti; 'kæʒʊəltɪ/ *noun* 名词 (*plural* 复数作 **casualties**)

a person who is hurt or killed in an accident or a war 在事故或战争中伤亡的人

casualty department /'kæʒuəlti dɪpɑ:tmənt; 'kæʒʊəltɪ dɪ'pɑrtmənt/, **casualty** *noun* 名词

the place in a hospital where doctors help people who have been hurt in an accident 急救室

cat 猫

cat /kæt; kæt/ *noun* 名词

1 an animal that people keep as a pet and to catch mice 猫 ✪ A young cat is called a **kitten**. 幼小的猫叫做 **kitten**。

2 the name of a group of large wild animals. Tigers and lions are cats. 猫科动物（老虎和狮子都是猫科动物。）

catch /kætʃ; kætʃ/ *verb* 动词 (**catches**, **catching**, **caught** /kɔ:t; kɔt/, **has caught**)

1 take and hold something that is moving 抓住或接住移动中的东西: *He threw the ball to me and I caught it.* 他把球扔给我，我接住了。

2 find and hold somebody or something 捉住或逮住某人或某物: *They caught a fish in the river.* 他们从河里抓到一条鱼。◇ *The man ran so fast that the police couldn't catch him.* 那个人跑得非常快，警方没抓着他。

3 see somebody when they are doing something wrong 看见某人正做坏事: *They caught the thief stealing the painting.* 他们看见有个贼正在偷那幅画儿。

4 be early enough for a bus, train, etc that is going to leave 赶上公共汽车、火车等: *You should run if you want to catch the bus.* 你要想赶上公共汽车，就得跑了。✪ opposite 反义词: **miss**

5 get an illness 得病: *She caught a cold.* 她感冒了。

6 let something be held tightly 使某物被夹住: *I caught my fingers in the door.* 我的手指让门给夹住了。

catch fire start to burn 烧着；着火: *The house caught fire.* 那所房子着火了。

catch up do something quickly so that you are not behind others 赶上: *If you miss a lesson, you can do some work at home to catch up.* 要是落下了功课，在家用些功也能赶上。◇ *Quick! Run after the others and catch them up.* 快！追上大家，赶上他们。

caterpillar /'kætəpɪlə(r); 'kætɚˌpɪlɚ/ *noun* 名词

a thing like a long hairy worm that will become a butterfly or moth 毛虫；蠋（蝴蝶的或蛾子的幼虫）

cathedral /kə'θi:drəl; kə'θidrəl/ *noun* 名词

a big important church 大教堂

Catholic /'kæθəlɪk; 'kæθəlɪk/ = **Roman Catholic**

cattle /'kætl; 'kætḷ/ *noun* 名词 (plural 复数)

cows and bulls 牛: *a herd of cattle* 一群牛

caught *form of* **catch** ✳ **catch** 的不同形式

cauliflower /'kɒliflaʊə(r); 'kɔləˌflaʊɚ/ *noun* 名词

cauliflower 菜花

a large vegetable with green leaves outside and a hard white part in the middle 菜花；花椰菜

cause[1] /kɔ:z; kɔz/ *noun* 名词

1 the thing or person that makes something happen 使某事物发生的事物或人；原因: *Bad driving is the cause of most road accidents.* 开车不小心是造成交通事故最主要的原因。

2 something that people care about and want to help 大家关心并愿意协助的事情；事业: *They gave the money to a good cause — it was used to build a new hospital.* 他们为慈善事业捐款——用以兴建一所新医院。

cause² /kɔ:z; kɔz/ *verb* 动词 (**causes**, **causing**, **caused** /kɔ:zd; kɔzd/)
be the reason why something happens 造成；引起；使发生；使产生: *Who caused the accident?* 是谁造成的这起事故？◇ *The fire was caused by a cigarette.* 这场火是由一枝香烟引起的。

caution /ˈkɔ:ʃn; ˈkɔʃən/ *noun* 名词 (no plural 无复数)
great care 小心；谨慎；慎重: *Caution! Wet floor.* 留心！地面很湿。

cautious /ˈkɔ:ʃəs; ˈkɔʃəs/ *adjective* 形容词
careful because there may be danger 小心的；谨慎的

cautiously *adverb* 副词
Cautiously, he pushed open the door and looked into the room. 他小心翼翼地推开门，向屋里看了看。

cave /keɪv; kev/ *noun* 名词
a large hole in the side of a mountain or under the ground 山洞；地洞: *Thousands of years ago, people lived in caves.* 千千万万年以前，人们住在山洞里。

CD /ˌsi: ˈdi:; ˌsi ˈdi/ *short for* **compact disc** ✱ **compact disc** 的缩略式

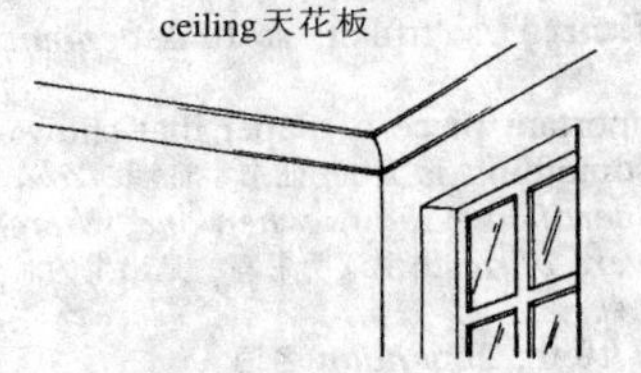

ceiling /ˈsi:lɪŋ; ˈsilɪŋ/ *noun* 名词
the part of a room over your head 天花板

celebrate /ˈseləbreɪt; ˈsɛləˌbret/ *verb* 动词 (**celebrates**, **celebrating**, **celebrated**)
enjoy yourself because you have a special reason to be happy 庆祝: *If you pass your exams, we'll have a party to celebrate.* 你要是考及格了，我们就开个庆祝会。

celebration /ˌseləˈbreɪʃn; ˌsɛləˈbreʃən/ *noun* 名词
a time when you enjoy yourself because you have a special reason to be happy 庆祝: *birthday celebrations* 生日庆祝会

cell /sel; sɛl/ *noun* 名词
1 a small room where a prisoner lives 牢房
2 the smallest part of any living thing 细胞

cellar /ˈselə(r); ˈsɛlɚ/ *noun* 名词
a room in the part of a building that is under the ground 地下室；地窖: *a wine cellar* 酒窖

cello /ˈtʃeləʊ; ˈtʃɛlo/ *noun* 名词 (*plural* 复数作 **cellos**)
a musical instrument like a big violin. You sit and hold it between your knees when you are playing it. 大提琴

Celsius /ˈselsiəs; ˈsɛlsɪəs/ *noun* 名词 (no plural 无复数)
a way of measuring temperature. Water freezes at 0°Celsius and boils at 100°Celsius. 摄氏温度（水在0摄氏度结冰，在100摄氏度沸腾。）✪ The short way of writing 'Celsius' is **C** ✱ Celsius 的缩写形式为 **C**: *52°C* ✱ 52摄氏度

cement /sɪˈment; səˈmɛnt/ *noun* 名词 (no plural 无复数)
grey powder that becomes hard like stone when you mix it with water and leave it to dry. Cement is used in building. 水泥（水泥用于建筑业。）

cemetery /ˈsemətri; ˈsɛməˌtɛrɪ/ *noun* 名词 (*plural* 复数作 **cemeteries**)
an area of ground where dead people are put under the earth 墓地；公墓

cent /sent; sɛnt/ *noun* 名词
a small coin that people use in the USA and some other countries. There are 100 cents in a **dollar**. 分（美国和某些国家的硬币。100分为1元，元叫做 **dollar**）

center *American English for* **centre** 美式英语，即 **centre**

centigrade /ˈsentɪgreɪd; ˈsɛntəˌgred/ *another word for* **Celsius** ✱ **Celsius** 的另一种说法

centiliter *American English for* **centilitre** 美式英语，即 **centilitre**

centilitre /ˈsentɪli:tə(r); ˈsɛntəˌlitɚ/ *noun* 名词
a measure of liquid. There are 100

centilitres in a **litre**. 厘升（100厘升为1升，升叫做 **litre**）✪ The short way of writing 'centilitre' is **cl** ✳ centilitre 的缩写形式为 **cl**: *250 cl* ✳ 250厘升

centimeter *American English for* **centimetre** 美式英语，即 **centimetre**

centimetre /ˈsentɪmiːtə(r); ˈsɛntə-ˌmitɚ/ *noun* 名词
a measure of length. There are 100 centimetres in a **metre**. 厘米（100厘米为1米，米叫做 **metre**。）✪ The short way of writing 'centimetre' is **cm** ✳ centimetre 的缩写形式为 **cm**: *98 cm* ✳ 98厘米

central /ˈsentrəl; ˈsɛntrəl/ *adjective* 形容词
in the middle part 在中心的；中央的: *central London* 伦敦中部

central heating /ˌsentrəl ˈhiːtɪŋ; ˌsɛntrəl ˈhitɪŋ/ *noun* 名词 (no plural 无复数)
a way of heating all the rooms in a house from one **boiler** 中央暖气系统；中央供热设备（热水器叫做 **boiler**）

centre /ˈsentə(r); ˈsɛntɚ/ *noun* 名词
1 the part in the middle 中心；中央: *the city centre* 市中心 ◇ *The flower has a yellow centre with white petals.* 这朵花花瓣是白的，中间是黄的。
2 a place where people come to do something special 人们进行某种活动的地方；中心: *a shopping centre* 购物中心 ◇ *Our town has a new sports centre.* 我们镇上有个新的体育中心。

century /ˈsentʃəri; ˈsɛntʃərɪ/ *noun* 名词 (*plural* 复数作 **centuries**)
1 100 years ✳ 100年
2 a time of 100 years, that we use in dates 世纪: *We are living at the end of the twentieth century.* 我们生活在二十世纪末。

cereal /ˈsɪəriəl; ˈsɪrɪəl/ *noun* 名词
1 (*plural* 复数作 **cereals**) a plant that farmers grow so that we can eat the seed 谷物: *Wheat and oats are cereals.* 小麦和燕麦都是谷物。
2 (no plural 无复数) special food made from rice, maize, wheat, etc that you can eat for breakfast（谷物做的）早餐食品: *a bowl of cereal with milk* 一碗加奶的谷物食品

ceremony /ˈserəməni; ˈsɛrəˌmonɪ/ *noun* 名词 (*plural* 复数作 **ceremonies**)
a time when you do something special and important 典礼；仪式: *the opening ceremony of the Olympic Games* 奥林匹克运动会开幕典礼 ◇ *a wedding ceremony* 婚礼

certain[1] /ˈsɜːtn; ˈsɝtn̩/ *adjective* 形容词
without any doubt; sure 无疑；肯定: *I am certain that I have seen her before.* 我以前确实见过她。◇ *It's not certain that they will come.* 他们来不来很难说。
for certain without any doubt 无疑地；确定地: *I don't know for certain where she is.* 我说不准她在哪里。
make certain check something so that you are sure about it 弄清楚；弄明白；弄确实: *Please make certain that the window is closed before you leave.* 请务必把窗户都关好了再走。

certain[2] /ˈsɜːtn; ˈsɝtn̩/ *adjective* 形容词
one or some that can be named 某；某些: *It's cheaper to telephone at certain times of the day.* 在一天中的某些时间打电话比较便宜。◇ *Do you want the work to be finished by a certain date?* 你是否要让这项工作在某日期之前完成？

certainly /ˈsɜːtnli; ˈsɝtn̩lɪ/ *adverb* 副词
1 without any doubt 无疑地；肯定地: *She is certainly the best swimmer in the team.* 她的确是队里游得最好的。
2 yes 是的: *'Will you open the door for me, please?' 'Certainly.'* "请给我开开门行吗？" "可以。"
certainly not no 不: *'Can I borrow your bicycle?' 'Certainly not!'* "我借一下你的自行车行吗？" "那可不行！"

certificate /səˈtɪfɪkət; sɚˈtɪfəkɪt/ *noun* 名词
an important piece of paper that shows that something is true 证书；证明: *Your birth certificate shows when and where you were born.* 出生证明书写的是出生的时间和地点。

chain /tʃeɪn; tʃen/ *noun* 名词
metal rings that are joined together 链子；链条: *Round her neck she wore a gold chain.* 她脖子上戴着个金链子。◇ *My bicycle chain is broken.* 我的自行车链子断了。

chain 链子

☞ picture at **bicycle** 见 **bicycle** 词条插图

chain *verb* 动词 (**chains**, **chaining**, **chained** /tʃeɪnd; tʃend/)

attach somebody or something to a place with a chain 用链子把某人或某物拴在某处: *The dog was chained to the fence.* 这条狗是用链子拴在篱笆上的。

chair /tʃeə(r); tʃɛr/ *noun* 名词

1 a piece of furniture with four legs, a seat and a back that one person can sit on 椅子: *a table and four chairs* 一张桌子和四把椅子

2 a person who controls a meeting (会议的) 主席 ✪ You can also say **chairman** /ˈtʃeəmən; ˈtʃɛrmən/, **chairwoman** /ˈtʃeəwʊmən; ˈtʃɛrˌwʊmən/ or **chairperson** /ˈtʃeəpɜːsn; ˈtʃɛrˌpɝsn̩/. 也可说 **chairman** /ˈtʃeəmən; ˈtʃɛrmən/、**chairwoman** /ˈtʃeəwʊmən; ˈtʃɛrˌwʊmən/ 或 **chairperson** /ˈtʃeəpɜːsn; ˈtʃɛrˌpɝsn̩/。

chalk /tʃɔːk; tʃɔk/ *noun* 名词 (no plural 无复数)

1 soft white rock 白垩: *The cliffs are made of chalk.* 这些悬崖都是白垩的。

2 a piece of this rock that you use for writing on a **blackboard** 粉笔 (黑板叫做 **blackboard**)

challenge /ˈtʃælɪndʒ; ˈtʃælɪndʒ/ *verb* 动词 (**challenges**, **challenging**, **challenged** /ˈtʃælɪndʒd; ˈtʃælɪndʒd/)

ask somebody to play a game with you or fight with you to see who wins 要求与某人比赛或打斗，看谁赢；向某人挑战: *The boxer challenged the world champion to a fight.* 那个拳击手向世界冠军挑战进行比赛。

challenge *noun* 名词

a new or difficult thing that makes you try hard 激励人努力去做新的或困难的事情；挑战: *Climbing the mountain will be a real challenge.* 攀登那座山可真了不起。

champagne /ʃæmˈpeɪn; ʃæmˈpen/ *noun* 名词 (no plural 无复数)

a French white wine with a lot of bubbles 香槟酒

champion /ˈtʃæmpiən; ˈtʃæmpɪən/ *noun* 名词

a person who is the best at a sport or game 冠军；优胜者: *a chess champion* 国际象棋冠军 ◇ *the world champion* 世界冠军

championship /ˈtʃæmpiənʃɪp; ˈtʃæmpɪənˌʃɪp/ *noun* 名词

a competition to find the champion 锦标赛: *Our team won the championship this year.* 我们队在今年锦标赛中获胜。

chance /tʃɑːns; tʃæns/ *noun* 名词

1 (*plural* 复数作 **chances**) a time when you can do something 能做某事的时间；机会；时机: *It was their last chance to escape.* 那次是他们最后一次逃跑的机会。◇ *I haven't had a chance to write to Jenny today. I'll do it tomorrow.* 我今天没来得及给珍妮写信。我明天写。

2 (*plural* 复数作 **chances**) a possibility that something may happen 某事发生的可能性: *He has a good chance of passing the exam because he has worked hard.* 他很有可能考试及格，因为他非常用功。

3 (no plural 无复数) something that happens that you cannot control; luck 碰运气的事物；运气

by chance not because you have planned it 偶然；意外地: *We met by chance at the station.* 我们在车站偶然相遇。

take a chance do something when it is possible that something bad may happen because of it 碰运气冒险做某事

change¹ /tʃeɪndʒ; tʃendʒ/ *verb* 动词 (**changes**, **changing**, **changed** /tʃeɪndʒd; tʃendʒd/)

1 become different 变；改变: *She has changed a lot since the last time I saw her—she looks much older.* 自从我上次见到她以来，她改变了很多——她很见老。◇ *Water changes into ice when it gets very cold.* 天很冷的时候，水就结成冰了。

2 make something different 改变某事物: *At this restaurant they change the menu every day.* 这个饭馆天天换菜单。

3 put or take something in place of another thing 用某事物换另一事物；替换；调换: *My new watch didn't work, so I took it back to the shop and changed it.* 我的新手表不走了，我拿回到商店换了一块。◇ *I went to the bank to change my francs into dollars.* 我去银行把法郎换成美元了。◇ *Can you change a £5 note please? I need some pound coins.* 请问，您能换开5英镑的钞票吗？我需要一些硬币。

4 put on different clothes 换衣物: *I must change before I go out.* 我得换换衣服再出门。✪ You can also say **get changed** 也可说 **get changed**: *I must get changed before I go out.* 我得换换衣服再出门。

5 get off a train or bus and get on another one 换车: *I have to change trains at Reading.* 我得在雷丁倒车。

C

change² /tʃeɪndʒ; tʃendʒ/ *noun* 名词
1 (no plural 无复数) money that you get when you have paid too much 找回的钱；找给的钱: *I gave the shop assistant £1. The sweets cost 75 pence, so he gave me 25 pence change.* 我付给店员1英镑。那些糖是75便士，他找给我25便士。
2 (no plural 无复数) small pieces of money; coins 零钱；硬币: *I haven't got any change.* 我没有零钱。
3 (*plural* 复数作 **changes**) a thing that is different now 改变；变化: *The new government has made a lot of changes.* 新政府进行了很多改革。
for a change because you want something different 为了有变化: *Today we had lunch in a restaurant for a change.* 今天我们和平常不同，是在饭馆吃的午饭。

C

channel /ˈtʃænl; ˈtʃænl̩/ *noun* 名词
1 a narrow place where water can go 航道；海峡: *the English Channel* (= the sea between England and France) 英吉利海峡（英国和法国之间的海道）
2 one of the things you can choose on television（电视的）频道: *Which channel are you watching?* 你正看的是哪个频道？

chapel /ˈtʃæpl; ˈtʃæpl̩/ *noun* 名词
a room or a small church where Christians go to pray 基督教徒礼拜用的房间或小教堂

chapter /ˈtʃæptə(r); ˈtʃæptɚ/ *noun* 名词
one of the parts of a book（书中的）章；篇；回: *You start reading a book at the beginning of Chapter 1.* 看书的时候是从第一章的开头看起。

character /ˈkærəktə(r); ˈkærɪktɚ/ *noun* 名词
1 (no plural 无复数) the way a person or thing is（人或物的）品质；特性: *He has a strong character.* 他个性很强。◇ *The new factory will change the character of the village.* 这座新工厂将要改变这个村子的特色。
2 (*plural* 复数作 **characters**) a person in a play, book or film（戏剧、书籍或影片中的）人物: *Tom and Jerry are famous cartoon characters.* 汤姆和杰里是著名的卡通人物。

charge¹ /tʃɑːdʒ; tʃɑrdʒ/ *verb* 动词 (**charges**, **charging**, **charged** /tʃɑːdʒd; tʃɑrdʒd/)
1 ask somebody to pay a certain price for something 要求某人为某事物付款；要价: *The garage charged me £200 for the repairs.* 汽车修理厂要我付200英镑修理费。
2 say that somebody has done something wrong 指控某人犯某错误；控告；指责: *The police have charged him with murder.* 警方控告他犯有谋杀罪。
3 move quickly and with a lot of force 迅猛地移动: *The bull charged.* 那头公牛向前猛冲。◇ *The children charged into the room.* 孩子们闯进房间里。

charge² /tʃɑːdʒ; tʃɑrdʒ/ *noun* 名词
1 the money that you must pay for something（需付的）费用: *There is a charge of £25 for the use of the hall.* 使用大厅的费用是25英镑。
2 a statement that somebody has done something wrong 指控；控告；指责: *a charge of murder* 指控谋杀
be in charge of somebody or 或 **something** look after or control somebody or something 照管或负责某人或某事物: *Tim is in charge of his baby brother while his mother is out.* 蒂姆在母亲出门时负责照看幼小的弟弟。◇ *The headmaster is in charge of the school.* 校长负责管理学校。

charity /ˈtʃærəti; ˈtʃærətɪ/ *noun* 名词
1 (*plural* 复数作 **charities**) a group of people who collect money to help people who need it 慈善团体: *The Red Cross is a charity.* 红十字会是慈善团体。
2 (no plural 无复数) being kind and helping other people 施舍；布施；赈济

charm /tʃɑːm; tʃɑrm/ *noun* 名词
1 (no plural 无复数) being able to make people like you 讨人喜欢的能力；魅力: *Anna has a lot of charm.* 安娜很有魅力。
2 (*plural* 复数作 **charms**) a small thing that you wear because you think it will bring good luck 护身符: *She wears a necklace with a lucky charm on it.* 她带着项链，上面还有个幸运护身符。
charm *verb* 动词 (**charms**, **charming**, **charmed** /tʃɑːmd; tʃɑrmd/)
make somebody like you 讨人喜欢: *The baby charmed everybody with her smile.* 那个幼小的女孩儿一笑，很讨人喜欢。

charming /ˈtʃɑːmɪŋ; ˈtʃɑrmɪŋ/ *adjective* 形容词
lovely; beautiful 可爱的；漂亮的: *a charming little village* 可爱的村庄

chart /tʃɑːt; tʃɑrt/ *noun* 名词
1 a drawing that gives information about something 图表：*a temperature chart* 体温图表
2 a map of the sea that sailors use 航海图

chase /tʃeɪs; tʃes/ *verb* 动词 (**chases**, **chasing**, **chased** /tʃeɪst; tʃest/)
run behind somebody or something and try to catch them 追赶某人或某事物：*The dog chased the cat around the garden.* 狗在花园四处追着猫。◇ *The police chased after the thief but he escaped.* 警方追捕那个窃贼，但是那个贼逃走了。
chase *noun* 名词
In that film there is an exciting car chase. 在那部影片里有个紧张的汽车追逐镜头。

chat /tʃæt; tʃæt/ *noun* 名词
a friendly talk 聊天；闲谈：*Let's have a chat about it later.* 咱们以后聊聊这件事。
chat *verb* 动词 (**chats**, **chatting**, **chatted**)
talk in a friendly way 聊天；闲谈

chatter /ˈtʃætə(r); ˈtʃætɚ/ *verb* 动词 (**chatters**, **chattering**, **chattered** /ˈtʃætəd; ˈtʃætɚd/)
talk quickly about things that are not very important 唠叨；喋喋不休：*Stop chattering and finish your work.* 别唠叨了，把工作做完吧。

cheap /tʃiːp; tʃip/ *adjective* 形容词 (**cheaper**, **cheapest**)
Something that is cheap does not cost a lot of money 廉价的；便宜的：*Tomatoes are cheaper in summer than in winter.* 西红柿夏天比冬天便宜。◇ *That restaurant is very good and quite cheap.* 这个饭馆价廉物美。✪ opposite 反义词：**expensive** or 或 **dear**

cheat /tʃiːt; tʃit/ *verb* 动词 (**cheats**, **cheating**, **cheated**)
do something that is not honest or fair 欺骗：*She cheated in the exam – she copied her friend's work.* 她考试作弊——她抄袭朋友的答卷。
cheat *noun* 名词
a person who cheats 欺骗别人的人

check[1] /tʃek; tʃɛk/ *verb* 动词 (**checks**, **checking**, **checked** /tʃekt; tʃɛkt/)
1 look at something to see that it is right, good, safe, etc 检查；核对；核实：*Do the sums and then use a calculator to check your answers.* 先做算数题，然后再用计算器检查答案。◇ *At the garage the man checked the oil and water.* 汽车加油站那个人检查了一下机油和水。◇ *Check that all the windows are closed before you leave.* 要检查一下所有的窗户都关好了再走。
2 *American English for* **tick 2** 美式英语，即 **tick 2**
check in tell the person at the desk in a hotel or an airport that you have arrived （在旅馆或机场柜台）办理登记手续：*I have to check in an hour before my flight.* 我得在班机起飞前一小时办理登机手续。
check out pay your bill at a hotel and leave 办理旅馆付账及退房手续

check[2] /tʃek; tʃɛk/ *noun* 名词
1 a look to see that everything is right, good, safe, etc 检查；核对；核实：*Have a quick check to see that you haven't forgotten anything.* 很快检查一下看看遗忘了什么没有。
2 *American English for* **cheque** 美式英语，即 **cheque**
3 *American English for* **bill 1** 美式英语，即 **bill 1**
4 *American English for* **tick 2** 美式英语，即 **tick 2**

check[3] /tʃek; tʃɛk/ *noun* 名词
a pattern of squares 方格图案
checked /tʃekt; tʃɛkt/ *adjective* 形容词
with a pattern of squares 有方格图形的：*a checked shirt* 方格的衬衫

check 方格图案

checked
有方格的

checkers /ˈtʃekəz; ˈtʃɛkɚz/ *American English for* **draughts** 美式英语，即 **draughts**

checkout /ˈtʃekaʊt; ˈtʃɛkˌaʊt/ *noun* 名词
one of the places in a supermarket where you pay for the things you are buying（超级市场的）付款处

check-up /ˈtʃek ʌp; ˈtʃɛkˌʌp/ *noun* 名词
an examination by a doctor to see if you are well 体格检查

cheek /tʃiːk; tʃik/ *noun* 名词
1 (*plural* 复数作 **cheeks**) one of the two round parts of your face under your eyes 面颊；脸蛋 ☞ picture on page C2 见第C2页图

2 (no plural 无复数) doing something without caring that it will make other people angry or unhappy 冒失；放肆；鲁莽: *What a cheek! Somebody has eaten my sandwiches.* 真没皮没脸！有人把我的三明治给吃了。

cheeky /'tʃi:ki; 'tʃikɪ/ *adjective* 形容词 (**cheekier, cheekiest**)
not polite 无礼的；厚脸皮的: *Don't be so cheeky!* 别那么没皮没脸！◇ *She was punished for being cheeky to a teacher.* 她对老师很无礼，因而受到惩罚。

C

cheer[1] /tʃɪə(r); tʃɪr/ *verb* 动词 (**cheers, cheering, cheered** /tʃɪəd; tʃɪrd/)
shout to show that you are pleased 欢呼；喝彩: *The crowd cheered loudly when the President arrived.* 总统抵达时，群众高声欢呼。

cheer up make somebody happier; become happier 使某人更愉快；高兴起来: *We gave Julie some flowers to cheer her up.* 我们送给朱莉一些花儿，让她高兴高兴。◇ *Cheer up! You will feel better soon.* 高兴点儿吧！你很快就感到好些了。

cheer[2] /tʃɪə(r); tʃɪr/ *noun* 名词
a shout that shows that you are pleased 欢呼；喝彩: *The crowd gave a loud cheer as the singer came onto the stage.* 歌手一上台，群众就大声欢呼起来。

three cheers for ... Hip, hip, hurray! words that you shout when somebody has done something good 为某人叫好的词语: *Three cheers for the winner! Hip, hip, hurray!* 祝贺比赛胜利！赢了，赢了，赢了！

cheerful /'tʃɪəfl; 'tʃɪrfəl/ *adjective* 形容词
happy 愉快的；快乐的: *a cheerful smile* 愉快的微笑 ◇ *You don't look very cheerful today. What's the matter?* 你今天不太高兴，怎么了？

cheers /tʃɪəz; tʃɪrz/
a word that you say to somebody when you have a drink together 祝酒用语 ✪ People sometimes say **cheers** instead of **thank you** or **goodbye**. 有时用**cheers**作**thank you**（谢谢）或**goodbye**（再见）的意思。

cheese /tʃi:z; tʃiz/ *noun* 名词
yellow or white food made from milk 奶酪；干酪: *bread and cheese* 面包和干酪

cheeseburger /'tʃi:zbɜ:gə(r); 'tʃizˌbɝgɚ/ *noun* 名词
a hamburger with cheese in it 干酪汉堡包

chef /ʃef; ʃɛf/ *noun* 名词
a person who cooks the food in a restaurant 厨师

chemical[1] /'kemɪkl; 'kɛmɪkḷ/ *noun* 名词
a solid or liquid substance that is used in chemistry or is made by chemistry 化学药品

chemical[2] /'kemɪkl; 'kɛmɪkḷ/ *adjective* 形容词
of chemistry or used in chemistry 化学的；用于化学的: *a chemical experiment* 化学实验

chemist /'kemɪst; 'kɛmɪst/ *noun* 名词
1 a person who makes and sells medicines 药剂师；药商 ✪ The shop where a chemist works is called a **chemist's**. 药店叫做 **chemist's**。It sells things like soap and perfume as well as medicines. 不仅卖药，还卖香皂和香水之类的东西。
2 a person who studies chemistry or who makes chemicals 化学家；制造化学药品的人

chemistry /'kemɪstri; 'kɛmɪstrɪ/ *noun* 名词 (no plural 无复数)
the science that studies gases, liquids and solids to find out what they are and what they do 化学

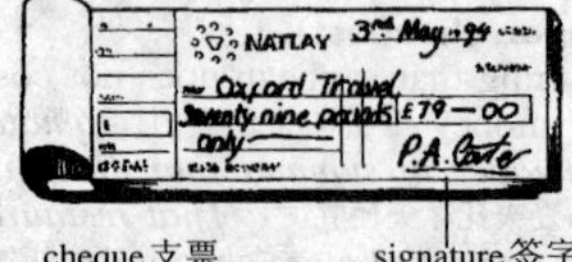

cheque 支票　　signature 签字

cheque /tʃek; tʃɛk/ *noun* 名词
a piece of paper from a bank that you can write on and use to pay for things 支票: *I gave him a cheque for £50.* 我给了他一张50英镑的支票。◇ *Can I pay by cheque?* 我付支票行吗？

cheque-book /'tʃek bʊk; 'tʃɛkˌbuk/ *noun* 名词
a book of cheques 支票簿

cherry 樱桃

cherry /'tʃeri; 'tʃɛrɪ/ *noun* 名词 (*plural* 复数作 **cherries**)
a small round red or black fruit 樱桃

chess /tʃes; tʃɛs/ *noun* 名词 (no plural 无复数)
a game that two people play with pieces called **chessmen** on a board that has black and white squares on it (called a **chessboard**) 国际象棋（棋子叫做 **chessman**，棋盘叫做 **chessboard**，为黑白方格的图案）

chest[1] /tʃest; tʃɛst/ *noun* 名词
the front part of your body below your shoulders and above your waist 胸部 ✪ picture on page C2 见第C2页图

chest[2] /tʃest; tʃɛst/ *noun* 名词
a large strong box with a lid 箱子

chest of drawers /ˌtʃest əv ˈdrɔ:z; ˌtʃɛst əv ˈdrɔrz/ *noun* 名词 (*plural* 复数作 **chests of drawers**)
a piece of furniture like a box with parts that you can pull out (**drawers**). A chest of drawers is usually used for keeping clothes in.（有抽屉的）柜橱；衣柜（抽屉叫做 **drawer**）

chew /tʃu:; tʃu/ *verb* 动词 (**chews, chewing, chewed** /tʃu:d; tʃud/)
use your teeth to make food soft 嚼；咀嚼

chewing-gum /ˈtʃu:ɪŋ gʌm; ˈtʃuɪŋ gʌm/ *noun* 名词 (no plural 无复数)
sweet stuff that you can chew for a long time 口香糖

chick /tʃɪk; tʃɪk/ *noun* 名词
a young bird, especially a young chicken（幼小的）鸟；（尤其指）小鸡: *a hen with her chicks* 母鸡和小鸡

chicken /ˈtʃɪkɪn; ˈtʃɪkɪn/ *noun* 名词
1 (*plural* 复数作 **chickens**) a bird that people keep on farms for its eggs and meat（饲养的）鸡

> ✪ A female chicken is called a **hen** and a male chicken is called a **cock**. 母鸡叫做 **hen**，公鸡叫做 **cock**。A young chicken is a **chick**. 幼小的鸡是 **chick**。

2 (no plural 无复数) meat from a chicken 鸡肉: *roast chicken* 烤鸡

chief[1] /tʃi:f; tʃif/ *adjective* 形容词
most important 最重要的；主要的；首要的: *Bad driving is one of the chief causes of road accidents.* 开车不小心是造成交通事故最主要的原因。

chiefly *adverb* 副词
mostly; mainly 首要地；主要地: *They didn't enjoy their holiday, chiefly because the weather was so bad.* 他们度假很不痛快，主要是因为天气太坏了。

chief[2] /tʃi:f; tʃif/ *noun* 名词
the leader or ruler of a group of people 领袖；统治者: *the chief of an African tribe* 非洲部落的酋长

child /tʃaɪld; tʃaɪld/ *noun* 名词 (*plural* 复数作 **children** /ˈtʃɪldrən; ˈtʃɪldrən/)
1 a boy or girl 儿童；孩子: *There are 30 children in the class.* 班上有30个孩子。
2 a daughter or son 女儿或儿子；子女；孩子: *One of her children got married last year.* 去年她有个孩子结婚了。☞ picture on page C3 见第C3页图

childhood /ˈtʃaɪldhʊd; ˈtʃaɪldˌhʊd/ *noun* 名词 (no plural 无复数)
the time when you are a child 童年；幼年时代: *She had a happy childhood.* 她童年很幸福。

childish /ˈtʃaɪldɪʃ; ˈtʃaɪldɪʃ/ *adjective* 形容词
like a child, or for children 像孩子的；为孩子的；幼稚的: *childish games* 儿童游戏

chilly /ˈtʃɪli; ˈtʃɪlɪ/ *adjective* 形容词 (**chillier, chilliest**)
cold 寒冷的: *a chilly morning* 寒冷的早晨

chime /tʃaɪm; tʃaɪm/ *verb* 动词 (**chimes, chiming, chimed** /tʃaɪmd; tʃaɪmd/)
make the sound that a bell makes 发出钟声: *The clock chimed midnight.* 那座钟发出午夜报时钟声。

chimney /ˈtʃɪmni; ˈtʃɪmnɪ/ *noun* 名词 (*plural* 复数作 **chimneys**)
a large pipe over a fire that lets smoke go outside into the air 烟囱；烟筒 ☞ picture at **house** 见 **house** 词条插图

chimpanzee /ˌtʃɪmpænˈzi:; ˌtʃɪmpænˈzi/ *noun* 名词
an African animal like a monkey with no tail 黑猩猩

chin /tʃɪn; tʃɪn/ *noun* 名词
the part of your face below your mouth 下巴；颏 ☞ picture on page C2 见第C2页图

china /ˈtʃaɪnə; ˈtʃaɪnə/ *noun* 名词 (no plural 无复数)
a hard white material made from earth, or things like plates and cups that are made from this 瓷器: *a china cup* 瓷茶杯

C

chip[1] /tʃɪp; tʃɪp/ *noun* 名词

1 a small piece of wood, stone, china, etc that has broken off a larger piece（木头、石头、瓷器等的）碎片；碎块

2 a piece of potato cooked in oil 炸土豆条儿: *We had fish and chips for lunch.* 我们午饭吃的是鱼和炸土豆条儿。

3 a microchip; a very small thing inside a computer, for example, that makes it work 微晶片；微型集成电路片（例如计算机中的）

4 *American English for* **crisp**[2] 美式英语，即 **crisp**[2]

chip[2] /tʃɪp; tʃɪp/ *verb* 动词 (**chips**, **chipping**, **chipped** /tʃɪpt; tʃɪpt/)
break a small piece from something 从某物上折下小块: *I chipped a cup.* 我把茶杯碰豁口了。

chirp /tʃɜ:p; tʃɝp/ *noun* 名词
the short high sound that a small bird makes（小鸟发出的）短而尖的叫声

chirp *verb* 动词 (**chirps**, **chirping**, **chirped** /tʃɜ:pt; tʃɝpt/)
make this sound（小鸟）发出短而尖的叫声

chocolate /ˈtʃɒklət; ˈtʃɑkəlɪt/ *noun* 名词

1 (no plural 无复数) dark brown sweet food that is made from cocoa 巧克力: *Do you like chocolate?* 你喜欢巧克力吗？◇ *a bar of chocolate* 一块巧克力 ◇ *a chocolate cake* 巧克力蛋糕

2 (*plural* 复数作 **chocolates**) a sweet made of chocolate 巧克力糖: *a box of chocolates* 一盒巧克力糖

choice /tʃɔɪs; tʃɔɪs/ *noun* 名词

1 deciding which one; choosing 挑选；选择: *You made the right choice.* 你的选择很正确。◇ *We have no choice. We must go immediately.* 我们没有别的办法。我们必须马上走。

2 the number of things that you can choose 可供选择的若干事物: *There is a big choice of vegetables in the market.* 市场上蔬菜种类齐全。

choir /ˈkwaɪə(r); kwaɪr/ *noun* 名词
a big group of people who sing together 合唱队；唱诗班: *a school choir* 学校的合唱队 ◇ *the church choir* 教堂的唱诗班

choke /tʃəʊk; tʃok/ *verb* 动词 (**chokes**, **choking**, **choked** /tʃəʊkt; tʃokt/)
not be able to breathe because something is in your throat 窒息

choose /tʃu:z; tʃuz/ *verb* 动词 (**chooses**, **choosing**, **chose** /tʃəʊz; tʃoz/, **has chosen** /ˈtʃəʊzn; ˈtʃozn̩/)
take the thing or person that you like best 选择；挑选: *Anna chose the biggest cake.* 安娜挑了一个最大的蛋糕。

chop[1] /tʃɒp; tʃɑp/ *verb* 动词 (**chops**, **chopping**, **chopped** /tʃɒpt; tʃɑpt/)
cut something with a knife or an axe（用刀或斧子）砍；剁；劈: *We chopped some wood for the fire.* 我们砍了些柴生火。◇ *Chop the meat up into small pieces.* 把肉剁碎。

chop[2] /tʃɒp; tʃɑp/ *noun* 名词
a thick slice of meat with a piece of bone in it 带骨的肉；排骨: *a lamb chop* 羊排骨

chorus /ˈkɔ:rəs; ˈkɔrəs/ *noun* 名词 (*plural* 复数作 **choruses**)
a part of a song that you repeat（歌曲的）副歌

christen /ˈkrɪsn; ˈkrɪsn̩/ *verb* 动词 (**christens**, **christening**, **christened** /ˈkrɪsnd; ˈkrɪsn̩d/)
give a first name to a baby and make him/her a member of the Christian church in a special ceremony 为婴儿举行命名及加入基督教的仪式

christening /ˈkrɪsnɪŋ; ˈkrɪsn̩ɪŋ/ *noun* 名词
the ceremony when a baby is christened 为婴儿命名及加入基督教的仪式

Christian /ˈkrɪstʃən; ˈkrɪstʃən/ *noun* 名词
a person who believes in Jesus Christ and what He taught 基督徒

Christian *adjective* 形容词
the Christian church 基督教

Christian name /ˈkrɪstʃən neɪm; ˈkrɪstʃən ˈnem/ *noun* 名词
a person's first name（人的）名字；教名: *Her surname is Baker and her Christian name is Susan.* 她姓贝克，名叫苏珊。☞ Note at **name** 见 **name** 词条注释

Christianity /ˌkrɪstiˈænəti; ˌkrɪstʃɪˈænətɪ/ *noun* 名词 (no plural 无复数)
the religion that follows what Jesus Christ taught 基督教

Christmas /ˈkrɪsməs; ˈkrɪsməs/ *noun* 名词
the special time when Christians remember the birth of Christ 圣诞节: *Merry Christmas!* 圣诞快乐！

C

✪ Christmas is a very important festival in Britain and the USA. 圣诞节是英国和美国最大的节日。**Christmas Day** is on 25 December (the day before this is called **Christmas Eve** and the day after is called **Boxing Day**). 圣诞节是在12月25日（其前一日是圣诞节前夕，叫做 **Christmas Eve**，其后一日是节礼日，叫做 **Boxing Day**）。Children believe that **Father Christmas** visits them at Christmas to bring **presents**, and we give presents and send **Christmas cards** to each other. 儿童认为圣诞老人 (**Father Christmas**) 在圣诞节送给他们礼物 (**present**)，而我们则互送礼物和圣诞卡 (**Christmas card**)。

Many people go to church at Christmas and sing **carols**. 很多人都在圣诞节去教堂做礼拜，唱圣诞颂歌 (**carol**)。We put special trees (**Christmas trees**) in our homes, and decorate them with coloured lights and other pretty things. 我们在家中摆放圣诞树 (**Christmas tree**)，上面装点着五颜六色的灯和其他小饰物。On Christmas Day, a special **Christmas dinner** is eaten, usually with roast **turkey** and hot **Christmas pudding** (a kind of cake made with dried fruit). 圣诞节吃的是圣诞大餐 (**Christmas dinner**)，通常有烤的火鸡 (**turkey**) 和热气腾腾的圣诞布丁 (**Christmas pudding**)一种带有干果的蛋糕。

church /tʃɜ:tʃ; tʃɝtʃ/ *noun* 名词 (*plural* 复数作 **churches**)
a building where Christians go to pray 教堂: *They go to church every Sunday.* 他们每星期日都到教堂去做礼拜。

churchyard /'tʃɜ:tʃjɑ:d; 'tʃɝtʃˌjɑrd/ *noun* 名词
a piece of land around a church 教堂的庭院

cigar /sɪ'gɑ:(r); sɪ'gɑr/ *noun* 名词
a roll of tobacco leaves that you can smoke 雪茄

cigarette /ˌsɪgə'ret; 'sɪgəˌrɛt/ *noun* 名词
small pieces of tobacco in a tube of paper that you can smoke 纸烟；香烟；烟卷

cinema /'sɪnəmə; 'sɪnəmə/ *noun* 名词
a place where you go to see a film 电影院: *Let's go to the cinema tonight.* 咱们今天晚上去看电影吧。

circle /'sɜ:kl; 'sɝkḷ/ *noun* 名词
a round shape 圆形；圆: *There are 360 degrees in a circle.* 一个圆有360度。☞ picture on page C5 见第C5页图

circular /'sɜ:kjələ(r); 'sɝkjəlɚ/ *adjec-tive* 形容词
with the shape of a circle; round 圆形的；圆的: *A wheel is circular.* 轮子是圆的。

circulate /'sɜ:kjəleɪt; 'sɝkjəˌlet/ *verb* 动词 (**circulates, circulating, circulated**)
move round 循环: *Blood circulates in our bodies.* 血液在我们体内循环。

circumference /sə'kʌmfərəns; sɚ-'kʌmfərəns/ *noun* 名词
the distance around a circle 圆周 ☞ picture on page C5 见第C5页图

circumstances /'sɜ:kəmstənsɪz; 'sɝkəmˌstænsɪz/ *noun* 名词 (plural 复数)
the facts that are true when something happens 环境；情形；情况

in or 或 **under the circumstances**
because things are as they are 在这种情况下；情形既然如此: *It was snowing, so under the circumstances we decided to stay at home.* 下雪了，在这种情况下我们决定呆在家里。

under no circumstances not at all; never 在任何情况下决不；无论如何不: *Under no circumstances should you go out alone at night.* 无论如何你也不要夜晚一个人出去。

circus /'sɜ:kəs; 'sɝkəs/ *noun* 名词 (*plural* 复数作 **circuses**)
a show in a big tent, with clowns, acrobats and animals 马戏表演

citizen /'sɪtɪzn; 'sɪtəzṇ/ *noun* 名词
a person who belongs to a country or a town 公民；市民: *She became a British citizen.* 她成了英国公民。

city /'sɪti; 'sɪtɪ/ *noun* 名词 (*plural* 复数作 **cities**)
1 a big and important town 城市；都市；市: *the city of Liverpool* 利物浦市 ◇ *the city centre* 市中心
2 the City (no plural 无复数) the part of London with a lot of banks and offices 伦敦商业区

civil /'sɪvl; 'sɪvḷ/ *adjective* 形容词
of the people of a country 公民的: *civil rights* 公民权

the Civil Service /ˌsɪvl ˈsɜːvɪs; ˌsɪvḷ ˈsɝvɪs/ *noun* 名词 (no plural 无复数)
the people who work for the government 全体公务员

civil war /ˌsɪvl ˈwɔː(r); ˌsɪvḷ ˈwɔr/ *noun* 名词
a war between groups of people in one country 内战

C

civilian /səˈvɪliən; səˈvɪljən/ *noun* 名词
a person who is not a soldier 平民；老百姓

civilization /ˌsɪvəlaɪˈzeɪʃn; ˌsɪvḷəˈzeʃən/ *noun* 名词
the way people live together in a certain place at a certain time 文明；文化：*ancient civilizations* 古代文化

cl *short way of writing* **centilitre** ＊ **centilitre** 的缩写形式

claim /kleɪm; klem/ *verb* 动词 (**claims, claiming, claimed** /kleɪmd; klemd/)
1 ask for something because it is yours 索取某事物（因为是属于自己的）: *If nobody claims the camera you found, you can have it.* 你拾的照相机，要是没人认领就可以归你。
2 say that something is true 声称某事物属实: *Manuel claims that he did the work without help.* 曼纽尔说工作全是他做的，没有人帮他忙。
claim *noun* 名词
The workers are making a claim for better pay. 工作人员要求加薪。

clang /klæŋ; klæŋ/ *noun* 名词
the loud sound that metal makes when you hit it with something 撞击金属的声音；当；哐: *The iron gates shut with a clang.* 铁门哐的一声关上了。

clap /klæp; klæp/ *verb* 动词 (**claps, clapping, clapped** /klæpt; klæpt/)
hit your hands together to make a noise, usually to show that you like something 拍手；（通常指）鼓掌: *At the end of the concert the audience clapped loudly.* 音乐会结束时，听众大声鼓掌。
clap *noun* 名词
the sound that you make when you hit your hands together 拍手声；鼓掌声

clash /klæʃ; klæʃ/ *verb* 动词 (**clashes, clashing, clashed** /klæʃt; klæʃt/)
1 fight or argue 争斗；争吵；冲突: *Police clashed with football fans outside the stadium last Saturday.* 警方与足球迷上星期六在体育馆外发生冲突。
2 be at the same time（指时间）冲突: *The match clashed with my swimming lesson, so I couldn't watch it.* 那场比赛和我的游泳课时间上冲突了，我没看成。
3 If colours clash, they do not look nice together（指颜色）不相配，不和谐: *Your tie clashes with your shirt!* 你的领带和你的衬衫颜色不和谐！

class /klɑːs; klæs/ *noun* 名词 (*plural* 复数作 **classes**)
1 a group of children or students who learn together 班级；班: *The whole class passed the exam.* 全班都及格了。◇ *There is a new girl in my class.* 我们班有个新来的女生。
2 the time when you learn something with a teacher 上课；课: *Classes begin at nine o'clock.* 九点钟上课。◇ *You mustn't eat in class.* 上课时不要吃东西。
3 a group of people or things that are the same in some way（人或事物的）种类；类别: *There are many different classes of animals.* 动物有很多种。
4 how good, comfortable, etc something is（事物好坏、舒适等程度的）等级；级别: *It costs more to travel first class.* 头等舱票价高。
classroom /ˈklɑːsruːm; ˈklæsˌrum/ *noun* 名词
a room where you have lessons in a school 教室

classic /ˈklæsɪk; ˈklæsɪk/ *noun* 名词
a book that is so good that people read it for many years after it was written 经典著作；名著: *'Alice in Wonderland' is a children's classic.*《艾丽思漫游奇境记》是儿童喜爱的名著。

classical /ˈklæsɪkl; ˈklæsɪkḷ/ *adjective* 形容词
1 in a style that people have used for a long time because they think it is good 古典的: *classical music* 古典音乐
2 of ancient Greece or Rome 古希腊或古罗马的: *classical Greek* 古希腊

clatter /ˈklætə(r); ˈklætɚ/ *noun* 名词 (no plural 无复数)
a loud noise that hard things make when they hit each other 硬物相撞时发出的响亮的声音: *the clatter of knives and forks* 刀叉碰撞的响声

clause /klɔːz; klɔz/ *noun* 名词

a part of a sentence that has a verb in it 从句；分句；子句

claw /klɔ:; klɔ/ *noun* 名词
one of the hard pointed parts on the feet of some animals and birds 爪（鸟兽的脚趾）: *Cats have sharp claws.* 猫的爪很尖。

clay /kleɪ; kle/ *noun* 名词 (no plural 无复数)
a kind of heavy earth that becomes hard when it is dry. Clay is used to make things like pots and tiles. 黏土（黏土可用以制造盆和瓦等。）

clean[1] /kli:n; klin/ *adjective* 形容词 (**cleaner, cleanest**)
not dirty 清洁的；干净的: *clean clothes* 干净的衣服 ◇ *clean air* 清新的空气 ☞ picture on page C27 见第C27页图

clean[2] /kli:n; klin/ *verb* 动词 (**cleans, cleaning, cleaned** /kli:nd; klind/)
take away the dirt or marks from something; make something clean 弄干净；除去污垢: *Sam helped his mother to clean the kitchen.* 萨姆帮助母亲把厨房打扫干净了。◇ *Don't forget to clean your teeth before you go to bed.* 别忘记了刷完牙再睡觉。

clean *noun* 名词 (no plural 无复数)
The car needs a clean. 汽车得擦洗了。

clear[1] /klɪə(r); klɪr/ *adjective* 形容词 (**clearer, clearest**)
1 easy to see, hear or understand 容易看见、听见或理解的；清楚的: *She spoke in a loud clear voice.* 她说话声音又洪亮又清楚。◇ *This photograph is very clear.* 这张照片很清晰。◇ *It's clear that Jenny is not happy.* 很明显，珍妮不高兴了。
2 that you can see through 清澈的: *clear glass* 透亮的玻璃
3 with nothing in the way; empty 无障碍的；通行无阻的: *The roads were very clear.* 道路畅通无阻。
4 bright; without clouds 晴朗的；无云的: *a clear day* 晴朗的一天

clear[2] /klɪə(r); klɪr/ *verb* 动词 (**clears, clearing, cleared** /klɪəd; klɪrd/)
1 take things away from a place because you do not need them there 清除某物: *They cleared the snow from the path.* 他们清除了路上的积雪。◇ *When you have finished your meal, clear the table.* 吃完饭把桌子收拾干净。
2 become clear 变得清楚、清澈、无障碍或晴朗: *It rained in the morning, but in the afternoon the sky cleared.* 上午下过雨，下午天就晴了。

clear off go away 走开: *He got cross and told them to clear off.* 他很生气，叫他们都走开。

clear out take everything out of a cupboard, room, etc so that you can clean it and make it tidy 把柜橱、房间等腾空以后清理

clear up make a place clean and tidy 使某处整洁: *She helped me to clear up after the party.* 聚会结束后，她帮我把地方收拾干净。

clearly /'klɪəli; 'klɪrlɪ/ *adverb* 副词
1 in a way that is easy to see, hear or understand 容易看、听或理解；清楚地: *Please speak louder—I can't hear you very clearly.* 请大点儿声说——我听得不大清楚。◇ *The notes explain very clearly what you have to do.* 你应该做的事，这个说明都解释得很清楚。
2 without any doubt 毫无疑问: *She is clearly very intelligent.* 她显然十分聪明。

clerk[1] /klɜ:rk; klɝk/ *American English for* **shop assistant** 美式英语，即 **shop assistant**

clerk[2] /klɑ:k; klɝk/ *noun* 名词
a person in an office or bank who does things like writing letters 文书；办事员；事务员

clever /'klevə(r); 'klɛvɚ/ *adjective* 形容词 (**cleverer, cleverest**)
able to learn, understand or do something quickly and well 机灵的；伶俐的；聪明的: *a clever student* 聪明的学生

cleverly *adverb* 副词
The book is cleverly written. 这本书写得很妙。

click /klɪk; klɪk/ *noun* 名词
a short sharp sound 短而尖的声音: *I heard a click as someone switched the light on.* 我听到有人咔嗒一声把灯打开了。

click *verb* 动词 (**clicks, clicking, clicked** /klɪkt; klɪkt/)
make this sound 发出短而尖的声音: *clicking cameras* 发出咔嗒声的照相机

client /'klaɪənt; 'klaɪənt/ *noun* 名词
a person who pays another person, for example a lawyer or an accountant, for help or advice 付款给某人（如律师或会计师）而获得帮助或意见的人；委托人

cliff /klɪf; klɪf/ *noun* 名词
the high steep side of a hill by the sea 峭壁；悬崖

C

climate /'klaɪmət; 'klaɪmɪt/ *noun* 名词
the sort of weather that a place has 气候: *Coffee will not grow in a cold climate.* 寒冷的地方不能生长咖啡。

climb /klaɪm; klaɪm/ *verb* 动词 (**climbs, climbing, climbed** /klaɪmd; klaɪmd/)
1 go up or down, walking or using your hands and feet 爬行；爬: *The cat climbed to the top of the tree.* 猫爬到树顶上去了。◇ *They climbed the mountain.* 他们爬上了这座山。
2 move to or from a place when it is not easy to do it（在不便行动之处）来或去: *The children climbed through a hole in the fence.* 孩子们钻过篱笆上的洞。
3 move to a higher place 到较高处；攀登: *The road climbs steeply.* 这条路上坡很陡。

climb *noun* 名词 (no plural 无复数)
It was a long climb from the village to the top of the mountain. 从村子到山顶要走很长的上坡路。

climbing *noun* 名词 (no plural 无复数)
the sport of climbing mountains or rocks 登山运动: *a pair of climbing boots* 一双登山靴子 ✪ We often say **go climbing** 常说 **go climbing**: *They usually go climbing in the Alps in the holidays.* 他们假期通常攀登阿尔卑斯山。

climber /'klaɪmə(r); 'klaɪmɚ/ *noun* 名词
a person who goes up and down mountains or rocks as a sport 登山运动员

cling /klɪŋ; klɪŋ/ *verb* 动词 (**clings, clinging, clung** /klʌŋ; klʌŋ/, **has clung**)
hold or stick tightly to somebody or something 抓住、抱住或附着于某人或某物: *The small child was crying and clinging to her mother.* 那个小孩儿哭着，还紧紧搂着她母亲。◇ *His wet clothes clung to his body.* 他一身湿透的衣服紧箍着身体。

clinic /'klɪnɪk; 'klɪnɪk/ *noun* 名词
a place where you can go to get special help from a doctor 诊所

clip /klɪp; klɪp/ *noun* 名词
a small piece of metal or plastic for holding things together 夹子；别针；回形针: *a paper-clip* 曲别针

clip *verb* 动词 (**clips, clipping, clipped** /klɪpt; klɪpt/)
join something to another thing with a clip 用夹子将某物夹在另一物上；用别针将某物别在另一物上: *I clipped the photo to the letter.* 我用曲别针把照片别在信上了。

cloak /kləʊk; klok/ *noun* 名词
a very loose coat that has no sleeves 斗篷；披风

cloakroom /'kləʊkru:m; 'klok,rʊm/ *noun* 名词
1 a place in a building where you can leave your coat or bag 衣帽间
2 a toilet in a public building（公共场所的）厕所

clock /klɒk; klɑk/ *noun* 名词
a thing that shows you what time it is. It stands in a room or hangs on a wall 时钟；座钟；挂钟: *an alarm clock* 闹钟 ✪ A thing that shows the time and that you wear on your wrist is called a **watch**. 手表叫做 **watch**。

> ✪ You say that a clock or watch is **fast** if it shows a time that is later than the real time. 如果钟表显示的时间比实际时间晚，叫做快 (**fast**)。You say that it is **slow** if it shows a time that is earlier than the real time. 如果显示的时间比实际时间早，叫做慢 (**slow**)。

clockwise /'klɒkwaɪz; 'klɑk,waɪz/ *adjective, adverb* 形容词，副词
in the direction that the hands of a clock move 顺时针方向（的）: *Turn the handle clockwise.* 沿顺时针方向转动手柄。✪ opposite 反义词: **anticlockwise**

close[1] /kləʊs; klos/ *adjective, adverb* 形容词，副词 (**closer, closest**)
1 near 接近；靠近: *We live close to the station.* 我们住的地方离车站很近。◇ *You're too close to the fire.* 你离火炉太近了。
2 If people are close, they like or love each other very much 亲近（的）；亲密（的）: *I'm very close to my sister.* 我和我妹妹很要好。◇ *John and I are close friends.* 我和约翰是亲密的朋友。
3 with only a very small difference 区别

很小（的）: *'Did David win the race?' 'No, but it was very close.'* "这场赛跑戴维赢了吗？" "没赢，只差一点儿。"

4 careful 留心（的）；密切（的）: *Keep a close watch on the children.* 仔细看好孩子。

close together with not much space between them 没什么空隙: *The photographer asked us to stand closer together.* 照相的人让我们彼此站得挨紧一些。

closely *adverb* 副词
in a close way 接近；亲近；区别很小；留心: *We watched her closely.* 我们注意地看着她。◇ *Paul entered, closely followed by Mike.* 保罗走进来，后面紧跟着迈克。

close² /kləʊz; kloz/ *verb* 动词 (**closes, closing, closed** /kləʊzd; klozd/)
1 shut 关闭: *Please close the window.* 请把窗户关上。◇ *Close your eyes!* 把眼睛闭上！◇ *The door closed quietly.* 门轻轻地关上了。
2 stop being open, so that people cannot go there 不再开放（大家不能再去）: *The banks close at 4.30 pm.* 银行4点30分关门。
✪ opposite 反义词: **open**

close down shut and stop working; make something shut and stop working（使某事物）关闭而不再经营；停业: *The shop closed down when the owner died.* 那个商店在店主死后就关门了。

closed *adjective* 形容词
not open; shut 不再开放；关闭: *The shops are closed on Sundays.* 商店星期日都不开门。☞ picture on page C27 见第C27页图

closet /'klɒzɪt; 'klɑzɪt/ *American English for* **cupboard** 美式英语，即 **cupboard**

cloth /klɒθ; klɔθ/ *noun* 名词
1 (no plural 无复数) material that is made of wool, cotton, etc and that we use for making clothes and other things 布（用毛、棉等制成的，可以做衣服或其他物件的材料）✪ **Material** is the word that we usually use. ✳ **material** 是常用词。
2 a piece of cloth that you use for a special job 作某种用途的布: *a tablecloth* (= for covering a table) 桌布 ◇ *Wipe the floor with a cloth.* 用布擦地板。

clothes /kləʊðz; kloz/ *noun* 名词 (plural 复数)
things like trousers, shirts and coats that you wear to cover your body 衣服；衣物: *She was wearing new clothes.* 她穿了一身新衣服。◇ *Take off those wet clothes.* 把湿衣服换下来吧。

clothing /'kləʊðɪŋ; 'kloðɪŋ/ *noun* 名词 (no plural 无复数)
clothes 衣服；衣物: *skirts, trousers and other pieces of clothing* 裙子、裤子以及其他衣物

cloud /klaʊd; klaʊd/ *noun* 名词
1 a white or grey shape in the sky that is made of small drops of water 云彩；云: *Look at those dark clouds. It's going to rain.* 看那些乌云，要下雨了。
2 dust or smoke that looks like a cloud（像云的）尘土或烟雾: *clouds of smoke* 一团团的烟

cloudy *adjective* 形容词 (**cloudier, cloudiest**)
with a lot of clouds 多云的: *a cloudy sky* 阴天

clown /klaʊn; klaʊn/ *noun* 名词
a person in a circus who wears funny clothes and makes people laugh（马戏团的）小丑

club¹ /klʌb; klʌb/ *noun* 名词
a group of people who do something together, or the place where they meet 俱乐部: *I belong to the tennis club.* 我是网球俱乐部的。☞ Look also at **nightclub**. 另见 **nightclub**。

club *verb* 动词 (**clubs, clubbing, clubbed** /klʌbd; klʌbd/)
club together give money so that a group of people can buy something 各人拿出若干钱合起来买东西；凑份子；出份子: *We all clubbed together to buy David and Lisa a wedding present.* 我们大家凑份子给戴维和莉萨买结婚礼物。

club² /klʌb; klʌb/ *noun* 名词
1 a heavy stick with a thick end（一端粗的）沉重棍棒
2 clubs (plural 复数) the playing-cards that have the shape ♣ on them 梅花（纸牌）: *the three of clubs* 梅花三

clue /klu:; klu/ *noun* 名词
something that helps to find the answer to a problem, or to know the truth 有助于找出问题的解决方法或了解事实真相的事物；线索: *The police have found a clue that may help them to catch the murderer.* 警方已经发现了捉拿谋杀者的线索。

not have a clue not know something,

or not know how to do something 对某事物一无所知或不知如何做某事: *'What's his name?' 'I haven't a clue.'* "他叫什么名字?""我完全不知道。"

clumsy /'klʌmzi; 'klʌmzɪ/ *adjective* 形容词 (**clumsier**, **clumsiest**)
If you are clumsy, you often drop things or do things badly because you do not move in an easy or careful way 动作笨拙的: *I'm so clumsy! I've just broken a glass.* 我真是笨手笨脚的!我刚打碎了一个玻璃杯。

clumsily /'klʌmzəli; 'klʌmzəlɪ/ *adverb* 副词
He clumsily knocked the cup off the table. 他笨手笨脚地把杯子碰到地上了。

clung *form of* **cling** * **cling** 的不同形式

clutch /klʌtʃ; klʌtʃ/ *verb* 动词 (**clutches**, **clutching**, **clutched** /klʌtʃt; klʌtʃt/)
hold something tightly 紧紧抱住或握住某物: *The child clutched his mother's hand.* 那个孩子紧紧抓住母亲的手。

cm *short way of writing* **centimetre** * **centimetre** 的缩写形式

Co /kəʊ; ko/ *short for* **company 1** * **company 1** 的缩略式

c/o
You use **c/o** (short for **care of**) when you are writing to somebody who is staying at another person's house 给住在别人家的人写信时,写 **c/o**（**care of** 的缩略式）请求转交: *Mrs Jenny Walker, c/o Miss P Smith* 请 P. 史密斯小姐转交珍妮·沃克夫人

coach[1] /kəʊtʃ; kotʃ/ *noun* 名词 (*plural* 复数作 **coaches**)
1 a bus for taking people on long journeys 长途汽车
2 a vehicle with four wheels that is pulled by horses 四轮马车: *The Queen travelled to the wedding in the royal coach.* 女王乘坐皇室马车光临婚礼。
3 one of the parts of a train where people sit（铁路的）客车厢

coach[2] /kəʊtʃ; kotʃ/ *noun* 名词 (*plural* 复数作 **coaches**)
a person who teaches a sport（体育的）教练: *a football coach* 足球教练

coach *verb* 动词 (**coaches**, **coaching**, **coached** /kəʊtʃt; kotʃt/)
teach somebody 辅导或训练某人: *She is coaching the British team for the Olympics.* 她正在训练准备参加奥林匹克运动会的英国队。

coal /kəʊl; kol/ *noun* 名词 (no plural 无复数)
hard black stuff that comes from under the ground and gives heat when you burn it 煤: *Put some more coal on the fire.* 往火里再加点儿煤。

coarse /kɔ:s; kɔrs/ *adjective* 形容词 (**coarser**, **coarsest**)
made of thick pieces so that it is not smooth 粗糙的: *coarse sand* 粗沙 ◇ *coarse material* 粗糙的材料

coast /kəʊst; kost/ *noun* 名词
the part of the land that is next to the sea 海岸: *Their house is near the coast.* 他们的房子离海岸很近。◇ *the west coast of France* 法国西海岸

coastguard /'kəʊstgɑ:d; 'kost,gɑrd/ *noun* 名词
a person whose job is to watch the sea and ships and help people who are in danger 海岸警卫队员

coastline /'kəʊstlaɪn; 'kost,laɪn/ *noun* 名词
the edge of the land next to the sea 海岸线: *a rocky coastline* 多岩石的海岸线

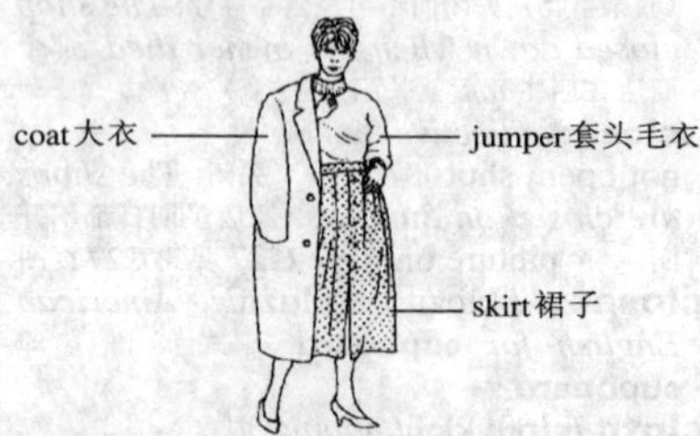

coat /kəʊt; kot/ *noun* 名词
1 a piece of clothing that you wear over your other clothes when you go outside in cold weather or rain 大衣；风雨衣: *Put your coat on—it's cold today.* 穿上大衣吧——今天冷。◇ *a raincoat* 雨衣
2 the hair or fur that covers an animal（动物的）皮毛: *A tiger has a striped coat.* 老虎的皮毛有条纹。

coat *verb* 动词 (**coats**, **coating**, **coated**)
put a thin covering of something over another thing 在某物上加上一薄层东西: *Their shoes were coated with mud.* 他们的鞋上粘着一层泥。

coat-hanger /ˈkəʊt hæŋə(r); ˈkot ˌhæŋɚ/ *noun* 名词
a piece of wood, metal or plastic with a hook. You use it for hanging clothes on. 衣架

coat-hanger 衣架

cobweb /ˈkɒbweb; ˈkɑbˌwɛb/ *noun* 名词
a net that a spider makes to catch insects 蜘蛛网

Coca-Cola /ˌkəʊkə ˈkəʊlə; ˌkokəˈkolə/ *noun* 名词
1 (no plural 无复数) a sweet brown drink with bubbles in it 可口可乐汽水（甜味，棕色）
2 (*plural* 复数作 **Coca-Colas**) a glass, bottle or can of Coca-Cola 一杯、一瓶或一罐可口可乐饮料
✪ **Coca-Cola** is a trade mark. ✳ **Coca-Cola** 是商标。

cock /kɒk; kɑk/ *noun* 名词
1 a male bird 雄鸟
2 a male chicken 公鸡

cockpit /ˈkɒkpɪt; ˈkɑkˌpɪt/ *noun* 名词
the part of a plane where the pilot sits （飞机驾驶员的）座舱

cocktail /ˈkɒkteɪl; ˈkɑkˌtel/ *noun* 名词
a drink made of alcohol, fruit juice, etc, mixed together 鸡尾酒

cocoa /ˈkəʊkəʊ; ˈkoko/ *noun* 名词 (no plural 无复数)
1 a brown powder from the beans of a tree, that is used to make chocolate 可可粉；巧克力粉
2 a drink of hot milk mixed with this powder 可可饮料: *a cup of cocoa* 一杯可可

coconut /ˈkəʊkənʌt; ˈkokəˌnʌt/ *noun* 名词
a very large brown nut that grows on trees in hot countries. Coconuts are hard and hairy on the outside, and they have sweet white food and liquid inside. 椰子

cod /kɒd; kɑd/ *noun* 名词 (*plural* 复数作 **cod**)
a large fish that lives in the sea and that you can eat 鳕

code /kəʊd; kod/ *noun* 名词
1 a way of writing secret messages, using letters, numbers or special signs 密码: *The list of names was written in code.* 名单是用密码写的。
2 a group of numbers or letters that helps you find something 代号: *What's the code* (= the telephone number) *for Paris?* 巴黎的代号（电话号码）是多少？
3 a set of rules for a group of people 规章；章程: *the Highway Code* (= rules for people who are driving on the road) 公路法规（= 在公路上开车的规则）

coffee /ˈkɒfi; ˈkɔfɪ/ *noun* 名词
1 (no plural 无复数) brown powder made from the beans of a tree that grows in hot countries. You use it for making a drink. 咖啡粉
2 (no plural 无复数) a drink of hot water mixed with this powder 热咖啡: *Would you like coffee or tea?* 您要咖啡还是要茶？ ◇ *a cup of coffee* 一杯咖啡
3 (*plural* 复数作 **coffees**) a cup of this drink 一杯咖啡: *Two coffees, please.* 请来两杯咖啡。✪ **White** coffee has milk in it and **black** coffee has no milk. 形容加奶的咖啡用的字是 **white**，不加奶的是 **black**。

coffee-table /ˈkɒfi teɪbl; ˈkɔfɪˌtebl̩/ *noun* 名词
a small low table 咖啡桌（小而矮的桌子）

coffin /ˈkɒfɪn; ˈkɔfɪn/ *noun* 名词
a box that you put a dead person's body in 棺材

coil /kɔɪl; kɔɪl/ *noun* 名词
a long piece of rope or wire that goes round in circles 缠成许多圈的绳子或金属丝；卷: *a coil of rope* 一卷绳子
coil *verb* 动词 (**coils**, **coiling**, **coiled** /kɔɪld; kɔɪld/)
make something into a lot of circles that are joined together 将某物卷成卷或盘成圈: *The snake coiled itself round a branch.* 蛇把身体缠绕在树枝上。

coin /kɔɪn; kɔɪn/ *noun* 名词
a round piece of money made of metal 硬币: *a pound coin* 一个一镑的硬币

coincidence /kəʊˈɪnsɪdəns; koˈɪnsədəns/ *noun* 名词
when things happen at the same time or in the same place by chance 巧合: *What a coincidence! I was thinking about you when you phoned!* 多巧哇！我正想着你呢，你就来电话了！

Coke /kəʊk; kok/ *another word for* **Coca-Cola** ✳ **Coca-Cola** 的另一种说法
✪ **Coke** is a trade mark. ✳ **Coke** 是商标。

cola /ˈkəʊlə; ˈkolə/ *noun* 名词

C

1 (no plural 无复数) a sweet brown drink with bubbles in it 可乐汽水（甜味，棕色）

2 (*plural* 复数作 **colas**) a glass, bottle or can of cola 一杯、一瓶或一罐可乐汽水

cold[1] /kəʊld; kold/ *adjective* 形容词 (**colder**, **coldest**)

1 not hot or warm; with a low temperature. Ice and snow are cold 冷的；凉的: *Put your coat on—it's cold outside.* 你把大衣穿上吧——外面很冷。◇ *I'm cold. Will you put the heater on?* 我很冷。你把暖气开开行吗？◇ *hot and cold water* 热水和冷水 ☞ picture on pageC27 见第C27页图

2 not friendly or kind 冷淡的；不友好的；不热情的: *a cold person* 不和气的人

coldly *adverb* 副词

in an unfriendly way 冷淡地；不友好地；不热情地: *She looked at me coldly.* 她冷冷地看着我。

cold[2] /kəʊld; kold/ *noun* 名词

1 (no plural 无复数) cold weather 冷天气；寒冷；冷: *Don't go out in the cold.* 天气冷，不要出去。

2 (*plural* 复数作 **colds**) an illness that makes you sneeze and cough 感冒；伤风: *I've got a cold.* 我感冒了。

catch a cold become ill with a cold 患感冒

collapse /kə'læps; kə'læps/ *verb* 动词 (**collapses**, **collapsing**, **collapsed** /kə'læpst; kə'læpst/)

fall down suddenly 突然倒下: *The building collapsed in the earthquake.* 那座楼在地震中倒塌了。◇ *She collapsed in the street and she was taken to hospital.* 她晕倒在街上，被送进了医院。

collapse *noun* 名词

the collapse of the bridge 桥的倒塌

collar /'kɒlə(r); 'kɑlɚ/ *noun* 名词

1 the part of your clothes that goes round your neck 领子；衣领

2 a band that you put round the neck of a dog or cat（猫狗的）项圈

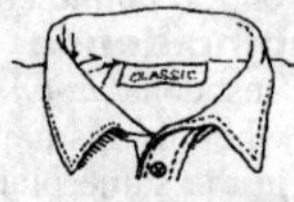

collar 领子

colleague /'kɒli:g; 'kɑlig/ *noun* 名词

a person who works with you 同事

collect /kə'lekt; kə'lɛkt/ *verb* 动词 (**collect**, **collecting**, **collected**)

1 take things from different people or places and put them together 把东西从各人或各处拿来放在一起；收集；敛: *The waiter collected the dirty glasses.* 服务员把脏玻璃杯都敛在一起了。

2 bring together things that are the same in some way, to study or enjoy them 把有某些共同之处的东西聚集在一起供研究或欣赏；收集: *My son collects stamps.* 我儿子收集邮票。

3 go and bring somebody or something from a place 到某处把某人或某物带来；领走；带走；取走: *She collects her children from school at 3.30.* 她在3点30分把她的孩子从学校接走。

collection /kə'lekʃn; kə'lɛkʃən/ *noun* 名词

1 a group of things that somebody has brought together 收集起来的东西；收藏物: *The Tate Gallery has a large collection of modern paintings.* 塔特陈列馆里收藏了大量现代绘画作品。◇ *a record collection* 收藏的一批唱片

2 taking something from a place or from people 从某处或各人处收集东西: *rubbish collection* 收集垃圾

collector /kə'lektə(r); kə'lɛktɚ/ *noun* 名词

a person who collects things as a hobby or as a job 收集人；收藏家: *a stamp collector* 集邮者 ◇ *a ticket collector at a railway station* 火车站的收票员

college /'kɒlɪdʒ; 'kɑlɪdʒ/ *noun* 名词

1 a place where people go to study more difficult subjects after they have left school 中学毕业以后上的学校；学院；专科学校；大学: *She's going to college next year.* 她明年就要上大学了。◇ *My brother is at college.* 我哥哥在大学读书。

2 a part of a university 大学的一部分；学院: *Kings College London* 伦敦大学金斯学院

collide /kə'laɪd; kə'laɪd/ *verb* 动词 (**collides**, **colliding**, **collided**)

move towards each other and hit each other 相撞: *The two lorries collided.* 两辆卡车相撞了。◇ *The lorry collided with a bus.* 卡车跟公共汽车撞上了。

collision /kə'lɪʒn; kə'lɪʒən/ *noun* 名词

when things or people collide（物体或人的）相撞: *The driver of the car was killed in the collision.* 小轿车司机在汽车相撞时死亡。

colon /'kəʊlən; 'kolən/ *noun* 名词
a mark (:) that you use in writing, for example before a list 冒号 (:)

colonel /'kɜ:nl; 'kɝnl̩/ *noun* 名词
an officer in the army（陆军）上校

colony /'kɒləni; 'kɑlənɪ/ *noun* 名词 (*plural* 复数作 **colonies**)
a country that is ruled by another country 殖民地: *Kenya was once a British colony.* 肯尼亚一度是英国的殖民地。

color *American English for* **colour** 美式英语，即 **colour**

colored *American English for* **coloured** 美式英语，即 **coloured**

colorful *American English for* **colourful** 美式英语，即 **colourful**

colour /'kʌlə(r); 'kʌlɚ/ *noun* 名词
Red, blue, yellow and green are all colours 颜色: *'What colour are your new shoes?' 'Black.'* "你的新鞋是什么颜色的？""黑的。" ◇ *The leaves change colour in autumn.* 叶子到秋天颜色就变了。

> ✪ Some words that we use to talk about colours are **light**, **pale**, **dark**, **deep** and **bright**. 用来修饰颜色的一些词有 **light**（浅的）、**pale**（淡的）、**dark**（深的）、**deep**（深的）、**bright**（鲜艳的）。

colour *verb* 动词 (**colours**, **colouring**, **coloured** /'kʌləd; 'kʌlɚd/)
put colours on something 给某物着色: *The children coloured their pictures with crayons.* 孩子们用蜡笔在图画上涂颜色。

coloured /'kʌləd; 'kʌlɚd/ *adjective* 形容词
with a colour 有色的: *She was wearing a brightly coloured jumper.* 她穿着鲜艳的毛衣。◇ *coloured paper* 有颜色的纸

colourful /'kʌləfl; 'kʌlɚfəl/ *adjective* 形容词
with a lot of bright colours 有很多鲜艳颜色的: *The garden is very colourful in summer.* 这个花园在夏天五彩缤纷。

column /'kɒləm; 'kɑləm/ *noun* 名词
1 a tall piece of stone that is part of a building 石柱
2 a long thin piece of writing on one side or part of a page（每页上的文字的）列，栏: *Each page of this dictionary has two columns.* 本词典每页有两栏。

comb /kəʊm; kom/ *noun* 名词
a flat piece of metal or plastic with a line of thin parts like teeth. You use it to make your hair tidy. 梳子

comb 梳子

comb *verb* 动词 (**combs**, **combing**, **combed** /kəʊmd; komd/)
make your hair tidy with a comb 用梳子梳头发: *Have you combed your hair?* 你梳头了吗？

combination /ˌkɒmbɪ'neɪʃn; ˌkɑmbə'neʃən/ *noun* 名词
two or more things mixed together（两个或两个以上事物）结合；混合；联合；合并: *The building is a combination of new and old styles.* 这座建筑物是新旧风格的结合体。

combine /kəm'baɪn; kəm'baɪn/ *verb* 动词 (**combined**, **combining**, **combined** /kəm'baɪnd; kəm'baɪnd/)
join or mix together 结合；混合；联合；合并: *The two schools combined and moved to a larger building.* 这两所学校合并后已迁往大校舍。

come /kʌm; kʌm/ *verb* 动词 (**comes**, **coming**, **came** /keɪm; kem/, **has come**)
1 move towards the person who is speaking or the place that you are talking about 向着说话的人或所提到的地方移动；来: *Come here, please.* 请过来。◇ *The dog came when I called him.* 这只狗我一叫它它就来。◇ *I'm sorry, but I can't come to your party.* 很抱歉，我不能参加您的聚会。
2 arrive 到达；抵达: *If you go along that road, you will come to the river.* 你顺着这条路走，就能到河边儿了。◇ *A letter came for you this morning.* 今天上午有您一封信。
3 be or happen 存在；出现；发生: *June comes after May.* 五月过后是六月。
4 go with the person who is speaking 与说话的人同行: *I'm going to a party tonight. Do you want to come?* 我今天晚上去参加一个聚会。你想跟我一起去吗？

come across something find something when you are not looking for it 偶然遇见或发现某物: *I came across these old photos yesterday.* 我昨天偶然发现了这些旧照片。

C

come apart break into pieces 破碎: *This old coat is coming apart.* 这件旧大衣都快破了。

come back return 回来；返回: *I'm going to Italy tomorrow and I'm coming back in January.* 我明天去意大利，一月份回来。

come from 1 be made from something 由某物制成: *Wool comes from sheep.* 羊毛取自羊的身上。**2** The place that you come from is where you were born or where you live 出生于或居住于某地；籍贯为: *I come from Japan.* 我是日本人。◇ *Where do you come from?* 您是哪儿的人？

come on!, come along! words that you use for telling somebody to hurry or to try harder 激励某人加速或努力的词语: *Come on! We'll be late!* 快点儿吧！我们都要晚了！

come out appear 出现: *The rain stopped and the sun came out.* 雨停了，太阳出来了。◇ *This book came out in 1996.* 本书于1996年出版。

how come ...? why or how...? 为什么或怎么…？: *How come you're here so early?* 你怎么来得这么早？

to come in the future 在将来: *I'll be very busy in the months to come.* 我这几个月要大忙一阵了。

comedian /kə'mi:diən; kə'midɪən/ *noun* 名词

a person whose job is to make people laugh 喜剧演员

comedy /'kɒmədi; 'kɑmədɪ/ *noun* 名词 (*plural* 复数作 **comedies**)

a funny play or film 喜剧（戏剧或影片）

comfort /'kʌmfət; 'kʌmfɚt/ *noun* 名词

1 (no plural 无复数) having everything your body needs; being without pain or problems 舒适；安逸: *They have enough money to live in comfort.* 他们有钱足以过舒适的日子。

2 (*plural* 复数作 **comforts**) a person or thing that helps you or makes life better 给予帮助或使生活愉快的人或事物: *Her children were a comfort to her when she was ill.* 她生病的时候，她的孩子很关心她。

comfort *verb* 动词 (**comforts, comforting, comforted**)

make somebody feel less unhappy or worried 安慰某人: *A mother was comforting her crying child.* 母亲正哄着啼哭的孩子。

comfortable /'kʌmftəbl; 'kʌmfɚtəbl̩/ *adjective* 形容词

1 nice to sit in, to be in, or to wear 使人舒适的: *This is a very comfortable bed.* 这个床很舒服。◇ *comfortable shoes* 舒适的鞋

2 with no pain or worry 舒适的；舒服的: *Sit down and make yourself comfortable.* 坐下，别拘束。

✪ opposite 反义词: **uncomfortable**

comfortably /'kʌmftəbli; 'kʌmfɚtəblɪ/ *adverb* 副词

Are you sitting comfortably? 你坐得舒服吗？

comic[1] /'kɒmɪk; 'kɑmɪk/, **comical** /'kɒmɪkl; 'kɑmɪkl̩/ *adjective* 形容词

funny 可笑的；滑稽的

comic[2] /'kɒmɪk; 'kɑmɪk/ *noun* 名词

a magazine for children, with pictures that tell a story（儿童的）连环画册

comma /'kɒmə; 'kɑmə/ *noun* 名词 (*plural* 复数作 **commas**)

a mark (,) that you use in writing to make a short stop in a sentence 逗号(，)

command /kə'mɑ:nd; kə'mænd/ *noun* 名词

1 (*plural* 复数作 **commands**) words that tell you that you must do something 命令；指示: *The soldiers must obey their general's commands.* 士兵必需服从将军的命令。

2 (no plural 无复数) the power to tell people what to do 指挥（权）: *Who is in command of this ship?* 谁负责指挥这艘船？

command *verb* 动词 (**commands, commanding, commanded**)

tell somebody that they must do something 命令某人做某事: *He commanded us to leave immediately.* 他命令我们立刻离开。✪ **Order** is the word that we usually use. ✳ **order**是常用词。

comment /'kɒment; 'kɑmɛnt/ *noun* 名词

words that you say about something to show what you think 意见；评论: *She made some interesting comments about the film.* 她对这部影片提出了一些有意思的看法。

comment *verb* 动词 (**comments, commenting, commented**)

say what you think about something 提出意见；评论: *A lot of people at school commented on my new watch.* 学校里很多人都谈论我的新手表。

commentary /ˈkɒməntri; ˈkɑmənˌtɛrɪ/ *noun* 名词 (*plural* 复数作 **commentaries**)
words that somebody says about something that is happening 评论: *We listened to the radio commentary on the football match.* 我们听了电台广播的那场足球赛的解说。

commentator /ˈkɒmənteɪtə(r); ˈkɑmənˌtetɚ/ *noun* 名词
a person who gives a commentary on radio or television（电台或电视的）解说员

commerce /ˈkɒmɜːs; ˈkɑmɝs/ *noun* 名词 (no plural 无复数)
the work of buying and selling things 商业；贸易

commercial /kəˈmɜːʃl; kəˈmɝʃəl/ *adjective* 形容词
for or about buying and selling things 商业的；贸易的: *a commercial vehicle* 商业用车

commercial *noun* 名词
a short film on television or radio that helps to sell something（电视或电台播出的）广告

commit /kəˈmɪt; kəˈmɪt/ *verb* 动词 (**commits**, **committing**, **committed**)
do something bad 做坏事；犯罪: *This man has committed a very serious crime.* 这个男子犯了很重的罪。

committee /kəˈmɪti; kəˈmɪtɪ/ *noun* 名词
a group of people that other people choose to plan or organize something 委员会: *The members of the club choose a new committee every year.* 这个俱乐部的成员每年选出新的委员会。

common[1] /ˈkɒmən; ˈkɑmən/ *adjective* 形容词 (**commoner**, **commonest**)
1 that you often see or that often happens 普通的；常见的；平常的: *Smith is a common name in England.* 在英国有很多人的名字都叫史密斯。
2 that everybody in a group does or has 共同的；共有的: *The English and Australians have a common language.* 英国人和澳洲人有共同的语言。
have something in common be like somebody in a certain way, or have the same interests as somebody 在某方面像某人；与某人有共同爱好: *Paul and I are good friends. We have a lot in common.* 我和保罗是好朋友。我们有很多共同的爱好。

common sense /ˌkɒmən ˈsens; ˈkɑmən ˈsɛns/ *noun* 名词 (no plural 无复数)
the ability to do the right thing and not make stupid mistakes, because of what you know about the world 常识；情理: *Jenny's got no common sense. She lay in the sun all day and got sunburnt.* 珍妮一点儿常识都没有。她晒了一整天太阳，把皮肤晒坏了。

common[2] /ˈkɒmən; ˈkɑmən/ *noun* 名词
a piece of land that everybody can use 公地（大家都可以使用的土地）: *We went for a walk on the common.* 我们到空地上去散了散步。

communicate /kəˈmjuːnɪkeɪt; kəˈmjunəˌket/ *verb* 动词 (**communicates**, **communicating**, **communicated**)
talk or write to somebody 与某人谈话或通信: *The pilots communicate with the airport by radio.* 飞行员用无线电和机场联系。

communication /kəˌmjuːnɪˈkeɪʃn; kəˌmjunəˈkeʃən/ *noun* 名词
1 (no plural 无复数) talking or writing to somebody（与某人的）通话或通信: *Communication is difficult when two people don't speak the same language.* 两个人语言不同就很难交往。
2 communications (plural 复数) ways of sending information or moving from one place to another 交流的方法；通讯；交通: *There are good communications with the islands.* 与各岛的联系畅通无阻。

community /kəˈmjuːnəti; kəˈmjunətɪ/ *noun* 名词 (*plural* 复数作 **communities**)
1 the people who live in a place 同一地区的居民；社区；社会: *Life in a small fishing community is very different from life in a big city.* 小片渔业区居民的生活与大城市的很不相同。
2 a group of people who join together, for example because they have the same interests or religion 团体；集体（如因有共同利益或宗教信仰的）: *the Asian community in Britain* 在英国的亚洲侨民团体

commute /kəˈmjuːt; kəˈmjut/ *verb* 动词 (**commutes**, **commuting**, **commuted**)
travel a long way from home to work

every day 通勤（从家至工作处每天乘坐长途车）: *She lives in the country and commutes to London.* 她住在郊外，通勤到伦敦。

commuter *noun* 名词
a person who commutes 通勤者

compact disc /ˌkɒmpækt ˈdɪsk; ˌkɑmpækt ˈdɪsk/ *noun* 名词
a small round piece of plastic, like a record. You play it on a special machine called a **compact disc player**. 激光唱片；光盘（用以播放的唱机叫做 **compact disc player**）✪ The short form is **CD**. 缩略式为 **CD**。

compact disc
激光唱片

companion /kəmˈpæniən; kəmˈpænjən/ *noun* 名词
a person who is with another person 同伴；伙伴

company /ˈkʌmpəni; ˈkʌmpənɪ/ *noun* 名词
1 (*plural* 复数作 **companies**) a group of people who work to make or sell things 公司；商行: *an advertising company* 广告公司
2 (no plural 无复数) being with other people 与他人在一起；交往: *She lives alone so she likes company at weekends.* 她独自生活，所以很喜欢周末和别人在一起。
keep somebody company be or go with somebody 与某人做伴；与某人同往；陪伴；结伴: *Please stay and keep me company for a while.* 请留下和我做会儿伴吧。

comparative /kəmˈpærətɪv; kəmˈpærətɪv/ *noun* 名词
in the form of an adjective or adverb that shows more of something（形容词或副词的）比较级形式: *The comparative of 'bad' is 'worse'.* ＊ bad 的比较级形式是 worse。
comparative *adjective* 形容词
'Longer' is the comparative form of 'long'. ＊ longer 是 long 的比较级形式。

compare /kəmˈpeə(r); kəmˈpɛr/ *verb* 动词 (**compares**, **comparing**, **compared** /kəmˈpeəd; kəmˈpɛrd/)
think about or look at people or things together so that you can see how they are different 比较；对比: *I've compared the prices in the two shops and the prices here are cheaper.* 我把两家商店的价格比较了一下，这儿的便宜。◇ *Compare your answers with those at the back of the book.* 把你的答案同书后的答案对照一下。
compared *adjective* 形容词
if you compare somebody or something 与某人或某事物相比: *Stephen is quite small, compared with his friends.* 斯蒂芬比他的朋友小得多。

comparison /kəmˈpærɪsn; kəmˈpærəsn̩/ *noun* 名词
seeing or understanding how things are different or the same 比较: *We made a comparison of prices in three different shops.* 我们对三家商店的价格做了比较。
in or 或 **by comparison with somebody or something** if you see or think about somebody or something together with another person or thing 与某人或某事物相比；相比之下；比较起来: *Britain is a small country in comparison with Australia.* 英国与澳大利亚相比，是个小国。

compartment /kəmˈpɑːtmənt; kəmˈpɑrtmənt/ *noun* 名词
1 a small room in a train（火车车厢中的）隔间: *The first-class compartments are at the front of the train.* 头等车室在列车前面。
2 a separate part inside a box or bag（箱子、盒子或袋子里的）小格，分隔层: *The suitcase had a secret compartment at the back.* 这个手提箱背面有个秘密夹层。

compass /ˈkʌmpəs; ˈkʌmpəs/ *noun* 名词 (*plural* 复数作 **compasses**)
a thing with a needle that always shows where north is 指南针；罗盘

compete /kəmˈpiːt; kəmˈpit/ *verb* 动词 (**competes**, **competing**, **competed**)
try to win a race or competition 竞争；对抗；比赛: *Teams from many countries compete in the World Cup.* 很多国家的球队参加世界杯比赛。

competition /ˌkɒmpəˈtɪʃn; ˌkɑmpəˈtɪʃən/ *noun* 名词
1 (*plural* 复数作 **competitions**) a game or test that people try to win 比赛或竞赛的项目: *I entered the painting competition and won first prize.* 我参加绘画比赛赢得了头奖。

2 (no plural 无复数) trying to win or be best 比赛；竞赛；较量: *We were in competition with a team from another school.* 我们同另一所学校的运动队比赛。

competitor /kəm'petɪtə(r); kəm'pɛtətɚ/ *noun* 名词
a person who is trying to win a competition 竞争者；比赛者；对手；敌手

complain /kəm'pleɪn; kəm'plen/ *verb* 动词 (**complains**, **complaining**, **complained** /kəm'pleɪnd; kəm'plend/)
say that you do not like something; say that you are unhappy or angry about something 说出不喜欢某事物；说出对某事物不愉快或感到气愤；抱怨；诉苦；发牢骚: *He complained to the waiter that his soup was cold.* 他不满地对服务员说汤是凉的。◇ *She was complaining about the weather.* 她抱怨天气太坏。

complaint /kəm'pleɪnt; kəm'plent/ *noun* 名词
saying that you do not like something (针对不喜欢的事物的）诉说；牢骚话；抱怨；诉苦；投诉: *We made a complaint to the hotel manager about the dirty rooms.* 我们向旅馆经理投诉房间太脏。

complete[1] /kəm'pli:t; kəm'plit/ *adjective* 形容词
1 with none of its parts missing 完整的；完全的；全部的；整个的: *I've got a complete set of Shakespeare's plays.* 我有一套莎士比亚戏剧全集。✪ opposite 反义词: **incomplete**
2 finished 完成: *The work is complete.* 这项工作已经做完了。
3 in every way; total 全面的；完全的: *Their visit was a complete surprise.* 他们的访问完全出人意外。

complete[2] /kəm'pli:t; kəm'plit/ *verb* 动词 (**completes**, **completing**, **completed**)
finish doing or making something 做完或完成某事物: *She was at university for two years but she did not complete her studies.* 她上了两年大学，但是没有上完。◇ *When will the new building be completed?* 这座新大厦什么时候建成？

completely /kəm'pli:tli; kəm'plitlɪ/ *adverb* 副词
totally; in every way 完全地；全部地；全面地: *The money has completely disappeared.* 钱全不见了。◇ *I completely forgot that it was your birthday!* 我把那天是你的生日忘得一干二净！

complex[1] /'kɒmpleks; kəm'plɛks/ *adjective* 形容词
difficult to understand because it has a lot of different parts 复杂难懂的: *a complex problem* 复杂的问题

complex[2] /'kɒmpleks; 'kɑmplɛks/ *noun* 名词 (*plural* 复数作 **complexes**)
a group of buildings 建筑群: *a sports complex* 综合体育馆场

complicated /'kɒmplɪkeɪtɪd; 'kɑmplə,ketɪd/ *adjective* 形容词
difficult to understand because it has a lot of different parts 复杂难懂的: *I can't explain how to play the game. It's too complicated.* 我解释不清楚这个游戏规则。太复杂了。

compliment /'kɒmplɪmənt; 'kɑmpləmənt/ *noun* 名词
pay somebody a compliment say something nice about somebody 称赞或夸奖某人: *Simon paid her a compliment on her speech.* 西蒙对她的讲话称赞了一番。
compliment *verb* 动词 (**compliments**, **complimenting**, **complimented**)
say something nice about somebody 称赞或夸奖某人: *They complimented Frank on his cooking.* 他们称赞弗兰克烹调手艺高。

compose /kəm'pəʊz; kəm'poz/ *verb* 动词 (**composes**, **composing**, **composed** /kəm'pəʊzd; kəm'pozd/)
write something, especially music 写作；（尤指）作曲: *Verdi composed many operas.* 威尔地创作了许多歌剧的曲子。
be composed of something be made of something; have something as parts 由某事物做成、构成或组成: *Water is composed of oxygen and hydrogen.* 水是由氧和氢结合而成的。

composer /kəm'pəʊzə(r); kəm'pozɚ/ *noun* 名词
a person who writes music 作曲者；作曲家: *My favourite composer is Mozart.* 我最喜爱的作曲家是莫扎特。

composition /ˌkɒmpə'zɪʃn; ˌkɑmpə'zɪʃən/ *noun* 名词
a piece of writing or music 作文；乐曲

compound /'kɒmpaʊnd; 'kɑmpaʊnd/ *noun* 名词
1 something that is made of two or

more parts 由至少两个部分做成、构成或组成的事物: *Salt is a chemical compound.* 盐是化合物。

2 a word that is made from other words 复合词: *'Fingernail' and 'waiting-room' are compounds.* ＊ fingernail 和 waiting-room 都是复合词。

comprehension /ˌkɒmprɪ'henʃn; ˌkɑmprɪ'hɛnʃən/ *noun* 名词 (no plural 无复数)

C

understanding something that you hear or read 理解（力）: *a test in listening comprehension* 听力测验

comprehensive school /ˌkɒmprɪ'hensɪv sku:l; ˌkɑmprɪ'hɛnsɪv 'skul/, **comprehensive** *noun* 名词

a school for pupils of all abilities between the ages of 11 and 18 综合中学（招收11岁至18岁不同程度的学生的学校）

compromise /'kɒmprəmaɪz; 'kɑmprəˌmaɪz/ *noun* 名词

an agreement with another person or group, when you both do part of what the other person or group wants 双方妥协或折衷的协议: *After long talks, the workers and management reached a compromise.* 经过长时间谈判，工人和管理阶层才达成折衷的协议。

compulsory /kəm'pʌlsəri; kəm'pʌlsərɪ/ *adjective* 形容词

If something is compulsory, you must do it 必须做的；强制的；义务的: *School is compulsory for all children between the ages of five and sixteen.* 五岁的儿童至十六岁的少年必须上学。

computer 计算机

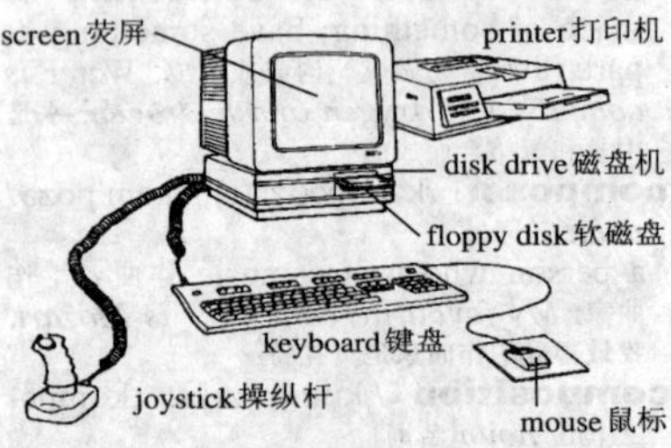

computer /kəm'pju:tə(r); kəm'pjutɚ/ *noun* 名词

a machine that stores information and finds answers very quickly 计算机；电脑

computer program /kəm'pju:tə prəʊgræm; kəm'pjutɚ 'progrəm/ *noun* 名词

information that tells a computer what to do 计算机程序

computer programmer /kəmˌpju:tə 'prəʊgræmə(r); kəm'pjutɚ 'progrəmɚ/ *noun* 名词

a person who writes computer programs 计算机程序设计员

computing *noun* 名词 (no plural 无复数)

using computers to do work 计算机的运算: *She is studying computing at college.* 她正在大学学习计算机运算。

conceal /kən'si:l; kən'sil/ *verb* 动词 (**conceals, concealing, concealed** /kən'si:ld; kən'sild/)

hide something 隐藏或隐瞒某事物: *They concealed the bomb in a suitcase.* 他们把炸弹藏在行李里了。✪ **Hide** is the word that we usually use. ＊ **hide** 是常用词。

conceited /kən'si:tɪd; kən'sitɪd/ *adjective* 形容词

too proud of yourself and what you can do 自负的；自高自大的

concentrate /'kɒnsntreɪt; 'kɑnsn̩ˌtret/ *verb* 动词 (**concentrates, concentrating, concentrated**)

think about what you are doing and not about anything else 全神贯注；精神集中: *Stop looking out of the window and concentrate on your work!* 别再往窗户外边看了，集中精神做你的工作！

concentration /ˌkɒnsn'treɪʃn; ˌkɑnsn̩'treʃən/ *noun* 名词 (no plural 无复数)

Concentration is very difficult when there's so much noise. 这么嘈杂，精神很难集中。

concern[1] /kən'sɜ:n; kən'sɝn/ *verb* 动词 (**concerns, concerning, concerned** /kən'sɜ:nd; kən'sɝnd/)

1 be important or interesting to somebody 对某人很重要或有关: *This notice concerns all passengers travelling to Manchester.* 这一通知关系到所有到曼彻斯特的乘客。

2 worry somebody 使某人担忧: *It concerns me that she is always late.* 我担心的是她总迟到。

3 be about something 关于某事物: *The story concerns a young boy and his* *parents.* 这个故事涉及的是一个小男孩儿和他的父母。

concerned *adjective* 形容词
worried 担心的；烦恼的；忧虑的: *They are very concerned about their son's illness.* 他们非常关心儿子的病。

concern² /kən'sɜ:n; kən'sɝn/ *noun* 名词
1 (no plural 无复数) worry 担心；忧虑: *There is a lot of concern about this problem.* 这个问题让人十分担心。
2 (*plural* 复数作 **concerns**) something that is important or interesting to somebody 对某人很重要或有关的事物: *Her problems are not my concern.* 她的问题我不闻不问。

concerning /kən'sɜ:nɪŋ; kən'sɝnɪŋ/ *preposition* 介词
about 关于: *Thank you for your letter concerning the date of the next meeting* ... 来函收悉，不胜感谢。关于下次会议日期…

concert /'kɒnsət; 'kɑnsɝt/ *noun* 名词
music played for a lot of people 音乐会: *a rock concert* 摇滚音乐会

conclusion /kən'klu:ʒn; kən'kluʒən/ *noun* 名词
what you believe or decide after thinking carefully 经过仔细思考后的看法或判断；结论: *We came to the conclusion* (= we decided) *that you were right.* 我们断定是你对。

concrete /'kɒŋkri:t; 'kɑnkrit/ *noun* 名词 (no plural 无复数)
hard grey material used for building things 混凝土: *a concrete path* 混凝土的小路

condemn /kən'dem; kən'dɛm/ *verb* 动词 (**condemns, condemning, condemned** /kən'demd; kən'dɛmd/)
1 say that somebody must be punished in a certain way 宣告某人必须受到某种惩罚；判某人刑: *The murderer was condemned to death.* 这个谋杀犯被判处死刑。
2 say strongly that somebody or something is bad or wrong 谴责某人或某事物恶劣或错误；指责；责备: *Many people condemned the government's decision.* 很多人指责政府的这一决定。

condition /kən'dɪʃn; kən'dɪʃən/ *noun* 名词
1 (no plural 无复数) how a person, animal or thing is 现状；状况: *The car was cheap and in good condition, so I bought it.* 这辆汽车很便宜，还用得过，所以我就买下了。
2 (*plural* 复数作 **conditions**) something that must happen before another thing can happen 条件: *One of the conditions of the job is that you agree to work on Saturdays.* 做这份工作的一个条件是得同意星期六上班。
3 conditions (plural 复数) how things are around you 环境；情况: *The prisoners lived in terrible conditions.* 囚犯在极恶劣的环境中生活。
on condition that only if 在…条件下: *You can go to the party on condition that you come home before midnight.* 你可以去参加聚会，可有一条，你得在午夜以前回来。

conduct /kən'dʌkt; kən'dʌkt/ *verb* 动词 (**conducts, conducting, conducted**)
1 stand in front of a group of musicians and control what they do 指挥（音乐）: *The orchestra was conducted by Peter Jones.* 这个管弦乐队是由彼得·琼斯指挥的。
2 show somebody where to go 为某人做向导；引导；带领: *She conducted us on a tour of the museum.* 她带领我们参观了博物馆。

conductor /kən'dʌktə(r); kən'dʌktɚ/ *noun* 名词
1 a person who stands in front of a group of musicians and controls what they do（乐队的）指挥
2 a person who sells tickets on a bus（公共汽车上的）售票员
3 *American English for* **guard² 2** 美式英语，即 **guard² 2**

cone /kəʊn; kon/ *noun* 名词
1 a shape with one flat round end and one pointed end 圆锥 ☞ picture on page C5 见第 C5 页图
2 the hard fruit of a **pine** or **fir** tree（松树 **pine** tree 或枞树 **fir** tree 的）球果: *a pine cone* 松果

cone 2 球果

conference /'kɒnfərəns; 'kɑnfərəns/ *noun* 名词
a time when many people meet to talk about a special thing 讨论（会）；协商（会）；会议: *an international conference* 国际会议

C

confess /kən'fes; kən'fɛs/ *verb* 动词 (**confesses**, **confessing**, **confessed** /kən'fest; kən'fɛst/)
say that you have done something wrong 承认（做错事）；供认；坦白: *She confessed that she had stolen the money.* 她招认偷了那笔钱。◇ *He confessed to the crime.* 他对罪行供认不讳。

confession /kən'feʃn; kən'fɛʃən/ *noun* 名词
something that you confess 承认；供认；坦白；交代: *She made a confession to the police.* 她向警方招供了。

confidence /'kɒnfɪdəns; 'kɑnfədəns/ *noun* 名词 (no plural 无复数)
the feeling that you can do something well 信心；自信；把握: *She answered the questions with confidence.* 她回答问题很有把握。

have confidence in somebody feel sure that somebody will do something well 对某人抱有信心: *I'm sure you'll pass the exam. I have great confidence in you.* 我担保你能考及格。我对你信心十足。

in confidence If somebody tells you something in confidence, it is a secret. 作为秘密

confident /'kɒnfɪdənt; 'kɑnfədənt/ *adjective* 形容词
sure that you can do something well, or that something will happen 有信心的；自信的；有把握的: *I'm confident that our team will win.* 我管保我们队赢。

confirm /kən'fɜ:m; kən'fɝm/ *verb* 动词 (**confirms**, **confirming**, **confirmed** /kən'fɜ:md; kən'fɝmd/)
say that something is true or that something will happen 说出某事属实或将发生；确认: *Please write and confirm the date of your arrival.* 请写出您到达的确切日期。

conflict /'kɒnflɪkt; 'kɑnflɪkt/ *noun* 名词
a fight or an argument 冲突；争斗；争吵

confuse /kən'fju:z; kən'fjuz/ *verb* 动词 (**confuses**, **confusing**, **confused** /kən'fju:zd; kən'fjuzd/)
1 mix somebody's ideas, so that they cannot think clearly or understand 把某人弄糊涂；使迷惑: *They confused me by asking so many questions.* 他们提了一大堆问题，把我都弄糊涂了。
2 think that one thing or person is another thing or person 把一事物或一人错当作另一事物或另一人；混淆: *Don't confuse the word 'weather' with 'whether'.* 不要把 weather（天气）这个字和 whether（是否）弄混了。

confused *adjective* 形容词
not able to think clearly 糊涂的；迷乱的: *The waiter got confused and brought everybody the wrong drink!* 服务员糊里糊涂，把大家要的饮料都上错了！

confusing *adjective* 形容词
difficult to understand 莫名其妙的；难以理解的: *This map is very confusing.* 这张地图真看不明白。

confusion /kən'fju:ʒn; kən'fjuʒən/ *noun* 名词 (no plural 无复数)
being confused 被弄糊涂: *He didn't speak any English and he looked at me in confusion when I asked him a question.* 他完全不会英语，我问他问题时他看着我不知所措。

congratulate /kən'grætʃuleɪt; kən'grætʃəˌlet/ *verb* 动词 (**congratulates**, **congratulating**, **congratulated**)
tell somebody that you are pleased about something that they have done 祝贺；庆贺: *I congratulated Susan on passing her exam.* 苏珊考及格了，我向她祝贺。

congratulations /kənˌgrætʃu'leɪʃnz; kənˌgrætʃə'leʃənz/ *noun* 名词 (plural 复数)
a word that shows you are pleased about something that somebody has done 向别人表示祝贺用的词: *Congratulations on your new job!* 祝贺你有了新工作！

congress /'kɒŋgres; 'kɑŋgrəs/ *noun* 名词
1 (*plural* 复数作 **congresses**) a meeting of many people to talk about important things 会议
2 Congress (no plural 无复数) a group of people who make the laws in some countries, for example in the United States 国会（例如美国的国会）

conjunction /kən'dʒʌŋkʃn; kən'dʒʌŋkʃən/ *noun* 名词
a word that joins other words or parts of a sentence 连词: *'And', 'or' and 'but' are conjunctions.* ＊and、or、but 都是连词。

conjuror /'kʌndʒərə(r); 'kʌndʒərə/ *noun* 名词

a person who does clever tricks that seem to be magic 变戏法的人；魔术师: *The conjuror pulled a rabbit out of a hat.* 魔术师从帽子里掏出一只兔子来。

connect /kəˈnekt; kəˈnɛkt/ *verb* 动词 (**connects, connecting, connected**)
join one thing to another thing 连接；联结；结合: *This wire connects the video recorder to the television.* 这条电线连接着录像机和电视机。◇ *The two cities are connected by a motorway.* 这两个城市之间有一条高速公路。

connection /kəˈnekʃn; kəˈnɛkʃən/ *noun* 名词
1 the way that one thing is joined to another 连接；联结；结合: *We had a bad connection on the phone so I couldn't hear him very well.* 我们的电话线接触不良，他的声音我听不清楚。◇ *Is there a connection between violence on TV and crime?* 电视中的暴力镜头和现实中的犯罪行为有没有关系？
2 a train, plane or bus that leaves a place soon after another arrives, so that people can change from one to the other（火车、飞机或公共汽车的）联运: *The train was late, so I missed my connection.* 火车误点了，所以我没赶上联运。
in connection with something about something 关于某事物: *The police want to talk to him in connection with the robbery.* 警方想找他谈谈那起劫案的事。

conscience /ˈkɒnʃəns; ˈkɑnʃəns/ *noun* 名词
the feeling inside you about what is right and wrong 良心；是非感
have a clear conscience feel that you have done nothing wrong 问心无愧
have a guilty conscience feel that you have done something wrong 问心有愧

conscious /ˈkɒnʃəs; ˈkɑnʃəs/ *adjective* 形容词
1 awake and able to think 清醒而能思考的: *The patient was conscious during the operation.* 病人在手术中始终很清醒。✪ opposite 反义词: **unconscious**
2 If you are conscious of something, you know about it 感觉到的；意识到的: *I was conscious that somebody was watching me.* 我意识到有人注视着我。

consciousness /ˈkɒnʃəsnəs; ˈkɑnʃəsnɪs/ *noun* 名词 (no plural 无复数)
lose consciousness stop being conscious 失去知觉: *As she fell, she hit her head and lost consciousness.* 她跌倒撞到头部，失去了知觉。

consent /kənˈsent; kənˈsɛnt/ *noun* 名词 (no plural 无复数)
agreeing to let somebody do something 同意让某人做某事: *Her parents gave their consent to the marriage.* 她父母答允了这门亲事。

consequence /ˈkɒnsɪkwəns; ˈkɑnsəˌkwɛns/ *noun* 名词
what happens because of something 结果；后果: *I've just bought a car and, as a consequence, I've got no money.* 我刚买了辆汽车，这样一来我就没钱了。◇ *The mistake had terrible consequences.* 这个错误造成严重后果。

consequently /ˈkɒnsɪkwəntli; ˈkɑnsəˌkwɛntlɪ/ *adverb* 副词
because of that; therefore 所以；因而: *He didn't do any work, and consequently failed the exam.* 他什么功课都不做，所以没考及格。

conservation /ˌkɒnsəˈveɪʃn; ˌkɑnsəˈveʃən/ *noun* 名词 (no plural 无复数)
taking good care of the world and its forests, lakes, plants, and animals 对大自然的保护；环境保护: *the conservation of the rain forests* 对热带雨林的保护

the Conservative Party /ðə kənˈsɜːvətɪv pɑːti; ðə kənˈsɝvətɪv pɑrtɪ/ *noun* 名词
one of the important political parties in Britain（英国的）保守党 ☞ Look at **the Labour Party** and **the Liberal Democrats**. 见 **the Labour Party** 和 **the Liberal Democrats**。

consider /kənˈsɪdə(r); kənˈsɪdɚ/ *verb* 动词 (**considers, considering, considered** /kənˈsɪdəd; kənˈsɪdɚd/)
1 think carefully about something 考虑；细想: *I'm considering going to Italy on holiday.* 我正在考虑到意大利去度假。◇ *We must consider what to do next.* 我们得考虑下一步怎么办。
2 think that something is true 认为；主张: *I consider her to be a good teacher.* 我认为她是个好老师。
3 think about the feelings of other people when you do something（做某事时）考虑到别人的感受: *I can't move to*

C

Australia next month! I have to consider my family. 我不能下个月就搬到澳大利亚去！我还得考虑我的家庭呢。

considerable /kən'sɪdərəbl; kən'sɪdərəbl̩/ *adjective* 形容词
great or large 相当多的；相当大的: *The car cost a considerable amount of money.* 这辆汽车价钱很高。
considerably /kən'sɪdərəbli; kən'sɪdərəblɪ/ *adverb* 副词
My flat is considerably smaller than yours. 我的公寓比你的小得多。

considerate /kən'sɪdərət; kən'sɪdərɪt/ *adjective* 形容词
A person who is considerate is kind, and thinks and cares about other people 为他人着想的；体贴别人的: *Please be more considerate and don't play loud music late at night.* 请多为别人着想，夜深时音乐声别太大。✪ opposite 反义词: **inconsiderate**

consideration /kən͵sɪdə'reɪʃn; kən͵sɪdə'reʃən/ *noun* 名词 (no plural 无复数)
1 thinking carefully about something 考虑；思考: *After a lot of consideration, I decided not to accept the job.* 我经再三考虑，决定不接受这份工作。
2 being kind, and caring about other people's feelings（对他人心情的）关切；照顾；体贴: *He shows no consideration for anybody else.* 他对谁都毫不关心。
take something into consideration think carefully about something when you are deciding（做决定时）考虑到某事物: *We must take the cost into consideration when choosing where to go on holiday.* 我们选择度假去处时要考虑到费用问题。

consist /kən'sɪst; kən'sɪst/ *verb* 动词 (**consists, consisting, consisted**)
consist of something be made of something; have something as parts 由某事物做成、构成或组成: *Jam consists of fruit and sugar.* 果酱是由水果和糖做的。

consistent /kən'sɪstənt; kən'sɪstənt/ *adjective* 形容词
always the same 一贯的；前后一致的: *His work isn't very consistent — sometimes it's good and sometimes it's terrible!* 他的工作状况不稳定——有时候很好，有时候很糟！✪ opposite 反义词: **inconsistent**

consonant /'kɒnsənənt; 'kɑnsənənt/ *noun* 名词
any letter of the alphabet that is not *a, e, i, o* or *u*, or the sound that you make when you say it 辅音字母；辅音 ☞ Look at **vowel**. 见 **vowel**。

constable /'kʌnstəbl; 'kɑnstəbl̩/ *noun* 名词
an ordinary police officer 警察

constant /'kɒnstənt; 'kɑnstənt/ *adjective* 形容词
Something that is constant happens all the time 不断发生的；不停的: *the constant noise of traffic* 车辆发出的不停的噪音
constantly *adverb* 副词
She talked constantly all evening. 她滔滔不绝地说了一晚上。

constituency /kən'stɪtjuənsi; kən'stɪtʃʊənsɪ/ *noun* 名词 (*plural* 复数作 **constituencies**)
a town or an area that chooses one **Member of Parliament** (a person in the government) 选区（选出的议员叫做 **Member of Parliament**）

constitution /͵kɒnstɪ'tju:ʃn; ͵kɑnstə'tuʃən/ *noun* 名词
the laws of a country 宪法: *the United States constitution* 美国宪法

construct /kən'strʌkt; kən'strʌkt/ *verb* 动词 (**constructs, constructing, constructed**)
build something 建筑或建造某物: *The bridge was constructed out of stone.* 这座桥是用石头修筑的。✪ **Build** is the word that we usually use. ＊ **build** 是常用词。
construction /kən'strʌkʃn; kən'strʌkʃən/ *noun* 名词
1 (no plural 无复数) building something 建筑或建造某物: *the construction of a new motorway* 新高速公路的修筑
2 (*plural* 复数作 **constructions**) something that people have built 建筑物

consult /kən'sʌlt; kən'sʌlt/ *verb* 动词 (**consults, consulting, consulted**)
ask somebody or look in a book when you want to know something 请教某人；查阅书籍: *If the pain doesn't go away, you should consult a doctor.* 要是疼痛不止，你就得找大夫看看了。

consume /kən'sju:m; kən'sum/ *verb* 动词 (**consumes, consuming, consumed** /kən'sju:md; kən'sumd/)
eat, drink or use something 吃、喝或用某

物；消费；消耗: *This car consumes a lot of petrol.* 这辆汽车很费油。

consumer *noun* 名词
a person who buys or uses something 消费者: *There are laws to protect consumers.* 有法律保护消费者。

consumption /kən'sʌmpʃn; kən'sʌmpʃən/ *noun* 名词 (no plural 无复数)
eating, drinking or using something 吃、喝或用某物；消费；消耗: *This car has a high petrol consumption* (= it uses a lot of petrol). 这辆汽车很费油。

contact¹ /'kɒntækt; 'kɑntækt/ *noun* 名词 (no plural 无复数)
meeting, talking to or writing to somebody 与某人会面、谈话或通信；交往: *Until Jenny went to school, she didn't have much contact with other children.* 珍妮在上学以前和别的孩子没什么来往。◇ *Are you still in contact with the people you met on holiday?* 你跟那些度假时候认识的人还有联系吗？◇ *Doctors come into contact with* (= meet) *a lot of people.* 医生接触的人很多。

contact² /'kɒntækt; 'kɑntækt/ *verb* 动词 (**contacts, contacting, contacted**)
telephone or write to somebody, or go to see them 与某人通话、通信或会面: *If you see this man, please contact the police.* 要是你看见这个男子，请与警方联系。

contact lens /'kɒntækt lenz; 'kɑntækt ˌlɛnz/ *noun* 名词 (*plural* 复数作 **contact lenses**)
a small round piece of plastic or glass that you wear in your eye so that you can see better 接触眼镜；隐形眼镜片

contain /kən'teɪn; kən'ten/ *verb* 动词 (**contains, containing, contained** /kən'teɪnd; kən'tend/)
have something inside it 包含；含有: *This box contains pens and pencils.* 这个盒子里盛着钢笔和铅笔。◇ *Chocolate contains a lot of sugar.* 巧克力里有很多糖分。

container /kən'teɪnə(r); kən'tenɚ/ *noun* 名词
a thing that you can put other things in. Boxes, bottles, bags and jars are all containers. 容器（箱子、盒子、瓶子、袋子、罐子都是容器）

content /kən'tent; kən'tɛnt/ *adjective* 形容词
happy with what you have 知足的；满足的；满意的: *She is not content with the money she has — she wants more.* 她不满足自己现有的钱——她还想要多些。

contented *adjective* 形容词
happy 愉快的: *a contented smile* 愉快的微笑 ✪ opposite 反义词: **discontented**

contents /'kɒntents; kən'tɛnts/ *noun* 名词 (plural 复数)
what is inside something 所容纳之物；所含之物；内容: *I poured the contents of the bottle into a bowl.* 我把瓶子里的东西倒到碗里了。◇ *The contents page of a book tells you what is in it.* 书中有目录的一页，说的是书中的内容。

contest /'kɒntest; 'kɑntɛst/ *noun* 名词
a game or competition that people try to win 比赛；竞赛: *a boxing contest* 拳击比赛

contestant /kən'testənt; kən'tɛstənt/ *noun* 名词

C

containers 容器

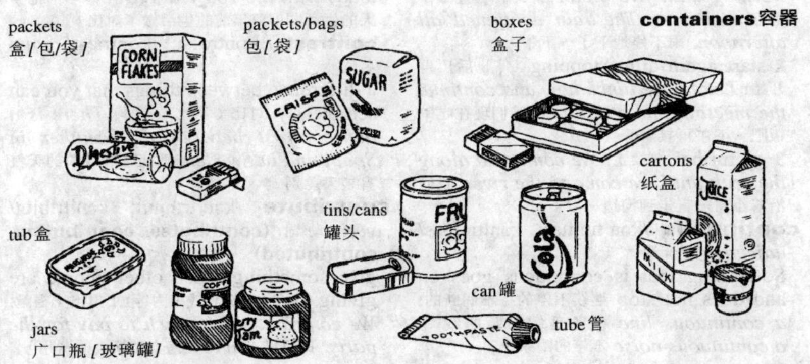

a person who tries to win a contest 比赛者；竞赛者: *There are six contestants in the race.* 有六个参赛者参加这场赛跑。

context /'kɒntekst; 'kɑntɛkst/ *noun* 名词
the words that come before and after another word or a sentence 上下文: *You can often understand the meaning of a word by looking at its context.* 看看一个词所在的上下文往往可以理解其含义。

C

continent /'kɒntɪnənt; 'kɑntənənt/ *noun* 名词
one of the seven big pieces of land in the world, for example Africa, Asia or Europe 洲（世界上的七大洲之一，如非洲、亚洲或欧洲）；大陆 ✪ In Britain, people sometimes say **the Continent** when they mean the main part of Europe. 在英国，有时说 **the Continent** 是指欧洲大陆。

continental /ˌkɒntɪ'nentl; ˌkɑntə'nɛntl̩/ *adjective* 形容词
a continental climate 大陆性气候

continual /kən'tɪnjuəl; kən'tɪnjʊəl/ *adjective* 形容词
that happens often 常发生的；频繁的: *We have had continual problems with this machine.* 我们这个机器常出问题。

continually /kən'tɪnjuəli; kən'tɪnjʊəlɪ/ *adverb* 副词
He is continually late for work. 他上班经常迟到。

continue /kən'tɪnju:; kən'tɪnjʊ/ *verb* 动词 (**continues**, **continuing**, **continued** /kən'tɪnju:d; kən'tɪnjʊd/)
1 not stop happening or doing something 继续做某事物: *We continued working until five o'clock.* 我们一直工作到五点钟。◇ *The rain continued all afternoon.* 雨不停地下了一下午。
2 start again after stopping（停止后）再开始: *Let's have lunch now and continue the meeting this afternoon.* 咱们现在吃午饭吧，下午再接着开会。
3 go further 继续走: *We continued along the path until we came to the river.* 我们沿着小路一直走到河边。

continuous /kən'tɪnjuəs; kən'tɪnjʊəs/ *adjective* 形容词
Something that is continuous goes on and does not stop 继续不停的；不间断的: *a continuous line* 一条延续不断的线 ◇ *a continuous noise* 不停的嘈杂声

continuously *adverb* 副词
It rained continuously for five hours. 雨一连下了五个小时。

contract /'kɒntrækt; 'kɑntrækt/ *noun* 名词
a piece of paper that says that somebody agrees to do something 合同；契约: *The company has signed a contract to build the new road.* 这家公司已经签约修建这条新路。

contradict /ˌkɒntrə'dɪkt; ˌkɑntrə'dɪkt/ *verb* 动词 (**contradicts**, **contradicting**, **contradicted**)
say that something is wrong or not true 说出某事物是错的或不属实；反驳；驳斥: *I said we didn't have any coffee, but Jill contradicted me.* 我说我们没有咖啡了，但是吉尔说我不了解情况。

contrary[1] /'kɒntrəri; 'kɑntrɛrɪ/ *noun* 名词 (no plural 无复数)
on the contrary the opposite is true 正相反；恰恰相反: *'You look ill, Ben.' 'On the contrary, I feel fine!'* "本，你气色不好。""不，我很好！"

contrary[2] /'kɒntrəri; 'kɑntrɛrɪ/ *adjective* 形容词
contrary to something very different from something; opposite to something 相反的；相对的: *He didn't stay in bed, contrary to the doctor's orders.* 他没有卧床，没听大夫的话。

contrast /kən'trɑ:st; kən'træst/ *verb* 动词 (**contrasts**, **contrasting**, **contrasted**)
look at or think about two or more things together and see the differences between them 对比；对照: *The book contrasts life today with life 100 years ago.* 这本书把今天的生活同100年前的生活做了对比。

contrast /'kɒntrɑ:st; 'kɑntræst/ *noun* 名词
a difference between things that you can see clearly 对比；相比；差异: *There is a big contrast between the weather in Spain and in Sweden.* 西班牙和瑞典的天气有很大差别。

contribute /kən'trɪbju:t; kən'trɪbjʊt/ *verb* 动词 (**contributes**, **contributing**, **contributed**)
give something when other people are giving too 出一份（钱、力等）；捐出；捐献: *We contributed £10 each to pay for the party.* 我们每人出10英镑支付聚会的费用。

contribution /ˌkɒntrɪˈbjuːʃn; ˌkɑntrəˈbjuʃən/ *noun* 名词
something that you give when other people are giving too 付出、捐出或捐献的东西: *We are sending contributions of food and clothing to people in poor countries.* 我们把捐献的食物和衣物送给贫穷国家的人民。

control¹ /kənˈtrəʊl; kənˈtrol/ *noun* 名词
1 (no plural 无复数) the power to make people or things do what you want 控制或操纵的能力或权力: *Who has control of the government?* 谁操纵着政府的大权? ◇ *A teacher must be in control of the class.* 教师必须要掌握住课堂情况。
2 controls (plural 复数) the parts of a machine that you press or move to make it work (机器的)操纵装置: *the controls of an aeroplane* 飞机的操纵装置
lose control not be able to make people or things do what you want 不能控制; 无法操纵: *The driver lost control and the bus went into the river.* 司机没能控制住公共汽车, 结果掉进河里了。
out of control If something is out of control, you cannot stop it or make it do what you want 失去控制; 无法止住: *The noise frightened the horse and it got out of control.* 响声把马吓惊了, 不受控制了。
under control If something is under control, it is doing what you want it to do 受控制; 受操纵: *The firemen have the fire under control.* 消防队把火势控制住了。

control² /kənˈtrəʊl; kənˈtrol/ *verb* 动词 (**controls, controlling, controlled** /kənˈtrəʊld; kənˈtrold/)
make people or things do what you want 控制; 操纵: *He can't control his dog.* 他管不住他的狗。◇ *This switch controls the heating.* 这个按钮是管暖气的。
controller *noun* 名词
a person who controls something 负责人; 管理员: *an air traffic controller* 航空调度员

convenience /kənˈviːniəns; kənˈvinjəns/ *noun* 名词 (no plural 无复数)
being easy to use; making things easy 方便; 便利; 省事: *For convenience, I usually do all my shopping in the same place.* 我图省事, 通常什么东西都在一个地方买。

convenient /kənˈviːniənt; kənˈvinjənt/ *adjective* 形容词
1 easy to use or go to 容易使用或到达的: *The house is very convenient for the station.* 这所房子离车站很近。
2 easy for somebody or something; suitable 方便的; 便利的; 合适的: *Let's meet on Friday. What's the most convenient time for you?* 咱们星期五见吧。几点钟对你最方便?
✪ opposite 反义词: **inconvenient**
conveniently *adverb* 副词
We live conveniently close to the shops. 我们住的地方到商店去很近便。

convent /ˈkɒnvənt; ˈkɑnvɛnt/ *noun* 名词
a place where religious women, called **nuns**, live, work and pray 女修道院 (其中的修女叫做 **nun**)

conversation /ˌkɒnvəˈseɪʃn; ˌkɑnvəˈseʃən/ *noun* 名词
a talk 谈话; 交谈: *She had a long conversation with her friend on the phone.* 她和朋友打电话说了很长时间。

conversion /kənˈvɜːʃn; kənˈvɝʒən/ *noun* 名词
changing something into another thing 转变; 转换: *the conversion of pounds into dollars* 把英镑兑换成美元

convert /kənˈvɜːt; kənˈvɝt/ *verb* 动词 (**converts, converting, converted**)
change into another thing 转变; 转换: *They converted the house into two flats.* 他们把那所房子改建成两个单元了。

convict /kənˈvɪkt; kənˈvɪkt/ *verb* 动词 (**convicts, convicting, convicted**)
decide in a court of law that somebody has done something wrong 宣判某人有罪: *She was convicted of murder and sent to prison.* 她被判有谋杀罪入狱。

convince /kənˈvɪns; kənˈvɪns/ *verb* 动词 (**convinces, convincing, convinced** /kənˈvɪnst; kənˈvɪnst/)
make somebody believe something 使某人确信某事: *I couldn't convince him that I was right.* 我无法让他相信我对。
convinced *adjective* 形容词
certain 确信的; 肯定的: *I'm convinced that I have seen her somewhere before.* 我肯定以前在哪儿见过她。

cook¹ /kʊk; kuk/ *verb* 动词 (**cooks, cooking, cooked** /kʊkt; kukt/)
make food ready to eat by heating it

烹调；做饭菜：*My father cooked the dinner.* 我父亲做好了这顿饭。◇ *I am learning to cook.* 我正在学烹饪。

> ✪ There are many words for ways of cooking food. 表达各种烹调方法有很多词语。Look at **bake**, **boil**, **fry**, **grill**, **roast**, **stew** and **toast**. 见 **bake**、**boil**、**fry**、**grill**、**roast**、**stew**、**toast** 各词条。

C

cooking *noun* 名词 (no plural 无复数)
1 making food ready to eat 烹调；做饭菜：*Who does the cooking in your family?* 你们家谁做饭？
2 what you cook 饭菜：*Italian cooking* 意大利饭

cook² /kʊk; kuk/ *noun* 名词
a person who cooks 做饭的人；厨师：*She works as a cook in a big hotel.* 她在一家大旅馆里当厨师。◇ *He is a good cook.* 他很会做饭。

cooker /'kʊkə(r); 'kʊkɚ/ *noun* 名词
a thing that you use in a kitchen for cooking food. It has an **oven** for cooking food inside it and places for heating pans on the top 炉具（其中有烤箱，叫做 **oven**，上面有炉架）：*an electric cooker* 电炉具

cookery /'kʊkəri; 'kʊkərɪ/ *noun* 名词 (no plural 无复数)
making food ready to eat, often as a subject that you can study 烹调技术；（常指）烹饪科目：*cookery lessons* 烹饪课

cookie /'kʊki; 'kʊkɪ/ *American English for* **biscuit** 美式英语，即 **biscuit**

cool¹ /ku:l; kul/ *adjective* 形容词 (**cooler**, **coolest**)
1 a little cold; not warm 凉的；不热的：*cool weather* 凉爽的天气 ◇ *I'd like a cool drink.* 我想要个冷饮。
2 calm; not excited 冷静的；不激动的

cool² /ku:l; kul/ *verb* 动词 (**cools**, **cooling**, **cooled** /ku:ld; kuld/)
make something less hot; become less hot 使某物凉；变凉：*Take the cake out of the oven and leave it to cool.* 把蛋糕从烤箱里拿出来凉一凉。
cool down **1** become less hot 变凉：*We swam in the river to cool down after our long walk.* 我们走了长路以后，到河里游泳凉快一下。 **2** become less excited or angry 冷静下来；消气

cooperate /kəʊ'ɒpəreɪt; ko'ɑpə͵ret/ *verb* 动词 (**cooperates**, **cooperating**, **cooperated**)
work together with someone else in a helpful way 合作；协作：*The two companies are cooperating with each other.* 这两个公司正在彼此合作。
cooperation /kəʊ͵ɒpə'reɪʃn; ko͵ɑpə'reʃən/ *noun* 名词 (no plural 无复数)
help 帮助；协助：*Thank you for your cooperation.* 感谢您的帮助。

cooperative /kəʊ'ɒpərətɪv; ko'ɑpərətɪv/ *adjective* 形容词
happy to help 乐于相助的；合作的：*The police asked her a lot of questions and she was very cooperative.* 警方问了她许多问题，她有问必答。

cope /kəʊp; kop/ *verb* 动词 (**copes**, **coping**, **coped** /kəʊpt; kopt/)
cope with somebody or 或 **something** do something well although it is difficult 对付；应付：*She has four young children. I don't know how she copes with them!* 她有四个小孩儿。我不知道她怎么带得了！

copied *form of* **copy²** ✳ **copy²** 的不同形式

copies
1 *plural of* **copy¹** ✳ **copy¹** 的复数形式
2 *form of* **copy²** ✳ **copy²** 的不同形式

copper /'kɒpə(r); 'kɑpɚ/ *noun* 名词 (no plural 无复数)
a metal with a colour between brown and red 铜：*copper wire* 铜丝

copy¹ /'kɒpi; 'kɑpɪ/ *noun* 名词 (*plural* 复数作 **copies**)
1 a thing that is made to look exactly like another thing 复制品：*This isn't a real painting by Van Gogh. It's only a copy.* 这不是凡·高的真品。只不过是个赝品罢了。◇ *The secretary made two copies of the letter.* 秘书把信复印了两份。
2 one example of a book or newspaper （书的）一本；（报纸的）一份：*Two million copies of the newspaper are sold every day.* 这种报纸每天卖二百万份。

copy² /'kɒpi; 'kɑpɪ/ *verb* 动词 (**copies**, **copying**, **copied** /'kɒpid; 'kɑpɪd/, **has copied**)
1 write or draw something so that it is exactly the same as another thing 抄写；描画：*The teacher asked us to copy the*

list of words into our books. 老师让我们把那些词语都抄到本子上。

2 try to look or do the same as another person 模仿: *Tom always copies what his brother does.* 汤姆总是模仿他哥哥的做法。

cord /kɔ:d; kɔrd/ *noun* 名词
strong thick string 绳索

core /kɔ:(r); kɔr/ *noun* 名词
the middle part of some kinds of fruit, where the seeds are 果心: *an apple core* 苹果核

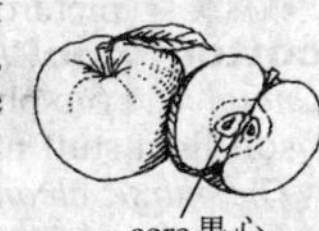

cork /kɔ:k; kɔrk/ *noun* 名词
1 (no plural 无复数) light strong stuff that comes from the outside of a special tree 软木
2 (*plural* 复数作 **corks**) a piece of cork that you put in a bottle to close it 软木塞

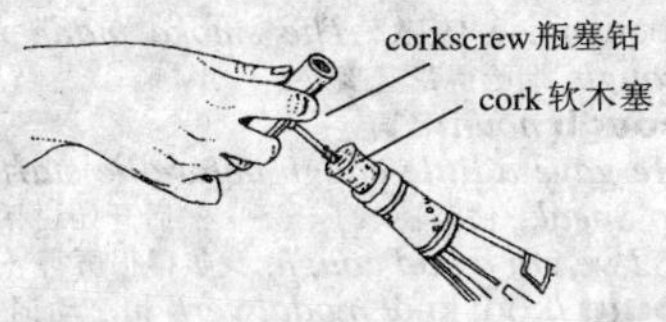

corkscrew /'kɔ:kskru:; 'kɔrk,skru/ *noun* 名词
a thing that you use for taking corks out of bottles 瓶塞钻（拔软木瓶塞用的）

corn /kɔ:n; kɔrn/ *noun* 名词 (no plural 无复数)
the seeds of plants like wheat or oats 谷物

corner 角儿

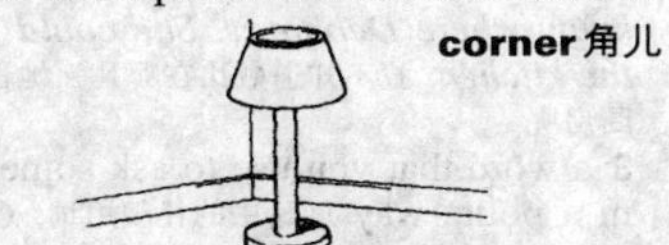
The lamp is in the **corner**. 灯在墙角儿那儿。

The bank is on the **corner**. 银行在拐角处。

corner /'kɔ:nə(r); 'kɔrnɚ/ *noun* 名词
a place where two lines, walls or roads meet 角儿；角落

cornflakes /'kɔ:nfleɪks; 'kɔrn,fleks/ *noun* 名词 (plural 复数)
food made from corn, that you eat with milk for breakfast. Cornflakes are a kind of **cereal**. 玉米片（加奶作早餐用，是一种用谷物做的早餐食品，叫做 **cereal**）

corporation /,kɔ:pə'reɪʃn; ,kɔrpə'reʃən/ *noun* 名词
1 a big company 大的公司: *the British Broadcasting Corporation* 英国广播公司
2 a group of people that the people in a town choose, who meet to decide things 市政当局

corpse /kɔ:ps; kɔrps/ *noun* 名词
the body of a dead person（人的）尸体

correct[1] /kə'rekt; kə'rɛkt/ *adjective* 形容词
right or true; with no mistakes 对的；正确的: *All your answers were correct.* 你全都答对了。◇ *What is the correct time, please?* 请问，现在准确时间是几点几分了？
✪ opposite 反义词: **incorrect**

correctly *adverb* 副词
Have I spelt your name correctly? 你的名字我拼得对不对？

correct[2] /kə'rekt; kə'rɛkt/ *verb* 动词 (**corrects, correcting, corrected**)
show where the mistakes are in something and make it right 改正；修改；纠正: *The class did the exercises and the teacher corrected them.* 全班同学做完练习，老师给他们修改。◇ *Please correct me if I make a mistake.* 要是我出了错儿，请您纠正。

correction /kə'rekʃn; kə'rɛkʃən/ *noun* 名词
the right word or answer that is put in the place of what was wrong 经改正的字或答案: *When the teacher gave my homework back to me it was full of corrections.* 老师把我的作业发还给我，批改之处比比皆是。

correspond /,kɒrə'spɒnd; ,kɔrə'spɑnd/ *verb* 动词 (**corresponds, corresponding, corresponded**)
be the same, or almost the same 相同的；相似的；相当的: *Does the name on the envelope correspond with the name inside the letter?* 信封上的名字和信瓤里的相符吗？

correspondence /,kɒrə'spɒndəns; ,kɔrə'spɑndəns/ *noun* 名词 (no plural 无复数)

writing letters; the letters that somebody writes or receives 通信；信件: *Her secretary reads all her correspondence.* 她的秘书阅读她所有的信件。

corridor /'kɒrɪdɔ:(r); 'kɔrədɚ/ *noun* 名词
a long narrow part inside a building with rooms on each side of it（建筑物中的）过道（两旁有房间）

C

cosmetics /kɒz'metɪks; kɑz'mɛtɪks/ *noun* 名词 (plural 复数)
special powders or creams that you use on your face or hair to make yourself more beautiful 化妆品

cost[1] /kɒst; kɔst/ *noun* 名词
1 the money that you must pay to have something 费用: *The cost of the repairs was very high.* 修理费非常高。
2 what you lose or give to have another thing 代价: *He saved the child at the cost of his own life.* 他以自己生命的代价救了那个孩子。
at all costs no matter what you must do to make it happen 不惜任何代价；无论如何: *We must win at all costs.* 我们无论如何必须赢。

cost[2] /kɒst; kɔst/ *verb* 动词 (**costs, costing, cost, has cost**)
1 have the price of 价钱为: *This plant cost £5.* 这种植物的价格是5英镑。◇ *How much did the book cost?* 那本书多少钱？
2 make you lose something 使失去某事物: *One mistake cost him his job.* 他这一个错误让他丢了工作。

costly /'kɒstli; 'kɔstlɪ/ *adjective* 形容词 (**costlier, costliest**)
expensive 昂贵的: *The repairs will be very costly.* 修理费非常高。

costume /'kɒstju:m; 'kɑstum/ *noun* 名词
the special clothes that people wear in a country or at a certain time（某国的或某时代的）服装: *The actors wore beautiful costumes.* 演员都穿着漂亮的服装。◇ *the national costume of Japan* 日本的民族服装 ☞ Look also at **swimming-costume**. 另见 **swimming-costume**。

cosy /'kəʊzi; 'kozɪ/ *adjective* 形容词 (**cosier, cosiest**)
warm and comfortable 暖和而舒适的: *a cosy room* 舒适的房间

cot /kɒt; kɑt/ *noun* 名词
a baby's bed with high sides（有高栏杆的）幼儿床

cottage /'kɒtɪdʒ; 'kɑtɪdʒ/ *noun* 名词
a small house in the country 村舍

cotton /'kɒtn; 'kɑtn̩/ *noun* 名词 (no plural 无复数)
cloth or thread that is made from the soft white stuff on the seeds of a plant that grows in hot countries 棉布或棉线: *a cotton shirt* 棉布衬衫 ◇ *a reel of cotton* 一轴棉线 ☞ picture at **sew** 见 **sew** 词条插图

cotton wool /ˌkɒtn 'wʊl; ˌkɑtn̩ 'wʊl/ *noun* 名词 (no plural 无复数)
soft light stuff made from cotton 脱脂棉: *The nurse cleaned the cut with cotton wool.* 护士用药棉擦伤口。

couch /kaʊtʃ; kaʊtʃ/ *noun* 名词 (*plural* 复数作 **couches**)
a long seat that you can sit or lie on（坐卧两用的）长沙发

cough /kɒf; kɔf/ *verb* 动词 (**coughs, coughing, coughed** /kɒft; kɔft/)
send air out of your throat with a sudden loud noise 咳嗽: *The smoke made me cough.* 烟呛得我直咳嗽。
cough *noun* 名词
He gave a little cough before he started to speak. 他轻轻咳了一下，然后开始讲话。◇ *I've got a bad cough.* 我咳得很厉害。

could /kʊd; kʊd/ *modal verb* 情态动词
1 the word for 'can' in the past ✳ can 的过去式: *He could run very fast when he was young.* 他小时候跑得很快。◇ *I could hear the birds singing.* 我听见鸟叫了。
2 a word that shows what will perhaps happen or what is possible 可能: *It could rain tomorrow.* 明天可能下雨。◇ *I don't know where Debbie is. She could be in the kitchen.* 我不知道戴比在哪儿。她也许在厨房呢。
3 a word that you use to ask something in a polite way 问话中的礼貌用词: *Could you open the door?* 您把门打开行吗？◇ *Could I have another drink, please?* 请再给我来一杯行吗？

✪ The negative form of 'could' is **could not** or the short form **couldn't** /'kʊdnt; 'kʊdn̩t/ ✳ could 的否定式是 **could not** 或缩略式 **couldn't** /'kʊdnt; 'kʊdn̩t/: *It was dark and I couldn't see anything.* 天很黑，我什么都看不见。

☞ Look at the Note on page 314 to find out more about **modal verbs**. 见第314页对 **modal verbs** 的进一步解释。

council /'kaʊnsl; 'kaʊnsl̩/ *noun* 名词
a group of people who are chosen to work together and to make rules and decide things 议会；政务会；委员会: *The city council is planning to build a new swimming-pool.* 市议会计划修建一个新游泳池。

councillor /'kaʊnsələ(r); 'kaʊnsl̩ɚ/ *noun* 名词
a member of a council 议员；政务会委员

council-house /'kaʊnsl haʊs; 'kaʊnsl̩ haʊs/ *noun* 名词
a house that a town or city owns, that you can rent 市、郡属有可供租用的房屋

count[1] /kaʊnt; kaʊnt/ *verb* 动词 (**counts, counting, counted**)
1 say numbers one after the other in the right order 数数: *The children are learning to count from one to ten.* 这些孩子正学着从一数到十。
2 look at people or things to see how many there are 数人或事物的数；计数: *I have counted the chairs—there are 32.* 我数了数椅子——有32把。
3 include somebody or something 包括某人或某事物: *There are five people in my family, counting me.* 我们家有五口人，包括我在内。
4 be important 有重要性；有价值: *He said that my ideas don't count because I'm only a child!* 他说我的主意不算数，因为我只是个孩子！
count on somebody feel sure that somebody will do something for you 信赖某人: *Can I count on you to help me?* 我全靠你帮忙了，行吗？

count[2] /kaʊnt; kaʊnt/ *noun* 名词
a time when you count things 计数: *After an election there is a count of all the votes.* 选举后要统计选票。
keep count of something know how many there are of something 知道某事物的数量: *Try to keep count of the number of tickets you sell.* 要记住你卖了多少票。
lose count of something not know how many there are of something 不知道某事物的数量

count[3] /kaʊnt; kaʊnt/ *noun* 名词
a man in some countries who has a special title 伯爵（某些国家男子的头衔）: *Count Dracula* 德拉库拉伯爵

counter /'kaʊntə(r); 'kaʊntɚ/ *noun* 名词
1 a long high table in a shop, bank or bar, that is between the people who work there and the people who want to buy things 柜台: *I put my money on the counter.* 我把钱放在柜台上了。
2 a small round thing that you use when you play some games （圆形的）筹码（用于某些游戏中的）

countess /'kaʊntəs; 'kaʊntɪs/ *noun* 名词 (*plural* 复数作 **countesses**)
a woman who has a special title. She may be married to a **count** or an **earl**. 女伯爵；伯爵夫人（嫁与伯爵 **count** 或 **earl** 者）

countless /'kaʊntləs; 'kaʊntlɪs/ *adjective* 形容词
very many 无数的；很多的: *I have tried to telephone him countless times.* 我给他打了多少次电话都打不通。

country /'kʌntri; 'kʌntrɪ/ *noun* 名词
1 (*plural* 复数作 **countries**) an area of land with its own people and government 国家: *France, Spain and Portugal are countries.* 法国、西班牙、葡萄牙都是国家。
2 the country (no plural 无复数) land that is not in a town 野外；郊野；乡村: *Do you live in the town or the country?* 你住在城里还是城外？

countryside /'kʌntrisaɪd; 'kʌntrɪˌsaɪd/ *noun* 名词 (no plural 无复数)
land with fields, woods, farms, etc, that is away from towns 野外；郊野；农村；乡村: *The countryside near York is very beautiful.* 约克一带的郊野非常漂亮。

county /'kaʊnti; 'kaʊntɪ/ *noun* 名词 (*plural* 复数作 **counties**)
one of the parts of Britain or Ireland（英国或爱尔兰的）郡: *Kent and Oxfordshire are counties in England.* 肯特郡和牛津郡都在英格兰。

couple /'kʌpl; 'kʌpl̩/ *noun* 名词
two people who are married, living together, etc（有婚姻、同居等关系的）两人；夫妻: *A young couple live next door.* 有一对年轻夫妇住在隔壁。
a couple of **1** two 两个: *I invited*

C

a couple of friends to lunch. 我请了两个朋友吃午饭。**2** a few 几个: *I'll be back in a couple of minutes.* 我几分钟后回来。

courage /ˈkʌrɪdʒ; ˈkɝɪdʒ/ *noun* 名词 (no plural 无复数)
not being afraid, or not showing that you are afraid when you do something dangerous or difficult 勇气: *She showed great courage when she went into the burning building to save the child.* 她进入燃烧着的大厦去抢救孩子，十分勇敢。

courageous /kəˈreɪdʒəs; kəˈredʒəs/ *adjective* 形容词
brave 勇敢的；英勇的；有胆量的: *a courageous young man* 勇敢的小伙子

courgette /kɔːˈʒet; kʊrˈʒɛt/ *noun* 名词
a long vegetable that is green on the outside and white on the inside 密生西葫芦

course /kɔːs; kɔrs/ *noun* 名词
1 a set of lessons on a certain subject 课程: *He's taking a course in computer programming.* 他正学习计算机程序设计课程。
2 one part of a meal 一道菜: *a three-course meal* 有三道菜的一顿饭 ◇ *I had chicken for the main course.* 我的主菜吃的是鸡。
3 a piece of ground for some kinds of sport（某类的）运动场: *a golf-course* 高尔夫球场 ◇ *a racecourse* 赛马场
4 the direction that something moves in 事物移动的方向: *We followed the course of the river.* 我们顺着河道走去。
5 the time when something is happening 某事发生的一段时间: *The telephone rang six times during the course of the evening.* 一晚上电话响了六次。
change course start to go in a different direction 改变方向: *The plane had to change course because of the storm.* 飞机因为遇到暴风雨而改变航向。
of course certainly 当然: *Of course I'll help you.* 我当然要帮助你。◇ *'Can I use your telephone?' 'Of course you can.'* "我用一用您的电话行吗？""当然可以。"◇ *'Are you angry with me?' 'Of course not!'* "你生我的气了吗？""绝对没有！"

court /kɔːt; kɔrt/ *noun* 名词
1 (*also* 亦作 **court of law**) a place where people (a **judge** or **jury**) decide if a person has done something wrong, and what the punishment will be 法庭；法院（法官叫做 **judge**，陪审团叫做 **jury**）: *The man will appear in court tomorrow.* 那个男子明天出庭。
2 a piece of ground where you can play a certain sport（某类的）运动场: *a tennis-court* 网球场

courtyard /ˈkɔːtjɑːd; ˈkɔrtˌjɑrd/ *noun* 名词
an open space without a roof, inside a building or between buildings 庭院；院子；天井

cousin /ˈkʌzn; ˈkʌzn̩/ *noun* 名词
the child of your aunt or uncle 堂（或表）兄、弟、姐或妹 ☞ picture on page C3 见第C3页图

cover[1] /ˈkʌvə(r); ˈkʌvɚ/ *verb* 动词 (**covers**, **covering**, **covered** /ˈkʌvəd; ˈkʌvɚd/)
1 put one thing over another thing to hide it or to keep it safe or warm 将一物放在另一物上（为安全或保暖）: *Cover the floor with a newspaper before you start painting.* 先把报纸铺在地上再粉刷。◇ *She covered her head with a scarf.* 她用头巾包着头。
2 be all over something 遍及某物: *Snow covered the ground.* 遍地都是雪。
be covered with or 或 **in something** have something all over yourself or itself 全身或全部都有某物: *The floor was covered in mud.* 地板上全是泥。

cover[2] /ˈkʌvə(r); ˈkʌvɚ/ *noun* 名词
1 a thing that you put over another thing, for example to keep it safe 遮盖住另一物之物（例如使之安全）；遮盖物；盖子；套子；罩子: *The computer has a plastic cover.* 这个计算机有个塑料罩儿。
2 the outside part of a book or magazine（书刊的）封面: *The book had a picture of a footballer on the cover.* 那本书的封面人物是个足球运动员。

coveralls /ˈkʌvərɔːlz; ˈkʌvəˌrɔlz/ *American English for* **overalls** 美式英语，即 **overalls**

covering /ˈkʌvərɪŋ; ˈkʌvərɪŋ/ *noun* 名词
something that covers another thing 遮盖住另一物之物；遮盖物: *There was a thick covering of snow on the ground.* 地上积着厚厚的雪。

cow /kaʊ; kaʊ/ *noun* 名词
a big female farm animal that gives milk 母牛

✪ The male is called a **bull** and a young cow is called a **calf**. 公牛叫做 **bull**，小牛叫做 **calf**。Meat from a cow is called **beef** and meat from a calf is called **veal**. 牛肉是 **beef**，小牛的肉是 **veal**。

coward /'kaʊəd; 'kaʊɚd/ *noun* 名词
a person who is afraid when there is danger or a problem 遇到危险或问题就害怕的人；胆小鬼

cowboy /'kaʊbɔɪ; 'kaʊˌbɔɪ/ *noun* 名词
a man who rides a horse and looks after cows on big farms in the USA 美国大农场中养马喂牛的男子；牛仔

crab /kræb; kræb/ *noun* 名词
an animal that lives in and near the sea. It has a hard shell and big claws. 螃蟹

crab 螃蟹

crack¹ /kræk; kræk/ *noun* 名词
1 a thin line on something where it is nearly broken 裂缝；裂纹: *There's a crack in this glass.* 这个玻璃杯上有个裂纹。
2 a sudden loud noise（突然发出的）大声: *a crack of thunder* 一声霹雳

crack² /kræk; kræk/ *verb* 动词 (**cracks**, **cracking**, **cracked** /krækt; krækt/)
break, but not into pieces 破裂（但没碎）: *The glass will crack if you pour boiling water into it.* 这只玻璃杯里倒进开水就会裂。◇ *This cup is cracked.* 这个杯子裂了。

cracker /'krækə(r); 'krækɚ/ *noun* 名词
1 a thin dry biscuit that you can eat with cheese 薄脆饼干（常与干酪一起食用）
2 a long round thing made of coloured paper with a small present inside. It makes a loud noise when two people pull the ends away from each other 彩包爆竹（彩色纸筒，内装小件礼物。两人各拉一端即劈啪作响）: *We often pull crackers at Christmas parties.* 我们在圣诞节聚会常常拉彩包爆竹玩儿。

crackle /'krækl; 'krækḷ/ *verb* 动词 (**crackles**, **crackling**, **crackled** /'krækld; 'krækḷd/)
make a lot of short sharp sounds 发出很多短而尖的声音: *Dry wood crackles when you burn it.* 干柴一燃烧就劈啪作响。

cradle /'kreɪdl; 'kredḷ/ *noun* 名词
a small bed for a baby 摇篮

craft /krɑ:ft; kræft/ *noun* 名词
a job in which you make things carefully and cleverly with your hands 手工艺；手艺；工艺: *Pottery and weaving are crafts.* 制陶和编织都是手工艺。

cram /kræm; kræm/ *verb* 动词 (**crams**, **cramming**, **crammed** /kræmd; kræmd/)
push too many people or things into something 把人或物塞进某处: *She crammed her clothes into a bag.* 她把衣服塞进袋子里了。

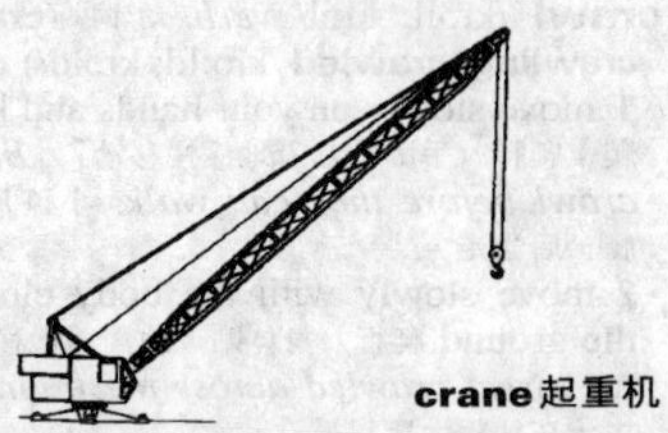

crane 起重机

crane /kreɪn; kren/ *noun* 名词
a big machine with a long part for lifting heavy things 起重机；吊车

crash¹ /kræʃ; kræʃ/ *noun* 名词 (*plural* 复数作 **crashes**)
1 an accident when something that is moving hits another thing 移动中的物体撞向另一物造成的事故: *He was killed in a car crash.* 他在汽车撞车事故中死亡。◇ *a plane crash* 飞机失事
2 a loud noise when something falls or hits another thing（一物落下或撞击另一物发出的）巨响: *I heard a crash as the tree fell.* 树倒的时候我听见咕咚一声。

crash² /kræʃ; kræʃ/ *verb* 动词 (**crashes**, **crashing**, **crashed** /kræʃt; kræʃt/)
1 have an accident; hit something 发生事故；撞击某物: *The bus crashed into a tree.* 公共汽车撞着树了。
2 make something hit another thing 使一物撞击另一物: *I crashed my father's car.* 我把父亲的汽车撞了。
3 fall or hit something with a loud noise

落下或撞击另一物发出巨响: *A tree crashed through the window.* 有棵树哗啦一声从窗外倒进屋里。

crash-helmet /ˈkræʃ helmɪt; ˈkræʃ-ˌhɛlmɪt/ *noun* 名词
a hard hat that you wear to keep your head safe 头盔: *Motor cyclists must wear crash-helmets in Britain.* 在英国骑摩托车必须戴头盔。

C

crate /kreɪt; kret/ *noun* 名词
a big box for carrying bottles or other things（运送瓶子等物品的）大箱子

crawl 爬

crawl /krɔːl; krɔl/ *verb* 动词 (**crawls, crawling, crawled** /krɔːld; krɔld/)
1 move slowly on your hands and knees 爬；爬行（手脚一起着地缓慢移动）: *Babies crawl before they can walk.* 小孩儿先会爬，后学走。
2 move slowly with the body close to the ground 爬行（身体贴近地面缓慢移动）: *An insect crawled across the floor.* 有个虫子在地板上爬过。
crawl *noun* 名词 (no plural 无复数)
a way of swimming on your front 爬泳；自由泳

crayon /ˈkreɪən; ˈkreən/ *noun* 名词
a soft thick coloured pencil 蜡笔: *The children were drawing pictures with crayons.* 孩子们正用蜡笔画画儿呢。

crazy /ˈkreɪzi; ˈkrezɪ/ *adjective* 形容词 (**crazier, craziest**)
mad or very stupid 疯狂的；愚蠢的: *You must be crazy to ride a bike at night with no lights.* 你夜里骑车不点灯，准是疯了。
crazy about somebody or 或 **something** If you are crazy about somebody or something, you like them very much 极爱某人或某事物；狂热的；热衷的: *She's crazy about football.* 她对足球着了迷。◇ *He's crazy about her.* 他爱她爱得不得了。
go crazy become very angry or excited 非常生气或激动: *My mum will go crazy if I get home late.* 我要是回家晚了，我妈妈就大发脾气。

creak /kriːk; krik/ *verb* 动词 (**creaks, creaking, creaked** /kriːkt; krikt/)
make a noise like a door that needs oil, or like an old wooden floor when you walk on it 发出嘎吱声（如门缺油或走在旧地板上发出的声音）
creak *noun* 名词
The door opened with a creak. 门吱的一声开了。

cream[1] /kriːm; krim/ *noun* 名词
1 (no plural 无复数) the thick liquid on the top of milk 奶油；乳脂: *Do you want cream in your coffee?* 你咖啡里要加奶油吗？
2 (*plural* 复数作 **creams**) a thick liquid that you put on your skin 乳霜；乳膏；润肤膏

cream[2] /kriːm; krim/ *adjective* 形容词
with a colour between white and yellow 奶油色: *She was wearing a cream dress.* 她穿着奶油色的连衣裙。

creamy /ˈkriːmi; ˈkrimɪ/ *adjective* 形容词
1 with cream in it: 含有奶油的 *a creamy sauce* 奶油沙司
2 like cream 像奶油的: *a creamy colour* 奶油色

crease /kriːs; kris/ *verb* 动词 (**creases, creasing, creased** /kriːst; krist/)
1 make untidy lines in paper or cloth by not being careful with it（纸或布）弄皱: *Don't sit on my jacket—you'll crease it.* 别坐在我的外衣上——看把它弄皱了。
2 become full of untidy lines 起皱: *This shirt creases easily.* 这件衬衫爱起皱。
crease *noun* 名词
a line in paper or cloth made by folding or pressing（纸或布折压成的）皱褶: *You need to iron this shirt—it's full of creases.* 你得熨熨这件衬衫了——满是褶子。

create /kriˈeɪt; krɪˈet/ *verb* 动词 (**creates, creating, created**)
make something new 创造；创作: *Do you believe that God created the world?* 你相信上帝创造世界的说法吗？◇ *The company has created a new kind of engine.* 这家公司研制了一个新型的发动机。

creation /kriˈeɪʃn; krɪˈeʃən/ *noun* 名词
1 (no plural 无复数) making something new 创造；创作: *the creation of the world* 创造世界
2 (*plural* 复数作 **creations**) a new thing that somebody has made 新创造的事物；

作品: *Mickey Mouse was the creation of Walt Disney.* 米老鼠是沃尔特·迪斯尼的作品。

creative /kri'eɪtɪv; krɪ'etɪv/ *adjective* 形容词
A person who is creative has a lot of new ideas or is good at making new things 有创造力的: *She's a very good painter—she's so creative.* 她是很出色的画家——很有创作能力。

creator /kri'eɪtə(r); krɪ'etɚ/ *noun* 名词
a person who makes something new 创造者；创作者: *Walt Disney was the creator of Mickey Mouse.* 沃尔特·迪斯尼是米老鼠的创作者。

creature /'kri:tʃə(r); 'kritʃɚ/ *noun* 名词
any living thing that is not a plant（除去植物以外的）一切生物: *birds, fish and other creatures* 鸟、鱼和其他动物 ◇ *This story is about creatures from another planet.* 这篇故事说的是从另一个星球来的生物。

credit[1] /'kredɪt; 'krɛdɪt/ *noun* 名词 (no plural 无复数)
buying something and paying for it later 先买东西，过后再付钱；赊购: *I bought the television on credit.* 我是用赊购方式买的这个电视机。

credit card /'kredɪt kɑ:d; 'krɛdɪt kɑrd/ *noun* 名词
a plastic card from a bank that you can use to buy something and pay for it later 信用卡: *Can I pay by credit card?* 我用信用卡付款行吗？

credit[2] /'kredɪt; 'krɛdɪt/ *noun* 名词 (no plural 无复数)
saying that somebody or something is good 称赞: *I did all the work but John got all the credit for it!* 工作都是我做的，可是受到称赞的都是约翰！

creep /kri:p; krip/ *verb* 动词 (**creeps, creeping, crept** /krept; krɛpt/, **has crept**)
move quietly and carefully so that nobody hears or sees you; move along close to the ground 悄悄地或小心地移动（以免被听见或看见）；紧贴地面移动；爬行: *The cat crept towards the bird.* 猫悄悄地向小鸟走去。◇ *I crept into the room where the children were sleeping.* 我一声不响地走进孩子们睡觉的屋子里。

crescent /'kreznt; 'krɛsn̩t/ *noun* 名词
1 the shape of the moon when it is less than half a circle 月牙；月牙形 ☞ picture on page C5 见第C5页图
2 a street or line of houses with a curved shape 成半圆形的街道或一排房屋: *I live at 34 Elgin Crescent.* 我住在埃尔金半圆路34号。

crew /kru:; kru/ *noun* 名词
all the people who work on a ship or an aeroplane（轮船或飞机上的）全体工作人员

cricket[1] /'krɪkɪt; 'krɪkɪt/ *noun* 名词
a small brown insect that makes a loud noise 蟋蟀；蛐蛐儿

cricket[2] /'krɪkɪt; 'krɪkɪt/ *noun* 名词 (no plural 无复数)
a game for two teams of eleven players who try to hit a small hard ball with a **bat** on a large field 板球运动（球板叫做**bat**）: *We watched a cricket match.* 我们观看了一场板球比赛。

cricketer *noun* 名词
a person who plays cricket 板球运动员

cried *form of* **cry**[1] ＊ **cry**[1] 的不同形式

cries
1 *form of* **cry**[1] ＊ **cry**[1] 的不同形式
2 *plural of* **cry**[2] ＊ **cry**[2] 的复数形式

crime /kraɪm; kraɪm/ *noun* 名词
something that somebody does that is against the law 罪；罪行: *Murder and robbery are serious crimes.* 谋杀和抢劫都是严重的罪行。

criminal[1] /'krɪmɪnl; 'krɪmən̩l/ *noun* 名词
a person who does something that is against the law 罪犯；犯人

criminal[2] /'krɪmɪnl; 'krɪmən̩l/ *adjective* 形容词
1 against the law 违法的；犯罪的: *Stealing is a criminal act.* 偷窃是犯罪行为。
2 of crime 关于犯罪的: *She is studying criminal law.* 她正在学习刑法。

crimson /'krɪmzn; 'krɪmzn̩/ *adjective* 形容词
with a dark red colour, like blood 深红色的

cripple /'krɪpl; 'krɪpl̩/ *verb* 动词 (**cripples, crippling, crippled** /'krɪpld; 'krɪpl̩d/)
hurt your legs or back badly so that you cannot walk 使双腿或腰背严重损伤而无法行走；使残废: *She was crippled in an accident.* 她在一次事故中身体残废了。

crisis /'kraɪsɪs; 'kraɪsɪs/ *noun* 名词 (*plural* 复数作 **crises** /'kraɪsi:z; 'kraɪsiz/)
a time when something very dangerous or serious happens 危机：*a political crisis* 政治危机

crisp¹ /krɪsp; krɪsp/ *adjective* 形容词 (**crisper**, **crispest**)
1 hard and dry 干而硬的；脆的：*If you keep the biscuits in a tin, they will stay crisp.* 饼干存放在罐子里就又酥又脆。
2 fresh and not soft 新鲜而不松软的；脆的：*crisp apples* 脆苹果

crisp² /krɪsp; krɪsp/ *noun* 名词
a very thin piece of potato cooked in hot oil 炸土豆片儿：*a packet of crisps* 一包炸土豆片儿

crisps 炸土豆儿片

critic /'krɪtɪk; 'krɪtɪk/ *noun* 名词
1 a person who says that somebody or something is wrong or bad 批评某人或某事物的人：*critics of the government* 批评政府的人
2 a person who writes about a book, film or play and says if he/she likes it or not（书刊、影片或戏剧的）评论者：*The critics liked his new film.* 影评人很喜欢他的新影片。

critical /'krɪtɪkl; 'krɪtɪkḷ/ *adjective* 形容词
1 If you are critical of somebody or something, you say that they are wrong or bad 批评的；指责的；非难的：*They were very critical of my work.* 他们对我的工作提出许多批评。
2 very serious or dangerous 非常严重的或危险的；危机的：*a critical illness* 极重的病
critically *adverb* 副词
She's critically ill. 她病得很重。

criticize /'krɪtɪsaɪz; 'krɪtəˌsaɪz/ *verb* 动词 (**criticizes**, **criticizing**, **criticized** /'krɪtɪsaɪzd; 'krɪtəˌsaɪzd/)
say that somebody or something is wrong or bad 批评：*He criticizes everything I do!* 我做什么事他都批评！
criticism /'krɪtɪsɪzəm; 'krɪtəˌsɪzəm/ *noun* 名词
what you think is bad about somebody or something 批评：*I listened to all their criticisms of my plan.* 我听着他们对我的计划提出的一切批评。

croak /krəʊk; krok/ *noun* 名词
the noise that a frog makes（青蛙的）呱呱叫声
croak *verb* 动词 (**croaks**, **croaking**, **croaked** /krəʊkt; krokt/)
make a noise like a frog makes 发出像青蛙的叫声

crockery /'krɒkəri; 'krɑkərɪ/ *noun* 名词 (no plural 无复数)
plates, cups and dishes 陶器（盘子、杯子、碟子）

crocodile /'krɒkədaɪl; 'krɑkəˌdaɪl/ *noun* 名词
a big long animal with sharp teeth. Crocodiles live in rivers in some hot countries 鳄；鳄鱼：*A crocodile is a reptile.* 鳄鱼是爬行动物。

crooked /'krʊkɪd; 'krʊkɪd/ *adjective* 形容词
not straight 歪斜的；扭曲的；弯曲的：*She has crooked teeth.* 她的牙不齐。

crop /krɒp; krɑp/ *noun* 名词
all the plants of one kind that a farmer grows at one time（一种作物一次的）收成；庄稼：*There was a good crop of potatoes last year.* 去年马铃薯收成很好。◇ *Rain is good for the crops.* 下雨对庄稼有好处。

cross¹ /krɒs; krɔs/ *noun* 名词 (*plural* 复数作 **crosses**)
1 a mark like + or X 十字形或叉形记号（如+或X）：*The cross on the map shows where I live.* 地图上打叉的就是我住的地方。
2 something with the shape + or X 十字形物或叉形物：*She wears a cross around her neck.* 她脖子上戴着一个十字坠儿。

cross² /krɒs; krɔs/ *verb* 动词 (**crosses**, **crossing**, **crossed** /krɒst; krɔst/)
1 go from one side of something to the other 从某物的一端走到另一端：*Be careful when you cross the road.* 过马路要小心。
2 put one thing over another thing 把一物放在另一物上：*She sat down and crossed her legs.* 她坐下以后双腿交叉着。
cross out draw a line through a word or words, for example because you have made a mistake 用划线方式把某词语（例如错的）除掉：*I crossed the word out and wrote it again.* 我把那个字划掉，又写了一个。

cross³ /krɒs; krɔs/ *adjective* 形容词
angry 生气的；恼怒的：*I was cross with*

her because she was late. 她晚了，我很生气。

crossing /'krɒsɪŋ; 'krɔsɪŋ/ *noun* 名词
a place where cars must stop for people to cross the road 人行横道

crossroads /'krɒsrəʊdz; 'krɔsˌrodz/ *noun* 名词 (*plural* 复数作 **crossroads**)
a place where two roads cross each other 十字路口；交叉路

crosswalk /'krɒswɔ:k; 'krɔsˌwɔk/ *American English for* **pedestrian crossing** 美式英语，即 **pedestrian crossing**

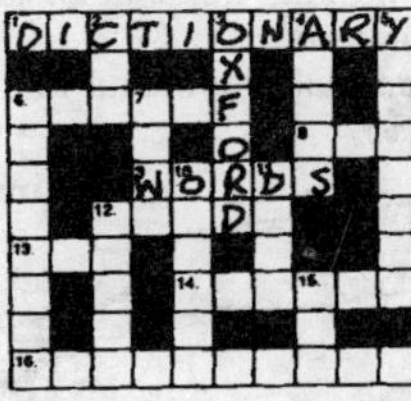

crossword 纵横字谜

crossword puzzle /'krɒswɜ:d pʌzl; 'krɔswɝd ˌpʌzḷ/, **crossword** /'krɒswɜ:d; 'krɔsˌwɝd/ *noun* 名词
a game on paper where you write words in squares 纵横字谜

crouch /kraʊtʃ; kraʊtʃ/ *verb* 动词 (**crouches**, **crouching**, **crouched** /kraʊtʃt; kraʊtʃt/)
bend your knees and back so that your body is close to the ground 蹲；蹲伏: *I crouched under the table to hide.* 我蹲在桌子底下藏着。

crow[1] /krəʊ; kro/ *noun* 名词
a large black bird that makes a loud noise 乌鸦

crow[2] /krəʊ; kro/ *verb* 动词 (**crows**, **crowing**, **crowed** /krəʊd; krod/)
make a loud noise like a male chicken (a **cock**) makes early in the morning（像公鸡般）啼叫（公鸡叫做 **cock**）

crowd /kraʊd; kraʊd/ *noun* 名词
a lot of people together 人群: *There was a large crowd at the football match.* 有一大群人正在看足球赛。

crowd *verb* 动词 (**crowds**, **crowding**, **crowded**)
come together in a big group 聚集: *The journalists crowded round the Prime Minister.* 新闻工作者把首相团团围住。

crowded *adjective* 形容词
full of people 人群拥挤的: *The streets were very crowded.* 街上人很挤。◇ *a crowded bus* 很挤的公共汽车

crown /kraʊn; kraʊn/ *noun* 名词
a special thing that a king or queen wears on his or her head at important times 王冠；皇冠

crown *verb* 动词 (**crowns**, **crowning**, **crowned** /kraʊnd; kraʊnd/)
put a crown on the head of a new king or queen 为新国王加冕: *Elizabeth II was crowned in 1952.* 伊丽莎白二世于1952年加冕。

crucial /'kru:ʃl; 'kruʃəl/ *adjective* 形容词
very important 极重要的: *a crucial moment* 紧要关头

cruel /'kru:əl; 'kruəl/ *adjective* 形容词 (**crueller**, **cruellest**)
A person who is cruel is unkind and likes to hurt other people or animals 残暴的；残忍的；残酷的: *I think it's cruel to keep animals in cages.* 我认为把动物关在笼子里很残忍。

cruelly /'kru:əli; 'kruəlɪ/ *adverb* 副词
in a cruel way 残暴地；残忍地；残酷地: *He was cruelly treated when he was a child.* 他小时候遭受残酷虐待。

cruelty /'kru:əlti; 'kruəltɪ/ *noun* 名词 (no plural 无复数)
being cruel 残暴；残忍；残酷: *cruelty to animals* 虐待动物

cruise /kru:z; kruz/ *noun* 名词
a holiday when you travel on a ship and visit a lot of different places 乘船旅游的假期: *They went on a world cruise.* 他们乘船环球旅游去了。

cruise *verb* 动词 (**cruises**, **cruising**, **cruised** /kru:zd; kruzd/)
travel on a ship as a holiday 乘船旅游度假: *They cruised around the Caribbean.* 他们乘船漫游加勒比海度假。

crumb /krʌm; krʌm/ *noun* 名词
a very small piece of bread, cake or biscuit（面包、蛋糕或饼干的）碎屑

crumble /'krʌmbl; 'krʌmbḷ/ *verb* 动词 (**crumbles**, **crumbling**, **crumbled** /'krʌmbld; 'krʌmbḷd/)
break into very small pieces 弄碎；碎成细屑: *The old castle walls are crumbling.* 那座古堡的城墙逐渐坍塌了。

crunch /krʌntʃ; krʌntʃ/ *verb* 动词 (**crunches**, **crunching**, **crunched** /krʌntʃt; krʌntʃt/)
1 make a loud noise when you eat something that is hard 嘎吱嘎吱地吃某硬物: *The dog was crunching a bone.* 狗啃着骨头。
2 make a noise like this when you press something hard（挤压时）发出嘎吱声: *The snow crunched under our feet as we walked.* 我们一边走，脚下的雪一边嘎吱嘎吱地响。

C

crush /krʌʃ; krʌʃ/ *verb* 动词 (**crushes**, **crushing**, **crushed** /krʌʃt; krʌʃt/)
press something very hard so that you break or damage it 把某物压碎或压坏: *She sat on my hat and crushed it.* 她把我的帽子坐扁了。

crust /krʌst; krʌst/ *noun* 名词
the hard part on the outside of bread 面包皮
crusty *adjective* 形容词
with a hard crust 有硬面包皮的: *crusty bread* 有硬皮的面包

crutch /krʌtʃ; krʌtʃ/ *noun* 名词 (*plural* 复数作 **crutches**)
a long stick that you put under your arm to help you walk when you have hurt your leg 腋夹拐杖: *He broke his leg and now he's on crutches* (= he walks using crutches). 他的腿断了，现在得撑着拐杖走路。

cry[1] /kraɪ; kraɪ/ *verb* 动词 (**cries**, **crying**, **cried** /kraɪd; kraɪd/, **has cried**)
1 have drops of water falling from your eyes, usually because you are unhappy 哭；流泪: *The baby cries a lot.* 那个小孩儿哭得很厉害。
2 shout or make a loud noise 喊；嚷；叫: *'Help!' he cried.* "救命啊！" 他喊着。◇ *She cried out in pain.* 她疼得喊叫起来。

cry[2] /kraɪ; kraɪ/ *noun* 名词 (*plural* 复数作 **cries**)
a loud noise that you make to show pain, fear or excitement, for example 喊；嚷；叫: *We heard her cries and ran to help.* 我们听见她喊就跑过去帮忙。◇ *the cry of a bird* 鸟的叫声

crystal /'krɪstl; 'krɪstḷ/ *noun* 名词
1 a kind of rock that looks like glass 水晶
2 a shape that some chemicals make when they are solid 结晶体: *salt crystals* 盐的结晶体

cub /kʌb; kʌb/ *noun* 名词
a young lion, bear, wolf, fox or tiger（狮子、熊、狼、狐狸或老虎的）幼兽

cube /kju:b; kjub/ *noun* 名词
a shape like a box with six square sides all the same size 立方形；立方体: *an ice-cube* 方形的冰块儿 ☞ picture on page C5 见第C5页图
cubic /'kju:bɪk; 'kjubɪk/ *adjective* 形容词
a cubic metre (= a space like a cube that is one metre long on each side) 一立方米（= 像每边一米的立方体的体积）

cuckoo /'kʊku:; 'kʊku/ *noun* 名词 (*plural* 复数作 **cuckoos**)
a bird that makes a sound like its name 布谷鸟；杜鹃

cucumber 黄瓜

cucumber /'kju:kʌmbə(r); 'kjukʌmbɚ/ *noun* 名词
a long vegetable with a green skin. You often eat it in salads. 黄瓜

cuddle /'kʌdl; 'kʌdḷ/ *verb* 动词 (**cuddles**, **cuddling**, **cuddled** /'kʌdld; 'kʌdḷd/)
hold somebody or something in your arms to show love 搂抱某人或某物（表示疼爱）: *He cuddled his baby.* 他抱着他的小孩儿。
cuddle *noun* 名词
give somebody a cuddle cuddle somebody 搂抱某人: *I gave her a cuddle.* 我拥抱了她一下。

cuff /kʌf; kʌf/ *noun* 名词
the end part of a sleeve, near your hand 袖口

cultivate /'kʌltɪveɪt; 'kʌltəˌvet/ *verb* 动词 (**cultivates**, **cultivating**, **cultivated**)
1 use land for growing plants 耕种: *Only a small area of the island was cultivated.* 岛上只有一小片地耕种过。
2 keep and care for plants 培育植物
cultivation /ˌkʌltɪ'veɪʃn; ˌkʌltə'veʃən/ *noun* 名词 (no plural 无复数)
cultivation of the land 种地

cultural /'kʌltʃərəl; 'kʌltʃərəl/ *adjective* 形容词

1 about the art, ideas and way of life of a group of people 文化的: *There are many cultural differences between Britain and Japan.* 英国和日本文化差异很大。
2 about things like art, music or theatre 艺术的

culture /'kʌltʃə(r); 'kʌltʃɚ/ *noun* 名词
the art, ideas and way of life of a group of people 文化: *She is studying the culture of the American Indians.* 她正在研究美洲印第安人的文化。

cunning /'kʌnɪŋ; 'kʌnɪŋ/ *adjective* 形容词
clever; good at making people believe something that is not true 狡猾的;善于欺骗人的;诡计多端的: *Their plan was quite cunning.* 他们的计划很狡猾。

cup /kʌp; kʌp/ *noun* 名词
1 a small round container with a handle, that you can drink from (有把儿的) 杯子: *a cup and saucer* 一套杯碟 ◇ *a cup of coffee* 一杯咖啡

2 a large metal thing like a cup, that you get for winning in a sport 奖杯

cupboard /'kʌbəd; 'kʌbɚd/ *noun* 名词
a piece of furniture with shelves and doors, where you keep things like clothes or food (存放衣物或食物的) 柜橱

cure[1] /kjʊə(r); kjʊr/ *verb* 动词 (**cures, curing, cured** /kjʊəd; kjʊrd/)
1 make an ill person well again 治愈病人: *The doctors can't cure her.* 大夫治不好她了。
2 make an illness go away 治愈疾病: *Can this disease be cured?* 这种病能治好吗?

cure[2] /kjʊə(r); kjʊr/ *noun* 名词
something that makes an illness go away 疗法;药物: *a cure for cancer* 治癌的疗法

curiosity /ˌkjʊəri'ɒsəti; ˌkjʊrɪ'ɑsətɪ/ *noun* 名词 (no plural 无复数)
wanting to know about things 好奇心: *I was full of curiosity about the letter.* 我对那封信十分好奇。

curious /'kjʊəriəs; 'kjʊrɪəs/ *adjective* 形容词
1 If you are curious, you want to know about something 好奇的: *I am curious to know where she found the money.* 我奇怪她在哪儿找到钱的。
2 strange or unusual 奇特的;不寻常的: *a curious noise* 奇怪的声音
curiously *adverb* 副词
'Where are you going?' she asked curiously. "你上哪儿去?" 她好奇地问。

curl[1] /kɜːl; kɝl/ *noun* 名词
a piece of hair in a round shape 鬈发
curly *adjective* 形容词 (**curlier, curliest**)
with a lot of curls 鬈发的: *He's got curly hair.* 他的头发是鬈的。 ☞ picture at **hair** 见 **hair** 词条插图

curl[2] /kɜːl; kɝl/ *verb* 动词 (**curls, curling, curled** /kɜːld; kɝld/)
bend into a round or curved shape 卷曲: *The leaves were brown and curled.* 叶子都黄了,卷了起来。
curl up put your arms, legs and head close to your body 蜷着身体: *The cat curled up by the fire.* 猫蜷着身体卧在炉子旁边。

currant /'kʌrənt; 'kɝənt/ *noun* 名词
1 a small sweet dried fruit 无子葡萄干
2 a small soft fruit 醋栗: *blackcurrants* 黑醋栗

currency /'kʌrənsi; 'kɝənsɪ/ *noun* 名词 (*plural* 复数作 **currencies**)
the money that a country uses 通货;货币: *The currency of the USA is the dollar.* 美国的货币是美元。

current[1] /'kʌrənt; 'kɝənt/ *adjective* 形容词
Something that is current is happening or used now 现在的;现行的: *current fashions* 当前的时装
currently *adverb* 副词
now 现在: *We are currently living in London.* 我们目前住在伦敦。

current[2] /'kʌrənt; 'kɝənt/ *noun* 名词
1 air or water that is moving 气流;水流: *It is dangerous to swim here because of the strong current.* 在这儿游泳很危险,水流太急。
2 electricity that is going through a wire 电流

curry /'kʌri; 'kɝɪ/ *noun* 名词 (*plural* 复数作 **curries**)
meat or vegetables cooked with spices. You often eat curry with rice 咖喱菜谱: *We had a curry in an Indian restaurant.* 我们在一家印度饭馆吃的是咖喱菜。

C

C

curse /kɜ:s; kɝs/ *noun* 名词
words that wish for something bad to happen to somebody 诅咒语: *The witch put a curse on him and he became a frog.* 女巫诅咒他，他就变成青蛙了。

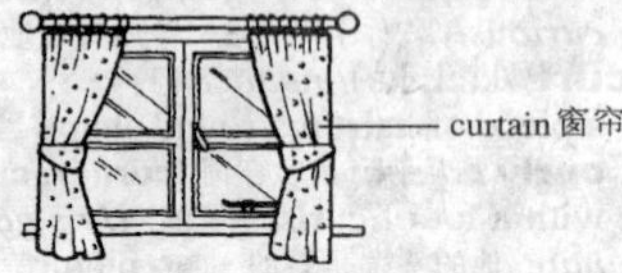
curtain 窗帘

curtain /'kɜ:tn; 'kɝtn̩/ *noun* 名词
a piece of cloth that you move to cover a window 窗帘

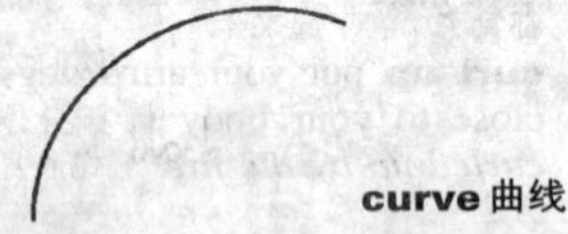
curve 曲线

curve /kɜ:v; kɝv/ *noun* 名词
a line that is not straight; a bend 曲线；弯处
curve *verb* 动词 (**curves**, **curving**, **curved** /kɜ:vd; kɝvd/)
make a round shape; bend 转变；形成圆形: *The road curves to the right.* 这条路转向右边。
curved *adjective* 形容词
a table with curved legs 弯腿的桌子 ◇ *a curved line* 曲线

cushion /'kʊʃn; 'kʊʃən/ *noun* 名词
a bag filled with something soft. You put it on a chair and sit on it or rest your body against it. 坐垫；靠垫；垫子

custard /'kʌstəd; 'kʌstɚd/ *noun* 名词 (no plural 无复数)
a sweet yellow sauce made with milk. You eat it with fruit or puddings. 蛋奶沙司（与水果或布丁一同食用）

custom /'kʌstəm; 'kʌstəm/ *noun* 名词
something that a group of people usually do 习俗；风俗: *It is a custom to give presents at Christmas.* 在圣诞节赠送礼物是一种习俗。

customer /'kʌstəmə(r); 'kʌstəmɚ/ *noun* 名词
a person who buys things from a shop 顾客

customs /'kʌstəmz; 'kʌstəmz/ *noun* 名词 (plural 复数)
the place at an airport or a port where you must show what you have brought with you from another country 海关: *a customs officer* 海关官员

cut[1] /kʌt; kʌt/ *verb* 动词 (**cuts**, **cutting**, **cut**, **has cut**)
1 break or make a hole in something with a knife or scissors, for example 切；剪: *I cut the string and opened the parcel.* 我把绳子剪断，打开包裹。◇ *I cut the apple in half* (= into two parts). 我把苹果切成两半。◇ *She cut her finger on some broken glass.* 她让碎玻璃把手指拉破了。
2 take one piece from something bigger（从较大物体上）切下或剪下: *Can you cut me a piece of cake, please?* 请给我切一块蛋糕行吗？
3 make something shorter with a knife or scissors, for example 削短或剪短: *Have you had your hair cut?* 你剪头发了吗？
be cut off be kept alone, away from other people 被孤立；与其他人隔离: *Our house was cut off from the village by the snow.* 大雪把我们的房子同村子的联系隔断了。
cut down **1** use, do or buy less of something 少用、少做或少买某事物: *The doctor told me to cut down on smoking.* 大夫让我少吸些烟。**2** cut something so that it falls down 将某物切、割或砍倒: *We cut down the old tree.* 我们把老树砍倒了。
cut off stop something 停止供应某物: *The workmen cut off the electricity.* 工人停止供电了。
cut out take something from the place where it was by using scissors, etc 切下或剪下某物: *I cut the picture out of the newspaper.* 我把那个画儿从报纸上剪下来了。
cut up break something into pieces with a knife or scissors, for example 切碎或剪碎

cut[2] /kʌt; kʌt/ *noun* 名词
a place where something has cut 破口: *I have a cut on my leg.* 我腿上有个口子。

cute /kju:t; kjut/ *adjective* 形容词 (**cuter**, **cutest**)
pretty 漂亮的: *What a cute little puppy!* 多漂亮的小狗哇！

cutlery /'kʌtləri; 'kʌtlərɪ/ *noun* 名词 (no plural 无复数)
knives, forks and spoons 刀子、叉子和勺儿

cycle /'saɪkl; 'saɪkḷ/ *noun* 名词
a bicycle 自行车；脚踏车: *a cycle shop* 自行车商店

cycle *verb* 动词 (**cycles**, **cycling**, **cycled** /'saɪkld; 'saɪkḷd/)
ride a bicycle 骑自行车: *I cycle to school every day.* 我每天骑自行车上学。✪ When you talk about cycling as a sport or for fun, you say **go cycling** 骑自行车运动或娱乐叫做 **go cycling**: *We went cycling in Holland last year.* 我们去年在荷兰骑自行车运动。

cyclist /'saɪklɪst; 'saɪklɪst/ *noun* 名词
a person who rides a bicycle 骑自行车的人

cylinder /'sɪlɪndə(r); 'sɪlɪndɚ/ *noun* 名词
a long round shape, like a tube or a tin of food 圆柱；圆柱体 ☞ picture on page C5 见第C5页图

cylindrical /sɪ'lɪndrɪkl; sɪ'lɪndrɪkḷ/ *adjective* 形容词
with this shape 圆柱形的

C

Dd

D

dab /dæb; dæb/ *verb* 动词 (**dabs**, **dabbing**, **dabbed** /dæbd; dæbd/)
touch something lightly and quickly 轻而快地触某物: *She dabbed the cut with cotton wool.* 她用药棉轻轻地按了按伤口。

dad /dæd; dæd/ *noun* 名词
father 爸爸；爹: *Hello, Dad.* 爸爸，您好。◇ *This is my dad.* 这是我爸爸。

daddy /'dædi; 'dædɪ/ *noun* 名词 (*plural* 复数作 **daddies**)
a word for 'father' that children use (儿语) 爸爸；爹爹

daffodil /'dæfədɪl; 'dæfəˌdɪl/ *noun* 名词
a yellow flower that grows in spring 水仙花

daft /dɑ:ft; dæft/ *adjective* 形容词 (**dafter**, **daftest**)
silly; stupid 傻的；愚蠢的: *I think you're daft to work for nothing!* 我认为你光干活儿不拿钱真傻！◇ *Don't be daft!* 别傻了你！

dagger /'dægə(r); 'dægɚ/ *noun* 名词
a short pointed knife that people use as a weapon 匕首

daily /'deɪli; 'delɪ/ *adjective*, *adverb* 形容词，副词
that happens or comes every day or once a day 每日的；每天一次的: *There are daily flights between London and New York.* 每天都有飞机来往于伦敦和纽约之间。◇ *a daily newspaper* 每日出版的报纸 ◇ *The museum is open daily from 9 a.m. to 5 p.m.* 博物馆开放时间是每天上午9时至下午5时。

dainty /'deɪnti; 'dentɪ/ *adjective* 形容词 (**daintier**, **daintiest**)
small and pretty 小巧精致的: *a dainty little girl* 娇小秀丽的女孩儿

dairy /'deəri; 'dɛrɪ/ *noun* 名词 (*plural* 复数作 **dairies**)
a place where milk is kept or where food like butter and cheese is made 牛奶场；奶制品场（如制造黄油和奶酪的）

daisy /'deɪzi; 'dezɪ/ *noun* 名词 (*plural* 复数作 **daisies**)
a small flower with white petals and a yellow middle 雏菊花

dam /dæm; dæm/ *noun* 名词
a wall that is built across a river to hold the water back 水坝；水堤；水闸

damage /'dæmɪdʒ; 'dæmɪdʒ/ *verb* 动词 (**damages**, **damaging**, **damaged** /'dæmɪdʒd; 'dæmɪdʒd/)
break or harm something 毁坏；伤害: *The house was badly damaged by fire.* 房子让大火给烧坏了。

damage *noun* 名词 (no plural 无复数)
He had an accident, but he didn't do any damage to his car. 他出事了，可是他的汽车倒一点也没撞坏。

damn /dæm; dæm/
a rude word that people sometimes use when they are angry (生气时有时用的粗话) 该死的；他妈的: *Damn! I've lost my key!* 倒霉！我钥匙丢了！

damp /dæmp; dæmp/ *adjective* 形容词 (**damper**, **dampest**)
a little wet 稍潮湿的: *a cold damp house* 又冷又潮的房子

dance[1] /dɑ:ns; dæns/ *verb* 动词 (**dances**, **dancing**, **danced** /dɑ:nst; dænst/)
move your body to music 跳舞: *Ian dances well.* 伊恩跳舞跳得好。◇ *I danced with her all night.* 我和她跳舞跳了一夜。

dancer *noun* 名词
a person who dances 跳舞的人；跳舞演员: *Nureyev was a famous ballet dancer.* 努里耶夫是个著名的芭蕾舞演员。◇ *I'm not a very good dancer.* 我不太会跳舞。

dancing *noun* 名词 (no plural 无复数)
moving to music 跳舞: *Will there be dancing at the party?* 在聚会上安排跳舞吗？

dance[2] /dɑ:ns; dæns/ *noun* 名词
1 movements that you do to music 跳舞；舞蹈
2 a party where people dance 舞会: *My parents are going to a dance tonight.* 我父母今天晚上去参加舞会。

danger /'deɪndʒə(r); 'dendʒɚ/ *noun* 名词
1 (no plural 无复数) the possibility that something bad may happen 危险: *You may be in danger if you travel alone late at night.* 深夜一个人出门可能有危险。
2 (*plural* 复数作 **dangers**) a person or thing that may bring harm or trouble 可能带来损伤或麻烦的人或事物: *Smoking is a danger to health.* 吸烟危害健康。

dangerous /'deɪndʒərəs; 'dendʒərəs/ *adjective* 形容词

A person or thing that is dangerous may hurt you（对人或事物）有危险的: *It's dangerous to drive a car at night without any lights.* 夜晚开车没有灯很危险。◇ *a dangerous illness* 重病

dangerously *adverb* 副词
She drives dangerously. 她车开得太危险了。

dare /deə(r); dɛr/ *verb* 动词 (**dares, daring, dared** /deəd; dɛrd/)

1 be brave enough to do something 敢；敢于；竟敢；胆敢: *I daren't tell Debbie that I've lost her book.* 我不敢告诉戴比我把她的书弄丢了。◇ *I didn't dare ask for more money.* 我不敢多要钱。

2 ask somebody to do something dangerous or silly to see if they are brave enough 激某人（看他敢不敢做危险的或愚蠢的事）: *I dare you to jump off that wall!* 我谅你不敢从那堵墙上跳下来！

don't you dare words that you use for telling somebody very strongly not to do something 严厉告诉某人不要做某事: *Don't you dare read my letters!* 你要是敢看我的信，哼！

how dare you words that show you are very angry about something that somebody has done 对某人已做的事感到愤怒的用语: *How dare you speak to me like that!* 你竟敢这样跟我说话！

daring /ˈdeərɪŋ; ˈdɛrɪŋ/ *adjective* 形容词
not afraid to do dangerous things 冒险的；大胆的

dark¹ /dɑːk; dɑrk/ *adjective* 形容词 (**darker, darkest**)

1 with no light, or not much light 黑暗的；暗的: *It was so dark that I couldn't see anything.* 天黑得我什么都看不见。◇ *It gets dark very early in the winter.* 冬天天黑得快。✪ opposite 反义词: **light**

2 A dark colour is nearer to black than to white 深色的: *a dark-green skirt* 深绿色的裙子 ◇ *He's got dark-brown eyes.* 他的眼睛是深棕色的。✪ opposite 反义词: **light** or 或 **pale**

3 A person who is dark has brown or black hair or skin（指人）毛发或皮肤棕色的或黑色的: *a thin, dark woman* 又黑又瘦的女子 ✪ opposite 反义词: **fair**

dark² /dɑːk; dɑrk/ *noun* 名词 (no plural 无复数)
where there is no light 黑暗；暗处: *Cats can see in the dark.* 猫在黑暗中也看得见东西。◇ *Are you afraid of the dark?* 你怕黑吗？

after dark after the sun goes down 太阳下山以后；天黑以后: *Don't go out alone after dark.* 天黑以后别一个人出去。

before dark before the sun goes down 太阳下山以前；天黑以前: *Make sure you get home before dark.* 你得天黑以前到家。

darkness /ˈdɑːknəs; ˈdɑrknɪs/ *noun* 名词 (no plural 无复数)
where there is no light 黑暗；暗处

in darkness with no light 黑暗的；在黑暗中: *The whole house was in darkness.* 房子里一片漆黑。

darling /ˈdɑːlɪŋ; ˈdɑrlɪŋ/ *noun* 名词
a name that you call somebody that you love 对心爱的人的称呼: *Are you all right, darling?* 你没事儿吧，亲爱的？

dart¹ /dɑːt; dɑrt/ *noun* 名词
a metal thing with a point at one end, that you throw at a round board in a game called **darts** 飞镖（掷镖游戏叫做 **darts**）

dart² /dɑːt; dɑrt/ *verb* 动词 (**darts, darting, darted**)
move quickly and suddenly 突然急速移动: *He darted across the road.* 他猛然冲过马路。

dash¹ /dæʃ; dæʃ/ *verb* 动词 (**dashes, dashing, dashed** /dæʃt; dæʃt/)
run quickly 飞跑: *I dashed into a shop when it started to rain.* 下起雨来了，我急忙跑进一家商店里。◇ *I must dash—I'm late for work.* 我得赶紧走了——上班已经晚了。

dash² /dæʃ; dæʃ/ *noun* 名词 (*plural* 复数作 **dashes**)

1 a mark (–) that you use in writing to show a short stop or to separate two parts of a sentence 破折号 (——)

2 a sudden short run 短距离的突然飞跑: *The robber made a dash for the door.* 劫匪向门口奔去。

data /ˈdeɪtə; ˈdætə/ *noun* 名词 (plural 复数)
facts or information 资料；数据: *We are studying the data that we have collected.* 我们正在研究我们搜集的资料。

date¹ /deɪt; det/ *noun* 名词
the number of the day, the month and

sometimes the year 日期；日子；（有时指）年份: *'What's the date today?' 'The first of February.'* "今天多少号？" "二月一号。" ◇ *Today's date is 11 September 1993.* 今天是1993年9月11日。◇ *What is your date of birth?* 你出生的日子是哪天？

out of date 1 not modern 非现时的；非现代的；陈旧的；过时的: *The machinery they use is completely out of date.* 他们用的机器全都是过时的。 **2** too old, so that you cannot use it 因过时而不能使用的: *This ticket is out of date.* 这张票已经过期了。

up to date 1 modern 现时的；现代的 **2** with the newest information 有最新信息的: *Is this list of names up to date?* 这份名单是新修正的吗？

D

date² /deɪt; det/ *noun* 名词

a small sweet brown fruit 枣

daughter /ˈdɔːtə(r); ˈdɔtɚ/ *noun* 名词

a girl or woman who is somebody's child 女儿: *They have two daughters and a son.* 他们有两个女儿一个儿子。◇ *My oldest daughter is a doctor.* 我的大女儿是医生。☞ picture on page C3 见第C3页图

daughter-in-law /ˈdɔːtər ɪn lɔː; ˈdɔtərɪnˌlɔ/ *noun* 名词 (*plural* 复数作 **daughters-in-law**)

the wife of your son 儿媳妇 ☞ picture on page C3 见第C3页图

dawn /dɔːn; dɔn/ *noun* 名词

the time when the sun comes up 黎明；拂晓

day /deɪ; de/ *noun* 名词 (*plural* 复数作 **days**)

1 a time of 24 hours from midnight to the next midnight 一天；一昼夜: *There are seven days in a week.* 一星期有七天。◇ *I went to Italy for a few days.* 我到意大利去了几天。◇ *'What day is it today?' 'Tuesday.'* "今天星期几？" "星期二。"

2 the time when it is light outside 白天: *Most people work during the day and sleep at night.* 大多数人白天工作夜里睡觉。

3 a time in the past 在过去的一段时期: *In my grandparents' day, not many people had cars.* 在我爷爷那个年头儿，有汽车的人不多。

one day 1 on a certain day in the past 在过去的某一天: *One day, a letter arrived.* 有一天来了一封信。✪ We often use **one day** at the beginning of a story. 讲故事常用 **one day** 开头。 **2** at some time in the future 将来的某时候: *I hope to visit Canada one day.* 我希望以后到加拿大去看看。

some day at some time in the future 将来的某时候: *Some day I'll be rich and famous.* 我总有一天能名利双收。

the day after tomorrow not tomorrow, but the next day 后天

the day before yesterday not yesterday, but the day before 前天

the other day a few days ago 几天前: *I went to London the other day.* 我前几天去了一趟伦敦。

these days now 目前: *A lot of people work with computers these days.* 很多人现在都使用计算机工作。

daylight /ˈdeɪlaɪt; ˈdeˌlaɪt/ *noun* 名词 (no plural 无复数)

the light from the sun during the day 日光: *These colours look different in daylight.* 这些颜色在阳光下看起来不一样。

day off /ˌdeɪ ˈɒf; ˈde ˈɔf/ *noun* 名词 (*plural* 复数作 **days off**)

a day when you do not go to work or school 不上班或不上学的日子；休息日

daytime /ˈdeɪtaɪm; ˈdeˌtaɪm/ *noun* 名词 (no plural 无复数)

the time when it is day and not night 白天；日间: *I prefer to study in the daytime and go out in the evening.* 我愿意白天学习晚上出去。

dazzle /ˈdæzl; ˈdæzl̩/ *verb* 动词 (**dazzles, dazzling, dazzled** /ˈdæzld; ˈdæzl̩d/)

If a light dazzles you, it shines brightly in your eyes so that you cannot see for a short time（因强光刺眼）一时看不见东西；眼花；目眩: *I was dazzled by the car's lights.* 汽车灯把我眼睛照花了。

dead¹ /ded; dɛd/ *adjective* 形容词

1 not living 死的: *All my grandparents are dead.* 我的祖父母和外祖父母都死了。◇ *Throw away those dead flowers.* 把那些谢了的花扔了吧。

2 very quiet 非常寂静的: *This town is dead: everywhere is closed after ten o'clock at night.* 这个镇十分寂静，晚上十点钟以后哪儿都关门了。

a dead end a street that is only open at one end 一端不通的街道；死胡同

the dead *noun* 名词 (plural 复数)

dead people 已死的人

dead² /ded; dɛd/ *adverb* 副词
completely or very 完全地；非常地：*I'm dead tired.* 我累得要命。

deadline /'dedlaɪn; 'dɛd,laɪn/ *noun* 名词
a day or time before which you must do something 截止的日期或时间：*The deadline for finishing this essay is next Tuesday.* 做完这篇文章的最后期限是下星期二。

deadly /'dedli; 'dɛdlɪ/ *adjective* 形容词 (**deadlier**, **deadliest**)
Something that is deadly may kill people or other living things （可能）致命的：*a deadly weapon* 致命的武器
deadly *adverb* 副词
extremely 极端地；非常地：*I'm deadly serious.* 我这可决不是闹着玩儿的。

deaf /def; dɛf/ *adjective* 形容词
not able to hear 聋的
the deaf *noun* 名词 (plural 复数)
people who are deaf 耳聋的人；聋子

deafen /'defn; 'dɛfən/ *verb* 动词 (**deafens**, **deafening**, **deafened** /'defnd; 'dɛfənd/)
make a very loud noise so that somebody cannot hear well 发出很大的声音震得某人听不清楚；使人感到震耳欲聋：*We were deafened by the sound of a plane flying over our heads.* 飞机从我们头上经过，震得我们什么都听不见了。

deafness /'defnəs; 'dɛfnɪs/ *noun* 名词 (no plural 无复数)
being deaf 聋

deal¹ /di:l; dil/ *noun* 名词
an agreement, usually about buying, selling or working 协议；（通常指）交易：*Let's make a deal—I'll help you today if you help me tomorrow.* 咱们来个协议——要是你明天帮助我，我今天就帮助你。

deal² /di:l; dil/ *noun* 名词
a good deal or 或 **a great deal** a lot; much 很多：*I saw a good deal of France on my holiday.* 我假期到过法国很多地方。◇ *We ate a great deal.* 我们吃了很多。

deal³ /di:l; dil/ *verb* 动词 (**deals**, **dealing**, **dealt** /delt; dɛlt/, **has dealt**)
deal in something buy and sell something in business 买卖；交易：*We deal in insurance.* 我们做保险业的生意。
deal out give something to each person 将某物分发给每个人：*I dealt out the cards for the next game.* 我发了下一轮的牌。
deal with somebody or 或 **something 1** look after something and do what is necessary 照料或处理某人或某事物：*I am too busy to deal with this problem now.* 我现在忙得顾不上这个问题。
2 tell about something 陈述某事：*The first chapter of the book deals with letter-writing.* 这本书的第一章说的是如何写信。
dealer *noun* 名词
a person who buys and sells things 商人：*drug dealers* 毒品贩子

dear /dɪə(r); dɪr/ *adjective* 形容词 (**dearer**, **dearest**)
1 a word that you use before a person's name at the beginning of a letter 用于书信开头的称谓之前：*Dear Mr Carter, …* 卡特先生台鉴：… ◇ *Dear Sir or Madam, …* 敬启者：…
2 that you love very much 非常爱的；亲爱的：*She was a dear friend.* 她原是我的好朋友。
3 that costs a lot of money ; expensive 价钱高的；贵的：*Those strawberries are too dear.* 那些草莓太贵了。✪ opposite 反义词：**cheap**
dear *noun* 名词
a word that you use when you are speaking to somebody that you know well or that you love （对熟人或所爱的人的称呼）亲爱的：*Hello, dear.* 喂，亲爱的。

death /deθ; dɛθ/ *noun* 名词
when a life finishes 死；死亡：*He became manager of the company after his father's death.* 他父亲死后他就成了公司的经理。◇ *There are thousands of deaths in car accidents every year.* 每年都有成千上万的人死于车祸。
deathly (**deathlier**, **deathliest**) *adjective* 形容词
like death 像死一样的：*There was a deathly silence.* 当时是死一般的寂静。

debate /dɪ'beɪt; dɪ'bet/ *noun* 名词
a public meeting where people talk about something important 争论；辩论；公开讨论重要事情的会议
debate *verb* 动词 (**debates**, **debating**, **debated**)
Parliament is debating the new law. 国会现在正在辩论这项新法规。

debt /det; dɛt/ *noun* 名词
money that you must pay back to some-

D

body 债；债务；欠款: *The company has borrowed a lot of money and it still has debts.* 这家公司借过很多钱而且仍有债务。

in debt If you are in debt, you must pay money to somebody. 欠债

decay /dɪ'keɪ; dɪ'ke/ *verb* 动词 (**decays, decaying, decayed** /dɪ'keɪd; dɪ'ked/)
become bad or fall to pieces 变坏；腐烂: *If you don't clean your teeth, they will decay.* 不刷牙就要有蛀牙了。

decay *noun* 名词 (no plural 无复数)
tooth decay 蛀牙

D

deceive /dɪ'si:v; dɪ'siv/ *verb* 动词 (**deceives, deceiving, deceived** /dɪ'si:vd; dɪ'sivd/)
make somebody believe something that is not true 欺骗某人: *Sophie's boyfriend deceived her—he didn't tell her he was already married.* 索菲的男朋友欺骗了她——他没告诉她他已经结婚了。◇ *She deceived me into thinking she was a police officer.* 她把我骗得还以为她是警察呢。

December /dɪ'sembə(r); dɪ'sɛmbɚ/ *noun* 名词
the twelfth month of the year 十二月

decent /'di:snt; 'disn̩t/ *adjective* 形容词
1 good enough; right 相当好的；合适的；体面的: *You can't wear jeans for a job interview—you should buy some decent clothes.* 不能穿着牛仔裤去参加求职面试——应该买些体面的衣服。
2 honest and good 诚实的；正派的: *decent people* 正直的人

decide /dɪ'saɪd; dɪ'saɪd/ *verb* 动词 (**decides, deciding, decided**)
choose something after thinking 决定: *I can't decide what colour to paint my room.* 我决定不了我的屋子刷什么颜色。◇ *We've decided to go to France for our holidays.* 我们决定到法国去度假。◇ *She decided that she didn't want to come.* 她决定不来了。

decimal /'desɪml; 'dɛsəml̩/ *noun* 名词
a part of a number, written after a dot (called a **decimal point**), for example 0.75 小数（如 0.75，小数点叫做 **decimal point**） ✪ We say '0.75' as 'nought point seven five'. ＊ 0.75读做 nought point seven five。

decision /dɪ'sɪʒn; dɪ'sɪʒən/ *noun* 名词
choosing something after thinking; deciding 决定；决心: *I must make a decision about what I'm going to do when I leave school.* 我中学毕业以后做什么，得有个打算。

deck /dek; dɛk/ *noun* 名词
the floor of a ship or bus 轮船或公共汽车的层面；甲板；层: *I always sit on the top deck when I travel by bus.* 我坐公共汽车总是坐上层。

deck-chair /'dek tʃeə(r); 'dɛkˌtʃɛr/ *noun* 名词
a chair that you use outside, for example on the beach. You can fold it up and carry it.（户外，如沙滩上用的）折叠椅

declare /dɪ'kleə(r); dɪ'klɛr/ *verb* 动词 (**declares, declaring, declared** /dɪ'kleəd; dɪ'klɛrd/)
1 say very clearly what you think or what you will do, often to a lot of people（常指向很多人）清楚说出自己的想法或要做的事；宣布；表明；声明: *He declared that he was not a thief.* 他郑重地说他不是贼。◇ *The country declared war on its enemy.* 该国已向敌人宣战。
2 In an airport or port you declare things that you have bought in another country so that you can pay tax on them 报关（向海关申报应纳税的物品）: *Have you anything to declare?* 你有要报关的东西吗？

declaration /ˌdeklə'reɪʃn; ˌdɛklə'reʃən/ *noun* 名词
a declaration of independence 独立宣言

decorate /'dekəreɪt; 'dɛkəˌret/ *verb* 动词 (**decorates, decorating, decorated**)
1 make something look nicer by adding beautiful things to it 装饰某物: *We decorated the room with flowers.* 我们用花朵把屋子装点了一下。
2 put paint or paper on the walls of a room 粉刷墙壁或糊墙纸: *I am decorating the kitchen.* 我正在粉刷厨房。

decorations /ˌdekə'reɪʃnz; ˌdɛkə'reʃənz/ *noun* 名词 (plural 复数)
beautiful things that you add to something to make it look nicer 装饰物: *Christmas decorations* 圣诞节的装饰品

decrease /dɪ'kri:s; dɪ'kris/ *verb* 动词 (**decreases, decreasing, decreased** /dɪ'kri:st; dɪ'krist/)
become smaller or less; make something smaller or less 变小或减少；使某物

变小或减少: *The number of people in the village has decreased from 200 to 100.* 村里的人数从200人减少到100人。

decrease /'di:kri:s; 'dikris/ *noun* 名词
There was a decrease in the number of people living in the village. 村里住的人减少了。
✪ opposite 反义词: **increase**

deep /di:p; dip/ *adjective* 形容词 (**deeper, deepest**)
1 Something that is deep goes down a long way（向下延伸）深的: *Be careful: the water is very deep.* 小心：水很深。◇ *There were deep cuts in his face.* 他脸上的伤口很深。✪ opposite 反义词: **shallow**
☞ picture on page C26 见第C26页图
2 You use 'deep' to say or ask how far something is from the top to the bottom 表达或询问从顶部到底部有多"深"的用词: *The hole was about six metres deep and three metres wide.* 这个洞有六米深、三米宽。✪ The noun is **depth**. 名词是 **depth**。
3 A deep colour is strong and dark（指颜色）深的: *She has deep-blue eyes.* 她的眼睛是深蓝色的。✪ opposite 反义词: **pale** or 或 **light**
4 A deep sound is low and strong（指声音）低沉的: *He has a deep voice.* 他声音低沉。
5 Deep feelings are very strong（指感情）强烈的: *deep sadness* 极度的悲哀
6 If you are in a deep sleep, it is difficult for somebody to wake you up（睡眠）不易醒的；酣睡的: *She was in such a deep sleep that she didn't hear me calling her.* 她睡得很熟，没听见我叫她。

deeply *adverb* 副词
strongly or completely 强烈地；完全地: *He is sleeping very deeply.* 他睡得正香。

deer 鹿

deer /dɪə(r); dɪr/ *noun* 名词 (*plural* 复数作 **deer**)
a wild animal that eats grass and can run fast 鹿

defeat /dɪ'fi:t; dɪ'fit/ *verb* 动词 (**defeats, defeating, defeated**)
win a fight or game against a person or group of people 战胜；击败: *Alexander the Great defeated the Persians in 334 BC.* 亚历山大（三世）大帝于公元前334年击败了波斯人。

defeat *noun* 名词
losing a game, fight or war（在竞赛、斗争或战争中的）失败

defence /dɪ'fens; dɪ'fɛns/ *noun* 名词
fighting against people who attack, or keeping away dangerous people or things 防御；防护；保卫: *They fought the war in defence of their country.* 他们为保卫祖国而战。

defend /dɪ'fend; dɪ'fɛnd/ *verb* 动词 (**defends, defending, defended**)
1 fight to keep away people or things that attack 保护；保卫: *They defended the city against the enemy.* 他们卫城抗敌。
2 say that somebody has not done something wrong 辩护: *My sister defended me when my father said I was lazy.* 我父亲说我懒，我姐姐为我辩护。◇ *He had a lawyer to defend him in court.* 他的律师在法庭上为他辩护。
3 try to stop another person or team scoring goals or points in a game（比赛中）防守，防卫

defense *American English for* **defence** 美式英语，即 **defence**

defied, defies *forms of* **defy** ＊ **defy**的不同形式

define /dɪ'faɪn; dɪ'faɪn/ *verb* 动词 (**defines, defining, defined** /dɪ'faɪnd; dɪ'faɪnd/)
say what a word means 给词语下定义: *How do you define 'rich'?* ＊ rich 是什么意思？

definite /'defɪnət; 'dɛfənɪt/ *adjective* 形容词
sure; certain 肯定的；确切的: *I want a definite answer, 'yes' or 'no'.* 我要一个明确的答复，"是"还是"不是"。◇ *I think it was Sally I saw but I'm not definite.* 我认为我看见的是萨莉，可是我没有把握。

definitely *adverb* 副词
certainly 肯定地；确实地: *I am definitely going to the theatre this evening – I have already bought my ticket.* 我今天晚上一定去看戏——我连票都买了。

definition /ˌdefɪ'nɪʃn; ˌdɛfə'nɪʃən/ *noun* 名词
a group of words that tell you what another word means（词语的）定义，释义

defy /dɪ'faɪ; dɪ'faɪ/ *verb* 动词 (**defies**, **defying**, **defied** /dɪ'faɪd; dɪ'faɪd/, **has defied**)
If you defy somebody or something, you do something that they say you should not do 违抗；抗拒；不服从: *She defied her parents and stayed out all night.* 她不听父母的话，整夜都没回家。

D

degree /dɪ'gri:; dɪ'gri/ *noun* 名词
1 a measurement of temperature（温度的量度单位）度；度数: *Water boils at 100 degrees Celsius (100°C).* 水在100摄氏度（100°C）时沸腾。
2 a measurement of angles（角度的量度单位）度；度数: *There are 90 degrees (90°) in a right angle.* 直角是90度（90°）。
3 Universities and colleges give degrees to students who have completed special courses there 学位: *She has a degree in Mathematics.* 她是数学学士。

delay[1] /dɪ'leɪ; dɪ'le/ *noun* 名词 (*plural* 复数作 **delays**)
a time when somebody or something is late 耽搁；延误；延迟: *There was a long delay at the airport.* 飞机误点了很长时间。
without delay immediately 立刻；马上: *You must pay the money without delay.* 你得马上付钱。

delay[2] /dɪ'leɪ; dɪ'le/ *verb* 动词 (**delays**, **delaying**, **delayed** /dɪ'leɪd; dɪ'led/)
1 make somebody or something late 使某人或某事物迟到；耽搁；延误: *My train was delayed for two hours because of the bad weather.* 因为天气不好，我坐的火车延误了两个小时。
2 not do something until a later time 推迟；延期: *I delayed my holiday because I was ill.* 我因病把假期推迟了。

deliberate /dɪ'lɪbərət; dɪ'lɪbərɪt/ *adjective* 形容词
that you want and plan to do, and do not do by mistake 故意的；蓄意的；有意的: *'Do you think it was an accident?' 'No, I'm sure it was deliberate.'* "你认为是意外吗？" "不，一定是成心的。"
deliberately *adverb* 副词
The police think that somebody started the fire deliberately. 警方认为是有人故意放的火。

delicate /'delɪkət; 'dɛləkət/ *adjective* 形容词
1 If something is delicate, you can break or damage it very easily 容易弄坏或弄伤的；易碎的；脆弱的: *I've got delicate skin, so I use special soap.* 我皮肤过敏，所以使用特殊肥皂。
2 pretty and fine; not strong 优美的；精巧的；不强的；柔和的；浅的；淡的: *delicate colours like pale pink and pale blue* 柔和的颜色，如粉红和浅蓝 ◇ *She had long, delicate fingers.* 她的手指修长而纤巧。

delicious /dɪ'lɪʃəs; dɪ'lɪʃəs/ *adjective* 形容词
very good to eat 美味的；可口的: *This soup is delicious.* 这个汤好喝。

delight[1] /dɪ'laɪt; dɪ'laɪt/ *verb* 动词 (**delights**, **delighting**, **delighted**)
make somebody very pleased or happy 使某人非常愉快或高兴
delighted *adjective* 形容词
very pleased or happy 非常愉快的或高兴的: *I'm delighted to meet you.* 能认识您，我很高兴。

delight[2] /dɪ'laɪt; dɪ'laɪt/ *noun* 名词 (no plural 无复数)
great happiness 喜悦；愉快；高兴
delightful /dɪ'laɪtfl; dɪ'laɪtfəl/ *adjective* 形容词
very nice; lovely 美好的；可爱的: *We stayed in a delightful little hotel.* 我们住的旅馆舒适宜人。

deliver /dɪ'lɪvə(r); dɪ'lɪvɚ/ *verb* 动词 (**delivers**, **delivering**, **delivered** /dɪ'lɪvəd; dɪ'lɪvɚd/)
take something to the place where it must go 递送；传送: *The postman delivered two letters this morning.* 邮递员今天上午送来了两封信。
delivery /dɪ'lɪvəri; dɪ'lɪvərɪ/ *noun* 名词 (*plural* 复数作 **deliveries**)
We are waiting for a delivery of bread. 我们正等着送面包来。

demand[1] /dɪ'mɑ:nd; dɪ'mænd/ *verb* 动词 (**demands**, **demanding**, **demanded**)
say strongly that you must have something（强烈地）要求: *The workers*

are demanding more money. 工人要求增加工资。◇ *She demanded to see the manager.* 她要求见经理。

demand² /dɪˈmɑːnd; dɪˈmænd/ *noun* 名词
saying strongly that you must have something（强烈的）要求
in demand wanted by a lot of people 有很多人需要或需求：*I'm in demand today—I've had eight telephone calls!* 今天很多人都找我——我已经接了八个电话了！

democracy /dɪˈmɒkrəsi; dəˈmɑkrəsɪ/ *noun* 名词 (*plural* 复数作 **democracies**)
1 a system of government where the people choose their leader (by **voting**) 民主制度（选举叫做 **voting**）
2 a country with a government that the people choose 民主制度的国家；民主政体：*Great Britain is a democracy.* 英国是民主的国家。

democrat /ˈdeməkræt; ˈdɛməˌkræt/ *noun* 名词
1 a person who wants democracy 民主主义者
2 Democrat a person in the Democratic Party in the USA 美国民主党的党员 ☞ Look at **Republican**. 见 **Republican**。

democratic /ˌdeməˈkrætɪk; ˌdɛməˈkrætɪk/ *adjective* 形容词
If a country, etc is democratic, all the people in it can choose its leaders or decide about the way it is organized. 民主政体的

demolish /dɪˈmɒlɪʃ; dɪˈmɑlɪʃ/ *verb* 动词 (**demolishes, demolishing, demolished** /dɪˈmɒlɪʃt; dɪˈmɑlɪʃt/)
break a building so that it falls down 拆除建筑物；拆毁：*They demolished six houses and built a supermarket in their place.* 他们拆掉了六所房子，在原地盖了一家超级市场。

demonstrate /ˈdemənstreɪt; ˈdɛmənˌstret/ *verb* 动词 (**demonstrates, demonstrating, demonstrated**)
1 show something clearly 表明；示范：*He demonstrated how to operate the machine.* 他示范使用这个机器的方法。
2 walk or stand in public with a group of people to show that you have strong feelings about something 进行示威游行或集会：*Thousands of people demonstrated against the war.* 成千上万的人参加了反战示威游行。

demonstration /ˌdemənˈstreɪʃn; ˌdɛmənˈstreʃən/ *noun* 名词
1 a group of people walking or standing together in public to show that they have strong feelings about something 示威游行或集会：*There were demonstrations all over Eastern Europe in 1989.* ✻ 1989年东欧各地都有示威游行或集会。
2 showing how to do something, or how something works 示范：*He gave us a cookery demonstration.* 他给我们做了烹饪示范。

den /den; dɛn/ *noun* 名词
the place where a wild animal lives 兽穴；（野兽的）窝

denied, denies *forms of* **deny** ✻ **deny** 的不同形式

denim /ˈdenɪm; ˈdɛnəm/ *noun* 名词 (no plural 无复数)
strong cotton material that is used for making jeans and other clothes. Denim is often blue 粗棉布（用以制牛仔裤等衣物，多为蓝色）：*a denim jacket* 粗布甲克

dense /dens; dɛns/ *adjective* 形容词
1 with a lot of things or people close together 密度大的；稠密的；密集的：*dense forests* 茂密的森林
2 thick and difficult to see through 因稠密而不易看透的；浓的：*dense fog* 浓雾

dent /dent; dɛnt / *noun* 名词
a hollow place in something flat, that comes when you hit it or press it hard 凹陷；凹部；凹痕：*There's a big dent in the side of my car.* 我的汽车车身瘪了一块。
dent *verb* 动词 (**dents, denting, dented**)
hit something and make a hollow place in it 撞击某物造成凹痕：*I dropped the tin and dented it.* 我把罐头给摔瘪了。

dentist /ˈdentɪst; ˈdɛntɪst/ *noun* 名词
a person whose job is to look after your teeth 牙医 ✪ When we talk about visiting the dentist, we say **go to the den-tist's** 去治牙叫做 **go to the dentist's**: *I've got toothache so I'm going to the dentist's.* 我牙疼，现在看牙去。☞ Note at **tooth** 见 **tooth** 词条注释

deny /dɪˈnaɪ; dɪˈnaɪ/ *verb* 动词 (**denies, denying, denied** /dɪˈnaɪd; dɪˈnaɪd/, **has denied**)
say that something is not true 否认；

D

否定: *He denied that he had stolen the car.* 他不承认偷了那辆汽车。◇ *They denied breaking the window.* 他们拒不承认窗户是他们打破的。✪ opposite 反义词: **admit**

depart /dɪ'pɑːt; dɪ'pɑrt/ *verb* 动词 (**departs**, **departing**, **departed**)
leave a place 离开: *The next train to Birmingham departs from platform 3.* 开往伯明翰的下一班火车从3号月台开出。✪ **Leave** is the word that we usually use. ✳ **leave** 是常用词。

department /dɪ'pɑːtmənt; dɪ'pɑrtmənt/ *noun* 名词
one of the parts of a university, school, government, shop, big company, etc (学校、政府、商店、大公司等的)部门;系;科;部;局;司;处: *The book department is on the second floor.* 图书部在三楼。◇ *Professor Jenkins is the head of the English department.* 詹金斯教授是英语系的系主任。

department store /dɪ'pɑːtmənt stɔː(r); dɪ'pɑrtmənt stɔr/ *noun* 名词
a big shop that sells a lot of different things 百货公司: *Harrods is a famous department store in London.* 哈罗德公司是伦敦著名的百货公司。

departure /dɪ'pɑːtʃə(r); dɪ'pɑrtʃɚ/ *noun* 名词
leaving a place 离开;离去: *A board inside the airport shows arrivals and departures.* 飞机场有个显示飞机抵达和起飞的时刻表。

depend /dɪ'pend; dɪ'pɛnd/ *verb* 动词 (**depends**, **depending**, **depended**)
depend on somebody or 或 **something 1** need somebody or something 需要或依靠某人或某事物;依赖: *She still depends on her parents for money because she hasn't got a job.* 她仍然靠父母的钱过活,因为她还没有工作。**2** trust somebody; feel sure that somebody or something will do what you want 信任或信赖某人或某事物: *I know I can depend on my friends to help me.* 我知道我能靠朋友帮忙。

it depends, that depends words that you use to show that something is not certain (用以表示不肯定的词语)那得看情况了: *'Do you want to play tennis tomorrow?' 'It depends on the weather.'* "你想明天去打网球吗?""那要看天气了。" ◇ *'Can you lend me some money?' 'That depends. How much do you want?'* "你能借给我点儿钱吗?""那得看借多少了。你要多少?"

dependent /dɪ'pendənt; dɪ'pɛndənt/ *adjective* 形容词
If you are dependent on somebody or something, you need them 需要某人或某事物支持的;需要或依靠某人或某事物的: *A baby is completely dependent on its parents.* 小孩儿完全离不开父母。

deposit /dɪ'pɒzɪt; dɪ'pɑzɪt/ *noun* 名词
1 money that you pay to show that you want something and that you will pay the rest later 定金;定钱: *I paid a deposit on a holiday.* 我交了度假费用的定金。
2 money that you pay into a bank 存进银行的钱;存款
3 extra money that you pay when you rent something. You get it back if you do not damage or lose what you have rented. 保证金;押金

deposit *verb* 动词 (**deposits**, **depositing**, **deposited**)
put something somewhere to keep it safe 把某物放在某处保存: *The money was deposited in the bank.* 钱存进银行了。

depress /dɪ'pres; dɪ'prɛs/ *verb* 动词 (**depresses**, **depressing**, **depressed** /dɪ'prest; dɪ'prɛst/)
make somebody feel unhappy 使某人忧愁或不愉快: *This cold winter weather really depresses me.* 大冬天这么冷,真让人不痛快。

depressed *adjective* 形容词
If you are depressed, you are very unhappy 忧愁的;消沉的;沮丧的: *He's been very depressed since he lost his job.* 他失去工作以后一直垂头丧气。

depressing *adjective* 形容词
Something that is depressing makes you very unhappy 使人忧愁、消沉或沮丧的: *That film about the war was very depressing.* 那部战争影片看了让人感到很沉痛。

depression /dɪ'preʃn; dɪ'prɛʃən/ *noun* 名词 (no plural 无复数)
a feeling of unhappiness 忧愁;消沉;沮丧

depth /depθ; dɛpθ/ *noun* 名词
how deep something is; how far it is from the top of something to the bottom 深;深度(从上至下的距离): *What is the depth of the swimming-pool?* 这个游泳池

有多深？◇ *The hole was 2 m in depth.* 这个洞有2米深。

deputy /ˈdepjəti; ˈdɛpjətɪ/ *noun* 名词 (*plural* 复数作 **deputies**)
the person in a company, school, etc, who does the work of the leader when he/she is not there（公司、学校等中负责人不在时）代行职务的人；任副职的人: *a deputy headmaster* 副校长

derivative /dɪˈrɪvətɪv; dəˈrɪvətɪv/ *noun* 名词
a word that is made from another word 派生词: *'Sadness' is a derivative of 'sad'.* ✳ sadness 是 sad 的派生词。

descend /dɪˈsend; dɪˈsɛnd/ *verb* 动词 (**descends**, **descending**, **descended**)
go down 下来；下去；下降: *The plane started to descend.* 飞机开始降落了。✪ It is more usual to say **go down**. ✳ **go down** 是常用词。

descendant /dɪˈsendənt; dɪˈsɛndənt/ *noun* 名词
Your descendants are your children, grandchildren and everybody in your family who lives after you 后代；后裔: *Queen Elizabeth II is a descendant of Queen Victoria.* 英国女王伊丽莎白二世是维多利亚女王的后代。

descent /dɪˈsent; dɪˈsɛnt/ *noun* 名词
going down 下来；下去；下降: *The plane began its descent to Munich airport.* 飞机在慕尼黑机场开始降落。

describe /dɪˈskraɪb; dɪˈskraɪb/ *verb* 动词 (**describes**, **describing**, **described** /dɪˈskraɪbd; dɪˈskraɪbd/)
say what somebody or something is like or what happened 描述某人或某事物；叙述；形容: *Can you describe the man you saw?* 你能不能形容一下你见过的那个男子？◇ *She described the accident to the police.* 她向警方讲述了出事的经过。

description /dɪˈskrɪpʃn; dɪˈskrɪpʃən/ *noun* 名词
words that tell what somebody or something is like or what happened（对某人或某事物的）描述；叙述；形容: *I have given the police a description of the thief.* 我向警方形容了那个贼的样子。

desert¹ /ˈdezət; ˈdɛzɚt/ *noun* 名词
a large area of land that is usually covered with sand. Deserts are very dry and not many plants can grow there 沙漠；荒漠；荒原: *the Sahara Desert* 撒哈拉沙漠

desert island /ˌdezət ˈaɪlənd; ˈdɛzɚt ˈaɪlənd/ *noun* 名词
an island where nobody lives, in a hot part of the world 热带地区无人居住的岛

desert² /dɪˈzɜːt; dɪˈzɝt/ *verb* 动词 (**deserts**, **deserting**, **deserted**)
leave a person or place when it is wrong to go 离弃某人或某地: *He deserted his wife and children.* 他抛弃了妻子和儿女。

deserted /dɪˈzɜːtɪd; dɪˈzɝtɪd/ *adjective* 形容词
empty, because all the people have left（因人都走了）无人的: *At night the streets are deserted.* 夜晚街道上空无一人。

deserve /dɪˈzɜːv; dɪˈzɝv/ *verb* 动词 (**deserves**, **deserving**, **deserved** /dɪˈzɜːvd; dɪˈzɝvd/)
be good or bad enough to have something（因好或坏）应得某事物: *You have worked very hard and you deserve a rest.* 你很努力，应该休息一下了。◇ *They stole money from old people, so they deserve to go to prison.* 他们偷了老年人的钱，活该得进监狱。

design¹ /dɪˈzaɪn; dɪˈzaɪn/ *verb* 动词 (**designs**, **designing**, **designed** /dɪˈzaɪnd; dɪˈzaɪnd/)
draw a plan that shows how to make something 设计；绘制图样: *The church was designed by a German architect.* 这座教堂是个德国建筑师设计的。

design² /dɪˈzaɪn; dɪˈzaɪn/ *noun* 名词
1 a drawing that shows how to make something 图样；设计图: *Have you seen the designs for the new shopping centre?* 你看过新购物中心的设计图了吗？
2 lines, shapes and colours on something 图案: *The wallpaper has a design of blue and green squares on it.* 壁纸上有蓝的和绿的格子图案。

designer /dɪˈzaɪnə(r); dɪˈzaɪnɚ/ *noun* 名词
a person whose job is to make drawings that show how something will be made 设计者；设计师: *a fashion designer* 时装设计家

desire /dɪˈzaɪə(r); dɪˈzaɪr/ *noun* 名词
a feeling of wanting something very much（对某事物的）渴望；欲望: *a desire for peace* 渴望和平

D

desk办公桌

desk /desk; dɛsk/ *noun* 名词
1 a table with drawers, where you sit to write or work 书桌；办公桌
2 a table or place in a building where somebody gives information, etc（供询问等的）柜台或类似的处所: *Ask at the information desk.* 在问讯处询问。

D

despair /dɪ'speə(r); dɪ'spɛr/ *noun* 名词 (no plural 无复数)
a feeling of not having hope 绝望: *He was in despair because he had no money and nowhere to live.* 他一无钱二无住处，已经绝望了。

desperate /'despərət; 'dɛspərɪt/ *adjective* 形容词
1 If you are desperate, you have no hope and you are ready to do anything to get what you want（因已绝望）为得到想要的事物，什么都愿意干的；不顾一切的: *She is so desperate for a job that she will work anywhere.* 她急切需要一份工作，在哪儿干都行。
2 very serious 极严重的: *There is a desperate need for food in some parts of Africa.* 非洲有些地区迫切需要食物。
desperately *adverb* 副词
He is desperately unhappy. 他非常不愉快。

desperation /ˌdespə'reɪʃn; ˌdɛspə'reʃən/ *noun* 名词 (no plural 无复数)
the feeling of having no hope, that makes you do anything to get what you want（为得到想要的事物，什么都愿意干的）绝望心情；不顾一切: *In desperation, she sold her ring to get money for food.* 她在绝望中把戒指卖了点儿钱买吃的。

despise /dɪ'spaɪz; dɪ'spaɪz/ *verb* 动词 (**despises**, **despising**, **despised** /dɪ'spaɪzd; dɪ'spaɪzd/)
hate somebody or something with contempt 厌恶或鄙视某人或某事物: *I despise people who tell lies.* 我讨厌说谎的人。

despite /dɪ'spaɪt; dɪ'spaɪt/ *preposition* 介词
although something is true; not noticing or not caring about something 尽管；不管；不顾: *We decided to go out despite the bad weather.* 尽管天气不好，我们还是决定出去。

dessert /dɪ'zɜ:t; dɪ'zɝt/ *noun* 名词
something sweet that you eat at the end of a meal（一顿饭最后吃的）甜食: *We had ice-cream for dessert.* 我们那顿饭最后吃的甜食是冰激凌。
dessertspoon /dɪ'zɜ:tspu:n; dɪ'zɝtˌspun/ *noun* 名词
a spoon that you use for eating desserts 点心勺

destination /ˌdestɪ'neɪʃn; ˌdɛstə'neʃən/ *noun* 名词
the place where somebody or something is going 目的地: *They were very tired when they finally reached their destination.* 他们终于到达目的地了，都累得不得了。

destroy /dɪ'strɔɪ; dɪ'strɔɪ/ *verb* 动词 (**destroys**, **destroying**, **destroyed** /dɪ'strɔɪd; dɪ'strɔɪd/)
break something completely so that you cannot use it again or so that it is gone 彻底毁坏某物（使之不能使用或不复存在）；摧毁；毁灭: *The house was destroyed by fire.* 房子让大火给烧毁了。

destruction /dɪ'strʌkʃn; dɪ'strʌkʃən/ *noun* 名词 (no plural 无复数)
breaking something completely so that you cannot use it again or so that it is gone（对某物的）彻底毁坏（因而不能使用或不复存在）；摧毁；毁灭: *the destruction of the city by bombs* 全城被炸弹摧毁

detached /dɪ'tætʃt; dɪ'tætʃt/ *adjective* 形容词
A detached house stands alone and is not joined to any other house.（指房屋）不与其他房屋相连的

detail /'di:teɪl; dɪ'tel/ *noun* 名词
1 one of the very small parts that make the whole of something 细节；枝节: *Tell me quickly what happened—I don't need to know all the details.* 简断截说告诉我怎么回事——我倒无需了解那些细节。
2 details (plural 复数) information about something 详情: *For more details, please telephone this number.* 欲知详情，请拨这个电话号码。

in detail with all the small parts 详细地: *Tell me about your plan in detail.* 把你的计划详细地告诉我。

detective /dɪ'tektɪv; dɪ'tɛktɪv/ *noun* 名词
a person whose job is to find out who did a crime. Detectives are usually police officers 侦探；（尤指）警探: *Sherlock Holmes is a famous detective in stories.* 故事中的福尔摩斯是著名的侦探。

detergent /dɪ'tɜ:dʒənt; dɪ'tɝdʒənt/ *noun* 名词
a powder or liquid that you use for washing things（粉状的或液状的）洗涤剂

determination /dɪˌtɜ:mɪ'neɪʃn; dɪˌtɝmə'neʃən/ *noun* 名词 (no plural 无复数)
being certain that you want to do something 决心；坚定性: *She has shown great determination to succeed.* 她表现出了争取成功的决心。

determined /dɪ'tɜ:mɪnd; dɪ'tɝmɪnd/ *adjective* 形容词
very certain that you want do something 有决心的；意志坚定的: *She is determined to win the match.* 她决心要在比赛中获胜。

detest /dɪ'test; dɪ'tɛst/ *verb* 动词 (**detests, detesting, detested**)
hate somebody or something very much 厌恶某人或某事物；憎恶: *I detest spiders.* 我很讨厌蜘蛛。

detour /'di:tʊə(r); dɪ'tʊr/ *noun* 名词
a longer way to a place when you cannot go by the usual way（道路不通时）绕行的路线: *The bridge was closed so we had to make a detour.* 桥给封住了，我们只好绕道而行。

develop /dɪ'veləp; dɪ'vɛləp/ *verb* 动词 (**develops, developing, developed** /dɪ'veləpt; dɪ'vɛləpt/)
1 become bigger or more complete; make something bigger or more complete（使某事物）发展；发育；发达；成长: *Children develop into adults.* 儿童能成长为成年人。
2 begin to have something 开始有某事物；出现；显露: *She developed the disease at the age of 27.* 她27岁时得的这种病。
3 When a photograph is developed, special chemicals are used on the film so that you can see the picture. 冲洗底片；使照片显影

development /dɪ'veləpmənt; dɪ'vɛləpmənt/ *noun* 名词
1 (no plural 无复数) becoming bigger or more complete; growing 发展；发育；发达；成长: *We studied the development of babies in their first year of life.* 我们研究了婴儿的生长过程。
2 (*plural* 复数作 **developments**) something new that happens 新发生的或新出现的事物: *There are new developments in science almost every day.* 科学上的新事物几乎每天都有。

device /dɪ'vaɪs; dɪ'vaɪs/ *noun* 名词
a tool or machine that you use for doing a special job 做某种工作用的工具或机器: *a device for opening tins* 开罐头的小器具

devil /'devl; 'dɛvl̩/ *noun* 名词
1 the Devil (no plural 无复数) the most powerful evil spirit, in the Christian religion（基督教所指的）魔鬼
2 an evil being or spirit 坏的人或灵魂

devote /dɪ'vəʊt; dɪ'vot/ *verb* 动词 (**devotes, devoting, devoted**)
give a lot of time or energy to something（为某事物）付出时间或精力；奉献: *She devoted her life to helping the poor.* 她一生致力于帮助穷人。
devoted *adjective* 形容词
If you are devoted to somebody or something, you love them very much（对某人某事物）非常爱的: *John is devoted to his wife and children.* 约翰深爱他的妻子儿女。

dew /dju:; du/ *noun* 名词 (no plural 无复数)
small drops of water that form on plants and grass in the night 露水: *In the morning, the grass was wet with dew.* 在早晨，青草沾满露水，湿漉漉的。

diagonal /daɪ'ægənl; daɪ'ægənl̩/ *adjective* 形容词
If you draw a diagonal line from one corner of a square to another, you make two triangles. 对角的；对角线的 ☞ picture on page C5 见第C5页图

diagram /'daɪəgræm; 'daɪəˌgræm/ *noun* 名词
a picture that explains something 图解；图表；示意图: *This diagram shows all the parts of an engine.* 这张图把发动机所有的部件都显示出来了。

dial /'daɪəl; 'daɪəl/ *noun* 名词
a circle with numbers or letters on it.

D

Some telephones and clocks have dials. 有数字或字母的圆盘；（某些电话的）拨号盘；（某些钟表的）表盘

dial *verb* 动词 (**dials**, **dialling**, **dialled** /'daɪəld; 'daɪəld/)

make a telephone call by moving a dial or pushing buttons 拨或按电话号码；打电话: *You have dialled the wrong number.* 你拨错号了。✪ In American English the spellings are **dialing** and **dialed**. 美式英语的拼法是 **dialing** 和 **dialed**。

dialog *American English for* **dialogue** 美式英语，即 **dialogue**

D

dialogue /'daɪəlɒg; 'daɪəˌlɔg/ *noun* 名词

words that people say to each other in a book, play or film（书、戏剧或电影中的）对话；对白

diameter /daɪ'æmɪtə(r); daɪ'æmətɚ/ *noun* 名词

a straight line across a circle, through the centre 直径 ☞ picture on page C5 见第C5页图

diamond /'daɪəmənd; 'daɪəmənd/ *noun* 名词

1 a hard stone that looks like clear glass and is very expensive 钻石；金刚石: *The ring has a large diamond in it.* 这枚戒指上镶着个大钻石。◇ *a diamond necklace* 钻石项链

2 the shape ◆ 菱形 ◆

3 diamonds (plural 复数) the playing-cards that have red shapes like diamonds on them 红方块花色的纸牌: *the eight of diamonds* 方块八

diary /'daɪəri; 'daɪərɪ/ *noun* 名词 (*plural* 复数作 **diaries**)

1 a book where you write what you are going to do 日程记事本（记录要做的事的本子）: *I'll look in my diary to see if I'm free tomorrow.* 我得查查我的日程记事本，看看明天有没有空儿。

2 a book where you write what you have done each day 日记本

keep a diary write in a diary every day 记日记

dice /daɪs; daɪs/ *noun* 名词 (*plural* 复数作 **dice**)

a small piece of wood or plastic with spots on the sides for playing games 色子；骰子: *Throw the dice.* 掷色子。

dice 色子

dictate /dɪk'teɪt; 'dɪktet/ *verb* 动词 (**dictates**, **dictating**, **dictated**)

1 say words so that another person can write them 口授词句（再由他人写出）；听写: *She dictated a letter to her secretary.* 她向秘书口授了信稿。

2 tell somebody that they must do something 向某人发号施令: *You can't dictate to me where I should go.* 你不能叫我去哪儿就去哪儿。

dictation /dɪk'teɪʃn; dɪk'teʃən/ *noun* 名词

words that you say so that another person can write them 口授（再由他人写出）的文字；听写的文字: *We had a dictation in English today* (= a test when we wrote what the teacher said). 我们今天测验了英语听写。

dictator /dɪk'teɪtə(r); 'dɪktetɚ/ *noun* 名词

a person who has complete control of a country 独裁者

dictionary /'dɪkʃənri; 'dɪkʃəˌnɛrɪ/ *noun* 名词 (*plural* 复数作 **dictionaries**)

a book that gives words from A to Z and explains what each word means 词典；字典

did *form of* **do** ✳ **do** 的不同形式

didn't /'dɪdnt; 'dɪdn̩t/ = **did not**

die /daɪ; daɪ/ *verb* 动词 (**dies**, **dying**, **died** /daɪd; daɪd/, **has died**)

stop living 死；死亡: *People, animals and plants die if they don't have water.* 人和动植物没有水就会死亡。

die down slowly become less strong 逐渐减弱: *The storm died down.* 风暴渐渐减弱了。

die of something stop living because of an illness 死于某种疾病: *She died of a heart attack.* 她因心脏病发作而死。

diesel /'diːzl; 'dizl̩/ *noun* 名词

1 (*plural* 复数作 **diesels**) (*also* 亦作 **diesel engine**) an engine in buses, trains and some cars that uses oil, not petrol 柴油机

2 (no plural 无复数) oil that is used in diesel engines 柴油

diet /'daɪət; 'daɪət/ *noun* 名词

1 the food that you usually eat 经常吃的食物；日常的饮食: *It is important to have a healthy diet.* 经常吃有益于健康的食物十分重要。

2 special foods that you eat when you are ill or when you want to get thinner （生病时的或为减轻体重时的）规定饮食

be or 或 **go on a diet** eat only special foods because you want to get thinner （为减轻体重）节食

difference /'dɪfrəns; 'dɪfrəns/ *noun* 名词 the way that one thing is not the same as another thing 差别；差异: *There is a big difference between British and German schools.* 英国的学校同德国的差别很大。◇ *What's the difference in price between these two bikes?* 这两辆自行车的价钱相差多少？

make a difference change something 改变某事物: *Your help has made a big difference—I understand the work much better now.* 有了你的帮助就大不相同了——这项工作我现在明白多了。

make no difference not change anything; not be important 没有变化；没有影响: *It makes no difference which train you catch—the price of the ticket is the same.* 你坐哪班火车都行——票价都一样。

tell the difference see how one thing or person is different from another thing or person 把一人与另一人或一事物与另一事物区分开: *Sarah looks exactly like her sister—I can't tell the difference (between them).* 萨拉跟她姐姐长得一模一样——我分不出（她俩）来。

different /'dɪfrənt; 'dɪfrənt/ *adjective* 形容词

1 not the same 不同的；不一样的: *These two shoes are different sizes!* 这两只鞋大小不一样。◇ *Cricket is different from baseball.* 板球与垒球不同。

2 many and not the same 多而不同的；各种的；各样的: *They sell 30 different sorts of ice-cream.* 他们出售30种冰激凌。

differently *adverb* 副词
He's very quiet at home but he behaves differently at school. 他在家一声不出，可是在学校里就完全不同了。

difficult /'dɪfɪkəlt; 'dɪfəkəlt/ *adjective* 形容词

1 not easy to do or understand 困难的；难做的；难懂的: *a difficult problem* 难题 ◇ *The exam was very difficult.* 这次考试很难。◇ *It's difficult to learn a new language.* 新学一种语言很不容易。✪ opposite 反义词: **easy**

2 A person who is difficult is not easy to please or will not do what you want （指人）不易取悦的；偏不按你的意思做的；跟你顶着干的: *She's a very difficult child.* 她是个处处跟你顶着的孩子。

difficulty /'dɪfɪkəlti; 'dɪfəˌkəltɪ/ *noun* 名词 (*plural* 复数作 **difficulties**)
a problem; something that is not easy to do or understand 困难；难做的或难懂的事物: *I have difficulty understanding German.* 我在理解德文方面有困难。

with difficulty not easily 困难地: *My grandfather walks with difficulty now.* 我祖父现在走路很困难。

dig /dɪg; dɪg/ *verb* 动词 (**digs, digging, dug** /dʌg; dʌg/, **has dug**)
move earth and make a hole in the ground 挖；刨；掘: *You need to dig the garden before you plant the seeds.* 要先把花园的土挖开再撒上种子。◇ *They dug a tunnel through the mountain for the new railway.* 他们为修新铁路挖掘了一条穿山隧道。

dig 挖

dig up take something from the ground by digging 从地里挖掘出某物: *They dug up some Roman coins in their field.* 他们从地里刨出了一些罗马硬币。

digest /daɪ'dʒest; daɪ'dʒɛst/ *verb* 动词 (**digests, digesting, digested**)
change food in your stomach so that your body can use it 消化

digestion /daɪ'dʒestʃən; daɪ'dʒɛstʃən/ *noun* 名词 (no plural 无复数)
changing food in your stomach so that your body can use it 消化

dignified /'dɪgnɪfaɪd; 'dɪgnəˌfaɪd/ *adjective* 形容词
calm, quiet and serious 从容、文静而严肃的；庄重的: *a dignified old lady* 庄重的老太太

dilute /daɪ'lju:t; daɪ'lut/ *verb* 动词 (**dilutes, diluting, diluted**)
add water to another liquid 在液体中搀水；稀释: *You need to dilute this paint before you use it.* 这种颜料要先稀释再使用。

dim /dɪm; dɪm/ *adjective* 形容词 (**dimmer, dimmest**)
not bright or clear 不光亮的；不清楚的：*The light was so dim that we couldn't see anything.* 光线很暗，我们什么都看不见。
dimly *adverb* 副词
The room was dimly lit. 屋里光线很暗。

din /dɪn; dɪn/ *noun* 名词 (no plural 无复数)
a very loud unpleasant noise（刺耳的）嘈杂声；喧闹声：*Stop making that terrible din!* 别那么吵啦！

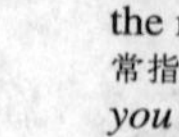

dinghy /ˈdɪŋi; ˈdɪŋgɪ/ *noun* 名词 (*plural* 复数作 **dinghies**)
a small boat 小船

dining-room /ˈdaɪnɪŋ ruːm; ˈdaɪnɪŋˌrum/ *noun* 名词
a room where people eat 饭厅；餐厅

dinner /ˈdɪnə(r); ˈdɪnɚ/ *noun* 名词
the largest meal of the day. You have dinner in the evening, or sometimes in the middle of the day（一天中的）主餐（通常指晚餐，有时也指午餐）：*What time do you usually have dinner?* 你一般以晚饭为主还是以午饭为主，几点钟吃？◇ *What's for dinner?* 晚饭吃什么？

dinosaur /ˈdaɪnəsɔː(r); ˈdaɪnəˌsɔr/ *noun* 名词
a big wild animal that lived a very long time ago 恐龙

dinosaur 恐龙

dip /dɪp; dɪp/ *verb* 动词 (**dips, dipping, dipped** /dɪpt; dɪpt/)
put something into a liquid for a short time and then take it out again 把某物放进液体中很快拿出；蘸：*Dip your hand in the water to see how hot it is.* 把手伸进水里试试看热不热。

diploma /dɪˈpləʊmə; dɪˈplomə/ *noun* 名词
a piece of paper that shows you have passed an examination or finished special studies 毕业证书；毕业文凭：*a teaching diploma* 教育文凭

diplomat /ˈdɪpləmæt; ˈdɪpləˌmæt/ *noun* 名词
a person whose job is to speak and do things for his/her country in another country 外交官；外交家

diplomatic /ˌdɪpləˈmætɪk; ˌdɪpləˈmætɪk/ *adjective* 形容词
diplomatic talks 外交会谈

direct[1] /dəˈrekt; dəˈrɛkt/ *adjective, adverb* 形容词，副词
1 as straight as possible, without turning or stopping 尽可能直的（不转弯也不停）；直通的；直达的：*Which is the most direct way to the town centre from here?* 从这儿到市中心哪条路最近？◇ *We flew direct from Paris to New York.* 我们从巴黎直接飞往纽约。◇ *The 6.45 train goes direct to Oxford.* 6点45分的火车直达牛津。
2 from one person or thing to another person or thing with nobody or nothing between them 从一人或一物到另一人或一物（中间不经他人或他物）；直接的：*You should keep this plant out of direct sunlight.* 这种植物不要直接受阳光照射。
☞ Look at **indirect**. 见 **indirect**。

direct[2] /dəˈrekt; dəˈrɛkt/ *verb* 动词 (**directs, directing, directed**)
1 tell somebody how to get to a place 为某人指路：*Can you direct me to the station, please?* 请问到车站怎么走？
2 tell or show somebody how to do something; control somebody or something 指导某人如何做某事；管理某人或某事物：*He has directed many plays at the National Theatre.* 他在国家剧院里导演了很多出话剧。

direction /dəˈrekʃn; dəˈrɛkʃən/ *noun* 名词
where a person or thing is going or looking 方向：*They got lost because they went in the wrong direction.* 他们走的方向错了，所以迷了路。

directions /dəˈrekʃnz; dəˈrɛkʃənz/ *noun* 名词 (plural 复数)
words that tell you how to get to a place or how to do something 指示如何到某处或如何做某事的词语；指南；说明书：*I couldn't find the school so I asked a woman for directions.* 我找不到那所学校，就向一个女子打听怎么走。◇ *I didn't read the directions on the packet before I made the cake.* 我做蛋糕之前没先看看包装盒上的说明。

directly /dəˈrektli; dəˈrɛktlɪ/ *adverb* 副词
1 exactly; in a direct way 直接地；径直地：*The teacher was looking directly at me.*

老师直盯着我。◇ *The post office is directly opposite the bank.* 邮局正对着银行。

2 very soon 很快地: *They left directly after breakfast.* 他们一吃完早饭就走了。

director /dəˈrektə(r); dəˈrɛktɚ/ *noun* 名词

1 a person who controls a business or a group of people（一企业或一部分人的）管理者；主管

2 a person who controls a film or play, for example by telling the actors what to do 导演

dirt /dɜːt; dɝt/ *noun* 名词 (no plural 无复数)

stuff that is not clean, for example mud or dust 污垢；污泥；灰尘: *The children came in from the garden covered in dirt.* 孩子们从花园进来，满身是泥。

dirty /ˈdɜːti; ˈdɝtɪ/ *adjective* 形容词 (**dirtier**, **dirtiest**)

not clean 脏的；肮脏的: *Your hands are dirty — go and wash them!* 你的手很脏，快洗去！☞ picture on page C27 见第C27页图

> **dis-** *prefix* 前缀
> You can add **dis-** to the beginning of some words to give them the opposite meaning, for example 在某些字之前加上 **dis-** 可构成反义词，如:
>
> **disagree** = not agree
>
> **dishonest** = not honest

disabled /dɪsˈeɪbld; dɪsˈebl̩d/ *adjective* 形容词

not able to use a part of your body well 丧失身体某部功能的；有残疾的: *Peter is disabled — he lost a leg in an accident.* 彼得有残疾——他在一次事故中失去了一条腿。

the disabled *noun* 名词 (plural 复数)

people who are disabled 残疾人；伤残人

disadvantage /ˌdɪsədˈvɑːntɪdʒ; ˌdɪsədˈvæntɪdʒ/ *noun* 名词

a problem that makes something difficult or less good 不利条件；不便之处: *One of the disadvantages of living in the countryside is that there is nowhere to go in the evenings.* 住在郊外的不便之处就是晚上没地方去。

disagree /ˌdɪsəˈgriː; ˌdɪsəˈgri/ *verb* 动词 (**disagrees**, **disagreeing**, **disagreed** /ˌdɪsəˈgriːd; ˌdɪsəˈgrid/)

say that another person's idea is wrong; not agree 说别人的意见不对；不同意: *I said it was a good film, but Jason disagreed with me.* 我说那部电影很好，可是贾森不以为然。◇ *My sister and I disagree about everything!* 我跟姐姐什么事儿意见都不一致！

disagreement /ˌdɪsəˈgriːmənt; ˌdɪsəˈgrimənt/ *noun* 名词

a talk between people with different ideas; an argument 意见不一致的谈话；争论: *My parents sometimes have disagreements about money.* 我父母有时候因为钱而意见不合。

disappear /ˌdɪsəˈpɪə(r); ˌdɪsəˈpɪr/ *verb* 动词 (**disappears**, **disappearing**, **disappeared** /ˌdɪsəˈpɪəd; ˌdɪsəˈpɪrd/)

If a person or thing disappears, they go away so people cannot see them 消失；失踪: *The sun disappeared behind the clouds.* 太阳消失在云层中。◇ *The police are looking for a woman who disappeared on Sunday.* 警方正在寻找星期日失踪的那个女子。

disappearance /ˌdɪsəˈpɪərəns; ˌdɪsəˈpɪrəns/ *noun* 名词

Everybody was worried about the child's disappearance. 大家都为孩子失踪的事发愁。

disappoint /ˌdɪsəˈpɔɪnt; ˌdɪsəˈpɔɪnt/ *verb* 动词 (**disappoints**, **disappointing**, **disappointed**)

make you sad because what you wanted did not happen 使人失望的或扫兴: *I'm sorry to disappoint you, but I can't come to your party.* 我不能参加您的聚会让您扫兴，非常抱歉。

disappointed *adjective* 形容词

If you are disappointed, you feel sad because what you wanted did not happen 失望的；失意的: *Susan was disappointed when she didn't win the prize.* 苏珊因未获奖而十分失望。

disappointing *adjective* 形容词

If something is disappointing, it makes you feel sad because it is not as good as you hoped 使人失望的或扫兴的: *disappointing exam results* 让人感到失望的考试成绩

disappointment /ˌdɪsəˈpɔɪntmənt; ˌdɪsəˈpɔɪntmənt/ *noun* 名词
1 (no plural 无复数) a feeling of sadness because what you wanted did not happen 失望；扫兴: *She couldn't hide her disappointment when she lost the match.* 她比赛输了，不禁流露出失望的神情。
2 (*plural* 复数作 **disappointments**) something that makes you sad because it is not what you hoped 使人失望或扫兴的事物: *Sarah's party was a disappointment—only four people came.* 萨拉的聚会真没劲，只来了四个人。

D

disapprove /ˌdɪsəˈpruːv; ˌdɪsəˈpruv/ *verb* 动词 (**disapproves**, **disapproving**, **disapproved** /ˌdɪsəˈpruːvd; ˌdɪsəˈpruvd/) think that somebody or something is bad 认为某人或某事物不好；不赞成: *Joe's parents disapproved of his new girlfriend.* 乔的父母看不上他的新女朋友。

disaster /dɪˈzɑːstə(r); dɪzˈæstɚ/ *noun* 名词
1 something very bad that happens and that may hurt a lot of people 灾难；灾祸；灾害: *Floods and earthquakes are disasters.* 洪水和地震都是灾难。
2 something that is very bad 极坏的事物: *Our holiday was a disaster! It rained all week!* 我们的假期可真糟糕！整个星期都下雨！

disastrous /dɪˈzɑːstrəs; dɪzˈæstrəs/ *adjective* 形容词
very bad; that causes great trouble 灾难性的；极坏的: *The heavy rain brought disastrous floods.* 这场大雨造成了大水灾。

disc /dɪsk; dɪsk/ *noun* 名词
1 a round flat thing 扁平的圆盘状物
2 a round flat thing that makes music when you play it on a record-player 唱片 ☞ Look also at **compact disc**, **floppy disk** and **hard disk**. 另见 **compact disc**、**floppy disk** 及 **hard disk**。

discipline /ˈdɪsəplɪn; ˈdɪsəplɪn/ *noun* 名词 (no plural 无复数)
teaching you to control yourself and follow rules 克制自己的训练及遵守规则的训练；纪律教育: *Children learn discipline at school.* 儿童在学校里学习遵守纪律。
discipline *verb* 动词 (**disciplines**, **disciplining**, **disciplined** /ˈdɪsəplɪnd; ˈdɪsəˌplɪnd/)
You must discipline yourself to work harder. 你必须严格要求自己，要更加努力。

disc jockey /ˈdɪsk dʒɒki; ˈdɪsk ˌdʒɑkɪ/ *noun* 名词
a person who plays records on the radio or at discos or nightclubs 在电台或迪斯科舞厅或夜总会里负责播唱片的人；唱片节目主持人 ✪ The short form is **DJ**. 缩略式为 **DJ**。

disco /ˈdɪskəʊ; ˈdɪsko/ *noun* 名词 (*plural* 复数作 **discos**)
a place where people dance and listen to pop music 迪斯科舞厅

disconnect /ˌdɪskəˈnekt; ˌdɪskəˈnɛkt/ *verb* 动词 (**disconnects**, **disconnecting**, **disconnected**)
stop electricity, gas, etc 停止供电、供煤气等: *Your phone will be disconnected if you don't pay the bill.* 你要是不付电话费，就要截断电话线了。

discount /ˈdɪskaʊnt; ˈdɪskaʊnt/ *noun* 名词
money that somebody takes away from the price of something to make it cheaper 从某物的价格中减去的钱数；折扣: *Students often get a discount on travel.* 学生的交通费大多有折扣。

discourage /dɪsˈkʌrɪdʒ; dɪsˈkɝɪdʒ/ *verb* 动词 (**discourages**, **discouraging**, **discouraged** /dɪsˈkʌrɪdʒd; dɪsˈkɝɪdʒd/)
make somebody not want to do something 使某人不愿做某事: *Jenny's parents tried to discourage her from leaving school.* 珍妮的父母想办法让她别退学。✪ opposite 反义词: **encourage**

discover /dɪˈskʌvə(r); dɪˈskʌvɚ/ *verb* 动词 (**discovers**, **discovering**, **discovered** /dɪˈskʌvəd; dɪˈskʌvɚd/)
find or learn something for the first time 发现；发觉: *Who discovered Australia?* 是谁发现的澳洲？◇ *I was in the shop when I discovered that I did not have any money.* 我到了商店里才发觉没带钱。

discovery /dɪˈskʌvəri; dɪˈskʌvərɪ/ *noun* 名词 (*plural* 复数作 **discoveries**)
finding or learning something for the first time 发现；发觉: *Scientists have made an important new discovery.* 科学家有个重大的新发现。

discriminate /dɪˈskrɪmɪneɪt; dɪˈskrɪməˌnet/ *verb* 动词 (**discriminates**, **discriminating**, **discriminated**) treat one person or a group in a different way to others 歧视某人或某些人: *This company discriminates against women—it pays them less than men for doing the same work.* 这家公司歧视女性——男女做同样的工作,可是给女的钱少。

discrimination /dɪˌskrɪmɪ'neɪʃn; dɪˌskrɪmə'neʃən/ *noun* 名词 (no plural 无复数)
religious discrimination (= treating somebody in an unfair way because their religion is not the same as yours) 宗教歧视(= 歧视与自己宗教信仰不同的人)

discuss /dɪ'skʌs; dɪ'skʌs/ *verb* 动词 (**discusses**, **discussing**, **discussed** /dɪ'skʌst; dɪ'skʌst/)
talk about something 谈论;讨论;议论;商量: *I discussed the problem with my parents.* 我跟父母谈了谈这个问题。

discussion /dɪ'skʌʃn; dɪ'skʌʃən/ *noun* 名词
We had an interesting discussion about politics. 我们讨论了政治问题,很有意思。

disease /dɪ'zi:z; dɪ'ziz/ *noun* 名词
an illness 疾病: *Cancer and measles are diseases.* 癌症和麻疹都是疾病。

disgrace /dɪs'greɪs; dɪs'gres/ *noun* 名词 (no plural 无复数)
when other people stop thinking well of you, because you have done something bad 出丑;丢脸: *He's in disgrace because he stole money from his brother.* 他真丢人,偷了他弟弟的钱。

disgraceful /dɪs'greɪsfl; dɪs'gresfəl/ *adjective* 形容词
Something that is disgraceful is very bad and makes you feel shame 可耻的;丢脸的: *The way the football fans behaved was disgraceful.* 那些足球球迷的行为很可耻。

disguise /dɪs'gaɪz; dɪs'gaɪz/ *verb* 动词 (**disguises**, **disguising**, **disguised** /dɪs'gaɪzd; dɪs'gaɪzd/)
make somebody or something different so that people will not know who or what they are 化装;伪装: *They disguised themselves as guards and escaped from the prison.* 他们化装成警卫从监狱逃走了。

disguise *noun* 名词
things that you wear so that people do not know who you are(供穿戴用而使别人认不出自己的)伪装物: *We went to the party in disguise.* 我们化了装去参加聚会。

disgust /dɪs'gʌst; dɪs'gʌst/ *noun* 名词 (no plural 无复数)
a strong feeling of not liking something 反感;厌恶: *They left the restaurant in disgust because the food was so bad.* 他们怀着厌恶的心情离开了那家饭馆,因为饭菜太差了。

disgust *verb* 动词 (**disgusts**, **disgusting**, **disgusted**)
make somebody have a strong feeling of not liking something 使某人反感或厌恶某事物

disgusted *adjective* 形容词
If you are disgusted, you have a strong feeling of not liking something 使人反感的或厌恶的: *I was disgusted to find a fly in my soup.* 我看见汤里有个苍蝇,非常恶心。

disgusting *adjective* 形容词
very bad 极坏的;讨厌的: *What a disgusting smell!* 多难闻的味儿!

dish /dɪʃ; dɪʃ/ *noun* 名词 (plural 复数作 **dishes**)
1 a container for food. You can use a dish to cook food in an oven, or to put food on the table. 碟子;盘子
2 a part of a meal 一道菜: *We had a fish dish and a vegetable dish.* 我们吃了一盘鱼和一盘青菜。
3 the dishes (plural 复数) all the plates, bowls, cups, etc that you must wash after a meal(饭后要洗的)锅碗瓢盆;餐具: *I'll wash the dishes.* 我来洗碗吧。

dishonest /dɪs'ɒnɪst; dɪs'ɑnɪst/ *adjective* 形容词
A person who is dishonest says things that are not true, or steals or cheats. 不诚实的;不正直的;骗人的

dishwasher /'dɪʃwɒʃə(r); 'dɪʃˌwɑʃɚ/ *noun* 名词
a machine that washes things like plates, glasses, knives and forks 洗碗机

disinfectant /ˌdɪsɪn'fektənt; ˌdɪsɪn'fɛktənt/ *noun* 名词
a liquid that you use for cleaning something very well 杀菌剂;消毒剂

disk /dɪsk; dɪsk/ *noun* 名词
a flat thing that stores information for computers(计算机的)磁盘: *a floppy disk* 软磁盘 ◇ *a hard disk* 硬磁盘

D

disk drive /'dɪsk draɪv; 'dɪsk ˌdraɪv/ *noun* 名词
the part of a computer where you can put **floppy disk** 磁盘机（可放入其中的软磁盘叫做 **floppy disk**）☞ picture at **computer** 见 **computer** 词条插图

dislike /dɪs'laɪk; dɪs'laɪk/ *verb* 动词 (**dislikes**, **disliking**, **disliked** /dɪs'laɪkt; dɪs'laɪkt/)
not like somebody or something 不喜欢某人或某事物: *I dislike getting up early.* 我不喜欢早起。
dislike *noun* 名词
a feeling of not liking somebody or something（对某人或某事物）不喜欢的心情；反感: *I have a strong dislike of hospitals.* 我很不喜欢医院。

D

dismal /'dɪzməl; 'dɪzml̩/ *adjective* 形容词
that makes you feel sad; not bright 使人悲伤的；阴沉的: *It was a wet, dismal day.* 那天下着雨，阴沉沉的。

dismay /dɪs'meɪ; dɪs'me/ *noun* 名词 (no plural 无复数)
a strong feeling of surprise and worry 惊愕而担忧的心情: *John looked at me in dismay when I told him about the accident.* 我把出事的消息告诉约翰时，他惊愕地看着我。
dismayed /dɪs'meɪd; dɪs'med/ *adjective* 形容词
I was dismayed to find that somebody had stolen my bike. 我突然发觉我的自行车让人给偷走了，十分着急。

dismiss /dɪs'mɪs; dɪs'mɪs/ *verb* 动词 (**dismisses**, **dismissing**, **dismissed** /dɪs'mɪst; dɪs'mɪsd/)
1 make somebody leave their job 解雇或开除某人: *He was dismissed for stealing money from the company.* 他偷了公司的钱，被开除了。✪ **Sack** and **fire** are the words that we usually use. ✳ **sack** 和 **fire** 是常用词。
2 allow somebody to leave a place 允许某人离开某处: *The lesson finished and the teacher dismissed the class.* 上完课老师准许学生走了。

disobey /ˌdɪsə'beɪ; ˌdɪsə'be/ *verb* 动词 (**disobeys**, **disobeying**, **disobeyed** /ˌdɪsə'beɪd; ˌdɪsə'bed/)
not do what somebody tells you to do; not obey 不按某人说的去做；不服从；不听话: *She disobeyed her parents and went to the party.* 她不听父母的话，参加聚会去了。
disobedient /ˌdɪsə'bi:diənt; ˌdɪsə'bidɪənt/ *adjective* 形容词
A person who is disobedient does not do what somebody tells him/her to do 不按某人说的去做的；不服从的；不听话的: *a disobedient child* 不听话的孩子
disobedience /ˌdɪsə'bi:diəns; ˌdɪsə'bidɪəns/ *noun* 名词 (no plural 无复数)
not doing what somebody tells you to do 不按某人说的去做；不服从；不听话

display /dɪ'spleɪ; dɪ'sple/ *verb* 动词 (**displays**, **displaying**, **displayed** /dɪ'spleɪd; dɪ'spled/)
show something so that people can see it 展示；陈列；展览: *All kinds of toys were displayed in the shop window.* 商店的橱窗里陈列着各种各样的玩具。
display *noun* 名词 (*plural* 复数作 **displays**)
something that people look at 供大家看的东西；陈列品；展览品: *a firework display* 烟火表演
on display in a place where people can look at it 在陈列处: *The paintings are on display in the museum.* 那些画儿正在博物馆展览。

dispose /dɪ'spəʊz; dɪ'spoz/ *verb* 动词 (**disposes**, **disposing**, **disposed** /dɪ'spəʊzd; dɪ'spozd/)
dispose of something throw something away or give something away because you do not want it 把（不要的）东西扔掉或给人: *Where can I dispose of this rubbish?* 我把这些垃圾扔到哪儿去？
disposal /dɪ'spəʊzl; dɪ'spozl̩/ *noun* 名词 (no plural 无复数)
the disposal of nuclear waste 核废料的处理

dispute /dɪ'spju:t; dɪ'spjut/ *noun* 名词
an angry talk between people with different ideas（愤怒的）争论，辩论: *There was a dispute about which driver caused the accident.* 大家争论的是哪个司机造成的事故。

dissatisfied /ˌdɪs'sætɪsfaɪd; dɪs'sætɪsˌfaɪd/ *adjective* 形容词
not pleased with something 不满意的；不满足的: *I am very dissatisfied with your work.* 我很不满意你的工作。

distance /ˈdɪstəns; ˈdɪstəns/ *noun* 名词
1 how far it is from one place to another place 距离: *It's a short distance from my house to the station.* 从我家到车站的距离很短。◇ *We usually measure distance in miles or kilometres.* 通常用英里或公里来测量距离。
2 a place that is far from somebody or something 远处: *From a distance, he looks quite young.* 他远看很年轻。
in the distance far away 远距离: *I could see a light in the distance.* 我看见远处有光。

distant /ˈdɪstənt; ˈdɪstənt/ *adjective* 形容词
far away in space or time（空间或时间）远的: *distant countries* 遥远的国家

distinct /dɪˈstɪŋkt; dɪˈstɪŋkt/ *adjective* 形容词
1 easy to hear, see or smell; clear 清楚的；清晰的；明显的；明确的: *There is a distinct smell of burning in this room.* 这屋里有股很大的烧东西的味儿。
2 clearly different 截然不同的: *English and Welsh are two distinct languages.* 英语和威尔士语完全不同。
distinctly *adverb* 副词
clearly 清楚地；清晰地；明显地；明确地: *I distinctly heard him say his name was Robert.* 我清清楚楚地听见他说他叫罗伯特。

distinguish /dɪˈstɪŋgwɪʃ; dɪˈstɪŋgwɪʃ/ *verb* 动词 (**distinguishes**, **distinguishing**, **distinguished** /dɪˈstɪŋgwɪʃt; dɪˈstɪŋgwɪʃt/)
see, hear, etc the difference between two things or people 辨别出（看出、听出等）两事物或两人之间的区别: *Some people can't distinguish between me and my twin sister.* 有的人分不出我和我的双生妹妹。◇ *Can you distinguish butter from margarine?* 你分得出纯黄油和人造黄油吗？

distinguished /dɪˈstɪŋgwɪʃt; dɪˈstɪŋgwɪʃt/ *adjective* 形容词
famous or important 著名的；重要的: *a distinguished actor* 有名的演员

distract /dɪˈstrækt; dɪˈstrækt/ *verb* 动词 (**distracts**, **distracting**, **distracted**)
If a person or thing distracts you, he/she/it stops you thinking about what you are doing 使某人分心；分散或扰乱某人的注意力: *The noise distracted me from my homework.* 那声音吵得我无法集中精神做功课。

distress /dɪˈstres; dɪˈstrɛs/ *noun* 名词 (no plural 无复数)
1 a strong feeling of pain or sadness 极大的痛苦或悲伤
2 being in danger and needing help 处于困境而需要帮助；危难: *a ship in distress* 遇险的船

distribute /dɪˈstrɪbju:t; dɪˈstrɪbjʊt/ *verb* 动词 (**distributes**, **distributing**, **distributed**)
give or send things to each person 分发或分配某事物: *New books are distributed on the first day of school.* 开学的第一天发新书。
distribution /ˌdɪstrɪˈbju:ʃn; ˌdɪstrəˈbjuʃən/ *noun* 名词 (no plural 无复数)
the distribution of newspapers 分发报纸

district /ˈdɪstrɪkt; ˈdɪstrɪkt/ *noun* 名词
a part of a country or town 国家或城镇的一部分；地区: *The Lake District is in the North-West of England.* 英国的湖区在英格兰的西北部。

disturb /dɪˈstɜ:b; dɪˈstɝb/ *verb* 动词 (**disturbs**, **disturbing**, **disturbed** /dɪˈstɜ:bd; dɪˈstɝbd/)
1 stop somebody doing something, for example thinking, working or sleeping 阻碍某人做某事（如思考、工作或睡眠）；打扰；干扰；骚扰: *My brother always disturbs me when I'm trying to do my homework.* 我一做功课我弟弟就来捣乱。◇ *Do not disturb.* (a notice that you put on a door to tell people not to come in) 请勿打扰。（门上的告示牌，请别人不要进来）
2 worry somebody 使某人烦恼或不安: *We were disturbed by the news that John was ill.* 我们听说约翰病了，都很不安。

disturbance /dɪˈstɜ:bəns; dɪˈstɝbəns/ *noun* 名词
1 a thing that stops you doing something, for example thinking, working or sleeping 阻碍某人做某事（如思考、工作或睡眠）的事物；打扰；干扰；骚扰
2 when a group of people fight or make a lot of noise and trouble 一批人的吵闹、打斗或制造的混乱；骚乱；动乱: *The football fans were causing a disturbance outside the stadium.* 足球球迷正在场外闹事。

ditch /dɪtʃ; dɪtʃ/ *noun* 名词 (*plural* 复数作 **ditches**)

D

a long narrow hole at the side of a road or field that carries away water 路边或田边的排水沟

dive 跳水

D

dive /daɪv; daɪv/ *verb* 动词 (**dives, diving, dived** /daɪvd; daɪvd/)
1 jump into water with your arms and head first (以手臂和头部先入水的方式) 跳水: *Sam dived into the pool.* 萨姆跳进了池中。
2 go under water 潜水: *The birds were diving for fish.* 小鸟潜入水中捉鱼。
diver /ˈdaɪvə(r); ˈdaɪvɚ/ *noun* 名词
a person who works under water 潜水员: *Police divers found a body in the lake.* 警方潜水人员在湖里找到一具尸体。
diving *noun* 名词 (no plural 无复数)
the sport of jumping into water or swimming under water 跳水或潜水运动

diversion /daɪˈvɜːʃn; daɪˈvɝʒən/ *noun* 名词
a way that you must go when the usual way is closed (因道路封住) 绕行的路: *There was a diversion around Chester because of a road accident.* 切斯特附近因出了交通事故而需改道绕行。

divert /daɪˈvɜːt; daɪˈvɝt/ *verb* 动词 (**diverts, diverting, diverted**)
make something go a different way 使某事物转换行进方向: *Our flight was diverted to another airport because of the bad weather.* 我们的班机因天气关系改变航线飞往另一机场。

divide /dɪˈvaɪd; dəˈvaɪd/ *verb* 动词 (**divides, dividing, divided**)
1 share or cut something into smaller parts 把某事物分开或割开 (成为小部分); 划分: *The teacher divided the class into groups of three.* 老师把学生分成三人一组。◇ *The book is divided into ten chapters.* 这本书共分为十章。
2 go into parts 分离开: *When the road divides, go left.* 在这条路的分岔口向左拐。
3 find out how many times one number goes into a bigger number 用某数除某数: *36 divided by 4 is 9* (36 ÷ 4 = 9). ✳ 36除以4等于9 (36 ÷ 4 = 9)。

divine /dɪˈvaɪn; dəˈvaɪn/ *adjective* 形容词
of, like or from God or a god 上帝或神的; 像上帝或神的; 上帝或神赐予的: *a divine message* 神谕

division /dɪˈvɪʒn; dəˈvɪʒən/ *noun* 名词
1 (no plural 无复数) finding out how many times one number goes into a bigger number 除法; 除
2 (no plural 无复数) sharing or cutting something into parts (对某事物的) 分开或割开 (成为小部分): *the division of Germany after the Second World War* 第二次世界大战后德国的分裂
3 (*plural* 复数作 **divisions**) one of the parts of a big company (大公司的) 部门: *He works in the sales division.* 他在营业部工作。

divorce /dɪˈvɔːs; dəˈvɔrs/ *noun* 名词
the end of a marriage by law 离婚: *She is getting a divorce.* 她正办理离婚手续。
divorce *verb* 动词 (**divorces, divorcing, divorced** /dɪˈvɔːst; dəˈvɔrst/)
He divorced his wife. 他跟太太离婚了。
✪ We often say **get divorced** ✳ **get divorced** 是常用词语: *They got divorced last year.* 他们去年离婚了。
divorced *adjective* 形容词
I'm not married—I'm divorced. 我现在单身——我离婚了。

DIY /ˌdiː aɪ ˈwaɪ; ˌdi aɪ ˈwaɪ/ *noun* 名词 (no plural 无复数)
making or repairing things in your house yourself. 'DIY' is short for **do-it-yourself** 自己干 (在家里自己制造或修理东西。DIY 是 **do-it-yourself** 的缩略式): *a DIY shop* 出售"自己干"材料的商店

dizzy /ˈdɪzi; ˈdɪzɪ/ *adjective* 形容词 (**dizzier, dizziest**)
If you feel dizzy, you feel that everything is turning round and round and that you are going to fall 头晕的; 眩晕的: *The room was very hot and I started to feel dizzy.* 屋里很热，我感到头晕了。

DJ /ˌdiː ˈdʒeɪ; ˌdi ˈdʒe/ *short for* **disc jockey** ✳ **disc jockey** 的缩略式

do[1] /duː, də; du/ *verb* 动词
1 a word that you use with another verb to make a question 与另一动词连用构成

do¹

present tense 现在时态		*negative short forms* 否定缩略式		*past tense* 过去时态	*present participle* 现在分词
I	**do**	I	**don't**	**did** /dɪd; dɪd/	**doing**
you	**do**	you	**don't**		
he/she/it	**does** /dʌz; dʌz/	he/she/it	**doesn't**	*past participle* 过去分词	
we	**do**	we	**don't**		
you	**do**	you	**don't**	**done** /dʌn; dʌn/	
they	**do**	they	**don't**		

问句: *Do you want an apple?* 你要苹果吗？

2 a word that you use with another verb when you are saying 'not' 与另一动词连用构成否定句: *I like football but I don't* (= do not) *like tennis.* 我喜欢足球，不喜欢网球。

3 a word that you use in place of saying something again 用以替代应重复的词语: *She doesn't speak English, but I do* (= I speak English). 她不会说英语，可是我会（= 我会说英语）。

4 a word that you use before another verb to make it stronger 用于另一动词前以加强语气: *You do look nice!* 你真的很帅。

do² /du:; du/ *verb* 动词 (**does** /dʌz; dʌz/, **doing**, **did** /dɪd; dɪd/, **has done** /dʌn; dʌn/)

1 carry out an action 进行一项活动: *What are you doing?* 你干什么呢？◇ *He did the cooking.* 是他做的饭。◇ *What did you do with my key?* (= where did you put it?) 你把我的钥匙放哪儿去了？

2 finish something; find the answer 做完某事；得到答案: *I have done my homework.* 我做完功课了。◇ *I can't do this sum — it's too difficult.* 我不会做这道算术题——太难了。

3 have a job or study something 有某职业；学某事: *'Tell me what he does.' 'He's a doctor.'* "告诉我他是干什么的。" "他是医生。" ◇ *She's doing Economics at Hull University.* 她在赫尔大学学经济。

4 be good enough; be enough 够好的；足够的: *Will this soup do for dinner?* 晚饭喝这个汤行吗？

be or 或 **have to do with somebody** or 或 **something** be connected with somebody or something 与某人或某事物有关: *I'm not sure what his job is — I think it's something to do with computers.* 我不太清楚他是做什么工作的——我想是跟计算机有点儿关系。◇ *Don't read that letter. It has nothing to do with you!* 别看那封信。跟你没关系！

could do with something want or need something 想要或需要某事物: *I could do with a drink.* 我想喝点什么。

do up 1 fasten something 把某物固定住；扣上；绑紧: *Do up the buttons on your shirt.* 把你衬衫的扣子系上。✪ opposite 反义词: **undo 2** clean and repair something to make it look newer 弄干净或修好某物（使之看起来新一些）: *They bought an old house and now they are doing it up.* 他们买了所旧房子，现在正在翻新呢。

dock /dɒk; dɑk/ *noun* 名词

a place by the sea or a river where ships go so that people can move things on and off them or repair them 码头；船坞

doctor /ˈdɒktə(r); ˈdɑktɚ/ *noun* 名词

1 a person whose job is to make sick people well again 医生；大夫: *Doctor Jones sees patients every morning.* 琼斯医生每天上午看病。✪ When we talk about visiting the doctor, we say **go to the doctor's** 去看病应说 **go to the doctor's**: *If you're feeling ill you should go to the doctor's.* 要是身体不舒服，就应该找大夫看看。

2 a person who has the highest degree from a university 博士

✪ When you write 'Doctor' as part of a person's name the short form is **Dr**. 若写在姓名之前，doctor 的缩略式 **Dr**。

document /ˈdɒkjumənt; ˈdɑkjəmənt/ *noun* 名词

a paper with important information on it 文件；公文: *a legal document* 法律文件

documentary /ˌdɒkjuˈmentri; ˌdɑkjəˈmɛntərɪ/ *noun* 名词 (*plural* 复数作 **documentaries**)

D

a film about true things 记录片: *I watched an interesting documentary about Japan on TV last night.* 我昨天晚上在电视上看了一部关于日本的记录片，很有意思。

dodge /dɒdʒ; dɑdʒ/ *verb* 动词 (**dodges**, **dodging**, **dodged** /dɒdʒd; dɑdʒd/)
move quickly to avoid something or somebody 躲避某物或某人；闪开；躲开: *He ran across the busy road, dodging the cars.* 他跑着穿过繁忙的马路，左闪右闪躲避汽车。

does *form of* **do** ✳ **do** 的不同形式

D

doesn't /ˈdʌznt; ˈdʌzn̩t/ = **does not**

dog /dɒg; dɔg/ *noun* 名词
an animal that many people keep as a pet or to do work 狗；犬 ✪ A young dog is called a **puppy**. 幼小的狗叫做 **puppy**。

doll /dɒl; dɔl/ *noun* 名词
a toy like a very small person 玩具娃娃；玩偶

dollar /ˈdɒlə(r); ˈdɑlɚ/ *noun* 名词
money that people use in the USA and some other countries. There are 100 **cents** in a dollar 元（美国和其他一些国家的货币，1元等于100分钱，分叫做 **cent**）: *Those jeans cost 45 dollars.* 那条牛仔裤45美元。✪ We write **$** 可写作 **$**: *This shirt costs $30.* 这件衬衫30美元。

dolphin 海豚

dolphin /ˈdɒlfɪn; ˈdɑlfɪn/ *noun* 名词
an intelligent animal that lives in the sea 海豚

dome /dəʊm; dom/ *noun* 名词
the round roof of a building 圆屋顶: *the dome of St Paul's Cathedral in London* 伦敦圣保罗大教堂的圆顶

domestic /dəˈmestɪk; dəˈmɛstɪk/ *adjective* 形容词
1 of or about the home or family 家的；家庭的；关于家的或家庭的: *Cooking and cleaning are domestic jobs.* 做饭和打扫卫生都是家务事。◇ *Many cats and dogs are domestic animals* (= animals that live in your home with you). 猫、狗大多是家畜。
2 of or inside a country 本国的；国内的: *a domestic flight* (= to a place in the same country) 国内班机

dominate /ˈdɒmɪneɪt; ˈdɑməˌnet/ *verb* 动词 (**dominates**, **dominating**, **dominated**)
control somebody or something because you are stronger or more important 控制或操纵某人或某事物: *He dominates his younger brother.* 他管着他弟弟。

donate /dəʊˈneɪt; ˈdonet/ *verb* 动词 (**donates**, **donating**, **donated**)
give something to people who need it 捐赠某物: *They donated £1 000 to the hospital.* 他们捐给医院1 000英镑。

donation /dəʊˈneɪʃn; doˈneʃən/ *noun* 名词
something that you give to people who need it 捐赠物品: *a donation of money* 捐的款

done *form of* **do** ✳ **do** 的不同形式

donkey /ˈdɒŋki; ˈdɑŋkɪ/ *noun* 名词 (*plural* 复数作 **donkeys**)
an animal like a small horse with long ears 驴

don't /dəʊnt; dont/ = **do not**

door /dɔ:(r); dɔr/ *noun* 名词
the way into a building or room; a piece of wood, glass or metal that you use to open and close the way in to a building, room, cupboard, car, etc 门口；门: *Can you close the door, please?* 请你把门关上行吗？◇ *Sophie knocked on the door. 'Come in,' Peter said.* 索菲敲了敲门。彼得说："请进。" ◇ *There is somebody at the door.* 门口有人。☞ picture at **house**. 见 **house** 词条插图。A house often has a **front door** and a **back door**. 房子一般都有前门（**front door**）和后门（**back door**）。
answer the door go to open the door when somebody knocks or rings the bell 应门（听见有人敲门或按铃后，去开门）
next door in the next house, room or building 在紧挨着的房子、屋子或大楼里；在隔壁: *Mary lives next door to us.* 玛丽住在我们隔壁。
out of doors outside; not in a building 在户外: *Farmers spend a lot of time out of doors.* 农民大部分时间都在户外。

doorbell /ˈdɔ:bel; ˈdɔrˌbɛl/ *noun* 名词
a bell outside a house that you ring to tell people inside that you want to go in 门铃

doorway /ˈdɔ:weɪ; ˈdɔrˌwe/ *noun* 名词
an opening for going into a building or

room 门口: *Mike was waiting in the doorway when they arrived.* 他们来的时候，迈克正在门口迎候。

dormitory /'dɔ:mətri; 'dɔrməˌtɔrɪ/ *noun* 名词 (*plural* 复数作 **dormitories**)
a big bedroom for a lot of people, usually in a school 宿舍（通常指学校的）

dose /dəʊs; dos/ *noun* 名词
an amount of medicine that you take at one time 一次剂量；一剂；一服: *Take a large dose of medicine before you go to bed.* 你临睡前要服一次大剂量的药。

dot /dɒt; dɑt/ *noun* 名词
a small round mark 小圆点: *The letter 'i' has a dot over it.* ＊i 这个字母上有个小圆点。
on the dot at exactly the right time 准时地: *Please be here at nine o'clock on the dot.* 请准时在九点整到这里来。

dotted line /ˌdɒtɪd 'laɪn; ˌdɑtɪd 'laɪn/ *noun* 名词
a line of dots that sometimes shows where you have to write something 点线；虚线: *Please sign* (= write your name) *on the dotted line.* 请在虚线上签名。

double /'dʌbl; 'dʌbl̩/ *adjective* 形容词
1 two times as much or as many; twice as much or as many 两倍的；双倍的: *a double portion of chips* 双份的炸土豆条儿
2 with two parts that are the same 有两个相同部分的: *double doors* 两扇的门
3 for two people 为两人的；供两人用的: *a double bed* 双人床 ◇ *a double room* 双人房间
4 You use 'double' before a letter or a number to show that it comes two times（用于一字母或数字前，表示该字母或数字出现两次）双；两个: *'How do you spell your name, Mr Coombe?' 'C, double O, M, B, E.'* "库姆先生，您的姓名用英文怎样拼写？" "C、O、O、M、B、E。" ◇ *My phone number is double four nine five one* (44951). 我的电话号码是四四九五一(44951)。
☞ Look at **single**. 见 **single**。

double *verb* 动词 (**doubles, doubling, doubled** /'dʌbld; 'dʌbl̩d/)
make something twice as much or as many; become twice as much or as many（使）某事物增加一倍: *The price has doubled: last year it was £10 and this year it's £20.* 价钱增加了一倍，去年是10英镑，今年是20英镑。

double-bass /ˌdʌbl 'beɪs; ˌdʌbl̩'bes/ *noun* 名词
a musical instrument like a very big violin 低音提琴

double-decker /ˌdʌbl 'dekə(r); ˌdʌbl̩-'dɛkɚ/ *noun* 名词
a bus with places to sit upstairs and downstairs 双层公共汽车

doubt[1] /daʊt; daʊt/ *noun* 名词
a feeling that you are not sure about something（对某事物的）怀疑；疑惑；疑问: *She says the story is true but I have my doubts about it.* 她说那件事是真事，我还是有点儿怀疑。
in doubt not sure 不肯定；不确信: *If you are in doubt, ask your teacher.* 你要是没有把握，问问老师吧。
no doubt I am sure 肯定；确信: *Paul isn't here yet, but no doubt he will come later.* 保罗还没来，但是他呆一会儿准来。

doubt[2] /daʊt; daʊt/ *verb* 动词 (**doubts, doubting, doubted**)
not feel sure about something; think that something is probably not true or probably will not happen 怀疑某事物；认为某事物可能不属实或不会产生；疑惑: *I doubt if he will come.* 我看他不一定来了。

doubtful /'daʊtfl; 'daʊtfəl/ *adjective* 形容词
not certain or not likely 不能确定的；不大可能的: *It is doubtful whether he will walk again.* 很难说他以后还能不能走路。

doubtless /'daʊtləs; 'daʊtlɪs/ *adverb* 副词
almost certainly 几乎可以肯定；大概: *Doubtless she'll be late!* 她准得晚了！

dough /dəʊ; do/ *noun* 名词 (no plural 无复数)
flour, water and other things mixed together, for making bread（做面包用的）生面团

dove /dʌv; dʌv/ *noun* 名词
a bird that is often used as a sign of peace 鸽子（常用做和平的象征）

down /daʊn; daʊn/ *preposition, adverb* 介词，副词
1 in or to a lower place; not up 下；在下；向下: *The sun goes down in the*

D

evening. 晚上太阳下山了。◇ *We ran down the hill.* 我们跑到山下。◇ *Put that box down on the floor.* 把箱子放在地上吧。☞ picture on page C4 见第C4页图

2 from standing to sitting or lying 坐下；躺下: *Sit down.* 坐下。◇ *Lie down on the bed.* 躺到床上去。

3 in a way that is smaller, less strong, etc 渐小；渐少；渐弱: *Prices are going down.* 价钱降低了。◇ *Turn that music down!* (= so that it is not so loud) 把音乐的音量调小点儿！（= 声音别那么大）

4 along 沿着；顺着: *'Can you tell me where the bank is, please?' 'Go down this road, then turn right at the end.'* "请问银行在哪儿？""沿着这条路走到头儿向右拐。"

5 on paper 在纸上；到纸上: *Write these words down.* 把这些字写下来。

downhill /ˌdaʊnˈhɪl; ˈdaunˌhɪl/ *adverb* 副词

down, towards the bottom of a hill 在山下；向山下: *My bicycle can go fast downhill.* 我的自行车下山很快。

downstairs /ˌdaʊnˈsteəz; ˈdaunˈstɛrz/ *adverb* 副词

to or on a lower floor of a building 到楼下；向楼下；在楼下: *I went downstairs to make breakfast.* 我到楼下做早饭去了。

downstairs *adjective* 形容词

She lives in the downstairs flat. 她住在楼下的公寓里。

✪ opposite 反义词: **upstairs**

downtown /ˌdaʊnˈtaʊn; ˈdaunˈtaun/ *American English for* **city centre** 美式英语，即 **city centre**: *She works downtown.* 她在城里工作。◇ *downtown Los Angeles* 洛杉矶市中心

downwards /ˈdaʊnwədz; ˈdaunwərdz/, **downward** /ˈdaʊnwəd; ˈdaunwərd/ *adverb* 副词

down; towards a lower place or towards the ground 下；向下；向地面: *She was lying face downward on the grass.* 她脸朝下趴在草地上。✪ opposite 反义词: **upwards**

doze /dəʊz; doz/ *verb* 动词 (**dozes, dozing, dozed** /dəʊzd; dozd/)

sleep lightly for a short time 小睡；打瞌睡；打盹儿: *My grandfather was dozing in his armchair.* 我爷爷在单座沙发上打起盹儿来了。

doze off start dozing 打起瞌睡；打起盹儿来: *I dozed off in front of the television.* 我在电视机前打起盹来了。

doze *noun* 名词

She had a doze after lunch. 她午饭后小睡了一会儿。

dozen /ˈdʌzn; ˈdʌzn̩/ *noun* 名词 (*plural* 复数作 **dozen**)

twelve（一）打（十二个）: *a dozen red roses* 一打红玫瑰 ◇ *two dozen boxes* 两打盒子 ◇ *half a dozen eggs* 半打鸡蛋

dozens of a lot of 很多: *They've invited dozens of people to the party.* 他们邀请了很多人参加聚会。

Dr *short way of writing* **Doctor** ✳ **Doctor** 的缩写形式

draft /dræft; dræft/, **drafty** /ˈdræfti; ˈdræftɪ/ *American English for* **draught, draughty** 美式英语，即 **draught**、**draughty**

drag /dræg; dræg/ *verb* 动词 (**drags, dragging, dragged** /drægd; drægd/)

1 pull something along the ground slowly, often because it is heavy 拖；拉；拽: *He couldn't lift the sack, so he dragged it out of the shop.* 他提不动那个袋子，只好把它拖出商店。

2 If something drags, it seems to go slowly because it is not interesting（因乏味）显得慢: *Time drags when you're waiting for a bus.* 等公共汽车的时候，时间好像过得很慢。

dragon /ˈdrægən; ˈdrægən/ *noun* 名词

a big dangerous animal with fire in its mouth, that you find only in stories 龙

drain[1] /dreɪn; dren/ *noun* 名词

a pipe that carries away dirty water from a building 排水管；下水道: *The drain is blocked.* 下水道堵塞了。

drain[2] /dreɪn; dren/ *verb* 动词 (**drains, draining, drained** /dreɪnd; drend/)

1 let liquid flow away from something, so that it becomes dry 让液体流走而使某物变干；控: *Wash the lettuce and then drain it.* 把莴苣先洗洗再控干。

2 become dry because liquid is flowing away（液体流走后）变干；控干: *Let the dishes drain.* 把碟子上的水控干。

3 flow away 流走: *The water drained away slowly.* 水慢慢流走了。

drama /ˈdrɑːmə; ˈdrɑmə/ *noun* 名词

1 (*plural* 复数作 **dramas**) a story that

you watch in the theatre or on television, or listen to on the radio 戏；剧；戏剧：*a TV drama* 电视剧

2 (no plural 无复数) the study of plays and acting 戏剧学：*She went to drama school.* 她上的是戏剧学校。

3 (*plural* 复数作 **dramas**) an exciting thing that happens 紧张刺激的事情：*There was a big drama at school when one of the teachers fell in the pond!* 有个老师掉进池塘里了，这件事轰动了全校。

dramatic /drə'mætɪk; drə'mætɪk/ *adjective* 形容词

1 of plays or the theatre 戏剧的；戏院的：*a dramatic society* 戏剧协会

2 sudden, great or exciting 突然的；巨大的；激动人心的；戏剧性的：*The finish of the race was very dramatic.* 这场速度比赛结局十分紧张刺激。

dramatically /drə'mætɪkli; drə'mætɪklɪ/ *adverb* 副词

Prices went up dramatically. 价格急剧上升。

dramatist /'dræmətɪst; 'dræmətɪst/ *noun* 名词

a person who writes plays 剧作家；编剧

drank *form of* **drink**[1] ＊ **drink**[1] 的不同形式

draught /drɑ:ft; dræft/ *noun* 名词

cold air that comes into a room（进入房间的）冷空气：*Can you shut the window? I can feel a draught.* 你把窗户关上行吗？我觉得有股冷风进来。

draughty /'drɑ:fti; 'dræftɪ/ *adjective* 形容词 (**draughtier**, **draughtiest**)

a draughty house 有穿堂风的房子

draughts /drɑ:fts; dræfts/ *noun* 名词 (plural 复数)

a game that two people play with round flat pieces on a board that has black and white squares on it 国际跳棋：*Do you want a game of draughts?* 你想下国际跳棋吗？

draw[1] /drɔ:; drɔ/ *verb* 动词 (**draws**, **drawing**, **drew** /dru:; dru/, **has drawn** /drɔ:n; drɔn/)

1 make a picture with a pencil, pen, chalk, etc（用铅笔、钢笔、粉笔等）画：*She drew a picture of a horse.* 她画了一匹马。◇ *He has drawn a car.* 他画了一辆汽车。◇ *My sister draws well.* 我姐姐很会画画儿。

2 pull or take something from a place 拉出或拿出某物；抽出；拔出：*He drew a knife from his pocket.* 他从口袋里掏出了一把刀。

3 move or come 移动；来：*The train drew into the station.* 火车进站了。

4 pull something to make it move 拉某物（使之移动）：*The carriage was drawn by two horses.* 这辆马车是用两匹马拉的。

5 end a game with the same number of points for both players or teams（比赛）打成平局；不分胜负：*Liverpool and Tottenham drew in last Saturday's match.* 上星期六的比赛利物浦队和托特纳姆队打成了平局。

6 open or close curtains 打开或合上帘子：*I switched on the light and drew the curtains.* 我开了灯，拉上了窗帘。

draw out take money out of a bank（从银行中）取钱；提款：*I drew out £50 before I went shopping.* 我从银行取出了50英镑去买东西。

draw up come to a place and stop 到达并停在某处：*A taxi drew up outside the house.* 有辆计程车来到房子外边停住了。

draw something up write something 写出；写下：*They drew up a list of people who they wanted to invite to the wedding.* 他们列出了打算邀请参加婚礼者的名单。

draw[2] /drɔ:; drɔ/ *noun* 名词

the result of a game when both players or teams have the same number of points（比赛的）平局，不分胜负：*The football match ended in a 1-1 draw.* 那场足球比赛踢成了一比一。

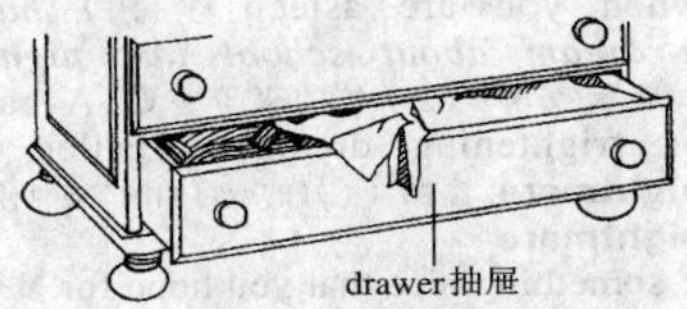

drawer /drɔ:(r); drɔr/ *noun* 名词

a thing like a box that you can pull out from a cupboard or desk, for example 抽屉

drawing /'drɔ:ɪŋ; 'drɔ·ɪŋ/ *noun* 名词

1 (*plural* 复数作 **drawings**) a picture made with a pencil, pen, chalk, etc（用铅笔、钢笔、粉笔等画的）画儿

2 (no plural 无复数) making pictures with a pencil, pen, chalk, etc（用铅笔、钢笔、粉笔等）画画儿：*Katherine is very good at drawing.* 凯瑟琳很会画画儿。

D

drawing-pin /ˈdrɔːɪŋ pɪn; ˈdrɔ·ɪŋˌpɪn/ *noun* 名词
a short pin with a flat round top, that you use for attaching paper to a wall or board 图钉: *I put the poster up with drawing-pins.* 我用图钉把海报钉上了。

drawn *form of* **draw**¹ ✳ **draw**¹ 的不同形式

dreadful /ˈdredfl; ˈdrɛdfəl/ *adjective* 形容词
very bad 非常坏的；糟糕的: *I had a dreadful journey—my train was two hours late!* 我一路上糟糕极了——火车误点两个小时！

D

dreadfully /ˈdredfəli; ˈdrɛdfəlɪ/ *adverb* 副词
very 非常: *I'm dreadfully sorry, but I must go now.* 十分抱歉，我现在得走了。

dream /driːm; drim/ *verb* 动词 (**dreams**, **dreaming**, **dreamt** /dremt; drɛmt/ or 或 **dreamed** /driːmd; drimd/, **has dreamt** or 或 **has dreamed**)
1 have a picture or idea in your mind when you are asleep 做梦；梦见: *I dreamt about you last night.* 我昨天夜里梦见你了。◇ *I dreamt that I met the Queen.* 我做梦梦见女王了。
2 hope for something nice in the future 梦想；向往: *She dreams of becoming a famous actress.* 她梦想成为名演员。

dream *noun* 名词
1 pictures or ideas in your mind when you are asleep 梦: *I had a dream about school last night.* 我昨天夜里梦见学校的事了。✪ A bad or frightening dream is called a **nightmare**. 噩梦（不好的或可怕的梦）叫做 **nightmare**。
2 something nice that you hope for 梦想

dress¹ /dres; drɛs/ *noun* 名词
1 (*plural* 复数作 **dresses**) a piece of clothing with a top part and a skirt, that a woman or girl wears 连衣裙
2 (no plural 无复数) clothes 衣物；衣服；服装: *The group of dancers wore national dress.* 这些舞蹈演员穿的是民族服装。

dress² /dres; drɛs/ *verb* 动词 (**dresses**, **dressing**, **dressed** /drest; drɛst/)
1 put clothes on yourself or another person（给某人）穿衣服: *She dressed quickly and went out.* 她匆匆穿上衣服出去了。◇ *He washed and dressed the baby.* 他给孩子洗了澡、穿上衣服。✪ opposite 反义词: **undress**
2 wear clothes 穿着衣服: *She dresses like a film star.* 她穿着打扮像个电影明星。
dressed in something wearing something 穿着某种衣服: *He was dressed in black.* 他穿着一身黑衣服。
dress up 1 put on your best clothes 穿上最好的衣服: *They dressed up to go to the theatre.* 他们穿上了最好的衣服去看戏去。**2** put on special clothes for fun, so that you look like another person or a thing（为娱乐）穿上特殊的衣服（装成别的人或东西）；化装: *The children dressed up as ghosts.* 孩子都化装成了鬼的样子。
get dressed put on your clothes 穿上衣服: *I got dressed and went downstairs for breakfast.* 我穿上衣服到楼下去吃早饭。✪ opposite 反义词: **get undressed**

dressing /ˈdresɪŋ; ˈdrɛsɪŋ/ *noun* 名词
1 a thing for covering a part of your body that is hurt 包扎伤口的用品: *You should put a dressing on that cut.* 你得把伤口包扎起来。
2 a mixture of oil, vinegar, etc that you put on a salad 拌色拉的调料

dressing-gown /ˈdresɪŋ gaʊn; ˈdrɛsɪŋˌgaʊn/ *noun* 名词
a piece of clothing like a coat that you wear over your pyjamas or nightdress 晨衣（在睡衣外面穿的长袍）

dressing-table /ˈdresɪŋ teɪbl; ˈdrɛsɪŋˌtebl̩/ *noun* 名词
a piece of bedroom furniture like a table with drawers and a mirror 梳妆台

drew *form of* **draw**¹ ✳ **draw**¹ 的不同形式

dried *form of* **dry**² ✳ **dry**² 的不同形式

drier¹ *form of* **dry**¹ ✳ **dry**¹ 的不同形式

drier² /ˈdraɪə(r); ˈdraɪɚ/ *noun* 名词
a machine for drying clothes 干衣机: *Take the clothes out of the washing-machine and put them in the drier.* 把衣服从洗衣机里拿出来再放进干衣机里。☞ Look also at **hair-drier**. 另见 **hair-drier**。

dries *form of* **dry**² ✳ **dry**² 的不同形式

driest *form of* **dry**¹ ✳ **dry**¹ 的不同形式

drift /drɪft; drɪft/ *verb* 动词 (**drifts, drifting, drifted**)
move slowly in the air or on water 飘移；漂流: *The empty boat drifted along on the sea.* 那条空船在海上漂来漂去。◇ *The balloon drifted away.* 气球飘走了。

drill /drɪl; drɪl/ *noun* 名词
a tool that you use for making holes 钻；钻床；钻机: *an electric drill* 电钻 ◇ *a dentist's drill* 牙钻

drill *verb* 动词 (**drills, drilling, drilled** /drɪld; drɪld/)
make a hole using a drill（用钻机）打眼；钻洞

drink 喝

drink[1] /drɪŋk; drɪŋk/ *verb* 动词 (**drinks, drinking, drank** /dræŋk; dræŋk/, **has drunk** /drʌŋk; drʌŋk/)
1 take in liquid, for example water, milk or coffee, through your mouth 喝: *What do you want to drink?* 您要喝什么？◇ *She was drinking a cup of tea.* 她喝着一杯茶。
2 drink alcohol 喝酒: *'Would you like some wine?' 'No, thank you. I don't drink.'* "您想喝点儿酒吗？""不，谢谢您。我不会喝酒。"

drink[2] /drɪŋk; drɪŋk/ *noun* 名词
1 liquid, for example water, milk or coffee, that you take in through your mouth 饮料（如水、牛奶或咖啡）: *Would you like a drink?* 您想喝点儿什么吗？◇ *Can I have a drink of water?* 我喝点儿水行吗？
2 drink with alcohol in it, for example beer or wine 含酒精的饮料（如啤酒或葡萄酒）: *There was lots of food and drink at the party.* 在这次聚会上有很多食物和酒。

drip /drɪp; drɪp/ *verb* 动词 (**drips, dripping, dripped** /drɪpt; drɪpt/)
1 fall slowly in small drops 缓慢滴下: *Water was dripping through the roof.* 水从屋顶滴下来。
2 have liquid falling from it in small drops 有液体从其中滴下: *The tap is dripping.* 水龙头滴着水。

drive[1] /draɪv; draɪv/ *verb* 动词 (**drives, driving, drove** /drəʊv; drov/, **has driven** /'drɪvn; 'drɪvən/)
1 control a car, bus, etc and make it go where you want to go 开车: *Can you drive?* 你会开车吗？◇ *She usually drives to work.* 她通常是开车去上班。
2 take somebody to a place in a car 开车送某人到某处: *My parents drove me to the airport.* 是我父母开车把我送到机场的。

drive[2] /draɪv; draɪv/ *noun* 名词
1 a journey in a car 乘坐汽车: *It's a long drive from Paris to Rome.* 从巴黎坐汽车到罗马要走很长时间。◇ *We went for a drive in my sister's car.* 我们坐我姐姐的汽车兜风去了。
2 a road that goes from the street to one house 私人车道（从街道通往一所房子的路）: *You can park your car in the drive.* 您可以把汽车停在这条私人车道上。

driver /'draɪvə(r); 'draɪvɚ/ *noun* 名词
a person who controls a car, bus, train, etc 驾驶机动车辆的人；司机；驾驶员: *John is a good driver.* 约翰开车开得很好。◇ *a taxi-driver* 计程车司机

driver's licence /'draɪvəz laɪsns; 'draɪvɚz ˌlaɪsṇs/ *American English for* **driving-licence** 美式英语，即 **driving-licence**

drive-in /'draɪv ɪn; 'draɪvˌɪn/ *noun* 名词
a place where you can go to eat or to watch a film while you are sitting in your car 免下车场所（顾客可安坐汽车中吃东西、看电影的去处）

driving /'draɪvɪŋ; 'draɪvɪŋ/ *noun* 名词 (no plural 无复数)
controlling a car, bus, etc 开车；驾驶: *Driving in the fog can be dangerous.* 在雾中开车很危险。

driving-licence /'draɪvɪŋ laɪsns; 'draɪvɪŋˌlaɪsṇs/ *noun* 名词
a piece of paper that shows that you are allowed to drive a car, etc 驾驶执照

driving test /'draɪvɪŋ test; 'draɪvɪŋ ˌtɛst/ *noun* 名词
a test that you have to pass before you get your **driving-licence** 驾驶考试（及格后获得的驾驶执照叫做 **driving-licence**）

D

droop /druːp; drup/ *verb* 动词 (**droops**, **drooping**, **drooped** /druːpt; drupt/)
bend or hang down 弯曲；下垂: *Flowers droop if you don't put them in water.* 花不放在水里就发蔫。

drop¹ /drɒp; drɑp/ *verb* 动词 (**drops**, **dropping**, **dropped** /drɒpt; drɑpt/)
1 let something fall 使某物掉下或落下: *I dropped my watch and it broke.* 我把手表掉在地上摔坏了。
2 fall 掉下；落下: *The glass dropped from her hands.* 玻璃杯从她手中掉了下来。

drop 掉下

3 become lower or less 变低；变少: *The temperature has dropped.* 温度下降了。
4 stop your car and let somebody get out 停住汽车好让某人下车: *Could you drop me at the station?* 您在车站停一下让我下车行吗？
5 stop doing something 不再做正做的事: *I'm going to drop geography at school next year.* 我打算明年不上地理课了。
drop in visit somebody who does not know that you are coming（未经预约）探望某人；串门儿: *Drop in to see me the next time you're in London.* 你下次来伦敦顺便到我这儿坐坐。
drop off fall asleep 打盹儿；打瞌睡: *She dropped off in front of the TV.* 她在电视机前打起盹儿来了。
drop out stop doing something with a group of people 不再与大家一起做正做的事: *I dropped out of the football team after I hurt my leg.* 我腿受伤以后就退出了足球队。

drop² /drɒp; drɑp/ *noun* 名词
1 a very small amount of liquid（液体的）一滴: *a drop of blood* 一滴血 ☞ picture on page C25 见第C25页图
2 a fall; going down 下降；降低: *a drop in temperature* 温度下降 ◇ *a drop in prices* 价格降低

drought /draʊt; draʊt/ *noun* 名词
a long time when there is not enough rain 干旱（时期）；旱灾: *Thousands of people died in the drought.* 成千上万的人在旱灾中死去。

drove *form of* **drive¹** ＊ **drive¹** 的不同形式

drown /draʊn; draʊn/ *verb* 动词 (**drowns**, **drowning**, **drowned** /draʊnd; draʊnd/)
1 die under water because you cannot breathe 淹死；溺死: *The boy fell in the river and drowned.* 那个男孩儿掉进河里淹死了。
2 make a person or an animal die by putting them under water so that they cannot breathe 把人或动物淹死: *They drowned the kittens.* 他们把小猫都淹死了。

drug /drʌg; drʌg/ *noun* 名词
1 something that makes you better when you are ill 药物；药品；药剂；药材
2 something that people eat, smoke or inject because it makes them feel happy or excited. In many countries it is against the law to use drugs 麻醉药；毒品（口服、吸食或注射后使人感到愉快或兴奋的药物。使用毒品在很多国家都是犯法的）: *She takes drugs.* 她吸毒。◇ *Heroin is a dangerous drug.* 海洛因是危险的麻醉药。

drug addict /ˈdrʌg ædɪkt; ˈdrʌg ædɪkt/ *noun* 名词
a person who cannot stop using drugs 有毒瘾的人；吸毒的人

drugstore /ˈdrʌgstɔː(r); ˈdrʌgˌstɔr/ *noun* 名词
a shop in the USA where you can buy medicines and a lot of other things（在美国的）药品杂货店（出售药品和各种杂物）

drums 鼓
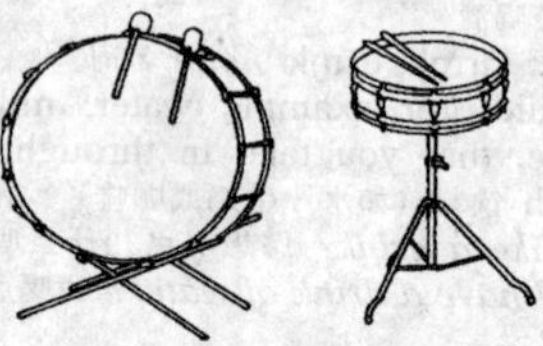

drum /drʌm; drʌm/ *noun* 名词
1 a musical instrument that you hit with sticks or with your hands 鼓: *He plays the drums in a band.* 他在乐队中打鼓。
2 a big round container for oil 装油的鼓状物: *an oil drum* 油桶

drummer /ˈdrʌmə(r); ˈdrʌmɚ/ *noun* 名词
a person who plays a drum 鼓手

drunk[1] *form of* **drink**[1] ＊ **drink**[1] 的不同形式

drunk[2] /drʌŋk; drʌŋk/ *adjective* 形容词
If a person is drunk, he/she has drunk too much alcohol. 醉的

dry[1] /draɪ; draɪ/ *adjective* 形容词 (**drier**, **driest**)
1 with no liquid in it or on it; not wet 干的；干燥的: *The washing isn't dry yet.* 洗的衣服还没干呢。☞ picture on page C27 见第C27页图
2 with no rain 少雨的；干旱的: *dry weather* 干燥的气候
3 not sweet 无甜味的；干的: *dry white wine* 干白葡萄酒

dry[2] /draɪ; draɪ/ *verb* 动词 (**dries**, **drying**, **dried** /draɪd; draɪd/, **has dried**)
1 become dry 变干: *Our clothes were drying in the sun.* 我们的衣服在太阳底下晾着呢。
2 make something dry 把某物弄干: *Dry your hands on this towel.* 用这条毛巾把手擦干。
dry out become completely dry 完全变干；干透: *Leave your shoes by the fire to dry out.* 把你的鞋放在火边烤干。
dry up **1** become completely dry 完全变干；干涸: *There was no rain for several months and all the rivers dried up.* 几个月没下雨了，所有的河都干了。**2** dry things like plates, knives and forks with a towel after you have washed them 用毛巾擦干（洗过的盘子、刀子、叉子等餐具）: *If I wash the dishes, could you dry up?* 要是我来洗碗，你来擦干行吗？✪ You can also say **do the drying-up**. 也可说 **do the drying-up**。

dry-clean /ˌdraɪ 'kli:n; 'draɪ'klin/ *verb* 动词 (**dry-cleans**, **dry-cleaning**, **dry-cleaned** /ˌdraɪ'kli:nd; 'draɪ'klind/)
make clothes clean by using chemicals, not water 干洗衣物: *I had my suit dry-cleaned.* 我把我的套装干洗了。
dry-cleaner's *noun* 名词
a shop where clothes and other things are dry-cleaned 干洗店

dryer /'draɪə(r); 'draɪə/ = **drier**[2]

dual carriageway /ˌdju:əl'kærɪdʒweɪ; ˌduəl 'kærɪdʒwe/ *noun* 名词
a wide road with grass or a fence between the two sides（中间有草丛或篱笆隔开的）双线车道

duchess /'dʌtʃəs; 'dʌtʃɪs/ *noun* 名词 (*plural* 复数作 **duchesses**)
1 a woman who has a special title 女公爵
2 the wife of a **duke** 公爵夫人（公爵叫做 **duke**）

duck 鸭子

duck[1] /dʌk; dʌk/ *noun* 名词
a bird that lives on and near water. You often see ducks on farms or in parks. 鸭子 ✪ A young duck is called a **duckling**. 雏鸭叫做 **duckling**。

duck[2] /dʌk; dʌk/ *verb* 动词 (**ducks**, **ducking**, **ducked** /dʌkt; dʌkt/)
move your head down quickly, so that something does not hit you or so that somebody does not see you 迅速低头（以免被打中或被看见）: *He saw the ball coming towards him and ducked.* 他看见球朝他飞来，赶紧低头闪开。

duckling /'dʌklɪŋ; 'dʌklɪŋ/ *noun* 名词
a young duck 雏鸭

due /dju:; du/ *adjective* 形容词
1 If something is due at a certain time, you expect it to happen or come then 到时候（该发生或该来）的: *What time is the train due?* 火车什么时候到？◇ *The new motorway is due to open in April.* 新高速公路四月通车。
2 If an amount of money is due, you must pay it（指应该付的款）到期的: *My rent is due at the beginning of the month.* 我月初交租钱。
due for something ready for something 该做某事物: *My car is due for a service.* 我的汽车该检修了。
due to something because of something 由于某事物: *The accident was due to bad driving.* 这起事故是由于驾驶不当造成的。

duet /dju'et; du'ɛt/ *noun* 名词
music for two people to sing or play on musical instruments 二重唱曲；二重奏曲: *James and Sarah sang a duet.* 詹姆斯和萨拉表演了二重唱。

dug *form of* **dig** ＊ **dig** 的不同形式

duke /dju:k; duk/ *noun* 名词
a man who has a special title 公爵 ☞ Look at **duchess**. 见 **duchess**。

D

dull /dʌl; dʌl/ *adjective* 形容词 (**duller**, **dullest**)
1 not bright 不晴朗的；不光亮的: *It was a dull, cloudy day.* 那天昏暗多云。
2 not strong or loud 不强的；声音不大的: *a dull pain* 隐约的疼痛
3 not interesting or exciting 乏味的；沉闷的: *Life is never dull in a big city.* 大城市里的生活是绝不会枯燥的。

dumb /dʌm; dʌm/ *adjective* 形容词
1 not able to speak 哑的: *There are special schools for children who are deaf and dumb.* 聋哑儿童有专门学校。
2 not intelligent; stupid 不聪明的；愚蠢的；笨的: *That was a dumb thing to do!* 那件事干得可真蠢！

D

dump /dʌmp; dʌmp/ *verb* 动词 (**dumps**, **dumping**, **dumped** /dʌmpt; dʌmpt/)
1 take something to a place and leave it there because you do not want it 丢掉不想要的东西: *They dumped their rubbish by the side of the road.* 他们把垃圾扔到路边了。
2 put something down without being careful 粗心地放下某物: *Don't dump your clothes on the floor!* 别把衣服胡乱扔到地上！

dump *noun* 名词
a place where you can take and leave things that you do not want 垃圾场；垃圾堆

dune /dju:n; dun/ *noun* 名词
a small hill of sand near the sea or in a desert 沙丘

dungarees /ˌdʌŋgə'ri:z; ˌdʌŋgə'riz/ *noun* 名词 (plural 复数)
trousers with a part that covers the top of your body 工装裤: *a new pair of dungarees* 一条新的工装裤

dungeon /'dʌndʒən; 'dʌndʒən/ *noun* 名词
a prison under the ground, for example in a castle 地牢（如城堡中的）

during /'djʊərɪŋ; 'dʊrɪŋ/ *preposition* 介词
1 all the time that something is happening 在…期间: *The sun gives us light during the day.* 太阳在白天供给我们光亮。
2 at some time while something else is happening 在有某情况的一段时间里: *She died during the night.* 她是夜里死的。◇ *I fell asleep during the film.* 我看着看着电影就睡着了。

dusk /dʌsk; dʌsk/ *noun* 名词 (no plural 无复数)
the time in the evening when it is nearly dark 黄昏；傍晚

dust /dʌst; dʌst/ *noun* 名词 (no plural 无复数)
dry dirt that is like powder 灰尘；尘土；尘埃: *The old table was covered in dust.* 旧桌子上满是灰尘。

dust *verb* 动词 (**dusts**, **dusting**, **dusted**)
take dust off something with a cloth（用布）擦掉某物上的灰尘: *I dusted the furniture.* 我把家具上的灰尘擦掉了。

dustbin 垃圾桶

dustbin /'dʌstbɪn; 'dʌstˌbɪn/ *noun* 名词
a thing that you put rubbish in outside your house（放置家门外的）垃圾桶

duster /'dʌstə(r); 'dʌstɚ/ *noun* 名词
a cloth that you use for taking the dust off furniture 掸布；抹布

dustman /'dʌstmən; 'dʌstmən/ *noun* 名词 (*plural* 复数作 **dustmen** /'dʌstmən; 'dʌstmən/)
a person whose job is to take away rubbish from outside people's houses 清除垃圾的工人

dusty /'dʌsti; 'dʌstɪ/ *adjective* 形容词 (**dustier**, **dustiest**)
covered with dust 有灰尘的: *The furniture was very dusty.* 家具上的灰尘很多。

duty¹ /'dju:ti; 'dutɪ/ *noun* 名词 (*plural* 复数作 **duties**)
something that you must do because it is part of your job or because you think it is right 责任；义务: *It's your duty to look after your parents when they get older.* 父母年老时子女有责任照顾他们。◇ *One of the duties of a secretary is to type letters.* 当秘书的要做的一件工作是打信。
off duty not working 不值班；歇班: *The police officer was off duty.* 那个警察歇班了。

on duty working 值班；上班：*Some nurses at the hospital are on duty all night.* 医院里有的护士整夜值班。

duty² /ˈdjuːti; ˈdutɪ/ *noun* 名词 (*plural* 复数作 **duties**)
money (a **tax**) that you pay to the government when you bring things into a country from another country 关税（税钱叫做 **tax**）

duty-free /ˌdjuːti ˈfriː; ˈdutɪˈfri/ *adjective, adverb* 形容词，副词
that you can bring into a country without paying money to the government. You can buy duty-free goods on planes or ships and at airports. 免税（的）（免税物品可在飞机上或轮船上以及机场中购买）

duvet /ˈduːveɪ; duˈve/ *noun* 名词
a thick warm cover for a bed. Duvets are often filled with feathers. 被子；（常指）羽绒被

dwarf /dwɔːf; dwɔrf/ *noun* 名词
a person who is much smaller than the usual size 侏儒

dye /daɪ; daɪ/ *noun* 名词
stuff that you use to change the colour of something, for example cloth or hair 染料

dye *verb* 动词 (**dyes, dyeing, dyed** /daɪd; daɪd/)
change the colour of something 漂染某物：*My parents were angry when I dyed my hair purple.* 我把头发染成了紫色，我父母很生气。

dying *form of* **die** ＊ **die** 的不同形式

be dying for something want to have something very much 极想要某物：*It's so hot! I'm dying for a drink.* 天气这么热！我真想喝点儿水。

be dying to want to do something very much 极想做某事：*My brother is dying to meet you.* 我哥哥很想见见您。

D

Ee

each /iːtʃ; itʃ/ *adjective, pronoun* 形容词，代词
every person or thing in a group 每；每个；各个：*Each student buys a book and a cassette.* 每个学生都买一本书和一盒录音带。◇ *He gave a present to each of the children.* 他送给孩子每人一份礼物。

They are looking at **each other**.
他们互相看着。

each *adverb* 副词
for one 每；每个；各个：*These peaches cost 25p each.* 这些桃儿25便士一个。
each other words that show that somebody does the same thing as another person 表示某人和另一人互相做同样的事的用语：*Gary and Susy looked at each other* (= Gary looked at Susy and Susy looked at Gary). 加里和苏西你看着我，我看着你（= 加里看着苏西，苏西看着加里）。

E

eager /ˈiːgə(r); ˈigɚ/ *adjective* 形容词
If you are eager to do something, you want to do it very much 热切的；热心的；渴望的：*She's eager to help with the party.* 她很想在聚会方面帮帮忙。
eagerly *adverb* 副词
The children were waiting eagerly for the film to begin. 孩子们都着急地等着电影开演。

eagle /ˈiːgl; ˈigḷ/ *noun* 名词
a large bird that catches and eats small birds and animals 雕；鹰

ear /ɪə(r); ɪr/ *noun* 名词
one of the two parts of a person or an animal that are used for hearing 耳朵：*Elephants have big ears.* 象的耳朵很大。
☞ picture on page C2 见第C2页图

earl /ɜːl; ɝl/ *noun* 名词
a British man who has a special title（英国的）伯爵

early /ˈɜːli; ˈɝlɪ/ *adjective, adverb* 形容词，副词 (**earlier, earliest**)
1 before the usual or right time 早（的）；提前（的）：*The train arrived ten minutes early.* 火车早到了十分钟。◇ *I was early for the lesson.* 我上课早来了一会儿。
2 near the beginning of a time 初；初期：*the early afternoon* 刚过中午 ◇ *She was in her early twenties* (= between the ages of 20 and about 23 or 24). 她二十出头（= 从20岁到23岁或24岁左右）。◇ *I have to get up early tomorrow.* 我明天得早起。
✪ opposite 反义词：**late**
an early night an evening when you go to bed earlier than usual 比平时睡得早的夜晚

earn /ɜːn; ɝn/ *verb* 动词 (**earns, earning, earned** /ɜːnd; ɝnd/)
1 get money by working 挣钱：*How much do teachers earn in your country?* 在你们国家教师挣多少钱？◇ *She earns about £900 a month.* 她每月大约挣900英镑。
2 get something because you have worked well or done something good（因做得好或做了好事）得到（应得的某事物）；获得；赢得：*You've earned a holiday!* 这次假期是你应得的！

earnings /ˈɜːnɪŋz; ˈɝnɪŋz/ *noun* 名词 (plural 复数)
money that you get for working 挣的钱；工资

earphones /ˈɪəfəʊnz; ˈɪrˌfonz/ *noun* 名词 (plural 复数)
things that you put over your head and ears for listening to a radio, cassette player, etc 耳机

earring /ˈɪərɪŋ; ˈɪrˌrɪŋ/ *noun* 名词
a pretty thing that you wear on your ear 耳环；耳饰

earring 耳饰

earth /ɜːθ; ɝθ/ 名词 *noun* (no plural 无复数)
1 this world; the planet that we live on 世界；地球：*The moon travels round the earth.* 月亮环绕地球运转。
2 what you grow plants in; soil 泥土；土壤：*Cover the seeds with earth.* 把种子用泥土埋起来。
on earth You use 'on earth' in questions with words like 'how' and 'what'

when you are very surprised or do not know what the answer will be (在问句中与 how 或 what 连用表示惊奇或疑问之意) 到底: *Where on earth is Paul? He's two hours late!* 保罗到底在哪儿呢？他已经晚了两个小时了！◇ *What on earth are you doing?* 你到底干什么呢？

earthquake /ˈɜːθkweɪk; ˈɝθˌkwek/ *noun* 名词
a sudden strong shaking of the ground 地震

ease /iːz; iz/ *noun* 名词 (no plural 无复数)
with ease with no difficulty 容易；无困难: *She answered the questions with ease.* 她毫无困难地回答了问题。

easily /ˈiːzəli; ˈizɪlɪ/ *adverb* 副词
with no difficulty 容易地；轻易地；无困难地: *The cinema was almost empty so we easily found a seat.* 电影院里的座位差不多都空着呢，我们很容易就找到了座位。

east /iːst; ist/ *noun* 名词 (no plural 无复数)
1 where the sun comes up in the morning 东；东方；东边: *Which way is east?* 哪边儿是东？☞ picture at **north** 见 **north** 词条插图
2 the East (no plural 无复数) the countries of Asia, for example China and Japan 东方国家；亚洲国家（如中国和日本）
east *adjective, adverb* 形容词，副词
They live on the east coast of Scotland. 他们住在苏格兰的东岸。◇ *an east wind* (= that comes from the east) 东风（= 从东方来的）◇ *We travelled east from San Francisco to New York.* 我们从旧金山向东走，到纽约去。
eastern /ˈiːstən; ˈistɚn/ *adjective* 形容词
in or of the east part of a place 东方的；东部的；东边的: *eastern Scotland* 苏格兰东部

Easter /ˈiːstə(r); ˈistɚ/ *noun* 名词 (no plural 无复数)
a Sunday in March or April, and the days around it, when Christians think about Christ coming back to life 复活节（三四月的一个星期日及其前后数日，基督徒用以纪念耶稣复活）: *I'm going on holiday at Easter.* 我打算在复活节度假。

> ✪ At Easter people often give eggs made of chocolate (**Easter eggs**) as presents. 在复活节大家常用巧克力做的蛋 (**Easter egg**) 送礼。

easy /ˈiːzi; ˈizɪ/ *adjective* 形容词 (**easier, easiest**)
1 If something is easy, you can do or understand it without any difficulty 容易的；不费力的；不难理解的: *The homework was very easy.* 这功课很容易做。◇ *English isn't an easy language to learn.* 英语不容易学。
2 without problems or pain 无困难的；无痛苦的；舒适的；安逸的: *He has had an easy life.* 他一直过着舒适安逸的生活。
✪ opposite 反义词: **difficult** or 或 **hard**
take it easy, take things easy not worry or work too much 不着急；不慌忙；不多做；不过分努力: *After my exams I'm going to take it easy for a few days.* 我考试以后要轻轻松松地过几天了。

eat /iːt; it/ *verb* 动词 (**eats, eating, ate** /et; et/, **has eaten** /ˈiːtn; ˈitn̩/)
take in food through your mouth 吃；喝: *Have you eaten all the chocolates?* 你把巧克力都吃了吗？◇ *Do you want something to eat?* 你想吃点儿东西吗？

echo /ˈekəʊ; ˈɛko/ *noun* 名词 (*plural* 复数作 **echoes**)
a sound that a wall sends back so that you hear it again 回声
echo *verb* 动词 (**echoes, echoing, echoed** /ˈekəʊd; ˈɛkod/)
His footsteps echoed in the empty hall. 他的脚步声在空荡荡的大堂里产生了回声。

eclipse /iˈklɪps; ɪˈklɪps/ *noun* 名词
1 a time when the moon comes between the earth and the sun so that we cannot see the sun's light 日食
2 a time when the earth comes between the sun and the moon so that we cannot see the moon's light 月食

ecology /iˈkɒlədʒi; iˈkɑlədʒɪ/ *noun* 名词 (no plural 无复数)
the study of the connection between living things and everything around them 生态学
ecological /ˌiːkəˈlɒdʒɪkl; ˌikəˈlɑdʒɪkl̩/ *adjective* 形容词
The destruction of the rain forests is causing serious ecological problems. 热带雨林遭到破坏，造成严重的生态问题。
ecologist /iˈkɒlədʒɪst; iˈkɑlədʒɪst/ *noun* 名词
a person who studies or knows a lot about ecology 生态学研究者；生态学家

E

economic /ˌiːkəˈnɒmɪk; ˌikəˈnɑmɪk/ *adjective* 形容词
about the way that a country spends its money and makes, buys and sells things 经济的: *The country is in serious economic difficulties.* 全国陷于严重的经济困难中。

economical /ˌiːkəˈnɒmɪkl; ˌikəˈnɑmɪkl̩/ *adjective* 形容词
If something is economical, it does not cost a lot of money to use it 节约的；节俭的；经济的: *This car is very economical to run* (= it does not use a lot of petrol). 这辆汽车很省油。

economics /ˌiːkəˈnɒmɪks; ˌikəˈnɑmɪks/ *noun* 名词 (no plural 无复数)
the study of the way that countries spend money and make, buy and sell things 经济学

economist /ɪˈkɒnəmɪst; ɪˈkɑnəmɪst/ *noun* 名词
a person who studies or knows a lot about economics 经济学研究者；经济学家

economy /ɪˈkɒnəmi; ɪˈkɑnəmɪ/ *noun* 名词 (*plural* 复数作 **economies**)
1 the way that a country spends its money and makes, buys and sells things 经济体制: *the economies of Japan and Germany* 日本和德国的经济体制
2 using money or things well and carefully（指使用钱或物）节约；节俭；节省

edge /edʒ; ɛdʒ/ *noun* 名词
the part along the end or side of something 边；边缘: *Don't sit on the edge of your chair—you might fall!* 不要坐在椅子边上——看把你摔着！

edition /ɪˈdɪʃn; ɪˈdɪʃən/ *noun* 名词
one form of a book, magazine or newspaper（书、杂志或报纸的）版本: *The story was in the evening edition of the newspaper.* 这件事刊登在这份报纸的晚报上。

editor /ˈedɪtə(r); ˈɛdɪtɚ/ *noun* 名词
a person whose job is to prepare or control a magazine, newspaper, book or film 编辑；编者；剪辑者

educate /ˈedʒukeɪt; ˈɛdʒʊˌket/ *verb* 动词 (**educates**, **educating**, **educated**)
teach somebody about things like reading, writing and mathematics at school or college 教育: *Where was she educated?* 她在哪儿受的教育？
education /ˌedʒuˈkeɪʃn; ˌɛdʒʊˈkeʃən/ *noun* 名词 (no plural 无复数)
teaching somebody about things like reading, writing and mathematics at school or college 教育: *He had a good education.* 他受过良好的教育。◇ *The government spends a lot of money on education.* 政府在教育方面开支很大。
educational /ˌedʒuˈkeɪʃənl; ˌɛdʒʊˈkeʃənl̩/ *adjective* 形容词
an educational video 富有教育意义的录像带

eel /iːl; il/ *noun* 名词
a long fish that looks like a snake 鳗；鳗鲡；白鳝

effect /ɪˈfekt; ɪˈfɛkt/ *noun* 名词
a change that happens because of something 效应；结果；后果: *We are studying the effects of heat on different metals.* 我们正在研究热对金属产生的各种效应。
have an effect on something make something change 使某事物起变化；对某事物产生影响: *His problems had a bad effect on his health.* 他的问题对他的健康有很大的影响。

effective /ɪˈfektɪv; ɪˈfɛktɪv/ *adjective* 形容词
Something that is effective works well 有效的: *Cycling is an effective way of keeping fit.* 骑自行车是一种有效的健身方法。

efficient /ɪˈfɪʃnt; ɪˈfɪʃənt/ *adjective* 形容词
A person or thing that is efficient works well and in the best way 效率高的；有能力的: *Our secretary is very efficient.* 我们的秘书很能干。✪ opposite 反义词: **inefficient**
efficiency /ɪˈfɪʃnsi; ɪˈfɪʃənsɪ/ *noun* 名词 (no plural 无复数)
being efficient 效率；能力
efficiently *adverb* 副词
You must use your time more efficiently. 你要更好地利用时间。

effort /ˈefət; ˈɛfɚt/ *noun* 名词
trying hard to do something; hard work 奋力；努力: *Thank you for all your efforts.* 感谢你多方面的努力。
make an effort try hard to do something 奋力；努力: *He made an effort to arrive on time.* 他已竭尽全力准时到达。

eg /ˌiː ˈdʒiː; ˈi ˈdʒi/ *short for* **for example** ✱ **for example** 的缩略式: *She travels to a lot of European countries,* *eg Spain, Greece and Italy.* 她到过欧洲很多国家，如西班牙、希腊、意大利。

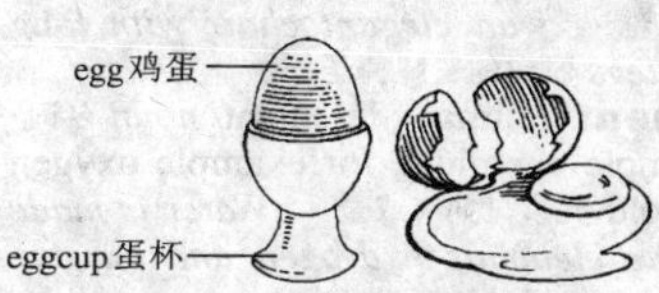

egg /eg; ɛg/ *noun* 名词
1 a round or oval thing that has a baby bird, fish, insect or snake inside it 蛋；卵: *The hen has laid an egg.* 母鸡下了一个蛋。
2 an egg from a hen that we eat 鸡蛋: *Do you want eggs and bacon for breakfast?* 你早饭要吃鸡蛋和腌肉吗？
eggcup /'egkʌp; 'ɛgˌkʌp/ *noun* 名词
a small cup that holds a boiled egg while you are eating it 蛋杯（吃煮鸡蛋用的小杯）

eight /eɪt; et/ *number* 数词
8 八
eighth /eɪtθ; etθ/ *adjective, adverb, noun* 形容词，副词，名词
1 8th 第8（个）；第八（个）
2 one of eight equal parts of something; ⅛ 八分之一

eighteen /ˌeɪ'ti:n; e'tin/ *number* 数词
18 十八
eighteenth /ˌeɪ'ti:nθ; e'tinθ/ *adjective, adverb, noun* 形容词，副词，名词
18th 第18（个）；第十八（个）

eighty /'eɪti; 'etɪ/ *number* 数词
1 80 八十
2 the eighties (plural 复数) the numbers, years or temperature between 80 and 89 ＊ 80至89（之间的数目、年数或温度）
in your eighties between the ages of 80 and 89 年岁在80至89之间；八十多岁
eightieth /'eɪtiəθ; 'etɪɪθ/ *adjective, adverb, noun* 形容词，副词，名词
80th 第80（个）；第八十（个）

either[1] /'aɪðə(r), 'i:ðə(r); 'iðɚ/ *adjective, pronoun* 形容词，代词
1 one of two things or people（指两事物或两人）其中之一: *There is cake and ice-cream. You can have either.* 有蛋糕和冰激凌。你要哪一样都行。◇ *Either of us will help you.* 我们俩有一个人来帮助你。
2 each 每（个）: *There are trees along either side of the street.* 这条街两边儿都有树。

either[2] / 'aɪðə(r), 'i:ðə(r); 'iðɚ/ *adverb* 副词
(used in sentences with 'not') also (用于含有 not 的句中) 也: *Lydia can't swim and I can't (swim) either.* 莉迪亚不会游泳，我也不会。
either ... or words that show two different things or people that you can choose 用以表示在两者之中可任择其一: *You can have either tea or coffee.* 你可以喝茶也可以喝咖啡。◇ *I will either write or telephone.* 我不是写信就是打电话。

elaborate /ɪ'læbəret; ɪ'læbərɪt/ *adjective* 形容词
not simple; with a lot of different parts 不简单的；复杂的: *The carpet has a very elaborate pattern on it.* 这块地毯的图案很复杂。

elastic /ɪ'læstɪk; ɪ'læstɪk/ *noun* 名词 (no plural 无复数)
material that becomes longer when you pull it and then goes back to its usual size 有松紧性的材料；松紧带: *His trousers have elastic in the top to stop them falling down.* 他的裤腰有松紧带防止掉裤子。
elastic *adjective* 形容词
elastic material 有松紧性的材料
elastic band /ɪˌlæstɪk 'bænd; ɪˌlæstɪk 'bænd/ *noun* 名词
a thin circle of rubber that you use for holding things together 橡皮筋；猴皮筋儿

elbow /'elbəʊ; 'ɛlˌbo/ *noun* 名词
the part in the middle of your arm where it bends 肘；胳膊肘儿 ☞ picture on page C2 见第C2页图

elder /'eldə(r); 'ɛldɚ/ *adjective* 形容词
older of two people（指两人中）年纪大的，年长的: *My elder brother lives in France and the younger one lives in London.* 我大哥住在法国，二哥住在伦敦。

elderly /'eldəli; 'ɛldɚlɪ/ *adjective* 形容词
quite old 上年纪的: *She is elderly and can't hear very well.* 她上了年纪耳朵有点儿背。

eldest /'eldɪst; 'ɛldɪst/ *adjective* 形容词
oldest of three or more people（指至少三人中）年纪最大的，最年长的: *Their eldest son is at university but the other two are at school.* 他们的大儿子上大学，两个小的上中小学。

E

elect /ɪ'lekt; ɪ'lɛkt/ *verb* 动词 (**elects, electing, elected**)
choose somebody to be a leader (by **voting**) 选举某人做领袖（投票方式叫做 **voting**）: *The new president was elected in 1990.* 新总统是在1990年选出的。

election /ɪ'lekʃn; ɪ'lɛkʃən/ *noun* 名词
a time when people choose somebody to be a leader by voting 选举: *The election will be held on Wednesday.* 选举将于星期三举行。

electric /ɪ'lektrɪk; ɪ'lɛktrɪk/ *adjective* 形容词
using electricity to make it work 用电力工作的；电动的: *an electric cooker* 电炉具 ◇ *an electric guitar* 电吉他

E

electrical /ɪ'lektrɪkl; ɪ'lɛktrɪkḷ/ *adjective* 形容词
of or using electricity 电的；使用电力的: *an electrical engineer* 电机工程师

electrician /ɪˌlek'trɪʃn; ɪˌlɛk'trɪʃən/ *noun* 名词
a person whose job is to work with electricity 电工: *This light isn't working — we need an electrician to mend it.* 这盏灯不亮了——咱们得找个电工来修理一下。

electricity /ɪˌlek'trɪsəti; ɪˌlɛk'trɪsətɪ/ *noun* 名词 (no plural 无复数)
power that comes through wires. Electricity can make heat and light and makes things work. 电；电力

electronic /ɪˌlek'trɒnɪk; ɪˌlɛk'trɑnɪk/ *adjective* 形容词
Things like computers, calculators and radios are electronic. They use **microchips** or **transistors** to make them work 电子的（如计算机、计算器、收音机等。所使用的微晶片叫做 **microchip**，晶体管叫做 **transistor**）: *an electronic typewriter* 电子打字机

electronics /ɪˌlek'trɒnɪks; ɪˌlɛk'trɑnɪks/ *noun* 名词 (no plural 无复数)
using **microchips** or **transistors** to make things like computers, calculators and radios 电子学的应用（用以制造计算机、计算器、收音机等的微晶片叫做 **microchip**，晶体管叫做 **transistor**）: *the electronics industry* 电子工业

elegant /'elɪgənt; 'ɛləgənt/ *adjective* 形容词
with a beautiful style or shape 优雅的；优美的；文雅的: *She looked very elegant in her black dress and diamond earrings.* 她穿着黑色的连衣裙，戴着钻石耳环，看起来很高雅。◇ *an elegant chair with long thin legs* 雅致的长腿椅子

element /'elɪmənt; 'ɛləmənt/ *noun* 名词
a simple chemical, for example oxygen or gold 元素（如氧或金）: *Water is made of the elements hydrogen and oxygen.* 水是由氢元素和氧元素组成的。

elementary /ˌelɪ'mentri; ˌɛlə'mɛntrɪ/ *adjective* 形容词
for beginners; not difficult to do or understand 初级的；不难做的；不难理解的: *an elementary dictionary* 初阶词典

elephant 象

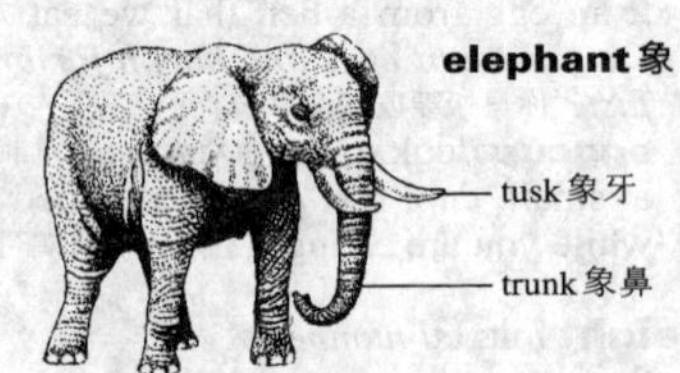

elephant /'elɪfənt; 'ɛləfənt/ *noun* 名词
a very big wild animal from Africa or Asia, with a long nose (called a **trunk**) that hangs down 象（象的鼻子叫做 **trunk**）

elevator /'eləveɪtə(r); 'ɛləˌvetɚ/ *American English for* **lift² 1** 美式英语，即 **lift² 1**

eleven /ɪ'levn; ɪ'lɛvən/ *number* 数词
11 十一

eleventh /ɪ'levnθ; ɪ'lɛvənθ/ *adjective, adverb, noun* 形容词，副词，名词
11th 第11（个）；第十一（个）

else /els; ɛls/ *adverb* 副词
1 more; extra 还有；再有；另外: *What else would you like?* 您还想要别的吗？◇ *Is anyone else coming to the party?* 还有其他人来参加这个聚会吗？
2 different; other 别的；其他的: *The Grand Hotel was full, so we stayed somewhere else.* 格兰德旅馆客满了，我们就到别处去住了。◇ *It's not mine — it must be somebody else's.* 这个不是我的——一定是别人的。◇ *There was nothing else to eat so we had pizza again.* 没有别的吃的，我们就又吃了一顿意大利饼。

✪ You use **else** after words like **anybody**, **nothing** and **somewhere**, and after question words like **where** and **who**. ＊ **else** 用于 **anybody**、**nothing**、

somewhere 之后，以及疑问词 **where** 和 **who** 之后。

or else if not, then 要不然；否则：*Go now, or else you'll be late.* 现在走吧，要不然你就晚了。

elsewhere /els'weə(r); 'ɛls,hwɛr/ *adverb* 副词
in or to another place 在别处；到别处：*He can't find a job in Liverpool so he's looking elsewhere for work.* 他在利物浦找不到工作，就又到别处去找了。

embarrass /ɪm'bærəs; ɪm'bærəs/ *verb* 动词 (**embarrasses**, **embarrassing**, **embarrassed** /ɪm'bærəst; ɪm'bærəst/)
make somebody feel shy or worried about what other people think of them 使人感到害羞或难为情：*Mark embarrassed his friends by singing very loudly on the bus.* 马克在公共汽车上大声唱歌，弄得朋友很不好意思。

embarrassed *adjective* 形容词
If you are embarrassed, you feel shy or worried about what other people think of you（指人）感到害羞的或难为情的：*Everyone laughed when I fell off my chair — I was really embarrassed!* 我从椅子上摔了下来，大家都笑了——我很不好意思！

embarrassing *adjective* 形容词
Something that is embarrassing makes you feel embarrassed（指事物）使人感到害羞的或难为情的：*I couldn't remember her name — it was so embarrassing!* 我想不起她的名字了——真不好意思！

embarrassment *noun* 名词
the feeling that you have when you are embarrassed; a person or thing that embarrasses you 害羞；难为情：*His face was red with embarrassment.* 他羞得满脸通红。

embassy /'embəsi; 'ɛmbəsɪ/ *noun* 名词 (*plural* 复数作 **embassies**)
a place where people work whose job is to speak and act for their government in another country 大使馆：*To get a visa to travel in America, you should apply to the American embassy.* 要领取到美国的签证，就得到美国大使馆申请。

embroider /ɪm'brɔɪdə(r); ɪm'brɔɪdɚ/ *verb* 动词 (**embroiders**, **embroidering**, **embroidered** /ɪm'brɔɪdəd; ɪm'brɔɪdɚd/)
make pictures with thread on cloth 刺绣

embroidered *adjective* 形容词
an embroidered blouse 绣花女衬衫

embroidery /ɪm'brɔɪdəri; ɪm'brɔɪdərɪ/ *noun* 名词 (no plural 无复数)
something that has been embroidered 刺绣制品

emerald /'emərəld; 'ɛmərəld/ *noun* 名词
a green jewel 绿宝石；翡翠：*an emerald ring* 翡翠戒指

emerald, emerald green *adjective* 形容词
bright green in colour 绿宝石色的；翡翠色的

emerge /ɪ'mɜ:dʒ; ɪ'mɝdʒ/ *verb* 动词 (**emerges**, **emerging**, **emerged** /ɪ'mɜ:dʒd; ɪ'mɝdʒd/)
come out from a place 从某处出来；现出；露出：*The moon emerged from behind the clouds.* 月亮从云层后露出来了。

emergency /ɪ'mɜ:dʒənsi; ɪ'mɝdʒənsɪ/ *noun* 名词 (*plural* 复数作 **emergencies**)
a sudden dangerous situation, when people must help quickly 突然出现的危险情形（大家得来帮忙）；紧急情况；紧急事件：*Come quickly, doctor! It's an emergency!* 快来呀，大夫！有急诊！◇ *I can lend you some money in an emergency.* 你急需用钱的时候，我能借给你一些。

emigrate /'emɪgreɪt; 'ɛmə,gret/ *verb* 动词 (**emigrates**, **emigrating**, **emigrated**)
leave your country to live in another country 移居外国：*They emigrated to Australia in the 1960s to find work.* 他们在60年代移居到澳大利亚寻找工作。

emigration /,emɪ'greɪʃn; ,ɛmə'greʃən/ *noun* 名词 (no plural 无复数)
the emigration of Soviet Jews to Israel 前苏联的犹太人移居到以色列

emotion /ɪ'məʊʃn; ɪ'moʃən/ *noun* 名词
a strong feeling, for example love or anger 强烈的感情（如爱或气愤）；情感；情绪

emotional /ɪ'məʊʃənl; ɪ'moʃənl̩/ *adjective* 形容词
1 about feelings 感情的；情感的：*She's got emotional problems — her boyfriend has left her.* 她有情感上的问题——她男朋友离开她了。
2 If you are emotional, you have strong feelings and you show them 感情强烈而外露的；易动感情的：*He got very emotional when we said goodbye.* 我们道别时他很激动。

E

emperor /ˈempərə(r); ˈɛmpərɚ/ *noun* 名词
a man who rules a group of countries (called an **empire**) 皇帝（帝国叫做 **empire**）: *the Emperor Napoleon* 拿破仑皇帝 ☞ Look at **empress**. 见 **empress**。

emphasize /ˈemfəsaɪz; ˈɛmfəˌsaɪz/ *verb* 动词 (**emphasizes**, **emphasizing**, **emphasized** /ˈemfəsaɪzd; ˈɛmfəˌsaɪzd/)
say something strongly to show that it is important 强调；着重: *She emphasized the importance of hard work.* 她强调努力的重要性。

empire /ˈempaɪə(r); ˈɛmpaɪr/ *noun* 名词
a group of countries that is controlled by one country 帝国: *the Roman Empire* 罗马帝国

E

employ /ɪmˈplɔɪ; ɪmˈplɔɪ/ *verb* 动词 (**employs**, **employing**, **employed** /ɪmˈplɔɪd; ɪmˈplɔɪd/)
pay somebody to do work for you 雇用某人: *The factory employs 800 workers.* 这个工厂雇用了800个工人。☞ Look at **unemployed**. 见 **unemployed**。

employee /ɪmˈplɔɪiː; ˌɛmplɔɪˈi/ *noun* 名词
a person who is paid to work 受雇者；雇员；雇工: *This company treats its employees very well.* 这家公司对待员工非常好。

employer /ɪmˈplɔɪə(r); ɪmˈplɔɪɚ/ *noun* 名词
a person or company that pays other people to do work 雇主

employment /ɪmˈplɔɪmənt; ɪmˈplɔɪmənt/ *noun* 名词 (no plural 无复数)
having a job that you are paid to do 受雇用: *She went to London and found employment as a taxi-driver.* 她到伦敦找到了职业，当上了计程车司机。☞ Look at **unemployment**. 见 **unemployment**。

empress /ˈemprəs; ˈɛmprɪs/ *noun* 名词 (*plural* 复数作 **empresses**)
a woman who rules a group of countries (called an **empire**), or the wife of an emperor 女皇；皇后（帝国叫做 **empire**）

empty¹ /ˈempti; ˈɛmptɪ/ *adjective* 形容词 (**emptier**, **emptiest**)
with nothing or nobody inside or on it 空的: *My glass is empty.* 我的玻璃杯是空的。◇ *The cinema was almost empty.* 这家电影院简直是空的。☞ picture at **full** 见 **full** 词条插图

empty² /ˈempti; ˈɛmptɪ/ *verb* 动词 (**empties**, **emptying**, **emptied** /ˈemptid; ˈɛmptɪd/, **has emptied**)
1 take everything out of something 把某物里的东西都取出来；弄空: *The waiter emptied the ashtrays.* 服务员把烟灰缸里的烟灰都倒了。◇ *We emptied our bags out onto the floor.* 我们把袋子里的东西都倒在地板上了。
2 become empty 变空: *The film finished and the cinema started to empty.* 电影演完了，观众纷纷离去。

enable /ɪˈneɪbl; ɪnˈebl̩/ *verb* 动词 (**enables**, **enabling**, **enabled** /ɪˈneɪbld; ɪnˈebl̩d/)
make it possible for somebody to do something 使某人能做某事: *Your help enabled me to finish the job.* 有了你的帮助我才做完这件工作。

enclose /ɪnˈkləʊz; ɪnˈkloz/ *verb* 动词 (**encloses**, **enclosing**, **enclosed** /ɪnˈkləʊzd; ɪnˈklozd/)
1 put something inside a letter or parcel 把某物放进信件或包裹中: *I enclose a cheque for £10.* 我随信附上一张10英镑的支票。
2 put something, for example a wall or fence, around a place on all sides 用某物（如墙或篱笆）围着某处: *The prison is enclosed by a high wall.* 这座监狱的四周有高墙围着。

encourage /ɪnˈkʌrɪdʒ; ɪnˈkʌrɪdʒ/ *verb* 动词 (**encourages**, **encouraging**, **encouraged** /ɪnˈkʌrɪdʒd; ɪnˈkɝɪdʒd/)
give somebody hope or help so that they do something or continue doing something 鼓励或帮助某人做某事: *We encouraged him to write a book about his adventures.* 我们鼓励他把他亲身经历的奇事写成书。

encouragement /ɪnˈkʌrɪdʒmənt; ɪnˈkɝɪdʒmənt/ *noun* 名词 (no plural 无复数)
giving somebody hope or help so that they do something or continue doing something（对某人做某事的）鼓励或帮助: *Kim's parents gave her a lot of encouragement when she was taking her exams.* 小金的父母在她考试期间给了她很多鼓励。

encouraging *adjective* 形容词
Something that is encouraging gives encouragement 令人鼓舞的: *Anna's school*

report is very encouraging. 从安娜的学生成绩报告单中看出她大有进步。

encyclopedia /ɪnˌsaɪkləˈpi:diə; ɪnˌsaɪkləˈpidɪə/ *noun* 名词 (*plural* 复数作 **encyclopedias**)
a book or set of books that gives information about a lot of different things from A to Z 百科全书: *an encyclopedia of world history* 世界历史百科全书

end[1] /end; ɛnd/ *noun* 名词
the furthest or last part of something 终极的或最后的部分；末端；尽头: *Turn right at the end of the street.* 在这条街的尽头向右拐。◇ *They were sitting at the other end of the room.* 他们坐在屋子的另一头儿。◇ *I'm going on holiday at the end of June.* 我六月底去度假。
come to an end stop 终止；结束: *The holiday was coming to an end and we started to think about going back to work.* 假期快结束了，我们也就想着回去工作的事了。
end to end in a line with the ends touching 首尾相接成一行: *They put the tables end to end.* 他们把桌子连起来排成一行。
for ... on end for a very long time 持续很长的时间: *He watches TV for hours on end.* 他一看电视就是几个小时。
in the end finally; at last 最后；终于: *I looked for the keys for hours and in the end I found them in the car.* 我找钥匙找了半天，结果在汽车里找到了。
make ends meet have enough money for your needs 有够用的钱；使收支相抵: *After her husband died it was difficult to make ends meet.* 她丈夫死后她很难维持生活。
put an end to something stop something happening 终止某事物: *We must put an end to this terrible war.* 我们必须遏止这场可怕的战争。

end[2] /end; ɛnd/ *verb* 动词 (**ends, ending, ended**)
1 stop 终止；结束: *What time does the film end?* 这场电影什么时候演完？◇ *The road ends here.* 这条路到这儿就到头儿了。◇ *Most adverbs in English end in '-ly'.* 英语的副词大多以 -ly 结尾。
2 finish something 终止或结束某事物: *We ended our holiday in France with a trip to Paris.* 我们到法国度假最后游览了巴黎，整个假期就结束了。
end up finally be in a place or doing something when you did not plan it (没想到) 最后到达某地或做某事: *If she continues to steal, she'll end up in prison.* 她要是再这么偷东西，终归得进监狱。◇ *He ended up as a teacher.* 他后来却当上了教师。

ending /ˈendɪŋ; ˈɛndɪŋ/ *noun* 名词
the last part of something, for example a word, story or film 某事物最后的部分 (如一个字的、故事的或电影的)；结尾；结局: *All these words have the same ending: criticize, organize and realize.* 下列字的结尾都是一样的: criticize、organize、realize。◇ *The film has a happy ending.* 这场电影的结局皆大欢喜。

endless /ˈendləs; ˈɛndlɪs/ *adjective* 形容词
never stopping or finishing; very long 不停的；无止境的；很长的: *The journey seemed endless.* 这个路程好像没完没了似的。
endlessly *adverb* 副词
He talks endlessly about nothing. 他滔滔不绝地说着空话。

enemy /ˈenəmi; ˈɛnəmɪ/ *noun* 名词 (*plural* 复数作 **enemies**)
1 a person who hates you 敌人；仇人；仇敌: *The President has many enemies.* 这个总统有很多仇敌。
2 the enemy (no plural 无复数) the army or country that your country is fighting against in a war 敌军；敌国: *The enemy is attacking from the north.* 敌军正在从北边进攻。
make enemies do things that make people hate you 做使人怀恨的事；树敌: *In business, you often make enemies.* 做生意常常得罪人。

energetic /ˌenəˈdʒetɪk; ˌɛnəˈdʒɛtɪk/ *adjective* 形容词
full of energy so that you can do a lot of things 精力充沛的；充满活力的

energy /ˈenədʒi; ˈɛnədʒɪ/ *noun* 名词 (no plural 无复数)
1 the power that your body has to do things 精力；气力；干劲: *You need a lot of energy to work with young children.* 做有关幼儿的工作需要充沛的精力。
2 the power from electricity, gas, coal, etc that is used to make machines work and to make heat and light (从电、煤气、

煤等产生的）能；能量: *It is important to try to save energy.* 节省能源十分重要。◇ *atomic energy* 原子能

engaged /ɪn'geɪdʒd; ɪn'gedʒd/ *adjective* 形容词

1 If two people are engaged, they have agreed to get married 已订婚的: *Louise is engaged to Michael.* 路易丝和迈克尔订婚了。◇ *They got engaged last year.* 他们去年订婚了。

2 (used about a telephone) being used （指电话线）使用着的；占线的: *I tried to phone him but his number was engaged.* 我给他打电话，可是他电话占着线呢。

engagement /ɪn'geɪdʒmənt; ɪn'gedʒmənt/ *noun* 名词

an agreement to marry somebody 订婚

E

engine /'endʒɪn; 'ɛndʒən/ *noun* 名词

1 a machine that makes things move 发动机；引擎: *a car engine* 汽车的发动机

2 the front part of a train which pulls the rest 机车；火车头

engineer /ˌendʒɪ'nɪə(r); ˌɛndʒə'nɪr/ *noun* 名词

a person whose job is to plan, make or repair things like machines, roads or bridges 以设计、制造或修理机器、道路或桥梁等为职业的人；工程师；建筑师；机械师: *My brother is an electrical engineer.* 我哥哥是电气工程师。

engineering /ˌendʒɪ'nɪərɪŋ; ˌɛndʒə'nɪrɪŋ/ *noun* 名词 (no plural 无复数)

planning and making things like machines, roads or bridges（机器、道路或桥梁等的）设计和制造；工程；工程学: *She's studying engineering at college.* 她在学院里学习工程学。◇ *He works in chemical engineering.* 他在化学工程部门工作。

enjoy /ɪn'dʒɔɪ; ɪn'dʒɔɪ/ *verb* 动词 (**enjoys**, **enjoying**, **enjoyed** /ɪn'dʒɔɪd; ɪn'dʒɔɪd/)

like something very much 非常喜爱某事物: *I enjoy playing football.* 我爱踢足球。◇ *Did you enjoy your dinner?* 这顿饭你喜欢吗？

enjoy yourself have a happy time; have fun 过得愉快；玩儿得痛快: *I really enjoyed myself at the party last night. Did you?* 我昨天晚上在聚会上玩儿得很高兴。你呢？

enjoyable /ɪn'dʒɔɪəbl; ɪn'dʒɔɪəbl̩/ *adjective* 形容词

Something that is enjoyable makes you happy 使人愉快的；令人快乐的: *Thank you for a very enjoyable evening.* 今天晚上过得非常愉快，谢谢您。

enjoyment /ɪn'dʒɔɪmənt; ɪn'dʒɔɪmənt/ *noun* 名词 (no plural 无复数)

a feeling of enjoying something; pleasure 愉快；欢乐；乐趣: *I get a lot of enjoyment from travelling.* 我从旅游中得到很多乐趣。

enlarge /ɪn'lɑ:dʒ; ɪn'lɑrdʒ/ *verb* 动词 (**enlarges**, **enlarging**, **enlarged** /ɪn'lɑ:dʒd; ɪn'lɑrdʒd/)

make something bigger（使某物）变大；扩大；增大: *Can you enlarge this photograph for me?* 您能给我把这张照片放大吗？

enlargement /ɪn'lɑ:dʒmənt; ɪn'lɑrdʒmənt/ *noun* 名词

a photograph that somebody has made bigger 放大的照片

enormous /ɪ'nɔ:məs; ɪ'nɔrməs/ *adjective* 形容词

very big 非常大的；巨大的: *an enormous dog* 很大的狗

enormously /ɪ'nɔ:məsli; ɪ'nɔrməslɪ/ *adverb* 副词

very or very much 很；非常: *London has changed enormously since my grandmother was a child.* 从我奶奶小时候到现在，伦敦已经发生了巨大的变化。

enough /ɪ'nʌf; ɪ'nʌf/ *adjective*, *adverb*, *pronoun* 形容词，副词，代词

as much or as many as you need 足够（的）；充足（的）；充分（的）: *There isn't enough food for ten people.* 食物不够十个人吃的。◇ *You're too thin—you don't eat enough.* 你太瘦了——你吃得太少了。◇ *Is she old enough to drive?* 她到了开车的年龄了吗？

enquire /ɪn'kwaɪə(r); ɪn'kwaɪr/, **enquiry** /ɪn'kwaɪəri; ɪn'kwaɪrɪ/ = **inquire**, **inquiry**

enrol /ɪn'rəʊl; ɪn'rol/ *verb* 动词 (**enrols**, **enrolling**, **enrolled** /ɪn'rəʊld; ɪn'rold/)

join a group, for example a school, college, course or club. You usually pay money (a **fee**) when you enrol 参加或加入某团体（如学校、课程或俱乐部。一般加入时要交的费用叫做 **fee**）；注册: *I've enrolled for English classes at the college.* 我已经注册参加学院的英语课程了。

ensure /ɪn'ʃʊə(r); ɪn'ʃʊr/ *verb* 动词

(**ensures**, **ensuring**, **ensured** /ɪn'ʃʊəd; ɪn'ʃʊrd/)
make certain 确保: *Please ensure that all the lights are switched off before you leave.* 请务必把所有的灯都关上再走。

enter /'entə(r); 'ɛntɚ/ *verb* 动词 (**enters**, **entering**, **entered** /'entəd; 'ɛntɚd/)
1 come or go into a place 进入某处；进来；进去: *They stopped talking when she entered the room.* 她一进屋他们就不再谈话了。◇ *Do not enter without knocking.* 进屋前先敲门。✪ In this sense, it is more usual to say **go in(to)** or **come in(to)**. 本词义通常用 **go in(to)** 或 **come in(to)** 来表达。
2 write a name or other information 填写姓名或其他资料；登记: *Please enter your name, address and date of birth at the bottom of the form.* 请把你的姓名、地址和出生日期填写在表格下方。
3 give your name to somebody because you want to do something like take an examination or run in a race 报名（例如参加考试或赛跑）: *I entered a competition last month and won £50.* 我上个月报名参加比赛赢了50英镑。

enterprise /'entəpraɪz; 'ɛntɚˌpraɪz/ *noun* 名词
a plan to do something new and difficult, often to get money（做新的和困难的事情的）计划（往往为获得金钱）: *a business enterprise* 企业规划

entertain /ˌentə'teɪn; ˌɛntɚ'ten/ *verb* 动词 (**entertains**, **entertaining**, **entertained** /ˌentə'teɪnd; ˌɛntɚ'tend/)
1 make somebody have a good time 使某人快乐: *She entertained us all with her funny stories.* 她给我们讲她那些有趣的故事让大家高兴。
2 give food and drink to visitors in your house 在家中招待客人饮食；款待；宴客: *We're entertaining friends this evening.* 我们今天晚上在家里请朋友吃饭。

entertaining /ˌentə'teɪnɪŋ; ˌɛntɚ'tenɪŋ/ *adjective* 形容词
funny or interesting 有趣的；有意思的: *The play was really entertaining.* 这出话剧可真有意思。

entertainment /ˌentə'teɪnmənt; ˌɛntɚ'tenmənt/ *noun* 名词
anything that entertains people, for example films, plays or concerts 使某人快乐的事物（如电影、戏剧或音乐会）；娱乐: *There isn't much entertainment for young people in this town.* 这个镇上没有什么为年轻人举办的娱乐活动。

enthusiasm /ɪn'θjuːziæzəm; ɪn'θuzɪˌæzəm/ *noun* 名词 (no plural 无复数)
a strong feeling of wanting to do something or liking something 想要做某事或喜爱某事物的强烈感情；热情；热心: *They didn't show much enthusiasm when I asked them to help me with the shopping.* 我叫他们帮忙买东西，他们兴趣不大。

enthusiastic /ɪnˌθjuːzi'æstɪk; ɪnˌθuzɪ'æstɪk/ *adjective* 形容词
full of enthusiasm 热情的；热心的: *She's starting a new job next week and she's very enthusiastic about it.* 她下星期就开始做新工作，觉得十分兴奋。

entire /ɪn'taɪə(r); ɪn'taɪr/ *adjective* 形容词
whole or complete; with no parts missing 全部的；完全的；整个的: *We spent the entire day on the beach.* 我们一整天都是在海滩上过的。

entirely /ɪn'taɪəli; ɪn'taɪrlɪ/ *adverb* 副词
completely 完全地: *She looks entirely different from her sister.* 她看起来和她姐姐完全不一样。◇ *I entirely agree with you.* 我完全同意你的意见。

entrance /'entrəns; 'ɛntrəns/ *noun* 名词
1 (*plural* 复数作 **entrances**) where you go into a place 入口处；门口: *I'll meet you at the entrance to the museum.* 我在博物馆门口和你见面。
2 (*plural* 复数作 **entrances**) coming or going into a place 进入某处；进来；进去: *He made his entrance onto the stage.* 他走上舞台。
3 (no plural 无复数) the right to go into a place 进入某处的权利: *They were refused entrance to the club because they were wearing jeans.* 人家不准他们进入俱乐部，因为他们穿的是牛仔裤。

entry /'entri; 'ɛntrɪ/ *noun* 名词 (*plural* 复数作 **entries**)
1 (no plural 无复数) the right to go into a place 进入某处的权利: *You can't go into that room—there's a sign on the door that says 'No Entry'.* 你不能进那个房间——门上有个牌子写着"禁止入内"。
2 (*plural* 复数作 **entries**) where you go into a place 入口处；门口

E

envelope /ˈenvələʊp; ˈɛnvəˌlop/ *noun* 名词
a paper cover for a letter 信封: *Have you written his address on the envelope?* 你把他的地址写在信封上了吗？☞ picture on page C31 见第C31页图

envied, envies *forms of* **envy** ✳ **envy** 的不同形式

envious /ˈenviəs; ˈɛnvɪəs/ *adjective* 形容词
wanting what somebody else has（对他人的事物）向往的；羡慕的；忌妒的: *She's envious of her sister's success.* 她羡慕她姐姐的成就。

environment /ɪnˈvaɪərənmənt; ɪnˈvaɪrənmənt/ *noun* 名词
1 everything around you 周围的一切；环境: *The children need a happy home environment.* 这些儿童需要有愉快的家庭环境。
2 the environment (no plural 无复数) the air, water, land, animals and plants around us 周围的空气、水、土地、动植物；自然环境: *We must do more to protect the environment.* 我们必须更加努力保护自然环境。

environmental /ɪnˌvaɪərənˈmentl; ɪnˌvaɪrənˈmɛntl̩/ *adjective* 形容词
We talked about pollution and other environmental problems. 我们谈论了污染问题以及其他自然环境问题。

envy /ˈenvi; ˈɛnvɪ/ *noun* 名词 (no plural 无复数)
a sad or angry feeling of wanting what another person has（向往他人事物的）难过的或气愤的心情；羡慕；忌妒: *I was filled with envy when I saw her new bike.* 我看到她的新自行车，心里十分羡慕。

envy *verb* 动词 (**envies**, **envying**, **envied** /ˈenvid; ˈɛnvɪd/, **has envied**)
I envy you! You always seem so happy! 我很羡慕你！你好像总是那么高兴！

epidemic /ˌepɪˈdemɪk; ˌɛpəˈdɛmɪk/ *noun* 名词
a disease that many people in a place have at the same time 在某处很多人同时得的病；流行病: *a flu epidemic* 流行性感冒

episode /ˈepɪsəʊd; ˈɛpəˌsod/ *noun* 名词
a programme on radio or television that is part of a longer story（电台或电视广播的）一集: *You can see the final episode of the series on Monday.* 星期一能看到这个片集的大结局。

equal[1] /ˈiːkwəl; ˈikwəl/ *adjective* 形容词
the same; as big, as much or as good as another 相同的；（大小、多少或好坏）同样的；同等的: *Women want equal pay for equal work.* 妇女要求同工同酬。◇ *I gave the two children equal numbers of sweets.* 我给两个孩子的糖果数目一样。

equal[2] /ˈiːkwəl; ˈikwəl/ *verb* 动词 (**equals**, **equalling**, **equalled** /ˈiːkwəld; ˈikwəld/)
1 be exactly the same amount as something 与某事物的量完全相同；等于: *Two plus two equals four* (2 + 2 = 4). 二加二等于四 (2 + 2 = 4)。
2 be as good as somebody or something（在好坏等程度上）与某人某事物相同；相等: *He ran the race in 21.2 seconds, equalling the world record.* 他以21.2秒的成绩跑完全程，平了世界纪录。

✪ In American English the spellings are **equaling** and **equaled**. 美式英语拼作 **equaling** 和 **equaled**。

equality /ɪˈkwɒləti; ɪˈkwɑlətɪ/ *noun* 名词 (no plural 无复数)
being the same or having the same rights 同等；平等；有相同的权利: *In some countries black people are still fighting for equality.* 在某些国家，黑人仍在争取和白人享有同等的权利。

equally /ˈiːkwəli; ˈikwəlɪ/ *adverb* 副词
1 in equal parts 每份相同；均等: *Don't eat all the chocolates yourself—share them out equally!* 别自己把巧克力都吃了——平分给大家！
2 in the same way 相同地；同样地: *You can wear the jacket with jeans but it looks equally good with a skirt.* 你可以穿外套配牛仔裤，可是配上裙子也一样好看。

equator /ɪˈkweɪtə(r); ɪˈkwetɚ/ *noun* 名词 (no plural 无复数)
the line on maps around the middle of the world. Countries near the equator are very hot. 赤道（赤道附近的国家非常热。）

equip /ɪˈkwɪp; ɪˈkwɪp/ *verb* 动词 (**equips**, **equipping**, **equipped** /ɪˈkwɪpt; ɪˈkwɪpt/)
give somebody, or put in a place, all the things that are needed for doing something 把为做某事所需要的所有东西给某人或放在某处；配备；装备: *Before you go climbing, you must equip yourselves*

with things like boots and ropes. 登山前得准备好靴子、绳子之类的东西。◇ *The kitchen is well equipped.* 这个厨房设备很齐全。

equipment /ɪ'kwɪpmənt; ɪ'kwɪpmənt/ *noun* 名词 (no plural 无复数)
special things that you need for doing something 为做某事所需要的专用物品；设备；装备: *sports equipment* 运动器材

eraser /ɪ'reɪzə(r); ɪ'resɚ/ *American English for* **rubber 2** 美式英语，即 **rubber 2**

error /'erə(r); 'ɛrɚ/ *noun* 名词
a thing that is done wrongly; a mistake 错误；差错: *The letter was sent to the wrong address because of a computer error.* 因为计算机出了差错，这封信地址送错了。

erupt /ɪ'rʌpt; ɪ'rʌpt/ *verb* 动词 (**erupts, erupting, erupted**)
When a **volcano** erupts, very hot liquid rock (called **lava**) suddenly comes out （指火山）爆发（火山叫做 **volcano**，岩浆叫做 **lava**）: *When Mount Vesuvius erupted, it buried Pompeii.* 维苏威火山爆发的时候把庞贝城埋没了。
eruption /ɪ'rʌpʃn; ɪ'rʌpʃən/ *noun* 名词
a volcanic eruption 火山爆发

escalator /'eskəleɪtə(r); 'ɛskəˌletɚ/ *noun* 名词
stairs that move and carry people up and down 可载人上下移动的阶梯；自动扶梯

escape /ɪ'skeɪp; ɪ'skep/ *verb* 动词 (**escapes, escaping, escaped** /ɪ'skeɪpt; ɪ'skept/)
1 get free from somebody or something 脱离某人或某事物；逃脱；逃走: *The bird escaped from the cage.* 鸟从笼子里逃走了。◇ *The prisoner escaped, but he was caught.* 那个囚犯越狱后又给抓着了。
2 If a liquid or gas escapes, it comes out of a place. （指液体或气体）流出；漏出；逸出
escape *noun* 名词
make your escape get free; get away from a place 逃脱；逃走: *They jumped out of a window and made their escape.* 他们跳窗户逃走了。

escort /ɪ'skɔ:t; ɪ'skɔrt/ *verb* 动词 (**escorts, escorting, escorted**)
go with somebody, for example to make sure that they arrive somewhere 陪送某人（如务必使之到达某处）；护送: *The police escorted him out of the building.* 警察护送他离开了大楼。

especially /ɪ'speʃəli; ə'spɛʃəlɪ/ *adverb* 副词
1 very; more than usual or more than others 很；尤其；格外: *I hate getting up early, especially in winter.* 我讨厌早起，尤其是冬天。◇ *The food in that restaurant is not especially good.* 那家餐厅的饭菜不太好。
2 for a particular person or thing 特别为某人或某事；特地: *I bought these flowers especially for you.* 这些花儿我是专为你买的。

essay /'eseɪ; 'ɛse/ *noun* 名词
a short piece of writing about a subject 关于某一专题的短篇文字；短文；小品文；散文: *Our teacher asked us to write an essay on our favourite author.* 我们老师叫我们作文，写我们最喜爱的作家。

essential /ɪ'senʃl; ə'senʃəl/ *adjective* 形容词
If something is essential, you must have or do it 不可缺少的；必要的: *It is essential that you work hard for this exam.* 你务必要用功迎接这次考试。

establish /ɪ'stæblɪʃ; ə'stæblɪʃ/ *verb* 动词 (**establishes, establishing, established** /ɪ'stæblɪʃt; ə'stæblɪʃt/)
start something new 成立某事物；建立；设立: *This company was established in 1852.* 这家公司是1852年成立的。

estate /ɪ'steɪt; ə'stet/ *noun* 名词
1 land with a lot of houses or factories on it（有很多房屋或工厂的）地区: *We live on a housing estate.* 我们住在住宅区。◇ *an industrial estate* 工业区
2 a large piece of land in the country that one person or family owns 个人或家族拥有的大片乡间土地
estate agent /ɪ'steɪt eɪdʒənt; ə'stet ˌedʒənt/ *noun* 名词
a person whose job is to sell buildings and land for other people 房地产经纪人（以代他人出售房地产为职业的人）
estate car /ɪ'steɪt kɑ:(r); ə'stet kɑr/ *noun* 名词
a long car with a door at the back and space behind the back seat for carrying things 客货两用轿车；旅行轿车（车身长，车后部有门，后座后部有载物空间）

E

estimate /'estɪmeɪt; 'ɛstə,met/ *verb* 动词 (**estimates**, **estimating**, **estimated**)
say how much you think something will cost, how big something is, how long it will take to do something, etc 估计；估价：*The builders estimated that it would take a week to repair the roof.* 建筑工人估计修理这个房顶要用一个星期。

estimate /'estɪmət; 'ɛstəmɪt/ *noun* 名词
The estimate for repairing the roof was £2 000. 修理这个房顶估价是2 000英镑。

estuary /'estʃuəri; 'ɛstʃʊ,ɛrɪ/ *noun* 名词 (*plural* 复数作 **estuaries**)
the wide part of a river where it goes into the sea 河口（河流入海处的宽阔部分）：*the Thames Estuary* 泰晤士河河口

E

etc /et'setərə; ,ɛt'sɛtərə/
You use 'etc' at the end of a list to show that there are other things but you are not going to name them all（用于一系列项目之后，表示列举未尽）等：*We bought coffee, milk, bread, etc at the shop.* 我们在商店买了咖啡、牛奶、面包等等。

ethnic /'eθnɪk; 'ɛθnɪk/ *adjective* 形容词
of or from another country or race 其他国家或种族的；来自其他国家或种族的：*There are a lot of different ethnic groups living in London.* 伦敦住着很多不同种族的人。

evacuate /ɪ'vækjueɪt; ɪ'vækjʊ,et/ *verb* 动词 (**evacuates**, **evacuating**, **evacuated**)
take people away from a dangerous place to a safer place 把人们从危险处移往较安全处；疏散：*The area near the factory was evacuated after the explosion.* 发生爆炸以后，工厂附近地区的人都疏散了。

evacuation /ɪ,vækju'eɪʃn; ɪ,vækjʊ'eʃən/ *noun* 名词
the evacuation of cities during the war 战时的城市人口疏散

evaporate /ɪ'væpəreɪt; ɪ'væpə,ret/ *verb* 动词 (**evaporates**, **evaporating**, **evaporated**)
If a liquid evaporates, it changes into a gas 蒸发（液体转变为气体）：*Water evaporates if you heat it.* 水受热则蒸发。

eve /i:v; iv/ *noun* 名词
the day before a special day（特殊日子的）前一天：*24 December is Christmas Eve.* 12月24日是圣诞节的前一天。◇ *I went to a party on New Year's Eve* (= 31 December). 我在除夕那天（12月31日）参加了一个聚会。

even[1] /'i:vn; 'ivən/ *adjective* 形容词
1 flat and smooth 平而光滑的：*I fell over because the floor wasn't even.* 地板不平，我摔倒了。✪ opposite 反义词：**uneven**
2 the same; equal 同样的；相等的：*Sara won the first game and I won the second, so we're even.* 萨拉赢了第一局，我赢了第二局；我们打平了。
3 Even numbers can be divided exactly by two 偶数的（可以用2整除的）：*4, 6 and 8 are even numbers.* * 4、6、8都是偶数。✪ opposite 反义词：**odd**

get even with somebody hurt somebody who has hurt you 伤害曾经伤害过自己的人；报复

even[2] /'i:vn; 'ivən/ *adverb* 副词
1 a word that you use to say that something is surprising 用以表示出乎意料的词；甚至；连；都：*The game is so easy that even a child can play it.* 这个游戏很容易，连小孩儿都会玩儿。◇ *He didn't laugh — he didn't even smile.* 他并没有笑出声来——脸上连笑容都没有。
2 a word that you use to make another word stronger 用作加强语气的词；更；还：*That car is big, but this one is even bigger.* 那辆汽车很大，这辆更大。

even if it does not change anything if 即使…也不会改变任何情况：*Even if you run, you won't catch the bus.* 你跑也没用，赶不上那辆公共汽车了。

even so although that is true 尽管如此：*I didn't have any lunch today, but even so I'm not hungry.* 我今天没吃午饭，然而并不饿。

even though although 尽管；虽然：*I went to the party, even though I was tired.* 我虽然很累，但还是参加聚会去了。

evening /'i:vnɪŋ; 'ivnɪŋ/ *noun* 名词
the part of the day between the afternoon and when you go to bed 从下午到就寝之间的时间；傍晚；晚上：*What are you doing this evening?* 你今天晚上做什么？◇ *We went for a long walk and in the evening we saw a film.* 我们散步走了很长时间，晚上又看了场电影。◇ *John came on Monday evening.* 约翰是星期一晚上来的。

event /ɪ'vent; ɪ'vɛnt/ *noun* 名词
1 something important that happens 重要的事情；事件：*My sister's wedding*

was a big event for our family. 我姐姐的婚礼是我们家的大事。

2 a race or competition 比赛；竞赛: *The next event will be the high-jump.* 下一项比赛是跳高。

eventually /ɪ'ventʃʊəli; ɪ'vɛntʃʊəlɪ/ *adverb* 副词

after a long time 经过很长时间之后；终于: *I waited for him for three hours, and eventually he came.* 我等了他三个小时，他终于来了。

ever /'evə(r); 'ɛvɚ/ *adverb* 副词

at any time 在任何时候；曾经: *'Have you ever been to Africa?' 'No, I haven't.'* "你到过非洲吗？""没有。" ◇ *Do you ever see Peter?* 你看见过彼得吗？

ever since in all the time since 自从: *I have known Lucy ever since we were children.* 我认识露西，我们从小就认识。

ever so, ever such a very 非常: *I'm ever so hot.* 我很热。◇ *It's ever such a good film.* 那部电影非常好。

for ever for all time; always 永远: *I will love you for ever.* 我永远爱你。

evergreen /'evəgri:n; 'ɛvɚˌgrin/ *noun* 名词

a tree that has green leaves all the year 常绿树（全年都有绿叶的树）

every /'evri; 'ɛvrɪ/ *adjective* 形容词

1 all of the people or things in a group（在一个整体中）所有的（人或事物）: *She knows every student in the school.* 她认识学校里所有的学生。

2 once in each 每一个；每一次: *He phones every evening.* 他每天晚上都打电话。

every now and then, every now and again, every so often sometimes, but not often 有的时候（并非常常）: *I see Robert every now and then.* 我有时候见到罗伯特。

every other alternate 交替的；隔: *She comes every other day* (= for example on Monday, Wednesday and Friday but not on Tuesday or Thursday). 她隔一天来一次（= 例如星期一、三、五来，二、四不来）。

everybody /'evribɒdi; 'ɛvrɪˌbɑdɪ/, **everyone** /'evriwʌn; 'ɛvrɪˌwʌn/ *pronoun* 代词

each person; all people 每一个人；所有的人；大家: *Everybody at school likes my coat.* 学校里谁都喜欢我的大衣。◇ *If everybody is here then we can start.* 要是大家都到齐了，咱们就能出发了。

everyday /'evrideɪ; 'ɛvrɪ'de/ *adjective* 形容词

normal; not special 日常的；平常的: *Computers are now part of everyday life.* 计算机现在已经是日常生活的一部分了。

everything /'evriθɪŋ; 'ɛvrɪˌθɪŋ/ *pronoun* 代词

each thing; all things 每个事物；所有的事物；一切事物: *Everything in that shop is very expensive.* 那家商店的东西什么都贵。

everywhere /'evriweə(r); 'ɛvrɪˌhwɛr/ *adverb* 副词

in all places or to all places 各处；到处: *I've looked everywhere for my pen, but I can't find it.* 我到处找我的钢笔，还是找不着。

evidence /'evɪdəns; 'ɛvədəns/ *noun* 名词 (no plural 无复数)

a thing that makes you believe that something has happened or that helps you know who did something 证据；根据: *The police searched the room, looking for evidence.* 警方搜查了那间屋子，寻找证据。◇ *a piece of evidence* 一项证据

give evidence tell what you know about somebody or something in a court of law（在法院）作证: *The man who saw the accident will give evidence in court.* 那个男子目睹了事故的经过，他将在法庭作证。

evident /'evɪdənt; 'ɛvədənt/ *adjective* 形容词

easy to see or understand 容易看见的；容易理解的；明显的；明白的: *It was evident that he was lying, because he didn't look at me when he was speaking.* 他显然是在撒谎，因为他说话的时候不看着我。

evidently *adverb* 副词

clearly 清楚地

evil /'i:vl; 'ivḷ/ *adjective* 形容词

very bad 极坏的: *an evil person* 坏人

exact /ɪg'zækt; ɪg'zækt/ *adjective* 形容词

completely correct; without any mistakes 完全正确的；准确的；精确的: *Have you got the exact time?* 你知道现在的准确时间吗？

exactly /ɪg'zæktli; ɪg'zæktlɪ/ *adverb* 副词

1 You use 'exactly' when you are

E

asking for or giving information that is completely correct 询问或陈述时，用以表示完全准确的词；准确地: *Can you tell me exactly what happened?* 你能不能如实地告诉我是怎么回事？◇ *It cost £10 exactly.* 花了整整十英镑。

2 just 正；恰恰: *This shirt is exactly what I wanted.* 这件衬衫正是我想要的。

3 You use 'exactly' to agree with somebody 用以表示同意某人的意见的词；完全正确: *'So you've never met this man before?' 'Exactly.'* "这么说，你以前从来没见过这个男的？""对。"

exaggerate /ɪɡˈzædʒəreɪt; ɪɡˈzædʒəˌret/ *verb* 动词 (**exaggerates**, **exaggerating**, **exaggerated**)

say that something is bigger, better, worse, etc than it really is 夸张；夸大: *Don't exaggerate! I was only two minutes late, not twenty.* 不要言过其实！我只是晚了两分钟，不是二十分钟。

exaggeration /ɪɡˌzædʒəˈreɪʃn; ɪɡˌzædʒəˈreʃən/ *noun* 名词

It's an exaggeration to say you don't know any English! 要说你一点儿英语都不会，那可是过甚其词！

examination /ɪɡˌzæmɪˈneɪʃn; ɪɡˌzæməˈneʃən/ *noun* 名词

1 (*also* 亦作 **exam**) a test of what you know or can do 考试: *We've got an exam in English next week.* 我们下星期考英语。

> ✪ You **sit** or **take** an examination. 参加考试，动词用 **sit** 或 **take**。If you do well, you **pass** and if you do badly, you **fail** 及格叫做 **pass**，不及格叫做 **fail**: *I took an examination at the end of the year.* 我年底参加了考试。◇ *Did she pass all her exams?* 她考试都及格了吗？

2 looking carefully at somebody or something（对某人或某事物的）仔细查看；检查: *She went into hospital for an examination.* 她到医院检查身体去了。

examine /ɪɡˈzæmɪn; ɪɡˈzæmɪn/ *verb* 动词 (**examines**, **examining**, **examined** /ɪɡˈzæmɪnd; ɪɡˈzæmɪnd/)

1 ask questions to find out what somebody knows or what they can do 考: *You will be examined on everything you have learnt this year.* 你们今年学的东西都要考。

2 look carefully at something or somebody 仔细查看某人或某事物；检查: *I had my chest examined by the doctor.* 医生检查了我的胸部。◇ *I examined the car before I bought it.* 我买这辆汽车之前仔细检查了一遍。

example /ɪɡˈzɑːmpl; ɪɡˈzæmpḷ/ *noun* 名词

something that shows what other things of the same kind are like 例子；实例: *This dictionary gives many examples of how words are used in sentences.* 这部词典列举很多例子，说明词语在句中的用法。

for example let me give you an example 例如；譬如: *Do you speak any other languages, for example French or German?* 你会说别的语言吗，例如法语或德语？

exceed /ɪkˈsiːd; ɪkˈsid/ *verb* 动词 (**exceeds**, **exceeding**, **exceeded**)

do or be more than something 超过: *The price will not exceed £50.* 价钱不会超过50英镑。

excellent /ˈeksələnt; ˈɛksḷənt/ *adjective* 形容词

very good 非常好的；优秀的: *She speaks excellent Japanese.* 她说日语说得非常漂亮。

except /ɪkˈsept; ɪkˈsɛpt/ *preposition* 介词

but not 除…之外（表示所说的不包括在内）: *The restaurant is open every day except Sunday.* 这家饭店除星期日外每天都营业。◇ *Everyone went to the party except for me.* 除了我以外，大家都参加聚会去了。

except that only that 只: *I don't know what he looks like, except that he's very tall.* 我不知道他的长相，只知道他很高。

exception /ɪkˈsepʃn; ɪkˈsɛpʃən/ *noun* 名词

a person or thing that is not the same as the others 与众不同的人或事物；例外: *Most of his films are good but this one is an exception.* 他的影片大多都很好，可是这部是个例外。

with the exception of somebody or 或 **something** if you do not count somebody or something 若不将某人或某事物计算在内的话: *I like all vegetables with the exception of cabbage.* 我什么菜都爱吃，就是不爱吃洋白菜。

exceptional /ɪkˈsepʃənl; ɪkˈsɛpʃənḷ/ *adjective* 形容词

1 not usual 异常的；罕见的: *It's exceptional to have such hot weather at this* *time of year.* 到这季节了天气还这么热，真少见。

2 very good 非常好的；优秀的: *She is an exceptional pianist.* 她是个杰出的钢琴家。

exceptionally /ɪk'sepʃənəli; ɪk'sɛpʃənl̩ɪ/ *adverb* 副词

He was an exceptionally good student. 他当时是个特别好的学生。

exchange /ɪks'tʃeɪndʒ; ɪks'tʃendʒ/ *verb* 动词 (**exchanges**, **exchanging**, **exchanged** /ɪks'tʃeɪndʒd; ɪks'tʃendʒd/)

give one thing and get another thing for it 换；交换；互换: *My new radio didn't work so I exchanged it for another one.* 我的新收音机坏了。我又换了一个。◇ *We exchanged telephone numbers at the end of the holiday.* 假期结束的时候，我们彼此记下了对方的电话号码。

exchange *noun* 名词

in exchange for something If you get one thing in exchange for another thing, you give one thing and get another thing for it 换取某事物: *I gave her English lessons in exchange for a room in her house.* 我借住她家一个房间，交换条件是教她英语。

exchange rate /ɪks'tʃeɪndʒ reɪt; ɪks'tʃendʒ ret/ *noun* 名词

how much money from one country you can buy with money from another country 兑换率: *The exchange rate is one pound to eight francs.* 兑换率是一镑换八法郎。

excite /ɪk'saɪt; ɪk'saɪt/ *verb* 动词 (**excites**, **exciting**, **excited**)

make somebody have strong feelings of happiness or interest so that they are not calm 使某人兴奋或激动: *Please don't excite the children too much or they won't sleep tonight.* 请不要把孩子弄得太兴奋了，要不他们今晚就睡不着觉了。

excited *adjective* 形容词

not calm, for example because you are happy about something that is going to happen 兴奋的；激动的: *He's getting very excited about his holiday.* 他对度假的事越来越兴奋了。

excitement /ɪk'saɪtmənt; ɪk'saɪtmənt/ *noun* 名词 (no plural 无复数)

a feeling of being excited 兴奋；激动: *There was great excitement in the stadium before the match began.* 比赛开始以前，体育馆里群情激奋。

exciting *adjective* 形容词

Something that is exciting makes you have strong feelings of happiness or interest 使人兴奋的；使人激动的: *an exciting film* 使人激动的影片 ◇ *She's got a very exciting job — she travels all over the world and meets lots of famous people.* 她找到一份很带劲的工作——能到世界各地旅行，还能见到很多名人。

exclaim /ɪk'skleɪm; ɪk'sklem/ *verb* 动词 (**exclaims**, **exclaiming**, **exclaimed** /ɪk'skleɪmd; ɪk'sklemd/)

say something suddenly and loudly because you are surprised, angry, etc（因惊奇、愤怒等）大叫；呼喊: *'I don't believe it!' she exclaimed.* "我不信！"她喊道。

exclamation /ˌeksklə'meɪʃn; ˌɛksklə'meʃən/ *noun* 名词

exclamation mark /ekslə'meɪʃn mɑ:k; ɛksklə'meʃən mɑrk/ *noun* 名词

a mark (!) that you use in writing to show loud or strong words or surprise 叹号；感叹号；惊叹号（!）

exclude /ɪk'sklu:d; ɪk'sklud/ *verb* 动词 (**excludes**, **excluding**, **excluded**)

shut or keep a person or thing out（把某人或某事物）排除在外: *We cannot exclude the students from the meeting. Their ideas are important.* 我们开会不能没有学生参加。他们的意见很重要。☞ Look at **include**. 见 **include**。

excluding *preposition* 介词

without; if you do not count 不包括: *The meal cost £35, excluding drinks.* 这顿饭35英镑，不包括饮料。

excursion /ɪk'skɜ:ʃn; ɪk'skɝʒən/ *noun* 名词

a short journey to see something interesting or to enjoy yourself 短途的旅行或游玩: *We're going on an excursion to the seaside on Sunday.* 我们星期日到海边儿去游玩儿。

excuse[1] /ɪk'skju:s; ɪk'skjus/ *noun* 名词

words you say or write to explain why you have done something wrong 解释为何做错事的言语；理由；借口: *You're late! What's your excuse this time?* 你迟到了！这次你怎么解释？

excuse[2] /ɪk'skju:z; ɪk'skjuz/ *verb* 动词 (**excuses**, **excusing**, **excused** /ɪk'skju:zd; ɪk'skjuzd/)

say that it is not important that a person

E

has done something wrong 原谅某人: *Please excuse us for being late.* 我们迟到了，请原谅。

excuse me You use 'excuse me' when you want to stop somebody who is speaking, or when you want to speak to somebody you don't know. You can also use 'excuse me' to say that you are sorry（打断别人谈话时用）对不起；（和陌生人谈话时用）请问；劳驾: *Excuse me, could you tell me the time, please?* 请问，现在几点钟了？◇ *Did I stand on your foot? Excuse me.* 我踩着您的脚了吧？对不起。

execute /'eksɪkju:t; 'ɛksɪˌkjut/ *verb* 动词 (**executes**, **executing**, **executed**)
kill somebody to punish them 处死某人；处决

execution /ˌeksɪ'kju:ʃn; ˌɛksɪ'kjuʃən/ *noun* 名词
the execution of prisoners 对囚犯的处决

executive /ɪg'zekjʊtɪv; ɪg'zɛkjutɪv/ *noun* 名词
an important businessman or businesswoman（企业中的）行政人员

exercise[1] /'eksəsaɪz; 'ɛksɚˌsaɪz/ *noun* 名词
1 (*plural* 复数作 **exercises**) a piece of work that you do to learn something 练习；训练: *The teacher asked us to do exercises 1 and 2 for homework.* 老师叫我们做的功课是练习1和练习2。
2 (no plural 无复数) moving your body to keep it strong and well（体育的）运动；锻炼: *Swimming is very good exercise.* 游泳是很好的运动。
3 (*plural* 复数作 **exercises**) a special movement that you do to keep your body strong and well（某类的）运动；体操: *Touch your toes and stand up 20 times. This exercise is good for your legs, stomach and back.* 先触脚趾然后再站起来，连续做20次。这一体操项目对腿部、腹部和背部都有好处。

exercise book /'eksəsaɪz bʊk; 'ɛksɚsaɪz bʊk/ *noun* 名词
a book with clean pages that you use at school for writing in 练习本

exercise[2] /'eksəsaɪz; 'ɛksɚˌsaɪz/ *verb* 动词 (**exercises**, **exercising**, **exercised** /'eksəsaɪzd; 'ɛksɚˌsaɪzd/)
move your body to keep it strong and well（指体育）运动；锻炼: *They exercise in the park every morning.* 他们每天早晨在公园里锻炼身体。

exhaust[1] /ɪg'zɔ:st; ɪg'zɔst/ *verb* 动词 (**exhausts**, **exhausting**, **exhausted**)
make somebody very tired 使某人非常疲倦: *The long journey exhausted us.* 旅途很长，把我们累坏了。

exhausted *adjective* 形容词
very tired 非常疲倦的: *I'm exhausted—I think I'll go to bed.* 我累极了——我看我还是睡觉去吧。

exhaust[2] /ɪg'zɔ:st; ɪg'zɔst/ *noun* 名词
a pipe that takes gas out from an engine, for example on a car（发动机的）排气管（如汽车的）

exhibition /ˌeksɪ'bɪʃn; ˌɛksə'bɪʃən/ *noun* 名词
a group of things in a place so that people can look at them 展览；陈列: *an exhibition of paintings by Monet* 莫奈的画展

exile /'eksaɪl; 'ɛksaɪl/ *noun* 名词
1 (no plural 无复数) having to live away from your own country, for example as a punishment 流放；放逐；充军: *Napoleon spent the last years of his life in exile.* 拿破仑晚年是在流放中度过的。
2 (*plural* 复数作 **exiles**) a person who must live away from his/her own country 被流放的人

exist /ɪg'zɪst; ɪg'zɪst/ *verb* 动词 (**exists**, **existing**, **existed**)
be real; live 存在；生存；生活: *Does life exist on other planets?* 别的星球上有生命吗？◇ *That word does not exist.* 根本没有这个字。

existence /ɪg'zɪstəns; ɪg'zɪstəns/ *noun* 名词 (no plural 无复数)
being real; existing 存在；生存；生活: *Do you believe in the existence of God?* 你相信有上帝吗？

exit /'eksɪt; 'ɛksɪt/ *noun* 名词
a way out of a building（建筑物的）出口处；太平门: *Where is the exit?* 出口儿在哪儿？

make an exit go out of a place 走出某处；出去；退场: *He made a quick exit.* 他匆匆地出去了。

exotic /ɪg'zɒtɪk; ɪg'zɑtɪk/ *adjective* 形容词
strange or interesting because it comes

E

from another country（因来自他国）奇怪的，有趣的: *exotic fruits* 外国的奇特水果

expand /ɪk'spænd; ɪk'spænd/ *verb* 动词 (**expands**, **expanding**, **expanded**)
become bigger or make something bigger（使某物）变大；扩大；扩展: *Metals expand when they are heated.* 金属受热则膨胀。

expansion /ɪk'spænʃn; ɪks'pænʃən/ *noun* 名词 (no plural 无复数)
getting bigger 变大；扩大；扩展: *The company needs bigger offices because of the expansion.* 这家公司因扩展业务而需要大些的办公室。

expect /ɪk'spekt; ɪk'spɛkt/ *verb* 动词 (**expects**, **expecting**, **expected**)
1 think that somebody or something will come or that something will happen 认为某人或某事物会来到；预料；预计: *I expect she'll be late. She usually is.* 我就知道她得迟到。她常常迟到。◇ *We expected it to be hot in San Francisco, but it was quite cold.* 我们原以为旧金山很热，其实很冷。◇ *She's expecting* (= she is going to have) *a baby in June.* 她六月份就要生孩子了。
2 think that something is probably true 认为某事物很可能属实；料想: *They haven't had lunch yet, so I expect they're hungry.* 他们还没吃午饭呢，我想他们准饿了。
3 If you are expected to do something, you must do it（被）要求做某事: *I am expected to work every Saturday.* 我每星期六都得上班。
I expect so You say 'I expect so' when you think that something will happen or that something is true 表达料想如此的用语: *'Is Ian coming?' 'Oh yes, I expect so.'* "伊恩来吗？" "来，他准来。"

expedition /ˌekspə'dɪʃn; ˌɛkspɪ'dɪʃən/ *noun* 名词
a journey to find or do something special（为寻找或做某事物的）远行；探险；考察: *Scott's expedition to the South Pole* 斯科特南极探险之行

expel /ɪk'spel; ɪk'spɛl/ *verb* 动词 (**expels**, **expelling**, **expelled** /ɪk'speld; ɪk'spɛld/)
send somebody away from a school or club（从学校或俱乐部里）驱逐某人；开除: *The boys were expelled from school for smoking.* 这些男生因吸烟而被开除。

expense /ɪk'spens; ɪk'spɛns/ *noun* 名词
1 the cost of something 花费；代价: *Having a car is a big expense.* 有汽车开销就大。
2 expenses (plural 复数) money that you spend on a certain thing（为某事）花费的钱: *The company pays our travelling expenses.* 公司给我们付路费。
at somebody's expense If you do something at somebody's expense, they pay for it 由某人付费: *We had dinner at the company's expense.* 公司付钱招待我们吃晚饭。

expensive /ɪk'spensɪv; ɪk'spɛnsɪv/ *adjective* 形容词
Something that is expensive costs a lot of money 费用大的；昂贵的: *expensive clothes* 很贵的衣服 ✪ opposite 反义词: **cheap** or 或 **inexpensive**

experience /ɪk'spɪəriəns; ɪk'spɪrɪəns/ *noun* 名词
1 (no plural 无复数) knowing about something because you have seen it or done it（因见过或做过某事物而获得的）认识；体验；经验: *She has four years' teaching experience.* 她有四年的教学经历。◇ *Do you have much experience of working with children?* 您做儿童方面的工作，经验多不多？
2 (*plural* 复数作 **experiences**) something that has happened to you 亲身经历过的事: *He wrote a book about his experiences in Africa.* 他把在非洲经历过的事写成了一本书。◇ *What's the most frightening experience you have ever had?* 你遇见过的最可怕的是什么事情？

experienced /ɪk'spɪəriənst; ɪk'spɪrɪənst/ *adjective* 形容词
If you are experienced, you know about something because you have done it many times before 有经验的；有阅历的: *She's an experienced driver.* 她开车很有经验。✪ opposite 反义词: **inexperienced**

experiment /ɪk'sperɪmənt; ɪk'spɛrəmənt/ *noun* 名词
You do an experiment to find out what will happen or to see if something is true 实验；试验: *They are doing experiments to find out if the drug is safe for humans.* 他们正在做实验研究这种药物对人体是否安全。

E

experiment *verb* 动词 (**experiments, experimenting, experimented**)
I don't think it's right to experiment on animals. 我认为用动物做试验是不对的。

expert /ˈekspɜːt; ˈɛkspɝt/ *noun* 名词
a person who knows a lot about something 精通某事物的人；专家: *He's an expert on Shakespeare.* 他是研究莎士比亚的专家。◇ *a computer expert* 计算机专家

explain /ɪkˈspleɪn; ɪkˈsplen/ *verb* 动词 (**explains, explaining, explained** /ɪkˈspleɪnd; ɪkˈsplend/)
1 tell somebody about something so that they understand it 给某人解释某事物；讲解；说明: *The teacher usually explains the new words to us.* 老师通常给我们解释生词的意思。◇ *He explained how to use the machine.* 他讲解了那台机器的使用方法。
2 give a reason for something 说明某事物的原因或理由: *I explained why we needed the money.* 我说明了我们需要那笔钱的原因。

E

explanation /ˌekspləˈneɪʃn; ˌɛkspləˈneʃən/ *noun* 名词
telling somebody about something so that they understand it, or giving a reason for something 解释；讲解；说明: *What explanation did they give for being late?* 他们对迟到一事作何解释？

explode /ɪkˈspləʊd; ɪkˈsplod/ *verb* 动词 (**explodes, exploding, exploded**)
burst suddenly with a very loud noise 爆炸: *A bomb exploded in the city centre, killing two people.* 在市中心有颗炸弹爆炸，炸死了两个人。✪ The noun is **explosion**. 名词是 **explosion**。

exploit /ɪkˈsplɔɪt; ɪkˈsplɔɪt/ *verb* 动词 (**exploits, exploiting, exploited**)
treat somebody badly to get what you want 为得到某事物而亏待某人；剥削: *People who work at home are often exploited—they work long hours for very little money.* 在家里工作的人往往吃亏——他们工作的时间长，得到的工钱少。

explore /ɪkˈsplɔː(r); ɪkˈsplɔr/ *verb* 动词 (**explores, exploring, explored** /ɪkˈsplɔːd; ɪkˈsplɔrd/)
travel around a new place to learn about it 在新地方四处察看（以了解情况）；考察: *Indiana Jones explored the jungles of South America.* 印第安纳·琼斯考察了南美洲的森林。

exploration /ˌekspləˈreɪʃn; ˌɛkspləˈreʃən/ *noun* 名词
the exploration of space 对宇宙空间的探索

explorer *noun* 名词
a person who travels around a new place to learn about it（为了解情况）在新地方四处察看的人；考察者: *The first European explorers arrived in America in the 15th century.* 在15世纪，欧洲第一批探险者到达美洲。

explosion /ɪkˈspləʊʒn; ɪkˈsploʒən/ *noun* 名词
bursting suddenly with a very loud noise 爆炸: *There was an explosion and pieces of glass flew everywhere.* 那场爆炸把玻璃炸得到处都是。✪ The verb is **explode**. 动词是 **explode**。

explosive /ɪkˈspləʊsɪv; ɪkˈsplosɪv/ *adjective* 形容词
Something that is explosive can cause an explosion 可引起爆炸的；爆炸性的: *an explosive gas* 可引起爆炸的气体

explosive *noun* 名词
a substance that can make things explode 爆炸物；炸药: *Dynamite is an explosive.* 炸药是爆炸物。

export /ɪkˈspɔːt; ɪksˈpɔrt/ *verb* 动词 (**exports, exporting, exported**)
sell things to another country 向他国出售物品；出口: *Japan exports cars to Britain.* 日本向英国出口汽车。

export /ˈekspɔːt; ˈɛkspɔrt/ *noun* 名词
1 (no plural 无复数) selling things to another country 向他国出售物品；出口: *These cars are made for export.* 这些汽车是为出口而生产的。
2 (*plural* 复数作 **exports**) something that you sell to another country 向他国出售的物品；出口商品: *The country's biggest exports are tea and cotton.* 这个国家的出口商品以茶叶和棉花为主。
✪ opposite 反义词: **import**

expose /ɪkˈspəʊz; ɪkˈspoz/ *verb* 动词 (**exposes, exposing, exposed** /ɪkˈspəʊzd; ɪkˈspozd/)
show something that is usually covered or hidden 把遮蔽或隐藏的事物显露出来；显示: *A baby's skin should not be exposed to the sun for too long.* 小孩儿的皮肤不应该晒得时间太长。◇ *The newspaper exposed his terrible secret.* 报纸揭露了他骇人听闻的秘密。

express[1] /ɪk'spres; ɪk'sprɛs/ *verb* 动词 (**expresses**, **expressing**, **expressed** /ɪk'sprest; ɪk'sprɛst/)
say or show how you think or feel 把想法或感觉说出来或表示出来；表达: *She expressed her ideas well.* 她的表达能力很强。

express[2] /ɪk'spres; ɪk'sprɛs/ *adjective* 形容词
that goes or is sent very quickly（行进得或被运送得）非常快的: *an express letter* 快信
express *adverb* 副词
I sent the parcel express. 那个包裹我是用快件邮寄的。

express[3] (*plural* 复数作 **expresses**), **express train** *noun* 名词
a fast train that does not stop at all stations（并非每站都停的）快速火车；快车

expression /ɪk'spreʃn; ɪk'sprɛʃən/ *noun* 名词
1 a word or group of words; a way of saying something 词；词语；表达方式: *The expression 'to drop off' means 'to fall asleep'.* ＊to drop off 这个词组的意思是 to fall asleep（入睡）。
2 the look on your face that shows how you feel 感情表现在面部上的样子；表情；神色: *an expression of surprise* 惊讶的神情

expressway /ɪk'spreswer; ɪk'sprɛsˌwe/ *American English for* **motorway** 美式英语，即 **motorway**

extend /ɪk'stend; ɪk'stɛnd/ *verb* 动词 (**extends**, **extending**, **extended**)
1 make something longer or bigger 使某事物更长或更大；伸长；延长；延展: *I'm extending my holiday for another week.* 我把假期又延长了一个星期。
2 continue or stretch 伸展；伸延: *The park extends as far as the river.* 这个公园一直伸展到河边。

extension /ɪk'stenʃn; ɪk'stɛnʃən/ *noun* 名词
1 a part that you add to something to make it bigger（为使某事物变大）增加的部分: *They've built an extension on the back of the house.* 他们在房子后面扩建出一部分来。
2 one of the telephones in a building that is connected to the main telephone（一座建筑物中的）电话分机: *Can I have extension 4110, please?* 请您替我接分机4110行吗？

extent /ɪk'stent; ɪk'stɛnt/ *noun* 名词 (no plural 无复数)
how big something is（某事物的）大小；范围: *I didn't know the full extent of the problem* (= how big it was) *until he explained it to me.* 我原来不知道问题究竟有多大，他向我解释以后才知道。✪ You use expressions like **to a certain extent** and **to some extent** to show that you do not think something is completely true 用 **to a certain extent** 或 **to some extent** 来表示认为某事物并非完全属实之意: *I agree with you to a certain extent.* 我在一定程度上同意你的意见。

exterior /ɪk'stɪəriə(r); ɪk'stɪrɪɚ/ *noun* 名词
the outside part 外面的部分；外部；外面；外表: *We painted the exterior of the house white.* 我们把房子的外墙刷成白色的了。
exterior *adjective* 形容词
an exterior door 通往房子外面的门
✪ opposite 反义词: **interior**

external /ɪk'stɜ:nl; ɪk'stɝnḷ/ *adjective* 形容词
on, of or from the outside 在外面的；外面的；来自外面的: *external walls* 外墙
✪ opposite 反义词: **internal**

extinct /ɪk'stɪŋkt; ɪk'stɪŋkt/ *adjective* 形容词
If a type of animal or plant is extinct, it does not exist now（指动植物）现已不存在的；绝种的: *Dinosaurs became extinct millions of years ago.* 千百万年以前恐龙就绝种了。

extra /'ekstrə; 'ɛkstrə/ *adjective*, *adverb* 形容词，副词
more than what is usual 额外（的）；外加（的）: *I have put an extra blanket on your bed because it's cold tonight.* 今天晚上很冷，我给你床上又加了一条毯子。◇ *The room costs £20 and you have to pay extra for breakfast.* 这个房间要20英镑，早餐另外收费。

extraordinary /ɪk'strɔ:dnri; ɪk'strɔrdṇˌɛrɪ/ *adjective* 形容词
very unusual or strange 很不寻常的；格外的；出奇的: *I had an extraordinary dream last night—I dreamt that I could fly.* 我昨天晚上做的梦很怪——我梦见我会飞了。

E

◇ *Have you seen that extraordinary building with the pink roof?* 你见过没见过那座挺别致的楼房，房顶是粉红色的那个？

extraordinarily /ɪk'strɔːdnrəli; ɪk'strɔrdn̩ˌɛrəlɪ/ *adverb* 副词
extremely 极端地；特殊地: *She's extraordinarily clever.* 她聪明极了。

extravagant /ɪk'strævəgənt; ɪk'strævəgənt/ *adjective* 形容词
1 If you are extravagant, you spend too much money. 奢侈的；挥霍的
2 Something that is extravagant costs too much money 昂贵的: *He buys her a lot of extravagant presents.* 他给她买很多昂贵的礼物。

extreme /ɪk'striːm; ɪk'strim/ *adjective* 形容词
1 very great or strong（指程度或强度）极大的；极强的: *the extreme cold of the Arctic* 北极的严寒
2 as far away as possible（指时间或空间）久远的；遥远的: *They came from the extreme north of Scotland.* 他们是苏格兰最北部的人。
3 If you say that a person is extreme, you mean that his/her ideas are too strong.（指人）思想偏激的
extremely *adverb* 副词
very 极端地；特殊地: *He's extremely good-looking.* 他好看极了。

eye /aɪ; aɪ/ *noun* 名词
one of the two parts in your head that you see with 眼睛: *She's got blue eyes.* 她的眼睛是蓝色的。◇ *Open your eyes!* 睁开眼睛！☞ picture on page C2 见第C2页图
catch somebody's eye 1 If you catch somebody's eye, you make them look at you 吸引某人的注意: *Try to catch the waiter's eye the next time he comes this way.* 服务员再往这边来的时候，你得想法让他看见你。 **2** If something catches your eye, you see it suddenly 突然看见某事物: *Her bright-yellow hat caught my eye.* 我突然看见她戴着一顶鲜艳的黄帽子。
in somebody's eyes as somebody thinks 在某人的心目中；在某人看来: *Richard is 42, but in his mother's eyes, he's still a little boy!* 理查德42岁了，但是在他母亲的眼里他仍是个小孩儿！
keep an eye on somebody or 或 **something** look after or watch somebody or something 照看或注视某人或某事物: *Will you keep an eye on my bag while I go to the toilet?* 我去厕所，你给我看着点包儿行吗？
see eye to eye with somebody agree with somebody 与某人看法一致: *Mr Harper doesn't always see eye to eye with his neighbours.* 哈珀先生并非总是跟邻居的看法一致。

eyebrow /'aɪbraʊ; 'aɪˌbraʊ/ *noun* 名词
one of the two lines of hair above your eyes 眉；眉毛 ☞ picture on page C2 见第C2页图

eyelash /'aɪlæʃ; 'aɪˌlæʃ/ *noun* 名词 (*plural* 复数作 **eyelashes**)
one of the hairs that grow in a line on your eyelid 睫毛: *She's got beautiful long eyelashes.* 她的长睫毛很漂亮。☞ picture on page C2 见第C2页图

eyelid /'aɪlɪd; 'aɪˌlɪd/ *noun* 名词
the piece of skin that can move to close your eye 眼睑；眼皮

eyesight /'aɪsaɪt; 'aɪˌsaɪt/ *noun* 名词 (no plural 无复数)
the power to see 视力: *Your eyesight is very good.* 你的视力很好。

Ff

F *short way of writing* **Fahrenheit** ＊ **Fahrenheit** 的缩写形式

fable /ˈfeɪbl; ˈfebl̩/ *noun* 名词
a short story, usually about animals, that teaches people something 寓言

fabulous /ˈfæbjʊləs; ˈfæbjələs/ *adjective* 形容词
very good; wonderful 极好的；绝妙的: *The food smells fabulous!* 这食物闻起来真香！

face[1] /feɪs; fes/ *noun* 名词
1 the front part of your head 脸；面孔: *Have you washed your face?* 你洗脸了吗？◇ *She had a smile on her face.* 她面露笑容。
2 the front or one side of something （物体的）正面或侧面: *a clock face* 表盘 ◇ *He put the cards face down on the table.* 他把纸牌扣着放在桌子上。
face to face If two people are face to face, they are looking straight at each other 面对面: *They stood face to face.* 他们面对面站着。
keep a straight face not smile or laugh when something is funny （该笑时）板着脸: *I couldn't keep a straight face when he dropped his watch in the soup!* 他把手表掉进汤里了，我忍不住笑了起来！
make or 或 **pull a face** move your mouth and eyes to show that you do not like something （不喜欢某事物时）做鬼脸；拉下脸: *She made a face when she saw what I had made for dinner.* 她一看我做的饭就做了个鬼脸。

face[2] /feɪs; fes/ *verb* 动词 (**faces, facing, faced** /feɪst; fest/)
1 have the face or the front towards something 面对或面向某物: *Can you all face the front of the class, please?* 请各位同学都向前看行吗？◇ *My bedroom faces the garden.* 我的卧室朝着花园。
2 be brave enough to meet somebody unfriendly or do something difficult 勇于面对难以应付的人或事物: *I can't face going to work today—I feel too ill.* 我今天上不了班了——我病得很厉害。
let's face it we must agree that it is true 我们得承认这是事实: *Let's face it—you're not very good at maths.* 我们得承认——你数学不太好。

facilities /fəˈsɪlətiz; fəˈsɪlətɪz/ *noun* 名词 (plural 复数)
things in a place for you to use 在一处所可供使用的物品；设备；设施: *Our school has very good sports facilities.* 我们学校运动设施非常好。

fact /fækt; fækt/ *noun* 名词
something that you know has happened or is true 事实；真相；实情: *It's a fact that the earth travels around the sun.* 地球围绕着太阳运行是事实。
in fact, in actual fact words that you use to show that something is true; really 事实上；实际上；其实: *I thought she was Swedish, but in actual fact she's from Norway.* 我以为她是瑞典人，其实她是挪威人。◇ *I think I saw him—I'm certain, in fact.* 我想我是看见他了——是看见了，实际上。

factory /ˈfæktəri; ˈfæktərɪ/ *noun* 名词 (*plural* 复数作 **factories**)
a place where people make things, usually with machines 工厂；制造厂: *He works at the car factory.* 他在汽车厂工作。

fade /feɪd; fed/ *verb* 动词 (**fades, fading, faded**)
become less bright and colourful 变得不光亮不鲜艳；褪色: *Will this shirt fade when I wash it?* 这件衬衫洗的时候掉色吗？◇ *faded jeans* 褪色的牛仔裤

Fahrenheit /ˈfærənhaɪt; ˈfærənˌhaɪt/ *noun* 名词 (no plural 无复数)
a way of measuring temperature. Water freezes at 32° Fahrenheit and boils at 212° Fahrenheit. 华氏温度（水在32华氏度结冰，在212华氏度沸腾。）✪ The short way of writing 'Fahrenheit' is **F** ＊ Fahrenheit 的缩写形式为 **F**: *110° F* ＊ 110 华氏度

fail /feɪl; fel/ *verb* 动词 (**fails, failing, failed** /feɪld; feld/)
1 not pass an exam or test 不及格；不合格: *She failed her driving test again.* 她驾驶测验又没及格。◇ *How many students failed last term?* 上学期多少学生不及格？
2 try to do something but not be able to do it 尽力做某事而未做成: *He played quite well but failed to win the match.* 他比赛时表现很好，可是没赢。

F

3 not do something that you should do 未做应做的事: *The driver failed to stop at a red light.* 司机在红灯前没停车。

fail *noun* 名词

without fail certainly 肯定；一定；必定: *Be there at twelve o'clock without fail!* 十二点钟务必到那里！

failure /'feɪljə(r); 'feljɚ/ *noun* 名词

1 (no plural 无复数) not being successful 失败；不成功: *The search for the missing children ended in failure.* 寻找失踪儿童的行动最后也未成功。

2 (*plural* 复数作 **failures**) a person or thing that does not do well 事情做不好的人或事物: *I felt that I was a failure because I didn't have a job.* 我认为我一事无成，连一份工作都没有。

faint[1] /feɪnt; fent/ *adjective* 形容词 (**fainter, faintest**)

1 not clear or strong 不清楚的或不强的；微弱的；模糊的；隐约的: *We could hear the faint sound of music in the distance.* 我们听见远处有隐约的音乐声。

2 If you feel faint, you feel that you are going to fall, for example because you are ill or tired. 要晕倒的（例如因病或疲倦）

faint[2] /feɪnt; fent/ *verb* 动词 (**faints, fainting, fainted**)

fall down suddenly, for example because you are weak, ill or shocked 晕倒；昏倒: *She almost fainted when she saw the blood on her leg.* 她看见腿上有血，险些晕倒。

fair[1] /feə(r); fɛr/ *adjective* 形容词 (**fairer, fairest**)

1 Somebody or something that is fair treats people equally or in the right way 公正的；公平的: *a fair judge* 公正的法官 ◇ *It's not fair! I have to go to bed but you can stay up and watch TV!* 这可不公平！我得去睡觉，你就能熬夜看电视！✪ opposite 反义词: **unfair**

2 with a light colour 浅色的: *He's got fair hair.* 他头发色浅。◇ *He is fair-haired.* 他头发色浅。✪ opposite 反义词: **dark**

3 quite good or quite large 尚好的；尚大的: *They've invited a fair number of people to their party.* 他们邀请了不少人参加聚会。

4 good, without rain 晴朗的；无雨的: *fair weather* 晴天

fair[2] /feə(r); fɛr/ *noun* 名词

a place outside where you can ride on big machines and play games to win prizes. Fairs usually travel from town to town.（露天的）游乐场；游乐会（有机械木马、有奖游戏。游乐会通常巡回到各地举办。）

fairly /'feəli; 'fɛrlɪ/ *adverb* 副词

1 in a way that is right and honest 公正而诚实地: *This company treats its workers fairly.* 这个公司对待工作人员很公正。✪ opposite 反义词: **unfairly**

2 quite; not very 相当的；颇: *She speaks French fairly well.* 她法语说得不错。◇ *I'm fairly certain it was him.* 我有几分把握，那是他。

fairy /'feəri; 'fɛrɪ/ *noun* 名词 (*plural* 复数作 **fairies**)

a very small person in stories. Fairies have wings and can do magic. 小仙子；小精灵（小仙子长着翅膀，会魔法）

fairy tale /'feəri teɪl; 'fɛrɪ tel/, **fairy story** /'feəri stɔ:ri; 'fɛrɪ 'stɔrɪ/ (*plural* 复数作 **fairy stories**) *noun* 名词

a story for children that is about magic 神话故事；童话

faith /feɪθ; feθ/ *noun* 名词

1 (no plural 无复数) feeling sure that somebody or something is good, right, honest, etc 信任；信心: *I've got great faith in your ability to do the job* (= I'm sure that you can do it). 我充分相信你有能力做好这项工作。

2 (*plural* 复数作 **faiths**) a religion 宗教信仰: *the Muslim faith* 伊斯兰教

faithful /'feɪθfl; 'feθfəl/ *adjective* 形容词

always ready to help your friends and to do what you have promised to do 忠实的；可信赖的: *a faithful friend* 忠实的朋友

faithfully /'feɪθfəli; 'feθfəlɪ/ *adverb* 副词

Yours faithfully words that you write at the end of a letter, before your name 用于信末署名前的客套话

fake /feɪk; fek/ *noun* 名词

a copy of something, made to trick people（用以骗人的）复制品；赝品: *This painting is not really by Van Gogh — it's a fake.* 这幅画不是凡·高的真迹——是件赝品。

fake *adjective* 形容词

a fake ten-pound note 一张十英镑的伪钞

fall[1] /fɔ:l; fɔl/ *verb* 动词 (**falls, falling, fell** /fel; fɛl/, **has fallen** /'fɔ:lən; 'fɔlən/)

1 go down quickly; drop 落下；跌落；

掉下: *The book fell off the table.* 书从桌子上掉下去了。◇ *She fell down the stairs and broke her arm.* 她从楼梯上跌下来，把胳膊摔断了。

2 (*also* 亦作 **fall over**) suddenly stop standing 跌倒；摔倒: *He slipped on the ice and fell.* 他在冰上滑倒了。◇ *I fell over and hurt my leg.* 我把腿摔坏了。

3 become lower or less 下降；减弱: *In the desert the temperature falls at night.* 在沙漠地区，夜晚气温下降。◇ *Prices have fallen again.* 又减价了。✪ opposite 反义词: **rise**

4 come or happen 来临；发生: *Darkness was falling.* 黑暗降临了。

fall apart break into pieces 破裂；破碎: *The chair fell apart when I sat on it.* 这把椅子我一坐就散架了。

fall asleep start sleeping 入睡: *She was so tired that she fell asleep in the armchair.* 她累得在单座沙发上睡着了。

fall behind become slower than others, or not do something when you should do it 落后: *She's falling behind with her school work because she goes out every evening.* 她功课落下了，因为她每天晚上都出去。

fall for somebody start to love somebody 爱上某人: *He has fallen for someone he met on holiday.* 他爱上了度假时认识的一个人。

fall out with somebody argue with somebody so that you stop being friends 与某人争吵而绝交: *John has fallen out with his girlfriend.* 约翰跟女朋友闹翻了。

fall through If a plan falls through, it does not happen. 落空；成为泡影

fall² /fɔːl; fɔl/ *noun* 名词

1 a sudden drop from a higher place to a lower place 落下；跌落；掉下: *He had a fall from his horse.* 他从马上摔下来了。

2 becoming lower or less 下降；减弱: *a fall in the price of oil* 油价的下降

3 falls (plural 复数) a place where water falls from a high place to a low place 瀑布: *the Victoria Falls* 维多利亚瀑布

4 *American English for* **autumn** 美式英语，即 **autumn**

false /fɔːls; fɔls/ *adjective* 形容词

1 not true; wrong 假的；与事实不符的；错误的: *A spider has eight legs—true or false?* 蜘蛛有八条腿——是对是错？◇ *She gave a false name to the police.* 她向警方供出的是假名字。

2 not real or not natural 假的；人造的: *People who have lost their own teeth wear false teeth* (= teeth that are made of plastic). 掉了牙的人就戴着假牙。

false alarm /ˌfɔːls əˈlɑːm; fɔls əˈlɑrm/ *noun* 名词

a warning about something bad, that does not happen 虚假的警报；虚惊: *Everyone thought there was a fire, but it was a false alarm.* 大家都以为失火了，却是虚惊一场。

fame /feɪm; fem/ *noun* 名词 (no plural 无复数)

being known by many people 名声；名气；声誉 ✪ The adjective is **famous**. 形容词是 **famous**。

familiar /fəˈmɪliə(r); fəˈmɪljɚ/ *adjective* 形容词

that you know well 熟悉的: *I heard a familiar voice in the next room.* 我听见隔壁有个熟人的声音。

be familiar with something know something well 熟悉；通晓: *I'm not familiar with this computer.* 我不熟悉这个计算机。

✪ opposite 反义词: **unfamiliar**

family /ˈfæməli; ˈfæməlɪ/ *noun* 名词 (*plural* 复数作 **families**)

1 parents and children 父母及其子女；家庭: *How many people are there in your family?* 你们家有几口人？◇ *My family have all got red hair.* 我们家的人头发都是红的。◇ *His family lives on a farm.* 他们家的人住在农场里。✪ Sometimes 'family' means not just parents and children but other people too, for example grandparents, aunts, uncles and cousins. 有时候 family 的含义不仅是父母及其子女，还包括其他的人，比如祖父母或外祖父母、姑母、姨母、伯母、婶母、舅母、伯父、叔父、舅父及堂（或表）兄弟姐妹。

2 a group of plants or animals（动植物的）科: *Lions belong to the cat family.* 狮子属于猫科动物。

family tree /ˌfæməli ˈtriː; ˈfæməlɪ tri/ *noun* 名词

a plan that shows all the people in a family 家谱图 ☞ picture on page C3 见第C3页图

F

famine /ˈfæmɪn; ˈfæmɪn/ *noun* 名词
A famine happens when there is not enough food in a country 饥荒: *There is a famine in many parts of Africa.* 非洲很多地区有饥荒。

famous /ˈfeɪməs; ˈfeməs/ *adjective* 形容词
known by many people 出名的；著名的: *Oxford is famous for its university.* 牛津市因其中的大学而闻名。◇ *Marilyn Monroe was a famous actress.* 梦露是著名的演员。✪ The noun is **fame**. 名词是 **fame**。

fans 扇子 *[* 电扇 *]*

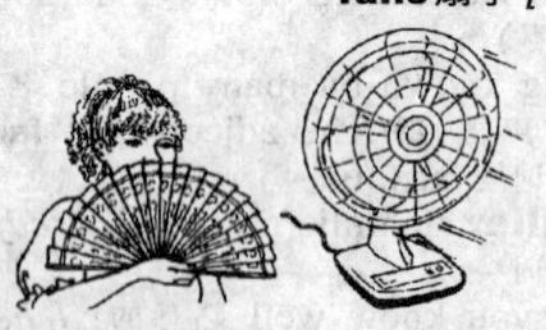

F

fan[1] /fæn; fæn/ *noun* 名词
a thing that moves the air to make you cooler 扇子: *an electric fan on the ceiling* 天花板上的电扇
fan *verb* 动词 (**fans**, **fanning**, **fanned** /fænd; fænd/)
make somebody or something cooler by moving the air 扇: *I fanned my face with the newspaper.* 我用报纸往脸上扇风凉快凉快。

fan[2] /fæn; fæn/ *noun* 名词
a person who likes somebody or something, for example a singer or a sport, very much 迷上某人或某事物的人（例如迷上某歌手或某项运动的人）: *She was a fan of the Beatles.* 她是披头士乐迷。◇ *football fans* 足球迷

fancy[1] /ˈfænsi; ˈfænsɪ/ *verb* 动词 (**fancies**, **fancying**, **fancied** /ˈfænsid; ˈfænsɪd/, **has fancied**)
1 feel that you would like something 想要某事物: *Do you fancy a drink?* 你想喝点儿什么吗？
2 a word that shows you are surprised （用以表示惊奇的词）想不到: *Fancy seeing you here!* 想不到在这儿见到你了！

fancy[2] /ˈfænsi; ˈfænsɪ/ *adjective* 形容词 (**fancier**, **fanciest**)
not simple or ordinary 精制的；不寻常的: *She wore a very fancy hat to the wedding.* 她戴着个很别致的帽子参加婚礼。

fancy dress /ˌfænsi ˈdres; ˈfænsɪ drɛs/ *noun* 名词 (no plural 无复数)
special clothes that you wear at a party so that you look like a different person or a thing （化装聚会穿的）奇装异服: *It was a fancy dress party so I went as Charlie Chaplin.* 那是一次化装聚会，所以我装扮成了卓别麟。

fantastic /fænˈtæstɪk; fænˈtæstɪk/ *adjective* 形容词
1 very good; wonderful 极好的；美妙的: *We had a fantastic holiday.* 我们的假期过得好极了。
2 strange or difficult to believe 离奇的；难以相信的: *He told us fantastic stories about his adventures.* 他给我们讲了一些他亲身经历的怪事。

fantasy /ˈfæntəsi; ˈfæntəsɪ/ *noun* 名词 (*plural* 复数作 **fantasies**)
something nice that you think about and that you hope will happen 想像中希望发生的好事；幻想

far[1] /fɑː(r); fɑr/ *adjective* 形容词 (**farther** /ˈfɑːðə(r); ˈfɑrðɚ/ or 或 **further** /ˈfɜːðə(r); ˈfɝðɚ/, **farthest** /ˈfɑːðɪst; ˈfɑrðɪst/ or 或 **furthest** /ˈfɜːðɪst; ˈfɝðɪst/)
1 a long way away 远的: *Let's walk—it's not far.* 咱们走着去吧——不远。
2 other 另外的: *They live on the far side of town.* 他们住在城的另一边。

far[2] /fɑː(r); fɑr/ *adverb* 副词 (**farther** /ˈfɑːðə(r); ˈfɑrðɚ/ or 或 **further** /ˈfɜːðə(r); ˈfɝðɚ/, **farthest** /ˈfɑːðɪst; ˈfɑrðɪst/ or 或 **furthest** /ˈfɜːðɪst; ˈfɝðɪst/)
1 a long way 远: *My house isn't far from the station.* 我家离车站不远。◇ *It's too far to drive in one day.* 那里很远，开车一天到不了。◇ *I walked much farther than you.* 我走得比你远得多。
2 You use 'far' to ask about the distance from one place to another place 用以询问两地间距离的词: *How far is it to Liverpool from here?* 从这儿到利物浦有多远？✪ We usually use 'far' only in questions and negative sentences, and after 'too' and 'so'. 通常 far 字仅用于问句和否定句中，还可用于 too 字和 so 字之后。In other sentences we use **a long way** 在其他句中要用 **a long way**: *It's a long way to walk —let's take the bus.* 走着去太远——咱们坐公共汽车吧。
3 very much 很；非常: *He's far taller*

than his brother. 他比他弟弟高得多。◇ *That's far too expensive.* 那可太贵了。

as far as to a place 直至某处: *We walked as far as the village and then came back.* 我们一直走到那个村子又回来了。

as far as I know words that you use when you think something is true but you are not certain 认为某事属实(但无把握);就我所知: *As far as I know, she's well, but I haven't seen her for a long time.* 就我所知,她病好了,可是我很长时间没见她了。

by far You use 'by far' to show that a person or thing is much better, bigger, etc than anybody or anything else 用以表示某人或某事物比其他的好得多或大得多等: *She's by far the best player in the team.* 她在队里比其他队员打得好得多。

far apart If two things or people are far apart, they are a long way from each other 相距很远: *I don't see him very often because we live too far apart.* 我不常见他,因为我们住得相隔很远。

far from not at all 毫不;一点儿也不: *I'm far from certain.* 我一点儿也没有把握。

so far until now 到现在为止: *So far the work has been easy.* 到现在为止,这件工作还算容易。

fare /feə(r); fɛr/ *noun* 名词
the money that you pay to travel by bus, train, plane, etc (公共汽车、火车、飞机等的)票钱: *How much is the train fare to Manchester?* 到曼彻斯特的火车票多少钱?

farewell /ˌfeə'wel; 'fɛr'wɛl/ *noun* 名词
saying goodbye 辞行;告别: *We are having a farewell party for Mike because he is going to live in Australia.* 我们给迈克举行告别聚会,因为他要到澳大利亚去生活了。

farm /fɑ:m; fɑrm/ *noun* 名词
land and buildings where people keep animals and grow crops 农田;农场;饲养场: *They work on a farm.* 他们在农场工作。◇ *farm animals* 农场饲养的动物

farm *verb* 动词 (**farms**, **farming**, **farmed** /fɑ:md; fɑrmd/)
He's farming in Scotland. 他正在苏格兰务农。

farmer *noun* 名词
a person who owns or looks after a farm 农场主;农民

farmhouse /'fɑ:mhaʊs; 'fɑrmˌhaʊs/ *noun* 名词
the house on a farm where the farmer lives 农场主或农民住的房子

farmyard /'fɑ:mjɑ:d; 'fɑrmˌjɑrd/ *noun* 名词
the outside space near a farmhouse. A farmyard has buildings or walls around it. 农家的庭院(农家庭院里有建筑物,四周有围墙。)

farther, farthest *forms of* **far** ∗ **far** 的不同形式

fascinating /'fæsɪneɪtɪŋ; 'fæsn̩ˌetɪŋ/ *adjective* 形容词
very interesting 极有趣的: *She told us fascinating stories about her journey through Africa.* 她给我们讲了她非洲之行中极有趣的见闻。

fashion /'fæʃn; 'fæʃən/ *noun* 名词
1 a way of dressing or doing something that people like and try to copy for a short time 一时流行的穿戴式样或做某事的方式;时尚;风尚;风气: *In the 1960s it was the fashion for women to wear very short skirts.* 在20世纪60年代,女子时兴穿超短裙。
2 the way you do something 做某事的方式、方法或样子: *He spoke in a very strange fashion.* 他说话样子很怪。

in fashion If something is in fashion, people like it at the moment 流行;入时;时兴: *Long hair is coming into fashion again.* 长发又流行起来了。

out of fashion If something is out of fashion, people do not like it at the moment 不再流行;过时: *Bright colours have gone out of fashion.* 大红大绿已经不时兴了。

fashionable /'fæʃnəbl; 'fæʃənəbl̩/ *adjective* 形容词
in the newest fashion 时兴的;时髦的;流行的: *She was wearing a fashionable black hat.* 她戴着一顶入时的黑帽子。✪ opposite 反义词: **unfashionable** or 或 **old-fashioned**

fashionably /'fæʃnəbli; 'fæʃənəblɪ/ *adverb* 副词
He was fashionably dressed. 他穿得很时髦。

fashion designer /'fæʃn dɪzaɪnə(r); 'fæʃən dɪ'zaɪnɚ/ *noun* 名词
a person whose job is to design clothes 服装设计师

F

fast[1] /fɑːst; fæst/ *adjective* 形容词 (**faster, fastest**)
1 A person or thing that is fast can move quickly 快的；迅速的: *a fast car* 速度快的汽车
2 If a clock or watch is fast, it shows a time that is later than the real time（指钟表）走得过快的: *My watch is five minutes fast.* 我的手表快了五分钟。
✪ opposite 反义词: **slow**
fast food /ˌfɑːst ˈfuːd; fæst ˈfud/ *noun* 名词 (no plural 无复数)
food like hamburgers and chips that can be cooked and eaten quickly 快餐食品（例如汉堡包和炸土豆条儿）

fast[2] /fɑːst; fæst/ *adverb* 副词 (**faster, fastest**)
quickly 快地；迅速地: *Don't talk so fast—I can't understand what you're saying.* 别说得那么快——我听不懂你的话。
✪ opposite 反义词: **slowly**
fast asleep sleeping very well 睡得很塌实: *The baby was fast asleep.* 孩子睡得很香。

fast[3] /fɑːst; fæst/ *verb* 动词 (**fasts, fasting, fasted**)
not eat food for a certain time 禁食（一段时间）: *Muslims fast during Ramadan.* 伊斯兰教徒在斋月白天禁食。

fasten /ˈfɑːsn; ˈfæsn̩/ *verb* 动词 (**fastens, fastening, fastened** /ˈfɑːsnd; ˈfæsn̩d/)
1 close something so that it will not come open 合起某物（不使打开）；系；扣；闩: *Please fasten your seat-belts.* 请系好安全带。◇ *Can you fasten this suitcase for me?* 你给我把这个手提箱盖好行吗？
2 join one thing to another thing 将某物联结在另一物上: *Fasten this badge to your jacket.* 把这个徽章别在你的外衣上。

fat[1] /fæt; fæt/ *adjective* 形容词 (**fatter, fattest**)
with a large round body 胖的；肥的；肥胖的: *You'll get fat if you eat too much chocolate.* 吃多了巧克力就发胖。
✪ opposite 反义词: **thin** ☞ picture on page C26 见第C26页图

fat[2] /fæt; fæt/ *noun* 名词
1 (no plural 无复数) the oily substance under the skins of animals and people 脂肪；肥肉: *Cut the fat off the meat.* 把这块肉上的膘切掉。
2 (*plural* 复数作 **fats**) oil that you use for cooking（烹调用的）油: *Heat some fat in a frying-pan.* 用煎锅把油加热。

fatal /ˈfeɪtl; ˈfetl̩/ *adjective* 形容词
1 Something that is fatal causes death 致命的: *a fatal car accident* 出人命的汽车事故
2 Something that is fatal has very bad results 后果严重的: *I made the fatal mistake of signing a paper I had not read properly.* 我没好好看文件就签了字，铸成大错。
fatally /ˈfeɪtəli; ˈfetl̩ɪ/ *adverb* 副词
She was fatally injured in the crash. 她在交通事故中受了重伤。

fate /feɪt; fet/ *noun* 名词
1 (no plural 无复数) the power that some people believe controls everything that happens 天数；天命
2 (*plural* 复数作 **fates**) what will happen to somebody or something 命运: *What will be the fate of the prisoners?* 这些囚犯命运如何？

father /ˈfɑːðə(r); ˈfɑðɚ/ *noun* 名词
a man who has a child 父亲；爸爸: *Where do your mother and father live?* 你母亲和父亲住在哪儿？☞ picture on page C3 见第C3页图 ☞ Look at **dad** and **daddy**. 见 **dad** 和 **daddy**。
Father Christmas /ˌfɑːðə ˈkrɪsməs; ˈfɑðɚ ˈkrɪsməs/ *noun* 名词
an old man with a red coat and a long white beard. Children believe that he brings presents at Christmas. 圣诞老人（留着白胡子穿着红外衣的老人。儿童以为圣诞老人在圣诞节时赠送礼物。）

father-in-law /ˈfɑːðər ɪn lɔː; ˈfɑðɚɪnˌlɔ/ *noun* 名词 (*plural* 复数作 **fathers-in-law**)
the father of your husband or wife 丈夫或妻子的父亲；公公；岳父 ☞ picture on page C3 见第C3页图

faucet /ˈfɔːsɪt; ˈfɔsɪt/ *American English for* **tap**[1] 美式英语，即 **tap**[1]

fault /fɔːlt; fɔlt/ *noun* 名词
1 (no plural 无复数) If something bad is your fault, you made it happen 错误；过失: *It's Sophie's fault that we are late.* 我们迟到是索菲的错儿。
2 (*plural* 复数作 **faults**) something that is wrong or bad in a person or thing 缺点；缺陷；毛病；瑕疵；故障: *There is*

a serious fault in the machine. 机器出了大毛病了。

faulty *adjective* 形容词

not working well 有缺点的；有故障的；不完善的: *This light doesn't work — the switch is faulty.* 这个灯不亮——电门有毛病。

favor *American English for* **favour** 美式英语，即 **favour**

favorite *American English for* **favourite** 美式英语，即 **favourite**

favour /ˈfeɪvə(r); ˈfevɚ/ *noun* 名词

something that you do to help somebody 为帮助某人而做的事；帮的忙；恩惠: *Would you do me a favour and open the door?* 帮个忙给我把门打开行吗？◇ *Could I ask you a favour — will you take me to the station this evening?* 求你件事行吗——今天晚上送我去车站行不行？

be in favour of something like or agree with something 喜爱或赞成某事物: *Are you in favour of higher taxes on cigarettes?* 你赞成增加对香烟的征税吗？

favourite /ˈfeɪvərɪt; ˈfevərɪt/ *adjective* 形容词

Your favourite person or thing is the one that you like more than any other 最喜爱的: *What's your favourite food?* 你最爱吃什么东西？

favourite *noun* 名词

a person or thing that you like more than any other 最喜爱的人或事物: *I like all chocolates but these are my favourites.* 凡是巧克力我都喜欢，但是最喜欢这种。

fax /fæks; fæks/ *verb* 动词 **(faxes, faxing, faxed** /fækst; fækst/)

send a copy of something like a letter or picture using telephone lines and a machine called a **fax machine** 用传真机送信件或图像（传真机叫做 **fax machine**）: *The drawings were faxed from New York.* 这些图是从纽约传送来的。

fax *noun* 名词 (*plural* 复数作 **faxes**)

a copy of something that is sent by a fax machine（由传真机传送的）传真件

fear /fɪə(r); fɪr/ *noun* 名词

the feeling that you have when you think that something bad might happen 害怕；恐惧: *I have a terrible fear of dogs.* 我特别怕狗。

fear *verb* 动词 **(fears, fearing, feared** /fɪəd; fɪrd/)

1 be afraid of somebody or something 害怕某人或某事物；惧怕: *We all fear illness and death.* 我们都害怕生病和死亡。

2 feel that something bad might happen 恐怕；担心: *I fear we will be late.* 恐怕我们要迟到了。

✪ It is more usual to say **be afraid (of)** or **be frightened (of)**. ✳ **be afraid (of)** 和 **be frightened (of)** 是常用词语。

feast /fi:st; fist/ *noun* 名词

a large special meal for a lot of people 盛宴；宴会: *a wedding feast* 婚宴

feat /fi:t; fit/ *noun* 名词

something you do that is clever, difficult or dangerous 费心思的、困难的或危险的事；功绩: *Climbing Mount Everest was an amazing feat.* 攀登埃佛勒斯峰（即珠穆朗玛峰）是了不起的事。

feather /ˈfeðə(r); ˈfɛðɚ/ *noun* 名词

Birds have feathers on their bodies to keep them warm and to help them fly. 羽毛

feather 羽毛

feature /ˈfi:tʃə(r); ˈfitʃɚ/ *noun* 名词

1 an important part of something 特征；特色；特点: *Pictures are a feature of this dictionary.* 本词典插图别具特色。

2 features (plural 复数) the parts of the face, for example the eyes, nose or mouth 面貌；容貌；五官（如眼睛、鼻子、嘴）

3 an important piece of writing in a magazine or newspaper, or a programme on TV（报刊或电视中的）特写或专题节目: *The magazine has a special feature on Paris on the centre pages.* 这份杂志的中间跨页上有个巴黎的特写。

February /ˈfebruəri; ˈfɛbruˌɛri/ *noun* 名词

the second month of the year 二月

fed *form of* **feed** ✳ **feed** 的不同形式

fed up /ˌfed ˈʌp; ˌfɛd ˈʌp/ *adjective* 形容词

unhappy or bored because you have had or done too much of something 厌倦；厌烦: *I'm fed up with watching TV — let's go out.* 电视我看腻了——咱们出去吧。

federal /ˈfedərəl; ˈfɛdərəl/ *adjective* 形容词

A federal country has several smaller countries or states that are joined to-

F

gether 联邦制的: *the Federal Government of the United States* 美国的联邦政府

federation /ˌfedəˈreɪʃn; ˌfɛdəˈreʃən/ *noun* 名词
a group of states or companies that work together 联邦；联合会；联合企业

fee /fi:; fi/ *noun* 名词
1 money that you pay to somebody for special work 服务费；酬金: *The lawyer's fee was £200.* 律师费是200英镑。
2 money that you pay to do something, for example to join a club 做某事的费用（如入会费）: *How much is the entrance fee?* 入场费多少钱？
3 fees (plural 复数) the money that you pay for lessons at school, college or university 学费: *Who pays your college fees?* 谁供你上大学？

feeble /ˈfi:bl; ˈfibḷ/ *adjective* 形容词 (**feebler**, **feeblest**)
not strong; weak 衰弱的；虚弱的；微弱的: *a feeble old man* 体弱的老翁

F

feed /fi:d; fid/ *verb* 动词 (**feeds**, **feeding**, **fed** /fed; fɛd/, **has fed**)
give food to a person or an animal 给人或动物食物；喂；饲养: *The baby's crying—I'll go and feed her.* 孩子哭了——我去喂喂她。

feel /fi:l; fil/ *verb* 动词 (**feels**, **feeling**, **felt** /felt; fɛlt/, **has felt**)
1 know something because your body tells you 感觉到；感受到；体会到；体验到: *How do you feel?* 你感觉怎样？◇ *I don't feel well.* 我觉得不舒服。◇ *I'm feeling tired.* 我感到很累。◇ *He felt somebody touch his arm.* 他觉着有人摸他的胳膊。
2 be rough, smooth, wet, dry, etc when you touch it 触摸时感觉粗糙、光滑、潮湿、干燥等: *The water felt cold.* 觉得出水很凉。◇ *This towel feels wet—can I have a dry one?* 这个毛巾摸着发潮——给我来个干的行吗？
3 think; believe 想；认为；以为: *I feel that we should talk about this.* 我认为我们应该谈谈这件事。
4 touch something to learn about it 触摸某物而获得了解: *Feel this wool—it's really soft.* 摸摸这种羊毛——真柔软。
feel for something If you feel for something, you try to get something you cannot see with your hands 摸着找某物: *She felt in her pocket for some matches.* 她在口袋里摸着，想找火柴。
feel like want something 想要某事物: *Do you feel like a cup of tea?* 你想要杯茶吗？◇ *I don't feel like going out tonight.* 我今天晚上不愿意出去。

feeling /ˈfi:lɪŋ; ˈfilɪŋ/ *noun* 名词
1 (*plural* 复数作 **feelings**) something that you feel inside yourself, like happiness or anger 心情；情绪；感情: *a feeling of sadness* 悲伤的心情
2 (no plural 无复数) the ability to feel in your body 知觉；感觉: *I was so cold that I had no feeling in my feet.* 我冻得脚都失去知觉了。
3 (*plural* 复数作 **feelings**) an idea that you are not certain about 无把握的想法: *I have a feeling that she isn't telling the truth.* 我看她是没说实话。
hurt somebody's feelings do or say something that makes somebody sad 做或说某事使人伤心；伤某人的感情: *Don't tell him you don't like his shirt—you'll hurt his feelings.* 别跟他说你不喜欢他的衬衫——你那么说就让他难受了。

feet *plural of* **foot** ＊ **foot** 的复数形式

fell *form of* **fall**[1] ＊ **fall**[1] 的不同形式

fellow[1] /ˈfeləʊ; ˈfɛlo/ *noun* 名词
a man 男子: *What is that fellow doing?* 那个男的干什么呢？

fellow[2] /ˈfeləʊ; ˈfɛlo/ *adjective* 形容词
a word that you use to talk about people who are the same as you（指和自己相同的人的用词）同伴的；同事的: *She doesn't know many of her fellow students.* 她认识的同学并不多。

felt *form of* **feel** ＊ **feel** 的不同形式

felt-pen /ˌfeltˈpen; ˌfɛltˈpɛn/, **felt-tip pen** /ˌfelt tɪpˈpen; ˌfɛlttɪp ˈpɛn/ *noun* 名词
a pen with a soft point 毡头笔

female /ˈfi:meɪl; ˈfimel/ *adjective* 形容词
A female animal or person belongs to the sex that can have babies. 雌性的；女性的
female *noun* 名词
My cat is a female. 我的猫是母猫。
☞ Look at **male**. 见 **male**。

feminine /ˈfemənɪn; ˈfɛmənɪn/ *adjective* 形容词
of or like a woman; right for a woman 女子的；像女子的；适合女性的: *feminine clothes* 女子服装 ☞ Look at **masculine**. 见 **masculine**。

fence /fens; fɛns/ *noun* 名词

fence 栅栏

a thing like a wall that is made of pieces of wood or metal. Fences are put round gardens and fields. 栅栏；篱笆；围墙

ferocious /fəˈrəʊʃəs; fəˈroʃəs/ *adjective* 形容词
very fierce and wild 非常凶猛而残暴的: *A rhinoceros is a ferocious animal.* 犀牛是猛兽。

ferry /ˈferi; ˈfɛrɪ/ *noun* 名词 (*plural* 复数作 **ferries**)
a boat that takes people or things on short journeys across a river or sea 渡船: *We travelled to France by ferry.* 我们乘渡船到法国。

fertile /ˈfɜ:taɪl; ˈfɝtl̩/ *adjective* 形容词
where plants grow well 肥沃的: *fertile soil* 肥沃的土壤 ✪ opposite 反义词: **infertile**

fertilizer /ˈfɜ:təlaɪzə(r); ˈfɝtl̩ˌaɪzɚ/ *noun* 名词
food for plants 肥料

festival /ˈfestɪvl; ˈfɛstəvl̩/ *noun* 名词
1 a time when people do special things because they are happy about something 节日；喜庆日子: *Christmas is an important Christian festival.* 圣诞节是基督教的重要节日。
2 a time when there are a lot of plays, concerts, etc in one place 众多戏剧、音乐会等聚集于一处演出；会演: *the Cannes Film Festival* 戛纳影展

fetch /fetʃ; fɛtʃ/ *verb* 动词 (**fetches**, **fetching**, **fetched** /fetʃt; fɛtʃt/)
1 go and bring back somebody or something 去接来某人；去取来某物: *Can you fetch me the books from the cupboard?* 你去把书从书架上给我拿来行吗？◇ *I went to fetch Andy from the station.* 我到车站去接安迪去了。☞ picture on page 58 见第58页图
2 If something fetches a certain price, somebody pays this price for it (指某物)卖得（某价钱）: *The house fetched £50 000.* 这所房子卖了50 000英镑。

fête /feɪt; fet/ *noun* 名词
a party outside where you can buy things and play games to win prizes. Schools and churches often have fêtes to get money（露天的）游乐会，义卖会（学校和教会常为筹款而举办）: *the summer fête* 暑期游乐会

fever /ˈfi:və(r); ˈfivɚ/ *noun* 名词
If you have a fever, your body is too hot because you are ill. 发烧

feverish /ˈfi:vərɪʃ; ˈfivərɪʃ/ *adjective* 形容词
If you are feverish, your body is too hot because you are ill. 发烧的

few /fju:; fju/ *adjective*, *pronoun* 形容词，代词 (**fewer**, **fewest**)
not many 不多；很少: *Few people live to the age of 100.* 很少有人活到100岁。◇ *There are fewer buses in the evenings.* 晚上公共汽车比较少。

a few some but not many 一些（但不多）: *Only a few people came to the meeting.* 只有几个人来开会。◇ *She has written a lot of books, but I have only read a few of them.* 她写过很多书，可是我只看过几本。

fiancé /fiˈɒnseɪ; fiˌɑnˈse/ *noun* 名词
A woman's fiancé is the man she is going to marry 未婚夫: *Can I introduce my fiancé, David? We've just got engaged.* 我来介绍一下我的未婚夫戴维，好吗？我们刚订婚。

fiancée /fiˈɒnseɪ; fiˈɑnse/ *noun* 名词
A man's fiancée is the woman he is going to marry. 未婚妻

fib /fɪb; fɪb/ *noun* 名词
something you say that you know is not true; a small lie 假话；小谎话: *Don't tell fibs!* 别说瞎话了！

fib *verb* 动词 (**fibs**, **fibbing**, **fibbed** /fɪbd; fɪbd/)
I was fibbing when I said I liked her hat. 我说我喜欢她的帽子，是骗她呢。

fibber *noun* 名词
a person who tells fibs 说小谎话的人

fiction /ˈfɪkʃn; ˈfɪkʃən/ *noun* 名词 (no plural 无复数)
stories that somebody writes and that are not true 虚构的故事；小说: *I enjoy reading fiction.* 我喜欢看小说。

fiddle /ˈfɪdl; ˈfɪdl̩/ *verb* 动词 (**fiddles**, **fiddling**, **fiddled** /ˈfɪdl̩d; ˈfɪdl̩d/)
touch something a lot with your fingers 用手指反复摆弄: *Stop fiddling with your*

F

pen and do some work! 别总摆弄钢笔了，干点儿活儿吧！

field /fi:ld; fild/ *noun* 名词

1 a piece of land that has a fence or hedge around it. Fields are used for growing crops or keeping animals in. 田地；农场

2 one thing that you study（学习或研究的）领域: *Dr Smith is one of the most famous scientists in his field.* 史密斯博士在他研究的领域中是位最著名的科学家。

3 a piece of land used for something special（作某种用途的）场地，场所: *a sports field* 运动场 ◇ *an airfield* (= a place where aeroplanes land and take off) 飞机场

4 a place where people find oil, coal, gold, etc（矿物）产地: *the oilfields of Texas* 得克萨斯油田 ◇ *a coalfield* 煤田

fierce /fɪəs; fɪrs/ *adjective* 形容词 (**fiercer, fiercest**)

1 angry and wild 愤怒而凶猛的: *a fierce dog* 恶狗

2 very strong 非常强劲的: *the fierce heat of the sun* 烈日

fifteen /ˌfɪfˈti:n; ˈfɪfˈtin/ *number* 数词

15 十五

fifteenth /ˌfɪfˈti:nθ; ˈfɪfˈtinθ/ *adjective, adverb, noun* 形容词，副词，名词

15th 第15（个）；第十五（个）

fifth /fɪfθ; fɪfθ/ *adjective, adverb, noun* 形容词，副词，名词

1 5th 第5（个）；第五（个）

2 one of five equal parts of something; ⅕ 五分之一

fifty /ˈfɪfti; ˈfɪftɪ/ *number* 数词

1 50 五十

2 the fifties (plural 复数) the numbers, years or temperature between 50 and 59 ＊ 50至59（之间的数目、年数或温度）: *He was born in the fifties* (= in the 1950s). 他是在五十年代出生的（= 20世纪50年代）。

in your fifties between the ages of 50 and 59 年岁在50至59之间；五十多岁

fiftieth /ˈfɪftiəθ; ˈfɪftɪɪθ/ *adjective, adverb, noun* 形容词，副词，名词

50th 第50（个）；第五十（个）

fig /fɪg; fɪg/ *noun* 名词

a soft sweet fruit that is full of small seeds 无花果

fight[1] /faɪt; faɪt/ *verb* 动词 (**fights, fighting, fought** /fɔ:t; fɔt/, **has fought**)

1 When people fight, they try to hurt or kill each other using their hands, knives or guns 打架；搏斗；打仗；作战: *What are the children fighting about?* 孩子们因为什么打起来了？

2 try very hard to stop something 尽力防止某事物: *He fought against the illness for two years.* 他跟疾病斗争了两年了。

3 talk in an angry way; argue 愤怒地说话；争吵；吵架

fight for something try very hard to do or get something 争取做或得到某事物；为…而斗争: *The workers are fighting for better pay.* 工人们正在为争取增加工资而斗争。

fighter *noun* 名词

1 a person who fights as a sport（某些运动的）运动员

2 a small aeroplane that shoots other aeroplanes 战斗机；歼击机

fight[2] /faɪt; faɪt/ *noun* 名词

an act of fighting 打架；搏斗；打仗；作战: *There was a fight outside the restaurant last night.* 昨天晚上饭馆外面有人打起来了。

figure /ˈfɪgə(r); ˈfɪgjɚ/ *noun* 名词

1 one of the symbols (0–9) that we use to show numbers（由0–9的一个）数字: *Shall I write the numbers in words or figures?* 数目字我写汉字还是写阿拉伯数字？

2 an amount or price 数额；价格: *What are our sales figures for Spain this year?* 我们今年对西班牙的销售额是多少？

3 the shape of a person's body 身材；体形；体态: *She's got a good figure.* 她身材好。

4 a shape of a person that you cannot see clearly 人体的模糊形象；身影: *I saw a tall figure outside the window.* 我看见窗户外边有个高大的身影。

5 figures (plural 复数) working with numbers to find an answer; arithmetic 计算；算术: *I'm not very good at figures.* 我的算术不太好。

figure of speech words that you use in an unusual way to make your meaning stronger（为加强语气而使用的）修辞手段；修辞格: *I didn't really mean that she was mad—it was just a figure of speech.* 我并不是说她真疯了——只不过是个夸张的说法而已。

file[1] /faɪl; faɪl/ *noun* 名词

1 a box or cover for keeping papers in（存放文件的）盒子、匣子、夹子或封皮；卷宗
2 a collection of information on a computer（计算机中的）文件

file 卷宗

file *verb* 动词 (**files**, **filing**, **filed** /faɪld; faɪld/)
put papers into a file 存档；归档: *Can you file these letters, please?* 劳驾，请把这些信归档行吗？

file² /faɪl; faɪl/ *noun* 名词
a tool with rough sides that you use for making things smooth 锉；锉刀: *a nail-file* 指甲锉
file *verb* 动词 (**files**, **filing**, **filed** /faɪld; faɪld/)
make something smooth with a file 把某物锉光滑: *She filed her nails.* 她把指甲锉光滑了。

file³ /faɪl; faɪl/ *verb* 动词 (**files**, **filing**, **filed** /faɪld; faɪld/)
walk in a line, one behind the other（一个跟着一个）排成一行走: *The students filed into the classroom.* 学生一个跟着一个走进了教室。
in single file in a line with each person following the one in front 一个人跟着一个人排成单行；鱼贯: *The children walked into the hall in single file.* 孩子们排成单行一个跟着一个走进了大厅。

fill /fɪl; fɪl/ *verb* 动词 (**fills**, **filling**, **filled** /fɪld; fɪld/)
1 make something full 使某物充满；装满；填满: *Can you fill this glass with water, please?* 请把这个玻璃杯倒满水行吗？
2 become full 变满；充满: *His eyes filled with tears.* 他眼里含着泪。
fill in write facts or answers in the spaces that have been left for them（在留出的空白处）填写内容或答案: *She gave me a form and told me to fill it in.* 她给我一份表格让我填写。
fill up become or make something completely full（使某物）完全变满或充满: *He filled up the tank with petrol.* 他把油箱灌满了汽油。

filling /ˈfɪlɪŋ; ˈfɪlɪŋ/ *noun* 名词
something that you put into a space or hole（放入空间或洞中的）填充物；馅: *I've got three fillings in my teeth.* 我的牙补了三处。◇ *What filling do you want in your sandwiches: cheese or ham?* 您要什么馅儿的三明治：干酪的还是火腿的？

film¹ /fɪlm; fɪlm/ *noun* 名词
1 moving pictures that you see at a cinema or on television 电影；影片: *There's a good film on at the cinema this week.* 这星期电影院有部好片子。
2 the special thin plastic that you use in a camera for taking photographs 胶卷；底片: *I bought a roll of black and white film.* 我买了一卷黑白胶卷。

film² /fɪlm; fɪlm/ *verb* 动词 (**films**, **filming**, **filmed** /fɪlmd; fɪlmd/)
use a camera to make moving pictures of a story, news, etc（用摄影机把故事、新闻等）拍成电影: *A TV company are filming outside my house.* 有家电视台正在我们家外面拍电影。

filter /ˈfɪltə(r); ˈfɪltɚ/ *noun* 名词
a thing used for holding back the solid parts in a liquid or gas 过滤器: *a coffee filter* 咖啡过滤器
filter *verb* 动词 (**filters**, **filtering**, **filtered** /ˈfɪltəd; ˈfɪltɚd/)
You should filter the water before you drink it. 你应该把水过滤后再喝。

filthy /ˈfɪlθi; ˈfɪlθɪ/ *adjective* 形容词 (**filthier**, **filthiest**)
very dirty 很脏的: *Go and wash your hands. They're filthy!* 去把你的手洗洗。多脏啊！

fin /fɪn; fɪn/ *noun* 名词
one of the thin flat parts on a fish that help it to swim 鳍 ☞ picture at **fish** 见 **fish** 词条插图

final¹ /ˈfaɪnl; ˈfaɪnḷ/ *adjective* 形容词
last; at the end 最后的；最终的: *The final word in this dictionary is 'zoom'.* 本词典最后的一个字是 zoom。

final² /ˈfaɪnl; ˈfaɪnḷ/ *noun* 名词
1 the last game in a competition to decide who wins 决赛
2 finals (plural 复数) the last examinations that you take at university（大学的）毕业考试

finally /ˈfaɪnəli; ˈfaɪnḷɪ/ *adverb* 副词
1 after a long time; in the end 最后；最终；终于: *After a long wait the bus finally arrived.* 等了很长时间公共汽车终于来了。

F

2 You use 'finally' before saying the last thing in a list 在列举最后一个项目之前用的词: *And finally, I would like to thank my parents for all their help.* 最后，我要感谢的是我父母对我各方面的帮助。

finance /ˈfaɪnæns; ˈfaɪnæns/ *noun* 名词

1 (no plural 无复数) money; planning how to get, save and use money for a business, country, etc 财务；金融；财政: *the French Minister of Finance* 法国财政部长

2 finances (plural 复数) the money you have that you can spend 可动用的钱；财务状况: *My finances aren't very good* (= I haven't got much money). 我的财务状况不佳（= 我没什么钱）。

finance *verb* 动词 (**finances**, **financing**, **financed** /ˈfaɪnænst; ˈfaɪnænst/)

give money to pay for something 支付某事物的钱；资助: *The building was financed by the government.* 这座建筑物是政府资助的。

F

financial /faɪˈnænʃl; faɪˈnænʃəl/ *adjective* 形容词

of or about money（关于）财务的；金融的；财政的: *financial problems* 财务问题

find /faɪnd; faɪnd/ *verb* 动词 (**finds**, **finding**, **found** /faʊnd; faund/, **has found**)

1 see or get something after looking or trying 找到或发现某事物: *I can't find my glasses.* 我找不到眼镜了。◇ *She hasn't found a job yet.* 她还没找到工作呢。◇ *Has anybody found the answer to this question?* 有人知道这个问题的答案了吗？

2 see or get something that you did not expect 偶然找到或发现某事物；遇到；碰到: *I found some money in the street.* 我在街上捡到一些钱。◇ *I woke up and found myself in hospital.* 我一醒来发觉自己是在医院里。

3 think or have an idea about something because you have felt, tried, seen it, etc（因感觉到、体验到、看到等）认为或有看法: *I didn't find that book very interesting.* 我认为那本书没什么意思。◇ *He finds it difficult to sleep at night.* 他感到夜晚很难入睡。

find out discover something, for example by asking or studying 发现某事物（如经过询问或研究）: *Can you find out what time the train leaves?* 你弄清楚火车什么时候开了吗？◇ *Has she found out that you broke the window?* 她知道窗户是你打碎的了吗？

fine[1] /faɪn; faɪn/ *adjective* 形容词 (**finer**, **finest**)

1 well or happy 健康的；愉快的: *'How are you?' 'Fine thanks. And you?'* "你好吗？" "很好，谢谢。你呢？"

2 good enough; okay 使人满意的；行: *'Let's meet on Monday.' 'Fine.'* "咱们星期一见吧。" "好。" ◇ *'Do you want some more milk in your coffee?' 'No, that's fine.'* "你咖啡里还要再加点儿奶吗？" "不要了，已经很好了。"

3 beautiful or of good quality 漂亮的；质量好的: *There's a fine view from the cathedral.* 从大教堂望去，风景很美。◇ *This is one of Monet's finest paintings.* 这是莫奈最好的一幅画儿。

4 (used about the weather) sunny; not raining（用于指天气）晴朗的；有阳光的；无雨的: *I hope it stays fine for our picnic.* 我希望到我们野餐的时候天气一直都这么好。

5 in very thin pieces 极细的；极稀的: *I've got very fine hair.* 我头发很稀。✪ opposite 反义词: **thick**

6 in very small pieces 颗粒极小的: *Salt is finer than sugar.* 盐比糖细。✪ opposite 反义词: **coarse**

fine[2] /faɪn; faɪn/ *noun* 名词

money that you must pay because you have done something wrong 因做错事而须付的钱；罚款；罚金: *You'll get a fine if you park your car there.* 要是把汽车停放在那儿就得罚款。

fine *verb* 动词 (**fines**, **fining**, **fined** /faɪnd; faɪnd/)

make somebody pay a fine 罚某人款: *I was fined £100 for speeding* (= driving too fast). 我因为超速（= 开车太快）被罚了100英镑。

finger /ˈfɪŋɡə(r); ˈfɪŋɡɚ/ *noun* 名词

one of the five parts at the end of each hand 手指: *She wears a ring on her little* (= smallest) *finger.* 她小手指上戴着个戒指。☞ picture on page C2 见第C2页图

keep your fingers crossed hope that somebody or something will be successful 祝愿某人或某事物顺利: *I'll keep my fingers crossed for you in your exams.* 我祝你考试顺利。

fingernail /ˈfɪŋɡəneɪl; ˈfɪŋɡɚˌnel/ *noun* 名词

the hard part at the end of your finger 手指甲 ☞ picture on page C2 见第C2页图

fingerprint /ˈfɪŋɡəprɪnt; ˈfɪŋɡɚˌprɪnt/ *noun* 名词
the mark that a finger makes when it touches something 手指纹: *The police found his fingerprints on the gun.* 警方发现枪上有他的指纹。

finish[1] /ˈfɪnɪʃ; ˈfɪnɪʃ/ *verb* 动词 (**finishes**, **finishing**, **finished** /ˈfɪnɪʃt; ˈfɪnɪʃt/)
1 stop happening 停止；结束: *School finishes at four o'clock.* 学校四点钟下课。
2 stop doing something; come to the end of something 停止做某事；结束某事物: *I finish work at half past five.* 我五点半下班。◇ *Hurry up and finish your dinner!* 快把饭吃完！◇ *Have you finished cleaning your room?* 你把你的房间打扫完了吗？
finish off do or eat the last part of something 把最后一部分做完或吃完: *He finished off all the milk.* 他把牛奶都喝完了。
finish with somebody or 或 **something** not want or need somebody or something any more 不再想要或不再需要某人或某事物: *Can I read this book when you've finished with it?* 你看完这本书给我看看行吗？

finish[2] /ˈfɪnɪʃ; ˈfɪnɪʃ/ *noun* 名词 (*plural* 复数作 **finishes**)
the last part of something; the end（某事物的）最后一部分；终结；终点: *the finish of a race* 赛跑的终点 ✪ opposite 反义词: **start**

fir /fɜ:(r); fɝ/, **fir-tree** /ˈfɜ: tri:; ˈfɝ tri/ *noun* 名词
a tall tree with thin sharp leaves (called **needles**) that do not fall off in winter 枞树；冷杉（其针叶叫做 **needle**）

fire[1] /ˈfaɪə(r); faɪr/ *noun* 名词
1 the heat and bright light that comes from burning things 火: *Many animals are afraid of fire.* 很多动物都怕火。◇ *There was a big fire at the factory last night.* 昨天夜里工厂失火了。
2 burning wood or coal that you use for keeping a place warm or for cooking（燃烧木柴或煤以取暖或做饭用的）炉火: *They lit a fire to keep warm.* 他们生了火取暖。
3 a thing that uses electricity or gas to keep a room warm（使用电力或煤气使房间保暖的）暖炉: *Switch on the fire.* 打开暖炉。
catch fire start to burn 烧着；着火: *She dropped her cigarette and the chair caught fire.* 她的烟卷掉下把椅子烧着了。
on fire burning 燃烧着: *My house is on fire!* 我的房子失火了！
put out a fire stop something from burning 灭火；救火: *We put out the fire with buckets of water.* 我们用一桶桶的水把火救灭了。
set fire to something, set something on fire make something start to burn 放火烧某物: *Somebody set the house on fire.* 有人放火把房子烧着了。

fire[2] /ˈfaɪə(r); faɪr/ *verb* 动词 (**fires**, **firing**, **fired** /ˈfaɪəd; faɪrd/)
1 shoot with a gun 用枪炮射击；开枪；开炮；开火: *The soldiers fired at the enemy.* 士兵向敌人开火了。
2 tell somebody to leave their job 解雇某人: *He was fired because he was always late for work.* 他因为上班总迟到而遭到解雇。

fire-alarm /ˈfaɪər əlɑ:m; ˈfaɪr əˌlɑrm/ *noun* 名词
a bell that rings to tell people that there is a fire 火警报警器

fire brigade /ˈfaɪə brɪˌɡeɪd; ˈfaɪr brɪˌɡed/ *noun* 名词
a group of people whose job is to stop fires 消防队: *Call the fire brigade!* 快叫消防队来！

fire-engine /ˈfaɪər endʒɪn; ˈfaɪrˌɛndʒən/ *noun* 名词
a vehicle that takes people and equipment to stop fires 救火车

fire-escape /ˈfaɪər ɪskeɪp; ˈfaɪrɪˌskep/ *noun* 名词
stairs on the outside of a building where people can leave quickly when there is a fire inside 太平梯（在建筑物外面供失火时逃生用的）

fire extinguisher /ˈfaɪər ɪkˌstɪŋɡwɪʃə(r); ˈfaɪr ɪkˌstɪŋɡwɪʃɚ/ *noun* 名词
a metal container full of chemicals for stopping a fire 灭火器

fireman /ˈfaɪəmən; ˈfaɪrmən/ (*plural* 复数作 **firemen** /ˈfaɪəmən; ˈfaɪrmən/), **fire-fighter** /ˈfaɪə faɪtə(r); ˈfaɪrˌfaɪtɚ/ *noun* 名词
a person whose job is to stop fires 消防队员

fireplace /ˈfaɪəpleɪs; ˈfaɪrˌples/ *noun* 名词
the place in a room where you can have a fire to make the room warm 壁炉

fire station /ˈfaɪə steɪʃn; ˈfaɪr ˌsteʃən/ *noun* 名词
a building where fire-engines are kept 消防站

firework /ˈfaɪəwɜ:k; ˈfaɪrˌwɝk/ *noun* 名词
a container with special powder in it that sends out coloured lights and smoke or makes a loud noise when you burn it 烟火（燃放时能发出各种颜色的火花供人观赏）: *We watched a firework display in the park.* 我们在公园里观看烟火表演。

firm¹ /fɜ:m; fɝm/ *adjective* 形容词 (**firmer, firmest**)
1 Something that is firm is quite hard or does not move easily 坚硬的或不易移动的；牢固的；结实的；稳固的: *Wait until the glue is firm.* 要等到胶粘结实了。◇ *The shelf isn't very firm, so don't put too many books on it.* 架子不太稳，上面别放太多书。
2 showing that you will not change your ideas 想法不改变的；坚定的；强硬的: *She's very firm with her children* (= she makes them do what she wants). 她对孩子很严格（= 她让他们做什么就得做什么）。◇ *a firm promise* 可靠的承诺
firmly *adverb* 副词
Nail the pieces of wood together firmly. 把木块牢牢钉在一起。

firm² /fɜ:m; fɝm/ *noun* 名词
a group of people working together in a business; a company 公司；商号: *My father works for a building firm.* 我父亲在建筑公司工作。

first¹ /fɜ:st; fɝst/ *adjective* 形容词
before all the others 第一的；最先的；最早的: *January is the first month of the year.* 一月是一年的第一个月份。
firstly *adverb* 副词
a word that you use when you are giving the first thing in a list 第一；首先: *We were angry firstly because he didn't come, and secondly because he didn't telephone.* 我们很生气，一是因为他没来，二是因为他也没打个电话。

first² /fɜ:st; fɝst/ *adverb* 副词
1 before all the others 第一；最先；最早: *I arrived at the house first.* 我是第一个到达那所房子那里的。
2 for the first time 第一次；最初: *I first met Paul in 1986.* 我初次见到保罗是在1986年。
3 before doing anything else 首先: *First fry the onions, then add the potatoes.* 先把洋葱炸了，然后再加进土豆儿。
at first at the beginning 起初: *At first she was afraid of the water, but she soon learned to swim.* 她起初怕水，但是不久就学会游泳了。
first of all before anything else 首先: *I'm going to cook dinner, but first of all I need to buy some food.* 我来做饭，可是得先去买点儿菜。

first³ /fɜ:st; fɝst/ *noun* 名词 (no plural 无复数)
a person or thing that comes earliest or before all others 来得最早的人或事物（或比其他的人或事物都早的）: *I was the first to arrive at the party.* 我是在聚会上到得最早的。◇ *Today is the first of May (May 1st).* 今天是五月一日。

first aid /ˌfɜ:st ˈeɪd; ˌfɝst ˈed/ *noun* 名词 (no plural 无复数)
quick simple help that you give to a person who is hurt, before a doctor comes 急救

first class /ˌfɜ:st ˈklɑ:s; ˈfɝst ˈklæs/ *noun* 名词 (no plural 无复数)
1 the part of a train, plane, etc that it is more expensive to travel in 第一等位；头等位（火车、飞机等席位较贵的部分）: *I got a seat in first class.* 我的座位是头等的。
2 the fastest, most expensive way of sending letters 第一类（最快、最贵的）邮寄方式
first-class /ˌfɜ:st ˈklɑ:s; ˈfɝstˈklæs/ *adjective, adverb* 形容词，副词
a first-class stamp 快信邮票 ◇ *It costs more to travel first-class.* 坐头等位比较贵。
☞ Look at **second class** and at the Note at **stamp**. 见 **second class** 及 **stamp** 词条注释。

first name /ˈfɜ:st neɪm; ˈfɝst ˌnem/ *noun* 名词
the name that your parents choose for you when you are born 名字（出生时

父母给取的）：*'What is Mr Carter's first name?' 'Paul.'* "卡特先生的名字叫什么？""叫保罗。" ☞ Note at **name** 见 **name** 词条注释

fish 鱼

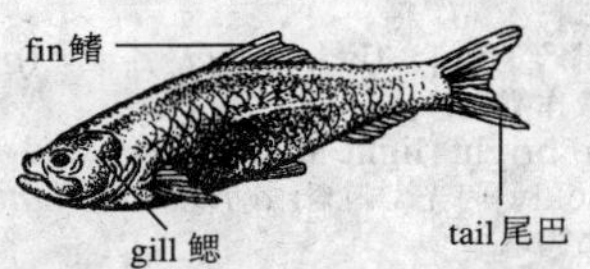

fish[1] /fɪʃ; fɪʃ/ *noun* 名词 (*plural* 复数作 **fish** or 或 **fishes**)
an animal that lives and breathes in water and uses its fins and tail for swimming 鱼: *I caught a big fish.* 我捉着了一条大鱼。◇ *We had fish and chips for dinner.* 我们晚饭吃的是鱼和炸土豆条儿。

fish[2] /fɪʃ; fɪʃ/ *verb* 动词 (**fishes, fishing, fished** /fɪʃt; fɪʃt/)
try to catch fish 捕鱼；钓鱼 ✪ When you talk about spending time fishing as a sport, you often say **go fishing** 以捕鱼作为运动或消遣叫做 **go fishing**: *I go fishing at weekends.* 我周末常去钓鱼。
fishing *noun* 名词 (no plural 无复数)
catching fish 捕鱼；钓鱼

fisherman /'fɪʃəmən; 'fɪʃɚmən/ *noun* 名词 (*plural* 复数作 **fishermen** /'fɪʃəmən; 'fɪʃɚmən/)
a person who catches fish as a job or sport 以捕鱼作为职业或作为运动的人；渔民；渔夫；钓鱼的人

fist /fɪst; fɪst/ *noun* 名词
a hand with the fingers closed tightly 拳；拳头: *She banged on the door with her fist.* 她用拳头砰砰地敲门。

fit[1] /fɪt; fɪt/ *adjective* 形容词 (**fitter, fittest**)
1 healthy and strong 健康而强壮: *I keep fit by going swimming every morning.* 我每天早晨游泳保持身体健康。
2 good enough; right 尚好的；合适的；适宜的: *This food isn't fit to eat.* 这种食物不适宜吃。◇ *Do you think she's fit for the job?* 你认为她适合做这项工作吗？
✪ opposite 反义词: **unfit**
fitness /'fɪtnəs; 'fɪtnəs/ *noun* 名词 (no plural 无复数)
being healthy and strong 健康而强壮

fit[2] /fɪt; fɪt/ *verb* 动词 (**fits, fitting, fitted**)
1 be the right size and shape for somebody or something 大小和形状对某人或某事物合适；合身: *These jeans don't fit me — they're too tight.* 这条牛仔裤我穿不合适——太瘦。◇ *This key doesn't fit the lock.* 这把钥匙打不开这把锁。
2 put something in the right place 把某物放在适当的地方: *Can you fit these pieces of the puzzle together?* 你能把这些拼图板拼在一起吗？
fit in 1 have space for somebody or something 有容纳某人或某物的地方: *I can only fit five people in the car.* 这辆汽车我只能载五个人。 **2** have time to do something or see somebody 有做某事或见某人的时间: *The doctor can fit you in at 10.30.* 医生能在10点30分见你。

fit[3] /fɪt; fɪt/ *noun* 名词
1 a sudden illness 突然生的病；（疾病的）发作
2 doing something suddenly that you cannot stop（自己控制不住）突然做出的事: *He was so funny — we were in fits of laughter.* 他太可笑了——逗得我们忍不住大笑起来。◇ *I had a coughing fit.* 我突然忍不住咳嗽起来了。

five /faɪv; faɪv/ *number* 数词
5 五

fix /fɪks; fɪks/ *verb* 动词 (**fixes, fixing, fixed** /fɪkst; fɪkst/)
1 put something in a place so that it will not move 把某物固定在某处；安装: *We fixed the shelf to the wall.* 我们把架子固定在墙上了。
2 repair something 修理某物: *The light isn't working — can you fix it?* 这个灯不亮了——你会修理吗？
3 decide something; make a plan for something 决定某事；为某事定计划: *They've fixed a date for the wedding.* 他们把举行婚礼的日子定下来了。◇ *Have you fixed up your holiday yet?* 你度假的事安排好了吗？
fixed *adjective* 形容词
Something that is fixed does not change or move 确定不变的；固定的: *a fixed price* 固定的价格

fizz /fɪz; fɪz/ *verb* 动词 (**fizzes, fizzing, fizzed** /fɪzd; fɪzd/)
If a drink fizzes, it makes a lot of small bubbles.（指液体）冒泡，起泡

F

fizzy *adjective* 形容词 (**fizzier**, **fizziest**)
Do you like fizzy drinks? 你爱喝汽水吗？

flag /flæg; flæg/ *noun* 名词
a piece of cloth with a special pattern on it joined to a stick (called a **flagpole**). Every country has its own flag. 旗；旗子（旗杆叫做 **flagpole**。各国都有自己的国旗。）

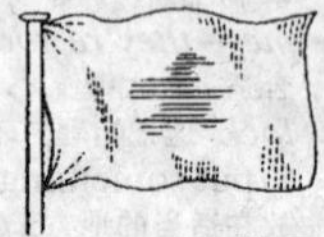
flag 旗子

flake /fleɪk; flek/ *noun* 名词
a small thin piece of something 小薄片: *snowflakes* 雪片 ◇ *Flakes of paint were coming off the wall.* 墙上的漆逐渐成片地剥落了。
flake *verb* 动词 (**flakes**, **flaking**, **flaked** /fleɪkt; flekt/)
Paint was flaking off the wall. 墙上的漆逐渐成片地剥落了。

F

flame /fleɪm; flem/ *noun* 名词
a hot bright pointed piece of fire 火焰 ☞ picture at **candle** 见 **candle** 词条插图
in flames burning 燃烧着: *The house was in flames.* 房子失火了。

flap[1] /flæp; flæp/ *noun* 名词
a flat piece of something that hangs down, for example to cover an opening. A flap is joined to something by one side（下垂的，例如遮住开口处的）扁平物（一边与他物相连）: *the flap of an envelope* 信封的封盖

flap[2] /flæp; flæp/ *verb* 动词 (**flaps**, **flapping**, **flapped** /flæpt; flæpt/)
move quickly up and down or from side to side 迅速地上下或左右移动；摇动；摆动: *Birds flap their wings when they fly.* 鸟类能鼓动着翅膀飞。◇ *The sails of the boat flapped in the wind.* 船帆随风摆动。

flare /fleə(r); flɛr/ *verb* 动词 (**flares**, **flaring**, **flared** /fleəd; flɛrd/)
flare up If a fire flares up, it suddenly burns more brightly or strongly. 火焰突然旺起来

flash[1] /flæʃ; flæʃ/ *verb* 动词 (**flashes**, **flashing**, **flashed** /flæʃt; flæʃt/)
1 send out a bright light that comes and goes quickly 发出闪光；闪耀: *The disco lights flashed on and off.* 迪斯科舞厅的灯光忽明忽暗。
2 make something send out a sudden bright light 使某物发出闪光: *She flashed a torch into the dark room.* 她用手电筒照射着黑暗的房间。
3 come and go very quickly 来去匆匆；一闪而过: *I saw something flash past the window.* 我看见有个东西在窗户那儿一闪而过。

flash[2] /flæʃ; flæʃ/ *noun* 名词 (*plural* 复数作 **flashes**)
1 a bright light that comes and goes quickly 闪光；闪耀: *a flash of lightning* 一道闪电
2 a bright light that you use with a camera for taking photographs 闪光灯（与照相机连用的）
in a flash very quickly 很快: *Wait for me—I'll be back in a flash.* 等我一会儿—我马上就来。

flashlight /ˈflæʃlaɪt; ˈflæʃˌlaɪt/ *American English for* **torch** 美式英语，即 **torch**

flat[1] /flæt; flæt/ *noun* 名词
a group of rooms for living in. A flat is usually on one floor of a house or big building. 公寓；单元房；一套房间（通常位于一所房子或一座大楼的一层）✪ A tall building with a lot of flats in it is called a **block of flats**. 公寓大楼叫做 **block of flats**。

flat[2] /flæt; flæt/ *adjective* 形容词 (**flatter**, **flattest**)
1 smooth, with no parts that are higher or lower than the rest 平坦的；平的: *The countryside in Holland is very flat.* 荷兰的旷野十分平坦。◇ *A table has a flat top.* 桌子的面是平的。
2 A tyre that is flat does not have enough air inside it.（指车胎）气不足的
flat *adverb* 副词
with no parts that are higher or lower than the rest 平着: *He lay flat on his back on the floor.* 他直挺挺地躺在地板上。

flatten /ˈflætn; ˈflætn̩/ *verb* 动词 (**flattens**, **flattening**, **flattened** /ˈflætnd; ˈflætn̩d/)
make something flat 把某物弄平: *I sat on the box and flattened it.* 我坐在那个盒子上，把它给坐扁了。

flatter /ˈflætə(r); ˈflætɚ/ *verb* 动词 (**flatters**, **flattering**, **flattered** /ˈflætəd; ˈflætɚd/)
1 try to please somebody by saying too many nice things about them that are

not completely true（说过多好话，夹杂不实之辞）讨好某人；恭维；奉承

2 If you are flattered by something, you like it because it makes you feel important（因觉得受重视）感到欢喜: *I felt flattered when she asked for my advice.* 她向我求教，我喜不自胜。

flattery /'flætəri; 'flætərɪ/ *noun* 名词 (no plural 无复数)

saying too many nice things about somebody to please them（讨好某人而说的）过多的好话；恭维；奉承

flavor *American English for* **flavour** 美式英语，即 **flavour**

flavour /'fleɪvə(r); 'flevɚ/ *noun* 名词

the taste of food（食物的）味道: *They sell 20 different flavours of ice-cream.* 他们出售20种味道各异的冰激凌。

flavour *verb* 动词 (**flavours**, **flavouring**, **flavoured** /'fleɪvəd; 'flevɚd/)

chocolate-flavoured milk 巧克力味的奶

flea /fli:; fli/ *noun* 名词

a very small insect without wings that can jump and that lives on and bites animals and people 跳蚤；蛇蚤: *Our cat has got fleas.* 我们的猫长蛇蚤了。

flee /fli:; fli/ *verb* 动词 (**flees**, **fleeing**, **fled** /fled; flɛd/, **has fled**)

run away from something bad or dangerous 逃离坏的或危险的环境: *During the war, thousands of people fled the country.* 在战争期间，成千上万的人逃离了祖国。

fleet /fli:t; flit/ *noun* 名词

a big group of ships 舰队；船队

flesh /fleʃ; flɛʃ/ *noun* 名词 (no plural 无复数)

the soft part of your body under your skin（身体上的）肉 ✪ The flesh of an animal that we eat is called **meat**. 供人吃的动物的肉叫做 **meat**。

flew *form of* **fly²** ＊ **fly²** 的不同形式

flex /fleks; flɛks/ *noun* 名词 (*plural* 复数作 **flexes**)

a long piece of wire covered with plastic that brings electricity to things like lamps, irons, etc（连接电灯、电熨斗等电器上的）一段电线

flexible /'fleksəbl; 'flɛksəbl̩/ *adjective* 形容词

1 that can bend easily without breaking 容易弯的；柔韧的

2 that can change easily 容易改变的；灵活的: *It's not important to me when we go — my plans are quite flexible.* 我们什么时候走对我来说无所谓——我的计划很灵活。

flies

1 *plural of* **fly¹** ＊ **fly¹** 的复数形式

2 *form of* **fly²** ＊ **fly²** 的不同形式

flight /flaɪt; flaɪt/ *noun* 名词

1 (*plural* 复数作 **flights**) a journey in an aeroplane 飞机的航行；航班；班机: *Our flight from New York leaves at 10 a.m.* 我们的班机上午10点自纽约启程。◇ *a direct flight from London to San Francisco* 从伦敦直飞旧金山

2 (no plural 无复数) flying 飞行: *Have you ever seen an eagle in flight?* 你看见过飞着的鹰吗？

flight of stairs /ˌflaɪt əv 'steəz; 'flaɪt əv ˌstɛrz/ *noun* 名词

a group of steps 一段楼梯

fling /flɪŋ; flɪŋ/ *verb* 动词 (**flings**, **flinging**, **flung** /flʌŋ; flʌŋ/, **has flung**)

throw something strongly or without care 猛力乱扔某物: *She flung a book and it hit me.* 她把书一扔结果打中我了。

flirt /flɜ:t; flɝt/ *verb* 动词 (**flirts**, **flirting**, **flirted**)

show somebody that you like them in a sexual way 调情；卖弄风情: *Who was that boy she was flirting with at the party?* 那个小伙子是谁，她在聚会上一个劲儿地跟他调情？

flirt *noun* 名词

a person who flirts a lot 爱调情的人；好卖弄风情的人

float /fləʊt; flot/ *verb* 动词 (**floats**, **floating**, **floated**)

1 stay on top of a liquid（在液面上）漂浮: *Wood floats on water.* 木头能在水上漂着。☞ Look at **sink**. 见 **sink**。

2 move slowly in the air（在空气中）飘动: *Clouds were floating across the sky.* 朵朵云彩在天空中飘来浮去。

flock /flɒk; flɑk/ *noun* 名词

a group of birds, sheep or goats（鸟或羊的）群: *a flock of seagulls* 一群海鸥

flood /flʌd; flʌd/ *noun* 名词

1 When there is a flood, a lot of water covers the land（地上的）大量的水；洪水；水灾: *Many homes were destroyed in the flood.* 这场水灾摧毁了很多家园。

2 a lot of something 大批；大量: *My dad had a flood of cards when he was in* *hospital.* 我爸爸住院的时候收到了很多慰问卡。

flood *verb* 动词 (**floods**, **flooding**, **flooded**)

A pipe burst and flooded the kitchen. 有个水管子裂了，流得厨房到处是水。

floor /flɔ:(r); flɔr/ *noun* 名词

1 the part of a room that you walk on 室内的地面；地板: *There weren't any chairs so we sat on the floor.* 屋子里没有椅子，我们就坐在地上了。

2 all the rooms at the same height in a building 一座大楼中同一层楼的所有房间；楼层: *I live on the top floor.* 我住在最上面的那层楼上。◇ *Our hotel room was on the sixth floor.* 我们旅馆的房间在六楼。☞ picture at **house** 见 **house** 词条插图

✪ The part of building that is on the same level as the street is called the **ground floor** in British English and the **first floor** in American English. 楼房地面与街道相平的楼层，在英式英语中叫做 **ground floor**，在美式英语中叫做 **first floor**。

floppy disk /ˌflɒpi ˈdɪsk; ˌflɑpɪ ˈdɪsk/ *noun* 名词

a small flat piece of plastic that stores information for a computer 软磁盘（用于计算机中的）☞ picture at **computer** 见 **computer** 词条插图

florist /ˈflɒrɪst; ˈflɔrɪst/ *noun* 名词

a person who sells flowers 卖花的人 ✪ A shop that sells flowers is called a **florist's**. 卖花的商店叫做 **florist's**。

flour /ˈflaʊə(r); flaʊr/ *noun* 名词 (no plural 无复数)

soft white or brown powder that we use to make bread, cakes, etc 面粉

flourish /ˈflʌrɪʃ; ˈflʌrɪʃ/ *verb* 动词 (**flourishes**, **flourishing**, **flourished** /ˈflʌrɪʃt; ˈflɝɪʃt/)

1 grow well 成长得好: *The garden flourished after all the rain.* 下了那么多雨，园子里郁郁葱葱。

2 become strong or successful 昌盛；旺盛；兴旺；繁荣: *Their business is flourishing.* 他们的生意十分兴隆。

flow /fləʊ; flo/ *verb* 动词 (**flows**, **flowing**, **flowed** /fləʊd; flod/)

move along like a river 流动: *This river flows into the North Sea.* 这条河流入北海。

flow *noun* 名词 (no plural 无复数)

I used a handkerchief to stop the flow of blood. 我用手绢止住血。

flower /ˈflaʊə(r); ˈflaʊɚ/ *noun* 名词

the brightly coloured part of a plant that comes before the seeds or fruit 花；花朵；花卉: *She gave me a bunch of flowers.* 她送给我一束花。☞ picture at **plant** 见 **plant** 词条插图

flowery /ˈflaʊəri; ˈflaʊərɪ/, **flowered** /ˈflaʊəd; ˈflaʊɚd/ *adjective* 形容词

with a pattern of flowers on it 有花朵图案的: *a flowery dress* 有花朵图案的连衣裙

flown *form of* **fly²** ＊ **fly²** 的不同形式

flu /flu:; flu/ *noun* 名词 (no plural 无复数)

an illness like a bad cold that makes you ache and feel very hot 流感（流行性感冒）: *I think I've got flu.* 我看我是得了流感了。

fluent /ˈflu:ənt; ˈfluənt/ *adjective* 形容词

1 able to speak easily and correctly（说话）流利而通顺的: *Ramon is fluent in English and French.* 拉蒙的英语和法语都很流利。

2 spoken easily and correctly（说得）流利而通顺的: *fluent German* 流利而通顺的德语

fluently *adverb* 副词

She speaks five languages fluently. 她会说五种语言，都十分流利而通顺。

fluff /flʌf; flʌf/ *noun* 名词 (no plural 无复数)

soft light stuff that comes off wool, animals, etc（从毛料、动物身上等落下的）绒毛

fluid /ˈflu:ɪd; ˈfluɪd/ *noun* 名词

anything that can flow; a liquid 流体；液体: *Water is a fluid.* 水是液体。

flung *form of* **fling** ＊ **fling** 的不同形式

flush /flʌʃ; flʌʃ/ *verb* 动词 (**flushes**, **flushing**, **flushed** /flʌʃt; flʌʃt/)

1 clean something by sending water through it 用水冲洗: *Please flush the toilet.* 请冲洗恭桶。

2 If you flush, your face becomes red（指人的面部）变红，发红: *He flushed with anger.* 他气得满脸通红。

flute /flu:t; flut/ *noun* 名词

a musical instrument with holes, that you blow 长笛

fly¹ /flaɪ; flaɪ/ *noun* 名词 (*plural* 复数作 **flies**)

a small insect with two wings 苍蝇

flute 长笛

fly² /flaɪ; flaɪ/ *verb* 动词 (**flies**, **flying**, **flew** /flu:; flu/, **has flown** /fləʊn; flon/)
1 move through the air 飞；飞行：*In autumn some birds fly to warmer countries.* 秋天有些鸟飞到暖和的地方去。
2 make an aircraft move through the air 使飞行器飞行；驾驶飞机：*A pilot is a person who flies an aircraft.* 飞机驾驶员是驾驶飞机飞行的人。
3 travel in an aeroplane 乘飞机：*I'm flying to Brussels tomorrow.* 我明天坐飞机去布鲁塞尔。
4 move quickly 迅速移动：*The door suddenly flew open and John came in.* 门突然开了，约翰进来了。◇ *A stone came flying through the window.* 有块石头从窗户外边飞进来。

fly 苍蝇

flying /'flaɪɪŋ; 'flaɪɪŋ/ *adjective* 形容词
able to fly 能飞的；会飞的: *flying insects* 飞虫
flying saucer /ˌflaɪɪŋ 'sɔ:sə(r); ˌflaɪɪŋ 'sɔsɚ/ *noun* 名词
a flying object that some people think they have seen, and that may come from another planet 飞碟（有人称曾见到的可能从其他星球来的飞行物体）

flyover /'flaɪəʊvə(r); 'flaɪˌovɚ/ *noun* 名词
a bridge that carries a road over other roads 立交桥（建筑在其他道路上方的道路桥梁）

foal /fəʊl; fol/ *noun* 名词
a young horse 幼小的马；驹

foam /fəʊm; fom/ *noun* 名词 (no plural 无复数)
a lot of very small white bubbles that you see when you move liquid quickly 泡沫

focus /'fəʊkəs; 'fokəs/ *verb* 动词 (**focuses**, **focusing**, **focused** /'fəʊkəst; 'fokəst/)
move parts of a camera, microscope, etc so that you can see things through it clearly 调整（照相机、显微镜等的）焦距；对焦
focus *noun* 名词 (no plural 无复数)
in focus If a photograph is in focus, it is clear. 在焦点上（照片清楚）
out of focus If a photograph is out of focus, it is not clear 不在焦点上（照片不清楚）：*Your face is out of focus in this photo.* 在这张照片上你的脸没照清楚。

fog /fɒg; fɔg/ *noun* 名词 (no plural 无复数)
thick cloudy air near the ground, that is difficult to see through 浓雾；大雾: *The fog will clear by late morning.* 快到中午的时候大雾就能消了。
foggy *adjective* 形容词 (**foggier**, **foggiest**)
a foggy day 有大雾的一天 ◇ *It was very foggy this morning.* 今天早晨雾很大。

foil /fɔɪl; fɔɪl/ *noun* 名词 (no plural 无复数)
metal that is very thin like paper. Foil is used for covering food 金属薄片；箔（用以包装食物）：*I wrapped the meat in foil and put it in the oven.* 我用铝箔把肉包起来放进烤箱里了。

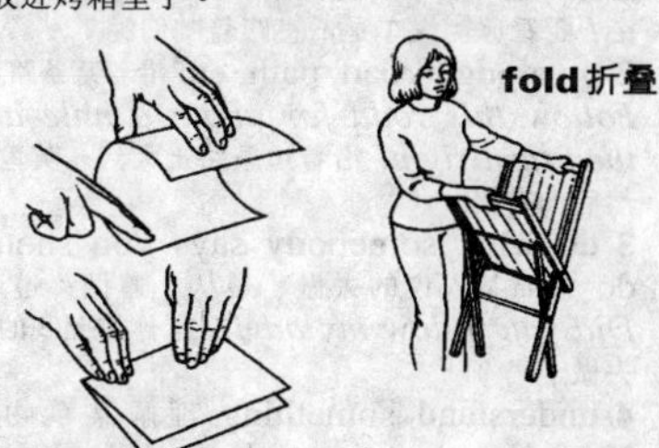
fold 折叠

fold¹ /fəʊld; fold/ *verb* 动词 (**folds**, **folding**, **folded**)
1 (*also* 亦作 **fold up**) bend something so that one part is on top of another part 折叠: *I folded the letter and put it in the envelope.* 我把信叠起来放进信封里了。◇ *Fold up your clothes.* 把你的衣服叠起来吧。✪ opposite 反义词: **unfold**
2 If you fold your arms, you cross them in front of your chest. 双臂在胸前交叉
folding *adjective* 形容词
that can be made flat 折的: *a folding bed* 折床

F

fold² /fəʊld; fold/ *noun* 名词
a line that is made when you bend cloth or paper（纸上的或布上的）折痕；折线

folder /'fəʊldə(r); 'foldɚ/ *noun* 名词
a cover made of cardboard or plastic for keeping papers in（硬纸板或塑料制的）文件夹；纸夹

folk /fəʊk; fok/ *noun* 名词 (plural 复数)
people 人们: *There are a lot of old folk living in this village.* 这个村子里住着很多老人。

folk-dance /'fəʊk dɑ:ns; 'fok,dæns/ *noun* 名词
an old dance of the people of a particular place 民间舞蹈: *the folk-dances of Turkey* 土耳其民间舞

folk-song /'fəʊk sɒg; 'foksɔŋ/ *noun* 名词
an old song of the people of a particular place 民歌

F

follow /'fɒləʊ; 'fɑlo/ *verb* 动词 (**follows**, **following**, **followed** /'fɒləʊd; 'fɑlod/)
1 come or go after somebody or something 跟随某人或某物来或去: *Follow me and I'll show you the way.* 跟我来，我告诉您怎么走。◇ *I think that car is following us!* 我看那辆汽车是一直跟着咱们呢！
2 go along a road, path, etc 沿着某条路走: *Follow this road for about a mile and then turn right.* 沿着这条路走大约一英里，然后向右拐。
3 do what somebody says you should do 按照某人说的去做；遵从；遵循；遵照: *Did you follow my advice?* 你按照我的话去做了吗？
4 understand something 理解某事物；领会: *Has everyone followed the lesson so far?* 大家是不是都明白现在讲的课了？
as follows as you will now hear or read 如下: *The dates of the meetings will be as follows: 21 March, 3 April, 19 April.* 开会的日期如下：3月21日、4月3日、4月19日。

following /'fɒləʊɪŋ; 'fɑləwɪŋ/ *adjective* 形容词
next 接着的；下一个: *I came back from holiday on Sunday and went to work on the following day.* 我星期日度假回来，第二天就上班了。

fond /fɒnd; fɑnd/ *adjective* 形容词 (**fonder**, **fondest**)
be fond of somebody or 或 **something** like somebody or something a lot 非常喜爱某人或某事物: *They are very fond of their uncle.* 他们非常喜欢他们的叔叔。

food /fu:d; fud/ *noun* 名词 (no plural 无复数)
People and animals eat food so that they can live and grow 食物；食品: *Let's go and get some food—I'm hungry.* 咱们去弄点儿吃的——我饿了。◇ *They gave the horses food and water.* 他们喂过了马又饮了马。

fool¹ /fu:l; ful/ *noun* 名词
a person who is silly or who does something silly 傻子；傻瓜；蠢人: *You fool! You forgot to lock the door!* 你这个傻瓜！你忘了锁门了！
make a fool of somebody do something that makes somebody look silly 使某人出丑: *He always makes a fool of himself at parties.* 他总是在聚会的时候出洋相。

fool² /fu:l; ful/ *verb* 动词 (**fools**, **fooling**, **fooled** /fu:ld; fuld/)
make somebody think something that is not true; trick somebody 使某人相信虚假的事；愚弄某人: *You can't fool me! I know you're lying!* 你别糊弄我！我知道你说的是瞎话！
fool about, **fool around** do silly things 做傻事；做蠢事: *Stop fooling about with that knife.* 别乱摆弄刀子。

foolish /'fu:lɪʃ; 'fulɪʃ/ *adjective* 形容词
stupid; silly 傻的；愚蠢的: *That was a foolish mistake.* 愚蠢的错误。
foolishly *adverb* 副词
I foolishly forgot to bring a coat. 我真笨，忘了带大衣了。

foot /fʊt; fʊt/ *noun* 名词
1 (*plural* 复数作 **feet** /fi:t; fit/) the part of your leg that you stand on 脚；足: *I've been walking all day and my feet hurt.* 我走了一整天的路，脚都走疼了。☞ picture on page C2 见第C2页图
2 (*plural* 复数作 **foot** or 或 **feet**) a measure of length (= 30.48 centimetres). There are twelve **inches** in a foot, and three feet in a **yard** 英尺（长度单位，= 30.48厘米。1英尺 = 12英寸。3英尺 = 1码。英寸叫做 **inch**，码叫做 **yard**。）: *'How tall are you?' 'Five foot six* (= five feet and six inches).' "你有多高？" "五英尺六英寸。" ✪ The short way of writing 'foot' is **ft**. ＊ foot 的缩写形式为 **ft**。

✪ In the past, people in Britain used **inches**, **feet**, **yards** and **miles** to measure distances, not **centimetres**, **metres** and **kilometres**. 过去英国人用英寸(**inch**)、英尺(**foot**)、码(**yard**)和英里(**mile**)来测量距离，而不用厘米(**centimetre**)、米(**metre**)和公里(**kilometre**)。Now many people use and understand both ways. 现在很多人两种方法都用。

3 the lowest part; the bottom 最下部；底部: *She was standing at the foot of the stairs.* 她站在楼梯最底层那里。

on foot walking 走着: *Shall we go by car or on foot?* 咱们坐汽车去还是走着去？

put your feet up rest 休息: *If you're tired, put your feet up and listen to the radio.* 你要是累了，就休息一会儿，听听收音机。

put your foot down say strongly that something must or must not happen 强烈坚持或反对某事: *My mum put her foot down when I asked if I could stay out all night.* 我问我妈妈我能不能在外面过夜，她说绝对不行。

football /ˈfʊtbɔːl; ˈfʊtˌbɔl/ *noun* 名词

1 (no plural 无复数) a game for two teams of eleven players who try to kick a ball into a **goal** on a field called a **pitch** 足球运动（球门叫做 **goal**，球场叫做 **pitch**）: *He plays football for England.* 他在英国足球队踢球。◇ *I'm going to a football match on Saturday.* 我星期六去看足球比赛。

2 (*plural* 复数作 **footballs**) a ball for playing this game 足球

footballer *noun* 名词

a person who plays football 足球运动员

footpath /ˈfʊtpɑːθ; ˈfʊtˌpæθ/ *noun* 名词

a path in the country for people to walk on（郊野的）人行小路

footprint /ˈfʊtprɪnt; ˈfʊtˌprɪnt/ *noun* 名词

a mark that your foot or shoe makes on the ground 脚印；足迹

footstep /ˈfʊtstep; ˈfʊtˌstɛp/ *noun* 名词

the sound of a person walking 脚步声: *I heard footsteps, and then a knock on the door.* 我听到有脚步声，接着是敲门声。

for¹ /fə(r), fɔː(r); fɚ, fɔr/ *preposition* 介词

1 a word that shows who will get or have something 表示谁将得到或将有某事物的词: *These flowers are for you.* 这些花是给你的。

2 a word that shows how something is used or why something is done 表示怎样使用某事物或为什么要做某事的词: *We had fish and chips for dinner.* 我们晚饭吃的是鱼和炸土豆条儿。◇ *Take this medicine for your cold.* 吃这种药治感冒。◇ *He was sent to prison for murder.* 他犯了谋杀罪被关进监狱了。

3 a word that shows how long 表示时间有多长的词: *She has lived here for 20 years.* 她在这儿住了20年了。☞ Note at **since** 见 **since** 词条注释

4 a word that shows how far 表示距离有多远的词: *We walked for miles.* 我们走了很远很远。

5 a word that shows where a person or thing is going 表示某人或某物要到何处去的词: *Is this the train for Glasgow?* 这是开往格拉斯哥的火车吗？

6 a word that shows the person or thing you are talking about 表示所涉及的人或事物的词: *It's time for us to go.* 我们该走了。

7 a word that shows how much something is 表示某事物多少钱的词: *I bought this book for £2.* 我买这本书花了2英镑。

8 a word that shows that you like an idea 表示赞成某意见的词: *Some people were for the strike and others were against it.* 有的人支持罢工，但也有人反对。

9 on the side of somebody or something 在某人或某事物的一方: *He plays football for Italy.* 他在意大利队踢足球。

10 with the meaning of 意思为…: *What is the word for 'table' in German?* "桌子"这个词用德语怎么说？

for² /fə(r); fɚ/ *conjunction* 连词

because 因为；由于: *She was crying, for she knew they could never meet again.* 她哭起来了，因为她知道他们再也不能相见了。

✪ **Because** and **as** are the words that we usually use. ✳ **because** 和 **as** 是常用词。

forbid /fəˈbɪd; fɚˈbɪd/ *verb* 动词 (**forbids**, **forbidding**, **forbade** /fəˈbæd; fɚˈbæd/, **has forbidden** /fəˈbɪdn; fɚˈbɪdn̩/)

say that somebody must not do something 不准某人做某事；不许；禁止: *My parents have forbidden me to see him again.* 我父母不准我再见他。◇ *Smoking is*

F

forbidden (= not allowed) *inside the building.* 大厦内禁止吸烟。

force¹ /fɔ:s; fɔrs/ *noun* 名词

1 (no plural 无复数) power or strength 力；力量: *He was killed by the force of the explosion.* 他被炸死了。

2 (*plural* 复数作 **forces**) a group of people, for example police or soldiers, who do a special job（警察或士兵等的）部队；军队: *the police force* 警察部队

by force using a lot of strength, for example by pushing, pulling or hitting 用很大力量（如推、拉或打击）: *I lost the key so I had to open the door by force.* 我把钥匙丢了，只好破门而入了。

force² /fɔ:s; fɔrs/ *verb* 动词 (**forces, forcing, forced** /fɔ:st; fɔrst/)

1 make somebody do something that they do not want to do 强迫某人做某事；迫使；逼: *They forced him to give them the money.* 他们强迫他给他们钱。

2 do something by using a lot of strength 用很大力量做某事: *The thief forced the window open.* 那个小偷破窗而入。

forecast /'fɔ:kɑ:st; fɔr'kæst/ *noun* 名词

what somebody thinks will happen 预报；预测: *The weather forecast said that it would snow today.* 天气预报说今天要下雪。

foreground /'fɔ:graʊnd; 'fɔrˌgraʊnd/ *noun* 名词

the part of a picture that seems nearest to you 画面的前部；前景: *The man in the foreground is my father.* 这张照片里前边的那个人是我父亲。✪ opposite 反义词: **background**

forehead /'fɔ:hed; 'fɔrˌhɛd/ *noun* 名词

the part of your face above your eyes 眼睛以上的部分；额；额头；脑门子 ☞ picture on page C2 见第C2页图

foreign /'fɒrən; 'fɔrɪn/ *adjective* 形容词

of or from another country 外国的；来自外国的: *We've got some foreign students staying at our house.* 我们家住着一些外国留学生。◇ *a foreign language* 外国语

foreigner *noun* 名词

a person from another country 外国人 ☞ Note at **stranger** 见 **stranger** 词条注释

forest /'fɒrɪst; 'fɔrɪst/ *noun* 名词

a big piece of land with a lot of trees 森林: *We went for a walk in the forest.* 我们在林中散步。

> ✪ A forest is larger than a **wood**. 森林比树林大。树林叫做 **wood**。A **jungle** is a forest in a very hot country. 热带的森林叫做 **jungle**。

forever /fər'evə(r); fə'ɛvə/ *adverb* 副词

1 for all time; always 永远: *I will love you forever.* 我永远爱你。

2 very often 总是；频频: *I can't read because he is forever asking me questions!* 他老问我问题，我都没法看书了！

forgave *form of* **forgive** ✳ **forgive** 的不同形式

forge /fɔ:dʒ; fɔrdʒ/ *verb* 动词 (**forges, forging, forged** /fɔ:dʒd; fɔrdʒd/)

make a copy of something because you want to trick people and make them think it is real 伪造某物（借以骗人）: *He was put in prison for forging money.* 他因伪造钱币而入狱。

forgery /'fɔ:dʒəri; 'fɔrdʒərɪ/ *noun* 名词

1 (no plural 无复数) making a copy of something to trick people 伪造物品借以骗人: *Forgery is a crime.* 伪造物品借以骗人是犯罪行为。

2 (*plural* 复数作 **forgeries**) a copy of something made to trick people（为行骗用的）伪造物品: *This painting is not really by Picasso — it's a forgery.* 这幅画不是毕加索的真迹——是个赝品。

forget /fə'get; fə'gɛt/ *verb* 动词 (**forgets, forgetting, forgot** /fə'gɒt; fə'gɑt/, **has forgotten** /fə'gɒtn; fə'gɑtn̩/)

1 not remember something; not have something in your mind any more 忘记；遗忘: *I've forgotten her name.* 我把她的名字忘了。◇ *Don't forget to feed the cat.* 别忘了喂猫。

2 not bring something with you 忘记携带某物: *I couldn't see the film very well because I had forgotten my glasses.* 那场电影我没看好，因为我忘带眼镜了。

3 stop thinking about something 不再想某事物；别再把某事放在心上: *Forget about your exams and enjoy yourself!* 别再想着考试的事了，玩儿玩儿吧！

forgive /fə'gɪv; fə'gɪv/ *verb* 动词 (**forgives, forgiving, forgave** /fə'geɪv; fə'gev/, **has forgiven** /fə'gɪvn; fə'gɪvən/)

stop being angry with somebody for a bad thing that they did 对某人做错事不再生

气；原谅；宽恕: *He never forgave me for forgetting his birthday.* 我把他的生日忘了，他一直都不原谅我。

fork /fɔ:k; fɔrk/ *noun* 名词

1 a thing with long points at one end, that you use for putting food in your mouth 叉子（餐具）

2 a large tool with points at one end, that you use for digging the ground 叉；耙子（农具）

3 a place where a road or river divides into two parts（道路或河流的）分岔处；岔口: *When you get to the fork in the road, go left.* 你见到岔口处就向左拐。

form¹ /fɔ:m; fɔrm/ *noun* 名词

1 a type of something 形式；种类: *Cars, trains and buses are all forms of transport.* 小轿车、火车、公共汽车是各种各样的交通工具。

2 a piece of paper with spaces for you to answer questions（需填写的）表格: *You need to fill in this form to get a new passport.* 你得填好这份表格才能领取新护照。

3 the shape of a person or thing（人或物的）形状；外形；样子: *For her birthday I made her a cake in the form of a cat.* 为了庆祝她的生日，我给她做了一个小猫形状的蛋糕。

4 one of the ways you write or say a word 字的书写或发音形式: *'Forgot' is a form of 'forget'.* ✻ forgot 是 forget 的另一形式。

5 a class in a school（中小学的）年级: *Which form are you in?* 你上几年级了？

form² /fɔ:m; fɔrm/ *verb* 动词 (**forms, forming, formed** /fɔ:md; fɔrmd/)

1 make something or give a shape to something 形成某事物；使某事物成为某种状态: *We formed a line outside the cinema.* 我们在电影院外边排着队。◇ *In English we usually form the past tense by adding 'ed'.* 英语一般是以加 ed 的方式构成过去式。

2 grow; take shape 构成；演变: *Ice forms when water freezes.* 水能冻成冰。

3 start a group, etc 建立组织: *They formed a club for French people living in London.* 他们为住在伦敦的法国侨民组织了一个俱乐部。

formal /'fɔ:ml; 'fɔrml̩/ *adjective* 形容词

You use formal language or behave in a formal way at important or serious times and with people you do not know very well 正式的；正规的；有礼貌的；庄重的: *'Yours faithfully' is a formal way of ending a letter.* 在书信的结尾处写上 Yours faithfully 较为郑重。◇ *I wore a suit and tie because it was a formal dinner.* 那次是个庄重的宴会，所以我穿着西装系着领带。✪ opposite 反义词: **informal**

formally /'fɔ:məli; 'fɔrml̩ɪ/ *adverb* 副词

They were dressed too formally for a disco. 他们参加迪斯科舞会穿得太郑重其事了。

former /'fɔ:mə(r); 'fɔrmɚ/ *adjective* 形容词

of a time before now 以前的: *the former Prime Minister, Mrs Thatcher* 前首相撒切尔夫人

former *noun* 名词 (no plural 无复数)

the first of two things or people（两事物或两人的）第一个；前者: *I have visited both Budapest and Vienna, and I prefer the former.* 我到过布达佩斯和维也纳这两个地方，我还是比较喜欢布达佩斯。☞ Look at **latter**. 见 **latter**。

formerly /'fɔ:məli; 'fɔrmɚlɪ/ *adverb* 副词

before this time 以前；从前: *Sri Lanka was formerly called Ceylon.* 斯里兰卡旧称锡兰。

formula /'fɔ:mjulə; 'fɔrmjələ/ *noun* 名词 (*plural* 复数作 **formulae** /'fɔ:mjuli:; 'fɔrmjə͵li/ or 或 **formulas**)

1 a group of letters, numbers or symbols that show a rule in mathematics or science 用字母、数字或符号表示的数学上的或其他学科上的式子；公式: *The formula for finding the area of a circle is πr^2.* 求圆面积的公式是 πr^2。

2 a list of the substances that you need to make something 做某物品所需材料的清单；配方；方子；处方: *a formula for a new drug* 新药的配方

fort /fɔ:t; fɔrt/ *noun* 名词
a strong building that was made to protect a place against its enemies 要塞；堡垒；碉堡

fortieth /ˈfɔ:tiəθ; ˈfɔrtɪɪθ/ *adjective, adverb, noun* 形容词，副词，名词
40th 第40（个）；第四十（个）

fortnight /ˈfɔ:tnaɪt; ˈfɔrtnaɪt/ *noun* 名词
two weeks 两星期: *I'm going on holiday for a fortnight.* 我要休假两个星期。

fortnightly *adjective, adverb* 形容词，副词
We have fortnightly meetings. 我们每两个星期开一次会。

fortress /ˈfɔ:trəs; ˈfɔrtrɪs/ *noun* 名词 (*plural* 复数作 **fortresses**)
a large strong building that was made to protect a place against its enemies 大的要塞；大堡垒

fortunate /ˈfɔ:tʃənət; ˈfɔrtʃənɪt/ *adjective* 形容词
lucky 幸运的: *I was very fortunate to get the job.* 我很运气得到了这份工作。
✪ opposite 反义词: **unfortunate**

fortunately *adverb* 副词
There was an accident but fortunately nobody was hurt. 出了一起事故，幸而无人受伤。

fortune /ˈfɔ:tʃu:n; ˈfɔrtʃən/ *noun* 名词
1 (no plural 无复数) things that happen that you cannot control; luck 机遇；运气；幸运: *I had the good fortune to get the job.* 我得到了这份工作，真有运气。
2 (*plural* 复数作 **fortunes**) a lot of money 大笔的钱；巨款: *He made a fortune selling old cars.* 他靠卖旧汽车发了财。

tell somebody's fortune say what will happen to somebody in the future 算命；看相: *The old lady said she could tell my fortune by looking at my hand.* 那个老太太说她能给我看手相。

forty /ˈfɔ:ti; ˈfɔrtɪ/ *number* 数词
1 40 四十
2 the forties (plural 复数) the numbers, years or temperature between 40 and 49 ＊40至49（之间的号码、数目、年份或温度）

in your forties between the ages of 40 and 49 年岁在40至49之间；四十多岁

forward[1] /ˈfɔ:wəd; ˈfɔrwɚd/, **forwards** /ˈfɔ:wədz; ˈfɔrwɚdz/ *adverb* 副词
1 in the direction that is in front of you 向前方: *Move forwards to the front of the train.* 向前走，到列车的前边去。
✪ opposite 反义词: **backwards**
2 to a later time 向较晚的时间: *When you travel from London to Paris, you need to put your watch forward.* 从伦敦到达巴黎，就要把手表的指针向前拨。

look forward to something wait for something with pleasure 愉快地等待某事物；殷切地期望；盼望: *We're looking forward to seeing you again.* 我们盼望着再见到你。

forward[2] /ˈfɔ:wəd; ˈfɔrwɚd/ *verb* 动词 (**forwards, forwarding, forwarded**)
send a letter to somebody at their new address 把信件投递到某人的新地址；转递: *Could you forward all my post to me while I'm in Liverpool?* 我在利物浦时，您把我所有的邮件都转递到利物浦来行吗？

> ✪ If you are writing to somebody who has moved to a new house but you do not know their address, you can write the old address and **please forward** on the envelope. 如果给某人写信而不知其搬迁后的新地址，可仍在信封上书写其旧地址再加上 **please forward**（请转递）字样。

fossil /ˈfɒsl; ˈfɑsḷ/ *noun* 名词
a part of a dead plant or an animal that has been in the ground for a very long time and has become hard 化石（古代动植物死亡后埋藏在地下变成像石头一样的东西）

fought *form of* **fight**[1] ＊ **fight**[1] 的不同形式

foul[1] /faʊl; faʊl/ *adjective* 形容词
1 dirty, or with a bad smell or taste 肮脏的；气味或味道不好的: *What a foul smell!* 多难闻哪！
2 very bad 非常坏的: *We had foul weather all week.* 我们整个星期天气糟糕极了。

foul[2] /faʊl; faʊl/ *noun* 名词
something you do that is against the rules of a game, for example football 违反游戏或比赛规则的事（如于足球比赛中）；犯规；违例: *He was sent off the field for a foul against the goalkeeper.* 他对守门员犯规而被罚出场。

foul *verb* 动词 (**fouls, fouling, fouled** /faʊld; faʊld/)
Johnson was fouled twice. 对方对约翰逊两次犯规。

found[1] *form of* **find** ✳ **find** 的不同形式

found[2] /faʊnd; faʊnd/ *verb* 动 词 (**founds**, **founding**, **founded**)
start something, for example a school or business 创办某事物（如学校或企业）；建立；创建；创立：*This school was founded in 1865.* 这所学校是1865年创建的。

founder *noun* 名词
a person who founds something 开创某事物的人；建立者；缔造者

foundation /faʊnˈdeɪʃn; faʊnˈdeʃən/ *noun* 名词
1 (no plural 无复数) starting a group, building, etc（组织、建筑物等的）建立；创建；创立：*the foundation of a new school* 新学校的创立
2 foundations (plural 复数) the strong parts of a building which you build first under the ground 地基；房基

fountain /ˈfaʊntən; ˈfaʊntn̩/ *noun* 名词
water that shoots up into the air and then falls down again. You often see fountains in gardens and parks. 喷泉（花园和公园中常见）

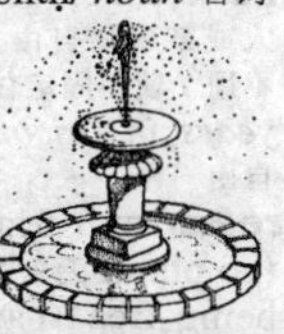

fountain 喷泉

fountain-pen /ˈfaʊntən pen; ˈfaʊntən-ˌpɛn/ *noun* 名词
a pen that you fill with ink 自来水笔

four /fɔː(r); fɔr/ *number* 数词
4 四
on all fours with your hands and knees on the ground 双手和双膝着地；趴着：*We went through the tunnel on all fours.* 我们爬着穿过了地道。

four-legged /ˌfɔː ˈlegɪd; ˈfɔrˈlɛgɪd/ *adjective* 形容词
with four legs. A horse is a four-legged animal. 有四条腿的（马是四足动物。）

fourth /fɔːθ; fɔrθ/ *adjective*, *adverb*, *noun* 形容词，副词，名词
4th 第4（个）；第四（个）

fourteen /ˌfɔːˈtiːn; fɔrˈtin/ *number* 数词
14 十四

fourteenth /ˌfɔːˈtiːnθ; fɔrˈtinθ/ *adjective*, *adverb*, *noun* 形容词，副词，名词
14th 第14（个）；第十四（个）

fox /fɒks; fɑks/ *noun* 名词 (*plural* 复数作 **foxes**)
a wild animal that looks like a dog and has a long thick tail and red fur 狐；狐狸

fraction /ˈfrækʃn; ˈfrækʃən/ *noun* 名词
1 an exact part of a number 分数；小数：¼ (= a quarter) *and* ⅓ (= a third) *are fractions.* ✳ ¼（= 四分之一）和⅓（= 三分之一）都是分数。
2 a very small part of something（某物的）很小的部分；一点儿：*For a fraction of a second I thought you were my sister.* 我猛然间还以为你是我妹妹呢。

fracture /ˈfræktʃə(r); ˈfræktʃɚ/ *verb* 动词 (**fractures**, **fracturing**, **fractured** /ˈfræktʃəd; ˈfræktʃɚd/)
break a bone in your body 骨折：*She fell and fractured her leg.* 她把腿摔折了。

fracture *noun* 名词
a fracture of the arm 胳臂骨折

fragile /ˈfrædʒaɪl; ˈfrædʒəl/ *adjective* 形容词
A thing that is fragile breaks easily 易碎的：*Be careful with those glasses. They're very fragile.* 小心那些玻璃杯。很容易碎。

fragment /ˈfrægmənt; ˈfrægmənt/ *noun* 名词
a very small piece that has broken off something（某物的）碎片：*The window broke and fragments of glass went everywhere.* 窗户破了，玻璃碎片崩得到处都是。

frail /freɪl; frel/ *adjective* 形容词 (**frailer**, **frailest**)
not strong or healthy 虚弱的；体弱的：*a frail old woman* 体弱的老太太

frame[1] /freɪm; frem/ *noun* 名词
1 a thin piece of wood or metal round the edge of a picture, window, mirror, etc（木制的或金属制的镶在画片、窗户、镜子等周围的）框架；框子；框儿
2 strong pieces of wood or metal that give something its shape（木制的或金属制的固定物体形状的结实的）框架，架子：*The frame of this bicycle was made in Britain and the wheels were made in Japan.* 这种自行车的车架子是英国制造的，车轮子是日本制造的。

frame of mind /ˌfreɪm əv ˈmaɪnd; ˌfrem əv ˈmaɪnd/ *noun* 名词
how you feel 心境；心情；情绪：*I'm not in the right frame of mind for a party.* 我没心思去参加聚会。

F

frame² /freɪm; frem/ *verb* 动词 (**frames, framing, framed** /freɪmd; fremd/)
put a picture in a frame 给画片镶框子: *She had her daughter's photograph framed.* 她把女儿的照片给镶上了框子。

framework /ˈfreɪmwɜ:k; ˈfremˌwɝk/ *noun* 名词
the strong part of something that gives it shape（固定物体形状的结实的）框架，架子；结构: *The bridge has a steel framework.* 这座桥是钢铁结构的。

frank /fræŋk; fræŋk/ *adjective* 形容词 (**franker, frankest**)
If you are frank, you say exactly what you think 直率的；坦率的；坦白的: *To be frank, I don't really like that shirt you're wearing.* 说老实话，我不太喜欢你穿的那件衬衫。

frankly *adverb* 副词
Tell me frankly what you think of my work. 你直截了当地告诉我，你认为我的工作怎么样。

fraud /frɔ:d; frɔd/ *noun* 名词
1 (no plural 无复数) doing things that are not honest to get money 用不诚实的手段获得钱的做法；骗钱；诈骗；欺诈: *Two of the company directors were sent to prison for fraud.* 公司里两个董事因犯欺诈罪入狱。
2 (*plural* 复数作 **frauds**) a person or thing that is not what he/she/it seems to be 冒充的人或事物: *He said he was a police officer but I knew he was a fraud.* 他说他是警察，可是我知道他是假冒的。

freckles /ˈfreklz; ˈfrɛkl̩z/ *noun* 名词 (plural 复数)
small light brown spots on a person's skin 雀斑（人的皮肤上的浅褐色的小斑点）: *A lot of people with red hair have freckles.* 红头发的人有雀斑的很多。

free¹ /fri:; fri/ *adjective, adverb* 形容词，副词 (**freer, freest**)
1 If you are free, you can go where you want and do what you want（指人）可任意走动或任意做事的；自由的: *After five years in prison she was finally free.* 她坐了五年牢后终于重获自由。
2 If something is free, you do not have to pay for it（指事物）不必付钱的；免费的: *We've got some free tickets for the concert.* 我们有几张音乐会的赠券。◇ *Children under five travel free on trains.* 五岁以下的儿童可免费乘坐火车。
3 not busy 不忙的；闲着的: *Are you free this afternoon?* 你今天下午有空吗？◇ *I don't have much free time.* 我没有什么空闲的时间。
4 not being used 暂时不用的: *Excuse me, is this seat free?* 请问这个座位有人坐吗？
5 not fixed 未固定住的: *Take the free end of the rope in your left hand.* 用你的左手握住绳子松着的一端。
free from something, free of something without something bad 没有某种坏事物的: *It's nice to be on holiday, free from all your worries.* 度假是件美事，免除了一切烦恼。
set free let a person or animal go out of a prison or cage 把人或动物放出监狱或牢笼: *We set the bird free and it flew away.* 我们把鸟放了，它就飞走了。

free² /fri:; fri/ *verb* 动词 (**frees, freeing, freed** /fri:d; frid/)
make somebody or something free 使某人或某事物自由；使某事物免费；使闲着或不用；使不固定住: *He was freed after ten years in prison.* 他坐了十年监狱后重获自由。

freedom /ˈfri:dəm; ˈfridəm/ *noun* 名词 (no plural 无复数)
being free 自由；不受束缚的状态: *They gave their children too much freedom.* 他们对孩子太放任了。

freeway /ˈfri:weɪ; ˈfriˌwe/ *American English for* **motorway** 美式英语，即 **motorway**

freeze /fri:z; friz/ *verb* 动词 (**freezes, freezing, froze** /frəʊz; froz/, **has frozen** /ˈfrəʊzn; ˈfrozn̩/)
1 become hard because it is so cold. When water freezes, it becomes ice. 遇冷而变硬；凝固；结冰（水遇冷能结冰。）
2 make food very cold so that it stays fresh for a long time 冷冻食物（保持新鲜）: *frozen food* 冷冻的食物
3 stop suddenly and stay very still 突然停住不动: *The cat froze when it saw the bird.* 猫看见鸟就突然停住不动了。
freeze to death be so cold that you die 冻死

freezer /ˈfri:zə(r); ˈfrizɚ/ *noun* 名词
a big metal box for making food very cold, like ice, so that you can keep it for a long time（冷冻食物使之保持新鲜的）冰柜；（冰箱中的）冷藏室

freezing /'fri:zɪŋ; 'frizɪŋ/ *adjective* 形容词
very cold 非常冷的: *Can you close the window? I'm freezing!* 你把窗户关上行吗？我冷极了！

freight /freɪt; fret/ *noun* 名词 (no plural 无复数)
things that lorries, ships, trains and aeroplanes carry from one place to another（卡车、轮船、火车、飞机运载的）货物: *a freight train* 货运列车

French fries /ˌfrentʃ 'fraɪz; ˌfrɛntʃ 'fraɪz/ *American English for* **chips**[1] **2** 美式英语，即 **chips**[1] **2**

frequent /'fri:kwənt; 'frikwənt/ *adjective* 形容词
Something that is frequent happens often 时常发生的；频繁的: *How frequent are the buses to the airport?* 到飞机场去的公共汽车多长时间一班？
frequently *adverb* 副词
often 时常；经常: *Simon is frequently late for school.* 西蒙上学常常迟到。

fresh /freʃ; frɛʃ/ *adjective* 形容词 (**fresher**, **freshest**)
1 made or picked not long ago; not old 新鲜的；新做的；新摘的: *I love the smell of fresh bread.* 我爱闻新鲜的面包的味儿。◇ *These flowers are fresh—I picked them this morning.* 这些花儿很新鲜——我今天早晨刚摘的。
2 new or different 新的；不同的: *fresh ideas* 新思想
3 not frozen or from a tin 非冷冻的；非罐头的: *fresh fruit* 新鲜的水果
4 clean and cool 清洁而凉爽的；清新的: *Open the window and let some fresh air in.* 把窗户打开，让新鲜空气进来。
fresh water /ˌfreʃ 'wɔ:tə; ˌfrɛʃ 'wɔtə/ *noun* 名词
not sea water 淡水（非海水）
freshly *adverb* 副词
freshly baked bread 新烤得的面包

Friday /'fraɪdeɪ; 'fraɪdɪ/ *noun* 名词
the sixth day of the week, next after Thursday 星期五

fridge /frɪdʒ; frɪdʒ/ *noun* 名词
a big metal box for keeping food and drink cold and fresh 冰箱: *Is there any milk in the fridge?* 冰箱里还有牛奶吗？

fried *form of* **fry** ∗ **fry** 的不同形式

friend /frend; frɛnd/ *noun* 名词
a person that you like and know very well 朋友: *David is my best friend.* 戴维是我最好的朋友。◇ *We are very good friends.* 我们是很要好的朋友。
make friends with somebody become a friend of somebody 与某人交朋友: *Have you made friends with any of the students in your class?* 你跟班上的同学交上朋友了吗？

friendly /'frendli; 'frɛndlɪ/ *adjective* 形容词 (**friendlier**, **friendliest**)
A person who is friendly is kind and helpful 友好的；和蔼可亲的: *My neighbours are very friendly.* 我的邻居非常和气。✪ opposite 反义词: **unfriendly**
be friendly with somebody If you are friendly with somebody, he/she is your friend 与某人很要好；与某人是朋友: *Jenny is friendly with a girl who lives in the same street.* 珍妮跟住在同一条街上的那个女孩儿很要好。

friendship /'frendʃɪp; 'frɛndʃɪp/ *noun* 名词
being friends with somebody 友情；友谊；友爱

fries *form of* **fry** ∗ **fry** 的不同形式

fright /fraɪt; fraɪt/ *noun* 名词
a sudden feeling of fear 惊吓: *Why didn't you knock on the door before you came in? You gave me a fright!* 你怎么不敲门就进来？把我吓了一跳！

frighten /'fraɪtn; 'fraɪtn̩/ *verb* 动词 (**frightens**, **frightening**, **frightened** /'fraɪtnd; 'fraɪtn̩d/)
make somebody feel afraid 使某人害怕；惊吓: *Sorry, did I frighten you?* 对不起，我吓着你了吗？
frightened *adjective* 形容词
If you are frightened, you are afraid of something 害怕的；受惊吓的: *He's frightened of spiders.* 他害怕蜘蛛。
frightening /'fraɪtnɪŋ; 'fraɪtn̩ɪŋ/ *adjective* 形容词
Something that is frightening makes you feel afraid 使人害怕的；可怕的；吓人的: *That was the most frightening film I have ever seen.* 那是我看过的最吓人的电影。

fringe /frɪndʒ; frɪndʒ/ *noun* 名词
1 the short hair that hangs down above your eyes 下垂至眼睛上部的短发；刘海儿 ☞ picture at **hair** 见 **hair** 词条插图

F

2 threads that hang from the edge of a piece of material（料子边缘的）穗子；毛边
3 the edge of a place（地方的）边缘: *We live on the fringes of town.* 我们住在小镇的边上。

fro /frəʊ; fro/ *adverb* 副词
to and fro first one way and then the other way, many times 来回地；往复地: *She travels to and fro between Oxford and London.* 她常在牛津和伦敦之间来来往往。

frog /frɒg; frɔg/ *noun* 名词
a small animal that lives in and near water. Frogs have long back legs and they can jump. 青蛙

frog 青蛙

from /frəm, frɒm; frəm, frɑm/ *preposition* 介词
1 a word that shows where something starts 表示某事物起始的词；从: *We travelled from New York to Boston.* 我们从纽约动身到波士顿。
2 a word that shows where somebody lives or was born 表示某人居住地或出生地的词: *I come from Spain.* 我是西班牙人。
3 a word that shows when somebody or something starts 表示某人或某事物开始的时间的词；从…起: *The shop is open from 9.30 until 5.30.* 这家商店从9点30分到5点30分营业。
4 a word that shows who gave or sent something 表示谁给或谁送某事物的词；来自: *I had a letter from Lyn.* 我收到林恩给我寄来的一封信。◇ *I borrowed a dress from my sister.* 我向姐姐借了一件连衣裙。
5 a word that shows the place where you find something 表示找到某事物之处的词；从: *He took the money from my bag.* 他从我的袋子里把钱拿走了。
6 a word that shows how far away something is 表示某事物多远的词；离: *The house is two miles from the village.* 这所房子离村子两英里。
7 a word that shows how something changes 表示某事物如何变化的词；从；由: *The sky changed from blue to grey.* 天空由蓝色变成了灰色。
8 a word that shows the lowest number or price 表示数目或价格起码的词；从: *The tickets cost from £5 to £15.* 票价从5英镑到15英镑。
9 a word that shows what is used to make something 表示用什么材料做成某物的词: *Paper is made from wood.* 纸是用木头做的。
10 a word that shows difference 表示事物间有区别的词: *My book is different from yours.* 我的书跟你的不一样。
11 a word that shows why 表示原因的词；由于；因为: *Children are dying from this disease.* 陆续有儿童死于这种疾病。

front /frʌnt; frʌnt/ *noun* 名词
the side or part of something that faces forwards and that you usually see first（物体的）正面；前面: *The book has a picture of a lion on the front.* 这本书封面上有个狮子的画面。◇ *John and I sat in the front of the car and the children sat in the back.* 我和约翰坐在汽车前边儿，孩子都坐在后边儿。☞ picture at **back** 见 **back** 词条插图
in front of somebody or 或 **something** **1** further forward than another person or thing 在某人或某物的前面: *Alice was sitting in front of the television.* 艾丽斯坐在电视机前边。☞ picture on page C1 见第C1页图 **2** when other people are there 当着其他人的面: *Please don't talk about it in front of my parents.* 请别当着我父母的面谈这件事。
front *adjective* 形容词
the front door 前门 ◇ *the front seat of a car* 汽车的前座

frontier /ˈfrʌntiə(r); frʌnˈtɪr/ *noun* 名词
the line where one country joins another country（国与国的）边界；边境；国界

frost /frɒst; frɔst/ *noun* 名词
ice like white powder that covers the ground when the weather is very cold 霜: *There was a frost last night.* 昨天夜里结霜了。
frosty *adjective* 形容词 (**frostier**, **frostiest**)
a frosty morning 霜晨

frown /fraʊn; fraʊn/ *verb* 动词 (**frowns**, **frowning**, **frowned** /fraʊnd; fraʊnd/)
move your eyebrows together to make lines on your forehead. You frown when you are worried, angry or thinking hard 皱眉，蹙额（于忧虑、生气或深思时）: *John frowned at me when I came in. 'You're late,' he said.* 我进来的时候约翰对我皱着眉。"你来晚了，"他说。

frown *noun* 名词
She looked at me with a frown. 她皱着眉看了我一下。

froze, frozen *forms of* **freeze** ✻ **freeze** 的不同形式

frozen food /ˌfrəʊzn ˈfuːd; ˌfrozn̩ ˈfud/ *noun* 名词 (no plural 无复数)
food that is very cold, like ice, when you buy it. You keep frozen food in a **freezer**. 冷冻的食物（冰柜或冰箱的冷藏室叫做 **freezer**。）

fruit /fruːt; frut/ *noun* 名词
the part of a plant or tree that holds the seeds and that you can eat. Bananas, oranges and apples are kinds of fruit. 水果（香蕉、橙子、苹果都属于水果类。）✪ Be careful! We do not usually say 'a fruit'. 注意！通常不说 a fruit。We say 'a piece of fruit' or 'some fruit' 要说 a piece of fruit 或 some fruit: *Would you like a piece of fruit?* 您想吃个水果吗？◇ *'Would you like some fruit?' 'Yes please — I'll have a pear.'* "您想吃点儿水果吗？" "好哇——我来个梨吧。"

frustrating /frʌˈstreɪtɪŋ; ˈfrʌstretɪŋ/ *adjective* 形容词
If something is frustrating, it makes you angry because you cannot do what you want to do（因不能做想做的事）使人生气的；使人灰心的；使人沮丧的: *It's very frustrating when you can't say what you mean in a foreign language.* 不能用外语说出想说的话，这种事真不痛快。

fry /fraɪ; fraɪ/ *verb* 动词 (**fries, frying, fried** /fraɪd; fraɪd/, **has fried**)
cook something or be cooked in hot oil 用热油烹饪某物；炸；煎；炒: *Fry the onions in butter.* 用黄油炸洋葱。◇ *fried eggs* 煎鸡蛋

fry-pan /ˈfraɪ pæn; ˈfraɪˌpæn/ *American English for* **frying-pan** 美式英语，即 **frying-pan**

frying-pan /ˈfraɪɪŋ pæn; ˈfraɪɪŋˌpæn/ *noun* 名词
a flat metal container with a long handle that you use for frying food（长柄的）煎锅

frying-pan 煎锅

ft *short way of writing* **foot 2** ✻ **foot 2** 的缩写形式

fuel /ˈfjuːəl; ˈfjuəl/ *noun* 名词 (no plural 无复数)
anything that you burn to make heat or power. Wood, coal and oil are kinds of fuel. 燃料（木柴、煤、石油都是燃料。）

fulfil /fʊlˈfɪl; fʊlˈfɪl/ *verb* 动词 (**fulfils, fulfilling, fulfilled** /fʊlˈfɪld; fʊlˈfɪld/)
do what you have planned or promised to do 做（所计划的或所承诺的）事情；履行；实现: *Jenny fulfilled her dream of travelling around the world.* 珍妮实现了环游世界的愿望。

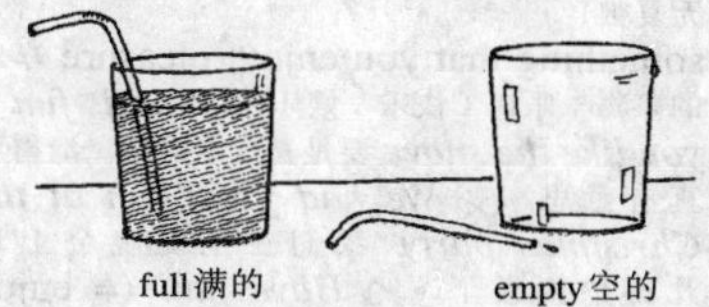
full 满的　　empty 空的

full /fʊl; fʊl/ *adjective* 形容词 (**fuller, fullest**)
1 with a lot of people or things in it, so that there is no more space 充满（人或物）的: *My glass is full.* 我的玻璃杯很满了。◇ *The bus was full so we waited for the next one.* 这辆公共汽车已经客满了，我们只好等下一辆。◇ *These socks are full of holes.* 这双袜子上净是窟窿。
2 complete; with nothing missing 完全的；完整的: *Please tell me the full story.* 请把这件事的详细情况告诉我。
3 as much, big, etc as possible 尽可能多的、大的…等: *The train was travelling at full speed.* 火车当时正在全速前进。
full up with no space for anything or anybody else 再没有多余的地方（容纳某物或某人）；全满；客满: *'Would you like anything else to eat?' 'No thank you, I'm full up.'* "您还想吃点儿什么吗？" "我已经很饱了，谢谢您。"
in full completely; with nothing missing 完全地；完整地: *Please write your name in full.* 请您把姓名写全了。

full stop /ˌfʊl ˈstɒp; ˌfʊl ˈstɑp/ *noun* 名词
a mark (.) that you use in writing to show the end of a sentence, or after the short form of a word 句号（.）（用于句末及缩写词之后）

full-time /ˌfʊl ˈtaɪm; ˌfʊlˈtaɪm/ *adjective, adverb* 形容词，副词
for all the normal working hours of the day or week（一天或一星期）全部工作时间（的）: *My mother has a full-time job.*

F

我母亲的工作是全职的。◇ *Do you work full-time?* 你的工作是全职的吗？☞ Look at **part-time**. 见 **part-time**。

fully /ˈfʊli; ˈfʊlɪ/ *adverb* 副词
completely; totally 完全地；全部地: *'Do you have a room for tonight, please?' 'No, I'm sorry, we're fully booked.'* "请问您这儿今天晚上有房间吗？""没有了，很抱歉，我们已经全部预订出去了。"

fun /fʌn; fʌn/ *noun* 名词 (no plural 无复数)
something that you enjoy; pleasure 享乐的事物；乐趣；快乐；娱乐: *Skiing is fun if you like the snow.* 要是喜欢雪的话，滑雪可真有意思。◇ *We had great fun at the Christmas party.* 我们在圣诞晚会上玩儿得热闹极了。◇ *Have fun!* (= enjoy yourself!) 高高兴兴地玩儿吧！
for fun to enjoy yourself 为了取乐: *I don't need English for my work — I'm learning it just for fun.* 我工作上倒并不需要英语——我就是学着玩儿。
make fun of somebody laugh about somebody in an unkind way 不怀好意地笑某人；拿某人取乐: *The other children make fun of him because he wears glasses.* 因为他戴眼镜，别的孩子就耍笑他。

function /ˈfʌŋkʃn; ˈfʌŋkʃən/ *noun* 名词
the special work that a person or thing does 作用；功能: *The function of the heart is to send blood round the body.* 心脏的功能就是向全身输送血液。
function *verb* 动词 (**functions, functioning, functioned** /ˈfʌŋkʃnd; ˈfʌŋkʃənd/)
work 起作用；运转: *The engine will not function without oil.* 发动机离开油就不能动了。

fund /fʌnd; fʌnd/ *noun* 名词
money that will be used for something special 用于指定的某项事务的钱；专款；基金: *The money from the concert will go into a fund to help homeless people.* 音乐会的收入将作为援助无家可归者的基金。

fundamental /ˌfʌndəˈmentl; ˌfʌndəˈmɛntl̩/ *adjective* 形容词
most important; basic 最重要的；基本的；基础的: *You are making a fundamental mistake.* 你犯了一个根本的错误。

funeral /ˈfjuːnərəl; ˈfjunərəl/ *noun* 名词
the time when a dead person is buried or burned 葬礼；出殡

funnel /ˈfʌnl; ˈfʌnl̩/ *noun* 名词
1 a tube that is wide at the top to help you pour things into bottles 漏斗
2 a large pipe on a ship or railway engine that smoke comes out of（轮船或火车头上的）烟筒

funny /ˈfʌni; ˈfʌnɪ/ *adjective* 形容词 (**funnier, funniest**)
1 A person or thing that is funny makes you laugh or smile（指人或事物）使人发笑的；有趣的: *a funny story* 好笑的故事
2 strange or surprising 奇怪的；使人惊奇的: *There's a funny smell in this room.* 这间屋子里有股怪味儿。

fur /fɜː(r); fɝ/ *noun* 名词
the soft thick hair on animals. Cats and rabbits have fur.（动物身上的）浓密的软毛（猫和兔子的身上都有毛。）
furry /ˈfɜːri; ˈfɝɪ/ *adjective* 形容词 (**furrier, furriest**)
a furry animal 毛茸茸的动物

furious /ˈfjʊəriəs; ˈfjʊrɪəs/ *adjective* 形容词
very angry 非常生气的；愤怒的: *My parents were furious with me when I came home late again.* 我又回家晚了，我父母对我大发脾气。

furnace /ˈfɜːnɪs; ˈfɝnɪs/ *noun* 名词
a very hot fire in a closed place, used for heating metals, making glass, etc 熔炉（熔炼金属或熔化玻璃等用的）

furnished /ˈfɜːnɪʃt; ˈfɝnɪʃt/ *adjective* 形容词
with furniture already in it 带有家具的: *I live in a furnished flat.* 我住在设有家具的公寓里。✪ opposite 反义词: **unfurnished**

furniture /ˈfɜːnɪtʃə(r); ˈfɝnɪtʃɚ/ *noun* 名词 (no plural 无复数)
tables, chairs, beds, etc 家具: *They've bought some furniture for their new house.* 他们买了些家具布置新房子。◇ *All the furniture is very old.* 所有的家具都很旧。◇ *The only piece of furniture in the room was a large bed.* 屋子里唯一的家具就是一张大床。

further /ˈfɜːðə(r); ˈfɝðɚ/ *adjective, adverb* 形容词，副词
1 more far 更远（的）: *Which is further — London or Birmingham?* 哪个城市远——是伦敦还是伯明翰？◇ *We couldn't go any further because the road was closed.* 我们无法再往前走了，因为路已经封住了。

2 more; extra 更多（的）；另外（的）: *Do you have any further questions?* 你还有别的问题吗？

further education /ˌfɜ:ðər edʒu-ˈkeɪʃn; ˌfɝðɚ ˌɛdʒʊˈkeʃən/ *noun* 名词
studying that you do after you leave school at the age of 16（16岁中学毕业以后的）继续教育

furthest *form of* **far** ＊ **far** 的不同形式

fuse /fju:z; fjuz/ *noun* 名词
a small piece of wire that stops too much electricity going through something. Plugs usually have fuses in them. 保险丝（可切断超负荷电路的金属丝。英国制造的插销中大多有保险丝。）

fuss[1] /fʌs; fʌs/ *noun* 名词 (no plural 无复数)
a lot of excitement or worry about small things that are not important（对琐事）兴奋、紧张或忧虑: *He makes a fuss when I'm five minutes late.* 我晚到了五分钟他就当成大事了。

make a fuss of somebody be kind to somebody; do a lot of small things for somebody 善待某人；对某人悉心照顾: *I like visiting my grandfather because he always makes a fuss of me.* 我喜欢去看我爷爷，因为他总是无微不至地照顾我。

fussy *adjective* 形容词 (**fussier**, **fussiest**)
A fussy person cares a lot about small things that are not important, and is difficult to please 过分注重琐事而难以取悦的；吹毛求疵的；挑剔的: *Rod is fussy about his food — he won't eat anything with onions in it.* 罗德对吃的东西很挑剔——有一点儿洋葱的他都不吃。

fuss[2] /fʌs; fʌs/ *verb* 动词 (**fusses, fussing, fussed** /fʌst; fʌst/)
worry and get excited about a lot of small things that are not important 对琐事忧虑而紧张: *Stop fussing!* 对小事别那么紧张！

future[1] /ˈfju:tʃə(r); ˈfjutʃɚ/ *noun* 名词
1 the time that will come 将来；未来: *Nobody knows what will happen in the future.* 谁也不知道将来怎么样。◇ *The company's future is uncertain.* 这家公司前途未卜。
2 the future (no plural 无复数) the form of a verb that shows what will happen after now（动词的）将来时态

in future after now 从今以后；今后: *You must work harder in future.* 你以后必须努力。

☞ Look at **past** and **present**. 见 **past** 和 **present**。

future[2] /ˈfju:tʃə(r); ˈfjutʃɚ/ *adjective* 形容词
of the time that will come 将来的；未来的: *Have you met John's future wife?* 你看见过约翰未来的妻子吗？

Gg

g *short way of writing* **gram** ＊ **gram** 的缩写形式

gadget /ˈgædʒɪt; ˈgædʒɪt/ *noun* 名词
a small machine or tool 小机械；小器具: *Their kitchen is full of electrical gadgets.* 他们家的厨房里有很多电动小器具。

gain /geɪn; gen/ *verb* 动词 (**gains**, **gaining**, **gained** /geɪnd; gend/)
1 get more of something 多得到某事物；增加: *She gained useful experience from her holiday job.* 她从假日的工作中获得了宝贵的经验。◇ *I have gained a lot of weight.* 我体重增加了很多。
2 get what you want or need 得到想要的或需要的；获得: *The police are trying to gain more information about the robbery.* 警方正在尽力搜集劫案的资料。

galaxy /ˈgæləksi; ˈgæləksɪ/ *noun* 名词 (*plural* 复数作 **galaxies**)
a very large group of stars and planets 星系

gale /geɪl; gel/ *noun* 名词
a very strong wind 大风: *The trees were blown down in the gale.* 树被大风刮倒了。

G

gallery /ˈgæləri; ˈgælərɪ/ *noun* 名词 (*plural* 复数作 **galleries**)
a building or room where people can go to look at paintings 美术馆；画廊: *We visited the art galleries in Florence.* 我们参观了佛罗伦萨艺术博物馆。

gallon /ˈgælən; ˈgælən/ *noun* 名词
a measure of liquid (= 4.5 litres). There are eight **pints** in a gallon 加仑（液量单位，= 4.5升；一加仑等于8品脱，品脱叫做 **pint**）: *a gallon of petrol* 一加仑汽油 ☞ Note at **pint** 见 **pint** 词条注释

gallop /ˈgæləp; ˈgæləp/ *verb* 动词 (**gallops**, **galloping**, **galloped** /ˈgæləpt; ˈgæləpt/)
When a horse gallops, it runs very fast with all its feet off the ground at the same time（指马）奔跑（四蹄同时离地）: *The horses galloped round the field.* 那些马在田野上到处奔驰。

gallop *noun* 名词
I took the horse for a gallop. 我骑马奔驰了一阵。

gamble /ˈgæmbl; ˈgæmbḷ/ *verb* 动词 (**gambles**, **gambling**, **gambled** /ˈgæmbld; ˈgæmbḷd/)
1 try to win money by playing games that need luck 赌；赌博: *He gambled a lot of money on the last race.* 他在赛马的最后一场赌了很多钱。
2 do something, although there is a chance that you might lose 冒着可能失败的风险做某事: *We bought the food for the picnic the day before, and gambled on the weather staying fine.* 我们前一天就买好了野餐食物，碰运气盼着一直有好天气。

gamble *noun* 名词
something that you do without knowing if you will win or lose 不知胜负的事；赌博

gambler /ˈgæmblə(r); ˈgæmblɚ/ *noun* 名词
a person who tries to win money by playing games that need luck 赌博的人

gambling /ˈgæmblɪŋ; ˈgæmblɪŋ/ *noun* 名词 (no plural 无复数)
playing games that need luck, to try to win money 赌博

game /geɪm; gem/ *noun* 名词
1 (*plural* 复数作 **games**) something you play that has rules 游戏；运动: *Shall we have a game of football?* 咱们踢一场足球好吗？◇ *We played a game of cards, and I won.* 我们玩儿纸牌游戏，我赢了。
2 (no plural 无复数) wild animals or birds that people shoot and sometimes eat 可供狩猎（有时食用）的禽兽；野味
3 games (plural 复数) sports that you play at school or in a competition 体育运动会；运动会: *the Olympic Games* 奥林匹克运动会

gang /gæŋ; gæŋ/ *noun* 名词
1 a group of people who do bad things together 一起做坏事的人；团伙；一帮: *a street gang* 一群流氓
2 a group of friends who often meet（经常见面的）一些朋友: *The whole gang is coming to the party tonight.* 这伙朋友今天晚上全都来参加聚会。
3 a group of workers 一批工作人员: *a gang of road menders* 一队修路工人

gang *verb* 动词 (**gangs**, **ganging**, **ganged** /gæŋd; gæŋd/)
gang up on or 或 **against somebody** join together against another

person 联合起来对付某人: *The other boys ganged up on Tim because he was much smaller than them.* 那些男孩子合伙欺负蒂姆，因为他比他们小得多。

gangster /'gæŋstə(r); 'gæŋstɚ/ *noun* 名词
one of a group of dangerous criminals 匪徒；歹徒: *Al Capone was a famous Chicago gangster.* 卡彭是芝加哥有名的歹徒。

gangway /'gæŋweɪ; 'gæŋˌwe/ *noun* 名词
1 a bridge from the side of a ship to the land so that people can go on and off（上下船用的）跳板
2 the long space between two rows of seats in a cinema, theatre, etc（电影院、剧院中的）座间过道

gaol /dʒeɪl; dʒel/ = **jail**

gap /gæp; gæp/ *noun* 名词
a space in something or between two things; a space where something should be（某物中的或两物间的）空间；间隔；（某物应在的）空位: *The sheep got out through a gap in the fence.* 羊从篱笆的豁口钻出去了。◇ *Write the correct word in the gap.* 在空白处填上正确的词。

gape /geɪp; gep/ *verb* 动词 (**gapes, gaping, gaped** /geɪpt; gept/)
look at somebody or something with your mouth open because you are surprised（因惊奇）张着嘴看某人或某事物: *She gaped at me when I said I was getting married.* 我说我要结婚了，她目瞪口呆地看着我。
gaping *adjective* 形容词
wide open 张开得很大的: *There was a gaping hole in the ground.* 地上有个很大的洞。

garage /'gærɑ:ʒ; gə'rɑʒ/ *noun* 名词
1 a building where you keep your car 汽车房；汽车库
2 a place where cars are repaired 汽车修车处；汽车修车厂
3 a place where you can buy petrol 加油站

garbage /'gɑ:bɪdʒ; 'gɑrbɪdʒ/ *American English for* **rubbish** 美式英语，即 **rubbish**

garbage can /'gɑ:bɪdʒ kæn; 'gɑrbɪdʒ kæn/ *American English for* **dustbin** 美式英语，即 **dustbin**

garden /'gɑ:dn; 'gɑrdn̩/ *noun* 名词
1 a piece of land by your house where you can grow flowers, fruit and vegetables（私人的）花园、果园或菜园: *Let's have lunch in the garden.* 咱们在花园里吃饭吧。
2 gardens (plural 复数) a public park 公园: *Kensington Gardens* 肯辛顿公园
garden *verb* 动词 (**gardens, gardening, gardened** /'gɑ:dnd; 'gɑrdn̩d/)
work in a garden 在花园里工作；做园艺活儿: *My mother was gardening all weekend.* 我母亲整个周末都在花园里干活儿。
gardener /'gɑ:dnə(r); 'gɑrdnɚ/ *noun* 名词
a person who works in a garden 园林工人；园丁
gardening /'gɑ:dnɪŋ; 'gɑrdnɪŋ/ *noun* 名词 (no plural 无复数)
My father does the gardening on Sundays. 我父亲星期日常常在花园里干活儿。

garlic /'gɑ:lɪk; 'gɑrlɪk/ *noun* 名词 (no plural 无复数)
a plant like a small onion with a strong taste and smell, that you use in cooking 蒜；大蒜；蒜头

gas /gæs; gæs/ *noun* 名词
1 (*plural* 复数作 **gases**) anything that is like air 气体: *Hydrogen and oxygen are gases.* 氢气和氧气都是气体。
2 (no plural 无复数) a gas with a strong smell, that you burn to make heat 用作燃料的气体；煤气；石油气: *Do you use electricity or gas for cooking?* 你做饭用电还是用煤气？◇ *a gas fire* 煤气暖炉
3 *American English for* **petrol** 美式英语，即 **petrol**

gas station /'gæs steɪʃn; 'gæs ˌsteʃən/ *American English for* **petrol station, service station, garage 3** 美式英语，即 **petrol station**、**service station**、**garage 3**

gasoline /'gæsəli:n; 'gæslˌin/ *American English for* **petrol** 美式英语，即 **petrol**

gasp /gɑ:sp; gæsp/ *verb* 动词 (**gasps, gasping, gasped** /gɑ:spt; gæspt/)
breathe in quickly and noisily through your mouth 用嘴吸入空气（快而有声）: *She gasped in surprise when she heard the news.* 她听到这个消息吃惊地倒抽了一口气。◇ *He was gasping for air when they pulled him out of the water.* 他们把他从水里拉出来的时候，他大口大口地吸着气。

G

gasp *noun* 名词
a gasp of surprise 吃惊地吸了一口气

gate 大门

gate /geɪt; get/ *noun* 名词
1 a kind of door in a fence or wall outside（篱笆或外墙的）门；大门: *We closed the gate to stop the cows getting out of the field.* 我们关上了栅栏门防止牛出去。
2 a door in an airport that you go through to reach the aeroplane（飞机场的）登机入口: *Please go to gate 15.* 请到第15号入口登机。

gateway /ˈgeɪtweɪ; ˈgetˌwe/ *noun* 名词
a way in or out of a place that has a gate to close it 大门口

gather /ˈgæðə(r); ˈgæðɚ/ *verb* 动词 (**gathers**, **gathering**, **gathered** /ˈgæðəd; ˈgæðɚd/)
1 come together in a group; meet 聚集；集合: *A crowd gathered to watch the fight.* 大家围在一起看他们吵架。
2 take things that are in different places and bring them together 把各处的东西收集在一起: *I gathered up all the books and papers and put them in my bag.* 我把书和文件收起来放进包里。
3 understand something 理解某事物: *I gather that you know my sister.* 我猜想你认识我妹妹。

gathering /ˈgæðərɪŋ; ˈgæðərɪŋ/ *noun* 名词
a time when people come together 集会；聚会: *There was a large gathering outside the palace.* 在宫殿外面聚集了很多人。

gauge /geɪdʒ; gedʒ/ *noun* 名词
an instrument that measures how much of something there is 计量器: *Where is the petrol gauge in this car?* 这辆汽车的汽油量表在哪儿？

gauge *verb* 动词 (**gauges**, **gauging**, **gauged** /geɪdʒd; gedʒd/)
measure something 测量某物

gave *form of* **give** ＊ **give** 的不同形式

G

gay /geɪ; ge/ *adjective* 形容词
1 attracted to people of the same sex; homosexual（指人）被同性吸引的；同性恋的
2 happy and full of fun 快乐的；愉快的 ✪ We do not often use 'gay' with this meaning now. 此义项现已不常用。

gaze /geɪz; gez/ *verb* 动词 (**gazes**, **gazing**, **gazed** /geɪzd; gezd/)
look at somebody or something for a long time 长时间看着某人或某物；凝视: *She sat and gazed out of the window.* 她坐在那里凝视着窗外。◇ *He was gazing at her.* 他目不转睛地看着她。

GCSE /ˌdʒiː siː es ˈiː; ˌdʒi si ɛs ˈi/ *noun* 名词
an examination in one subject that children at schools in England, Wales and Northern Ireland take when they are 16 普通中等教育证书考试（英格兰、威尔士、北爱尔兰年满16岁的学生参加的一科考试）✪ 'GCSE' is short for **General Certificate of Secondary Education**. ＊ GCSE 是 **General Certificate of Secondary Education** 的缩略式。

gear /gɪə(r); gɪr/ *noun* 名词
1 (*plural* 复数作 **gears**) a set of wheels that work together in a machine to pass power from one part to another. The gears of a car or bicycle help to control it when it goes up and down hills and help it to go faster or slower 齿轮组；（汽车的）排挡: *You need to change gear to go round the corner.* 转弯的时候需要换挡。
2 (no plural 无复数) special clothes or things that you need for a job or sport（做某工作或运动所需要的）特殊衣物或装备: *camping gear* 野营用品

geese *plural of* **goose** ＊ **goose** 的复数形式

gem /dʒem; dʒɛm/ *noun* 名词
a beautiful stone that is very valuable; a jewel 宝石

general[1] /ˈdʒenrəl; ˈdʒɛnərəl/ *adjective* 形容词
1 of, by or for most people or things 普遍的；一般的；全体的；整体的: *Is this car park for general use?* 这个停车场是公用的吗？
2 not in detail 非详细的；概括的；大体上的: *The back cover gives you a general idea of what the book is about.* 书的封底介绍的是全书的梗概。

in general usually 总的说来；大体上: *I don't eat much meat in general.* 我一般很少吃肉。

general election /ˌdʒenrəl ɪ'lekʃn; ˌdʒɛnərəl ɪ'lɛkʃən/ *noun* 名词
a time when people choose a new government 大选；普选: *Did you vote in the last general election?* 上次大选你投票了吗？

general knowledge /ˌdʒenrəl 'nɒlɪdʒ; ˌdʒɛnərəl 'nɑlɪdʒ/ *noun* 名词 (no plural 无复数)
what you know about a lot of different things 一般的知识；常识

general² /'dʒenrəl; 'dʒɛnərəl/ *noun* 名词
a very important officer in the army 将军

generally /'dʒenrəli; 'dʒɛnərəlɪ/ *adverb* 副词
usually; mostly 通常地；一般地: *I generally get up at about eight o'clock.* 我一般在八点钟左右起床。

generate /'dʒenəreɪt; 'dʒɛnəˌret/ *verb* 动词 (**generates**, **generating**, **generated**)
make heat, electricity, etc 产生热量、电流等: *Power stations generate electricity.* 发电厂是发电的。

generation /ˌdʒenə'reɪʃn; ˌdʒɛnə'reʃən/ *noun* 名词
1 the children, or the parents, or the grandparents, in a family (家族的) 代；辈分: *This photo shows three generations of my family.* 这张照片是我们家三代同堂的合影。
2 all the people who were born at about the same time 一代人: *The older and the younger generations listen to different music.* 年老的一代和年轻的一代听的音乐不一样。

generosity /ˌdʒenə'rɒsəti; ˌdʒɛnə'rɑsətɪ/ *noun* 名词 (no plural 无复数)
liking to give things to other people 慷慨；大方

generous /'dʒenərəs; 'dʒɛnərəs/ *adjective* 形容词
1 always ready to give things or to spend money 慷慨的；大方的: *She is very generous—she often buys me presents.* 她很大方——常常给我买礼物。
2 large 大量的；丰富的: *generous amounts of food* 丰盛的食物

generously *adverb* 副词
Please give generously. 请慷慨施与。

genius /'dʒi:niəs; 'dʒinjəs/ *noun* 名词 (*plural* 复数作 **geniuses**)
a very clever person 天才人物: *Einstein was a genius.* 爱因斯坦是个天才。

gentle /'dʒentl; 'dʒɛntḷ/ *adjective* 形容词 (**gentler**, **gentlest**)
quiet and kind; not rough 文静而和蔼的；不粗暴的: *Be gentle with the baby.* 对幼儿要温柔体贴。◇ *a gentle voice* 温和的声音 ◇ *It was a hot day, but there was a gentle breeze* (= a soft wind). 天气很热，倒有些微风。

gently /'dʒentli; 'dʒɛntlɪ/ *adverb* 副词
Close the door gently or you'll wake the children up. 要轻轻关门，不然就把孩子吵醒了。

gentleman /'dʒentlmən; 'dʒɛntḷmən/ *noun* 名词 (*plural* 复数作 **gentlemen** /'dʒentlmən; 'dʒɛntḷmən/)
1 a polite way of saying 'man' 对男子的尊称；先生: *There is a gentleman here to see you.* 有位先生要见您。
2 a man who is polite and kind to other people 和蔼可亲的男子
☞ Look at **lady**. 见 **lady**。

Gents /dʒents; dʒɛnts/ *noun* 名词 (no plural 无复数)
a public toilet for men 男用公共厕所；男厕: *Do you know where the Gents is, please?* 请问，您知道男厕所在哪儿吗？

genuine /'dʒenjuɪn; 'dʒɛnjuɪn/ *adjective* 形容词
real and true 真的；真实的: *Those aren't genuine diamonds—they're pieces of glass!* 那不是真钻石——是玻璃！

genuinely *adverb* 副词
really 真正: *Do you think he's genuinely sorry?* 你认为他是真抱歉吗？

geography /dʒi'ɒgrəfi; dʒi'ɑgrəfɪ/ *noun* 名词 (no plural 无复数)
the study of the earth and its countries, mountains, rivers, weather, etc 地理学

geographical /ˌdʒi:ə'græfɪkl; ˌdʒiə'græfɪkḷ/ *adjective* 形容词
geographical names (= names of countries, seas, cities, etc) 地名

geology /dʒi'ɒlədʒi; dʒi'ɑlədʒɪ/ *noun* 名词 (no plural 无复数)
the study of rocks and soil and how they were made 地质学

geologist /dʒiˈɒlədʒɪst; dʒiˈɑlədʒɪst/ *noun* 名词
a person who studies or knows a lot about geology 地质学研究者；地质学家

geometry /dʒiˈɒmətri; dʒiˈɑmətrɪ/ *noun* 名词 (no plural 无复数)
the study of things like lines, angles and shapes 几何学

geranium /dʒəˈreɪniəm; dʒəˈrenɪəm/ *noun* 名词
a plant with red, white or pink flowers 老鹳草；天竺葵（花呈红色、白色或粉色）

germ /dʒɜːm; dʒɝm/ *noun* 名词
a very small living thing that can make you ill 细菌；病菌: *flu germs* 感冒病菌

gesture /ˈdʒestʃə(r); ˈdʒɛstʃɚ/ *noun* 名词
a movement of your head or hand to show how you feel or what you want 用头或手表达情感或愿望的动作；姿势；手势

get /get; gɛt/ *verb* 动词 (**gets**, **getting**, **got** /gɒt; gɑt/, **has got**)
1 buy or take something 买到或取得某事物: *Will you get some bread when you go shopping?* 你去买东西的时候带回点儿面包来行吗？
2 receive something 得到某事物: *I got a lot of presents for my birthday.* 我过生日的时候收到很多礼物。
3 become 变成；变得: *He is getting fat.* 他发胖了。◇ *Mum got angry.* 妈妈生气了。◇ *It's getting cold.* 天气越来越冷了。
4 go and bring back somebody or something 接回某人；取回某物: *Jenny will get the children from school.* 珍妮要到学校去把孩子都接回来。
5 arrive somewhere 到达某处: *We got to London at ten o'clock.* 我们到伦敦的时候是十点钟。
6 start to have an illness 生病；得病: *I think I'm getting a cold.* 我看我是得了感冒了。
7 understand or hear something 理解或听到某事物: *I don't get the joke.* 我听不懂这个笑话。
8 a word that you use with part of another verb to show that something happens to somebody or something 与另一动词连用，表示某人或某事物发生某事: *She got caught by the police.* 她让警察给抓住了。
9 travel on a train, bus, etc 乘坐火车、公共汽车等: *I didn't walk—I got the train.* 我不是步行——我坐的是火车。
10 make somebody do something 使某人做某事: *I got Peter to help me.* 我让彼得来帮助我。

get away with something do something bad and not be punished for it 做坏事而未受惩罚: *He lied but he got away with it.* 他撒了谎也没人把他怎么样。

get back return 回来；回去: *When did you get back from your holiday?* 你什么时候放完假回来？

get in come to a place 来到某处；抵达: *My train got in at 7.15.* 我坐的火车是7点15分到的。

get in, get into something climb into a car 上汽车: *Tom got into the car.* 汤姆上了汽车了。

get off leave a train, bus, bicycle, etc 下火车、公共汽车、自行车等: *Where did you get off the bus?* 你是在哪儿下的公共汽车？

get on **1** words that you use to say or ask how well somebody does something 用以表达或询问某人做某事的情况的词语: *Patrick is getting on well at school.* 帕特里克上学情况很好。◇ *How did you get on in the exam?* 你考试考得怎么样？ **2** become late（指时间）渐晚: *I must go home—the time is getting on.* 我得回家了——时间不早了。 **3** become old（指人）渐老: *My grandfather is getting on—he's nearly 80.* 我祖父上年纪了——他都快80了。

get on, get onto something climb onto a bus, train or bicycle 上公共汽车、火车或自行车: *I got on the train.* 我上了火车。

get on with somebody live or work in a friendly way with somebody 与某人和睦生活或工作: *We get on well with our neighbours.* 我们跟邻居的关系很好。

get out leave a car, etc（从汽车等处）出来: *I opened the door and got out.* 我打开门走了出来。

get out of something not do something that you do not like 避开不喜欢做的事: *I'll come swimming with you if I can get out of cleaning my room.* 我要是能不打扫我的房间，我就跟你一起去游泳。

get something out take something from the place where it was 从某处取某物: *She opened her bag and got out a pen.* 她把包打开拿出了一枝钢笔。

G

get over something become well or happy again after you have been ill or sad（生病或烦恼过后）又健康或愉快起来: *He still hasn't got over his wife's death.* 他还没有摆脱妻子死亡的悲伤。

get through be able to speak to somebody on the telephone; be connected 能与某人在电话中通话；（电话）打通: *I tried to ring Kate but I couldn't get through.* 我给凯特打过电话，可是没打通。

get through something **1** use or finish a certain amount of something 用完或做完某数量的事物: *I got through a lot of work today.* 我今天做了很多工作。 **2** pass an examination, etc（考试等）及格；合格

get together meet; come together in a group 会见；聚会；聚集: *The whole family got together for Christmas.* 全家聚集在一起过圣诞节。

get up stand up; get out of bed 站起来；起床: *What time do you usually get up?* 你平时几点钟起床？

get up to something **1** do something, usually something bad 做某事（通常指坏事）: *I must go and see what the children are getting up to.* 我得去看看孩子们搞什么鬼呢。 **2** come as far as a place in a book, etc（阅读）到（书等的）某处: *I've got up to page 180.* 我读到第180页了。

have got have something 有某事物: *She has got brown eyes.* 她的眼睛是棕色的。◇ *Have you got any money?* 你有钱吗？

have got to If you have got to do something, you must do it 必须；不得不: *I have got to leave soon.* 我马上得走了。

ghost /gəʊst; gost/ *noun* 名词
the form of a dead person that a living person thinks he/she sees 鬼: *Do you believe in ghosts?* 你相信有鬼吗？

ghostly *adjective* 形容词
of or like a ghost 鬼的；像鬼的: *ghostly noises* 像鬼发出的声音

giant /ˈdʒaɪənt; ˈdʒaɪənt/ *noun* 名词
a very big tall person in stories (故事中的)巨人: *Goliath was a giant.* 歌利亚是巨人。

giant *adjective* 形容词
very big 巨大的: *a giant insect* 很大的虫子

gift /gɪft; gɪft/ *noun* 名词
1 something that you give to or get from somebody; a present 礼物: *wedding gifts* 结婚礼物
2 something that you can do well or learn easily 天赋；才能: *She has a gift for languages.* 她有语言天才。

gigantic /dʒaɪˈgæntɪk; dʒaɪˈgæntɪk/ *adjective* 形容词
very big 巨大的

giggle /ˈgɪgl; ˈgɪgl̩/ *verb* 动词 (**giggles**, **giggling**, **giggled** /ˈgɪgld; ˈgɪgl̩d/)
laugh in a silly way 傻笑: *The children couldn't stop giggling.* 孩子们不停地傻笑。

giggle *noun* 名词
There was a giggle from the back of the class. 教室后面发出了傻笑声。

gill /gɪl; gɪl/ *noun* 名词
the part on each side of a fish that it breathes through 鳃 ☞ picture at **fish** 见 **fish** 词条插图

ginger[1] /ˈdʒɪndʒə(r); ˈdʒɪndʒɚ/ *noun* 名词 (no plural 无复数)
a plant with a very hot strong taste, that is used in cooking 姜: *a ginger biscuit* 姜味饼干

gingerbread /ˈdʒɪndʒəbred; ˈdʒɪndʒɚˌbrɛd/ *noun* 名词 (no plural 无复数)
a dark brown cake with ginger in it 姜味饼

ginger[2] /ˈdʒɪndʒə(r); ˈdʒɪndʒɚ/ *adjective* 形容词
with a colour between brown and orange 姜黄色的（介于棕色与橙色之间的）: *My brother has got ginger hair.* 我弟弟的头发是姜黄色的。◇ *a ginger cat* 黄猫

gipsy /ˈdʒɪpsi; ˈdʒɪpsɪ/ = **gypsy**

giraffe /dʒəˈrɑːf; dʒəˈræf/ *noun* 名词
a big animal from Africa with a very long neck and long legs 长颈鹿

girl /gɜːl; gɝl/ *noun* 名词
a female child; a young woman 女孩子；少女

girlfriend /ˈgɜːlfrend; ˈgɝlˌfrɛnd/ *noun* 名词
a girl or woman who is somebody's special friend 女朋友: *Have you got a girlfriend?* 你有女朋友吗？

Girl Guide /ˌgɜːl ˈgaɪd; ˌgɝl ˈgaɪd/ *noun* 名词
a member of a special club for girls 女童子军

give /gɪv; gɪv/ *verb* 动词 (**gives**, **giving**, **gave** /geɪv; gev/, **has given** /ˈgɪvn; ˈgɪvən/)

G

1 let somebody have something 给某人某事物: *She gave me a watch for my birthday.* 我过生日她送给我一块手表。◇ *I gave my ticket to the man at the door.* 我把票给了站在门口的那个男子了。◇ *I gave John £60 for his old bike.* 我给约翰60英镑买了他那辆旧自行车。

2 make somebody have or feel something 使某人有某事物或感到有某事物: *That noise is giving me a headache.* 那种噪音吵得我头很疼。

3 make a sound, movement, etc 发出声音或做出动作等: *Jo gave me an angry look.* 乔生气地看了我一眼。◇ *He gave a shout.* 他大叫了一声。◇ *She gave him a kiss.* 她吻了他一下。

give away give something to somebody without getting money for it 把某物赠送给某人: *I've given all my old clothes away.* 我把我的旧衣服都送给别人了。

give somebody back something, give something back to somebody return something to somebody 把某物还给某人: *Can you give me back the cassette I lent you last week?* 你把我上星期借给你的录音带还给我行吗？

G

give in say that you will do something that you do not want to do, or agree that you will not win 让步；屈服: *My parents finally gave in and said I could go to the party.* 我父母最后让步了，说我可以去参加聚会。

give something in give work, etc to somebody 把作业等交给某人: *The teacher asked us to give in our essays today.* 老师让我们今天交作文。

give out give something to many people 把某物分发给很多人: *Could you give out these books to the class, please?* 请你把这些本子发给全班行吗？

give up stop trying to do something, because you know that you cannot do it (因自知无能力) 不再做某事: *I give up—what's the answer?* 我认输了——答案是什么？

give something up stop doing or having something 不再做某事物；不再有某事物: *I'm trying to give up smoking.* 我正想办法戒烟呢。

glacier /'glæsiə(r); 'gleʃɚ/ *noun* 名词
a large river of ice that moves slowly down a mountain 冰川；冰河

glad /glæd; glæd/ *adjective* 形容词
happy; pleased 高兴；愉快: *He was glad to see us.* 他看见我们后非常高兴。

gladly *adverb* 副词
If you do something gladly, you are happy to do it 高兴地；愉快地: *I'll gladly help you.* 我很乐意帮助你。

glance /glɑ:ns; glæns/ *verb* 动词 (**glances**, **glancing**, **glanced** /glɑ:nst; glænst/)
look quickly at somebody or something 很快看一下某人或某物: *Susan glanced at her watch.* 苏珊看了看手表。

glance *noun* 名词
a glance at the newspaper 看看报

at a glance with one look 看一眼: *I could see at a glance that he was ill.* 我一眼就看出他病了。

glare /gleə(r); glɛr/ *verb* 动词 (**glares**, **glaring**, **glared** /gleəd; glɛrd/)
1 look angrily at somebody 怒视某人: *He glared at the children.* 他生气地瞪着那些孩子。
2 shine with a strong light that hurts your eyes 发出刺眼的光: *The sun glared down.* 太阳放出刺眼的光芒。

glare *noun* 名词
1 (no plural 无复数) strong light that hurts your eyes 刺眼的光: *the glare of the car's headlights* 汽车前大灯发出的刺眼的光
2 (*plural* 复数作 **glares**) a long angry look 长时间怒目而视: *I tried to say something, but he gave me a glare.* 我想说句话，可是他一直狠狠地瞪着我。

glass /glɑ:s; glæs/ *noun* 名词
1 (no plural 无复数) hard stuff that you can see through. Bottles and windows are made of glass 玻璃 (瓶子和窗户都是玻璃做的): *I cut myself on some broken glass.* 我让玻璃给拉破了。◇ *a glass jar* 玻璃罐子

glass 玻璃杯

2 (*plural* 复数作 **glasses**) a thing made of glass that you drink from 玻璃杯: *Could I have a glass of milk, please?* 请问，我喝一杯牛奶行吗？◇ *a wineglass* 玻璃酒杯

glasses /'glɑ:sɪz; 'glæsɪz/ *noun* 名词 (plural 复数)
two pieces of special glass (called

lenses) in a frame that people wear over their eyes to help them see better 眼镜（镜片叫做 **lens**）: *Does she wear glasses?* 她戴眼镜吗？ ☞ Look also at **sunglasses**. 另见 **sunglasses**。

✪ Be careful! You cannot say 'a glasses'. 注意！不可说 a glasses。You can say **a pair of glasses** 可以说 **a pair of glasses**: *I need a new pair of glasses.* 我需要配一副新眼镜了。(or 也可说: *I need (some) new glasses.*)

gleam /gli:m; glim/ *verb* 动词 (**gleams, gleaming, gleamed** /gli:md; glimd/)
shine with a soft light 用微弱的光线照射: *The lake gleamed in the moonlight.* 那片湖水在月光下闪闪发光。
gleam *noun* 名词
I could see a gleam of light through the trees. 我看到树林中有个微弱的亮光。

glide /glaɪd; glaɪd/ *verb* 动词 (**glides, gliding, glided**)
move smoothly and silently 滑动；滑行: *The bird glided through the air.* 那只鸟在空中滑翔。

glider /ˈglaɪdə(r); ˈglaɪdɚ/ *noun* 名词
an aeroplane without an engine 滑翔机（无发动机的飞机）
gliding *noun* 名词 (no plural 无复数)
flying in a glider as a sport 滑翔运动

glimmer /ˈglɪmə(r); ˈglɪmɚ/ *verb* 动词 (**glimmers, glimmering, glimmered** /ˈglɪməd; ˈglɪmɚd/)
shine with a small, weak light 发出微弱的闪光
glimmer *noun* 名词
the glimmer of a candle 蜡烛发出的微弱的闪光

glimpse /glɪmps; glɪmps/ *verb* 动词 (**glimpses, glimpsing, glimpsed** /glɪmpst; glɪmpst/)
see somebody or something quickly, but not clearly 很快地看一下某人或某物；瞥见: *I just glimpsed a plane between the clouds.* 我瞥见了云层中有一架飞机。
glimpse *noun* 名词
catch a glimpse of somebody or 或 **something** see somebody or something quickly, but not clearly 很快地看一下某人或某物；瞥见: *I caught a glimpse of myself in the mirror as I walked past.* 我从镜子旁边经过，向里边看了自己一眼。

glisten /ˈglɪsn; ˈglɪsn̩/ *verb* 动词 (**glistens, glistening, glistened** /ˈglɪsnd; ˈglɪsn̩d/)
shine because it is wet or smooth（因有液体或因光滑）反光；闪光: *His eyes glistened with tears.* 他的泪眼晶莹地闪着光。

glitter /ˈglɪtə(r); ˈglɪtɚ/ *verb* 动词 (**glitters, glittering, glittered** /ˈglɪtəd; ˈglɪtɚd/)
shine brightly with a lot of small flashes of light 闪烁；闪耀；闪光: *The broken glass glittered in the sun.* 碎玻璃在阳光下闪闪发光。◇ *glittering diamonds* 闪闪发光的宝石
glitter *noun* 名词 (no plural 无复数)
the glitter of jewels 宝石的闪光

global /ˈgləʊbl; ˈglobl̩/ *adjective* 形容词
of or about the whole world 整个地球的；关于全世界的: *Pollution is a global problem.* 污染问题是全球的问题。

globe /gləʊb; glob/ *noun* 名词
1 a ball with a map of the world on it 地球仪
2 the globe (no plural 无复数) the earth 地球；世界: *He's travelled all over the globe.* 他到过世界各地。

gloomy /ˈglu:mi; ˈglumɪ/ *adjective* 形容词 (**gloomier, gloomiest**)
1 dark and sad 黑暗（而使人悲伤）的: *What a gloomy day!* 多么阴暗而让人难受的一天！
2 sad and without hope 悲伤而无希望的: *He's feeling very gloomy because he can't get a job.* 他找不到工作又伤心又失望。
gloomily /ˈglu:mɪli; ˈglumɪlɪ/ *adverb* 副词
She looked gloomily out of the window at the rain. 她伤感地看着窗外下着的雨。

glorious /ˈglɔ:riəs; ˈglɔrɪəs/ *adjective* 形容词
1 wonderful or beautiful 美妙的；美丽的；极好的: *The weather was glorious.* 天气好极了。
2 famous and full of glory 显赫而荣誉的；光荣的: *a glorious history* 光辉的历史

glory /ˈglɔ:ri; ˈglɔrɪ/ *noun* 名词 (no plural 无复数)
1 fame and respect that you get when you do great things 做大好事而获得的名声

和尊敬；光荣；荣誉: *the glory of winning at the Olympics* 在奥林匹克运动会赢得的荣誉

2 great beauty 美丽；壮观: *Autumn is the best time to see the forest in all its glory.* 秋天观赏气象万千的森林是最佳时节。

glossy /ˈglɒsi; ˈglɔsɪ/ *adjective* 形容词 (**glossier, glossiest**)

smooth and shiny 光滑而发亮的: *glossy hair* 有光泽的毛发

glove /glʌv; glʌv/ *noun* 名词

a thing that you wear to keep your hand warm or safe 手套: *I need a new pair of gloves.* 我需要一副新手套了。◇ *rubber gloves* 橡胶手套

gloves 手套

glow /gləʊ; glo/ *verb* 动词 (**glows, glowing, glowed** /gləʊd; glod/)

send out soft light or heat without flames or smoke 发出微弱的光或热量（无火焰或烟）: *His cigarette glowed in the dark.* 他的香烟在黑暗中发出微弱的亮光。

glow *noun* 名词

the glow of the sky at sunset 天空中落日的余晖

glue /glu:; glu/ *noun* 名词 (no plural 无复数)

a thick liquid that you use for sticking things together 胶水

glue *verb* 动词 (**glues, gluing, glued** /glu:d; glud/)

stick one thing to another thing with glue 用胶水把一物粘到另一物上: *Glue the two pieces of wood together.* 把两块木头粘在一起。

gnaw /nɔ:; nɔ/ *verb* 动词 (**gnaws, gnawing, gnawed** /nɔ:d; nɔd/)

bite something for a long time 长时间咬某物；啃: *The dog was gnawing a bone.* 狗啃着骨头。

go[1] /gəʊ; go/ *verb* 动词 (**goes, going, went** /went; wɛnt/, **has gone** /gɒn; gɔn/)

1 move from one place to another 从一个地方到另一个地方: *I went to London by train.* 我是坐火车到伦敦去的。◇ *Her new car goes very fast.* 她的新汽车非常快。

2 travel to a place to do something 到一个地方去做某事: *Paul has gone shopping.* 保罗买东西去了。◇ *Are you going to Dave's party?* 你去参加戴夫的聚会吗？◇ *I'll go and make some coffee.* 我去煮点咖啡。

3 leave a place 离开一个地方: *What time does the train go?* 火车什么时候开？◇ *I must go now—it's four o'clock.* 我得走了——已经四点钟了。

4 become 变为；变成；成为: *Her hair has gone grey.* 她的头发已经花白了。

5 have as its place 在应在的地方: *'Where do these plates go?' 'In that cupboard.'* “这些盘子是放在哪儿的？”“在那个柜子里。”

6 lead to a place 通往某处: *Does this road go to the station?* 这条路能到车站吗？

7 work 运转: *Jenny dropped the clock and now it doesn't go.* 珍妮把钟给摔了，现在不走了。

8 happen in a certain way 呈现某种状态: *How is your new job going?* 你的新工作怎么样？◇ *The week went very quickly.* 这个星期过得真快。

9 disappear 消失: *My headache has gone.* 我的头已经不疼了。

10 be or look good with something else 与其他事物在一起相称或好看；相配: *Does this jumper go with my skirt?* 这件套头毛衣跟我的裙子相称吗？

11 make a certain sound 发出某种声音: *Cows go 'moo'.* 牛的叫声是“哞哞”。

go ahead begin or continue to do something 开始或继续做某事: *'Can I borrow your pen?' 'Yes, go ahead.'* “我借用一下你的钢笔行吗？”“可以，拿去用吧。”

go away leave 离开: *Go away! I'm doing my homework.* 走开！我正做功课呢。◇ *They have gone away for the weekend.* 他们度周末去了。

go back go again to a place where you were before; return 回到原来的地方: *We're going back to school tomorrow.* 我们明天返校。

go by pass（指时间）过去: *The holidays went by very quickly.* 假期过得真快。

go down well be something that people like 成为受大家欢迎的事物: *The film went down very well in America.* 这部影片在美国大受欢迎。

go off 1 explode 爆炸: *A bomb went off in the station today.* 今天车站有颗炸弹爆

炸了。**2** When food or drink goes off, it becomes too old to eat or drink（指食物或饮料）腐坏: *This milk has gone off—it smells horrible.* 牛奶已经变质了——难闻极了。

go off somebody or 或 **something** stop liking somebody or something 不再喜欢某人或某事物

go on **1** happen 发生: *What's going on?* 出什么事了？**2** continue; not stop 继续；不停止: *I went on working.* 我一直工作着。**3** words that you use when you want somebody to do something 用作要某人做某事的词语: *Oh, go on! Come to the party with me!* 嘿，来吧！跟我去参加聚会去吧！

go out **1** leave the place where you live or work 暂时离开住的或工作的地方；外出: *I went out for a walk.* 我出去散了散步。◇ *We're going out tonight.* 我们今天晚上出门。**2** stop shining or burning 不再发光；不再燃烧: *The fire has gone out.* 火灭了。

go out with somebody have somebody as a boyfriend or girlfriend 结交某人作男朋友或女朋友: *She's going out with a boy at school.* 她跟学校里的一个男生谈上恋爱了。

go over something look at or explain something carefully from the beginning to the end 从头到尾仔细检查或解释某事物: *Go over your work before you give it to the teacher.* 把功课认真检查一遍再交给老师。

go round **1** be enough for everybody 足够每人一份: *Is there enough wine to go round?* 葡萄酒够不够每人一份？**2** go to somebody's home 到某人的家去: *We're going round to Jo's this evening.* 我们今天晚上到乔家去。

go through something **1** look at or explain something carefully from the beginning to the end 从头到尾仔细检查或解释某事物: *The teacher went through our homework.* 老师细心批改我们的家庭作业。**2** suffer something 遭受某种困苦: *She went through a difficult time when her husband was ill.* 她丈夫生病的时候，她吃了很多苦。

go up become higher or more 变高；变多: *The price of petrol has gone up again.* 汽油又涨价了。

been or **gone**? 用 **been** 还是用 **gone**？

If somebody has **been** to a place, they have travelled there and come back again 用 has **been** 表达某人到某处，意思是说他到那里以后又回来了:

*I've **been** to Italy three times.* 我去过意大利三次。

If somebody has **gone** to a place, they have travelled there and they are there now 用 has **gone** 表达某人到某处，意思是说他到了那里而且还在那里:

*Judy isn't here. She has **gone** to Italy.* 朱迪没在这儿。她到意大利去了。

go² /gəʊ; go/ *noun* 名词 (*plural* 复数作 **goes**)

the time when you can or should do something 能够或应该做某事的时候；轮到某人的机会: *Get off the bike—it's my go!* 你从自行车上下来吧——该轮到我骑了！

have a go try to do something 尽力做某事: *I'll have a go at mending your bike.* 我尽量给你修修这辆自行车。

in one go with one try 一下子；一次: *There are too many books here to carry in one go.* 这儿的书这么多，一下子拿不了。

goal /gəʊl; gol/ *noun* 名词

1 the place where the ball must go to win a point in a game like football（足球等球类运动的）球门: *He kicked the ball into the goal.* 他把球踢进了球门。

2 a point that a team wins in a game like football when the ball goes into the goal（球进入球门而得的）分: *Liverpool won by three goals to two.* 利物浦队以三比二获胜。◇ *Jones has scored another goal.* 琼斯又得一分。

goalkeeper /ˈgəʊlkiːpə(r); ˈgolˌkipɚ/ *noun* 名词

G

a player in a game like football who must stop the ball from going into the goal（足球等球类运动的）守门员

goat 山羊

goat /gəʊt; got/ *noun* 名词
an animal with horns. People keep goats for their milk. 山羊；奶羊（专门用来产奶的）✪ A young goat is called a **kid**. 幼小的山羊叫做 **kid**。

god /gɒd; gɑd/ *noun* 名词
1 (*plural* 复数作 **gods**) a being that people believe controls them and nature 神：*Mars was the Roman god of war.* 马尔斯是罗马的战神。
2 God (no plural 无复数) the one great being that Christians, Jews and Muslims believe made the world and controls everything（基督教徒、犹太教徒和伊斯兰教徒信奉的）上帝；天主；主；真主

goddess /ˈgɒdes; ˈgɑdɪs/ *noun* 名词 (*plural* 复数作 **goddesses**)
a female god 女神：*Venus was the Roman goddess of love.* 维纳斯是罗马的爱神。

goes *form of* **go¹** ＊ **go¹** 的不同形式

goggles /ˈgɒglz; ˈgɑgl̩z/ *noun* 名词 (plural 复数)
big glasses that you wear so that water, dust, wind, etc cannot get in your eyes. Swimmers, skiers and motor cyclists often wear goggles 护目镜（游泳、滑雪、骑摩托车的人常戴的）：*a pair of goggles* 一副护目镜

going *form of* **go¹** ＊ **go¹** 的不同形式
be going to 1 words that show what you plan to do in the future 用以表示打算做某事的词语：*Joe's going to cook the dinner tonight.* 乔要做今天晚上这顿饭。
2 words that you use when you are sure that something will happen 用以表示某事肯定要发生的词语：*It's going to rain.* 要下雨了。

gold /gəʊld; gold/ *noun* 名词 (no plural 无复数)
a yellow metal that is very valuable 金；黄金：*Is your ring made of gold?* 你的戒指是金的吗？◇ *a gold watch* 金表
gold *adjective* 形容词
with the colour of gold 金色的：*gold paint* 金漆

golden /ˈgəʊldən; ˈgoldn̩/ *adjective* 形容词
1 made of gold 金制的：*a golden crown* 金冠
2 with the colour of gold 金色的：*golden hair* 金发

goldfish /ˈgəʊldfɪʃ; ˈgold,fɪʃ/ *noun* 名词 (*plural* 复数作 **goldfish**)
a small orange fish that people keep as a pet 金鱼

golf /gɒlf; gɑlf/ *noun* 名词 (no plural 无复数)
a game that you play by hitting a small ball into holes with a long stick (called a **golf club**) 高尔夫球运动（高尔夫球棒叫做 **golf club**）：*My mother plays golf on Sundays.* 我母亲星期日经常打高尔夫球。

golf-course /ˈgɒlf kɔːs; ˈgɑlf,kors/ *noun* 名词
a large piece of land, covered in grass, where people play golf 高尔夫球场

gone *form of* **go¹** ＊ **go¹** 的不同形式

good¹ /gʊd; gʊd/ *adjective* 形容词 (**better, best**)
1 that does what you want; done or made very well 满意的；做得好的：*It's a good knife — it cuts very well.* 这把刀真好——很好用。◇ *The film was really good.* 这部影片可真好。
2 that you enjoy; nice 使人喜爱的；晴朗的；好的：*Have a good evening!* 晚上玩儿个痛快吧！◇ *The weather was very good.* 天气非常好。
3 able to do something well 能把某事做好的：*She's a good driver.* 她汽车开得很好。
4 kind, or doing the right thing 和蔼可亲的；做得对的：*It's good of you to help.* 感谢你的帮助。◇ *The children were very good while you were out.* 你出门的时候孩子们都很乖。
5 right or suitable 适当的；合适的：*This is a good place for a picnic.* 这是适合野餐的地方。
6 big, long, complete, etc 大的、长的、完全的等等：*Take a good look at this photo.* 好好看看这张照片吧。

7 a word that you use when you are pleased 用以表示愉快或满意的词: *Is everyone here? Good. Now let's begin.* 大家都到齐了吗？好。咱们开始吧。

✪ The adverb is **well**. 副词是 **well**。

good at something able to do something well 能把某事做好的: *James is very good at tennis.* 詹姆斯网球打得好。

good for you If something is good for you, it makes you well, happy, etc 对某人（健康、愉快等等）有好处: *Fresh fruit and vegetables are good for you.* 你吃新鲜的水果和蔬菜有好处。

good² /ɡʊd; ɡud/ *noun* 名词 (no plural 无复数)
something that is right or helpful 正确的或有益的事物

be no good, not be any good not be useful 没有用处: *This jumper isn't any good. It's too small.* 这件套头毛衣不行。太小。◇ *It's no good asking mum for money — she hasn't got any.* 找妈妈要钱也没用——她根本没有。

do somebody good make somebody well or happy 使某人健康或愉快；对某人有益: *It will do you good to go to bed early tonight.* 你今天晚上早点儿睡觉有好处。

for good for all time; for ever 永久；永远: *She has gone to Australia for good.* 她到澳大利亚不再回来了。

good afternoon /ˌɡʊd ɑːftəˈnuːn; ɡud ˌæftɚˈnun/
words that you say when you see or speak to somebody in the afternoon ✪ Often we just say **Afternoon**（下午见面时的问候语，往往只说 **Afternoon**）您好；你好: *'Good afternoon, Laura.' 'Afternoon, Mike.'* "劳拉，你好。""迈克，你好。"

goodbye /ˌɡʊdˈbaɪ; ɡudˈbaɪ/
a word that you say when somebody goes away, or when you go away（用于分手时的客套话）再见: *Goodbye! See you tomorrow.* 再见！明天见。

good evening /ˌɡʊd ˈiːvnɪŋ; ɡud ˈivnɪŋ/
words that you say when you see or speak to somebody in the evening ✪ Often we just say **Evening**（晚上见面时的问候语，往往只说 **Evening**）您好；你好: *'Good evening, Mr James.' 'Evening, Miss Evans.'* "詹姆斯先生，您好。""埃文斯小姐，您好。"

Good Friday /ˌɡʊd ˈfraɪdeɪ; ˌɡud ˈfraɪdɪ/ *noun* 名词
the Friday before Easter when Christians remember the death of Christ 耶稣受难节（复活节前的星期五，基督徒用以纪念耶稣受难日）

good-looking /ˌɡʊd ˈlʊkɪŋ; ˌɡudˈlʊkɪŋ/ *adjective* 形容词
nice to look at; handsome 好看的；漂亮的: *He's a good-looking boy.* 这个男孩儿很漂亮。☞ Note at **beautiful** 见 **beautiful** 词条注释

good morning /ˌɡʊd ˈmɔːnɪŋ; ɡud ˈmɔrnɪŋ/
words that you say when you see or speak to somebody in the morning ✪ Often we just say **Morning**（早晨见面时的问候语，往往只说 **Morning**）您好；你好: *'Good morning, Jack.' 'Morning.'* "杰克，你好。""你好。"

good-natured /ˌɡʊd ˈneɪtʃəd; ˈɡudˈnetʃɚd/ *adjective* 形容词
friendly and kind 和善的；和蔼的

goodness /ˈɡʊdnəs; ˈɡudnɪs/ *noun* 名词 (no plural 无复数)
1 something in food that is good for your health（食物中的）养分；营养: *Fresh vegetables have a lot of goodness in them.* 新鲜的蔬菜中有很多营养。
2 being good or kind 美德；善良

for goodness' sake words that show anger 表示气愤的词语: *For goodness' sake, hurry up!* 天哪，快点儿吧！

goodness, goodness me words that show surprise 表示惊奇的词语: *Goodness! What a big cake!* 嚄，好大的蛋糕哇！

thank goodness words that show you are happy because a problem or danger has gone away 经过困难或危险以后，表示愉快的词语: *Thank goodness it's stopped raining.* 谢天谢地，雨停了。

good night /ˌɡʊd ˈnaɪt; ˌɡud ˈnaɪt/
words that you say when you leave somebody in the evening（晚上分手时的告别语）再见

goods /ɡʊdz; ɡudz/ *noun* 名词 (plural 复数)
1 things that you buy or sell 商品: *That shop sells electrical goods.* 那个商店卖电器用品。

G

2 things that a train or lorry carries (火车或卡车运载的）货物: *a goods train* 货运列车

good-tempered /ˌgʊd ˈtempəd; ˈgʊd-ˈtɛmpɚd/ *adjective* 形容词
not often angry 脾气好的；不爱生气的: *My dad is very good-tempered.* 我爸爸脾气非常好。

goose /guːs; gus/ *noun* 名词 (*plural* 复数作 **geese** /giːs; gis/)
a big bird with a long neck. People keep geese on farms for their eggs and meat. 鹅

gooseberry /ˈgʊzbəri; ˈgusˌbɛrɪ/ *noun* 名词 (*plural* 复数作 **gooseberries**)
a small green fruit with hairs 醋栗（绿色多毛的小果实）

gorgeous /ˈgɔːdʒəs; ˈgɔrdʒəs/ *adjective* 形容词
very good; wonderful 非常好的；美妙的: *The weather was gorgeous!* 天气好极了！◇ *What a gorgeous dress!* 多漂亮的连衣裙哪！

gorilla /gəˈrɪlə; gəˈrɪlə/ *noun* 名词
an African animal like a very big black monkey 大猩猩（产于非洲）

gosh /gɒʃ; gɑʃ/
a word that shows surprise 表示惊奇的词语: *Gosh! What a big house!* 嘎！多大的房子啊！

gossip /ˈgɒsɪp; ˈgɑsəp/ *noun* 名词 (no plural 无复数)
talk about other people that is often unkind（常指对别人非善意的）闲话；流言蜚语: *Don't believe all the gossip you hear.* 别听见什么闲话就信什么。

gossip *verb* 动词 (**gossips**, **gossiping**, **gossiped** /ˈgɒsɪpt; ˈgɑsəpt/)
They were gossiping about Jenny's new boyfriend. 他们议论着珍妮新交的男朋友。

got *form of* **get** ✱ **get** 的不同形式

govern /ˈgʌvn; ˈgʌvɚn/ *verb* 动词 (**governs**, **governing**, **governed** /ˈgʌvnd; ˈgʌvɚnd/)
control a country or part of a country 治理或统治国家（或地区）: *Britain is governed by Parliament.* 英国是由国会治理的。

government /ˈgʌvənmənt; ˈgʌvɚn-mənt/ *noun* 名词
a group of people who control a country 政府: *The leaders of all the European governments will meet today in Brussels.* 欧洲各国政府的领袖将于今日在布鲁塞尔召开会议。◇ *The Government have discussed the plan.* 政府已经研究了这一计划。

governor /ˈgʌvənə(r); ˈgʌvənɚ/ *noun* 名词
1 a person who controls part of a country 管辖一地区的人；省长；州长；总督: *the Governor of California* 加利福尼亚州州长
2 a person who controls a place like a prison or hospital 管理监狱或医院等机构的人；典狱长；院长

gown /gaʊn; gaun/ *noun* 名词
1 a long dress that a woman wears at a special time（在特殊场合穿的）女长服
2 a long loose piece of clothing that people wear to do a special job. Judges and university teachers sometimes wear gowns.（做特殊工作时穿的）长服（法官和大学教师有时穿长袍）

grab /græb; græb/ *verb* 动词 (**grabs**, **grabbing**, **grabbed** /græbd; græbd/)
take something quickly and roughly 迅速而粗暴地拿走某物；抢；夺: *The thief grabbed her bag and ran away.* 那个强盗抢走她的提包就跑了。

grace /greɪs; gres/ *noun* 名词 (no plural 无复数)
1 a beautiful way of moving（动作的）优美: *She dances with grace.* 她舞姿优美。
2 thanks to God that people say before or after they eat（饭前或饭后对上帝的）感恩祷告

graceful /ˈgreɪsfl; ˈgresfəl/ *adjective* 形容词
A person or thing that is graceful moves in a beautiful way（动作）优美的: *a graceful dancer* 动作优美的舞蹈演员

gracefully /ˈgreɪsfəli; ˈgresfəlɪ/ *adverb* 副词
He moves very gracefully. 他动作非常优美。

grade[1] /greɪd; gred/ *noun* 名词
1 how good something is; the level or quality of something（事物好坏的）等级，级别: *Which grade of petrol does your car use?* 你的汽车用的是哪一级的汽油？
2 a number or letter that a teacher gives for your work to show how good it is（教师给的）分数: *She got very good grades in all her exams.* 她所有考试成绩都非常好。

3 a class in a school in the USA where all the children are the same age（美国小学的）年级: *My sister is in the fifth grade.* 我妹妹上五年级。

grade² /ˈgreɪd; gred/ *verb* 动词 (**grades, grading, graded**)
sort things or people into sizes, kinds, etc 把事物或人（按大小、种类等）进行分类，分级: *The eggs are graded by size.* 鸡蛋按大小分类。

grade crossing /ˈgreɪd krɒsɪŋ; ˈgred ˌkrɔsɪŋ/ *American English for* **level crossing** 美式英语，即 **level crossing**。

gradual /ˈgrædʒuəl; ˈgrædʒuəl/ *adjective* 形容词
Something that is gradual happens slowly 逐渐的；缓慢的: *I am making gradual progress with my work.* 我的工作渐渐有些进展。

gradually /ˈgrædʒuəli; ˈgrædʒulɪ/ *adverb* 副词
We all become gradually older. 我们的年纪都越来越大。

graduate¹ /ˈgrædʒuət; ˈgrædʒuɪt/ *noun* 名词
a person who has finished studying at a university or college and who has passed his/her last exams（高等院校的）毕业生: *an Oxford graduate* 牛津大学毕业生

graduate² /ˈgrædʒueɪt; ˈgrædʒuˌet/ *verb* 动词 (**graduates, graduating, graduated**)
finish your studies at a university or college and pass your last exams（高等院校）毕业: *I graduated from Exeter University in 1994.* 我1994年于埃克塞特大学毕业。

graffiti /grəˈfiːti; grəˈfitɪ/ *noun* 名词 (plural 复数)
funny, rude or angry words or pictures that people write or draw on walls（在墙上涂写的）可笑的、粗俗的或气愤的词语或图画: *The walls of the old building were covered with graffiti.* 那座旧楼的墙上到处是胡写乱画的东西。

grain /greɪn; gren/ *noun* 名词
1 (no plural 无复数) the seeds of a plant like wheat or rice that we eat 谷物（我们吃的小麦或稻米等的种子）
2 (*plural* 复数作 **grains**) a seed or a small hard piece of something 种子或小粒硬物: *grains of rice* 米粒 ◇ *a grain of sand* 沙粒

gram, gramme /græm; græm/ *noun* 名词
a measure of weight. There are 1 000 grams in a **kilogram**. 克（重量单位。1 000克等于1公斤，公斤叫做 **kilogram**。）✪ The short way of writing 'gram' is **g** ✳ gram 的缩写形式为 **g**: *30 g of butter* ✳ 30克黄油

grammar /ˈgræmə(r); ˈgræmɚ/ *noun* 名词 (no plural 无复数)
the rules that tell you how to put words together when you speak or write 语法

grammar school /ˈgræmə skʊl; ˈgræmɚ skul/ *noun* 名词
a school for children between the ages of 11 and 18 who are good at studying 文法学校（为11至18岁学业优良的学生而设的）

grammatical /grəˈmætɪkl; grəˈmætɪkḷ/ *adjective* 形容词
1 of or about grammar 语法的；关于语法的: *What is the grammatical rule for making plural in English?* 英语中构成复数的语法规则是怎样的？
2 correct because it follows the rules of grammar（语法上）正确的；符合语法规则的: *The sentence 'They is happy' is not grammatical.* ✳ They is happy 这句话不符合语法规则。✪ opposite 反义词: **ungrammatical**

grammatically /grəˈmætɪkli; grəˈmætɪklɪ/ *adverb* 副词
The sentence is not grammatically correct. 这句话语法上不正确。

gran /græn; græn/ *noun* 名词
grandmother 奶奶；姥姥

grand /grænd; grænd/ *adjective* 形容词 (**grander, grandest**)
very big, important, rich, etc 非常大的、重要的、富有的等等: *They live in a grand house in the centre of London.* 他们住在伦敦中部一所深宅大院里。

grandad /ˈgrændæd; ˈgrænˌdæd/ *noun* 名词
grandfather 爷爷；姥爷（外祖父）

grandchild /ˈgræntʃaɪld; ˈgrænˌtʃaɪld/ *noun* 名词 (*plural* 复数作 **grandchildren** /ˈgræntʃɪldrən; ˈgrænˌtʃɪldrən/)
the child of your child 孙子；孙女；外孙子；外孙女 ☞ picture on page C3 见第C3页图

G

granddaughter /ˈgrændɔ:tə(r); ˈgræn-ˌdɔtɚ/ *noun* 名词
the daughter of your child 孙女；外孙女 ☞ picture on page C3 见第C3 页图

grandfather /ˈgrænfɑ:ðə(r); ˈgræn-ˌfɑðɚ/ *noun* 名词
the father of your mother or father 外祖父（姥爷）；祖父（爷爷） ☞ picture on page C3 见第C3 页图

grandma /ˈgrænmɑ:; ˈgrænmɑ/ *noun* 名词
grandmother 姥姥（外祖母）；奶奶（祖母）

grandmother /ˈgrænmʌðə(r); ˈgræn-ˌmʌðɚ/ *noun* 名词
the mother of your mother or father 外祖母（姥姥）；祖母（奶奶） ☞ picture on page C3 见第C3 页图

grandpa /ˈgrænpɑ:; ˈgrænpɑ/ *noun* 名词
grandfather 姥爷（外祖父）；爷爷（祖父）

grandparents /ˈgrænpeərənts; ˈgræn-ˌpɛrənts/ *noun* 名词 (plural 复数)
the mother and father of your mother or father 外祖母和外祖父；祖母和祖父 ☞ picture on page C3 见第C3 页图

grandson /ˈgrænsʌn; ˈgrænˌsʌn/ *noun* 名词
the son of your child 孙子；外孙子 ☞ picture on page C3 见第C3 页图

grandstand /ˈgrændstænd; ˈgræn-ˌstænd/ *noun* 名词
lines of seats, with a roof over them, where you sit to watch a sport 看台（运动场上有顶盖的观众座席）

granny, **grannie** /ˈgræni; ˈgrænɪ/ *noun* 名词 (*plural* 复数作 **grannies**)
grandmother 姥姥（外祖母）；奶奶（祖母）

grant[1] /grɑ:nt; grænt/ *noun* 名词
money that you give for a special reason 为某种原因而赠予的钱：*The government gives grants to some young people so they can study at university.* 政府给某些年轻人奖学金，好让他们上大学。

grant[2] /grɑ:nt; grænt/ *verb* 动词 (**grants, granting, granted**)
give somebody what they have asked for 给予某人所要求的事物：*They granted him a visa to leave the country.* 他们给他办理了出国签证。

grape /greɪp; grep/ *noun* 名词
a small green or purple fruit that we eat or make into wine 葡萄：*a bunch of grapes* 一串葡萄

a bunch of grapes 一串葡萄

grapefruit /ˈgreɪpfru:t; ˈgrepˌfrut/ *noun* 名词 (*plural* 复数作 **grapefruit** or 或 **grapefruits**)
a fruit that looks like a big orange, but is yellow 葡萄柚

grapevine /ˈgreɪpvaɪn; ˈgrepˌvaɪn/ *noun* 名词
the grapevine the way that news is passed from one person to another（指消息）人人相传的途径：*I heard it on the grapevine that you are getting married.* 我听人说你要结婚了。

graph 图表

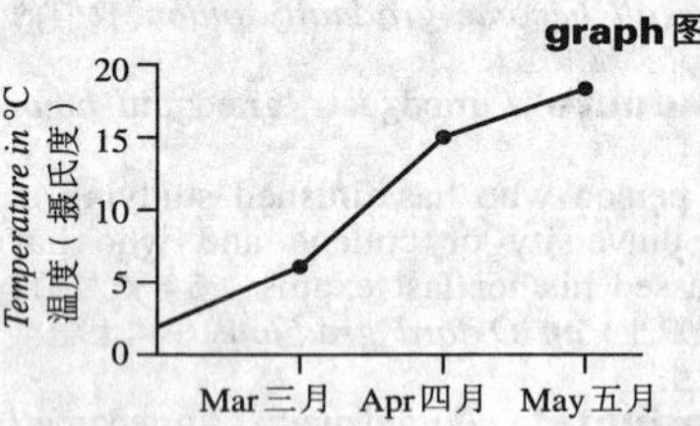

graph /grɑ:f; græf/ *noun* 名词
a picture that shows how numbers, amounts, etc are different from each other 图表

grasp /grɑ:sp; græsp/ *verb* 动词 (**grasps, grasping, grasped** /grɑ:spt; græspt/)
1 hold something tightly 抓住某物：*Claire grasped my arm to stop herself from falling.* 克莱尔抓住了我的胳膊她才没摔倒。
2 understand something 理解某事物：*He could not grasp what I was saying.* 他无法领会我说的话。

grasp *noun* 名词 (no plural 无复数)
The ball fell from my grasp. 那个球我没抓住。

grass /grɑ:s; græs/ *noun* 名词 (no plural 无复数)
a plant with thin green leaves that covers fields and gardens. Cows and

sheep eat grass 草: *Don't walk on the grass.* 勿踏草地。

grassy *adjective* 形容词
covered with grass 长着草的

grate /greɪt; gret/ *verb* 动词 (**grates, grating, grated**)
If you grate food you rub it over a metal tool (called a **grater**) so that it is in very small pieces 把食物擦成细丝儿（使用的器具叫做礤床儿 **grater**）: *Can you grate some cheese?* 你把干酪擦成丝儿行吗？◇ *grated carrot* 擦成的胡萝卜丝儿

grateful /'greɪtfl; 'gretfəl/ *adjective* 形容词
If you are grateful, you feel or show thanks to somebody 感激的；感谢的: *We are grateful to you for the help you have given us.* 我们感谢您的帮助。✪ opposite 反义词: **ungrateful**

gratitude /'grætɪtju:d; 'grætəˌtud/ *noun* 名词 (no plural 无复数)
the feeling of being grateful 感激；感谢: *We gave David a present to show our gratitude for all his help.* 我们送给戴维一份礼物，对他的大力帮助表示感谢。

grave[1] /greɪv; grev/ *adjective* 形容词 (**graver, gravest**)
very bad or serious 非常坏的；极严重的 ✪ **Serious** is the word that we usually use. ＊ **serious** 是常用词。

grave[2] /greɪv; grev/ *noun* 名词
a hole in the ground where a dead person's body is put 墓穴；坟墓: *We put flowers on the grave.* 我们把花摆放在坟上。

gravestone /'greɪvstəʊn; 'grevˌston/ *noun* 名词
a piece of stone on a grave that shows the name of the dead person 墓碑

graveyard /'greɪvjɑ:d; 'grevˌjɑrd/ *noun* 名词
a piece of land near a church where dead people are put in the ground 墓地；坟场；公墓

gravel /'grævl; 'grævḷ/ *noun* 名词 (no plural 无复数)
very small stones that are used for making roads（铺路用的）碎石

gravity /'grævəti; 'grævətɪ/ *noun* 名词 (no plural 无复数)
the force that pulls everything towards the earth 地心引力

gravy /'greɪvi; 'grevɪ/ *noun* 名词 (no plural 无复数)
a hot brown liquid that you eat with meat and vegetables（棕色，热的，浇在肉和蔬菜上食用的）调味汁

gray *American English for* **grey** 美式英语，即 **grey**

graze[1] /greɪz; grez/ *verb* 动词 (**grazes, grazing, grazed** /greɪzd; grezd/)
hurt your skin by rubbing it against something rough 擦伤皮肤: *He fell and grazed his arm.* 他跌倒后把胳臂擦伤了。

graze *noun* 名词
Her legs were covered with grazes. 她的双腿擦伤了很多处。

graze[2] /greɪz; grez/ *verb* 动词 (**grazes, grazing, grazed** /greɪzd; grezd/)
eat grass 吃草: *The sheep were grazing in the fields.* 羊群在地里吃着草。

grease /gri:s; gris/ *noun* 名词 (no plural 无复数)
fat from animals, or any thick stuff that is like oil（动物的）油脂；（像油的）黏稠物质: *You will need very hot water to get the grease off these plates.* 你得用很烫的水才能把这些盘子上的油洗掉。

greasy /'gri:si; 'grisɪ/ *adjective* 形容词 (**greasier, greasiest**)
with a lot of grease on or in it 有很多（动物）油脂的；有很多（像油的）黏稠物质的: *Greasy food is not good for you.* 吃油腻的食物不利于健康。◇ *greasy hair* 油性的头发

great[1] /greɪt; gret/ *adjective* 形容词 (**greater, greatest**)
1 very large or very much 非常大的；非常多的: *It's a great pleasure to meet you.* 与您见面非常愉快。
2 important or special 重要的；伟大的: *Einstein was a great scientist.* 爱因斯坦是位伟大的科学家。
3 very; very good 非常的；非常好的: *They are great friends.* 他们是非常好的朋友。◇ *There's a great big dog in the garden!* 花园里有条很大的狗！
4 very good; wonderful 非常好的；美妙的: *I had a great weekend.* 我周末过得好极了。◇ *It's great to see you!* 能看见你可太好了！

a great many very many 很多的: *He knows a great many people.* 他认识很多人。

great-² /greɪt; gret/ *prefix* 前缀
a word that you put before other words to show some parts of a family. 用于表示家族称谓的某些词之前，指再隔一代的亲属关系。For example, your **great-grandmother** is the mother of your grandmother or grandfather, and your **great-grandson** is the son of your grandson or granddaughter. 例如 **great-grandmother**（曾祖母或外曾祖母）是祖母或外祖母或祖父或外祖父的母亲，**great-grandson**（曾孙或外曾孙）是孙子或外孙或孙女或外孙女的儿子。

greatly /ˈgreɪtli; ˈgretlɪ/ *adverb* 副词
very much 非常；很：*I wasn't greatly surprised to see her.* 见到她我并不太吃惊。

greed /gri:d; grid/ *noun* 名词 (no plural 无复数)
the feeling that you want more of something than you need 对某事物超出需要的要求；贪心；贪婪

greedy *adjective* 形容词 (**greedier**, **greediest**)
A person who is greedy wants or takes more of something than he/she needs 贪心的；贪婪的：*She's so greedy—she's eaten all the chocolates!* 她太贪嘴了——把所有的巧克力都吃了！

green /gri:n; grin/ *adjective* 形容词 (**greener**, **greenest**)
with the colour of leaves and grass 绿色的：*My brother has green eyes.* 我弟弟眼睛是绿的。◇ *dark green* 深绿色的

green *noun* 名词
1 the colour of leaves and grass 绿色：*She was dressed in green.* 她穿着一身绿色的衣服。
2 a place in the centre of a village that is covered with grass（村子中心的）绿草地

greengrocer /ˈgri:ngrəʊsə(r); ˈgrinˌgrosɚ/ *noun* 名词
a person who sells fruit and vegetables in a small shop (called a **greengrocer's**) 在小商店中卖水果和蔬菜的人；果菜商（这类商店叫做 **greengrocer's**）

greenhouse /ˈgri:nhaʊs; ˈgrinˌhaus/ *noun* 名词 (*plural* 复数作 **greenhouses** /ˈgri:nhaʊzɪz; ˈgrinˌhaʊzɪz/)
a building made of glass, where plants grow 温室（培育植物的玻璃建筑物）

greet /gri:t; grit/ *verb* 动词 (**greets**, **greeting**, **greeted**)
say or do something when you meet somebody（见某人时）问候；打招呼：*He greeted me with a smile.* 他见到我时向我微笑致意。

greeting /ˈgri:tɪŋ; ˈgritɪŋ/ *noun* 名词
1 words that you say when you meet somebody（见到某人时说的）问候语；寒暄：*'Hello' and 'Good morning' are greetings.* "喂"和"您早"都是问候语。
2 greetings (plural 复数) words that you write to somebody at a special time（在某些时候写的）问候语；贺词：*a greetings card* (= a card that you send at Christmas or on a birthday, for example) 贺卡（= 例如圣诞贺卡或生日贺卡）

grew *form of* **grow** ＊ **grow** 的不同形式

grey /greɪ; gre/ *adjective* 形容词 (**greyer**, **greyest**)
with a colour like black and white mixed together 灰色的：*My grandmother has grey hair.* 我奶奶头发是灰色的。◇ *a grey-haired old man* 头发花白的老翁 ◇ *The sky was grey.* 天空灰暗。

grey *noun* 名词
He was dressed in grey. 他穿着一身灰色的衣服。

grid /grɪd; grɪd/ *noun* 名词
lines that cross each other to make squares, for example on a map 格子（如地图上的）

grief /gri:f; grif/ *noun* 名词 (no plural 无复数)
great sadness 悲痛；忧伤

grieve /gri:v; griv/ *verb* 动词 (**grieves**, **grieving**, **grieved** /gri:vd; grivd/)
feel great sadness 感到悲痛：*She is grieving for her dead son.* 她儿子死了，她万分悲痛。

grill /grɪl; grɪl/ *verb* 动词 (**grills**, **grilling**, **grilled** /grɪld; grɪld/)
cook meat, fish, etc on metal bars under or over heat（在金属烤架上）烤肉、鱼等：*grilled steak* 烤牛排

grill *noun* 名词
the part of a cooker, or a special metal thing, where you grill food 烤架（炉具中的或专做烤食物用的）

grin /grɪn; grɪn/ *verb* 动词 (**grins**,

grinning, **grinned** /grɪnd; grɪnd/)
have a big smile on your face 露齿而笑: *She grinned at me.* 她朝我咧着嘴笑。
grin *noun* 名词
He had a big grin on his face. 他咧着大嘴笑。

grind /graɪnd; graɪnd/ *verb* 动词 (**grinds**, **grinding**, **ground** /graʊnd; graʊnd/, **has ground**)
make something into very small pieces or powder by crushing it 磨碎；碾碎: *They ground the wheat into flour.* 他们把小麦磨成了面粉。◇ *ground coffee* 磨成的咖啡粉末

grip /grɪp; grɪp/ *verb* 动词 (**grips**, **gripping**, **gripped** /grɪpt; grɪpt/)
hold something tightly 抓住某物: *Marie gripped my hand as we crossed the road.* 玛丽和我横过马路的时候，她紧紧抓着我的手。
grip *noun* 名词 (no plural 无复数)
He kept a tight grip on the rope. 他紧紧抓住绳子。

grit /grɪt; grɪt/ *noun* 名词 (no plural 无复数)
very small pieces of stone 小石子；沙粒

groan /grəʊn; gron/ *verb* 动词 (**groans**, **groaning**, **groaned** /grəʊnd; grond/)
make a deep sad sound, for example because you are unhappy or in pain 发出低沉难过的声音（如因不愉快或痛苦）；呻吟；叹息: *'I've got a headache,' he groaned.* "我头疼，"他哼哼着说。
groan *noun* 名词
'I've got to do my homework,' she said with a groan. "我还得做功课呢，"她叹了一口气。

groceries /ˈgrəʊsəriz; ˈgrosərɪz/ *noun* 名词 (plural 复数)
food that you buy in packets, tins, jars, etc（论包、罐、瓶等购买的）食品

groom /gru:m; grum/ *noun* 名词
1 a person whose job is to look after horses 马夫
2 a man on the day of his wedding; a bridegroom 新郎

groove /gru:v; gruv/ *noun* 名词
a long thin cut 槽（物体细长的凹下部分）: *The needle moves along a groove in the record.* 唱针沿着唱片上的纹路移动。

grope /grəʊp; grop/ *verb* 动词 (**gropes**, **groping**, **groped** /grəʊpt; gropt/)
try to find something by using your hands, when you cannot see（因看不见）用手摸索寻找东西: *I groped in the dark for the door.* 我在黑暗中摸索着寻找门口。

ground¹ *form of* **grind** ✳ **grind** 的不同形式

ground² /graʊnd; graʊnd/ *noun* 名词
1 (no plural 无复数) the top part of the earth 地面: *We sat on the ground to eat our picnic.* 我们坐在地上吃野餐。
2 (*plural* 复数作 **grounds**) a piece of land that is used for something special（作某种用途的）场地: *a sports ground* 运动场 ◇ *a playground* (= a place where children play) 游戏场
3 grounds (plural 复数) the land around a large building（建筑物周围的）场地: *the grounds of the hospital* 医院的大院子

ground floor /ˌgraʊnd ˈflɔ:(r); ˌgraʊnd ˈflɔr/ *noun* 名词
the part of a building that is at the same height as the street 楼房地面与街道相平的楼层；一楼: *My office is on the ground floor.* 我的办公室在一楼。☞ picture at **house** 见 **house** 词条插图

group /gru:p; grup/ *noun* 名词
1 a number of people or things together 在一起的一些人或事物；群；批；堆: *A group of people were standing outside the shop.* 商店外面站着一群人。
2 people who play pop music together（演奏流行歌曲的）乐队

grow /grəʊ; gro/ *verb* 动词 (**grows**, **growing**, **grew** /gru:; gru/, **has grown** /grəʊn; gron/)
1 become bigger 变大；成长；发育: *Children grow very quickly.* 孩子们长得很快。
2 When a plant grows somewhere, it lives there（指植物）生长: *Oranges grow in warm countries.* 柑橘生长在热带国家。
3 plant something in the ground and look after it 种植；栽种: *We grow potatoes and carrots in our garden.* 我们在园子里种了些土豆儿和胡萝卜。
4 let something grow 使某物生长: *Mark has grown a beard.* 马克留胡子了。
5 become 变成；变得: *It was growing dark.* 天渐渐黑了。✪ In this sense, it is more usual to say **get** or **become**. 这一义通常用 **get** 或 **become** 表达。

G

grow into something get bigger and become something 长大而成为某物: *Kittens grow into cats.* 小猫能长成大猫。

grow out of something become too big to do or wear something（因长大）不宜做某事或不宜穿戴某物: *She's grown out of her shoes.* 她的鞋已经小了。

grow up become an adult; change from a child to a man or woman 长到成年；从儿童长到成人: *I want to be a doctor when I grow up.* 我想长大以后当医生。

growl /graʊl; graʊl/ *verb* 动词 (**growls, growling, growled** /graʊld; graʊld/)
If an animal growls, it makes a low angry sound（指动物愤怒时）吼叫；怒吼: *The dog growled at the stranger.* 那条狗对着生人狂吠。

growl *noun* 名词
The dog gave a fierce growl. 狗吼叫了一声。

grown-up /ˈgrəʊnʌp; ˈgronˌʌp/ *noun* 名词
a man or woman, not a child; an adult 成人: *Ask a grown-up to help you.* 找个成年人来帮助你。

grown-up /ˈgrəʊnʌp; ˈgronˌʌp/ *adjective* 形容词
She has a grown-up son. 她有个儿子已经长大成人了。

growth /grəʊθ; groθ/ *noun* 名词 (no plural 无复数)
getting bigger; growing 长大；成长；发育: *the growth of a baby* 幼儿的发育成长

grubby /ˈgrʌbi; ˈgrʌbɪ/ *adjective* 形容词 (**grubbier, grubbiest**)
dirty 肮脏的: *grubby hands* 脏手

grumble /ˈgrʌmbl; ˈgrʌmbḷ/ *verb* 动词 (**grumbles, grumbling, grumbled** /ˈgrʌmbld; ˈgrʌmbḷd/)
say many times that you do not like something 一再说不喜欢某事物；发怨言；抱怨: *The children often grumble about the food at school.* 孩子们常常抱怨学校饭菜不好。

grumpy /ˈgrʌmpi; ˈgrʌmpɪ/ *adjective* 形容词 (**grumpier, grumpiest**)
a little angry; bad-tempered 稍微生气的；脾气坏的: *She gets grumpy when she's tired.* 她一累就发脾气。

grunt /grʌnt; grʌnt/ *verb* 动词 (**grunts, grunting, grunted**)
make a short rough sound, like a pig makes 发出短促刺耳的声音（像猪发出的声音）

grunt *noun* 名词
She didn't say anything—she just gave a grunt. 她什么都没说——只是咕哝了一声。

guarantee /ˌgærənˈtiː; ˌgærənˈti/ *noun* 名词
1 a special promise on paper that a company will repair a thing you have bought, or give you a new one, if it goes wrong（公司给顾客的）产品保修或退换证书；保修单: *This watch has a two-year guarantee.* 这种手表有两年保修证明。
2 a promise that something will happen（对某事一定发生的）保证: *I want a guarantee that you will do the work today.* 我需要你保证今天一定做这件事。

guarantee *verb* 动词 (**guarantees, guaranteeing, guaranteed** /ˌgærənˈtiːd; ˌgærənˈtid/)
1 say that you will repair a thing that somebody buys, or give them a new one, if it goes wrong 保证对产品保修或退换: *The television is guaranteed for three years.* 这种电视机有三年保修期。
2 promise something 保证某事物: *I can't guarantee that I will be able to help you, but I'll try.* 我不能保证一定能帮助你，但是我一定尽力而为。

guard[1] /gɑːd; gɑrd/ *verb* 动词 (**guards, guarding, guarded**)
keep somebody or something safe from other people, or stop somebody from escaping 保卫某人或某事物的安全；看守某人不使逃跑: *The house was guarded by two large dogs.* 这所房子有两条大狗看着。

guard[2] /gɑːd; gɑrd/ *noun* 名词
1 a person who keeps somebody or something safe from other people, or who stops somebody from escaping 警卫；看守: *There are guards outside the palace.* 宫殿外面有警卫人员。
2 a person whose job is to look after people and things on a train（火车上的）列车长

on guard guarding 保卫着；看守着: *The soldiers were on guard outside the airport.* 士兵在机场外面戒备着。

guardian /ˈgɑːdiən; ˈgɑrdɪən/ *noun* 名词
a person who looks after a child with no parents（无父母的儿童的）监护人

G

guerrilla /gəˈrɪlə; gəˈrɪlə/ *noun* 名词
a person who is not in an army but who fights secretly against the government or an army 游击队员

guess /ges; gɛs/ *verb* 动词 (**guesses**, **guessing**, **guessed** /gest; gɛst/)
give an answer when you do not know if it is right 猜；猜测: *Can you guess how old he is?* 你能猜出他有多少岁吗？
guess *noun* 名词 (*plural* 复数作 **guesses**)
If you don't know the answer, have a guess! 你要是不知道答案，那就猜猜吧！

guest /gest; gɛst/ *noun* 名词
1 a person that you invite to your home, to a party, etc 客人；来宾: *There were 200 guests at the wedding.* 有200宾客参加了婚礼。
2 a person who is staying in a hotel（住在旅馆里的）客人
guest-house /ˈgest haʊs; ˈgɛstˌhaʊs/ *noun* 名词 (*plural* 复数作 **guest-houses** /ˈgest haʊzɪz; ˈgɛstˌhaʊzɪz/)
a small hotel 小旅馆

guidance /ˈgaɪdns; ˈgaɪdn̩s/ *noun* 名词 (no plural 无复数)
help and advice 指导；指引: *I want some guidance on how to find a job.* 我想请教怎样找工作。

guide¹ /gaɪd; gaɪd/ *noun* 名词
1 a person who shows other people where to go and tells them about a place 导游；向导: *The guide took us round the castle.* 导游带领我们参观了城堡。
2 (*also* 亦作 **guidebook**) a book that tells you about a town, country, etc 介绍某城镇、国家等的书；旅游手册
3 a book that tells you about something, or how to do something 指导如何做某事物的书: *a guide to skiing* 滑雪指南
4 Guide = Girl Guide

guide² /gaɪd; gaɪd/ *verb* 动词 (**guides**, **guiding**, **guided**)
show somebody where to go or what to do 指导某人去某处或做某事: *He guided us through the busy streets to our hotel.* 他带领我们穿过繁忙的街道找到了我们的旅馆。

guilt /gɪlt; gɪlt/ *noun* 名词 (no plural 无复数)
1 having done something wrong 罪；有罪: *The police could not prove his guilt.* 警方无法证明他有罪。✪ opposite 反义词: **innocence**
2 the feeling that you have when you know that you have done something wrong 自知做错了事；内疚: *She felt terrible guilt after stealing the money.* 她偷了钱以后极度内疚。

guilty /ˈgɪlti; ˈgɪltɪ/ *adjective* 形容词 (**guiltier**, **guiltiest**)
1 If you are guilty, you have done something wrong 有罪的；犯罪的: *He is guilty of murder.* 他犯有谋杀罪。✪ opposite 反义词: **innocent**
2 If you feel guilty, you feel that you have done something wrong 自知做错了事的；内疚的: *I feel guilty about lying to her.* 我向她撒了谎，十分惭愧。

guinea-pig /ˈgɪni pɪg; ˈgɪnɪˌpɪg/ *noun* 名词
1 a small animal that people keep as a pet 天竺鼠；豚鼠（可作宠物）
2 a person who is used in an experiment 供作实验的人

guitar 吉他

guitar /gɪˈtɑ:(r); gɪˈtɑr/ *noun* 名词
a musical instrument with strings 吉他: *I play the guitar in a band.* 我在乐队里弹吉他。
guitarist /gɪˈtɑ:rɪst; gɪˈtɑrɪst/ *noun* 名词
a person who plays the guitar 弹吉他的人；吉他手

gulf /gʌlf; gʌlf/ *noun* 名词
a large part of the sea that has land almost all the way around it 海湾: *the Gulf of Mexico* 墨西哥湾

gull /gʌl; gʌl/ *noun* 名词
a large grey or white bird that lives by the sea; a seagull 鸥；海鸥

gulp /gʌlp; gʌlp/ *verb* 动词 (**gulps**, **gulping**, **gulped** /gʌlpt; gʌlpt/)
eat or drink something quickly 匆匆吃或喝某物: *He gulped down a cup of tea and left.* 他一口气喝了一杯茶就走了。
gulp *noun* 名词
She took a gulp of coffee. 她喝了一大口咖啡。

G

gum /gʌm; gʌm/ *noun* 名词

1 (*plural* 复数作 **gums**) Your gums are the hard pink parts of your mouth that hold the teeth. 齿龈；牙龈；牙床

2 (no plural 无复数) thick liquid that you use for sticking pieces of paper together 胶水

☞ Look also at **chewing-gum**. 另见 **chewing-gum**。

gun /gʌn; gʌn/ *noun* 名词

a thing that shoots out pieces of metal (called **bullets**) to kill or hurt people or animals 枪（子弹叫做 **bullet**）: *He pointed the gun at the bird and fired.* 他把枪对准了鸟开了一枪。

gun 枪

gunman /ˈgʌnmən; ˈgʌnmən/ *noun* 名词 (*plural* 复数作 **gunmen** /ˈgʌnmən; ˈgʌnˌmən/)

a man who shoots another person with a gun 用枪杀人的人

gunpowder /ˈgʌnpaʊdə(r); ˈgʌnˌpaʊdɚ/ *noun* 名词 (no plural 无复数)

powder that explodes. It is used in guns and fireworks. 火药（用于枪炮和烟火中）

gush /gʌʃ; gʌʃ/ *verb* 动词 (**gushes, gushing, gushed** /gʌʃt; gʌʃt/)

flow out suddenly and strongly 猛然流出；涌出；喷出: *Blood was gushing from the cut in her leg.* 她腿上的伤口血流如注。

gust /gʌst; gʌst/ *noun* 名词

a sudden strong wind 一阵狂风: *A gust of wind blew his hat off.* 一阵狂风把他的帽子刮掉了。

gutter /ˈgʌtə(r); ˈgʌtɚ/ *noun* 名词

1 a pipe under the edge of a roof to carry away rainwater（房上的）排水檐沟

2 the part at the edge of a road where water is carried away（路边的）排水沟；路边沟

guy /gaɪ; gaɪ/ *noun* 名词

1 a man 男子: *He's a nice guy!* 他是个好人！

2 a big doll that children make and burn on **Guy Fawkes Night** 盖伊（儿童做的高大的模拟人像，在福克斯日晚焚烧）

✪ In Britain, **Guy Fawkes Night** or **Bonfire Night** is the evening of 5 November, when people have a party outside with a **bonfire** and **fireworks**. 在英国，11月5日晚叫做 **Guy Fawkes Night** 或 **Bonfire Night**，大家在户外点燃篝火（**bonfire**）和烟火（**firework**）。＊ Guy Fawkes was a man who tried to destroy the **Houses of Parliament** in 1605. 盖伊·福克斯是1605年图谋炸毁国会大厦（**Houses of Parliament**）的人。

gymnasium /dʒɪmˈneɪziəm; dʒɪmˈnezɪəm/ *noun* 名词

a room where you do exercises for your body 体育馆；健身房 ✪ The short form is **gym**. 缩略式为 **gym**。

gymnastics /dʒɪmˈnæstɪks; dʒɪmˈnæstɪks/ *noun* 名词 (plural 复数)

exercises for your body 体操 ✪ The short form is **gym**. 缩略式为 **gym**。

gypsy /ˈdʒɪpsi; ˈdʒɪpsɪ/ *noun* 名词 (*plural* 复数作 **gypsies**)

Gypsies are people who live in **caravans** and travel around from one place to another. 吉卜赛人（所用的篷车叫做 **caravan**）

Hh

habit /'hæbɪt; 'hæbɪt/ *noun* 名词
something that you do very often 个人常常做的某种事；习惯: *Smoking is a bad habit.* 吸烟是一种坏习惯。◇ *She's got a habit of phoning me when I'm in bed.* 她常常在我睡觉的时候给我打电话。

habitat /'hæbɪtæt; 'hæbəˌtæt/ *noun* 名词
the natural place where a plant or animal lives（动物或植物生长的）自然环境

had *form of* **have** ＊ **have** 的不同形式

hadn't /'hædnt; 'hædn̩t/ = **had not**

ha! ha! /ˌhɑ: 'hɑ:; 'hɑ ˌhɑ/
words that you write to show that somebody is laughing (用书面语表示的人的笑声) 哈！哈！

hail /heɪl; hel/ *noun* 名词 (no plural 无复数)
frozen rain that falls in small hard balls (called **hailstones**) 雹；冰雹（雹粒叫做 **hailstone**）
hail *verb* 动词 (**hails**, **hailing**, **hailed** /heɪld; held/)
It's hailing. 现在下雹子了。

hair 头发

She's got straight hair.
她的头发是直的。

He's got curly hair.
他的头发是鬈的。

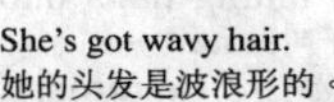

She's got wavy hair.
她的头发是波浪形的。

He's bald.
他秃顶了。

hair /heə(r); hɛr/ *noun* 名词
1 (*plural* 复数作 **hairs**) one of the long thin things that grow on the skin of people and animals（人和动物身上的）毛；汗毛；毛发: *There's a hair in my soup.* 我的汤里有根毛。
2 (no plural 无复数) all the hairs on a person's head 头发: *She's got long black hair.* 她的头发又黑又长。☞ picture on page C2 见第C2页图

> ✪ You wash your hair with **shampoo** and make it tidy with a **hairbrush** or a **comb**. 洗头发用的洗涤剂叫做 **shampoo**，梳头的发刷叫做 **hairbrush**，梳子叫做 **comb**。Some words that you can use to talk about the colour of a person's hair are **black, dark, brown, ginger, red, fair, blond** and **grey**. 用以形容头发颜色的词有 **black**（黑色）、**dark**（深色）、**brown**（棕色）、**ginger**（黄色）、**red**（红色）、**fair**（浅色）、**blond**（金色）、**grey**（灰色）等。

hairbrush /'heəbrʌʃ; 'hɛrˌbrʌʃ/ *noun* 名词 (*plural* 复数作 **hairbrushes**)
a brush that you use to make your hair tidy 发刷

haircut /'heəkʌt; 'hɛrˌkʌt/ *noun* 名词
1 when somebody cuts your hair 理发: *I need a haircut.* 我该理发了。
2 the way that your hair is cut 发式；发型: *I like your new haircut.* 我喜欢你的新发型。

hairdresser /'heədresə(r); 'hɛrˌdrɛsɚ/ *noun* 名词
a person whose job is to wash, cut and arrange hair 理发师 ✪ The place where a hairdresser works is called a **hairdresser's** 理发师工作的地方叫做理发店 **(hairdresser's)**: *I'm going to the hairdresser's to get my hair cut.* 我要到理发店去理发。

hair-drier, hair-dryer /'heə draɪə(r); 'hɛrˌdraɪɚ/ *noun* 名词
a machine that dries hair by blowing hot air on it（吹干头发用的）吹风机

hairstyle /'heəstaɪl; 'hɛrˌstaɪl/ *noun* 名词
the way that your hair is cut and arranged 发式；发型

hairy /'heəri; 'hɛrɪ/ *adjective* 形容词 (**hairier**, **hairiest**)
covered with hair 多毛的: *He has got hairy legs.* 他的腿上有很多毛。

H

half /hɑːf; hæf/ *noun* 名词 (*plural* 复数作 **halves** /hɑːvz; hævz/) *adjective*, *pronoun* 形容词，代词
one of two equal parts of something; ½ 半；一半: *Half of six is three.* 六的一半是三。◇ *I lived in Rome for two and a half years.* 我在罗马住了两年半。◇ *The journey takes an hour and a half.* 路上用了一个半小时。◇ *She gave me half of her apple.* 她把她的那个苹果给了我一半。
in half so that there are two equal parts 成为相等的两半: *Cut the cake in half.* 把蛋糕切成两半。
half *adverb* 副词
50%; partly 半；一半；部分地: *The bottle is half empty.* 这个瓶子半瓶是空的。
half past 30 minutes after an hour on the clock（钟表上的）半点钟；…点半: *It's half past nine.* 现在九点半了。☞ picture on page C8 见第C8页图

half-price /ˌhɑːf ˈpraɪs; ˈhæfˈpraɪs/ *adjective*, *adverb* 形容词，副词
for half the usual price 半价(的): *Children travel half-price on most trains and buses.* 儿童乘坐火车和公共汽车大多半价。

half-term /ˌhɑːf ˈtɜːm; ˌhæfˈtɝm/ *noun* 名词
a short school holiday in the middle of a term 期中假（学校一个学期中间的短假）

H

half-time /ˌhɑːf ˈtaɪm; ˈhæfˌtaɪm/ *noun* 名词 (no plural 无复数)
a short time in the middle of a game like football, when you are not playing（足球等运动的）中场休息

halfway /ˌhɑːfˈweɪ; ˈhæfˈwe/ *adverb* 副词
in the middle 半路上；中途；在中间: *They live halfway between London and Oxford.* 他们住在伦敦和牛津的中间。◇ *She went out halfway through the lesson.* 她上着一半课就出去了。

hall /hɔːl; hɔl/ *noun* 名词
1 a big room or building where a lot of people meet 可供很多人聚会的房间或建筑物；大厅；礼堂: *a concert hall* 音乐厅 ◇ *We did our exams in the school hall.* 我们考试是在学校大礼堂举行的。
2 the room in a house that is near the front door and has doors to other rooms 房子里靠近前门可通往其他房间的房间；门厅；正门走廊: *You can leave your coat in the hall.* 你可以把大衣放在大厅里。

hallo = **hello**

Hallowe'en /ˌhæləʊˈiːn; ˌhæloˈin/ *noun* 名词 (no plural 无复数)
31 October. Some people believe that at Hallowe'en, witches and ghosts appear. 万圣节前夕（10月31日，有人认为女巫和鬼到时都会出现）

halt /hɔːlt; hɔlt/ *noun* 名词 (no plural 无复数)
come to a halt stop 停止；停住: *The car came to a halt.* 汽车停住了。

halve /hɑːv; hæv/ *verb* 动词 (**halves**, **halving**, **halved** /hɑːvd; hævd/)
divide something into two parts that are the same 把某事物分成相等的两半；对半分: *There were two of us, so I halved the orange.* 我们是两个人，所以我把那个橙子分成一人一半。

halves *plural of* **half** ＊ **half** 的复数形式

ham /hæm; hæm/ *noun* 名词 (no plural 无复数)
meat from a pig's leg that you can keep for a long time because salt or smoke was used to prepare it 火腿（腌制的猪腿）☞ Note at **pig** 见 **pig** 词条注释

hamburger /ˈhæmbɜːgə(r); ˈhæmbɝgɚ/ *noun* 名词
meat cut into very small pieces and made into a flat round shape, that you eat between two pieces of bread 汉堡肉饼儿（用肉末做的饼儿，常夹在面包中间吃）；汉堡包: *A hamburger and chips, please.* 请来个汉堡包和炸土豆条儿。

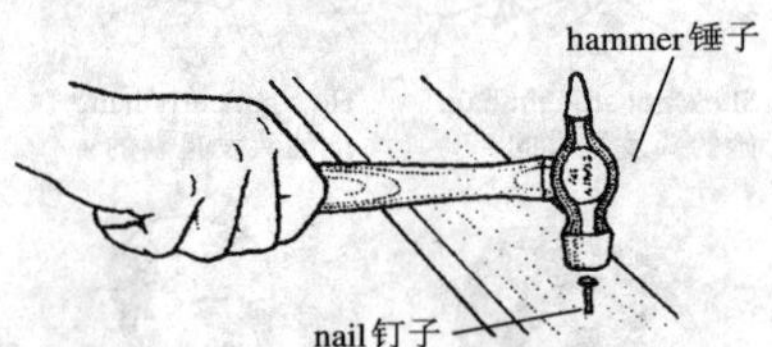

hammer /ˈhæmə(r); ˈhæmɚ/ *noun* 名词
a tool with a handle and a heavy metal part, that you use for hitting **nails** into things 锤子；榔头（钉子叫做 **nail**）
hammer *verb* 动词 (**hammers**, **hammering**, **hammered** /ˈhæməd; ˈhæmɚd/)
1 hit something with a hammer 用锤子敲打某物: *I hammered the nail into the wood.* 我把钉子钉进木头里去了。

2 hit something hard 用力敲打某物: *He hammered on the door until somebody opened it.* 他使劲敲门才有人把门打开。

hammock /ˈhæmək; ˈhæmək/ *noun* 名词
a bed made of cloth or rope that you hang up at the two ends 吊床（用布或绳子制成两端挂起来的床）

hamster /ˈhæmstə(r); ˈhæmstɚ/ *noun* 名词
a small animal that people keep as a pet. Hamsters can keep food in the sides of their mouths. 仓鼠（供玩赏的一种小鼠，嘴两旁有颊囊可藏食物）

hand[1] /hænd; hænd/ *noun* 名词
1 the part at the end of your arm 手: *She held the letter in her hand.* 她手里拿着信。 ☞ picture on page C2 见第C2页图
2 one of the parts of a clock or watch that move to show the time（钟表的）指针
a hand some help 一些帮助；帮些忙: *Could you give me a hand with my homework?* 你帮帮我做功课行吗？
by hand without using a machine 用手（不用机器）；以手工: *The curtains were made by hand.* 这些帘子是手工制造的。
get out of hand become difficult to control 变得难以控制: *The party got out of hand.* 那个聚会失去控制了。
hand in hand with your hand in another person's hand 手拉手
hands up **1** put one hand in the air if you can answer the question 举手（回答问题） **2** put your hands in the air because somebody has a gun 举手（投降）
hold hands have another person's hand in your hand 握手；拉手
in good hands well looked after 受到很好的照顾: *Don't worry—your daughter is in good hands.* 不必担心——您的女儿受到很好的照顾。
on hand near and ready to help 随时提供帮助: *There is a doctor on hand 24 hours a day.* 一天24小时都有医生值班。

hold hands 拉着手

on the one hand ... on the other hand words that show the good and bad things about an idea 用以表示一件事有好坏两个方面: *On the one hand the hotel has a lovely view, but on the other hand it doesn't have a restaurant.* 这家旅馆的优点是风景好，缺点是没有餐厅。

hand[2] /hænd; hænd/ *verb* 动词 (**hands, handing, handed**)
put something into somebody's hand 把某物放到某人手中: *Can you hand me the scissors, please?* 请把剪子递给我行吗？◇ *I handed the money to the shop assistant.* 我把钱交给商店的服务员了。
hand down pass a thing, story, etc from an older person to a younger one 年长的人把事物传给年轻的人: *He never had new clothes—they were handed down from his older brothers.* 他从来没有新衣服——都是穿几个哥哥剩下的。
hand in give something to somebody 把某物交给某人: *The teacher asked us to hand in our homework.* 老师让我们交作业。
hand out give something to many people 把某物分发给很多人: *Please hand out these books.* 请把这些书发给大家。
hand over give something to somebody 把某物交给某人: *'Hand over that knife!' said the police officer.* "把刀子交出来!"警察说。

handbag /ˈhændbæg; ˈhændˌbæg/ *noun* 名词
a small bag for carrying things like money and keys 小手提包（放钱和钥匙的）

handcuffs /ˈhændkʌfs; ˈhændˌkʌfs/ *noun* 名词 (plural 复数)
two metal rings with a chain that are put on a prisoner's arms so that he/she cannot use his/her hands 手铐

handful /ˈhændfʊl; ˈhændfʊl/ *noun* 名词
1 as much as you can hold in one hand 一只手能握住的量；一把: *a handful of stones* 一把石子
2 a small number 少量；一小撮: *Only a handful of people came to the meeting.* 来开会的人很少。

handicap /ˈhændikæp; ˈhændɪˌkæp/ *noun* 名词
something that stops you doing well 阻碍把事情做好的事物；不利条件: *a school for children with physical handicaps* 为残疾儿童创办的学校

H

handicapped /'hændikæpt; 'hændɪˌkæpt/ *adjective* 形容词
not able to use a part of your body well 身体有残疾的: *They have a handicapped son.* 他们有个儿子身体有残疾。

handkerchief /'hæŋkətʃɪf; 'hæŋkətʃɪf/ *noun* 名词
a square piece of cloth or paper that you use for cleaning your nose 用来擦鼻涕的方形的布或纸；手绢儿；手帕；纸巾

handles 把手

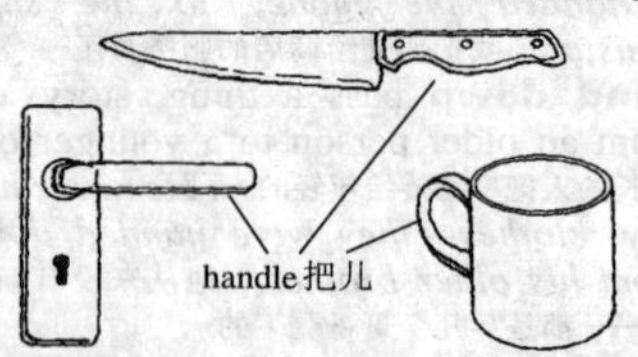

handle[1] /'hændl; 'hændl̩/ *noun* 名词
the part of a thing that you hold in your hand 器物上手拿的地方；把手；柄: *I turned the handle and opened the door.* 我转了一下把手，门就开了。◇ *Hold that knife by the handle.* 握着刀把儿。

handle[2] /'hændl; 'hændl̩/ *verb* 动词 (**handles**, **handling**, **handled** /'hændld; 'hændl̩d/)
1 touch something with your hands 触；摸；拿；抓: *Please wash your hands before you handle the food.* 请洗洗手再拿食物。
2 control somebody or something 控制某人或某事物: *That dog is too big for a small child to handle.* 那条狗很大，小孩儿管不了它。
3 look after something and do what is necessary 照看并处理某事物: *My secretary handles all letters.* 我的秘书处理所有的信件。

handlebars /'hændlbɑːz; 'hændl̩bɑrz/ *noun* 名词 (plural 复数)
the part at the front of a bicycle or motor cycle that you hold when you are riding it（自行车或摩托车的）把手；车把 ☞ picture at **bicycle** 见 **bicycle** 词条插图

hand-luggage /'hænd lʌgɪdʒ; 'hændˌlʌgɪdʒ/ *noun* 名词 (no plural 无复数)
a small bag or anything that you carry with you on an aeroplane（可随身携带登机的）小件行李

handmade /ˌhænd'meɪd; 'hænd'med/ *adjective* 形容词
made by a person, not by a machine 手工制造的（非机器生产的）: *handmade chocolates* 手工制造的巧克力

handsome /'hænsəm; 'hænsəm/ *adjective* 形容词
good-looking 好看的；漂亮的: *a handsome man* 漂亮的男子 ☞ Note at **beautiful** 见 **beautiful** 词条注释

handwriting /'hændraɪtɪŋ; 'hændˌraɪtɪŋ/ *noun* 名词 (no plural 无复数)
the way you write 个人写的字的样子；笔迹；字迹: *Her handwriting is difficult to read.* 她写的字很难认。

handy /'hændi; 'hændɪ/ *adjective* 形容词 (**handier**, **handiest**)
1 useful 有用的；便利的: *This bag will be handy for carrying my books.* 用这个袋子装我的书一定很方便。
2 near and easy to find or reach 近便的；在手头上的: *Have you got a pen handy?* 你手边儿有钢笔吗？
come in handy be useful 能有用: *Don't throw that box away—it might come in handy for something.* 别把这个箱子扔了——没准儿装什么东西的时候用得着。

hang /hæŋ; hæŋ/ *verb* 动词
1 (**hangs**, **hanging**, **hung** /hʌŋ; hʌŋ/, **has hung**) fix something, or be fixed at the top so that the lower part is free 悬挂；吊: *Hang your coat (up) on the hook.* 把你的大衣挂在衣钩上。◇ *I hung the washing on the line to dry.* 我把洗好的衣服挂在绳子上晾干。
2 (**hangs**, **hanging**, **hanged** /hæŋd; hæŋd/, **has hanged**) kill somebody by holding them above the ground by a rope around the neck 绞死某人；上吊: *She was hanged for murder.* 她因犯谋杀罪被处以绞刑。
hang about, **hang around** stay somewhere with nothing special to do 无所事事地待在某处；闲荡: *My plane was late so I had to hang about in the airport all morning.* 我要等的飞机误点了，所以我一上午都在机场闲待着。
hang on wait 等着: *Hang on—I'm not ready.* 等一等——我还没准备好呢。
hang on to somebody or 或 **something** hold something firmly 抓紧某物: *Hang on to your purse.* 你把钱包攥住了。

hang up end a telephone call by putting the telephone down 挂断电话（把话筒放回原处）

hanger /ˈhæŋə(r); ˈhæŋɚ/ *noun* 名词
a coat-hanger; a piece of metal, wood or plastic with a hook. You use it for hanging clothes on. 衣架 ☞ picture at **coat-hanger** 见 **coat-hanger** 词条插图

hang-glider /ˈhæŋ glaɪdə(r); ˈhæŋˌglaɪdɚ/ *noun* 名词
a thing made of a very large piece of material on a frame, which you hang from and fly through the air 悬挂式滑翔机
hang-gliding *noun* 名词 (no plural 无复数)
the sport of flying in a hang-glider 悬挂式滑翔运动

hanky, hankie /ˈhæŋki; ˈhæŋkɪ/ *noun* 名词 (*plural* 复数作 **hankies**)
a handkerchief 手绢儿；手帕；纸巾

happen /ˈhæpən; ˈhæpən/ *verb* 动词 (**happens**, **happening**, **happened** /ˈhæpənd; ˈhæpənd/)
take place 发生: *How did the accident happen?* 事故是怎么发生的？◇ *Did you hear what happened to me yesterday?* 你听见我昨天怎么了吗？
happen to do something by chance 偶然做某事: *I happened to meet Tim yesterday.* 我昨天碰见蒂姆了。

happy /ˈhæpi; ˈhæpɪ/ *adjective* 形容词 (**happier**, **happiest**)
1 If you are happy, you feel very pleased. People often laugh or smile when they are happy 愉快；高兴；快乐: *She looks very happy.* 她看起来很高兴。◇ *That was one of the happiest days of my life.* 那天是我一生中最快乐的一天。✪ opposite 反义词: **unhappy** or 或 **sad** ☞ picture on page C26 见第C26页图
2 a word that you use to say that you hope somebody will enjoy a special time 祝愿某人在某场合过得愉快的用语: *Happy New Year!* 新年快乐！◇ *Happy Christmas!* 圣诞快乐！◇ *Happy Birthday!* 生日快乐！✪ **Many happy returns (of the day)** means the same as **Happy Birthday**. ＊ **many happy returns (of the day)** 的意思和 **Happy Birthday** 一样。
happily /ˈhæpɪli; ˈhæpḷɪ/ *adverb* 副词
1 in a happy way 愉快地；高兴地；快乐地
2 it is lucky that 幸运地: *Happily, the accident was not serious.* 幸好事故不太严重。
happiness /ˈhæpinəs; ˈhæpɪnɪs/ *noun* 名词 (no plural 无复数)
being happy 愉快；高兴；快乐；幸福

harbor *American English for* **harbour** 美式英语，即 **harbour**

harbour /ˈhɑːbə(r); ˈhɑrbɚ/ *noun* 名词
a place where ships can stay safely in the water 港；港口；港湾

hard[1] /hɑːd; hɑrd/ *adjective* 形容词 (**harder**, **hardest**)
1 not soft; firm 硬的；坚实的；坚固的: *These apples are very hard.* 这些苹果真硬。◇ *I couldn't sleep because the bed was too hard.* 我没睡着觉，因为床太硬了。✪ opposite 反义词: **soft** ☞ picture on page C27 见第C27页图
2 difficult to do or understand 困难的；难做的；难懂的: *The exam was very hard.* 这次考试非常难。◇ *hard work* 困难的工作 ☞ Look at **easy**. 见 **easy**。
3 full of problems 有很多难题的；艰难的；困苦的: *He's had a hard life.* 他当时生活很苦。
4 not kind or gentle 无情的；严厉的: *She is very hard on her children.* 她对孩子很严。

hard[2] /hɑːd; hɑrd/ *adverb* 副词
1 a lot 努力地；辛勤地: *She works very hard.* 她很努力。◇ *You must try harder!* 你得再加把劲！
2 strongly 强劲地；猛烈地: *It's raining hard.* 雨下得很大。◇ *She hit him hard.* 她狠狠打了他一顿。

hardback /ˈhɑːdbæk; ˈhɑrdbæk/ *noun* 名词
a book with a hard cover 精装书 ☞ Look at **paperback**. 见 **paperback**。

hard disk /ˌhɑːd ˈdɪsk; hɑrd ˈdɪsk/ *noun* 名词
a plastic part inside a computer that stores information 硬磁盘

harden /ˈhɑːdn; ˈhɑrdn̩/ *verb* 动词 (**hardens**, **hardening**, **hardened** /ˈhɑːdnd; ˈhɑrdn̩d/)
become hard 变硬: *Wait for the cement to harden.* 要等到水泥变硬。

hardly /ˈhɑːdli; ˈhɑrdlɪ/ *adverb* 副词
almost not; only just 几乎没有；几乎不；刚刚；仅仅: *She spoke so quietly that I could hardly hear her.* 她说话声音很低，

H

我简直听不清。◇ *There's hardly any (= almost no) coffee left.* 咖啡差不多一点儿都没剩。

hare /heə(r); hɛr/ *noun* 名词
an animal like a big rabbit. Hares have long ears and can run very fast. 野兔

harm¹ /hɑ:m; hɑrm/ *noun* 名词 (no plural 无复数)
hurt or damage 损害；伤害
come to harm be hurt or damaged 受到损害: *Make sure the children don't come to any harm.* 一定不能让孩子们受到任何伤害。
there is no harm in nothing bad will happen if you do something 做某事并无害处: *I don't know if she'll help you, but there's no harm in asking.* 我不知道她是否帮助你，你不妨问问她。

harm² /hɑ:m; hɑrm/ *verb* 动词 (**harms, harming, harmed** /hɑ:md; hɑrmd/)
hurt or damage somebody or something 损害或伤害某人或某事物: *The dog won't harm you.* 这条狗不咬人。

harmful /'hɑ:mfl; 'hɑrmfəl/ *adjective* 形容词
Something that is harmful can hurt or damage people or things 可造成损害或伤害的；有害的: *Strong sunlight can be harmful to young babies.* 强烈的阳光对幼儿有害处。

harmless /'hɑ:mləs; 'hɑrmlɪs/ *adjective* 形容词
not dangerous 无害的；无危险的: *Don't be frightened—these insects are harmless.* 别害怕——这些虫子不伤人。

harmony /'hɑ:məni; 'hɑrmənɪ/ *noun* 名词
1 (no plural 无复数) having the same ideas, etc, with no arguments（指意见、想法等）一致（无争论）: *The different races live together in harmony.* 不同种族的人和睦相处。
2 (*plural* 复数作 **harmonies**) musical notes that sound nice together（指乐音）和声: *They sang in harmony.* 他们用和声演唱。

harsh /hɑ:ʃ; hɑrʃ/ *adjective* 形容词 (**harsher, harshest**)
1 rough and unpleasant to see or hear 刺眼的；刺耳的: *a harsh voice* 难听的嗓音
2 not kind; cruel 不善良的；残忍的: *a harsh punishment* 酷刑

harvest /'hɑ:vɪst; 'hɑrvɪst/ *noun* 名词
1 the time when fruit, corn or vegetables are ready to cut or pick 水果、谷物或蔬菜的收获时期；收割；摘取: *The apple harvest is in September.* 苹果的收获期是九月份。
2 all the fruit, corn or vegetables that are cut or picked 收获的水果、谷物或蔬菜；收获；收成: *We had a good harvest this year.* 我们今年收成很好。
harvest *verb* 动词 (**harvests, harvesting, harvested**)
When does the farmer harvest his wheat? 这个农民什么时候收割小麦？

has *form of* **have** ✻ **have** 的不同形式

hasn't /'hæznt; 'hæzn̩t/ = **has not**

haste /heɪst; hest/ *noun* 名词 (no plural 无复数)
doing things too quickly 急忙；匆忙: *In his haste to get up, he knocked over the chair.* 他匆忙起身，把椅子碰倒了。
in haste quickly; in a hurry 急忙；匆忙: *The letter was written in haste.* 那封信是匆匆忙忙写的。

hasty /'heɪsti; 'hestɪ/ *adjective* 形容词 (**hastier, hastiest**)
1 If you are hasty, you do something too quickly 做某事过快的: *Don't be too hasty. This is a very important decision.* 不要仓促行事。这个决定非同小可。
2 said or done quickly 说得或做得很快的: *We ate a hasty lunch, then left.* 我们匆匆地吃了午饭就走了。
hastily /'heɪstɪli; 'hestl̩ɪ/ *adverb* 副词
He put the money hastily into his pocket. 他赶紧把钱装进衣袋里了。

hats 帽子

hat /hæt; hæt/ *noun* 名词
a thing that you wear on your head 帽子: *She's wearing a hat.* 她戴着顶帽子。

hatch /hætʃ; hætʃ/ *verb* 动词 (**hatches, hatching, hatched** /hætʃt; hætʃt/)
When baby birds, insects, fish, etc hatch, they come out of an egg.（指小鸟、小虫、小鱼等从卵中）孵出

hate /heɪt; het/ *verb* 动词 (**hates, hating, hated**)
have a very strong feeling of not liking

somebody or something 极不喜欢某人或某事物；讨厌；恨: *Most cats hate water.* 猫大多不喜欢水。◇ *I hate waiting for buses.* 我最讨厌等公共汽车了。

hate, hatred /'heɪtrɪd; 'hetrɪd/ *noun* 名词 (no plural 无复数)
a very strong feeling of not liking somebody or something（对某人或某事物的）厌恶；仇恨

haul /hɔ:l; hɔl/ *verb* 动词 (**hauls, hauling, hauled** /hɔ:ld; hɔld/)
pull something heavy 拉很重的东西；拖；拽: *They hauled the boat out of the river.* 他们把船从河里拖了出来。

haunt /hɔ:nt; hɔnt/ *verb* 动词 (**haunts, haunting, haunted**)
1 If a ghost haunts a place, it visits it often（指鬼魂）常出没于某处: *A ghost haunts the castle.* 那座城堡常闹鬼。
2 If something sad or unpleasant haunts you, you often think of it（指悲伤的或不愉快的事）萦绕心头: *Her unhappy face still haunts me.* 我一直想着她那不高兴的样子。

haunted *adjective* 形容词
often visited by ghosts 鬼魂经常出没的: *a haunted house* 常闹鬼的房子

have¹ /həv, hæv; həv, 'hæv/ *verb* 动词
a word that you use with parts of other verbs to show that something happened or started in the past 与另一动词的过去分词连用构成完成时态，表示某事物已经发生或以前已经开始: *I have seen that film.* 我看过那部电影。◇ *We have been in England for six months.* 我们在英格兰已经住了半年了。◇ *When we arrived, Paul had already left.* 我们到的时候，保罗已经走了。☞ verb table on next page 见下页动词表

have² /hæv; 'hæv/ *verb* 动词 (**has** /hæz; 'hæz/, **having, had** /hæd; 'hæd/, **has had**)
1 (*also* 亦作 **have got**) own or keep something 有某事物: *She has blue eyes.* 她眼睛是蓝的。◇ *They have got a big car.* 他们有辆大汽车。◇ *Do you have any brothers and sisters?* 你有兄弟姐妹吗？
2 be ill with something; feel something 患某种疾病: *She has got a headache.* 她头疼。
3 eat or drink something 吃或喝某物: *What time do you have breakfast?* 您几点钟吃早饭？
4 a word that shows that something happens to somebody or something 表示某人或某事物发生某事的词: *I had a shower.* 我冲了个淋浴。◇ *He has had an accident.* 他出了事故了。◇ *Did you have a good holiday?* 您假期过得好吗？
5 (*also* 亦作 **have got**) a word that you use with some nouns 与某些名词连用的词: *I have an idea.* 我有个主意。◇ *Have you got time to help me?* 您有时间帮我个忙吗？

have to, have got to must 必须: *I have to/have got to go to school tomorrow.* 我明天得上学。◇ *We don't have to/haven't got to get up early tomorrow.* 我们明天不必早起。◇ *Do we have to/have we got to pay for this now?* 我们必须现在付款吗？

have something done let somebody do something for you 让某人为你做某事: *I had my hair cut yesterday.* 我昨天理发了。◇ *Have you had your car mended?* 你的汽车修理了吗？

haven't /'hævnt; 'hævn̩t/ = **have not**

hawk /hɔ:k; hɔk/ *noun* 名词
a big bird that catches and eats other birds and small animals 鹰

hay /heɪ; he/ *noun* 名词 (no plural 无复数)
dry grass that is used as food for farm animals 干草（用做牲畜饲料）

hay fever /'heɪ fi:və(r); 'he ˌfivɚ/ *noun* 名词 (no plural 无复数)
an illness like a cold. Grass and other plants can cause hay fever. 枯草热（类似感冒的病，由草和其他植物引起）

hazard /'hæzəd; 'hæzɚd/ *noun* 名词
a danger 危险: *Ice is a hazard for drivers.* 路上有冰能给开车的人造成危险。

hazardous /'hæzədəs; 'hæzɚdəs/ *adjective* 形容词
dangerous 危险的: *Motor racing is a hazardous sport.* 汽车速度比赛是危险的运动。

hazelnut /'heɪzlnʌt; 'hezl̩ˌnʌt/ *noun* 名词
a small nut that you can eat 榛子

he /hi:; hi/ *pronoun* 代词 (*plural* 复数作 **they**)
the man or boy that the sentence is about（用作主语）（指男性）他；（指雄性动物）它: *I saw Mike when he arrived.* 迈克来的时候我看见他了。◇ *'Where is John?' 'He's* (= he is) *at home.'* "约翰在哪儿呢？""他在家呢。"

have¹

present tense 现在式		*short forms* 缩略式	*negative short forms* 否定缩略式	
I	**have**	I**'ve**	I	**haven't**
you	**have**	you**'ve**	you	**haven't**
he/she/it	**has** /hæz; 'hæz/	he**'s**/she**'s**/it**'s**	he/she/it	**hasn't**
we	**have**	we**'ve**	we	**haven't**
you	**have**	you**'ve**	you	**haven't**
they	**have**	they**'ve**	they	**haven't**

past tense 过去式 **had** /hæd; 'hæd/
present participle 现在分词 **having**
past participle 过去分词 **had**

past tense short forms 缩略过去式
I**'d**
you**'d**
he**'d**/she**'d**/it**'d**
we**'d**
you**'d**
they**'d**

head¹ /hed; hɛd/ *noun* 名词
1 the part of your body above your neck, that has your eyes, ears, nose and mouth in it 头；头部: *She turned her head to look at me.* 她转过头来看着我。☞ picture on page C2 见第C2页图
2 what you use for thinking 头脑；脑海: *A strange thought came into his head.* 他脑海里产生了一个奇怪的念头。
3 the top, front or most important part 顶端；前面；最重要的部分: *She sat at the head of the table.* 她坐在桌子的上座一端。
4 the most important person 最重要的人；首脑；首领；首长: *The Pope is the head of the Roman Catholic church.* 教皇是天主教的元首。
5 heads (plural 复数) the side of a coin that has the head of a person on it 漫儿，漫面（硬币有人头像的一面）✪ You say **heads or tails** when you are throwing a coin in the air to decide something, for example who will start a game. 掷硬币做决定（如比赛谁先开始）时，说"要字儿，要漫儿（**heads or tails**）"。
a head, per head for one person 对于每个人: *The meal cost £12 a head.* 这顿饭每人12英镑。
go to your head make you too pleased with yourself 使自己过于得意；冲昏头脑: *Winning a prize for his painting went to his head, and he began to think he was a great artist.* 他的画儿得了奖他就头脑发胀，以为自己成了大艺术家了。
head first with your head before the rest of your body 从头部开始

✪ In Britain, you **nod** your head (move it up and down) to say 'yes' or to show that you agree, and you **shake** your head (move it from side to side) to say 'no' or to show that you disagree.在英国，点头（表示同意）叫做 **nod** your head，摇头（表示不同意）叫做 **shake** your head。

head² /hed; hɛd/ *verb* 动词 (**heads, heading, headed**)
1 be at the front or top of a group 在一群体的前部或顶端: *Michael's name heads the list.* 迈克尔的名字在名单的最上端。
2 hit a ball with your head 用头部顶球
head for go towards a place 向某处行进: *Let's head for home.* 咱们回家吧。
headache /'hedeɪk; 'hɛdˌek/ *noun* 名词
a pain in your head 头痛: *I've got a headache.* 我头疼。
heading /'hedɪŋ; 'hɛdɪŋ/ *noun* 名词
the words at the top of a piece of writing

to show what it is about; a title 在篇章上端标明其内容的简短语句；标题

headlight /'hedlaɪt; 'hɛd,laɪt/, **headlamp** /'hedlæmp; 'hɛd,læmp/ *noun* 名词
one of the two big strong lights on the front of a car（汽车的）前灯 ☞ picture at **car** 见 **car** 词条插图

headline /'hedlaɪn; 'hɛd,laɪn/ *noun* 名词
1 words in big letters at the top of a newspaper story（报纸页首的）大字标题
2 the headlines (plural 复数) the most important news on radio or television（无线电或电视广播的）新闻内容提要: *Here are the news headlines.* 以下是新闻内容提要。

headmaster /,hed'mɑːstə(r); 'hɛd'mæstɚ/ *noun* 名词
a man who is in charge of a school（中小学的）（男）校长

headmistress /,hed'mɪstrəs; 'hɛd'mɪstrɪs/ *noun* 名词 (*plural* 复数作 **headmistresses**)
a woman who is in charge of a school（中小学的）（女）校长

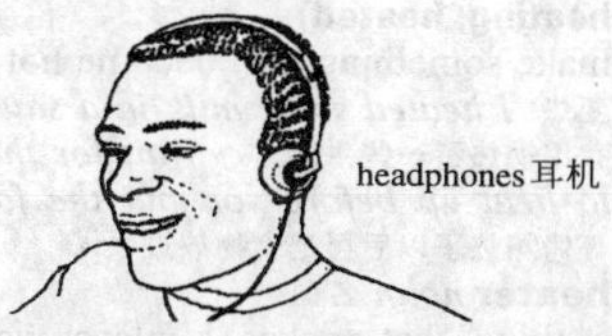
headphones 耳机

headphones /'hedfəʊnz; 'hɛd,fonz/ *noun* 名词 (plural 复数)
things that you put over your head and ears for listening to a radio, cassette player, etc 头戴式收话器；耳机

headquarters /,hed'kwɔːtəz; 'hɛd'kwɔrtɚz/ *noun* 名词 (plural 复数)
the main offices where the leaders work 总部；司令部；指挥部: *The company's headquarters are in London.* 这家公司的总公司在伦敦。✪ The short form is **HQ**. 缩略式是 **HQ**。

headway /'hedweɪ; 'hɛd,we/ *noun* 名词 (no plural 无复数)
make headway go forward 向前行进；取得进步或进展: *We haven't made much headway in our discussions.* 我们的讨论无大进展。

heal /hiːl; hil/ *verb* 动词 (**heals, healing, healed** /hiːld; hild/)
become well again; make something well again（使）康复: *The cut on his leg healed slowly.* 他腿上的伤口慢慢痊愈了。

health /helθ; hɛlθ/ *noun* 名词 (no plural 无复数)
how well your body is; how you are 健康；健康状况: *Smoking is bad for your health.* 吸烟对健康不利。

healthy /'helθi; 'hɛlθɪ/ *adjective* 形容词 (**healthier, healthiest**)
1 well; not ill 健康的；强健的: *healthy children* 健康的儿童
2 that helps to make or keep you well 有益健康的: *healthy food* 保健食品
✪ opposite 反义词: **unhealthy**

heap /hiːp; hip/ *noun* 名词
1 a lot of things on top of one another in an untidy way; a large amount of something 堆: *She left her clothes in a heap on the floor.* 她把衣服扔在地板上堆成一堆。
2 heaps (plural 复数) a lot 许多；大量: *heaps of time* 充裕的时间

heap *verb* 动词 (**heaps, heaping, heaped** /hiːpt; hipt/)
put a lot of things on top of one another 堆积；堆聚: *She heaped food onto my plate.* 她把食物堆在我的盘子上。

hear /hɪə(r); hɪr/ *verb* 动词 (**hears, hearing, heard** /hɜːd; hɝd/, **has heard**)
1 get sounds with your ears 听到: *Can you hear that noise?* 你听见那个声音了吗？◇ *I heard somebody laughing in the next room.* 我听见隔壁有笑声。

hear or **listen**? 用 **hear** 还是用 **listen**？

Hear and **listen** are used in different ways. ✻ **hear** 和 **listen** 的用法不同。
When you **hear** something, sounds come to your ears ✻ **hear** 指客观上声音传到耳朵里:

I **heard** *the door close.* 我听到关门的声音。

When you **listen to** something, you are trying to hear it ✻ **listen to** 指主观上想要去听:

I **listen to** *the radio every morning.* 我每天早晨收听无线电广播。

2 learn about something with your ears 听到而得知某事物: *Have you heard the news?* 你听到那个消息了吗？

hear from somebody get a letter or a phone call from somebody 接获某人的信件或电话: *Have you heard from your sister?* 你收到你妹妹的信了吗？

hear of somebody or 或 **something** know about somebody or something 听到或知道某人或某事物: *Who is he? I've never heard of him.* 他是谁？我从来没听说过他。

will not hear of something will not agree to something 不同意某事物: *My father wouldn't hear of me paying for the meal.* 我父亲不让我给饭钱。

hearing /'hɪərɪŋ; 'hɪrɪŋ/ *noun* 名词 (no plural 无复数)

the power to hear 听力: *Speak louder—her hearing isn't very good.* 说话大点声——她听力不大好。

heart /hɑ:t; hɑrt/ *noun* 名词

1 the part of a person's or animal's body that makes the blood go round inside 心；心脏: *Your heart beats faster when you run.* 一跑起来心脏跳动就快。☞ picture on page C2 见第C2页图

2 your feelings 心地；心肠: *She has a kind heart.* 她心地善良。

3 the centre; the middle part 中心；中央；中间的部分: *They live in the heart of the countryside.* 他们住在郊外青树翠蔓之中。

4 the shape ♥ 心形 ♥

5 hearts (plural 复数) the playing-cards that have red shapes like hearts on them (纸牌的)红桃: *the six of hearts* 红桃六

break somebody's heart make somebody very sad 使某人很伤心: *It broke his heart when his wife died.* 他妻子死时他肝肠痛断。

by heart so that you know every word 记住每一个字；背诵: *I have learned the poem by heart.* 我把这首诗背下来了。

lose heart stop hoping 失望: *Don't lose heart—you can still win if you try.* 别灰心——你再加把劲还是能赢的。

your heart sinks you suddenly feel unhappy 突然感到不愉快: *My heart sank when I saw the first question on the exam paper.* 我一看到试卷上的第一题心就凉了。

heart attack /'hɑ:t ətæk; 'hɑrt əˌtæk/ *noun* 名词

a sudden dangerous illness, when your heart stops working properly 心脏病: *She had a heart attack and died.* 她患心脏病死去。

heartbeat /'hɑ:tbi:t; 'hɑrtˌbit/ *noun* 名词

the movement or sound of your heart as it pushes blood around your body 心搏；心跳声: *The doctor listened to my heartbeat.* 医生听了听我的心脏。

heartless /'hɑ:tləs; 'hɑrtlɪs/ *adjective* 形容词

not kind; cruel 无情的；残忍的

heat /hi:t; hit/ *noun* 名词

1 (no plural 无复数) the feeling of something hot 热: *the heat of the sun* 太阳的热力

2 (*plural* 复数作 **heats**) one of the first parts of a race or competition (比赛的)预赛: *The winner of this heat will play in the final.* 这次预赛的优胜者可进入决赛。

heat, heat up *verb* 动词 (**heats, heating, heated**)

make something hot; become hot 加热；变热: *I heated some milk in a saucepan.* 我用锅热了一些牛奶。◇ *Wait for the oven to heat up before you put the food in.* 等烤箱热了以后再把食物放进去。

heater *noun* 名词

a thing that makes a place warm or heats water 把处所或水加热的装置；加热器；炉子: *Switch on the heater if you feel cold.* 要是觉得冷就把暖气打开。◇ *a water-heater* 热水器

heath /hi:θ; hiθ/ *noun* 名词

a big piece of wild land where there are no farms 荒地

heating /'hi:tɪŋ; 'hitɪŋ/ *noun* 名词 (no plural 无复数)

the way you make a building warm (建筑物的)供热系统；供热装置: *What kind of heating do you have?* 你们使用什么暖气设备？

heave /hi:v; hiv/ *verb* 动词 (**heaves, heaving, heaved** /hi:vd; hivd/)

lift or pull something heavy 提；拉；拖；拽重物: *We heaved the suitcase up the stairs.* 我们把衣箱拖到了楼梯上。

heaven /'hevn; 'hɛvən/ *noun* 名词 (no plural 无复数)

Many people believe that God lives in heaven and that good people go to heaven when they die.（很多人认为）上帝所在的地方和好人死后去的地方；天堂；天国 ☞ Look at **hell**. 见 **hell**。

Good Heavens! words that you use to show surprise 表示惊奇的词语：*Good Heavens! I've won £100!* 老天爷！我赢了100英镑！

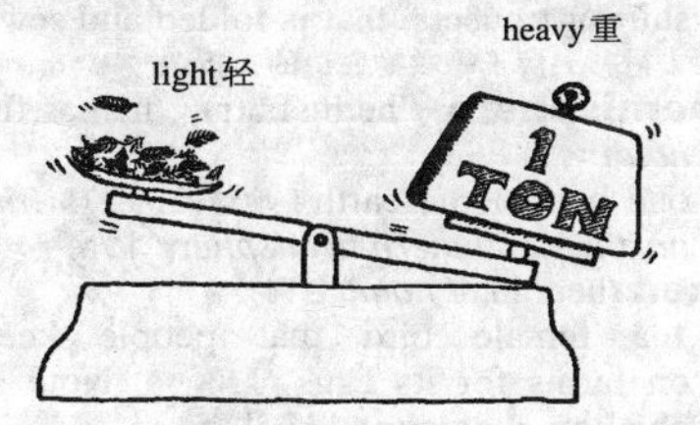

heavy /'hevi; 'hɛvɪ/ *adjective* 形容词 (**heavier, heaviest**)

1 with a lot of weight, so it is difficult to lift or move 难以抬起或移动的；重的：*I can't carry this bag — it's too heavy.* 我拿不动这个袋子——太重了。

2 larger, stronger or more than usual（比一般的）大的，强的，多的：*heavy rain* 大雨 ◇ *The traffic was very heavy this morning.* 今天上午路上非常拥挤。

✪ opposite 反义词：**light**

heavy metal /ˌhevi 'metl; 'hɛvɪ 'mɛtl̩/ *noun* 名词 (no plural 无复数)

a kind of very loud rock music 一种音量很大的摇滚乐

heavily /'hevəli; 'hɛvl̩ɪ/ *adverb* 副词

It was raining heavily. 雨下得很大。

hectare /'hekteə(r); 'hɛktɛr/ *noun* 名词

a measure of land. There are 10 000 **square metres** in a hectare. 公顷（测量土地的单位，等于10 000平方米。平方米叫做 **square metre**）

hectic /'hektɪk; 'hɛktɪk/ *adjective* 形容词

very busy 非常忙的；忙碌的：*I had a hectic day at work.* 我今天工作特别忙。

he'd /hi:d; hid/

1 = he had

2 = he would

hedge /hedʒ; hɛdʒ/ *noun* 名词

a line of small trees that makes a kind of wall around a garden or field（花园或场地周围的）树篱

hedgehog /'hedʒhɒg; 'hɛdʒˌhɔg/ *noun* 名词

a small animal covered with hairs that are like sharp needles 刺猬

heel /hi:l; hil/ *noun* 名词

1 the back part of your foot（脚的）后跟 ☞ picture on page C2 见第C2页图

2 the back part of a shoe under the heel of your foot（鞋的）后跟

3 the part of a sock that covers the heel of your foot（袜子的）后跟

height /haɪt; haɪt/ *noun* 名词

1 (*plural* 复数作 **heights**) how far it is from the bottom to the top of somebody or something 高度；身高：*What is the height of this mountain?* 这座山有多高？◇ *The wall is two metres in height.* 这堵墙有两米高。◇ *She asked me my height, weight and age.* 她问了问我的身高、体重和年龄。☞ picture on page C5 见第C5页图

2 (*plural* 复数作 **heights**) a high place 高处：*I'm afraid of heights.* 我怕登高。

3 (no plural 无复数) the strongest or most important part of something（某事物的）最强的或最重要的部分；顶点；极度：*the height of summer* 盛夏时节

heir /eə(r); ɛr/ *noun* 名词

a person who receives money, goods, etc when another person dies 继承人：*Prince Charles is Queen Elizabeth's heir.* 查尔斯王储是伊丽莎白女王的继承人。

heiress /'eəres; 'ɛrɪs/ *noun* 名词 (*plural* 复数作 **heiresses**)

an heir who is a woman（女）继承人

held *form of* **hold**[1] ＊ **hold**[1] 的不同形式

helicopter 直升飞机

helicopter /'helɪkɒptə(r); 'hɛlɪˌkɑptɚ/ *noun* 名词

a kind of small aircraft that can go straight up in the air. It has long metal parts on top that turn to help it fly. 直升飞机

hell /hel; hɛl/ *noun* 名词 (no plural 无复数)

Some people believe that bad people go

H

to hell when they die.（有的人认为）坏人死后去的地方；地狱。☞ Look at **heaven**. 见 **heaven**。

he'll /hi:l; hil/ = **he will**

hello /hə'ləʊ; hə'lo/
a word that you say when you meet somebody or when you answer the telephone 与某人打招呼或接电话时的用语；喂

helmet /'helmɪt; 'hɛlmɪt/ *noun* 名词
a hard hat that keeps your head safe 头盔: *Motor cyclists in Britain must wear helmets.* 在英国骑摩托车必须戴头盔。

help /help; hɛlp/ *verb* 动词 (**helps, helping, helped** /helpt; hɛlpt/)
1 do something useful for somebody; make somebody's work easier 帮助某人；协助；援助: *Will you help me with the washing-up?* 你帮助我刷碗好吗？◇ *She helped me to carry the box.* 她帮我提着箱子。
2 a word that you shout when you are in danger 遇危险时喊叫的用语；救命: *Help! I can't swim!* 救命！我不会游泳！
can't help If you can't help doing something, you can't stop yourself doing it 控制不住自己而做某事: *It was so funny that I couldn't help laughing.* 太有意思了，我忍不住笑了起来。
help yourself take what you want 随便取用自己想要的东西: *Help yourself to a drink.* 您自己随便取用饮品吧。◇ *'Can I have a sandwich?' 'Of course. Help yourself!'* "我吃一份三明治行吗？""太可以了。请便！"
help *noun* 名词 (no plural 无复数)
1 helping somebody（对某人的）帮助；协助: *Thank you for all your help.* 感谢您大力协助。◇ *Do you need any help?* 您需要帮忙吗？
2 a person or thing that helps 提供帮助的人或事物；助手；帮手: *He was a great help to me when I was ill.* 我生病的时候他可帮了大忙了。

helpful /'helpfl; 'hɛlpfəl/ *adjective* 形容词
A person or thing that is helpful gives help 有帮助的；有用的: *The woman in the shop was very helpful.* 商店里的那个女子非常热心。◇ *helpful advice* 有益的建议 ✪ opposite 反义词: **unhelpful**

helping /'helpɪŋ; 'hɛlpɪŋ/ *noun* 名词
the amount of food on your plate 一盘食物的量: *I had a big helping of pie.* 我吃了一大盘的馅饼。

helpless /'helpləs; 'hɛlplɪs/ *adjective* 形容词
not able to do things without help 不能自助的: *Babies are totally helpless.* 幼儿完全不能照顾自己。

hem /hem; hɛm/ *noun* 名词
the bottom edge of something like a shirt or trousers, that is folded and sewn（衬衫、裤子等衣物底边的）折边

hemisphere /'hemɪsfɪə(r); 'hɛməs,fɪr/ *noun* 名词
one half of the earth（地球的）半球: *the northern/southern hemisphere* 北/南半球

hen /hen; hɛn/ *noun* 名词
1 a female bird that people keep on farms for its eggs 母鸡 ☞ Note at **chicken** 见 **chicken** 词条注释
2 any female bird（任何的）雌鸟
✪ A male bird is a **cock**. 雄鸟叫做 **cock**。

her[1] /hɜ:(r); hɝ/ *pronoun* 代词 (*plural* 复数作 **them**)
a word that shows a woman or a girl（用作宾语）（指女性）她；（指雌性动物）它: *Tell Jenny that I'll see her tonight.* 告诉珍妮我今天晚上见她。◇ *I wrote to her yesterday.* 我昨天给她写了封信。

her[2] /hɜ:(r); hɝ/ *adjective* 形容词
the woman or girl that you have just talked about（指女性）她的；（指雌性动物）它的: *That's her book.* 那是她的书。◇ *Jill has hurt her leg.* 吉尔把她的腿弄伤了。

herb /hɜ:b; ɝb/ *noun* 名词
a plant that people use to make food taste good, or in medicine 用做佐料或药物的植物；药草；芳草

herd /hɜ:d; hɝd/ *noun* 名词
a big group of animals of the same kind（同类动物的）一群: *a herd of cows* 一群牛 ◇ *a herd of elephants* 一群象

here /hɪə(r); hɪr/ *adverb* 副词
in, at or to this place 在这里；向这里: *Your glasses are here.* 您的眼镜在这儿呢。◇ *Come here, please.* 请到这里来。◇ *Here's my car.* 我的车在这儿呢。◇ *Where's Bill? Oh, here he is.* 比尔在哪儿呢？噢，他在这儿呢。
here and there in different places 在各处；到处: *There were groups of people here and there along the beach.* 海滩上到处都是一群群的人。

here goes words that you say before you do something exciting or dangerous 在做刺激或惊险事情之前说的话: *'Here goes,' said Susan, and jumped into the river.* 苏珊说"瞧着啊"，说完就跳进河里去了。

here you are words that you say when you give something to somebody 把某物给某人时说的话: *'Can I borrow a pen, please?' 'Yes, here you are.'* "请问，我借枝钢笔行吗？""行，给你"。

here's /hɪəz; hɪrz/ = **here is**

hero /ˈhɪərəʊ; ˈhɪro/ *noun* 名词 (*plural* 复数作 **heroes**)

1 a person who has done something brave or good 做了勇敢的事或好事的人；英雄: *Everybody said that Mark was a hero after he rescued his sister from the fire.* 马克从火场中把他妹妹救出来以后，大家都说他是个勇士。

2 the most important man or boy in a book, play or film（书、戏剧或影片中的）男主角；男主人公

heroic /hɪˈrəʊɪk; hɪˈro·ɪk/ *adjective* 形容词

very brave 英勇的

heroin /ˈherəʊɪn; ˈhɛro·ɪn/ *noun* 名词 (no plural 无复数)

a very strong drug that can be dangerous 海洛因

heroine /ˈherəʊɪn; ˈhɛro·ɪn/ *noun* 名词

1 a woman who has done something brave or good 做了勇敢的事或好事的女子；女英雄

2 the most important woman or girl in a book, play or film（书、戏剧或影片中的）女主角；女主人公

hers /hɜːz; hɝz/ *pronoun* 代词

something that belongs to her（指女性）她的；（指雌性动物）它的: *Gina says this book is hers.* 吉纳说这本书是她的。◇ *Are these keys hers?* 这些钥匙是她的吗？

herself /hɜːˈself; hɝˈsɛlf/ *pronoun* 代词 (*plural* 复数作 **themselves** /ðəmˈselvz; ðəmˈsɛlvz/)

1 a word that shows the same woman or girl that you have just talked about（用作反身代词）（指女性）她自己；（指雌性动物）它自己: *She fell and hurt herself.* 她摔伤了。

2 a word that makes 'she' stronger（用作反身强调代词）（指女性）她自己，她本人；（指雌性动物）它自己: *'Who told you that Jenny was married?' 'She told me herself.'* "谁告诉你珍妮结婚了？""她自己告诉我的。"

by herself **1** alone; without other people 她独自地；她单独地（没有别人相伴）: *She lives by herself.* 她独自一人生活。 **2** without help 她独自地；她单独地（没有别人帮助）: *She can carry the box by herself.* 她自己能拿得动这个箱子。

he's /hiːz; hiz/

1 = **he is**

2 = **he has**

hesitate /ˈhezɪteɪt; ˈhɛzəˌtet/ *verb* 动词 (**hesitates, hesitating, hesitated**)

stop for a moment before you do or say something because you are not sure about it 犹豫；踌躇: *He hesitated before answering the question.* 他犹豫了一下才回答这个问题。

hesitation /ˌhezɪˈteɪʃn; ˌhɛzəˈteʃən/ *noun* 名词 (no plural 无复数)

They agreed without hesitation. 他们毫不犹豫地同意了。

hexagon /ˈheksəgən; ˈhɛksəˌgɑn/ *noun* 名词

a shape with six sides 六边形；六角形

hexagonal /heksˈægənl; hɛksˈægənḷ/ *adjective* 形容词

with six sides 六边形的；六角形的: *a hexagonal box* 六边形的盒子

hey /heɪ; he/

a word that you shout to make somebody listen to you, or when you are surprised 让别人听你说话或表示惊奇的用语；喂；嘿: *Hey! Where are you going?* 嘿！你上哪儿去？

hi /haɪ; haɪ/

a word that you say when you meet somebody; hello 遇见某人时打招呼的用语；喂；嘿: *Hi Tony! How are you?* 喂，托尼！你好吗？

hiccup, hiccough /ˈhɪkʌp; ˈhɪkʌp/ *noun* 名词

a sudden noise that you make in your throat. You sometimes get hiccups when you have eaten or drunk too quickly. 嗝；呃逆（喉咙突然发出的声音，有时因吃喝过急所致。）

hide /haɪd; haɪd/ *verb* 动词 (**hides, hiding, hid** /hɪd; hɪd/, **has hidden** /ˈhɪdn; ˈhɪdṇ/)

1 put something where people cannot

H

find it 隐藏某物（不让别人发现）: *I hid the money under the bed.* 我把钱藏在床底下了。

2 be or get in a place where people cannot see or find you 躲藏起来（使别人看不见你或找不到你）: *Somebody was hiding behind the door.* 有人藏在门后边。

3 not tell or show something to somebody 不把某事物告诉某人；不向某人表露某事物: *She tried to hide her feelings.* 她尽力不使感情外露。

hide-and-seek /ˌhaɪdnˈsiːk; ˈhaɪdn̩ˈsik/ *noun* 名词 (no plural 无复数)

a game that children play. Some children hide and one child tries to find them. 捉迷藏（儿童游戏）

hideous /ˈhɪdiəs; ˈhɪdɪəs/ *adjective* 形容词

very ugly 丑陋的: *That shirt is hideous!* 那件衬衫真难看！

hiding /ˈhaɪdɪŋ; ˈhaɪdɪŋ/ *noun* 名词 (no plural 无复数)

be in hiding, go into hiding be in, or go into a place where people will not find you 躲藏起来（使别人找不到你）: *The prisoners escaped and went into hiding.* 犯人越狱后都躲藏起来了。

hi-fi /ˈhaɪ faɪ; ˈhaɪˈfaɪ/ *noun* 名词

a machine for playing records, cassettes and compact discs 高保真度唱机（可播放普通唱片、录音带、激光唱片等）

high /haɪ; haɪ/ *adjective* 形容词 (**higher**, **highest**)

1 Something that is high goes up a long way（指物体从下向上距离）高的: *a high wall* 高墙 ◇ *Mount Everest is the highest mountain in the world.* 埃佛勒斯峰（即珠穆朗玛峰）是世界上最高的山峰。✪ opposite 反义词: **low** ☞ picture on page C26 见第C26页图

2 You use 'high' to say or ask how far something is from the bottom to the top 表示或询问某物有多高的词: *The table is 80 cm high.* 这张桌子80厘米高。☞ picture on page C5 见第C5页图

✪ We use **tall**, not **high**, to talk about people 指人的高矮用 **tall** 字而不用 **high** 字: *How tall are you?* 你身高多少？◇ *He's 1.72 metres tall.* 他身高1.72米。

3 far from the ground（指离地面远）高的: *a high shelf* 高的搁板

4 great（指度数大）高的: *The car was travelling at high speed.* 那辆汽车正以高速行驶。◇ *high temperatures* 高温

5 at the top of sound; not deep（指音调）高的: *I heard the high voice of a child.* 我听到小孩儿的尖嗓音。

☞ Look at **low**. 见 **low** 。

high *adverb* 副词

a long way above the ground（指离地面远）高: *The plane flew high above the clouds.* 飞机在云层上飞行。

high and low everywhere 到处；各处: *I've looked high and low for my keys, but I can't find them anywhere.* 我到处找钥匙，哪儿都找不到。

high-jump /ˈhaɪ dʒʌmp; ˈhaɪˌdʒʌmp/ *noun* 名词 (no plural 无复数)

a sport where people jump over a high bar 跳高（运动）

highlands /ˈhaɪləndz; ˈhaɪləndz/ *noun* 名词 (plural 复数)

the part of a country with hills and mountains 有丘陵和山的地区；高地: *the Scottish Highlands* 苏格兰高地

highlight /ˈhaɪlaɪt; ˈhaɪˌlaɪt/ *noun* 名词

the best or most exciting part of something 最好的或最精彩的部分: *The highlight of our holiday was a visit to the palace.* 我们假期最有意思的活动就是参观那座宫殿。

highly /ˈhaɪli; ˈhaɪlɪ/ *adverb* 副词

1 very or very much 很；非常；高度地: *Their children are highly intelligent.* 他们的孩子都特别聪明。◇ *She has a highly paid job.* 她的工作薪水非常高。

2 very well 非常好: *I think very highly of your work* (= I think it is very good). 我认为你的工作好极了。

Highness /ˈhaɪnəs; ˈhaɪnɪs/ *noun* 名词 (*plural* 复数作 **Highnesses**)

a word that you use when speaking to or about a royal person（用作对皇室成员的尊称）殿下: *His Highness the Prince of Wales* 威尔士亲王殿下

high school /ˈhaɪ skuːl; ˈhaɪ ˌskul/ *noun* 名词

1 a school in Britain for children between the ages of 11 and 18（英国11至18岁学生就读的）中学

2 a school in the USA for children between the ages of 15 and 18（美国15至18岁学生就读的）中学

high street /ˈhaɪ striːt; ˈhaɪ ˌstrit/ *noun* 名词

the biggest or most important street in a town（一城镇中最大的或最主要的）大街: *There is a bookshop on the High Street.* 在最主要的大街上有个书店。

highway /'haɪweɪ; 'haɪˌwe/ *noun* 名词
a big road between towns（城镇之间的）公路 ✪ **Highway** is used mostly in American English. ✳ **highway** 一词多用于美式英语。

hijack /'haɪdʒæk; 'haɪˌdʒæk/ *verb* 动词 (**hijacks, hijacking, hijacked** /'haɪdʒækt; 'haɪˌdʒækt/)
take control of an aeroplane or a car and make the pilot or driver take you somewhere 劫持飞机或汽车
hijacker *noun* 名词
a person who hijacks a plane or car 劫持飞机或汽车的人

hill /hɪl; hɪl/ *noun* 名词
a high piece of land that is not as high as a mountain 山冈；小山: *I pushed my bike up the hill.* 我推着自行车上山坡。◇ *Their house is at the top of the hill.* 他们家在那座山顶上。☞ Look also at **uphill** and **downhill**. 另见 **uphill** 和 **downhill**。
hilly *adjective* 形容词 (**hillier, hilliest**)
with a lot of hills 有很多小山的: *The countryside is very hilly where I live.* 我住的地方是丘陵地带。

him /hɪm; hɪm/ *pronoun* 代词 (*plural* 复数作 **them**)
a word that shows a man or boy（用作宾语）（指男性）他；（指雄性动物）它: *Where's Andy? I can't see him.* 安迪在哪儿呢？我找不着他。◇ *I spoke to him yesterday.* 我昨天和他谈过话。

himself /hɪm'self; hɪm'sɛlf/ *pronoun* 代词 (*plural* 复数作 **themselves** /ðəm'selvz; ðəm'sɛlvz/)
1 a word that shows the same man or boy that you have just talked about（用作反身代词）（指男性）他自己；（指雄性动物）它自己: *Paul looked at himself in the mirror.* 保罗照了照镜子。
2 a word that makes 'he' stronger（用作反身强调代词）（指男性）他自己，他本人；（指雄性动物）它自己: *Did he make this cake himself?* 这个蛋糕是他自己做的吗？
by himself **1** alone; without other people 他独自地；他单独地（没有别人相伴）: *Dad went shopping by himself.* 爸爸自己买东西去了。**2** without help 他独自地；他单独地（没有别人帮助）: *He did it by himself.* 他自己做的。

Hindu /'hɪndu:; 'hɪndu/ *noun* 名词
a person who follows one of the religions of India, called **Hinduism** 印度教徒（印度教叫做 **Hinduism**）

hinge /hɪndʒ; hɪndʒ/ *noun* 名词
a piece of metal that joins two sides of a box, door, etc together so that it can open and close 铰链；合叶（连接箱子、门等两个部分的金属片，使之可以开合）

hint /hɪnt; hɪnt/ *verb* 动词 (**hints, hinting, hinted**)
say something, but not in a direct way 暗示；示意: *Sarah looked at her watch, hinting that she wanted to go home.* 萨拉看了看手表，表示她要回家了。
hint *noun* 名词
1 something that you say, but not in a direct way 暗示；示意: *When he said he had no money, it was a hint that he wanted you to pay for his dinner.* 他说他没钱，意思是他希望你请他吃晚饭。
2 a small amount of something 少量的某事物: *There's a hint of garlic in this soup.* 这个汤里有点蒜味儿。

hip /hɪp; hɪp/ *noun* 名词
the place where your leg joins the side of your body 胯；髋部（人的两腿与躯干连接的部分）☞ picture on page C2 见第C2页图

hippopotamus /ˌhɪpə'pɒtəməs; ˌhɪpə'pɑtəməs/ *noun* 名词 (*plural* 复数作 **hippopotamuses** or 或 **hippopotami** /ˌhɪpə'pɒtəmaɪ; ˌhɪpə'pɑtəˌmaɪ/)
a large African animal with thick skin that lives near water 河马（产于非洲）✪ The short form is **hippo**. 缩略式是 **hippo**。

hire /'haɪə(r); haɪr/ *verb* 动词 (**hires, hiring, hired** /'haɪəd; haɪrd/)
1 pay to use something for a short time 付钱而短期使用某物；租用: *We hired a car when we were on holiday.* 我们度假的时候租了一辆汽车。
2 pay somebody to do a job for you 付钱让某人给自己做事；雇用: *We hired somebody to mend the roof.* 我们雇了个人来修理房顶。
hire out let somebody hire something from you 出租: *They hire out bicycles.* 他们出租自行车。

H

hire *noun* 名词 (no plural 无复数)
Have you got any boats for hire? 您这儿有小船出租吗？

his /hɪz; hɪz/ *adjective* 形容词
of him（指男性）他的；（指雄性动物）它的: *John came with his sister.* 约翰跟他妹妹一起来了。◇ *He has hurt his arm.* 他把胳臂弄伤了。

his *pronoun* 代词
something that belongs to him（指男性）他的；（指雄性动物）它的: *Are these books yours or his?* 这些书是你的还是他的？

hiss /hɪs; hɪs/ *verb* 动词 (**hisses**, **hissing**, **hissed** /hɪst; hɪst/)
make a noise like a very long **S** 发出很长的"嘶"声: *The cat hissed at me.* 猫对我发出"嘶嘶"声。

hiss *noun* 名词 (*plural* 复数作 **hisses**)
the hiss of steam 蒸汽发出的"嘶嘶"声

historic /hɪˈstɒrɪk; hɪsˈtɔrɪk/ *adjective* 形容词
important in history 历史上重要的；有历史意义的: *It was a historic moment when man first walked on the moon.* 人类初次在月球上行走，这是具有历史意义的时刻。

historical /hɪˈstɒrɪkl; hɪsˈtɔrɪkḷ/ *adjective* 形容词
of or about past times 历史的；关于历史的: *She writes historical novels.* 她写的是历史小说。

history /ˈhɪstri; ˈhɪstrɪ/ *noun* 名词 (no plural 无复数)
1 the study of things that happened in the past 历史学: *History is my favourite subject at school.* 我最喜欢上历史课了。
2 all the things that happened in the past 历史: *It was an important moment in history.* 那是历史上的重要时刻。

hit[1] /hɪt; hɪt/ *verb* 动词 (**hits**, **hitting**, **hit**, **has hit**)
touch somebody or something hard 重重触及某人或某物；打；击；碰；撞: *He hit me on the head with a book.* 他用书打我的头。◇ *The car hit a wall.* 汽车撞墙了。

hit[2] /hɪt; hɪt/ *noun* 名词
1 touching somebody or something hard 重重触及某人或某物；打；击；碰；撞: *That was a good hit!* (in a game of cricket or baseball, for example) 打得好！（例如板球或棒球比赛中）
2 a person or a thing that a lot of people like 很多人喜爱的人或事物: *This song was a hit in America.* 这首歌在美国风靡一时。

hitchhike /ˈhɪtʃhaɪk; ˈhɪtʃˌhaɪk/, **hitch** *verb* 动词 (**hitchhikes**, **hitchhiking**, **hitchhiked** /ˈhɪtʃhaɪkt; ˈhɪtʃˌhaɪkt/, **hitches**, **hitching**, **hitched** /hɪtʃt; hɪtʃt/)
travel by asking for free rides in cars and lorries 经要求免费乘搭他人的轿车或卡车；搭便车: *We hitchhiked across Europe.* 我们搭便车横贯欧洲。

hitchhiker *noun* 名词
a person who hitchhikes 搭便车的人

hive /haɪv; haɪv/ *noun* 名词
a box where bees live 蜂箱；蜂房

hoard /hɔːd; hɔrd/ *noun* 名词
a secret store of something, for example food or money 秘密储藏的东西（例如食物或钱）

hoard *verb* 动词 (**hoards**, **hoarding**, **hoarded**)
save and keep things secretly 秘密存储东西: *The old man hoarded the money in a box under his bed.* 老翁把钱放在盒子里藏在床底下。

hoarse /hɔːs; hɔrs/ *adjective* 形容词
If your voice is hoarse, it is rough and quiet, for example because you have a cold.（指嗓音）嘶哑的（如因感冒）

hoax /həʊks; hoks/ *noun* 名词 (*plural* 复数作 **hoaxes**)
a trick that makes somebody believe something that is not true 使某人信以为真的把戏；恶作剧: *There wasn't really a bomb in the station—it was a hoax.* 车站并没有炸弹——只是一场恶作剧。

hobby /ˈhɒbi; ˈhɑbɪ/ *noun* 名词 (*plural* 复数作 **hobbies**)
something that you like doing when you are not working 业余爱好: *My hobbies are reading and swimming.* 我的业余爱好是看书和游泳。

hockey /ˈhɒki; ˈhɑkɪ/ *noun* 名词 (no plural 无复数)
a game for two teams of eleven players who hit a small ball with long curved sticks on a field (called a **pitch**) 曲棍球（球场叫做 **pitch**）

hold[1] /həʊld; hold/ *verb* 动词 (**holds**, **holding**, **held** /held; hɛld/, **has held**)
1 have something in your hand or arms 用手或用手臂持有某物；握；抱；搂: *She was*

holding a gun. 她拿着枪。◇ *He held the baby in his arms.* 他抱着孩子。

2 keep something in a certain way 保持某状况: *Hold your hand up.* 把手举起来。

3 have space for a certain number or amount 有容纳某数量的空间；装；盛: *The car holds five people.* 这辆汽车能坐五个人。

4 make something happen 使某事物发生: *The meeting was held in the town hall.* 会议是在城镇礼堂举行的。

5 have something 持有某物: *He holds a Swiss passport.* 他有瑞士护照。

hold somebody or 或 **something back** stop somebody or something from moving forwards 阻止某人或某事物前进: *The police held back the crowd.* 警察把人群拦住了。

Hold it! Wait! Don't move! 等一等！不要动！

hold on **1** wait 等一等: *Hold on, I'm coming.* 等一等，我这就来。 **2** not stop holding something tightly 抓住某物不放: *The child held on to her mother's hand.* 孩子紧紧抓住母亲的手。

hold up **1** make somebody or something late 使某人或某事物晚到: *The plane was held up for 40 minutes.* 飞机误点40分钟。**2** try to steal from a place, using a gun（用枪）抢劫某处: *Two men held up a bank in Bristol today.* 有两个男子今日持枪抢劫布里斯托尔一家银行。

hold² /həʊld; hold/ *noun* 名词 (no plural 无复数)

having something in your hand 用手拿住或握住某物: *Can you get hold of* (= take and hold) *the other end of the table and help me move it?* 你抬着桌子那一头帮我挪挪行吗？

get hold of somebody find somebody so that you can speak to them 找某人谈话: *I'm trying to get hold of Peter but he's not at home.* 我想找彼得谈谈，可是他不在家。

get hold of something find something 找某物: *I can't get hold of the book I need.* 我找不到我需要的那本书。

hold³ /həʊld; hold/ *noun* 名词

the part of a ship or an aeroplane where you keep the goods（轮船的或飞机的）货舱

hole /həʊl; hol/ *noun* 名词

an empty space or opening in something 洞；孔；坑；窟窿: *I'm going to dig a hole in the garden.* 我要在花园里挖一个坑。◇ *The dentist filled the hole in my tooth.* 牙医填好了我牙上的一个洞。◇ *My socks are full of holes.* 我袜子上净是窟窿。

holiday /'hɒlədeɪ; 'hɑlə,de/ *noun* 名词

a day or days when you do not go to work or school, and when you may go and stay away from home 假日；假期（不上班或不上学的一日或多日，也可以出门）: *The school holidays start next week.* 下星期学校就开始放假了。◇ *We're going to France for our summer holidays.* 我们打算到法国去过暑假。✪ A day when everybody in a country has a holiday is called a **bank holiday** or a **public holiday** in Britain. 在英国，全国的人都放假的公众假期叫做 **bank holiday** 或 **public holiday**。

on holiday not at work or school 不上班或不上学；放假: *Mrs Smith isn't here this week. She's on holiday.* 史密斯夫人这个星期不在这儿。她放假了。

hollow /'hɒləʊ; 'hɑlo/ *adjective* 形容词

with an empty space inside 中间空的；空心的: *A drum is hollow.* 鼓的中间是空的。

holly /'hɒli; 'hɑlɪ/ *noun* 名词

a tree that has leaves with a lot of sharp points, and red berries 冬青（树，叶子有尖，果实红色）✪ People often put holly in their houses at Christmas. 圣诞节常在家中摆设。

holy /'həʊli; 'holɪ/ *adjective* 形容词 (**holier**, **holiest**)

1 very special because it is about God or a god 关于上帝的；关于神的；神圣的: *The Bible is the holy book of Christians.* 《圣经》是基督徒的关于上帝的书。

2 A holy person lives a good and religious life.（指人）圣洁的；善良而有宗教信仰的

home¹ /həʊm; hom/ *noun* 名词

1 the place where you live 家: *Simon left home at the age of 18.* 西蒙18岁的时候离开家了。

2 a place where they look after people, for example children who have no parents, or old people 为需要受到照顾的人而设的机构（如孤儿院或养老院等）: *My grandmother lives in a home.* 我奶奶住在养老院里。

at home in your house or flat 在家: *I stayed at home yesterday.* 我昨天在家。◇ *Is Sara at home?* 萨拉在家吗？

home² /həʊm; hom/ *adverb* 副词
to the place where you live 回家；到家 ✪ Be careful! We do not use **to** before **home** 注意！**home** 字之前不要加 **to** 字: *Let's go home.* 咱们回家吧。◇ *What time did you arrive home last night?* 昨天晚上你几点钟回家的？

home³ /həʊm; hom/ *adjective* 形容词
of your home or your country 家的；国家的: *What is your home address?* 你家的地址在哪儿？

homeless /ˈhəʊmləs; ˈhomlɪs/ *adjective* 形容词
If you are homeless, you have nowhere to live 无家的: *The floods made many people homeless.* 闹水灾很多人无家可归。

home-made /ˌhəʊmˈmeɪd; ˈhomˈmed/ *adjective* 形容词
made in your house, not bought in a shop 自家做的（并非在商店买的）: *home-made bread* 自家做的面包

homesick /ˈhəʊmsɪk; ˈhomˌsɪk/ *adjective* 形容词
sad because you are away from home 因离家而难过的；想家的

homework /ˈhəʊmwɜːk; ˈhomˌwɝk/ *noun* 名词 (no plural 无复数)
work that a teacher gives to you to do at home（教师留给学生的）家庭作业；功课: *Have you done your French homework?* 你做法语作业了吗？☞ Note at **housework** 见 **housework** 词条注释

homosexual /ˌhəʊməˈsekʃuəl; ˌhoməˈsɛkʃuəl/ *adjective* 形容词
attracted to people of the same sex 同性恋的

honest /ˈɒnɪst; ˈɑnɪst/ *adjective* 形容词
A person who is honest says what is true and does not steal or cheat（指人）诚实的，老实的: *She's a very honest person.* 她非常诚实。◇ *Be honest—do you really like this dress?* 说实话——你是不是真喜欢这件连衣裙？✪ opposite 反义词: **dishonest**

honestly *adverb* 副词
Try to answer the questions honestly. 要老老实实回答问题。◇ *Honestly, I don't know where your money is.* 老实说，我并不知道你的钱在哪儿呢。

honesty /ˈɒnəsti; ˈɑnəstɪ/ *noun* 名词 (no plural 无复数)
being honest 诚实；老实

honey /ˈhʌni; ˈhʌnɪ/ *noun* 名词 (no plural 无复数)
the sweet food that bees make 蜂蜜

honeymoon /ˈhʌnimuːn; ˈhʌnɪˌmun/ *noun* 名词
a holiday that a man and woman have just after they get married 蜜月

honor *American English for* **honour** 美式英语，即 **honour**

honour /ˈɒnə(r); ˈɑnɚ/ *noun* 名词 (no plural 无复数)
1 something that makes you proud and pleased 光荣；荣幸: *It was a great honour to be invited to Buckingham Palace.* 受到邀请到白金汉宫是很大的光荣。
2 the respect from other people that a person or country gets because of something very good that they have done 荣誉: *They are fighting for the honour of their country.* 他们正在为祖国的荣誉而战斗。

in honour of somebody to show that you respect somebody 出于对某人的敬意: *There is a party tonight in honour of our visitors.* 今天有个欢迎来宾的晚会。

hood /hʊd; hʊd/ *noun* 名词
1 the part of a coat or jacket that covers your head and neck 风帽；兜帽
2 *American English for* **bonnet 1** 美式英语，即 **bonnet 1**

hood 风帽

hoof /huːf; huf/ *noun* 名词 (*plural* 复数作 **hoofs** or 或 **hooves** /huːvz; hʊvz/)
the hard part of the foot of horses and some other animals（马和其他动物的）蹄 ☞ picture at **horse** 见 **horse** 词条插图

hook /hʊk; hʊk/ *noun* 名词
a curved piece of metal or plastic for hanging things on, or for catching something 钩；钩子: *Hang your coat on that hook.* 您把大衣挂在那个钩子上。◇ *a fish-hook* 鱼钩

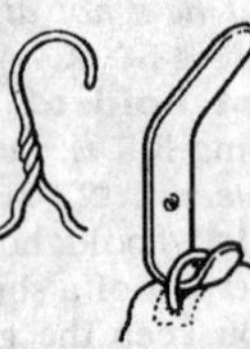
hooks 钩

off the hook If a telephone is off the hook, the part that you speak into (the **receiver**) is not in place so that the telephone will not ring. 电话的听筒（叫做 **receiver**）未放在原位上（铃不响）

hooligan /'hu:lɪgən; 'hulɪgən/ *noun* 名词
a young person who behaves in a noisy way and fights other people 小流氓；阿飞: *football hooligans* 足球迷小流氓

hoot /hu:t; hut/ *noun* 名词
the sound that an owl or a car's horn makes 猫头鹰的叫声或汽车的喇叭声
hoot *verb* 动词 (**hoots, hooting, hooted**)
make this sound 发出猫头鹰的叫声或汽车的喇叭声: *The driver hooted at the dog.* 司机对着狗响喇叭。

Hoover /'hu:və(r); 'huvɚ/ *noun* 名词
a machine that cleans carpets by sucking up dirt 吸尘器 ✪ **Hoover** is a trade mark. ✳ **Hoover** 是商标。

hooves *plural of* **hoof** ✳ **hoof** 的复数形式

hop /hɒp; hɑp/ *verb* 动词 (**hops, hopping, hopped** /hɒpt; hɑpt/)
1 jump on one foot 单脚跳
2 jump with two or all feet together 双足跳或齐足跳: *The frog hopped onto the stone.* 青蛙跳到石头上去了。

hop 单脚跳

hope¹ /həʊp; hop/ *noun* 名词
1 a feeling of wanting something to happen and thinking that it will 希望: *He hasn't worked very hard so there is not much hope that he will pass the exam.* 他没怎么用功，所以考及格的希望不大。
2 a person or thing that gives you hope 给人以希望的人或事物: *Can you help me? You're my only hope.* 你帮帮我行吗？我全靠你了。
give up hope stop thinking that what you want will happen 失去希望: *Don't give up hope. The letter may come tomorrow.* 不要觉得没希望了。也许明天信就来了。

hope² /həʊp; hop/ *verb* 动词 (**hopes, hoping, hoped** /həʊpt; hopt/)
want something that may happen 希望: *I hope you have a nice holiday.* 我希望你假期愉快。◇ *I hope to see you tomorrow.* 我希望明天能见您。◇ *We're hoping that Dave will come to the party.* 我们希望戴夫来参加聚会。◇ *She's hoping for a bike for her birthday.* 她希望过生日那天能得到一辆自行车。
I hope not I do not want that to happen 我希望不要发生那种事: *'Do you think it will rain?' 'I hope not.'* "你看能下雨吗？" "但愿别下。"
I hope so I want that to happen 我希望能有那种事: *'Will you be at the party?' 'I'm not sure—I hope so.'* "你参加那个聚会吗？" "我还说不好——我希望能去。"

hopeful /'həʊpfl; 'hopfəl/ *adjective* 形容词
If you are hopeful, you think that something that you want will happen（指人对某事物）怀着希望；抱有希望: *I'm hopeful about getting a job.* 我很希望能找到工作。
hopefully /'həʊpfəli; 'hopfəlɪ/ *adverb* 副词
1 in a hopeful way 怀着希望地；抱有希望地: *The cat looked hopefully at our plates.* 猫眼馋地看着我们的盘子。
2 I hope 我希望: *Hopefully he won't be late.* 但愿他别迟到。

hopeless /'həʊpləs; 'hoplɪs/ *adjective* 形容词
1 very bad 没有希望的；非常坏的: *I'm hopeless at tennis.* 我打网球简直糟糕透了。
2 useless 没用的；无益的: *It's hopeless trying to work when my brother is here—he's so noisy!* 我弟弟在这儿你就别想干活儿了——他太闹了。
hopelessly *adverb* 副词
We got hopelessly lost in the forest. 我们在森林里完全迷了路了。

horizon /hə'raɪzn; hə'raɪzn̩/ *noun* 名词
the line between the earth or sea and the sky 天跟地或海交界的线；地平线: *We could see a ship on the horizon.* 我们看见在天水交接处有一艘船。

horizontal /ˌhɒrɪ'zɒntl; ˌhɔrə'zɑntl̩/ *adjective* 形容词
Something that is horizontal goes from side to side, not up and down 水平的；横的: *a horizontal line* 水平线 ☞ picture on page C5 见第C5页图

H

horn /hɔ:n; hɔrn/ *noun* 名词

1 one of the hard pointed things that some animals have on their heads（某些动物的）角 ☞ picture at **goat** 见 **goat** 词条插图

2 a thing in a car, ship, etc that makes a loud sound to warn people（汽车、轮船等的）喇叭: *Don't sound your horn late at night.* 深夜开车不要按喇叭。

3 a musical instrument that you blow（乐器中的）号

horoscope /ˈhɒrəskəʊp; ˈhɔrəˌskop/ *noun* 名词

something that tells you what will happen, using the planets and your date of birth 占星术；星座运程（以星象和人的生日来预测某事物的方法）: *Have you read your horoscope today?* (in a newspaper, for example) 你今天看你的星座运程了吗？（例如在报纸上刊载的）

horrible /ˈhɒrəbl; ˈhɔrəbl̩/ *adjective* 形容词

1 Something that is horrible makes you feel afraid or shocked 可怕的；使人震惊的: *There was a horrible murder here last week.* 上星期这里发生了一起骇人听闻的凶杀案。

2 very bad 非常坏的；糟糕的: *What horrible weather!* 天气可真坏！

H

horrid /ˈhɒrɪd; ˈhɔrɪd/ *adjective* 形容词

very bad or unkind 非常坏的；不善良的: *Don't be so horrid!* 别那么凶！

horrify /ˈhɒrɪfaɪ; ˈhɔrəˌfaɪ/ *verb* 动词 (**horrifies**, **horrifying**, **horrified** /ˈhɒrɪfaɪd; ˈhɔrəˌfaɪd/, **has horrified**)

shock and frighten somebody 惊吓某人: *We were horrified by the photos of the car crash.* 我们看见那些汽车撞毁的照片，害怕极了。

horror /ˈhɒrə(r); ˈhɔrɚ/ *noun* 名词 (no plural 无复数)

a feeling of fear or shock 恐惧；惊恐: *They watched in horror as the child ran in front of the bus.* 他们一见孩子在公共汽车前面跑，吓得不知所措。

horror film /ˈhɒrə fɪlm; ˈhɔrɚ ˌfɪlm/ *noun* 名词

a film that shows frightening things 恐怖影片

horse /hɔ:s; hɔrs/ *noun* 名词

a big animal that can carry people and pull heavy things 马: *Can you ride a horse?* 你会骑马吗？✪ A young horse is called a **foal**. 幼小的马叫做 **foal**。

horse 马

hoof 蹄

on horseback sitting on a horse 骑马: *We saw a lot of policemen on horseback.* 我们看见很多骑马的警察。

horseshoe /ˈhɔ:s ʃu:; ˈhɔrsˌʃu/ *noun* 名词

a piece of metal like a U that a horse wears on its foot 马蹄铁；马掌

hose /həʊz; hoz/, **hose-pipe** /ˈhəʊzpaɪp; ˈhozˌpaɪp/ *noun* 名词

a long soft tube that you use to bring water, for example in the garden or when there is a fire（软的）水管；水龙（如花园中的或救火用的）

hospital /ˈhɒspɪtl; ˈhɑspɪtl̩/ *noun* 名词

a place where doctors and nurses look after people who are ill or hurt 医院: *My brother is in hospital—he's broken his leg.* 我哥哥住院了——他腿折了。◇ *The ambulance took her to hospital.* 救护车把她送到医院去了。

> ✪ A room in a hospital where people sleep is called a **ward**. 病房叫做 **ward**。A person who is staying in hospital is called a **patient**. 病人叫做 **patient**。

hospitality /ˌhɒspɪˈtæləti; ˌhɑspɪˈtælətɪ/ *noun* 名词 (no plural 无复数)

being friendly to people who are visiting you, and looking after them well 殷勤待客；好客: *We thanked them for their hospitality.* 我们感谢他们的盛情款待。

host /həʊst; host/ *noun* 名词

a person who invites guests, for example to a party（待客的）主人: *The host offered me a drink.* 主人向我敬酒。

hostage /ˈhɒstɪdʒ; ˈhɑstɪdʒ/ *noun* 名词

a prisoner that you keep until people give you what you want 人质（被拘留的人，用以迫使别人就范）: *The hijackers have freed all the hostages.* 劫持者把所有人质都放了。

hold somebody hostage keep somebody as a hostage 扣押某人作为人质: *They held his daughter hostage until he paid them the money.* 他们扣住他女儿当人质，逼他付款。

take somebody hostage catch somebody and keep them as a hostage 抓住某人作为人质

hostel /ˈhɒstl; ˈhɑstl̩/ *noun* 名词
a place like a cheap hotel where people can stay 类似廉价旅馆的住所；寄宿舍；招待所: *a youth hostel* 青年招待所

hostess /ˈhəʊstəs; ˈhostɪs/ *noun* 名词 (*plural* 复数作 **hostesses**)
a woman who invites guests, for example to a party（待客的）（女的）主人 ☞ Look also at **air-hostess**. 另见 **air-hostess**。

hostile /ˈhɒstaɪl; ˈhɑstl̩/ *adjective* 形容词
very unfriendly 极不友好的；含敌意的: *a hostile army* 敌军

hot /hɒt; hɑt/ *adjective* 形容词 (**hotter, hottest**)
1 not cold. A fire is hot 热的: *I'm hot. Can you open the window?* 我很热。您把窗户打开行吗？◇ *It's hot today, isn't it?* 今天很热，是吧？◇ *hot water* 热水 ☞ picture on page C27 见第C27页图
2 Food that is hot has a strong, burning taste（指食物）辣的: *a hot curry* 咖喱

hotel /həʊˈtel; hoˈtɛl/ *noun* 名词
a place where you pay to sleep and eat 旅馆；旅店: *I stayed at a hotel near the airport.* 我住在飞机场附近的一家旅馆里。

hour /ˈaʊə(r); aʊr/ *noun* 名词
1 a measure of time. There are 60 **minutes** in an hour 小时（一小时有60分钟，分叫做 **minute**）: *The journey took two hours.* 路上用了两个小时。◇ *I've been waiting for an hour.* 我等了一个小时。◇ *half an hour* 半小时
2 hours (plural 复数) the time when somebody is working, or when a shop or office is open（指人工作的或商店营业的或办公的）时间: *Our office hours are 9 a.m. to 5 p.m.* 我们的办公时间是上午9时至下午5时。

hourly /ˈaʊəli; ˈaʊrlɪ/ *adjective*, *adverb* 形容词，副词
that happens or comes once an hour 每小时一次（的）: *There is an hourly bus to Oxford.* 开往牛津的公共汽车每小时一班。

house 房子

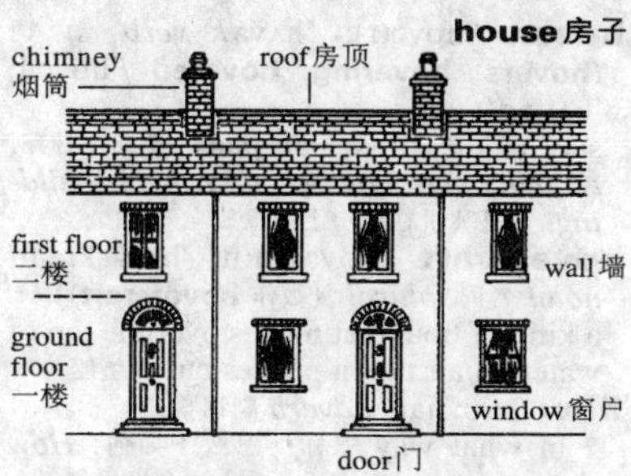

house /haʊs; haʊs/ *noun* 名词 (*plural* 复数作 **houses** /ˈhaʊzɪz; ˈhaʊzɪz/)
1 a building where a person or a family lives. A house has more than one floor（一个人或一家人居住的）楼房；（不止一层的）住宅，房子: *How many rooms are there in your house?* 你们家的小楼有几个房间？◇ *We're having dinner at Jenny's house tonight.* 我们今天晚上在珍妮家吃饭。☞ Look at **bungalow**, **cottage** and **flat**. 见 **bungalow**、**cottage** 和 **flat**。
2 a building for a special use 有某种用途的房子: *a warehouse* 货仓

housewife /ˈhaʊswaɪf; ˈhaʊsˌwaɪf/ *noun* 名词 (*plural* 复数作 **housewives** /ˈhaʊswaɪvz; ˈhaʊsˌwaɪvz/)
a woman who works for her family in the house 家庭主妇；家庭妇女

housework /ˈhaʊswɜːk; ˈhaʊsˌwɝk/ *noun* 名词 (no plural 无复数)
work that you do in your house, for example cleaning and washing 家务劳动（例如打扫卫生和洗衣服）✪ Be careful! Work that a teacher gives you to do at home is called **homework**. 注意！教师留的家庭作业叫做 **homework**。

housing /ˈhaʊzɪŋ; ˈhaʊzɪŋ/ *noun* 名词 (no plural 无复数)
flats and houses for people to live in 供人居住的房屋；住宅: *We need more housing for young people.* 我们需要为年轻人提供更多的住宅。

housing estate /ˈhaʊzɪŋ ɪsteɪt; ˈhaʊzɪŋ əˌstet/ *noun* 名词
a big group of houses that were built at the same time 同时建造的一片住宅区；住宅小区: *We live on a housing estate.* 我们住在住宅小区。

hover /ˈhɒvə(r); ˈhʌvɚ/ *verb* 动词 (**hovers**, **hovering**, **hovered** /ˈhɒvəd; ˈhʌvɚd/)
stay in the air in one place 盘旋；翱翔: *A helicopter hovered above the building.* 直升飞机在楼房上空盘旋。

hovercraft /ˈhɒvəkrɑ:ft; ˈhʌvɚˌkræft/ *noun* 名词 (*plural* 复数作 **hovercraft**)
a kind of boat that moves over the top of water on air that it pushes out 气垫船

how /haʊ; haʊ/ *adverb* 副词
1 in what way 怎样；怎么；如何: *How does this machine work?* 这个机器是怎么工作的？◇ *She told me how to get to the station.* 她把到车站去的方法告诉我了。◇ *Do you know how to spell 'elementary'?* 你知道 elementary 这个字怎么拼吗？
2 a word that you use to ask if somebody is well 用以问候别人身体健康的词: *'How is your sister?' 'She's very well, thank you.'* "你姐姐身体好吗？" "她很好，谢谢您。" ✪ You use 'how' only when you are asking about somebody's health. ＊ how 字只用以问候某人健康状况怎么样。When you are asking somebody to describe another person or a thing you use **what ... like?** 若问某人或某物什么样，要用 **what ... like?**: *'What is your sister like?' 'She's tall with brown hair.'* "你妹妹什么样？" "她个子很高，头发是棕色的。"
3 a word that you use to ask if something is good 用以询问某事物好坏的词: *How was the film?* 那部影片好不好？
4 a word that you use to ask questions about amount, etc 用以询问数量多少的词: *How old are you?* 您多少岁？◇ *How many brothers and sisters have you got?* 你有几个兄弟姐妹？◇ *How much does this cost?* 这个多少钱？◇ *How long have you lived here?* 您在这儿住了多长时间了？
5 a word that shows surprise or strong feeling 用以表示惊奇或加强语气的词: *How kind of you to help!* 多谢您帮忙！
how about ...? words that you use when you suggest something 用以提出建议的词: *How about a drink?* 喝点儿东西怎么样？◇ *How about going for a walk?* 出去散散步好不好？
how are you? do you feel well? 您好吗？；你好吗？: *'How are you?' 'Fine, thanks.'* "您好吗？" "我很好，谢谢您。"
how do you do? polite words that you say when you meet somebody for the first time 与某人初次见面时的问候语；您好 ✪ When somebody says 'How do you do?', you also answer 'How do you do?' 问候的人说 How do you do?，回答的人也要说 How do you do?

however[1] /haʊˈevə(r); haʊˈɛvɚ/ *adverb* 副词
1 it does not matter how 不管多么；无论如何: *I never win, however hard I try.* 我无论怎么努力也赢不了。
2 a way of saying 'how' more strongly ＊ how 字的加强语气的说法: *However did you find me?* 你究竟是怎么找到我的？

however[2] /haʊˈevə(r); haʊˈɛvɚ/ *conjunction* 连词
but 可是；但是；然而: *She's very intelligent. However, she's quite lazy.* 她非常聪明。但是她很懒。

howl /haʊl; haʊl/ *noun* 名词
a long loud sound, like a dog makes（像狗发出的）长而大的声音；嗥叫
howl *verb* 动词 (**howls**, **howling**, **howled** /haʊld; haʊld/)
make this sound 发出（像狗发出的）长而大的声音；嗥叫: *The dogs howled all night.* 那些狗叫了一夜。◇ *The wind howled around the house.* 大风在房子周围呼呼作声。

HQ /ˌeɪtʃ ˈkju:; ˌetʃ ˈkju/ *short for* **headquarters** ＊ **headquarters** 的缩略式

hug /hʌg; hʌg/ *verb* 动词 (**hugs**, **hugging**, **hugged** /hʌgd; hʌgd/)
put your arms around somebody to show that you love them 拥抱某人（示爱）: *She hugged her parents and said goodbye.* 她搂着父母说再见。
hug *noun* 名词
He gave his brother a hug. 他拥抱他弟弟一下。

huge /hju:dʒ; hjudʒ/ *adjective* 形容词
very big 极大的；巨大的: *They live in a huge house.* 他们住着一所很大的楼房。

hullo = **hello**

hum /hʌm; hʌm/ *verb* 动词 (**hums**, **humming**, **hummed** /hʌmd; hʌmd/)
1 make a sound like bees（像蜜蜂般）发嗡嗡声
2 sing with your lips closed 哼歌曲（嘴唇合着）: *If you don't know the words of the song, hum it.* 你要是不知道歌词，就哼着唱吧。

human /'hju:mən; 'hjumən/ *adjective* 形容词
of or like people, not animals or machines 人的；像人的（并非动物的，也并非机器的）: *the human body* 人体
human, human being *noun* 名词
a person 人: *Human beings have lived on earth for thousands of years.* 人在地球上已经生存了千百万年。
the human race /ðə ˌhju:mən 'reɪs; ðə ˌhjumən 'res/ *noun* 名词 (no plural 无复数)
all the people in the world 人类
humble /'hʌmbl; 'hʌmbl̩/ *adjective* 形容词
1 A humble person does not think he/she is better or more important than other people 谦虚的: *Becoming rich and famous has not changed her—she is still very humble.* 她富贵成名之后也没有丝毫改变——她还是那么谦虚。
2 simple or poor 简朴的；低劣的: *a humble cottage* 简朴的村舍
humor *American English for* **humour** 美式英语，即 **humour**
humorous /'hju:mərəs; 'hjumərəs/ *adjective* 形容词
A person or thing that is humorous makes you smile or laugh 幽默的；诙谐的；滑稽的: *a humorous story* 幽默的故事
humour /'hju:mə(r); 'hjumə˞/ *noun* 名词 (no plural 无复数)
being funny 幽默；诙谐；滑稽: *a story full of humour* 非常幽默的故事
have a sense of humour be able to laugh and make other people laugh at funny things 有幽默感: *Dave has a good sense of humour.* 戴夫很有幽默感。
hump /hʌmp; hʌmp/ *noun* 名词
a round lump 圆形的隆起物: *A camel has a hump on its back.* 骆驼的背上有驼峰。
hundred /'hʌndrəd; 'hʌndrəd/ *number* 数词
100 一百: *We invited a hundred people to the party.* 我们邀请了一百人参加聚会。◇ *two hundred pounds* 二百磅 ◇ *four hundred and twenty* 四百二十 ◇ *hundreds of people* 数以百计的人
hundredth /'hʌndrədθ; 'hʌndrədθ/ *adjective, adverb, noun* 形容词，副词，名词
100th 第100（个）；第一百（个）

hung *form of* **hang1** ∗ **hang1** 的不同形式
hunger /'hʌŋgə(r); 'hʌŋgə˞/ *noun* 名词 (no plural 无复数)
the feeling that you want or need to eat 饿；饥饿 ✪ Be careful! You cannot say 'I have hunger' in English. You must say 'I am hungry'. 注意！不可以说 I have hunger，应该说 I am hungry。
hungry /'hʌŋgri; 'hʌŋgrɪ/ *adjective* 形容词 (**hungrier, hungriest**)
If you are hungry, you want to eat 饿；饥饿: *Let's eat soon—I'm hungry!* 咱们快吃饭吧——我饿了！
hunt /hʌnt; hʌnt/ *verb* 动词 (**hunts, hunting, hunted**)
chase animals to kill them as a sport or for food 猎逐鸟兽（作为运动或为用作食物）；打猎: *Young lions have to learn to hunt.* 幼小的狮子得学会捕食。✪ When you talk about spending time hunting, you say **go hunting** 狩猎活动叫做 **go hunting**: *They went hunting in the forest.* 他们到森林里打猎去了。
hunt for something try to find something 寻找某事物: *I've hunted everywhere for my watch but I can't find it.* 我到处找我的手表，就是找不到。
hunt *noun* 名词
a fox-hunt 猎狐 ◇ *a hunt for my keys* 找我的钥匙
hunter *noun* 名词
a person who chases and kills animals 狩猎者；猎人
hunting *noun* 名词 (no plural 无复数)
chasing and killing animals 猎逐鸟兽；打猎
hurl /hɜ:l; hɝl/ *verb* 动词 (**hurls, hurling, hurled** /hɜ:ld; hɝld/)
throw something strongly 用力扔某物: *She hurled the book across the room.* 她把那本书从房间的一头扔到另一头。
hurray, hooray /hə'reɪ; hʊ're/, **hurrah** /hə'rɑ:; hʊ'rɑ/
a word that you shout when you are very pleased about something 非常愉快时的喊叫声: *Hurray! She's won!* 好哇！她赢了。
hurricane /'hʌrɪkən; 'hʌrɪˌken/ *noun* 名词
a storm with very strong winds 飓风
hurry[1] /'hʌri; 'hʌrɪ/ *noun* 名词
in a hurry If you are in a hurry, you

need to do something quickly 迅速地；匆忙地: *I can't talk to you now — I'm in a hurry.* 我现在不能跟你谈话——我有急事。

hurry² /ˈhʌri; ˈhʌrɪ/ *verb* 动词 (**hurries, hurrying, hurried** /ˈhʌrid; ˈhɝɪd/)
move or do something quickly 行动快或做某事快: *We hurried home after school.* 我们一放学就急急忙忙回家了。
hurry up move or do something more quickly 更快地行动或做某事: *Hurry up or we'll be late!* 快点儿，要不然我们就晚了。

hurt /hɜːt; hɝt/ *verb* 动词 (**hurts, hurting, hurt, has hurt**)
1 make somebody or something feel pain 使某人或某物感到疼痛；弄疼；弄伤: *I fell and hurt my leg.* 我把腿摔疼了。◇ *Did you hurt yourself?* 你把自己弄伤了吗？◇ *You hurt her feelings* (= made her unhappy) *when you said she was fat.* 你说她胖可伤了她的感情了。◇ *These shoes hurt — they are too small.* 这双鞋挤脚——太小了。
2 feel pain 感到疼痛: *My leg hurts.* 我腿疼。

husband /ˈhʌzbənd; ˈhʌzbənd/ *noun* 名词
the man that a woman is married to 丈夫 ☞ picture on page C3 见第C3页图

H

hut /hʌt; hʌt/ *noun* 名词
a small building with one room. Huts are usually made of wood or metal. （只有一间屋子的）小房子（常为木制的或金属制的）

hydrogen /ˈhaɪdrədʒən; ˈhaɪdrədʒən/ *noun* 名词 (no plural 无复数)
a light gas that you cannot see or smell 氢: *Water is made of hydrogen and oxygen.* 水是由氢和氧构成的。

hygiene /ˈhaɪdʒiːn; ˈhaɪdʒin/ *noun* 名词 (no plural 无复数)
keeping yourself and things around you clean 卫生: *Good hygiene is very important when you are preparing food.* 做吃的东西的时候，要特别讲卫生。

hygienic /haɪˈdʒiːnɪk; ˌhaɪdʒɪˈɛnɪk/ *adjective* 形容词
clean 卫生的；清洁的 ✪ opposite 反义词: **unhygienic**

hymn /hɪm; hɪm/ *noun* 名词
a song that Christians sing in church 圣歌（基督徒做礼拜时唱的）

hyphen /ˈhaɪfn; ˈhaɪfən/ *noun* 名词
a mark (–) that you use in writing. It joins words together (for example *ice-cream*) or shows that a word continues on the next line. 连接号（–）（把词连接在一起的符号，例如ice-cream字中的短横，或作书写时的移行符号）

Ii

I /aɪ; aɪ/ *pronoun* 代词 (*plural* 复数作 **we**) the person who is speaking 我: *I am German.* 我是德国人。◇ *I'll* (= I will) *see you tomorrow.* 我明天见你。◇ *I'm early, aren't I?* 我很早吧，是不是？

ice /aɪs; aɪs/ *noun* 名词 (no plural 无复数) water that has become hard because it is very cold 冰: *Do you want ice in your drink?* 您的饮品里要加冰吗？

iceberg /'aɪsbɜ:g; 'aɪsˌbɝg/ *noun* 名词 a very big piece of ice in the sea 浮在海洋中的巨大冰块；冰山

ice-cream /ˌaɪs'kri:m; 'aɪs'krim/ *noun* 名词 very cold sweet food made from milk 冰激凌；冰淇淋: *Do you like ice-cream?* 你喜欢吃冰激凌吗？◇ *Two chocolate ice-creams, please.* 请来两份巧克力冰激凌。

ice-cube /'aɪs kju:b; 'aɪsˌkjub/ *noun* 名词 a small piece of ice that you put in a drink to make it cold（加入饮料中用的）小冰块

iced /aɪst; aɪst/ *adjective* 形容词
1 very cold 极冷的；冰冷的: *iced water* 冰水
2 covered with **icing** 覆有糖霜的（糖霜叫做 **icing**）: *iced cakes* 有一层糖霜的蛋糕

ice hockey /'aɪs hɒki; 'aɪs ˌhɑkɪ/ *noun* 名词 (no plural 无复数) a game that two teams play on ice 冰球运动

ice lolly /ˌaɪs 'lɒli; 'aɪs 'lɑlɪ/ *noun* 名词 (*plural* 复数作 **ice lollies**) a piece of sweet ice on a stick 冰棍儿

ice-rink /'aɪs rɪŋk; 'aɪsˌrɪŋk/ *noun* 名词 a special place where you can skate 冰场

ice-skating /'aɪs skeɪtɪŋ; 'aɪsˌsketɪŋ/ *noun* 名词 (no plural 无复数) moving on ice in special boots (called **ice-skates**) that have long sharp pieces of metal on the bottom 滑冰（冰鞋叫做 **ice-skate**）

icicle /'aɪsɪkl; 'aɪsɪkḷ/ *noun* 名词 a long piece of ice that hangs down from something 从某物处垂下的冰柱；冰锥

icing /'aɪsɪŋ; 'aɪsɪŋ/ *noun* 名词 (no plural 无复数) sweet stuff that you use for covering cakes（用于覆在糕点上的）糖霜: *a cake with pink icing* 有一层粉红色糖霜的蛋糕

icy /'aɪsi; 'aɪsɪ/ *adjective* 形容词 (**icier, iciest**)
1 covered with ice 覆有冰的: *icy roads* 结了冰的路
2 very cold 冰冷的；极冷的: *an icy wind* 凛冽的风

ID /ˌaɪ'di:; 'aɪ'di/ *short for* **identification 2** ∗ **identification 2** 的缩略式

I'd /aɪd; aɪd/
1 = **I had**
2 = **I would**

idea /aɪ'dɪə; aɪ'dɪə/ *noun* 名词
1 a plan or new thought 计划或新的想法；主意: *It was a good idea to give Martin a pen for his birthday.* 马丁过生日，送他一枝钢笔是个好主意。◇ *I've got an idea. Let's have a party!* 我有个想法。咱们开个聚会吧！
2 a picture in your mind 印象；想像: *The film gives you a good idea of what Iceland is like.* 这部影片中冰岛的情景给人留下清晰的印象。◇ *I've got no idea* (= I do not know) *where she is.* 我不知道她在哪里。
3 what you believe 意见；信念: *My parents have very strict ideas about who I go out with.* 我跟什么样的人谈恋爱，我父母有十分严格的要求。

ideal /aɪ'di:əl; aɪ'dɪəl/ *adjective* 形容词 the best or exactly right 最好的或最确切的；理想的: *This is an ideal place for a picnic.* 在这个地方野餐非常理想。

identical /aɪ'dentɪkl; aɪ'dɛntɪkḷ/ *adjective* 形容词 exactly the same 完全相同的: *These two cameras are identical.* 这两个照相机完全一样。◇ *identical twins* 一模一样的双胞胎

identify /aɪ'dentɪfaɪ; aɪ'dɛntəˌfaɪ/ *verb* 动词 (**identifies, identifying, identified** /aɪ'dentɪfaɪd; aɪ'dɛntəˌfaɪd/, **has identified**) say or know who somebody is or what something is 认出某人或某物；识别: *The police have not identified the dead man yet.* 警方尚未辨认出男死者的身分。

I

identification /aɪˌdentɪfɪˈkeɪʃn; aɪˌdɛntəfəˈkeʃən/ *noun* 名词 (no plural 无复数)

1 identifying somebody or something (对某人或某物的) 辨认；识别: *The identification of bodies after the accident was difficult.* 这次事故发生后，辨认尸体的工作十分困难。

2 something that shows who you are, for example a passport 证明身分的事物 (例如护照)；身分证明: *Do you have any identification?* 您有身分证件吗？✪ The short form is **ID**. 缩略式为 **ID**。

identity /aɪˈdentəti; aɪˈdɛntətɪ/ *noun* 名词 (*plural* 复数作 **identities**)

who or what a person or thing is 本身；本体；身分: *The identity of the killer is not known.* 现在还不知道是谁杀害的。

identity card /aɪˈdentəti kɑːd; aɪˈdɛntətɪ kɑrd/ *noun* 名词

a card that shows who you are 身分证

idiom /ˈɪdiəm; ˈɪdɪəm/ *noun* 名词

a group of words with a special meaning 有特殊含义的词组；习语；惯用语；成语: *The idiom 'break somebody's heart' means 'make somebody very unhappy'.* ＊break somebody's heart 这一习语的意思是"使某人非常难过"。

idiomatic /ˌɪdiəˈmætɪk; ˌɪdɪəˈmætɪk/ *adjective* 形容词

using idioms 使用习语的: *idiomatic English* 使用习语的英语说法

idiot /ˈɪdiət; ˈɪdɪət/ *noun* 名词

a person who is stupid or does something silly 愚蠢的或做傻事的人；傻瓜；笨蛋: *I was an idiot to forget my key.* 我真糊涂，忘带钥匙了。

idol /ˈaɪdl; ˈaɪdl̩/ *noun* 名词

1 something that people worship as a god 敬奉如神的事物；神像

2 a famous person that people love 受爱戴的名人: *Madonna is the idol of millions of teenagers.* 麦当娜是千千万万青少年的偶像。

ie /ˌaɪ ˈiː; ˌaɪ ˈi/

this is what I mean 就是；即: *You can buy hot drinks, ie tea and coffee, on the train.* 在火车上可以买到热的饮品，也就是茶和咖啡。✪ **ie** is usually used in writing. ＊**ie** 这个词通常用于书面语。

if /ɪf; ɪf/ *conjunction* 连词

1 a word that you use to say what is possible or true when another thing happens or is true 如果；要是；假如: *If you press this button, the machine starts.* 如果按这个钮，机器就开动了。◇ *If you see him, give him this letter.* 您要是见到他，就把这封信交给他。◇ *If your feet were smaller, you could wear my shoes.* 你的脚要是小一点儿，就能穿我的鞋了。◇ *If I had a million pounds, I would buy a big house.* 假如我有一百万英镑，我就买一座大房子。◇ *I may see you tomorrow. If not, I'll see you next week.* 我可能明天见你，不行的话，就得下星期见了。

2 a word that shows a question; whether 是否: *Do you know if Paul is at home?* 你知道不知道保罗在不在家？◇ *She asked me if I wanted to go to a party.* 她问我想不想去参加聚会。

as if in a way that makes you think something 好像；似乎；仿佛: *She looks as if she has been on holiday.* 看她那样子，好像刚放过假似的。

if only words that show that you want something very much 但愿；要是…就好了: *If only I could drive!* 我要是会开车多好哇！

ignorance /ˈɪgnərəns; ˈɪgnərəns/ *noun* 名词 (no plural 无复数)

not knowing about something 不知道（某事物）；（对某事物）无知: *Her ignorance surprised me.* 她一无所知，叫我吃惊。

ignorant /ˈɪgnərənt; ˈɪgnərənt/ *adjective* 形容词

If you are ignorant, you do not know about something（对某事物）不知道的；无知的: *I'm very ignorant about computers.* 我对计算机一窍不通。

ignore /ɪgˈnɔː(r); ɪgˈnɔr/ *verb* 动词 (**ignores, ignoring, ignored** /ɪgˈnɔːd; ɪgˈnɔrd/)

know about somebody or something, but do not do anything about it 知道某人或某事物，但不采取任何行动；不理会；忽视: *He ignored the warning and put his head in the lion's cage.* 他不理会那种警告，硬是把头伸进狮子笼里。◇ *I said hello to her, but she ignored me!* 我跟她打招呼，她不理我！

il- *prefix* 前缀

You can add **il-** to the beginning of some words to give them the opposite meaning, for example 在某些字前可加 **il-** 构成反义词，如:

illegal = not legal

ill /ɪl; ɪl/ *adjective* 形容词

1 not well; not in good health 有病的；不健康的: *Mark is in bed because he is ill.* 马克因病躺在床上。◇ *I feel too ill to go to work.* 我不舒服，不能去上班了。✪ The noun is **illness**. 名词是 **illness**。

2 bad 坏的；不好的: *ill health* 不健康

be taken ill become ill 生病: *Josie was taken ill on holiday.* 乔西放假的时候病了。

I'll /aɪl; aɪl/ = **I shall, I will**

illegal /ɪ'li:gl; ɪ'ligl̩/ *adjective* 形容词

not allowed by the law; not legal 不合法的；违法的: *It is illegal to drive a car in Britain if you are under the age of 17.* 在英国，17岁以下的人开车是违法的。

illegally /ɪ'li:gəli; ɪ'ligl̩ɪ/ *adverb* 副词

She came into the country illegally. 她是通过非法途径入境的。

illness /'ɪlnəs; 'ɪlnɪs/ *noun* 名词 (*plural* 复数作 **illnesses**)

being ill 病；疾病: *Cancer is a serious illness.* 癌症是重病。◇ *He could not come to the meeting because of illness.* 他因病不能来开会。

ill-treat /ˌɪl 'tri:t; ɪl'trit/ *verb* 动词 (**ill-treats, ill-treating, ill-treated**)

do unkind things to a person or an animal 虐待（人或动物）: *This dog has been ill-treated.* 这条狗受过虐待。

illustrate /'ɪləstreɪt; 'ɪləstret/ *verb* 动词 (**illustrates, illustrating, illustrated**)

add pictures to show something more clearly 用插图说明某事物: *The book is illustrated with colour photographs.* 这本书里有很多彩色插图。

illustration /ˌɪlə'streɪʃn; ˌɪləs'treʃən/ *noun* 名词

a picture 插图: *This dictionary has a lot of illustrations.* 本词典有很多插图。

> **im-** *prefix* 前缀
> you can add **im-** to the beginning of some words to give them the opposite meaning, for example 在某些字前可加 **im-** 构成反义词，如:
> **impatient** = not patient

I'm /aɪm; aɪm/ = **I am**

image /'ɪmɪdʒ; 'ɪmɪdʒ/ *noun* 名词

1 a picture in people's minds of somebody or something 人的头脑中对某人或某事物的图像；印象；想像: *A lot of people have an image of London as cold and rainy.* 很多人对伦敦的印象是寒冷多雨。

2 a picture on paper or in a mirror 纸上的或镜中的图像: *images of war* 反映战争的图片

imaginary /ɪ'mædʒɪnəri; ɪ'mædʒəˌnɛrɪ/ *adjective* 形容词

not real; only in your mind 非真实的；仅在脑海中的；想像中的: *The film is about an imaginary country.* 这部影片描述的是个虚构的国家。

imagination /ɪˌmædʒɪ'neɪʃn; ɪˌmædʒə'neʃən/ *noun* 名词

being able to think of new ideas or make pictures in your mind 能产生新的想法或形象；想像力；想像: *You need a lot of imagination to write stories for children.* 写儿童故事需要有丰富的想像力。◇ *You didn't really see a ghost—it was just your imagination.* 你并没有真正看见鬼——只不过是你的想像而已。

imagine /ɪ'mædʒɪn; ɪ'mædʒɪn/ *verb* 动词 (**imagines, imagining, imagined** /ɪ'mædʒɪnd; ɪ'mædʒɪnd/)

1 make a picture of something in your mind 想像: *Can you imagine life without electricity?* 你能想像出生活中没有电的情形吗？◇ *I closed my eyes and imagined I was lying on a beach.* 我闭上眼睛，想像到我躺在海滩上的情景。

2 think that something will happen or that something is true 料想；设想: *I imagine Mehmet will come by car.* 我设想穆罕默德将坐着汽车来。

imitate /'ɪmɪteɪt; 'ɪməˌtet/ *verb* 动词 (**imitates, imitating, imitated**)

try to do the same as somebody or something; copy somebody or something 模仿某人或某事物；仿效: *He imitated his teacher's voice.* 他模仿老师的声音。

imitation /ˌɪmɪ'teɪʃn; ˌɪmə'teʃən/ *noun* 名词

something that you make to look like another thing; a copy 仿制的事物；仿造品；仿效: *It's not a diamond, it's only a glass imitation.* 这不是钻石，是用玻璃仿制的。◇ *imitation leather* 人造革

immediate /ɪ'mi:diət; ɪ'midɪɪt/ *adjective* 形容词

happening at once 立即的；即刻的: *I can't wait—I need an immediate answer.* 我不能等——需要马上给我答复。

immediately /ɪ'mi:diətli; ɪ'midɪɪtlɪ/ *adverb* 副词
now; at once 立刻；马上: *Come to my office immediately!* 马上到我的办公室来！

immense /ɪ'mens; ɪ'mɛns/ *adjective* 形容词
very big 极大的；巨大的: *immense problems* 很大的困难

immensely /ɪ'mensli; ɪ'mɛnslɪ/ *adverb* 副词
very or very much 很；非常: *We enjoyed the party immensely.* 我们在聚会上非常愉快。

immigrant /'ɪmɪgrənt; 'ɪməgrənt/ *noun* 名词
a person who comes to another country to live there 到外国居住的人；移民: *Many immigrants to Britain have come from Asia.* 到英国来的移民有很多是亚洲人。

immigration /ˌɪmɪ'greɪʃn; ˌɪmə'greʃən/ *noun* 名词 (no plural 无复数)
coming to another country to live there 移民

immune /ɪ'mju:n; ɪ'mjun/ *adjective* 形容词
safe, so that you cannot get a disease 有免疫力的（不得某种疾病的）: *You're immune to measles if you've had it before.* 得过麻疹的人就有免疫力了。

impatience /ɪm'peɪʃns; ɪm'peʃəns/ *noun* 名词 (no plural 无复数)
not being calm when you are waiting 无耐性；不耐烦: *He showed his impatience by looking at his watch five or six times.* 他看手表看了五六次，显出不耐烦的样子。

impatient /ɪm'peɪʃnt; ɪm'peʃənt/ *adjective* 形容词
If you are impatient, you do not want to wait for something 无耐性的；不耐烦的: *Don't be so impatient! The bus will be here soon.* 别那么没耐性！公共汽车马上就来了。
impatiently *adverb* 副词
'Hurry up!' she said impatiently. "快点儿吧！"她不耐烦地说。

imperative /ɪm'perətɪv; ɪm'pɛrətɪv/ *noun* 名词
the form of a verb that you use for telling somebody to do something 祈使语气的动词形式: *'Listen!' and 'Go away!' are in the imperative.* "听！"和"走开！"都是祈使语气。

imply /ɪm'plaɪ; ɪm'plaɪ/ *verb* 动词 (**implies**, **implying**, **implied** /ɪm'plaɪd; ɪm'plaɪd/, **has implied**)
mean something without saying it 虽未说出但含有某意思；暗示；暗指: *He asked if I had any work to do. He was implying that I was lazy.* 他问我有没有事情做。言外之意是我懒惰。

import /ɪm'pɔ:t; ɪm'pɔrt/ *verb* 动词 (**imports**, **importing**, **imported**)
buy things from another country and bring them into your country 从外国买东西进入自己的国家；进口: *Britain imports oranges from Spain.* 英国从西班牙进口橙子。✪ opposite 反义词: **export**
import /'ɪmpɔ:t; 'ɪmpɔrt/ *noun* 名词
a thing that is imported 进口货 ✪ opposite 反义词: **export**
importer /ɪm'pɔ:tə(r); ɪm'pɔrtɚ/ *noun* 名词
a person, company or country that imports things 从事进口货物的人、公司或国家

important /ɪm'pɔ:tnt; ɪm'pɔrtn̩t/ *adjective* 形容词
1 If something is important, you must do, have or think about it 必须做的、必须有的或必须想到的；重要的: *It is important to sleep well the night before an exam.* 考试前夕一定要睡好觉。◇ *I think that happiness is more important than money.* 我认为幸福比金钱重要。
2 powerful or special 有权力的或特殊的；重要的: *The prime minister is a very important person.* 总理是十分重要的人物。
✪ opposite 反义词: **unimportant**
importance /ɪm'pɔ:tns; ɪm'pɔrtn̩s/ *noun* 名词 (no plural 无复数)
being important; value 重要；重要性；有价值: *Oil is of great importance to industry.* 石油在工业上非常重要。

impossible /ɪm'pɒsəbl; ɪm'pɑsəbl̩/ *adjective* 形容词
If something is impossible, you cannot do it, or it cannot happen 不可能的；做不到的；不能发生的: *It is impossible to finish this work by five o'clock.* 五点钟以前不可能做完这项工作。◇ *The house was impossible to find.* 那所房子是找不到的。
impossibility /ɪmˌpɒsə'bɪləti; ˌɪmpɑsə'bɪlətɪ/ *noun* 名词 (*plural* 复数作 **impossibilities**)

I can't lend you £1000. It's an impossibility! 我无法借给你1 000英镑。这是不可能的事！

impress /ɪm'pres; ɪm'prɛs/ *verb* 动词 (**impresses**, **impressing**, **impressed** /ɪm'prest; ɪm'prɛst/)
make somebody have good feelings or thoughts about you or about something that is yours 使某人对你或你的事物有好的感想；给某人留下好印象: *He was so impressed by Cindy's singing that he asked her to sing on the radio.* 他很爱听辛迪唱的歌，所以请她到电台演唱。

impressive /ɪm'presɪv; ɪm'prɛsɪv/ *adjective* 形容词
If something is impressive, it impresses people, for example because it is very good or very big 使人有好感的；给人留下深刻印象的（例如因为非常好或非常大）: *an impressive building* 壮观的建筑物 ◇ *Your work is very impressive.* 您的工作真了不起。

impression /ɪm'preʃn; ɪm'prɛʃən/ *noun* 名词
feelings or thoughts you have about somebody or something 对某人或某事物的感想；印象: *My first impressions of London were not very good.* 我对伦敦的初步印象并不太好。◇ *What's your impression of the new teacher?* 你对新老师的印象怎么样？

make an impression give somebody a certain idea of yourself（把自己的表现）给某人留下某种印象: *He made a good impression on his first day at work.* 他第一天上班就给人留下了很好的印象。

imprison /ɪm'prɪzn; ɪm'prɪzn̩/ *verb* 动词 (**imprisons**, **imprisoning**, **imprisoned** /ɪm'prɪznd; ɪm'prɪzn̩d/)
put somebody in prison 监禁某人；关押: *He was imprisoned for killing his wife.* 他因杀死妻子而入狱。

imprisonment /ɪm'prɪznmənt; ɪm'prɪzn̩mənt/ *noun* 名词 (no plural 无复数)
being in prison 监禁；关押；坐牢: *two years' imprisonment* 两年监禁

improve /ɪm'pru:v; ɪm'pruv/ *verb* 动词 (**improves**, **improving**, **improved** /ɪm'pru:vd; ɪm'pruvd/)
become better or make something better （使某事物）变得更好；改进；改善: *Your English has improved a lot this year.* 你的英语今年有很大进步。◇ *You must improve your spelling.* 你得减少拼写错误。

improvement /ɪm'pru:vmənt; ɪm'pruvmənt/ *noun* 名词
a change that makes something better than it was before 改良；改进；改善: *There has been a big improvement in Sam's work.* 萨姆的功课有很大进步。

impulse /'ɪmpʌls; 'ɪmpʌls/ *noun* 名词
a sudden strong wish to do something 突然想做某事物的强烈愿望；突如其来的念头: *She felt an impulse to run away.* 她突然想到要跑开。

in[1] /ɪn; ɪn/ *adverb* 副词
1 to a place, from outside 向里；进入: *I opened the door and went in.* 我开门进去了。
2 at home or at work 在家；在工作: *'Can I speak to Helen, please?' 'I'm sorry — she's not in.'* "请问，可以跟海伦说话吗？""很抱歉——她不在。"

in[2] /ɪn; ɪn/ *preposition* 介词
1 a word that shows where 表示在何处的词；在…: *Glasgow is in Scotland.* 格拉斯哥在苏格兰。◇ *He put his hand in the water.* 他把手伸进水里。◇ *Julie is in bed.* 朱莉在床上。☞ picture on page C1 见第C1页图
2 a word that shows when 表示在何时的词；在…: *My birthday is in May.* 我的生日在五月。◇ *He started school in 1987.* 他1987年开始上学。☞ picture on page C29 见第C29页图
3 a word that shows how long; after 表示时间有多长的词；在…以后: *I'll be ready in ten minutes.* 我十分钟后就准备好。
4 a word that shows how somebody or something is 表示某人或某事物如何的词: *This room is in a mess.* 这个房间乱七八糟。◇ *Jenny was in tears* (= she was crying). 珍妮哭了。
5 a word that shows what clothes somebody is wearing 表示某人穿着什么样的衣服的词: *He was dressed in a suit.* 他穿着一套西装。
6 a word that shows what way, what language, etc 表示用什么方法、什么语言的词: *Write your name in capital letters.* 把您的名字用大写字母写出。◇ *They were speaking in French.* 他们正在用法语谈话。
7 a word that shows somebody's job 表示某人从事的工作的词: *He's in the army.* 他在陆军服役。

I

8 making something 构成某事物: *There are 100 centimetres in a metre.*＊100厘米等于1米。◇*Sit in a circle.* 围成一圈坐着。

in-[3] *prefix* 前缀
You can add **in-** to the beginning of some words to give them the opposite meaning, for example 在某些字前加上 **in-** 可构成反义词，如:
incomplete = not complete

inability /ˌɪnəˈbɪləti; ˌɪnəˈbɪlətɪ/ *noun* 名词 (no plural 无复数)
not being able to do something 不能做某事；无能力: *He has an inability to talk about his problems.* 他不能谈出自己的问题。

inaccurate /ɪnˈækjərət; ɪnˈækjərɪt/ *adjective* 形容词
not correct; with mistakes in it 不正确的；不准确的；有错误的: *The report in the newspaper was inaccurate.* 报纸上的这篇报道有误。

inadequate /ɪnˈædɪkwət; ɪnˈædəkwɪt/ *adjective* 形容词
not as much as you need, or not good enough 不足的；不够的；不够好的: *These shoes are inadequate for cold weather.* 这种鞋冷天穿不够暖。◇ *inadequate food* 不够吃的食物

inch /ɪntʃ; ɪntʃ/ *noun* 名词 (*plural* 复数作 **inches**)
a measure of length (= 2.54 centimetres). There are twelve inches in a **foot** 英寸（= 2.54厘米。12英寸等于1英尺，英尺叫做 **foot**。）: *I am five foot six inches tall.* 我身高五英尺六英寸。◇ *a twelve-inch ruler* 十二英寸的尺子 ☞ Note at **foot** 见 **foot** 词条注释

incident /ˈɪnsɪdənt; ˈɪnsədənt/ *noun* 名词
something that happens 发生的事: *Josie told us about a funny incident at school, when her teacher fell in the pond!* 乔西告诉我们一件学校里可笑的事，她们老师掉进池塘里了！

incidentally /ɪnsɪˈdentəli; ˌɪnsəˈdɛntḷɪ/ *adverb* 副词
a word that you say when you are going to talk about something different 改变话题用的词；顺便提一下: *Charles helped us to move the table. Incidentally, he has a new car.* 查尔斯帮我们搬的那张桌子。顺便提一句，他有一辆新汽车。

inclined /ɪnˈklaɪnd; ɪnˈklaɪnd/ *adjective* 形容词
be inclined to **1** be likely to do something 很有可能做某事: *I don't want to tell Susy about this—she's inclined to get angry.* 我不想告诉苏西——她动不动就生气。**2** want to do something 想要做某事: *I'm inclined to agree with you.* 我趋向于同意你的意见。

include /ɪnˈklu:d; ɪnˈklud/ *verb* 动词 (**includes, including, included**)
1 have somebody or something as one part of the whole 包括某人或某事物: *The price of the room includes breakfast.* 房间的租金包括早餐在内。
2 make somebody or something part of a group 把某人或某事物包括在内: *Have you included tea on the list of things to buy?* 你把茶叶加在购物单里了吗？
☞ Look at **exclude**. 见 **exclude**。
including *preposition* 介词
with; if you count 包括；算在内: *There were five people in the car, including the driver.* 汽车里有五个人，包括司机。

income /ˈɪnkʌm; ˈɪnˌkʌm/ *noun* 名词
all the money that you receive for your work, for example 收到的所有的钱（例如工作所得）；收入: *What was your income last year?* 您去年的收入是多少？
income tax /ˈɪnkʌm tæks; ˈɪnkʌm tæks/ *noun* 名词 (no plural 无复数)
the money that you pay to the government from the money that you earn 所得税

incomplete /ˌɪnkəmˈpli:t; ˌɪnkəmˈplit/ *adjective* 形容词
not finished; with parts missing 未完成的；不完全的；不完整的: *This list is incomplete.* 这份清单不完全。

inconsiderate /ˌɪnkənˈsɪdərət; ˌɪnkənˈsɪdərɪt/ *adjective* 形容词
A person who is inconsiderate does not think or care about other people and their feelings 不替别人着想的；不体贴别人的: *It's inconsiderate of you to make so much noise when people are asleep.* 人家都睡了，你这么大声音，太不顾及别人了。

inconsistent /ˌɪnkənˈsɪstənt; ˌɪnkənˈsɪstənt/ *adjective* 形容词
not always the same 并非始终一样: *She's very inconsistent—sometimes her work*

is good and sometimes it's bad. 她反复无常——工作时好时坏。

inconvenience /ˌɪnkən'vi:niəns; ˌɪnkən'vinjəns/ *noun* 名词 (no plural 无复数)
problems or difficulty 不方便；困难: *The snow caused a lot of inconvenience to drivers.* 这场雪给司机造成极大不便。

inconvenient /ˌɪnkən'vi:niənt; ˌɪnkən-'vinjənt/ *adjective* 形容词
If something is inconvenient, it gives you problems or difficulty 不方便的；困难的: *She came at an inconvenient time — I was on the telephone.* 她来得不是时候——我正打电话呢。

incorrect /ˌɪnkə'rekt; ˌɪnkə'rɛkt/ *adjective* 形容词
not correct; not right or true 不正确的；不对的；不真实的: *It is incorrect to say that two plus two equals five.* 说二加二等于五是不对的。
incorrectly *adverb* 副词
The name was incorrectly spelt. 这个名字拼写得不对。

increase /ɪn'kri:s; ɪn'kris/ *verb* 动词 (**increases**, **increasing**, **increased** /ɪn-'kri:st; ɪn'krist/)
become bigger or more; make something bigger or more（使某事物）变大或变多；增大；增加: *The number of women who go to work has increased.* 女子就业人数多了。
increase /'ɪnkri:s; 'ɪnkris/ *noun* 名词
There has been an increase in road accidents. 交通事故增多了。◇ *a price increase* 涨价
✪ opposite 反义词: **decrease**

incredible /ɪn'kredəbl; ɪn'krɛdəbḷ/ *adjective* 形容词
1 surprising and very difficult to believe 使人惊奇而难以置信的；不可思议的: *Mike told us an incredible story about his grandmother catching a thief.* 迈克告诉我们他祖母抓住个小偷，简直不可思议。
2 very great 非常大的: *She earns an incredible amount of money.* 她挣的钱多极了。
incredibly /ɪn'kredəbli; ɪn'krɛdəblɪ/ *adverb* 副词
extremely 极端地: *He's incredibly clever.* 他极其聪明。

indeed /ɪn'di:d; ɪn'did/ *adverb* 副词
1 a word that makes 'very' stronger 用以增强 very 一词的语气的词: *Thank you very much indeed.* 多谢您。◇ *She's very happy indeed.* 她实在非常愉快。
2 really; certainly 的确；确实: *'Did you have a good holiday?' 'I did indeed.'* "您假期过得愉快吗？" "愉快极了。"

indefinite /ɪn'defɪnət; ɪn'dɛfənɪt/ *adjective* 形容词
not definite; not clear or certain 不确切的；不明确的；不肯定的: *They are staying for an indefinite length of time.* 他们逗留的时间长短未定。
indefinitely /ɪn'defɪnətlɪ; ɪn'dɛfənɪtlɪ/ *adverb* 副词
for a long time, perhaps for ever 长时间地（可能无限期）: *I can't wait indefinitely.* 我不能一直等下去。

independence /ˌɪndɪ'pendəns; ˌɪndɪ-'pɛndəns/ *noun* 名词 (no plural 无复数)
being free from another person, thing or country 不受他人、他事物或他国束缚；自主；独立: *America declared its independence from Britain in 1776.* 美国于1776年脱离英国而宣告独立。

independent /ˌɪndɪ'pendənt; ˌɪndɪ-'pɛndənt/ *adjective* 形容词
1 not controlled by another person, thing or country 不受他人、他事物或他国控制的；自主的；独立的: *Zimbabwe has been independent since 1980.* 津巴布韦已于1980年独立。
2 A person who is independent does not need help（指人）不需要别人帮助的；自立的: *She lives alone now and she is very independent.* 她现在独自生活，完全不用别人帮助。

index /'ɪndeks; 'ɪndɛks/ *noun* 名词 (*plural* 复数作 **indexes**)
a list of words from A to Z at the end of a book. It tells you what things are in the book and where you can find them.（列于书后的）索引

indicate /'ɪndɪkeɪt; 'ɪndəˌket/ *verb* 动词 (**indicates**, **indicating**, **indicated**)
1 show something, usually by pointing with your finger 表明某事物（通常用手指）: *Can you indicate your school on this map?* 你能在地图上指出你们学校的位置吗？
2 give a sign about something 象征某事物；预示: *Black clouds indicate that it's going to rain.* 乌云滚滚预示着要下雨。

3 show that your car is going to turn by using a light（指汽车的指示灯）显示要转向: *You should indicate left now.* 你现在应该打出左转指示灯。

indication /ˌɪndɪˈkeɪʃn; ˌɪndəˈkeʃən/ *noun* 名词
something that shows something 指示；显示: *He gave no indication that he was angry.* 他当时并没流露出他已经生气了。

indicator /ˈɪndɪkeɪtə(r); ˈɪndəˌketɚ/ *noun* 名词
a light on a car that shows that it is going to turn left or right（汽车向左或向右转的）指示灯

indignant /ɪnˈdɪgnənt; ɪnˈdɪgnənt/ *adjective* 形容词
angry because somebody has done or said something that you do not like or agree with 愤怒的（因不满某人说的话或做的事）: *She was indignant when I said she was lazy.* 我说她懒，她火儿了。

indignantly *adverb* 副词
'I'm not late,' he said indignantly. "我并没迟到，"他愤愤不平地说。

indignation /ˌɪndɪgˈneɪʃn; ˌɪndɪgˈneʃən/ *noun* 名词 (no plural 无复数)
a feeling of anger and surprise 愤怒而吃惊的情绪；气愤；愤慨

indirect /ˌɪndəˈrekt; ˌɪndəˈrɛkt / *adjective* 形容词
not straight or direct 不直的或不直接的；间接的；迂回的: *We came an indirect way to avoid the city centre.* 我们来的时候绕道避开了市中心。

indirectly *adverb* 副词
in an indirect way 不直或不直接地；间接地；迂回地

individual¹ /ˌɪndɪˈvɪdʒuəl; ˌɪndəˈvɪdʒuəl/ *adjective* 形容词
1 for only one person or thing 仅供一人或一事物的；单独的；个别的: *He had individual lessons to help him learn to read.* 他上单独课补习阅读。
2 single and different 单一而不同的；独特的；特有的: *Each individual country has its own flag.* 各个国家都有自己的国旗。

individually /ˌɪndɪˈvɪdʒuəli; ˌɪndəˈvɪdʒuəlɪ/ *adverb* 副词
separately; alone; not together 分别地；独自地；个别地: *The teacher spoke to each student individually.* 老师和每个学生个别谈话。

individual² /ˌɪndɪˈvɪdʒuəl; ˌɪndəˈvɪdʒuəl/ *noun* 名词
one person 个人；个体: *Teachers must treat each child as an individual.* 教师必须把每个学生当作独立的个体。

indoor /ˈɪndɔ:(r); ˈɪnˌdɔr/ *adjective* 形容词
done or used inside a building 在建筑物内做的或用的；室内的: *an indoor swimming-pool* 室内游泳池 ◇ *indoor games* 室内游戏
✪ opposite 反义词: **outdoor**

indoors /ˌɪnˈdɔ:z; ˈɪnˈdɔrz/ *adverb* 副词
in or into a building 在建筑物内或进入建筑物内: *Let's go indoors. I'm cold.* 咱们进屋去吧。我冷了。✪ opposite 反义词: **outdoors**

industrial /ɪnˈdʌstriəl; ɪnˈdʌstrɪəl/ *adjective* 形容词
1 of or about making things in factories 工业的；关于工业生产的；产业的: *industrial machines* 工业机器
2 with a lot of factories 有很多工厂的；工业的: *Leeds is an industrial city.* 利兹是个工业城市。

industry /ˈɪndəstri; ˈɪndəstrɪ/ *noun* 名词
1 (no plural 无复数) the work of making things in factories 工业: *Is there much industry in your country?* 你们国家工业发达吗？
2 (*plural* 复数作 **industries**) all the companies that make the same thing 行业: *Japan has a big car industry.* 日本汽车业规模很大。

inefficient /ˌɪnɪˈfɪʃnt; ˌɪnəˈfɪʃənt/ *adjective* 形容词
A person or thing that is inefficient does not work well or in the best way 做得不好的或方法不好的；效率低的: *This machine is very old and inefficient.* 这个机器很陈旧，效率又低。

inevitable /ɪnˈevɪtəbl; ɪnˈɛvətəbḷ/ *adjective* 形容词
If something is inevitable, it will certainly happen 必然发生的；不可避免的: *The accident was inevitable — he was driving too fast.* 这起事故无可避免——他开车开得太快了。

inevitably /ɪnˈevɪtəbli; ɪnˈɛvətəblɪ/ *adverb* 副词
Building the new hospital inevitably cost a lot of money. 修建这座新医院不免花了很多钱。

I

inexperienced /ˌɪnɪk'spɪəriənst; ˌɪnɪk-'spɪrɪənst/ *adjective* 形容词
If you are inexperienced, you do not know about something because you have not done it many times before 无经验的；缺乏经验的: *a young inexperienced driver* 无经验的年轻司机

infant school /'ɪnfənt sku:l; 'ɪnfənt skul/ *noun* 名词
a school for children between the ages of five and seven 幼儿学校（为五岁至七岁儿童设置的学校）

infect /ɪn'fekt; ɪn'fɛkt/ *verb* 动词 (**infects**, **infecting**, **infected**)
give a disease to somebody 传染；感染: *He infected the other children in the class with his cold.* 他的感冒传染给班上其他同学了。

infected *adjective* 形容词
full of small living things (called **germs**) that can make you ill 受感染的（细菌叫做 **germ**）: *Clean that cut or it could become infected.* 把那个伤口消消毒，否则可能感染。

infection /ɪn'fekʃn; ɪn'fɛkʃən/ *noun* 名词
a disease 传染病: *Mike has an ear infection.* 迈克的耳朵受细菌感染了。

infectious /ɪn'fekʃəs; ɪn'fɛkʃəs/ *adjective* 形容词
that goes easily from one person to another 传染的；感染的: *This disease is infectious.* 这种病是传染病。

inferior /ɪn'fɪəriə(r); ɪn'fɪrɪɚ/ *adjective* 形容词
not as good or important as another person or thing 没有他人或他事物那么好或那么重要的；差的；次要的: *Lisa's work is so good that she makes the other students feel inferior.* 利萨的作业非常好，别的同学都觉得比不上她。✪ opposite 反义词: **superior**

infinite /'ɪnfɪnət; 'ɪnfənɪt/ *adjective* 形容词
with no end; too much or too many to count or measure 无尽的；无穷的；无数的: *There is an infinite number of stars in the sky.* 天上有无数的星星。

infinitive /ɪn'fɪnətɪv; ɪn'fɪnətɪv/ *noun* 名词
the simple form of a verb 动词的原形；不定式: *'Eat', 'go' and 'play' are all infinitives.* ＊eat、go、play 都是动词的原形。

inflate /ɪn'fleɪt; ɪn'flet/ *verb* 动词 (**inflates**, **inflating**, **inflated**)
fill something with air or gas to make it bigger 使某物充气膨胀: *He inflated the tyre.* 他给轮胎充了气。✪ It is more usual to say **blow up** or **pump up**. 常用词语是 **blow up** 或 **pump up**。

inflation /ɪn'fleɪʃn; ɪn'fleʃən/ *noun* 名词 (no plural 无复数)
a general rise in prices in a country 通货膨胀: *The government is trying to control inflation.* 政府正在设法遏止通货膨胀。

influence /'ɪnfluəns; 'ɪnflʊəns/ *noun* 名词
1 (no plural 无复数) the power to change what somebody believes or does（改变别人的思想或行动的）影响力；影响: *Television has a strong influence on people.* 电视对人有很大的影响。
2 (*plural* 复数作 **influences**) a person or thing that can change somebody or something 影响他人或他事物的人或事物: *Paul's new girlfriend is a good influence on him.* 保罗的新女朋友对他有好的影响。

influence *verb* 动词 (**influences**, **influencing**, **influenced** /'ɪnfluənst; 'ɪnflʊənst/)
change somebody or something; make somebody do what you want 影响某人或某事物；支配某人: *She is easily influenced by her friends.* 她很容易受朋友的影响。

inform /ɪn'fɔ:m; ɪn'fɔrm/ *verb* 动词 (**informs**, **informing**, **informed** /ɪn-'fɔ:md; ɪn'fɔrmd/)
tell something to somebody 把某事告诉某人；通知: *You should inform the police of the accident.* 你应该向警方报告这起事故。

informal /ɪn'fɔ:ml; ɪn'fɔrml/ *adjective* 形容词
You use informal language or behave in an informal way in situations that are friendly and easy, not serious or important, and with people that you know well. You do not usually use informal words when you write (except in letters to people that you know well)（指言语或行为）不拘礼节的；不讲究形式的（用于随便与熟人相处的环境中，而不用于严肃的或重要的场合。在书面语中，除了与熟人通信以外，一般不使用这类词语）: *I wear a suit when I'm at work, but more informal clothes,*

I

like jeans and T-shirts, at weekends. 我上班的时候穿着套装，可是在周末就穿牛仔裤和短袖汗衫之类较为随便的衣服。◇ *an informal letter* 口语体的信

informally /ɪn'fɔːməli; ɪn'fɔrmḷɪ/ *adverb* 副词
The students talked informally to each other. 同学们无拘无束地互相交谈。

information /ˌɪnfə'meɪʃn; ˌɪnfɚ'meʃən/ *noun* 名词 (no plural 无复数)
what you tell somebody; facts 信息；资料；事实: *Can you give me some information about trains to London?* 您能不能给我一些开往伦敦的列车的资料？✪ Be careful! You cannot say 'an information'. 注意！不可说 an information。You can say 'some information' or 'a piece of information' 可以说 some information 或 a piece of information: *She gave me an interesting piece of information.* 她给我一份很有趣的资料。

ingredient /ɪn'griːdiənt; ɪn'gridɪənt/ *noun* 名词
one of the things that you put in when you make something to eat（烹调用的）材料；成分: *The ingredients for this cake are flour, butter, sugar and eggs.* 做这种蛋糕的材料是面粉、黄油、糖、鸡蛋。

inhabitant /ɪn'hæbɪtənt; ɪn'hæbɪtənt/ *noun* 名词
a person or an animal that lives in a place 生活在某一地方的人或动物；居民；栖息的动物: *The town has 30 000 inhabit-ants.* 这个镇上住着30 000居民。

I

inhabited /ɪn'hæbɪtɪd; ɪn'hæbɪtɪd/ *adjective* 形容词
be inhabited have people or animals living there 有人居住的或有动物栖息的: *The South Pole is inhabited by penguins.* 南极有企鹅栖息。

inherit /ɪn'herɪt; ɪn'hɛrɪt/ *verb* 动词 (**inherits**, **inheriting**, **inherited**)
receive something from somebody who has died 继承某物: *Sabine inherited some money from her grandmother.* 萨拜因继承了她祖母的一些钱。

inheritance /ɪn'herɪtəns; ɪn'hɛrɪtəns/ *noun* 名词
something that you inherit 继承之物

initial /ɪ'nɪʃl; ɪ'nɪʃəl/ *adjective* 形容词
first 最初的；开始的；第一个的: *Our initial idea was to go to Greece, but then we decided to go to Spain.* 我们最初的想法是去希腊，可是后来又决定去西班牙了。

initially /ɪ'nɪʃəli; ɪ'nɪʃəlɪ/ *adverb* 副词
in the beginning; at first 最初；开头；首先: *Initially hated living in England, but now I love it!* 最初我很不喜欢英格兰，但是现在我很喜欢了！

initials /ɪ'nɪʃlz; ɪ'nɪʃəlz/ *noun* 名词 (plural 复数)
the first letters of your names（姓名的）首字母: *Julie Ann Smith's initials are J.A.S.* ＊ Julie Ann Smith 的首字母是 J.A.S.

inject /ɪn'dʒekt; ɪn'dʒɛkt/ *verb* 动词 (**injects**, **injecting**, **injected**)
use a special needle to put a drug into a person's body 给某人注射

injection /ɪn'dʒekʃn; ɪn'dʒɛkʃən/ *noun* 名词
The doctor gave the baby an injection. 医生给那个小孩儿打了一针。

injure /'ɪndʒə(r); 'ɪndʒɚ/ *verb* 动词 (**injures**, **injuring**, **injured** /'ɪndʒəd; 'ɪndʒɚd/)
hurt somebody or something 伤害某人或某物: *She injured her arm when she was playing tennis.* 她打网球的时候把胳膊弄伤了。◇ *Joe was injured in a car accident.* 乔在汽车事故中受了伤。

injured *adjective* 形容词
The injured woman was taken to hospital. 那个受伤的女子已被送往医院。

injury /'ɪndʒəri; 'ɪndʒərɪ/ *noun* 名词 (*plural* 复数作 **injuries**)
damage to the body of a person or an animal（指对人或动物身体的）伤害: *He had serious head injuries.* 他头部受了重伤。

injustice /ɪn'dʒʌstɪs; ɪn'dʒʌstɪs/ *noun* 名词 (no plural 无复数)
not being fair or right 不公正；不公平；非正义: *People are angry about the injustice of the new tax.* 大家认为新税制不公平，都很气愤。

ink /ɪŋk; ɪŋk/ *noun* 名词
a coloured liquid for writing and printing 墨水；油墨: *The words on this page are printed in black ink.* 本页的字是用黑色油墨印刷的。

inland /'ɪnlənd; 'ɪnlənd/ *adjective* 形容词
in the middle of a country, not near the sea 内陆的；内地的: *an inland lake* 内陆的湖

inland /ˌɪnˈlænd; ˈɪnˌlænd/ *adverb* 副词
in or towards the middle of a country 在内陆；向内地

inn /ɪn; ɪn/ *noun* 名词
a house or small hotel where you can buy drinks and food 客栈；小旅馆：*We went to the 'Bear Inn' for lunch.* 我们到Bear Inn 小馆去吃午饭。✪ **Inn** is an old word that we do not use much now, except in names. ＊ **inn** 是个较旧的字，除作店名外已不常用。The usual words are **pub** or **hotel**. 现在通常用 **pub** 或 **hotel**。

inner /ˈɪnə(r); ˈɪnɚ/ *adjective* 形容词
of the inside; in the centre 内部的；中心的：*the inner city* 市中心 ✪ opposite 反义词：**outer**

innocent /ˈɪnəsnt; ˈɪnəsn̩t/ *adjective* 形容词
If you are innocent, you have not done wrong 无辜的；无罪的；清白的：*The police say John stole the money, but I think he's innocent.* 警方说约翰偷钱，可是我认为他是无辜的。✪ opposite 反义词：**guilty**
innocence /ˈɪnəsns; ˈɪnəsn̩s/ *noun* 名词 (no plural 无复数)
The prisoner's family are sure of her innocence. 这个女犯人的家属认定她没有罪。
✪ opposite 反义词：**guilt**

inquire /ɪnˈkwaɪə(r); ɪnˈkwaɪr/ *verb* 动词 (**inquires, inquiring, inquired** /ɪnˈkwaɪəd; ɪnˈkwaɪrd/)
ask 询问；问：*I inquired about trains to Leeds.* 我查问了开往利兹的列车的情况。◇ *'Are you hungry?' he inquired.* "你饿吗？"他问道。✪ **Ask** is the word that we usually use. ＊ **ask** 是常用词。
inquire into something try to find out more about something that happened 调查；查问：*The police are inquiring into the murder.* 警方正在调查这起谋杀案。

inquiry /ɪnˈkwaɪəri; ˈɪnkwərɪ/ *noun* 名词 (*plural* 复数作 **inquiries**)
a question that you ask about something（询问的）问题：*The police are making inquiries about the robbery.* 警方正在查问这一劫案的情况。

insane /ɪnˈseɪn; ɪnˈsen/ *adjective* 形容词
mad 疯狂的

insect /ˈɪnsekt; ˈɪnsɛkt/ *noun* 名词
a very small animal that has six legs 昆虫：*Ants, flies, butterflies and beetles are all insects.* 蚂蚁、苍蝇、蝴蝶、甲虫都是昆虫。

insecure /ˌɪnsɪˈkjʊə(r); ˌɪnsɪˈkjʊr/ *adjective* 形容词
1 not safe or firm 不安全的；不牢固的：*An actor's job is very insecure.* 演员工作很不稳定。
2 worried and not sure about yourself 担心而无主意的；缺乏安全感的：*Since their father left, the children have felt very insecure.* 孩子们在父亲离开后，感到六神无主。
insecurity /ˌɪnsɪˈkjʊərəti; ˌɪnsɪˈkjʊrətɪ/ *noun* 名词 (no plural 无复数)
She had feelings of insecurity. 她觉得没有安全感。

insert /ɪnˈsɜːt; ɪnˈsɝt/ *verb* 动词 (**inserts, inserting, inserted**)
put something into something or between two things 插入某物中或两物之间：*Insert the key into the lock.* 把钥匙插进锁孔里。

inside[1] /ɪnˈsaɪd; ˈɪnˈsaɪd/ *noun* 名词
the part near the middle of something 里面；内部：*The inside of a pear is white and the outside is green or yellow.* 梨的里面是白色的，外面是绿色的或黄色的。◇ *He did not see the inside of the house before he bought it.* 他买这所房子之前也没进去看看里面是什么样的。
inside out with the wrong side on the outside 里面朝外：*You've got your jumper on inside out.* 你的套头毛衣里外穿反了。

inside out 里面朝外

inside[2] /ˈɪnsaɪd; ˈɪnˈsaɪd/ *adjective* 形容词
in or near the middle 里面的；内部的：*the inside pages of a newspaper* 报纸的内页

inside[3] /ɪnˈsaɪd; ɪnˈsaɪd/ *preposition, adverb* 介词，副词
in or to the inside of something 在里面；向内部：*What's inside the box?* 箱子里面有什么？◇ *It's raining—let's go inside* (= into the building). 下雨了——咱们进去吧。☞ picture on page C1 见第C1页图

insist /ɪnˈsɪst; ɪnˈsɪst/ *verb* 动词 (**insists, insisting, insisted**)
1 say very strongly that you must do

or have something or that something must happen 坚持或坚决要求某事物: *I said I would walk to the station, but Paul insisted on driving me there.* 我说我要走到车站去，可是保罗一定要开车送我去。

2 say very strongly that something is true, when somebody does not believe you 坚持说某事属实（尤指有人不相信时）: *Mum insists that she saw a ghost.* 妈妈硬说她看见鬼了。

inspect /ɪn'spekt; ɪn'spɛkt/ *verb* 动词 (**inspects**, **inspecting**, **inspected**)

1 look at something carefully 检查某事物: *I inspected the car before I bought it.* 我买这辆汽车之前把它仔细检查了一遍。

2 visit a place or a group of people to see that work is done well 视察某处或检查工作: *The kitchens are inspected every week.* 厨房每星期都要检查一次。

inspection /ɪn'spekʃn; ɪn'spɛkʃən/ *noun* 名词

The police made an inspection of the house. 警方把房子检查了一遍。

inspector /ɪn'spektə(r); ɪn'spɛktɚ/ *noun* 名词

1 a person whose job is to see that things are done correctly 检查员；视查员: *On the train, the inspector asked to see my ticket.* 在列车上，检票员要查看我的车票。◇ *a factory inspector* 工厂的检验员

2 a police officer（警察）巡官

inspiration /ˌɪnspə'reɪʃn; ˌɪnspə'reʃən/ *noun* 名词

a person or thing that gives you ideas which help you do something good, for example write or paint 灵感: *The beauty of the mountains is a great inspiration to many artists.* 群山的美景启发了很多艺术家的灵感。

inspire /ɪn'spaɪə(r); ɪn'spaɪr/ *verb* 动词 (**inspires**, **inspiring**, **inspired** /ɪn'spaɪəd; ɪn'spaɪrd/)

1 give somebody ideas that help them do something good, for example write or paint 给某人以灵感: *His wife inspired him to write this poem.* 他妻子激发了他的灵感创作出了这首诗。

2 make somebody feel or think something 使某人感觉到或联想到某事物: *Her words inspired us all with hope.* 她的话使我们觉得又有了希望。

install /ɪn'stɔ:l; ɪn'stɔl/ *verb* 动词 (**installs**, **installing**, **installed** /ɪn'stɔ:ld; ɪn'stɔld/)

put a new thing in its place so it is ready to use 安装；设置: *She installed a new washing-machine.* 她安装了一个新的洗衣机。

installment *American English for* **instalment** 美式英语，即 **instalment**

instalment /ɪn'stɔ:lmənt; ɪn'stɔlmənt/ *noun* 名词

1 one part of a long story on radio or television, or in a magazine（电台或电视台播放的，或杂志刊载的长篇故事的）一集: *Did you read the last instalment?* 你看最后一集了吗？

2 a part of the cost of something that you pay each week or month, for example（分期付款的）一期付款: *She's paying for her new car in twelve monthly instalments.* 她买这辆新汽车分十二个月付款。

instance /'ɪnstəns; 'ɪnstəns/ *noun* 名词

an example 例子；实例；事例: *There have been many instances of forests fires this year.* 今年有很多起森林火灾。

for instance as an example 例如: *There are many things to see in London—for instance Big Ben and Buckingham Palace.* 伦敦有很多东西可看——例如大本钟和白金汉宫。

instant[1] /'ɪnstənt; 'ɪnstənt/ *adjective* 形容词

1 that happens very quickly; immediate 立即的；立刻的: *The film was an instant success.* 这部影片一上映就大获成功。

2 quick and easy to prepare 很快就容易做好的: *an instant meal* 方便快餐

instant coffee /ˌɪnstənt 'kɒfi; ˌɪnstənt 'kɔfɪ/ *noun* 名词 (no plural 无复数)

coffee that you make quickly with coffee powder and hot water 速溶咖啡

instantly *adverb* 副词

immediately; at once 立刻；马上: *I asked him a question and he replied instantly.* 我问他一个问题，他立刻回答出来了。

instant[2] /'ɪnstənt; 'ɪnstənt/ *noun* 名词

a very short time; a moment 瞬间；片刻: *She thought for an instant before she answered.* 她想了一下才回答。

instead /ɪn'sted; ɪn'stɛd/ *adverb* 副词

in the place of somebody or something

代替（某人或某事物）: *We haven't got any coffee. Would you like tea instead?* 我们没有咖啡。您喝茶行吗？◇ *Stuart can't go to the meeting so I will go instead.* 斯图尔特不能去开会，所以我替他去。

instead of *preposition* 介词
in the place of 代替…；而不…: *He's been playing football all afternoon instead of studying.* 他踢了一下午足球而没念书。◇ *Can you come at 7.30 instead of 8.00?* 您别8点钟来了，改在7点30分行吗？

instinct /'ɪnstɪŋkt; 'ɪnstɪŋkt/ *noun* 名词
something that makes people and animals do certain things without thinking or learning about them 本能: *Birds build their nests by instinct.* 鸟天生会筑巢。

instinctive /ɪn'stɪŋktɪv; ɪn'stɪŋktɪv/ *adjective* 形容词
Animals have an instinctive fear of fire. 动物生来就怕火。

institute /'ɪnstɪtju:t; 'ɪnstəˌtut/ *noun* 名词
a group of people who meet to study or talk about a special thing; the building where they meet 协会；会所；会址: *the Institute of Science* 科学研究会

institution /ˌɪnstɪ'tju:ʃn; ˌɪnstə'tuʃən/ *noun* 名词
a big building like a bank, hospital, prison or school, and all the people in it（银行、医院、监狱或学校等）机构: *Most of the hospitals and schools in Britain are government institutions* (= the government controls them). 英国多数医院和学校都是政府主办的机构。

instruct /ɪn'strʌkt; ɪn'strʌkt/ *verb* 动词 (**instructs, instructing, instructed**)
1 tell somebody what they must do 指示或指导某人做某事: *He instructed the driver to take him to the palace.* 他吩咐司机把他送到宫殿去。
2 teach somebody 教授或教导某人: *She instructed me in how to use the computer.* 她教我使用计算机。

instruction /ɪn'strʌkʃn; ɪn'strʌkʃən/ *noun* 名词
1 (*plural* 复数作 **instructions**) words that tell you what you must do or how to do something（做法或用法等的）说明；指示: *Read the instructions on the box before you make the cake.* 先阅读盒子上的蛋糕做法说明，然后再动手做。
2 (no plural 无复数) teaching or being taught something（对知识的）教授；传授: *driving instruction* 驾驶训练

instructor /ɪn'strʌktə(r); ɪn'strʌktɚ/ *noun* 名词
a person who teaches you how to do something 教员；教练；指导员: *a driving instructor* 驾驶教练

instrument /'ɪnstrəmənt; 'ɪnstrəmənt/ *noun* 名词
1 a thing that you use for doing a special job 工具；器具；仪器: *A telescope is an instrument used for looking at things that are a long way away.* 望远镜是用以观察远距离物体的仪器。◇ *medical instruments* (= used by doctors) 医疗器械（= 医生使用的）
2 a thing that you use for playing music 乐器: *Violins and trumpets are musical instruments.* 小提琴和小号都是乐器。◇ *What instrument do you play?* 您是演奏什么乐器的？

insult /ɪn'sʌlt; ɪn'sʌlt/ *verb* 动词 (**insults, insulting, insulted**)
be rude to somebody 侮辱某人；辱骂；侮慢: *She insulted my brother by saying he was fat.* 她侮辱我哥哥，说他肥胖。

insult /'ɪnsʌlt; 'ɪnsʌlt/ *noun* 名词
something rude that you say or do to somebody 侮辱人的言语或行动；辱骂；侮慢: *The boys shouted insults at each other.* 那些男孩子互相对骂。

insurance /ɪn'ʃʊərəns; ɪn'ʃurəns/ *noun* 名词 (no plural 无复数)
an agreement where you pay money to a company so that it will give you a lot of money if something bad happens（保险公司的）保险合同；保险单: *When I crashed my car, the insurance paid for the repairs.* 我撞了汽车以后，保险公司给付了修理费。

insure /ɪn'ʃʊə(r); ɪn'ʃur/ *verb* 动词 (**insures, insuring, insured** /ɪn'ʃʊəd; ɪn'ʃurd/)
1 pay money to a company, so that it will give you money if something bad happens（向保险公司）投保（缴纳保险费用，遇到损失可获得赔偿）；买保险: *Have you insured your house against fire?* 您的房子投保火险了吗？◇ *My car isn't insured.* 我的汽车没买保险。
2 *American English for* **ensure** 美式英语，即 **ensure**。

I

intelligence /ɪn'telɪdʒəns; ɪn'tɛlədʒəns/ *noun* 名词 (no plural 无复数)
being able to think, learn and understand quickly and well 思维、学习和理解得快而好的能力；智慧；聪明: *He is a man of great intelligence.* 他是个很有智慧的人。◇ *an intelligence test* 智力测验

intelligent /ɪn'telɪdʒənt; ɪn'tɛlədʒənt/ *adjective* 形容词
able to think, learn and understand quickly and well 思维、学习和理解得快而好的；有智慧的；聪明的: *Their daughter is very intelligent.* 他们的女儿非常聪明。

intend /ɪn'tend; ɪn'tɛnd/ *verb* 动词 (**intends**, **intending**, **intended**)
plan to do something 打算；想要: *When do you intend to go to London?* 您打算什么时候去伦敦？
be intended for somebody or 或 **something** be for somebody or something 为某人或某事物的: *This dictionary is intended for elementary learners of English.* 本词典是为初学英语的人编写的。

intense /ɪn'tens; ɪn'tɛns/ *adjective* 形容词
very great or strong 非常大的或非常强的: *intense pain* 剧痛 ◇ *The heat from the fire was intense.* 这个暖炉的热力很强。

intention /ɪn'tenʃn; ɪn'tɛnʃən/ *noun* 名词
what you plan to do 意图；用意；打算: *They have no intention of getting married.* 他们无意结婚。
intentional /ɪn'tenʃənl; ɪn'tɛnʃənl̩/ *adjective* 形容词
that you want and plan to do, and do not do by mistake 有意的；故意的: *I'm sorry I upset you—it wasn't intentional!* 对不起让您不痛快了——我不是成心的！✪ opposite 反义词: **unintentional**
intentionally /ɪn'tenʃənəli; ɪn'tɛnʃnəlɪ/ *adverb* 副词
They broke the window intentionally—it wasn't an accident. 他们是故意把窗户打破的——不是意外。

interest[1] /'ɪntrəst; 'ɪntrɪst/ *noun* 名词
1 (no plural 无复数) wanting to know or learn about somebody or something 想要知道或了解某人或某事物；关心；好奇心；兴趣: *He read the story with interest.* 他津津有味地看那部小说。
2 (*plural* 复数作 **interests**) something that you like doing or learning about 喜欢做的或喜欢学的事物；爱好: *His interests are computers and rock music.* 他爱好计算机和摇滚乐。
3 (no plural 无复数) the extra money that you pay back if you borrow money or that you receive if you put money in a bank 利息
take an interest in somebody or 或 **something** want to know about somebody or something 想要了解某人或某事物: *He takes no interest in politics.* 他对政治不感兴趣。

interest[2] /'ɪntrəst; 'ɪntrɪst/ *verb* 动词 (**interests**, **interesting**, **interested**)
make somebody want to know more 使某人想多了解些；使某人感兴趣: *Religion doesn't interest her.* 宗教问题不能引起她的兴趣。
interested *adjective* 形容词
If you are interested in somebody or something, you want to know more about them（指本人对某人或某事物）想多了解些的；感兴趣的: *Are you interested in cars?* 您对汽车有兴趣吗？✪ opposite 反义词: **uninterested**
interesting *adjective* 形容词
A person or thing that is interesting makes you want to know more about him/her/it（指某人或某事物）使人想多了解些的；使人感兴趣的: *This book is very interesting.* 这本书很吸引人。◇ *That's an interesting idea!* 这个主意真有意思！✪ opposite 反义词: **uninteresting** or 或 **boring**

interfere /ˌɪntə'fɪə(r); ˌɪntɚ'fɪr/ *verb* 动词 (**interferes**, **interfering**, **interfered** /ˌɪntə'fɪəd; ˌɪntɚ'fɪrd/)
1 try to do something with or for somebody, when they do not want your help 干预；干涉；干扰: *Don't interfere! Let John decide what he wants to do.* 别打扰他！让约翰自己决定他想做什么。
2 stop something from being done well 阻碍；妨碍；妨害: *His interest in football often interferes with his studies.* 他喜爱足球因而常常影响了学习。
3 change or touch something without asking if you can（未经允许）改动或触摸某物: *Who's been interfering with the clock? It's stopped.* 谁乱动这个钟了？已经停了。

interference /ˌɪntəˈfɪərəns; ˌɪntɚˈfɪrəns/ *noun* 名词
Go away! I don't want any interference when I'm working! 走开！我工作的时候不愿意有人打扰！

interior /ɪnˈtɪəriə(r); ɪnˈtɪrɪɚ/ *noun* 名词
the inside part 内部；里面: *We painted the interior of the house white.* 我们把房子里面刷成白色的了。
interior *adjective* 形容词
interior walls 里面的墙
✪ opposite 反义词: **exterior**

intermediate /ˌɪntəˈmi:diət; ˌɪntɚˈmidɪɪt/ *adjective* 形容词
that comes between two people or things; in the middle 在两人或两事物之间的；中间的: *She's in an intermediate class.* 她在中级班。

internal /ɪnˈtɜ:nl; ɪnˈtɝnl̩/ *adjective* 形容词
of or on the inside 内部的；在内部的: *He has internal injuries* (= inside his body). 他有内伤（＝体内）。✪ opposite 反义词: **external**
internally /ɪnˈtɜ:nəli; ɪnˈtɝnl̩ɪ/ *adverb* 副词
on the inside 内部；在内部

international /ˌɪntəˈnæʃnəl; ˌɪntɚˈnæʃənl̩/ *adjective* 形容词
between different countries 国与国之间的；国际的: *an international football match* 国际足球比赛 ◇ *an international flight* 国际航班

interpret /ɪnˈtɜ:prɪt; ɪnˈtɝprɪt/ *verb* 动词 (**interprets**, **interpreting**, **interpreted**)
say in one language what somebody has said in another language 口头翻译；口译: *I can't speak Italian –interpret for me.* 我不会说意大利语——您给我翻译一下行吗？
interpreter *noun* 名词
a person who interprets 做口头翻译的人；口译者: *The President had an interpreter when he went to China.* 那位会长到中国去的时候带着个口译人员。

interrupt /ˌɪntəˈrʌpt; ˌɪntəˈrʌpt/ *verb* 动词 (**interrupts**, **interrupting**, **interrupted**)
1 stop somebody speaking or doing something by saying or doing something yourself 用言语或动作中止某人的话或动作；打扰: *Please don't interrupt me when I'm speaking.* 请不要打断我的话。
2 stop something for a time 暂时中止某事物: *The war interrupted travel between the two countries.* 这场战争中断了两国之间的交通。
interruption /ˌɪntəˈrʌpʃn; ˌɪntəˈrʌpʃən/ *noun* 名词
I can't do my homework here. There are too many interruptions. 我无法在这里做功课。干扰太多了。

interval /ˈɪntəvl; ˈɪntɚvl̩/ *noun* 名词
a short time between two parts of a play or concert（戏剧、音乐会的）中间休息；幕间休息: *We bought drinks in the interval.* 我们在幕间休息的时候买了些饮品。

interview /ˈɪntəvju:; ˈɪntɚˌvju/ *noun* 名词
1 a meeting when somebody asks you questions to decide if you will have a job（申请工作时接受的）面试: *I've got an interview for a new job tomorrow.* 我找新工作，明天有个面试。
2 a meeting when somebody answers questions for a newspaper or for a television or radio programme（报纸、电视或电台对某人的）采访: *There was an interview with the Prime Minister on TV last night.* 昨天晚上有个采访首相的电视节目。
interview *verb* 动词 (**interviews**, **interviewing**, **interviewed** /ˈɪntəvju:d; ˈɪntɚˌvjud/)
ask somebody questions in an interview 进行面试或采访；面试；采访: *They interviewed six people for the job.* 他们面试了六个申请这份工作的人。
interviewer *noun* 名词
a person who asks questions in an interview 面试或采访的主持人: *The interviewer asked me why I wanted the job.* 面试主持人问我为什么要做这份工作。

into /ˈɪntə, ˈɪntu, ˈɪntu:; ˈɪntə, ˈɪntu/ *preposition* 介词
1 to the middle or the inside of something 到某物的中间或内部: *Come into the house.* 到房子里来。◇ *I went into town.* 我进城了。◇ *He fell into the river.* 他掉进河里了。☞ picture on page C4 见第C4页图
2 a word that shows how somebody or something changes 表示某人或某事物产生变化的词: *When it is very cold, water changes into ice.* 非常冷的时候水就结成冰了。

I

◇ *They made the room into a bedroom.* 他们把这个房间改成卧室了。

3 against something 触及某事物: *The car crashed into a tree.* 汽车撞到树上了。

4 a word that you use when you divide a number（用以表示把一个数分成若干等份的词）除: *4 into 12 is 3.* 用4除12得3。

be into something like something; be interested in something 喜爱某事物: *What sort of music are you into?* 您喜欢什么音乐？

introduce /ˌɪntrəˈdju:s; ˌɪntrəˈdus/ *verb* 动词 (**introduces, introducing, introduced** /ˌɪntrəˈdju:st; ˌɪntrəˈdjust/)

1 bring people together for the first time and tell each of them the name of the other 为他人相互介绍（使彼此认识）: *She introduced me to her brother.* 她把我介绍给她的哥哥。

2 bring in something new 开始采用新事物: *This law was introduced in 1990.* 这项法规是在1990年开始实施的。

introduce yourself tell somebody your name 自我介绍: *He introduced himself to me.* 他向我做了自我介绍。

introduction /ˌɪntrəˈdʌkʃn; ˌɪntrəˈdʌkʃən/ *noun* 名词

1 (*plural* 复数作 **introductions**) bringing people together to meet each other（为他人相互认识而做的）介绍

2 (*plural* 复数作 **introductions**) a piece of writing at the beginning of a book that tells you about the book（书的）前言；序言

3 (no plural 无复数) bringing in something new 开始采用的新事物: *the introduction of computers into schools* 学校开始使用计算机

invade /ɪnˈveɪd; ɪnˈved/ *verb* 动词 (**invades, invading, invaded**)

go into another country to attack it 武装侵入他国；侵略: *They invaded the country with tanks and guns.* 他们使用坦克和枪炮侵入了那个国家。

invader *noun* 名词

a person who invades 侵略者

invalid /ˈɪnvəlɪd; ˈɪnvəlɪd/ *noun* 名词

a person who is very ill and needs another person to look after him/her（需他人照顾的）病弱者: *She has been an invalid since the accident.* 她出了事故以后就一直需要别人照顾。

invaluable /ɪnˈvæljuəbl; ɪnˈvæljuəbḷ/ *adjective* 形容词

very useful 极其宝贵的；非常有用的: *Your help was invaluable.* 您的帮助是非常宝贵的。

invariably /ɪnˈveəriəbli; ɪnˈvɛrɪəblɪ/ *adverb* 副词

almost always 几乎总是: *He invariably arrives late.* 他差不多每次都迟到。

invasion /ɪnˈveɪʒn; ɪnˈveʒən/ *noun* 名词

a time when an army from one country goes into another country to attack it 对他国的武装侵入；侵略: *Germany's invasion of Poland in 1939* 德国于1939年入侵波兰

invent /ɪnˈvent; ɪnˈvɛnt/ *verb* 动词 (**invents, inventing, invented**)

1 make or think of something for the first time 发明；创造: *Who invented the bicycle?* 自行车是谁发明的？

2 tell something that is not true 捏造；虚构: *She invented a story about where she was last night.* 她胡编出她昨天晚上去的地方。

inventor /ɪnˈventə(r); ɪnˈvɛntɚ/ *noun* 名词

a person who makes or thinks of something new 发明者；创造者

invention /ɪnˈvenʃn; ɪnˈvɛnʃən/ *noun* 名词

1 (*plural* 复数作 **inventions**) a thing that somebody has made for the first time 发明或创造的事物

2 (no plural 无复数) inventing something 发明；创造: *The invention of the telephone changed the world.* 电话的发明改变了世界。

inverted commas /ɪnˌvɜ:tɪd ˈkɒməz; ɪnˌvɝtɪd ˈkɑməz/ *noun* 名词 (plural 复数)

the signs " " or ' ' that you use in writing before and after words that somebody said 引号" "或' '

invest /ɪnˈvest; ɪnˈvɛst/ *verb* 动词 (**invests, investing, invested**)

give money to a business or bank so that you will get more money back 投资: *He invested all his money in the company.* 他把钱都投资在这家公司里了。

investment /ɪnˈvestmənt; ɪnˈvɛstmənt/ *noun* 名词

investing money; money that you invest

I

投资；（投资的）资金: *an investment of £10 000* ＊ 10 000英镑的投资

investigate /ɪn'vestɪgeɪt; ɪn'vɛstə͵get/ *verb* 动词 (**investigates**, **investigating**, **investigated**)
try to find out about something 调查；侦查: *The police are investigating the murder.* 警方正在调查这起凶杀案。

investigation /ɪn͵vestɪ'geɪʃn; ɪn͵vɛstə'geʃən/ *noun* 名词
The police are holding an investigation into the fire. 警方正在调查这一起火事件。

invisible /ɪn'vɪzəbl; ɪn'vɪzəbḷ/ *adjective* 形容词
If something is invisible, you cannot see it 看不见的: *Wind is invisible.* 风是看不见的。

invitation /͵ɪnvɪ'teɪʃn; ͵ɪnvə'teʃən/ *noun* 名词
If you have an invitation to go somewhere, somebody has spoken or written to you and asked you to go 邀请: *Joe sent me an invitation to his party.* 乔给我寄来请帖，邀请我参加他的聚会。

invite /ɪn'vaɪt; ɪn'vaɪt/ *verb* 动词 (**invites**, **inviting**, **invited**)
ask somebody to come to a party or a meeting, for example 邀请: *Anna invited me to her party.* 安娜邀请我去参加她的聚会。◇ *Let's invite them for dinner.* 咱们请他们吃顿饭吧。

invoice /'ɪnvɔɪs; 'ɪnvɔɪs/ *noun* 名词
a list that shows how much you must pay for things that somebody has sold you, or for work that somebody has done for you 发票；发货票

involve /ɪn'vɒlv; ɪn'vɑlv/ *verb* 动词 (**involves**, **involving**, **involved** /ɪn'vɒlʌd; ɪn'vɑlvd/)
1 have something as a part 包含某事物: *The job involves using a computer.* 做这份工作需要使用计算机。
2 make somebody take part in something 使很多人参与某活动: *A lot of people were involved in planning the wedding.* 有很多人参与筹备这一婚礼。

inward /'ɪnwəd; 'ɪnwəd/, **inwards** /'ɪnwədz; 'ɪnwədz/ *adverb* 副词
towards the inside or centre 向内；向中心: *The doors open inwards.* 这些门都是向里开的。✪ opposite 反义词: **outward** or 或 **outwards**

> **ir-** *prefix* 前缀
> You can add **ir-** to the beginning of some words to give them the opposite meaning, for example 在某些字前可加 **ir-** 构成反义词，如:
> **irregular** = not regular

iron /'aɪən; 'aɪən/ *noun* 名词
1 (no plural 无复数) a strong hard metal 铁: *The gates are made of iron.* 这些大门是铁的。◇ *an iron bar* 铁棍
2 (*plural* 复数作 **irons**) an electrical thing that gets hot and that you use for making clothes smooth 电熨斗

iron *verb* 动词 (**irons**, **ironing**, **ironed** /'aɪənd; 'aɪənd/)
make clothes smooth with an iron（用电熨斗）熨平衣物: *Can you iron this shirt for me?* 您给我熨熨这件衬衫行吗？✪ When we talk about ironing a lot of clothes, we often say **do the ironing** 熨很多衣物，常说 **do the ironing**: *I've done the ironing.* 我把这批衣服熨完了。

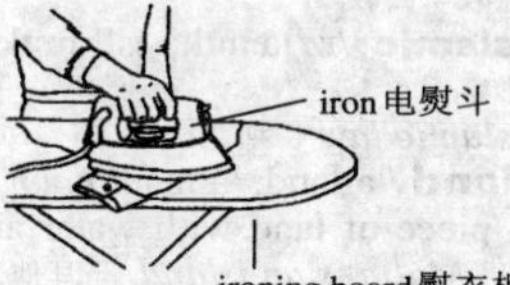

ironing *noun* 名词 (no plural 无复数)
clothes that you must iron 待熨的衣物: *There's a pile of ironing on the chair.* 椅子上有一堆要熨的衣服。

ironing-board /'aɪənɪŋ bɔ:d; 'aɪənɪŋ ͵bɔrd/ *noun* 名词
a special long table where you iron clothes 熨衣板

irregular /ɪ'regjələ(r); ɪ'rɛgjələ/ *adjective* 形容词
1 that happens again and again, but with different amounts of time in between 一次又一次，但时间间隔不一的；不定期发生的: *Their visits were irregular.* 他们到访的时间不定。
2 A word that is irregular does not have the usual verb forms or plural（指词，因时态、复数等）形式不规则的: *'Catch' is an irregular verb.* ＊ catch 是个不规则动词。

I

irrelevant /ɪ'reləvənt; ɪ'rɛləvənt/ *adjective* 形容词
not connected with something and not important 与某事物无关而且不重要: *We are good friends. She is older than me, but that is irrelevant.* 我们是好朋友。她比我大，却也并不妨事。

irritate /'ɪrɪteɪt; 'ɪrəˌtet/ *verb* 动词 (**irritates**, **irritating**, **irritated**)
1 make somebody quite angry 使某人愤怒: *He irritates me when he asks so many questions.* 他问了那么多问题，把我问火儿了。
2 make a part of your body hurt a little 使身体某部不适: *Cigarette smoke irritates my eyes.* 香烟的烟雾熏得我的眼睛难受。
irritation /ˌɪrɪ'teɪʃn; ˌɪrə'teʃən/ *noun* 名词
This plant causes irritation to your skin. 这种植物能刺激皮肤引起不适。

is *form of* **be** ✳ **be** 的不同形式

Islam /'ɪzlɑːm; 'ɪsləm/ *noun* 名词 (no plural 无复数)
the religion of Muslim people. Islam teaches that there is only one God and that Muhammad is his messenger. 伊斯兰教；回教
Islamic /ɪz'læmɪk; ɪs'lɑmɪk/ *adjective* 形容词
Islamic law 伊斯兰教规

island /'aɪlənd; 'aɪlənd/ *noun* 名词
a piece of land with water all around it 岛: *Malta is an island.* 马耳他是个岛。

Isle /aɪl; aɪl/ *noun* 名词
an island 岛: *the British Isles* 不列颠群岛
✪ **Isle** is usually used in names of islands. ✳ **isle** 一词常用做岛屿的名称。

isn't /'ɪznt; 'ɪzn̩t/ = **is not**

isolated /'aɪsəleɪtɪd; 'aɪsl̩ˌetɪd/ *adjective* 形容词
far from other people or things 远离他人或他事物的；隔离的: *an isolated house in the mountains* 群山中与外界隔绝的一所房子
isolation /ˌaɪsə'leɪʃn; ˌaɪsl̩'eʃən/ *noun* 名词 (no plural 无复数)
being away from other people or things 远离他人或他事物；隔离: *A lot of old people live in isolation.* 有很多老人过着孤独的生活。

issue¹ /'ɪʃuː; 'ɪʃʊ/ *noun* 名词
1 an important problem that people talk about（人们议论的）重大问题: *Pollution is a serious issue.* 环境污染是个严重问题。
2 a magazine or newspaper of a particular day, week, or month（杂志或报纸的）一期: *Have you read this week's issue of the magazine?* 这份杂志本星期的这一期您看过吗？

issue² /'ɪʃuː; 'ɪʃʊ/ *verb* 动词 (**issues**, **issuing**, **issued** /'ɪʃuːd; 'ɪʃʊd/)
give something to people 把某物发给大家: *The soldiers were issued with uniforms.* 士兵都发制服了。

it /ɪt; ɪt/ *pronoun* 代词 (*plural* 复数作 **they**, **them**)
1 a word that shows a thing or animal 称事、物或动物的词；它: *I've got a new shirt. It's (= it is) blue.* 我有件新衬衫。是蓝色的。◇ *Where is the coffee? I can't find it.* 咖啡在哪里？我找不着。
2 a word that points to an idea that follows 预指下文的词: *It is difficult to learn Japanese.* 日语很难学。
3 a word that shows who somebody is 表明某人是谁的词: *'Who's on the telephone?' 'It's Jo.'* "打电话的是谁？" "是乔。"
4 a word at the beginning of a sentence about time, the weather, distance, etc 用于句首，指时间、天气、距离等的词: *It's six o'clock.* 六点钟了。◇ *It's hot today.* 今天很热。◇ *It's 100 kilometres to London.* 到伦敦是100公里。

italics /ɪ'tælɪks; ɪ'tælɪks/ *noun* 名词 (plural 复数)
letters that lean to the side 斜体字母: *This sentence is in italics.* 本句的（英文）文字是斜体字。

itch /ɪtʃ; ɪtʃ/ *verb* 动词 (**itches**, **itching**, **itched** /ɪtʃt; ɪtʃt/)
have a feeling on your skin that makes you want to rub or scratch it 痒: *My nose itches.* 我的鼻子发痒。◇ *This jumper makes me itch.* 我穿这件套头毛衣很痒。
itch *noun* 名词 (*plural* 复数作 **itches**)
I've got an itch. 我很痒。
itchy *adjective* 形容词
If something is itchy, it itches or it makes you itch（使人）发痒的: *itchy skin* 发痒的皮肤

it'd /'ɪtəd; 'ɪtəd/
1 = **it had**
2 = **it would**

item /'aɪtəm; 'aɪtəm/ *noun* 名词
1 one thing in a list or group of things

（清单中或一些事物中的）一项，一件，一个: *She had the most expensive item on the menu.* 她吃的是菜谱上最贵的菜。◇ *an item of clothing* 一件衣服

2 a piece of news 一条消息: *There was an interesting item on TV about South Africa.* 电视上有个关于南非的很有意思的消息。

it'll /'ɪtl; 'ɪtḷ/ = **it will**

its /ɪts; ɪts/ *adjective* 形容词

of the thing or animal that you have just talked about（指事、物或动物）它的: *The dog has hurt its leg.* 这条狗的腿受伤了。◇ *The company has its factory in Hull.* 这家公司在赫尔设有工厂。

it's /ɪts; ɪts/

1 = it is

2 = it has

itself /ɪt'self; ɪt'sɛlf/ *pronoun* 代词 (*plural* 复数作 **themselves** /ðəm'selvz; ðəm'sɛlvz/)

1 a word that shows the same thing or animal that you have just talked about 它自己；它本身: *The cat was washing itself.* 猫自己洗身体呢。

2 a word that makes 'it' stronger 用以增强 it 一词的语气的词: *The hotel itself was nice but I didn't like the town.* 旅馆本身倒不错，可是我不喜欢这个镇。

by itself **1** alone 独自地；单独地: *The house stands by itself in the forest.* 那所房子孤零零地坐落在森林之中。 **2** without being controlled by a person 不用人操纵；自动地: *The machine will start by itself.* 这个机器能自动开启。

I've /aɪv; aɪv/ = **I have**

ivory /'aɪvəri; 'aɪvərɪ/ *noun* 名词 (no plural 无复数)

the hard white stuff that an elephant's **tusks** are made of 象牙物质（象牙叫做 **tusk**）

ivy /'aɪvi; 'aɪvɪ/ *noun* 名词 (no plural 无复数)

a plant with dark green leaves, that climbs up walls or trees 常春藤（可缘墙壁或树木攀爬的植物，叶呈深绿色）

I

Jj

jack /dʒæk; dʒæk/ *noun* 名詞
the playing-card that has a picture of a young man on it（纸牌中的）杰克，J: *the jack of hearts* 红桃J

jacket /ˈdʒækɪt; ˈdʒækɪt/ *noun* 名词
a short coat with sleeves 短上衣；甲克 ☞ picture at **suit** 见 **suit** 词条插图

jacket potato /ˌdʒækɪt pəˈteɪtəʊ; ˈdʒækɪt pəˌteto/ *noun* 名词 (*plural* 复数作 **jacket potatoes**)
a potato that you cook in the oven without taking the skin off 带皮烤熟的土豆

jagged /ˈdʒægɪd; ˈdʒægɪd/ *adjective* 形容词
rough, with a lot of sharp points 粗糙而有很多尖的: *jagged rocks* 犬牙交错的岩石

jaguar /ˈdʒægjuə(r); ˈdʒægjʊˌɑr/ *noun* 名词
a wild animal like a big cat. It has yellow fur with black spots. 美洲豹；美洲虎

jail /dʒeɪl; dʒel/ *noun* 名词
a prison 监狱: *He was sent to jail for two years.* 他入狱两年。

jail *verb* 动词 (**jails**, **jailing**, **jailed** /dʒeɪld; dʒeld/)
put somebody in prison 把某人关进监狱: *She was jailed for killing her husband.* 她因杀死丈夫而入狱。

jam[1] /dʒæm; dʒæm/ *noun* 名词 (no plural 无复数)
food made from fruit and sugar. You eat jam on bread 果酱: *a jar of strawberry jam* 一罐草莓酱

jam[2] /dʒæm; dʒæm/ *verb* 动词 (**jams**, **jamming**, **jammed** /dʒæmd; dʒæmd/)
1 push something into a place where there is not much space 把某物塞进或挤进某处: *She jammed all her clothes into a suitcase.* 她把所有的衣服都塞进手提箱里了。
2 fix something or become fixed so that you cannot move it（使某物）卡住（不能活动）: *I can't open the window. It's jammed.* 我打不开这个窗户。卡住了。

jam[3] /dʒæm; dʒæm/ *noun* 名词
a lot of people or things in a place, so that it is difficult to move 很多人或事物聚于一处难以活动；拥挤；拥塞: *a traffic jam* 交通阻塞

January /ˈdʒænjuəri; ˈdʒænjʊˌɛrɪ/ *noun* 名词
the first month of the year 一月（份）

jar /dʒɑ:(r); dʒɑr/ *noun* 名词
a glass container for food（盛食物的）玻璃罐；广口瓶: *a jar of coffee* 一罐咖啡 ◇ *a jamjar* 果酱瓶 ☞ picture at **container** 见 **container** 词条插图

javelin /ˈdʒævəlɪn; ˈdʒævlɪn/ *noun* 名词
a long pointed stick that people throw as a sport 标枪

jaw /dʒɔ:; dʒɔ/ *noun* 名词
one of the two bones in the head of a person or an animal that hold the teeth 颌 ☞ picture on page C2 见第C2页图

jazz /dʒæz; dʒæz/ *noun* 名词 (no plural 无复数)
a kind of music with a strong beat 爵士乐

jealous /ˈdʒeləs; ˈdʒɛləs/ *adjective* 形容词
1 angry or sad because you want what another person has（因想要别人有的事物而气愤或悲伤）忌妒的: *Benjamin was jealous of his brother's new car.* 本杰明忌妒哥哥有辆新汽车。
2 angry or sad because you are afraid of losing somebody's love（因怕失去别人的爱而气愤或悲伤）忌妒的: *Sarah's boyfriend gets jealous if she speaks to other boys.* 萨拉要是跟别的小伙子说话，她男朋友就忌妒。

jealousy /ˈdʒeləsi; ˈdʒɛləsɪ/ *noun* 名词 (no plural 无复数)
being jealous 忌妒

jeans /dʒi:nz; dʒinz/ *noun* 名词 (plural 复数)
trousers made of strong cotton material, called **denim**. Jeans are usually blue 牛仔裤（多为蓝色，其布料叫做 **denim**）: *a pair of jeans* 一条牛仔裤 ◇ *She wore jeans and a T-shirt.* 她穿着牛仔裤和短袖汗衫。

Jeep /dʒi:p; dʒip/ *noun* 名词
a strong car that can go well over rough land 吉普车 ✪ **Jeep** is a trade mark. ✳ **Jeep**是商标。

jelly /ˈdʒeli; ˈdʒɛlɪ/ *noun* 名词 (*plural* 复数作 **jellies**)
a soft food made from fruit juice and sugar, that shakes when you move it 果冻

J

jellyfish /'dʒelifɪʃ; 'dʒɛlɪˌfɪʃ/ *noun* 名词 (*plural* 复数作 **jellyfish** or 或 **jellyfishes**)
a sea animal like jelly, that you can see through 水母；海蜇: *I saw a jellyfish on the beach.* 我在海滩上看见一个水母。

jerk /dʒɜ:k; dʒɝk/ *noun* 名词
a sudden pull or other movement 突然的拖拉或其他活动: *The bus started with a jerk.* 公共汽车开车的时候猛抻了一下。

jerk *verb* 动词 (**jerks, jerking, jerked** /dʒɜ:kt; dʒɝkt/)
The car jerked forward. 汽车一颠一颠地往前开。◇ *She jerked the door open.* 她猛然把门拉开了。

jet /dʒet; dʒɛt/ *noun* 名词
1 an aeroplane that flies when its engines push out hot gas 喷气式飞机
2 liquid or gas that is coming very fast out of a small hole（从小孔中）喷出的液体或气体；喷射: *a jet of gas* 喷气 ◇ *jets of water* 喷水

jet lag /'dʒet læg; 'dʒɛt læg/ *noun* 名词 (no plural 无复数)
a very tired feeling that you may have after a long journey by aeroplane 喷气飞行时差反应（长途飞行后身体可能出现的疲劳感觉）

Jew /dʒu:; dʒu/ *noun* 名词
a person who follows the old religion of Israel, called **Judaism** 犹太教徒（犹太教叫做 **Judaism**）

Jewish /'dʒu:ɪʃ; 'dʒuɪʃ/ *adjective* 形容词
She is Jewish. 她是犹太人。

jewel /'dʒu:əl; 'dʒuəl/ *noun* 名词
a beautiful stone, for example a diamond, that is very valuable 宝石（例如钻石）

jeweller *noun* 名词
a person who sells, makes or repairs jewellery and watches 出售、制造或修理珠宝和钟表的人 ✪ A shop that sells jewellery and watches is called a **jeweller's**. 出售珠宝和钟表的商店叫做 **jeweller's**。

jewellery /'dʒu:əlri; 'dʒuəlrɪ/ *noun* 名词 (no plural 无复数)
things like rings, bracelets and necklaces 首饰（例如戒指、手镯、项链等）: *She wears a lot of jewellery.* 她戴着很多首饰。

jeweler, jewelry *American English for* **jeweller, jewellery** 美式英语，即 **jeweller**、**jewellery**

jigsaw puzzle 拼图玩具

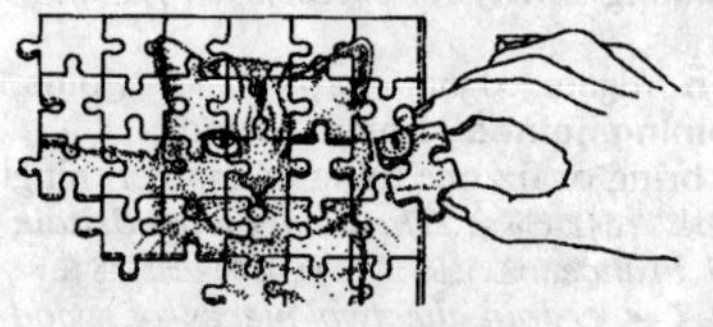

jigsaw, jigsaw puzzle /'dʒɪgsɔ: pʌzl; 'dʒɪgsɔ ˌpʌzḷ/ *noun* 名词
a picture in many pieces that you must put together 拼图玩具

job /dʒɒb; dʒɑb/ *noun* 名词
1 the work that you do for money（为得到钱而做的）工作: *He has left school but he hasn't got a job.* 他中学毕业了，可是还没有工作。◇ *She's looking for a new job.* 她正在找新的工作。
2 a piece of work that you must do（必须做的）事情: *I have a lot of jobs to do in the house.* 我家里还有很多事要做呢。

a good job a good or lucky thing 好的或幸运的事: *It's a good job that I was at home when you phoned.* 您打电话来的时候，我正好在家。

make a good job of something do something well 把某事做好: *You made a good job of the painting.* 你粉刷得很好。

out of a job If you are out of a job, you do not have work that you are paid to do. 失业

jockey /'dʒɒki; 'dʒɑkɪ/ *noun* 名词 (*plural* 复数作 **jockeys**)
a person who rides horses in races 职业赛马骑师

jog /dʒɒg; dʒɑg/ *verb* 动词 (**jogs, jogging, jogged** /dʒɒgd; dʒɑgd/)
1 run slowly for exercise 慢跑（作为运动）: *I jogged round the park.* 我在公园各处慢跑。✪ We often say **go jogging** 常说 **go jogging**: *I go jogging every morning.* 我每天早晨都慢跑。
2 push or touch something a little, so that it moves 轻推或轻触某物: *She jogged my arm and I spilled my drink.* 她碰了我胳膊一下，我就把饮品洒了。

jog *noun* 名词 (no plural 无复数)
a slow run for exercise（作为运动的）慢跑: *I went for a jog.* 我去锻炼慢跑了。

jogger *noun* 名词
a person who jogs（为运动）慢跑的人

J

jogging *noun* 名词 (no plural 无复数)
running slowly for exercise（作为运动的）慢跑

join /dʒɔɪn; dʒɔɪn/ *verb* 动词 (**joins, joining, joined** /dʒɔɪnd; dʒɔɪnd/)
1 bring or fix one thing to another thing 连结；结合；联合: *The tunnel joins Britain to France.* 这个隧道把英国和法国连在一起了。◇ *Join the two pieces of wood together.* 把这两块木头连接在一起。
2 come together with somebody or something 与某人或某事物相聚或会合: *This road joins the motorway soon.* 这条路很快就要跟高速公路会合了。◇ *Will you join us for dinner?* 您来跟我们一起吃饭好吗？
3 become a member of a group 成为某群体的成员: *He joined the army.* 他参军了。
join in do something with other people 与他人一起做某事: *We're playing football. Do you want to join in?* 我们踢足球。你也来吗？

joint[1] /dʒɔɪnt; dʒɔɪnt/ *noun* 名词
1 a part of the body where two bones come together. Elbows and knees are joints. 骨头互相连接的部位；关节
2 a place where two parts of something join together 两个物体相连接的地方: *the joints of a pipe* 管子的接头
3 a big piece of meat that you cook（烹饪用的）大块肉: *a joint of beef* 一大块牛肉

joint[2] /dʒɔɪnt; dʒɔɪnt/ *adjective* 形容词
that people do or have together 大家共同做的或共同有的: *Paul and Ian gave a joint party.* 保罗和伊恩合着举办了个聚会。

joke[1] /dʒəʊk; dʒok/ *noun* 名词
something that you say or do to make people laugh 使人发笑的话或事；笑话: *She told us a joke.* 她给我们讲了个笑话。
play a joke on somebody do something to somebody to make other people laugh; trick somebody 拿某人取笑；戏弄某人: *They played a joke on their teacher — they hid his books.* 他们跟老师开个玩笑——把他的书藏起来了。

joke[2] /dʒəʊk; dʒok/ *verb* 动词 (**jokes, joking, joked** /dʒəʊkt; dʒokt/)
say things that are not serious; say funny things 开玩笑；说笑话: *I didn't really mean what I said — I was only joking.* 我说的话其实并不是那个意思——不过是说着玩的。

jolly /ˈdʒɒli; ˈdʒɑlɪ/ *adjective* 形容词 (**jollier, jolliest**)
happy and full of fun 愉快而有趣的
jolly *adverb* 副词
very 非常；很: *It was a jolly good meal.* 那顿饭好极了。

jolt /dʒəʊlt; dʒolt/ *noun* 名词
a sudden movement 突然的移动: *The train stopped with a jolt.* 火车停的时候摇晃了一下。
jolt *verb* 动词 (**jolts, jolting, jolted**)
move or move something suddenly and quickly 突然迅速地移动（某物）: *The van jolted along the rough road.* 客货车在凹凸不平的路上颠簸前行。

jot /dʒɒt; dʒɑt/ *verb* 动词 (**jots, jotting, jotted**)
jot down write something quickly 迅速写下: *I jotted down his phone number.* 我匆匆写下了他的电话号码。

journal /ˈdʒɜːnl; ˈdʒɝnl̩/ *noun* 名词
a magazine about one special thing 专题杂志: *a medical journal* 医学杂志

journalism /ˈdʒɜːnəlɪzəm; ˈdʒɝnl̩ˌɪzəm/ *noun* 名词 (no plural 无复数)
the work of writing about the news for newspapers, magazines, television or radio 为报刊、电视或电台写新闻稿的工作；新闻业

journalist /ˈdʒɜːnəlɪst; ˈdʒɝnl̩ɪst/ *noun* 名词
a person whose job is to write about the news for newspapers, magazines, television or radio 为报刊、电视或电台写新闻稿的人；新闻工作者

journey /ˈdʒɜːni; ˈdʒɝnɪ/ *noun* 名词 (*plural* 复数作 **journeys**)
going from one place to another（从一处到另一处的）行走；路程；旅行: *Did you have a good journey?* 您一路上顺利吗？◇ *The plane journey from London to Paris takes an hour.* 坐飞机从伦敦到巴黎的航程需要一个小时。

joy /dʒɔɪ; dʒɔɪ/ *noun* 名词 (no plural 无复数)
a very happy feeling 快乐；愉快；喜悦: *Their children give them so much joy.* 他们的孩子给了他们很大乐趣。

joystick /ˈdʒɔɪstɪk; ˈdʒɔɪˌstɪk/ *noun* 名词
a handle that you move to control something, for example a computer or an aeroplane 操纵杆（例如计算机或飞机上的）

☞ picture at **computer** 见 **computer** 词条插图

Judaism /ˈdʒuːdeɪɪzəm; ˈdʒudɪˌɪzəm/ *noun* 名词 (no plural 无复数)
the religion of the Jewish people 犹太教

judge[1] /dʒʌdʒ; dʒʌdʒ/ *noun* 名词
1 the person in a court of law who decides how to punish somebody 审判官；法官：*The judge sent the man to prison for 20 years for killing his wife.* 法官判处那个杀死妻子的男子入狱20年。
2 a person who chooses the winner of a competition（比赛的）裁判员

judge[2] /dʒʌdʒ; dʒʌdʒ/ *verb* 动词 (**judges, judging, judged** /dʒʌdʒd; dʒʌdʒd/)
1 decide if something is good or bad, right or wrong, for example 判断；审判；评定（某事物的好坏、对错等）
2 decide who or what wins a competition 评判；裁判（比赛的优胜者）：*The headmaster judged the painting competition.* 校长任绘画比赛的评判。

judgement /ˈdʒʌdʒmənt; ˈdʒʌdʒmənt/ *noun* 名词
1 what a judge in a court of law decides（法官的）判决；裁决
2 what you think about somebody or something（对某人或某事物的）想法；看法：*In my judgement, she will do the job very well.* 我认为她能做好这件事。

judo /ˈdʒuːdəʊ; ˈdʒudo/ *noun* 名词 (no plural 无复数)
a sport where two people fight and try to throw each other onto the floor 柔道

jug 大罐

jug /dʒʌg; dʒʌg/ *noun* 名词
a container with a handle that you use for holding or pouring water or milk, for example（有柄的）大罐；壶（例如盛奶或倒水等用的）

juggle /ˈdʒʌgl; ˈdʒʌgl̩/ *verb* 动词 (**juggles, juggling, juggled** /ˈdʒʌgld; ˈdʒʌgl̩d/)
keep two or more things in the air by throwing and catching them quickly

juggle 玩抛接杂耍

玩抛接杂耍：*The clown juggled three oranges.* 小丑用三个橙子玩抛接杂耍。

juggler /ˈdʒʌglə(r); ˈdʒʌglɚ/ *noun* 名词
a person who juggles 玩抛接杂耍的人

juice /dʒuːs; dʒus/ *noun* 名词 (no plural 无复数)
the liquid from fruit and vegetables（水果和蔬菜的）汁：*a glass of orange juice* 一杯橙汁 ◇ *lemon juice* 柠檬汁

juicy /ˈdʒuːsi; ˈdʒusɪ/ *adjective* 形容词 (**juicier, juiciest**)
with a lot of juice 多汁的：*big juicy tomatoes* 多汁的大西红柿

jukebox /ˈdʒuːkbɒks; ˈdʒukˌbɑks/ *noun* 名词 (*plural* 复数作 **jukeboxes**)
a machine in a café or bar that plays music when you put money in it 自动点唱机（在小餐馆或酒吧中可投币选择歌曲的）

July /dʒuˈlaɪ; dʒuˈlaɪ/ *noun* 名词
the seventh month of the year 七月

jumble /ˈdʒʌmbl; ˈdʒʌmbl̩/ *verb* 动词 (**jumbles, jumbling, jumbled** /ˈdʒʌmbld; ˈdʒʌmbl̩d/)
jumble up mix things so that they are untidy or in the wrong place 把东西胡乱混在一起：*I can't find the photo I was looking for — they are all jumbled up in this box.* 我找不到我想找的那张照片——都混在这个盒子里了。

jumble *noun* 名词 (no plural 无复数)
a lot of things that are mixed together in an untidy way 胡乱混在一起的很多东西：*a jumble of old clothes and books* 一堆旧的衣服和书

jumble sale /ˈdʒʌmbl seɪl; ˈdʒʌmbl̩ sel/ *noun* 名词
a sale of things that people do not want any more. Clubs, churches and schools often have jumble sales to get money.

J

旧杂物义卖（俱乐部、教堂和学校常为筹款而举办）

jump 跳

jump /dʒʌmp; dʒʌmp/ *verb* 动词 (**jumps, jumping, jumped** /dʒʌmpt; dʒʌmpt/)

1 move quickly off the ground, using your legs to push you up 跳: *The cat jumped onto the table.* 猫跳到桌子上去了。◇ *The horse jumped over the wall.* 马跳过墙了。

2 move quickly 迅速移动: *He jumped into the car and drove away.* 他匆匆上了汽车就开走了。

3 move suddenly because you are surprised or frightened（因吃惊或害怕）跳动: *A loud noise made me jump.* 有一个大声音把我吓了一跳。

jump *noun* 名词

With one jump, the horse was over the fence. 马一下子就跳过了篱笆。

jumper /ˈdʒʌmpə(r); ˈdʒʌmpɚ/ *noun* 名词

a warm piece of clothing with sleeves, that you wear on the top part of your body. Jumpers are often made of wool. 厚的上衣；（常指）套头毛衣 ☞ picture at **coat** 见 **coat** 词条插图

jump-rope /ˈdʒʌmp rəʊp; ˈdʒʌmpˌrop/ *American English for* **skipping-rope** 美式英语，即 **skipping-rope**

J

junction /ˈdʒʌŋkʃn; ˈdʒʌŋkʃən/ *noun* 名词

a place where roads or railway lines meet 公路或铁路的交叉点；交叉路口: *Turn right at the next junction.* 在下一个路口向右拐。

June /dʒu:n; dʒun/ *noun* 名词

the sixth month of the year 六月

jungle /ˈdʒʌŋgl; ˈdʒʌŋgl̩/ *noun* 名词

a thick forest in a hot part of the world（热带的）丛林: *There are jungles in South America.* 南美洲有茂密的丛林。

junior /ˈdʒu:niə(r); ˈdʒunjɚ/ *adjective* 形容词

1 less important（地位或身分）较低的: *He's a junior officer in the army.* 他是陆军低级军官。

2 younger（年纪）较小的: *a junior pupil* 低班的小学生

✪ opposite 反义词: **senior**

junior school /ˈdʒu:niə sku:l; ˈdʒunjɚ skul/ *noun* 名词

a school for children between the ages of seven and eleven 小学校（为七岁至十一岁儿童设置的）

junk /dʒʌŋk; dʒʌŋk/ *noun* 名词 (no plural 无复数)

things that are old or useless 旧的或无用的东西: *The cupboard is full of junk.* 柜子里净是没用的东西。

junk food /ˈdʒʌŋk fu:d; ˈdʒʌŋk fud/ *noun* 名词

food that is not very good for you, but that is easy to prepare or ready to eat 不利健康的小吃（指易做的或现成的）

jury /ˈdʒʊəri; ˈdʒʊrɪ/ *noun* 名词 (*plural* 复数作 **juries**)

a group of people in a court of law who decide if somebody has done something wrong or not 陪审团: *The jury decided that the woman was guilty of killing her husband.* 陪审团裁决那个杀死丈夫的女子有罪。

just[1] /dʒʌst; dʒʌst/ *adverb* 副词

1 a very short time before 在很短时间以前；刚刚；刚才: *Jim isn't here — he's just gone out.* 吉姆不在这里——他刚出去。

2 at this or that moment; now or very soon 在这时或在那时；现在或马上: *I'm just going to make some coffee.* 我这就去煮些咖啡。◇ *She phoned just as I was going to bed.* 我正要睡觉的时候她来电话了。

3 only 只是；仅仅: *It's just a small present.* 这只不过是个小小的礼物。

4 almost not 几乎不: *I ran to the station and I just caught the train.* 我跑到车站，险些没赶上火车。

5 a word that makes what you say stronger 加强语气的词: *Just look at that funny little dog!* 快看看这只有趣的小狗吧！

just a minute, just a moment wait for a short time 等一等；等一会儿: *Just a minute — there's someone at the door.* 等一下——门那儿有个人。

just now 1 at this time; now 这时；现在: *I can't talk to you just now. I'm* *busy.* 我现在没法跟你谈话——我很忙。

2 a short time before 在很短时间以前；刚刚；刚才: *Where's Liz? She was here just now.* 利兹在哪儿呢？她刚才还在这儿呢。

just² /dʒʌst; dʒʌst/ *adjective* 形容词

fair and right 公平而正确的: *a just punishment* 应有的惩罚 ✪ opposite 反义词: **unjust**

justice /ˈdʒʌstɪs; ˈdʒʌstɪs/ *noun* 名词 (no plural 无复数)

1 being fair and right 公平而正确；公道；正义: *Justice for all!* 要公正对待所有的人！ ✪ opposite 反义词: **injustice**

2 the law 法律；司法: *British justice* 英国的法律

justify /ˈdʒʌstɪfaɪ; ˈdʒʌstəˌfaɪ/ *verb* 动词 (**justifies, justifying, justified** /ˈdʒʌstɪfaɪd; ˈdʒʌstəˌfaɪd/, **has justified**)

be or give a good reason for something 作为合理解释；提出正当理由: *Can you justify what you did?* 你能说出你这样做的理由吗？

J

Kk

kangaroo 袋鼠

kangaroo /ˌkæŋgəˈruː; ˌkæŋgəˈru/ *noun* 名词 (*plural* 复数作 **kangaroos**)
an animal in Australia that jumps on its strong back legs 袋鼠（产于澳洲）

karate /kəˈrɑːti; kəˈrɑtɪ/ *noun* 名词 (no plural 无复数)
a Japanese sport where people fight with their hands and feet 空手道（日本式徒手武术）

keen /kiːn; kin/ *adjective* 形容词 (**keener, keenest**)
1 If you are keen, you want to do something and are interested in it 热切的；热心的: *Ian was keen to go out but I wanted to stay at home.* 伊恩很愿意出去，可是我想呆在家里。◇ *Louise is a keen swimmer.* 路易丝喜好游泳。
2 very good or strong 很好的；很强的: *keen eyesight* 很强的视力
be keen on somebody or 或 **something** like somebody or something very much 非常喜爱某人或某事物: *Katie is keen on football.* 凯蒂特别喜欢足球。

keep /kiːp; kip/ *verb* 动词 (**keeps, keeping, kept** /kept; kɛpt/, **has kept**)
1 have something and not give it to another person 有某事物而不给别人；保有；保存；保留: *You can keep that book—I don't need it.* 你可以留下那本书——我不用了。
2 continue in the same way and not change 保持不变: *Keep still—I want to take your photograph.* 别动——我来给你照张相。
3 make somebody or something stay the same and not change 使某人或某事物保持不变: *Keep this door closed.* 这扇门要经常关着。◇ *You must keep the baby warm.* 不要让孩子冻着。
4 have something in a special place 在某处存放某物: *Where do you keep the coffee?* 您把咖啡放在哪儿了？
5 not stop doing something; do something many times 不停地做某事；一再地做某事: *Keep driving until you see the cinema, then turn left.* 开着车一直向前，看见电影院就向左拐。◇ *She keeps forgetting my name.* 她总也记不住我的名字。
6 look after and buy food and other things for a person or an animal 养活（人或动物）: *It costs a lot to keep a family of four.* 要养活一个四口人的家庭花费很大。◇ *They keep sheep and pigs on their farm.* 他们在农场上饲养羊和猪。
7 stay fresh 保持新鲜: *Will this fish keep until tomorrow?* 这条鱼明天还能新鲜吗？
keep away from somebody or 或 **something** not go near somebody or something 不接近某人或某事物: *Keep away from the river please, children.* 孩子们，请不要靠近河边。
keep somebody from stop somebody from doing something 不让某人做某事: *You can't keep me from going out!* 你不能不让我出去！
keep going continue; not stop 继续；不停: *I was very tired but I kept going to the end of the race.* 我已经很累了，可是仍然坚持下去而到达了终点。
keep off something not go on something 不要在某处走: *Keep off the grass!* 不要在草地上走！
keep on not stop doing something; do something many times 不停地做某事；一再地做某事: *We kept on driving all night!* 我们开车开了一夜！◇ *That man keeps on looking at me.* 那个男的总看着我。
keep out stay outside 留在外边；不进入: *The sign on the door said 'Danger. Keep out!'* 门上的字写着“危险，不准进入！”
keep somebody or 或 **something out** stop somebody or something from going in 不让某人或某物进入: *We put a fence round the garden to keep the sheep out.* 我们在花园周围修了个篱笆，怕羊进来。
keep up with somebody or 或 **something** go as fast as another person or thing so that you are together 跟上某人或某事物: *Don't walk so quickly—I can't keep up with you.* 别走那么快——我跟不上你们了。

K

keeper /'ki:pə(r); 'kipɚ/ *noun* 名词
a person who looks after something 照看某事物的人: *He's a keeper at the zoo — he looks after the lions.* 他是动物园的饲养员——管喂狮子。☞ Look also at **goalkeeper**. 另见 **goalkeeper**。

kennel /'kenl; 'kɛnl̩/ *noun* 名词
a small house where a dog sleeps 狗窝

kept *form of* **keep** ✳ **keep** 的不同形式

kerb /kɜ:b; kɝb/ *noun* 名词
the edge of a path next to a road（靠近马路的）便道边缘: *They stood on the kerb waiting to cross the road.* 他们站在便道边儿上，等着过马路。

ketchup /'ketʃəp; 'kɛtʃəp/ *noun* 名词 (no plural 无复数)
a cold sauce made from tomatoes 番茄酱: *Do you want ketchup on your chips?* 你的炸土豆条儿要加番茄酱吗？

kettle /'ketl; 'kɛtl̩/ *noun* 名词
a metal or plastic pot that you use for making water hot（坐水的）壶: *Put the kettle on* (= fill it with water and make it start to get hot). 坐壶水吧（＝把水注入壶中加热）。

kettle 壶

key[1] /ki:; ki/ *noun* 名词
1 a piece of metal that opens or closes a lock 钥匙: *He turned the key and opened the door.* 他转动钥匙把门打开了。

key 钥匙

2 one of the parts of a typewriter, computer, piano, etc that you press with your fingers（打字机、计算机、钢琴等的）键: *Pianos have black and white keys.* 钢琴上有黑的和白的键。
3 answers to questions 答案: *Check your answers with the key at the back of the book.* 用书后的答案来核对一下你自己的答案。

key[2] /ki:; ki/ *verb* 动词 (**keys**, **keying**, **keyed** /ki:d; kid/)
key in put words or numbers into a computer by pressing the keys 用键盘把数据输入计算机中；键入: *Key in your name.* 键入您的名字。

keyboard /'ki:bɔ:d; 'kiˌbord/ *noun* 名词
1 all the keys on a piano, computer or typewriter, for example（钢琴、计算机或打字机的）键盘 ☞ picture at **computer** 见 **computer** 词条插图
2 a musical instrument like a small electrical piano 键盘琴（似小型电子钢琴的乐器）: *a keyboard player* 键盘琴演奏者

keyhole /'ki:həʊl; 'kiˌhol/ *noun* 名词
a hole in a lock where you put a key 锁孔；钥匙孔

kg *short way of writing* **kilogram** ✳ **kilogram** 的缩写形式

kick[1] /kɪk; kɪk/ *verb* 动词 (**kicks**, **kicking**, **kicked** /kɪkt; kɪkt/)
1 hit somebody or something with your foot 踢: *I kicked the ball to Chris.* 我把球踢给克里斯了。
2 move your foot or feet up quickly 蹬；踩脚: *The child was kicking and screaming.* 那个孩子边踩脚边喊叫。
kick off start a game of football（足球比赛）开球
kick somebody out make somebody leave a place 把某人赶走: *The boys were kicked out of the cinema because they were noisy.* 那些男孩子太闹，被轰出电影院了。

kick[2] /kɪk; kɪk/ *noun* 名词
1 hitting something or somebody with your foot, or moving your foot or feet up quickly 踢；蹬；踩脚: *Jenny gave the ball a kick.* 珍妮踢了球一下。
2 a feeling of excitement 兴奋；快感；快乐

kick-off /'kɪk ɒf; 'kɪkˌɔf/ *noun* 名词
the start of a game of football（足球比赛的）开球: *The kick-off is at 2.30.*（这场足球比赛的）开球时间是2时30分。

kid /kɪd; kɪd/ *noun* 名词
1 a child 小孩儿: *How old are your kids?* 您的小孩儿都几岁了？✪ This is an informal word. 这是个口语用词。
2 a young goat 幼小的山羊 ☞ picture at **goat** 见 **goat** 词条插图

kidnap /'kɪdnæp; 'kɪdnæp/ *verb* 动词 (**kidnaps**, **kidnapping**, **kidnapped** /'kɪdnæpt; 'kɪdnæpt/)
take somebody away and hide them, so that their family or friends will pay you money to free them 绑架；诱拐: *The son of a rich businessman was kidnapped today.* 有个富商的儿子今天被绑架了。
kidnapper *noun* 名词
a person who kidnaps somebody 进行绑架的人

kidney /'kɪdni; 'kɪdnɪ/ *noun* 名词 (*plural* 复数作 **kidneys**)
one of two parts inside your body 肾；肾脏 ☞ picture on page C2 见第C2页图

kill /kɪl; kɪl/ *verb* 动词 (**kills**, **killing**, **killed** /kɪld; kɪld/)
make somebody or something die 杀死某人或某生物: *The police do not know who killed the old man.* 警方不知道杀死老翁的是谁。◇ *Three people were killed in the accident.* 事故中有三人死亡。
killer *noun* 名词
a person, animal or thing that kills 杀生的人、动物或事物

kilogram, kilogramme /'kɪləgræm; 'kɪləˌgræm/, **kilo** /'ki:ləʊ; 'kilo/ (*plural* 复数作 **kilos**) *noun* 名词
a measure of weight. There are 1 000 **grams** in a kilogram 公斤；千克（1公斤等于1 000克，克叫做 **gram**）: *I bought two kilos of potatoes.* 我买了两公斤土豆儿。✪ The short way of writing 'kilogram' is **kg** ✳ kilogram 的缩写形式为 **kg**: *1 kg of bananas* ✳ 1公斤香蕉

kilometer *American English for* **kilometre** 美式英语，即 **kilometre**

kilometre /'kɪləmi:tə(r), kɪ'lɒmɪtə(r); 'kɪləˌmitɚ/ *noun* 名词
a measure of length. There are 1 000 **metres** in a kilometre. 公里；千米（1公里等于1 000米，米叫做 **metre**。）✪ The short way of writing 'kilometre' is **km** ✳ kilometre 的缩写形式为 **km**: *They live 100 km from Paris.* 他们住在离巴黎100公里的地方。

kilt /kɪlt; kɪlt/ *noun* 名词
a skirt that men in Scotland sometimes wear（苏格兰男子有时穿的）短裙

kind[1] /kaɪnd; kaɪnd/ *adjective* 形容词 (**kinder**, **kindest**)
friendly and good to other people 友好的；亲切的；和蔼的: *'Can I carry your bag?' 'Thanks. That's very kind of you.'* "我替您拿着袋子好吗？" "谢谢你。" ◇ *Be kind to animals.* 要善待动物。✪ opposite 反义词: **unkind**
kind-hearted /ˌkaɪnd 'hɑ:tɪd; ˌkaɪnd-'hɑrtɪd/ *adjective* 形容词
A person who is kind-hearted is kind and gentle to other people. 好心的；善良的
kindness /'kaɪndnəs; 'kaɪndnɪs/ *noun* 名词 (no plural 无复数)
being kind 友好；亲切；和蔼；好意: *Thank you for your kindness.* 谢谢您的好意。

kind[2] /kaɪnd; kaɪnd/ *noun* 名词
a group of things or people that are the same in some way; a sort or type 某方面相同的事物或人；种类: *What kind of car do you have?* 您的汽车是哪种的？◇ *The shop sells ten different kinds of bread.* 这个商店出售十种面包。
kind of words that you use when you are not sure about something 用以表示对某事物无把握的词语: *He looks kind of tired.* 他看起来好像累了。

kindly[1] /'kaɪndli; 'kaɪndlɪ/ *adverb* 副词
in a kind way 友好地；亲切地；和蔼地: *She kindly drove me to the station.* 她很热情地开车把我送到车站。

kindly[2] /'kaɪndli; 'kaɪndlɪ/ *adjective* 形容词 (**kindlier**, **kindliest**)
kind and friendly 亲切友好的；和蔼的: *a kindly old man* 慈祥的老先生

king /kɪŋ; kɪŋ/ *noun* 名词
a man who rules a country and who is from a royal family 国王: *King Juan Carlos of Spain* 西班牙国王胡安·卡洛斯 ☞ Look at **queen**. 见 **queen**。

kingdom /'kɪŋdəm; 'kɪŋdəm/ *noun* 名词
a country where a king or queen rules 王国: *the United Kingdom* 英国

kiosk /'ki:ɒsk; kɪ'ɑsk/ *noun* 名词
a small shop in a street where you can buy things like sweets and newspapers through an open window（通过窗口出售糖果和报纸的）街边小商店；售货亭 ☞ Look also at **telephone kiosk**. 另见 **telephone kiosk**。

kiss /kɪs; kɪs/ *verb* 动词 (**kisses**, **kissing**, **kissed** /kɪst; kɪst/)
touch somebody with your lips to show love or to say hello or goodbye 吻；亲吻: *She kissed me on the cheek.* 她吻了吻我的面颊。◇ *Mark and Lucy were kissing in the park.* 马克和露西在公园里接吻。
kiss (*plural* 复数作 **kisses**) *noun* 名词
Give me a kiss! 亲我一下吧！

kit /kɪt; kɪt/ *noun* 名词
1 all the clothes or other things that you need to do something or to play a sport（做某事时或运动时需要的）全套衣物或其他用具: *Where is my football kit?* 我的足球用品在哪里呢？◇ *a tool kit* 一套工具
2 a set of small pieces that you put

together to make something 配套元件（可用以装配成某物）: *a kit for making a model aeroplane* 一套飞机模型拼具

kitchen /ˈkɪtʃɪn; ˈkɪtʃɪn/ *noun* 名词
a room where you cook food 厨房

kite /kaɪt; kaɪt/ *noun* 名词
a light toy made of paper or cloth on a long string. You can make a kite fly in the wind 风筝: *The children were flying kites on the hill.* 孩子们在山冈上放风筝。

kitten /ˈkɪtn; ˈkɪtn̩/ *noun* 名词
a young cat 幼小的猫 ☞ picture at **cat** 见 **cat** 词条插图

km *short way of writing* **kilometre** ＊ **kilometre** 的缩写形式

knee /niː; ni/ *noun* 名词
the part in the middle of your leg where it bends 膝；膝盖: *I fell and cut my knee.* 我把膝盖摔破了。☞ picture on page C2 见第C2页图

kneel /niːl; nil/ *verb* 动词 (**kneels, kneeling, knelt** /nelt; nɛlt/ or 或 **kneeled** /niːld; nild/, **has knelt** or 或 **has kneeled**)
go down or stay with your knees on the ground 跪下；跪: *He knelt down to pray.* 他跪着祈祷。◇ *Jenny was kneeling on the floor.* 珍妮跪在地板上。

kneel 跪

knew *form of* **know** ＊ **know** 的不同形式

knickers /ˈnɪkəz; ˈnɪkɚz/ *noun* 名词 (plural 复数)
a small piece of clothing that a woman or girl wears under her other clothes, between the middle of her body and the top of her legs（女用）内裤: *a pair of knickers* 一条女用内裤

knife 刀

knife /naɪf; naɪf/ *noun* 名词 (*plural* 复数作 **knives** /naɪvz; naɪvz/)
a sharp metal thing with a handle, that you use to cut things or to fight 刀

knight /naɪt; naɪt/ *noun* 名词
1 a man who has a special title and who can use 'Sir' in front of his name 爵士（其名前可用 Sir 字头衔）
2 a soldier who rode a horse and fought a long time ago（中古时代的）骑士

knit /nɪt; nɪt/ *verb* 动词 (**knits, knitting, knitted**)
use long sticks (called **knitting-needles**) to make clothes from wool 编织；编结（织针叫做 **knitting-needle**）: *My grandmother knitted this hat for me.* 这顶帽子是我奶奶给我织的。

knitting *noun* 名词 (no plural 无复数)
1 making clothes from wool 用毛线编织衣物: *Her hobbies are knitting and football.* 她的业余爱好是织毛衣还有足球。
2 something that you are knitting 编织物

knit 编织

knitting-needle /ˈnɪtɪŋ niːdl; ˈnɪtɪŋ ˌnidl/ *noun* 名词
a long metal or plastic stick that you use for knitting 织针

knives *plural of* **knife** ＊ **knife** 的复数形式

knob /nɒb; nɑb/ *noun* 名词
1 a round handle on a door or drawer（门上的或抽屉上的）球形拉手: *a wooden doorknob* 木制的球形门拉手
2 a round thing that you turn to control part of a machine（机器上的）球形按钮

knock¹ /nɒk; nɑk/ *verb* 动词 (**knocks, knocking, knocked** /nɒkt; nɑkt/)
1 hit something to make a noise 撞击某物发出声音；敲；打: *I knocked on the door, but nobody answered.* 我敲了敲门，可是没人应声。
2 hit something hard 碰；撞: *I knocked my head on the car door.* 我的头撞在汽车门上了。◇ *She knocked a glass off the table.* 她把玻璃杯从桌子上碰掉了。

knock somebody down, knock somebody over hit somebody so that they fall onto the ground 把某人击倒或撞倒在地上: *The little boy was knocked down by a car.* 那个小男孩儿让汽车给撞倒了。

knock something down break a building so that it falls down 拆除建筑物: *They knocked down the old houses and built a supermarket in their place.* 他们把那些旧房子拆了，在原处盖了一座超级市场。

knock somebody out hit somebody hard so that they cannot get up again for a while 把某人打得倒下，一时起不来

knock something over hit something so that it falls 把某物撞倒或碰掉: *I knocked over a vase of flowers.* 我把花瓶碰倒了。

knock² /nɒk; nɑk/ *noun* 名词
hitting something hard or the sound that this makes 撞击某物或撞击某物发出的声音；敲；打: *I heard a knock at the door.* 我听见有人敲门。

knot /nɒt; nɑt/ *noun* 名词
a place where you have tied two ends of rope, string, etc tightly together（绳索等的）结: *I tied a knot in the rope.* 我在绳子上打了个结。◇ *Can you undo this knot* (= make it loose)? 你能把这个结解开吗？

knot 结

knot *verb* 动词 (**knots**, **knotting**, **knotted**)
tie a knot in something 在某物上打结: *He knotted the ends of the rope together.* 他把绳子两头系在一起了。

know /nəʊ; no/ *verb* 动词 (**knows**, **knowing**, **knew** /nju:; nu/, **has known** /nəʊn; non/)
1 have something in your head, because you have learned it（经过学习）会，知道: *I don't know her name.* 我不知道她的名字。◇ *He knows a lot about cars.* 他对汽车很在行。◇ *Do you know how to use this machine?* 你会使用这个机器吗？◇ *'You're late!' 'Yes, I know.'* "你晚了！" "是啊，我知道。"
2 have met or seen somebody or something before, perhaps many times 见过某人或某事（可能多次）；认识；熟悉: *I have known Mario for six years.* 我认识马里奥已经六年了。◇ *I know Paris quite well.* 我很熟悉巴黎。

get to know somebody start to know somebody well 开始熟悉某人: *I liked him when I got to know him.* 我跟他一熟了就喜欢他了。

let somebody know tell somebody 告诉某人: *Let me know if you need any help.* 您要是需要帮忙的话就告诉我一声。

you know words that you use when you are thinking about what to say next 用作说话思索时的口头语

✪ You use expressions like **God knows** and **Heaven knows** to show very strongly that you do not know something 表示不知道某事物时，加强语气的词语是 **God knows** 和 **Heaven knows** 等: *'Where is Lisa?' 'God knows!'* "莉萨在哪儿呢？" "天知道！"

knowledge /'nɒlɪdʒ; 'nɑlɪdʒ/ *noun* 名词 (no plural 无复数)
what you know and understand about something 了解；理解: *He has a good knowledge of European history.* 他精通欧洲历史。

knuckle /'nʌkl; 'nʌkl̩/ *noun* 名词
the bones where your fingers join your hand and where your hands bend 指节；指关节

koala /kəʊ'ɑ:lə; ko'ɑlə/ *noun* 名词
a wild animal, like a small bear, that lives in Australia 树袋熊（产于澳洲）

kph
a way of measuring how fast something is moving. 'Kph' is short for **kilometres per hour**. 千米/小时；公里/小时 (kph 是 **kilometres per hour** 的缩略式。)

Ll

l *short way of writing* **litre** ✳ **litre** 的缩写形式

lab /læb; læb/ *short for* **laboratory** ✳ **laboratory** 的缩略式

labels 标记

label /ˈleɪbl; ˈlebl̩/ *noun* 名词
a piece of paper or plastic on something that tells you about it 标签；标记：*The label on the bottle says 'Made in Mexico'.* 瓶子上的标签写的是"墨西哥制造"。
label *verb* 动词 (**labels**, **labelling**, **labelled** /ˈleɪbld; ˈlebl̩d/)
put a label on something 在某物上加标签或标记：*I labelled all the boxes with my name and address.* 我把所有的箱子上都写上了我的姓名和地址。✪ In American English the spellings are **labeling** and **labeled**. 美式英语的拼法是 **labeling** 和 **labeled**。

labor *American English for* **labour** 美式英语，即 **labour**

laboratory /ləˈbɒrətri; ˈlæbrəˌtorɪ/ *noun* 名词 (*plural* 复数作 **laboratories**)
a special room where scientists work 实验室 ✪ The short form of 'laboratory' is **lab**. ✳ laboratory 的缩略式为 **lab**。

laborer *American English for* **labourer** 美式英语，即 **labourer**

labour /ˈleɪbə(r); ˈlebɚ/ *noun* 名词 (no plural 无复数)
hard work that you do with your hands and body（体力的）劳动
the Labour Party /ðəˈleɪbə pɑːti; ðə ˈlebɚ ˌpɑrtɪ/ *noun* 名词
one of the important political parties in Britain（英国的）工党 ☞ Look at **the Conservative Party** and **the Liberal Democrats**. 见 **the Conservative Party** 和 **the Liberal Democrats**。

labourer /ˈleɪbərə(r); ˈlebərɚ/ *noun* 名词
a person who does hard work with his/her hands and body（体力的）劳动者；工人：*a farm labourer* 农业工人

lace /leɪs; les/ *noun* 名词

1 (no plural 无复数) thin pretty material with a pattern of very small holes in it 带有精美图案的薄的透孔织品：*lace curtains* 网眼纱帘 ◇ *a handkerchief with lace round the edge* 带网眼花边的手帕
2 (*plural* 复数作 **laces**) a string that you tie to close a shoe 鞋带

lack /læk; læk/ *verb* 动词 (**lacks**, **lacking**, **lacked** /lækt; lækt/)
not have something, or not have enough of something 没有或缺少某事物：*The children lacked the food they needed.* 这些儿童缺少食物。
be lacking be needed 不足；不够：*Money is lacking for a new school.* 兴办新学校的资金不足。
lack *noun* 名词 (no plural 无复数)
There is a lack of good teachers. 缺乏优秀教师。

lad /læd; læd/ *noun* 名词
a boy or young man 男孩儿；小伙子

ladder 梯子

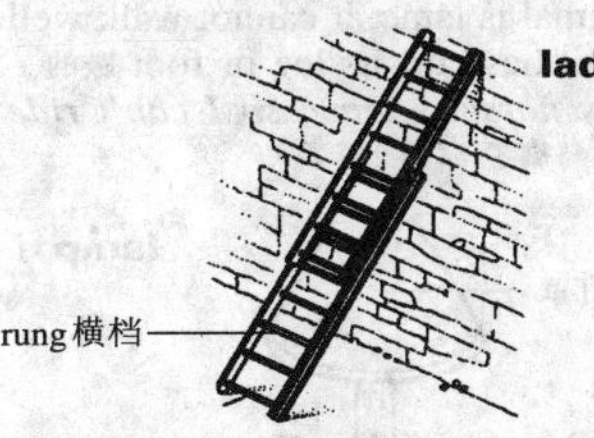

ladder /ˈlædə(r); ˈlædɚ/ *noun* 名词
two tall pieces of metal or wood with shorter pieces (called **rungs**) between them. You use a ladder for climbing up something. 梯子（梯子的横档叫做 **rung**）

Ladies /ˈleɪdiz; ˈledɪz/ *noun* 名词 (no plural 无复数)
a public toilet for women 女厕所：*Where is the Ladies, please?* 请问，女厕所在哪里？

lady /ˈleɪdi; ˈledɪ/ *noun* 名词 (*plural* 复数作 **ladies**)
1 a polite way of saying 'woman'（对女子的尊称）女士；小姐；夫人：*an old lady*

老夫人 ☞ Look at **gentleman**. 见 **gentleman**。

2 Lady a woman with a special title (对有某种头衔的女子的尊称) 阁下；女士；小姐；夫人: *Before she married Charles, her name was Lady Diana Spencer.* 戴安娜·斯潘塞小姐是她嫁给查尔斯之前用的名字。☞ Look at **Lord**. 见 **Lord**。

lager /'lɑ:gə(r); 'lɑgɚ/ *noun* 名词

1 (no plural 无复数) a light beer 贮藏啤酒 (一种淡啤酒): *I'll have a pint of lager, please.* 请给我一品脱贮藏啤酒。

2 (*plural* 复数作 **lagers**) a glass, bottle or can of lager 一杯、一瓶或一罐贮藏啤酒

laid *form of* **lay²** ＊ **lay²** 的不同形式

lain *form of* **lie²** ＊ **lie²** 的不同形式

lake /leɪk; lek/ *noun* 名词

a big area of water with land all around it 湖: *Lake Victoria* 维多利亚湖 ◇ *We went swimming in the lake.* 我们到湖里去游泳了。

lamb /læm; læm/ *noun* 名词

1 (*plural* 复数作 **lambs**) a young sheep 幼小的绵羊 ☞ picture at **sheep** 见 **sheep** 词条插图

2 (no plural 无复数) meat from a lamb 羊肉: *We had roast lamb for lunch.* 我们中午吃的是烤羊肉。

lame /leɪm; lem/ *adjective* 形容词

If an animal is lame, it cannot walk well because it has hurt its leg or foot 跛的；瘸的: *My horse is lame, so I can't ride her.* 我的马瘸了，不能骑了。

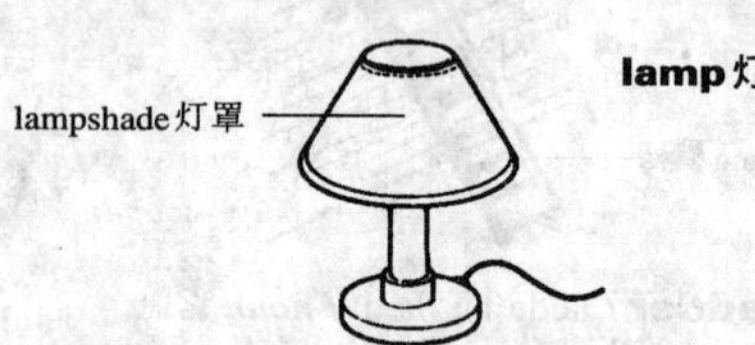

lamp /læmp; læmp/ *noun* 名词

a thing that gives light 灯: *It was dark, so I switched on the lamp.* 天黑了，我把灯打开了。

L

lamppost /'læmp pəʊst; 'læmpˌpost/ *noun* 名词

a tall thing in the street with a light on the top 路灯柱

lampshade /'læmpʃeɪd; 'læmpˌʃed/ *noun* 名词

a cover for a lamp 灯罩

land¹ /lænd; lænd/ *noun* 名词

1 (no plural 无复数) the part of the earth that is not the sea 陆地；大地: *After two weeks in a boat, we were happy to see land.* 我们坐了两个星期的船以后，看见陆地非常高兴。

2 (no plural 无复数) a piece of ground 一块土地；地皮: *They have bought some land and they are going to build a house on it.* 他们买了些地，打算盖一所房子。◇ *farming land* 耕地

3 (*plural* 复数作 **lands**) a country 国土；国家: *She returned to the land where she was born.* 她又回到了祖国。✪ In this sense, **country** is the word that we usually use. 这一义项的常用词是 **country**。

land² /lænd; lænd/ *verb* 动词 (**lands, landing, landed**)

1 come onto the ground from the air or from the sea (从空中或海上) 来到陆上；着陆；降落；登陆；上岸: *The plane landed at Heathrow airport.* 飞机降落在希思罗机场。◇ *The boat has landed.* 船已抵岸。

2 bring an aircraft down onto the ground 使飞机着陆: *The pilot landed the plane safely.* 飞行员驾驶飞机安全着陆。

landing /'lændɪŋ; 'lændɪŋ/ *noun* 名词

1 coming down onto the ground 来到陆上；着陆；降落: *The plane made a safe landing in a field.* 飞机在田地里安全着陆。

2 a flat place at the top of stairs in a building 楼梯平台: *There's a telephone on the landing.* 在楼梯平台处有个电话。

landlady /'lændleɪdi; 'lændˌledɪ/ *noun* 名词 (*plural* 复数作 **landladies**)

1 a woman who has a house and lets you live there if you pay her money (女的) 房东

2 a woman who has a pub or a small hotel (酒店或小旅馆的) (女的) 店主

landlord /'lændlɔ:d; 'lændˌlɔrd/ *noun* 名词

1 a man who has a house and lets you live there if you pay him money (男的) 房东

2 a man who has a pub or a small hotel (酒店或小旅馆的) (男的) 店主

landmark /'lændmɑ:k; 'lændˌmɑrk/ *noun* 名词

a big building or another thing that you can see easily from far away (从远处易看

出的）大的建筑物或其他标志物: *Big Ben is one of London's most famous landmarks.* 大本钟是伦敦最著名的一个标志物。

landscape /'lændskeɪp; 'lændskep/ *noun* 名词
everything you can see in an area of land（陆上的）风景；景色: *The Scottish landscape is very beautiful.* 苏格兰的风景非常漂亮。

lane /leɪn; len/ *noun* 名词
1 a narrow road in the country 乡间小路
2 one part of a wide road（宽阔道路上的）单行车道: *We were driving in the middle lane of the motorway.* 我们在高速公路的中间车道上行驶。

language /'læŋgwɪdʒ; 'læŋgwɪdʒ/ *noun* 名词
1 (no plural 无复数) words that people say or write 语言
2 (*plural* 复数作 **languages**) words that a certain group of people say and write（某种）语言: *'Do you speak any foreign languages?' 'Yes, I speak French and Italian.'* "您会说外国语吗？""我会说法语和意大利语。"

lap¹ /læp; læp/ *noun* 名词
the flat part at the top of your legs when you are sitting（人坐着时）大腿的上方: *The child sat on his mother's lap.* 那个孩子坐在母亲的腿上。

lap² /læp; læp/ *noun* 名词
going once round the track in a race（跑道的）一圈: *The runner fell on the last lap.* 那个参赛者在最后一圈摔倒了。

large /lɑ:dʒ; lɑrdʒ/ *adjective* 形容词 (**larger, largest**)
big 大的: *They live in a large house.* 他们住在一所大房子里。◇ *She has a large family.* 她的家庭是个大家庭。◇ *Have you got this shirt in a large size?* 这种衬衫你们有大号的吗？✪ opposite 反义词: **small**
☞ picture on page C26 见第C26页图

largely /'lɑ:dʒli; 'lɑrdʒlɪ/ *adverb* 副词
mostly; mainly 大体上；主要地: *The room is largely used for meetings.* 这个房间大多开会时用。

laser /'leɪzə(r); 'lezə/ *noun* 名词
an instrument that makes a very strong line of light (called a **laser beam**). Some lasers are used to cut metal and others are used by doctors in operations. 激光器（激光叫做 **laser beam**）

last¹ /lɑ:st; læst/ *adjective* 形容词
1 after all the others 最后的: *December is the last month of the year.* 十二月是一年中最后的一个月。
2 just before now 刚过去的: *It's June now, so last month was May.* 现在是六月，所以上个月是五月。◇ *I was at school last week, but this week I'm on holiday.* 我上星期上课，这个星期放假。
3 only one left 唯一剩下的: *Who wants the last cake?* 谁要最后这块蛋糕？
last night yesterday in the evening or in the night 昨天晚上: *Did you go out last night?* 您昨天晚上出去了吗？
lastly *adverb* 副词
finally, as the last thing 最后；作为最后一点: *Lastly, I want to thank my parents for all their help.* 最后，我要感谢我父母对我各方面的帮助。

last² /lɑ:st; læst/ *adverb* 副词
1 after all the others 最后: *He finished last in the race.* 他赛跑落得了最后。
2 at a time that is nearest to now 最近一次；上次: *I last saw Penny in 1993.* 我上一次见到彭尼是在1993年。

last³ /lɑ:st; læst/ *noun* 名词 (no plural 无复数)
a person or thing that comes after all the others; what comes at the end 最后一个人或事物: *I was the last to arrive at the party.* 我是聚会上最后一个到的。
at last in the end; after some time 最后；终于: *She waited all week, and at last the letter arrived.* 她等了一个星期，信终于到了。

last⁴ /lɑ:st; læst/ *verb* 动词 (**lasts, lasting, lasted**)
1 continue for a time 延续；持续；维持: *The film lasted for three hours.* 那部电影演了三个小时。◇ *I hope the good weather will last until the weekend.* 我希望到周末天气都一直这么好。
2 be enough for a certain time 足够维持某段时间: *We have enough food to last us till next week.* 我们的食物够吃到下星期的。

late /leɪt; let/ *adjective, adverb* 形容词，副词 (**later, latest**)
1 after the usual or right time 在一般的或正常的时间之后；晚的；迟的: *I went to bed late last night.* 我昨天睡得晚。◇ *I was late for school today* (= I arrived late). 我今天上课迟到了。◇ *My train was late.*

L

我坐的火车误点了。✪ opposite 反义词: **early**

2 near the end of a time 接近某时间的末尾；在末期；将尽时的: *They arrived in the late afternoon.* 他们是傍晚到的。◇ *She's in her late twenties* (= between the ages of about 25 and 29). 她快三十岁了。✪ opposite 反义词: **early**

3 no longer alive; dead 已故；去世的: *Her late husband was a doctor.* 她已故的丈夫是个医生。

a late night an evening when you go to bed later than usual 比平时睡得晚的夜晚

at the latest not later than 不迟于: *Please be here by twelve o'clock at the latest.* 请最晚在十二点钟来到这里。

later on at a later time 以后；其后: *Bye — I'll see you later on.* 再见——以后见。

lately /'leɪtli; 'letlɪ/ *adverb* 副词

not long ago; recently 不久前；近来: *Have you seen Mark lately?* 您最近见过马克吗？◇ *The weather has been very bad lately.* 近来天气很不好。

latest /'leɪtɪst; 'letəst/ *adjective* 形容词

newest 最新的: *the latest fashions* 最新的时装

latter /'lætə(r); 'lætɚ/ *adjective* 形容词

last 最后的: *She lived in Liverpool in the latter part of her life.* 她晚年是在利物浦度过的。

latter *noun* 名词 (no plural 无复数)

the second of two things or people（两事物或两人中的）后者: *I study both French and German, but I prefer the latter.* 我学法语也学德语，其实我比较喜欢德语。☞ Look at **former**. 见 **former**。

laugh /lɑ:f; læf/ *verb* 动词 (**laughs, laughing, laughed** /lɑ:ft; læft/)

make sounds that show you are happy or that you think something is funny 笑；发笑: *His jokes always make me laugh.* 他说的笑话总是逗得我哈哈大笑。

laugh at somebody or 或 **something** laugh to show that you think somebody or something is funny or silly 因觉得某人有趣或笨拙而发笑: *The children laughed at the clown.* 孩子们看着那个小丑，都笑了起来。◇ *They all laughed at me when I said I was frightened of dogs.* 我说我怕狗，他们都笑话我。

laugh *noun* 名词

My brother has a loud laugh. 我哥哥笑声很大。◇ *She told us a joke and we all had a good laugh.* 她给我们讲了个笑话，我们都大笑起来。

for a laugh as a joke; for fun 开玩笑；为了取笑: *The boys put a spider in her bed for a laugh.* 那些男孩儿闹着玩，把蜘蛛放在她床上了。

laughter /'lɑ:ftə(r); 'læftɚ/ *noun* 名词 (no plural 无复数)

the sound of laughing 笑声: *I could hear laughter in the next room.* 我听到隔壁有笑声。

launch /lɔ:ntʃ; lɔntʃ/ *verb* 动词 (**launches, launching, launched** /lɔ:ntʃt; lɔntʃt/)

1 put a ship into the water or a spacecraft into the sky 使船下水或使航天器升空: *This ship was launched in 1967.* 这艘船于1967年下水。

2 start something new 开始新事物: *The magazine was launched last year.* 这份杂志是去年创办的。

launderette /ˌlɔ:ndə'ret; ˌlɔndə'rɛt/ *noun* 名词

a shop where you pay to wash and dry your clothes in machines（付款后可使用机器洗衣、干衣的）自助洗衣店

laundromat /'lɔ:ndrəmæt; 'lɔndrəˌmæt/ *American English for* **launderette** 美式英语，即 **launderette**

laundry /'lɔ:ndri; 'lɔndrɪ/ *noun* 名词

1 (no plural 无复数) clothes that you must wash or that you have washed 待洗的或已洗的衣物: *a laundry basket* 存放洗的衣服的篮子

2 (*plural* 复数作 **laundries**) a place where you send things like sheets and clothes so that somebody can wash them for you 洗衣店

lava /'lɑ:və; 'lɑvə/ *noun* 名词 (no plural 无复数)

hot liquid rock that comes out of a **volcano**（火山喷出的）熔岩（火山叫做 **volcano**）

lavatory /'lævətri; 'lævəˌtorɪ/ *noun* 名词 (*plural* 复数作 **lavatories**)

a large bowl with a seat that you use when you need to empty waste from your body. The room that it is in is also called a **lavatory** 抽水马桶（有抽水马桶的厕所也叫做 **lavatory**）: *Where's your* *lavatory, please?* 请问，您这儿的厕所在哪里？ ✪ **Toilet** is the word that we usually use. ✳ **toilet** 是常用词。

law /lɔ:; lɔ/ *noun* 名词

1 a rule of a country that says what people may and may not do（具体的）法律: *There is a law against stealing.* 盗窃是违法的。☞ Look at **legal**. 见 **legal**。

2 the law (no plural 无复数) all the laws of a country（整体的）法律；法令；法规

against the law not allowed by the rules of a country 犯法；违法: *Murder is against the law.* 故意杀人是犯法的。

break the law do something that the laws of a country say you must not do 做违法的事: *I have never broken the law.* 我从来没做过违法的事。

lawcourt /'lɔ:kɔ:t; 'lɔˌkɔrt/ *noun* 名词

a place where people (a **judge** or 或 **jury**) decide if somebody has done something wrong, and what the punishment will be 法庭；法院（法官叫做 **judge**，陪审团叫做 **jury**）

lawn /lɔ:n; lɔn/ *noun* 名词

a piece of short grass in a garden or park（花园或公园里的）草地；草坪: *They were sitting on the lawn.* 他们坐在草坪上。

lawnmower /'lɔ:nməʊə(r); 'lɔnˌmoɚ/ *noun* 名词

a machine that cuts grass 刈草机

lawyer /'lɔ:jə(r); 'lɔjɚ/ *noun* 名词

a person who has studied the law and who helps people or talks for them in a court of law 律师

lay[1] *form of* **lie**[2] ✳ **lie**[2] 的不同形式

lay[2] /leɪ; le/ *verb* 动词 (**lays, laying, laid** /leɪd; led/, **has laid**)

1 put something carefully on another thing 把某物小心放在另一物上: *I laid the papers on the desk.* 我把文件放在办公桌上了。

2 make an egg 下蛋；产卵: *Birds and insects lay eggs.* 鸟和昆虫都能产卵。

layer /'leɪə(r); 'leɚ/ *noun* 名词

something flat that lies on another thing or that is between other things 层: *The table was covered with a thin layer of dust.* 桌子上有一层尘土。◇ *The cake has a layer of jam in the middle.* 这块蛋糕中间有一层果酱。

lazy /'leɪzi; 'lezɪ/ *adjective* 形容词 (**lazier, laziest**)

A person who is lazy does not want to work 懒；懒惰: *Don't be so lazy—come and help me!* 别那么懒了——过来帮帮我吧！◇ *My teacher said I was lazy.* 我们老师说我懒散。

lazily /'leɪzɪli; 'lezəlɪ/ *adverb* 副词

in a slow, lazy way 缓慢而懒惰地: *She walked lazily across the room.* 她在屋子里懒洋洋地从一边走到另一边。

laziness /'leɪzinəs; 'lezɪnɪs/ *noun* 名词 (no plural 无复数)

being lazy 懒惰

lb *short way of writing* **pound 2** ✳ **pound 2** 的缩写形式

lead[1] /led; lɛd/ *noun* 名词

1 (no plural 无复数) a soft grey metal that is very heavy. Lead is used to make things like water-pipes and roofs. 铅

2 (*plural* 复数作 **leads**) the grey part inside a pencil 铅笔心

lead[2] /li:d; lid/ *verb* 动词 (**leads, leading, led** /led; lɛd/, **has led**)

1 take a person or an animal somewhere by going in front 带领某人或动物到某处: *He led me to my room.* 他把我领到我的房间。

2 be the first or the best, for example in a race or game（在径赛或游戏中）领先；居首位: *Who's leading in the race?* 现在谁跑在最前面？

3 go to a place 通往某处: *This path leads to the river.* 这条小路通到河边。

4 control a group of people 带领或领导一个群体: *The team was led by Gary Hollis.* 这个队是由加里·霍利斯带队。

lead to something make something happen 引致或导致某事物: *Smoking can lead to heart disease.* 吸烟能引起心脏病。

lead[3] /li:d; lid/ *noun* 名词 (no plural 无复数)

going in front or doing something first 带领；领头

be in the lead be in front 领先: *At the start of the race her horse was in the lead.* 她下注的马刚一起跑就领先。

lead[4] /li:d; lid/ *noun* 名词

1 a long piece of leather or a chain that you tie to a dog's neck so that it walks with you（牵狗用的）皮带或链子

2 a long piece of wire that brings

electricity to things like lamps and machines（输送电流到电灯和机器等处的）导线

leader /ˈli:də(r); ˈlidɚ/ *noun* 名词

1 a person who controls a group of people 领导者；领袖: *They chose a new leader.* 他们选出了新领袖。

2 a person or group that is the first or the best 领先的或最好的人或群体: *The leader is ten metres in front of the other runners.* 跑在最前面的比其余的领先十米。

leadership /ˈli:dəʃɪp; ˈlidɚˌʃɪp/ *noun* 名词 (no plural 无复数)

controlling a group of people（对群体的）领导: *The country is under new leadership* (= has new leaders). 国家有了新的领袖。

leading /ˈli:dɪŋ; ˈlidɪŋ/ *adjective* 形容词

best or very important 最好的或非常重要的: *a leading writer* 第一流的作家

leaf /li:f; lif/ *noun* 名词 (*plural* 复数作 **leaves** /li:vz; livz/)

one of the flat green parts that grow on a plant or tree 叶子: *Leaves fall from the trees in autumn.* 秋天树叶就落了。☞ pictures at **plant** and **tree** 见 **plant** 和 **tree** 词条插图

leaflet /ˈli:flət; ˈliflɪt/ *noun* 名词

a piece of paper with writing on it that tells you about something 传单: *The man at the tourist information office gave me a leaflet about buses to the airport.* 旅游咨询处的男职员给了我一份公共汽车到飞机场的宣传单。

league /li:g; lig/ *noun* 名词

1 a group of teams that play against each other in a sport（参赛运动队的）联合会: *the football league* 足球联合会

2 a group of people or countries that work together to do something 联盟；同盟: *the League of Nations* 国际联盟

leak /li:k; lik/ *verb* 动词 (**leaks, leaking, leaked** /li:kt; likt/)

1 have a hole that liquid or gas can go through 漏液体或气体: *The roof of our house leaks when it rains.* 我们房顶一下雨就漏。◇ *The boat is leaking.* 船漏了。

2 go out through a hole 漏出: *Water is leaking from the pipe.* 水从管子里漏出了。

leak *noun* 名词

There's a leak in the roof. 房顶上有个漏洞。

lean¹ /li:n; lin/ *adjective* 形容词 (**leaner, leanest**)

1 thin but strong 瘦而强壮的: *He is tall and lean.* 他又高又瘦。

2 Lean meat does not have very much fat. 瘦肉

lean 依靠或探身

She is **leaning** against a tree.
她靠着树站着。

He is **leaning** out of a window.
他探身窗外。

lean² /li:n; lin/ *verb* 动词 (**leans, leaning, leant** /lent; lɛnt/ or 或 **leaned** /li:nd; lind/, **has leant** or 或 **has leaned**)

1 not be straight; bend forwards, backwards or to the side 倾斜；歪斜

2 put your body or a thing against another thing 使身体或某物靠在另一物上: *Lean your bike against the wall.* 把自行车靠在墙上吧。

leap /li:p; lip/ *verb* 动词 (**leaps, leaping, leapt** /lept; lɛpt/ or 或 **leaped** /li:pt; lipt/, **has leapt** or 或 **has leaped**)

make a big jump 跳；跳跃: *The cat leapt onto the table.* 猫跳到桌子上去了。

leap *noun* 名词

a big jump 跳；跳跃: *With one leap, he was over the wall.* 他一跳就跳到墙上去了。

leap year /ˈli:p jɪə(r); ˈlip ˌjɪr/ *noun* 名词

a year when February has 29 days. Leap years happen every four years. 闰年

learn /lɜ:n; lɝn/ *verb* 动词 (**learns, learning, learnt** /lɜ:nt; lɝnt/ or 或 **learned** /lɜ:nd; lɝnd/, **has learnt** or 或 **has learned**)

1 find out something, or how to do something, by studying or by doing it often 学；学习: *Jodie is learning to swim.* 乔迪正在学游泳。◇ *I learnt English at school.* 我上学的时候学的是英语。◇ *Learn this list of words for homework* (= so you can remember them). 家庭作业是要求学会这些词语（= 不要忘记）。☞ Look at **teach**. 见 **teach**。

L

2 hear about something 听说；获悉：*I was sorry to learn of your father's death.* 听说您父亲去世了，我非常难过。

learner /ˈlɜːnə(r); ˈlɝnɚ/ *noun* 名词
a person who is learning 学习的人：*This dictionary is for learners of English.* 本词典是为学习英语的人编写的。

leash /liːʃ; liʃ/ *American English for* **lead⁴ 1** 美式英语，即 **lead⁴ 1**

least¹ /liːst; list/ *adjective, pronoun* 形容词，代词
the smallest amount of something 最小（的）；最少（的）：*Susan has a lot of money, Jenny has less, and Kate has the least.* 苏珊有很多钱，珍妮的钱少，凯特的钱最少。☞ Look at **less**. 见 **less**。

least² /liːst; list/ *adverb* 副词
less than all others 最小；最少：*This is the least expensive camera in the shop.* 这是这家商店里最便宜的照相机。
at least **1** not less than 至少；起码：*It will cost at least £150.* 这至少得150英镑。 **2** although other things are bad 尽管其他方面都不好，但是…：*We're not rich, but at least we're happy.* 我们虽然并不富裕，但是我们很愉快。
not in the least not at all 一点也不；毫不：*'Are you angry?' 'Not in the least!'* "你生气了吗？""一点儿都没生气！"

leather /ˈleðə(r); ˈlɛðɚ/ *noun* 名词 (no plural 无复数)
the skin of an animal that is used to make things like shoes, jackets or bags 皮革；皮子：*a leather jacket* 皮甲克

leave¹ /liːv; liv/ *verb* 动词 (**leaves, leaving, left** /left; lɛft/, **has left**)
1 go away from somebody or something 离开某人或某事物：*The train leaves at 8.40.* 火车8点40分开。◇ *She left home when she was 18.* 她18岁时离开了家。◇ *I left my job in May.* 我五月份离职了。
2 let somebody or something stay in the same place or in the same way 使某人或某事物留在原地或保持原状：*John left the door open.* 约翰让门开着。
3 not bring something with you 不携带某物：*I left my books at home.* 我把书留在家里了。
4 make something stay; not use something 使某事物留着；不使用某事物：*Leave some cake for me!* 给我留些蛋糕！
leave somebody alone not speak to or touch somebody 不与某人说话或不接触某人：*Leave me alone—I'm busy!* 别打扰我——我正忙着呢。
leave something alone not touch or take something 不接触或不拿某物：*Leave that bag alone—it's mine!* 别动那个袋子——那是我的！
leave somebody or 或 **something behind** not take somebody or something with you 不携带某人或某物：*She went shopping and left the children behind.* 她去买东西，没带着孩子。
leave for start a journey to a place 起程到某地：*Jenny is leaving for France tomorrow.* 珍妮明天到法国去。
leave out not put in or do something; not include somebody or something 不把某人或某事物包括在内或不做某事物：*The other children left him out of the game.* 别的孩子都不带他玩儿。◇ *I left out question 3 in the exam because it was too difficult.* 我没做第3道试题，难极了。
leave something to somebody **1** let somebody do a job for you 让某人为你做某事：*I left the cooking to John.* 我把做饭的事交给约翰去做。 **2** give something to somebody when you die 死后把某事物留给某人：*She left all her money to her sons.* 她死后把钱都留给几个儿子了。

leave² /liːv; liv/ *noun* 名词 (no plural 无复数)
a time when you do not go to work 假期：*I have 25 days' leave each year.* 我每年有25天假。
on leave having a holiday from your job 休假中：*He's on leave from the army.* 他离开了部队正在度假。

leaves *plural of* **leaf** ＊ **leaf** 的复数形式

lecture /ˈlektʃə(r); ˈlɛktʃɚ/ *noun* 名词
a talk to a group of people to teach them about something 演讲；讲课：*She gave an interesting lecture on Spanish history.* 她讲了关于西班牙历史的很有意思的一课。
lecture *verb* 动词 (**lectures, lecturing, lectured** /ˈlektʃəd; ˈlɛktʃɚd/)
Professor Sims lectures on Modern Art. 西姆斯教授讲现代艺术课。
lecturer *noun* 名词
a person whose job is to lecture 讲师：*He is a university lecturer.* 他是大学讲师。

led *form of* **lead²** ＊ **lead²** 的不同形式

ledge /ledʒ; lɛdʒ/ *noun* 名词
a long narrow flat place, for example under a window or on the side of a mountain 长条的窄而平的地方（例如窗户下边的或山边的）: *a window-ledge* 窗台

leek /li:k; lik/ *noun* 名词
a vegetable like a long white onion with green leaves韭葱: *leek and potato soup* 韭葱土豆汤

left[1] *form of* **leave**[1] ✳ **leave**[1] 的不同形式
be left be there after the rest has gone 剩下: *There is only a small piece of cake left.* 只剩下一小块蛋糕。

left[2] /left; lɛft/ *adjective, adverb* 形容词，副词
opposite of right 左: *Turn left at the church.* 在教堂处向左转。◇ *My left leg hurts.* 我左腿疼。
left *noun* 名词 (no plural 无复数)
The house is on your left. 那所房子在您左边。◇ *In Britain we drive on the left.* 在英国我们靠左侧行驶。

left-hand /'left hænd; 'lɛft'hænd/ *adjective* 形容词
of or on the left 左边的: *Your heart is on the left-hand side of your body.* 心脏在身体的左侧。
left-handed /ˌleft 'hændɪd; 'lɛft-'hændɪd/ *adjective* 形容词
If you are left-handed, you use your left hand more easily than your right-hand, for example when you write. 习惯用左手的（例如写字）

leg /leg; lɛg/ *noun* 名词
1 one of the long parts of the body of a person or an animal that is used for walking and standing（人或动物的）腿: *A dog has four legs.* 狗有四条腿。☞ picture on page C2 见第C2页图
2 one of the parts of a pair of trousers that covers your leg 裤腿
3 one of the long parts that a table or chair stands on（桌子或椅子的）腿
pull somebody's leg try to make somebody believe something that is not true, for fun（开玩笑）使某人信以为真: *I didn't really see an elephant—I was only pulling your leg!* 我并没有真看见大象——说着玩儿骗你呢！

legal /'li:gl; 'ligḷ/ *adjective* 形容词
1 allowed by the law 合法的: *In many parts of America, it is legal to carry a gun.* 在美国很多地方，带枪是合法的。✪ opposite 反义词: **illegal** or 或 **against the law**
2 of or about the law 法律上的: *legal advice* 法律方面的意见
legally /'li:gəli; 'ligḷɪ/ *adverb* 副词
They are not legally married. 他们未经法律程序结婚。

legend /'ledʒənd; 'lɛdʒənd/ *noun* 名词
an old story that is perhaps not true 传奇；传说: *the legend of Robin Hood* 罗宾汉传奇

leisure /'leʒə(r); 'liʒɚ/ *noun* 名词 (no plural 无复数)
the time when you are not working and can do what you want 空闲；闲暇
leisure centre /'leʒə sentə(r); 'lɛʒɚ ˌsɛntɚ/ *noun* 名词
a place where you can play sports and do other things in your free time 业余活动中心

lemon /'lemən; 'lɛmən/ *noun* 名词
a yellow fruit with a sour taste 柠檬

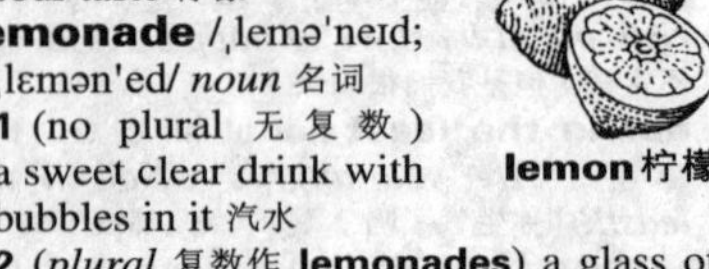
lemon 柠檬

lemonade /ˌlemə'neɪd; ˌlɛmən'ed/ *noun* 名词
1 (no plural 无复数)
a sweet clear drink with bubbles in it 汽水
2 (*plural* 复数作 **lemonades**) a glass of this drink 一杯汽水

lend /lend; lɛnd/ *verb* 动词 (**lends, lending, lent** /lent; lɛnt/, **has lent**)
give something to somebody for a short time 把某物借给某人: *Rick lent me his car for an hour.* 里克把汽车借给我一个小时。☞ picture at **borrow** 见 **borrow** 词条插图

length /leŋθ; lɛŋθ/ *noun* 名词 (no plural 无复数)
how long something is 长度: *The table is two metres in length.* 这张桌子两米长。◇ *We measured the length of the garden.* 我们测量了花园的长度。☞ picture on page C5 见第C5页图

lengthen /'leŋθn; 'lɛŋθən/ *verb* 动词 (**lengthens, lengthening, lengthened** /'leŋθnd; 'lɛŋθənd/)
become longer or make something longer（使某物）变长；加长

lengthy /'leŋθi; 'lɛŋθɪ/ *adjective* 形容词 (**lengthier, lengthiest**)
long 长的: *a lengthy meeting* 很长的会议

L

lens /lenz; lɛnz/ *noun* 名词 (*plural* 复数作 **lenses**)
a special piece of glass in things like cameras, microscopes or glasses 透镜；镜片 ☞ Look also at **contact lens**. 另见 **contact lens**。

lent *form of* **lend** ＊ **lend** 的不同形式

lentil /'lentl; 'lɛntḷ/ *noun* 名词
a small round dried seed. You cook lentils in water before you eat them 小扁豆: *lentil soup* 小扁豆汤

leopard /'lepəd; 'lɛpɚd/ *noun* 名词
a wild animal like a big cat with yellow fur and dark spots 豹

less[1] /les; lɛs/ *adjective*, *pronoun* 形容词，代词
a smaller amount of something; not so much 较少；更少: *A poor person has less money than a rich person.* 穷人比富人钱少。◇ *I'm too fat—I should eat less.* 我太胖了——应该少吃点儿了。☞ Look at **least**. 见 **least**。

less[2] /les; lɛs/ *adverb* 副词
not so much 较少；更少: *It rains less in summer.* 夏天雨下得少。◇ *He's less intelligent than his sister.* 他不如妹妹聪明。☞ Look at **least**. 见 **least**。

lesson /'lesn; 'lɛsṇ/ *noun* 名词
a time when you learn something with a teacher 课: *We have a French lesson after lunch.* 我们午饭后上法语课。

let[1] /let; lɛt/ *verb* 动词 (**lets**, **letting**, **let**, **has let**)
allow somebody or something to do something 让某人或某事物做某事: *Her parents won't let her go out with her boyfriend.* 她父母不让她跟男朋友谈恋爱。◇ *Let me carry your bag.* 我来给您提着包吧。◇ *Don't let the fire go out.* 可别让火灭了。◇ *Let the dog in* (= let it come in). 把狗放进来吧。

let somebody down not do something that you promised to do for somebody 承诺为某人做某事而不做；使某人失望: *Claire has let me down. We agreed to meet at eight o'clock but she didn't come.* 克莱尔让我很失望。我们说好了八点钟见面，她没来。

let go of somebody or 或 **something, let somebody** or 或 **something go** stop holding somebody or something 放开某人或某事物: *Let go of my hand!* 把我的手放开！◇ *Hold the rope and don't let go.* 抓住绳子，别松手。

let somebody off not punish somebody 不惩罚某人: *He wasn't sent to prison—the judge let him off.* 没把他关进监狱——法官饶了他了。

let's You use 'let's' to ask somebody to do something with you 用以要求某人一起做某事；咱们: *Let's go to the theatre this evening.* 咱们今天晚上一起看戏去吧。

let[2] /let; lɛt/ *verb* 动词 (**lets**, **letting**, **let**, **has let**)
allow somebody to use your house or land if they pay you 出租房屋或土地: *Have you got any rooms to let?* 您这儿有房间出租吗？

letter /'letə(r); 'lɛtɚ/ *noun* 名词
1 a sign in writing 字母: *Z is the last letter in the English alphabet.* ＊Z是英语字母表中的最后一个字母。

> ✪ A, B and C are **capital** letters, and a, b, and c are **small** letters. ＊ A、B、C这样的大写字母叫做 **capital** letters，a、b、c 这样的小写字母叫做 **small** letters。

2 a piece of writing that one person sends to another person 信件: *Did you post my letter?* 您把我的信寄出去了吗？◇ *She wrote a letter to her mother.* 她给母亲写了封信。

letter-box /'letə bɒks; 'lɛtɚ,bɑks/ *noun* 名词 (*plural* 复数作 **letter-boxes**)
1 a hole for letters in the door of a house（住宅门上的）投信口
2 a box for letters outside a house（收信人住宅外的）信箱
3 a box in the street where you put letters that you want to send（设于街道上为投寄信件的）信箱

lettuce /'letɪs; 'lɛtɪs/ *noun* 名词
a plant with big leaves that you eat without cooking, in salads 莴苣；生菜（拌色拉中生吃的）

level[1] /'levl; 'lɛvḷ/ *adjective* 形容词
1 with no part higher than another part; flat 水平的；平的；平坦的: *We need level ground to play football on.* 我们需要有块平地踢足球。◇ *This shelf isn't level.* 这块搁板不平。
2 with the same heights, points or

L

positions, for example 一样高的；等高的（例如高度、点数或位置等）: *The two teams are level with 40 points each.* 两队各得40分打成平局。◇ *His head is level with his mother's shoulder.* 他的头部和母亲的肩膀一般高。

level² /ˈlevl; ˈlɛvl̩/ *noun* 名词
how high something is（某事物的）高度；水平；级别: *The town is 500 metres above sea level.* 这个镇子海拔500米。◇ *an elementary-level English class* 初级英语班

level crossing /ˌlevl ˈkrɒsɪŋ; ˌlɛvl̩ ˈkrɔsɪŋ/ *noun* 名词
a place where a railway line goes over a road 平交道（铁路和公路的平面交叉处）

lever /ˈliːvə(r); ˈlɛvɚ/ *noun* 名词
1 a bar for lifting something heavy or opening something. You put one end under the thing you want to lift or open, and push the other end. 杠杆
2 a thing that you pull or push to make a machine work（机器的）操作杆: *Pull this lever.* 拉这个操作杆。

liable /ˈlaɪəbl; ˈlaɪəbl̩/ *adjective* 形容词
If you are liable to do something, you usually do it or you will probably do it（因通常做某事）很可能仍做某事: *He's liable to get angry if you don't do what he says.* 要是不按他的话去做，他可爱生气。

liar /ˈlaɪə(r); ˈlaɪɚ/ *noun* 名词
a person who says or writes things that are not true 说谎的人: *I don't believe her—she's a liar.* 我不信她的话——她常撒谎。

liberal /ˈlɪbərəl; ˈlɪbərəl/ *adjective* 形容词
A person who is liberal lets other people do and think what they want（对于别人的思想行为）宽容的；思想开放的: *Kim's parents are very liberal, but mine are quite strict.* 小金的父母很随和，可是我的父母非常严。

the Liberal Democrats /ðə ˌlɪbərəl ˈdeməkræts; ðə ˌlɪbərəl ˈdɛməkræts/ *noun* 名词 (plural 复数)
one of the important political parties in Britain（英国的）自由民主党 ☞ Look at **the Conservative Party** and **the Labour Party**. 见 **the Conservative Party** 和 **the Labour Party**。

liberate /ˈlɪbəreɪt; ˈlɪbəˌret/ *verb* 动词 (**liberates, liberating, liberated**)
make somebody or something free 使某人或某事物自由；解放: *France was liberated in 1945.* 法国于1945年解放。

liberty /ˈlɪbəti; ˈlɪbɚtɪ/ *noun* 名词 (no plural 无复数)
being free to go where you want and do what you want 自由

library /ˈlaɪbrəri; ˈlaɪˌbrɛrɪ/ *noun* 名词 (*plural* 复数作 **libraries**)
a room or building where you go to borrow or read books 图书馆 ✪ Be careful! You cannot buy books from a **library**. 注意！不能在图书馆（**library**）里买书。The place where you buy books is called a **bookshop**.买书的地方是书店，叫做 **bookshop**。

librarian /laɪˈbreəriən; laɪˈbrɛrɪən/ *noun* 名词
a person who works in a library 图书馆管理员

licence /ˈlaɪsns; ˈlaɪsn̩s/ *noun* 名词
1 a piece of paper that shows you are allowed to do or have something 执照；许可证: *Do you have a driving-licence?* 您有驾驶执照吗？
2 *American English for* **license** 美式英语，即 **license**

license /ˈlaɪsns; ˈlaɪsn̩s/ *verb* 动词 (**licenses, licensing, licensed** /ˈlaɪsnst; ˈlaɪsn̩st/)
1 give somebody a licence 给某人执照或许可证: *This shop is licensed to sell guns.* 这个商店有售枪执照。
2 *American English for* **licence** 美式英语，即 **licence**

license plate /ˈlaɪsns pleɪt; ˈlaɪsn̩s plet/ *American English for* **number-plate** 美式英语，即 **number-plate**

lick /lɪk; lɪk/ *verb* 动词 (**licks, licking, licked** /lɪkt; lɪkt/)
move your tongue over something 舔某物: *The cat was licking its paws.* 猫正在舔自己的爪子。

lick *noun* 名词
Can I have a lick of your ice-cream? 我舔一口你的冰激凌行吗？

lids 盖子

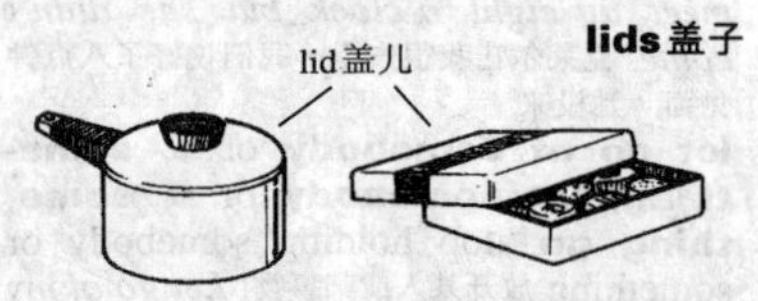

lid /lɪd; lɪd/ *noun* 名词
the top part of a box, pot or other container that covers it and that you can take off 盖子；盖儿 ☞ Look also at **eyelid**. 另见 **eyelid**。

lie[1] /laɪ; laɪ/ *verb* 动词 (**lies, lying, lied** /laɪd; laɪd/, **has lied**)
say something that you know is not true 说谎: *He lied about his age. He said he was 16 but really he's 14.* 他谎报年龄。他说他16岁，其实他14岁。
lie *noun* 名词
something you say that you know is not true 谎话: *She told me a lie.* 她向我撒了个谎。
☞ A person who lies is a **liar**. 说谎的人叫做 **liar**。

lie[2] /laɪ; laɪ/ *verb* 动词 (**lies, lying, lay** /leɪ; le/, **has lain** /leɪn; len/)
1 put your body flat on something so that you are not sitting or standing 平卧；躺: *He lay on the bed.* 他躺在床上就睡着了。
2 have your body flat on something 以某种姿势躺: *The baby was lying on its back.* 那个幼儿仰卧着。
3 be or stay on something 存在或停留在某物上: *Snow lay on the ground.* 地上有积雪。
lie down put or have your body flat on something 躺下: *She lay down on the bed.* 她躺在床上。

lieutenant /lefˈtenənt; luˈtɛnənt/ *noun* 名词
an officer in the army or navy 陆军中尉；海军上尉

life /laɪf; laɪf/ *noun* 名词
1 (no plural 无复数) People, animals and plants have life, but things like stone, metal and water do not 生命: *Do you believe there is life after death?* 你相信不相信死后还有生命？◇ *Is there life on the moon?* 月球上有生命吗？
2 (*plural* 复数作 **lives** /laɪvz; laɪvz/) being alive 性命: *Many people lost their lives* (= died) *in the fire.* 很多人在这场大火中丧了命。◇ *The doctor saved her life* (= stopped her dying). 医生挽救了她的性命。
3 (*plural* 复数作 **lives**) the time that you have been alive 一生；终生: *He has lived here all his life.* 他一生都住在这里。
4 (no plural 无复数) the way that you live 生活: *an unhappy life* 不愉快的生活
5 (no plural 无复数) energy; being busy and interested 活力；生命力: *Young children are full of life.* 儿童都是朝气蓬勃的。
lead a life live in a certain way 过某种生活: *She leads a busy life.* 她过着忙忙碌碌的日子。

lifebelt /ˈlaɪfbelt; ˈlaɪfˌbɛlt/ *noun* 名词
a big ring that you hold or wear if you fall into water to stop you from drowning 救生圈

lifeboat /ˈlaɪfbəʊt; ˈlaɪfˌbot/ *noun* 名词
a boat that goes to help people who are in danger at sea 救生艇

life-jacket /ˈlaɪf dʒækɪt; ˈlaɪfˌdʒækɪt/ *noun* 名词
a special jacket that you wear in a boat to stop you from drowning if you fall in the water 救生衣

lifestyle /ˈlaɪfstaɪl; ˈlaɪfˈstaɪl/ *noun* 名词
the way that you live 生活方式: *They have a healthy lifestyle.* 他们的生活方式十分健康。

lifetime /ˈlaɪftaɪm; ˈlaɪfˌtaɪm/ *noun* 名词
all the time that you are alive 一生；终生: *There have been a lot of changes in my grandmother's lifetime.* 我祖母一生中经历过很多变化。

lift[1] /lɪft; lɪft/ *verb* 动词 (**lifts, lifting, lifted**)
move somebody or something up 把某人或某物抬起或举起: *I can't lift this box. It's too heavy.* 我举不起这个箱子。太重了。◇ *Lift your arm.* 把您的胳膊抬起来。

lift[2] /lɪft; lɪft/ *noun* 名词
1 a machine that takes people and things up and down in a high building 电梯；升降机: *Shall we use the stairs or take the lift?* 我们是走楼梯还是坐电梯？
2 a free journey in another person's car 免费乘搭他人的汽车；坐他人的顺路车: *Can you give me a lift to the station?* 您能让我顺便坐您的汽车到车站去吗？

light[1] /laɪt; laɪt/ *noun* 名词
1 (no plural 无复数) Light comes from the sun, fire and lamps. It makes us able to see things 光线；光；阳光；火光；灯光: *sunlight* 日光 ◇ *The light was not very good so it was difficult to read.* 当时光线不好，很难阅读。

2 (*plural* 复数作 **lights**) a thing that gives light, for example an electric lamp 灯（例如电灯）☞ Look also at **traffic-lights**. 另见 **traffic-lights**。

✪ A light can be **on** or **off**. 灯开着叫做 **on**，关着叫做 **off**。You can **put**, **turn** or **switch** a light **on**, **off** or **out** 开灯或关灯叫做 **put**、**turn** 或 **switch** a light **on**、**off** 或 **out**: *Turn the lights off before you go to bed.* 临睡前要关灯。◇ *It's getting dark. Shall I switch the light on?* 天黑了。我把灯打开好吗？

3 (no plural 无复数) something, for example a match, that you use to start a cigarette burning 点火物（例如火柴，用以点香烟）: *Have you got a light?* 您有火儿吗？

set light to something make something start to burn 点燃某物

light² /laɪt; laɪt/ *adjective* 形容词 (**lighter**, **lightest**)

1 with a lot of light; not dark 明亮的: *In summer it's light until about ten o'clock.* 夏天到了十点钟左右天色才暗下来。◇ *The room has a lot of windows so it's very light.* 这个房间有很多窗户所以很亮。

2 with a pale colour; not dark 浅色的: *a light-blue shirt* 浅蓝色的衬衫

3 easy to lift or move; not heavy 轻的；不重的: *Will you carry this bag for me? It's very light.* 你给我提这个袋子行吗？非常轻。☞ picture at **heavy** 见 **heavy** 词条插图

4 not very much or not very strong 不太多或不太强: *light rain* 小雨 ◇ *I had a light breakfast.* 我吃的早饭不太多。

lightly *adverb* 副词

She touched me lightly on the arm. 她轻轻触摸我的胳膊。

light³ /laɪt; laɪt/ *verb* 动词 (**lights**, **lighting**, **lit** /lɪt; lɪt/ or 或 **lighted**, **has lit** or 或 **has lighted**)

1 make something start to burn 点燃某物: *Will you light the fire?* 您点上火好吗？

2 give light to something 照亮某物: *The room is lit by two big lamps.* 这间屋子点着两盏很大的灯。

light-bulb /ˈlaɪt bʌlb; ˈlaɪtˌbʌlb/ *noun* 名词

the glass part of an electric lamp that gives light 电灯泡

L

lighter /ˈlaɪtə(r); ˈlaɪtɚ/ *noun* 名词

a thing for lighting cigarettes 打火机

lighthouse /ˈlaɪthaʊs; ˈlaɪtˌhaʊs/ *noun* 名词 (*plural* 复数作 **lighthouses** /ˈlaɪthaʊzɪz; ˈlaɪtˌhaʊzɪz/)

a tall building by or in the sea, with a strong light to show ships that there are rocks 灯塔

lighting /ˈlaɪtɪŋ; ˈlaɪtɪŋ/ *noun* 名词 (no plural 无复数)

the kind of lights that a place has 照明设备: *street lighting* 街道照明设备

lightning /ˈlaɪtnɪŋ; ˈlaɪtnɪŋ/ *noun* 名词 (no plural 无复数)

a sudden bright light in the sky when there is a storm 闪电: *He was struck (= hit) by lightning.* 他遭雷电击中。☞ Look at **thunder**. 见 **thunder**。

like¹ /laɪk; laɪk/ *verb* 动词 (**likes**, **liking**, **liked** /laɪkt; laɪkt/)

feel that somebody or something is good or nice; enjoy something 喜欢或喜爱某人或某事物: *Do you like Jenny's new boyfriend?* 你喜欢珍妮的新男朋友吗？◇ *I don't like carrots.* 我不爱吃胡萝卜。◇ *I like playing tennis.* 我喜欢打网球。✪ opposite 反义词: **dislike**

if you like if you want 你要是愿意的话: *'Shall we go out?' 'Yes, if you like.'* "咱们出去好吗？""好哇，听你的。"

✪ **Would like** is a more polite way of saying **want** 用 **would like** 表达 **want**（想要）较为客气: *Would you like some coffee?* 您想来点儿咖啡吗？◇ *I'd like to speak to the manager.* 我很想跟经理谈谈。

like² /laɪk; laɪk/ *preposition*, *conjunction* 介词，连词

1 the same as somebody or something 与某人或某事物相像；类似；相似: *She is wearing a dress like mine.* 她穿着一件连衣裙，跟我的一样。◇ *John looks like his father.* 约翰长得像父亲。☞ Look at **unlike**. 见 **unlike**。

2 in the same way as somebody or something 像某人或某事物那样: *She acted like a child.* 她举动像个孩子。

3 for example 例如；比方: *I bought a lot of things, like books and clothes.* 我买了很多东西，比如书和衣服。

what is ... like? words that you say when you want to know more about somebody or something 想进一步了解某人

或某事物的用语: *'What's that book like?' 'It's very interesting.'* "那本书怎么样？" "很有意思。"

likely /'laɪkli; 'laɪklɪ/ *adjective* 形容词 (**likelier**, **likeliest**)
If something is likely, it will probably happen 可能发生的；有可能的: *It's likely that she will agree.* 她很可能同意。◇ *They are likely to be late.* 他们要晚了。✪ opposite 反义词: **unlikely**

likeness /'laɪknəs; 'laɪknɪs/ *noun* 名词 (no plural 无复数)
being or looking the same（情况或样子）相像；相似: *There's a strong likeness between John and his brother.* 约翰跟他哥哥长得非常像。

likewise /'laɪkwaɪz; 'laɪk͵waɪz/ *adverb* 副词
the same 同样地；照样地: *I sat down and John did likewise.* 我坐下了，约翰也坐下了。

lily /'lɪli; 'lɪlɪ/ *noun* 名词 (*plural* 复数作 **lilies**)
a plant with big flowers 百合；百合花

limb /lɪm; lɪm/ *noun* 名词
an arm or a leg 一条胳膊或腿；肢

lime /laɪm; laɪm/ *noun* 名词
a small green fruit like a lemon 酸橙

limit /'lɪmɪt; 'lɪmɪt/ *noun* 名词
the most that is possible or allowed 极限；限度: *What is the speed limit?* (= how fast are you allowed to go?) 车速限制是多少？

limit *verb* 动词 (**limits**, **limiting**, **limited**)
do or have no more than a certain amount or number 限制；限定: *The theatre only has 100 seats, so we must limit the number of tickets we sell.* 剧院里只有100个座位，所以我们得限制售票的数量。

limp /lɪmp; lɪmp/ *verb* 动词 (**limps**, **limping**, **limped** /lɪmpt; lɪmpt/)
walk with difficulty because you have hurt your foot or leg 跛行；一拐一拐地走

limp *noun* 名词 (no plural 无复数)
She walks with a limp. 她走路一瘸一拐的。

line¹ /laɪn; laɪn/ *noun* 名词
1 a long thin mark like this __________ (像原文定义中所标示的__________) 线；线条: *Draw a straight line.* 画一条直线。◇ *Two yellow lines at the side of the road mean that you can't park there.* 路边的双黄线标记表示不准在该处停车。
2 people or things beside each other or one after the other 排成队的人或事物: *Stand in a line.* 站成一排。
3 all the words that are beside each other on a page（字的）一行: *How many lines are there on this page?* 这一页上有多少行字？◇ *I don't know the next line of the poem.* 我不知道这首诗的下一行是怎么写的。
4 a long piece of string or rope 绳索: *Hang the washing on the line to dry.* 把洗好的衣服晾在绳子上。
5 what a train moves along（铁路的）轨道；铁轨
6 a very long wire for telephones or electricity 电话线；线路: *I tried to phone him but the line was busy.* 我给他打过电话，但是线路占线。

line² /laɪn; laɪn/ *verb* 动词 (**lines**, **lining**, **lined** /laɪnd; laɪnd/)
1 stand or be in lines along something 站成队；排成行: *People lined the street to watch the race.* 人们在街上站成一排观看速度比赛。
2 cover the inside of something with a different material 给某物安衬里: *The boots are lined with fur.* 这双靴子有毛皮衬里。
line up stand in a line or make a line 站成队；排成行: *We lined up to buy tickets.* 我们排队买票。

linen /'lɪnɪn; 'lɪnɪn/ *noun* 名词 (no plural 无复数)
1 a kind of strong cloth 亚麻布: *a white linen jacket* 亚麻外套
2 things like tablecloths and sheets that are made of cotton or linen 棉布的或亚麻的桌布、床单等

liner /'laɪnə(r); 'laɪnɚ/ *noun* 名词
1 a big ship that carries people a long way 班轮；邮轮
2 a bag that you put inside something to keep it clean（放在某物内用以保持清洁的）衬袋: *a dustbin liner* 垃圾桶里的塑料衬袋

linger /'lɪŋgə(r); 'lɪŋgɚ/ *verb* 动词 (**lingers**, **lingering**, **lingered** /'lɪŋgəd; 'lɪŋgɚd/)
stay somewhere for a long time 逗留；徘徊: *They lingered in the park after the end of the concert.* 他们在音乐会结束后还在公园里徘徊。

lining /ˈlaɪnɪŋ; ˈlaɪnɪŋ/ *noun* 名词
material that covers the inside of something 衬里；里子: *My coat has a thick lining so it's very warm.* 我的大衣衬里很厚，所以很暖和。

link /lɪŋk; lɪŋk/ *noun* 名词
1 something that joins things or people together 把人或事物联系起来的事物；联系；关系: *There's a link between smoking and heart disease.* 吸烟和心脏病有关联。
2 one of the round parts in a chain（链条的）一环
link *verb* 动词 (**links, linking, linked** /lɪŋkt; lɪŋkt/)
join two people or things 把两人或两事物联系或连结起来: *The new tunnel links Britain to France.* 新的隧道把英法两国连结起来了。

lion /ˈlaɪən; ˈlaɪən/ *noun* 名词
a wild animal like a big cat with yellow fur. Lions live in Africa and parts of Asia. 狮子（产于非洲和南亚）

✪ A female lion is called a **lioness** and a young lion is called a **cub**. 母狮子叫做 **lioness**，幼小的狮子叫做 **cub**。

lip /lɪp; lɪp/ *noun* 名词
one of the two soft red parts above and below your mouth 嘴唇 ☞ picture on page C2 见第C2页图

lipstick /ˈlɪpstɪk; ˈlɪpˌstɪk/ *noun* 名词
colour that you put on your lips 口红；唇膏: *I put on some lipstick.* 我涂了一些口红。

liquid /ˈlɪkwɪd; ˈlɪkwɪd/ *noun* 名词
anything that is not a solid or a gas. Water, oil and milk are liquids. 液体
liquid *adjective* 形容词
liquid gold 装饰陶瓷用的金水

list /lɪst; lɪst/ *noun* 名词
a lot of names or other things that you write, one after another 一览表；清单: *a shopping list* (= of things that you must buy) 购物单
list *verb* 动词 (**lists, listing, listed**)
make a list 列出单子；造表: *The teacher listed all our names.* 老师把我们大家的名字都列了出来。

listen /ˈlɪsn; ˈlɪsn̩/ *verb* 动词 (**listens, listening, listened** /ˈlɪsnd; ˈlɪsn̩d/)
hear something when you are trying to hear it（有意识地）听；倾听: *I was listening to the radio.* 我听着收音机。◇ *Listen! I want to tell you something.* 听着！我想告诉你们一件事。☞ Note at **hear** 见 **hear** 词条注释

lit *form of* **light³** ✳ **light³** 的不同形式

liter *American English for* **litre** 美式英语，即 **litre**

literature /ˈlɪtrətʃə(r); ˈlɪtərəˌtʃʊr/ *noun* 名词 (no plural 无复数)
books, plays and poetry 文学: *He is studying English literature.* 他正在学习英国文学。

litre /ˈliːtə(r); ˈlitɚ/ *noun* 名词
a measure of liquid. There are 100 **centilitres** in a litre 升（容量单位，1升等于100厘升，厘升叫做 **centilitre**）: *ten litres of petrol* 十升汽油 ✪ The short way of writing 'litre' is **l** ✳ litre 的缩写形式为 **l**: *20 l* ✳ 20升

litter¹ /ˈlɪtə(r); ˈlɪtɚ/ *noun* 名词
1 (no plural 无复数) pieces of paper and other things that people leave on the ground（弃置在地上的）纸张等杂物；垃圾: *The park was full of litter after the concert.* 音乐会过后，公园里到处都是乱扔的垃圾。
2 (*plural* 复数作 **litters**) all the baby animals that are born to the same mother at the same time（一胎生的）小动物: *Our dog had a litter of six puppies.* 我们的狗一窝生了六个小狗。

litter² /ˈlɪtə(r); ˈlɪtɚ/ *verb* 动词 (**litters, littering, littered** /ˈlɪtəd; ˈlɪtɚd/)
be or make something untidy with litter 有纸张等杂物使某处凌乱: *My desk was littered with papers.* 我的办公桌上有很多乱七八糟的纸。

little¹ /ˈlɪtl; ˈlɪtl̩/ *adjective* 形容词
1 not big; small 小的: *a little village* 小村子 ☞ picture on page C26 见第C26页图
2 young 幼小的: *a little girl* 小姑娘
3 not much 少量的: *We have very little money.* 我们的钱很少。

L

a little some but not much 一些（但不多）；少量；一点儿: *I speak a little French.* 我会说一点儿法语。

little² /ˈlɪtl; ˈlɪtḷ/ *adverb* 副词
not much 少量；少许；稍微: *I'm tired — I slept very little last night.* 我很疲倦——昨天睡得很少。
a little quite; rather 有些；有几分；颇: *This skirt is a little too short for me.* 这条裙子我穿有点儿太短了。
little by little slowly 慢慢地；逐渐地: *Little by little she started to feel better.* 她慢慢觉得好起来了。

little³ /ˈlɪtl; ˈlɪtḷ/ *pronoun* 代词
a small amount; not much 少量；少许；一点儿: *I've got some ice-cream. Would you like a little?* 我有些冰激凌。您想来点儿吗？◇ *I did very little today.* 我今天做得很少。

live¹ /lɪv; lɪv/ *verb* 动词 (**lives, living, lived** /lɪvd; lɪvd/)
1 be or stay alive 活着；活；生存: *You can't live without water.* 没有水就不能活。◇ *He lived to the age of 93.* 他活到93岁。
2 have your home somewhere 居住；住: *Where do you live?* 您住在哪里？
3 spend your life in a certain way（以某种方式）生活；过（某种）日子: *They live a quiet life in the country.* 他们在郊外过着宁静的生活。
live on something **1** eat or drink only one thing 仅靠吃或喝某物维持生命: *Cows live on grass.* 牛靠吃草维持生命。
2 have a certain amount of money 靠某些钱生活: *They live on £70 a week.* 他们靠每周70英镑维持生活。

live² /laɪv; laɪv/ *adjective* 形容词
1 not dead 有生命的；活的: *The snake ate a live mouse.* 那条蛇吃了一只活老鼠。
2 If a radio or television programme is live, you see or hear it at the same time as it happens（指广播）现场直播的: *a live football match* 现场直播的足球比赛
3 with electricity passing through it（指电线等）带电的: *Don't touch that wire — it's live!* 别碰那条电线——有电！

lively /ˈlaɪvli; ˈlaɪvlɪ/ *adjective* 形容词 (**livelier, liveliest**)
full of life; always moving or doing things 有生气的；活跃的: *The children are very lively.* 儿童都非常活跃。

liver /ˈlɪvə(r); ˈlɪvɚ/ *noun* 名词
the part inside the body of a person or an animal that cleans the blood 肝；肝脏 ☞ picture on page C2 见第C2页图

lives *plural of* **life** ✻ **life** 的复数形式

living¹ /ˈlɪvɪŋ; ˈlɪvɪŋ/ *adjective* 形容词
alive; not dead 活的；活着的: *Some people say he is the greatest living writer.* 有人说他是在世的最伟大的作家。

living² /ˈlɪvɪŋ; ˈlɪvɪŋ/ *noun* 名词
1 the way that you get money 谋生之道；生计: *What do you do for a living?* 您靠做什么事维持生活？
2 the way that you live 生活方式

living-room /ˈlɪvɪŋ ruːm; ˈlɪvɪŋ ˌrum/ *noun* 名词
a room in a house where people sit and watch television or talk, for example 起居室；客厅

lizard 蜥蜴

lizard /ˈlɪzəd; ˈlɪzɚd/ *noun* 名词
a small animal that has four legs, a long tail and rough skin 蜥蜴

load¹ /ləʊd; lod/ *noun* 名词
1 something that is carried 负荷物；载荷物: *The lorry brought another load of wood.* 卡车又运来一车木头。
2 loads (plural 复数) a lot 大量；许多: *We've got loads of time.* 我们有很多时间。

load² /ləʊd; lod/ *verb* 动词 (**loads, loading, loaded**)
1 put things in or on something, for example a car or ship, that will carry them 装载；装货: *Two men loaded the furniture into the van.* 有两个人把家具装到运货车上了。◇ *They're loading the plane now.* 他们现在正在往飞机上装货。✪ opposite 反义词: **unload**
2 put bullets in a gun or film in a camera 把子弹装进枪里；把胶卷装进照相机里

loaf /ləʊf; lof/ *noun* 名词 (*plural* 复数作 **loaves** /ləʊvz; lovz/)
a big piece of bread 大面包: *a loaf of bread* 一个大面包 ☞ picture at **bread** 见 **bread** 词条插图

loan /ləʊn; lon/ *noun* 名词
money that somebody lends you 借到的

钱；借款: *The bank gave me a loan of £1 000 to buy a new car.* 银行借给我1 000英镑买新汽车。

loan *verb* 动词 (**loans**, **loaning**, **loaned** /ləʊnd; lond/)
lend something 借出某物: *This book is loaned from the library.* 这本书是从图书馆借的。

lobster /'lɒbstə(r); 'lɑbstɚ/ *noun* 名词
a sea animal with a hard shell, two big claws, eight legs and a long tail 龙虾

local /'ləʊkl; 'lokḷ/ *adjective* 形容词
of a place near you 当地的；本地的；地方的: *Her children go to the local school.* 她的孩子都在当地学校上学。◇ *a local newspaper* 本地报纸 ◇ *local government* 地方政府

locally /'ləʊkəli; 'lokəlɪ/ *adverb* 副词
Do you work locally? 您是在本地工作吗？

located /ləʊ'keɪtɪd; lo'ketɪd/ *adjective* 形容词
in a place 在某处: *The factory is located near Glasgow.* 那座工厂位于格拉斯哥附近。

location /ləʊ'keɪʃn; lo'keʃən/ *noun* 名词
a place 地方；位置: *The house is in a quiet location on top of a hill.* 那所小楼坐落在幽静的山顶上。

lock¹ /lɒk; lɑk/ *noun* 名词
a metal thing that keeps a door, gate, box, etc closed so that you cannot open it without a key 锁

lock 锁

lock² /lɒk; lɑk/ *verb* 动词 (**locks**, **locking**, **locked** /lɒkt; lɑkt/)
close with a key 锁住: *Don't forget to lock the door when you leave.* 您走的时候别忘了把门锁上。✪ opposite 反义词: **unlock**

lock away put something in a place that you close with a key 把某物锁好: *The paintings are locked away at night.* 这些画儿夜里都锁起来了。

lock in lock a door so that somebody cannot go out 把门锁住不让某人出去: *The prisoners are locked in.* 囚犯都锁进了牢房。

lock out lock a door so that somebody cannot go in 把门锁住不让某人进来

lock up lock all the doors and windows of a building 把建筑物的所有门窗都锁好

locker /'lɒkə(r); 'lɑkɚ/ *noun* 名词
a small cupboard, with a lock, for keeping things in, for example in a school or at a station（带锁的）小柜（如学校或车站中的）

lodge /lɒdʒ; lɑdʒ/ *verb* 动词 (**lodges**, **lodging**, **lodged** /lɒdʒd; lɑdʒd/)
pay to live in another person's house 在某人家中付费寄宿: *I lodged with a family when I was studying in Oxford.* 我在牛津读书时，在别人家里付费寄宿。

lodger *noun* 名词
a person who pays to live in another person's house 在某人家中付费寄宿的人

loft /lɒft; lɔft/ *noun* 名词
the room or space under the roof of a house 阁楼；顶楼: *My old books are in a box in the loft.* 我的旧书在阁楼的箱子里。

log /lɒg; lɔg/ *noun* 名词
a thick round piece of wood from a tree 原木: *Put another log on the fire.* 往炉子里再添一条木柴。

log 原木

lollipop /'lɒlipɒp; 'lɑlɪˌpɑp/, **lolly** /'lɒli; 'lɑlɪ/ (*plural* 复数作 **lollies**) *noun* 名词
a big sweet on a stick 棒糖 ☞ Look also at **ice lolly**. 另见 **ice lolly**。

lonely /'ləʊnli; 'lonlɪ/ *adjective* 形容词 (**lonelier**, **loneliest**)
1 unhappy because you are not with other people 因不与他人在一起而不愉快的；孤寂的；寂寞的: *I was very lonely when I first came to London.* 我刚到伦敦的时候非常寂寞。
2 far from other places 远离其他地方的；偏僻的；偏远的: *a lonely house in the hills* 山中孤零零的一所小楼

loneliness /'ləʊnlinəs; 'lonlɪnəs/ *noun* 名词 (no plural 无复数)
being lonely 孤寂；寂寞

long¹ /lɒŋ; lɔŋ/ *adjective* 形容词 (**longer** /'lɒŋgə(r); 'lɔŋgɚ/, **longest** /'lɒŋgɪst; 'lɔŋgɪst/)
1 far from one end to the other 长的: *This is the longest road in Britain.* 这是英国最长的公路。◇ *She has long black hair.* 她的头发又长又黑。✪ opposite 反义词: **short** ☞ picture on page C26 见第C26页图

L

2 You use 'long' to say or ask how far something is from one end to the other 陈述或询问某物长短的词: *How long is the table?* 这张桌子有多长？◇ *The wall is 5 m long.* 这堵墙5米长。☞ picture on page C5 见第C5页图

3 that continues for a lot of time（指时间）长的: *a long film* 一部长的影片 ✪ opposite 反义词: **short**

4 You use 'long' to say or ask about the time from the beginning to the end of something 陈述或询问时间长短的词: *How long is the lesson?* 这节课有多长时间？

long² /lɒŋ; lɔŋ/ *adverb* 副词

for a lot of time 长久；长期地: *I can't stay long.* 我在这儿呆不长。

as long as, so long as if 只要；如果: *You can borrow the book as long as you promise not to lose it.* 这本书你要保证别丢了，你就能借走。

long after at a time much after（指某时）之后很久

long ago many years in the past 很久以前: *Long ago there were no cars.* 很久以前没有汽车。

long before at a time much before（指某时）之前很久: *My grandfather died long before I was born.* 我出生的时候，祖父早已去世了。

no longer, not any longer not now; not as before 不再；已不: *She doesn't live here any longer.* 她已不住在这里了。

long³ /lɒŋ; lɔŋ/ *noun* 名词 (no plural 无复数)

a lot of time 很长时间；很久: *She went shopping but she was not out for long.* 她买东西去了，可是出去的时间不长。

long⁴ /lɒŋ; lɔŋ/ *verb* 动词 (**longs, longing, longed** /lɒŋd; lɔŋd/)

want something very much 非常想要某事物；渴望: *I long to see my family again.* 我很想再见到我家里的人。◇ *She's longing for a letter from her boyfriend.* 她一直在盼望着男朋友的来信。

longing *noun* 名词

a strong feeling of wanting something 渴望；热望

long-jump /'lɒŋ dʒʌmp; 'lɔŋˌdʒʌmp/ *noun* 名词 (no plural 无复数)

a sport where you try to jump as far as you can 跳远运动

loo /lu:; lu/ *noun* 名词 (*plural* 复数作 **loos**)

toilet 厕所: *I need to go to the loo.* 我要去厕所。✪ This is an informal word. 这是口语用词。

look¹ /lʊk; lʊk/ *verb* 动词 (**looks, looking, looked** /lʊkt; lʊkt/)

1 turn your eyes towards somebody or something and try to see them（有意识地）看: *Look at this picture.* 看看这张画儿。◇ *You should look both ways before you cross the road.* 横过马路前，应该先看看左右两边路面情况。☞ Note at **see** 见 **see** 词条注释

2 seem to be; appear 看起来；看上去；似乎；显得: *You look tired!* 你看起来很累了。

3 You say 'look' to make somebody listen to you 招呼别人注意听的词: *Look, I need some money.* 我说，我需要点儿钱。

look after somebody or 或 **something** take care of somebody or something 照看或照料某人或某事物: *Can you look after my cat when I'm on holiday?* 我度假的时候，您给照看着我的猫行吗？

look as if, look as though seem or appear 看来好像；似乎: *It looks as if it's going to rain.* 好像要下雨了。

look for somebody or 或 **something** try to find somebody or something 寻找某人或某事物: *I'm looking for my keys.* 我正在找我的钥匙。

look forward to something wait for something with pleasure（怀着愉快的心情）等待；盼望: *I'm looking forward to seeing you again.* 我盼望着再见到您。

look into something study something carefully 仔细研究某事物；调查: *We will look into the problem.* 我们要把这个问题认真研究一下。

look like somebody or 或 **something 1** seem to be something 看起来像；似乎: *That looks like a good film.* 那部电影好像不错。**2** words that you use to ask about somebody's appearance 询问某人相貌的词: *'What does he look like?' 'He's tall with dark hair.'* "他长相什么样？""他很高，头发是黑的。"

3 have the same appearance as somebody or something 与某人或某物相像: *She looks like her mother.* 她长得像她母亲。

look out! be careful! 小心！；当心！: *Look out! There's a car coming!* 小心！汽车来了！

look out for somebody or 或 **something** pay attention and try to see somebody or something 警惕或留心某人或某事物: *Look out for thieves!* 留神有小偷！

look round visit a place 参观某处: *We looked round the cathedral.* 我们参观了大教堂。

look² /lʊk; lʊk/ *noun* 名词

1 turning your eyes towards somebody or something; looking（指有意识的动作）看: *Paula gave me an angry look!* 葆拉气愤地看了我一眼！

2 the way something seems 外貌；样子: *I don't like the look of this weather. I think it's going to rain.* 我不喜欢这样的天气。我看是要下雨了。

3 looks (plural 复数) how a person's face and body is 相貌和身材；长相: *good looks* 一表人才

have a look 1 see something 看: *Can I have a look at your photos?* 我看看您的照片行吗？**2** try to find something 寻找: *I've had a look for your pen, but I can't find it.* 我找过您的钢笔，但是没找到。

have a look round see many parts of a place 参观某处: *We had a look round the museum.* 我们参观了博物馆。

loop /lu:p; lup/ *noun* 名词

a round shape made by something like string or rope（绳索等绕成的）圈；环

loop 绳圈

loose /lu:s; lus/ *adjective* 形容词 (**looser, loosest**)

1 not tied or fixed 松开的；不牢固的: *The dog broke its chain and got loose.* 狗挣脱了链子跑了。◇ *One of his teeth is loose.* 他有颗牙活动了。

2 not tight 不紧的；宽松的: *a loose white dress* 白色宽松的连衣裙 ☞ picture on page C27 见第C27页图

loosely *adverb* 副词

not tightly or firmly 不紧地；不牢固地: *The rope was tied loosely round a tree.* 那条绳子松松地系在树上。

loosen /'lu:sn; 'lusn̩/ *verb* 动词 (**loosens, loosening, loosened** /'lu:snd; 'lusn̩d/)

become looser or make something looser（使某物）变松: *Can you loosen this knot? It's too tight.* 你能把这个结儿解开吗？太紧了。✪ opposite 反义词: **tighten**

Lord /lɔ:d; lɔrd/ *noun* 名词

1 Lord a man who has a special title（对有某种头衔的男子的尊称）勋爵；阁下；大人: *Lord Fraser* 弗雷泽大臣 ☞ Look at **Lady**. 见 **Lady**。

2 the Lord (no plural 无复数) God or Jesus Christ 上帝；基督

lorry 卡车

lorry /'lɒri; 'lɔrɪ/ *noun* 名词 (*plural* 复数作 **lorries**)

a big vehicle for carrying heavy things 卡车

lose /lu:z; luz/ *verb* 动词 (**loses, losing, lost** /lɒst; lɔst/, **has lost**)

1 not be able to find something 找不到某物；丢失；遗失: *I can't open the door because I've lost my key.* 我把钥匙丢了，所以开不开门了。

2 not have somebody or something that you had before 失去原有的某人或某事物: *I lost my job when the factory closed.* 工厂一倒闭我就失业了。

3 not win 输；失败: *Our team lost the match.* 这场比赛我们队输了。

loser /'lu:zə(r); 'luzɚ/ *noun* 名词

a person who does not win a game, race or competition（游戏、径赛或竞争中）输者；失败者 ✪ opposite 反义词: **winner**

loss /lɒs; lɔs/ *noun* 名词 (*plural* 复数作 **losses**)

1 losing something 丢失；遗失；失去；失败: *Has she told the police about the loss of her car?* 她丢失汽车的事报警了吗？◇ *job losses* 失去工作

2 how much money a business loses（生意等的）亏损的钱: *The company made a loss of £5 million.* 这家公司损失了500万英镑。

at a loss If you are at a loss, you do not know what to do or say. 不知道做什么或说什么；不知所措

lost¹ *form of* **lose** ∗ **lose** 的不同形式

lost² /lɒst; lɔst/ *adjective* 形容词
1 If you are lost, you do not know where you are 不知道身在何处的；迷路的: *I took the wrong road and now I'm lost.* 我走错了路，现在迷路了。◇ *Take this map so that you don't get lost!* 带着这张地图，你就迷不了路了！
2 If something is lost, you cannot find it. 丢失的；失去的
lost property /ˌlɒst ˈprɒpəti; ˌlɔst ˈprɑpɚtɪ/ *noun* 名词 (no plural 无复数)
things that people have lost 人们遗失的物品: *I left my bag on the train, so I went to the lost property office at the station.* 我把提包落在火车上了，所以到车站失物招领处去找。

lot¹ /lɒt; lɑt/ *noun* 名词
a lot very much; a big amount or number 许多；大量: *We ate a lot.* 我们吃了很多。
a lot of, lots of a big number or amount of something 许多的；大量的: *She's got a lot of friends.* 她有很多朋友。◇ *Lots of love from Jenny* (= words at the end of a letter 写信结尾的热情问候语).

lot² /lɒt; lɑt/ *adverb* 副词
a lot very much or often 很；非常；经常: *Your flat is a lot bigger than mine.* 您的公寓比我的大得多。◇ *I go to the cinema a lot.* 我常常看电影。

lotion /ˈləʊʃn; ˈloʃən/ *noun* 名词
liquid that you put on your skin（外用的）护肤液: *suntan lotion* 防晒液

loud /laʊd; laʊd/ *adjective, adverb* 形容词，副词 (**louder, loudest**)
that makes a lot of noise; not quiet 喧闹的；响亮的: *I couldn't hear what he said because the music was too loud.* 音乐的声音很大，我听不见他说的话。◇ *loud voices* 洪亮的嗓音 ◇ *Please speak a bit louder—I can't hear you.* 请大点儿声说——我听不清您说的话。☞ picture on page C27 见第C27页图
out loud so that other people can hear it 使别人能听见；出声地；大声地: *I read the story out loud.* 我朗读了那篇故事。
loudly *adverb* 副词
She laughed loudly. 她大笑起来。

loudspeaker /ˌlaʊdˈspiːkə(r); ˈlaʊdˈspikɚ/ *noun* 名词
an instrument for making sounds louder 扩音器；扬声器: *Music was coming from the loudspeakers.* 从扩音器里传来了音乐声。

lounge /laʊndʒ; laʊndʒ/ *noun* 名词
a room in a house or hotel where you can sit in comfortable chairs（住宅或旅馆中的）休息室

love¹ /lʌv; lʌv/ *verb* 动词 (**loves, loving, loved** /lʌvd; lʌvd/)
1 have a strong warm feeling for somebody（指对人）爱，疼爱，热爱，爱戴: *I love him very much.* 我非常爱他。◇ *She loves her parents.* 她爱她的父母。
2 like something very much（指对事物）非常喜欢，喜爱: *I love skiing.* 我爱滑雪。◇ *I would love to go to America.* 我很乐意到美国去。

love² /lʌv; lʌv/ *noun* 名词
1 (no plural 无复数) a strong warm feeling of liking somebody or something（对某人或某事物的）爱；喜爱；热爱: *Their love for each other was very strong.* 他们真诚相爱。◇ *a love of football* 喜爱足球
2 (*plural* 复数作 **loves**) a person that you love 所爱的人: *Yes, my love.* 是的，亲爱的。
3 (no plural 无复数) (*also* 亦作 **love from**) a way of ending a letter to somebody that you know well 给熟人写信结尾的热情问候语: *Lots of love from Peter.*
4 (no plural 无复数) a word in tennis that means zero（网球用语）零分: *The score is 15-love.* 比分是15比0。
be in love with somebody love somebody 热恋着某人: *He says he is in love with her and they are going to get married.* 他说他热恋着她，并且打算结婚了。
fall in love with somebody begin to love somebody 爱上某人: *He fell in love with Anna the first time they met.* 他对安娜一见钟情。

lovely /ˈlʌvli; ˈlʌvlɪ/ *adjective* 形容词 (**lovelier, loveliest**)
beautiful or very nice 可爱的；美丽的；漂亮的: *That's a lovely dress.* 这件连衣裙真漂亮。◇ *We had a lovely holiday.* 我们假期过得好极了。◇ *It's lovely to see you again.* 又见到您，多高兴啊。

lover /ˈlʌvə(r); ˈlʌvɚ/ *noun* 名词
a person who you have sex with, but who is not your husband or wife（有性关系的）情人（但并非夫妻）

L

loving /ˈlʌvɪŋ; ˈlʌvɪŋ/ *adjective* 形容词
feeling or showing love 爱的；表示爱的：*loving parents* 对子女疼爱的父母

low /ləʊ; lo/ *adjective* 形容词 (**lower**, **lowest**)
1 near the ground; not high 低的；矮的：*There was a low wall round the garden.* 花园四周有矮墙。◇ *a low bridge* 低矮的桥 ☞ picture on page C26 见第C26页图
2 less than usual 低于一般的；比通常少的：*low temperatures* 低温 ◇ *low pay* 低工资
3 soft and quiet 温和而悄悄的：*I heard low voices in the next room.* 我听见隔壁有人小声说话。
4 deep; not high 低沉的；不高的：*a low sound* 低沉的声音
low *adverb* 副词
near the ground 离地面近；低：*The plane flew low over the fields.* 飞机在田地上空低飞。

lower¹ /ˈləʊə(r); ˈloɚ/ *verb* 动词 (**lowers**, **lowering**, **lowered** /ˈləʊəd; ˈloɚd/)
1 move somebody or something down 把某人或某事物移至低处：*They lowered the flag.* 他们降下了旗子。
2 make something less 减低或减少某事物：*Please lower your voice* (= speak more quietly). 请您把说话声音降低些。
✪ opposite 反义词：**raise**

lower² /ˈləʊə(r); ˈloɚ/ *adjective* 形容词
that is under another; bottom 在下面的；最底下的：*the lower lip* 下唇 ✪ opposite 反义词：**upper**

loyal /ˈlɔɪəl; ˈlɔɪəl/ *adjective* 形容词
A person who is loyal does not change his/her friends or beliefs 忠诚的；忠贞的：*a loyal friend* 忠实的朋友 ◇ *He is loyal to the company he works for.* 他忠于他们的公司。
loyalty /ˈlɔɪəlti; ˈlɔɪəltɪ/ *noun* 名词 (no plural 无复数)
being loyal 忠诚；忠贞：*Loyalty to your friends is very important.* 对朋友忠心耿耿十分重要。

LP /ˌel ˈpiː; ˌɛl ˈpi/ *noun* 名词
a record with about 25 minutes of music on each side 密纹唱片 ☞ Look at **single**. 见 **single**。

L-plate /ˈel pleɪt; ˈɛl plet/ *noun* 名词
a sign with a big red letter L on it, that you put on your car when you are learning to drive ✳ L字牌（有红色L字母的牌子，英国学习驾驶的人置于汽车上的）

luck /lʌk; lʌk/ *noun* 名词 (no plural 无复数)
1 things that happen to you that you cannot control; chance 运气；机会
2 good things that happen to you that you cannot control 好运；幸运：*Wish me luck for my exams!* 祝我考试运气好吧！
bad luck, hard luck words that you say to somebody when you are sorry that they did not have good luck 对运气不好的人说的同情话
be in luck have good things happen to you 运气好；走运：*I was in luck—the shop had the book I wanted.* 我真运气——书店里有我要的那本书。
good luck words that you say to somebody when you hope that they will do well 希望某人把事做好的祝颂话：*Good luck! I'm sure you'll get the job.* 万事如意！我保证你能得到这份工作。

lucky /ˈlʌki; ˈlʌkɪ/ *adjective* 形容词 (**luckier**, **luckiest**)
1 If you are lucky, you have good luck 幸运的；有好运的：*She had a bad accident and she is lucky to be alive.* 她大难不死是不幸中的万幸。
2 Something that is lucky brings good luck 带来好运的：*My lucky number is 3.* 我的幸运号码是3。
✪ opposite 反义词：**unlucky**
luckily /ˈlʌkɪli; ˈlʌkɪlɪ/ *adverb* 副词
it is lucky that 幸好；幸而：*I was late, but luckily they waited for me.* 我迟到了，幸好他们还都等着我呢。

luggage /ˈlʌgɪdʒ; ˈlʌgɪdʒ/ *noun* 名词 (no plural 无复数)
bags and suitcases that you take with you when you travel 行李：*'How much luggage have you got?' 'Only one suitcase.'* "您有多少行李？""只有一个手提箱。"

lump /lʌmp; lʌmp/ *noun* 名词
1 a hard piece of something（硬物的）块：*two lumps of sugar* 两块方糖 ◇ *a lump of coal* 一块煤 ☞ picture on page C25 见第C25页图
2 a part in or on your body which has become hard and bigger（身体上的）包，疙瘩：*I've got a lump on my head where I hit it.* 我的头上撞出了个包。

lunch /lʌntʃ; lʌntʃ/ *noun* 名词 (*plural* 复数作 **lunches**)
a meal that you eat in the middle of the day 午饭；午餐: *What would you like for lunch?* 您午餐想吃什么？◇ *What time do you usually have lunch?* 您平常什么时候吃午饭？

lunch-time /ˈlʌntʃ taɪm; ˈlʌntʃˌtaɪm/ *noun* 名词
the time when you eat lunch 午饭时间: *I'll meet you at lunch-time.* 我午饭时间见你。

lung /lʌŋ; lʌŋ/ *noun* 名词
one of the two parts inside your body that you use for breathing 肺 ☞ picture on page C2 见第C2页图

luxurious /lʌgˈʒʊəriəs; lʌgˈʒʊrɪəs/ *adjective* 形容词
very comfortable and expensive 极舒适昂贵的；豪华的: *a luxurious hotel* 豪华的旅馆

luxury /ˈlʌkʃəri; ˈlʌkʃərɪ/ *noun* 名词
1 (no plural 无复数) a way of living when you have all the expensive and beautiful things that you want 豪华: *They live in luxury in a beautiful house in the West Indies.* 他们住在西印度群岛一所漂亮的小楼里，过着豪华的生活。◇ *a luxury hotel* 豪华的旅馆
2 (*plural* 复数作 **luxuries**) something that is very nice and expensive that you do not really need 极好而贵但并非真正需要的事物；奢侈: *Eating in a restaurant is a luxury for most people.* 在饭馆里吃饭对大多数人来说是奢侈的事。

lying *form of* **lie** ＊ **lie** 的不同形式

L

Mm

m *short way of writing* **metre** ✳ **metre** 的缩写形式

mac /mæk; mæk/ *noun* 名词
a light coat that you wear when it rains 雨衣

machine /mə'ʃi:n; mə'ʃin/ *noun* 名词
a thing with parts that move to do work or to make something. Machines often use electricity 机器（机器常用电力驱动）: *a washing-machine* 洗衣机 ◇ *This machine does not work.* 这个机器不动了。

machine-gun /mə'ʃi:n gʌn; mə'ʃin-ˌgʌn/ *noun* 名词
a gun that can send out a lot of bullets very quickly 机关枪

machinery /mə'ʃi:nəri; mə'ʃinərɪ/ *noun* 名词 (no plural 无复数)
1 the parts of a machine 机器的部件；机件: *the machinery inside a clock* 时钟内部的机件
2 a group of machines 机器（总称）: *The factory has bought some new machinery.* 这家工厂买了些新机器。

mad /mæd; mæd/ *adjective* 形容词 (**madder, maddest**)
1 ill in your mind 患精神病的；疯的
2 very stupid; crazy 愚蠢的；疯狂的: *I think you're mad to go out in this snow!* 这样的大雪天你还出去，我看你是疯了！
3 very angry 气愤的；愤怒的: *He was mad at me for losing his watch.* 我把他的手表弄丢了，他对我大发脾气。
be mad about somebody or 或 **something** like somebody or something very much 非常喜爱某人或某事物: *Mina is mad about computer games.* 米纳对电脑游戏着迷了。◇ *He's mad about her.* 他爱她爱得如醉如痴。
drive somebody mad make somebody very angry 使某人非常气愤: *This noise is driving me mad!* 这种噪音吵得我难受极了！
go mad **1** become ill in your mind 患精神病；发疯: *He went mad and killed himself.* 他患精神病把自己杀死了。
2 become very angry 非常气愤；愤怒: *Mum will go mad when she finds out what you did at school.* 妈妈要是知道了你在学校里的事，一定得大发雷霆。

madam /'mædəm; 'mædəm/ *noun* 名词 (no plural 无复数)
1 a polite way of speaking to a woman, instead of using her name 对女子的尊称（不与姓名连用）: *'Can I help you, madam?' asked the shop assistant.* "小姐，您要买点儿什么？"售货员问道。
2 Madam a word that you use at the beginning of a business letter to a woman 在商务信件的开头称呼女子的用词: *Dear Madam ...* 敬启者…
☞ Look at **sir**. 见 **sir**。

made *form of* **make**[1] ✳ **make**[1] 的不同形式
made of something from this material 由这种材料做成的: *This shirt is made of cotton.* 这件衬衫是棉布制的。

madness /'mædnəs; 'mædnɪs/ *noun* 名词 (no plural 无复数)
being ill in your mind 精神病；精神失常

magazine /ˌmægə'zi:n; 'mægəˌzin/ *noun* 名词
a kind of thin book with a paper cover that you can buy every week or every month. It has a lot of different stories and pictures inside. 杂志；期刊

magic /'mædʒɪk; 'mædʒɪk/ *noun* 名词 (no plural 无复数)
1 a special power that can make strange or impossible things happen 魔法；巫术: *The witch changed the prince into a frog by magic.* 女巫用魔法把王子变成了青蛙。
2 clever tricks that somebody can do to surprise people 魔术；戏法
magic, magical /'mædʒɪkl; 'mædʒɪkḷ/ *adjective* 形容词
magic tricks 魔术 ◇ *The witch had magical powers.* 女巫有魔法。

magician /mə'dʒɪʃn; mə'dʒɪʃən/ *noun* 名词
1 a man in stories who has strange, unusual powers 男巫: *The magician turned the boy into a dog.* 巫师把那个男孩儿变成了一条狗。
2 a person who does clever tricks to surprise people 魔术师

magistrate /'mædʒɪstreɪt; 'mædʒɪsˌtret/ *noun* 名词
a judge in a court of law who decides

how to punish people for small crimes 地方法官

magnet /'mægnət; 'mægnɪt/ *noun* 名词
a piece of metal that can make other metal things move towards it 磁铁

magnetic /mæg'netɪk; mæg'nɛtɪk/ *adjective* 形容词
with the power of a magnet 有磁性的: *Is this metal magnetic?* 这种金属有磁性吗？

magnificent /mæg'nɪfɪsnt; mæg-'nɪfəsn̩t/ *adjective* 形容词
very good or beautiful 壮丽的；宏伟的: *What a magnificent cathedral!* 多么宏伟壮观的大教堂啊！

magnify /'mægnɪfaɪ; 'mægnəˌfaɪ/ *verb* 动词 (**magnifies**, **magnifying**, **magnified** /'mægnɪfaɪd; 'mægnəˌfaɪd/, **has magnified**)
make something look bigger than it really is 放大某物: *We magnified the insect under a microscope.* 我们看到昆虫在显微镜下放大了。

magnifying glass /'mægnɪfaɪɪŋ glɑːs; 'mægnəfaɪɪŋ glæs/ *noun* 名词 (*plural* 复数作 **magnifying glasses**)
a special piece of glass that you hold in your hand. It makes things look bigger than they really are. 放大镜

maid /meɪd; med/ *noun* 名词
a woman who does work like cleaning in a hotel or large house 女仆；女用人（如在旅馆或大宅中做清洁工作的）

mail /meɪl; mel/ *noun* 名词 (no plural 无复数)
1 the way of sending and receiving letters, parcels, etc; post 邮政（方式）: *airmail* 空邮
2 letters and parcels that you send or receive; post 邮件；信件；邮包: *Is there any mail for me?* 有我的信吗？

mail *verb* 动词 (**mails**, **mailing**, **mailed** /meɪld; meld/)
send something in the mail 邮寄某物: *I'll mail the money to you.* 我将把钱寄给您。
✪ **Mail** is more usual in American English. 美式英语多用 **mail**。In British English you usually say **post**. 英式英语一般说 **post**。

mailbox /'meɪlbɒks; 'melˌbɑks/ *American English for* **letter-box, pillar-box, postbox** 美式英语，即 **letter-box**、**pillar-box**、**postbox**

mailman /'meɪlmæn; 'melˌmæn/ *American English for* **postman** 美式英语，即 **postman**

main /meɪn; men/ *adjective* 形容词
most important 主要的；最重要的: *My main reason for learning English is to get a better job.* 我学英语主要是想找份更好的工作。

ˌmain course /ˌmeɪn 'kɔːs; 'men kors/ *noun* 名词
the most important part of a meal（一顿饭的）主菜: *I had fish for the main course.* 我主菜吃的是鱼。

main road /ˌmeɪn 'rəʊd; ˌmen 'rod/ *noun* 名词
a big important road between towns（城镇之间的）大路；公路

mainly *adverb* 副词
mostly 主要地；大体上: *The students here are mainly from Japan.* 这里的学生大多来自日本。◇ *She eats mainly vegetables.* 她以蔬菜为主食。

maintain /meɪn'teɪn; men'ten/ *verb* 动词 (**maintains**, **maintaining**, **maintained** /meɪn'teɪnd; men'tend/)
1 continue with something 保持或维持某事物: *If he can maintain this speed, he'll win the race.* 他在比赛中要是能保持这种速度就能赢。
2 keep something working well 保养或维修某物: *The roads are well maintained.* 这些路保养得很好。

maintenance /'meɪntənəns; 'mentə-nəns/ *noun* 名词 (no plural 无复数)
things that you do to keep something working well 保养；维修: *maintenance of a machine* 机器的维修

maize /meɪz; mez/ *noun* 名词 (no plural 无复数)
a tall plant with big yellow seeds that you can eat 玉米；玉蜀黍

Majesty /'mædʒəsti; 'mædʒəstɪ/ *noun* 名词 (*plural* 复数作 **Majesties**)
a word that you use to talk to or about a king or queen 陛下（对君主的尊称）: *Her Majesty Queen Elizabeth II* 伊丽莎白二世女王陛下

major¹ /'meɪdʒə(r); 'medʒɚ/ *adjective* 形容词
very large, important or serious 非常大的、重要的或严重的: *There are airports in all the major cities.* 各大城市都有飞机场。

◇ *major problems* 严重的问题 ✪ opposite 反义词: **minor**

major² /'meɪdʒə(r); 'medʒɚ/ *noun* 名词
an officer in the army 陆军少校

majority /mə'dʒɒrəti; mə'dʒɔrətɪ/ *noun* 名词 (no plural 无复数)
most things or people in a group（在一些事物或人中的）大多数: *The majority of families in Japan have a colour television.* 日本大多数家庭都有彩色电视机。☞ Look at **minority**. 见 **minority**。

make¹ /meɪk; mek/ *verb* 动词 (**makes, making, made** /meɪd; med/, **has made**)
1 put things together so that you have a new thing 做某物；制造；建造: *They make cars in that factory.* 那家工厂制造汽车。◇ *He made a box out of some pieces of wood.* 他用些木料做了个箱子。
2 cause something to be or to happen; produce something 造成某事物；引起；产生: *The plane made a loud noise when it landed.* 飞机着陆时发出了很大的声音。◇ *Chocolates make you fat.* 吃巧克力能让人发胖。◇ *That film made me cry.* 那部电影把我感动得直流泪。◇ *I made a mistake.* 我犯了个错误。
3 force somebody to do something 迫使某人做某事；强迫；逼迫；逼: *My father made me stay at home.* 我父亲让我呆在家里。
4 a word that you use with money, numbers and time 与钱、数目和时间连用的词: *She makes* (= earns) *a lot of money.* 她挣的钱很多。◇ *Five and seven make twelve.* 五加七等于十二。◇ *'What's the time?' 'I make it six o'clock.'* "几点钟了？""我的表六点钟。"
5 give somebody a job 给某人一项工作；选举；指派: *They made him President.* 他们让他当会长。
6 be able to go somewhere 能去某处: *I'm sorry, but I can't make the meeting on Friday.* 很抱歉，我不能参加星期五的会议。
make do with something use something that is not very good, because there is nothing better 用某事物勉强应付（因无更好的）；将就；凑合: *We didn't have a table, but we made do with some boxes.* 我们没有桌子，就用些箱子凑合着。
make something into something change something so that it becomes a different thing 把某事物变成另一事物: *They made the bedroom into an office.* 他们把卧室改成办公室了。
make out be able to see or understand something that is not clear 能辨认出或理解（原来并不清楚的）某事物: *It was dark and I couldn't make out the words on the sign.* 因为光线很暗，我看不清牌子上写的是什么字。
make up 1 tell something that is not true 捏造或虚构某事物: *Nobody believes that story—he made it up!* 谁也不相信那件事——是他瞎编的！**2** end a quarrel with somebody 与某人和解或和好: *Jenny and Tom had an argument last week, but they've made up now.* 珍妮跟汤姆上星期吵了一架，可是现在和好了。

make² /meɪk; mek/ *noun* 名词
the name of the company that made something（制造某物的）厂家名称: *'What make is your car?' 'It's a Ford.'* "您的汽车是哪个厂子出的？""是福特牌的。"

maker /'meɪkə(r); 'mekɚ/ *noun* 名词
a person or company that makes something 制造某物的人或公司；制造者: *a film maker* 制片人

make-up /'meɪk ʌp; 'mek,ʌp/ *noun* 名词 (no plural 无复数)
special powders and creams that you put on your face to make yourself more beautiful. Actors also wear make-up to make themselves look different 化妆品（使容貌美丽的脂粉）；化装用品（演员扮演角色用的物品）: *She put on her make-up.* 她搽了些化妆品。

male /meɪl; mel/ *adjective* 形容词
A male animal or person belongs to the sex that cannot have babies 男的；雄的: *A cock is a male chicken.* 公鸡是雄性的鸡。
male *noun* 名词
If you look at these fish you can see that the males are bigger than the females. 要是看看这些鱼，就能看出雄的比雌的大。
☞ Look at **female**. 见 **female**。

mammal /'mæml; 'mæml̩/ *noun* 名词
any animal that drinks milk from its mother's body when it is young 哺乳动物: *Dogs, horses, whales and people are all mammals.* 狗、马、鲸和人都是哺乳动物。

man /mæn; mæn/ *noun* 名词
1 (*plural* 复数作 **men** /men; mɛn/)

M

a grown-up male person 男人；成年男子: *I saw a tall man with dark hair.* 我看见个身材高大、头发乌黑的成年男子。

2 (*plural* 复数作 **men**) any person（任何的）人: *All men must have water to live.* 人必须有水才能活。

3 (no plural 无复数) all human beings; people 人类: *How long has man lived on the earth?* 人类在地球上生存多久了？

manage /ˈmænɪdʒ; ˈmænɪdʒ/ *verb* 动词 (**manages**, **managing**, **managed** /ˈmænɪdʒd; ˈmænɪdʒd/)

1 be able to do something that is difficult 能做成某种（困难的）事: *The box was heavy but she managed to carry it to the car.* 箱子很重，她却设法把它搬到汽车上了。

2 control somebody or something 管理或控制某人或某事物: *She manages a department of 30 people.* 她掌管一个有30人的部门。

management /ˈmænɪdʒmənt; ˈmænɪdʒmənt/ *noun* 名词

1 (no plural 无复数) control of something, for example a business, and the people who work in it（对企业及其工作人员的）管理: *good management* 良好的企业管理

2 (*plural* 复数作 **management**) all the people who control a business（企业的）全体主管人员；管理部门；资方: *The management have decided to close the factory.* 主管部门决定把工厂关闭。

manager /ˈmænɪdʒə(r); ˈmænɪdʒɚ/ *noun* 名词

a person who controls a business, bank or hotel, for example 经理；管理人（例如公司、银行或旅馆的）: *Clive is the manager of a shoe shop.* 克莱夫是鞋店的经理。◇ *a bank manager* 银行经理

manageress /ˌmænɪdʒəˈres; ˈmænɪdʒərɪs/ *noun* 名词

a woman who controls a shop or restaurant（女的）经理

managing director /ˌmænɪdʒɪŋ dəˈrektə(r); ˌmænɪdʒɪŋ dəˈrɛktɚ/ *noun* 名词

the person who controls a big business（大企业的）管理人，总经理

mane /meɪn; men/ *noun* 名词

the long hair on the neck of a horse or lion 鬃，鬣（马或狮子颈上的长毛）

mango /ˈmæŋgəʊ; ˈmæŋgo/ *noun* 名词 (*plural* 复数作 **mangoes** or 或 **mangos**)

a fruit that is yellow or red on the outside and yellow on the inside. Mangoes grow in hot countries. 芒果（热带水果）

mankind /mænˈkaɪnd; mænˈkaɪnd/ *noun* 名词 (no plural 无复数)

all the people in the world 人类

man-made /ˌmæn ˈmeɪd; ˌmænˈmed/ *adjective* 形容词

made by people; not natural 人造的；人工的: *man-made materials* 人造材料

manner /ˈmænə(r); ˈmænɚ/ *noun* 名词

1 the way that you do something or the way that something happens 方式；方法: *Don't get angry. Let's try to talk about this in a calm manner.* 别生气。咱们心平气和地谈谈这件事。

2 manners (plural 复数) the way you behave when you are with other people 礼貌；规矩: *It's bad manners to talk with your mouth full.* 嘴里含着东西说话是不礼貌的。

mansion /ˈmænʃn; ˈmænʃən/ *noun* 名词

a very big house 宅第；公馆；大厦

mantelpiece /ˈmæntlpiːs; ˈmæntḷˌpis/ *noun* 名词

a long flat piece of wood, etc above a fireplace 壁炉台: *She has photographs of her children on the mantelpiece.* 她在壁炉台上摆着孩子的照片。

manual[1] /ˈmænjuəl; ˈmænjʊəl/ *adjective* 形容词

that you do with your hands 手工的；用手的: *Do you prefer manual work or office work?* 您喜欢体力劳动还是脑力劳动？

manually /ˈmænjuəli; ˈmænjʊəlɪ/ *adverb* 副词

using your hands 用手；用手操作: *This machine is operated manually.* 这部机器是用手操作的。

manual[2] /ˈmænjuəl; ˈmænjʊəl/ *noun* 名词

a book that tells you how to do something 介绍做某事物的书；手册: *Do you have a manual for this video recorder?* 您有这部录像机的使用手册吗？

manufacture /ˌmænjuˈfæktʃə(r); ˌmænjəˈfæktʃɚ/ *verb* 动词 (**manufactures**, **manufacturing**, **manufactured** /ˌmænjuˈfæktʃəd; ˌmænjəˈfæktʃɚd/)

make things in a factory using machines（用机器）制造物品: *The company manufactures radios.* 这家工厂是制造收音机的。

manufacture *noun* 名词 (no plural 无复数)
the manufacture of plastic from oil 用石油制成塑料

manufacturer *noun* 名词
If it doesn't work, send it back to the manufacturers. 要是还不行的话，就把它送回厂家去吧。

many /'meni; 'mɛnɪ/ *adjective* 形容词 (**many**, **more**, **most**), *pronoun* 代词
a large number of people or things 许多的（人或事物）: *Many people in this country are very poor.* 这个国家很多人都很穷。◇ *There aren't many students in my class.* 我们班学生不多。◇ *Many of these books are very old.* 这些书有很多是古籍。◇ *There are too many mistakes in your homework.* 你的家庭作业里错误太多了。
as many as the same number that 像…一样多: *Take as many cakes as you want.* 你想吃多少蛋糕就吃多少蛋糕。
how many ...? words that you use to ask about the number of people or things 用以询问多少人或事物的词: *How many brothers and sisters have you got?* 你有几个兄弟姐妹？
☞ Look at **much**. 见 **much**。

map /mæp; mæp/ *noun* 名词
a drawing of a town, a country or the world. It shows things like mountains, rivers and roads 地图: *Can you find Glasgow on the map?* 你能在地图上找到格拉斯哥吗？◇ *a street map of Exeter* 埃克塞特街道图 ✪ A book of maps is called an **atlas**. 地图集叫做 **atlas**。

marathon /'mærəθən; 'mærəˌθɑn/ *noun* 名词
a very long race when people run about 42 kilometres 马拉松赛跑（约42公里）

marble /'mɑ:bl; 'mɑrbl̩/ *noun* 名词
1 (no plural 无复数) very hard stone that is used to make buildings and statues 大理石: *Marble is always cold when you touch it.* 大理石摸上去总是凉的。
2 (*plural* 复数作 **marbles**) a small glass ball that you use in a children's game（儿童玩的）玻璃弹球: *They are playing marbles.* 他们正在弹玻璃球玩儿呢。

M

March /mɑ:tʃ; mɑrtʃ/ *noun* 名词
the third month of the year 三月

march /mɑ:tʃ; mɑrtʃ/ *verb* 动词 (**marches**, **marching**, **marched** /mɑ:tʃt; mɑrtʃt/)
1 walk like a soldier（像士兵般）行进；齐步走: *The soldiers marched along the road.* 士兵沿公路行进。
2 walk with a large group of people to show that you have strong feelings about something（在示威游行中）行进: *They marched through the town shouting 'Stop the war!'* 他们在城里进行示威游行，高喊着"停止战争！"

march *noun* 名词 (*plural* 复数作 **marches**)
1 marching 行军；行进: *The soldiers were tired after the long march.* 士兵长途行军后都疲倦了。
2 a long walk by a large group of people to show that they have strong feelings about something 示威游行: *a peace march* 为争取和平的游行

margarine /ˌmɑ:dʒə'ri:n; 'mɑrdʒəˌrɪn/ *noun* 名词 (no plural 无复数)
soft yellow food that looks like butter, but is not made of milk. You put it on bread or use it in cooking. 人造黄油

margin /'mɑ:dʒɪn; 'mɑrdʒɪn/ *noun* 名词
the space at the side of a page that has no writing or pictures in it 页边空白

mark[1] /mɑ:k; mɑrk/ *noun* 名词
1 a spot or line that makes something less good than it was before 污点；痕迹: *There's a dirty mark on the front of your shirt.* 你衬衫前面有块污迹。
2 a shape or special sign on something 记号；符号；标记: *This mark shows that the ring is made of silver.* 这一标记表明这个戒指是银的。
3 a number or letter that a teacher gives for your work to show how good it is（教师给的）分数，等级符号: *She got very good marks in the exam.* 她考试得的分数很高。

mark[2] /mɑ:k; mɑrk/ *verb* 动词 (**marks**, **marking**, **marked** /mɑ:kt; mɑrkt/)
1 put a sign on something by writing or drawing on it 在某物上做记号；标出: *The price is marked on the bottom of the box.* 价钱标在盒子底面。
2 put a tick (✓) or cross (✗) on school work to show if it is right or wrong, or write a number or letter to show how good it is 给（学习成绩）判对（✓）或错（✗），评分数或等级: *The teacher marked all my answers wrong.* 老师在我的答案上都打了错号。

3 show where something is 表明某物的位置: *This cross marks the place where he died.* 这个十字符号标明他死去的地点。

market /'mɑ:kɪt; 'mɑrkɪt/ *noun* 名词

1 a place where people go to buy and sell things, usually outside 集市；市场（通常在外面）: *There is a fruit and vegetable market in the town square.* 镇上的广场有个蔬果市场。

2 the people who want to buy something 想购买某物的一批人；消费者市场: *There is a big market for personal computers in the USA.* 在美国，个人计算机有很大的市场。

marmalade /'mɑ:məleɪd; 'mɑrml̩,ed/ *noun* 名词 (no plural 无复数)

soft sweet food made from oranges or lemons（用橙子或柠檬做的）果酱: *We had toast and marmalade for breakfast.* 我们早饭吃的是烤面包片和橙子酱。

marriage /'mærɪdʒ; 'mærɪdʒ/ *noun* 名词

1 the time when two people are together as husband and wife 婚姻: *They had a long and happy marriage.* 他们的婚姻长久而幸福。

2 the time when a man and woman become husband and wife; a wedding 结婚；婚礼: *The marriage will take place in church.* 婚礼将在教堂举行。

marry /'mæri; 'mærɪ/ *verb* 动词 (**marries**, **marrying**, **married** /'mærid; 'mærɪd/, **has married**)

take somebody as your husband or wife 与某人结婚；娶；嫁: *Will you marry me?* 你愿意和我结婚吗？◇ *They married when they were very young.* 他们结婚的时候十分年轻。✪ It is more usual to say **get married**. 通常说 **get married**。

married *adjective* 形容词

How long have you been married? 你结婚多久了？◇ *Ian is married to Helen.* 伊恩和海伦结婚了。✪ opposite 反义词: **single** or 或 **unmarried**

get married take somebody as your husband or wife 结婚: *Susan and Mike got married last year.* 苏珊和迈克去年结婚了。

marsh /mɑ:ʃ; mɑrʃ/ *noun* 名词 (*plural* 复数作 **marshes**)

soft wet ground 沼泽

marvelous *American English for* **marvellous** 美式英语，即 **marvellous**

marvellous /'mɑ:vələs; 'mɑrvl̩əs/ *adjective* 形容词

very good; wonderful 极好的；绝妙的: *I had a marvellous holiday.* 我假期过得太美了。

masculine /'mæskjʊlɪn; 'mæskjəlɪn/ *adjective* 形容词

of or like a man; right for a man 男性的；像男子的；适合男子的: *a masculine voice* 男性的声音 ☞ Look at **feminine**. 见 **feminine**。

mash /mæʃ; mæʃ/ *verb* 动词 (**mashes**, **mashing**, **mashed** /mæʃt; mæʃt/)

press and mix food to make it soft 把食物压碎搅烂成糊状: *mashed potatoes* 土豆泥

masks 口罩或面罩

mask /mɑ:sk; mæsk/ *noun* 名词

a thing that you wear over your face to hide or protect it 面罩；面具；口罩: *The thieves were wearing masks.* 那些窃贼都戴着面具。◇ *The doctors and nurses all wore a mask.* 所有医生和护士都戴着口罩。

Mass /mæs; mæs/ *noun* 名词 (*plural* 复数作 **Masses**)

a service in the Roman Catholic church 弥撒

mass /mæs; mæs/ *noun* 名词 (*plural* 复数作 **masses**)

a large amount or number of something 大量；大批；众多: *a mass of rock* 很多岩石 ◇ *masses of people* 群众

massacre /'mæsəkə(r); 'mæsəkɚ/ *noun* 名词

the cruel killing of a lot of people 大批残杀人；屠杀

massacre *verb* 动词 (**massacres**, **massacring**, **massacred** /'mæsəkəd; 'mæsəkɚd/)

The army massacred hundreds of women and children. 军队屠杀了数以百计的妇女儿童。

massive /'mæsɪv; 'mæsɪv/ *adjective* 形容词

very big 巨大的: *The house is massive — it has 16 bedrooms!* 这所房子非常大——有16个卧室！

mast /mɑːst; mæst/ *noun* 名词

1 a tall piece of wood or metal that holds the sails on a boat 桅杆；樯（船上挂帆的杆子）

2 a very tall metal thing that sends out sounds or pictures for radio or television 天线塔（无线电或电视播出声音或画面的）

master¹ /ˈmɑːstə(r); ˈmæstɚ/ *noun* 名词

a man who has people or animals in his control 管理人或动物的人；主管人；主人: *The dog ran to its master.* 狗向主人跑去。

master² /ˈmɑːstə(r); ˈmæstɚ/ *verb* 动词 (**masters, mastering, mastered** /ˈmɑː-stəd; ˈmæstɚd/)

learn how to do something well 学会做好某事物；掌握；精通: *It takes a long time to master a foreign language.* 掌握一门外语要用很长时间。

masterpiece /ˈmɑːstəpiːs; ˈmæstɚˌpis/ *noun* 名词

a very good painting, book, film, etc 极好的画儿、书、影片等；杰作: *'War and Peace' was Tolstoy's masterpiece.*《战争与和平》是托尔斯泰的名著。

mat /mæt; mæt/ *noun* 名词

1 a small thing that covers a part of the floor（室内地面上的）小垫子: *Wipe your feet on the doormat before you go in.* 你把脚在门口蹭鞋垫上蹭蹭再进去。

2 a small thing that you put on a table under a hot dish or cup or a glass（放在桌子上垫热碟子或茶杯或玻璃杯的）小垫子: *a table-mat* 碗盘垫

match¹ /mætʃ; mætʃ/ *noun* 名词 (*plural* 复数作 **matches**)

a special short thin piece of wood that makes fire when you rub it on something rough 火柴: *He struck a match and lit his cigarette.* 他划着了火柴点香烟。◇ *a box of matches* 一盒火柴

matches 火柴

matchbox /ˈmætʃbɒks; ˈmætʃˌbɑks/ *noun* 名词

a small box for matches 火柴盒

match² /mætʃ; mætʃ/ *noun* 名词 (*plural* 复数作 **matches**)

a game between two people or teams 比赛；竞赛: *a football match* 足球赛 ◇ *a boxing match* 拳击赛

match³ /mætʃ; mætʃ/ *verb* 动词 (**matches, matching, matched** /mætʃt; mætʃt/)

1 have the same colour, shape or pattern as something else, or look good with something else 与某物（颜色、形状或图案）相同或相配: *That scarf doesn't match your blouse.* 那条头巾跟您的衬衫不相配。

2 find something that is like another thing or that you can put with it 找到与某事物相似或相配的另一事物: *Match the word with the right picture.* 找出与这个词相关的图来。

match *noun* 名词 (no plural 无复数)

something that looks good with something else, for example because it has the same colour, shape or pattern（一事物与另一事物的）相同或相配（如颜色、形状或图案）: *Your shoes and dress are a good match.* 您的鞋和连衣裙很相配。

matching *adjective* 形容词

She was wearing a blue skirt and matching jacket. 她穿着蓝裙子和相配的短上衣。

mate /meɪt; met/ *noun* 名词

1 a friend 朋友: *He went out with his mates last night.* 他昨天晚上跟朋友出去了。

✪ This is an informal word. 这是个俗语词。

2 a person who lives, works or studies with you 一起生活、工作或学习的人；伙伴；同事；同学: *André is one of my classmates.* 安德烈是我同班同学。◇ *a flatmate* 同住一公寓的人

3 one of two animals that come together to make young animals 交配的一个动物: *The bird is looking for a mate.* 这只鸟正在寻找适合交配的鸟。

mate *verb* 动词 (**mates, mating, mated**)

When animals mate, they come together to make young animals.（指动物）交配

material /məˈtɪəriəl; məˈtɪrɪəl/ *noun* 名词

1 what you use for making or doing something 材料；原料: *Wood and stone are building materials.* 木材和石头都是建筑材料。◇ *writing materials* (= pens, pencils and paper, for example) 用于书写的材料（= 钢笔、铅笔、纸等）

2 stuff that is made of wool, cotton, etc and that you use for making clothes and other things; cloth（用以做衣物等的毛、

M

棉等的）料子；布: *I don't have enough material to make a dress.* 我的料子不够做一件连衣裙的。

math /mæθ; mæθ/ *American English for* **maths** 美式英语，即 **maths**

mathematics /ˌmæθəˈmætɪks; ˌmæθəˈmætɪks/, **maths** /mæθs; mæθs/ *noun* 名词 (no plural 无复数)
the study of numbers, measurements and shapes 数学: *Maths is my favourite subject.* 数学是我最喜欢的科目。
mathematical /ˌmæθəˈmætɪkl; ˌmæθəˈmætɪkl̩/ *adjective* 形容词
a mathematical problem 数学题

matter[1] /ˈmætə(r); ˈmætɚ/ *noun* 名词
something that you must talk about or do（要谈论的或要做的）事情；事务: *There is a matter I would like to discuss with you.* 有件事我想和您谈谈。
as a matter of fact words that you use when you say something true, important or interesting 事实上；实际上；其实: *I'm going home early today. As a matter of fact, it's my birthday.* 今天我得早点儿回家。说实话，今天是我生日。
be the matter with somebody or 或 **something** be the reason for problems or unhappiness, for example 是（问题、不幸事情等的）原因或理由: *Julie is crying. What's the matter with her?* 朱莉哭了。她怎么了？◇ *There is something the matter with my eye.* 我的眼睛出毛病了。
no matter how, what, when, who, etc however, whatever, whenever, whoever, etc 无论如何；无论什么；无论何时；无论谁: *No matter how hard I try, I can't open the door.* 我不管怎么用力也开不开这个门。

matter[2] /ˈmætə(r); ˈmætɚ/ *verb* 动词 (**matters, mattering, mattered** /ˈmætəd; ˈmætɚd/)
be important 关系重大；要紧: *It doesn't matter if you're late—we'll wait for you.* 您来晚了也不要紧——我们一定等着您。

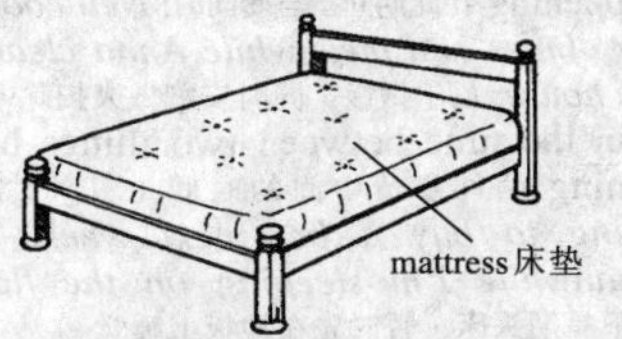
mattress 床垫

mattress /ˈmætrəs; ˈmætrɪs/ *noun* 名词 (*plural* 复数作 **mattresses**)
the thick soft part of a bed 床垫

mature /məˈtjʊə(r); məˈtʊr/ *adjective* 形容词
like an adult; fully grown 成年的；成熟的

mauve /məʊv; mov/ *adjective* 形容词
purple 紫色的

maximum /ˈmæksɪməm; ˈmæksəməm/ *noun* 名词 (no plural 无复数)
the most; the biggest possible size, amount or number 最大限度；最大的体积或数量: *This plane can carry a maximum of 150 people.* 这架飞机最多能载150人。
maximum *adjective* 形容词
We drove at a maximum speed of 110 kilometres per hour. 我们以每小时110公里的最高速度驾驶。
✪ opposite 反义词: **minimum**

May /meɪ; me/ *noun* 名词
the fifth month of the year 五月

may /meɪ; me/ *modal verb* 情态动词
1 a word that shows what will perhaps happen or what is possible 也许；可能: *I may go to Spain next year.* 我明年可能到西班牙去。◇ *He may not be here.* 他也许不在这里。
2 be allowed to do something 允许；可以: *May I open the window?* 我可以打开窗户吗？◇ *You may stay here tonight.* 您今天可以在这里过夜。
3 I hope that this will happen 祝愿；但愿: *May God be with you.* 上帝保佑您。
☞ Look at the Note on page 314 to find out more about **modal verbs.** 见第314页对 **modal verbs** 的进一步解释。

maybe /ˈmeɪbi; ˈmebi/ *adverb* 副词
perhaps; possibly 也许；可能；大概: *'Are you going out tonight?' 'Maybe.'* "您今天晚上出去吗？""可能吧。"◇ *Maybe you should phone him.* 你也许应该给他打个电话了。

mayor /meə(r); ˈmeɚ/ *noun* 名词
the leader of a **council** (a group of people who control a town or city) 市长（市议会叫做 **council**）
mayoress /meəˈres; ˈmeərəs/ *noun* 名词 (*plural* 复数作 **mayoresses**)
a mayor who is a woman, or the wife of a mayor（女的）市长；市长的妻子

me /miː; mi/ *pronoun* 代词 (*plural* 复数作 **us**)

the person who is speaking 我: *When he saw me he told me about the accident.* 他一看见我就把出事的情况告诉我了。◇ *'Who broke the window?' 'It was me.'* "谁把窗户打破了？""是我。"

meadow /'medəʊ; 'mɛdo/ *noun* 名词
a field of grass 草地

meal /mi:l; mil/ *noun* 名词
food that you eat at a certain time of the day 餐；饭食；一顿饭: *Breakfast is the first meal of the day.* 早饭是一天的第一顿饭。

> ✪ **Breakfast**, **lunch** and **dinner** (and sometimes **tea** and **supper**) are the usual meals of the day. 一天的饭通常是早饭(**breakfast**)、午饭(**lunch**)、晚饭(**dinner**)。有时有下午茶点(**tea**)，晚饭又叫做 **supper**。

mean¹ /mi:n; min/ *verb* 动词 (**means**, **meaning**, **meant** /ment; mɛnt/, **has meant**)

1 say or show something in a different way; have as a meaning 意味；意思是: *What does 'medicine' mean?* ＊ medicine 是什么意思？◇ *The red light means that you have to stop here.* 红灯表示要在这里停下。

2 plan or want to say something 打算或想要说某事: *She said 'yes' but she really meant 'no'.* 她嘴里同意，其实心里不同意。◇ *I don't understand what you mean.* 我不明白您的意思。

3 plan or want to do something 打算或想要做某事: *I didn't mean to hurt you.* 我并没有要伤害你的意思。◇ *I meant to phone you, but I forgot.* 我是想给你打电话来着，可是忘了。

4 make something happen 使某事物发生；造成: *This snow means there will be no sport today.* 下了这场雪，今天就没有体育活动了。

be meant to **1** If you are meant to do something, you should do it 应该: *You're not meant to smoke on the train.* 在列车上不应该吸烟。**2** If something is meant to be true, people say it is true 据说: *This is meant to be a good film.* 据说这部影片很好。

mean something to somebody be important to somebody 对某人很重要: *My family means a lot to me.* 我把家庭放在第一位。

mean² /mi:n; min/ *adjective* 形容词 (**meaner**, **meanest**)

1 A person who is mean does not like to give things or to spend money 吝啬的；小气的: *Jim is very mean — he never buys anybody a drink.* 吉姆很小气——他从来不请人喝点儿东西。✪ opposite 反义词: **generous**

2 unkind 不善良的；不友好的: *It was mean of you to say that Peter was fat.* 你说彼得很胖，这么说可太刻薄了。

meaning /'mi:nɪŋ; 'minɪŋ/ *noun* 名词
what something means or shows 意思；意义；含义: *This word has two different meanings.* 这个词有两个意思。

means /mi:nz; minz/ *noun* 名词 (*plural* 复数作 **means**)
a way of doing something; a way of going somewhere（做某事的）方法；手段；（到某处的）途径: *I don't have a car and there are no trains, so I haven't got any means of getting to London.* 我没有汽车，现在又没有火车，没办法到伦敦去了。

by means of something by using something 用某办法；借助于某事物: *We crossed the river by means of a small bridge.* 我们经小桥过的河。

by no means not at all 绝不；一点儿都不: *I am by no means certain that I can come.* 我能不能来，现在一点儿把握都没有。

meant *form of* **mean¹** ＊ **mean¹** 的不同形式

meantime /'mi:ntaɪm; 'minˌtaɪm/ *noun* 名词 (no plural 无复数)

in the meantime in the time between two things happening 两件事情中间的时间；其间: *The police will be here soon, in the meantime you should stay calm.* 警察马上就到——这个时候你要镇静。

meanwhile /'mi:nwaɪl; 'minˌhwaɪl/ *adverb* 副词

1 at the same time as another thing is happening 在此期间；与此同时: *Neil cooked the dinner and meanwhile Anna cleaned the house.* 尼尔做饭，同时安娜做大扫除。

2 in the time between two things happening 两件事情中间的时间；其间: *I'm going to buy a bed next week, but meanwhile I'm sleeping on the floor.* 我下星期买床，暂时先在地板上睡觉。

M

measles /ˈmi:zlz; ˈmizḷz/ *noun* 名词 (no plural 无复数)
an illness that makes small red spots come on your skin 麻疹: *My little brother has got measles.* 我弟弟得麻疹了。

measure¹ /ˈmeʒə(r); ˈmɛʒɚ/ *verb* 动词 (**measures**, **measuring**, **measured** /ˈmeʒəd; ˈmɛʒɚd/)
1 find the size, weight or amount of somebody or something 量度；测量: *I measured the box with a ruler.* 我用尺子量了量这个箱子。
2 be a certain size or amount 为某体积或数量: *This room measures six metres across.* 这个房间宽六米。

measure² /ˈmeʒə(r); ˈmɛʒɚ/ *noun* 名词
a way of showing the size or amount of something 量度法；计量制: *A metre is a measure of length.* 米是长度单位。

measurement /ˈmeʒəmənt; ˈmɛʒɚmənt/ *noun* 名词
how long, wide, high, etc something is (量得某物的) 长度、宽度、高度等: *What are the measurements of the kitchen?* 这个厨房的面积是多少？

meat /mi:t; mit/ *noun* 名词 (no plural 无复数)
the parts of an animal's body that you can eat (食用的) 肉: *You can buy meat at a butcher's.* 在肉铺可以买到肉。

mechanic /məˈkænɪk; məˈkænɪk/ *noun* 名词
a person whose job is to repair or work with machines 修理或操纵机器的人；技工: *a car mechanic* 汽车修理工

mechanical /məˈkænɪkl; məˈkænɪkḷ/ *adjective* 形容词
moved, done or made by a machine 机械的；用机械的；机械制造的: *a mechanical toy* 机械玩具

mechanics /məˈkænɪks; məˈkænɪks/ *noun* 名词 (no plural 无复数)
the study of how machines work 力学；机械学

medal /ˈmedl; ˈmɛdḷ/ *noun* 名词
a piece of metal with words and pictures on it that is given to somebody who has done something very good 奖章；勋章: *She won a gold medal in the Olympic Games.* 她在奥林匹克运动会上获得一枚金牌。

media /ˈmi:diə; ˈmidɪə/ *noun* 名词 (plural 复数)
the media television, radio and newspapers 大众传播媒介（电视、电台和报纸）: *The media are always interested in the lives of film stars.* 大众传播媒介总是非常关注影星的生活。

medical /ˈmedɪkl; ˈmɛdɪkḷ/ *adjective* 形容词
of or about medicine, hospitals or doctors 医学的；医术的；医疗的: *a medical student* 医学院的学生 ◇ *medical treatment* 医疗

medicine /ˈmedsn; ˈmɛdəsn̩/ *noun* 名词
1 (no plural 无复数) the science of understanding illnesses and making sick people well again 医学: *He studied medicine for five years before becoming a doctor.* 他学了五年医学，才当上医生。
2 (*plural* 复数作 **medicines**) pills or special drinks that help you to get better when you are ill 药: *Take this medicine every morning.* 每天早晨要吃这种药。

medieval /ˌmediˈi:vl; ˌmidɪˈivḷ/ *adjective* 形容词
of the years between about 1100 and 1500 in Europe 中世纪的（欧洲历史上1100年至1500年期间的）: *a medieval castle* 中世纪的城堡 ☞ Look at **the Middle Ages**. 见 **the Middle Ages**。

medium /ˈmi:diəm; ˈmidɪəm/ *adjective* 形容词
not big and not small; middle 不大不小的；中等的: *Would you like a small, medium or large coke?* 您想要大的、中的还是小的可口可乐？◇ *He is of medium height.* 他是中等身材。

meet /mi:t; mit/ *verb* 动词 (**meets**, **meeting**, **met** /met; mɛt/, **has met**)
1 come together at a certain time and place when you have planned it (预先约定) 相会；会见；相见: *Let's meet outside the cinema at eight o'clock.* 咱们八点钟在电影院外面见。
2 see and say hello to somebody 看见某人并打招呼；遇见: *I met Kate in the library today.* 我今天在图书馆碰见凯特了。
3 see and speak to somebody for the first time 第一次见某人并谈话；结识: *Have you met Anne?* 您认识安娜吗？
4 go to a place and wait for somebody to arrive 到某处去接某人: *Can you meet me at the airport?* 您能到飞机场接我吗？

5 join together with something 与某事物聚集到一起: *The two rivers meet in Oxford.* 这两条河在牛津汇合。

meeting /ˈmiːtɪŋ; ˈmitɪŋ/ *noun* 名词

1 a time when a group of people come together for a special reason 会议；集会: *We had a meeting to talk about the plans for the new swimming-pool.* 我们开了个会，研究修建新游泳池的计划。

2 two or more people coming together 相会；会见；相见: *Do you remember your first meeting with your husband?* 你还记得你和你丈夫初次见面的情形吗？

melody /ˈmelədi; ˈmɛlədɪ/ *noun* 名词 (*plural* 复数作 **melodies**)

a group of musical notes that make a nice sound when you play or sing them together; a tune 优美的音调；曲调；旋律: *This song has a lovely melody.* 这首歌调子很美。

melon /ˈmelən; ˈmɛlən/ *noun* 名词

a big round yellow or green fruit with a lot of seeds inside 瓜

melt /melt; mɛlt/ *verb* 动词 (**melts, melting, melted**)

warm something so that it becomes liquid; get warmer so that it becomes liquid（使某物）加热变成液体；融化；熔化: *Melt the butter in a saucepan.* 把黄油放在锅里溶化。◇ *The snow melted in the sunshine.* 雪在阳光下融化了。

member /ˈmembə(r); ˈmɛmbɚ/ *noun* 名词

a person who is in a group（群体中的）成员；会员: *I'm a member of the school football team.* 我是学校足球队的队员。

Member of Parliament /ˌmembər əv ˈpɑːləmənt; ˌmɛmbɚ əv pɑrləmənt/ *noun* 名词

a person that the people of a town or city choose to speak for them in politics 议员 ✪ The short form is **MP**. 缩略式为 **MP**。

membership /ˈmembəʃɪp; ˈmɛmbɚˌʃɪp/ *noun* 名词 (no plural 无复数)

being in a group（群体中的）成员身分；会员资格: *Membership of the club costs £20 a year.* 俱乐部会费每年20英镑。

memo /ˈmeməʊ; ˈmɛmo/ (*plural* 复数作 **memos**), **memorandum** /ˌmeməˈrændəm; ˌmɛməˈrændəm/ (*plural* 复数作 **memoranda**) *noun* 名词

a note that you write to a person who works with you（给一道工作的人写的）便条；通知；备忘录: *I sent you a memo about the meeting on Friday.* 我给您发出了一份星期五会议纪要。

memorable /ˈmemərəbl; ˈmɛmərəbl̩/ *adjective* 形容词

easy to remember because it is special in some way（因与众不同）容易记住的: *Their wedding was a very memorable day.* 他们的婚礼是个难忘的日子。

memorial /məˈmɔːriəl; məˈmɔrɪəl/ *noun* 名词

something that people build or do to help us remember somebody, or something that happened 纪念碑；纪念仪式: *The statue is a memorial to all the soldiers who died in the war.* 这尊雕像是纪念全体阵亡将士的。

memorize /ˈmeməraɪz; ˈmɛməˌraɪz/ *verb* 动词 (**memorizes, memorizing, memorized** /ˈmeməraɪzd; ˈmɛməˌraɪzd/)

learn something so that you can remember it exactly 记住某事物；熟记: *We have to memorize a poem for homework.* 我们的家庭作业是要背诵一首诗。

memory /ˈmeməri; ˈmɛmərɪ/ *noun* 名词 (*plural* 复数作 **memories**)

1 the power to remember things 记忆力；记性: *She's got a very good memory—she never forgets people's names.* 她记性非常好——别人的名字她从来不忘。

2 something that you remember 记忆的事物；回忆: *I have very happy memories of that holiday.* 我记忆中那个假期十分愉快。

3 the part of a computer that holds information（计算机的）存储器

men *plural of* **man** ✳ **man** 的复数形式

mend /mend; mɛnd/ *verb* 动词 (**mends, mending, mended**)

make something good again when it was broken; repair something 修理或修补某物: *Can you mend this chair?* 您能修好这把椅子吗？

mental /ˈmentl; ˈmɛntl̩/ *adjective* 形容词

of or in your mind 精神的；心理的: *mental illness* 精神病

mentally /ˈmentəli; ˈmɛntl̩ɪ/ *adverb* 副词

He is mentally ill. 他有精神病。

M

mention /ˈmenʃn; ˈmɛnʃən/ *verb* 动词 (**mentions**, **mentioning**, **mentioned** /ˈmenʃnd; ˈmɛnʃənd/)
speak or write a little about something 说到或写到某事物；提到: *When Liz telephoned, she mentioned that she was going to buy a new car.* 利兹来电话时提到她要买辆新汽车。◇ *He didn't mention Anna in his letter.* 他信中没提到安娜。
don't mention it polite words that you say when somebody says 'thank you'（表示不必道谢的客气话）不用谢，别客气: *'Thanks very much.' 'Don't mention it.'* "谢谢。" "不用谢。"
mention *noun* 名词
There was no mention of the accident in the newspaper. 报纸上没有提到这次事故。

menu /ˈmenju:; ˈmɛnju/ *noun* 名词 (*plural* 复数作 **menus**)
1 a list of the food that you can choose in a restaurant（饭馆的）菜单: *What's on the menu tonight?* 今天晚上菜单上有什么菜？◇ *Can I have the menu, please?* 请给我看看菜单行吗？
2 a list on the screen of a computer that shows what you can do（计算机荧光屏上显示的）项目单，选择单

merchant /ˈmɜ:tʃənt; ˈmɝtʃənt/ *noun* 名词
a person who buys and sells things, especially from and to other countries 商人（尤指外贸商人）: *She's a wine merchant.* 她是批发葡萄酒的商人。

mercy /ˈmɜ:si; ˈmɝsɪ/ *noun* 名词 (no plural 无复数)
being kind and not hurting somebody who has done wrong 仁慈；宽恕；宽容: *The prisoners asked the king for mercy.* 囚犯们请求国王开恩。
be at the mercy of somebody or 或 **something** have no power against somebody or something 任由某人或某事物摆布；无力对抗: *Farmers are at the mercy of the weather.* 农民靠天吃饭。

mere /mɪə(r); mɪr/ *adjective* 形容词
only; not more than 仅仅；不超过: *She was a mere child when her parents died.* 她父母死时她只不过是个孩子。
merely *adverb* 副词
only 仅；只: *I don't want to buy the book—I am merely asking how much it costs.* 我并不想买这本书——只不过问问价钱。

merge /mɜ:dʒ; mɝdʒ/ *verb* 动词 (**merges**, **merging**, **merged** /mɜ:dʒd; mɝdʒd/)
join together with something else 与另一事物合并: *The two small companies merged into one large one.* 这两家小公司合并成一家大公司了。

merit /ˈmerɪt; ˈmɛrɪt/ *noun* 名词
what is good about somebody or something（某人或某事物的）优点；长处: *What are the merits of this plan?* 这个计划有什么好处？

mermaid /ˈmɜ:meɪd; ˈmɝˌmed/ *noun* 名词
a woman in stories who has a fish's tail and lives in the sea（故事中的）美人鱼（长着鱼尾的女子，生活在海中）

merry /ˈmeri; ˈmɛrɪ/ *adjective* 形容词 (**merrier**, **merriest**)
happy and full of fun 愉快的；欢乐的: *Merry Christmas!* 圣诞快乐！

merry-go-round /ˈmeri gəʊ raʊnd; ˈmɛrɪ goˌraʊnd/ *noun* 名词
a big round machine at a fair. It has model animals or cars on it that children can ride on as it turns. 旋转木马

mess[1] /mes; mɛs/ *noun* 名词 (no plural 无复数)
1 a lot of untidy or dirty things all in the wrong place（胡乱放置的）许多脏的或乱的东西: *There was a terrible mess after the party.* 聚会过后，到处弄得乱七八糟。
2 a person or thing that is untidy or dirty 不整齐的或不清洁的人或物: *My hair is a mess!* 我的头发太乱了！
be in a mess **1** be untidy 不整齐: *My bedroom is in a mess.* 我的卧室凌乱不堪。
2 have problems 有困难: *She's in a mess—she's got no money and nowhere to live.* 她很狼狈——又没钱又没住处。

mess[2] /mes; mɛs/ *verb* 动词 (**messes**, **messing**, **messed** /mest; mɛst/)
mess about, mess around do something in a silly way; play when you should be working 胡闹；（该工作时）闲玩: *Stop messing around and finish your work!* 别瞎闹了，把工作做完吧！
mess up **1** do something badly or make something go wrong 胡乱做某事物或把某事物弄糟: *The bad weather messed up our plans for the weekend.* 天气不好，把我们周末的安排打乱了。 **2** make some-

M

thing untidy or dirty 把某物弄得不整齐或不清洁

message /ˈmesɪdʒ; ˈmɛsɪdʒ/ *noun* 名词

words that one person sends to another (向他人传送的) 信息；消息: *Could you give a message to Jenny, please? Please tell her I will be late.* 请您给珍妮捎个口信行吗？请告诉她我得迟到。◇ *Mr Willis is not here at the moment. Can I take a message?* 威利斯先生现在不在这里。有什么事需要我转达吗？

messenger /ˈmesɪndʒə(r); ˈmɛsṇdʒə˞/ *noun* 名词

a person who brings a message 传达信息的人；通信员；信差

messy /ˈmesi; ˈmɛsɪ/ *adjective* 形容词 (**messier, messiest**)

1 untidy or dirty 不整齐的或不清洁的: *a messy kitchen* 脏乱的厨房

2 that makes you untidy or dirty 把人弄得不整齐或不清洁的: *Painting is a messy job.* 画画儿的时候往往把自己弄得很脏。

met *form of* **meet** ＊ **meet** 的不同形式

metal /ˈmetl; ˈmɛtl̩/ *noun* 名词

Iron, lead, tin and gold are all metals 金属: *This chair is made of metal.* 这把椅子是金属的。◇ *a metal box* 金属的盒子

meter /ˈmiːtə(r); ˈmitə˞/ *noun* 名词

1 a machine that measures or counts something (测量或计数的) 仪表，仪器: *An electricity meter shows how much electricity you have used.* 电表是显示用电度数的仪器。

2 *American English for* **metre** 美式英语，即 **metre**

method /ˈmeθəd; ˈmɛθəd/ *noun* 名词

a way of doing something 方法；方式；办法: *What is the best method of cooking beef?* 用什么方法烹调牛肉最好？

metre /ˈmiːtə(r); ˈmitə˞/ *noun* 名词

a measure of length. There are 100 **centimetres** in a metre 米；公尺 (1米等于100厘米，厘米叫做 **centimetre**)：*The wall is eight metres long.* 这堵墙长八米。

✪ The short way of writing 'metre' is **m** ＊ metre 的缩写形式为 **m**: *2 m* ＊ 2米

metric /ˈmetrɪk; ˈmɛtrɪk/ *adjective* 形容词

using metres, grams, litres, etc to measure things 公制的；十进制的

M

miaow /miˈaʊ; mɪˈaʊ/ *noun* 名词

a sound that a cat makes 喵 (猫叫声)

miaow *verb* 动词 (**miaows, miaowing, miaowed** /miˈaʊd; mɪˈaʊd/)

make this sound 作猫叫声；作喵喵声

mice *plural of* **mouse** ＊ **mouse** 的复数形式

microchip /ˈmaɪkrəʊtʃɪp; ˈmaɪkrotʃɪp/ *noun* 名词

a very small thing inside a computer, for example, that makes it work 微晶片 (如计算机中的)

microcomputer /ˈmaɪkrəʊkəmpjuː-tə(r); ˌmaɪkrokəmˈpjutə˞/ *noun* 名词

a small computer 微型计算机

microphone 话筒

microphone /ˈmaɪkrəfəʊn; ˈmaɪkrə-ˌfon/ *noun* 名词

an electrical thing that makes sounds louder or records them so you can listen to them later 微音器；话筒；麦克风

microscope /ˈmaɪkrəskəʊp; ˈmaɪkrə-ˌskop/ *noun* 名词

an instrument with special glass in it, that makes very small things look much bigger 显微镜: *The scientist looked at the hair under the microscope.* 科学家在显微镜下观察毛发。

microwave /ˈmaɪkrəweɪv; ˈmaɪkrəˌwev/, **microwave oven** /ˌmaɪkrəweɪv ˈʌvn; ˌmaɪkrəwev ˈʌvən/ *noun* 名词

a special oven that cooks food very quickly 微波炉

mid, mid- /mɪd; mɪd/ *adjective* 形容词

(in) the middle of (在) 中间的: *I'm going on holiday in mid July.* 我打算七月中度假。◇ *mid-morning coffee* 上午中间喝的咖啡

midday /ˌmɪdˈdeɪ; ˈmɪdˌde/ *noun* 名词 (no plural 无复数)

twelve o'clock in the day 白天12点钟；正午；中午: *We met at midday.* 我们是在中午见的面。

middle /ˈmɪdl; ˈmɪdl̩/ *noun* 名词

1 the part that is the same distance from the sides, edges or ends of something (指部位) 中间；中部；中央: *A peach has a stone in the middle.* 桃儿的中心有个核。

2 the time after the beginning and before the end（指时间）中间；其间: *The phone rang in the middle of the night.* 半夜的时候电话响了。

be in the middle of be busy doing something 正忙着做某事物: *I can't speak to you now—I'm in the middle of cooking dinner.* 我现在不能跟你说话——我正做着饭呢。

middle *adjective* 形容词
There are three houses and ours is the middle one. 那里有三座小楼，我们的是中间的那座。

middle-aged /ˌmɪdl ˈeɪdʒd; ˈmɪdl̩ˈedʒd/ *adjective* 形容词
not old and not young; between the ages of about 40 and 60 中年的；40岁至60岁之间的: *a middle-aged man* 中年男子

the Middle Ages /ðə ˌmɪdl ˈeɪdʒɪz; ðə ˌmɪdl̩ ˈedʒɪz/ *noun* 名词 (plural 复数)
the years between about 1100 and 1500 in Europe 中世纪（欧洲历史上1100年至1500年期间）☞ Look at **medieval**. 见 **medieval**。

middle school /ˈmɪdl skuːl; ˈmɪdl̩ skul/ *noun* 名词
a school for children between the ages of 9 and 13 中间学校（为9岁至13岁儿童而设的）

midnight /ˈmɪdnaɪt; ˈmɪdˌnaɪt/ *noun* 名词 (no plural 无复数)
twelve o'clock at night 午夜；子夜；半夜12点钟: *We left the party at midnight.* 我们在午夜离开了聚会的地方。

midway /ˌmɪdˈweɪ; ˈmɪdˈwe/ *adverb* 副词
in the middle 在中途；在中间: *The village is midway between London and Birmingham.* 这个村子在伦敦和伯明翰的中间。

might /maɪt; maɪt/ *modal verb* 情态动词
1 a word for 'may' in the past ✳ may 的过去时态: *He said he might be late, but he was early.* 他说他可能迟到，其实他来早了。

2 a word that shows what will perhaps happen or what is possible 用以表示可能发生或有可能性的词: *Don't run because you might fall.* 别跑，看摔着。◇ *'Where's Anne?' 'I don't know — she might be in the kitchen.'* "安妮在哪儿呢？""我不知道——可能在厨房呢。"

3 a word that you use to ask something in a very polite way 表示请求的礼貌用词: *Might I say something?* 我可以说句话吗？
☞ Look at the Note on page 314 to find out more about **modal verbs**. 见第314页对 **modal verbs** 的进一步解释。

mighty /ˈmaɪti; ˈmaɪtɪ/ *adjective* 形容词 (**mightier, mightiest**)
very great, strong or powerful 巨大的；强大的；有力的: *a mighty ocean* 浩瀚的海洋

mild /maɪld; maɪld/ *adjective* 形容词 (**milder, mildest**)
1 gentle; not strong or rough 柔和的；不强烈的；不粗糙的: *This cheese has a mild taste.* 这种奶酪味道很淡。
2 not too hot and not too cold 不冷不热的；温和的: *a mild winter* 暖和的冬天

mile /maɪl; maɪl/ *noun* 名词
a measure of length that is used in Britain and the USA (= 1.6 kilometres) 英里（英美的量度单位，等于1.6公里）: *We live three miles from the sea.* 我们住的地方离海边三英里。☞ Note at **foot** 见 **foot** 词条注释

military /ˈmɪlətri; ˈmɪləˌtɛrɪ/ *adjective* 形容词
of or for soldiers or the army 军人的；军事的；陆军的: *a military camp* 军营 ◇ *military action* 作战

milk /mɪlk; mɪlk/ *noun* 名词 (no plural 无复数)
the white liquid that a mother makes in her body to give to her baby. People drink the milk that cows and some other animals make 奶，乳（尤指供人饮用的牛奶或其他动物的奶）: *Do you want milk in your coffee?* 您的咖啡里要加牛奶吗？

milk *verb* 动词 (**milks, milking, milked** /mɪlkt; mɪlkt/)
take milk from a cow or another animal 挤（牛的或其他动物的）奶

milkman /ˈmɪlkmən; ˈmɪlkˌmæn/ *noun* 名词 (*plural* 复数作 **milkmen** /ˈmɪlkmən; ˈmɪlkˌmɛn/)
a person who brings milk to your house 送牛奶的人

milky /ˈmɪlki; ˈmɪlkɪ/ *adjective* 形容词
with a lot of milk in it 有很多奶的: *milky coffee* 牛奶咖啡

mill /mɪl; mɪl/ *noun* 名词
1 a building where a machine makes corn into flour 磨粉厂；磨坊 ☞ Look also at **windmill**. 另见 **windmill**。

2 a factory for making things like steel or paper（制造钢铁或纸等的）工厂: *a paper-mill* 造纸厂

millimeter *American English for* **millimetre** 美式英语，即 **millimetre**

millimetre /ˈmɪlɪmiːtə(r); ˈmɪləˌmitɚ/ *noun* 名词
a measure of length. There are ten millimetres in a **centimetre**. 毫米（长度单位，10毫米等于1厘米，厘米叫做 **centimetre**。）
✪ The short way of writing 'millimetre' is **mm** ✳ millimetre的缩写形式为 **mm**: *60 mm* ✳ 60毫米

million /ˈmɪljən; ˈmɪljən/ *number* 数词
1 000 000; one thousand thousand ✳ 100万；兆: *About 56 million people live in this country.* 本国大约有5 600万人。◇ *millions of dollars* 数百万元 ◇ *six million pounds* 六百万镑
millionth /ˈmɪljənθ; ˈmɪljənθ/ *adjective, adverb, noun* 形容词，副词，名词
1 000 000th 第100万（个）；第一百万（个）

millionaire /ˌmɪljəˈneə(r); ˌmɪljənˈɛr/ *noun* 名词
a very rich person who has more than a million pounds, dollars, etc 百万富翁

mime /maɪm; maɪm/ *verb* 动词 (**mimes, miming, mimed** /maɪmd; maɪmd/)
tell something by your actions, not by speaking 用动作把某事告诉某人（不用言语）

mince /mɪns; mɪns/ *verb* 动词 (**minces, mincing, minced** /mɪnst; mɪnst/)
cut meat into very small pieces, using a special machine 把肉切碎、剁碎或绞碎（用绞肉机）: *minced beef* 绞碎的牛肉
mince *noun* 名词 (no plural 无复数)
meat in very small pieces 绞碎的肉；肉末

mind[1] /maɪnd; maɪnd/ *noun* 名词
the part of you that thinks and remembers 人体中管思维和记忆的部分；头脑；脑筋；脑子: *He has a very quick mind.* 他头脑敏锐。
change your mind have an idea, then decide to do something different 改变主意: *I planned a holiday in France and then changed my mind and went to Italy.* 我原打算到法国度假，后来改变主意到意大利去了。
have something on your mind be worried about something 担忧某事物: *I've got a lot on my mind at the moment.* 我现在有很多操心的事。
make up your mind decide something 决定某事物: *Shall I buy the blue shirt or the red one? I can't make up my mind.* 我是买蓝衬衫还是买红衬衫？我还拿不定主意。

mind[2] /maɪnd; maɪnd/ *verb* 动词 (**minds, minding, minded**)
1 feel unhappy or angry about something 对某事物感到不愉快或气愤；介意: *'Do you mind if I smoke?' 'No, I don't mind.'* (= you may smoke) "我要是吸烟，您不介意吧？""不介意。"（= 您可以吸烟）
2 be careful of somebody or something 照看或留心某人或某事物: *Mind the step!* 当心台阶！◇ *Mind! There's a dog in the road.* 小心！路上有条狗。
do you mind ...?, would you mind ...? please could you...? 请您…行吗？: *It's cold—would you mind closing the window?* 这里很冷——请您关上窗户行吗？
I don't mind it is not important to me which thing 我对哪个都无所谓: *'Do you want tea or coffee?' 'I don't mind.'* "您要茶还是要咖啡？""什么都行。"
never mind don't worry; there is no problem; it doesn't matter 不必担心；没问题；没关系: *'I forgot your book.' 'Never mind, I don't need it today.'* "我忘了把你的书带来了""没关系，我今天不用。"

mine[1] /maɪn; maɪn/ *noun* 名词
a very big hole in the ground where people work to get things like coal, gold or diamonds 矿井；矿坑: *a coalmine* 煤矿
mine *verb* 动词 (**mines, mining, mined** /maɪnd; maɪnd/)
dig in the ground for things like coal or gold 开矿；采矿
miner *noun* 名词
a person who works in a mine 矿工: *His father was a miner.* 他父亲是矿工。

mine[2] /maɪn; maɪn/ *pronoun* 代词
something that belongs to me 我的事物: *That bike is mine.* 那辆自行车是我的。◇ *Are those books mine or yours?* 那些书是你的还是我的？

mineral /ˈmɪnərəl; ˈmɪnərəl/ *noun* 名词
Minerals are things like coal, gold, salt or oil that come from the ground and that people use. 矿物（例如煤、金、盐或石油）
mineral water /ˈmɪnərəl wɔːtə(r); ˈmɪnərəl ˌwɔtɚ/ *noun* 名词

water with minerals in it, that comes from the ground 矿泉水: *a bottle of mineral water* 一瓶矿泉水

mini- /'mɪni; 'mɪnɪ/ *prefix* 前缀
very small 非常小的: *The school has a minibus that can carry twelve people.* 这所学校有辆小型客车，可以载十二个人。

miniature /'mɪnətʃə(r); 'mɪnɪətʃɚ/ *noun* 名词
a very small copy of something larger 微型复制品；微小模型: *a miniature railway* 小铁路

minimum /'mɪnɪməm; 'mɪnəməm/ *noun* 名词 (no plural 无复数)
the smallest size, amount or number that is possible 最低限度；最小的体积或数量: *We need a minimum of six people to play this game.* 我们起码要有六个人做这个游戏。
minimum *adjective* 形容词
What is the minimum age for leaving school in your country? 在你们国家，中学毕业的最低年龄是多少岁？
✪ opposite 反义词: **maximum**

minister /'mɪnɪstə(r); 'mɪnɪstɚ/ *noun* 名词
1 one of the most important people in a government 部长；大臣: *the Minister of Education* 教育部长
2 a priest in some Christian churches（基督教某些教派的）牧师

ministry /'mɪnɪstri; 'mɪnɪstrɪ/ *noun* 名词 (*plural* 复数作 **ministries**)
a part of the government that controls one special thing（政府的）部: *the Ministry of Defence* 国防部

minor /'maɪnə(r); 'maɪnɚ/ *adjective* 形容词
not very big or important 不太大的；不太重要的: *Don't worry — it's only a minor problem.* 别担心——只是个小问题。◇ *a minor road* 辅助道路 ✪ opposite 反义词: **major**

minority /maɪ'nɒrəti; maɪ'nɔrətɪ/ *noun* 名词 (no plural 无复数)
the smaller part of a group（群体中的）小部分，少数: *Only a minority of the students speak English.* 只有少数学生会说英语。☞ Look at **majority**. 见 **majority**。

mint /mɪnt; mɪnt/ *noun* 名词
1 (no plural 无复数) a small plant with a strong fresh taste and smell, that you put in food and drinks 薄荷: *mint chewing-gum* 薄荷口香糖
2 (*plural* 复数作 **mints**) a sweet made from this 薄荷糖

minus /'maɪnəs; 'maɪnəs/ *preposition* 介词
1 less; when you take away 减；减去: *Six minus two is four* (6 – 2 = 4). 六减二等于四 (6 – 2 = 4)。☞ Look at **plus**. 见 **plus**。
2 below zero 零下: *The temperature will fall to minus ten degrees.* 温度将要降到零下十度。

minute[1] /'mɪnɪt; 'mɪnɪt/ *noun* 名词
a measure of time. There are 60 **seconds** in a minute and 60 minutes in an **hour** 分（时间单位。1分钟等于60秒，秒叫做 **second**；60分钟等于1小时，小时叫做 **hour**）: *It's nine minutes past six.* 现在是六点零九分。◇ *The train leaves in ten minutes.* 火车还有十分钟就要开了。
in a minute very soon 马上；立刻: *I'll be ready in a minute.* 我马上就准备好。
the minute as soon as 一…就…: *Phone me the minute you arrive.* 你一到就给我打个电话。

minute[2] /maɪ'nju:t; maɪ'nut/ *adjective* 形容词
very small 极小的；极少的: *I can't read his writing — it's minute.* 我看不清他的笔迹——写得太小了。

miracle /'mɪrəkl; 'mɪrəkl̩/ *noun* 名词
a wonderful and surprising thing that happens and that you cannot explain 奇迹: *It's a miracle that he wasn't killed when he fell from the window.* 他从窗户上摔下来而没有死，真是个奇迹。
miraculous /mɪ'rækjʊləs; mə'rækjələs/ *adjective* 形容词
wonderful and surprising 奇妙的；使人惊奇的: *a miraculous escape* 神奇的逃脱

mirror /'mɪrə(r); 'mɪrɚ/ *noun* 名词
a piece of special glass where you can see yourself 镜子: *Look in the mirror.* 照照镜子吧。

M

mis- *prefix* 前缀
You can add **mis-** to the beginning of some words to show that something is done wrong or badly, for example 在某些字前可加 **mis-** 表示做错某事物或没有做好，如:

misbehave = behave badly

misunderstand = not understand correctly

miserable /ˈmɪzrəbl; ˈmɪzrəbl̩/ *adjective* 形容词
1 If you are miserable, you are very sad (指人) 痛苦的: *I waited in the rain for an hour, feeling cold, wet and miserable.* 我冒雨等候了一个小时，感到又冷、又湿、又难受。
2 If something is miserable, it makes you very sad (指事物) 使人难受的: *miserable weather* 叫人难受的天气

misery /ˈmɪzəri; ˈmɪzərɪ/ *noun* 名词 (no plural 无复数)
great unhappiness 大不幸；痛苦；悲惨

misfortune /ˌmɪsˈfɔːtʃuːn; mɪsˈfɔrtʃən/ *noun* 名词
something bad that happens; bad luck 灾祸；不幸: *She had the misfortune to crash her car and lose her job on the same day.* 她很不幸，同一天里把汽车撞了又失去了工作。

mislead /ˌmɪsˈliːd; mɪsˈlid/ *verb* 动词 (**misleads**, **misleading**, **misled** /ˌmɪsˈled; mɪsˈlɛd/, **has misled**)
make somebody believe something that is not true 使某人相信不确的事；误导某人: *You misled me when you said you could give me a job.* 你说你能给我一份工作，误使我信以为真。

Miss /mɪs; mɪs/
a word that you use before the name of a girl or woman who is not married 用作未婚女子姓名之前的称谓语；小姐: *Dear Miss Smith, ...* 史密斯小姐… ☞ Look at **Mrs** and **Ms**. 见 **Mrs** 和 **Ms**。

miss /mɪs; mɪs/ *verb* 动词 (**misses**, **missing**, **missed** /mɪst; mɪst/)
1 not hit or catch something 未击中或未抓住某事物: *I tried to hit the ball but I missed.* 我没打着那个球。
2 feel sad about somebody or something that has gone 想念或怀念某人或某事物: *I'll miss you when you go to Canada.* 你到加拿大以后，我一定很想你。
3 be too late for a train, bus, plane or boat 未赶上火车、公共汽车、飞机或船: *I just missed my bus.* 我只差一步而没赶上公共汽车。
4 not see, hear, etc something 未看见、未听见…某事物；错过: *You missed a good programme on TV last night.* 你错过了昨天晚上电视的好节目。
miss out not put in or do something; not include something 未放进或未包括某事物: *I didn't finish the exam — I missed out two questions.* 我没答完试卷——落了两道题。

missile /ˈmɪsaɪl; ˈmɪsl̩/ *noun* 名词
a thing that you throw or send through the air to hurt somebody 扔出的或放出的伤害人的东西；投掷物: *The boys were throwing stones, bottles and other missiles.* 那些男孩子扔石头、瓶子之类的东西。◇ *nuclear missiles* 核导弹

missing /ˈmɪsɪŋ; ˈmɪsɪŋ/ *adjective* 形容词
lost, or not in the usual place 失去的或未在原处的: *The police are looking for the missing child.* 警方正在找寻那个失踪的孩子。◇ *My purse is missing. Have you seen it?* 我的钱包不见了。你看见了吗？

mission /ˈmɪʃn; ˈmɪʃən/ *noun* 名词
a journey to do a special job 去做某工作之行: *They were sent on a mission to the moon.* 他们被送往月球执行任务。

missionary /ˈmɪʃənri; ˈmɪʃənˌɛrɪ/ *noun* 名词 (*plural* 复数作 **missionaries**)
a person who goes to another country to teach people about a religion (到他国去的) 传教士

mist /mɪst; mɪst/ *noun* 名词
thin cloud near the ground, that is difficult to see through 薄雾: *Early in the morning, the fields were covered in mist.* 清晨，田野笼罩在薄雾之中。
misty *adjective* 形容词 (**mistier**, **mistiest**)
a misty morning 雾霭朦胧的早晨

mistake[1] /mɪˈsteɪk; məˈstek/ *noun* 名词
something that you think or do that is wrong 错误；过失: *You have made a lot of spelling mistakes in this letter.* 你信中

有很多拼写错误。◇ *It was a mistake to go by bus — the journey took two hours!* 坐公共汽车去是不对的——这一趟用了两个小时！

by mistake when you did not plan to do it 错误地；并非有意地: *I took your book by mistake — I thought it was mine.* 我错拿了你的书——还以为是我的呢。

mistake² /mɪ'steɪk; mə'stek/ *verb* 动词 (**mistakes**, **mistaking**, **mistook** /mɪ'stʊk; mɪs'tʊk/, **has mistaken** /mɪ'steɪkən; mə'stekən/)
think that somebody or something is a different person or thing 认错某人或某物: *I'm sorry — I mistook you for my cousin.* 很抱歉——我把您看成我表弟了。

mistaken *adjective* 形容词
wrong 错误的: *I said she was Spanish but I was mistaken — she's Portuguese.* 我原来说她是西班牙人，我弄错了——她其实是葡萄牙人。

misunderstand /ˌmɪsˌʌndə'stænd; ˌmɪsʌndɚ'stænd/ *verb* 动词 (**misunderstands**, **misunderstanding**, **misunderstood** /ˌmɪsˌʌndə'stʊd; ˌmɪsʌndɚ'stʊd/, **has misunderstood**)
not understand something correctly 误会；误解: *I'm sorry, I misunderstood what you said.* 对不起，我误解了您的话。

misunderstanding *noun* 名词
not understanding something correctly 误会；误解: *I think there's been a misunderstanding. I ordered two tickets, not four.* 我看我们有些误会。我订的是两张票，不是四张票。

mitten /'mɪtn; 'mɪtn̩/ *noun* 名词
a thing that you wear to keep your hand warm. It has one part for your thumb and another part for your other fingers. 连指手套（拇指与另四指分开的）

mix /mɪks; mɪks/ *verb* 动词 (**mixes**, **mixing**, **mixed** /mɪkst; mɪkst/)
1 put different things together to make something new 把不同的东西混合或搀合在一起: *Mix yellow and blue paint together to make green.* 把黄的和蓝的颜料混合在一起配成绿色的。
2 join together to make something new 混合或搀合在一起: *Oil and water don't mix.* 油和水不能混合。
3 be with and talk to other people 与他人相处；交往: *In my job, I mix with a lot of different people.* 我在工作中常和各种人打交道。

mix up 1 think that one person or thing is a different person or thing 认错某人或某物: *People often mix Mark up with his brother.* 很多人常把马克和他的弟弟弄混了。**2** make things untidy 弄乱某事物: *Don't mix up my papers!* 别把我的文件弄乱了！

mixed /mɪkst; mɪkst/ *adjective* 形容词
of different kinds 混合的: *a mixed salad* 什锦色拉 ◇ *a mixed class* (of boys and girls together) 男女合班

mixer /'mɪksə(r); 'mɪksɚ/ *noun* 名词
a machine that mixes things 搅拌机: *a food-mixer* 食物搅拌器

mixture /'mɪkstʃə(r); 'mɪkstʃɚ/ *noun* 名词
something that you make by mixing different things together 混合之物: *Air is a mixture of gases.* 空气是多种气体的混合物。◇ *a cake mixture* 做蛋糕的混合料

mm *short way of writing* **millimetre** ✳ **millimetre** 的缩写形式

moan /məʊn; mon/ *verb* 动词 (**moans**, **moaning**, **moaned** /məʊnd; mond/)
1 make a long sad sound when you are hurt or very unhappy 发出呻吟声（受伤或痛苦时）: *He was moaning with pain.* 他痛苦地呻吟着。
2 talk a lot about something that you do not like 抱怨；发牢骚: *He's always moaning about the weather.* 他总是抱怨天气不好。

moan *noun* 名词
I heard a loud moan. 我听见很大的呻吟声。

mob /mɒb; mɑb/ *noun* 名词
a big noisy group of people who are shouting or fighting 大吵大闹的人群；暴民

mobile /'məʊbaɪl; 'mobl̩/ *adjective* 形容词
able to move easily from place to place 易于移动的: *A mobile library visits the village every week.* 流动图书馆每星期都到这个村子里来。

modal verb /ˌməʊdl 'vɜːb; ˌmodl̩ 'vɝb/ *noun* 名词
a verb, for example 'might', 'can' or 'must', that you use with another verb 情态动词（might、can 或 must 等与另一动词连用的动词）

Modal verbs

Can, could, may, might, should, must, will, shall, would and **ought to** are modal verbs. ＊ **can**、**could**、**may**、**might**、**should**、**must**、**will**、**shall**、**would**、**ought to** 都是情态动词。

Modal verbs do not have an 's' in the 'he/she' form 情态动词与 he/she 连用时没有s词尾形式:

She can drive. (NOT 不作: *She cans drive.*)

After modal verbs （except **ought to**），you use the infinitive without 'to' 在情态动词后面用动词原形，不用 to（**ought to** 例外）:

I must go now. (NOT 不作: *I must to go.*)

You make questions and negative sentences without 'do' or 'did' 在疑问句和否定句中不用 do 或 did:

Will you come with me? (NOT 不作: *Do you will come?*)

They might not know. (NOT 不作: *They don't might know.*)

model[1] /'mɒdl; 'mɑdḷ/ *noun* 名词

1 a small copy of something（比实物小的）模型: *a model of the Taj Mahal* 泰吉·马哈尔陵墓模型 ◇ *a model aeroplane* 模型飞机

2 a person who wears clothes at a special show or for photographs, so that people will see them and buy them（为推销时装进行表演或供拍摄的）模特儿

3 one of the cars, machines, etc that a certain company makes（汽车、机器等的）型号: *Have you seen the latest model of the Ford Sierra?* 你看见过最新型号的福特牌汽车吗？

4 a person who sits or stands so that an artist can draw, paint or photograph him/her（供艺术工作者画的或拍摄的）模特儿

model[2] /'mɒdl; 'mɑdḷ/ *verb* 动词 (**models, modelling, modelled** /'mɒdld; 'mɑdḷd/)

wear and show clothes as a model（当模特儿）作时装表演: *Kate modelled swimsuits at the fashion show.* 凯特穿着游泳衣进行时装表演。

moderate /'mɒdərət; 'mɑdərɪt/ *adjective* 形容词

in the middle; not too much and not too little; not too big and not too small 中等的；不多不少的；不大不小的: *Cook the vegetables over a moderate heat.* 用文火烹调蔬菜。

modern /'mɒdn; 'mɑdən/ *adjective* 形容词

of the present time; of the kind that is usual now 现代的；时髦的: *modern art* 现代艺术 ◇ *The airport is very modern.* 这个机场是最新式的。

modest /'mɒdɪst; 'mɑdɪst/ *adjective* 形容词

A person who is modest does not talk much about good things that he/she has done or about things that he/she can do well 谦逊的；谦虚的: *You didn't tell me you could sing so well—you're very modest!* 你没告诉过我你能唱得这么好——你太谦虚了！

modestly *adverb* 副词

He spoke quietly and modestly about his success. 他很谦和地谈了谈自己的成绩。

modesty /'mɒdəsti; 'mɑdəstɪ/ *noun* 名词 (no plural 无复数)

being modest 谦逊；谦虚

moist /mɔɪst; mɔɪst/ *adjective* 形容词

a little wet 潮湿的；湿润的: *Keep the earth moist or the plant will die.* 要保持土壤潮湿以免植物枯死。

moisture /'mɔɪstʃə(r); 'mɔɪstʃɚ/ *noun* 名词 (no plural 无复数)

small drops of water on something or in the air 潮湿；湿气

mold, **moldy** *American English for* **mould, mouldy** 美式英语，即 **mould**、**mouldy**

mole[1] /məʊl; mol/ *noun* 名词

a small grey or brown animal that lives under the ground and makes tunnels 鼹；鼹鼠

mole[2] /məʊl; mol/ *noun* 名词

a small dark spot on a person's skin 痣

mom /mɒm; mɑm/ *American English for* **mum** 美式英语，即 **mum**

moment /'məʊmənt; 'momənt/ *noun* 名词

a very short time 一会儿；片刻：

M

He thought for a moment before he answered. 他想了一下才回答。◇ *Can you wait a moment?* 您等一会儿行吗？

at the moment now 现在；此刻: *She's on holiday at the moment, but she'll be back next week.* 她现在放着假呢，可是下星期就回来。

in a moment very soon 一会儿；立刻；马上: *He'll be here in a moment.* 他这就来。

the moment as soon as 一…就…: *Tell Jim to phone me the moment he arrives.* 告诉吉姆，让他一到就给我来个电话。

momma /ˈmɒmə; ˈmɑmə/, **mommy** /ˈmɒmi; ˈmɑmɪ/ *American English for* **mummy** 美式英语，即 **mummy**

monarch /ˈmɒnək; ˈmɑnɚk/ *noun* 名词
a king or queen 君主

monarchy /ˈmɒnəki; ˈmɑnɚkɪ/ *noun* 名词 (*plural* 复数作 **monarchies**)
a country that has a king or queen 君主国

monastery /ˈmɒnəstri; ˈmɑnəsˌtɛrɪ/ *noun* 名词 (*plural* 复数作 **monasteries**)
a place where religious men, called **monks**, live, work and pray（修士的）隐修院（修士叫做 **monk**）

Monday /ˈmʌndeɪ; ˈmʌndɪ/ *noun* 名词
the second day of the week, next after Sunday 星期一

money /ˈmʌni; ˈmʌnɪ/ *noun* 名词 (no plural 无复数)
small round metal things (called **coins**) and pieces of paper (called **notes**) that you use when you buy or sell something 钱；货币（硬币叫做 **coin**，纸币叫做 **note**）: *How much money did you spend?* 你花了多少钱？◇ *This jacket cost a lot of money.* 这件外衣很值钱。

make money get or earn money 赚钱；挣钱

monk /mʌŋk; mʌŋk/ *noun* 名词
a religious man who lives with other religious men in a **monastery** 修士（隐修院叫做 **monastery**）

monkey 猴

monkey /ˈmʌŋki; ˈmʌŋkɪ/ *noun* 名词 (*plural* 复数作 **monkeys**)
an animal with a long tail, that can climb trees 猴；猿

monster /ˈmɒnstə(r); ˈmɑnstɚ/ *noun* 名词
an animal in stories that is big, ugly and frightening（故事中的）巨大、丑陋、可怕的怪物: *A dragon is a kind of monster.* 龙是一种巨大的怪物。

month /mʌnθ; mʌnθ/ *noun* 名词
1 one of the twelve parts of a year 月份；月: *December is the last month of the year.* 十二月是一年中最后的一个月。◇ *We went on holiday last month.* 我们上个月度假去了。◇ *My exams start at the end of the month.* 我月底开始考试。
2 about four weeks 一个月的时间: *She was in hospital for a month.* 她住院住了一个月。

monthly /ˈmʌnθli; ˈmʌnθlɪ/ *adjective, adverb* 形容词，副词
that happens or comes every month or once a month 每月的；每月一次的: *a monthly magazine* 月刊杂志 ◇ *I am paid monthly.* 我按月领工资。

monument /ˈmɒnjumənt; ˈmɑnjəmənt/ *noun* 名词
a thing that is built to help people remember a person or something that happened 为纪念某人或某事物的建筑物；纪念碑: *This is a monument to Queen Victoria.* 这是维多利亚女王纪念碑。

moo /mu:; mu/ *noun* 名词
the sound that a cow makes 哞（牛叫的声音）

moo *verb* 动词 (**moos, mooing, mooed** /mu:d; mud/)
make this sound 作牛叫声；发哞声

mood /mu:d; mud/ *noun* 名词
how you feel 心境；情绪: *Dad is in a bad mood because he's lost his glasses.* 爸爸心情不好，因为他把眼镜丢了。◇ *Our teacher was in a very good mood today.* 我们老师今天情绪非常好。

be in the mood for something feel that you want something 有做某事的心情: *I'm not in the mood for a party.* 我没有心思参加聚会。

moon /mu:n; mun/ *noun* 名词
the moon (no plural 无复数)
the big thing that shines in the sky at night 月亮

M

full moon /ˌfʊl ˈmu:n; ˌfʊl ˈmun/ *noun* 名词
the time when you can see all of the moon 望月，满月（月亮圆的时候）

new moon /ˌnju: ˈmu:n; ˌnju ˈmun/ *noun* 名词
the time when you can see only the first thin part of the moon 新月，朔月（月亮形状如钩的时候）

moonlight /ˈmu:nlaɪt; ˈmunˌlaɪt/ *noun* 名词 (no plural 无复数)
the light from the moon 月光

moor[1] /mʊə(r); mʊr/ *noun* 名词
wild land on hills that has grass and low plants, but not many trees 有草和灌木而少乔木的高地；漠泽；高沼: *the Yorkshire moors* 约克郡漠泽 ◇ *We went walking on the moor.* 我们在高沼地散了散步。

moor[2] /mʊə(r); mʊr/ *verb* 动词 (**moors, mooring, moored** /mʊəd; mʊrd/)
tie a boat or ship to something so that it will stay in one place 把船系住；停泊

mop /mɒp; mɑp/ *noun* 名词
a thing with a long handle that you use for washing floors 拖把；墩布

mop *verb* 动词 (**mops, mopping, mopped** /mɒpt; mɑpt/)
clean something with a cloth or mop 用布或拖把擦净某物: *I mopped the floor.* 我把地板擦了。

moped /ˈməʊped; ˈmopɛd/ *noun* 名词
a thing like a bicycle with a small engine 摩托自行车

moral[1] /ˈmɒrəl; ˈmɔrəl/ *adjective* 形容词
about what you think is right or wrong 道德的；伦理的: *Some people do not eat meat for moral reasons.* 有些人出于道德原因而不吃肉。◇ *a moral problem* 有关伦理的问题

morally /ˈmɒrəli; ˈmɔrəlɪ/ *adverb* 副词
It's morally wrong to tell lies. 说谎是不道德的。

moral[2] /ˈmɒrəl; ˈmɔrəl/ *noun* 名词
a lesson about what is right and wrong, that you can learn from a story or from something that happens（从故事或实事中可汲取的）道德方面的教训；教益: *The moral of the story is that we should be kind to animals.* 这个故事的寓意是教育我们要善待动物。

more[1] /mɔ:(r); mɔr/ *adjective, pronoun* 形容词，代词
a bigger amount or number of something 更大（的）；更多（的）: *You've got more money than I have.* 你的钱比我的多。◇ *Can I have some more sugar in my tea?* 我的茶里再多加些糖行吗？◇ *We need two more chairs.* 我们需要再加两把椅子。◇ *There aren't any more chocolates.* 再也没有巧克力了。☞ Look at **most**. 见 **most**。

more[2] /mɔ:(r); mɔr/ *adverb* 副词
1 a word that makes an adjective or adverb stronger 用作加强形容词或副词的语气的词；更；更加: *Your book was more expensive than mine.* 你的书比我的贵。◇ *Please speak more slowly.* 请说得再慢一些。
2 a bigger amount or number 更大；更多；更甚: *I like Anna more than her brother.* 我喜欢安娜甚于她哥哥。
☞ Look at **most**. 见 **most**。

more or less almost, but not exactly 差不多；或多或少: *We are more or less the same age.* 我们年纪相仿。

not any more not as before; not any longer 不再；再也不: *They don't live here any more.* 他们不在这里住了。

once more again 再一次: *Spring will soon be here once more.* 春天又快到了。

morning /ˈmɔ:nɪŋ; ˈmɔrnɪŋ/ *noun* 名词
the first part of the day, between the time when the sun comes up and midday 从日出到中午的时间；上午；早晨: *I went swimming this morning.* 我今天早上游泳去了。◇ *I'm going to London tomorrow morning.* 我明天上午到伦敦去。◇ *The letter arrived on Tuesday morning.* 这封信是星期二上午到的。◇ *I felt ill all morning.* 我病了一上午。

in the morning **1** not in the afternoon or evening 在上午；在早晨: *I start work at nine o'clock in the morning.* 我早上九点钟开始工作。 **2** tomorrow during the morning 明天上午；明天早晨: *I'll see you in the morning.* 我明天上午见您。

mortgage /ˈmɔ:gɪdʒ; ˈmɔrgɪdʒ/ *noun* 名词
money that you borrow to buy a house（买房子的）抵押贷款

Moslem /ˈmɒzləm; ˈmɑzləm/ = **Muslim**

mosque /mɒsk; mɑsk/ *noun* 名词
a building where Muslims go to pray 清真寺

mosquito /mə'ski:təʊ; mə'skito/ *noun* 名词 (*plural* 复数作 **mosquitoes**)
a small flying insect that bites people and animals and drinks their blood 蚊子

moss /mɒs; mɔs/ *noun* 名词 (no plural 无复数)
a soft green plant that grows like a carpet on things like trees and stones 藓；苔

most[1] /məʊst; most/ *adjective, pronoun* 形容词，代词
the biggest amount or number of something 最大（的）；最多（的）: *Jo did a lot of work, but I did the most.* 乔做了很多工作，可是我做得最多。◇ *He was ill for most of last week.* 他上星期病了好几天。☞ Look at **more**. 见 **more**。
at most, at the most not more than; but not more 不超过；至多: *We can stay two days at the most.* 我们顶多能住两天。
make the most of something use something in the best way 充分利用某事物: *We only have one free day, so let's make the most of it.* 咱们只有一天自由时间，得好好利用。

most[2] /məʊst; most/ *adverb* 副词
more than all others 最: *It's the most beautiful garden I have ever seen.* 这是我见过的最漂亮的花园。◇ *Which part of your holiday did you most enjoy?* 你假期过得最愉快的是哪段时间？

mostly /'məʊstli; 'mostlɪ/ *adverb* 副词
almost all 几乎全部；大多: *The students in my class are mostly Japanese.* 我们班大部分学生都是日本人。

motel /məʊ'tel; mo'tɛl/ *noun* 名词
a hotel for people who are travelling by car 汽车旅馆（为开车的人设的）

moth /mɒθ; mɔθ/ *noun* 名词
an insect with big wings that flies at night 蛾

mother /'mʌðə(r); 'mʌðɚ/ *noun* 名词
a woman who has a child 母亲；妈妈: *My mother is a doctor.* 我母亲是医生。☞ picture on page C3. 见第C3页图。Look at **mum** and **mummy**. 见 **mum** 和 **mummy**。

mother-in-law /'mʌðər ɪn lɔ:; 'mʌðərɪn,lɔ/ *noun* 名词 (*plural* 复数作 **mothers-in-law**)
the mother of your husband or wife 丈夫或妻子的母亲；婆婆；岳母 ☞ picture on page C3 见第C3页图

motion /'məʊʃn; 'moʃən/ *noun* 名词 (no plural 无复数)
in motion moving 在移动中: *Don't put your head out of the window while the train is in motion.* 火车开着的时候不要把头伸出窗外。

motive /'məʊtɪv; 'motɪv/ *noun* 名词
a reason for doing something 做某事物的原因；动机: *Was there a motive for the murder?* 这一谋杀有动机吗？

motor /'məʊtə(r); 'motɚ/ *noun* 名词
the part inside a machine that makes it move or work 发动机；马达: *an electric motor* 电动机

motor bike 摩托车

motor bike /'məʊtə baɪk; 'motɚ,baɪk/, **motor cycle** /'məʊtə saɪkl; 'motɚ,saɪkl/ *noun* 名词
a large bicycle with an engine 摩托车
motor cyclist /'məʊtə saɪklɪst; 'motɚ,saɪklɪst/ *noun* 名词
a person who rides a motor cycle 骑摩托车的人

motor boat /'məʊtə bəʊt; 'motɚ,bot/ *noun* 名词
a small fast boat that has an engine 摩托船

motorist /'məʊtərɪst; 'motərɪst/ *noun* 名词
a person who drives a car 开汽车的人

motor racing /'məʊtə reɪsɪŋ; 'motɚ,resɪŋ/ *noun* 名词 (no plural 无复数)
a sport where people drive cars very fast on a special road (called a **track**) to try to win races 汽车比赛（赛车道叫做 **track**）: *He watched motor racing on TV.* 他观看了电视上的汽车比赛。

motorway /'məʊtəweɪ; 'motɚ,we/ *noun* 名词
a wide road where cars, lorries and coaches can travel a long way fast 高速公路: *The motorway around London is called the M25.* 环绕伦敦的高速公路叫做M25。

mould[1] /məʊld; mold/ *noun* 名词 (no plural 无复数)
soft green, grey or blue stuff that grows on food that is too old 霉；霉菌
mouldy *adjective* 形容词
covered with mould 发霉的：*mouldy cheese* 发霉的乳酪

mould[2] /məʊld; mold/ *verb* 动词 (**moulds, moulding, moulded**)
make something soft into a certain shape 使软材料成形: *The children moulded the animals out of clay.* 孩子们用泥做了一些小动物。
mould *noun* 名词
an empty container for making things into a certain shape 模子；铸模: *They poured the hot metal into the mould.* 他们把熔化的金属倒进模子里。

mound /maʊnd; maund/ *noun* 名词
1 a small hill 小丘；小土岗
2 a pile of things（东西的）一堆: *a mound of newspapers* 一堆报纸

Mount /maʊnt; maunt/ *noun* 名词
You use 'Mount' before the name of a mountain 用于山名之前: *Mount Everest* 埃佛勒斯峰（即珠穆朗玛峰）✪ The short way of writing 'Mount' is **Mt** ✳ Mount 的缩写形式为 **Mt**: *Mt Etna* 埃特纳火山

mountain /'maʊntən; 'mauntn̩/ *noun* 名词
a very high hill 山；山岳: *Everest is the highest mountain in the world.* 埃佛勒斯峰（即珠穆朗玛峰）是世界上最高的山峰。◇ *We climbed the mountain.* 我们攀登过那座山。

mountaineer /ˌmaʊntə'nɪə(r); ˌmauntn̩'ɪr/ *noun* 名词
a person who climbs mountains 登山的人
mountaineering /ˌmaʊntə'nɪərɪŋ; ˌmauntn̩'ɪrɪŋ/ *noun* 名词 (no plural 无复数)
the sport of climbing mountains 登山运动

mourn /mɔ:n; mɔrn/ *verb* 动词 (**mourns, mourning, mourned** /mɔ:nd; mɔrnd/)
feel very sad, usually because somebody has died 悲痛；（通常指因有人死亡）哀悼: *She is still mourning for her husband.* 她仍因丈夫死亡而哀伤不已。

mourning /'mɔ:nɪŋ; 'mɔrnɪŋ/ *noun* 名词 (no plural 无复数)
a time when people are very sad because somebody has died（因有人死亡）哀悼；悼念: *They are in mourning for their son.* 他们悲悼着死去的儿子。

mouse /maʊs; maus/ *noun* 名词 (*plural* 复数作 **mice** /maɪs; maɪs/)

mouse 老鼠

1 a small animal with a long tail 鼠；耗子: *Our cat caught a mouse.* 我们的猫捉住了一只老鼠。
2 a thing that you move with your hand to tell a computer what to do（计算机的）鼠标，滑鼠 ☞ picture at **computer** 见 **computer** 词条插图

moustache /mə'stɑ:ʃ; mə'stæʃ/ *noun* 名词
the hair above a man's mouth, below his nose 髭（嘴上边的胡子）: *He has got a moustache.* 他嘴上边留着小胡子。

moustache 髭

mouth /maʊθ; maʊθ/ *noun* 名词 (*plural* 复数作 **mouths** /maʊðz; maʊðz/)
1 the part of your face below your nose that you use for eating and speaking 嘴: *Open your mouth, please!* 请张开嘴！☞ picture on page C2 见第C2页图
2 the place where a river goes into the sea 河口

mouthful /'maʊθfʊl; 'maʊθˌfʊl/ *noun* 名词
the amount of food or drink that you can put in your mouth at one time 一口（食物或饮料）的量: *a mouthful of food* 一口的食物

move[1] /mu:v; muv/ *verb* 动词 (**moves, moving, moved** /mu:vd; muvd/)
1 go from one place to another; change the way you are standing or sitting 走；改变站着或坐着的姿势: *Don't get off the bus while it's moving.* 公共汽车未停稳时不要下车。◇ *We moved to the front of the cinema.* 我们向电影院的前部走去。
2 put something in another place or another way 移动或挪动某物: *Can you move your car, please?* 请您移动一下汽车行吗？
3 go to live in another place 迁居；搬家: *They sold their house in London and moved to Liverpool.* 他们把伦敦的房子卖了，搬到利物浦去了。◇ *We are moving house soon.* 我们快搬家了。

move in go to live in a house or flat 搬进住宅: *I've got a new flat — I'm moving in next week.* 我有了个新公寓——下星期搬进去。

move out leave a house or flat where you were living 搬出住宅

move² /mu:v; muv/ *noun* 名词

1 going from one place to another; changing the way you are standing or sitting 走；改变站着或坐着的姿势: *The police are watching every move she makes.* 警方密切注视着她的一举一动。

2 going to live in a new place 迁居；搬家: *We need a big van for the move.* 我们搬家需要一辆大客货车。

get a move on hurry 赶快；加紧: *Get a move on or you'll be late for work!* 快点儿，你上班要迟到了！

movement /'mu:vmənt; 'muvmənt/ *noun* 名词

1 moving or being moved 移动；运动；活动: *The old man's movements were slow and painful.* 那个老翁行动缓慢而痛苦。

2 a group of people who have the same ideas or beliefs (有共同思想或信念的)团体；(群众)运动: *a political movement* 政治运动

movie /'mu:vi; 'muvɪ/ *noun* 名词

1 a film that you see at the cinema 电影；影片: *Would you like to see a movie?* 你想去看电影吗？

2 the movies (plural 复数) the cinema 电影院: *We went to the movies last night.* 我们昨天晚上看电影去了。

✪ **Movie** is the American English word. ＊ **movie** 是美式英语用词。In British English we usually use **film** and **cinema**. 英式英语中用 **film** 和 **cinema**。

mow /məʊ; mo/ *verb* 动词 (**mows, mowing, mowed** /məʊd; mod/, **has mown** /məʊn; mon/)

cut grass 割草: *Sally is mowing the grass.* 萨莉正在割草。

mower *noun* 名词

a machine that cuts grass; a lawnmower 割草机；草坪刈草机

MP /ˌem 'pi:; ˌɛm 'pi/ *short for* **Member of Parliament** ＊ **Member of Parliament** 的缩略式

mph

a way of measuring how fast something is moving. 'Mph' is short for **miles per hour** 英里/小时（每小时英里数。mph 为 **miles per hour** 的缩略式）: *The train was travelling at 125 mph.* 那列火车行驶的速度是每小时125英里。

Mr /'mɪstə(r); 'mɪstɚ/

a word that you use before the name of a man 用作男子姓名前的称谓；先生: *Mr John Smith* 约翰·史密斯先生 ◇ *Mr Major* 梅杰先生

Mrs /'mɪsɪz; 'mɪsɪz/

a word that you use before the name of a woman who is married 用作已婚女子姓名前的称谓；夫人；太太: *Mrs Sandra Williams* 桑德拉·威廉斯夫人 ◇ *Mrs Mills* 米尔斯太太 ☞ Look at **Miss** and **Ms**. 见 **Miss** 和 **Ms**。

Ms /məz, mɪz; mɪz/

a word that you use before the name of any woman, instead of **Mrs** or **Miss** 用作任何女子姓名前的称谓，可代替 **Mrs** 或 **Miss** 使用；女士: *Ms Fiona Green* 菲奥纳·格林女士

Mt *short way of writing* **Mount** ＊ **Mount** 的缩写形式

much¹ /mʌtʃ; mʌtʃ/ *adjective* 形容词 (**much, more, most**), *pronoun* 代词

a big amount of something; a lot of something 大量的；许多: *I haven't got much money.* 我的钱不多。◇ *There was so much food that we couldn't eat it all.* 食物多得我们吃不完。◇ *'Do you like it?' 'No, not much.'* "你喜欢这个吗？" "不太喜欢。" ✪ We usually use 'much' only in negative sentences, in questions, and after 'too', 'so', 'as' and 'how'. ＊ much 一般只用于否定句、疑问句，以及 too、so、as、how 等词之后。In other sentences we use **a lot (of)** 在其他情况下要用 **a lot (of)**: *She's got a lot of money.* 她有很多钱。☞ Look at **many**. 见 **many**。

as much as the same amount that 像…一样多: *Eat as much as you can.* 你能吃多少就吃多少。

how much ...? 1 what amount? 多少: *How much paper do you want?* 您要多少纸？ **2** what price? 价钱是多少？: *How much is this shirt?* 这件衬衫多少钱？

much² /mʌtʃ; mʌtʃ/ *adverb* 副词

a lot 很；甚: *I don't like him very much.* 我不太喜欢他。◇ *Your flat is much bigger than mine.* 您的公寓比我的大得多。

mud /mʌd; mʌd/ *noun* 名词 (no plural 无复数)

soft wet earth 泥（软而含水的土）: *Phil came home from the football match covered in mud.* 菲尔赛完足球回到家里，浑身是泥。

muddle /'mʌdl; 'mʌdḷ/ *verb* 动词 (**muddles**, **muddling**, **muddled** /'mʌdld; 'mʌdḷd/)

muddle somebody up mix somebody's ideas so that they cannot understand or think clearly 使某人糊涂: *Don't ask so many questions—you're muddling me up.* 别问那么多问题——都把我弄糊涂了。

muddle somebody or 或 **something up** think that one person or thing is a different person or thing 把一人或一事物误作另一人或另一事物: *I always muddle Jenny up with her sister.* 我总是把珍妮错认为是她妹妹。

muddle something up make something untidy 把某事物弄乱: *You've muddled all my papers up!* 你把我的文件都弄乱了！

muddle *noun* 名词

in a muddle untidy or not thinking clearly 凌乱；糊涂: *Your room is in a terrible muddle.* 你的房间简直乱七八糟。◇ *I was in such a muddle that I couldn't find anything.* 我真是糊涂，什么都找不着。

muddy /'mʌdi; 'mʌdɪ/ *adjective* 形容词 (**muddier**, **muddiest**)

covered with mud（覆）有泥的: *When it rains, the roads get very muddy.* 一下雨道路就很泥泞。

mug[1] /mʌg; mʌg/ *noun* 名词

a big cup with straight sides 圆筒形大杯子；缸子: *a mug of tea* 一缸子茶

mug 缸子

mug[2] /mʌg; mʌg/ *verb* 动词 (**mugs**, **mugging**, **mugged** /mʌgd; mʌgd/)

attack somebody in the street and take their money 拦路抢钱

mugger *noun* 名词

a person who mugs somebody 拦路抢钱的人

mule /mju:l; mjul/ *noun* 名词

an animal whose parents were a horse and a donkey 骡；骡子

multicoloured /ˌmʌlti'kʌləd; ˌmʌltɪ'kʌlɚd/ *adjective* 形容词

with many colours 有多种颜色的: *multicoloured birds* 五颜六色的小鸟

multiply /'mʌltɪplaɪ; 'mʌltəˌplaɪ/ *verb* 动词 (**multiplies**, **multiplying**, **multiplied** /'mʌltɪplaɪd; 'mʌltəˌplaɪd/, **has multiplied**)

make a number bigger by a certain number of times（指乘法运算）乘: *Two multiplied by three is six* (2 × 3 = 6). 二乘三等于六（2 × 3 = 6）。◇ *Multiply three and seven together.* ＊3与7相乘。

multiplication /ˌmʌltɪplɪ'keɪʃn; ˌmʌltəplə'keʃən/ *noun* 名词 (no plural 无复数)

multiplying a number（指乘法运算的）乘

multi-storey /ˌmʌlti 'stɔ:ri; ˌmʌltɪ'storɪ/ *adjective* 形容词

with many floors（指楼层）多层的: *a multi-storey car park* 多层停车场

mum /mʌm; mʌm/ *noun* 名词

mother 妈妈: *This is my mum.* 这是我妈妈。◇ *Can I have an apple, Mum?* 妈妈，我吃个苹果行吗？

mumble /'mʌmbl; 'mʌmbḷ/ *verb* 动词 (**mumbles**, **mumbling**, **mumbled** /'mʌmbld; 'mʌmbḷd/)

speak quietly in a way that is not clear, so that people cannot hear you well 含糊地说某事（使人听不清）；叽咕: *She mumbled something about a party, but I didn't hear what she said.* 她叽叽咕咕地说了些聚会的事，我听不清她说的是什么。

mummy /'mʌmi; 'mʌmɪ/ *noun* 名词 (*plural* 复数作 **mummies**)

a word for 'mother' that children use 妈妈（儿语）

murder /'mɜ:də(r); 'mɝdɚ/ *verb* 动词 (**murders**, **murdering**, **murdered** /'mɜ:dəd; 'mɝdɚd/)

kill somebody when you have decided to do it 故意杀人；谋杀: *She was murdered with a knife.* 她是被人用刀杀死的。

murder *noun* 名词

murdering somebody 故意杀人；谋杀: *He was sent to prison for the murder of a police officer.* 他因谋杀警察而入狱。

murderer *noun* 名词

a person who has murdered somebody 故意杀人的人；谋杀者: *The police have caught the murderer.* 警方捉住了谋杀犯。

murmur /'mɜ:mə(r); 'mɝmɚ/ *verb* 动词 (**murmurs**, **murmuring**, **murmured** /'mɜ:məd; 'mɝmɚd/)

speak in a low quiet voice or make

a low sound that is not very clear 用低而轻的声音说或发出低而不清的声音: *'I love you,' she murmured in his ear.* "我爱你，" 她对他喃喃耳语。

murmur *noun* 名词

I heard the murmur of voices from the next room. 我听见隔壁传来喃喃细语声。◇ *the murmur of the wind in the trees* 风吹拂树木发出的萧萧飒飒声

muscle /'mʌsl; 'mʌsl̩/ *noun* 名词

one of the parts inside your body that become tight or loose to help you move 肌肉

museum /mju'zi:əm; mju'zɪəm/ *noun* 名词

a building where people can look at old or interesting things 博物馆: *Have you ever been to the British Museum?* 你去过不列颠博物馆吗？

mushroom /'mʌʃrum; 'mʌʃrum/ *noun* 名词

a plant that you can eat, with a flat top and no leaves 蘑菇

mushroom 蘑菇

music /'mju:zɪk; 'mjuzɪk/ *noun* 名词 (no plural 无复数)

1 the sounds that you make by singing, or by playing instruments 音乐: *What sort of music do you like?* 您喜欢什么音乐？

2 signs on paper to show people what to sing or play 乐谱: *Can you read music?* 你识乐谱吗？

✪ Some types of music are **pop**, **rock**, **jazz**, **soul**, **reggae**, **rap** and **classical**. 音乐中的一些种类是：流行音乐（**pop**）、摇滚乐（**rock**）、爵士乐（**jazz**）、灵乐（**soul**）、雷盖乐（**reggae**）、说唱乐（**rap**）、古典音乐（**classical**）等。

musical /'mju:zɪkl; 'mjuzɪkl̩/ *adjective* 形容词

1 of music 音乐的: *musical instruments* (= the piano, the guitar or the trumpet, for example) 乐器（例如钢琴、吉他或小号等）

2 good at making music 精于音乐的: *She's a very musical child—she plays the piano and the violin.* 她是个有音乐资质的孩子——她又会弹钢琴又会拉小提琴。

musical *noun* 名词

a play or film that has singing and dancing in it 有音乐和舞蹈的戏剧或影片

musician /mju'zɪʃn; mju'zɪʃən/ *noun* 名词

a person who writes music or plays a musical instrument 作曲的或演奏乐曲的人；作曲家；音乐家

Muslim /'mʊzlɪm; 'mʌzləm/ *noun* 名词

a person who follows the religion of **Islam** 穆斯林；伊斯兰教徒（伊斯兰教叫做 **Islam**）

Muslim *adjective* 形容词

the Muslim way of life 穆斯林的生活方式

must /məst, mʌst; məst, mʌst/ *modal verb* 情态动词

1 a word that you use to tell somebody what to do or what is necessary 必须；需要: *You must look before you cross the road.* 横过马路一定要先看看来往车辆。

✪ You use **must not** or the short form **mustn't** to tell people not to do something 告诉别人不要做某事时，用 **must not** 或用其缩略式 **mustn't**:

You ***mustn't*** *be late.* 你不得迟到。

When you want to say that somebody can do something if they want, but that it is not necessary, you use **don't have to** 要是想告诉某人他想做某事他就可以去做，但并非不做不行，这个意思可用 **don't have to** 来表达:

You ***don't have to*** *do your homework today* (= you can do it if you want, but it is not necessary). 你今天不必做家庭作业（= 你愿意做也可以，但并不是非做不可）。

2 a word that shows that you are sure something is true 用以表示确信某事物属实的词；一定: *You must be tired after your long journey.* 你走了这么长的路一定很累了。◇ *I can't find my keys. I must have left them at home.* 我找不着钥匙了。我准是把钥匙落在家里了。

☞ Look at the Note on page 314 to find out more about **modal verbs**. 见第314页对 **modal verbs** 的进一步解释。

mustache *American English for* **moustache** 美式英语，即 **moustache**

M

mustard /ˈmʌstəd; ˈmʌstɚd/ *noun* 名词 (no plural 无复数)
a thick yellow sauce with a very strong taste, that you eat with meat 芥末酱

mustn't /ˈmʌsnt; ˈmʌsn̩t/ = **must not**

mutter /ˈmʌtə(r); ˈmʌtɚ/ *verb* 动词 (**mutters, muttering, muttered** /ˈmʌtəd; ˈmʌtɚd/)
speak in a low quiet voice that is difficult to hear 低声说话（难以听见）；叽咕: *He muttered something about going home, and left the room.* 他叽叽咕咕地说要回家，然后就离开房间了。

my /maɪ; maɪ/ *adjective* 形容词
of me 我的: *Where is my watch?* 我的手表在哪儿呢？◇ *These are my books, not yours.* 这都是我的书，不是你的。◇ *I've hurt my arm.* 我把胳膊弄伤了。

myself /maɪˈself; maɪˈsɛlf/ *pronoun* 代词 (*plural* 复数作 **ourselves**)
1 a word that shows the same person as the one who is speaking（用做反身代词）我自己: *I hurt myself.* 我把自己弄伤了。◇ *I bought myself a new shirt.* 我买了件新衬衫。
2 a word that makes 'I' stronger（用做反身强调代词）我自己，我本人: *'Did you buy this cake?' 'No, I made it myself.'* "这个蛋糕是你买的吗？""不是，是我自己做的。"

by myself **1** alone; without other people 我独自地，我单独地（没有别人相伴）: *I live by myself.* 我自己一个人生活。
2 without help 我独自地，我单独地（没有别人帮助）: *I made dinner by myself.* 我自己做的晚饭。

mysterious /mɪˈstɪəriəs; mɪsˈtɪrɪəs/ *adjective* 形容词
Something that is mysterious is strange and you do not know about it or understand it 神秘的；奇怪的；难以理解的: *The house is empty but some people say they have seen mysterious lights there in the night.* 这所房子是空的，可是有人说晚上他们看见里面有神秘的亮光。

mysteriously *adverb* 副词
The plane disappeared mysteriously. 飞机神秘地失踪了。

mystery /ˈmɪstri; ˈmɪstərɪ/ *noun* 名词 (*plural* 复数作 **mysteries**)
something strange that you cannot understand or explain 不可理解或不可解释的事物；神秘的事物: *The police say that the man's death is still a mystery.* 警方说那男子的死亡仍是个谜。

myth /mɪθ; mɪθ/ *noun* 名词
1 a very old story 神话
2 a story or belief that is not true 不真实的事情或信念

Nn

nail /neɪl; nel/ *noun* 名词

1 the hard part at the end of a finger or toe 指甲；趾甲: *toenails* 趾甲 ◇ *fingernails* 指甲 ☞ picture on page C2 见第C2页图

2 a small thin piece of metal with one sharp end which you hit into wood (with a **hammer**) to fix things together 钉子（锤子叫做 **hammer**）☞ picture at **hammer** 见 **hammer** 词条插图

nail *verb* 动词 (**nails**, **nailing**, **nailed** /neɪld; neld/)

fix something to another thing with a nail 用钉子钉住: *I nailed the pieces of wood together.* 我把木头都钉在一起了。

naked /'neɪkɪd; 'nekɪd/ *adjective* 形容词

If you are naked, you are not wearing any clothes. 裸体的

name[1] /neɪm; nem/ *noun* 名词

a word or words that you use to call or talk about a person or thing 名字；名称: *My name is Chris Eaves.* 我名叫克里斯·伊夫斯。◇ *What's your name?* 您叫什么名字？◇ *Do you know the name of this flower?* 您知道这种花叫什么名字吗？

> ✪ Your **first name** is the name that your parents give you when you are born. 出生时父母给起的名字叫做 **first name**。In Christian countries this is also called your **Christian name**. 在信奉基督的国家中这个名字又可称为教名 **(Christian name)**。Your **surname** is the name that everybody in your family has. 姓叫做 **surname**。A **nickname** is a name that your friends or family sometimes call you instead of your real name. 除本名外，朋友或家人有时另给起的外号或昵称叫做 **nickname**。

call somebody names say bad, unkind words about somebody 辱骂某人: *Joe cried because the other children were calling him names.* 小乔哭了，因为别的孩子骂他。

name[2] /neɪm; nem/ *verb* 动词 (**names**, **naming**, **named** /neɪmd; nemd/)

1 give a name to somebody or something 给某人或某事物起名；取名；命名: *They named their baby Sophie.* 他们给孩子起名叫索菲。◇ *They named him Michael after his grandfather* (= gave him the same name as his grandfather). 他们给他按祖父的名字取名叫迈克尔。

2 know and say the name of somebody or something 说出某人或某事物的名字: *The headmaster could name every one of his 600 pupils.* 这600个学生每个人的名字校长都叫得出来。

namely /'neɪmli; 'nemlɪ/ *adverb* 副词

You use 'namely' when you are going to name a person or thing that you have just said something about 即；也就是: *Only two students were late, namely Sergio and Antonio.* 只有两个学生迟到，就是塞尔希奥和安东尼奥。

nanny /'næni; 'nænɪ/ *noun* 名词 (*plural* 复数作 **nannies**)

a woman whose job is to look after the children of a family （儿童的）保姆

nap /næp; næp/ *noun* 名词

a short sleep that you have during the day（白天的）小睡: *I had a nap after lunch.* 我午饭后睡了一小觉。

napkin /'næpkɪn; 'næpkɪn/ *noun* 名词

a piece of cloth or paper that you use when you are eating to clean your mouth and hands and to keep your clothes clean（布的或纸的）餐巾

nappy /'næpi; 'næpɪ/ *noun* 名词 (*plural* 复数作 **nappies**)

a piece of cloth or strong paper that a baby wears around its bottom and between its legs（布的或纸的）尿布

narrow /'nærəʊ; 'næro/ *adjective* 形容词 (**narrower**, **narrowest**)

not far from one side to the other（指宽度）窄的；狭窄的: *The road was too narrow for two cars to pass.* 路很窄，两辆汽车开不过去。✪ opposite 反义词: **wide** or 或 **broad** ☞ picture on page C26 见第C26页图

have a narrow escape If you have a narrow escape, something bad almost happens to you 险些遭殃: *You had a very narrow escape—your car nearly hit a tree.* 你真万幸——你的汽车险些撞到树上。

N

narrowly *adverb* 副词
only just 仅仅；勉强地: *The car narrowly missed hitting me.* 汽车差一点儿撞着我。

nasty /ˈnɑːsti; ˈnæstɪ/ *adjective* 形容词 (**nastier**, **nastiest**)
bad; not nice 很坏的；讨厌的: *There's a nasty smell in this room.* 这间屋子里有些坏味。◇ *Don't be so nasty!* 别那么讨厌！

nation /ˈneɪʃn; ˈneʃən/ *noun* 名词
a country and all the people who live in it 国家及其全体人民

national /ˈnæʃnəl; ˈnæʃənḷ/ *adjective* 形容词
of or for all of a country 全国的；全民的；国家的；国民的: *She wore the national costume of Greece.* 她穿着希腊的民族服装。◇ *national newspapers* 发行全国的报纸

national anthem /ˌnæʃnəl ˈænθəm; ˈnæʃnəḷ ˈænθəm/ *noun* 名词
the song of a country 国歌

national park /ˌnæʃnəl ˈpɑːk; ˈnæʃnəḷ ˈpɑrk/ *noun* 名词
a large area of beautiful land that the government looks after 国立公园

nationality /ˌnæʃəˈnæləti; ˌnæʃənˈælətɪ/ *noun* 名词 (*plural* 复数作 **nationalities**)
belonging to a certain country 国籍: *'What nationality are you?' 'I'm French.'* "您是哪国人？""我是法国人。"

native /ˈneɪtɪv; ˈnetɪv/ *adjective* 形容词
(of) the place where you were born 出生地的: *I returned to my native country.* 我回到了我的祖国。

native *noun* 名词
a person who was born in a place 当地人；本国人: *He lives in London but he's a native of Liverpool.* 他住在伦敦，原籍利物浦。

natural /ˈnætʃrəl; ˈnætʃrəl/ *adjective* 形容词
1 made by nature, not by people 天然的；自然的: *This part of Scotland is an area of great natural beauty.* 苏格兰这一带是天然胜景。◇ *Earthquakes and floods are natural disasters.* 地震和水灾都是天灾。
2 normal or usual 正常的；经常的: *It's natural for parents to feel sad when their children leave home.* 孩子离开家，父母自然很难过。✪ opposite 反义词: **unnatural**

naturally /ˈnætʃrəli; ˈnætʃrəlɪ/ *adverb* 副词
1 in a way that is not made or caused by people 天然；非人为地: *Is your hair naturally curly?* 您的头发是天生鬈曲的吗？
2 of course 当然；必然: *You didn't answer the telephone, so I naturally thought you were out.* 您没有接电话，我当然以为您出去了。
3 in a normal way 自然；正常地: *Try to stand naturally while I take a photo.* 我拍照的时候，你站的姿势要自然些。

nature /ˈneɪtʃə(r); ˈnetʃɚ/ *noun* 名词
1 (no plural 无复数) everything in the world that was not made by people 自然界；大自然: *the beauty of nature* 大自然的美景
2 (*plural* 复数作 **natures**) the way a person or thing is 本性；天性: *Our cat has a very friendly nature.* 我们的猫天生很温顺。

naughty /ˈnɔːti; ˈnɔtɪ/ *adjective* 形容词 (**naughtier**, **naughtiest**)
You say that a child is naughty when he/she does bad things or does not do what you ask him/her to do（指儿童）调皮的，不听话的: *She's the naughtiest child in the class.* 她是班上最调皮捣蛋的学生。

naval /ˈneɪvl; ˈnevḷ/ *adjective* 形容词
of a navy 海军的: *a naval officer* 海军军官

navigate /ˈnævɪgeɪt; ˈnævəˌget/ *verb* 动词 (**navigates**, **navigating**, **navigated**)
use a map, etc to find which way a ship, an aeroplane or a car should go 依照地图等驾驶（轮船、飞机或汽车）；导航: *Long ago, explorers used the stars to navigate.* 很久以前，探险家依靠观察星星来导航。

navigator /ˈnævɪgeɪtə(r); ˈnævəˌgetɚ/ *noun* 名词
a person who navigates 导航者；领航员；司机的引路人

navy /ˈneɪvi; ˈnevɪ/ *noun* 名词 (*plural* 复数作 **navies**)
the ships that a country uses when there is a war, and the people who work on them 海军: *Mark is in the navy.* 马克在海军服役。

navy blue /ˌneɪvi ˈbluː; ˌnevɪ ˈblu/ *adjective* 形容词
dark blue 海军蓝；深蓝色

N

near /nɪə(r); nɪr/ *adjective, adverb* 形容词，副词 (**nearer, nearest**)
not far; close 不远；很近: *Let's walk to my house. It's quite near.* 咱们走着到我家去吧。离这里很近。◇ *Where's the nearest hospital?* 离这里最近的医院在哪儿？◇ *My parents live quite near.* 我父母住的地方离这里很近。

near *preposition* 介词
close to somebody or something 接近某人或某事物；靠近: *I don't need a car because I live near the city centre.* 我不需要汽车，我住的地方离市中心很近。

nearby /ˈnɪəbaɪ; ˈnɪrˌbaɪ/ *adjective* 形容词
not far away; close 不远；很近: *We took her to a nearby hospital.* 我们把她送到附近的医院里。

nearby /nɪəˈbaɪ; ˈnɪrˈbaɪ/ *adverb* 副词
Let's go and see Tim — he lives nearby. 咱们去看看蒂姆吧——他住的地方离这里很近。

nearly /ˈnɪəli; ˈnɪrlɪ/ *adverb* 副词
almost; not quite 几乎；差不多: *I'm nearly 16 — it's my birthday next week.* 我快16岁了——我下星期过生日。◇ *She was so ill that she nearly died.* 她病得很厉害，都快死了。

not nearly not at all 相差很远: *The book wasn't nearly as good as the film.* 这本书远远不如那部影片。

neat /niːt; nit/ *adjective* 形容词 (**neater, neatest**)
with everything in the right place; tidy 整齐的: *Keep your room neat and tidy.* 房间里的东西要整整齐齐。

neatly *adverb* 副词
Write your name neatly. 把你的名字写工整。

necessarily /ˌnesəˈserəli; ˈnɛsəˌsɛrəlɪ/ *adverb* 副词
not necessarily not always 不总是；不见得: *Big men aren't necessarily strong.* 大个子不一定强壮。

necessary /ˈnesəsəri; ˈnɛsəˌsɛrɪ/ *adjective* 形容词
If something is necessary, you must have or do it 必须的；必要的: *Warm clothes are necessary in winter.* 冬天一定要有防寒的衣服。

necessity /nəˈsesəti; nəˈsɛsətɪ/ *noun* 名词 (*plural* 复数作 **necessities**)
something that you must have 必需品: *Food and clothes are necessities of life.* 食物和衣服都是生活必需品。

neck /nek; nɛk/ *noun* 名词
1 the part of your body between your shoulders and your head 脖子；颈: *Helen wore a thick scarf round her neck.* 海伦脖子上围着一条厚围巾。☞ picture on page C2 见第C2页图
2 the part of a jumper, T-shirt, etc that goes round your neck（套头毛衣、短袖汗衫等的）领口
3 the thin part at the top of a bottle 瓶口

necklace /ˈnekləs; ˈnɛklɪs/ *noun* 名词
a pretty thing that you wear round your neck 项链: *a diamond necklace* 钻石项链

necklace 项链

need¹ /niːd; nid/ *verb* 动词 (**needs, needing, needed**)
1 must have something; want something important and necessary that is not there 需要: *All plants and animals need water.* 所有的植物和动物都需要水。◇ *You don't need your coat — it's not cold.* 你不需要大衣——天气不冷。
2 If you need to do something, you must do it, or it is very important to do it 必需；必须: *James is very ill. He needs to go to hospital.* 詹姆斯病得很重。他得去医院。◇ *'Do we need to pay now, or can we pay next week?' 'You needn't pay now.'/'You don't need to pay now.'* "我们是不是得现在付款，还是可以下星期付款？" "您不必现在付款。"

need² /niːd; nid/ *noun* 名词
be in need of something 需要某事物 want something important and necessary that is not there 需要: *She's in need of a rest.* 她需要休息。

needle /ˈniːdl; ˈnidl̩/ *noun* 名词
1 a small thin piece of metal with a hole at one end and a sharp point at the other. You use a needle for sewing（缝纫用的）针: *If you give me a needle and cotton, I'll sew the button on your shirt.* 你要是给我针线，我就把衬衫扣子给你钉上。☞ picture at **sew** 见 **sew** 词条插图
2 something that is like a needle 针状物: *the needle of a compass* 罗盘的指针

N

3 a very thin pointed leaf. **Pine trees** and **fir-trees** have needles. 针叶（松树 **pine tree** 和枞树 **fir-tree** 都长着针叶）☞ Look also at **knitting-needle**. 另见 **knitting-needle**。

needn't /'ni:dnt; 'nidn̩t/ = **need not**

negative /'negətɪv; 'nɛgətɪv/ *adjective* 形容词
using words like 'no', 'not' and 'never' 否定的（用 no、not、never 等否定词的）: *'I don't like British food' is a negative sentence.* "我不喜欢英国饭菜"是个否定句。
negative *noun* 名词
a piece of film that you use to make a photograph. On a negative, dark things are light and light things are dark. 负片；底片（拍摄过的胶片，用来印制相片）

neglect /nɪ'glekt; nɪ'glɛkt/ *verb* 动词 (**neglects**, **neglecting**, **neglected**)
not take care of somebody or something 疏忽某人或某事物；忽略: *The dog was dirty and thin because its owner had neglected it.* 那条狗又脏又瘦，因为主人疏于照顾。
neglect *noun* 名词 (no plural 无复数)
The house was in a state of neglect. 这所楼房无人照管。

neigh /neɪ; ne/ *noun* 名词
the sound that a horse makes 马的嘶叫声
neigh *verb* 动词 (**neighs**, **neighing**, **neighed** /neɪd; ned/)
make this sound（马）嘶叫

neighbor, neighboring *American English for* **neighbour, neighbouring** 美式英语，即 **neighbour**、**neighbouring**

neighborhood *American English for* **neighbourhood** 美式英语，即 **neighbourhood**

neighbour /'neɪbə(r); 'nebɚ/ *noun* 名词
a person who lives near you 邻居: *Don't make so much noise or you'll wake the neighbours.* 别那么大声，看把邻居吵醒了。
✪ Your **next-door neighbour** is the person who lives in the house next door to your house. 隔壁（的邻居）叫做 **next-door neighbour**。
neighbouring *adjective* 形容词
that is near 相邻的；邻近的: *We played football against a team from the neighbouring village.* 我们跟邻村的球队赛了一场足球。

neighbourhood /'neɪbəhʊd; 'nebɚˌhʊd/ *noun* 名词
a part of a town 附近地区；四邻: *They live in a friendly neighbourhood.* 他们四邻相处和睦。

neither[1] /'naɪðə(r), 'ni:ðə(r); 'niðɚ/ *adjective, pronoun* 形容词，代词
not one and not the other of two things or people（二者）都不: *Neither book was very interesting.* 这两本书都没什么意思。◇ *Neither of the children liked the film.* 两个孩子都不喜欢那部影片。

neither[2] /'naɪðə(r), 'ni:ðə(r); 'niðɚ/ *adverb* 副词
(used in sentences with 'not' 用于含有 not 的句中) also not 也不: *Lydia can't swim and neither can I.* 莉迪亚不会游泳，我也不会。◇ *'I don't like rice.' 'Neither do I.'* "我不喜欢吃米饭。""我也不喜欢。"
neither ... nor not ... and not 既不…也不…: *Neither Paul nor I went to the party.* 保罗和我都没去参加聚会。

nephew /'nefju:; 'nɛfju/ *noun* 名词
the son of your brother or sister 兄弟的或姐妹的儿子；侄子；外甥 ☞ picture on page C3 见第C3页图

nerve /nɜ:v; nɝv/ *noun* 名词
1 (*plural* 复数作 **nerves**) one of the long thin things inside your body that carry feelings and messages to and from your brain 神经
2 nerves (plural 复数) being worried or afraid 担忧或害怕；神经紧张: *John breathed deeply to calm his nerves.* 约翰深深地呼吸定了定神。
3 (no plural 无复数) being brave or calm when there is danger（遇危险时）有勇气，镇静: *You need a lot of nerve to be a racing driver.* 当赛车手得很有胆量。
get on somebody's nerves annoy somebody 烦扰某人: *Stop making that noise — you're getting on my nerves!* 别弄出那种声音——你把人扰得心烦意乱！

nervous /'nɜ:vəs; 'nɝvəs/ *adjective* 形容词
1 worried or afraid 担忧或害怕的；神经紧张的: *I'm quite nervous about starting my new job.* 我开始做新工作心情十分紧张。
2 of the nerves in your body 神经的: *the nervous system* 神经系统
nervously *adverb* 副词
He laughed nervously because he didn't know what to say. 他不知道说什么好，所以神经质地笑了起来。

nervousness /ˈnɜːvəsnəs; ˈnɝvəsnɪs/ *noun* 名词 (no plural 无复数)
being nervous 担忧或害怕；神经紧张

nest /nest; nɛst/ *noun* 名词
a place where a bird, a snake, an insect, etc lives and lays its eggs or keeps its babies（鸟、蛇、昆虫等的）窝；巢: *a bird's nest* 鸟窝

nest *verb* 动词 (**nests, nesting, nested**)
make and live in a nest（指鸟、蛇、昆虫等）做窝或筑巢栖居: *The ducks are nesting by the river.* 那些鸭子正在河边筑巢。

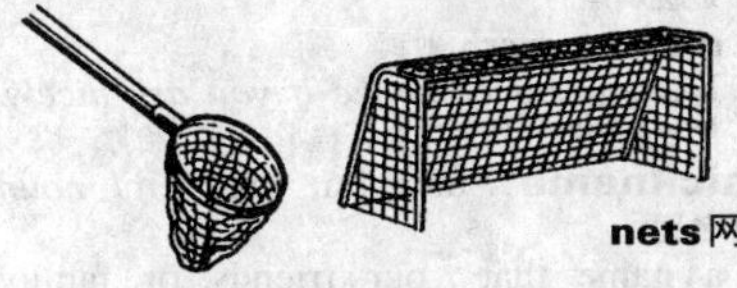
nets 网

net /net; nɛt/ *noun* 名词
material that is made of long pieces of string, etc with holes between them 网: *a fishing net* 鱼网 ◇ *a tennis net* 网球网

netball /ˈnetbɔːl; ˈnɛtˌbɔl/ *noun* 名词 (no plural 无复数)
a game where two teams of seven players try to throw a ball through a high round net 无挡板篮球

nettle /ˈnetl; ˈnɛtl̩/ *noun* 名词
a wild plant covered with hairs that can hurt you if you touch them 荨麻

network /ˈnetwɜːk; ˈnɛtˌwɝk/ *noun* 名词
a large group of things that are connected to one another across a country, etc 网状系统: *the railway network* 铁路网

never /ˈnevə(r); ˈnɛvɚ/ *adverb* 副词
not at any time; not ever 从来没有；决不: *She never works on Saturdays.* 星期六她向来不工作。◇ *I've never been to America.* 我从来没去过美国。◇ *I will never forget you.* 我决忘不了你。

nevertheless /ˌnevəðəˈles; ˌnɛvɚðəˈlɛs/ *conjunction, adverb* 连词，副词
but; however; although that is true 但是；然而；虽然如此: *They played very well. Nevertheless, they didn't win.* 他们在比赛中表现得非常好。但是他们并没有赢。

new /njuː; nu/ *adjective* 形容词 (**newer, newest**)
1 Something that is new has just been made or bought 新的（刚做的或刚买的）: *I bought a new pair of shoes yesterday.* 我昨天买了双新鞋。◇ *Have you seen Spike Lee's new film?* 你看过斯派克·李的新影片吗？ ☞ picture on page C27 见第C27页图
2 that you have not seen, had, learnt, etc before 新的（以前没见过的、没有过的、没学过的等）: *Our new flat is much bigger than our old one.* 我们的新公寓比旧的大得多。◇ *The teacher usually explains the new words to us.* 老师通常给我们解释生词。

new to something If you are new to something, you are at a place or doing something for the first time 第一次到某处或做某事: *They are new to the town and they don't have any friends there.* 他们新到这座城镇，什么朋友也没有。

new year the beginning of the year; the time around 1 January 新年: *Happy New Year!* 新年快乐！✪ 1 January is called **New Year's Day** and 31 December is called **New Year's Eve**. 1月1日是元旦，叫做 **New Year's Day**；12月31日是除夕，叫做 **New Year's Eve**。

newcomer /ˈnjuːkʌmə(r); ˈnjuˌkʌmɚ/ *noun* 名词
a person who has just come to a place 新来的人

newly /ˈnjuːli; ˈnjulɪ/ *adverb* 副词
not long ago; recently 不久以前；新近: *Our school is newly built.* 我们学校是新建的。

news /njuːz; nuz/ *noun* 名词 (no plural 无复数)
1 words that tell people about things that have just happened 消息；新闻: *Have you heard the news? Stewart is getting married.* 你听说了吗？斯图尔特要结婚了。◇ *I've got some good news for you.* 我告诉你个好消息。✪ Be careful! You cannot say 'a news'. 注意！不可说 a news。You can say 'some news' or 'a piece of news' 可以说 some news 或 a piece of news: *Julie told us an interesting piece of news.* 朱莉告诉我们一个有趣的消息。
2 the news (no plural 无复数) a programme on television or radio that tells people about important things that have just happened（电视或电台的）新闻广播: *We heard about the plane crash on the news.* 我们从新闻广播中听到飞机失事的消息。

N

break the news tell somebody about something important that has happened 告诉某人重要的消息: *Have you broken the news to your wife?* 你把这件大事告诉你妻子了吗?

newsagent /ˈnju:zeɪdʒənt; ˈnjuzˌedʒənt/ *noun* 名词
a person who has a shop that sells things like newspapers, magazines, sweets and cigarettes 报刊经销人（设有店铺，出售报纸、杂志、糖果、香烟等）
✪ The shop where a newsagent works is called a **newsagent's**. 这种店铺叫做 **newsagent's**。

newspaper /ˈnju:speɪpə(r); ˈnuzˌpepə˞/ *noun* 名词
large pieces of paper with news, advertisements and other things printed on them, that you can buy every day or every week 报纸

next[1] /nekst; nɛkst/ *adjective* 形容词
1 that comes after this one 下一个: *I'm going on holiday next week.* 我下星期放假。◇ *Go straight on, then take the next road on the right.* 一直走，到下一个路口向右拐。
2 nearest to this one 离这里最近的；邻近的: *I live in the next village.* 我住在邻近的村子里。
next to at the side of somebody or something; beside 在某人或某物的旁边；紧挨着的: *The bank is next to the post office.* 银行在邮局旁边。☞ picture on page C1 见第C1页图

next[2] /nekst; nɛkst/ *adverb* 副词
after this; then 在这之后；然后: *I've finished this work. What shall I do next?* 我把这件工作做完了。我下一步做什么呢?

next[3] /nekst; nɛkst/ *noun* 名词 (no plural 无复数)
the person or thing that comes after this one 下一个人或事物: *Susy came first and Paul was the next to arrive.* 苏西是第一个来的，保罗是跟着到的。

next door /ˌnekst ˈdɔ:(r); ˌnɛkst ˈdɔr/ *adjective*, *adverb* 形容词，副词
in or to the nearest house 隔壁（的）: *Who lives next door?* 谁住在隔壁? ◇ *next-door neighbours* 隔壁的邻居

nibble /ˈnɪbl; ˈnɪbl̩/ *verb* 动词 (**nibbles**, **nibbling**, **nibbled** /ˈnɪbld; ˈnɪbl̩d/)
eat something in very small bites 小口咬某物；啃: *The mouse nibbled the cheese.* 老鼠把奶酪啃了。

nice /naɪs; naɪs/ *adjective* 形容词 (**nicer**, **nicest**)
pleasant, good or kind 愉快的、好的或善良的: *Did you have a nice holiday?* 您假期过得愉快吗? ◇ *I met a nice boy at the party.* 我在聚会上认识了一个很好的男孩儿。◇ *It's nice to see you.* 见到你，我很高兴。
nice and ... words that show that you like something 用以表示喜爱某事物的词: *It's nice and warm by the fire.* 在火炉边真是暖烘烘的。
nicely *adverb* 副词
You can have a cake if you ask nicely. 你要是很有礼貌地说要蛋糕，就可以给你一块。

nickname /ˈnɪkneɪm; ˈnɪkˌnem/ *noun* 名词
a name that your friends or family sometimes call you instead of your real name 外号；昵称（除本名外，朋友或家人有时另给起的名字）

niece /ni:s; nis/ *noun* 名词
the daughter of your brother or sister 兄弟的或姐妹的女儿；侄女；外甥女 ☞ picture on page C3 见第C3页图

night /naɪt; naɪt/ *noun* 名词
1 the time when it is dark because there is no light from the sun 夜间: *Most people sleep at night.* 大多数人都在夜里睡觉。◇ *She stayed at my house last night.* 她昨天在我家过夜。◇ *The baby cried all night.* 那个小孩儿哭了一夜。
2 the part of the day between the afternoon and when you go to bed 晚上: *We went to a party on Saturday night.* 我们星期六晚上参加了个聚会。
✪ **Tonight** means the night or evening of today. ＊ **tonight** 指的是今天夜里或今天晚上。

nightclub /ˈnaɪtklʌb; ˈnaɪtˌklʌb/ *noun* 名词
a place where you can go late in the evening to drink and dance, for example 夜总会

nightdress /ˈnaɪtdres; ˈnaɪtˌdrɛs/ (*plural* 复数作 **nightdresses**), **nightie** /ˈnaɪti; ˈnaɪtɪ/ *noun* 名词
a loose dress that a woman or girl wears in bed（女子的）长睡衣；睡袍

nightly /ˈnaɪtli; ˈnaɪtlɪ/ *adjective*, *adverb* 形容词，副词

that happens or comes every night 每夜（的）；每晚（的）: *a nightly TV show* 每晚播放的电视节目

nightmare /ˈnaɪtmeə(r); ˈnaɪtˌmɛr/ *noun* 名词

1 a dream that frightens you 噩梦: *I had a nightmare last night.* 我昨天夜里做了个噩梦。

2 something that is very bad or frightening 非常坏的或可怕的事情: *Travelling through the snow was a nightmare.* 那次雪中之行十分可怕。

night-time /ˈnaɪt taɪm; ˈnaɪtˌtaɪm/ *noun* 名词 (no plural 无复数)

the time when it is dark 夜间: *She is afraid to go out at night-time.* 她害怕在夜里出去。

nil /nɪl; nɪl/ *noun* 名词 (no plural 无复数)

nothing 无；零: *Our team won the match by two goals to nil.* 我们队以二比零赢了那场比赛。

nine /naɪn; naɪn/ *number* 数词

9 九

ninth /naɪnθ; naɪnθ/ *adjective, adverb, noun* 形容词，副词，名词

1 9th 第9（个）；第九（个）

2 one of nine equal parts of something; ⅑ 九分之一

nineteen /ˌnaɪnˈtiːn; naɪnˈtin/ *number* 数词

19 十九

nineteenth /ˌnaɪnˈtiːnθ; naɪnˈtinθ/ *adjective, adverb, noun* 形容词，副词，名词

19th 第19（个）；第十九（个）

ninety /ˈnaɪnti; ˈnaɪntɪ/ *number* 数词

1 90 九十

2 the nineties (plural 复数) the numbers, years or temperatures between 90 and 99 ＊ 90至99（之间的数目、年数或温度）

in your nineties between the ages of 90 and 99 年岁在90至99之间；九十多岁: *My grandmother is in her nineties.* 我祖母九十多岁了。

ninetieth /ˈnaɪntiəθ; ˈnaɪntɪəθ/ *adjective, adverb, noun* 形容词，副词，名词

90th 第90（个）；第九十（个）

nitrogen /ˈnaɪtrədʒən; ˈnaɪtrədʒən/ *noun* 名词 (no plural 无复数)

a gas in the air 氮

no[1], **No** *short way of writing* **number 1** ＊ **number** 词条中第1义项的缩写形式

no[2] /nəʊ; no/ *adjective* 形容词

1 not one; not any 没有；无: *I have no money — my purse is empty.* 我没有钱——我的钱包是空的。

2 a word that shows you are not allowed to do something（表示不准做某事的词）不准，禁止: *The sign said 'No Smoking'.* 牌子上写着"禁止吸烟"。

no *adverb* 副词

not any 不: *My flat is no bigger than yours.* 我的公寓不比你的大。

no[3] /nəʊ; no/

a word that you use to show that something is not right or true, or that you do not want something; not yes（表示某事物不对或不确，或自己不想要某事物的词）不，不是: *'Do you want a drink?' 'No, thank you.'* "您想喝点儿东西吗？""不喝，谢谢您。"◇ *'He's Italian.' 'No he isn't. He's French.'* "他是意大利人。""不是，他是法国人。"

oh no! words that you say when something bad happens 出现坏事时说的词语: *Oh no! I've broken my watch!* 糟糕！我把手表弄坏了！

noble /ˈnəʊbl; ˈnobl̩/ *adjective* 形容词 (**nobler, noblest**)

1 of a rich important family 出身高贵的；贵族的: *a noble prince* 出身高贵的王子

2 good, honest and not selfish 良好、诚实而不自私的；高尚的: *noble thoughts* 崇高的思想

nobody /ˈnəʊbədi; ˈnobədɪ/ *pronoun* 代词

no person; not anybody 没有人；无人: *Nobody in our class speaks Greek.* 我们班没有人会说希腊语。◇ *There was nobody at home.* 家里没有人。

nod /nɒd; nɑd/ *verb* 动词 (**nods, nodding, nodded**)

move your head down and up again quickly as a way of saying 'yes' or 'hello' to somebody 点头（表示同意或打招呼）: *'Do you understand?' asked the teacher, and everybody nodded.* "你们明白吗？"老师问，大家都点了点头。

nod *noun* 名词

Jim gave me a nod when I arrived. 我一到，吉姆就向我点了点头。

noise /nɔɪz; nɔɪz/ *noun* 名词

1 something that you hear; a sound 听到的声音；响声: *I heard a noise upstairs.* 我听见楼上有声音。

2 a loud sound that you do not like 大的刺耳的声音；噪音；噪声: *Don't make so much noise!* 别弄出那么难听的声音！◇ *What a terrible noise!* 多讨厌的声音！

noisy /'nɔɪzi; 'nɔɪzɪ/ *adjective* 形容词 (**noisier, noisiest**)

1 full of loud noise 嘈杂的；喧闹的: *The restaurant was too noisy.* 这个饭馆太吵了。

2 If a person or thing is noisy, he/she/it makes a lot of noise（指人或物）发出嘈杂或喧闹声的: *The children are very noisy.* 这些孩子太吵了。

✪ opposite 反义词: **quiet**

noisily /'nɔɪzɪli; 'nɔɪzɪlɪ/ *adverb* 副词 *He ate his dinner noisily.* 他吃饭的时候发出很大的声音。

non- /nɒn; nɑn/ *prefix* 前缀

You can add **non-** to the beginning of some words to give them the opposite meaning, for example 在某些字前可加 **non-** 构成反义词，如:

a **non-smoker** = a person who does not smoke 不吸烟的人

a **non-stop** train = a train that goes from one place to another without stopping at the other stations between 直通车

none /nʌn; nʌn/ *pronoun* 代词

not any; not one 毫无；一个也没有: *She has eaten all the chocolates — there are none in the box.* 她把巧克力都吃了——盒子里一块都没有了。◇ *I went to every bookshop, but none of them had the book I wanted.* 我到过所有的书店，全都没有我要的书。

nonsense /'nɒnsns; 'nɑnsɛns/ *noun* 名词 (no plural 无复数)

words or ideas that have no meaning or that are not true 无意义的或不属实的言语或想法；胡说；废话；荒唐念头: *It's nonsense to say that Jackie is lazy.* 说杰基这个人懒惰，那可是胡说八道。

noodles /'nu:dlz; 'nudl̩z/ *noun* 名词 (plural 复数)

long thin pieces of food made from flour, eggs and water 面条

noon /nu:n; nun/ *noun* 名词 (no plural 无复数)

twelve o'clock in the middle of the day 白天12点钟；正午；中午: *I met Sally at noon.* 我是在中午遇见萨莉的。

no one /'nəʊ wʌn; 'no ˌwʌn/ *pronoun* 代词

no person; not anybody 没有人；无人: *There was no one in the classroom.* 教室里没有人。◇ *No one saw me go into the house.* 谁也没看见我走进那所房子。

nor /nɔ:(r); nɔr/ *conjunction* 连词

(used after 'neither' and 'not' 用于 neither 和 not 之后) also not 也不；也没: *If Alan doesn't go, nor will Lucy.* 要是艾伦不去，露西也不去。◇ *'I don't like eggs.' 'Nor do I.'* "我不爱吃鸡蛋。""我也不爱吃。" ◇ *Neither Tom nor I eat meat.* 汤姆和我都不吃肉。

normal /'nɔ:ml; 'nɔrml̩/ *adjective* 形容词

usual and ordinary; not different or special 正常的；通常的；普通的: *I will be home at the normal time.* 我还是在平常的时候到家。

normally /'nɔ:məli; 'nɔrml̩ɪ/ *adverb* 副词

1 usually 通常: *I normally go to bed at about eleven o'clock.* 我一般约在十一点钟睡觉。

2 in a normal way 正常: *He isn't behaving normally.* 他现在举止不正常。

north 北

west 西

east 东

south 南

north /nɔ:θ; nɔrθ/ *noun* 名词 (no plural 无复数)

the direction that is on your left when you watch the sun come up in the morning 北；北方；北边: *the north of England* 英格兰的北部

north *adjective, adverb* 形容词，副词 *They live in North London.* 他们住在伦敦北部。◇ *a north wind* (= that comes from the north) 北风（= 从北方来的）◇ *We travelled north from London to Scotland.* 我们从伦敦北行至苏格兰。

northern /'nɔ:ðən; 'nɔrðɚn/ *adjective* 形容词

in or of the north part of a place 北方的；北部的；北边的: *Newcastle is in northern England.* 纽卡斯尔在英格兰北部。

nose /nəʊz; noz/ *noun* 名词
1 the part of your face, above your mouth, that you use for breathing and smelling 鼻子 ☞ picture on page C2 见第C2页图
2 the front part of a plane （飞机的）机首
blow your nose blow air through your nose to empty it, into a piece of cloth or paper (a **handkerchief** or a **tissue**) 擤鼻子（所用的手绢叫做 **handkerchief**，纸巾叫做 **tissue**）

nostril /ˈnɒstrəl; ˈnɑstrəl/ *noun* 名词
one of the two holes in your nose 鼻孔 ☞ picture on page C2 见第C2页图

nosy /ˈnəʊzi; ˈnozɪ/ *adjective* 形容词 (**nosier**, **nosiest**)
too interested in other people's lives and in things that you should not be interested in 爱打听别人的闲事的: *'Where are you going?' 'Don't be so nosy!'* "你到哪儿去？""少管闲事！"

not /nɒt; nɑt/ *adverb* 副词
a word that gives the opposite meaning to another word or a sentence 不；没: *I'm not hungry.* 我不饿。◇ *They did not arrive.* 他们没来。◇ *I can come tomorrow, but not on Tuesday.* 我明天能来，但是星期二不行。◇ *'Are you angry with me?' 'No, I'm not.'* "你生我的气了吗？""没有哇，我没生气。" ✪ We often say and write **n't** 在口语和书面语中均可略作 **n't**: *John isn't* (= is not) *here.* 约翰没在这儿。◇ *I haven't* (= have not) *got any sisters.* 我没有姐姐和妹妹。
not at all **1** no; not a little bit 无；一点儿也不: *'Are you tired?' 'Not at all.'* "您累吗？""一点儿也不累。" **2** polite words that you say when somebody has said 'thank you' 回应别人道谢的礼貌用语: *'Thanks for your help.' 'Oh, not at all.'* "谢谢您帮了我的忙。""噢，没什么。"

note[1] /nəʊt; not/ *noun* 名词
1 some words that you write quickly to help you remember something 笔记；摘记: *I made a note of her address.* 我把她的地址记了下来。
2 a short letter 短信；便条: *Dave sent me a note to thank me for the present.* 戴夫寄给我一封短信，感谢我送给他礼物。
3 a piece of paper money 纸币: *He gave me a £10 note.* 他给我一张10英镑的纸币。
4 a short piece of extra information about something in a book （书中的）注释；注解: *Look at the note on page 39.* 见39页注释。
5 one sound in music, or a mark on paper that shows a sound in music （音乐的）单音；（乐谱上的）音符: *I can play a few notes of this song.* 我能奏出这个歌的几个音。
take notes write when somebody is speaking so that you can remember their words later 记笔记: *The teacher asked us to take notes in the lesson.* 老师让我们上课记笔记。

note[2] /nəʊt; not/ *verb* 动词 (**notes**, **noting**, **noted**)
notice and remember something 注意并记住某事物: *Please note that all the shops are closed on Mondays.* 请注意所有商店星期一都不开门。
note down write something so that you can remember it 记下: *The police officer noted down my name and address.* 警察把我的姓名和地址都记了下来。

notebook /ˈnəʊtbʊk; ˈnot͵bʊk/ *noun* 名词
a small book where you write things that you want to remember 笔记本；记事本

notepad /ˈnəʊtpæd; ˈnotpæd/ *noun* 名词
some pieces of paper that are joined together at one edge, where you write things that you want to remember 便条本

notepaper /ˈnəʊtpeɪpə(r); ˈnot͵pepɚ/ *noun* 名词 (no plural 无复数)
paper that you write letters on 信纸

nothing /ˈnʌθɪŋ; ˈnʌθɪŋ/ *pronoun* 代词
not anything; no thing 什么也没有；无物: *There's nothing in this bottle — it's empty.* 瓶子里什么都没有——是空的。◇ *I've finished all my work and I've got nothing to do.* 我把工作都做完了，没有什么可做了。
for nothing **1** for no money; free 不用钱；免费: *You can have these books for nothing. I don't want them.* 这些书你愿意要就给你。我不要了。 **2** without a good

N

result 无结果；徒劳: *I went to the station for nothing—she wasn't on the train.* 我白去车站一趟——她没坐那班火车。

have nothing on If you have nothing on, you are not wearing any clothes. 没穿衣服；光着身子

nothing but only 仅仅: *He eats nothing but salad.* 他仅以色拉为食。

nothing like not the same as somebody or something in any way 完全不像某人或某事物: *He's nothing like his brother.* 他一点儿也不像他哥哥。

notice[1] /ˈnəʊtɪs; ˈnotɪs/ *noun* 名词

1 (*plural* 复数作 **notices**) a piece of writing that tells people something 布告；公告；启事: *The notice on the wall says 'NO SMOKING'.* 墙上的告示上写着"禁止吸烟"。

2 (no plural 无复数) a warning that something is going to happen 通知；警告: *Our teacher gave us two weeks' notice of the history exam.* 我们老师通知我们两星期后考历史。

at short notice with not much time to get ready 没有充足准备时间: *We left for Scotland at very short notice and I forgot to take my coat.* 我们前往苏格兰十分仓促，我忘记带上大衣了。

give in or 或 **hand in your notice** tell the person you work for that you are going to leave your job 向负责人递交辞呈

take no notice of somebody or 或 **something** not listen to or look at somebody or something; not pay attention to somebody or something 不理会或不注意某人或某事物: *Take no notice of what she said—she's not feeling well.* 别理会她的话——她身体不舒服。

notice[2] /ˈnəʊtɪs; ˈnotɪs/ *verb* 动词 (**notices**, **noticing**, **noticed** /ˈnəʊtɪst; ˈnotɪst/)

see somebody or something 看到或注意到某人或某事物: *Did you notice what she was wearing?* 你看见她穿着什么衣服了吗？◇ *I noticed that he was driving a new car.* 我看见他开着新汽车。

noticeable /ˈnəʊtɪsəbl; ˈnotɪsəbḷ/ *adjective* 形容词

easy to see 容易看见的: *I've got a mark on my shirt. Is it noticeable?* 我衬衫上有个斑点。看得出来吗？

notice-board /ˈnəʊtɪs bɔːd; ˈnotɪsˌbɔrd/ *noun* 名词

a flat piece of wood on a wall. You put papers on a notice-board so everybody can read them 布告牌: *The teacher put the exam results on the notice-board.* 老师在布告牌上公布了考试成绩。

nought /nɔːt; nɔt/ *noun* 名词

the number 0 零；0: *We say 0.5 as 'nought point five'.* 我们把0.5读做"零点五"。

noun /naʊn; naʊn/ *noun* 名词

a word that is the name of a person, place, thing or idea 名词: *'Anne', 'London', 'cat' and 'happiness' are all nouns.* ＊Anne、London、cat、happiness 都是名词。

novel /ˈnɒvl; ˈnɑvḷ/ *noun* 名词

a book that tells a story about people and things that are not real 小说: *'David Copperfield' is a novel by Charles Dickens.* 《大卫·科波菲尔》是狄更斯写的小说。

novelist /ˈnɒvəlɪst; ˈnɑvḷɪst/ *noun* 名词

a person who writes novels 写小说的人；小说家

November /nəʊˈvembə(r); noˈvɛmbɚ/ *noun* 名词

the eleventh month of the year 十一月

now[1] /naʊ; naʊ/ *adverb* 副词

1 at this time 现在；目前: *I can't see you now—can you come back later?* 我现在无法见你——你等一会儿再来行吗？◇ *She was in Paris but she's living in Rome now.* 她原来在巴黎，可是目前住在罗马。◇ *Don't wait—do it now!* 别等着——现在就做！

2 a word that you use when you start to talk about something new, or to make people listen to you 用以引起新话题或引起别人注意听的词: *I've finished writing this letter. Now, what shall we have for dinner?* 我把这封信写完了。那么，咱们晚饭吃什么？◇ *Be quiet, now!* 安静吧！

from now on after this time; in the future 从此以后；今后: *From now on your teacher will be Mr Hancock.* 今后给你们上课的老师就是汉考克先生了。

now and again, now and then sometimes, but not often 有时（但不经常）；偶尔: *We go to the cinema now and again.* 我们偶尔看看电影。

now² /naʊ; naʊ/ *conjunction* 连词
because something has happened 由于；既然: *Now that Mark has arrived we can start dinner.* 既然马克已经来了，咱们可以开饭了。

nowadays /ˈnaʊədeɪz; ˈnaʊəˌdez/ *adverb* 副词
at this time 时下；现今: *A lot of people work with computers nowadays.* 很多人如今使用计算机工作。

nowhere /ˈnəʊweə(r); ˈnoˌhwɛr/ *adverb* 副词
not anywhere; at, in or to no place 无处: *There's nowhere to stay in this village.* 这个村子里没有地方住。
nowhere near not at all 绝不: *Ruichi's English is nowhere near as good as yours.* 鲁伊吉的英语远远没有你的好。

nuclear /ˈnju:kliə(r); ˈnuklɪɚ/ *adjective* 形容词
1 of or about the inside part of **atoms** 原子核的（原子叫做 **atom**）: *nuclear physics* 核物理学
2 using the great power that is made by breaking or joining parts of atoms 使用核能的: *nuclear energy* 核能 ◇ *nuclear weapons* 核武器

nudge /nʌdʒ; nʌdʒ/ *verb* 动词 (**nudges, nudging, nudged** /nʌdʒd; nʌdʒd/)
touch or push somebody or something with your elbow 用肘碰或推某人或某物: *Nudge me if I fall asleep in the film.* 我看电影时要是睡着了你就碰碰我。
nudge *noun* 名词
Liz gave me a nudge. 利兹用肘碰了碰我。

nuisance /ˈnju:sns; ˈnusn̩s/ *noun* 名词
a person or thing that causes you trouble 引起麻烦的人或事物: *I've lost my keys. What a nuisance!* 我把钥匙丢了。真讨厌！

numb /nʌm; nʌm/ *adjective* 形容词
not able to feel anything 失去感觉的；麻木的: *My fingers were numb with cold.* 我的手指都冻木了。

number /ˈnʌmbə(r); ˈnʌmbɚ/ *noun* 名词
1 a word like 'two' or 'fifteen', or a symbol or group of symbols like 7 or 130 数字；数目: *Choose a number between ten and one hundred.* 从十到一百之间选出一个数字来。◇ *My phone number is Oxford 56767.* 我的电话号码是牛津56767。
✪ We sometimes write **No** or **no** 有时可写做 **No** 或 **no**: *I live at no 47.* 我住在47号。
2 a group of more than one person or thing 若干；一批；一群: *A large number of our students come from Japan.* 我们学生中有很多日本人。◇ *There are a number of ways you can cook an egg.* 鸡蛋有很多吃法。
number *verb* 动词 (**numbers, numbering, numbered** /ˈnʌmbəd; ˈnʌmbɚd/)
give a number to something 给某事物编号: *Number the pages from one to ten.* 把这些书页从一到十编上号码。

number-plate /ˈnʌmbə pleɪt; ˈnʌmbɚˌplet/ *noun* 名词
the flat piece of metal on the front and back of a car that has numbers and letters on it (its **registration number**)（汽车前后的）号码牌（上面的牌照号码叫做 **registration number**）☞ picture at **car** 见 **car** 词条插图

numerous /ˈnju:mərəs; ˈnumərəs/ *adjective* 形容词
very many 很多: *He writes a lot of letters because he has numerous friends.* 他写了很多信，因为他有很多朋友。

nun /nʌn; nʌn/ *noun* 名词
a religious woman who lives with other religious women in a **convent** 修女（女修道院叫做 **convent**）

nurse¹ /nɜ:s; nɝs/ *noun* 名词
a person whose job is to look after people who are sick or hurt 护士: *My sister works as a nurse in a hospital.* 我姐姐在医院里当护士。

nurse² /nɜ:s; nɝs/ *verb* 动词 (**nurses, nursing, nursed** /nɜ:st; nɝst/)
look after somebody who is sick or hurt 照看生病或受伤的人: *I nursed my father when he was ill.* 我父亲生病时我护理他。

nursery /ˈnɜ:səri; ˈnɝsərɪ/ *noun* 名词 (*plural* 复数作 **nurseries**)
1 a place where young children can stay when their parents are at work 托儿所；保育院
2 a place where people grow and sell plants 苗圃；育苗场
nursery rhyme /ˈnɜ:səri raɪm; ˈnɝsərɪ raɪm/ *noun* 名词
a song or poem for young children 儿歌
nursery school /ˈnɜ:səri sku:l; ˈnɝsərɪ skul/ *noun* 名词

N

a school for children between the ages of three and five 幼儿园

nursing /ˈnɜːsɪŋ; ˈnɝsɪŋ/ *noun* 名词 (no plural 无复数)
the job of being a nurse 护理: *He has decided to go into nursing when he leaves school.* 他打算中学毕业以后做护理工作。

nut /nʌt; nʌt/ *noun* 名词
1 the hard fruit of a tree or bush 坚果: *walnuts, hazelnuts and peanuts* 胡桃、榛子和花生

nuts 坚果

2 a small piece of metal with a hole in the middle that you put on the end of a long piece of metal (called a **bolt**). You use nuts and bolts for fixing things together. 螺母；螺帽（螺栓叫做 **bolt**）

nylon /ˈnaɪlɒn; ˈnaɪlɑn/ *noun* 名词 (no plural 无复数)
very strong material made by machines. Nylon is used for making clothes and other things 尼龙: *a nylon brush* 尼龙刷子

Oo

O /əʊ; o/
1 = **Oh**
2 a way of saying the number '0' 零（"0" 的一种说法）

oak /əʊk; ok/ *noun* 名词
1 (*plural* 复数作 **oaks**) a kind of large tree 栎树；橡树
2 (no plural 无复数) the wood of an oak tree 栎木: *an oak table* 栎木桌子

OAP /ˌəʊ eɪ ˈpiː; ˌo e ˈpi/ *short for* **old-age pensioner** ✳ **old-age pensioner** 的缩略式

oar /ɔː(r); ɔr/ *noun* 名词
a long piece of wood with one flat end. You use oars to move a small boat through water (to **row**). 桨（划桨叫做 **row**）。☞ picture at **row** 见 **row** 词条插图

oasis /əʊˈeɪsɪs; oˈesɪs/ *noun* 名词 (*plural* 复数作 **oases** /əʊˈeɪsiːz; oˈesiz/)
a place in a desert that has trees and water（沙漠中的）绿洲

oath /əʊθ; oθ/ *noun* 名词
a serious promise 誓言；誓词；誓约: *I took an oath in front of a lawyer.* 我在律师面前宣了誓。

oats /əʊts; ots/ *noun* 名词 (plural 复数)
a plant with seeds that we use as food for people and animals 燕麦: *We make porridge from oats.* 我们用燕麦片做粥。

obedient /əˈbiːdiənt; əˈbidɪənt/ *adjective* 形容词
An obedient person does what somebody tells him/her to do 服从的；顺从的；听话的: *He was an obedient child.* 他原是个听话的孩子。✪ opposite 反义词: **disobedient**
obedience /əˈbiːdiəns; əˈbidɪəns/ *noun* 名词 (no plural 无复数)
being obedient 服从；顺从；听话
obediently *adverb* 副词
I called the dog and it followed me obediently. 我一叫那条狗，它就很听话地跟着我。

obey /əˈbeɪ; əˈbe/ *verb* 动词 (**obeys**, **obeying**, **obeyed** /əˈbeɪd; əˈbed/)
do what somebody or something tells you to do 服从；顺从；听话: *You must obey the law.* 必须遵守法律。

object¹ /ˈɒbdʒɪkt; ˈɑbdʒɪkt/ *noun* 名词
1 a thing that you can see and touch 可见到及可触摸的实物；物体: *There was a small round object on the table.* 桌子上有个小的圆形物体。
2 what you plan to do 打算做的事；目标；目的: *His object in life is to become as rich as possible.* 他生活的目标就是越阔气越好。
3 In the sentence 'Jane painted the door', the object of the sentence is 'the door'. 宾语（在 Jane painted the door 一句中，the door 是句子的宾语。）

object² /əbˈdʒekt; əbˈdʒɛkt/ *verb* 动词 (**objects**, **objecting**, **objected**)
not like something or not agree with something 不喜欢或不赞成某事物；反对：*I object to the plan.* 我不同意这个方案。
objection /əbˈdʒekʃn; əbˈdʒɛkʃən/ *noun* 名词
saying or feeling that you do not like something or that you do not agree with something（对某事物）不喜欢或不赞成；反对: *I have no objections to the plan.* 我不反对这个计划。

obligation /ˌɒblɪˈgeɪʃn; ˌɑbləˈgeʃən/ *noun* 名词
something that you must do 必须做的事；责任；义务: *We have an obligation to help.* 我们有责任予以援助。

oblige /əˈblaɪdʒ; əˈblaɪdʒ/ *verb* 动词 (**obliges**, **obliging**, **obliged** /əˈblaɪdʒd; əˈblaɪdʒd/)
be obliged to If you are obliged to do something, you must do it 必须做某事: *You are not obliged to come if you do not want to.* 您要是不想来，就不一定非来不可。

oblong /ˈɒblɒŋ; ˈɑblɔŋ/ *noun* 名词
a shape with two long sides, two short sides and four angles of 90 degrees 长方形 ☞ picture on page C5 见第C5页图
oblong *adjective* 形容词
This page is oblong. 这一页是长方形的。

observation /ˌɒbzəˈveɪʃn; ˌɑbzɚˈveʃən/ *noun* 名词 (no plural 无复数)
watching or being watched carefully 观察；注视

be under observation be watched carefully 被观察；被监视: *The police kept the house under observation.* 警方监视着这所房子。

O

observe /ə'bzɜ:v; əb'zɝv/ *verb* 动词 (**observes**, **observing**, **observed** /ə'bzɜ:vd; əb'zɝvd/)
watch somebody or something carefully; see somebody or something 观察或注视某人或某事物: *The police observed a man leaving the house.* 警察看见有个男子离开那所房子。

obsess /əb'ses; əb'sɛs/ *verb* 动词 (**obsesses**, **obsessing**, **obsessed** /əb'sest; əb'sɛst/)
be obsessed with somebody or 或 **something** think about somebody or something all the time 一直想着某人或某事物: *Debbie is obsessed with football.* 戴比迷上足球了。
obsession /əb'seʃn; əb'sɛʃən/ *noun* 名词
a person or thing that you think about all the time 一直想着的人或事物: *Cars are his obsession.* 他心里总是想着汽车。

obstacle /'ɒbstəkl; 'ɑbstəkḷ/ *noun* 名词
1 something that is in front of you, that you must go over or round before you can go on 障碍物: *The horse jumped over the obstacle.* 那匹马跳过了障碍物。
2 a problem that stops you doing something 障碍

obstinate /'ɒbstɪnət; 'ɑbstənɪt/ *adjective* 形容词
An obstinate person does not change his/her ideas or do what other people want him/her to do 固执的；顽固的: *He's too obstinate to say he's sorry.* 他很固执，就是不道歉。

obstruct /əb'strʌkt; əb'strʌkt/ *verb* 动词 (**obstructs**, **obstructing**, **obstructed**)
be in the way so that somebody or something cannot go past 阻塞通路: *Please move your car—you're obstructing the traffic.* 请移动一下您的汽车——您阻塞交通了。
obstruction /əb'strʌkʃn; əb'strʌkʃən/ *noun* 名词
a thing that stops somebody or something from going past 阻塞物: *The train had to stop because there was an obstruction on the line.* 因为铁轨上有障碍物，火车只好停了下来。

obtain /əb'teɪn; əb'ten/ *verb* 动词 (**obtains**, **obtaining**, **obtained** /əb'teɪnd; əb'tend/)
get something 得到某事物: *Where can I obtain tickets for the play?* 这出戏的票在哪儿买？ ✪ **Get** is the word that we usually use. ＊ **get** 是常用词。

obvious /'ɒbviəs; 'ɑbvɪəs/ *adjective* 形容词
very clear and easy to see or understand 清楚的；明显的；易懂的: *It's obvious that she's not happy.* 她显然很不愉快。
obviously *adverb* 副词
it is easy to see or understand that; clearly 显然；易懂地；清楚地: *He obviously learned English at school—he speaks it very well.* 他显然在学校学过英语——他说得非常好。

occasion /ə'keɪʒn; ə'keʒən/ *noun* 名词
1 a time when something happens（事情发生的）时刻；场合: *I've been to Paris on three or four occasions.* 我去过巴黎三四次。
2 a special time（特殊的）时刻；时机: *A wedding is a big family occasion.* 婚礼是全家的大事。

occasional /ə'keɪʒənl; ə'keʒənḷ/ *adjective* 形容词
that happens sometimes, but not very often 时而发生的（但不经常）；偶尔的: *We get the occasional visitor.* 我们偶尔有客人来。
occasionally /ə'keɪʒənəli; ə'keʒənəlɪ/ *adverb* 副词
sometimes, but not often 有时（但不经常）；偶尔: *I go to London occasionally.* 我偶尔到伦敦去。

occupation /ˌɒkju'peɪʃn; ˌɑkjə'peʃən/ *noun* 名词
1 (*plural* 复数作 **occupations**) a job 职业；工作: *What is your mother's occupation?* 您母亲做什么工作？ ✪ **Job** is the word that we usually use. ＊ **job** 是常用词。
2 (*plural* 复数作 **occupations**) something that you do in your free time 空闲时做的事；业余活动；消遣: *Fishing is his favourite occupation.* 钓鱼是他最喜爱的消遣。
3 (no plural 无复数) living in a house, room, etc（在一所房子里、一间屋子里等的）居住: *The new house is now ready for occupation.* 这所新房子现在可以准备住人了。

4 (no plural 无复数) taking and keeping a town or country in war（战时对城镇或国家的）占领；占据

occupy /ˈɒkjupaɪ; ˈɑkjəˌpaɪ/ *verb* 动词 (**occupies**, **occupying**, **occupied** /ˈɒkjupaɪd; ˈɑkjəˌpaɪd/, **has occupied**)

1 live or be in a place 在某处居住；在某处: *Who occupies the house next door?* 谁住在隔壁的房子里？

2 make somebody busy; take somebody's time 使某人忙碌；占用某人的时间: *The children occupy most of her free time.* 孩子们把她大部分空余时间都占去了。

3 take and keep control of a country, town, etc in a war（战时）占领一国家、城镇等: *The Normans occupied England from 1066.* 诺曼人从1066年起占领了英格兰。

occupied *adjective* 形容词

1 busy 忙碌的: *This work will keep me occupied all week.* 这项工作能让我忙一个星期。

2 being used 被使用；已占用: *Excuse me — is this seat occupied?* 请问——这个座位有人坐吗？

occur /əˈkɜː(r); əˈkɝ/ *verb* 动词 (**occurs**, **occurring**, **occurred** /əˈkɜːd; əˈkɝd/)

happen 发生: *The accident occurred this morning.* 这起事故是今天上午发生的。

occur to somebody come into somebody's mind 想到；想起: *It occurred to me that she didn't know our new address.* 我突然想到她不知道我们的新地址。

ocean /ˈəʊʃn; ˈoʃən/ *noun* 名词

a very big sea 洋；海洋；大海: *the Atlantic Ocean* 大西洋

o'clock /əˈklɒk; əˈklɑk/ *adverb* 副词

a word that you use after the numbers one to twelve for saying what time it is（说钟点时用于1至12数字之后）…点钟 ✪ Be careful! 'O'clock' is only used with full hours 注意！o'clock 只能与整数钟点连用: *I left home at four o'clock and arrived in London at half past five.* 我四点钟离开家，五点半到达伦敦。(*NOT* 不可作 *at half past five o'clock*) ☞ Look at page C8. 见第C8页。

October /ɒkˈtəʊbə(r); ɑkˈtobɚ/ *noun* 名词

the tenth month of the year 十月

octopus /ˈɒktəpəs; ˈɑktəpəs/ *noun* 名词 (*plural* 复数作 **octopuses**)

a sea animal with eight arms 章鱼

odd /ɒd; ɑd/ *adjective* 形容词 (**odder**, **oddest**)

1 strange or unusual 奇怪的；不寻常的: *It's odd that he left without telling anybody.* 他走的时候谁也没告诉，真奇怪。

2 Odd numbers cannot be divided exactly by two 奇数的（不能被2整除的数）: *1, 3, 5 and 7 are all odd numbers.* ＊1、3、5、7都是奇数。✪ opposite 反义词: **even**

3 part of a pair when the other one is not there（一双中的）单个的（缺另一个）: *You're wearing odd socks! One is black and the other is green!* 你穿的两只袜子不是一双！一只黑一只绿！

the odd one out one that is different from all the others 与众不同的人或物；落单的: *'Apple', 'orange', 'cabbage' — which is the odd one out?* 苹果、橙子、洋白菜——哪一个与其他两个不属一类？

oddly *adverb* 副词

strangely 奇怪地: *She behaved very oddly.* 她表现得非常奇怪。

odds and ends /ˌɒdz ənd ˈendz; ˌɑdz ənd ˈɛndz/ *noun* 名词 (plural 复数)

different small things that are not important 琐碎物品: *Sarah went out to buy a few odds and ends for the party.* 萨拉为举办聚会出去买些零星杂物。

of /əv, ɒv; əv, ɑv/ *preposition* 介词

1 a word that shows who or what has or owns something（表示领属关系的词）…的: *the back of the chair* 椅子的背 ◇ *What's the name of this mountain?* 这座山的名字叫什么？◇ *the plays of Shakespeare* 莎士比亚的戏剧

2 a word that you use after an amount, etc 用于数量等之后的词: *a litre of water* 一升水 ◇ *the fourth of July* 七月四日

3 a word that shows what something is or what is in something 表示某物是什么或使用什么的词: *a piece of wood* 一块木头 ◇ *a cup of tea* 一杯茶 ◇ *Is this shirt made of cotton?* 这件衬衫是棉的吗？

4 a word that shows who 表明某人的词: *That's very kind of you.* 非常感谢您。

5 a word that shows that somebody or something is part of a group 表示整体中某人或某事物的词: *One of her friends is a doctor.* 她有个朋友是医生。

6 a word that you use with some adjectives and verbs 与某些形容词或动词连用的词: *I'm proud of you.* 我为你感到骄傲。

O

◇ *This perfume smells of roses.* 这种香水有玫瑰味。

off /ɒf; ɔf/ *preposition, adverb* 介词，副词

1 down or away from something 从某处向下或离开: *He fell off the roof.* 他从房上摔了下来。◇ *We got off the bus.* 我们下了公共汽车。◇ *The thief ran off.* 那个小偷跑了。

2 away from the place where it was 离开原处: *If you're hot, take your coat off.* 您要是热，就把大衣脱了。◇ *Can you clean that paint off the carpet?* 你能把地毯上的这块油漆弄掉吗？

3 not working; not being used 不工作；不被使用: *All the lights are off.* 所有的灯都关着。

4 away 离；远离: *My birthday is not far off.* 我的生日快到了。

5 not at work or school 不工作；不上学: *I had the day off yesterday.* 我昨天放假。

6 joined to something 与某物相连: *The bathroom is off the bedroom.* 浴室通着卧室。

7 not fresh 不新鲜: *This milk is off.* 牛奶不新鲜了。

offence /ə'fens; ə'fɛns/ *noun* 名词

something you do that is against the law 违法行为；罪行: *It is an offence to drive at night without lights.* 夜晚无灯行车是违法的。

take offence become angry or unhappy 生气；不愉快: *He took offence because I said his spelling was bad.* 我说他拼写很差，他就生了气了。

offend /ə'fend; ə'fɛnd/ *verb* 动词 (**offends**, **offending**, **offended**)

make somebody feel angry or unhappy; hurt somebody's feelings 使某人生气或不愉快；触怒；冒犯: *She was offended when you said she was fat.* 你说她胖，她生了气了。

offense *American English for* **offence** 美式英语，即 **offence**

offer /'ɒfə(r); 'ɔfɚ/ *verb* 动词 (**offers**, **offering**, **offered** /'ɒfəd; 'ɔfɚd/)

say or show that you will do or give something if another person wants it 说出或表示出愿意做某事物或愿意给某事物（若对方要的话）；请人接受: *She offered me a cake.* 她让我吃蛋糕。◇ *I offered to help her.* 我向她表示愿意帮助她。

offer *noun* 名词

Thanks for the offer, but I don't need any help. 我并不需要帮助，但您的好意我心领了。

office /'ɒfɪs; 'ɔfɪs/ *noun* 名词

1 a room or building with desks and telephones, where people work 办公室；办公楼；办事处: *I work in an office.* 我在办事处上班。

2 a room or building where you can buy something or get information 购买某物的处所；询问处: *The ticket office is at the front of the station.* 售票处在车站前边。◇ *the post office* 邮政局

3 one part of the government 政府的部门: *the Foreign Office* 外交部

officer /'ɒfɪsə(r); 'ɔfəsɚ/ *noun* 名词

1 a person in the army, navy or air force who gives orders to other people 军官: *a naval officer* 海军军官

2 a person who does important work, especially for the government 做重要工作的人（尤指为政府工作的）；官员: *a prison officer* 监狱看守 ◇ *police officers* 警察

official[1] /ə'fɪʃl; ə'fɪʃəl/ *adjective* 形容词

of or from the government or somebody who is important （来自）政府或重要人物的；官方的；正式的: *an official report* 官方的报道 ◇ *The news is now official — they are getting married!* 这个消息现在已经作准——他们快结婚了！✪ opposite 反义词: **unofficial**

officially *adverb* 副词

I think I've got the job, but they will tell me officially on Friday. 我算是得到这份工作了，可是他要到星期五再正式通知我。

official[2] /ə'fɪʃl; ə'fɪʃəl/ *noun* 名词

a person who does important work, especially for the government 做重要工作的人（尤指为政府工作的）；官员: *government officials* 政府官员

off-licence /'ɒf laɪsns; 'ɔf,laɪsn̩s/ *noun* 名词

a shop where you can buy drinks like beer and wine 卖酒的铺子；酒店

often /'ɒfn; 'ɔfən/ *adverb* 副词

many times 常常；经常；时常: *We often play football on Sundays.* 我们星期日常常踢足球。◇ *I've often seen her on the train.* 我常在火车上碰见她。◇ *I don't write to him very often.* 我不常给他写信。◇ *How often do you visit her?* 你多长时间去探望她一次？

O

every so often sometimes, but not often 有时（但不经常）: *Every so often she phones me.* 她偶尔给我来个电话。

oh /əʊ; o/

1 a word that shows a strong feeling, like surprise or fear 表示强烈感情的词（例如惊奇或害怕）: *Oh no! I've lost my keys!* 糟糕！我把钥匙丢了！

2 a word that you say before other words 用于其他词语之前的词: *'What time is it?' 'Oh, about two o'clock.'* "现在几点钟了？""噢，大约两点钟了。"

Oh dear words that show you are surprised or unhappy 表示惊奇或不愉快的词: *Oh dear — have you hurt yourself?* 哎呀——你受伤了吗？

Oh well words that you use when you are not happy about something, but you cannot change it 表示不喜欢某事物（却又无法改变）的词: *'I'm too busy to go out tonight.' 'Oh well, I'll see you tomorrow then.'* "我很忙，今天晚上不能出去。""哟，那么我明天再见你吧。"

oil /ɔɪl; ɔɪl/ *noun* 名词 (no plural 无复数)

1 a thick liquid that comes from plants or animals and that you use in cooking（得自动植物的，可食用的）油；食油: *Fry the onions in oil.* 把洋葱炸一下。

2 a thick liquid that comes from under the ground or the sea. We burn oil or use it in machines.（得自陆地或海洋的）油；石油（用作燃料或用于机器）

oil-painting /ˈɔɪl peɪntɪŋ; ˈɔɪlˌpentɪŋ/ *noun* 名词

a picture that has been done with paint made from oil 油画

oil rig /ˈɔɪl rɪɡ; ˈɔɪl ˌrɪɡ/ *noun* 名词

a special building with machines that dig for oil under the sea or on land 石油钻塔

oily /ˈɔɪli; ˈɔɪlɪ/ *adjective* 形容词 (**oilier**, **oiliest**)

like oil or covered with oil 像油的；有油的: *I don't like oily food.* 我不爱吃油腻的食物。◇ *an oily liquid* 油状的液体

OK, okay /ˌəʊˈkeɪ; ˈoˈke/

yes; all right 好吧；行: *'Do you want to go to a party?' 'OK.'* "你想去参加聚会吗？""好哇。"

OK, okay *adjective* , *adverb* 形容词，副词

all right; good or well enough 行；好的: *Is it okay to sit here?* 坐这儿行吗？

old /əʊld; old/ *adjective* 形容词 (**older**, **oldest**)

1 If you are old, you have lived for a long time 年老的: *My grandfather is very old.* 我祖父很老了。◇ *My sister is older than me.* 我姐姐比我大。✪ opposite 反义词: **young** ☞ picture on page C26 见第C26页图

2 made or bought a long time ago 很久以前做的或买的；旧的: *an old house* 旧房子 ✪ opposite 反义词: **new** ☞ picture on page C27 见第C27页图

3 You use 'old' to show the age of somebody or something 用以表示年龄的词: *He's nine years old.* 他九岁了。◇ *How old are you?* 您多少岁了？◇ *a six-year-old boy* 六岁的男孩儿

4 that you did or had before now 以前干的或有的；原先的: *My old job was more interesting than this one.* 我以前的那份工作比现在的有意思。✪ opposite 反义词: **new**

5 that you have known for a long time 相识很久的: *Jenny is an old friend — we were at school together.* 珍妮是老朋友了—我们同过学。

the old *noun* 名词 (plural 复数)

old people 老人（总称）

old age /ˌəʊld ˈeɪdʒ; ˌold ˈedʒ/ *noun* 名词 (no plural 无复数)

the part of your life when you are old 老年；晚年

old-age pension /ˌəʊld eɪdʒ ˈpenʃn; ˌoldedʒ ˈpɛnʃən/ *noun* 名词 (no plural 无复数)

money that you get from a government or a company when you are old and do not work any more (when you are **retired**) 养老金（年老退休叫做 **retire**）

old-age pensioner /ˌəʊld eɪdʒ ˈpenʃənə(r); ˌoldedʒ ˈpɛnʃənɚ/ *noun* 名词

a person who has an old-age pension 领取养老金的人 ✪ The short form is **OAP**. 缩略式为 **OAP**。

old-fashioned /ˌəʊld ˈfæʃnd; ˈold-ˈfæʃənd/ *adjective* 形容词

not modern; that people do not often use or wear now 过时的；老式的: *Clothes from the 1970s look old-fashioned now.* ＊20世纪70年代的衣服现在看来已经过时了。

olive /ˈɒlɪv; ˈɑlɪv/ *noun* 名词

a small green or black fruit, that people eat or make into oil 橄榄

omelette /ˈɒmlət; ˈɑmlɪt/ *noun* 名词
eggs that you mix together and cook in oil 煎蛋（打匀后煎的）: *a cheese omelette* 干酪煎蛋

O

omit /əˈmɪt; əˈmɪt/ *verb* 动词 (**omits, omitting, omitted**)
not include something; leave something out 不包括某事物；遗漏: *Omit question 2 and do question 3.* 不要做第2题，要做第3题。✪ It is more usual to say **leave out**. ✳ **leave out** 是常用词语。

on /ɒn; ɑn/ *preposition, adverb* 介词，副词
1 a word that shows where 表示在何处的词；在…上: *Your book is on the table.* 您的书在桌子上。◇ *The number is on the door.* 号数在门上。◇ *There is a good film on TV tonight.* 今天晚上电视上有个好影片。◇ *I've got a cut on my hand.* 我手上有个伤口。☞ picture on page C1 见第C1页图
2 a word that shows when 表示在何时的词: *My birthday is on 6 May.* 我的生日是5月6日。◇ *I'll see you on Monday.* 我星期一见你。☞ Look at page C29. 见第C29页。
3 a word that shows that somebody or something continues 表示某人或某事物继续进行: *You can't stop here—drive on.* 您不能停在这里——把车往前开。
4 about 关于: *a book on cars* 关于汽车的书
5 working; being used 正在工作；正被使用: *Is the light on or off?* 灯是开着还是关着？
6 using something 使用某事物: *I spoke to Jenny on the telephone.* 我跟珍妮通过电话。◇ *I came here on foot* (= walking). 我是走着来的。
7 covering your body 遮蔽身体；穿着；戴着: *Put your coat on.* 你把大衣穿上。
8 happening 发生: *What's on at the cinema?* 电影院演什么？
9 when something happens 当某事发生时: *She telephoned me on her return from New York.* 她从纽约一回来就给我打了个电话。
on and on without stopping 不停地；不断地: *He went* (= talked) *on and on about his girlfriend.* 他滔滔不绝地谈论着他的女朋友。

once /wʌns; wʌns/ *adverb* 副词
1 one time 一次: *I've only been to Spain once.* 我只去过一次西班牙。◇ *He phones us once a week* (= once every week). 他每星期给我们打一次电话。
2 at some time in the past 在过去的某时；曾经: *This house was once a school.* 这座楼以前是学校。
at once 1 immediately; now 立刻；马上: *Come here at once!* 马上到这里来！
2 at the same time 同时: *I can't do two things at once!* 我无法同时做两件事！
for once this time only 仅此一次: *For once I agree with you.* 只有这一次我同意你的意见。
once again, once more again, as before 再一次: *Can you explain it to me once more?* 您再给我解释一次行吗？
once or twice a few times; not often 一两次；几次；不常: *I've only met them once or twice.* 我只见过他们一两次。

once *conjunction* 连词
as soon as 一…就…: *Once you've finished your homework you can go out.* 你一做完家庭作业就能出去。

one[1] /wʌn; wʌn/ *noun, adjective* 名词，形容词
1 the number 1 一: *One and one make two* (1 + 1 = 2). 一加一等于二 (1 + 1 = 2)。◇ *Only one person spoke.* 只有一个人讲过话。◇ *One of my friends is an actress.* 我有个朋友是（女）演员。
2 a 某一: *I saw her one day last week.* 我上星期有一天见过她。
3 only 唯一的: *You are the one person I can trust.* 你是我唯一能够信任的人。
4 the same 同一的: *All the birds flew in one direction.* 鸟都朝着同一个方向飞走了。
one by one first one, then the next, etc; one at a time 一个一个地；逐一: *Please come in one by one.* 请一个一个地进来。

one[2] /wʌn; wʌn/ *pronoun* 代词
a word that you say instead of the name of a person or thing 用以代替所说的人或事物的名称的词: *I've got some bananas. Do you want one?* 我有些香蕉。你要一个吗？◇ *'Which shirt do you prefer?' 'This one.'* "您喜欢哪件衬衫？""这一件。" ◇ *Here are some books—take the ones you want.* 这里有些书——你随便拿几本吧。
one another words that show that somebody does the same thing as another person 相互；彼此: *John and*

Mark looked at one another (= John looked at Mark and Mark looked at John). 约翰和马克面面相觑（= 约翰看马克，马克看约翰）。

one³ /wʌn; wʌn/ *pronoun* 代词
any person; a person 任何人；一个人: *One can fly to New York in three hours.* 坐飞机三小时就可以到纽约。✪ It is formal to use 'one' in this way. 在这种情况下用 one 字显得庄重些。We often use **you**. 一般用 **you** 字。

oneself /wʌn'self; wʌn'sɛlf/ *pronoun* 代词
1 a word that shows the same person as 'one' in a sentence 自己；本身: *to hurt oneself* 把自己弄伤了
2 a word that makes 'one' stronger 用以加强 one 的语气的词: *One can do it oneself.* 任何人自己都可以做。
by oneself **1** alone; without other people 独自地；单独地（没有别人相伴） **2** without help 独自地；单独地（没有别人帮助）

one-way /ˌwʌn 'weɪ; 'wʌn'we/ *adjective* 形容词
1 A one-way street is a street where you can drive in one direction only.（指道路）单行的
2 A one-way ticket is a ticket to travel to a place, but not back again.（指票）单程的 ✪ opposite 反义词: **return**

onion /'ʌniən; 'ʌnjən/ *noun* 名词
a round vegetable with a strong taste and smell 洋葱；葱头: *onion soup* 洋葱汤 ◇ *Cutting onions can make you cry.* 切洋葱有时能流眼泪。

onion 洋葱

only¹ /'əʊnli; 'onlɪ/ *adjective* 形容词
with no others 唯一的；仅有的: *She's the only girl in her class—all the other students are boys.* 她是班上唯一的女同学——其他都是男生。
an only child a child who has no brothers or sisters 独生子女

only² /'əʊnli; 'onlɪ/ *adverb* 副词
and nobody or nothing else; no more than 只；仅；仅仅: *I invited twenty people to the party, but only five came.* 我邀请了二十人参加聚会，可是只来了五个人。◇ *We can't have dinner now. It's only four o'clock!* 我们不能现在吃晚饭。现在才四点钟！◇ *We only waited five minutes.* 我们只等了五分钟。
only just **1** a short time before 刚刚: *We've only just arrived.* 我们刚刚到。 **2** almost not 差一点儿没；几乎不: *We only just had enough money to pay for the meal.* 我们的钱几乎不够付那顿饭的。

only³ /'əʊnli; 'onlɪ/ *conjunction* 连词
but 但是: *I like this bag, only it's too expensive.* 我很喜欢这个提包，可是太贵了。

onto, on to /'ɒntə, 'ɒntu, 'ɒntu:; 'ɑntə, 'ɑntu/ *preposition* 介词
to a place on somebody or something 向某人或某事物处: *The cat jumped on to the table.* 猫跳到桌子上去了。◇ *The bottle fell onto the floor.* 瓶子掉到地上了。

onwards /'ɒnwədz; 'ɑnwədz/, **onward** /'ɒnwəd; 'ɑnwəd/ *adverb* 副词
1 and after 以及以后: *I shall be at home from eight o'clock onwards.* 我在八点钟以后都在家。
2 forward; further 向前: *The soldiers marched onwards until they came to a bridge.* 士兵齐步前进来到一座桥前。

open¹ /'əʊpən; 'opən/ *adjective* 形容词
1 not closed, so that people or things can go in or out 开着的（人或物可以出入）: *Leave the windows open.* 让窗户都开着吧。☞ picture on page C27 见第C27页图
2 not closed or covered, so that you can see inside 开着的（可以看到里面）: *The book lay open on the table.* 那本书在桌上摊开放着。◇ *an open box* 开着的盒子
3 ready for people to go in 敞开的（大家可以进入）: *The bank is open from 9 a.m. to 4 p.m.* 银行从上午9点到下午4点营业。
4 that anybody can do or visit, for example 公开的；开放的（例如任何人均可做或参观）: *The competition is open to all children under the age of 14.* ✳ 14岁以下儿童均可参加这一竞赛。
5 with not many buildings, trees, etc 建筑物、树木等不多的；空旷的: *open fields* 空旷的田地
in the open air outside 露天的；在户外: *We had our lunch in the open air.* 我们是在户外吃的午饭。

open² /'əʊpən; 'opən/ *verb* 动词 (**opens, opening, opened** /'əʊpənd; 'opənd/)
1 move so that people or things can go

in, out or through 打开（人或物可以出入或穿过）: *It was hot, so I opened a window.* 天气很热，我把窗户打开了。◇ *The door opened and a man came in.* 门开了，进来了一个男子。

O

2 move so that something is not closed or covered 张开（使某物不遮住）: *Open your eyes!* 睁开眼睛！

3 fold something out or back, to show what is inside 翻开；掀开（展示内容）: *Open your books.* 把书打开。

4 be ready for people to use; start 准备好供人使用；开始: *Banks don't open on Sundays.* 银行星期日不开门。

5 say that something can start or is ready 宣布某事物开始或已准备好: *The President opened the new hospital.* 主席宣布新医院开始营业。

✪ opposite 反义词: **close** or 或 **shut**

open³ /ˈəʊpən; ˈopən/ *noun* 名词 (no plural 无复数)

in the open outside 露天的；在户外: *I like to be out in the open at weekends.* 我喜欢周末到户外活动。

open-air /ˈəʊpən ˈeə(r); ˈopənˈɛr/ *adjective* 形容词

outside 露天的；户外的: *an open-air concert* 露天音乐会

opener /ˈəʊpnə(r); ˈopənɚ/ *noun* 名词

a thing that you use for opening tins or bottles 开罐头或瓶盖的工具；开瓶器；开罐器: *a tin-opener* 开罐器

opening /ˈəʊpnɪŋ; ˈopənɪŋ/ *noun* 名词

1 a hole or space in something where people or things can go in and out; a hole（人或物可以出入的）洞；开口；通道: *The sheep got out of the field through an opening in the fence.* 羊从篱笆的豁口跑到牧场外面去了。

2 when something is opened 开始；开端: *the opening of the new theatre* 新剧院开始营业

openly /ˈəʊpənli; ˈopənlɪ/ *adverb* 副词

not secretly; without trying to hide anything 公开地；坦率地: *She told me openly that she didn't agree.* 她直率地告诉我她不同意。

opera /ˈɒprə; ˈɑpərə/ *noun* 名词

a play where the actors sing most of the words 歌剧: *Do you like opera?* 您喜欢歌剧吗？◇ *We went to see an opera by Verdi.* 我们去看了一出威尔地的歌剧。

opera-house /ˈɒprə haʊs; ˈɑpərə haus/ *noun* 名词

a building where you can see operas 歌剧院

operate /ˈɒpəreɪt; ˈɑpəˌret/ *verb* 动词 (**operates, operating, operated**)

1 work or make something work 工作或使某事物工作；运转；操纵: *How do you operate this machine?* 怎样操纵这台机器？◇ *I don't know how this computer operates.* 我不知道这个计算机是怎样工作的。

2 cut a person's body to take out or mend a part inside 动手术: *The doctor will operate on her leg tomorrow.* 医生明天给她做腿部手术。

> ✪ A doctor who operates is called a **surgeon**. 外科医生叫做 **surgeon**。A surgeon's work is called **surgery**. 手术叫做 **surgery**。

operation /ˌɒpəˈreɪʃn; ˌɑpəˈreʃən/ *noun* 名词

1 cutting a person's body to take out or mend a part inside 手术: *He had an operation on his eye.* 他的眼睛动过手术。

2 something that happens, that needs a lot of people or careful planning 需要很多人的或需要周密计划的行动: *a military operation* 军事行动

operator /ˈɒpəreɪtə(r); ˈɑpəˌretɚ/ *noun* 名词

1 a person who makes a machine work 操纵机器的人；操作员: *She's a computer operator.* 她是计算机操作员。

2 a person who works for a telephone company and helps people to make calls 话务员；接线生: *In Britain, you dial 100 for the operator.* 在英国，可拨100找话务员。

opinion /əˈpɪniən; əˈpɪnjən/ *noun* 名词

what you think about something 意见；看法: *What's your opinion of his work?* 您对他的工作有什么意见？◇ *In my opinion,* (= I think that) *she's wrong.* 我认为她不对。

opponent /əˈpəʊnənt; əˈponənt/ *noun* 名词

a person that you fight or argue with, or play a game against（打斗或争论或比赛的）对手，对方: *The team beat their opponents easily.* 这个队轻易把对手都打败了。

O

opportunity /ˌɒpəˈtjuːnəti; ˌɑpɚˈtunətɪ/ *noun* 名词 (*plural* 复数作 **opportunities**)
a time when you can do something that you want to do; a chance 想做某事而能做到的时候；机会: *I was only in Paris for two days and I didn't get the opportunity to visit the Louvre.* 我在巴黎只呆了两天，没有机会参观罗浮宫博物馆。

oppose /əˈpəʊz; əˈpoz/ *verb* 动词 (**opposes**, **opposing**, **opposed** /əˈpəʊzd; əˈpozd/)
try to stop or change something because you do not like it 尽力阻止或改变某事物；反对: *A lot of people opposed the new law.* 很多人反对这项新法规。
as opposed to something words that you use to show that you are talking about one thing, not something different 用以表示谈论的是一件事（而不是其他事）的词语: *She teaches at the college, as opposed to the university.* 她在学院任教，不是在大学任教。
be opposed to something disagree strongly with something 强烈反对某事物: *I am opposed to the plan.* 我很反对这个计划。

opposite[1] /ˈɒpəzɪt; ˈɑpəzɪt/ *adjective, adverb, preposition* 形容词，副词，介词
1 across from where somebody or something is; on the other side 另一侧（的）；相对着（的）: *The church is on the opposite side of the road from my flat.* 教堂是在我住的公寓一侧马路的对面。◇ *You sit here, and I'll sit opposite.* 你坐在这儿，我坐在对面。◇ *The bank is opposite the supermarket.* 银行在超级市场的对面。☞ picture on page C1 见第C1页图
2 as different as possible 相反的: *North is the opposite direction to south.* 北和南的方向相反。

opposite[2] /ˈɒpəzɪt; ˈɑpəzɪt/ *noun* 名词
a word or thing that is as different as possible from another word or thing 反义词；相反的事物: *'Hot' is the opposite of 'cold'.* "热"是"冷"的反义词。

opposition /ˌɒpəˈzɪʃn; ˌɑpəˈzɪʃən/ *noun* 名词 (no plural 无复数)
disagreeing with something and trying to stop it 反对；对抗: *There was a lot of opposition to the plan.* 有很多人反对这个计划。

optician /ɒpˈtɪʃn; ɑpˈtɪʃən/ *noun* 名词
a person who finds out how well you can see and sells you glasses（兼配制眼镜的）验光师 ✪ The place where an optician works is called an **optician's**. 有验光师工作的眼镜店叫做 **optician's**。

optimism /ˈɒptɪmɪzəm; ˈɑptəˌmɪzəm/ *noun* 名词 (no plural 无复数)
thinking that good things will happen 乐观 ✪ opposite 反义词: **pessimism**
optimist /ˈɒptɪmɪst; ˈɑptəmɪst/ *noun* 名词
a person who always thinks that good things will happen 乐观的人；乐观主义者

optimistic /ˌɒptɪˈmɪstɪk; ˌɑptəˈmɪstɪk/ *adjective* 形容词
If you are optimistic, you think that good things will happen 乐观的；乐观主义的: *I'm optimistic about winning.* 我对获胜抱乐观态度。

option /ˈɒpʃn; ˈɑpʃən/ *noun* 名词
a thing that you can choose 可供选择的事物: *If you're going to France, there are two options—you can go by plane or by boat.* 要想到法国去有两个途径可供选择——可以坐飞机或者坐轮船。

optional /ˈɒpʃənl; ˈɑpʃənl̩/ *adjective* 形容词
that you can choose or not choose 选取或不选取均可的: *All students must learn English, but German is optional.* 所有学生必须学习英语，但是德语可以选修。✪ opposite 反义词: **compulsory**

or /ɔː(r); ɔr/ *conjunction* 连词
1 a word that joins the words for different things that you can choose（用于陈述句中）或者；（用于疑问句中）还是: *Is it blue or green?* 是蓝的还是绿的？◇ *Are you coming or not?* 你来不来？◇ *You can have soup, salad or sandwiches.* 您可以要汤、色拉或者三明治。
2 if not, then 否则；要不然: *Go now, or you'll be late.* 现在走吧，要不然你就迟到了。

oral /ˈɔːrəl; ˈɔrəl/ *adjective* 形容词
spoken, not written 口头的；口述的: *an oral test in English* 英语口试

orange[1] /ˈɒrɪndʒ; ˈɔrɪndʒ/ *noun* 名词
a round fruit with a colour between red and yellow, and a thick skin 柑橘；橙子: *orange juice* 橙子汁

orange 柑橘

O

orange[2] /ˈɒrɪndʒ; ˈɔrɪndʒ/ *adjective* 形容词
with a colour that is between red and yellow 橘红色的；橙黄色的: *orange paint* 橘红色的涂料
orange *noun* 名词
Orange is my favourite colour. 橙黄色是我最喜欢的颜色。

orbit /ˈɔːbɪt; ˈɔrbɪt/ *noun* 名词
the path of one thing that is moving round another thing in space（天体运行的）轨道
orbit *verb* 动词 (**orbits**, **orbiting**, **orbited**)
move round something in space 在太空环绕某物的轨道上运行: *The spacecraft is orbiting the moon.* 航天器在环绕月球的轨道上运行着。

orchard /ˈɔːtʃəd; ˈɔrtʃɚd/ *noun* 名词
a place where a lot of fruit trees grow 果园

orchestra /ˈɔːkɪstrə; ˈɔrkɪstrə/ *noun* 名词
a big group of people who play different musical instruments together 管弦乐队

ordeal /ɔːˈdiːl; ɔrˈdil/ *noun* 名词
a very bad or painful thing that happens to somebody 苦难经历；严峻考验: *He was lost in the mountains for a week without food or water — it was a terrible ordeal.* 他在山里迷了路，一个星期既没有食物又没有水——受尽了痛苦的折磨。

order[1] /ˈɔːdə(r); ˈɔrdɚ/ *noun* 名词
1 (no plural 无复数) the way that you place people or things together 次序；顺序: *The names are in alphabetical order* (= with the names that begin with A first, then B, then C, etc). 名字是按字母顺序排列的（= 先是名字开头字母是A的、然后是B的、然后是C的，以此类推）。
2 (no plural 无复数) when everything is in the right place or everybody is doing the right thing 整齐；有条理: *Our teacher likes order in the classroom.* 我们老师喜欢教室里井井有条。
3 (*plural* 复数作 **orders**) words that tell somebody to do something 命令: *Soldiers must always obey orders.* 军人必须永远服从命令。
4 (*plural* 复数作 **orders**) asking somebody to make, send or bring you something 指示；定货: *The waiter came and took our order* (= we told him what we wanted to eat). 服务员前来听取我们的要求（= 我们把我们要吃的东西告诉他）。
in order with everything in the right place 整齐地；有条理: *Are these papers in order?* 这些文件整理好了吗？
in order to so that you can do something 以便做某事: *We arrived early in order to buy our tickets.* 我们到得很早好买到票。
out of order not working 不工作；出故障: *I couldn't ring you – the phone was out of order.* 我没法给你打电话——电话坏了。

order[2] /ˈɔːdə(r); ˈɔrdɚ/ *verb* 动词 (**orders**, **ordering**, **ordered** /ˈɔːdəd; ˈɔrdɚd/)
1 tell somebody that they must do something 命令；吩咐: *The doctor ordered me to stay in bed.* 医生吩咐我卧床。
2 say that you want something to be made, sent, brought, etc 指示；定货: *The shop didn't have the book I wanted, so I ordered it.* 书店没有我要的书，所以我预订了一本。◇ *When the waiter came I ordered an omelette.* 服务员来的时候我点了一份煎鸡蛋。

ordinary /ˈɔːdnri; ˈɔrdnɛrɪ/ *adjective* 形容词
normal; not special or unusual 平常的；正常的；通常的: *Simon was wearing a suit, but I was in my ordinary clothes.* 西蒙穿着套装，而我穿着平日穿的衣服。
out of the ordinary unusual; strange 不正常的；奇怪的: *Did you see anything out of the ordinary?* 你看见有什么反常现象吗？

ore /ɔː(r); ɔr/ *noun* 名词
rock or earth from which you get metal 矿石；矿砂: *iron ore* 铁矿石

organ /ˈɔːgən; ˈɔrgən/ *noun* 名词
1 a part of the body that has a special purpose, for example the heart or the liver 器官（例如心脏或肝脏）
2 a big musical instrument like a piano, with pipes that air goes through to make sounds 风琴: *She plays the organ in church.* 她在教堂里弹奏风琴。

organic /ɔːˈgænɪk; ɔrˈgænɪk/ *adjective* 形容词
1 of living things 有机的: *organic chemistry* 有机化学

2 grown in a natural way, without using chemicals 自然生长的（不使用化学肥料的）: *organic vegetables* 不施化肥的蔬菜

organization /ˌɔːɡənaɪˈzeɪʃn; ˌɔrɡənəˈzeʃən/ *noun* 名词

1 (*plural* 复数作 **organizations**) a group of people who work together for a special purpose 组织；机构；团体: *He works for an organization that helps old people.* 他在一所协助老年人的机构里工作。

2 (no plural 无复数) planning or arranging something 计划；安排；组织: *She's busy with the organization of her daughter's wedding.* 她忙着筹备女儿的婚礼。

organize /ˈɔːɡənaɪz; ˈɔrɡənˌaɪz/ *verb* 动词 (**organizes**, **organizing**, **organized** /ˈɔːɡənaɪzd; ˈɔrɡənˌaɪzd/)

plan or arrange something 计划或安排某事物；组织: *Our teacher has organized a visit to the museum.* 我们老师组织了参观博物馆的活动。

oriental /ˌɔːriˈentl; ˌɔrɪˈɛntl̩/ *adjective* 形容词

of or from eastern countries, for example China or Japan 东方国家的（例如中国或日本）: *oriental art* 东方美术

origin /ˈɒrɪdʒɪn; ˈɑrədʒɪn/ *noun* 名词

the beginning; the start of something 开端；起始: *Many English words have Latin origins.* 英语有很多词来自拉丁语。

original /əˈrɪdʒənl; əˈrɪdʒənl̩/ *adjective* 形容词

1 first; earliest 最初的；原先的: *I have the car now, but my sister was the original owner.* 这辆汽车原来是我姐姐的，现在是我的了。

2 new and different 新颖的；不一般的: *His poems are very original.* 他的诗别具一格。

3 real, not copied 真正的；非复制的: *original paintings* 真正原作的画儿

original *noun* 名词

This is a copy of the painting — the original is in the National Gallery. 这幅画儿是复制品——原作藏于国立美术馆。

originally /əˈrɪdʒənəli; əˈrɪdʒənl̩ɪ/ *adverb* 副词

in the beginning; at first 最初；原先: *This building was originally the home of a rich family, but now it's a hotel.* 这座楼原来是个富家的住宅，现在是旅馆了。

ornament /ˈɔːnəmənt; ˈɔrnəmənt/ *noun* 名词

a thing that we have because it is beautiful, not because it is useful 装饰物: *Their house is full of china ornaments.* 他们家有很多瓷器摆设。

ornamental /ˌɔːnəˈmentl; ˌɔrnəˈmɛntl̩/ *adjective* 形容词

There is an ornamental pond in the garden. 花园里有个观赏水池。

orphan /ˈɔːfn; ˈɔrfən/ *noun* 名词

a child whose mother and father are dead 孤儿

ostrich /ˈɒstrɪtʃ; ˈɔstrɪtʃ/ *noun* 名词 (*plural* 复数作 **ostriches**)

a very big bird from Africa. Ostriches have very long legs and can run fast, but they cannot fly. 鸵鸟

other /ˈʌðə(r); ˈʌðɚ/ *adjective, pronoun* 形容词，代词

as well as or different from the one or ones I have said 其他的；另外的；别的: *Carmen and Maria are Spanish, but the other students in my class are Japanese.* 我们班上卡门和玛丽亚是西班牙人，其余的学生都是日本人。◇ *I can only find one shoe. Have you seen the other one?* 我只找到一只鞋。你看见另一只了吗？◇ *I saw her on the other side of the road.* 我看见她在马路对面。◇ *John and Claire arrived at nine o'clock, but the others* (= the other people) *were late.* 约翰和克莱尔是九点钟到的，别的人都迟到了。

other than except; apart from 除了（表示所说的不包括在内）: *I haven't told anybody other than you.* 除了你以外，我谁也没告诉。

some ... or other words that show you are not sure 表示无把握的词语: *I can't find my glasses. I know I put them somewhere or other.* 我找不着眼镜了。我好像把它放在什么地方了。

the other day not many days ago 不久前的一天: *I saw your brother the other day.* 我前几天看见你哥哥了。

otherwise /ˈʌðəwaɪz; ˈʌðɚˌwaɪz/ *adverb* 副词

1 in all other ways 在其他方面；除此以外: *The house is a bit small, but otherwise it's very nice.* 这所房子小一点儿，除此之外倒都很好。

2 in a different way 不同地: *Most people*

agreed, but Rachel thought otherwise. 大多数人都同意了，可是雷切尔却不以为然。

otherwise *conjunction* 连词

if not 要不然；否则: *Hurry up, otherwise you'll be late.* 快点儿吧，要不你就迟到了。

ouch /aʊtʃ; aʊtʃ/

You say 'ouch' when you suddenly feel pain 表示突然疼痛的词: *Ouch! That hurts!* 哎哟！真疼！

ought to /'ɔ:t tə, 'ɔ:t tu, 'ɔ:t tu:; 'ɔttə, 'ɔttu/ *modal verb* 情态动词

1 words that you use to tell or ask somebody what is the right thing to do 应该: *It's late — you ought to go home.* 天晚了——你得回家了。◇ *Ought I to ring her?* 我应当给她打个电话吗？

2 words that you use to say what you think will happen or what you think is true 表示推测的词: *Tim has worked very hard, so he ought to pass the exam.* 蒂姆非常用功，所以他准能考及格。◇ *That film ought to be good.* 那部影片一定很好。

☞ Look at the Note on page 314 to find out more about **modal verbs**. 见第314页对 **modal verbs** 的进一步解释。

ounce /aʊns; aʊns/ *noun* 名词

a measure of weight (= 28.35 grams). There are 16 ounces in a **pound** 盎司（重量单位，等于28.35克。16盎司等于1磅，磅叫做 **pound**）: *four ounces of flour* 四盎司的面粉 ✪ The short way of writing 'ounce' is **oz** ✳ ounce 的缩写形式为 **oz**: *6 oz butter* ✳ 6盎司的黄油

☞ Note at **pound** 见 **pound** 词条注释

our /ɑ:(r), 'aʊə(r); ɑr, aʊr/ *adjective* 形容词

of us 我们的: *This is our house.* 这是我们的房子。

ours /ɑ:z, 'aʊəz; ɑrz, aʊrz/ *pronoun* 代词

something that belongs to us 我们的: *Your car is the same as ours.* 你们的汽车跟我们的一样。

ourselves /ɑ:'selvz, aʊə'selvz; ɑr-'sɛlvz, aʊr'sɛlvz/ *pronoun* 代词 (plural 复数)

1 a word that shows the same people that you have just talked about（用做反身代词）我们自己: *We made ourselves some coffee.* 我们煮了些咖啡喝。

2 a word that makes 'we' stronger（用做反身强调代词）我们自己；我们本身: *We built the house ourselves.* 这所房子是我们自己盖的。

by ourselves **1** alone; without other people 我们独自地；我们单独地（没有别人相伴）: *We went on holiday by ourselves.* 我们独自过的假日。**2** without help 我们独自地；我们单独地（没有别人帮助）

out /aʊt; aʊt/ *adjective, adverb* 形容词，副词

1 away from a place; from inside 不在某地（的）；向外（的）: *When you go out, please close the door.* 您出去的时候请把门关上。◇ *She opened the box and took out a gun.* 她把箱子打开，取出了一枝枪。

2 not at home or not in the place where you work 不在家；不在工作地点: *I phoned Steve but he was out.* 我给史蒂夫打过电话，他不在。◇ *I went out to the cinema last night.* 我昨天晚上看电影去了。

3 not burning or shining 熄灭: *The fire went out.* 火灭了。

4 not hidden; that you can see 显露出: *Look! The sun is out!* 嘿！太阳出来了！◇ *All the flowers are out* (= open). 花全都开了。

5 in a loud voice 大声地: *She cried out in pain.* 她疼得大叫起来。

outbreak /'aʊtbreɪk; 'aʊtˌbrek/ *noun* 名词

the sudden start of something 突然发生；爆发；发作: *There have been outbreaks of fighting in the city.* 城里突然打了起来。

outdoor /'aʊtdɔ:(r); 'aʊtˌdɔr/ *adjective* 形容词

done or used outside a building 户外的；露天的: *Football and cricket are outdoor games.* 足球和板球都是户外运动。✪ opposite 反义词: **indoor**

outdoors /ˌaʊt'dɔ:z; aʊt'dɔrz/ *adverb* 副词

outside a building 在户外；在露天: *In summer we sometimes eat outdoors.* 我们夏天有时候在户外吃饭。✪ opposite 反义词: **indoors**

outer /'aʊtə(r); 'aʊtɚ/ *adjective* 形容词

on the outside; far from the centre 外部的；远离中心的: *I live in outer London.* 我住在伦敦郊外。✪ opposite 反义词: **inner**

outfit /'aʊtfɪt; 'aʊtˌfɪt/ *noun* 名词

a set of clothes that you wear together 一套衣服: *I've bought a new outfit for the party.* 我为参加这次聚会买了一套新衣服。

outing /'aʊtɪŋ; 'aʊtɪŋ/ *noun* 名词

a short journey to enjoy yourself 短途旅行；远足: *We went on an outing to the zoo last Saturday.* 我们上星期六到动物园去玩儿了。

outline /ˈaʊtlaɪn; ˈaʊtˌlaɪn/ *noun* 名词
a line that shows the shape or edge of something 轮廓；外形: *It was dark, but we could see the outline of the castle on the hill.* 天黑，可是我们还能看见山上城堡的轮廓。

outlook /ˈaʊtlʊk; ˈaʊtˌlʊk/ *noun* 名词
what will probably happen 可能发生的情况；展望: *The outlook for the weekend: dry and sunny weather in all parts of Britain.* 周末预测：英国各地天气晴朗干燥。

out of /ˈaʊt əv; ˈaʊt əv/ *preposition* 介词
1 words that show where from 表示从某处出来的词: *She took a cake out of the box.* 她从盒子里拿出一块蛋糕来。◇ *She got out of bed.* 她起床了。☞ picture on page C4 见第C4页图
2 not in 不在内: *Fish can't live out of water.* 鱼离开水就不能活。
3 by using something; from 用某事物；以: *He made a table out of some old pieces of wood.* 他用些旧木料做了个桌子。
4 from that number 从某数目中: *Nine out of ten people think that the government is right.* 十个人里有九个认为政府做得对。
5 because of 由于: *Anna helped us out of kindness.* 安娜出于好心帮助了我们。
6 without 没有: *She's been out of work for six months.* 她已经失业六个月了。

output /ˈaʊtpʊt; ˈaʊtˌpʊt/ *noun* 名词 (no plural 无复数)
the amount of things that somebody or something has made or done 产量: *What was the factory's output last year?* 这家工厂去年的产量是多少？

outside[1] /ˌaʊtˈsaɪd; ˈaʊtˈsaɪd/ *noun* 名词
the part of something that is away from the middle 外面；外部: *The outside of a pear is green or yellow and the inside is white.* 梨的外部是绿的或黄的，里面是白的。

outside[2] /ˌaʊtˈsaɪd; ˈaʊtˈsaɪd/ *adjective* 形容词
away from the middle of something 外面的；外部的: *The outside walls of a house were painted white.* 房子的外墙漆成了白色。

outside[3] /ˌaʊtˈsaɪd; aʊtˈsaɪd/ *preposition, adverb* 介词，副词
not in; in or to a place that is not inside a building 在外面；向外部: *I left my bicycle outside the shop.* 我把自行车放在商店外面了。◇ *Come outside and see the garden!* 出来到花园看看吧！

outskirts /ˈaʊtskɜːts; ˈaʊtˌskɝts/ *noun* 名词 (plural 复数)
the parts of a town or city that are far from the centre 市郊: *The airport is on the outskirts of the city.* 飞机场在市郊。

outstanding /ˌaʊtˈstændɪŋ; ˈaʊtˈstændɪŋ/ *adjective* 形容词
very good; much better than others 优秀的；杰出的: *Her work is outstanding.* 她的工作很突出。

outward /ˈaʊtwəd; ˈaʊtwɚd/, **outwards** /ˈaʊtwədz; ˈaʊtwɚdz/ *adverb* 副词
towards the outside 向外: *The windows open outwards.* 这些窗户是向外开的。✪ opposite 反义词: **inward** or 或 **inwards**

O

oval /ˈəʊvl; ˈovl̩/ *noun* 名词
a shape like an egg 卵形；椭圆形 ☞ picture on page C5 见第C5页图
oval *adjective* 形容词
with a shape like an egg 卵形的；椭圆形的: *an oval mirror* 椭圆形的镜子

oven /ˈʌvn; ˈʌvən/ *noun* 名词
the part of a cooker that has a door. You put food inside an oven to cook it. 烤箱

over[1] /ˈəʊvə(r); ˈovɚ/ *adverb, preposition* 副词，介词
1 above something; higher than something 在某物上方；比某物高: *A plane flew over our heads.* 飞机从我们头顶上空飞过。◇ *There is a picture over the fireplace.* 壁炉上方有一幅画儿。
2 on somebody or something so that it covers them 遮盖住某人或某物: *She put a blanket over the sleeping child.* 她给睡着的孩子盖上了毯子。
3 down 向下: *I fell over in the street.* 我在街上摔倒了。
4 across; to the other side of something 横越；到某物的另一边: *The dog jumped over the wall.* 狗跳过了墙。◇ *a bridge over a river* 架在河上的桥 ☞ picture on page C4 见第C4页图
5 so that the other side is on top 翻转过来: *Turn the cassette over.* 把盒式带翻过来。
6 more than a number, price, etc 超过一数目、价钱等: *She lived in Spain for over 20 years.* 她在西班牙住了20多年。◇ *This*

game is for children of ten and over. 这个游戏是十岁以上儿童玩儿的。

7 not used 未使用；剩余: *There are a lot of cakes left over from the party.* 这次聚会剩下很多蛋糕。

8 from one place to another 从一处到另一处: *Come over and see us on Saturday.* 星期六到我们这儿来坐坐。

9 a word that shows that you repeat something 表示重复的词: *He said the same thing over and over again* (= many times). 他反复说着同一件事。◇ *The audience liked the song so much that she sang it all over again* (= again, from the beginning). 听众非常喜欢那首歌，所以她又唱了一遍。

10 finished 结束；完结: *My exams are over.* 我考试都考完了。

all over in every part 各处: *She travels all over the world.* 她到全世界去旅行。

over here here 这里: *Come over here!* 到这儿来！

over there there 那里: *Go over there and see if you can help.* 到那儿看看你能不能帮些忙。

over-[2] /ˈəʊvə(r); ˈovɚ/ *prefix* 前缀
You can add **over-** to the beginning of a lot of words to give them the meaning 'too much', for example 在很多字前可加 **over-**，赋予"过多"或"过度"之意，如:

overeat = eat too much

oversleep = sleep too long

overall[1] /ˌəʊvərˈɔ:l; ˈovɚˌɔl/ *adjective* 形容词
of everything; total 全部的；总计的: *The overall cost of the repairs will be about £350.* 全部修理费大约是350英镑。

overall *adverb* 副词
How much will it cost overall? 一共要多少钱？

overall[2] /ˈəʊvərɔ:l; ˈovɚˌɔl/ *noun* 名词
a kind of coat that you wear over your clothes to keep them clean when you are working 长罩衣（大衣式工作服）

overalls /ˈəʊvərɔ:lz; ˈovɚˌɔlz/ *noun* 名词 (plural 复数)
a piece of clothing that covers your legs, body and arms. You wear it over your other clothes to keep them clean when you are working. 工装裤

overboard /ˈəʊvəbɔ:d; ˈovɚˌbɔrd/ *adverb* 副词
over the side of a boat and into the water 越过船舷进入水中: *She fell overboard.* 她从船上掉进水里了。

overcoat /ˈəʊvəkəʊt; ˈovɚˌkot/ *noun* 名词
a long thick coat that you wear in cold weather（厚的）大衣

overcome /ˌəʊvəˈkʌm; ˌovɚˈkʌm/ *verb* 动词 (**overcomes**, **overcoming**, **overcame** /ˌəʊvəˈkeɪm; ˌovɚˈkem/, **has overcome**)
find an answer to a difficult thing in your life; control something 克服；解决: *He overcame his fear of flying.* 他克服了飞行恐惧心理。

overcrowded /ˌəʊvəˈkraʊdɪd; ˌovɚˈkraʊdɪd/ *adjective* 形容词
too full of people 过度拥挤的: *The trains are overcrowded on Friday evenings.* 星期五晚上火车上拥挤不堪。

overdue /ˌəʊvəˈdju:; ˈovɚˈdu/ *adjective* 形容词
late 迟的: *Our landlady is angry because the rent is overdue.* 我们逾期未付房租，（女）房东很生气。

overflow /ˌəʊvəˈfləʊ; ˌovɚˈflo/ *verb* 动词 (**overflows**, **overflowing**, **overflowed** /ˌəʊvəˈfləʊd; ˌovɚˈflod/)
come over the edge of something because there is too much in it 溢出: *After the rain, the river overflowed its banks.* 下过雨后，河水漫出了河岸。

overgrown /ˌəʊvəˈgrəʊn; ˈovɚˈgron/ *adjective* 形容词
covered with plants that have grown too big 杂草丛生的: *The house was empty and the garden was overgrown.* 那所房子空着，花园里杂草丛生。

overhead /ˈəʊvəhed; ˈovɚˌhɛd/ *adjective* 形容词
above your head 头顶上方的: *an overhead light* 头顶上方的灯

overhead /ˌəʊvəˈhed; ˈovɚˈhɛd/ *adverb* 副词
A plane flew overhead. 飞机从头顶上空飞过。

overhear /ˌəʊvəˈhɪə(r); ˌovɚˈhɪr/ *verb* 动词 (**overhears**, **overhearing**, **over-**

heard /ˌəʊvəˈhɜːd; ˌovɚˈhɝd/, **has overheard**)
hear what somebody is saying when they are speaking to another person, not to you 从旁听到: *I overheard Louise saying that she was unhappy.* 我无意中听到路易丝说她自己很不愉快。

overlap /ˌəʊvəˈlæp; ˌovɚˈlæp/ *verb* 动词 (**overlaps**, **overlapping**, **overlapped** /ˌəʊvəˈlæpt; ˌovɚˈlæpt/)
When two things overlap, part of one thing covers part of the other thing 部分重迭: *The tiles on the roof overlap.* 房上的瓦相互重迭着。

overlook /ˌəʊvəˈlʊk; ˌovɚˈlʊk/ *verb* 动词 (**overlooks**, **overlooking**, **overlooked** /ˌəʊvəˈlʊkt; ˌovɚˈlʊkt/)
1 look down on something from above 从高处往下看；俯视: *My room overlooks the garden.* 从我的房间可以看到下面的花园。
2 not see or notice something 未看到或未注意到某事物: *He overlooked a spelling mistake.* 他没看出有个拼写错误。

overnight /ˌəʊvəˈnaɪt; ˈovɚˈnaɪt/ *adjective*, *adverb* 形容词，副词
for or during the night 在夜晚（的）: *They stayed at our house overnight.* 他们在我家过了一夜。◇ *an overnight journey* 夜间的行程

overpass /ˈəʊvəpɑːs; ˈovɚˌpæs/ *American English for* **flyover** 美式英语，即 **flyover**

overseas /ˌəʊvəˈsiːz; ˈovɚˈsiz/ *adjective*, *adverb* 形容词，副词
in, to or from another country across the sea 海外（的）: *There are many overseas students in Britain.* 英国有很多外国留学生。◇ *She travels overseas a lot.* 她经常到国外去。

oversleep /ˌəʊvəˈsliːp; ˈovɚˈslip/ *verb* 动词 (**oversleeps**, **oversleeping**, **overslept** /ˌəʊvəˈslept; ˈovɚˈslɛpt/, **has overslept**)
sleep too long and not wake up at the right time 睡得太久；睡过头: *I overslept and was late for work.* 我睡过了头，上班迟到了。

overtake /ˌəʊvəˈteɪk; ˌovɚˈtek/ *verb* 动词 (**overtakes**, **overtaking**, **overtook** /ˌəʊvəˈtʊk; ˌovɚˈtʊk/, **has overtaken** /ˌəʊvəˈteɪkən; ˌovɚˈtekən/)
go past somebody or something that is going more slowly 超越某人或某事物: *The car overtook a bus.* 那辆轿车超越了公共汽车。

overtime /ˈəʊvətaɪm; ˈovɚˌtaɪm/ *noun* 名词 (no plural 无复数)
extra time that you spend at work 加班: *I have done a lot of overtime this week.* 我这星期多次加班。

overweight /ˌəʊvəˈweɪt; ˈovɚˈwet/ *adjective* 形容词
too heavy or fat 过重的；过胖的: *The doctor said I was overweight and that I should eat less.* 医生说我过胖应该少吃点儿东西。

overwhelming /ˌəʊvəˈwelmɪŋ; ˌovɚˈhwɛlmɪŋ/ *adjective* 形容词
very great or strong 巨大的；强烈的: *an overwhelming feeling of loneliness* 极其孤单的心绪

ow /aʊ; aʊ/
You say 'ow' when you suddenly feel pain 表示突然疼痛的词: *Ow! You're standing on my foot.* 哎哟！你踩我脚了。

owe /əʊ; o/ *verb* 动词 (**owes**, **owing**, **owed** /əʊd; od/)
1 have to pay money to somebody because they have given you something 欠某人钱: *I lent you £5 last week and £5 the week before, so you owe me £10.* 我上星期借给你5英镑，上上星期借给你5英镑，所以你欠我10英镑。
2 feel that you have something because of what another person has done 感激某人: *She owes her life to the man who pulled her out of the river.* 她感激那个男子救命之恩，是他把她从河里救出来的。

owing to /ˈəʊɪŋ tu; ˈo·ɪŋ tʊ/ *preposition* 介词
because of 由于；因为: *The train was late owing to the bad weather.* 那班列车因天气恶劣而误点。

owl /aʊl; aʊl/ *noun* 名词
a bird that flies at night and eats small animals 猫头鹰

owl 猫头鹰

own[1] /əʊn; on/ *adjective*, *pronoun* 形容词，代词
You use 'own' to say that something belongs to a person or thing 属于某人或某事物的: *Is that your own camera or did you borrow it?* 那个照相机是你的，还是你借的？

◇ *I have my own room* (= for me and nobody else). 我有自己的屋子。✪ Be careful! You cannot use 'own' after 'a' or 'the'. 注意！不可以在 a 或 the 之后用 own。You cannot say 不可以说: *I would like an own room.* You say 应该说: *I would like my own room.* (*or* 或者说: *I would like a room of my own.*)

get your own back on somebody do something bad to somebody who has done something bad to you 报复: *He said he would get his own back on me for breaking his watch.* 他说我把他手表弄坏了，他得向我报复。

of your own that belongs to you and not to anybody else 属于自己的: *I want a home of my own.* 我想有个属于自己的家。

on your own **1** alone 独自: *She lives on her own.* 她独自生活。**2** without help 独力地；无人相助: *I can't move this box on my own—can you help me?* 我一个人搬不动这个箱子——你帮我搬行吗？

own² /əʊn; on/ *verb* 动词 (**owns**, **owning**, **owned** /əʊnd; ond/)
have something that is yours 有某事物（属于自己的）: *We don't own our flat—we rent it.* 我们自己没有房子——这个公寓是租的。

own up say that you have done something wrong 承认有错: *Nobody owned up to breaking the window.* 没有人承认把窗户打破了。

owner /ˈəʊnə(r); ˈonɚ/ *noun* 名词
a person who has something 某物的所有者；物主: *Who is the owner of that red car?* 那辆红色汽车是谁的？

ox /ɒks; ɑks/ *noun* 名词 (*plural* 复数作 **oxen** /ˈɒksn; ˈɑksn̩/)
a male cow. Oxen are sometimes used to pull or carry heavy things on farms. 公牛（有时用作农场力畜）

oxygen /ˈɒksɪdʒən; ˈɑksədʒən/ *noun* 名词 (no plural 无复数)
a gas in the air. Plants and animals need oxygen to live. 氧气

oz *short way of writing* **ounce** ✱ **ounce** 的缩写形式

ozone /ˈəʊzəʊn; ˈozon/ *noun* 名词 (no plural 无复数)
a gas in the air 臭氧

Pp

P

p
1 /piː; pi/ *short for* **pence** ✱ **pence** 的缩略式
2 *short way of writing* **page 1** ✱ **page 1** 的缩写形式

pace /peɪs; pes/ *noun* 名词
1 a step 一步: *Take two paces forward!* 向前两步走！
2 how fast you do something or how fast something happens 速度: *The race began at a fast pace.* 比赛一开始速度就很快。
keep pace with somebody or 或 **something** go as fast as somebody or something 与某人或某事物齐头并进: *She couldn't keep pace with the other runners.* 她跟不上其他参赛者的步伐。

pack[1] /pæk; pæk/ *noun* 名词
1 a group of things that you buy together（一起买的）一批物品: *I bought a pack of five exercise books.* 我买了一沓装的五个练习本。
2 a group of animals that hunt together（一起猎食的）一群动物: *a pack of wolves* 一群狼
3 *American English for* **packet** 美式英语，即 **packet**
pack of cards /ˌpæk əv ˈkɑːdz; ˈpæk əv ˌkɑrdz/ *noun* 名词
a set of 52 playing-cards 一副纸牌（52张）☞ Look at **card**. 见 **card**。

pack[2] /pæk; pæk/ *verb* 动词 (**packs, packing, packed** /pækt; pækt/)
1 put things into a bag or suitcase before you go somewhere（为去某处）把东西装进提包或衣箱中；收拾行李: *Have you packed your suitcase?* 你把衣箱装好了吗？◇ *Don't forget to pack your toothbrush.* 别忘了把牙刷放进提包里。
2 put things into a box, bag, etc 把东西装进盒子、袋子等容器里: *Pack all these books into boxes.* 把这些书都装进箱子里。
✪ opposite 反义词: **unpack**
pack up 1 stop doing something 不再做某事: *At two o'clock we packed up and went home.* 我们两点钟的时候收工回家了。
2 If a machine packs up, it stops working.（指机器）停止工作

packed lunch /ˌpækt ˈlʌntʃ; ˌpækt ˈlʌntʃ/ *noun* 名词
sandwiches and other things that you take with you to eat at school or work 上学或上班带去吃的三明治之类的食物

package /ˈpækɪdʒ; ˈpækɪdʒ/ *noun* 名词
something that is wrapped in paper; a small parcel 用纸包着的东西

package holiday /ˌpækɪdʒ ˈhɒlədeɪ; ˈpækɪdʒ ˌhɑləde/, **package tour** /ˈpækɪdʒ tʊə(r); ˈpækɪdʒ ˌtʊr/ *noun* 名词
a complete holiday where a travel company sells you your hotel, flight, etc together 代办旅游（由旅行社安排，旅馆、航班等费用在内的）: *We went on a package tour to Spain last year.* 去年我们参加了代办旅游团去西班牙。

packaging /ˈpækɪdʒɪŋ; ˈpækɪdʒɪŋ/ *noun* 名词 (no plural 无复数)
material like paper, cardboard or plastic that is used to wrap things that you buy or that you send 包装材料（买东西或寄东西包装用的，如纸、硬纸板或塑料）

packed /pækt; pækt/ *adjective* 形容词
full 满的；挤满的: *The train was packed.* 火车里挤满了人。

packet /ˈpækɪt; ˈpækɪt/ *noun* 名词
a small box or bag that you buy things in（包装商品的）小盒，小包，小袋: *a packet of cigarettes* 一包香烟 ◇ *an empty cigarette packet* 空的香烟盒 ◇ *a packet of biscuits* 一包饼干 ☞ picture at **container** 见 **container** 词条插图

pact /pækt; pækt/ *noun* 名词
an important agreement to do something 契约；公约；协议: *The two countries signed a peace pact.* 两国签订了和约。

pad /pæd; pæd/ *noun* 名词
1 some pieces of paper that are joined together at one end（纸的一边粘住，便于撕下的）便笺本；拍纸簿: *a writing pad* 拍纸簿
2 a thick flat piece of soft material 一块厚而软的材料；垫料: *Footballers wear pads on their legs to protect them.* 足球运动员戴着护腿。◇ *I used a pad of cotton wool to clean the cut.* 我用一块药棉擦了擦伤口。

paddle[1] /ˈpædl; ˈpædl̩/ *noun* 名词
a piece of wood with a flat end, that you

use for moving a small boat through water 短桨

paddle *verb* 动词 (**paddles**, **paddling**, **paddled** /ˈpædld; ˈpædl̩d/)

move a small boat through water with a paddle 划桨；划船: *We paddled up the river.* 我们乘着小船向上游划去。

paddle² /ˈpædl; ˈpædl̩/ *verb* 动词 (**paddles**, **paddling**, **paddled** /ˈpædld; ˈpædl̩d/)

walk in water that is not deep, with no shoes on your feet（光着脚）蹚水；涉水: *The children were paddling in the sea.* 孩子们在海边蹚着水玩儿。

padlock /ˈpædlɒk; ˈpædˌlɑk/ *noun* 名词

a lock that you use on things like gates and bicycles 挂锁；扣锁

page /peɪdʒ; pedʒ/ *noun* 名词

1 one side of a piece of paper in a book, magazine or newspaper 页（书刊的一张纸的一面）；版（报纸的一面）: *Please turn to page 120.* 请翻到第120页。◇ *What page is the story on?* 这件事是在第几版上登的？ ✪ The short way of writing 'page' is **p**. ✳ page 的缩写形式为 **p**。

2 one piece of paper in a book, magazine or newspaper 页（书或报刊的一张纸）

paid *form of* **pay¹** ✳ **pay¹** 的不同形式

pain /peɪn; pen/ *noun* 名词

1 (*plural* 复数作 **pains**) the feeling that you have in your body when you are hurt or ill 疼；疼痛: *I've got a pain in my leg.* 我腿疼。◇ *He's in pain.* 他感到疼痛。

2 (no plural 无复数) unhappiness 不愉快；痛苦

painful /ˈpeɪnfl; ˈpenfəl/ *adjective* 形容词

Something that is painful gives pain 疼的；疼痛的；痛苦的: *I've cut my leg—it's very painful.* 我把腿弄破了——疼极了。

paint 用颜料涂或画

paint 1 涂颜料　　paint 2 做画

paint /peɪnt; pent/ *noun* 名词

a coloured liquid that you put on things with a brush, to change the colour or to make a picture 液体的颜料；涂料: *red paint* 红色的涂料 ◇ *Is the paint dry yet?* 油漆干了吗？

paint *verb* 动词 (**paints**, **painting**, **painted**)

1 put paint on something to change the colour 在某物上涂（液体的）颜料: *We painted the walls grey.* 我们把墙刷成灰色的了。

2 make a picture of somebody or something with paints 用（液体的）颜料做画: *I'm painting some flowers.* 我正在用水彩画花。◇ *My sister paints very well.* 我姐姐油画画得非常好。

paintbrush /ˈpeɪntbrʌʃ; ˈpentˌbrʌʃ/ *noun* 名词 (*plural* 复数作 **paintbrushes**)

a brush that you use for painting（涂液体颜料用的）刷子；（用液体颜料做画或写字的）画笔，毛笔

painter /ˈpeɪntə(r); ˈpentɚ/ *noun* 名词

1 a person whose job is to paint things like walls or houses 粉刷工；油漆工

2 a person who paints pictures 用液体颜料做画的人；（用水彩或油彩做画的）画家: *Picasso was a famous painter.* 毕加索是著名的画家。

painting /ˈpeɪntɪŋ; ˈpentɪŋ/ *noun* 名词

a picture that somebody makes with paint 水彩画；油画: *a painting by Rembrandt* 伦勃朗的画

pair /peə(r); pɛr/ *noun* 名词

1 two things of the same kind that you use together 两件一起使用的同类东西；一双；一对: *a pair of shoes* 一双鞋 ◇ *a pair of earrings* 一对耳环 ☞ picture on page C25 见第C25页图

2 a thing with two parts that are joined together 由两部分组成的单件物品: *a pair of glasses* 一副眼镜 ◇ *a pair of scissors* 一把剪子 ◇ *I bought two pairs of trousers.* 我买了两条裤子。

3 two people or animals together 在一起的两个人或两个动物: *a pair of ducks* 一对鸭子

in pairs with two things or people together（指东西或人）两个在一起；成双的；成对的: *Shoes are only sold in pairs.* 鞋都是按双卖的。

pajamas *American English for* **pyjamas** 美式英语，即 **pyjamas**

palace /ˈpæləs; ˈpælɪs/ *noun* 名词

a very large house where a king, queen or another important person lives 宫殿；

皇宫；（要人的）宅第：*The Queen lives at Buckingham Palace.* 女王住在白金汉宫里。

pale /peɪl; pel/ *adjective* 形容词 (**paler, palest**)
1 with not much colour in your face; white（指面色）苍白的：*Are you ill? You look pale.* 你病了吗？你气色不好。
2 with a light colour; not strong or dark（指颜色）浅的；淡的：*a pale-blue dress* 浅蓝色的连衣裙 ✪ opposite 反义词：**dark** or 或 **deep**

palm /pɑːm; pɑm/ *noun* 名词
1 the flat part of the front of your hand 掌；手掌；掌心；手心 ☞ picture on page C2 见第C2页图
2 (*also* 亦作 **palm-tree**) a tree that grows in hot countries, with no branches and a lot of big leaves at the top 棕榈树：*a coconut palm* 椰子树

pan /pæn; pæn/ *noun* 名词
a metal pot that you use for cooking 锅：*a frying-pan* 煎锅 ◇ *a saucepan* 长柄炖锅

pancake /ˈpænkeɪk; ˈpæŋˌkek/ *noun* 名词
a very thin round thing that you eat. You make pancakes with flour, eggs and milk and cook them in a frying-pan. 烙饼；薄饼

panda /ˈpændə; ˈpændə/ *noun* 名词
a large black and white animal like a bear, that lives in China 大熊猫；大猫熊

pane /peɪn; pen/ *noun* 名词
a piece of glass in a window（窗户上的）玻璃

panel /ˈpænl; ˈpænl̩/ *noun* 名词
1 a flat piece of wood, metal or glass that is part of a door, wall or ceiling（门、墙或天花板上的）镶板，嵌板
2 a flat part on a machine, where there are things to help you control it（机器上的）仪表板：*the control panel of a TV* 电视机控制板

panic /ˈpænɪk; ˈpænɪk/ *noun* 名词
a sudden feeling of fear that you cannot control and that makes you do things without thinking carefully 恐慌；惊惶：*There was panic in the shop when the fire started.* 商店失火时，里面的人一片恐慌。

panic *verb* 动词 (**panics, panicking, panicked** /ˈpænɪkt; ˈpænɪkt/)
Don't panic! 不要惊慌！

pant /pænt; pænt/ *verb* 动词 (**pants, panting, panted**)
take in and let out air quickly through your mouth, for example after running or because you are very hot 喘；气喘：*The dog was panting.* 那条狗急促地喘着气。

panther /ˈpænθə(r); ˈpænθɚ/ *noun* 名词
a wild animal like a big cat. Panthers are usually black. 豹；（尤指）黑豹

pantomime /ˈpæntəmaɪm; ˈpæntəˌmaɪm/ *noun* 名词
a funny play for children, with singing and dancing. You can usually see pantomimes at Christmas. 童话剧（通常于圣诞节演出）

pants /pænts; pænts/ *noun* 名词 (plural 复数)
1 a small piece of clothing that you wear under your other clothes, between the middle of your body and the top of your legs（贴身的）裤衩；短内裤：*a pair of pants* 一条短内裤
2 *American English for* **trousers** 美式英语，即 **trousers**

paper /ˈpeɪpə(r); ˈpepɚ/ *noun* 名词
1 (no plural 无复数) thin material for writing or drawing on or for wrapping things in 纸：*The pages of this book are made of paper.* 这本书的书页是纸做的。◇ *a sheet of paper* 一张纸 ◇ *a paper bag* 纸袋
2 (*plural* 复数作 **papers**) a newspaper 报纸：*Have you seen today's paper?* 你看见今天的报纸了吗？
3 papers (plural 复数) important pieces of paper with writing on them 文件；证件：*The police officer asked to see my papers* (= for example, a passport or an identity card). 警察要求看我的证件（例如护照或身分证）。
4 (*plural* 复数作 **papers**) a group of questions in an examination 试卷：*The English paper was easy.* 英语试卷很容易。

paperback /ˈpeɪpəbæk; ˈpepɚˌbæk/ *noun* 名词
a book with a paper cover 简装书；平装书 ☞ Look at **hardback**. 见 **hardback**。

paper-clip /ˈpeɪpə klɪp; ˈpepɚˌklɪp/ *noun* 名词
a small metal thing that you use for holding pieces of paper together 回形针；曲别针

paper-clip 曲别针

parachute降落伞

parachute /'pærəʃu:t; 'pærəˌʃut/ *noun* 名词
a thing like a big umbrella that you have on your back when you jump out of an aeroplane and that opens, so that you will fall to the ground slowly 降落伞

parade /pə'reɪd; pə'red/ *noun* 名词
a line of people who are walking together for a special reason, while other people watch them（人群的）游行: *a military parade* 阅兵

paradise /'pærədaɪs; 'pærəˌdaɪs/ *noun* 名词 (no plural 无复数)
the place where some people think good people go after they die; heaven 天堂；天国

paragraph /'pærəgrɑ:f; 'pærəˌgræf/ *noun* 名词
a group of lines of writing. A paragraph always begins on a new line. 段落

parallel /'pærəlel; 'pærəˌlɛl/ *adjective* 形容词
Parallel lines are straight lines that are always the same distance from each other. 平行的 ☞ picture on page C5 见第C5页图

paralysed /'pærəlaɪzd; 'pærəˌlaɪzd/ *adjective* 形容词
If you are paralysed, you cannot move your body or a part of it 瘫痪的；麻痹的: *After the accident she was paralysed in both legs.* 发生事故后她双腿就瘫痪了。

paralyzed *American English for* **paralysed** 美式英语，即 **paralysed**

parcel /'pɑ:sl; 'pɑrsḷ/ *noun* 名词
something with paper around it, that you send or carry 纸包；包裹: *She sent a parcel of books to her aunt.* 她给姑姑寄去了一包书。

parcel包裹

pardon /'pɑ:dn; 'pɑrdṇ/ *verb* 动词 (**pardons**, **pardoning**, **pardoned** /'pɑ:dnd; 'pɑrdṇd/)
forgive somebody for something bad that they have done 宽恕或原谅某人 ✪ **Forgive** is the word that we usually use. ✳ **forgive** 是常用词。

pardon? What did you say? 您刚才说什么？

pardon me **1** What did you say? 您刚才说什么？ **2** I am sorry. 对不起。

parent /'peərənt; 'pɛrənt/ *noun* 名词
a mother or father 母亲或父亲: *Her parents live in Italy.* 她父母住在意大利。 ☞ picture on page C3 见第C3页图

parish /'pærɪʃ; 'pærɪʃ/ *noun* 名词 (*plural* 复数作 **parishes**)
an area that has its own church and priest（宗教的）牧区

park[1] /pɑ:k; pɑrk/ *noun* 名词
a large place with grass and trees, where anybody can go to walk, play games, etc 公园: *We had a picnic in the park.* 我们在公园里吃了一顿野餐。◇ *Hyde Park* 海德公园

park[2] /pɑ:k; pɑrk/ *verb* 动词 (**parks**, **parking**, **parked** /pɑ:kt; pɑrkt/)
stop and leave a car, lorry, etc somewhere for a time 停放汽车: *You can't park in this street.* 这条街上不准停放汽车。◇ *My car is parked opposite the bank.* 我的汽车停放在银行对面了。

parking *noun* 名词 (no plural 无复数)
The sign says 'No Parking'. 牌子上写着"不准停放汽车"。◇ *I can't find a parking space.* 我找不到停放汽车的地方。

parking-lot /'pɑ:kɪŋ lɒt; 'pɑrkɪŋˌlɑt/ *American English for* **car park** 美式英语，即 **car park**

parking-meter /'pɑ:kɪŋ mi:tə(r); 'pɑrkɪŋˌmitɚ/ *noun* 名词
a machine that you put money into to pay for parking a car next to it 停车计时收费器

parliament /'pɑ:ləmənt; 'pɑrləmənt/ *noun* 名词
the people who make the laws in a country 议会；国会: *the French parliament* 法国议会

✪ In the United Kingdom, the group of people who make the laws meet in the **Houses of Parliament** in London. 在英国，议员在伦敦开会的国会两院叫做 **Houses of Parliament**。The two parts of the Houses of Parliament are called the **House of Commons** (where the **Members of Parliament** meet) and the **House of Lords**. 其中一个是下议院，叫做 **House of Commons**（是议员，即 **Members of Parliament**，开会的处所）；另一个是上议院，叫做 **House of Lords**。

parrot /'pærət; 'pærət/ *noun* 名词
a bird with very bright feathers that can copy what people say 鹦鹉

parsley /'pɑ:sli; 'pɑrslɪ/ *noun* 名词 (no plural 无复数)
a small plant that you use in cooking 欧芹（类似芫荽或香菜的作料）

part[1] /pɑ:t; pɑrt/ *noun* 名词
1 some, but not all of something; one of the pieces of something 部分: *We spent part of the day on the beach.* 我们这一天部分时间是在海滩上度过的。◇ *Which part of Spain do you come from?* 您是西班牙什么地方的人？
2 a piece of a machine（机器的）零件: *Is there a shop near here that sells bicycle parts?* 附近有没有卖自行车零件的商店？
3 the person you are in a play or film（戏剧或影片的）角色: *She played the part of Ophelia.* 她扮演奥菲莉亚这个角色。
take part in something do something together with other people 参加；参与: *All the students took part in the concert.* 所有学生都参加了这次音乐会。

part[2] /pɑ:t; pɑrt/ *verb* 动词 (**parts, parting, parted**)
go away from each other 别离；分手: *We parted at the station. John got on the train and I went home.* 我们在车站分手了。约翰上了火车，我回家了。

participate /pɑ:'tɪsɪpeɪt; pɑr'tɪsə͵pet/ *verb* 动词 (**participates, participating, participated**)
do something together with other people 参加；参与: *Ten countries participated in the discussions.* 有十个国家参加了会谈。

participant /pɑ:'tɪsɪpənt; pɑr'tɪsəpənt/ *noun* 名词
a person who does something together with other people 参加者；参与者

participation /pɑ:͵tɪsɪ'peɪʃn; pɑr͵tɪsə'peʃən/ *noun* 名词 (no plural 无复数)
doing something together with other people 参加；参与

participle /'pɑ:tɪsɪpl; 'pɑrtə͵sɪpl̩/ *noun* 名词
a form of a verb 分词（动词的一种形式）: *The present participle of 'eat' is 'eating' and the past participle is 'eaten'.* ✳ eat 这一动词的现在分词是 eating，过去分词是 eaten。

particular /pə'tɪkjələ(r); pɚ'tɪkjəlɚ/ *adjective* 形容词
1 one only, and not any other 特定的: *You need a particular kind of flour to make bread.* 做面包需要用特定的面粉。
2 special or more than usual 特别的；非一般的: *The road is very icy, so take particular care when you are driving.* 这条路上结了很多冰，开车要特别小心。
3 If you are particular, you want something to be exactly right 讲究的；挑剔的: *He's very particular about the food he eats.* 他对吃的东西非常讲究。
in particular more than others 尤其；特别地: *Is there anything in particular you want to do this weekend?* 这个周末你有什么特别要做的事情吗？

particularly /pə'tɪkjələli; pɚ'tɪkjəlɚlɪ/ *adverb* 副词
more than others; especially 尤其；特别地；特殊地: *I'm particularly tired today.* 我今天特别累。◇ *I don't particularly like fish.* 我不那么喜欢鱼。

parties *plural of* **party** ✳ **party** 的复数形式

parting /'pɑ:tɪŋ; 'pɑrtɪŋ/ *noun* 名词
1 a line that you make on your head by combing your hair in different directions（头发的）分缝
2 when people leave each other 别离；分手: *It was a sad parting for Sarah and Tom.* 萨拉和汤姆分手时非常难过。

partly /'pɑ:tli; 'pɑrtlɪ/ *adverb* 副词
not completely but in some way 部分地；不完全地: *The window was partly open.* 窗户半开着。◇ *The accident was partly my fault and partly the other driver's.*

P

这次事故一部分是我的错，另一个司机也有一部分责任。

partner /ˈpɑːtnə(r); ˈpɑrtnɚ/ *noun* 名词
1 your husband, wife, boyfriend or girlfriend 丈夫、妻子、男朋友或女朋友
2 a person you are dancing with, or playing a game with 舞伴；（游戏的）伙伴
3 one of the people who owns a business（生意上的）合伙人

partnership /ˈpɑːtnəʃɪp; ˈpɑrtnɚˌʃɪp/ *noun* 名词
being partners 丈夫、妻子、男朋友、女朋友、舞伴、伙伴或合伙人等的身分或关系: *The two sisters went into partnership and opened a shop.* 他们姐俩合伙开了个商店。

part of speech /ˌpɑːt əv ˈspiːtʃ; ˌpɑrt əv ˈspitʃ/ *noun* 名词
'Noun', 'verb', 'adjective' and 'adverb' are parts of speech. 词类（名词、动词、形容词、副词等）

part-time /ˌpɑːt ˈtaɪm; ˌpɑrtˈtaɪm/ *adjective, adverb* 形容词，副词
for only a part of the day or week（一天或一星期）部分工作时间（的）: *I've got a part-time job as a secretary.* 我找到个兼职工作，担任秘书。◇ *Jenny works part-time.* 珍妮只是部分时间工作。☞ Look at **full-time**. 见 **full-time**。

party /ˈpɑːti; ˈpɑrtɪ/ *noun* 名词 (*plural* 复数作 **parties**)
1 a meeting of friends, often in somebody's house, to eat, drink and perhaps dance（朋友的）聚会（常指在某人家中吃、喝或许跳舞）: *We're having a party this Saturday. Can you come?* 我们这个星期六有个聚会。你能来吗？◇ *a birthday party* 生日聚会
2 a group of people who have the same ideas about politics 政党；党派: *the Labour Party* 工党
3 a group of people who are travelling or working together 一起旅行或工作的一批人；组；团: *a party of tourists* 旅行团

pass[1] /pɑːs; pæs/ *noun* 名词 (*plural* 复数作 **passes**)
1 a special piece of paper or card that says you can go somewhere or do something 通行证；许可证: *You need a pass to get into the factory.* 需要有通行证才能进入这个工厂。
2 kicking, throwing or hitting a ball to somebody in a game（某些球类运动的）传球
3 doing well enough in an examination（考试）及格: *How many passes did you get in your exams?* 你考试有几门功课及格？
4 a road or way through mountains 山路；山道: *the Brenner Pass* 布伦纳罗山口

pass[2] /pɑːs; pæs/ *verb* 动词 (**passes, passing, passed** /pɑːst; pæst/)
1 go by somebody or something 在某人或某物旁走过；经过；路过: *She passed me in the street.* 她在街上从我身旁经过。◇ *Do you pass any shops on your way to the station?* 你到车站去路过商店吗？
2 give something to somebody 把某物交给某人；传给；递给: *Could you pass me the salt, please?* 请您把盐递给我行吗？
3 go by（指时间）消逝，过去: *A week passed before his letter arrived.* 过了一个星期他的信才到。
4 do well enough in an examination or test（考试或测验）及格: *Did you pass your driving test?* 你驾驶测验及格了吗？✪ opposite 反义词: **fail**
5 spend time 度过或消磨时间: *How did you pass the time in hospital?* 你住院时是怎样打发时间的？
pass on give or tell something to another person 转交；转告；转达: *Will you pass on a message to Mike for me?* 您替我向迈克转告一句话行吗？
pass through go through a place 经过某处: *The train passes through Oxford on its way to London.* 列车在开往伦敦的路上经过牛津。

passage /ˈpæsɪdʒ; ˈpæsɪdʒ/ *noun* 名词
1 a short part of a book or speech（书或讲话的）一段，一节: *We studied a passage from the story for homework.* 我们学习了故事中的一个段落作为家庭作业。
2 a narrow way, for example between two buildings 通路；通道（例如两座楼之间的）

passenger /ˈpæsɪndʒə(r); ˈpæsn̩dʒɚ/ *noun* 名词
a person who is travelling in a car, bus, train, plane, etc, but not the person who is driving it（汽车、火车、飞机等的）乘客: *The plane was carrying 200 passengers.* 那架飞机运载着200名旅客。

passer-by /ˌpɑːsə ˈbaɪ; ˈpæsɚˈbaɪ/ *noun* 名词 (*plural* 复数作 **passers-by**) a person who is walking past you in the street 过路人: *I asked a passer-by where the museum was.* 我向一个过路的人打听博物馆的地点。

passion /ˈpæʃn; ˈpæʃən/ *noun* 名词
a very strong feeling, usually of love, but sometimes of anger or hate 强烈的感情（通常指爱，但有时也指怒或恨）；激情

passionate /ˈpæʃənət; ˈpæʃənɪt/ *adjective* 形容词
with very strong feelings 有强烈的感情的；怀有激情的: *a passionate kiss* 热恋的吻

passive /ˈpæsɪv; ˈpæsɪv/ *noun* 名词 (no plural 无复数)
the form of a verb that shows that the action is done by a person or thing to another person or thing 被动语态（动词的一种形式）: *In the sentence 'The car was stolen by thieves', the verb is in the passive.* 在 The car was stolen by thieves 一句中，动词是被动语态。✪ opposite 反义词: **active**

passport /ˈpɑːspɔːt; ˈpæsˌpɔrt/ *noun* 名词
a small book with your name and photograph in it. You must take it with you when you travel to other countries. 护照

password /ˈpɑːswɜːd; ˈpæsˌwɝd/ *noun* 名词
a secret word that you must say to enter a place（进入某处必须说出的）暗号，口令

past¹ /pɑːst; pæst/ *noun* 名词 (no plural 无复数)
1 the time before now, and the things that happened then 过去；以前；往事: *We learn about the past in history lessons.* 我们在历史课上了解到了过去的事。◇ *In the past, many people had large families.* 从前很多人的家庭都是大家庭。
2 (*also* 亦作 **past tense**) the form of a verb that you use to talk about the time before now（动词的）过去式: *The past tense of the verb 'go' is 'went'.* 动词 go 的过去式是 went。
☞ Look at **present** and **future**. 见 **present** 和 **future**。

past *adjective* 形容词
1 of the time that has gone 过去的；以前的: *We will forget your past mistakes.* 我们不再计较你过去的错误。
2 last; just before now 刚过去的: *He has been ill for the past week.* 他病了一个星期了。

past² /pɑːst; pæst/ *preposition, adverb* 介词，副词
1 a word that shows how many minutes after the hour 表示（在小时之后的）多少分钟的词: *It's two minutes past four.* 现在是四点零二分。◇ *It's half past seven.* 现在是七点半。☞ Look at page C8. 见第C8页。
2 from one side of somebody or something to the other; by; on the other side of somebody or something 从某人或某物的一边到另一边；经过；路过: *Go past the cinema, then turn left.* 走过电影院以后向左拐。◇ *The bus went past without stopping.* 公共汽车没停站就开过去了。

paste /peɪst; pest/ *noun* 名词
soft wet stuff, sometimes used for sticking paper to things 糨糊: *Mix the powder with water to make a paste.* 把这种粉加水调成糨糊。

pastime /ˈpɑːstaɪm; ˈpæsˌtaɪm/ *noun* 名词
something that you like doing when you are not working 消遣；娱乐: *Painting is her favourite pastime.* 绘画是她喜爱的消遣。

pastry /ˈpeɪstri; ˈpestrɪ/ *noun* 名词
1 (no plural 无复数) a mixture of flour, fat and water that is used for making pies 油酥面团（做糕饼用的）
2 (*plural* 复数作 **pastries**) a small cake made with pastry 酥皮糕点

pat /pæt; pæt/ *verb* 动词 (**pats, patting, patted**)
touch somebody or something lightly with your hand flat 轻拍某人或某物: *She patted the dog on the head.* 她轻轻拍了拍狗的头部。

pat *noun* 名词
He gave me a pat on the shoulder. 他轻轻拍了拍我的肩膀。

patch /pætʃ; pætʃ/ *noun* 名词 (*plural* 复数作 **patches**)
1 a piece of cloth that you use to cover a hole in things like clothes 补丁；补片；补块: *I sewed a patch on my jeans.* 我在我的牛仔裤上打了个补丁。
2 a small piece of something that is not the same as the other parts（与周围不同的）小片，小块；斑: *a black cat with a white patch on its back* 背上有块白毛的黑猫

pâté /ˈpæteɪ; pɑˈte/ *noun* 名词 (no plural 无复数)
thick food made from meat, fish or vegetables, that you eat on bread（肉、鱼或蔬菜等做的）酱

path /pɑːθ; pæθ/ *noun* 名词 (*plural* 复数作 **paths** /pɑːðz; pæðz/)
a way across a piece of land, where people can walk 小路；小径：*a path through the woods* 穿过树林的小路

P

patience /ˈpeɪʃns; ˈpeʃəns/ *noun* 名词 (no plural 无复数)
staying calm and not getting angry when you are waiting for something, or when you have problems 耐性；耐心：*Learning to play the piano takes hard work and patience.* 学弹钢琴要刻苦还要有耐性。✪ opposite 反义词: **impatience**
lose patience with somebody become angry with somebody 对某人忍无可忍；发怒: *She was walking so slowly that her sister finally lost patience with her.* 她走得非常慢，她姐姐忍不住发起脾气来。

patient[1] /ˈpeɪʃnt; ˈpeʃənt/ *adjective* 形容词
able to stay calm and not get angry when you are waiting for something or when you have problems 有耐性的；有耐心的: *Just sit there and be patient. Your mum will be here soon.* 你坐在那儿再忍一会儿。你妈妈马上就来了。✪ opposite 反义词: **impatient**
patiently *adverb* 副词
She waited patiently for the bus. 她很有耐性地等着公共汽车。

patient[2] /ˈpeɪʃnt; ˈpeʃənt/ *noun* 名词
a sick person that a doctor is looking after 病人

patrol /pəˈtrəʊl; pəˈtrol/ *noun* 名词
a group of people, ships, aircraft, etc that go round a place to see that everything is all right 巡逻的人、船、飞机等: *an army patrol* 陆军的巡逻队
on patrol going round a place to see that everything is all right 巡逻: *During the carnival there will be 30 police cars on patrol.* 在狂欢节期间，将有30辆警车执行巡逻任务。
patrol *verb* 动词 (**patrols**, **patrolling**, **patrolled** /pəˈtrəʊld; pəˈtrold/)
A guard patrols the gate at night. 夜晚有个警卫在大门口巡逻。

patter /ˈpætə(r); ˈpætɚ/ *verb* 动词 (**patters**, **pattering**, **pattered** /ˈpætəd; ˈpætɚd/)
make quick light sounds 发出快而轻的声音: *Rain pattered against the window.* 雨点轻轻拍打着窗户。
patter *noun* 名词
the patter of children's feet on the stairs 孩子们在楼梯上发出的快而轻的脚步声

pattern /ˈpætn; ˈpætɚn/ *noun* 名词
1 shapes and colours on something 图案；花样: *The curtains had a pattern of flowers and leaves.* 帘子上有花和叶子的图案。
2 a thing that you copy when you make something（用以制造某物的）样式；图样: *I bought some material and a pattern to make a new skirt.* 我买了些料子和一个纸样来做新裙子。
patterned /ˈpætnd; ˈpætɚnd/ *adjective* 形容词
with shapes and colours on it 有图案或花样的: *a patterned shirt* 有图案的衬衫

pause /pɔːz; pɔz/ *noun* 名词
a short stop 暂停: *She played for 30 minutes without a pause.* 她不停地演奏了30分钟。
pause *verb* 动词 (**pauses**, **pausing**, **paused** /pɔːzd; pɔzd/)
stop for a short time 暂停: *He paused before answering my question.* 他停了一下才回答我的问题。

pavement /ˈpeɪvmənt; ˈpevmənt/ *noun* 名词
the part at the side of a road where people can walk 人行道

paw /pɔː; pɔ/ *noun* 名词
the foot of an animal, for example a dog, cat or bear 爪子（例如狗、猫或熊的）
☞ picture at **cat** 见 **cat** 词条插图

pay[1] /peɪ; pe/ *verb* 动词 (**pays**, **paying**, **paid** /peɪd; ped/, **has paid**)
1 give money to get something 付钱（得到某事物）: *She paid £4 000 for her car.* 她付了4 000英镑买了辆汽车。◇ *Are you paying in cash or by cheque?* 您是付现款还是给支票？
2 give money for work that somebody does 付钱（作为酬金）: *I paid the builder for mending the roof.* 我付给建造商修房顶的钱。
pay back give back the money that somebody has lent to you 还（曾借的）钱:

Can you lend me £5? I'll pay you back (= pay it back to you) *next week.* 你借给我5英镑行吗？我下星期还给你。

pay somebody back hurt somebody who has hurt you 报复: *One day I'll pay her back for lying to me!* 她向我撒谎，总有一天我得治她一下。

pay for something give money for what you buy 付钱（买东西）: *Have you paid for your hotel room yet?* 您付了旅馆的房钱了吗？

pay² /peɪ; pe/ *noun* 名词 (no plural 无复数)
the money that you get for work 工资；薪金

payment /ˈpeɪmənt; ˈpemənt/ *noun* 名词
1 (no plural 无复数) paying or being paid 付钱；报酬: *This cheque is in payment for the work you have done.* 这张支票是给您的酬金。
2 (*plural* 复数作 **payments**) an amount of money that you pay 付出的钱数: *I make monthly payments of £50.* 我每月付50英镑。

pay phone /ˈpeɪ fəʊn; ˈpeˌfon/ *noun* 名词
a telephone that you put money in to make a call（投币式）公用电话

PC /ˌpiː ˈsiː; ˌpi ˈsi/ *noun* 名词
1 a small computer. 'PC' is short for **personal computer**. 个人用计算机；个人电脑（PC是 **personal computer** 的缩略式。）
2 a policeman. 'PC' is short for **police constable** 警察（PC是 **police constable** 的缩略式。）: *PC Smith* 史密斯警察

PE /ˌpiː ˈiː; ˌpi ˈi/ *short for* **physical education** ＊ **physical education** 的缩略式

pea /piː; pi/ *noun* 名词
a very small round green vegetable. Peas grow in **pods**. 豌豆（豆荚叫做 **pod**）

peace /piːs; pis/ *noun* 名词 (no plural 无复数)
1 a time when there is no war, fighting or trouble between people or countries 和平；太平；和睦
2 being quiet and calm 安静；平静: *the peace of the countryside at night* 夜晚郊野的宁静 ◇ *Go away and leave me in peace!* 走开，别打扰我！

make peace agree to end a war or fight 停战；和解: *The two countries made peace.* 两国已经停战了。

peaceful /ˈpiːsfl; ˈpisfəl/ *adjective* 形容词
1 with no fighting 和平的；太平的；和睦的: *a peaceful demonstration* 和平的游行
2 quiet and calm 安静的；平静的: *a peaceful evening* 宁静的晚间

peacefully /ˈpiːsfəli; ˈpisfəlɪ/ *adverb* 副词
She's sleeping peacefully. 她安安静静地睡着觉。

peach /piːtʃ; pitʃ/ *noun* 名词 (*plural* 复数作 **peaches**)
a soft round fruit with a yellow and red skin and a large stone in the centre 桃

peach 桃

peacock /ˈpiːkɒk; ˈpiˌkɑk/ *noun* 名词
a large bird with beautiful long blue and green feathers in its tail 孔雀

peak /piːk; pik/ *noun* 名词
1 the pointed top of a mountain 山峰
2 the time when something is highest, biggest, etc 高峰；顶峰: *The traffic is at its peak between five and six in the evening.* 傍晚五六点钟是交通的高峰时间。
3 the pointed front part of a hat that is above your eyes 帽舌

peanut /ˈpiːnʌt; ˈpiˌnʌt/ *noun* 名词
a nut that you can eat 花生

pear /peə(r); pɛr/ *noun* 名词
a fruit that is green or yellow on the outside and white on the inside 梨

pear 梨

pearl /pɜːl; pɝl/ *noun* 名词
a small round white thing that comes from an **oyster** (a kind of shellfish). Pearls are used to make things like necklaces and earrings 珍珠（产自牡蛎，牡蛎叫做 **oyster**）: *a pearl necklace* 珍珠项链

peasant /ˈpeznt; ˈpɛznt̩/ *noun* 名词
a poor person who lives in the country and works on a small piece of land 农民

pebble /ˈpebl; ˈpɛbl̩/ *noun* 名词
a small round stone 卵石

peck /pek; pɛk/ *verb* 动词 (**pecks, pecking, pecked** /pekt; pɛkt/)
When a bird pecks something, it eats or bites it with its beak 啄: *The hens were pecking at the corn.* 母鸡正啄着玉米。

peculiar /pɪˈkjuːliə(r); pɪˈkjuljɚ/ *adjective* 形容词

strange; not usual 奇怪的；不寻常的：*What's that peculiar smell?* 那是什么怪味儿？

pedal /ˈpedl; ˈpɛdl̩/ *noun* 名词
a part of a bicycle or other machine that you move with your feet 踏板；脚蹬子（自行车或其他机器的）☞ picture at **bicycle** 见 **bicycle** 词条插图

P

pedestrian /pəˈdestriən; pəˈdɛstrɪən/ *noun* 名词
a person who is walking in the street 行人

pedestrian crossing /pəˌdestriən ˈkrɒsɪŋ; pəˌdɛstrɪən ˈkrɔsɪŋ/ *noun* 名词
a place where cars must stop so that people can cross the road 人行横道

pedestrian precinct /pəˌdestriən ˈpriːsɪŋkt; pəˌdɛstrɪən ˈprisɪŋkt/ *noun* 名词
a part of a town where there are a lot of shops and where cars cannot go 行人区（禁止车辆通行的商业区）

peel /piːl; pil/ *noun* 名词 (no plural 无复数)
the outside part of some fruit and vegetables（蔬菜和水果的）皮：*orange peel* 橙子皮

peel *verb* 动词 (**peels**, **peeling**, **peeled** /piːld; pild/)
1 take the outside part off a fruit or vegetable 去掉蔬菜和水果的皮：*Can you peel the potatoes?* 你来削土豆皮行吗？
2 come off in thin pieces 成片脱落：*The paint is peeling off the walls.* 墙皮脱落了。

peep /piːp; pip/ *verb* 动词 (**peeps**, **peeping**, **peeped** /piːpt; pipt/)
1 look at something quickly or secretly 很快地或偷偷地看：*I peeped through the window and saw her.* 我隔着窗户偷看了她一眼。
2 come out for a short time 出来片刻：*The moon peeped out from behind the clouds.* 月亮从云层中探了探头。

peer /pɪə(r); pɪr/ *verb* 动词 (**peers**, **peering**, **peered** /pɪəd; pɪrd/)
look closely at something because you cannot see well 仔细看（因看不清楚）：*I peered outside but I couldn't see anything because it was dark.* 我向外张望，可是因为天黑什么也看不见。

peg /peg; pɛg/ *noun* 名词
1 a small thing on a wall or door where you can hang clothes（在墙上或门上可挂衣物的）钉，钩：*Your coat is on the peg.* 您的大衣挂在衣钩上呢。
2 a small wooden or plastic thing that holds wet clothes on a line when they are drying（晾衣绳上的木制的或塑料的）夹子：*a clothes-peg* 晾衣夹

pen¹ /pen; pɛn/ *noun* 名词
a thing that you use for writing with a coloured liquid (called **ink**) 钢笔（墨水叫做 **ink**）

pen² /pen; pɛn/ *noun* 名词
a small place with a fence around it for keeping animals in（饲养动物的有围栏的）圈

penalty /ˈpenlti; ˈpɛnl̩tɪ/ *noun* 名词 (*plural* 复数作 **penalties**)
a punishment 处罚；惩罚：*The penalty for travelling without a ticket is £300* (= you must pay £300). 无票搭乘交通工具的惩罚是300英镑。

pence *plural of* **penny** ＊ **penny** 的复数形式

pencil /ˈpensl; ˈpɛnsl̩/ *noun* 名词
a thin piece of wood with grey or coloured stuff inside it. Pencils are used for writing or drawing. 铅笔

pen-friend /ˈpen frend; ˈpɛnˌfrɛnd/, **pen-pal** /ˈpen pæl; ˈpɛnˌpæl/ *noun* 名词
a person that you write to but have probably never met 笔友（与之通信而可能未见过面的人）

penguin 企鹅

penguin /ˈpeŋgwɪn; ˈpɛŋgwɪn/ *noun* 名词
a black and white bird that lives in very cold places. Penguins can swim but they cannot fly. 企鹅

penknife /ˈpen naɪf; ˈpɛnˌnaɪf/ *noun* 名词 (*plural* 复数作 **penknives** /ˈpen naɪvz; ˈpɛnˌnaɪvz/)
a small knife that you can carry in your pocket 小折刀

penny /'peni; 'pɛnɪ/ *noun* 名词 (*plural* 复数作 **pence** /pens; pɛns/ or 或 **pennies**)
a small coin that people use in Britain. There are 100 pence in a **pound** 便士(英国硬币。100便士等于1镑，镑叫做 **pound**)：*These pencils cost 40 pence each.* 这些铅笔40便士一枝。✪ The short form of 'pence' is **p** ✳ pence 的缩略式为 **p**: *Can you lend me 50p?* 你借给我50便士行吗？

pension /'penʃn; 'pɛnʃən/ *noun* 名词
money that you get from a government or a company when you are old and do not work any more (when you are **retired**) 养老金；退休金（退休叫做 **retire**）
pensioner /'penʃənə(r); 'pɛnʃənɚ/ *noun* 名词
a person who has a pension 领养老金或退休金的人

people /'pi:pl; 'pipl̩/ *noun* 名词 (plural 复数)
more than one person（不止一个）人：*How many people came to the meeting?* 有多少人来开会了？◇ *People often arrive late at parties.* 有的人参加聚会经常迟到。

pepper /'pepə(r); 'pɛpɚ/ *noun* 名词
1 (no plural 无复数) powder with a hot taste that you put on food 胡椒粉: *salt and pepper* 盐和胡椒粉
2 (*plural* 复数作 **peppers**) a red, green or yellow vegetable with a lot of white seeds inside 辣椒

peppermint /'pepəmɪnt; 'pɛpɚˌmɪnt/ *noun* 名词
1 (no plural 无复数) a plant with a strong fresh taste and smell. It is used to make things like sweets and medicines. 胡椒薄荷
2 (*plural* 复数作 **peppermints**) a sweet made from this 薄荷糖

per /pə(r); pɚ/ *preposition* 介词
for each; in each 每；每一: *These apples cost 40p per pound.* 这些苹果40便士一磅。◇ *I was driving at 60 miles per hour.* 我当时开车的速度是每小时60英里。

per cent /pə 'sent; pɚ'sɛnt/ *noun* 名词 (no plural 无复数)
%; in each hundred ✳ %；每一百个之中: *90 per cent of the people who work here are men* (= in 100 people there are 90 men). 在这里工作的人百分之九十都是男的。
percentage /pə'sentɪdʒ; pɚ'sɛntɪdʒ/ *noun* 名词
'What percentage of students passed the exam?' 'Oh, about eighty per cent.' "学生及格人数的百分比是多少？""噢，大约是百分之八十。"

perch /pɜ:tʃ; pɝtʃ/ *noun* 名词 (*plural* 复数作 **perches**)
a place where a bird sits 鸟的栖息处
perch *verb* 动词 (**perches, perching, perched** /pɜ:tʃt; pɝtʃt/)
sit on something narrow 坐在窄物上: *The bird perched on a branch.* 那只鸟停在树枝上了。

perfect /'pɜ:fɪkt; 'pɝfɪkt/ *adjective* 形容词
1 so good that it cannot be better; with nothing wrong 完美的；无瑕的: *Her English is perfect.* 她的英语非常地道。◇ *The weather is perfect for a picnic.* 这种天气去野餐十分理想。
2 made from 'has', 'have' or 'had' and the **past participle** of a verb 完成式的（由 has、have 或 had 加上动词的过去分词 **past participle** 构成）：*perfect tenses* 完成时态

perfectly /'pɜ:fɪktli; 'pɝfɪktlɪ/ *adverb* 副词
1 completely; very 完全；非常: *I'm perfectly all right.* 我现在好极了。
2 in a perfect way 完美地；完满地: *She played the piece of music perfectly.* 那首音乐她演奏得十分精彩。

perform /pə'fɔ:m; pɚ'fɔrm/ *verb* 动词 (**performs, performing, performed** /pə'fɔ:md; pɚ'fɔrmd/)
1 do a piece of work 做一项工作: *The doctor performed an operation to save her life.* 医生动手术挽救她的生命。
2 be in a play, concert, etc 表演；演奏；演唱: *The band is performing at the Odeon tonight.* 那个乐队今晚在音乐厅演出。
performer *noun* 名词
a person who is in a play, concert, etc 表演者；演奏者；演唱者

P

performance /pəˈfɔːməns; pɚˈfɔrməns/ *noun* 名词

1 (*plural* 复数作 **performances**) a time when a play, etc. is shown, or music is played in front of a lot of people 表演；演奏；演唱: *We went to the evening performance of the play?* 我们去看了那出戏的晚场演出。

2 (no plural 无复数) how well you do something 做某事的表现: *My parents were pleased with my performance in the exam.* 我父母对我的考试成绩很满意。

P

perfume /ˈpɜːfjuːm; ˈpɝfjum/ *noun* 名词

1 a nice smell 香味

2 a liquid with a nice smell that you put on your body 香水: *a bottle of perfume* 一瓶香水

perhaps /pəˈhæps; pɚˈhæps/ *adverb* 副词

a word that you use when you are not sure about something 表示对某事物不很肯定的词；也许；可能；大概: *I don't know where she is — perhaps she's still at work.* 我不知道她在哪里——大概还在工作呢。◇ *There were three men, or perhaps four.* 有三个男的，也许是四个。

period /ˈpɪəriəd; ˈpɪrɪəd/ *noun* 名词

1 an amount of time 一段时间；期间: *He was ill four times in a period of six months.* 他在六个月这段时间里病了四次。

2 a certain time in the life of a person or the history of a country（个人一生的或国家历史上的）某段时间；时期: *What period of history are you studying?* 您正在研究哪一时期的历史？

3 a lesson 课时；学时: *We have five periods of German a week.* 我们一星期有五堂德语课。

4 the time when a woman loses blood from her body each month 月经

5 *American English for* **full stop** 美式英语，即 **full stop**

permanent /ˈpɜːmənənt; ˈpɝmənənt/ *adjective* 形容词

Something that is permanent continues for ever or for a very long time and does not change 永久的；长期的: *I'm looking for a permanent job.* 我正在找一份固定的工作。

☞ Look at **temporary**. 见 **temporary**。

permanently *adverb* 副词

Has he left permanently or is he coming back? 他是永远离开了，还是以后再回来？

permission /pəˈmɪʃn; pɚˈmɪʃən/ *noun* 名词 (no plural 无复数)

allowing somebody to do something 许可；准许；允许: *She gave me permission to leave early.* 她允许我早点儿走。

permit[1] /pəˈmɪt; pɚˈmɪt/ *verb* 动词 (**permits**, **permitting**, **permitted**)

allow somebody to do something 许可；准许；允许: *You are not permitted to smoke in the hospital.* 医院里不准许吸烟。

✪ **Allow** is the word that we usually use. ✳ **allow**是常用词。

permit[2] /ˈpɜːmɪt; ˈpɝmɪt/ *noun* 名词

a piece of paper that says you can do something or go somewhere 许可证；通行证: *Have you got a work permit?* 您得到工作许可证了吗？

person /ˈpɜːsn; ˈpɝsn̩/ *noun* 名词 (*plural* 复数作 **people** /ˈpiːpl; ˈpipl̩/)

a man or woman 人: *I think she's the best person for the job.* 我认为她是最适合做这项工作的人。

in person seeing somebody, not just speaking on the telephone or writing a letter 亲身；亲自；本人: *I want to speak to her in person.* 我想跟她本人谈谈。

personal /ˈpɜːsənl; ˈpɝsn̩l/ *adjective* 形容词

of or for one person; private 个人的；私人的: *This letter is personal, so I don't want anyone else to read it.* 这封是私人信，我不想让别人看。

personal stereo /ˌpɜːsənl ˈsteriəʊ; ˌpɝsn̩l ˈstɛrɪo/ *noun* 名词 (*plural* 复数作 **personal stereos**)

a small cassette player or radio with **headphones**, that is easy to carry（便携式的）个人用的立体声唱机或收音机（使用的头戴式收话器叫做 **headphones**）

personality /ˌpɜːsəˈnæləti; ˌpɝsn̩ˈælətɪ/ *noun* 名词 (*plural* 复数作 **personalities**)

1 what sort of person you are; your character 人格；品格；个性: *Mark has a great personality.* 马克的品格很高尚。

2 a famous person 名人: *a television personality* 电视圈中的名人

personally /ˈpɜːsənəli; ˈpɝsn̩lɪ/ *adverb* 副词

You say 'personally' when you are saying what you think about something 就我来说；就自己而言: *Personally, I like*

P

her, but a lot of people don't. 就我个人来说，我喜欢她，可是有很多人并不喜欢她。

persuade /pə'sweɪd; pɚ'swed/ *verb* 动词 (**persuades**, **persuading**, **persuaded**)
make somebody think or do something by talking to them 劝说或说服某人做某事: *The man in the shop persuaded me to buy the most expensive pen.* 商店里的男子劝我买最贵的钢笔。

persuasion /pə'sweɪʒn; pɚ'sweʒən/ *noun* 名词 (no plural 无复数)
persuading somebody or being persuaded 劝说；说服: *After a lot of persuasion she agreed to come.* 好说歹说，她才同意来。

pessimism /'pesɪmɪzəm; 'pɛsəˌmɪzəm/ *noun* 名词 (no plural 无复数)
thinking that bad things will happen 悲观 ✪ opposite 反义词: **optimism**

pessimist /'pesɪmɪst; 'pɛsəmɪst/ *noun* 名词
a person who always thinks that bad things will happen 悲观的人；悲观主义者

pessimistic /ˌpesɪ'mɪstɪk; ˌpɛsə'mɪstɪk/ *adjective* 形容词
If you are pessimistic, you think that bad things will happen 悲观的；悲观主义的: *Don't be so pessimistic!* 别那么悲观！

pest /pest; pɛst/ *noun* 名词
1 an insect or animal that damages plants or food 害虫、害兽、害鸟等有害动物
2 a person or thing that makes you a little angry 讨厌的人或事物: *My sister won't leave me alone when I'm working — she's a real pest!* 我妹妹就是不能让我清清静静地工作——太讨厌了！

pet /pet; pɛt/ *noun* 名词
1 an animal that you keep in your home 玩赏动物；宠物: *I've got two pets — a cat and a goldfish.* 我养了两个小宠物——一只猫和一条金鱼。
2 a child that a teacher or a parent likes best 受教师或父母宠爱的孩子: *She's the teacher's pet.* 她是受老师宠爱的学生。

petal /'petl; 'pɛtl/ *noun* 名词
one of the coloured parts of a flower 花瓣

petition /pə'tɪʃn; pə'tɪʃən/ *noun* 名词
a special letter, from a group of people, that asks for something 请愿书: *Hundreds of people signed the petition for a new pedestrian crossing.* 数以百计的人签名请愿要求设置新的人行横道。

petrol /'petrəl; 'pɛtrəl/ *noun* 名词 (no plural 无复数)
a liquid that you put in a car to make the engine work 汽油

petrol station /'petrəl steɪʃn; 'pɛtrəl ˌsteʃən/ *noun* 名词
a place where you can buy petrol 汽车加油站

phantom /'fæntəm; 'fæntəm/ *noun* 名词
a ghost 鬼魂

pharmacist /'fɑːməsɪst; 'fɑrməsɪst/ *another word for* **chemist 1** ✳ **chemist 1** 的另一种说法

phase /feɪz; fez/ *noun* 名词
a time when something is changing or growing（某事物正在变化或发展的）阶段；时期: *My first year at university was a very exciting phase of my life.* 我上大学的第一年是我一生中最兴奋的时候。

philosophy /fə'lɒsəfi; fə'lɑsəfɪ/ *noun* 名词
1 (no plural 无复数) the study of ideas about the meaning of life 哲学
2 (*plural* 复数作 **philosophies**) what one person thinks about life 人生观；人生哲学: *Enjoy yourself today and don't worry about tomorrow — that's my philosophy!* 且享今朝乐，莫管明日愁——这就是我的人生哲学！

philosopher /fə'lɒsəfə(r); fə'lɑsəfɚ/ *noun* 名词
a person who studies philosophy 哲学家

phone /fəʊn; fon/ *noun* 名词
a telephone; an instrument that you use for talking to somebody who is in another place 电话: *The phone's ringing — can you answer it?* 电话铃响了——你接听行吗？◇ *What's your phone number?* 您的电话号码是多少？◇ *I need to make a phone call.* 我需要打个电话。

on the phone using a telephone to speak to somebody 用电话交谈；通话: *Anna was on the phone for an hour.* 安娜已经通话一个小时了。

phone *verb* 动词 (**phones**, **phoning**, **phoned** /fəʊnd; fond/)
use a telephone 打电话: *I phoned Di last night.* 我昨天晚上给戴打了个电话。

phone book /'fəʊn bʊk; 'fon bʊk/ *noun* 名词
a book of people's names, addresses and telephone numbers 电话簿

phone box /ˈfəʊn bɒks; ˈfon ˌbɑks/ (*plural* 复数作 **phone boxes**), **phone booth** /ˈfəʊn bu:ð; ˈfon ˌbuθ/ *noun* 名词
a public telephone in the street 电话亭

phonecard /ˈfəʊnkɑ:d; ˈfonˌkɑrd/ *noun* 名词
a small plastic card that you can use to pay for a call to somebody from a **phone box** 电话卡（在电话亭 **phone box** 中代替现金使用的塑料卡）

P

phonetics /fəˈnetɪks; fəˈnɛtɪks/ *noun* 名词 (no plural 无复数)
the study of the sounds that people make when they speak 语音学

phonetic *adjective* 形容词
using special signs to show how to say words 使用音标的: *The phonetic alphabet is printed at the bottom of this page.* 语音字母印在本页的下端。

photocopy /ˈfəʊtəʊkɒpi; ˈfotoˌkɑpɪ/ *noun* 名词 (*plural* 复数作 **photocopies**)
a copy of something on paper that you make with a special machine (called a **photocopier**) 影印件；影印本（影印机叫做 **photocopier**）

photocopy *verb* 动词 (**photocopies**, **photocopying**, **photocopied** /ˈfəʊtəʊkɒpid; ˈfotoˌkɑpɪd/, **has photocopied**)
Can you photocopy this letter for me? 您把这封信给我影印一份行吗？

photograph /ˈfəʊtəgrɑ:f; ˈfotəˌgræf/, **photo** /ˈfəʊtəʊ; ˈfoto/ (*plural* 复数作 **photos**) *noun* 名词
a picture that you take with a camera 照片；相片: *I took a photo of the Eiffel Tower.* 我照了一张埃菲尔铁塔的照片。

photograph *verb* 动词 (**photographs**, **photographing**, **photographed** /ˈfəʊtəgrɑ:ft; ˈfotəˌgræft/)
take a photograph of somebody or something 照相；拍照: *The winner was photographed holding his prize.* 优胜者拿着他的奖品照了一张相。

photographer /fəˈtɒgrəfə(r); fəˈtɑgrəfɚ/ *noun* 名词
a person who takes photographs 摄影者；摄影师

photographic /ˌfəʊtəˈgræfɪk; ˌfotəˈgræfɪk/ *adjective* 形容词
about photographs or photography 摄影的；摄影术的: *photographic equipment* 摄影器材

photography /fəˈtɒgrəfi; fəˈtɑgrəfɪ/ *noun* 名词 (no plural 无复数)
taking photographs 摄影；摄影术

phrase /freɪz; frez/ *noun* 名词
a group of words that you use together as part of a sentence 词组；短语: *'First of all' and 'a bar of chocolate' are phrases.* ＊ first of all 和 a bar of chocolate 都是词组。

physical /ˈfɪzɪkl; ˈfɪzɪkḷ/ *adjective* 形容词
You use 'physical' about things that you feel or do with your body 身体的；肉体的: *physical exercise* 体育活动

physically /ˈfɪzɪkli; ˈfɪzɪkḷɪ/ *adverb* 副词
I'm not physically fit. 我身体不舒服。

physical education /ˌfɪzɪkl edʒuˈkeɪʃn; ˌfɪzɪkḷ ɛdʒəˈkeʃən/ *noun* 名词 (no plural 无复数)
sports that you do at school（学校中的）体育 ✪ The short form is **PE**. 缩略式为 **PE**。

physics /ˈfɪzɪks; ˈfɪzɪks/ *noun* 名词 (no plural 无复数)
the study of things like heat, light and sound 物理学

physicist /ˈfɪzɪsɪst; ˈfɪzəsɪst/ *noun* 名词
a person who studies or knows a lot about physics 物理学研究者；物理学家

piano /piˈænəʊ; pɪˈæno/ *noun* 名词 (*plural* 复数作 **pianos**)
a big musical instrument that you play by pressing black and white bars (called **keys**) 钢琴（琴键叫做 **key**）: *Can you play the piano?* 您会弹钢琴吗？

pianist /ˈpi:ənɪst; ˈpiənɪst/ *noun* 名词
a person who plays the piano 钢琴演奏者；钢琴家

pick[1] /pɪk; pɪk/ *verb* 动词 (**picks**, **picking**, **picked** /pɪkt; pɪkt/)
1 take the person or thing you like best; choose 挑选；选择: *They picked Simon as their captain.* 他们选出西蒙当队长。
2 take a flower, fruit or vegetable from the place where it grows 采摘花朵、水果或蔬菜: *I've picked some flowers for you.* 我给你采了些花。

pick out be able to see somebody or something in a lot of others（在一些人或事物中）分辨出某人或某事物: *Can you pick out my father in this photo?* 你能在这张照片里认出我父亲吗？

pick up **1** take and lift somebody or something 举起或抬起某人或某物: *She picked up the bags and put them on the table.* 她把袋子都拿起来放在桌子上。◇ *The phone stopped ringing just as I picked it up.* 我刚一拿起话筒，电话就不响了。**2** come to take somebody or something away 来接某人或取某物: *My father picks me up from school.* 我父亲到学校来接我。**3** learn something without really studying it（并非特意地）学会某事物: *Did you pick up any Japanese while you were in Tokyo?* 你在东京的时候，学点儿日语了吗？

pick² /pɪk; pɪk/ *noun* 名词 (no plural 无复数)

what you choose; your choice 挑选的事物；选择

take your pick choose what you like 任意挑选: *We've got orange juice, lemonade or milk. Take your pick.* 我们有橙子汁、汽水或牛奶。您随便挑吧。

picket /'pɪkɪt; 'pɪkɪt/ *verb* 动词 (**pickets, picketing, picketed**)

stand outside the place where you work when there is a **strike**, and try to stop other people going to work（罢工时）任纠察队员（守在工作地点外面阻拦他人上班）（罢工叫做 **strike**）

picket *noun* 名词

a person or group of people who picket（罢工时的）纠察队员（守在工作地点外面阻拦他人上班的人）: *There was a picket outside the hospital.* 医院外面有罢工纠察队。

pickpocket /'pɪkpɒkɪt; 'pɪk,pɑkɪt/ *noun* 名词

a person who steals things from people's pockets 扒手

picnic /'pɪknɪk; 'pɪknɪk/ *noun* 名词

a meal that you eat outside, away from home 野餐: *We had a picnic by the river.* 我们在河边吃了一顿野餐。

picnic *verb* 动词 (**picnics, picnicking, picnicked** /'pɪknɪkt; 'pɪknɪkt/)

have a picnic 野餐: *We picnicked on the beach yesterday.* 我们昨天在海滩上吃了一顿野餐。

picture /'pɪktʃə(r); 'pɪktʃɚ/ *noun* 名词

1 a drawing, painting or photograph 图画、图片或照片: *Julie drew a picture of her dog.* 朱莉画了一张她的狗的图画。◇ *They showed us some pictures of their wedding.* 他们给我们看了他们结婚时候的一些照片。

2 the pictures (plural 复数) the cinema 电影院: *We're going to the pictures this evening.* 我们今天晚上去看电影。

take a picture photograph something 照相；拍照: *I took a picture of the house.* 我照了一张那所房子的照片。

pie /paɪ; paɪ/ *noun* 名词

meat, fruit, vegetables, etc with pastry 排（一种点心，用油酥面团做成浅盘子形状的底，在上面加肉、水果、蔬菜等制成）: *an apple pie* 苹果排

pie 排

piece /pi:s; pis/ *noun* 名词

1 a part of something 某物的一部分；一块；一片: *Would you like another piece of cake?* 您再来一块蛋糕好吗？◇ *a piece of broken glass* 一块碎玻璃 ☞ picture on page C25 见第C25页图

2 one single thing 一个完整的东西；一件: *Have you got a piece of paper?* 你有一张纸吗？◇ *That's an interesting piece of news.* 这个消息很有意思。

3 a coin 硬币: *a 50p piece* 一个50便士的硬币

fall to pieces break into pieces 碎成块: *The chair fell to pieces when I sat on it.* 这把椅子我一坐就散了。

in pieces broken 破碎: *The teapot lay in pieces on the floor.* 地上是那把茶壶的碎片。

take something to pieces divide something into its parts 拆开: *I took the bed to pieces because it was too big to go through the door.* 因为床太大不能通过这道门，我就把它拆开了。

pier /pɪə(r); pɪr/ *noun* 名词

a long thing that is built from the land into the sea, where people can walk or get on and off boats（伸入海中的）码头

pierce /pɪəs; pɪrs/ *verb* 动词 (**pierces, piercing, pierced** /pɪəst; pɪrst/)

make a hole in something with a sharp point 用尖物刺入某物；穿孔: *The nail pierced her skin.* 钉子把她的皮肤扎破了。

piercing /'pɪəsɪŋ; 'pɪrsɪŋ/ *adjective* 形容词

A piercing sound is very loud and sharp（指声音）大而尖的；刺耳的: *a piercing cry* 刺耳的叫声

P

pig /pɪg; pɪg/ *noun* 名词

1 a fat animal that people keep on farms for its meat 猪

✪ A young pig is called a **piglet**. 幼小的猪叫做 **piglet**。Meat from a pig is called **pork**, **bacon** or **ham**. 猪肉叫做 **pork**，腌猪肉叫做 **bacon**，火腿叫做 **ham**。

P

2 an unkind person or a person who eats too much 不和善的人；残忍的人；贪婪的人: *You've eaten all the biscuits, you pig!* 你把饼干都吃了，你这个贪吃鬼！

pigeon /ˈpɪdʒɪn; ˈpɪdʒən/ *noun* 名词

a grey bird that you often see in towns 鸽子

piglet /ˈpɪglət; ˈpɪglɪt/ *noun* 名词

a young pig 幼小的猪

pigsty /ˈpɪgstaɪ; ˈpɪgstaɪ/ *noun* 名词 (*plural* 复数作 **pigsties**)

a small building where pigs live 猪圈

pile /paɪl; paɪl/ *noun* 名词

a lot of things on top of one another; a large amount of something 堆；摞；大量: *There's a pile of clothes on the floor.* 地板上有一堆衣服。◇ *a pile of earth* 一大堆土 ☞ picture on page C25 见第C25页图

pile *verb* 动词 (**piles**, **piling**, **piled** /paɪld; paɪld/)

put a lot of things on top of one another 堆放；堆积: *She piled the boxes on the table.* 她把盒子都摞在桌子上了。

pilgrim /ˈpɪlgrɪm; ˈpɪlgrəm/ *noun* 名词

a person who travels a long way to a place because it has a special religious meaning 朝圣者；香客

pilgrimage /ˈpɪlgrɪmɪdʒ; ˈpɪlgrəmɪdʒ/ *noun* 名词

a journey that a pilgrim makes（朝圣者或香客的）朝圣之行

pill /pɪl; pɪl/ *noun* 名词

a small round hard piece of medicine that you swallow 药丸；药片: *Take one of these pills before every meal.* 每顿饭前吃一片这种药。

pillar /ˈpɪlə(r); ˈpɪlɚ/ *noun* 名词

a tall strong piece of stone, wood or metal that holds up a building 柱子

pillar-box /ˈpɪlə bɒks; ˈpɪlɚˌbɑks/ *noun* 名词 (*plural* 复数作 **pillar-boxes**)

a tall red box in the street for sending letters 邮筒；信筒（呈柱形，红色）

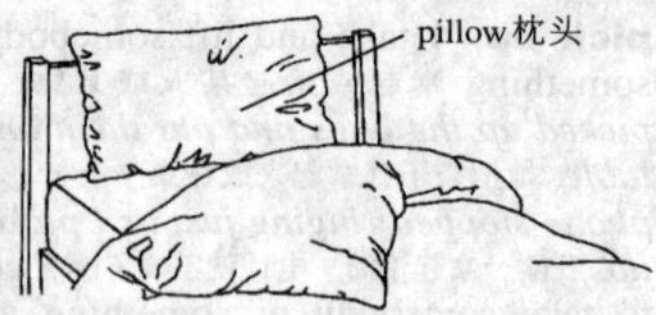

pillow /ˈpɪləʊ; ˈpɪlo/ *noun* 名词

a soft thing that you put your head on when you are in bed 枕头

pillowcase /ˈpɪləʊkeɪs; ˈpɪloˌkes/ *noun* 名词

a cover for a pillow 枕套

pilot /ˈpaɪlət; ˈpaɪlət/ *noun* 名词

1 a person who flies an aircraft（飞行器的）驾驶员；飞行员

2 a person who guides a ship along a river, into a harbour, etc（船舶的）领航员；领港员

pin[1] /pɪn; pɪn/ *noun* 名词

a small thin piece of metal with a flat part at one end and a sharp point at the other. You use a pin for holding pieces of cloth or paper together. 大头针 ☞ Look also at **drawing-pin** and **safety pin**. 另见 **drawing-pin** 和 **safety pin**。

pins and needles /ˌpɪnz ən ˈni:dlz; ˌpɪnz ənd ˈnidl̩z/ *noun* 名词 (plural 复数)

the feeling that you sometimes get in a part of your body when you have not moved it for a long time 麻（身体某部分由于长时间不活动，有时发生的麻木的感觉）

pin[2] /pɪn; pɪn/ *verb* 动词 (**pins**, **pinning**, **pinned** /pɪnd; pɪnd/)

1 fix things together with a pin or pins 用大头针钉住或别住某物: *Pin the pieces of material together before you sew them.* 先把料子用大头针别住，然后再缝起来。◇ *Could you pin this notice to the board?* 您把这份通知用大头针钉在布告板上行吗？

2 hold somebody or something so that they cannot move 束缚住某人或某物使之不能动: *He tried to get away, but they pinned him against the wall.* 他想溜走，可是他们把他按在墙上使他不能动弹。

pinch /pɪntʃ; pɪntʃ/ *verb* 动词 (**pinches**, **pinching**, **pinched** /pɪntʃt; pɪntʃt/)

1 press somebody's skin tightly between your thumb and finger 用拇指和别的手指夹住某人的皮肤；捏；掐；拧: *Don't pinch me—it hurts!* 别掐我——很疼！

2 steal something 偷东西: *Who's pinched my pen?* 谁把我的钢笔偷走了？✪ This is an informal use. 这是个俗语词。

pinch *noun* 名词 (*plural* 复数作 **pinches**)

1 pinching something 用拇指和别的手指夹住某人的皮肤；捏；掐；拧: *He gave my leg a pinch.* 他掐了我的腿一下。

2 how much of something you can hold between your thumb and finger 能用拇指和别的手指夹住的量；一捏: *Add a pinch of salt to the soup.* 往汤里放一捏盐。

pine /paɪn; paɪn/, **pine tree** /ˈpaɪn triː; ˈpaɪn ˌtri/ *noun* 名词

a tall tree with thin sharp leaves (called **needles**) that do not fall off in winter 松树（针叶叫做 **needle**）

pineapple /ˈpaɪnæpl; ˈpaɪnˌæpl̩/ *noun* 名词

a big fruit that has a rough brown skin and a yellow inside part 菠萝

pineapple 菠萝

ping-pong /ˈpɪŋ pɒŋ; ˈpɪŋˌpɑŋ/ *noun* 名词 (no plural 无复数)

a game where players use a round **bat** to hit a small light ball over a net on a big table; table tennis 乒乓球运动（球拍叫做 **bat**）

pink /pɪŋk; pɪŋk/ *adjective* 形容词

with a light red colour 粉红色的: *a pink jumper* 粉红色的套头毛衣

pink *noun* 名词

She was dressed in pink. 她穿着粉红色的衣服。

pint /paɪnt; paɪnt/ *noun* 名词

a measure of liquid (= 0.57 litres). There are eight pints in a **gallon** 品脱（液量单位，= 0.57升；8品脱等于1加仑，加仑叫做 **gallon**）; *a pint of beer* 一品脱啤酒 ◇ *two pints of milk* 两品脱牛奶 ✪ The short way of writing 'pint' is **pt**. ＊ pint 的缩写形式为 **pt**。

✪ In the past, people in Britain used **pints** and **gallons** to measure liquids, not **litres**. 从前，英国人用品脱（**pint**）和加仑（**gallon**）来量度液体，而不用升（**litre**）。Now, many people use and understand both ways. 现在许多人都可使用这两种液量单位。

pioneer /ˌpaɪəˈnɪə(r); ˌpaɪəˈnɪr/ *noun* 名词

a person who goes somewhere or does something before other people 最先（史无前例）到某处或做某事的人；拓荒者: *the pioneers of the American West* 开发美国西部的人

pip /pɪp; pɪp/ *noun* 名词

the seed of some fruits. Lemons, oranges and apples have pips.（某些水果的）种子，子儿（例如柠檬、柑橘、苹果等的）

pipe /paɪp; paɪp/ *noun* 名词

1 a long tube that takes water, oil, gas, etc from one place to another 管子

2 a thing that you put tobacco in to smoke it 烟斗

3 a musical instrument that you blow 管乐器

pipeline /ˈpaɪplaɪn; ˈpaɪpˌlaɪn/ *noun* 名词

a big pipe that carries oil or gas a long way（长距离输送油、气的）管道

pirate /ˈpaɪrət; ˈpaɪrət/ *noun* 名词

a person on a ship who robs other ships 海盗

pistol /ˈpɪstl; ˈpɪstl̩/ *noun* 名词

a small gun 手枪

pit /pɪt; pɪt/ *noun* 名词

1 a deep hole in the ground（深入地下的）坑

2 a deep hole that people make in the ground to take out coal（深入地下的）煤矿；矿坑

pitch¹ /pɪtʃ; pɪtʃ/ *noun* 名词 (*plural* 复数作 **pitches**)

1 a piece of ground where you play games like football or cricket（足球或板球等的）球场

2 how high or low a sound is（声音的）高度；音高

pitch² /pɪtʃ; pɪtʃ/ *verb* 动词 (**pitches, pitching, pitched** /pɪtʃt; pɪtʃt/)

put up a tent 搭帐篷: *We pitched our tent under a big tree.* 我们在一棵大树下搭起了帐篷。

pitcher /ˈpɪtʃə(r); ˈpɪtʃɚ/ *American English for* **jug** 美式英语，即 **jug**

pity¹ /ˈpɪti; ˈpɪtɪ/ *noun* 名词 (no plural 无复数)

sadness for a person or an animal who is in pain or who has problems 同情；怜悯: *I felt pity for the old dog so I gave*

P

him some food. 我很可怜那条老狗，所以喂了它一些食物。

it's a pity, what a pity it is sad 很遗憾；真可惜: *It's a pity you can't come to the party.* 您不能来参加聚会，真遗憾。

take pity on somebody help somebody because you feel sad for them 出于同情或怜悯而帮助某人: *I took pity on her and gave her some money.* 我很同情她，就给了她些钱。

P

pity² /ˈpɪti; ˈpɪtɪ/ *verb* 动词 (**pities, pitying, pitied** /ˈpɪtid; ˈpɪtɪd/, **has pitied**)
feel sad for somebody who is in pain or who has problems 同情或怜悯某人: *I really pity people who haven't got anywhere to live.* 我非常同情那些无家可归的人。

pizza /ˈpiːtsə; ˈpitsə/ *noun* 名词 (*plural* 复数作 **pizzas**)
a flat round piece of bread with tomatoes, cheese and other things on top, that is cooked in an oven 意大利饼（饼上覆西红柿、奶酪等，在烤箱中烘制而成）

place¹ /pleɪs; ples/ *noun* 名词

1 where somebody or something is 地方；场所: *Put the book back in the right place.* 把书放回原处。

2 a building, town, country, etc 建筑物、城镇、国家等: *Budapest is a very interesting place.* 布达佩斯是个很有趣的地方。◇ *Do you know a good place to have lunch?* 您能介绍个好地方吃午饭吗？

3 a seat or space for one person（容一个人的）座位或空间: *An old man was sitting in my place.* 有个老翁坐在我的位子上了。

4 where you are in a race, test, etc（在比赛、测验等中的）名次: *Alice finished in second place.* 艾丽斯得了第二名。

in place where it should be; in the right place 在应在的地方: *She tied her hair with a ribbon to keep it in place.* 她用一条带子把头发固定住了。

in place of somebody or 或 **something** instead of somebody or something 代替某人或某事物: *Joe became goalkeeper in place of Martin, who had broken his leg.* 马丁的腿骨折了，乔代替他担任守门员。

take place happen 发生: *The wedding of John and Sara will take place on 22 May.* 约翰和萨拉的婚礼将于5月22日举行。

place² /pleɪs; ples/ *verb* 动词 (**places, placing, placed** /pleɪst; plest/)
put something somewhere 把某物放在某处: *The waiter placed the meal in front of me.* 服务员把饭菜放在我的面前。

plain¹ /pleɪn; plen/ *adjective* 形容词 (**plainer, plainest**)

1 with no pattern; all one colour 没有图案的；一种颜色的: *She wore a plain blue dress.* 她穿着一身素的蓝色连衣裙。

2 simple and ordinary 简单而普通的: *plain food* 普通的食物

3 easy to see, hear or understand; clear 容易看见、听见或理解的；清楚的: *It's plain that he's unhappy.* 他显然很不愉快。

4 not pretty 不漂亮的: *She was a plain child.* 她是个长相普通的孩子。

plainly *adverb* 副词
clearly 清楚地；显然: *They were plainly very angry.* 他们显然十分生气。

plain² /pleɪn; plen/ *noun* 名词
a large piece of flat land 平原

plait /plæt; plet/ *verb* 动词 (**plaits, plaiting, plaited**)
put long pieces of hair, rope, etc over and under each other to make one thick piece 编（辫子、绳子等）: *Her hair is plaited.* 她把头发编成辫子了。

plait *noun* 名词
a long piece of hair that somebody has plaited 辫子: *She wears her hair in plaits.* 她留着辫子。

plan¹ /plæn; plæn/ *noun* 名词

1 something that you have decided to do, and how to do it 计划；规划；方案: *What are your holiday plans?* 您假期有什么安排？◇ *They have plans to build a new school.* 他们计划修建一所新学校。

2 a map 地图: *a street plan of London* 伦敦街道图

3 a drawing for a new building, machine, etc 设计图（为建造新建筑物、机器等的）: *Have you seen the plans for the new shopping centre?* 您看过新购物中心的设计图了吗？

plan² /plæn; plæn/ *verb* 动词 (**plans, planning, planned** /plænd; plænd/)
decide what you are going to do and how you are going to do it 计划；打算: *They're planning a holiday in Australia next summer.* 他们正计划夏天一到就去澳大利亚度假。◇ *I'm planning to go to university.* 我打算上大学。

plane /pleɪn; plen/ *noun* 名词
an aeroplane 飞机: *I like travelling by plane.* 我爱坐飞机。◇ *What time does your plane land?* 您坐的飞机什么时候着陆? ☞ picture at **aeroplane** 见 **aeroplane** 词条插图

planet /'plænɪt; 'plænɪt/ *noun* 名词
a large round thing in space that moves around the sun 行星: *Earth, Mars and Venus are planets.* 地球、火星、金星都是行星。

plank /plæŋk; plæŋk/ *noun* 名词
a long flat piece of wood 木板

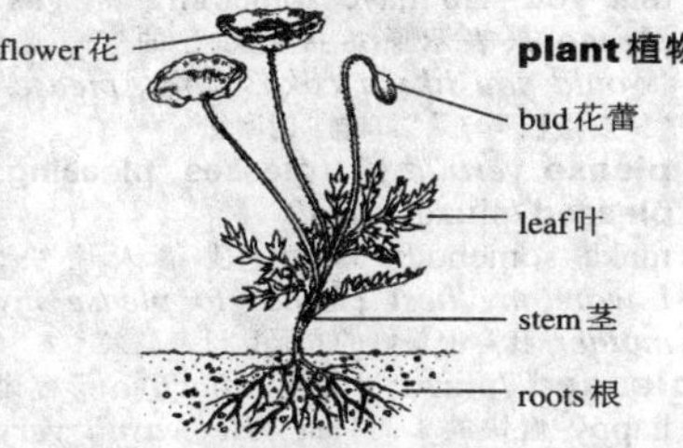

plant[1] /plɑ:nt; plænt/ *noun* 名词
anything that grows from the ground 植物: *Don't forget to water the plants.* 别忘了给植物浇水。

plant[2] /plɑ:nt; plænt/ *verb* 动词 (**plants, planting, planted**)
put plants or seeds in the ground to grow 种植;栽种: *We planted some roses in the garden.* 我们在花园里种了些玫瑰。

plantation /plɑ:n'teɪʃn; plæn'teʃən/ *noun* 名词
a piece of land where things like tea, cotton or tobacco grow 种植园: *a sugar plantation* 甘蔗园

plaster /'plɑ:stə(r); 'plæstɚ/ *noun* 名词
1 (no plural 无复数) soft stuff that becomes hard and smooth when it is dry. Plaster is used for covering walls. 灰泥(用来涂墙的)
2 (*plural* 复数作 **plasters**) a small piece of sticky material that you put over a cut on your body to keep it clean 橡皮膏
3 (no plural 无复数) white stuff that you put round a broken arm or leg. It becomes hard and keeps the arm or leg safe until it is better 石膏: *When I broke my leg it was in plaster for two months.* 我腿骨折的时候打了两个月的石膏。

plastic /'plæstɪk; 'plæstɪk/ *noun* 名词 (no plural 无复数)
a strong light material that is made in factories. Plastic is used for making a lot of different things 塑料: *These chairs are made of plastic.* 这些椅子是塑料的。◇ *plastic cups* 塑料杯

plate /pleɪt; plet/ *noun* 名词
a round flat thing that you put food on 盘子;碟子 ☞ Look also at **number-plate**. 另见 **number-plate**。

plate 盘子

platform /'plætfɔ:m; 'plæt͵fɔrm/ *noun* 名词
1 the part of a railway station where you stand to wait for a train (火车站的)站台;月台: *The train to London leaves from platform 5.* 开往伦敦的火车在第5号站台。
2 a place that is higher than the floor, where people stand so that other people can see and hear them (高出地面的)台;讲台;舞台: *The headmaster went up to the platform to make his speech.* 校长走上讲台讲话。

play[1] /pleɪ; ple/ *verb* 动词 (**plays, playing, played** /pleɪd; pled/)
1 have fun; do something to enjoy yourself 玩儿;玩耍: *The children were playing with their toys.* 孩子们正在玩儿着玩具。
2 take part in a game 参加比赛: *I like playing tennis.* 我爱打网球。◇ *Do you know how to play chess?* 你会下国际象棋吗?
3 make music with a musical instrument 演奏乐器: *My sister plays the piano very well.* 我姐姐弹钢琴弹得非常好。✪ We always use **the** before the names of musical instruments 乐器名称之前要用 **the**: *I'm learning to play the violin.* 我正在学习拉小提琴。
4 put a record, tape or compact disc in a machine and listen to it 播放普通唱片、磁带或激光唱片等: *Shall I play the tape again?* 我把磁带再放一遍好吗?
5 be somebody in a play in the theatre or on television or radio 扮演某角色(在戏院、电视或电台演出): *Hamlet was played by Michael Kent.* 哈姆雷特这个角色是由迈克尔·肯特扮演的。

P

play² /pleɪ; ple/ *noun* 名词

1 (*plural* 复数作 **plays**) a story that you watch in the theatre or on television, or listen to on the radio 戏剧: *We went to see a play at the National Theatre.* 我们在国家剧院看了一出戏。

2 (no plural 无复数) games; what children do for fun 游戏: *work and play* 工作和游戏 ✪ Be careful! We **play** football, cards, etc or we **have a game of** football, cards, etc (NOT **a play**). 注意！踢足球、打扑克等活动，可以用 **play** 这个动词，也可以用 **have a game of** 这个词组（但不可作 **a play**）。

player /ˈpleɪə(r); ˈpleɚ/ *noun* 名词

1 a person who plays a game 游戏者；运动员: *football players* 足球运动员

2 a person who plays a musical instrument 乐器演奏者: *a trumpet player* 吹奏小号的人

playground /ˈpleɪgraʊnd; ˈpleˌgraʊnd/ *noun* 名词

a piece of land where children can play 游戏场；运动场

playing-cards /ˈpleɪɪŋ kɑ:dz; ˈpleɪŋˌkɑrdz/ *noun* 名词

a set of 52 cards that you use for playing games 纸牌；扑克牌 ☞ Look at **card**. 见 **card**。

playing-field /ˈpleɪɪŋ fi:ld; ˈpleɪŋˌfild/ *noun* 名词

a field for sports like football and cricket（足球、板球等的）球场；运动场

plea /pli:; pli/ *noun* 名词

asking for something with strong feeling 恳求；请求: *He made a plea for help.* 他请求帮助。

plead /pli:d; plid/ *verb* 动词 (**pleads, pleading, pleaded**)

ask for something in a very strong way 恳求；请求: *He pleaded with his parents to buy him a guitar.* 他央求父母给他买个吉他。

plead guilty say in a court of law that you did something wrong 承认有罪: *She pleaded guilty to murder.* 她承认犯有谋杀罪。

plead not guilty say in a court of law that you did not do something wrong 不承认有罪

pleasant /ˈpleznt; ˈplɛzn̩t/ *adjective* 形容词

nice, enjoyable or friendly 美好的；可喜的；友好的: *The weather here is very pleasant.* 这里天气宜人。◇ *He's a very pleasant person.* 他很讨人喜欢。✪ opposite 反义词: **unpleasant**

pleasantly *adverb* 副词

She smiled pleasantly. 她亲切地微笑着。

please /pli:z; pliz/

a word that you use when you ask politely 用于要求对方做某事的敬词；请: *What's the time, please?* 请问现在几点钟了？◇ *Two cups of coffee, please.* 请来两杯咖啡。✪ You use **yes, please** to say that you will have something 用 **yes, please** 来表示愿意接受好意的客气话: *'Would you like a cake?' 'Yes, please.'* "您要蛋糕吗？" "好哇，谢谢您。"

please *verb* 动词 (**pleases, pleasing, pleased** /pli:zd; plizd/)

make somebody happy 使某人愉快: *I wore my best clothes to please my mother.* 我穿上最好的衣服让母亲高兴。

pleased /pli:zd; plizd/ *adjective* 形容词

happy 愉快的；高兴的: *He wasn't very pleased to see me.* 他并不那么乐意见我。◇ *Are you pleased with your new watch?* 你的新手表合意吗？

pleasure /ˈpleʒə(r); ˈplɛʒɚ/ *noun* 名词

1 (no plural 无复数) the feeling of being happy or enjoying something 愉快；快乐: *I go sailing for pleasure.* 我做帆船运动取乐。

2 (*plural* 复数作 **pleasures**) something that makes you happy 使人愉快的事物: *It was a pleasure to meet you.* 能认识您非常高兴。

it's a pleasure You say 'it's a pleasure' as a polite way of answering somebody who thanks you 答应对方道谢的礼貌用语: *'Thank you for your help.' 'It's a pleasure.'* "谢谢您帮忙。" "不客气。"

with pleasure You say 'with pleasure' to show in a polite way that you are happy to do something 表示乐意做某事的礼貌用语: *'Can you help me move these boxes?' 'Yes, with pleasure.'* "您帮我搬搬这些箱子行吗？" "好，我来帮您。"

pleat /pli:t; plit/ *noun* 名词

a fold in a piece of cloth（布上的）褶

pled /pled; plɛd/ *American English for* **pleaded** 美式英语，即 **pleaded**

plenty /'plenti; 'plɛntɪ/ *pronoun* 代词
as much or as many as you need; a lot 充裕；大量: *Do you want to stay for dinner? There's plenty of food.* 你在这儿吃饭吗？有的是吃的。

pliers /'plaɪəz; 'plaɪɚz/ *noun* 名词 (plural 复数)
a tool for holding things tightly or for cutting wire 钳子；老虎钳: *Have you got a pair of pliers?* 您有钳子吗？

plod /plɒd; plɑd/ *verb* 动词 (**plods, plodding, plodded**)
walk slowly in a heavy tired way 迈着沉重的脚步行走: *We plodded up the hill in the rain.* 我们冒着雨吃力地往山坡上走。

plot /plɒt; plɑt/ *noun* 名词
1 a secret plan to do something that is wrong 阴谋: *a plot to kill the President* 杀害总统的阴谋
2 what happens in a story, play or film（故事、戏剧或影片中的）情节: *This book has a very exciting plot.* 这部书的故事情节非常紧张。

plot *verb* 动词 (**plots, plotting, plotted**)
make a secret plan to do something that is wrong 密谋；策划: *They plotted to rob the bank.* 他们密谋抢劫银行。

plough /plaʊ; plaʊ/ *noun* 名词
a machine used on farms for digging and turning over the soil. Ploughs are usually pulled by tractors. 犁（通常用拖拉机牵引）

plough *verb* 动词 (**ploughs, ploughing, ploughed** /plaʊd; plaʊd/)
use a plough to dig and turn over the soil 犁地；耕地: *The farmer ploughed his fields.* 那个农民把地耕了。

plow *American English for* **plough** 美式英语，即 **plough**

plugs 插头或塞子

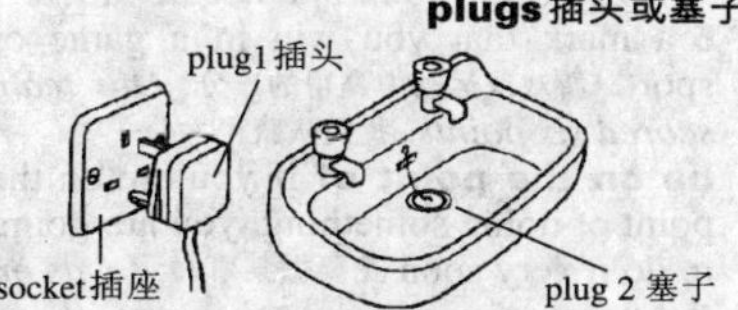

plug /plʌg; plʌg/ *noun* 名词
1 a thing that joins a lamp, machine, etc to a place in the wall (called a **socket**) where there is electricity 插头（插座叫做 **socket**）
2 a round thing that you put in the hole in a wash-basin or bath, to stop the water going out 塞子

plug *verb* 动词 (**plugs, plugging, plugged** /plʌgd; plʌgd/)
fill a hole with something 用某物塞住洞: *I plugged the hole in the pipe with plastic.* 我用塑料堵住了管子上的洞。

plug in put an electric plug into a place in the wall where there is electricity 插上插头: *Can you plug the radio in, please?* 请您把收音机的插头插上行吗？◇ *The lamp isn't plugged in.* 这个灯的插头没插上。✪ opposite 反义词: **unplug**

plum /plʌm; plʌm/ *noun* 名词
a soft round fruit with a stone in the middle 李子；梅子

plumber /'plʌmə(r); 'plʌmɚ/ *noun* 名词
a person whose job is to put in and repair things like water-pipes and baths 铅管工；管子工

plump /plʌmp; plʌmp/ *adjective* 形容词 (**plumper, plumpest**)
quite fat, in a nice way 胖的；丰满的: *a plump baby* 胖乎乎的小孩儿

plunge /plʌndʒ; plʌndʒ/ *verb* 动词 (**plunges, plunging, plunged** /plʌndʒd; plʌndʒd/)
1 jump or fall suddenly into something 突然跳入或落入某处: *She plunged into the pool.* 她跳进游泳池里。
2 push something suddenly and strongly into something else 突然而猛力把某物推入某处: *I plunged my hand into the water.* 我一下子把手伸进水里。

plural /'plʊərəl; 'plʊrəl/ *noun* 名词
the form of a word that shows there is more than one 复数（形式）: *The plural of 'child' is 'children'.* ✳ child 的复数形式是 children。

plural *adjective* 形容词
Most plural nouns in English end in 's'. 英语的复数名词多以 s 结尾。
☞ Look at **singular**. 见 **singular**。

plus /plʌs; plʌs/ *preposition* 介词
added to; and 加；加上: *Two plus three is five* (2 + 3 = 5). 二加三等于五 (2 + 3 = 5)。◇ *We have invited twelve friends to the party, plus my brother and his girlfriend.* 我们请了十二个朋友参加聚会，加上我哥哥和他的女朋友。☞ Look at **minus**. 见 **minus**。

P

p.m. /ˌpiː ˈem; ˌpi ˈɛm/
You use p.m. after a time to show that it is between midday and midnight 用于表示时间的词之后，指从正午到午夜的时间；下午；午后: *The plane leaves at 3 p.m.* 飞机下午3时起飞。✪ We use **a.m.** for times between midnight and midday. 从午夜到正午的时间，用 **a.m.** 表示。

pneumonia /njuːˈməʊniə; nuˈmonjə/ *noun* 名词 (no plural 无复数)
a serious illness of the lungs 肺炎

poach[1] /pəʊtʃ; potʃ/ *verb* 动词 (**poaches**, **poaching**, **poached** /pəʊtʃt; potʃt/)
cook food gently in or over water or milk 用文火在水或奶中煮或蒸食物: *a poached egg* 煮荷包蛋

poach[2] /pəʊtʃ; potʃ/ *verb* 动词 (**poaches**, **poaching**, **poached** /pəʊtʃt; potʃt/)
kill and steal animals, birds or fish from another person's land 在他人地界偷猎或偷捕兽、鸟或鱼

poacher *noun* 名词
a person who poaches 在他人地界偷猎或偷捕兽、鸟或鱼的人

PO Box /ˌpiː ˈəʊ bɒks; ˌpɪo ˈbɑks/ *noun* 名词 (*plural* 复数作 **PO Boxes**)
a box in a post office for keeping the letters of a person or office 邮政信箱: *The address is PO Box 63, Bristol BS7 1JN.* 地址是布里斯托尔BS7 1JN，邮政信箱63号。

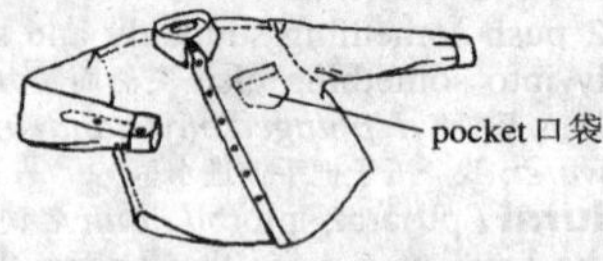

pocket /ˈpɒkɪt; ˈpɑkɪt/ *noun* 名词
a small bag in your clothes for carrying things（衣服上的）口袋；衣袋；兜儿: *I put the key in my pocket.* 我把钥匙放进衣袋里了。

pick somebody's pocket steal money from somebody's pocket or bag 从别人衣袋或提包中偷窃；扒窃

pocketbook /ˈpɒkɪtbʊk; ˈpɑkɪtˌbʊk/
American English for **wallet** 美式英语，即 **wallet**

pocket money /ˈpɒkɪt mʌni; ˈpɑkɪt ˌmʌnɪ/ *noun* 名词 (no plural 无复数)
money that parents give to a child each week to buy things（父母给子女的）零花钱: *How much pocket money do you get?* 你有多少零花钱？

pod /pɒd; pɑd/ *noun* 名词
the long green part of some plants, that has seeds inside it. Peas grow in pods. 荚；豆荚

poem /ˈpəʊɪm; ˈpo·ɪm/ *noun* 名词
a piece of writing, usually with short lines that may rhyme. Poems try to show feelings or ideas 诗；韵文: *I have written a poem.* 我写了一首诗。

poet /ˈpəʊɪt; ˈpo·ɪt/ *noun* 名词
a person who writes poems 诗人: *Keats was a famous English poet.* 济慈是著名的英国诗人。

poetic /pəʊˈetɪk; poˈɛtɪk/ *adjective* 形容词
of or like poets or poetry 诗的；诗人的；有诗意的: *poetic language* 富诗意的语言

poetry /ˈpəʊətri; ˈpo·ɪtrɪ/ *noun* 名词 (no plural 无复数)
poems 诗（总称）: *Wordsworth wrote beautiful poetry.* 华兹华斯写下了优美的诗篇。

point[1] /pɔɪnt; pɔɪnt/ *noun* 名词

1 a small round mark (.) that shows part of a number 小数点（.）: *2.5* (two point five) ✳ 2.5（二点五）

2 a certain time or place 某一时刻或地方: *It started to rain and at that point we decided to go home.* 那时下起雨来了，我们当时就决定回家了。

3 the most important idea; the purpose or reason 要点；目的或理由: *The point of going to school is to learn.* 上学的目的就是要学习。◇ *What's the point of phoning her? She's not at home.* 给她打电话有什么用？她不在家呀。

4 the sharp end of something（物体的）尖端；尖儿: *the point of a needle* 针尖儿

5 a mark that you win in a game or sport（游戏或运动中赢得的）分: *Our team scored six points.* 我们队获得六分。

be on the point of If you are on the point of doing something, you are going to do it very soon 正要做某事时: *I was on the point of going out when the phone rang.* 我正要出去，电话铃就响了。

point of view your way of thinking about something 观点；看法: *I understand your point of view.* 我明白您的观点。

there's no point in there is no good reason to do something 没有充分理由做某事: *There's no point in waiting for Julie — she isn't coming.* 没有必要再等朱莉了——她不来了。

point² /pɔɪnt; pɔɪnt/ *verb* 动词 (**points, pointing, pointed**)
show where something is using your finger, a stick, etc（用手指、棍等）指出或指示某物的位置: *I asked him where the bank was and he pointed across the road.* 我问他银行在哪里，他指向马路的对面。◇ *There was a sign pointing towards the city centre.* 有个指示到市中心去的路标。

point something at somebody or 或 **something** hold something towards somebody or something 持某物瞄准或对着某人或某物: *She was pointing a gun at his head.* 她用枪瞄准他的头部。

point out tell or show something 说出；指出: *Eva pointed out that my bag was open.* 伊娃说我的手提包的口开着呢。

pointed /'pɔɪntɪd; 'pɔɪntɪd/ *adjective* 形容词
with a sharp end 有尖的；尖的: *a long pointed nose* 又高又尖的鼻子

pointless /'pɔɪntləs; 'pɔɪntlɪs/ *adjective* 形容词
with no use or purpose 无用的；无目标的: *It's pointless telling Paul anything — he never listens.* 跟保罗说什么都没用——他根本不听。

poison /'pɔɪzn; 'pɔɪzn̩/ *noun* 名词 (no plural 无复数)
something that will kill you or make you very ill if you eat or drink it 毒药；毒物: *rat poison* 老鼠药

poison *verb* 动词 (**poisons, poisoning, poisoned** /'pɔɪznd; 'pɔɪzn̩d/)
use poison to kill or hurt somebody or something 用毒药杀害或伤害某人或某物；毒死

poisonous /'pɔɪzənəs; 'pɔɪzn̩əs/ *adjective* 形容词
Something that is poisonous will kill you or make you very ill if you eat or drink it 有毒的: *Some berries are poisonous.* 有些浆果有毒。

poke /pəʊk; pok/ *verb* 动词 (**pokes, poking, poked** /pəʊkt; pokt/)
1 push somebody or something hard with your finger or another long thin thing（用手指或细长物）捅；戳: *She poked me in the eye with a pencil.* 她用铅笔把我的眼睛捅了。
2 push something quickly somewhere 很快把某物推向或伸向某处: *Jeff poked his head out of the window.* 杰夫把头伸出窗外。

poke *noun* 名词
I gave her a poke to wake her up. 我捅了捅她，好让她醒来。

polar /'pəʊlə(r); 'polɚ/ *adjective* 形容词
of the North or South Pole 北极的；南极的

polar bear /ˌpəʊlə 'beə(r); ˌpolɚ 'bɛr/ *noun* 名词
a white bear that lives near the North Pole 北极熊

pole¹ /pəʊl; pol/ *noun* 名词
a long thin piece of wood or metal. Poles are often used to hold something up 杆；竿；棒: *a flag-pole* 旗杆 ◇ *tent poles* 帐篷支柱

pole² /pəʊl; pol/ *noun* 名词
one of two places at the top and bottom of the earth 地极: *the North Pole* 北极 ◇ *the South Pole* 南极

police /pə'li:s; pə'lis/ *noun* 名词 (plural 复数)
a group of people whose job is to make sure that people do not break the laws of a country 警方；警察部门: *Have the police found the murderer?* 警方找到凶手了吗？◇ *a police car* 警车

police force /pə'li:s fɔ:s; pə'lis ˌfors/ *noun* 名词
all the police officers in a country or part of a country（一国或一地区的全体的）警察，警察部队

policeman /pə'li:smən; pə'lismən/ *noun* 名词 (*plural* 复数作 **policemen** /pə'li:smən; pə'lismən/)
a man who works in the police（男的）警察

police constable /pəˌli:s 'kʌnstəbl; pə'lis 'kɑnstəbl̩/ *noun* 名词
an ordinary police officer（普通的）警察
✪ The short form is **PC**. 缩略式为 **PC**。

police officer /pə'li:s ɒfɪsə(r); pə'lis ɔˌfəsɚ/ *noun* 名词
a policeman or policewoman（男的或女的）警察

police station /pə'li:s steɪʃn; pə'lis ˌsteʃən/ *noun* 名词
an office where police officers work 警察局；派出所

policewoman /pə'li:swʊmən; pə'lis-ˌwʊmən/ *noun* 名词 (*plural* 复数作 **policewomen**)
a woman who works in the police（女的）警察

P

policy /'pɒləsi; 'pɑləsɪ/ *noun* 名词 (*plural* 复数作 **policies**)
the plans of a group of people 方针；政策: *What is the government's policy on education?* 政府的教育政策是怎样的？

polish /'pɒlɪʃ; 'pɑlɪʃ/ *verb* 动词 (**polishes, polishing, polished** /'pɒlɪʃt; 'pɑlɪʃt/)
rub something so that it shines 磨光或擦亮某物: *Have you polished your shoes?* 你擦鞋了吗？

polish *noun* 名词 (no plural 无复数)
stuff that you put on something to make it shine 擦光剂；上光剂: *furniture polish* 家具上光蜡

polite /pə'laɪt; pə'laɪt/ *adjective* 形容词
If you are polite, you are helpful and kind to other people and you do not do or say things that make people sad or angry 有礼貌的；客气的: *It is polite to say 'please' when you ask for something.* 向别人要东西时，要说声"请"才算有礼貌。
✪ opposite 反义词: **impolite** or 或 **rude**

politely *adverb* 副词
He asked politely for a glass of water. 他很有礼貌地要一杯水。

politeness /pə'laɪtnəs; pə'laɪtnɪs/ *noun* 名词 (no plural 无复数)
being polite 有礼貌；客气

political /pə'lɪtɪkl; pə'lɪtɪkḷ/ *adjective* 形容词
of or about the work of government 政治的: *A political party is a group of people who have the same ideas about how to control their country.* 政党就是在治理国家方面有共同观点的一批人。◇ *political beliefs* 政治信仰

politically /pə'lɪtɪkli; pə'lɪtɪklɪ/ *adverb* 副词
a politically powerful country 在政治方面强大的国家

politician /ˌpɒlə'tɪʃn; ˌpɑlə'tɪʃən/ *noun* 名词
a person who works in the government or who wants to work in the government 政治家: *Members of Parliament are politicians.* 国会议员都是政治人物。

politics /'pɒlətɪks; 'pɑləˌtɪks/ *noun* 名词 (no plural 无复数)
1 the work of government 政治活动: *Are you interested in politics?* 您喜欢政治活动吗？
2 the study of government 政治学: *She studied politics at university.* 她在大学学习政治。

pollen /'pɒlən; 'pɑlən/ *noun* 名词 (no plural 无复数)
the yellow powder in flowers 花粉

pollute /pə'lu:t; pə'lut/ *verb* 动词 (**pollutes, polluting, polluted**)
make air, rivers, etc dirty and dangerous 污染空气、河流等: *Many of Britain's rivers are polluted with chemicals from factories.* 英国很多河流都遭到工厂排出的化学废料的污染。

pollution /pə'lu:ʃn; pə'luʃən/ *noun* 名词 (no plural 无复数)
1 polluting air, rivers, etc（对空气、河流等的）污染: *We must stop the pollution of our beaches.* 我们必须制止对海滩的污染。
2 dirty and dangerous stuff from cars, factories, etc（从汽车、工厂等处排出的）污染物

pond /pɒnd; pɑnd/ *noun* 名词
a small area of water 池塘: *We have a fish-pond in our garden.* 我们花园里有个鱼塘。

pony /'pəʊni; 'ponɪ/ *noun* 名词 (*plural* 复数作 **ponies**)
a small horse 小马

pony-tail /'pəʊniteɪl; 'ponɪˌtel/ *noun* 名词
long hair that you tie at the back of your head so that it hangs down 马尾发型

pool /pu:l; pul/ *noun* 名词
1 a little liquid or light on the ground 地上的一小片液体或亮光: *After the rain there were pools of water on the road.* 下过雨后，路上有许多水洼儿。◇ *She was lying in a pool of blood.* 她躺在血泊中。
2 a place for swimming 游泳池: *Karen dived into the pool.* 卡伦头朝下跳入水中。

poor /pɔ:(r); pʊr/ *adjective* 形容词 (**poorer, poorest**)
1 with very little money 贫穷的；贫困的: *She was too poor to buy clothes for her*

children. 她很穷，没钱给孩子买衣服。✪ opposite 反义词：**rich**. The noun is **poverty**. 名词是 **poverty**。

2 a word that you use when you feel sad because somebody has problems 因他人有困难而感到难过的词；可怜的: *Poor Tina! She's feeling ill.* 可怜的蒂娜！她身体不舒服了。

3 not good 不好的；差劲的: *My grandfather is in very poor health.* 我祖父身体很糟糕。

the poor *noun* 名词 (plural 复数)
people who do not have much money 穷人

poorly /ˈpɔːli; ˈpʊrlɪ/ *adverb* 副词
not well; badly 不好；坏: *The street is poorly lit.* 这条街道的光线很差。

pop[1] /pɒp; pɑp/ *noun* 名词 (no plural 无复数)
modern music that a lot of young people like 流行音乐: *What's your favourite pop group?* 你最喜欢的流行歌曲歌星是哪些人？ ◇ *pop music* 流行音乐 ◇ *a pop singer* 演唱流行歌曲的歌星

pop[2] /pɒp; pɑp/ *noun* 名词
a short sharp sound 短促而清脆的声音: *The cork came out of the bottle with a loud pop.* 瓶塞砰的一声拔了出来。

pop[3] /pɒp; pɑp/ *verb* 动词 (**pops, popping, popped** /pɒpt; pɑpt/)

1 make a short sharp sound; make something make a short sharp sound（使某物）发出短促而清脆的声音: *The balloon will pop if you put a pin in it.* 气球用针一扎就砰的一声爆了。

2 go somewhere quickly 迅速到某处: *She has popped into the shop to buy a newspaper.* 她匆匆到商店买了一份报纸。

3 put or take something somewhere quickly 迅速把某物放到或拿到某处: *Katie popped a sweet into her mouth.* 凯蒂一下子就把糖放进嘴里了。◇ *He popped his head round the door to say goodbye.* 他在门口探了一下头，说了声再见。

pop in go somewhere for a short time 到某处作短暂逗留: *We were near Tim's house so we popped in for a cup of coffee.* 我们当时在蒂姆家附近，就到他家串门儿喝杯咖啡。

pop up appear suddenly 突然出现: *Fast food restaurants are popping up everywhere.* 快餐店转眼间到处都是。

pope /pəʊp; pop/ *noun* 名词
the most important person in the Roman Catholic Church（天主教的）教皇；教宗: *Pope John Paul* 约翰·保罗教皇

popular /ˈpɒpjələ(r); ˈpɑpjələ˞/ *adjective* 形容词
liked by a lot of people 大家都喜爱的；大众化的: *Football is a popular sport in Britain.* 在英国，大家都很喜欢足球运动。✪ opposite 反义词: **unpopular**

popularity /ˌpɒpjuˈlærəti; ˌpɑpjəˈlærətɪ/ *noun* 名词 (no plural 无复数)
being liked by a lot of people 大家都喜爱的现象；通俗性；普及

population /ˌpɒpjuˈleɪʃn; ˌpɑpjəˈleʃən/ *noun* 名词
the number of people who live in a place 人口: *What is the population of your country?* 你们国家人口有多少？

pork /pɔːk; pɔrk/ *noun* 名词 (no plural 无复数)
meat from a pig 猪肉: *pork sausages* 猪肉香肠 ☞ Note at **pig** 见 **pig** 词条注释

porridge /ˈpɒrɪdʒ; ˈpɔrɪdʒ/ *noun* 名词 (no plural 无复数)
soft food made from oats cooked with milk or water, that people eat for breakfast 用燕麦片加牛奶或水做的粥（用作早餐）；麦片粥

port /pɔːt; pɔrt/ *noun* 名词
a town or city by the sea, where ships arrive and leave 港口城镇；口岸: *Liverpool is a large port in the North of England.* 利物浦是英国北部一个大的港口城市。

portable /ˈpɔːtəbl; ˈpɔrtəbl̩/ *adjective* 形容词
that you can move or carry easily 容易移动或携带的；便携式的；手提式的；轻便的: *a portable television* 便携式电视机

porter /ˈpɔːtə(r); ˈpɔrtə˞/ *noun* 名词

1 a person whose job is to carry people's bags in places like railway stations and hotels（火车站和旅馆等处的）搬运工

2 a person whose job is to look after the entrance of a hotel or other large building（旅馆或其他大建筑物的）门卫；守门人

portion /ˈpɔːʃn; ˈpɔrʃən/ *noun* 名词
a part of something that one person gets（一个人得到的某物的）一部分: *He gave a portion of the money to each of his*

children. 他给他的孩子每人一部分钱。◇ *a large portion of chips* 一大份的炸土豆条儿

portrait /ˈpɔːtreɪt; ˈpɔrtret/ *noun* 名词
a painting or picture of a person (人的) 画像或照片

position /pəˈzɪʃn; pəˈzɪʃən/ *noun* 名词
1 the place where somebody or something is (某人或某物所处的) 位置: *Can you show me the position of your village on the map?* 你告诉我你们村子在地图上的位置行吗?
2 the way a person is sitting or lying, or the way a thing is standing (指人坐着或躺着的) 姿势; (指物体存在的) 状态: *She was still sitting in the same position when I came back.* 我回来的时候,她还是像原来那样坐着。
3 how things are at a certain time (事物在某段时间的) 情势; 处境: *He's in a difficult position — he hasn't got enough money to finish his studies.* 他处境困难——他的钱不够,无法完成学业。
in position in the right place 在适当的位置: *The dancers were in position, waiting for the music to start.* 舞蹈演员都已各就各位,等候音乐一开始就翩翩起舞。

positive /ˈpɒzətɪv; ˈpɑzətɪv/ *adjective* 形容词
1 completely certain 完全肯定的; 明确的: *Are you positive that you closed the door?* 你肯定把门关上了吗?
2 that helps you or gives you hope 有助益的; 带来希望的: *The teacher was very positive about my work.* 老师对我的功课进步满怀信心。
positively *adverb* 副词
really; certainly 真正地; 肯定地: *The idea is positively stupid.* 这种想法愚蠢到家了。

possess /pəˈzes; pəˈzɛs/ *verb* 动词 (**possesses**, **possessing**, **possessed** /pəˈzest; pəˈzɛst/)
have or own something 领有或持有某事物: *He lost everything that he possessed in the fire.* 这场大火把他所有的一切都化为乌有。✪ **Have** and **own** are the words that we usually use. ✳ **have** 和 **own** 是常用词。

possession /pəˈzeʃn; pəˈzɛʃən/ *noun* 名词
1 (no plural 无复数) having or owning something 领有或持有某事物: *The possession of drugs is a crime.* 藏有毒品是犯罪行为。
2 possessions (plural 复数) the things that you have or own 所有物; 财产

possibility /ˌpɒsəˈbɪləti; ˌpɑsəˈbɪlətɪ/ *noun* 名词 (*plural* 复数作 **possibilities**)
something that might happen 可能发生的事; 可能性: *There's a possibility that it will rain, so take your umbrella.* 可能要下雨,你带着雨伞吧。

possible /ˈpɒsəbl; ˈpɑsəbl̩/ *adjective* 形容词
If something is possible, it can happen or you can do it 可能发生的; 可能做到的: *Is it possible to get to Birmingham by train?* 到伯明翰能坐火车去吗? ◇ *I'll phone you as soon as possible.* 我尽快给您打电话。✪ opposite 反义词: **impossible**

possibly /ˈpɒsəbli; ˈpɑsəblɪ/ *adverb* 副词
1 perhaps 大概; 也许; 或许: *'Will you be free tomorrow?' 'Possibly.'* "您明天有空吗?" "可能有空。"
2 in a way that can be done 可能地: *I'll come as soon as I possibly can.* 只要我能早来我就一定早来。

post[1] /pəʊst; post/ *noun* 名词
a tall piece of wood or metal that stands in the ground to hold something or to show where something is (地上树立的) 桩; 柱子; 杆子 (用以固着某物或指示某处的): *Can you see a signpost anywhere?* 你看看附近有路标吗?

post[2] /pəʊst; post/ *noun* 名词 (no plural 无复数)
1 the way of sending and receiving letters, parcels, etc (信件、包裹等的) 邮寄: *I sent your present by post.* 我寄给您一件礼物。
2 letters and parcels that you send or receive (邮寄的) 信件、包裹等: *Did you get any post this morning?* 您今天早晨收到信了吗?
postage /ˈpəʊstɪdʒ; ˈpostɪdʒ/ *noun* 名词 (no plural 无复数)
money that you must pay when you send a letter or parcel 邮费; 邮资
postal /ˈpəʊstl; ˈpostl̩/ *adjective* 形容词
of the post 邮政的; 邮务的; 邮寄的: *postal collections* 邮递员定时收取信件的次数
postbox /ˈpəʊstbɒks; ˈpostˌbɑks/ *noun* 名词 (*plural* 复数作 **postboxes**)

a box in the street where you put letters that you want to send（邮局设置于街道上的供人投寄信件的）信箱

postcard 明信片

postcard /'pəʊstkɑ:d; 'post,kɑrd/ *noun* 名词
a card with a picture on one side, that you write on and send by post 明信片

postcode /'pəʊstkəʊd; 'post,kod/ *noun* 名词
a group of numbers and letters that you write at the end of an address 邮政编码 ☞ picture on page C31 见第C31页图

postman /'pəʊstmən; 'postmən/ *noun* 名词 (*plural* 复数作 **postmen** /'pəʊstmən; 'postmən/)
a man who takes (**delivers**) letters and parcels to people（男的）邮递员；邮差（投递叫做 **deliver**）

post office /'pəʊst ɒfɪs; 'post ,ɔfɪs/ *noun* 名词
a building where you go to send letters and parcels and to buy stamps 邮政局

postwoman /'pəʊstwʊmən; 'post-,wʊmən/ *noun* 名词 (*plural* 复数作 **post-women**)
a woman who takes (**delivers**) letters and parcels to people（女的）邮递员；邮差（投递叫做 **deliver**）

post[3] /pəʊst; post/ *verb* 动词 (**posts, posting, posted**)
1 send a letter or parcel 邮寄信件、包裹等: *Could you post this letter for me?* 您给我把这封信寄出去行吗？
2 send somebody to a place to do a job 派某人到某处做事: *Sara's company have posted her to Japan for two years.* 萨拉的公司派她到日本工作两年。

poster /'pəʊstə(r); 'postɚ/ *noun* 名词
a big piece of paper on a wall, with a picture or words on it 招贴；海报

postpone /pə'spəʊn; pos'pon/ *verb* 动词 (**postpones, postponing, post-poned** /pə'spəʊnd; pos'pond/)
say that something will happen at a later time, not now 使某事物延期；推迟某事物: *It's raining, so we will postpone the game until tomorrow.* 下雨了，所以我们把比赛推迟到明天举行。

pot /pɒt; pɑt/ *noun* 名词
1 a deep round container for cooking（烹饪用的）锅: *a big pot of soup* 一大锅汤
2 a container that you use for a special thing 有某种用途的容器: *a teapot* 茶壶 ◇ *a pot of paint* 一罐涂料 ◇ *a plant pot* 花盆

potato /pə'teɪtəʊ; pə'teto/ *noun* 名词 (*plural* 复数作 **potatoes**)
a round vegetable that grows under the ground, that is white on the inside and brown or yellow on the outside. You cook it before you eat it 土豆；马铃薯: *a baked potato* 烤的土豆

pottery /'pɒtəri; 'pɑtərɪ/ *noun* 名词 (no plural 无复数)
1 cups, plates and other things made from **clay** (heavy earth that becomes hard when it dries) 陶器（陶土叫做 **clay**）: *This shop sells beautiful pottery.* 这个商店出售精美的陶器。
2 making cups, plates and other things from clay 陶器制造（术）: *Her hobby is pottery.* 她的爱好是做陶器。

poultry /'pəʊltri; 'poltrɪ/ *noun* 名词 (plural 复数)
birds that people keep on farms for their eggs or their meat. Hens, ducks and geese are poultry. 家禽

pounce /paʊns; paʊns/ *verb* 动词 (**pounces, pouncing, pounced** /paʊnst; paʊnst/)
jump on somebody or something suddenly 突然向某人或某物猛扑: *The cat pounced on the bird.* 猫向鸟扑去。

pound /paʊnd; paʊnd/ *noun* 名词
1 money that people use in Britain. There are 100 **pence** in a pound 镑（英国货币单位。1镑等于100便士，便士叫做 **penny**，复数作 **pence**）: *The computer cost six hundred pounds.* 这台计算机价值六百英镑。◇ *a ten-pound note* 一张十英镑的纸币 ◇ *a pound coin* 一枚一英镑的硬币
✪ We write **£** 书写时略作 **£**: *I spent £40 today.* 我今天花了40英镑。
2 a measure of weight (= 0.454 kilograms). There are 16 **ounces** in a pound 磅（重量单位，等于0.454公斤。1磅等于16盎司，盎司叫做 **ounce**）: *Half*

P

a pound of mushrooms, please. 请给我半磅的蘑菇。◇ *two pounds of sugar* 两磅糖 ◇ *These apples cost 40p a pound.* 这些苹果40便士一磅。✪ The short way of writing 'pound' is **lb**. ✳ pound 的缩写形式为 **lb**。

> ✪ In the past, people in Britain used **ounces, pounds** and **stones** to measure weight, not **grams** and **kilograms**. 从前，英国人用盎司（**ounce**）、磅（**pound**）和吩（**stone**）来量度重量，而不用克（**gram**）和公斤（**kilogram**）。Now, many people use and understand both ways. 现在许多人都会使用这两种重量单位。

pour 倒

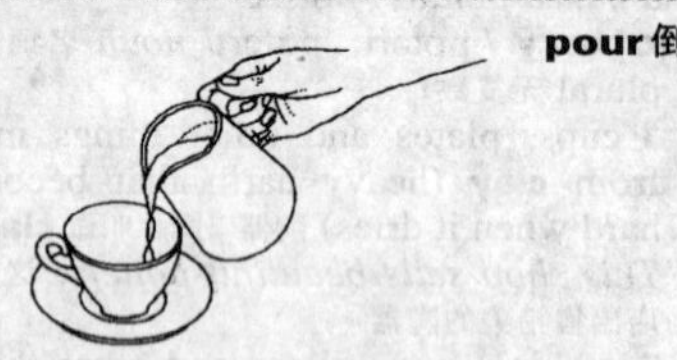

pour /pɔ:(r); pɔr/ *verb* 动词 (**pours, pouring, poured** /pɔ:d; pɔrd/)

1 make liquid flow out of or into something 使液体流出或流入某处: *She poured wine into my glass.* 她把葡萄酒倒进我的酒杯里。◇ *She poured me a glass of wine.* 她给我倒了一杯葡萄酒。

2 flow quickly 涌流: *Oil poured out of the damaged ship.* 油从毁坏的船里涌了出来。

it's pouring it is raining very hard 大雨如注

poverty /'pɒvəti; 'pɑvətɪ/ *noun* 名词 (no plural 无复数)

being poor 贫穷；贫困: *There are many people living in poverty in this city.* 在这座城市里有很多人生活贫困。

powder /'paʊdə(r); 'paʊdə/ *noun* 名词

dry stuff that is made of a lot of very small pieces 粉末: *washing-powder* (= for washing clothes) 洗衣粉 ◇ *face-powder* (= that you put on your face) 扑面粉

power /'paʊə(r); 'paʊə/ *noun* 名词

1 (no plural 无复数) being strong; being able to do something 力量；能力: *the power of the storm* 风暴的力量 ◇ *I did everything in my power* (= everything I could do) *to help her.* 我已竭尽全力帮助她。

2 (no plural 无复数) being able to make people do what you want 影响力；势力: *The president has a lot of power.* 这个会长很有影响力。

3 (no plural 无复数) what makes things work; energy 动力: *nuclear power* 核动力

4 (*plural* 复数作 **powers**) the right to do something 权力: *Police officers have the power to arrest people.* 警察有逮捕人的权力。

5 (*plural* 复数作 **powers**) a strong person or country 强有力的人或国家: *There is a meeting of world powers in Rome next week.* 下星期在罗马召开世界强国会议。

power point /'paʊə pɔɪnt; 'paʊə,pɔɪnt/ *noun* 名词

a place in a wall where you can push an electric plug（墙上的）电源插座

power station /'paʊə steɪʃn; 'paʊə ,steʃən/ *noun* 名词

a place where electricity is made 发电站；发电厂

powerful /'paʊəfl; 'paʊəfəl/ *adjective* 形容词

1 very strong; with a lot of power 强有力的；力量大的: *The car has a very powerful engine.* 这辆汽车发动机功率很大。◇ *The president is very powerful.* 这个主席势力很大。

2 that you can smell or hear clearly, or feel strongly 气味浓的；声音大的；感觉强烈的: *a powerful drug* 强力的药

practical /'præktɪkl; 'præktɪkḷ/ *adjective* 形容词

1 that is about doing or making things, not just about ideas 实践的；实际的: *Have you got any practical experience of teaching?* 您有实际教学经验吗？

2 able to do useful things 有实际用途的；实用的: *I'm not a very practical person.* 我不大会做实际工作。

3 possible to do easily 可能容易做的；可行的: *Your plan isn't practical.* 你的计划谈何容易。

practically /'præktɪkli; 'præktɪkḷɪ/ *adverb* 副词

almost; nearly 几乎；差不多: *Don't go out — lunch is practically ready!* 别出去了——午饭都差不多做好了！◇ *It rained practically every day.* 几乎每天都下雨。

practice /'præktɪs; 'præktɪs/ *noun* 名词 (no plural 无复数)

1 doing something many times so that you will do it well（反复的）练习；实践: *You need lots of practice when you're learning to play a musical instrument.* 学会弹奏一种乐器需要多多练习。

2 *American English for* **practise** 美式英语，即 **practise**

out of practice not good at something, because you have not done it for a long time 疏于练习或实践

practise /'præktɪs; 'præktɪs/ *verb* 动词 (**practises, practising, practised** /'præktɪst; 'præktɪst/)

do something many times so that you will do it well 反复练习；实践: *If you want to play the piano well, you must practise every day.* 要想把钢琴弹好就得每天练习。

praise /preɪz; prez/ *verb* 动词 (**praises, praising, praised** /preɪzd; prezd/)

say that somebody or something is good 称赞某人或某事物: *She was praised for her hard work.* 她因为努力而受到表扬。

praise *noun* 名词 (no plural 无复数)

The book has received a lot of praise. 这本书大获好评。

pram 婴儿车

pram /præm; præm/ *noun* 名词

a thing that a baby lies in to go out. It has wheels so that you can push it.（手推的）婴儿车

prawn /prɔ:n; prɔn/ *noun* 名词

a small pink sea animal that you can eat 大虾；对虾

pray /preɪ; pre/ *verb* 动词 (**prays, praying, prayed** /preɪd; pred/)

speak to God or a god 祈祷；祷告: *They prayed for help.* 他们祈求上帝保佑。

prayer /preə(r); prɛr/ *noun* 名词

words that you say when you speak to God or a god 祈祷文: *They said a prayer for peace.* 他们为和平做祷告。

preach /pri:tʃ; pritʃ/ *verb* 动词 (**preaches, preaching, preached** /pri:tʃt; pritʃt/)

talk about God or a god to a group of people 讲道；布道

precaution /prɪ'kɔ:ʃn; prɪ'kɔʃən/ *noun* 名词

something that you do so that bad things will not happen 预防措施: *I took the precaution of locking all the windows when I went out.* 我出门时把窗户都扣好了以防万一。

precious /'preʃəs; 'prɛʃəs/ *adjective* 形容词

1 very valuable 贵重的；宝贵的: *Diamonds are precious stones.* 钻石是一种宝石。

2 that you love very much 受到珍爱的: *My family is very precious to me.* 我的家庭在我心中占着十分重要的地位。

precise /prɪ'saɪs; prɪ'saɪs/ *adjective* 形容词

exactly right 精确的；准确的: *I gave him precise instructions on how to get to my house.* 我已经把到我家的途径给他讲得一清二楚。

precisely *adverb* 副词

exactly 精确地；准确地: *They arrived at two o'clock precisely.* 他们是两点整到达的。

predict /prɪ'dɪkt; prɪ'dɪkt/ *verb* 动词 (**predicts, predicting, predicted**)

say what you think will happen 预言；预告: *She predicted that it would rain, and she was right.* 她早说要下雨，果不其然。

prediction /prɪ'dɪkʃn; prɪ'dɪkʃən/ *noun* 名词

His predictions were not correct. 他的预言并不正确。

prefer /prɪ'fɜ:(r); prɪ'fɝ/ *verb* 动词 (**prefers, preferring, preferred** /prɪ'fɜ:d; prɪ'fɝd/)

like one thing or person better than another（在相比较下）喜欢某事物或某人: *Would you prefer tea or coffee?* 您爱喝茶还是爱喝咖啡？◇ *Jenny wants to go to the cinema but I would prefer to stay at home.* 珍妮要去看电影，我倒是比较喜欢呆在家里。◇ *He prefers going out to studying.* 他喜欢出去，不喜欢学习。

preference /'prefrəns; 'prɛfrəns/ *noun* 名词

P

liking one thing or person better than another（在相比较下）喜欢某事物或某人: *We have lemonade and orange juice — do you have a preference?* 我们有汽水和橙子汁——您喜欢哪样？

preferable /'prefrəbl; 'prɛfrəbl̩/ *adjective* 形容词
better; that you like more 更好的；更称心的: *I think living in the country is preferable to living in the city.* 我认为在乡村生活比在城市生活好。

preferably /'prefrəbli; 'prɛfrəblɪ/ *adverb* 副词
Phone me on Sunday morning, but preferably not too early! 星期日早上给我打个电话，可是也别太早哇！

prefix /'pri:fɪks; 'pri,fɪks/ *noun* 名词 (*plural* 复数作 **prefixes**)
a group of letters that you add to the beginning of a word to make another word 前缀（加在一个词前面的几个字母，用以构成另一个词）: *The prefix 'im-' means 'not', so 'impossible' means 'not possible'.* ＊ im- 这个前缀的意思是 not，所以 impossible 的意思是 not possible。☞ Look at **suffix**. 见 **suffix**。

pregnant /'pregnənt; 'prɛgnənt/ *adjective* 形容词
If a woman is pregnant, she has a baby growing in her body. 怀孕的；妊娠的

prejudice /'predʒədɪs; 'prɛdʒədɪs/ *noun* 名词
a feeling of not liking somebody or something, before you know much about them 偏见；成见: *She has a prejudice against foreigners.* 她对外国人有偏见。

prejudiced /'predʒədɪst; 'prɛdʒədɪst/ *adjective* 形容词
with strong and unfair ideas about somebody or something, before you know much about them 有偏见的；有成见的: *He is prejudiced against me because I'm a woman.* 他对我有偏见，因为我是女的。

preparation /,prepə'reɪʃn; ,prɛpə'reʃən/ *noun* 名词
1 (no plural 无复数) making something ready 预备；准备: *the preparation of food* 准备食物
2 preparations (plural 复数) what you do to get ready for something 准备工作: *wedding preparations* 婚礼的准备工作
in preparation for something to get ready for something 为某事做准备: *I packed my bags in preparation for the journey.* 我打好了包准备出门。

prepare /prɪ'peə(r); prɪ'pɛr/ *verb* 动词 (**prepares**, **preparing**, **prepared** /prɪ'peəd; prɪ'pɛrd/)
make somebody or something ready; make yourself ready 使某人有准备；把某事物准备好: *Martin is in the kitchen preparing the dinner.* 马丁正在厨房做饭。◇ *I prepared well for the exam.* 我已充分准备好迎接考试。

prepared for something ready for something difficult or bad 对困难或坏事做好准备: *I wasn't prepared for all these problems.* 我对于这些难题感到措手不及。

prepared to happy to do something 乐于做某事物: *I'm not prepared to give you any money.* 我可不愿意给你钱。

preposition /,prepə'zɪʃn; ,prɛpə'zɪʃən/ *noun* 名词
a word that you use before a noun or pronoun to show where, when, how, etc 介词（用于名词或代词前，表示处所、时间、方法等的词）: *'In,' 'for,' 'after' and 'above' are all prepositions.* ＊ in、for、after、above 都是介词。◇ *In the sentence 'He travelled from London to Munich', 'from' and 'to' are prepositions.* 在 He travelled from London to Munich 一句中，from 和 to 是介词。

prescribe /prɪ'skraɪb; prɪ'skraɪb/ *verb* 动词 (**prescribes**, **prescribing**, **prescribed** /prɪ'skraɪbd; prɪ'skraɪbd/)
say that somebody must take a medicine 开药方；处方: *The doctor prescribed some tablets for her cough.* 医生给她开了些咳嗽药。

prescription /prɪ'skrɪpʃn; prɪ'skrɪpʃən/ *noun* 名词
a piece of paper where a doctor writes what medicine you need. You take it to a **chemist's** and get the medicine there. 药方；处方（药房叫做 **chemist's**）

presence /'prezns; 'prɛzn̩s/ *noun* 名词 (no plural 无复数)
being in a place 存在；出席；出场: *She was so quiet that I didn't notice her presence.* 她一声不吭，我都没注意到她在那儿。

in the presence of somebody with another person or other people there 当着某人；有某人在场: *She signed the papers in the presence of a lawyer.* 她在有律师的情况下签署了文件。

present[1] /ˈpreznt; ˈprɛzn̩t/ *adjective* 形容词

1 in a place 存在的；出席的；出场的: *There were 200 people present at the meeting.* 有200人出席了会议。

2 being or happening now 现存的；现有的: *What is your present job?* 您现在做什么工作？

present[2] /ˈpreznt; ˈprɛzn̩t/ *noun* 名词 (no plural 无复数)

1 the time now 现在；此刻: *I can't help you at present — I'm too busy.* 我现在无法帮助你——我太忙了。

2 (*also* 亦作 **present tense**) the form of a verb that you use to talk about now（动词的）现在式

☞ Look at **past** and **future**. 见 **past** 和 **future**。

present[3] /ˈpreznt; ˈprɛzn̩t/ *noun* 名词

something that you give to or get from somebody 礼物；赠品: *a birthday present* 生日礼物

present[4] /prɪˈzent; prɪˈzɛnt/ *verb* 动词 (**presents**, **presenting**, **presented**)

give something to somebody 把某物交给或送给某人: *Who presented the prizes to the winners?* 谁给优胜者颁奖？

presentation /ˌprezn̩ˈteɪʃn; ˌprizɛnˈteʃən/ *noun* 名词

presenting something 交出或送出某物: *The presentation of the prizes will take place at 7.30.* 颁奖仪式于7点30分举行。

presently /ˈpreznt̩li; ˈprɛzn̩tlɪ/ *adverb* 副词

1 soon 不久: *He will be here presently.* 他马上就来。

2 now 现在: *She's presently working in a café.* 她现在在一家小餐馆工作。

preservation /ˌprezəˈveɪʃn; ˌprɛzɚˈveʃən/ *noun* 名词 (no plural 无复数)

keeping something safe; making something stay the same 保护；保存: *the preservation of rare birds* 保护稀有鸟类

preserve /prɪˈzɜːv; prɪˈzɝv/ *verb* 动词 (**preserves**, **preserving**, **preserved** /prɪˈzɜːvd; prɪˈzɝvd/)

keep something safe; make something stay the same 保护；保存: *Parts of the town are new, but they have preserved many of the old buildings.* 这个镇子有些地方是新建的，可是还保存了许多旧的建筑物。

president /ˈprezɪdənt; ˈprɛzədənt/ *noun* 名词

1 the leader in many countries that do not have a king or queen 总统；国家主席: *the President of the United States of America* 美国总统

2 the most important person in a big company, club, etc 公司、俱乐部等的负责人；总裁；董事长；会长

presidential /ˌprezɪˈdenʃl; ˌprɛzəˈdɛnʃəl/ *adjective* 形容词

of a president or his/her work 总统、主席、总裁、董事长、会长等的（职务的）: *the presidential elections* 总统选举

press[1] /pres; prɛs/ *verb* 动词 (**presses**, **pressing**, **pressed** /prest; prɛst/)

1 push something 按；压: *If you press this button, the door will open.* 一按这个钮，门就开了。◇ *She pressed her face against the window.* 她把脸贴在窗户上。

2 make clothes flat and smooth using an iron（用熨斗）熨平衣物: *This suit needs pressing.* 这套衣服需要熨。

press[2] /pres; prɛs/ *noun* 名词

1 the press (no plural 无复数) newspapers and magazines and the people who write them 报刊和记者；新闻界: *She told her story to the press.* 她把她的事告诉新闻界了。

2 (*plural* 复数作 **presses**) pushing something 按；压: *Give the doorbell a press.* 按一下门铃。

3 (*plural* 复数作 **presses**) a machine for printing things like books and newspapers 印刷机

pressure /ˈpreʃə(r); ˈprɛʃɚ/ *noun* 名词

1 the force that presses on something（物体承受的）压力: *the air pressure in a car tyre* 汽车轮胎里空气的压力

2 a feeling of worry or unhappiness, for example because you have too many things to do（精神上或工作中的）压力: *the pressures of city life* 城市生活的压力

presume /prɪˈzjuːm; prɪˈzum/ *verb* 动词 (**presumes**, **presuming**, **presumed** /prɪˈzjuːmd; prɪˈzjumd/)

think that something is true but not be certain 认为某事物属实（但无把握）；推测:

P

She's not home yet so I presume she's still at work. 她还没回家，看来她还在工作呢。

pretend /prɪ'tend; prɪ'tɛnd/ *verb* 动词 (**pretends, pretending, pretended**)
try to make somebody believe something that is not true 尽力使别人信以为真；假装: *He didn't want to talk, so he pretended to be asleep.* 他不想说话，就假装睡着了。

P

pretty[1] /'prɪti; 'prɪtɪ/ *adjective* 形容词 (**prettier, prettiest**)
nice to look at 好看的；漂亮的: *a pretty little girl* 漂亮的小姑娘 ◇ *These flowers are very pretty.* 这些花非常好看。☞ Note at **beautiful** 见 **beautiful** 词条注释

pretty[2] /'prɪti; 'prɪtɪ/ *adverb* 副词
quite; fairly 相当；颇: *It's pretty cold today.* 今天天气够冷的。

prevent /prɪ'vent; prɪ'vɛnt/ *verb* 动词 (**prevents, preventing, prevented**)
stop somebody from doing something or stop something happening 阻止某人做某事；防止某事物: *Her parents want to prevent her from getting married.* 她父母想阻止她结婚。◇ *It is easier to prevent disease than to cure it.* 预防疾病比治疗疾病容易些。

prevention /prɪ'venʃn; prɪ'vɛnʃən/ *noun* 名词 (no plural 无复数)
preventing something 防止某事物: *the prevention of crime* 防止犯罪行为

previous /'pri:viəs; 'privɪəs/ *adjective* 形容词
that happened or came before or earlier (发生得或来得）在前的；较早的: *Who was the previous owner of the car?* 这辆汽车前一个车主是谁？

previously *adverb* 副词
I work in a factory now, but previously I was a secretary. 我现在在工厂工作，可是我以前当秘书。

prey /preɪ; pre/ *noun* 名词 (no plural 无复数)
an animal or bird that another animal or bird kills for food 被捕食的动物: *Zebra are prey for lions.* 斑马是狮子捕食的动物。

price /praɪs; praɪs/ *noun* 名词
how much money you pay to buy something 价格；价钱: *The price is £15.* 价钱是15英镑。◇ *Prices in this country are very high.* 这个国家的物价非常高。

prick /prɪk; prɪk/ *verb* 动词 (**pricks, pricking, pricked** /prɪkt; prɪkt/)
make a very small hole in something, or hurt somebody, with a sharp point 在某物上穿孔；用尖物刺某人: *I pricked my finger on a needle.* 我手指让针给扎了。◇ *Prick the potatoes with a fork before you cook them.* 先把土豆用叉子扎一下然后再做熟。

prick *noun* 名词
a small sharp pain（轻微的）刺痛: *She felt the prick of a needle.* 她感到针刺的疼痛。

prickle /'prɪkl; 'prɪkl̩/ *noun* 名词
a sharp point on a plant or an animal（动植物表面的）刺: *A hedgehog has prickles.* 刺猬身上有刺。

prickly /'prɪkli; 'prɪklɪ/ *adjective* 形容词
covered with prickles（指动植物表面）多刺的: *a prickly bush* 多刺的灌木

pride /praɪd; praɪd/ *noun* 名词 (no plural 无复数)
1 being pleased about something that you or others have done or about something that you have; being proud 得意；自豪: *She showed us her painting with great pride.* 她十分得意地给我们看她的油画。
2 the feeling that you are better than other people 骄傲；自大

priest /pri:st; prist/ *noun* 名词
a person who leads people in their religion 神职人员: *a Buddhist priest* 佛教神职人员

primary /'praɪməri; 'praɪˌmɛrɪ/ *adjective* 形容词
first; most important 最初的；最重要的: *What is the primary cause of the illness?* 这个病是怎样引起的？

primary school /'praɪməri sku:l; 'praɪmɛrɪ ˌskul/ *noun* 名词
a school for children between the ages of five and eleven 小学（为五岁至十一岁儿童而设的）

prime minister /ˌpraɪm 'mɪnɪstə(r); ˌpraɪm 'mɪnɪstɚ/ *noun* 名词
the leader of the government in some countries, for example in Britain 首相；总理

prince /prɪns; prɪns/ *noun* 名词
1 a man in a royal family, especially the son of a king or queen 君王家族（除国王外）的男性成员；（尤指）王子: *the Prince of Wales* 威尔士王储

2 a man who is the ruler of a small country（小国家的男性的）国王

princess /ˌprɪnˈses; ˈprɪnsɪs/ *noun* 名词 (*plural* 复数作 **princesses**)
a woman in a royal family, especially the daughter of a king or queen or the wife of a prince 君王家族（除王后外）的女性成员；（尤指）公主或王子的妻子

principal[1] /ˈprɪnsəpl; ˈprɪnsəpl̩/ *adjective* 形容词
most important 最重要的；首要的: *My principal reason for going to Rome was to learn Italian.* 我到罗马去主要是想学习意大利语。

principal[2] /ˈprɪnsəpl; ˈprɪnsəpl̩/ *noun* 名词
a person who is in charge of a school or college（某些学校或学院的）校长，院长

principally /ˈprɪnsəpli; ˈprɪnsəpl̩ɪ/ *adverb* 副词
mainly; mostly 首要地；主要地: *She sometimes travels to Europe, but she works principally in Africa.* 她有时候到欧洲去，可是工作主要在非洲。

principle /ˈprɪnsəpl; ˈprɪnsəpl̩/ *noun* 名词
1 a rule about how you should live 原则: *He has very strong principles.* 他很有原则。
2 a rule or fact about how something happens or works 原理: *scientific principles* 科学原理

print /prɪnt; prɪnt/ *verb* 动词 (**prints, printing, printed**)
1 put words or pictures onto paper using a machine. Books, newspapers and magazines are printed. 印刷
2 write with letters that are not joined together 用印刷体写: *Please print your name and address clearly.* 请用印刷体把姓名和地址写清楚。

print *noun* 名词
1 (no plural 无复数) letters that a machine makes on paper 印出的字: *The print is too small to read.* 印出来的字太小，看不清楚。
2 (*plural* 复数作 **prints**) a mark where something has pressed 物体压出的痕迹: *footprints in the snow* 雪中的足迹
3 (*plural* 复数作 **prints**) a copy on paper of a painting or photograph 印出的图片或照片

printer /ˈprɪntə(r); ˈprɪntɚ/ *noun* 名词
1 a person or company that prints things like books or newspapers 印刷工；印刷商
2 a machine that prints words from a computer（计算机的）打印机 ☞ picture at **computer** 见 **computer** 词条插图

prison /ˈprɪzn; ˈprɪzn̩/ *noun* 名词
a place where people must stay when they have done something that is wrong 监狱: *He was sent to prison for robbing a bank.* 他因抢劫银行而入狱。◇ *She was in prison for 15 years.* 她在狱中关了15年。

prisoner /ˈprɪznə(r); ˈprɪzn̩ɚ/ *noun* 名词
a person who is in prison or any person who is not free 囚犯；无自由的人

private /ˈpraɪvət; ˈpraɪvɪt/ *adjective* 形容词
1 for one person or a small group of people only, and not for anybody else 私人的；小群体的: *The house has a private swimming-pool* (= that only the people who live in the house can use). 这座宅院有个私人游泳池。◇ *You shouldn't read his letters—they're private.* 你不应该看他的信——那些都是私人信件。
2 alone; without other people there 单独的；无他人在场的: *I would like a private meeting with the manager.* 我想跟经理单独谈谈。
3 not of your job 非工作上的；个人的: *She never talks about her private life with the people at work.* 她从不跟同事说她个人生活的事。
4 not controlled by the government 不受政府控制的；私营的: *a private hospital* (= you must pay to go there) 私立医院 ◇ *private schools* 私立学校
in private alone; without other people there 单独的；无他人在场的: *Can I speak to you in private?* 我想跟您单独谈谈行吗？

privately *adverb* 副词
Let's go into my office—we can talk more privately there. 咱们到我的办公室去吧——可以清静地谈谈话。

privilege /ˈprɪvəlɪdʒ; ˈprɪvl̩ɪdʒ/ *noun* 名词
something special that only one person or a few people may do or have 特权；特别待遇: *Prisoners who behave well have special privileges.* 表现好的犯人可获特别优待。

P

P

privileged /'prɪvəlɪdʒd; 'prɪvlɪdʒd/ *adjective* 形容词
I felt very privileged when I was invited to Buckingham Palace. 我受到白金汉宫的邀请，感到非常荣幸。

prize /praɪz; praɪz/ *noun* 名词
something that you give to the person who wins a game, race, etc（给予获胜者的）奖；奖品；奖金: *I won first prize in the painting competition.* 我获得了绘画竞赛的一等奖。

probable /'prɒbəbl; 'prɑbəbl̩/ *adjective* 形容词
If something is probable, it will almost certainly happen or it is almost certainly true 几乎肯定的；很可能的: *It is probable that he will be late.* 他八成要晚了。✪ opposite 反义词: **improbable**

probably /'prɒbəbli; 'prɑbəblɪ/ *adverb* 副词
almost certainly 几乎肯定；很可能；大概: *I will probably see you on Thursday.* 我星期四大概能见你。

problem /'prɒbləm; 'prɑbləm/ *noun* 名词
1 something that is difficult; something that makes you worry 困难的事物；使人担忧的事物: *She has a lot of problems. Her husband is ill and her son is in prison.* 她有很多难处。她丈夫病了，儿子又进了监狱。◇ *There is a problem with my telephone—it doesn't work.* 我的电话出毛病了——不能用了。
2 a question that you must answer by thinking about it 问题；难题: *I can't solve this problem.* 我无法解决这个问题。

proceed /prə'si:d; prə'sid/ *verb* 动词 (**proceeds, proceeding, proceeded**)
continue; go on 继续进行；继续下去: *If everyone is here, then we can proceed with the meeting.* 要是大家都在这儿，咱们就接着开会吧。✪ **Continue** and **go on** are the words that we usually use. ✳ **continue** 和 **go on** 是常用词。

process /'prəʊses; 'prɑsɛs/ *noun* 名词 (*plural* 复数作 **processes**)
a number of actions, one after the other for doing or making something 步骤；程序；过程: *He explained the process of building a boat.* 他解释了造船的步骤。◇ *Learning a language is usually a slow process.* 学习语言通常要经历一个缓慢的过程。

procession /prə'seʃn; prə'sɛʃən/ *noun* 名词
a line of people or cars that are moving slowly along（指人、汽车等）缓慢行进的行列: *We watched the carnival procession.* 我们观看了狂欢节的游行。

produce[1] /prə'dju:s; prə'dus/ *verb* 动词 (**produces, producing, produced** /prə'dju:st; prə'djust/)
1 make or grow something 制造或生产某物: *This factory produces cars.* 这家工厂是制造汽车的。◇ *What does the farm produce?* 这个农场出产什么？
2 make something happen 使某事物发生；产生: *His hard work produced good results.* 他很努力，因而取得了很好的成绩。
3 bring something out to show it 把某物拿出来或展示出来: *She produced a ticket from her pocket.* 她从口袋里掏出一张票来。
4 organize something like a play or film 组织上演戏剧或制作影片等等；监制；编导: *The play was produced by Peter Gordon.* 这出戏是由彼得·戈登编导的。

produce[2] /'prɒdju:s; 'prɑdus/ *noun* 名词 (no plural 无复数)
food that you grow on a farm or in a garden to sell（农场或园圃里生产的）农产品: *fresh farm produce* 新鲜的农产品

producer /prə'dju:sə(r); prə'dusɚ/ *noun* 名词
1 a person who organizes something like a play or film 组织上演戏剧或制作影片等的人；监制；编导: *a television producer* 电视节目制作人
2 a company or country that makes or grows something 制造或生产某物的公司或国家: *Brazil is an important producer of coffee.* 巴西是很重要的咖啡产地。

product /'prɒdʌkt; 'prɑdʌkt/ *noun* 名词
something that people make or grow to sell 为出售而制造或生产的产品: *Coffee is Brazil's main product.* 咖啡是巴西的主要产品。

production /prə'dʌkʃn; prə'dʌkʃən/ *noun* 名词
1 (no plural 无复数) making or growing something 制造或生产某物: *the production of oil* 采油
2 (*plural* 复数作 **productions**) a play, film, etc 戏剧或影片等

profession /prə'feʃn; prə'fɛʃən/ *noun* 名词

a job that needs a lot of studying and special training（需要深入学习和专业训练的）职业: *She's a doctor by profession.* 她的职业是医生。

professional /prəˈfeʃənl; prəˈfɛʃənl̩/ *adjective* 形容词

1 of or about somebody who has a profession 专业人员的: *I got professional advice from a lawyer.* 我得到了律师的内行指导。

2 who does something for money as a job 职业性的: *a professional footballer* 职业足球运动员 ☞ Look at **amateur**. 见 **amateur**。

professionally /prəˈfeʃənəli; prəˈfɛʃənl̩ɪ/ *adverb* 副词

He plays the piano professionally. 他以弹钢琴为职业。

professor /prəˈfesə(r); prəˈfɛsɚ/ *noun* 名词

an important teacher at a university 教授: *Professor Hall* 霍尔教授

profile /ˈprəʊfaɪl; ˈprofaɪl/ *noun* 名词

the shape of a person's face when you see it from the side 人面部的侧面轮廓

profit /ˈprɒfɪt; ˈprɑfɪt/ *noun* 名词

money that you get when you sell something for more than it cost to buy or make 利润；赢利: *If you buy a bike for £70 and sell it for £80, you make a profit of £10.* 要是用70英镑买了一辆自行车，转手卖了80英镑，所赚的利润就是10英镑。

profitable /ˈprɒfɪtəbl; ˈprɑfɪtəbl̩/ *adjective* 形容词

If something is profitable, it brings you money 有利润的: *a profitable business* 赚钱的生意

program /ˈprəʊgræm; ˈprogrəm/ *noun* 名词

1 a list of instructions that you give to a computer（计算机的）编码指令，程序

2 *American English for* **programme** 美式英语，即 **programme**

program *verb* 动词 (**programs**, **programming**, **programmed** /ˈprəʊgræmd; ˈprogræmd/)

give instructions to a computer 用程序指示计算机工作 ✪ In American English the spellings are **programing** and **programed**. 美式英语的拼法为 **programing** 和 **programed**。

programmer *noun* 名词

a person whose job is to write programs for a computer（计算机）程序编制员，程序设计师

programer *American English for* **programmer** 美式英语，即 **programmer**

programme /ˈprəʊgræm; ˈprogrəm/ *noun* 名词

1 something on television or radio（电视或电台的）节目: *Did you watch that programme about Japan on TV last night?* 你昨天晚上看了关于日本的电视节目了吗？

2 a piece of paper or a little book that tells people at a play or concert what they are going to see or hear（戏剧或音乐会的）演出说明书，节目单

3 a plan of things to do（要做的）计划: *What is your programme for tomorrow?* 你明天有什么安排？

progress[1] /ˈprəʊgres; ˈprɑgrɛs/ *noun* 名词 (no plural 无复数)

moving forward or becoming better 前进；进步；进展: *Jo has made good progress in maths this year.* 乔今年数学进步很大。

in progress happening 进行中: *Silence! Examination in progress.* 安静！现在正在考试。

progress[2] /prəˈgres; prəˈgrɛs/ *verb* 动词 (**progresses**, **progressing**, **progressed** /prəˈgrest; prəˈgrɛst/)

move forward or become better 前进；进步；进展: *I felt more tired as the day progressed.* 我这一天过得越发疲倦了。

prohibit /prəˈhɪbɪt; proˈhɪbɪt/ *verb* 动词 (**prohibits**, **prohibiting**, **prohibited**)

say that people must not do something 禁止大家做某事: *Smoking is prohibited in the theatre.* 戏院里禁止吸烟。

project /ˈprɒdʒekt; ˈprɑdʒɛkt/ *noun* 名词

1 a big plan to do something（做某事的）大的计划；工程: *a project to build a new airport* 修建新机场的规划

2 a piece of work that you do at school. You find out a lot about something and write about it（学校的）习作项目；课题: *We did a project on Africa.* 我们做了关于非洲的一项研究。

projector /prəˈdʒektə(r); prəˈdʒɛktɚ/ *noun* 名词

a machine that shows films or pictures on a wall or screen 电影放映机；幻灯机

prominent /ˈprɒmɪnənt; ˈprɑmənənt/ *adjective* 形容词
1 easy to see, for example because it is bigger than usual 惹人注目的；突出的（例如因为比普通的大）: *prominent teeth* 龅牙
2 important and famous 重要而有名的；著名的；杰出的: *a prominent writer* 杰出的作家

P

promise¹ /ˈprɒmɪs; ˈprɑmɪs/ *verb* 动词 (**promises, promising, promised** /ˈprɒmɪst; ˈprɑmɪst/)
say that you will certainly do or not do something 承诺；许诺: *She promised to give me the money today.* 她答应今天把钱给我。◇ *I promise I'll come.* 我保证我一定来。◇ *Promise me that you won't be late!* 答应我你一定不迟到！

promise² /ˈprɒmɪs; ˈprɑmɪs/ *noun* 名词
saying that you will certainly do or not do something 承诺；许诺
break a promise not do what you promised 违背诺言
keep a promise do what you promised 履行诺言
make a promise say that you will certainly do or not do something 作出允诺

promote /prəˈməʊt; prəˈmot/ *verb* 动词 (**promotes, promoting, promoted**)
give somebody a more important job 提升某人（做更重要的工作）: *She worked hard, and after a year she was promoted to manager.* 她工作努力，一年后就提升为经理了。
promotion /prəˈməʊʃn; prəˈmoʃən/ *noun* 名词
The new job is a promotion for me. 这份新工作对我来说是晋升。

prompt /prɒmpt; prɑmpt/ *adjective* 形容词
quick 迅速的；及时的: *She gave me a prompt answer.* 她答复我很及时。
promptly *adverb* 副词
quickly; not late 迅速地；及时地: *We arrived promptly at two o'clock.* 我们在两点钟及时到达。

pronoun /ˈprəʊnaʊn; ˈpronaʊn/ *noun* 名词
a word that you use in place of a noun 代词（代替名词的词）: *'He', 'it', 'me' and 'them' are all pronouns.* "他"、"它"、"我"、"他们"都是代词。

pronounce /prəˈnaʊns; prəˈnaʊns/ *verb* 动词 (**pronounces, pronouncing, pronounced** /prəˈnaʊnst; prəˈnaʊnst/)
make the sound of a letter or word 发字母的或字的音: *How do you pronounce your name?* 您名字的读音是怎样的？◇ *You don't pronounce the 'b' at the end of 'comb'.* ＊comb 这个字的最后一个字母b不发音。

pronunciation /prəˌnʌnsiˈeɪʃn; prəˌnʌnsɪˈeʃən/ *noun* 名词
how you say a word or words（字或词组的）发音；发音法: *There are two different pronunciations for this word.* 这个字有两种发音方法。◇ *His pronunciation is very good.* 他的发音非常好。

proof /pru:f; pruf/ *noun* 名词 (no plural 无复数)
something that shows that an idea is true 证明；证据: *Do you have any proof that you are the owner of this car?* 你有证据证明这辆汽车是你的吗？✪ The verb is **prove**. 动词是 **prove**。

propeller /prəˈpelə(r); prəˈpɛlɚ/ *noun* 名词
a thing that is joined to the engine on a ship or an aeroplane. It turns round fast to make the ship or aeroplane move.（轮船或飞机的发动机的）推进器；螺旋桨

proper /ˈprɒpə(r); ˈprɑpɚ/ *adjective* 形容词
1 right or correct 适合的；适当的: *I haven't got the proper tools to mend the car.* 我没有修理汽车的适当工具。
2 real 真正的: *He hasn't got any proper friends.* 他没有真正的朋友。
properly *adverb* 副词
well or correctly（做得）好或正确: *Close the door properly.* 把门关好。

property /ˈprɒpəti; ˈprɑpətɪ/ *noun* 名词
1 (no plural 无复数) something that you have or own 所有物；财产: *This book is the property of James Gray.* 这本书是詹姆斯·格雷的财物。
2 (*plural* 复数作 **properties**) a building and the land around it 建筑物及其周围的土地；房地产

prophet /ˈprɒfɪt; ˈprɑfɪt/ *noun* 名词
a person that God chooses to give his message to people（某些宗教的）先知

proportion /prəˈpɔ:ʃn; prəˈpɔrʃən/ *noun* 名词
1 a part of something（某事物的）部分:

A large proportion of people leave school when they are 16. 大部分人16岁时中学毕业。

2 the amount or size of one thing compared to another thing（一物与另一物在数量或大小的）比例: *What is the proportion of men to women in the factory?* 这家工厂男女比例是多少？

proposal /prəˈpəʊzl; prəˈpozl̩/ *noun* 名词

1 a plan or idea about how to do something 计划；方案；提案: *a proposal to build a new station* 修建新火车站的方案

2 asking somebody to marry you 向某人求婚

propose /prəˈpəʊz; prəˈpoz/ *verb* 动词 (**proposes**, **proposing**, **proposed** /prəˈpəʊzd; prəˈpozd/)

1 say what you think should happen or be done 提议；建议: *I proposed that we should meet again on Monday.* 我建议我们星期一再开一次会。

2 ask somebody to marry you 向某人求婚: *Melissa proposed to Mike.* 梅利莎向迈克求婚。

protect /prəˈtekt; prəˈtɛkt/ *verb* 动词 (**protects**, **protecting**, **protected**)

keep somebody or something safe 保护某人或某事物: *Wear a hat to protect your head against the sun.* 戴上帽子以免头部晒着。◇ *Parents try to protect their children from danger.* 父母尽量保护子女不要受到危害。

protection /prəˈtekʃn; prəˈtɛkʃən/ *noun* 名词 (no plural 无复数)

keeping somebody or something safe 保护某人或某事物: *protection against disease* 预防疾病

protest /prəˈtest; prəˈtɛst/ *verb* 动词 (**protests**, **protesting**, **protested**)

say or show strongly that you do not like something 强烈反对；抗议: *They protested against the government's plans.* 他们强烈反对政府的计划。

protest /ˈprəʊtest; ˈprotɛst/ *noun* 名词

They made a protest against the new tax. 他们对新税制提出了强烈抗议。

Protestant /ˈprɒtɪstənt; ˈprɑtɪstənt/ *noun* 名词

a person who believes in the Christian God and who is not a Roman Catholic 新教徒（信仰基督教而非天主教的成员）

proud /praʊd; praud/ *adjective* 形容词 (**prouder**, **proudest**)

1 If you feel proud, you are pleased about something that you or others have done or about something that you have 感到得意的；自豪的: *They are very proud of their new house.* 他们为自己的新房子而感到非常自豪。

2 A person who is proud thinks that he/she is better than other people 骄傲的；自大的: *She was too proud to say she was sorry.* 她傲慢得都不肯陪个不是。

✪ The noun is **pride**. 名词是 **pride**。

proudly *adverb* 副词

'I made this myself,' he said proudly. "这是我自己做的，"他自豪地说。

prove /pruːv; pruv/ *verb* 动词 (**proves**, **proving**, **proved** /pruːvd; pruvd/, **has proved** or 或 **has proven** /ˈpruːvn; ˈpruvən/)

show that something is true 证明某事物属实: *The blood on his shirt proves that he is the murderer.* 他衬衫上的血迹证明他就是凶手。✪ The noun is **proof**. 名词是 **proof**。

proverb /ˈprɒvɜːb; ˈprɑvɝb/ *noun* 名词

a short sentence that people often say, that gives help or advice 谚语；格言: *'The early bird catches the worm' is an English proverb.* "早起的鸟能捉到虫"是句英国谚语。

provide /prəˈvaɪd; prəˈvaɪd/ *verb* 动词 (**provides**, **providing**, **provided**)

give something to somebody who needs it 把某物给有需要的人；提供；供应: *I'll provide the food for the party.* 我为聚会准备了食物。◇ *The company have provided me with a car.* 公司为我提供了一辆汽车。

provided /prəˈvaɪdɪd; prəˈvaɪdɪd/, **providing** /prəˈvaɪdɪŋ; prəˈvaɪdɪŋ/ *conjunction* 连词

only if 在…情况或条件下；如果；倘若: *Phone me when you get home, providing it's not too late.* 您一到家就给我打个电话，要是不太晚的话。◇ *I'll go provided that the children can come with me.* 要是孩子都跟我一起去我就去。

province /ˈprɒvɪns; ˈprɑvɪns/ *noun* 名词

a part of a country（指国家的地区）省；州: *Canada has ten provinces.* 加拿大有十个省。

provincial /prə'vɪnʃl; prə'vɪnʃəl/ *adjective* 形容词
of a province（指国家的地区）省的；州的: *the provincial government* 省政府

PS /ˌpi: 'es; ˌpi 'ɛs/
You write 'PS' at the end of a letter, after your name, when you want to add something 又及（信写完并已署名后另作补述时的用语）: *... Love from Paul. PS I'll bring the car.* …此问近好。保罗
我把汽车开来。又及。

psychiatrist /saɪ'kaɪətrɪst; saɪ'kaɪətrɪst/ *noun* 名词
a doctor who helps people who are ill in the mind 精神科医生

psychology /saɪ'kɒlədʒi; saɪ'kɑlədʒɪ/ *noun* 名词 (no plural 无复数)
the study of the mind and how it works 心理学

psychologist /saɪ'kɒlədʒɪst; saɪ'kɑlədʒɪst/ *noun* 名词
a person who studies or knows a lot about psychology 心理学研究者；心理学家

pt *short way of writing* **pint** ＊ **pint** 的缩写形式

PTO /ˌpi: ti: 'əʊ; ˌpi ti 'o/
please turn over; words at the bottom of a page that tell you to turn to the next page 请翻过来；见下页（页末字样）

pub /pʌb; pʌb/ *noun* 名词
a place where people go to have a drink and meet their friends 酒馆；酒店

> ✪ In Britain, you can buy **alcoholic** drinks like beer and wine in a pub if you are over the age of 18. 在英国，18岁以上的人可以在酒馆里买到啤酒和葡萄酒等含酒精的 **(alcoholic)** 饮品。In a lot of pubs you can also buy food. 在许多酒馆里还能买到食物。

public[1] /'pʌblɪk; 'pʌblɪk/ *adjective* 形容词
of or for everybody 公众的；公共的；公用的: *a public telephone* 公用电话 ◇ *Smoking is not allowed in public places.* 在公共场所不准吸烟。

public convenience /ˌpʌblɪk kən'vi:niəns; ˌpʌblɪk kən'vinjəns/ *noun* 名词
a building or room with a toilet for everybody to use, for example in the street 公共厕所

public school /ˌpʌblɪk 'sku:l; 'pʌblɪk ˌskul/ *noun* 名词
a school for pupils between the age of 13 and 18. Parents must pay to send their children to a public school. 公学（为13岁至18岁学生而设的私立付费学校）

public transport /ˌpʌblɪk 'trænspɔ:t; ˌpʌblɪk 'trænsport/ *noun* 名词
buses and trains that everybody can use 公共交通工具: *I usually travel by public transport.* 我出门通常乘坐公共交通工具。

publicly *adverb* 副词
to everybody; not secretly 对大家；公开地；非秘密地: *She spoke publicly about her friendship with the Prince.* 她公开谈论跟王子的友谊。

public[2] /'pʌblɪk; 'pʌblɪk/ *noun* 名词
the public (no plural 无复数)
all people 公众；民众: *The palace is open to the public between 10 a.m. and 4 p.m.* 这座宫殿从上午10时至下午4时向公众开放。
in public when other people are there 有别人在场；公开地: *I don't want to talk about it in public.* 我不想当着外人谈这件事。

publication /ˌpʌblɪ'keɪʃn; ˌpʌblɪ'keʃən/ *noun* 名词
1 (no plural 无复数) making and selling a book, magazine, etc 出版: *He became very rich after the publication of his first book.* 他在他第一本书出版以后就非常富了。
2 (*plural* 复数作 **publications**) a book, magazine, etc 出版物

publicity /pʌb'lɪsəti; pʌb'lɪsətɪ/ *noun* 名词 (no plural 无复数)
giving information about something so that people know about it 提供某事的信息让公众知道；宣传: *There was a lot of publicity for the new film.* 这部新影片已广为宣传。

publish /'pʌblɪʃ; 'pʌblɪʃ/ *verb* 动词 (**publishes**, **publishing**, **published** /'pʌblɪʃt; 'pʌblɪʃt/)
prepare and print a book, magazine or newspaper for selling 出版；发行: *This dictionary was published by Oxford University Press.* 这本词典是牛津大学出版社出版的。

publisher *noun* 名词
a person or company that publishes

books, magazines or newspapers 出版者；出版商；出版社

pudding /ˈpʊdɪŋ; ˈpʊdɪŋ/ *noun* 名词
1 something sweet that you eat at the end of a meal（在餐末吃的）甜食: *What's for pudding today?* 今天的餐末甜食是什么？
2 a kind of cake that you usually eat hot at the end of a meal（通常在餐末吃的）热布丁

puddle /ˈpʌdl; ˈpʌdl̩/ *noun* 名词
a little water on the ground（地面上的）小片水

puff /pʌf; pʌf/ *noun* 名词
a small amount of air, wind, smoke, etc that blows 一阵（气、风、烟等）: *a puff of smoke* 一股烟

puff *verb* 动词 (**puffs**, **puffing**, **puffed** /pʌft; pʌft/)
1 come out in puffs（气、风、烟等）冒出；刮起；喷出: *Smoke was puffing out of the chimney.* 烟筒正冒着烟。
2 breathe quickly 喘气: *She was puffing as she ran up the hill.* 她气喘吁吁地往小山上跑。

pull 拉

pull[1] /pʊl; pʊl/ *verb* 动词 (**pulls**, **pulling**, **pulled** /pʊld; pʊld/)
1 move somebody or something strongly towards you 用力使某人或某物朝自己所在的方向移动；拉；拽: *She pulled the drawer open.* 她把抽屉拉开了。
2 go forward, moving something behind you 使某物跟在自己后面移动；拖；牵: *The cart was pulled by two horses.* 那辆大车用两匹马拉着。
3 move something somewhere 把某物向某处移动: *He pulled up his trousers.* 他把裤子提上了。

pull down destroy a building 拆毁建筑物: *The old school has been pulled down.* 那所旧学校已经拆了。

pull in drive a car to the side of the road and stop 把汽车开到路边停住: *I pulled in to look at the map.* 我把汽车开到路边停下来查看地图。

pull yourself together control your feelings after being upset（心情烦乱之后）控制感情: *Pull yourself together and stop crying.* 你控制一下情绪，别哭了。

pull up stop a car 把汽车停住: *The driver pulled up at the traffic lights.* 司机在交通灯处把汽车停住。

pull[2] /pʊl; pʊl/ *noun* 名词
pulling something 拉；拽；拖；牵: *Give the rope a pull.* 把绳子拉一拉。

pullover /ˈpʊləʊvə(r); ˈpʊlˌovɚ/ *noun* 名词
a warm piece of clothing with sleeves, that you wear on the top part of your body. Pullovers are often made of wool. 厚上衣；（常指）套头毛衣

pulse /pʌls; pʌls/ *noun* 名词
the beating of your heart that you feel in different parts of your body, especially in your wrist 脉搏: *The nurse felt his pulse.* 护士给他诊了诊脉。

pump /pʌmp; pʌmp/ *noun* 名词
a machine that moves a liquid or gas into or out of something 泵；抽水机；抽气机；打气筒: *a bicycle-pump* 自行车打气筒 ◇ *a petrol pump* 汽油泵

pump *verb* 动词 (**pumps**, **pumping**, **pumped** /pʌmpt; pʌmpt/)
move a liquid or gas with a pump 用泵抽出或压入液体或气体: *Your heart pumps blood around your body.* 心脏把血液压送到全身。

pump up fill something with air, using a pump 用泵给某物充气: *I pumped up my bicycle tyres.* 我给自行车车胎打了打气。

pumpkin /ˈpʌmpkɪn; ˈpʌmpkɪn/ *noun* 名词
a very large round vegetable with a thick orange skin 南瓜

pun /pʌn; pʌn/ *noun* 名词
a funny use of a word that has two meanings, or that sounds the same as another word 双关语

punch /pʌntʃ; pʌntʃ/ *verb* 动词 (**punches**, **punching**, **punched** /pʌntʃt; pʌntʃt/)
1 hit somebody or something hard with your closed hand (your **fist**) 用拳头打某人或某物（拳头叫做 **fist**）: *She punched me in the stomach.* 她用拳头打我的肚子。
2 make a hole in something with a special tool 用某种工具在某物上打孔: *He punched my ticket.* 他在我的票上打了孔。

P

punch *noun* 名词 (*plural* 复数作 **punches**)
a punch on the chin 打在下巴上的一拳

punctual /'pʌŋktʃuəl; 'pʌŋktʃuəl/ *adjective* 形容词
If you are punctual, you come or do something at the right time 准时的；守时的: *Please try to be punctual for your classes.* 请尽量准时上课。

punctually /'pʌŋktʃuəli; 'pʌŋktʃuəlɪ/ *adverb* 副词
They arrived punctually at seven o'clock. 他们在七点钟准时到达。

punctuate /'pʌŋktʃueɪt; 'pʌŋktʃuˌet/ *verb* 动词 (**punctuates**, **punctuating**, **punctuated**)
put marks like commas, full stops and question marks in writing（在文字中）加标点符号

punctuation /ˌpʌŋktʃu'eɪʃn; ˌpʌŋktʃʊ-'eʃən/ *noun* 名词 (no plural 无复数)
using punctuation marks when you are writing 使用标点符号

punctuation mark /pʌŋktʃu'eɪʃn mɑ:k; ˌpʌŋktʃʊ'eʃən mɑrk/ *noun* 名词
one of the signs that you use when you are writing. Commas (,), full stops (.) and colons (:) are all punctuation marks. 标点符号

puncture /'pʌŋktʃə(r); 'pʌŋktʃɚ/ *noun* 名词
a hole in a tyre, that lets the air go out（轮胎上的）孔（漏气）: *My bike has got a puncture.* 我的自行车轮胎扎了个洞。

puncture *verb* 动词 (**punctures**, **puncturing**, **punctured** /'pʌŋktʃəd; 'pʌŋktʃɚd/)
make a puncture in something 在某物上穿孔: *A piece of glass punctured the tyre.* 有块玻璃把轮胎扎破了。

punish /'pʌnɪʃ; 'pʌnɪʃ/ *verb* 动词 (**punishes**, **punishing**, **punished** /'pʌnɪʃt; 'pʌnɪʃt/)
make somebody suffer because they have done something wrong 处罚或惩罚某人: *The children were punished for telling lies.* 孩子们因为说谎而受到处罚。

punishment /'pʌnɪʃmənt; 'pʌnɪʃmənt/ *noun* 名词
What is the punishment for murder in your country? 在你们国家谋杀罪处以什么惩罚？◇ *The child was sent to bed as a punishment for being naughty.* 那个孩子淘气，罚他上床睡觉去了。

pupil /'pju:pl; 'pjupḷ/ *noun* 名词
a person who is learning at school（中小学的）学生: *There are 30 pupils in the class.* 这个班有30个学生。

puppet /'pʌpɪt; 'pʌpɪt/ *noun* 名词
a doll that you move by pulling strings or by putting your hand inside it and moving your fingers（可操纵的）木偶；布袋木偶；提线木偶

puppy /'pʌpi; 'pʌpɪ/ *noun* 名词 (*plural* 复数作 **puppies**)
a young dog 幼小的狗

purchase /'pɜ:tʃəs; 'pɝtʃəs/ *verb* 动词 (**purchases**, **purchasing**, **purchased** /'pɜ:tʃəst; 'pɝtʃəst/)
buy something 购买: *The company has purchased three new shops.* 这家公司收购了三个新商店。✪ **Buy** is the word that we usually use. ＊ **buy** 是常用词。

purchase *noun* 名词
buying something; something that you have bought 购买；购买的物品: *She made several purchases and then left.* 她买了几件东西就走了。

pure /pjʊə(r); pjʊr/ *adjective* 形容词 (**purer**, **purest**)
1 not mixed with anything else; clean 纯粹的；纯净的: *This shirt is pure cotton.* 这件衬衫是纯棉的。◇ *pure mountain air* 山区清新的空气
2 complete or total 完全的；全部的: *What she said was pure nonsense.* 她说的全是废话。

purely *adverb* 副词
completely or only 纯粹地；完全地；仅仅: *He doesn't like his job—he does it purely for the money.* 他并不喜欢自己的工作，只是为了挣那份钱。

purple /'pɜ:pl; 'pɝpḷ/ *adjective* 形容词
with a colour between red and blue 紫的

purple *noun* 名词
She often wears purple. 她常常穿紫色衣服。

purpose /'pɜ:pəs; 'pɝpəs/ *noun* 名词
the reason for doing something 目的；意图: *What is the purpose of your visit?* 您这次到访的目的是什么？

on purpose because you want to; not by accident 特意地；故意地: *'You've broken my pen!' 'I'm sorry, I didn't do* *it on purpose.*'"你把我的钢笔弄坏了!""对不起,我不是成心的。"

purr /pɜ:(r); pɝ/ *verb* 动词 (**purrs, purring, purred** /pɜ:d; pɝd/)
When a cat purrs, it makes a low sound that shows that it is happy. (指猫快活时)发出低沉的呼噜声

purse 钱包

purse /pɜ:s; pɝs/ *noun* 名词
1 a small bag that you keep money in 钱包
2 *American English for* **handbag** 美式英语,即 **handbag**

pursue /pəˈsju:; pɚˈsu/ *verb* 动词 (**pursues, pursuing, pursued** /pəˈsju:d; pɚˈsud/)
follow somebody or something because you want to catch them 追赶某人或某物(想捉住): *The police pursued the stolen car for several kilometres.* 警察追赶那辆被偷的汽车,追了好几公里。✪ **Chase** is the word that we usually use. ✳ **chase** 是常用词。

push 推

push /pʊʃ; pʊʃ/ *verb* 动词 (**pushes, pushing, pushed** /pʊʃt; pʊʃt/)
1 move somebody or something strongly away from you 用力使某人或某物朝离开自己的方向移动;推: *The car broke down so we had to push it to a garage.* 汽车坏了,我们只好把它推到修车处去。
2 press something with your finger 用手指压;按: *Push the red button to stop the bus.* 按那个红色的钮就能让公共汽车停住。
push *noun* 名词 (*plural* 复数作 **pushes**) *She gave him a push and he fell.* 她把他推倒了。

pushchair /ˈpʊʃtʃeə(r); ˈpʊʃˌtʃɛr/ *noun* 名词

pushchair 幼儿车

a chair on wheels for a small child 幼儿车

pussy /ˈpʊsi; ˈpʊsɪ/ *noun* 名词 (*plural* 复数作 **pussies**)
a word for 'cat' that children use (儿语)猫;猫咪

put /pʊt; pʊt/ *verb* 动词 (**puts, putting, put, has put**)
move something to a place 把某物置于某处;放置: *She put the book on the table.* 她把书放在桌子上了。◇ *He put his hand in his pocket.* 他一只手插在口袋里。◇ *Put* (= write) *your name at the top of the page.* 把你的名字写在这页纸的上端。
put away put something in its usual place 把某物放在原处: *She put the box away in the cupboard.* 她把盒子放回柜子里。
put down put something on another thing, for example on the floor or a table 把某物放在另一物上(例如放在地板上或桌子上)
put somebody off make you feel that you do not like somebody or something, or that you do not want to do something 使某人厌恶某人或(做)某事物: *The accident put me off driving.* 出了事故以后我就不愿意开车了。
put something off not do something until a later time 推迟某事物: *He put off his holiday because the children were ill.* 他把假期推迟了,因为孩子都病了。
put on 1 take clothes and wear them 穿戴衣物: *Put on your coat.* 把你的大衣穿上。✪ opposite 反义词: **take off**
2 press or turn something to make an electrical thing start working 按或拧开关(开动电器): *I put on the TV.* 我把电视机打开了。◇ *Put the lights on.* 把电灯打开。**3** make a record, cassette or compact disc start to play 播放普通唱片、磁带或激光唱片等: *Let's put my new cassette on.* 咱们播放我的新磁带听听吧。

P

put out stop a fire or stop a light shining 把火熄灭；把灯关上: *She put out the fire with a bucket of water.* 她用一桶水把火浇灭了。

put somebody through connect somebody on the telephone to the person that they want to speak to 为某人接通电话: *Can you put me through to the manager, please?* 劳驾请经理接电话行吗？

put somebody up let somebody sleep in your home 留某人在家中住: *Can you put me up for the night?* 您让我在您家过一夜行吗？

put up with somebody or 或 **something** suffer pain or problems without complaining 容忍；忍受: *We can't change the bad weather, so we have to put up with it.* 天气坏我们没有办法，只好忍着吧。

puzzle[1] /'pʌzl; 'pʌzl̩/ *noun* 名词

1 something that is difficult to understand or explain 难以理解的或难以解释的事物: *Janet's reason for leaving her job is a puzzle to me.* 珍妮特为什么辞职，我无法理解。

2 a game that is difficult and makes you think a lot 困难的智力游戏；谜: *a crossword puzzle* 纵横字谜 ☞ Look also at **jigsaw puzzle**. 另见 **jigsaw puzzle**。

puzzle[2] /'pʌzl; 'pʌzl̩/ *verb* 动词 (**puzzles**, **puzzling**, **puzzled** /'pʌzld; 'pʌzl̩d/)

make you think a lot because you cannot understand or explain it 让某人动脑筋；使困惑: *Tim's illness puzzled his doctors.* 蒂姆的病把医生难住了。

puzzled *adjective* 形容词

If you are puzzled, you cannot understand or explain something（指人对某事物）无法理解或解释；困惑的；茫然的: *She was puzzled when he didn't answer her letter.* 她想不通为什么他不给她回信。

puzzling /'pʌzlɪŋ; 'pʌzlɪŋ/ *adjective* 形容词

If something is puzzling, you cannot understand or explain it.（指某事物）使人无法理解或解释的；使人困惑的

pyjamas /pə'dʒɑ:məz; pə'dʒæməz/ *noun* 名词 (plural 复数)

a loose jacket and trousers that you wear in bed 睡衣裤

pyramid /'pɪrəmɪd; 'pɪrəmɪd/ *noun* 名词

a shape with a flat bottom and three or four sides that come to a point at the top 锥体: *the pyramids of Egypt* 埃及的金字塔 ☞ picture on page C5 见第C5页图

Qq

quack /kwæk; kwæk/ *noun* 名词
the sound that a duck makes（鸭子叫的）嘎嘎声
quack *verb* 动词 (**quacks**, **quacking**, **quacked** /kwækt; kwækt/)
make this sound 发出（鸭子叫的）嘎嘎声

qualification /ˌkwɒlɪfɪˈkeɪʃn; ˌkwɑləfəˈkeʃən/ *noun* 名词
an examination that you have passed, or training or knowledge that you need to do a special job 资格；资历: *He left school with no qualifications.* 他中学肄业。

qualify /ˈkwɒlɪfaɪ; ˈkwɑləˌfaɪ/ *verb* 动词 (**qualifies**, **qualifying**, **qualified** /ˈkwɒlɪfaɪd; ˈkwɑləˌfaɪd/, **has qualified**)
get the right knowledge and training and pass exams so that you can do a certain job 获得资格: *Anna has qualified as a doctor.* 安娜具备做医生的资格。
qualified *adjective* 形容词
a qualified nurse 合格的护士

quality /ˈkwɒləti; ˈkwɑlətɪ/ *noun* 名词 (no plural 无复数)
how good or bad something is 某事物好坏的程度；质量；品质: *This furniture isn't very good quality.* 这种家具质量不太好。

quantity /ˈkwɒntəti; ˈkwɑntətɪ/ *noun* 名词 (*plural* 复数作 **quantities**)
how much of something there is; amount 数量: *I only bought a small quantity of cheese.* 我只买了少量的奶酪。

quarrel /ˈkwɒrəl; ˈkwɔrəl/ *verb* 动词 (**quarrels**, **quarrelling**, **quarrelled** /ˈkwɒrəld; ˈkwɔrəld/)
talk angrily with somebody because you do not agree 争吵；吵架；吵嘴: *They quarrelled because they both wanted to use the car.* 他们吵架了，因为他们都想用那辆汽车。✪ In American English the spellings are **quarreling** and **quarreled**. 美式英语拼作 **quarreling** 和 **quarreled**。
quarrel *noun* 名词
a fight with words; an argument 争吵；吵架；吵嘴: *He had a quarrel with his wife about who should do the housework.* 为了谁做家务事，他跟妻子吵了一架。

quarry /ˈkwɒri; ˈkwɔrɪ/ *noun* 名词 (*plural* 复数作 **quarries**)
a place where people cut stone out of the ground to make things like buildings or roads 采石场

quarter /ˈkwɔ:tə(r); ˈkwɔrtɚ/ *noun* 名词
1 one of four equal parts of something; ¼ 四分之一: *a mile and a quarter* 一又四分之一英里 ◇ *The film starts in three-quarters of an hour.* 电影在三刻钟以后开演。
2 three months 三个月；季度: *You get a telephone bill every quarter.* 电话费账单每个季度收到一次。
3 a part of a town 城镇的一部分；区: *the student quarter* 学生居住区
(a) quarter past 15 minutes after the hour（某个钟点的）过15分钟；过一刻: *It's quarter past two.* 现在是两点一刻。◇ *I'll meet you at a quarter past.* 我在（某个钟点的）过一刻钟的时候见你。✪ In American English you say **a quarter after** 美式英语说 **a quarter after**: *It's a quarter after seven.* 现在是七点一刻。✪ Look at page C8. 见第C8页。
(a) quarter to 15 minutes before the hour 差15分钟到，差一刻到（某个钟点）: *quarter to nine* 差一刻九点 ✪ In American English you say **a quarter of**. 美式英语说 **a quarter of**。✪ Look at page C8. 见第C8页。
quarter-final /ˌkwɔ:tə ˈfaɪnl; ˌkwɔrtɚ-ˈfaɪnḷ/ *noun* 名词
In a competition, a quarter-final is one of the four games that are played to choose who will play in the **semifinals**.（比赛的）四分之一决赛（半决赛叫做 **semi-final**）

quay /ki:; ki/ *noun* 名词 (*plural* 复数作 **quays**)
a place in a harbour where ships go so that people can move things on and off them 码头

queen /kwi:n; kwin/ *noun* 名词
1 a woman who rules a country and who is from a royal family 女王: *Queen Elizabeth II* (= the second), *the Queen of England* 伊丽莎白二世女王，英国女王
2 the wife of a king 王后

query /ˈkwɪəri; ˈkwɪrɪ/ *noun* 名词 (*plural* 复数作 **queries**)
a question 疑问；问题: *Phone me if you have any queries.* 您要是有疑问就给我打电话。

query *verb* 动词 (**queries**, **querying**, **queried** /ˈkwɪərid; ˈkwɪrɪd/)
ask a question about something that you think is wrong（怀疑某事物有错误）提出疑问: *We queried the bill but the waitress said it was correct.* 我们提出账单有问题，可是那个女服务员说单据正确无误。

Q

question[1] /ˈkwestʃən; ˈkwɛstʃən/ *noun* 名词
1 something that you ask（提出的）问题: *They asked me a lot of questions.* 他们问了我很多问题。◇ *She didn't answer my question.* 她没有回答我的问题。◇ *What is the answer to question 3?* 第3个问题的答案是什么？
2 a problem that needs an answer（需解决的）难题: *We need more money. The question is, where are we going to get it from?* 我们还需要些钱。问题是我们从哪儿弄来呀？

in question that we are talking about 谈论中的: *On the day in question I was in London.* 我们谈到的那一天，当时我正在伦敦。

out of the question not possible 不可能的: *No, I won't give you any more money. It's out of the question!* 不行，我不再给你钱了。决不可能了！

question mark /ˈkwestʃən mɑːk; ˈkwɛstʃən mɑrk/ *noun* 名词
the sign (?) that you write at the end of a question 问号（?）

question tag /ˈkwestʃən tæɡ; ˈkwɛstʃən tæɡ/ *noun* 名词
words that you put on the end of a sentence to make a question 疑问句附加词语（加在陈述句或祈使句后构成疑问句的词语）: *In the sentence 'You are French, aren't you?', 'aren't you' is a question tag.* 在 You are French，aren't you？这句话里，aren't you 就是疑问句附加词语。

question[2] /ˈkwestʃən; ˈkwɛstʃən/ *verb* 动词 (**questions**, **questioning**, **questioned** /ˈkwestʃənd; ˈkwɛstʃənd/)
ask somebody questions about something 问某人问题: *The police questioned him about the stolen car.* 警方查问他那辆被偷的汽车的事。

questionnaire /ˌkwestʃəˈneə(r); ˌkwɛstʃənˈɛr/ *noun* 名词
a list of questions for people to answer 问卷；调查表: *Please fill in* (= write the answers on) *the questionnaire.* 请填写这份问卷。

queue /kjuː; kju/ *noun* 名词
a line of people who are waiting to do something（等待做某事的人排的）队: *There's a long queue outside the cinema.* 电影院外面排着长队。☞ picture on page C25 见第C25页图

queue, **queue up** *verb* 动词 (**queues**, **queuing**, **queued** /kjuːd; kjud/)
stand in a queue 排成队: *We queued for a bus.* 我们排着队等候公共汽车。

quick /kwɪk; kwɪk/ *adjective*, *adverb* 形容词，副词 (**quicker**, **quickest**)
fast; that takes little time 快；迅速（的）: *It's quicker to travel by plane than by train.* 坐飞机比坐火车快。◇ *Can I make a quick telephone call?* 我很快打个电话行吗？☞ Look at **slow**. 见 **slow**。

quickly *adverb* 副词
Come as quickly as you can! 你尽快来。

quid /kwɪd; kwɪd/ *noun* 名词 (*plural* 复数作 **quid**)
a pound in money 一英镑: *It costs five quid.* 价钱是五英镑。✪ This is an informal word. 这是个俗语词。

quiet /ˈkwaɪət; ˈkwaɪət/ *adjective* 形容词 (**quieter**, **quietest**)
1 with little sound or no sound 轻声的；无声的；安静的: *Be quiet — the baby's asleep.* 小声点儿——孩子睡着呢。◇ *a quiet voice* 轻轻的嗓音 ✪ opposite 反义词: **loud** or 或 **noisy** ☞ picture on page C27 见第C27页图
2 without many people or without many things happening 人不多的；发生的事情不多的；平静的: *London is very quiet on Sundays.* 伦敦星期日非常宁静。

quiet *noun* 名词 (no plural 无复数)
being quiet 安静: *I need quiet when I'm working.* 我工作的时候需要安静。

quietly *adverb* 副词
Please close the door quietly. 请轻轻关门。

quilt /kwɪlt; kwɪlt/ *noun* 名词
a soft thick cover for a bed. Quilts often have feathers inside. 被褥；被子；褥子

quit /kwɪt; kwɪt/ *American English for* **leave**[1] **1** 美式英语，即 **leave**[1] **1**

quite /kwaɪt; kwaɪt/ *adverb* 副词
1 not very; rather; fairly 不很；颇为；相当: *It's quite warm today, but it's not hot.* 今天相当暖和，但是并不热。◇ *He plays the guitar quite well.* 他弹吉他弹得很不错。◇ *We waited quite a long time.* 我们等了有一段时间了。
2 completely 完全；十分: *Dinner is not quite ready.* 饭还没完全做好。
quite a few or 或 **quite a lot of** a lot of something 相当多: *There were quite a few people at the party.* 参加聚会的人可真不少。◇ *They drank quite a lot of wine.* 他们喝了很多葡萄酒。

quiz /kwɪz; kwɪz/ *noun* 名词 (*plural* 复数作 **quizzes**)
a game where you try to answer questions 问答竞赛: *a quiz on television* 电视问答竞赛

quotation /kwəʊ'teɪʃn; kwo'teʃən/, **quote** /kwəʊt; kwot/ *noun* 名词
words that you say or write, that another person said or wrote before 语录；引文: *That's a quotation from a poem by Keats.* 那个引文是从济慈诗中摘录的。
quotation marks /kwəʊ'teɪʃn mɑːks; kwo'teʃən ˌmɑrks/, **quotes** *noun* 名词 (plural 复数)
the signs " " or ' ' that you use in writing before and after words that someone has said 引号（" " 或 ' '）

quote /kwəʊt; kwot/ *verb* 动词 (**quotes, quoting, quoted**)
say or write something that another person said or wrote before 引用他人的语言或文字: *She quoted from the Bible.* 她引用了《圣经》的词句。

Rr

rabbi /ˈræbaɪ; ˈræbaɪ/ *noun* 名词 (*plural* 复数作 **rabbis**)
a teacher or leader of the Jewish religion 拉比（犹太教的导师或教士）

rabbit /ˈræbɪt; ˈræbɪt/ *noun* 名词
a small animal with long ears. Rabbits live in holes under the ground. 兔子

rabbit 兔子

race[1] /reɪs; res/ *noun* 名词
1 a competition to see who can run, drive, ride, etc fastest 速度竞赛（赛跑、赛车、赛马等）: *Who won the race?* 这场比赛最快的是谁？◇ *a horse-race* 赛马
2 the races (plural 复数) a time when there are a lot of horse-races in one place 赛马大会（在一处有多次赛事的期间）

racecourse /ˈreɪskɔːs; ˈresˌkɔrs/, **racetrack** /ˈreɪstræk; ˈresˌtræk/ *noun* 名词
a place where you go to see horse-races 赛马场

race[2] /reɪs; res/ *verb* 动词 (**races, racing, raced** /reɪst; rest/)
run, drive, ride, etc in a competition to see who is the fastest 参加速度竞赛（赛跑、赛车、赛马等）: *The cars raced round the track.* 汽车围着跑道比赛。

race[3] /reɪs; res/ *noun* 名词
a group of people of the same kind, for example with the same colour of skin 人种；种族: *People of many different races live together in this country.* 在这个国家里，各种族的人民在一起生活。

racial /ˈreɪʃl; ˈreʃəl/ *adjective* 形容词
of race 人种的；种族的: *racial differences* 种族的差异

racing /ˈreɪsɪŋ; ˈresɪŋ/ *noun* 名词 (no plural 无复数)
a sport where horses, cars, etc race against each other 速度竞赛（赛跑、赛车、赛马等）: *a racing car* 供比赛用的汽车

racism /ˈreɪsɪzəm; ˈresɪzəm/ *noun* 名词 (no plural 无复数)
the belief that some groups (**races**) of people are better than others 种族主义（种族叫做 **race**）

racist /ˈreɪsɪst; ˈresɪst/ *noun* 名词
a person who believes that some races of people are better than others 种族主义者

racist *adjective* 形容词
a racist comment 含有种族主义偏见的评论

rack /ræk; ræk/ *noun* 名词
a kind of shelf, made of bars, that you put things in or on（条形结构的）架子（可放东西或挂东西等）: *Put your bag in the luggage rack* (= on a bus or train). 把你的包放在行李架上（= 在公共汽车或火车上）。

racket 球拍

racket, racquet /ˈrækɪt; ˈrækɪt/ *noun* 名词
a thing that you use for hitting the ball in tennis, badminton and squash（网球、羽毛球、软式墙网球的）球拍

radar /ˈreɪdɑː(r); ˈredɑr/ *noun* 名词 (no plural 无复数)
a way of finding where a ship or an aircraft is and how fast it is travelling by using radio waves 雷达

radiation /ˌreɪdiˈeɪʃn; ˌredɪˈeʃən/ *noun* 名词 (no plural 无复数)
dangerous energy that some substances send out 放射线（某些物质放射出来的有危险的能量）

radiator /ˈreɪdieɪtə(r); ˈredɪˌetɚ/ *noun* 名词
1 a metal thing with hot water inside that you use to make a room warm 散热器（金属装置，内有热水可使室温增高）
2 a part of a car that has water in it to keep the engine cold 冷却器（汽车零件，内有水可使发动机降温）

radio /ˈreɪdiəʊ; ˈredɪˌo/ *noun* 名词
1 (no plural 无复数) sending or receiving sounds that travel a long way through the air by special waves 无线电传送: *The captain of the ship sent a message by radio.* 船长用无线电发出信号。

2 (*plural* 复数作 **radios**) an instrument that brings voices or music from far away so that you can hear them 收音机；无线电: *We listened to an interesting programme on the radio.* 我们从收音机里听到个很有意思的节目。

radius /ˈreɪdiəs; ˈredɪəs/ *noun* 名词 (*plural* 复数作 **radii** /ˈreɪdiaɪ; ˈredɪˌaɪ/)
the length of a straight line from the centre of a circle to the outside 半径 ☞ picture on page C5 见第C5页图

raft /rɑːft; ræft/ *noun* 名词
a flat boat with no sides and no engine 筏子

rag /ræg; ræg/ *noun* 名词
1 a small piece of old cloth that you use for cleaning 抹布；搌布
2 rags (plural 复数) clothes that are very old and torn 破旧衣服: *She was dressed in rags.* 当时她穿得很破烂。

rage /reɪdʒ; redʒ/ *noun* 名词
strong anger 大怒；狂怒

raid /reɪd; red/ *noun* 名词
a sudden attack on a place 突袭；突击: *a bank raid* 抢劫银行
raid *verb* 动词 (**raids**, **raiding**, **raided**)
Police raided the house looking for drugs. 警方突然搜查了这所房子，寻找毒品。

rail /reɪl; rel/ *noun* 名词
1 (*plural* 复数作 **rails**) a long piece of wood or metal that is fixed to a wall or to something else（固定在墙上或其他地方的）横杆: *There's a rail in the bathroom for hanging your towel on.* 浴室里有个挂毛巾的横杆。
2 rails (plural 复数) the long pieces of metal that trains go on 铁轨；轨道
3 (no plural 无复数) trains as a way of travelling 铁路（交通）；铁路运输: *British Rail* 英国铁路 ◇ *I travelled from London to Leeds by rail* (= in a train). 我从伦敦坐火车到利兹。

railings /ˈreɪlɪŋz; ˈrelɪŋz/ *noun* 名词 (plural 复数)
a fence made of long pieces of metal 栏杆；栅栏

railroad /ˈreɪlrəʊd; ˈrelˌrod/ *American English for* **railway** 美式英语，即 **railway**

railway /ˈreɪlweɪ; ˈrelˌwe/ *noun* 名词
1 (*also* 亦作 **railway line**) the metal lines that trains go on from one place to another 铁路；铁道
2 a train service that carries people and things 铁路运输: *a railway timetable* 列车时刻表

railway station /ˈreɪlweɪ steɪʃn; ˈrelwe ˌsteʃən/ *noun* 名词
a place where trains stop so that people can get on and off 火车站

rain /reɪn; ren/ *noun* 名词 (no plural 无复数)
the water that falls from the sky 雨
rain *verb* 动词 (**rains**, **raining**, **rained** /reɪnd; rend/)
When it rains, water falls from the sky 下雨: *It's raining.* 下雨了。◇ *It rained all day.* 下了一整天的雨。

rainbow /ˈreɪnbəʊ; ˈrenˌbo/ *noun* 名词
a half circle of bright colours that you sometimes see in the sky when rain and sun come together 虹；彩虹

raincoat /ˈreɪnkəʊt; ˈrenˌkot/ *noun* 名词
a light coat that you wear when it rains 雨衣

rain forest /ˈreɪn fɒrɪst; ˈren ˌfɔrɪst/ *noun* 名词
a forest in a hot part of the world where there is a lot of rain 雨林

rainy /ˈreɪni; ˈrenɪ/ *adjective* 形容词 (**rainier**, **rainiest**)
with a lot of rain 多雨的；下雨的: *a rainy day* 雨天

raise /reɪz; rez/ *verb* 动词 (**raises**, **raising**, **raised** /reɪzd; rezd/)
1 move something or somebody up 使某物或某人向上移动；举起；升起；抬起: *Raise your hand if you want to ask a question.* 要想问问题就举手。✪ opposite 反义词: **lower**
2 make something bigger, higher, stronger, etc 使某事物更大、更高、更强等；增加；提高；加强: *They've raised the price of petrol.* 汽油涨价了。◇ *She raised her voice* (= spoke louder). 她把嗓门提高了。
3 get money from other people 筹款；募捐: *We raised £1 000 for the hospital.* 我们为医院筹集了1 000英镑。
4 start to talk about something 开始谈论某事: *He raised an interesting question.* 他提出个很有意思的问题。

raisin /ˈreɪzn; ˈrezn̩/ *noun* 名词
a dried grape 葡萄干

rake /reɪk; rek/ *noun* 名词
a tool with a long handle that you use in

a garden for collecting leaves or for making the soil flat 耙子

rake *verb* 动词 (**rakes**, **raking**, **raked** /reɪkt; rekt/)

Rake up the dead leaves. 把枯叶耙到一起。

rally /ˈræli; ˈrælɪ/ *noun* 名词 (*plural* 复数作 **rallies**)

1 a group of people walking or standing together to show that they feel strongly about something（表达强烈意见的）游行或集会: *a peace rally* 争取和平的群众大会

2 a race for cars or motor cycles（汽车或摩托车）比赛

ramp /ræmp; ræmp/ *noun* 名词

a path that goes to a higher or lower place 斜路；斜坡: *I pushed the wheel-chair up the ramp.* 我把轮椅推上斜坡。

R

ran *form of* **run¹** ✳ **run¹** 的不同形式

random /ˈrændəm; ˈrændəm/ *adjective* 形容词

at random without any special plan 无计划的；任意的: *She chose a few books at random.* 她随便选了几本书。

rang *form of* **ring²** ✳ **ring²** 的不同形式

range¹ /reɪndʒ; rendʒ/ *noun* 名词

1 different things of the same kind 同类的各种事物: *This shop sells a range of bicycles.* 这家商店出售各种各样的自行车。

2 how far you can see, hear, shoot, travel, etc（能够看到、听到、射到、达到的）最远距离: *The gun has a range of five miles.* 这种炮的射程是五英里。

3 the amount between the highest and the lowest（最高与最低之间的）限度；幅度；程度: *The age range of the children is between eight and twelve.* 儿童年龄范围介于八岁至十二岁之间。

4 a line of mountains or hills 山脉

range² /reɪndʒ; rendʒ/ *verb* 动词 (**ranges**, **ranging**, **ranged** /reɪndʒd; rendʒd/)

be at different points between two things 在两事物之间的各处: *The ages of the students in the class range from 18 to 50.* 班上学生的年龄介于18岁至50岁之间。

rank /ræŋk; ræŋk/ *noun* 名词

how important somebody is in a group of people, for example in an army（人在群体中的）等级；级别（例如军阶）: *General is one of the highest ranks in the army.* 将军是军队中的高级将领。

ransom /ˈrænsəm; ˈrænsəm/ *noun* 名词

money that you must pay so that a criminal will free a person that he/she has taken（需付给劫匪的）赎金（使人质获释）: *The kidnappers have demanded a ransom of a million pounds.* 劫匪要求一百万英镑的赎金。

rap /ræp; ræp/ *noun* 名词

1 a quick knock 很快的敲击（声）: *I heard a rap at the door.* 我听见有急促的敲门声。

2 a kind of music in which singers speak the words of a song very quickly 说唱乐（一种音乐，演唱者急速念出唱词）

rap *verb* 动词 (**raps**, **rapping**, **rapped** /ræpt; ræpt/)

1 hit something quickly and lightly 快而轻地敲击某物: *She rapped on the door.* 她快而轻地敲着门。

2 speak the words of a song very quickly 急速念出唱词

rape /reɪp; rep/ *verb* 动词 (**rapes**, **raping**, **raped** /reɪpt; rept/)

make somebody have sex when they do not want to 强奸

rape *noun* 名词

He was sent to prison for rape. 他因犯强奸罪而入狱。

rapid /ˈræpɪd; ˈræpɪd/ *adjective* 形容词

quick; fast 迅速的；快的: *rapid changes* 急速的变化

rapidly *adverb* 副词

The snow rapidly disappeared. 雪很快就不见了。

rare /reə(r); rɛr/ *adjective* 形容词 (**rarer**, **rarest**)

1 If something is rare, you do not find or see it often 稀有的；罕见的: *Pandas are rare animals.* 大熊猫是稀有动物。◇ *It's rare to see snow in April.* 四月份下雪很少见。

2 Meat that is rare is only cooked a little.（指肉）半熟的

rarely *adverb* 副词

not often 不常: *I rarely go to London.* 我很少到伦敦去。

rash¹ /ræʃ; ræʃ/ *noun* 名词 (*plural* 复数作 **rashes**)

a lot of small red spots on your skin 疹；皮疹

rash² /ræʃ; ræʃ/ *adjective* 形容词 (**rasher**, **rashest**)

If you are rash, you do things too quickly, without thinking 轻率的；不经考

虑的: *You were very rash to leave your job before you had found a new one.* 你没找到新工作就辞职，未免太轻率了。

raspberry /ˈrɑːzbəri; ˈræzˌbɛrɪ/ *noun* 名词 (*plural* 复数作 **raspberries**)
a small soft red fruit 悬钩子（红色小果）: *raspberry jam* 悬钩子果酱

rat /ræt; ræt/ *noun* 名词
an animal like a big mouse 大鼠

rate /reɪt; ret/ *noun* 名词
1 the speed of something or how often something happens 速度；率: *The crime rate was lower in 1993 than in 1992.* ＊ 1993年的犯罪率比1992年低。
2 the amount that something costs or that somebody is paid 价格；费用: *My rate of pay is £5 an hour.* 我的工作报酬是每小时5英镑。
at any rate anyway; whatever happens 无论如何；不管怎样: *I hope to be back before ten o'clock—I won't be late at any rate.* 我希望十点钟以前回来——反正我不会迟到。

rather /ˈrɑːðə(r); ˈræðɚ/ *adverb* 副词
more than a little but not very; quite 颇；相当: *We were rather tired after our long journey.* 我们走了很长的路，有些累了。◇ *It's rather a small room.* 那间屋子比较小。
rather than in the place of; instead of 而不: *Could I have beer rather than wine?* 我喝啤酒不喝葡萄酒行吗？
would rather would prefer to do something 较喜欢: *I would rather go by train than by bus.* 我比较喜欢坐火车，不那么喜欢坐公共汽车。

ration /ˈræʃn; ˈræʃən/ *noun* 名词
a small amount of something that you are allowed to have when there is not enough for everybody to have what they want（某物短缺时的）配给限额，定量: *food rations* 食物配给量

rattle /ˈrætl; ˈrætḷ/ *verb* 动词 (**rattles, rattling, rattled** /ˈrætld; ˈrætḷd/)
1 make a lot of short sounds because it is shaking 接连发出短促的声音（因为颤动）: *The windows were rattling all night in the wind.* 风把窗户刮得整夜格格作响。
2 shake something so that it makes a lot of small sounds 摇动某物接连发出短促的声音: *She rattled the money in the tin.* 她把铁盒里的钱摇动得格格作响。

rattle *noun* 名词
1 the noise of things hitting each other 物体相碰发出的声音: *the rattle of empty bottles* 空瓶子相碰发出的哐当哐当的声音
2 a toy that a baby can shake to make a noise 摇动而发出声音的儿童玩具；拨浪鼓

raw /rɔː; rɔ/ *adjective* 形容词
1 not cooked 未经烹调的；生的: *raw meat* 生肉
2 natural; as it comes from the soil, from plants, etc 自然状态的；得自土壤、植物等的: *raw sugar* 粗糖

ray /reɪ; re/ *noun* 名词 (*plural* 复数作 **rays**)
a line of light or heat（光或热形成的）线；光线；辐射线: *the rays of the sun* 太阳的光线

razor /ˈreɪzə(r); ˈrezɚ/ *noun* 名词
a sharp thing that people use to cut hair off their bodies (to **shave**) 剃刀；刮脸刀（剃或刮叫做 **shave**）: *an electric razor* 电动剃胡刀
razor-blade /ˈreɪzə bleɪd; ˈrezɚˌbled/ *noun* 名词
the thin metal part of a razor that cuts 剃刀刀片

Rd *short way of writing* **road** ＊ **road** 的缩写形式

re- *prefix* 前缀
You can add **re-** to the beginning of some words to give them the meaning 'again', for example 在某些字前可加 **re-** 赋予“再”、“又”或“重新”之意，如:

rebuild = build again: *We rebuilt the fence after the storm.* 在风暴过后我们重新修了篱笆。

redo = do again: *Your homework is all wrong. Please redo it.* 你的家庭作业全都错了。请你重做一遍吧。

reach /riːtʃ; ritʃ/ *verb* 动词 (**reaches, reaching, reached** /riːtʃt; ritʃt/)
1 arrive somewhere 达到或到达某处: *It was dark when we reached Paris.* 我们抵达巴黎的时候，天已经黑了。◇ *Have you reached the end of the book yet?* 这本书你读到末尾处了吗？
2 put out your hand to do or get something; be able to touch something 伸手做某事或能触摸到某物: *I reached for*

R

the telephone. 我伸手去拿电话。◇ *Can you get that book from the top shelf for me? I can't reach.* 你给我把架子顶上的书拿下来行吗？我够不着。

reach *noun* 名词 (no plural 无复数)

beyond reach, out of reach too far away to touch 够不着：*Keep this medicine out of the reach of children.* 把这个药放在儿童够不着的地方。

within reach near enough to touch or go to 够得着或在附近: *Is the beach within reach of the hotel?* 海滩就在旅馆附近吗？

react /ri'ækt; rɪ'ækt/ *verb* 动词 (**reacts, reacting, reacted**)

say or do something when another thing happens 作出反应；回应: *How did Jo react to the news?* 乔对这个消息有什么反应？

reaction /ri'ækʃn; rɪ'ækʃən/ *noun* 名词

what you say or do because of something that has happened（作出的）反应；回应: *What was her reaction when you told her about the accident?* 你告诉她这起事故后，她当时有什么反应？

read /ri:d; rid/ *verb* 动词 (**reads, reading, read** /red; rɛd/, **has read**)

1 look at words and understand them 阅读；默读: *Have you read this book? It's very interesting.* 这本书你看过吗？非常有意思。

2 say words that you can see 念出声来；朗读: *I read a story to the children.* 我给孩子们读了一篇故事。

read out read something to other people 把内容读给别人听: *The teacher read out the list of names.* 老师宣读了名单。

reading *noun* 名词 (no plural 无复数)

My interests are reading and football. 我的爱好是看书和足球。

reader /'ri:də(r); 'ridɚ/ *noun* 名词

1 a person who reads something 读者

2 a book for reading at school 阅读教材；读本

ready /'redi; 'rɛdɪ/ *adjective* 形容词

1 prepared so that you can do something 准备好（做某事）: *I'll be ready to leave in five minutes.* 我再准备五分钟就可以走。

2 prepared so that you can use it 准备好（用某物）: *Dinner will be ready soon.* 饭很快就要做好了。

3 happy to do something 乐意（做某事）: *He's always ready to help.* 他随时都愿意帮助别人。

get ready make yourself ready for something 做好准备（做某事）: *I'm getting ready to go out.* 我正准备好要出门。

ready-made /ˌredi 'meɪd; 'rɛdɪ'med/ *adjective* 形容词

prepared and ready to use 准备好而随时可用的；现成的: *ready-made meals* 事先做好的饭菜

real /rɪəl; 'rɪəl/ *adverb* 副词

1 not just in the mind; that really exists 实际存在的（并非头脑中的）；实在的: *The film is about something that happened in real life.* 这部电影反映的是实际生活中发生的事。

2 true 真实的；确实的: *The name he gave to the police wasn't his real name.* 他告诉警方的名字并不是他的真名字。

3 natural; not a copy 自然状态的；并非仿制的: *This ring is real gold.* 这个戒指是真金的。

4 big or complete 大的或完全的: *I've got a real problem.* 我有个大难题。

reality /ri'æləti; rɪ'ælətɪ/ *noun* 名 (*plural* 复数作 **realities**)

the way that something really is 现实；真实: *People think I have an interesting job, but in reality it's quite boring.* 别人还以为我的工作很有意思，其实相当枯燥。

realize /'rɪəlaɪz; 'rɪəˌlaɪz/ *verb* 动词 (**realizes, realizing, realized** /'rɪəlaɪzd; 'riəˌlaɪzd/)

understand or know something 了解到或认识到某事物: *When I got home, I realized that I had lost my key.* 我回到家才知道我把钥匙丢了。◇ *I didn't realize you were American.* 我没有意识到您是美国人。

realization /ˌrɪəlaɪ'zeɪʃn; ˌrɪələ'zeʃən/ *noun* 名词 (no plural 无复数)

understanding or knowing something（对某事物的）了解或认识

really /'rɪəli; 'rɪəlɪ/ *adverb* 副词

1 in fact; truly 实际上；真正地: *Do you really love him?* 你真爱他吗？

2 very or very much 很；非常: *I'm really hungry.* 我饿极了。◇ *'Do you like this music?' 'Not really.'* "你喜欢这首乐曲吗？" "不太喜欢。"

3 a word that shows you are interested or surprised 表示有兴趣或表示惊奇的词:

'I'm going to China next year.' 'Really?' "我明年到中国去。""真的吗？"

rear /rɪə(r); rɪr/ *noun* 名词 (no plural 无复数)
the back part 后部；后面；背后: *The kitchen is at the rear of the house.* 厨房在房子的后部。
rear *adjective* 形容词
at the back 后部的；后面的；背后的: *the rear window* 汽车的后窗

reason /'ri:zn; 'riznฺ/ *noun* 名词
why you do something or why something happens 原因；理由: *The reason I didn't come to the party was that I was ill.* 我没有参加聚会是因为我病了。◇ *Is there any reason why you were late?* 你来晚了，有理由吗？

reasonable /'ri:znəbl; 'riznəbl̩/ *adjective* 形容词
1 fair and willing to listen to what other people say 讲理的；明事理的: *Be reasonable! You can't ask one person to do all the work!* 得讲道理呀！所有的工作总不能都让一个人做吧！
2 fair or right 公道的；合理的: *I think £20 is a reasonable price.* 我认为20英镑价钱还算公道。
✪ opposite 反义词: **unreasonable**
reasonably /'ri:znəbli; 'riznəblɪ/ *adverb* 副词
1 quite, but not very 相当地；尚可: *The food was reasonably good.* 食物还算不错。
2 in a reasonable way 按照讲理的方式；合理地: *Don't get angry—let's talk about this reasonably.* 别生气——咱们平心静气地谈谈这件事。

reassure /ˌri:ə'ʃʊə(r); ˌriə'ʃʊr/ *verb* 动词 (**reassures**, **reassuring**, **reassured** /ˌri:ə'ʃʊəd; ˌriə'ʃʊrd/)
say or do something to make somebody feel safer or happier 说或做某事使某人放心或愉快些: *The doctor reassured her that she was not seriously ill.* 医生让她放心，说她的病不太严重。
reassurance /ˌri:ə'ʃʊərəns; ˌriə'ʃʊrəns/ *noun* 名词
what you say to make somebody feel safer or happier 使某人放心的或愉快些的言语: *He needs reassurance that he is right.* 他需要别人说他做得对。

rebel[1] /'rebl; 'rɛbl̩/ *noun* 名词
a person who fights against the people in control 反抗当权者的人；造反者

rebel[2] /rɪ'bel; rɪ'bɛl/ *verb* 动词 (**rebels**, **rebelling**, **rebelled** /rɪ'beld; rɪ'bɛld/)
fight against the people in control 反抗当权者；造反: *She rebelled against her parents by refusing to go to university.* 她违抗父母的意愿，不去上大学。
rebellion /rɪ'beliən; rɪ'bɛljən/ *noun* 名词
a time when a lot of people fight against the people in control（众人对当权者采取的）反抗行动；造反: *Hundreds of people died in the rebellion.* 在叛乱过程中丧生者数以百计。

recall /rɪ'kɔ:l; rɪ'kɔl/ *verb* 动词 (**recalls**, **recalling**, **recalled** /rɪ'kɔ:ld; rɪ'kɔld/)
remember something 回想起某事物；回忆: *I can't recall the name of the hotel.* 那个旅馆的名字我想不起来了。✪ **Remember** is the word that we usually use. ✳ **remember** 是常用词。

receipt /rɪ'si:t; rɪ'sit/ *noun* 名词
a piece of paper that shows you have paid for something 收据；收条: *Can I have a receipt?* 给我个收据行吗？

receive /rɪ'si:v; rɪ'siv/ *verb* 动词 (**receives**, **receiving**, **received** /rɪ'si:vd; rɪ'sivd/)
get something that somebody has given or sent to you 得到或收到某物（赠送的或邮寄的）: *Did you receive my letter?* 您收到我的信了吗？✪ **Get** is the word that we usually use. ✳ **get** 是常用词。

receiver /rɪ'si:və(r); rɪ'sivɚ/ *noun* 名词
the part of a telephone that you use for listening and speaking（电话机的）听筒
☞ picture on page C32 见第C32页图

recent /'ri:snt; 'risn̩t/ *adjective* 形容词
that happened a short time ago 不久前的；近来的: *Is this a recent photo of your son?* 这是您儿子的近照吗？
recently *adverb* 副词
not long ago 不久前；近来: *She's been on holiday recently—that's why she's so brown.* 她最近刚放过假——难怪她晒得那么黑。

reception /rɪ'sepʃn; rɪ'sɛpʃən/ *noun* 名词
1 (no plural 无复数) the place where you go first when you arrive at a hotel, company, etc（旅馆、公司等处的）接待处:

R

Leave your key at reception if you go out. 您出去时把钥匙交到接待处。

2 (*plural* 复数作 **receptions**) a big important party 招待会；宴会: *a wedding reception* 婚宴

receptionist /rɪ'sepʃənɪst; rɪ'sɛpʃənɪst/ *noun* 名词

a person in a hotel, company, etc who helps you when you arrive and who may also answer the telephone（旅馆、公司等处的）接待员

recipe /'resəpi; 'rɛsəpɪ/ *noun* 名词

a piece of writing that tells you how to cook something（介绍菜肴等制作方法的）食谱

reckless /'rekləs; 'rɛklɪs/ *adjective* 形容词

A person who is reckless does dangerous things without thinking about what could happen 不考虑后果的；鲁莽的: *reckless driving* 鲁莽驾驶

reckon /'rekən; 'rɛkən/ *verb* 动词 (**reckons**, **reckoning**, **reckoned** /'rekənd; 'rɛkənd/)

believe something because you have thought about it 认为: *I reckon the holiday will cost us £500.* 我看我们度假得用500英镑。

recognize /'rekəgnaɪz; 'rɛkəg,naɪz/ *verb* 动词 (**recognizes**, **recognizing**, **recognized** /'rekəgnaɪzd; 'rɛkəg,naɪzd/)

1 know again somebody or something that you have seen or heard before 认出；辨认: *I didn't recognize you without your glasses.* 你没戴眼镜，我都没认出你来。

2 know that something is true 认为某事属实: *They recognize that there is a problem.* 他们承认确实有问题。

recognition /ˌrekəg'nɪʃn; ˌrɛkəg'nɪʃən/ *noun* 名词 (no plural 无复数)

recognizing somebody or something 认出某人某事物；承认

recommend /ˌrekə'mend; ˌrɛkə'mɛnd/ *verb* 动词 (**recommends**, **recommending**, **recommended**)

1 tell somebody that a person or thing is good or useful 推荐某人或某事物: *Can you recommend a hotel near the airport?* 您给我介绍个离机场近的旅馆行吗？

2 tell somebody in a helpful way what you think they should do 建议某人做某事: *I recommend that you see a doctor.* 我看你还是找大夫看看吧。

recommendation /ˌrekəmen'deɪʃn; ˌrɛkəmɛn'deʃən/ *noun* 名词

We stayed at the Grand Hotel on Kurt's recommendation (= because he said it was good). 我们根据库尔特的推荐住在格兰德旅馆。

record[1] /'rekɔ:d; 'rɛkɚd/ *noun* 名词

1 notes about things that have happened（对发生的事情的）记录；记载: *Keep a record of all the money you spend.* 把你花的钱都记录下来。

2 a round plastic thing that makes music when you play it on a **record-player** 唱片（唱机叫做 **record-player**）: *Put another record on.* 再放另一张唱片。

3 the best, fastest, highest, lowest, etc that has been done in a sport（运动方面最好的）记录: *She holds the world record for long jump.* 她保持着跳远世界记录。◇ *He crossed the Atlantic in record time.* 他以创记录的时间横越了大西洋。

break a record do better in a sport than anybody has done before（在运动方面）打破记录

record[2] /rɪ'kɔ:d; rɪ'kɔrd/ *verb* 动词 (**records**, **recording**, **recorded**)

1 write notes about or make pictures of things that happen so you can remember them later 以文字或图像记录或记载某事物: *In his diary he recorded everything that he did.* 他在日记中把做的事情都记下来了。

2 put music or a film on a tape or record so that you can listen to or watch it later 录音；录像: *I recorded a concert from the radio.* 我从收音机里录制了音乐会的节目。

recorder /rɪ'kɔ:də(r); rɪ'kɔrdɚ/ *noun* 名词

a musical instrument that you blow. Children often play recorders. 竖笛（多为儿童乐器）☞ Look also at **tape recorder** and **video recorder**. 另见 **tape recorder** 和 **video recorder**。

recording /rɪ'kɔ:dɪŋ; rɪ'kɔrdɪŋ/ *noun* 名词

sounds or pictures on a tape, record or film（录制的）音像；录音；录像: *a new recording of Mozart's 'Don Giovanni'* 新录制的莫扎特的《唐·乔万尼》录音

record-player /ˈrekɔ:d pleɪə(r); ˈrɛkɚdˌpleɚ/ *noun* 名词
a machine that makes music come out of records 唱机

recover /rɪˈkʌvə(r); rɪˈkʌvɚ/ *verb* 动词 (**recovers, recovering, recovered** /rɪˈkʌvəd; rɪˈkʌvɚd/)
1 become well or happy again after you have been ill or sad 恢复健康或情绪: *She is slowly recovering from her illness.* 她病后正在慢慢康复。
2 get back something that you have lost 重新得到失去的东西: *Police recovered the stolen car.* 警方找到了被偷的汽车。

recovery /rɪˈkʌvəri; rɪˈkʌvərɪ/ *noun* 名词 (no plural 无复数)
He made a quick recovery after his illness. 他病后迅速恢复了健康。

rectangle /ˈrektæŋgl; ˈrɛktæŋgḷ/ *noun* 名词
a shape with two long sides, two short sides and four angles of 90 degrees 长方形；矩形 ☞ picture on page C5 见第C5页图

rectangular /rekˈtæŋgjələ(r); rɛkˈtæŋgjəlɚ/ *adjective* 形容词
with the shape of a rectangle 长方形的；矩形的: *This page is rectangular.* 本页是长方形的。

recycle /ˌri:ˈsaɪkl; riˈsaɪkḷ/ *verb* 动词 (**recycles, recycling, recycled** /ˌri:ˈsaɪkld; riˈsaɪkḷd/)
do something to materials like paper and glass so that they can be used again 用废旧材料（如纸和玻璃等）再造某物: *Old newspapers can be recycled.* 废报纸可以回收再造纸。

red /red; rɛd/ *adjective* 形容词 (**redder, reddest**)
1 with the colour of blood 红色的: *She's wearing a bright red dress.* 她穿着鲜红色的连衣裙。◇ *red wine* 红葡萄酒
2 Red hair has a colour between red, orange and brown. （指毛发）发红色、橙色、棕色的

red *noun* 名词
Lucy was dressed in red. 露西穿着红色的衣服。

reduce /rɪˈdju:s; rɪˈdus/ *verb* 动词 (**reduces, reducing, reduced** /rɪˈdju:st; rɪˈdjust/)
make something smaller or less 使某物小些或少些；缩小；减少: *I bought this shirt because the price was reduced from £20 to £12.* 我买这件衬衫是因为价钱从20英镑减到了12英镑。◇ *Reduce speed now* (= words on a road sign). 开始减速（道路标示牌上的文字）。

reduction /rɪˈdʌkʃn; rɪˈdʌkʃən/ *noun* 名词
price reductions 减价
✪ opposite 反义词: **increase**

redundant /rɪˈdʌndənt; rɪˈdʌndənt/ *adjective* 形容词
without a job because you are not needed any more（因所做的工作不再需要人做）失业的，被解雇的: *When the factory closed, 300 people were made redundant.* 因工厂倒闭造成300人失业。

reed /ri:d; rid/ *noun* 名词
a tall plant, like grass, that grows in or near water 芦苇

reel /ri:l; ril/ *noun* 名词
a thing with round sides that holds cotton for sewing, film for cameras, etc（线、胶卷等的）卷轴；卷筒；卷盘: *a reel of cotton* 一轴棉线

reel 卷轴

refer /rɪˈfɜ:(r); rɪˈfɝ/ *verb* 动词 (**refers, referring, referred** /rɪˈfɜ:d; rɪˈfɝd/)
refer to somebody or 或 **something** **1** talk about somebody or something 提到或说到某人或某事物: *When I said that some people are stupid, I wasn't referring to you!* 我说有人很愚蠢，我并没有说你呀！ **2** be used to mean something 用以指某事物；意为: *The word 'child' refers here to anybody under the age of 16.* 此处"孩子"一词指16岁以下的任何人。
3 look in a book or ask somebody for information（为了解某事）参看某书或请教某人: *If you don't understand a word, you may refer to your dictionaries.* 要是不明白某个词的意思，可以查词典。

referee /ˌrefəˈri:; ˌrɛfəˈri/ *noun* 名词
a person in a sport like football or boxing who controls the match（足球或拳击等比赛的）裁判员

reference /ˈrefrəns; ˈrɛfərəns/ *noun* 名词
1 what somebody says or writes about something 谈到某事的言语或文字: *There are many references to Stratford in this*

R

book about Shakespeare. 在关于莎士比亚的这本书里，有很多地方都谈到了斯特拉特福。

2 If somebody gives you a reference, they write about you to somebody who may give you a new job（帮助某人获得新工作的）证明文书；介绍信；推荐书: *Did your boss give you a good reference?* 你的老板给你写的介绍信好不好？

reference book /'refrəns bʊk; 'rɛfrəns bʊk/ *noun* 名词
a book where you look for information 参考书；工具书: *A dictionary is a reference book.* 词典是工具书。

reflect /rɪ'flekt; rɪ'flɛkt/ *verb* 动词 (**reflects, reflecting, reflected**)
send back light, heat or sound 反射光、热或声音；反映: *A mirror reflects a picture of you when you look in it.* 照镜子的时候，镜子里就能反映出自己的形象。

reflection /rɪ'flekʃn; rɪ'flɛkʃən/ *noun* 名词
1 (*plural* 复数作 **reflections**) a picture that you see in a mirror or in water（镜中的或水中的）映像；倒影: *He looked into the pool and saw a reflection of himself.* 他看见水池里有自己的倒影。
2 (no plural 无复数) sending back light, heat or sound（对光、热或声音的）反射，反映

reform /rɪ'fɔ:m; rɪ'fɔrm/ *verb* 动词 (**reforms, reforming, reformed** /rɪ'fɔ:md; rɪ'fɔrmd/)
change something to make it better 改善；改进；改良；改革: *The government wants to reform the education system in this country.* 政府准备改革教育制度。

reform *noun* 名词
a change to make something better 改善；改进；改良；改革: *political reform* 政治改革

refresh /rɪ'freʃ; rɪ'frɛʃ/ *verb* 动词 (**refreshes, refreshing, refreshed** /rɪ'freʃt; rɪ'frɛʃt/)
make somebody feel cooler, stronger or less tired 使某人感到凉爽、强壮或恢复精力: *A sleep will refresh you after your long journey.* 走了长路以后睡一觉就能恢复体力了。

refreshing *adjective* 形容词
a cool, refreshing drink 清凉饮料

refreshments /rɪ'freʃmənts; rɪ'frɛʃmənts/ *noun* 名词 (plural 复数)
food and drinks that you can buy in a place like a cinema or theatre（影剧院等处出售的）食物和饮料: *Refreshments will be sold in the interval.* 在演出中间休息时将有食物和饮料出售。

refrigerator /rɪ'frɪdʒəreɪtə(r); rɪ'frɪdʒəˌretɚ/ *noun* 名词
a big metal box for keeping food and drink cold and fresh 冰箱 ✪ **Fridge** is the word that we usually use. ✳ **fridge** 是常用词。

refuge /'refju:dʒ; 'rɛfjudʒ/ *noun* 名词
a place where you are safe from somebody or something（离开某人或某事物的）安全地方；避难处；庇护所

take refuge from something go to a safe place to get away from something bad or dangerous 到安全的地方去（离开坏的或危险的环境）；到避难处或庇护所: *We took refuge from the hot sun under a tree.* 我们到树底下去免得晒着。

refugee /ˌrefju'dʒi:; ˌrɛfjʊ'dʒi/ *noun* 名词
a person who must leave his/her country because of danger 难民

refund /ri'fʌnd; rɪ'fʌnd/ *verb* 动词 (**refunds, refunding, refunded**)
pay back money 退钱: *I took the camera back to the shop and they refunded my money.* 我把照相机拿到商店，他们把钱退给我了。

refund /'ri:fʌnd; 'riˌfʌnd/ *noun* 名词
money that is paid back to you 退回的钱；退款: *The watch I bought was broken so I asked for a refund.* 我买的手表坏了，我让他们退我钱。

refuse /rɪ'fju:z; rɪ'fjuz/ *verb* 动词 (**refuses, refusing, refused** /rɪ'fju:zd; rɪ'fjuzd/)
say 'no' when somebody asks you to do or have something 拒绝: *I asked Matthew to help, but he refused.* 我请马修帮忙，可是他不愿意。◇ *The shop assistant refused to give me my money back.* 售货员不肯把钱退给我。

refusal /rɪ'fju:zl; rɪ'fjuzl̩/ *noun* 名词
saying 'no' when somebody asks you to do or have something 拒绝: *a refusal to pay* 拒不付钱

regard[1] /rɪ'gɑ:d; rɪ'gɑrd/ *verb* 动词 (**regards, regarding, regarded**)
think of somebody or something in a certain way 认为某人或某事物是；把某人

或某事物看成: *I regard her as my best friend.* 我把她当作我最好的朋友。

regard[2] /rɪ'gɑ:d; rɪ'gɑrd/ *noun* 名词

1 (no plural 无复数) what you think about somebody or something (对某人或某事物的)看法: *I have a high regard for his work* (= I think it is very good). 我认为他工作很出色。

2 (no plural 无复数) care 关心: *She shows no regard for other people's feelings.* 她不顾及别人的感情。

3 regards (plural 复数) kind wishes 致意;问候: *Please give my regards to your parents.* 请代我向您父母致意。

reggae /'regeɪ; 'rɛge/ *noun* 名词 (no plural 无复数)

a type of West Indian music 雷盖乐(西印度群岛的一种音乐)

regiment /'redʒɪmənt; 'rɛdʒəmənt/ *noun* 名词

a group of soldiers in an army 团(军队的编制单位)

region /'ri:dʒən; 'ridʒən/ *noun* 名词

a part of a country or of the world 地区;区域: *There will be snow in northern regions today.* 今天北部地区将有雪。

regional /'ri:dʒənl; 'ridʒənl̩/ *adjective* 形容词

of a certain region 地区的;区域的

register[1] /'redʒɪstə(r); 'rɛdʒɪstɚ/ *noun* 名词

a list of names 登记表;注册簿: *The teacher keeps a register of all the students in the class.* 老师记录着全班学生的考勤情况。

register[2] /'redʒɪstə(r); 'rɛdʒɪstɚ/ *verb* 动词 (**registers, registering, registered** /'redʒɪstəd; 'rɛdʒɪstɚd/)

1 put a name on a list 登记姓名: *I would like to register for the English course.* 我想登记学习英语课程。

2 show a number or amount 显示出数量: *The thermometer registered 30°C.* 温度计显示着30°C(三十摄氏度)。

registration /ˌredʒɪ'streɪʃn; ˌrɛdʒɪ'streʃən/ *noun* 名词 (no plural 无复数)

putting a name on a list 登记;注册: *registration of births, marriages and deaths* 出生、婚姻、死亡登记

registration number /redʒɪ'streɪʃn nʌmbə(r); rɛdʒɪ'streʃən ˌnʌmbɚ/ *noun* 名词

the numbers and letters on the front and back of a car, etc (汽车等的)登记号码;牌照号码

regret /rɪ'gret; rɪ'grɛt/ *verb* 动词 (**regrets, regretting, regretted**)

feel sorry about something that you did 后悔;抱歉: *He regrets selling his car.* 他后悔把汽车给卖了。◇ *I don't regret what I said to her.* 我跟她说了那些话我并不后悔。

regret *noun* 名词

I don't have any regrets about leaving my job. 我辞去那份工作一点儿都不后悔。

regular /'regjələ(r); 'rɛgjəlɚ/ *adjective* 形容词

1 that happens again and again with the same amount of space or time in between 有规律的;定期的;定时的: *We have regular meetings every Monday morning.* 我们每星期一上午都开会。◇ *regular breathing* 均匀的呼吸

2 who goes somewhere or does something often 常到某处或常做某事的: *I've never seen him before — he's not one of my regular customers.* 我以前从来没见过他——他不是我这儿的老主顾。

3 usual 经常的: *Who is your regular doctor?* 经常给您看病的是哪位医生?

4 A word that is regular has the usual verb forms or plural (指词形或复数)规则的: *'Work' is a regular verb.* * work 是规则动词。

☞ Look at **irregular**. 见 **irregular**。

regularly *adverb* 副词

We meet regularly every Friday. 我们每星期五都见面。

regulation /ˌregju'leɪʃn; ˌrɛgjə'leʃən/ *noun* 名词

something that controls what people do; a rule or law 规章;规则;条例: *You can't smoke here — it's against fire regulations.* 这里不准吸烟——在这里吸烟是违反防火条例的。

rehearse /rɪ'hɜ:s; rɪ'hɝs/ *verb* 动词 (**rehearses, rehearsing, rehearsed** /rɪ'hɜ:st; rɪ'hɝst/)

do or say something again and again before you do it in front of other people 排练;排演: *We are rehearsing for the concert.* 我们为音乐会演出正在排练。

rehearsal /rɪ'hɜ:sl; rɪ'hɝsl̩/ *noun* 名词

a time when you rehearse 排练;排演: *There's a rehearsal for the play tonight.* 为今天晚上演出这出戏,现在正在排练。

R

reign /reɪn; ren/ *noun* 名词
a time when a king or queen rules a country 君主统治时期: *The reign of Queen Elizabeth II began in 1952.* 伊丽莎白二世女王于1952年即位。

reign *verb* 动词 (**reigns**, **reigning**, **reigned** /reɪnd; rend/)
be king or queen of a country 成为君主: *Queen Victoria reigned for a long time.* 维多利亚女王在位时期很长。

rein /reɪn; ren/ *noun* 名词
a long thin piece of leather that a horse wears on its head so that a rider can control it 缰绳

reindeer /'reɪndɪə(r); 'renˌdɪr/ *noun* 名词 (*plural* 复数作 **reindeer**)
a big animal that lives in very cold countries 驯鹿

reject /rɪ'dʒekt; rɪ'dʒɛkt/ *verb* 动词 (**rejects**, **rejecting**, **rejected**)
say that you do not want somebody or something 拒绝接受某人或某事物: *He rejected my offer of help.* 我主动提出帮忙，他拒不接受。

related /rɪ'leɪtɪd; rɪ'letɪd/ *adjective* 形容词
in the same family; connected 属于同一家的；有亲属关系的；相联系的: *'Are those two boys related?' 'Yes, they're brothers.'* "那两个男孩儿是亲戚吗？""是啊，他们是哥俩。"

relation /rɪ'leɪʃn; rɪ'leʃən/ *noun* 名词
1 a person in your family 亲戚；亲属
2 a connection between two things 关系；联系: *There is no relation between the size of the countries and the number of people who live there.* 国家的大小与其居民人数并无关系。

relationship /rɪ'leɪʃnʃɪp; rɪ'leʃənˌʃɪp/ *noun* 名词
how people, things or ideas are connected to each other; feelings between people 关系；关联: *I have a good relationship with my parents.* 我跟我父母的关系很好。◇ *The book is about the relationship between an Indian boy and an English girl.* 这本书写的是一个印度男孩儿和一个英国女孩儿的故事。

relative /'relətɪv; 'rɛlətɪv/ *noun* 名词
a person in your family 亲戚；亲属

relatively /'relətɪvli; 'rɛlətɪvlɪ/ *adverb* 副词
quite 相当地: *This room is relatively small.* 这个屋子比较小。

relax /rɪ'læks; rɪ'læks/ *verb* 动词 (**relaxes**, **relaxing**, **relaxed** /rɪ'lækst; rɪ'lækst/)
1 rest and be calm; become less worried or angry 休息；缓和；轻松: *After a hard day at work I spent the evening relaxing in front of the television.* 我工作累了一天，晚上轻松地看看电视。
2 become less tight or make something become less tight（使某事物）松弛；放松: *Let your body relax.* 你要把身体放松。

relaxation /ˌri:læk'seɪʃn; ˌrilæks'eʃən/ *noun* 名词 (no plural 无复数)
You need more rest and relaxation. 您需要多休息，松弛一下。

relaxed *adjective* 形容词
She felt relaxed after her holiday. 她放过假以后感到轻松多了。

release /rɪ'li:s; rɪ'lis/ *verb* 动词 (**releases**, **releasing**, **released** /rɪ'li:st; rɪ'list/)
let a person or an animal go free 放走人或动物: *We opened the cage and released the bird.* 我们打开笼子把鸟放了。

release *noun* 名词
the release of the prisoners 放出囚犯

relevant /'reləvənt; 'rɛləvənt/ *adjective* 形容词
connected with what you are talking or writing about; important（与所说的或所写的）有关的；切题的: *We need somebody who can do the job well — your age is not relevant.* 我们需要个能把这项工作做好的人——您的年龄没有关系。✪ opposite 反义词: **irrelevant**

reliable /rɪ'laɪəbl; rɪ'laɪəbl̩/ *adjective* 形容词
that you can trust 可信赖的；可靠的: *My car is very reliable.* 我的汽车很靠得住。◇ *He is a reliable person.* 他很可靠。✪ opposite 反义词: **unreliable**

relied *form of* **rely** ✳ **rely** 的不同形式

relief /rɪ'li:f; rɪ'lif/ *noun* 名词 (no plural 无复数)
1 what you feel when pain or worry stops（痛苦或忧愁等的）消除，解除: *It was a great relief to know she was safe.* 知道她很安全也就放心了。
2 food or money for people who need it 救援物资；救济食品；救济金: *Many countries sent relief to the people who*

had lost their homes in the floods. 很多国家都给在水灾中无家可归的人送去救援物资。

relies *form of* **rely** ＊ **rely** 的不同形式

relieved /rɪ'li:vd; rɪ'livd/ *adjective* 形容词

pleased because a problem or danger has gone away（消除困难或危险后）宽慰的；放心的：*I was relieved to hear that you weren't hurt in the accident.* 听说您在事故中并没有受伤，我就放了心了。

religion /rɪ'lɪdʒən; rɪ'lɪdʒən/ *noun* 名词

1 (no plural 无复数) believing in a god 宗教信仰

2 (*plural* 复数作 **religions**) one of the ways of believing in a god, for example Christianity, Islam or Buddhism 宗教（例如基督教、伊斯兰教、佛教）

religious /rɪ'lɪdʒəs; rɪ'lɪdʒəs/ *adjective* 形容词

1 of religion 宗教的：*a religious leader* 宗教领袖

2 with a strong belief in a religion 笃信宗教的；虔诚的：*I'm not very religious.* 我不太信仰宗教。

reluctant /rɪ'lʌktənt; rɪ'lʌktənt/ *adjective* 形容词

If you are reluctant to do something, you do not want to do it 不情愿的；勉强的：*Ian was reluctant to give me the money.* 伊恩不太愿意把钱给我。

reluctance /rɪ'lʌktəns; rɪ'lʌktəns/ *noun* 名词 (no plural 无复数)

being reluctant 不情愿；勉强：*He agreed, but with great reluctance.* 他同意是同意了，可是非常勉强。

reluctantly *adverb* 副词

Anna reluctantly agreed to help with the washing-up. 安娜勉勉强强同意去帮助洗碗了。

rely /rɪ'laɪ; rɪ'laɪ/ *verb* 动词 (**relies**, **relying**, **relied** /rɪ'laɪd; rɪ'laɪd/, **has relied**)

rely on somebody or 或 **something**

1 feel sure that somebody or something will do what they should do 指望或依赖某人或某事物：*You can rely on him to help you.* 你可以依靠他来帮助你。 **2** need somebody or something 需要某人或某事物：*I rely on my parents for money.* 我的钱都是靠父母给的。✪ The adjective is **reliable**. 形容词是 **reliable**。

remain /rɪ'meɪn; rɪ'men/ *verb* 动词 (**remains**, **remaining**, **remained** /rɪ'meɪnd; rɪ'mend/)

1 stay after other people or things have gone 留下；剩下；遗留：*After the fire, very little remained of the house.* 这场大火过后，房子已经没剩下什么了。

2 stay in the same way; not change 保持原状；仍然是：*I asked her a question but she remained silent.* 我问她一个问题，可是她一直默不作声。

remains /rɪ'meɪnz; rɪ'menz/ *noun* 名词 (plural 复数)

what is left when most of something has gone 剩余物；残余：*the remains of an old church* 古老教堂的遗迹

remark /rɪ'mɑ:k; rɪ'mɑrk/ *verb* 动词 (**remarks**, **remarking**, **remarked** /rɪ'mɑ:kt; rɪ'mɑrkt/)

say something 说；谈论：*'It's cold today,' he remarked.* "今天很冷，" 他说。

remark *noun* 名词

something that you say 说的话；评论：*He made a remark about the food.* 他对这种食物议论了一番。

remarkable /rɪ'mɑ:kəbl; rɪ'mɑrkəbl̩/ *adjective* 形容词

unusual and surprising in a good way 不寻常的；非凡的：*a remarkable discovery* 异乎寻常的发现

remarkably /rɪ'mɑ:kəbli; rɪ'mɑrkəblɪ/ *adverb* 副词

She speaks French remarkably well. 她说法语说得好极了。

remedy /'remədi; 'rɛmədɪ/ *noun* 名词 (*plural* 复数作 **remedies**)

a way of making something better 使某事物改良的方法：*a remedy for toothache* 牙疼的疗法

remember /rɪ'membə(r); rɪ'mɛmbɚ/ *verb* 动词 (**remembers**, **remembering**, **remembered** /rɪ'membəd; rɪ'mɛmbɚd/)

keep something in your mind or bring something back into your mind; not forget something 记着；想起；记住：*Can you remember his name?* 他的名字您记得吗？◇ *I remember posting the letter.* 我还记着寄信这件事。◇ *Did you remember to go to the bank?* 你记得去银行了吗？

remind /rɪ'maɪnd; rɪ'maɪnd/ *verb* 动词 (**reminds, reminding, reminded**)

make somebody remember somebody

R

or something 使某人记住或想起某人或某事；提醒：*This song reminds me of my holiday in France.* 我一听这首歌就想起了我在法国度假的情形。◇ *I reminded her to buy some bread.* 我提醒她买些面包。

reminder *noun* 名词
something that makes you remember 帮助记忆的东西

remote /rɪˈməʊt; rɪˈmot/ *adjective* 形容词 (**remoter**, **remotest**)
far from other places 遥远的；偏远的：*They live in a remote farmhouse in Scotland.* 他们住在苏格兰偏远的农舍里。

remove /rɪˈmu:v; rɪˈmuv/ *verb* 动词 (**removes**, **removing**, **removed** /rɪˈmu:vd; rɪˈmuvd/)
take somebody or something away or off 移开或除去某人或某物：*The statue was removed from the museum.* 那座塑像已经从博物馆搬走了。◇ *Please remove your shoes before entering the temple.* 请先脱鞋再进入庙宇。✪ It is more usual to use other words, for example **take out** or **take off**. 一般常用其他的词语，如 **take out** 或 **take off**。

removal /rɪˈmu:vl; rɪˈmuvl̩/ *noun* 名词
removing something 移动；迁移；去除：*a removal van* (= a lorry that is used for moving furniture to a new house) 搬迁用车（= 搬家用的卡车）

renew /riˈnju:; rɪˈnu/ *verb* 动词 (**renews**, **renewing**, **renewed** /riˈnju:d; rɪˈnjud/)
get or give something new in the place of something old 把某物换成新的；更新某物：*If you want to stay in America for another month you must renew your visa.* 您要想在美国多住一个月就得办理延期签证。

rent /rent; rɛnt/ *verb* 动词 (**rents**, **renting**, **rented**)
1 pay to live in a place or to use something that belongs to another person 租住某处或租用某物：*I rent a flat in the centre of town.* 我在市中心租了一个公寓。
2 let somebody live in a place or use something that belongs to you, if they pay you 把住处或某物出租给别人：*Mr Hodges rents out rooms to students.* 霍奇斯先生把那些房间租给学生了。

rent *noun* 名词
the money that you pay to live in a place or to use something that belongs to another person 房租；租金：*My rent is £300 a month.* 我的租金是每月300英镑。

repair /rɪˈpeə(r); rɪˈpɛr/ *verb* 动词 (**repairs**, **repairing**, **repaired** /rɪˈpeəd; rɪˈpɛrd/)
make something that is broken good again; mend something 修理或修补某物：*Can you repair my bike?* 您给我修修自行车行吗？

repair *noun* 名词
The shop is closed for repairs to the roof. 这家商店修理房顶停止营业。

repay /riˈpeɪ; rɪˈpe/ *verb* 动词 (**repays**, **repaying**, **repaid** /riˈpeɪd; rɪˈped/, **has repaid**)
1 pay back money to somebody 付还某人钱；偿还
2 do something for somebody to show your thanks 报答某人；酬谢：*How can I repay you for all your help?* 您帮助我无微不至，我怎么报答您呢？

repayment /riˈpeɪmənt; rɪˈpemənt/ *noun* 名词
paying somebody back 付还；偿还：*monthly repayments* 按月还款

repeat /rɪˈpi:t; rɪˈpit/ *verb* 动词 (**repeats**, **repeating**, **repeated**)
1 say or do something again 重复说或做某事：*He didn't hear my question, so I repeated it.* 他没听见我的问题，所以我又重复了一遍。
2 say what another person has said 复述他人的话：*Repeat this sentence after me.* 跟着我说这句话。

repeat *noun* 名词
something that is done again 重复做的事物：*There are a lot of repeats of old programmes on TV.* 电视上有很多旧节目反复播放。

repetition /ˌrepəˈtɪʃn; ˌrɛpɪˈtɪʃən/ *noun* 名词
saying or doing something again 重复的言语或重复做某事：*This book is boring — it's full of repetition.* 这本书很枯燥——净是翻来覆去的话。

replace /riˈpleɪs; rɪˈples, ˌriˈples/ *verb* 动词 (**replaces**, **replacing**, **replaced** /riˈpleɪst; rɪˈplest, ˌriˈplest/)
1 put something back in the right place 把某物放回原处：*Please replace the books on the shelf when you have finished with them.* 书看完后请放回架子上。

2 take the place of somebody or something 取代某人或某事物；替代: *John Major replaced Margaret Thatcher as Prime Minister.* 约翰·梅杰接替了玛格丽特·撒切尔担任首相。

3 put a new or different person or thing in the place of another 更换某人或某事物: *The watch was broken so the shop replaced it with a new one.* 那块手表坏了，商店又给换了一块新的。

replacement /ri'pleɪsmənt; rɪ'plesmənt/ *noun* 名词

1 (*plural* 复数作 **replacements**) a new or different person or thing that takes the place of another 代替者；替换物: *Susan is leaving the company next month so we need to find a replacement.* 苏珊下月离开本公司，我们得再找个人做这份工作。

2 (no plural 无复数) putting a new or different person or thing in the place of another 代替；替换

reply /rɪ'plaɪ; rɪ'plaɪ/ *verb* 动词 (**replies, replying, replied** /rɪ'plaɪd; rɪ'plaɪd/, **has replied**)

answer 回答；答复: *I have written to Jenny but she hasn't replied.* 我给珍妮写了封信，她还没回信呢。

reply *noun* 名词 (*plural* 复数作 **replies**) an answer 回答；答复: *Have you had a reply to your letter?* 您收到回信了吗？

in reply as an answer 作为回答: *What did you say in reply to his question?* 他的问题你是怎样回答的？

report[1] /rɪ'pɔ:t; rɪ'pɔrt/ *verb* 动词 (**reports, reporting, reported**)

tell or write about something that has happened 报告；报道；汇报: *We reported the accident to the police.* 我们向警方报告了这起事故的情况。

report[2] /rɪ'pɔ:t; rɪ'pɔrt/ *noun* 名词

1 something that somebody says or writes about something that has happened 报告；报道；汇报: *Did you read the newspaper reports about the earthquake?* 报纸上关于地震的报道你看了吗？

2 something that teachers write about a student's work（教师评定学生的）成绩报告单

reporter /rɪ'pɔ:tə(r); rɪ'pɔrtɚ/ *noun* 名词

a person who writes in a newspaper or speaks on the radio or television about things that have happened 记者；新闻通讯员

represent /ˌreprɪ'zent; ˌrɛprɪ'zɛnt/ *verb* 动词 (**represents, representing, represented**)

1 be a sign for something 代表或象征某事物: *The yellow lines on the map represent roads.* 这张地图上黄色的线代表道路。

2 speak or do something for another person or other people 代表他人说话或做事: *Christie will represent Britain at the next Olympic Games.* 克里斯蒂将代表英国参加下一届奥运会。

representative /ˌreprɪ'zentətɪv; ˌrɛprɪ'zɛntətɪv/ *noun* 名词

a person who speaks or does something for a group of people 代表（代他人说话或做事的人）: *There were representatives from every country in Europe at the meeting.* 欧洲各国的代表都参加了会议。

reproduce /ˌri:prə'dju:s; ˌriprə'dus/ *verb* 动词 (**reproduces, reproducing, reproduced** /ˌri:prə'dju:st; ˌriprə'djust/)

When animals or plants reproduce, they have young ones. 生殖；繁殖

reproduction /ˌri:prə'dʌkʃn; ˌriprə'dʌkʃən/ *noun* 名词 (no plural 无复数)

We are studying plant reproduction at school. 我们正在学校上植物繁殖课。

reptile /'reptaɪl; 'rɛptl̩/ *noun* 名词

an animal with cold blood, that lays eggs. Snakes, lizards, crocodiles and tortoises are reptiles. 爬行动物（冷血，卵生，例如蛇、蜥蜴、鳄鱼、陆龟等）

republic /rɪ'pʌblɪk; rɪ'pʌblɪk/ *noun* 名词

a country where people choose the government and the leader (the **president**) 共和国（总统叫做 **president**）: *the Republic of Ireland* 爱尔兰共和国

republican /rɪ'pʌblɪkən; rɪ'pʌblɪkən/ *noun* 名词

1 a person who wants a republic 拥护共和政体的人

2 Republican a person in the Republican Party in the USA（美国）共和党党员 ☞ Look at **Democrat**. 见 **Democrat**。

reputation /ˌrepju'teɪʃn; ˌrɛpjə'teʃən/ *noun* 名词

what people think or say about somebody or something 名声；名誉；

R

名气：*This restaurant has a good reputation.* 这家饭馆享有盛名。

request /rɪ'kwest; rɪ'kwɛst/ *verb* 动词 (**requests, requesting, requested**)
ask for something 要求或请求某事物：*Passengers are requested not to smoke* (= a notice in a bus). 请勿吸烟（公共汽车中的告示）。✪ It is more usual to say **ask (for)**. ＊ **ask (for)** 较常用。

request *noun* 名词
asking for something 要求或请求某事物：*They made a request for money.* 他们请求要钱。

require /rɪ'kwaɪə(r); rɪ'kwaɪr/ *verb* 动词 (**requires, requiring, required** /rɪ'kwaɪəd; rɪ'kwaɪrd/)
need something 需要某事物：*Do you require anything else?* 您还需要什么别的吗？✪ **Need** is the word that we usually use. ＊ **need** 是常用词。

requirement /rɪ'kwaɪəmənt; rɪ'kwaɪrmənt/ *noun* 名词
something that you need 需要的事物

rescue /'reskju:; 'rɛskjʊ/ *verb* 动词 (**rescues, rescuing, rescued**)
save somebody or something from danger 搭救某人或某物（脱险）：*She rescued the child when he fell in the river.* 她把掉进河里的孩子抢救出来了。

rescue *noun* 名词

come or 或 **go to somebody's rescue**
try to help somebody 尽力援救或帮助某人：*The police came to his rescue.* 警察尽力帮助他。

research /rɪ'sɜ:tʃ; rɪ'sɝtʃ/ *noun* 名词 (no plural 无复数)
studying something carefully to find out more about it 研究；探讨；调查：*scientific research* 科学研究

research *verb* 动词 (**researches, researching, researched** /rɪ'sɜ:tʃt; rɪ'sɝtʃt/)
study something carefully to find out more about it 研究；探讨；调查：*Scientists are researching the causes of the disease.* 科学家正在研究这种疾病的病因。

resemble /rɪ'zembl; rɪ'zɛmbḷ/ *verb* 动词 (**resembles, resembling, resembled** /rɪ'zembld; rɪ'zɛmbḷd/)
look like somebody or something 与某人或某物相似：*Lisa resembles her mother.* 莉萨长得像她母亲。✪ It is more usual to say **look like.** ＊ **look like** 较常用。

resemblance /rɪ'zembləns; rɪ'zɛmbləns/ *noun* 名词
There's no resemblance between my two brothers. 我两个哥哥长得一点儿都不像。

resent /rɪ'zent; rɪ'zɛnt/ *verb* 动词 (**resents, resenting, resented**)
feel angry about something because it is not fair（因某事不公平）感到气愤或怨恨：*I resent Alan getting the job. He got it because he's the manager's son!* 艾伦得到那份工作我很生气。就因为他是经理的儿子！

resentment /rɪ'zentmənt; rɪ'zɛntmənt/ *noun* 名词 (no plural 无复数)
a feeling of anger about something that is not fair（因某事不公平而感到的）气愤或怨恨

reserve[1] /rɪ'zɜ:v; rɪ'zɝv/ *verb* 动词 (**reserves, reserving, reserved** /rɪ'zɜ:vd; rɪ'zɝvd/)
keep something for a special reason or to use later; ask somebody to keep something for you 保留或储备某物；要求某人为你保留某物：*I would like to reserve a single room for tomorrow night, please.* 劳驾，我想预订个明天晚上的单人房间。◇ *Those seats are reserved.* 这些座位已经有人预订了。

reservation /ˌrezə'veɪʃn; ˌrɛzɚ'veʃən/ *noun* 名词
a room, seat or another thing that you have reserved 预订或保留的房间、座位等物：*I made a reservation for a table for two.* 我预订了一个双座的桌位。

reserve[2] /rɪ'zɜ:v; rɪ'zɝv/ *noun* 名词
1 something that you keep to use later 储备物：*reserves of food* 储备的食物
2 a person who will play in a game if another person cannot play（准备参赛的）替补队员

in reserve for using later 留以备用；储备；储存：*Don't spend all the money – keep some in reserve.* 别把钱都花了——留点儿积蓄。

reservoir /'rezəvwɑ:(r); 'rɛzɚˌvwɑr/ *noun* 名词
a big lake where a town or city keeps water to use later（城镇储备水的）蓄水池；水库

residence /'rezɪdəns; 'rɛzədəns/ *noun* 名词
1 (no plural 无复数) living in a place

居住: *a university hall of residence* (= a place where students live) 大学生宿舍楼 **2** (*plural* 复数作 **residences**) the place where an important or famous person lives（要人或名人的）住宅；宅邸；官邸: *the Prime Minister's residence* 首相官邸

resident /ˈrezɪdənt; ˈrɛzədənt/ *noun* 名词
a person who lives in a place 居民

resign /rɪˈzaɪn; rɪˈzaɪn/ *verb* 动词 (**resigns, resigning, resigned** /rɪˈzaɪnd; rɪˈzaɪnd/)
leave your job 辞职: *The director has resigned.* 该董事已经辞职了。
resign yourself to something accept something that you do not like 忍受某事物: *There were a lot of people at the doctor's so John resigned himself to a long wait.* 医生那里有很多人候诊，所以约翰只好慢慢等候。

resignation /ˌrezɪgˈneɪʃn; ˌrɛzɪgˈneʃən/ *noun* 名词
saying that you want to leave your job 辞职
hand in your resignation tell the person you work for that you are going to leave your job 提交辞呈

resist /rɪˈzɪst; rɪˈzɪst/ *verb* 动词 (**resists, resisting, resisted**)
1 fight against somebody or something; try to stop somebody or something 抵抗；对抗: *If he has a gun, don't try to resist.* 要是他有枪就不要反抗。
2 refuse to do or have something that you want to do or have（对想要做或想要有的事物）不做或不要: *I can't resist chocolate.* 我总忍不住得吃巧克力。
resistance /rɪˈzɪstəns; rɪˈzɪstəns/ *noun* 名词 (no plural 无复数)
resisting somebody or something 抵抗；对抗: *There was a lot of resistance to the plan to build a new motorway.* 有很多人反对修建高速公路的计划。

resolution /ˌrezəˈluːʃn; ˌrɛzəˈluʃən/ *noun* 名词
something that you decide to do 决定；决心: *Julie made a resolution to stop smoking.* 朱莉已经下决心戒烟了。

resort /rɪˈzɔːt; rɪˈzɔrt/ *noun* 名词
a place where a lot of people go on holiday 度假胜地: *St Tropez is a seaside resort.* 圣特罗佩是海滨度假胜地。
a last resort the only person or thing left that can help 唯一可求助的人；最后的手段: *Nobody else will lend me the money, so I am asking you as a last resort.* 谁都不肯借给我钱，我最后只好向您求助了。

resources /rɪˈsɔːsɪz; rɪˈsorsɪz/ *noun* 名词 (plural 复数)
things that a person or a country has and can use 个人或国家所有的且可使用的东西；人力或物力资源: *Oil is one of our most important natural resources.* 石油是我们最重要的一种自然资源。

respect[1] /rɪˈspekt; rɪˈspɛkt/ *noun* 名词 (no plural 无复数)
1 thinking that somebody is very good or clever 尊敬；敬重: *I have a lot of respect for your father.* 我非常尊敬您父亲。
2 being polite to somebody 有礼貌；客气: *You should treat old people with more respect.* 对待老人应该更有礼貌。

respect[2] /rɪˈspekt; rɪˈspɛkt/ *verb* 动词 (**respects, respecting, respected**)
think that somebody is good or clever 尊敬；敬重: *The students respect their teacher.* 这些学生很尊敬老师。

respectable /rɪˈspektəbl; rɪˈspɛktəbḷ/ *adjective* 形容词
If a person or thing is respectable, people think he/she/it is good or correct 受尊重的；正派的: *She comes from a respectable family.* 她出身于有社会地位的家庭。

respond /rɪˈspɒnd; rɪˈspɑnd/ *verb* 动词 (**responds, responding, responded**)
do or say something to answer somebody or something 回答；回应；反应: *I said 'hello' and he responded by smiling.* 我跟他打招呼，他对我笑了笑。

response /rɪˈspɒns; rɪˈspɑns/ *noun* 名词
an answer to somebody or something 回答；回应；反应: *I wrote to them but I've had no response.* 我给他们去过信，但一直没有回音。

responsible /rɪˈspɒnsəbl; rɪˈspɑnsəbḷ/ *adjective* 形容词
1 If you are responsible for somebody or something, you must look after them（对某人或某事物）须负责任；承担责任: *The driver is responsible for the lives of the people on the bus.* 公共汽车司机要对乘客的生命负责。

2 A responsible person is somebody that you can trust（指人）可信赖的，可靠的: *We need a responsible person to look after our son.* 我们需要个可靠的人照看我们的儿子。✪ opposite 反义词: **irresponsible**

be responsible for something be the person who made something bad happen 是使坏事发生的人: *Who was responsible for the accident?* 这起事故是谁造成的？

responsibility /rɪˌspɒnsəˈbɪləti; rɪˌspɑnsəˈbɪlətɪ/ *noun* 名词

1 (no plural 无复数) being responsible for somebody or something; having to look after somebody or something 责任；负责: *She has responsibility for the whole department.* 她负责整个部门的工作。

2 (*plural* 复数作 **responsibilities**) something that you must do; somebody or something that you must look after 职责；任务: *The dog is my brother's responsibility.* 照管这条狗是我哥哥的事。

rest[1] /rest; rɛst/ *verb* 动词 (**rests**, **resting**, **rested**)

1 sleep or be still and quiet 睡觉或休息: *We worked all morning and then rested for an hour before starting work again.* 我们工作了一上午，然后休息了一小时便又接着干起来了。

2 be on something; put something on or against another thing 在某物上；把某物放在或靠在某物上: *His arms were resting on the table.* 他把手臂放在桌子上。

rest[2] /rest; rɛst/ *noun* 名词

sleeping or being still and quiet 睡眠或休息: *After walking for an hour, we stopped for a rest.* 我们走了一小时，停下来歇了一会儿。

rest[3] /rest; rɛst/ *noun* 名词 (no plural 无复数)

the rest 1 what is there when a part has gone 剩余部分；其余: *If you don't want the rest, I'll eat it.* 剩下的如果你不要了，我就吃了。◇ *I liked the beginning, but the rest of the film wasn't very good.* 这部电影我喜欢开头的部分，其余的没什么劲。

2 the other people or things 其他的人或事物: *Jason watched TV and the rest of us went for a walk.* 贾森看电视，我们其余的人都去散步了。

restaurant /ˈrestrɒnt; ˈrɛstərənt/ *noun* 名词

a place where you buy a meal and eat it 饭店；餐馆；餐厅

restless /ˈrestləs; ˈrɛstlɪs/ *adjective* 形容词

not able to be still 静不下来的；不能安宁的: *The children always get restless on long journeys.* 出远门的时候，孩子们总是闲不住。

restore /rɪˈstɔː(r); rɪˈstɔr/ *verb* 动词 (**restores**, **restoring**, **restored** /rɪˈstɔːd; rɪˈstord/)

make something as good as it was before 使某事物恢复原状: *The old palace was restored.* 那座旧宫殿已经修复了。

restrain /rɪˈstreɪn; rɪˈstren/ *verb* 动词 (**restrains**, **restraining**, **restrained** /rɪˈstreɪnd; rɪˈstrend/)

stop somebody or something from doing something; control somebody or something 抑制或遏制某人或某事物；管制；约束: *I couldn't restrain my anger.* 我当时抑制不住愤怒。

restrict /rɪˈstrɪkt; rɪˈstrɪkt/ *verb* 动词 (**restricts**, **restricting**, **restricted**)

allow only a certain amount, size, sort, etc 只能允许某数量、体积、种类等；限制；限定: *Our house is very small, so we had to restrict the number of people we invited to the party.* 我们的房子很小，所以得限制邀请来参加聚会的人数。

restriction /rɪˈstrɪkʃn; rɪˈstrɪkʃən/ *noun* 名词

a rule to control somebody or something（对某人某事物的）限制规则；约束: *There are a lot of parking restrictions in the city centre.* 在市中心停放汽车有很多限制。

rest room /ˈrest ruːm; ˈrɛst rum/ *American English for* **public convenience** 美式英语，即 **public convenience**

result[1] /rɪˈzʌlt; rɪˈzʌlt/ *noun* 名词

1 what happens because something else has happened 结果: *The accident was a result of bad driving.* 这起事故是驾驶不当的结果。

2 the score or mark at the end of a game, competition or exam（运动、竞赛或考试的）成绩，分数: *football results*

足球赛的积分 ◇ *When will you know your exam results?* 你们什么时候知道考试成绩？

as a result because of something 因为某事物；因而: *I got up late, and as a result I missed the train.* 我起晚了，所以误了火车。

result² *verb* 动词 (**results**, **resulting**, **resulted**)

result in something make something happen 使某事物发生；产生某种结果: *The accident resulted in the death of two drivers.* 这起事故造成两个司机死亡。

retire /rɪ'taɪə(r); rɪ'taɪr/ *verb* 动词 (**retires**, **retiring**, **retired** /rɪ'taɪəd; rɪ'taɪrd/)

stop working because you are a certain age 退休: *My grandfather retired when he was 65.* 我祖父65岁时退休了。

retired *adjective* 形容词

a retired teacher 退休的教师

retirement /rɪ'taɪəmənt; rɪ'taɪrmənt/ *noun* 名词 (no plural 无复数)

the time when a person stops working because he/she is a certain age 退休: *What is the age of retirement in your country?* 你们国家退休年龄是多少岁？

retreat /rɪ'tri:t; rɪ'trit/ *verb* 动词 (**retreats**, **retreating**, **retreated**)

move back or away from somebody or something, for example because you have lost a fight 退后；撤退；退却（例如因战败）: *The enemy is retreating.* 敌人正在撤退。

retreat *noun* 名词

retreating 退后；撤退；退却: *The army is now in retreat.* 军队现在正在撤退。

return¹ /rɪ'tɜ:n; rɪ'tɝn/ *verb* 动词 (**returns**, **returning**, **returned** /rɪ'tɜ:nd; rɪ'tɝnd/)

1 come or go back to a place 返回；回来；回去: *They returned from Italy last week.* 他们上星期从意大利回来了。

2 give, put, send or take something back 把某物归还、放回、送回或拿回: *Will you return this book to the library?* 您把这本书还给图书馆好吗？

return² /rɪ'tɜ:n; rɪ'tɝn/ *noun* 名词

1 (no plural 无复数) coming or going back to a place 返回；回来；回去: *They met me at the airport on my return to Britain.* 我回到英国的时候，他们在飞机场接我。

2 (no plural 无复数) giving, putting, sending or taking something back 归还、放回、送回或拿回某物: *the return of the stolen money* 归还偷去的钱

3 (*plural* 复数作 **returns**) (*also* 亦作 **return ticket**) a ticket to travel to a place and back again 来回票；往返票；双程票: *A return to London, please.* 请给我到伦敦的往返票。☞ Look at **single**. 见 **single**。

in return If you do something in return for something else, you do it because somebody has helped you or given you something 作为回报: *We have bought you a present in return for all your help.* 我们为感谢您的帮助给您买了一件礼物。

returns /rɪ'tɜ:nz; rɪ'tɝnz/ *noun* 名词 (plural 复数)

many happy returns words that you say on somebody's birthday 作生日祝贺用语

reunion /ri:'ju:niən; ri'junjən/ *noun* 名词

a meeting of people who have not seen each other for a long time（久别重逢的）重聚；团聚: *We had a family reunion on my aunt's birthday.* 我们在我姑姑生日那天阖家团聚在一起。

reveal /rɪ'vi:l; rɪ'vil/ *verb* 动词 (**reveals**, **revealing**, **revealed** /rɪ'vi:ld; rɪ'vild/)

tell something that was a secret or show something that was hidden 透露；揭露；显露: *She refused to reveal any names to the police.* 她不肯向警方透露任何名字。

revenge /rɪ'vendʒ; rɪ'vɛndʒ/ *noun* 名词 (no plural 无复数)

get, have or 或 **take your revenge on somebody** do something bad to somebody who has done something bad to you 报复；报仇: *He says he will take his revenge on the judge who sent him to prison.* 他说他要向把他关进监狱的法官报仇。

reverse¹ /rɪ'vɜ:s; rɪ'vɝs/ *verb* 动词 (**reverses**, **reversing**, **reversed** /rɪ'vɜ:st; rɪ'vɝst/)

1 make a car, etc go backwards 使汽车等倒退行驶: *I reversed the car into the garage.* 我把汽车倒着开进车房里了。

2 turn something the other way round 使某物翻转: *Writing is reversed in a mirror.* 从镜子里看字是反着的。

R

reverse the charges make a telephone call that the person you are telephoning will pay for 由接电话的人付电话费

reverse[2] /rɪ'vɜːs; rɪ'vɝs/ *noun* 名词 (no plural 无复数)
the opposite thing or way 相反的事物或方法
in reverse in the opposite way; starting at the end and finishing at the beginning 顺序相反；反向: *We ate our dinner in reverse — we started with the ice-cream and finished with the soup!* 我们吃饭时与正常顺序相反——先吃冰激凌最后喝汤！

review /rɪ'vjuː; rɪ'vju/ *noun* 名词
1 a piece of writing in a newspaper or magazine that says what somebody thinks about a book, film, play, etc（报纸或杂志上的）书评、影评、剧评等: *The film got very good reviews.* 这部影片大获好评。
2 thinking again about something that happened before 回顾: *a review of all the important events of the year* 全年大事回顾
review *verb* 动词 (**reviews**, **reviewing**, **reviewed** /rɪ'vjuːd; rɪ'vjud/)
1 write a review about a book, film, play, etc 写书评、影评、剧评等
2 think again about something that happened before 回顾: *Let's review what we have learned in this lesson.* 咱们把本课所学的内容复习一下。

revise /rɪ'vaɪz; rɪ'vaɪz/ *verb* 动词 (**revises**, **revising**, **revised** /rɪ'vaɪzd; rɪ'vaɪzd/)
1 study again something that you have learnt, before an exam（考试前）复习功课: *I'm revising for the Geography test.* 我正在为地理测验复习功课。
2 change something to make it better or more correct 把某事物改好或改对；复核；校订: *The book was revised.* 这本书已经过修订。

revision /rɪ'vɪʒn; rɪ'vɪʒən/ *noun* 名词 (no plural 无复数)
studying again something that you have learnt, before an exam（考试前的）复习功课: *I haven't done any revision for the maths exam.* 我数学考试还没有复习呢。

revive /rɪ'vaɪv; rɪ'vaɪv/ *verb* 动词 (**revives**, **reviving**, **revived** /rɪ'vaɪvd; rɪ'vaɪvd/)
become or make somebody or something well or strong again 使某人或某事物再好起来或再次强盛；康复；复兴: *They pulled the boy out of the river and tried to revive him, but he was already dead.* 大家把那个男孩儿从河里拉上来抢救，可是他已经死了。

revolt /rɪ'vəʊlt; rɪ'volt/ *verb* 动词 (**revolts**, **revolting**, **revolted**)
fight against the people in control 反叛当权者；造反；叛乱: *The army is revolting against the government.* 军队哗变反抗政府。
revolt *noun* 名词
when people fight against the people in control（对当权者的）反叛；造反；叛乱

revolting /rɪ'vəʊltɪŋ; rɪ'voltɪŋ/ *adjective* 形容词
horrible; so bad that it makes you feel sick 讨厌的；让人作呕的: *This meat tastes revolting.* 这肉尝一口就恶心。

revolution /ˌrevə'luːʃn; ˌrɛvə'luʃən/ *noun* 名词
1 a fight by people against their government, to put a new government in its place 推翻政府建立新政权；革命: *The French Revolution was in 1789.* 法国大革命发生在1789年。
2 a big change in the way of doing things 根本改革；革命: *the Industrial Revolution* 产业革命

reward /rɪ'wɔːd; rɪ'wɔrd/ *noun* 名词
a present or money that you give to thank somebody for something that they have done 报酬；酬金: *She is offering a £50 reward to anyone who finds her dog.* 她提出愿给找到她的狗的人酬金50英镑。
reward *verb* 动词 (**rewards**, **rewarding**, **rewarded**)
give a reward to somebody 给某人报酬；奖赏某人: *Jason's parents bought him a bike to reward him for passing his exam.* 贾森的父母为奖励他考试及格给他买了一辆自行车。

rewind /riː'waɪnd; rɪ'waɪnd/ *verb* 动词 (**rewinds**, **rewinding**, **rewound** /riː'waʊnd; rɪ'waʊnd/, **has rewound**)
make a tape (in a **tape recorder** or **video recorder**) go backwards 使（录

音机 **tape recorder** 或录像机 **video recorder** 的）磁带绕回，倒回: *Rewind the tape and play it again.* 把带子倒回来再放一遍。

rhinoceros 犀牛

rhinoceros /raɪˈnɒsərəs; raɪˈnɑsərəs/ *noun* 名词 (*plural* 复数作 **rhinoceros** or 或 **rhinoceroses**)
a big wild animal with thick skin and a horn on its nose. Rhinoceroses live in Africa and Asia. 犀牛（产于非洲和亚洲）✪ The short form is **rhino**. 缩略式为 **rhino**。

rhyme¹ /raɪm; raɪm/ *noun* 名词
1 when two words have the same sound, for example 'bell' and 'well' 韵；韵脚；同韵词（例如 bell 和 well）: *Her poetry is written in rhyme.* 她写的诗押韵。
2 a short piece of writing where the lines end with the same sounds 韵文

rhyme² /raɪm; raɪm/ *verb* 动词 (**rhymes**, **rhyming**, **rhymed** /raɪmd; raɪmd/)
1 have the same sound as another word 使词押韵: *'Moon' rhymes with 'spoon' and 'chair' rhymes with 'bear'.* ✳ moon 和 spoon 押韵，chair 和 bear 押韵。
2 have lines that end with the same sounds（指诗句）押韵: *This poem doesn't rhyme.* 这首诗不押韵。

rhythm /ˈrɪðəm; ˈrɪðəm/ *noun* 名词
a regular pattern of sounds that come again and again 节奏: *This music has a good rhythm.* 这支乐曲的节奏很好。

rib /rɪb; rɪb/ *noun* 名词
one of the bones around your chest 肋骨 ☞ picture on page C2 见第C2页图

ribbon /ˈrɪbən; ˈrɪbən/ *noun* 名词
a long thin piece of pretty material for tying things（漂亮的）捆扎带；装饰带: *She wore a ribbon in her hair.* 她头发上扎着饰带。

ribbon 捆扎带

rice /raɪs; raɪs/ *noun* 名词 (no plural 无复数)
white or brown seeds from a plant that grows in hot countries, that we use as food 稻米；大米: *Would you like rice or potatoes with your chicken?* 您这盘鸡肉里是配米饭还是配土豆儿？

rich /rɪtʃ; rɪtʃ/ *adjective* 形容词 (**richer**, **richest**)
1 with a lot of money 富的；富有的: *a rich family* 富裕的家庭 ✪ opposite 反义词: **poor**
2 with a lot of something（指某物）丰富的: *This country is rich in oil.* 这个国家盛产石油。
3 Food that is rich has a lot of fat or sugar in it（指食物）油腻的或多糖的: *a rich chocolate cake* 油腻的巧克力蛋糕
the rich *noun* 名词 (plural 复数)
people who have a lot of money 富人；有钱人

rid /rɪd; rɪd/ *verb* 动词
get rid of somebody or 或 **something** throw something away or become free of somebody or something 扔掉某物或摆脱某人或某事物: *I got rid of my old coat and bought a new one.* 我把旧大衣扔了，又买了一件新的。◇ *This dog is following me — I can't get rid of it.* 这条狗老跟着我——没办法把它甩开。

riddle /ˈrɪdl; ˈrɪdl̩/ *noun* 名词
a question that has a clever or funny answer 谜语: *Here's a riddle: What has four legs but can't walk? The answer is a chair!* 猜猜这个谜语：尽管有四条腿，可是不会走路，是什么呢？谜底是椅子。

ride /raɪd; raɪd/ *verb* 动词 (**rides**, **riding**, **rode** /rəʊd; rod/, **has ridden** /ˈrɪdn; ˈrɪdn̩/)
1 sit on a horse or bicycle and control it as it moves 骑马；骑自行车: *I'm learning to ride* (= a horse). 我正在学骑马呢。◇ *Don't ride your bike on the grass!* 别在草地上骑自行车！✪ When you talk about spending time riding a horse, you say **go riding** 骑马消遣的说法是 **go riding**: *I went riding today.* 我今天骑马玩儿了。
2 travel in a car, bus or train 乘坐小轿车、公共汽车或火车: *We rode in the back of the car.* 我们坐在汽车的后面。✪ When you control a car, bus or train, you **drive** it. 驾驶小轿车、公共汽车或火车叫做 **drive**。

R

ride *noun* 名词
a journey on a horse or bicycle, or in a car, bus or train 骑马；骑自行车；乘坐小轿车、公共汽车或火车: *We went for a ride in the woods.* 我们在树林里骑马玩儿。◇ *I had a ride in his new car.* 我坐了一次他的新汽车。

rider *noun* 名词
a person who rides a horse or bicycle 骑马或骑自行车的人

riding *noun* 名词 (no plural 无复数)
the sport of riding a horse 骑马运动

ridge /rɪdʒ; rɪdʒ/ *noun* 名词
a long thin part of something that is higher than the rest, for example along the top of hills or mountains 狭长的隆起部分（例如山脊）: *We walked along the ridge looking down at the valley below.* 我们沿着山脊走，俯视着下面的山谷。

ridiculous /rɪ'dɪkjələs; rɪ'dɪkjələs/ *adjective* 形容词
so silly that it makes people laugh 可笑的；荒谬的: *You can't play tennis with a football — that's ridiculous!* 谁也不能拿足球当网球打——太荒唐了！

rifle /'raɪfl; 'raɪfl̩/ *noun* 名词
a long gun that you hold against your shoulder when you fire it 步枪；来复枪

right[1] /raɪt; raɪt/ *adjective, adverb* 形容词，副词
opposite of left. Most people write with their right hand 右: *Turn right at the end of the street.* 在这条街的尽头向右转。

right *noun* 名词 (no plural 无复数)
We live in the first house on the right. 我们住在右边第一所房子里。

right[2] /raɪt; raɪt/ *adjective* 形容词
1 correct or true 正确的；属实的: *That's not the right answer.* 那个答案不正确。◇ *'Are you Mr Johnson?' 'Yes, that's right.'* "您是约翰逊先生吧？""对，是我。"
2 good; fair or what the law allows 正当的；恰当的；合法的: *It's not right to leave young children alone in the house.* 把幼小的儿童单独留在家里是不合法的。
3 best 最好的: *Is she the right person for the job?* 她是最适合做这项工作的人吗？
✪ opposite 反义词: **wrong**

right[3] /raɪt; raɪt/ *adverb* 副词
1 correctly 正确地: *Have I spelt your name right?* 我拼写您的名字拼得对吗？✪ opposite 反义词: **wrong**
2 exactly 准确地；正好: *He was sitting right next to me.* 他紧挨着我坐着。
3 all the way 一直（由始至终）: *Go right to the end of the road.* 一直走到这条路的尽头。
4 immediately 立即；马上: *We left right after dinner.* 我们一吃完饭就走了。
5 yes, I agree; yes, I will 我同意: *'I'll see you tomorrow.' 'Right.'* "我明天见你。""行。"
6 You say 'right' to make somebody listen to you 用 right 作招呼别人注意听的用语: *Are you ready? Right, let's go.* 你准备好了吗？喂，咱们走吧。

right away immediately; now 立即；马上；现在: *Phone the doctor right away.* 马上给大夫打电话。

right[4] /raɪt; raɪt/ *noun* 名词
1 (no plural 无复数) what is good or fair 好；正确: *Young children have to learn the difference between right and wrong.* 小孩儿得学会分辨正确与错误。
2 (*plural* 复数作 **rights**) what you are allowed to do, especially by law 允许做的事；（尤指法律规定的）权利: *In Britain, everyone has the right to vote at 18.* 在英国，年满18岁的人都有选举权。

right angle /'raɪt æŋgl; 'raɪt ˌæŋgl̩/ *noun* 名词
an angle of 90 degrees. A square has four right angles. 直角（90度的角。正方形有四个直角）☞ picture on page C5 见第C5页图

right-hand /'raɪt hænd; 'raɪt'hænd/ *adjective* 形容词
of or on the right 右边的: *The supermarket is on the right-hand side of the road.* 超级市场在这条路的右边。

right-handed /ˌraɪt'hændɪd; 'raɪt-'hændɪd/ *adjective* 形容词
If you are right-handed, you use your right hand more easily than your left hand. 习惯用右手的

rightly /'raɪtli; 'raɪtlɪ/ *adverb* 副词
correctly 正确地: *If I remember rightly, the party was on 15 June.* 要是我没记错的话，那次聚会是在6月15日。

rigid /'rɪdʒɪd; 'rɪdʒɪd/ *adjective* 形容词
1 hard and not easy to bend or move 坚硬而不易弯曲或不易移动的
2 not able to be changed; strict 不能改变的；严格的: *My school has very rigid rules.* 我们学校校规很严。

rim /rɪm; rɪm/ *noun* 名词
the edge of something round（圆形物体的）边缘: *the rim of a cup* 杯子的边

rind /raɪnd; raɪnd/ *noun* 名词
the thick hard skin of some fruits, or of bacon or cheese（某些水果的，或腌猪肉的或干酪的）厚而硬的皮: *lemon rind* 柠檬皮

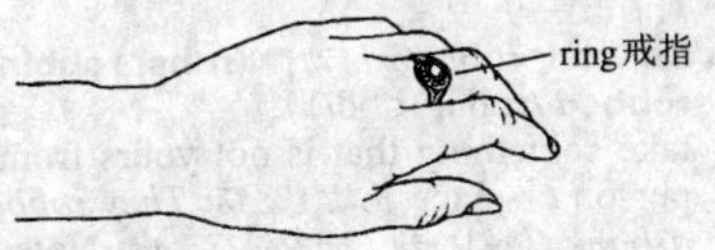

ring[1] /rɪŋ; rɪŋ/ *noun* 名词
1 a circle of metal that you wear on your finger 指环；戒指
2 a circle 圆圈: *Please stand in a ring.* 请站成一个圆圈。
3 a space with seats around it, for a circus or boxing match（为马戏表演或拳击比赛的）周围有座位的场地

ring[2] /rɪŋ; rɪŋ/ *verb* 动词 (**rings, ringing, rang** /ræŋ; ræŋ/, **has rung** /rʌŋ; rʌŋ/)
1 make a sound like a bell 发出像铃声的声音: *The telephone is ringing.* 电话铃响了。
2 press or move a bell so that it makes a sound 按铃或摇铃使之发出声响: *We rang the doorbell again but nobody answered.* 我们又按了一次门铃，可是没有人应门。
3 telephone somebody 给某人打电话: *I'll ring you on Sunday.* 我星期日给你打电话。
ring somebody back telephone somebody again 再次给某人打电话；给某人回电话: *I wasn't at home when Jo called, so I rang her back later.* 乔给我打电话的时候我不在家，我后来给她回了个电话。
ring up telephone somebody 给某人打电话: *Your brother rang up while you were out.* 你出去的时候你哥哥给你来了个电话。

ring[3] /rɪŋ; rɪŋ/ *noun* 名词
the sound that a bell makes 铃声: *There was a ring at the door.* 门铃响了。
give somebody a ring telephone somebody 给某人打电话: *I'll give you a ring later.* 我等一会儿给你打电话。

rinse /rɪns; rɪns/ *verb* 动词 (**rinses, rinsing, rinsed** /rɪnst; rɪnst/)
wash something with water to take away dirt or soap 用水洗掉污垢或肥皂沫: *Wash your hair and rinse it well.* 洗完头后再冲洗干净。

riot /ˈraɪət; ˈraɪət/ *noun* 名词
when a group of people fight and make a lot of noise and trouble 暴乱；骚乱: *There were riots in the streets after the football match.* 在足球比赛结束后，街道上发生了骚乱。
riot *verb* 动词 (**riots, rioting, rioted**)
The prisoners are rioting. 囚犯们正在闹事。

rip /rɪp; rɪp/ *verb* 动词 (**rips, ripping, ripped** /rɪpt; rɪpt/)
pull or tear quickly and roughly 拉；撕；扯: *I ripped my shirt on a nail.* 我的衬衫让钉子给刷破了。◇ *Joe ripped the letter open.* 乔把信撕开了。
rip up tear something into small pieces 把某物撕碎: *She ripped the photo up.* 她把照片撕碎了。

ripe /raɪp; raɪp/ *adjective* 形容词 (**riper, ripest**)
Fruit that is ripe is ready to eat（指水果）成熟的: *These bananas aren't ripe — they're still green.* 这些香蕉不熟——还绿着呢。

rise /raɪz; raɪz/ *verb* 动词 (**rises, rising, rose** /rəʊz; roz/, **has risen** /ˈrɪzn; ˈrɪzn̩/)
go up; become higher or more 上升；增高或增多: *The sun rises in the east and sets (= goes down) in the west.* 太阳从东方升起，至西方落下。◇ *Prices are rising.* 涨价了。
rise *noun* 名词
becoming higher or more 增高或增多: *a rise in the price of oil* 油价上涨 ◇ *a pay rise* 增加工资

risk /rɪsk; rɪsk/ *noun* 名词
the possibility that something bad may happen; danger 坏事发生的可能性；风险；危险: *Do you think there's any risk of rain?* 你看这个天儿保不住要下雨吧？
at risk in danger 有危险: *Children are at risk from this disease.* 儿童有得这种病的危险。
take a risk or 或 **risks** do something when it is possible that something bad may happen because of it 不顾可能出现坏结果而做某事；冒险做某事: *Don't take risks when you're driving.* 开车的时候可别干冒险的事。
risk *verb* 动词 (**risks, risking, risked** /rɪskt; rɪskt/)
1 put somebody or something in danger

R

使某人或某事物面临危险: *He risked his life to save the child from the burning house.* 他冒着生命危险把孩子从着火的房子里抢救出来。

2 do something when there is a possibility that something bad may happen because of it 不顾可能出现坏结果而做某事；冒险做某事: *If you don't work harder, you risk failing the exam.* 你要是不用功，就别怕考试不及格。

risky /'rɪski; 'rɪskɪ/ *adjective* 形容词 (**riskier**, **riskiest**)
dangerous 有危险的；冒险的

rival /'raɪvl; 'raɪvl̩/ *noun* 名词
a person who wants to do better than you or who is trying to take what you want 竞争者；对手: *John and Lucy are rivals for the manager's job.* 约翰和露西竞争经理这份工作。

R

river /'rɪvə(r); 'rɪvɚ/ *noun* 名词
a long wide line of water that flows into the sea 河；江；水道: *the River Amazon* 亚马孙河

road /rəʊd; rod/ *noun* 名词
the way from one place to another, where cars can go（可通行汽车的）路；道路；公路: *Is this the road to Brighton?* 这条公路是通往布赖顿的吗？◇ *My address is 47 Ridley Road, London NW10.* 我的地址是伦敦里德利路47号，邮政编码NW10。

✪ The short way of writing 'Road' in addresses is **Rd** ＊ Road 用于地址的缩写形式为 **Rd**: *30 Welton Rd* 韦尔敦路30号

by road in a car, bus, etc 乘小汽车、公共汽车等；由公路: *It's a long journey by road — the train is faster.* 由公路走路程很长——坐火车快。

roam /rəʊm; rom/ *verb* 动词 (**roams**, **roaming**, **roamed** /rəʊmd; romd/)
walk or travel with no special plan 无计划地走；漫游；闲逛: *Dogs were roaming the streets looking for food.* 狗在街上各处走来走去找东西吃。

roar /rɔ:(r); rɔr/ *verb* 动词 (**roars**, **roaring**, **roared** /rɔ:d; rɔrd/)
make a loud deep sound 发出大而低沉的声音；吼叫: *The lion roared.* 狮子吼叫着。◇ *Everybody roared with laughter.* 大家都哈哈大笑。

roar *noun* 名词
the roar of an aeroplane's engines 飞机发动机的隆隆声

roast /rəʊst; rost/ *verb* 动词 (**roasts**, **roasting**, **roasted**)
cook or be cooked in an oven or over a fire 烤或烘食物: *Roast the chicken in a hot oven.* 用烤箱高温烤鸡。

roast *adjective* 形容词
roast beef and roast potatoes 烤的牛肉和烤的土豆儿

rob /rɒb; rɑb/ *verb* 动词 (**robs**, **robbing**, **robbed** /rɒbd; rɑbd/)
take something that is not yours from a person or place 抢劫；盗窃: *They robbed a bank.* 他们抢劫了一家银行。☞ Note at **steal** 见 **steal** 词条注释

robber *noun* 名词
a person who robs 劫匪；强盗；窃贼

robbery /'rɒbəri; 'rɑbərɪ/ *noun* 名词 (*plural* 复数作 **robberies**)
taking something that is not yours from a bank, etc 抢劫；盗窃: *What time did the robbery take place?* 劫案是什么时候发生的？

robin /'rɒbɪn; 'rɑbɪn/ *noun* 名词
a small brown bird with a red front 鸲；欧洲鸲（褐色小鸟，胸部红色）

robot /'rəʊbɒt; 'robɑt/ *noun* 名词
a machine that can work like a person 机器人: *This car was built by robots.* 这辆汽车是机器人制造的。

rock[1] /rɒk; rɑk/ *noun* 名词
1 (no plural 无复数) the very hard stuff that is in the ground and in mountains 岩；岩层

2 (*plural* 复数作 **rocks**) a big piece of this 岩石；礁石: *The ship hit the rocks.* 轮船触礁了。

rock[2] /rɒk; rɑk/, **rock music** /'rɒk mju:zɪk; 'rɑk ˌmjuzɪk/ *noun* 名词 (no plural 无复数)
a sort of modern music 摇滚乐: *a rock concert* 摇滚乐音乐会

rock[3] /rɒk; rɑk/ *verb* 动词 (**rocks**, **rocking**, **rocked** /rɒkt; rɑkt/)
move slowly backwards and forwards or from side to side; make somebody or something do this（使某人或某物）摆动；摇动；摇晃: *The boat was rocking gently on the lake.* 小船在湖面微微摇晃。◇ *I rocked the baby until she went to sleep.* 我摇晃着孩子把她摇得睡着了。

rocket /'rɒkɪt; 'rɑkɪt/ *noun* 名词
1 an engine with long round sides that pushes a spacecraft up into space 火箭

2 a thing with long round sides that carries a bomb through the air 火箭弹

3 a **firework** that goes up into the air and then explodes（发射到空中爆炸的）烟火

rocky /ˈrɒki; ˈrɑkɪ/ *adjective* 形容词 (**rockier**, **rockiest**)
with a lot of rocks 多岩石的: *a rocky path* 多岩石的小路

rod /rɒd; rɑd/ *noun* 名词
a thin straight piece of wood or metal 杆；竿；棍；棒: *a fishing-rod* 鱼竿

rode *form of* **ride** ✳ **ride** 的不同形式

role /rəʊl; rol/ *noun* 名词

1 the person you are in a play or film 角色: *The role of the King was played by Bob Lewis.* 国王这一角色是由鲍勃·刘易斯扮演的。

2 what a person does 任务；工作: *Your role is to tell other people what to do.* 你的任务是给别人布置工作。

roll¹ /rəʊl; rol/ *verb* 动词 (**rolls**, **rolling**, **rolled** /rəʊld; rold/)

1 move along, turning over and over; make something go over and over（使某物）滚动: *The pencil rolled off the table on to the floor.* 铅笔从桌子上滚到地上去了。◇ *We rolled the rock down the path.* 我们把石头沿小路滚下去。

2 move on wheels（由轮子转动）移动，行进: *The car rolled down the hill.* 汽车顺山坡而下。

3 make something flat by moving something heavy on top of it 碾平；轧平；擀平: *Roll the pastry into a large circle.* 把油酥面团擀成一个大圆片。

roll over turn your body a different way when you are lying down（躺着时）翻身: *She rolled over.* 她翻了个身。

roll up make something into a long round shape or the shape of a ball 把某物卷起或团成球形: *Can you help me to roll up this carpet?* 你帮我把地毯卷起来行吗？

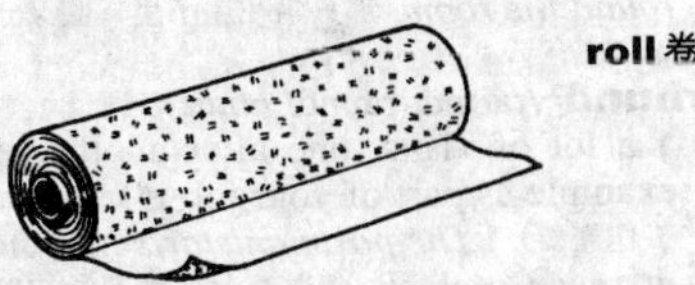

roll 卷

roll² /rəʊl; rol/ *noun* 名词

1 something made into a long round shape by rolling it around itself many times 成卷的东西: *a roll of material* 一卷材料 ◇ *a roll of film* 一卷胶卷

2 a small round piece of bread made for one person 小圆面包: *a roll and butter* 小圆面包和黄油

roller-skate /ˈrəʊlə skeɪt; ˈrolɚ ˌsket/ *noun* 名词
a shoe with wheels on the bottom, for moving quickly on smooth ground 旱冰鞋；轱辘鞋

roller-skate 旱冰鞋

roller-skating *noun* 名词 (no plural 无复数)
moving on roller-skates 滑旱冰

Roman Catholic /ˌrəʊmən ˈkæθəlɪk; ˈromən ˈkæθəlɪk/ *noun* 名词
a member of the Christian church that follows the Pope 天主教

romance /rəʊˈmæns; roˈmæns/ *noun* 名词

1 a time when two people are in love 两人相爱（期间）；恋爱: *a romance between a doctor and a nurse* 医生与护士的恋爱

2 a story about love 爱情故事: *She writes romances.* 她写的是爱情故事。

romantic /rəʊˈmæntɪk; roˈmæntɪk/ *adjective* 形容词
about love; full of feelings of love 爱情的；多情的: *a romantic film* 爱情故事片

roof /ruːf; ruf/ *noun* 名词 (*plural* 复数作 **roofs**)
the top of a building or car, that covers it（建筑物或汽车的）顶部；屋顶；车顶 ☞ picture at **house** 见 **house** 词条插图

room /ruːm; rum/ *noun* 名词

1 (*plural* 复数作 **rooms**) one of the spaces with walls round it in a building 房间；室: *How many rooms has your flat got?* 你们公寓有几个房间？◇ *a classroom* 教室

✪ A house or flat usually has a **living-room** (or **sitting-room** or **lounge**), **bedrooms**, a **bathroom**, a **toilet**, a **kitchen**, a **hall** and perhaps a **dining-room**. 一所房子或一套公寓一般有起居室（**living-room**）（或称 **sitting-room** 或 **lounge**）、卧室（**bedroom**）、浴室（**bathroom**）、厕所（**toilet**）、厨房（**kitchen**）、门厅（**hall**），也许还有个饭厅（**dining-room**）。

R

2 (no plural 无复数) space; enough space 空间；（够用的）地方: *There's no room for you in the car.* 汽车里没有你坐的地方了。

root /ruːt; rut/ *noun* 名词
the part of a plant that is under the ground（植物的）根 ☞ picture at **plant** 见 **plant** 词条插图

rope /rəʊp; rop/ *noun* 名词
very thick strong string 绳子

rope 绳子

rose¹ *form of* **rise** ✳ **rise** 的不同形式

rose² /rəʊz; roz/ *noun* 名词
a flower with a sweet smell. It grows on a bush that has sharp points (called **thorns**) on it. 蔷薇花；玫瑰花（刺叫做 **thorn**）

rosy /ˈrəʊzi; ˈrozɪ/ *adjective* 形容词 (**rosier, rosiest**)
pink 粉红色的；玫瑰红的: *rosy cheeks* 红润的脸颊

rot /rɒt; rɑt/ *verb* 动词 (**rots, rotting, rotted**)
become bad and soft, as things do when they die 腐烂；腐坏: *Nobody picked the apples so they rotted.* 苹果没有人摘，结果都烂了。

rotate /rəʊˈteɪt; ˈrotet/ *verb* 动词 (**rotates, rotating, rotated**)
move in circles 旋转；转动: *The earth rotates around the sun.* 地球围着太阳转。

rotten /ˈrɒtn; ˈrɑtn̩/ *adjective* 形容词
1 old and not fresh; bad 腐烂的；变质的；坏的: *These eggs are rotten — they smell horrible!* 这些蛋已经坏了——臭极了！
2 very bad; not nice or kind 极坏的；糟糕的；讨厌的: *The weather was rotten all week.* 这一星期天气糟透了。

rough /rʌf; rʌf/ *adjective* 形容词 (**rougher, roughest**)
1 not smooth or flat 粗糙的；不平的: *It was difficult to walk on the rough ground.* 在高低不平的地面上很难走。
2 not gentle or calm 不平静的；粗鲁的；粗暴的；粗野的: *rough seas* 波涛汹涌的海面
3 not exactly correct; made or done quickly 粗略的；粗率的；很快做成的: *Can you give me a rough idea how much it will cost?* 您告诉我个大略的价钱行吗？◇ *a rough drawing* 草草画成的画儿

roughly /ˈrʌfli; ˈrʌflɪ/ *adverb* 副词
1 not gently 粗鲁地；粗暴地；粗野地: *He pushed me roughly away.* 他很粗鲁地把我推开了。
2 about; not exactly 大约；大概: *The bike cost roughly £150.* 这辆自行车大约要150英镑。

round¹ /raʊnd; raʊnd/ *adjective* 形容词
with the shape of a circle or a ball 圆形的；球形的: *a round plate* 圆的盘子

round² /raʊnd; raʊnd/ *adverb, preposition* 副词，介词
1 on or to all sides of something, often in a circle 围绕；环绕: *The earth moves round the sun.* 地球围着太阳转。◇ *We sat round the table.* 我们围着桌子坐着。◇ *He tied a scarf round his neck.* 他脖子上围着围巾。☞ picture on page C4 见第C4页图
2 in the opposite direction or in another direction 相反方向；转过来: *I turned round and went home again.* 我转身又回家了。◇ *Turn your chair round.* 把您的椅子转过来。
3 in or to different parts of a place 在各处；到各处: *We travelled round France last summer.* 我们去年夏天周游了法国。
4 from one person to another 从一人到另一人: *Pass these photos round the class.* 把这些照片交给全班传阅。
5 to somebody's house 到某人的家: *Come round* (= to my house) *at eight o'clock.* 八点钟到我家来吧。
6 to or on the other side of something 到另一边；在另一边: *There's a bank just round the corner.* 拐弯处就有一家银行。
go round be enough for everybody 够每人一份: *Are there enough cakes to go round?* 蛋糕够每人一份吗？
round about nearly; not exactly 差不多；大约: *It will cost round about £90.* 这大约要90英镑。
round and round round many times 一圈又一圈: *The bird flew round and round the room.* 那只鸟在屋子里一圈又一圈地飞着。

round³ /raʊnd; raʊnd/ *noun* 名词
1 a lot of visits, one after another, for example as part of your job 巡回（例如因工作需要）: *The postman starts his round at seven o'clock.* 邮递员七点钟开始按路线到各处投递信件。
2 one part of a game or competition（游戏或比赛的）一轮，一局，一场，一个回合:

the third round of the boxing match 拳击比赛的第三个回合

3 drinks for all the people in a group 每人一份的饮品: *I'll buy this round. What would you like?* 这次每人一份饮品我请客。您喝什么？

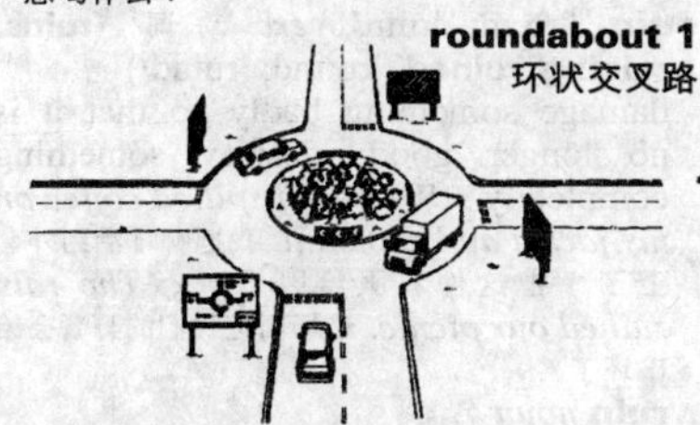

roundabout 1 环状交叉路

roundabout /ˈraʊndəbaʊt; ˈraʊndəˌbaʊt/ *noun* 名词

1 a place where roads meet, where cars must drive round in a circle 环状交叉路（车辆须按同一方向绕行）

2 a big round machine at a fair. It has model animals or cars on it that children can ride on as it turns. 旋转木马（儿童游乐场的）

round trip /ˌraʊndˈtrɪp; ˈraʊnd ˈtrɪp/ *noun* 名词

a journey to a place and back again 往返旅程

route /ruːt; raʊt/ *noun* 名词

a way from one place to another（从一处到另一处的）路线；路程: *What is the quickest route from London to Edinburgh?* 从伦敦到爱丁堡走哪条路最快？

routine /ruːˈtiːn; ruˈtin/ *noun* 名词

your usual way of doing things 通常做事的方式；例行公事: *My morning routine is to get up at seven, have breakfast, then leave home at eight.* 我早晨一贯是七点钟起床，吃早饭，然后八点钟出门。

row[1] /rəʊ; ro/ *noun* 名词

a line of people or things 成排或成行的人或事物: *We sat in the front row of the theatre* (= the front line of seats). 我们坐在戏院的前排。◇ *a row of houses* 一排房子 ☞ picture on page C25 见第C25页图

rowing 划船

row[2] /rəʊ; ro/ *verb* 动词 (**rows, rowing, rowed** /rəʊd; rod/)

move a boat through water using long pieces of wood with flat ends (called **oars**) 划船（桨叫做 **oar**）: *We rowed across the lake.* 我们在湖上划船。✪ When you talk about spending time rowing as a sport, you say **go rowing** 划船运动的说法是 **go rowing**: *We went rowing on the river.* 我们在河里划船玩儿。

rowing-boat /ˈrəʊɪŋ bəʊt; ˈroɪŋˌbot/ *noun* 名词

a small boat that you move through water using oars 划艇

row[3] /raʊ; raʊ/ *noun* 名词

1 (*plural* 复数作 **rows**) a noisy talk between people who do not agree about something 争吵；吵闹: *She had a row with her boyfriend.* 她跟男朋友吵了一架。

2 (no plural 无复数) loud noise 大的噪声: *The children were making a terrible row.* 孩子们吵闹的声音太大了。

royal /ˈrɔɪəl; ˈrɔɪəl/ *adjective* 形容词

of or about a king or queen 国王的或王后的；女王的: *the royal family* 王室

royalty /ˈrɔɪəlti; ˈrɔɪəltɪ/ *noun* 名词 (no plural 无复数)

kings, queens and their families 王室成员；王族

rub /rʌb; rʌb/ *verb* 动词 (**rubs, rubbing, rubbed** /rʌbd; rʌbd/)

move something backwards and forwards on another thing 用某物擦另一物；磨；抹: *I rubbed my hands together to keep them warm.* 我来回搓着手取暖。◇ *The cat rubbed its head against my leg.* 猫用脑袋蹭我的腿。

rub out take writing or marks off something by using a rubber or a cloth 用橡皮或布擦掉某物: *I rubbed the word out and wrote it again.* 我把字擦掉了，又写了一个。

rub *noun* 名词 (no plural 无复数)

Give your shoes a rub. 把你的鞋擦擦吧。

rubber /ˈrʌbə(r); ˈrʌbɚ/ *noun* 名词

1 (no plural 无复数) material that we use to make things like car tyres 橡胶

2 (*plural* 复数作 **rubbers**) a small piece of rubber that you use for taking away marks that you have made with a pencil（擦铅笔痕迹的）橡皮

R

rubber band /ˌrʌbə(r)ˈbænd; ˈrʌbɚ ˈbænd/ *noun* 名词
a thin circle of rubber that you use for holding things together 橡皮筋；橡皮圈

rubbish /ˈrʌbɪʃ; ˈrʌbɪʃ/ *noun* 名词 (no plural 无复数)
1 things that you do not want any more 垃圾；废物: *old boxes, bottles and other rubbish* 旧盒子、瓶子之类的废物 ◇ *Throw this rubbish in the bin.* 把这些垃圾扔进垃圾箱里吧。
2 something that is bad, stupid or wrong 坏的、蠢的或错的事物: *You're talking rubbish!* 你胡说八道！

rucksack /ˈrʌksæk; ˈrʌkˌsæk/ *noun* 名词
a bag that you carry on your back, for example when you are walking or climbing 背包（例如走路或登山时用的）

rudder /ˈrʌdə(r); ˈrʌdɚ/ *noun* 名词
a flat piece of wood or metal at the back of a boat or an aeroplane. It moves to make the boat or aeroplane go left or right.（船的）舵；（飞机的）方向舵

rude /ru:d; rud/ *adjective* 形容词 (**ruder, rudest**)
1 not polite 无礼的；粗野的: *It's rude to walk away when someone is talking to you.* 人家跟你说话时你走开了，这是很不礼貌的。
2 about things like sex or using the toilet（指言语）低级趣味的（例如关于性或大小便等）: *rude words* 粗俗的话

rudely *adverb* 副词
'Shut up!' she said rudely. "闭上嘴！"她粗鲁地说。

rug 小地毯

rug /rʌg; rʌg/ *noun* 名词
1 a small piece of thick material that you put on the floor（小块的厚的）地毯
2 a thick piece of material that you put round your body to keep you warm（盖在身上用的）厚毯子

rugby /ˈrʌgbi; ˈrʌgbɪ/ *noun* 名词 (no plural 无复数)
a game like football for two teams of 13 or 15 players. In rugby, you can kick and carry the ball.（英式的）橄榄球运动（两队各13或15人参赛，用手脚均可）

ruin /ˈru:ɪn; ˈruɪn/ *verb* 动词 (**ruins, ruining, ruined** /ˈru:ɪnd; ˈruɪnd/)
damage something badly so that it is no longer good; destroy something completely 毁坏；毁灭: *I spilled coffee on my jacket and ruined it.* 我把咖啡洒到外套上了，把这件衣服给毁了。◇ *The rain ruined our picnic.* 这场雨把我们的野餐会给破坏了。

ruin *noun* 名词
a building that has been badly damaged 遭到严重破坏的建筑物；废墟: *The old castle is now a ruin.* 那座旧城堡现在已经成了废墟了。

in ruins badly damaged or destroyed 遭到毁坏或毁灭: *The city was in ruins after the war.* 战争过后，那座城市已经成了颓垣断壁。

rule[1] /ru:l; rul/ *noun* 名词
1 (*plural* 复数作 **rules**) something that tells you what you must or must not do 规则；规章；条例: *It's against the school rules to smoke.* 吸烟是违反校规的。◇ *break the rules* (= do something that you should not do) 犯规
2 (no plural 无复数) government 统治；管辖: *India was once under British rule.* 印度曾受英国统治。

rule[2] /ru:l; rul/ *verb* 动词 (**rules, ruling, ruled** /ru:ld; ruld/)
control a country 统治或治理国家: *Queen Victoria ruled for many years.* 维多利亚女王统治了很多年。

ruler 尺

ruler /ˈru:lə(r); ˈrulɚ/ *noun* 名词
1 a long piece of plastic, metal or wood that you use for drawing straight lines or for measuring things 尺（画直线或量长度的器具）
2 a person who rules a country 统治者

rum /rʌm; rʌm/ *noun* 名词
a strong alcoholic drink 朗姆酒

rumble /'rʌmbl; 'rʌmbḷ/ *verb* 动词 (**rumbles**, **rumbling**, **rumbled** /'rʌmbld; 'rʌmbḷd/)
make a long deep sound 发出长而低沉的声音: *I'm so hungry that my stomach is rumbling.* 我饿得肚子咕咕叫。
rumble *noun* 名词 (no plural 无复数)
the rumble of thunder 雷声隆隆

rumor *American English for* **rumour** 美式英语，即 **rumour**

rumour /'ru:mə(r); 'rumɚ/ *noun* 名词
something that a lot of people are talking about that is perhaps not true 传闻；谣言: *There's a rumour that our teacher is leaving.* 有谣传说我们老师要走了。

run[1] /rʌn; rʌn/ *verb* 动词 (**runs**, **running**, **ran** /ræn; ræn/, **has run**)
1 move very quickly on your legs 跑: *I was late, so I ran to the bus-stop.* 我已经晚了，所以得跑着去公共汽车站。
2 go; make a journey 行进；行驶: *The buses don't run on Sundays.* 公共汽车星期日停开。
3 control something and make it work 管理或经营: *Who runs the company?* 谁经管这家公司？
4 pass or go somewhere 经过或通到某处: *The road runs across the fields.* 这条路经过那些田地。
5 flow 流动: *The river runs into the North Sea.* 这条河流入北海。
6 work 工作: *The car had stopped but the engine was still running.* 汽车已经停了，可是发动机还在转动。
7 move something somewhere 使某物移动: *He ran his fingers through his hair.* 他用手拢着头发。
run after somebody or 或 **something** try to catch a person or an animal 追赶某人或某动物: *The dog ran after a rabbit.* 狗追着兔子。
run away go quickly away from a place 逃走: *She ran away from home when she was 14.* 她14岁的时候就离家出走了。
run out of something have no more of something 不再有某事物: *We've run out of coffee. Will you go and buy some?* 我们没有咖啡了，你去买点儿行吗？
run over somebody or 或 **something** drive over somebody or something（指汽车）轧过某人或某物: *The dog was run over by a bus.* 那条狗让公共汽车给轧死了。

run[2] /rʌn; rʌn/ *noun* 名词
moving very quickly on your legs 跑步: *I go for a run every morning.* 我每天早晨都跑步。

rung[1] *form of* **ring**[2] ＊ **ring**[2] 的不同形式

rung[2] /rʌŋ; rʌŋ/ *noun* 名词
one of the steps of a ladder（梯子的）横档，梯级 ☞ picture at **ladder** 见 **ladder** 词条插图

runner /'rʌnə(r); 'rʌnɚ/ *noun* 名词
a person who runs 奔跑的人

runner-up /ˌrʌnər 'ʌp; 'rʌnɚ'ʌp/ *noun* 名词 (*plural* 复数作 **runners-up** /ˌrʌnəz'ʌp; 'rʌnɚz'ʌp/)
a person or team that comes second in a race or competition（竞赛中的）第二名；亚军

running[1] /'rʌnɪŋ; 'rʌnɪŋ/ *noun* 名词 (no plural 无复数)
the sport of running 赛跑: *running shoes* 跑鞋

running[2] /'rʌnɪŋ; 'rʌnɪŋ/ *adjective* 形容词
one after another 一个接一个: *We won the competition for three years running.* 我们连续三年都赢得这项比赛。

runway /'rʌnweɪ; 'rʌnˌwe/ *noun* 名词 (*plural* 复数作 **runways**)
a long piece of ground where aeroplanes take off and land（飞机的）跑道

rural /'rʊərəl; 'rurəl/ *adjective* 形容词
of the country, not the town 乡村的: *The book is about life in rural France.* 这本书写的是法国乡村的生活。

rush /rʌʃ; rʌʃ/ *verb* 动词 (**rushes**, **rushing**, **rushed** /rʌʃt; rʌʃt/)
1 go or come very quickly 急速去或来: *The children rushed out of school.* 孩子们飞快地跑出学校。
2 do something quickly or make somebody do something quickly（使某人）仓促行事: *We rushed to finish the work on time.* 我们准时把工作赶完了。
3 take somebody or something quickly to a place 急速把某人或某物送到某处: *She was rushed to hospital.* 她立即被送到医院。
rush *noun* 名词 (no plural 无复数)
1 a sudden quick movement 急速的动作；冲；奔: *At the end of the film there*

was a rush for the exits. 电影一结束，大家都涌向出口处。

2 a need to move or do something very quickly 急速行动或做某事: *I can't stop now — I'm in a rush.* 我现在不能停下来——我正忙着呢。

the rush hour /ðə ˈrʌʃ aʊə(r); ðə ˈrʌʃ ˌaʊr/ *noun* 名词
the time when a lot of people are going to or coming from work（上下班时的）交通拥挤时间

rust /rʌst; rʌst/ *noun* 名词 (no plural 无复数)
red-brown stuff that you sometimes see on metal that has been wet 铁锈

rust *verb* 动词 (**rusts**, **rusting**, **rusted**)
become covered with rust 生锈: *My bike rusted because I left it out in the rain.* 我的自行车生锈了，因为我把它放在外边让雨浇了。

rusty *adjective* 形容词 (**rustier**, **rustiest**)
covered with rust 生锈的: *a rusty nail* 生锈的钉子

rustle /ˈrʌsl; ˈrʌsl̩/ *verb* 动词 (**rustles**, **rustling**, **rustled** /ˈrʌsld; ˈrʌsl̩d/)
make a sound like dry leaves moving together; make something make this sound（使某物）发出像干叶子相互摩擦的声音: *Stop rustling your newspaper — I can't hear the film!* 别把报纸弄得沙沙响——我都听不见电影的声音了！

rustle *noun* 名词 (no plural 无复数)
the rustle of leaves 叶子的沙沙声

Ss

sack[1] /sæk; sæk/ *noun* 名词
a big strong bag for carrying heavy things 大口袋（装重东西的用具）: *a sack of potatoes* 一袋马铃薯

sack[2] /sæk; sæk/ *verb* 动词 (**sacks, sacking, sacked** /sækt; sækt/)
say that somebody must leave their job 解雇某人: *The manager sacked her because she was always late.* 因为她总迟到，经理把她解雇了。
sack *noun* 名词 (no plural 无复数)
get the sack lose your job 被解雇
give somebody the sack say that somebody must leave their job 解雇某人

sacred /'seɪkrɪd; 'sekrɪd/ *adjective* 形容词
with a special religious meaning 宗教的；神圣的: *A church is a sacred building.* 教堂是举行宗教活动的处所。

sacrifice /'sækrɪfaɪs; 'sækrəˌfaɪs/ *verb* 动词 (**sacrifices, sacrificing, sacrificed** /'sækrɪfaɪst; 'sækrəˌfaɪst/)
1 kill an animal as a present to a god 宰杀动物祭祀；献祭: *They sacrificed a lamb.* 他们用羊羔祭神。
2 stop doing or having something important so that you can help somebody or to get something else（为助人或为得到某事物）牺牲某事物: *During the war, many people sacrificed their lives for their country.* 在那次战争中有许多人为国捐躯。
sacrifice *noun* 名词
They made a lot of sacrifices to pay for their son to go to university. 他们为供儿子上大学作了很多牺牲。

sad /sæd; sæd/ *adjective* 形容词 (**sadder, saddest**)
1 unhappy 悲哀的；难过的: *The children were very sad when their dog died.* 孩子们因为狗死了而伤心。☞ picture on page C26 见第C26页图
2 that makes you feel unhappy 使人悲哀的或难过的: *a sad story* 让人伤心的事
sadly *adverb* 副词
She looked sadly at the empty house. 她看着空荡荡的房子，心里十分难过。
sadness /'sædnəs; 'sædnɪs/ *noun* 名词 (no plural 无复数)
the feeling of being sad 悲哀；难过

saddle /'sædl; 'sædḷ/ *noun* 名词
a seat on a horse or bicycle（马的）鞍子；（自行车的）车座 ☞ picture at **bicycle** 见 **bicycle** 词条插图

safari /sə'fɑ:ri; sə'fɑrɪ/ *noun* 名词 (*plural* 复数作 **safaris**)
a journey to look at or hunt wild animals, usually in Africa 游猎（通常指在非洲的）

safe[1] /seɪf; sef/ *adjective* 形容词 (**safer, safest**)
1 not in danger; not hurt 不遇到危险的；不受到伤害的；安全的；平安的: *Don't go out alone at night—you won't be safe.* 夜晚不要独自出门——不安全。
2 not dangerous 不造成危险的；安全的: *Is it safe to swim in this river?* 在这条河里游泳安全吗？◇ *Always keep medicines in a safe place.* 药品一定要放在安全的地方。
safe and sound not hurt or broken 没受伤害或没坏；平安无事: *The child was found safe and sound.* 那个孩子平安无事。
safely *adverb* 副词
Phone your parents to tell them you have arrived safely. 给你父母打个电话，告诉他们你平安到达了。

safe[2] /seɪf; sef/ *noun* 名词
a strong metal box with a lock where you keep money or things like jewellery 保险箱

safety /'seɪfti; 'seftɪ/ *noun* 名词 (no plural 无复数)
being safe 安全；平安: *He is worried about the safety of his children.* 他为子女的安全担心。

safety-belt /'seɪfti belt; 'seftɪˌbɛlt/ *noun* 名词
a long thin piece of material that you put round your body in a car or an aeroplane to keep you safe in an accident 安全带（坐汽车或坐飞机时用的）

safety pin /'seɪfti pɪn; 'seftɪ ˌpɪn/ *noun* 名词
a pin that you use for joining things together. It has a cover over the point so that it is not dangerous. 别针

safety pin 别针

S

sag /sæg; sæg/ *verb* 动词 (**sags, sagging, sagged** /sægd; sægd/)
bend or hang down 向下凹或向下陷: *The bed is very old and it sags in the middle.* 这张床很旧，中间已经陷下去了。

said *form of* **say**[1] ＊ **say**[1] 的不同形式

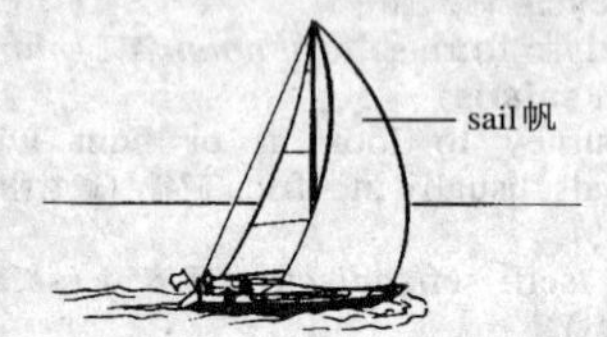

sail[1] /seɪl; sel/ *noun* 名词
a big piece of cloth on a boat. The wind blows against the sail and moves the boat along. 帆

sail[2] /seɪl; sel/ *verb* 动词 (**sails, sailing, sailed** /seɪld; seld/)
1 travel on water 在水中行驶: *The ship sailed along the coast.* 船沿着海岸行驶。
2 control a boat with sails 驾驶帆船: *We sailed the yacht down the river.* 我们在河中驾驶帆船顺流而下。✪ When you talk about spending time sailing a boat, you say **go sailing** 驾驶帆船消遣的说法是 **go sailing**: *We often go sailing on the Thames at weekends.* 我们周末常在泰晤士河上驾驶帆船玩儿。
sailing *noun* 名词 (no plural 无复数)
the sport of controlling a boat with sails 驾驶帆船运动

sailor /ˈseɪlə(r); ˈselɚ/ *noun* 名词
a person who works on a ship 海员；水手

saint /seɪnt; sent/ *noun* 名词
a very good and holy person 圣人；圣徒: *Saint Nicholas* 圣尼古拉 ✪ You usually say /sənt; sent/ before names. 这个字用在名字前一般读作 /sənt; sent/。The short way of writing ‘Saint’ before names is **St** ＊ Saint 用在名字前的缩写形式为 **St**: *St George's church* 圣乔治教堂

sake /seɪk; sek/ *noun* 名词
for the sake of somebody or 或 **something, for somebody's** or 或 **something's sake** to help somebody or something; because of somebody or something 为了某人或某事物；由于某人或某事物的缘故: *Chris and Jackie stayed together for the sake of their children.* 克里斯和杰基是为了他们的孩子才没分手。
✪ You use expressions like **for goodness' sake, for God's sake** and **for Heaven's sake** to show that you are angry 可用 **for goodness' sake**、**for God's sake**、**for Heaven's sake** 等词语表示气愤: *For goodness' sake, be quiet!* 天哪，安静点儿吧！

salad /ˈsæləd; ˈsæləd/ *noun* 名词
a dish of cold, usually raw vegetables 色拉；凉拌菜: *Do you want chips or salad with your chicken?* 您这盘鸡肉里要配炸土豆条儿还是配色拉？

salary /ˈsæləri; ˈsælərɪ/ *noun* 名词 (*plural* 复数作 **salaries**)
money that you receive every month for the work that you do（按月领的）薪金；薪水

sale /seɪl; sel/ *noun* 名词
1 (no plural 无复数) selling something 卖；出售
2 (*plural* 复数作 **sales**) a time when a shop sells things for less money than usual（商店的）减价（出售货物期间）: *In the sale, everything is half-price.* 在大减价的时候，所有物品都半价出售。
for sale If something is for sale, its owner wants to sell it 待售: *Is this house for sale?* 这所房子卖吗？
on sale If something is on sale, you can buy it in shops 在商店出售: *The magazine is on sale at most newsagents.* 这份杂志在大多数报刊经销店里都有卖的。

salesclerk /ˈseɪlzklɜ:rk; ˈselzˌklɝk/ *American English for* **shop assistant** 美式英语，即 **shop assistant**

salesman /ˈseɪlzmən; ˈselzmən/ *noun* 名词 (*plural* 复数作 **salesmen** /ˈseɪlzmən; ˈselzmən/), **saleswoman** /ˈseɪlzwʊmən; ˈselzˌwʊmən/ (*plural* 复数作 **saleswomen**), **salesperson** /ˈseɪlzpɜ:sn; ˈselzˌpɝsn/ (*plural* 复数作 **salespeople**)
a person whose job is selling things 售货员；推销员

salmon /ˈsæmən; ˈsæmən/ *noun* 名词 (*plural* 复数作 **salmon**)
a big fish that lives in the sea and in rivers and that you can eat 鲑；大马哈鱼

salt /sɔ:lt; sɔlt/ *noun* 名词 (no plural 无复数)
white stuff that comes from sea water and from the earth. We put it on food to

make it taste better 盐: *Add a little salt and pepper.* 加点儿盐和胡椒粉。

salty *adjective* 形容词 (**saltier, saltiest**)
with salt in it 含盐的；咸的: *Sea water is salty.* 海水是咸的。

salute /sə'lu:t; sə'lut/ *verb* 动词 (**salutes, saluting, saluted**)
make the special sign that soldiers make, by lifting your hand to your head (指军人) 敬礼；行举手礼: *The soldiers saluted as the Queen walked past.* 女王走过时，士兵行礼致敬。

salute *noun* 名词
The soldier gave a salute. 士兵敬了个礼。

same /seɪm; sem/ *adjective* 形容词
the same not different; not another 同一的: *Emma and I like the same kind of music.* 我跟埃玛都喜欢同一种音乐。◇ *I've lived in the same town all my life.* 我一辈子都住在一个镇子上。◇ *He went to the same school as me.* 他和我在同一所学校上学。

same *pronoun* 代词
all or 或 **just the same** anyway 尽管如此；仍然: *I understand why you're angry. All the same, I think you should say sorry.* 我理解你为什么生气。即便这样，我认为你还是应该陪个不是。
same to you words that you use for saying to somebody what they have said to you 用对方说的话反过来回答对方: *'Have a good weekend.' 'Same to you.'* "祝你周末愉快。" "也祝你周末愉快。"
the same not a different person or thing 同样的人或事物: *Do these two words mean the same?* 这两个词意思一样吗？◇ *Your watch is the same as mine.* 您的手表跟我的一样。

sample /'sɑ:mpl; 'sæmpḷ/ *noun* 名词
a small amount of something that shows what the rest is like 样品；货样；标本: *a free sample of perfume* 免费的香水样品 ◇ *a blood sample* 血样

sand /sænd; sænd/ *noun* 名词 (no plural 无复数)
powder made of very small pieces of rock, that you find next to the sea and in deserts 沙子

sandy *adjective* 形容词 (**sandier, sandiest**)
with sand 有沙子的: *a sandy beach* 沙滩

sandal /'sændl; 'sændḷ/ *noun* 名词
a light open shoe that you wear in warm weather 凉鞋

sandals 凉鞋

sandwich /'sænwɪdʒ; 'sænwɪtʃ/ *noun* 名词 (*plural* 复数作 **sandwiches**)
two pieces of bread with other food between them 三明治；夹心面包片: *a cheese sandwich* 干酪三明治

sane /seɪn; sen/ *adjective* 形容词 (**saner, sanest**)
with a normal healthy mind; not mad 心智健全的；神志正常的 ✪ opposite 反义词: **insane**

sang *form of* **sing** ✳ **sing** 的不同形式

sank *form of* **sink²** ✳ **sink²** 的不同形式

Santa Claus /'sæntə klɔ:z; 'sæntə ˌklɔz/ *another word for* **Father Christmas** ✳ **Father Christmas** 的另一种说法

sarcastic /sɑ:'kæstɪk; sɑr'kæstɪk/ *adjective* 形容词
If you are sarcastic, you say the opposite of what you mean, in an unkind way. 讽刺的；挖苦的

sardine /sɑ:'di:n; sɑr'din/ *noun* 名词
a very small fish that you can eat. You often buy sardines in tins. 沙丁鱼（通常制成罐头）

sari /'sɑ:ri; 'sɑri/ *noun* 名词 (*plural* 复数作 **saris**)
a long piece of material that Indian women wear around their bodies as a dress 莎丽（印度女子裹在身上的长条布，用作外衣）

sat *form of* **sit** ✳ **sit** 的不同形式

satchel /'sætʃəl; 'sætʃəl/ *noun* 名词
a bag that children use for carrying books to and from school 书包

satellite /'sætəlaɪt; 'sætḷˌaɪt/ *noun* 名词
1 a thing in space that moves round a planet 卫星: *The moon is a satellite of the earth.* 月球是地球的卫星。
2 a thing that people have sent into space. Satellites travel round the earth and send back pictures or television and radio signals 人造卫星: *satellite television* 卫星电视

satin /'sætɪn; 'sætṇ/ *noun* 名词 (no plural 无复数)
very shiny smooth cloth 缎子

satisfaction /ˌsætɪsˈfækʃn; ˌsætɪsˈfækʃən/ *noun* 名词 (no plural 无复数)
being pleased with what you or other people have done 满意；满足：*She finished painting the picture and looked at it with satisfaction.* 她画完了那张画儿，看了看觉得很满意。

satisfactory /ˌsætɪsˈfæktəri; ˌsætɪsˈfæktərɪ/ *adjective* 形容词
good enough, but not very good 够好的（但不十分好）；尚可的：*Her work is not satisfactory.* 她的工作不那么好。✪ opposite 反义词：**unsatisfactory**

satisfy /ˈsætɪsfaɪ; ˈsætɪsˌfaɪ/ *verb* 动词 (**satisfies**, **satisfying**, **satisfied** /ˈsætɪsfaɪd; ˈsætɪsˌfaɪd/, **has satisfied**)
give somebody what they want or need; be good enough to make somebody pleased 使某人满意或满足：*Nothing he does satisfies his father.* 他做什么事他父亲都不满意。

satisfied *adjective* 形容词
pleased because you have had or done what you wanted 满意的；满足的：*The teacher was not satisfied with my work.* 老师对我的功课很不满意。

satisfying *adjective* 形容词
Something that is satisfying makes you pleased because it is what you want 使人满意或满足的：*a satisfying result* 让人满意的结果

Saturday /ˈsætədeɪ; ˈsætədɪ/ *noun* 名词
the seventh day of the week, next after Friday 星期六

sauce /sɔːs; sɔs/ *noun* 名词
a thick liquid that you eat on or with other food 沙司；调味汁；酱：*tomato sauce* 番茄酱

saucepan /ˈsɔːspən; ˈsɔsˌpæn/ *noun* 名词
a round metal container for cooking 锅（通常指有盖及柄的）

saucepan 锅

saucer /ˈsɔːsə(r); ˈsɔsɚ/ *noun* 名词
a small round plate that you put under a cup 茶托；茶杯碟 ☞ picture at **cup** 见 **cup** 词条插图

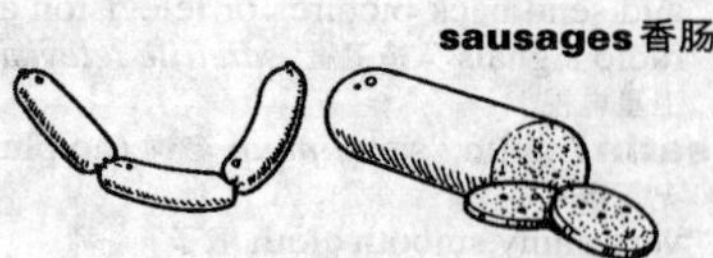
sausages 香肠

sausage /ˈsɒsɪdʒ; ˈsɔsɪdʒ/ *noun* 名词
meat that is cut into very small pieces and made into a long, thin shape 香肠：*garlic sausage* 蒜味香肠 ◇ *sausages and chips* 香肠和炸土豆条儿

savage /ˈsævɪdʒ; ˈsævɪdʒ/ *adjective* 形容词
wild or fierce 野性的；凶猛的：*a savage attack by a large dog* 凶猛的大狗的攻击

save /seɪv; sev/ *verb* 动词 (**saves**, **saving**, **saved** /seɪvd; sevd/)
1 take somebody or something away from danger 救；拯救；抢救：*He saved me from the fire.* 他把我从大火中救出。◇ *The doctor saved her life.* 医生救了她的命。
2 keep something, especially money, to use later 储蓄；（尤指）存钱：*I've saved enough money to buy a car.* 我已经存够了买汽车的钱。◇ *Save some of the meat for tomorrow.* 留下点儿肉明天吃。
3 use less of something 节省某物：*She saves money by making her own clothes.* 她自己做衣服省下些钱。
4 stop somebody from scoring a goal, for example in football 阻止某人射门得分（例如足球比赛中）；救球
save up for something keep money to buy something later 存钱买某物：*I'm saving up for a new bike.* 我正攒钱买新自行车呢。

savings /ˈseɪvɪŋz; ˈsevɪŋz/ *noun* 名词 (plural 复数)
money that you are keeping to use later 储蓄金；存款；积蓄：*I keep my savings in the bank.* 我把储蓄的钱存在银行里了。

saw[1] *form of* **see** ＊ **see** 的不同形式

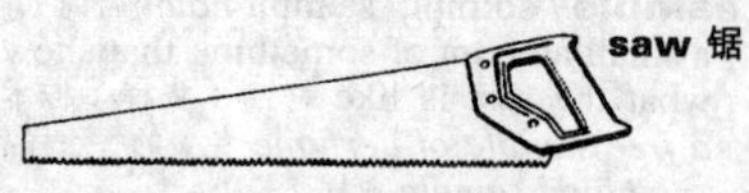
saw 锯

saw[2] /sɔː; sɔ/ *noun* 名词
a metal tool for cutting wood 锯
saw *verb* 动词 (**saws**, **sawing**, **sawed** /sɔːd; sɔd/, **has sawn** /sɔːn; sɔn/)
She sawed a branch off the tree. 她锯下了一截树枝。

sawdust /ˈsɔːdʌst; ˈsɔˌdʌst/ *noun* 名词 (no plural 无复数)
powder that falls when you saw wood 锯末

saxophone 萨克管

saxophone /ˈsæksəfəʊn; ˈsæksəˌfon/ *noun* 名词
a musical instrument made of metal that you play by blowing into it 萨克管

say¹ /seɪ; se/ *verb* 动词 (**says** /sez; sɛz/, **saying**, **said** /sed; sɛd/, **has said**)
1 make words with your mouth 用嘴表达意思；说: *You say 'please' when you ask for something.* 表示请求的时候要说"请"字。◇ *'This is my room,' he said.* "这是我的屋子，"他说。◇ *She said that she was cold.* 她说她冷。

> **say** or **tell**? 用 **say** 还是用 **tell**？
>
> **Say** and **tell** are not used in the same way. ＊ **say** 和 **tell** 的使用方法不同。Look at these sentences 请看以下例句:
>
> *Jo **said** 'I'm ready.'* 乔说："我准备好了。"
>
> *Jo **said** (that) she was ready.* 乔说她准备好了。
>
> *Jo **said** to me that she was ready.* 乔对我说她准备好了。
>
> *Jo **told** me (that) she was ready.* 乔告诉我说她准备好了。
>
> *Jo **told** me to close the door.* 乔让我把门关上。

2 give information 表达信息: *The notice on the door said 'Private'.* 门上的告示上写着"私用房间"。◇ *The clock says half past three.* 时钟显示着时间是三点半。
that is to say what I mean is … 也就是说…；我的意思是…：*I'll see you in a week, that's to say next Monday.* 我一个星期后见你，也就是下星期一。

say² /seɪ; se/ *noun* 名词
have a say have the right to help decide something（对某事）有协助做决定的权利: *I would like to have a say in who we invite to the party.* 咱们要请谁来参加聚会，我希望我的意见也能算数。

saying /ˈseɪɪŋ; ˈseɪŋ/ *noun* 名词
a sentence that people often say, that gives advice about something 谚语；格言；俗话: *'Look before you leap' is an old saying.* "三思而后行"是句古谚。

scab /skæb; skæb/ *noun* 名词
a hard covering that grows over your skin where it is cut or broken 痂

scaffolding /ˈskæfəldɪŋ; ˈskæfḷdɪŋ/ *noun* 名词 (no plural 无复数)
metal bars and pieces of wood joined together, where people like painters and builders can stand when they are working on high parts of a building 脚手架；施工架

scald /skɔːld; skɔld/ *verb* 动词 (**scalds**, **scalding**, **scalded**)
burn somebody or something with very hot liquid 液体烫伤某人或某物

scale /skeɪl; skel/ *noun* 名词
1 a set of marks on something for measuring 标度；刻度: *This ruler has one scale in centimetres and one scale in inches.* 这把尺上有厘米的刻度和英寸的刻度。
2 how distances are shown on a map 比例尺；比例；比率: *This map has a scale of one centimetre to ten kilometres.* 这张地图的比例是一厘米比十公里。
3 one of the flat hard things that cover the body of animals like fish and snakes 鳞；鳞片（鱼和蛇等动物身上的）

scales /skeɪlz; skelz/ *noun* 名词 (plural 复数)
a machine for showing how heavy people or things are 天平；台秤；磅秤

scales 台秤

scalp /skælp; skælp/ *noun* 名词
the skin on the top of your head, under your hair 头皮（头顶上的皮肤）

scan /skæn; skæn/ *verb* 动词 (**scans**, **scanning**, **scanned** /skænd; skænd/)
1 look carefully because you are trying to find something（为找某物）细看；仔细检查: *They scanned the sea, looking for a boat.* 他们仔细巡视海面，寻找一艘船。

S

2 read something quickly 匆匆阅读某段文字: *Jenny scanned the list until she found her name.* 珍妮粗略地看了看名单，很快就找到了自己的名字。

scanner *noun* 名词
a machine that gives a picture of the inside of something. Doctors use one kind of scanner to look inside people's bodies. 扫描器（医生用一种扫描器可检查人体内部）

scandal /'skændl; 'skændḷ/ *noun* 名词
1 (*plural* 复数作 **scandals**) something that makes a lot of people talk about it, perhaps in an angry way 大家谈论的（也许引起公愤的）事情；丑事；丑闻: *There was a big scandal when the Prince decided to get married again.* 王子决定再婚，一时满城风雨。
2 (no plural 无复数) unkind talk about somebody that gives you a bad idea of them 流言蜚语；闲话

S

scar /skɑ:(r); skɑr/ *noun* 名词
a mark on your skin, that an old cut has left 伤痕；疤

scar *verb* 动词 (**scars**, **scarring**, **scarred** /skɑ:d; skɑrd/)
make a scar on skin 留下伤痕或疤: *His face was badly scarred by the accident.* 他出事以后脸上留下很多疤。

scarce /skeəs; skɛrs/ *adjective* 形容词 (**scarcer**, **scarcest**)
difficult to find; not enough 罕见的；不足的: *Food for birds and animals is scarce in the winter.* 冬天鸟兽的食物很少。

scarcely /'skeəsli; 'skɛrslɪ/ *adverb* 副词
almost not; only just 几乎不；仅仅: *He was so frightened that he could scarcely speak.* 他吓得几乎说不出话来。

scare /skeə(r); skɛr/ *verb* 动词 (**scares**, **scaring**, **scared** /skeəd; skɛrd/)
make somebody frightened 使某人害怕；吓: *That noise scared me!* 那响声把我吓坏了！

scare *noun* 名词
a feeling of being frightened 惊恐；恐慌: *You gave me a scare!* 你吓了我一跳！

scared *adjective* 形容词
frightened 受惊吓的；感到害怕的: *Claire is scared of the dark.* 克莱尔很怕黑。

scarecrow /'skeəkrəʊ; 'skɛrˌkro/ *noun* 名词
a thing that looks like a person, that farmers put in their fields to frighten birds 稻草人（农民用以吓走鸟的）

scarves 围巾或头巾

scarf /skɑ:f; skɑrf/ *noun* 名词 (*plural* 复数作 **scarves** /skɑ:vz; skɑrvz/)
a piece of material that you wear around your neck or head 围巾；头巾

scarlet /'skɑ:lət; 'skɑrlət/ *adjective* 形容词
with a bright red colour 猩红的；鲜红的

scatter /'skætə(r); 'skætɚ/ *verb* 动词 (**scatters**, **scattering**, **scattered** /'skætəd; 'skætɚd/)
1 move quickly in different directions 迅速散开: *The crowd scattered when it started to rain.* 雨一下起来，大家就都散了。
2 throw things so that they fall in a lot of different places 撒；散布: *She scattered the pieces of bread on the grass for the birds.* 她往草地上撒了些碎面包喂鸟。

scene /si:n; sin/ *noun* 名词
1 a place where something happened 事发地点: *The police arrived at the scene of the crime.* 警方来到了案发现场。
2 what you see in a place; a view 情景；景色: *He painted scenes of life in the countryside.* 他画的是郊野的写生画儿。
3 part of a play or film（戏剧或影片中的）场，场面，片段: *Act 1, Scene 2 of 'Hamlet'* 《哈姆雷特》第一幕第二场

scenery /'si:nəri; 'sinərɪ/ *noun* 名词 (no plural 无复数)
1 the things like mountains, rivers and forests that you see around you in the countryside（郊野山水、树木等的）景象；风景: *What beautiful scenery!* 风景多漂亮啊！
2 things on the stage of a theatre that make it look like a real place（舞台上的）场景，布景

scent /sent; sɛnt/ *noun* 名词
1 (*plural* 复数作 **scents**) a smell 鼻子可以闻到的味儿；气味: *This flower has no scent.* 这种花没有味儿。

2 (no plural 无复数) a liquid with a nice smell, that you put on your body 香水: *a bottle of scent* 一瓶香水

scented *adjective* 形容词
with a nice smell 有香味的: *scented soap* 香皂

schedule /ˈʃedjuːl; ˈskɛdʒʊl/ *noun* 名词
a plan or list of times when things will happen or be done 计划表；进度表: *I've got a busy schedule next week.* 我下星期的事情安排得很满。

behind schedule late 比预定计划晚: *We're behind schedule with the work.* 我们未能按时完成工作计划。

on schedule with everything happening at the right time 按计划中的进度: *We are on schedule to finish the work in May.* 我们按计划于五月份完成工作。

scheme /skiːm; skim/ *noun* 名词
a plan 计划；方案: *a scheme to build more houses* 多建房屋的计划

scholar /ˈskɒlə(r); ˈskɑlɚ/ *noun* 名词
a person who has learned a lot about something 学者: *a famous history scholar* 研究历史的著名学者

scholarship /ˈskɒləʃɪp; ˈskɑlɚˌʃɪp/ *noun* 名词
money that is given to a good student to help him/her to continue studying 奖学金: *Adrian won a scholarship to Cambridge.* 阿德里安荣获剑桥大学的奖学金。

school /skuːl; skul/ *noun* 名词
1 (*plural* 复数作 **schools**) a place where children go to learn（小学或中学的）学校: *Lucy is at school.* 露西正在学校。◇ *Which school do you go to?* 你上的是哪所中学？
2 (no plural 无复数) being at school 上小学或中学: *I hate school!* 我讨厌上学！◇ *He left school when he was 16.* 他16岁时中学毕业。◇ *School starts at nine o'clock.* 九点钟上课。
3 (*plural* 复数作 **schools**) a place where you go to learn a special thing（专科的）学校: *a language school* 语言学校

schoolboy /ˈskuːlbɔɪ; ˈskulˌbɔɪ/, **schoolgirl** /ˈskuːlgɜːl; ˈskulˌgɝl/, **schoolchild** /ˈskuːltʃaɪld; ˈskulˌtʃaɪld/ (*plural* 复数作 **schoolchildren**) *noun* 名词
a boy or girl who goes to school（中小学的）学生

school-days /ˈskuːldeɪz; ˈskulˌdez/ *noun* 名词 (plural 复数)
the time in your life when you are at school（中小学的）学生时代

☞ Look at **nursery school**, **primary school**, **junior school**, **middle school**, **secondary school**, **grammar school** and **comprehensive school** to find out more about schools in Britain. 参看 **nursery school**、**primary school**、**junior school**、**middle school**、**secondary school**、**grammar school**、**comprehensive school**，可对英国的学校有进一步的了解。You must pay to go to a **private school** or a **public school**. 在私立学校（**private school**）或公学（**public school**）上学须付学费。A **boarding-school** is a school where the pupils live. 寄宿学校叫做 **boarding-school**。When you leave school, you may go to a **college** or **university**. 中学毕业可升读学院（**college**）或大学（**university**）。

science /ˈsaɪəns; ˈsaɪəns/ *noun* 名词
the study of natural things 科学；自然科学；理科: *I'm interested in science.* 我喜欢自然科学。◇ *Biology, chemistry and physics are all sciences.* 生物、化学、物理都属于理科。

science fiction /ˌsaɪəns ˈfɪkʃn; ˈsaɪəns ˈfɪkʃən/ *noun* 名词 (no plural 无复数)
stories about things like travel in space, life on other planets or life in the future 科学幻想小说

scientific /ˌsaɪənˈtɪfɪk; ˌsaɪənˈtɪfɪk/ *adjective* 形容词
of or about science 科学的；自然科学的；理科的: *a scientific experiment* 科学实验

scientist /ˈsaɪəntɪst; ˈsaɪəntɪst/ *noun* 名词
a person who studies science or works with science 研究自然科学的人；自然科学家

scissors /ˈsɪzəz; ˈsɪzɚz/ *noun* 名词 (plural 复数)
a tool for cutting that has two sharp parts that are joined together 剪刀；剪子: *These scissors aren't very sharp.* 这把剪子不快。✪ Be careful! You cannot say 'a scissors'. 注意！不可说 a scissors。

S

scissors 剪刀

You can say a **pair of scissors** 可以说 a **pair of scissors**: *I need a pair of scissors.* 我需要一把剪子。(or 也可作: *I need some scissors.*)

scoop /sku:p; skup/ *verb* 动词 (**scoops, scooping, scooped** /sku:pt; skupt/)
use a spoon or your hands to take something up or out（用勺或双手）铲起；舀出: *I scooped some ice-cream out of the bowl.* 我从小桶里舀出些冰激凌来。

scooter /'sku:tə(r); 'skutɚ/ *noun* 名词
a light motor cycle with a small engine 小型摩托车

S

score /skɔ:(r); skɔr/ *noun* 名词
the number of points, goals, etc that you win in a game or competition（比赛中得的）分数: *The winner got a score of 320.* 优胜者获得320分。

score *verb* 动词 (**scores, scoring, scored** /skɔ:d; skɔrd/)
win a point in a game or competition（在比赛中）得分: *Italy scored three goals against France.* 意大利队以三分战胜法国队。

scorn /skɔ:n; skɔrn/ *noun* 名词 (no plural 无复数)
the strong feeling you have when you think that somebody or something is not good enough 鄙视；轻蔑: *He was full of scorn for my idea.* 他十分看不起我的主意。

Scout /skaʊt; skaut/ = **Boy Scout**

scramble /'skræmbl; 'skræmbl̩/ *verb* 动词 (**scrambles, scrambling, scrambled** /'skræmbld; 'skræmbl̩d/)
move quickly up or over something, using your hands to help you 爬上或爬过；攀登: *They scrambled over the wall.* 他们爬过了墙。

scrambled eggs /ˌskræmbld 'egz; ˌskræmbl̩d 'ɛgz/ *noun* 名词 (plural 复数)
eggs that you mix together with milk and cook in a pan with butter（加牛奶和黄油的）炒鸡蛋

scrap /skræp; skræp/ *noun* 名词
1 (*plural* 复数作 **scraps**) a small piece of something 碎片；碎屑；小块: *a scrap of paper.* 一片纸
2 (no plural 无复数) something you do not want any more but that is made of material that can be used again（仍有利用价值的）废材料: *scrap paper* 便条纸（废纸利用）

scrape /skreɪp; skrep/ *verb* 动词 (**scrapes, scraping, scraped** /skreɪpt; skrept/)
1 move a rough or sharp thing across something 擦；削；磨: *I scraped the mud off my shoes with a knife.* 我用刀把我鞋上的泥刮掉了。
2 hurt or damage something by moving it against a rough or sharp thing 擦伤；刮坏: *I fell and scraped my knee on the wall.* 我跌倒时碰到墙把膝盖擦破了。

scratch[1] /skrætʃ; skrætʃ/ *verb* 动词 (**scratches, scratching, scratched** /skrætʃt; skrætʃt/)
1 cut or make a mark on something with a sharp thing 刮破；划开；抓坏: *The cat scratched me!* 猫把我抓破了！
2 move your fingernails across your skin 挠皮肤；搔痒: *She scratched her head.* 她挠了挠头。

scratch[2] /skrætʃ; skrætʃ/ *noun* 名词 (*plural* 复数作 **scratches**)
a cut or mark that a sharp thing makes（刮、划、抓的）伤或痕: *Her hands were covered in scratches from the rose bush.* 她的手让那株玫瑰刮伤多处。
from scratch from the beginning 从头开始: *I threw away the letter I was writing and started again from scratch.* 我把正写着的信给扔了，又重新写一封。

scream /skri:m; skrim/ *verb* 动词 (**screams, screaming, screamed** /skri:md; skrimd/)
make a loud high cry that shows you are afraid or hurt 尖声喊叫: *She saw the snake and screamed.* 她看见了蛇就尖叫起来。◇ *He screamed for help.* 他高声叫喊救命。

scream *noun* 名词
a loud high cry 尖声的喊叫: *a scream of pain* 疼痛的叫喊声

screech /skri:tʃ; skritʃ/ *verb* 动词 (**screeches, screeching, screeched** /skri:tʃt; skritʃt/)
make a loud high sound 发出尖厉的声音:

The car's brakes screeched as it stopped suddenly. 汽车突然停住，刹车发出刺耳的声音。

screen /skri:n; skrin/ *noun* 名词
1 the flat square part of a television or computer where you see pictures or words（电视机或计算机的）荧屏；屏幕 ☞ picture at **computer** 见 **computer** 词条插图
2 the flat thing on the wall of a cinema, where you see films 银幕
3 a kind of thin wall that you can move around. Screens are used to keep away cold, light, etc or to stop people from seeing something 屏风；帘；帐：*The nurse put a screen around the bed.* 护士在床的四周围上了屏风。

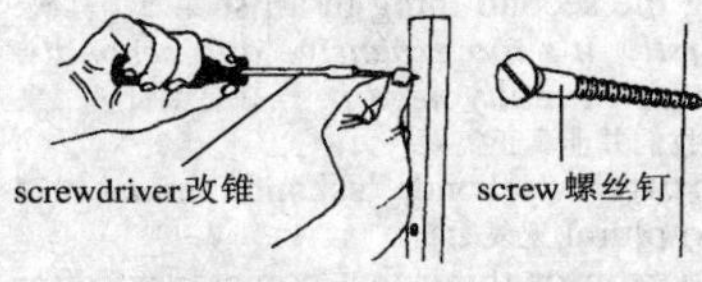

screw /skru:; skru/ *noun* 名词
a small metal thing with a sharp end, that you use for fixing things together. You push it into something by turning it with a **screwdriver**. 螺丝钉；螺钉（改锥叫做 **screwdriver**）
screw *verb* 动词 (**screws**, **screwing**, **screwed** /skru:d; skrud/)
1 fix something to another thing using a screw 用螺丝钉把一物固定到另一物上
2 turn something to fix it to another thing 把一物拧到另一物上: *Screw the lid on the jar.* 把盖儿拧到罐子上。✪ opposite 反义词: **unscrew**
screw up make paper or material into a ball with your hand 把纸或其他材料揉成团: *He screwed up the letter and threw it in the bin.* 他把信揉成团扔进垃圾箱里去了。

screwdriver /ˈskru:draɪvə(r); ˈskru-ˌdraɪvɚ/ *noun* 名词
a tool for turning screws 改锥；螺丝刀

scribble /ˈskrɪbl; ˈskrɪbḷ/ *verb* 动词 (**scribbles**, **scribbling**, **scribbled** /ˈskrɪbld; ˈskrɪbḷd/)
write something or make marks on paper quickly and without care 匆匆地胡乱写或画: *The children scribbled in my book.* 孩子们在我的书上乱写乱画。

script /skrɪpt; skrɪpt/ *noun* 名词
the written words that actors speak in a play or film（戏剧或电影的）脚本

scrub /skrʌb; skrʌb/ *verb* 动词 (**scrubs**, **scrubbing**, **scrubbed** /skrʌbd; skrʌbd/)
rub something hard to clean it, usually with a brush and soap and water 用力刷洗某物: *He scrubbed the floor.* 他把地板刷了。

scruffy /ˈskrʌfi; ˈskrʌfɪ/ *adjective* 形容词 (**scruffier**, **scruffiest**)
untidy and perhaps dirty 不整齐而且也许不清洁的；邋遢的: *She was wearing scruffy jeans.* 她穿着一条邋遢的牛仔裤。

sculptor /ˈskʌlptə(r); ˈskʌlptɚ/ *noun* 名词
a person who makes shapes from things like stone or wood 做雕塑的人

sculpture /ˈskʌlptʃə(r); ˈskʌlptʃɚ/ *noun* 名词
1 (no plural 无复数) making shapes from things like stone or wood 雕塑
2 (*plural* 复数作 **sculptures**) a shape made from things like stone or wood 雕塑品

sea /si:; si/ *noun* 名词
1 (no plural 无复数) the salty water that covers large parts of the earth 海；海洋: *We went for a swim in the sea.* 我们到海里游泳去了。◇ *The sea is very rough today.* 今天海面风浪很大。
2 (*plural* 复数作 **seas**) a big area of salty water（某处的）海: *the Black Sea* 黑海
at sea travelling on the sea 航海: *We spent three weeks at sea.* 我们在海上航行了三个星期。

seafood /ˈsi:fu:d; ˈsiˌfud/ *noun* 名词 (no plural 无复数)
fish and small animals from the sea that you can eat 海味

seagull /ˈsi:gʌl; ˈsiˌgʌl/ *noun* 名词
a big grey or white bird with a loud cry, that lives near the sea 海鸥

seal[1] /si:l; sil/ *noun* 名词
an animal with short fur that lives in and near the sea, and that eats fish 海豹

seal[2] /si:l; sil/ *verb* 动词 (**seals**, **sealing**, **sealed** /si:ld; sild/)
close something tightly by sticking two parts together 把两部分粘合以封住某物: *She sealed the envelope.* 她把信封封上了。

seam /si:m; sim/ *noun* 名词
a line where two pieces of cloth are joined together（两块布接合的）缝

search /sɜ:tʃ; sɝtʃ/ *verb* 动词 (**searches**, **searching**, **searched** /sɜ:tʃt; sɝtʃt/)
look carefully because you are trying to find somebody or something 搜查或细查某人或某物: *I searched everywhere for my pen.* 我到处寻找我的钢笔。

search *noun* 名词 (*plural* 复数作 **searches**)
I found my key after a long search. 我找了半天才找到我的钥匙。

in search of somebody or 或 **something** looking for somebody or something 寻找某人或某物: *We drove round the town in search of a cheap hotel.* 我们为找个便宜旅馆开着车跑遍了全城。

sea shell /'si: ʃel; 'si ˌʃɛl/ *noun* 名词
the hard outside part of a small animal that lives in the sea 海贝壳

sea shells 海贝壳

seashore /'si:ʃɔ:(r); 'siˌʃor/ *noun* 名词 (no plural 无复数)
the land next to the sea; the beach 海岸；海滨

seasick /'si:sɪk; 'siˌsɪk/ *adjective* 形容词
If you are seasick, you feel ill in your stomach because the boat you are on is moving a lot. 晕船的

seaside /'si:saɪd; 'siˌsaɪd/ *noun* 名词 (no plural 无复数)
a place by the sea where people go on holiday（作度假去处的）海边，海滨: *Let's go to the seaside.* 咱们到海边去吧。

season /'si:zn; 'sizn̩/ *noun* 名词
1 one of the four parts of the year. The four seasons are **spring**, **summer**, **autumn** and **winter**. 季；季节（四季的名称是春 **spring**、夏 **summer**、秋 **autumn**、冬 **winter**。）
2 a special time of the year for something 一年中有某事物的时期: *The football season starts in August.* 从八月份就开始进入足球联赛期。

seat /si:t; sit/ *noun* 名词
something that you sit on 座位: *the back seat of a car* 汽车的后排座位 ◇ *We had seats at the front of the theatre.* 我们的座位在戏院的前排。

take a seat sit down 坐下: *Please take a seat.* 请坐。

seat-belt /'si:t belt; 'sitˌbɛlt/ *noun* 名词
a long thin piece of material that you put round your body in a car or an aeroplane to keep you safe in an accident（汽车或飞机的）座位安全带

seaweed /'si:wi:d; 'siˌwid/ *noun* 名词 (no plural 无复数)
a plant that grows in the sea 海藻；海草

second[1] /'sekənd; 'sɛkənd/ *adjective*, *adverb* 形容词，副词
next after first 第二（的）: *February is the second month of the year.* 二月是一年里的第二个月。

secondly *adverb* 副词
a word that you use when you are giving the second thing in a list 第二；其次: *Firstly, it's too expensive and secondly, we don't really need it.* 一来是太贵，二来是我们并非真正需要。

second[2] /'sekənd; 'sɛkənd/ *noun* 名词 (no plural 无复数)
a person or thing that comes next after the first 第二个人或事物: *Today is the second of April* (*April 2nd*). 今天是四月二日。◇ *I was the first to arrive, and Jim was the second.* 我是第一个到的，吉姆是第二个到的。

second[3] /'sekənd; 'sɛkənd/ *noun* 名词
1 a measure of time. There are 60 seconds in a **minute**. 秒（时间的计量单位。60秒等于1分钟，分叫做 **minute**。）
2 a very short time 很短的时间；一会儿: *Wait a second!* 等一会儿！◇ *I'll be ready in a second.* 我马上就准备好了。

secondary school /'sekəndri sku:l; 'sɛkəndɛrɪ ˌskul/ *noun* 名词
a school for pupils between the ages of 11 and 18 中学（为11岁至18岁的学生而设的）

second class /ˌsekənd 'klɑ:s; 'sɛkənd 'klæs/ *noun* 名词 (no plural 无复数)
1 the part of a train, plane, etc that it is cheaper to travel in（火车、飞机等的）二等座位: *We sat in second class.* 我们坐的是二等座位。
2 the cheapest but the slowest way of sending letters 二等邮件（最便宜但最慢的）

second-class *adjective*, *adverb* 形容词，副词
a second-class ticket 二等票 ◇ *I sent the letter second-class.* 我是按二等邮件寄的信。

☞ Look at **first class** and at the Note at **stamp**. 见 **first class** 及 **stamp** 词条注释。

second-hand /ˌsekənd 'hænd; 'sɛkənd'hænd/ *adjective, adverb* 形容词，副词
not new; used by another person before 二手（的）；别人用过（的）: *second-hand books* 旧书 ◇ *I bought this car second-hand.* 我买的这辆汽车是二手货。

secrecy /'si:krəsi; 'sikrəsɪ/ *noun* 名词 (no plural 无复数)
not telling other people 保密: *They worked in secrecy.* 他们的工作是保密的。

secret[1] /'si:krət; 'sikrɪt/ *adjective* 形容词
If something is secret, other people do not or must not know about it 秘密的；保密的；机密的: *They kept their wedding secret* (= they did not tell anybody about it). 他们的婚礼是秘密举行的。◇ *a secret meeting* 秘密的会议
secretly *adverb* 副词
without other people knowing 秘密地；保密: *We are secretly planning a big party for her.* 我们正偷偷为她准备一个盛大的聚会。

secret[2] /'si:krət; 'sikrɪt/ *noun* 名词
something that you do not or must not tell other people 秘密；机密: *I can't tell you where I'm going—it's a secret.* 我不能告诉你我到哪儿去——这是秘密。
in secret without other people knowing 秘密的；保密: *They met in secret.* 他们秘密会晤。
keep a secret not tell other people a secret 保密: *Can you keep a secret?* 你能保守秘密吗？

secretary /'sekrətri; 'sɛkrəˌtɛrɪ/ *noun* 名词 (*plural* 复数作 **secretaries**)
1 a person who types letters, answers the telephone and does other things in an office 秘书
2 an important person in the government 大臣；部长: *the Secretary of State for Education* 教育大臣
3 *American English for* **minister 1** 美式英语，即 **minister 1**
secretarial /ˌsekrə'teəriəl; ˌsɛkrə'tɛrɪəl/ *adjective* 形容词
of or about the work of a secretary 秘书的；大臣的；部长的: *a secretarial college* 秘书学院

secretive /'si:krətɪv; 'sikrətɪv/ *adjective* 形容词
If you are secretive, you do not like to tell other people about yourself or your plans 不愿把自己的事告诉别人；爱保密的: *Mark is very secretive about his job.* 马克对自己的工作讳莫如深。

section /'sekʃn; 'sɛkʃən/ *noun* 名词
one of the parts of something 部分: *This section of the road is closed.* 这条路的这一段已经封闭了。

secure /sɪ'kjʊə(r); sɪ'kjʊr/ *adjective* 形容词
1 safe 安全的；稳妥可靠的: *Don't climb that ladder—it's not very secure* (= it may fall). 别爬那个梯子——不稳（= 可能倒）。◇ *Her job is secure* (= she will not lose it). 她的工作很保险（= 她不会失去这份工作）。
2 If you are secure, you feel safe and you are not worried 无忧虑的: *Do you feel secure about the future?* 你对前途担心不担心？ ✪ opposite 反义词: **insecure**
3 well locked or protected so that nobody can go in or out 锁住的或受保护的（无人能出入）: *This gate isn't very secure.* 这个大门不太管用。
securely *adverb* 副词
Are all the windows securely closed? 那些窗户都关好了吗？

security /sɪ'kjʊərəti; sɪ'kjʊrətɪ/ *noun* 名词 (no plural 无复数)
1 the feeling of being safe 安全感: *Children need love and security.* 儿童需要疼爱，需要有安全感。
2 things that you do to keep a place safe 安全措施: *We need better security at airports.* 我们需要在机场加强保卫工作。

see /si:; si/ *verb* 动词 (**sees, seeing, saw** /sɔ:; sɔ/, **has seen** /si:n; sin/)
1 know something using your eyes 看见；看: *It was so dark that I couldn't see anything.* 周围黑得我什么都看不见。◇ *Can you see that plane?* 你看得见那架飞机吗？◇ *I'm going to see a film tonight.* 我今天晚上去看电影。

see or **look**? 用 **see** 还是用 **look**？

See and **look** are used in different ways. ＊ **see** 和 **look** 的用法不同。When you **see** something, you know about it with your eyes, without trying ＊ **see** 指不费力而看见:

S

Suddenly I **saw** *a bird fly past the window.* 突然我看见有只鸟从窗口飞过。

When you **look at** something, you turn your eyes towards it because you want to see it ✻ **look at** 指有意将视线转移到某物上而看见:

Look at *this picture carefully. Can you* **see** *the bird?* 仔细看看这张画儿。你看见鸟了吗？

2 visit or meet somebody 看望或遇见某人: *I'll see you outside the station at ten o'clock.* 我十点钟在车站外边见你。

3 understand something 理解某事物: *'You have to turn the key this way.' 'I see.'* "这把钥匙得这样拧才行。""明白了。"

4 find out about something 找出某事物: *Look in the newspaper to see what time the film starts.* 看看报纸，看这场电影什么时候开演。

S

5 make certain about something 使某事物落实: *Please see that everybody is here.* 请务必让大家都到这儿来。

I'll see I will think about what you have said and tell you what I have decided later 我要考虑一下再告诉你: *'Will you lend me the money?' 'I'll see.'* "您把这笔钱借给我行吗？""我先考虑一下再说吧。"

seeing that, seeing as because 由于；因为: *Seeing that you've got nothing to do, you can help me!* 你现在什么事儿也没有，就来帮我个忙吧！

see somebody off go to an airport or a station to say goodbye to somebody who is leaving 到机场或车站为某人送行

see to somebody or 或 **something** do what you need to do for somebody or something 照看某人或某事物: *Sit down—I'll see to the dinner.* 你先坐下——我去看看饭怎么样了。

see you, see you later goodbye 再见

seed /siːd; sid/ *noun* 名词
the small hard part of a plant from which a new plant grows 种子

seek /siːk; sik/ *verb* 动词 (**seeks, seeking, sought** /sɔːt; sɔt/, **has sought**)
try to find or get something 寻找或找到某事物: *You should seek help.* 你应该找人帮帮忙。

seem /siːm; sim/ *verb* 动词 (**seems, seeming, seemed** /siːmd; simd/)
make you think that something is true 似乎；好像: *She seems tired.* 她好像累了。◇ *My mother seems to like you.* 我母亲似乎很喜欢你。◇ *Helen seems like* (= seems to be) *a nice girl.* 海伦像是个不错的姑娘。

seen *form of* **see** ✻ **see** 的不同形式

see-saw /ˈsiː sɔː; ˈsiˌsɔ/ *noun* 名词
a special piece of wood that can move up and down when a child sits on each end 跷跷板（儿童游戏用具）

seize /siːz; siz/ *verb* 动词 (**seizes, seizing, seized** /siːzd; sizd/)
take something quickly and strongly 抓住；攫取: *The thief seized my bag and ran away.* 那个贼把我的提包抢跑了。

seldom /ˈseldəm; ˈsɛldəm/ *adverb* 副词
not often 不常: *It seldom snows in Athens.* 雅典很少下雪。

select /sɪˈlekt; səˈlɛkt/ *verb* 动词 (**selects, selecting, selected**)
take the person or thing that you like best; choose 选择；挑选；选拔: *The manager has selected two new players for the team.* 经理挑选了两个新队员加入这个队。✪ **Choose** is the word that we usually use. ✻ **choose** 是常用词。

selection /sɪˈlekʃn; səˈlɛkʃən/ *noun* 名词
1 (no plural 无复数) taking the person or thing you like best 选择；挑选；选拔: *the selection of a new president* 挑选新会长
2 (*plural* 复数作 **selections**) a group of people or things that somebody has chosen, or a group of things that you can choose from 挑选出的或可供挑选的人或事物: *This shop has a good selection of cassettes and compact discs.* 这家商店有些精选的录音带和激光唱片。

self- /self; sɛlf/ *prefix* 前缀
by yourself; for yourself 由自己；为自己: *He is self-taught—he never went to university.* 他是自学成材的——他从没上过大学。

self-confident /ˌself ˈkɒnfɪdənt; ˈsɛlfˈkɑnfədənt/ *adjective* 形容词
sure about yourself and what you can do 自信的

self-conscious /ˌself ˈkɒnʃəs; ˈsɛlf-ˈkɑnʃəs/ *adjective* 形容词
worried about what other people think of you（因顾虑别人有何看法）拘谨不自然的: *She walked into her new school feeling very self-conscious.* 她走进新学校，感到非常局促不安。

self-employed /ˌself ɪmˈplɔɪd; ˌsɛlfɪmˈplɔɪd/ *adjective* 形容词
If you are self-employed, you work for yourself, not for somebody else's company 自己经营的；个体户的: *He's a self-employed electrician.* 他是个体户电工。

selfish /ˈselfɪʃ; ˈsɛlfɪʃ/ *adjective* 形容词
If you are selfish, you think too much about what you want and not about what other people want 自私的；不顾别人的: *It was selfish of you to go out when your mother was ill.* 你母亲病了你还出去，太自私了。✪ opposite 反义词: **unselfish**

selfishly *adverb* 副词
He behaved very selfishly. 他表现得很自私。

selfishness /ˈselfɪʃnəs; ˈsɛlfɪʃnɪs/ *noun* 名词 (no plural 无复数)
Her selfishness made me very angry. 她很自私，我为此十分生气。

self-service /ˌself ˈsɜːvɪs; ˈsɛlfˈsɝvɪs/ *adjective* 形容词
In a self-service shop or restaurant you take what you want and then pay for it.（指商店或饭馆）自我服务的；自助式的

sell /sel; sɛl/ *verb* 动词 (**sells, selling, sold** /səʊld; sold/, **has sold**)
give something to somebody who pays you money for it 卖；出售: *I sold my guitar for £200.* 我把吉他卖了200英镑。◇ *He sold me a ticket.* 他卖给我一张票。◇ *Newsagents usually sell chocolates and cigarettes.* 经销报刊的人一般也出售巧克力和香烟。☞ Look at **buy**.见 **buy**。

sell out be sold completely so that there are no more left 卖光；售完: *I went to the shop to buy a newspaper, but they had all sold out.* 我到商店去买报纸，可是都卖光了。

sell out of something sell all that you have of something 卖光存货: *We have oranges, but we have sold out of apples.* 我们有橙子，可是苹果都卖光了。

Sellotape /ˈseləʊteɪp; ˈsɛloˌtep/ *noun* 名词 (no plural 无复数)
clear paper or plastic that you buy in a narrow roll. You use it for sticking things like paper and cardboard together.（透明的）胶带（可用以粘纸的）✪ **Sellotape** is a trade mark. ✳ **Sellotape** 是商标。

semi- /semi; ˈsɛmɪ/ *prefix* 前缀
half 半: *A semicircle is a half circle.* 半圈是半个圆圈。

semicolon /ˌsemiˈkəʊlən; ˈsɛməˌkolən/ *noun* 名词
a mark (;) that you use in writing to separate parts of a sentence 分号（；）

semi-detached /ˌsemi dɪˈtætʃt; ˌsɛmədɪˈtætʃt/ *adjective* 形容词
A semi-detached house is joined to another house on one side.（指房子）半独立式的（与另一所房子共用一堵墙的）

S

semifinal /ˌsemiˈfaɪnl; ˌsɛməˈfaɪnl̩/ *noun* 名词
In a competition, a semifinal is one of the two games that are played to find out who will play in the **final**.（竞赛中的）半决赛（决赛叫做 **final**）

senate /ˈsenət; ˈsɛnɪt/ *noun* 名词
1 one of the parts of the government in some countries（某些国家的）参议院
2 the Senate (no plural 无复数) the more important part of the government in the USA（美国的）参议院

senator /ˈsenətə(r); ˈsɛnətɚ/ *noun* 名词
a member of a senate 参议员

send /send; sɛnd/ *verb* 动词 (**sends, sending, sent** /sent; sɛnt/, **has sent**)
1 make something go somewhere 送或寄某物: *I sent a letter to John.* 我寄给约翰一封信。◇ *Have you sent your parents a postcard?* 你给父母寄明信片了吗？
2 make somebody go somewhere 派或遣某人: *My company is sending me to New York.* 我们公司要把我派到纽约去。◇ *He was sent to prison for ten years.* 他被监禁十年。

send for somebody or 或 **something** ask for somebody or something to come to you 要求某人来；要求把某物送来: *Send for an ambulance!* 叫救护车来！

send off post something 寄出某物: *I'll send the letter off today.* 我今天要把信寄出去。

senior /ˈsiːniə(r); ˈsinjɚ/ *adjective* 形容词
1 more important（级别或权位等）较高的: *a senior officer in the army* 陆军的高级军官
2 older 年长的: *a senior pupil* 高年级学生
✪ opposite 反义词: **junior**
senior citizen /ˌsiːniə ˈsɪtɪzn; ˈsinjɚ ˈsɪtəzn̩/ *noun* 名词
an old person 老人

sensation /senˈseɪʃn; sɛnˈseʃən/ *noun* 名词
1 a feeling 感觉；感受: *I felt a burning sensation on my skin.* 我皮肤上有灼热的感觉。
2 great excitement or interest; something that makes people very excited 轰动；群情激动: *The new film caused a sensation in Hollywood.* 这部新影片在好莱坞引起了轰动。

sensational /senˈseɪʃənl; sɛnˈseʃənl̩/ *adjective* 形容词
very exciting or interesting 轰动的；群情激动的: *sensational news* 耸人听闻的消息

sense¹ /sens; sɛns/ *noun* 名词
1 (*plural* 复数作 **senses**) the power to see, hear, smell, taste or touch 感觉官能（视觉、听觉、嗅觉、味觉或触觉）: *Dogs have a good sense of smell.* 狗的嗅觉很灵敏。
2 (no plural 无复数) the ability to feel or understand something 理解力；领悟力: *The boy had no sense of right and wrong.* 那个男孩儿没有分辨是非的能力。
3 (no plural 无复数) the ability to think carefully about something and to do the right thing 仔细思考并采取正确行动的能力；行事有理智: *Did anybody have the sense to call the police?* 当时有没有明白人想到把警察找来？
4 (*plural* 复数作 **senses**) a meaning 意思；意义: *This word has four senses.* 这个词有四个意思。
make sense be possible to understand 有意义；有道理；讲得通: *What does this sentence mean? It doesn't make sense to me.* 这句话是什么意思？我看讲不通。

sense² /sens; sɛns/ *verb* 动词 (**senses, sensing, sensed** /senst; sɛnst/)
understand or feel something 意识到或感觉到某事物: *I sensed that he was worried.* 我意识到他有愁事。

sensible /ˈsensəbl; ˈsɛnsəbl̩/ *adjective* 形容词
1 able to think carefully about something and to do the right thing 仔细思考后能采取正确行动的；行事有理智的: *It was very sensible of you to call the police when you saw the accident.* 你一看见出了事故就去找警察，真是精明能干。
2 right and good 合适的；实用的: *We are going for a long walk, so wear some sensible shoes.* 咱们要走很长的路，得穿舒适的鞋。
sensibly /ˈsensəbli; ˈsɛnsəblɪ/ *adverb* 副词
She was sensibly dressed. 她穿得很合时宜。

sensitive /ˈsensətɪv; ˈsɛnsətɪv/ *adjective* 形容词
1 If you are sensitive about something, you easily become worried or unhappy about it（指人对某事物）易担忧或不悦的；神经质的: *Don't say anything bad about her work — she's very sensitive about it.* 千万别说她的工作不好——她就怕提这件事。
✪ opposite 反义词: **insensitive**
2 A person who is sensitive understands and is careful about other people's feelings（指人对他人的感情）体贴人的: *He's a very sensitive man.* 他这个人很能体谅别人。✪ opposite 反义词: **insensitive**
3 If something is sensitive, it is easy to hurt or damage（指某事物）易受伤害或损坏的: *sensitive skin* 过敏的皮肤

sent *form of* **send** ✳ **send** 的不同形式

sentence¹ /ˈsentəns; ˈsɛntəns/ *noun* 名词
a group of words that tells you something or asks a question. When a sentence is written, it always begins with a capital letter and usually ends with a full stop. 句子

sentence² /ˈsentəns; ˈsɛntəns/ *noun* 名词
the punishment that a judge gives to somebody in a court of law（对给予某种惩罚的）判决或宣判；判刑
sentence *verb* 动词 (**sentences, sentencing, sentenced** /ˈsentənst; ˈsɛntənst/)
tell somebody in a court of law what their punishment will be 判决或宣判某种

惩罚: *The judge sentenced the man to two years in prison.* 法官判决那个男子入狱两年。

separate¹ /ˈseprət; ˈsɛprɪt/ *adjective* 形容词

1 away from something; not together or not joined 分开的；不在一起的；不相连的: *Cut the cake into eight separate pieces.* 把蛋糕切成八块。◇ *In my school, the older children are separate from the younger ones.* 我们学校年龄大的学生跟年龄小的不在一起。

2 different; not the same 不同的；有区别的: *We stayed in separate rooms in the same hotel.* 我们在同一家旅馆里，各住各的房间。

separately *adverb* 副词

Shall we pay separately or together? 我们付款是分开付还是合在一起付？

separate² /ˈsepəreɪt; ˈsɛpəˌret/ *verb* 动词 (**separates, separating, separated**)

1 stop being together 不再在一起；分开: *My parents separated when I was a baby.* 我很小的时候父母就分居了。

2 divide people or things; keep people or things away from each other（使人或事物）不在一起；分开: *The teacher separated the class into two groups.* 老师把全班分成两组。

3 be between two things 在两者之间；从中隔开: *The Mediterranean separates Europe and Africa.* 欧洲和非洲之间隔着地中海。

separation /ˌsepəˈreɪʃn; ˌsɛpəˈreʃən/ *noun* 名词

The separation from my family and friends made me very unhappy. 我离开亲友十分难过。

September /sepˈtembə(r); sɛpˈtɛmbɚ/ *noun* 名词

the ninth month of the year 九月

sergeant /ˈsɑːdʒənt; ˈsɑrdʒənt/ *noun* 名词

an officer in the army or the police（陆军的）中士；（警察的）巡佐

serial /ˈsɪəriəl; ˈsɪrɪəl/ *noun* 名词

a story that is told in parts on television or radio, or in a magazine（电视、电台或杂志的）连续故事集

series /ˈsɪəriːz; ˈsɪriz/ *noun* 名词 (*plural* 复数作 **series**)

1 a number of things of the same kind that come one after another 一系列的事物: *I heard a series of shots and then silence.* 我听到了连续的枪声，然后就没声音了。

2 a number of television or radio programmes, often on the same subject, that come one after another（电视或电台的）系列节目: *a TV series on dinosaurs* 关于恐龙的电视系列节目

serious /ˈsɪəriəs; ˈsɪrɪəs/ *adjective* 形容词

1 very bad 极坏的；严重的: *That was a serious mistake.* 这是个大错。◇ *They had a serious accident.* 他们出了个严重事故。

2 important 重大的: *a serious decision* 重大的决定

3 not funny 并非可笑的；严肃认真的: *a serious film* 主题严肃的影片

4 If you are serious, you are not joking or playing 并非开玩笑或闹着玩的；正经的: *Are you serious about going to live in Spain?* 你要搬到西班牙去住，是真的吗？◇ *You look very serious. Is something wrong?* 你表情很严肃。怎么了？

seriously *adverb* 副词

She's seriously ill. 她病得很重。

take somebody or 或 **something seriously** show that you know somebody or something is important 表示某人或某事物很重要；认真对待: *Don't take what he says too seriously—he is always joking.* 别把他说的话太当真——他总开玩笑。

seriousness /ˈsɪəriəsnəs; ˈsɪrɪəsnɪs/ *noun* 名词 (no plural 无复数)

The boy didn't understand the seriousness of his crime. 那个男孩儿不明白自己罪行的严重性。

sermon /ˈsɜːmən; ˈsɝmən/ *noun* 名词

a talk that a priest gives in church 讲道（教士做的）

servant /ˈsɜːvənt; ˈsɝvənt/ *noun* 名词

a person who works in another person's house, doing work like cooking and cleaning 用人；仆人

serve /sɜːv; sɝv/ *verb* 动词 (**serves, serving, served** /sɜːvd; sɝvd/)

1 do work for other people 为别人工作或服务: *During the war he served in the army.* 在战争期间，他在陆军服役。

2 give food or drink to somebody 给某人食物或饮料: *Breakfast is served from 7.30 to 9.00 a.m.* 早餐供应时间是7时30分至9时。

3 help somebody in a shop to buy things 在商店中接待顾客: *Excuse me, Madam. Are you being served?* 请问，小姐。有售货员接待您吗？

it serves you right it is right that this bad thing has happened to you 你出了坏事是应该的；活该: *'I feel ill.' 'It serves you right for eating so much!'* "我不舒服。""谁让你吃那么多，活该！"

service /'sɜːvɪs; 'sɝvɪs/ *noun* 名词

1 (*plural* 复数作 **services**) a business that does useful work for all the people in a country or an area（为国家或地区全民服务的）企业；公用事业: *This town has a good bus service.* 这个镇上的公共汽车服务非常好。◇ *the postal service* 邮政业务

2 (no plural 无复数) help or work that you do for somebody（对某人的）协助；（为某人做的）工作: *She left the company after ten years of service.* 她在公司工作了十年以后就走了。

S

3 (no plural 无复数) the work that somebody does for customers in a shop, restaurant or hotel（在商店、饭馆或旅馆招待顾客的）工作；服务: *The food was good but the service was very slow.* 饭菜很好，就是上菜太慢。

4 (*plural* 复数作 **services**) a meeting in a church with prayers and singing（教堂的）礼拜；祈祷会: *We went to the evening service.* 我们去参加了晚祷。

5 (*plural* 复数作 **services**) the time when somebody looks at a car or machine to see that it is working well（汽车或机器的）维修: *She takes her car to the garage for a service every six months.* 她每隔半年就把汽车送到车厂检修一次。

6 services (plural 复数) a place by a motorway where you can stop to buy petrol and food and use the toilets（高速公路旁的）汽车服务站（可购买汽油、食物及使用厕所）

7 the services (plural 复数) the army, navy and air force 三军（陆军、海军、空军）

service station /'sɜːvɪs steɪʃn; 'sɝvɪs ˌsteʃən/ *noun* 名词

a place where you can buy petrol 汽车加油站

serviette /ˌsɜːvi'et; ˌsɝvɪ'ɛt/ *noun* 名词

a piece of cloth or paper that you use when you are eating to clean your mouth and hands and to keep your clothes clean 餐巾

session /'seʃn; 'sɛʃən/ *noun* 名词

a time when people meet to do something（大家开会或做某事的）一段时间: *The first swimming session is at nine o'clock.* 第一段游泳时间是在九点钟。

set[1] /set; sɛt/ *noun* 名词

a group of things of the same kind, or a group of things that you use together 同类的一批东西或一起使用的一套东西: *a set of six glasses* 六个一套的玻璃杯 ◇ *a set of tools* 一套工具

set[2] /set; sɛt/ *verb* 动词 (**sets**, **setting**, **set**, **has set**)

1 put something somewhere 把某物放在某处: *Dad set the plate in front of me.* 爸爸把盘子摆在我的面前。

2 make something ready to use or to start working 把某物准备好（以便使用或开动）: *I set my alarm clock for seven o'clock.* 我把闹钟调到七点钟。◇ *I set the table* (= put knives, forks, etc on it). 我铺好了桌子（＝摆上刀叉等）。

3 make something happen 使某事物发生: *They set the school on fire* (= made it start to burn). 他们放火把学校烧了。

4 When the sun sets, it goes down from the sky.（指太阳）落下 ✪ opposite 反义词: **rise**

5 decide what something will be; fix something 决定某事；固定某物: *Let's set a date for the meeting.* 咱们把会议时间定下来吧。

6 give somebody work to do 给某人工作做: *Our teacher set us a lot of homework.* 我们老师给我们留了很多家庭作业。

7 become hard or solid 变硬或变成固体: *Wait for the cement to set.* 要等一段时间水泥才能凝固变硬。

set off, set out start a journey 出发；动身: *We set off for Oxford at two o'clock.* 我们两点钟动身到牛津去。

set up start something 建立或开创某事物: *The company was set up in 1981.* 这家公司建于1981年。

settee /se'tiː; sɛ'ti/ *noun* 名词

a long soft seat for more than one person（不止一人坐的）长沙发

setting /'setɪŋ; 'sɛtɪŋ/ *noun* 名词

the place where something is or where something happens（某事物存在或发生的）

环境: *The house is in a beautiful setting on top of a hill.* 那所房子在山顶上，风景优美。

settle /'setl; 'sɛtl̩/ *verb* 动词 (**settles, settling, settled** /'setld; 'sɛtl̩d/)

1 go to live in a new place and stay there 到某处定居；落户: *Ruth left England and went to settle in America.* 鲁思已离开英国到美国定居。

2 decide something after talking with somebody; end a discussion or argument（与某人商谈之后）决定某事；结束讨论或争论: *Have you settled your argument with Rajit?* 你跟拉吉特的争论解决了吗？

3 come down and rest somewhere 落下而停在某处: *The bird settled on a branch.* 鸟落在树枝上了。

4 pay something 付某事物的钱: *Have you settled your bill?* 您结账了吗？

settle down 1 sit down or lie down so that you are comfortable 舒适地坐下或躺下: *I settled down in front of the television.* 我在电视机前边舒舒服服地坐着。 **2** become calm and quiet 平静下来: *The children settled down and went to sleep.* 孩子都安静下来睡着了。 **3** begin to have a calm life in one place 开始在某处过平静的日子: *When are you going to get married and settle down?* 你什么时候结婚，过个消停日子？

settle in start to feel happy in a new place 开始在某处感到愉快: *We only moved to this flat last week and we haven't settled in yet.* 我们上星期才搬到这所公寓来，还没安顿下来呢。

settlement /'setlmənt; 'sɛtl̩mənt/ *noun* 名词

1 an agreement about something after talking or arguing（在商谈或争论之后的）决定；解决；和解: *After long talks about pay, the workers and their boss reached a settlement.* 工人同老板在工资方面经过长时间的谈判达成了协议。

2 a group of homes in a place where no people have lived before（在以前无人居住处建立的）居民点: *a settlement in the forest* 林区的居民点

seven /'sevn; 'sɛvən/ *number* 数词

7 七

seventh /'sevnθ; 'sɛvənθ/ *adjective, adverb, noun* 形容词，副词，名词

1 7th 第7（个）；第七（个）

2 one of seven equal parts of something; 1/7 七分之一

seventeen /ˌsevn'ti:n; ˌsɛvən'tin/ *number* 数词

17 十七

seventeenth /ˌsevn'ti:nθ; ˌsɛvən'tinθ/ *adjective, adverb, noun* 形容词，副词，名词

17th 第17（个）；第十七（个）

seventy /'sevnti; 'sɛvəntɪ/ *number* 数词

1 70 七十

2 the seventies (plural 复数) the numbers, years or temperature between 70 and 79 ＊ 70至79（之间的数目、年数或温度）

in your seventies between the ages of 70 and 79 年岁在70至79之间；七十多岁

seventieth /'sevntiəθ; 'sɛvəntɪəθ/ *adjective, adverb, noun* 形容词，副词，名词

70th 第70（个）；第七十（个）

several /'sevrəl; 'sɛvrəl/ *adjective, pronoun* 形容词，代词

more than two but not many 两个以上（但不很多）；几个: *I've read this book several times.* 这本书我已经看了几遍了。◇ *Several letters arrived this morning.* 今天上午来了几封信。◇ *If you need a pen, there are several on the table.* 您要是需要钢笔的话，桌上有几枝。

severe /sɪ'vɪə(r); sə'vɪr/ *adjective* 形容词 (**severer, severest**)

1 not kind or gentle 严格的；严厉的；苛刻的: *severe punishment* 严厉的惩罚

2 very bad 非常恶劣的: *a severe headache* 剧烈的头痛 ◇ *a severe* (= very cold) *winter* 严冬

severely *adverb* 副词

They punished him severely. 他们很严厉地惩罚了他。◇ *She was severely injured in the accident.* 她在事故中受了重伤。

sew 缝

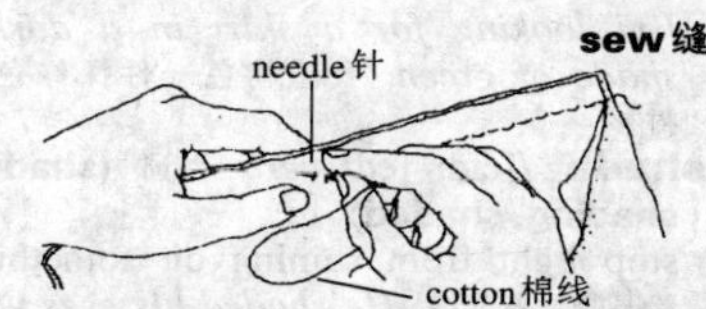

sew /səʊ; so/ *verb* 动词 (**sews, sewing, sewed** /səʊd; sod/, **has sewed** or 或 **has sewn** /səʊn; son/)

use a needle and cotton to join pieces of material together or to join something to

S

material（用针线）缝: *He sewed a button on his shirt.* 他把扣子钉在衬衫上了。◇ *Can you sew?* 你会做针线活儿吗？

sewing *noun* 名词 (no plural 无复数) something that you sew 针线活儿

sewing-machine /ˈsəʊɪŋ məʃiːn; ˈsoɪŋ məˌʃin/ *noun* 名词 a machine that you use for sewing 缝纫机

sex /seks; sɛks/ *noun* 名词

1 (*plural* 复数作 **sexes**) being a male or a female 性别: *What sex is your dog?* 你的狗是公的还是母的？◇ *the male sex* 男性

2 (no plural 无复数) when two people put their bodies together, sometimes to make a baby 性交: *She had sex with him.* 她跟他发生了性关系。

sh! /ʃ; ʃ/ be quiet! 安静！: *Sh! You'll wake the baby up!* 安静点儿！看把孩子吵醒了！

S

shabby /ˈʃæbi; ˈʃæbɪ/ *adjective* 形容词 (**shabbier, shabbiest**) old and untidy or dirty because you have used it a lot 破旧而不整洁的: *a shabby coat* 破旧的大衣

shabbily /ˈʃæbɪli; ˈʃæbl̩ɪ/ *adverb* 副词 *She was shabbily dressed.* 她穿得破破烂烂。

shade¹ /ʃeɪd; ʃed/ *noun* 名词

1 (no plural 无复数) a place where it is dark and cool because the sun doesn't shine there 荫；阴凉处: *We sat in the shade of a big tree.* 我们在大树阴下坐着。

2 (*plural* 复数作 **shades**) a thing that keeps strong light from your eyes（防强光刺眼的）遮光物: *I bought a new shade for the lamp.* 我买了个新灯罩。

3 (*plural* 复数作 **shades**) how light or dark a colour is 色度（颜色深浅的程度）: *I'm looking for a shirt in a darker shade of green.* 我想物色一件深绿色的衬衫。

shade² /ʃeɪd; ʃed/ *verb* 动词 (**shades, shading, shaded**) stop light from shining on something 给某物遮着光线: *He shaded his eyes with his hand.* 他把手放在眼睛上方挡住光线。

shadow /ˈʃædəʊ; ˈʃædo/ *noun* 名词 a dark shape that you see near somebody or something that is in front of the light 影子

shady /ˈʃeɪdi; ˈʃedɪ/ *adjective* 形容词 (**shadier, shadiest**) not in bright sunshine 遮阳的；背阴的: *We sat in a shady part of the garden.* 我们坐在花园背阴的地方。

shake /ʃeɪk; ʃek/ *verb* 动词 (**shakes, shaking, shook** /ʃʊk; ʃuk/, **has shaken** /ˈʃeɪkən; ˈʃekən/)

1 move quickly from side to side or up and down 急速摇动或颠簸: *The house shakes when trains go past.* 火车经过时房子震得直颤。◇ *He was shaking with fear.* 他吓得直发抖。

2 make something move quickly from side to side or up and down 使某物急速摇动或颠簸: *Shake the bottle before opening it.* 把瓶子摇一摇再打开。◇ *An explosion shook the windows.* 那次爆炸把窗户震得直颤。

shake hands hold somebody's hand and move it up and down as a greeting 握手（表示问候或祝贺）

shake your head move your head from side to side to say 'no' 摇头（表示不同意）

shaky /ˈʃeɪki; ˈʃekɪ/ *adjective* 形容词 (**shakier, shakiest**)

1 shaking because you are ill or frightened（因病或害怕）发抖的；颤抖的: *You've got shaky hands.* 你的手直发抖。

2 not firm; not strong 不坚定的；不稳定的；不结实的: *Don't sit in that chair—it's a bit shaky.* 那把椅子不能坐——不太稳。

shall /ʃəl, ʃæl; ʃəl, ʃæl/ *modal verb* 情态动词

1 a word that you use instead of 'will' with 'I' and 'we' to show the future 与 I 和 we 连用表示将来的词: *I shall see you tomorrow.* 我明天见你。

2 a word that you use when you ask what is the right thing to do 用以表示征求意见的词: *Shall I close the window?* 我关上窗户好吗？◇ *What shall we do tomorrow?* 我们明天做什么呢？

✪ The negative form of 'shall' is **shall not** or the short form **shan't** /ʃɑ:nt; ʃænt/ ✳ shall 的否定式是 **shall not** 或其缩略式 **shan't** /ʃɑ:nt; ʃænt/:

I shan't be there. 我（将）不在那儿。

The short form of 'shall' is **'ll**. ✳ shall 的缩略式为 **'ll**。We often use this 一般多用这一缩略式:

I'll (= I shall) *see you tomorrow.* 我明天见你。

☞ Look at the Note on page 314 to find out more about **modal verbs.** 见第 314页对 **modal verbs** 的进一步解释。

shallow /'ʃæləʊ; 'ʃælo/ *adjective* 形容词 (**shallower, shallowest**)
not deep; with not much water 浅的: *This part of the river is shallow — we can walk across.* 这条河这部分水浅——我们可以蹚水过去。☞ picture on page C26 见第C26页图

shame /ʃeɪm; ʃem/ *noun* 名词 (no plural 无复数)
the unhappy feeling that you have when you have done something wrong or stupid 羞耻；羞愧；惭愧: *I was filled with* (= felt a lot of) *shame after I lied to my parents.* 我向父母撒了谎，感到非常羞愧。✪ The adjective is **ashamed**. 形容词是 **ashamed**。
it's a shame, what a shame it is sad; I am sorry 遗憾的事；可惜: *It's a shame that you can't come to our party.* 您不能来参加我们的聚会，非常遗憾。

shampoo /ʃæm'pu:; ʃæm'pu/ *noun* 名词 (*plural* 复数作 **shampoos**)
a special liquid for washing your hair 洗发液；洗发膏: *a bottle of shampoo* 一瓶洗发液

shan't /ʃɑ:nt; ʃænt/ = **shall not**

shape¹ /ʃeɪp; ʃep/ *noun* 名词
1 (*plural* 复数作 **shapes**) what you see if you draw a line round something; the form of something 外形；形状；样子: *What shape is the table — round or square?* 那张桌子是什么形状的——是圆的还是方的？◇ *I bought a bowl in the shape of a fish.* 我买了一个形状像鱼的盘子。◇ *Circles, squares and triangles are all different shapes.* 圆的、方的、三角的，都是各种各样的形状。
2 (no plural 无复数) how good or bad something is; how healthy somebody is 事物好坏的程度；人的健康的状况: *He was in bad shape after the accident.* 他出事以后身体很不好。
out of shape not in the right shape 变形；走样: *My jumper went out of shape when I washed it.* 我的套头毛衣洗过以后走样子了。

shape² /ʃeɪp; ʃep/ *verb* 动词 (**shapes, shaping, shaped** /ʃeɪpt; ʃept/)
give a certain shape to something 做成某种形状: *She shaped the clay into a pot.* 她用黏土做成了一个盆。
shaped *adjective* 形容词
with a certain shape 具有某种形状的: *He gave me a birthday card shaped like a cat.* 他送给我一个小猫形状的生日贺卡。◇ *a heart-shaped box of chocolates* 一个心形盒的巧克力

share¹ /ʃeə(r); ʃɛr/ *verb* 动词 (**shares, sharing, shared** /ʃeəd; ʃɛrd/)
1 give parts of something to different people 把某物分给大家: *Share these sweets with your friends.* 把这些糖分给你的朋友吃。◇ *We shared a large pizza between three of us.* 我们三个人吃了一大个意大利饼。
2 have or use something with another person 与别人共有或共用某物；分享: *I share a bedroom with my sister.* 我跟我姐姐共用一间卧室。

share² /ʃeə(r); ʃɛr/ *noun* 名词
a part of something bigger that each person has（每个人的）一份: *Here is your share of the money.* 这份钱是你的。◇ *I did my share of the work.* 我做完了分给我的那份工作。

shark 鲨鱼

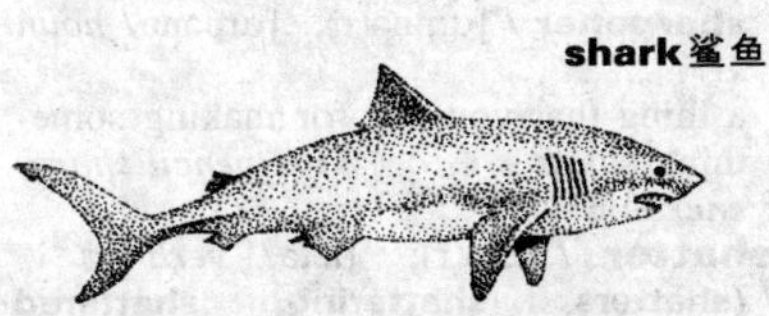

shark /ʃɑ:k; ʃɑrk/ *noun* 名词
a big fish that lives in the sea. Some sharks have sharp teeth and are dangerous. 鲨鱼

S

sharp[1] /ʃɑ:p; ʃɑrp/ *adjective* 形容词 (**sharper**, **sharpest**)

1 with an edge or point that cuts or makes holes easily 尖锐的；锋利的：*a sharp knife* 一把快刀 ◇ *a sharp needle* 尖的针 ✪ opposite 反义词：**blunt**

2 strong and sudden 强烈而突然的：*a sharp bend in the road* 路上的急转弯 ◇ *I felt a sharp pain in my leg.* 我感到腿上一阵剧烈疼痛。

3 clear and easy to see 清楚而易见的：*We could see the sharp outline of the mountains against the sky.* 我们看见天空衬托的群山，轮廓十分清晰。

4 with a taste like lemons or vinegar 酸味的：*If your drink tastes too sharp, add some sugar.* 您要是觉得这个饮品太酸就加点儿糖。

5 able to see, hear or learn well 指视力、听力或领悟力良好的；灵敏的；敏锐的：*She's got a very sharp mind.* 她头脑非常敏锐。◇ *sharp eyes* 灵敏的眼睛

6 sudden and angry 突然而气愤的；尖刻的：*sharp words* 刻薄的言语

sharply *adverb* 副词

The road bends sharply to the left. 这是条向左急转弯的路。◇ *'Go away!' he said sharply.* "走开！"他怒气冲冲地说。

sharp[2] /ʃɑ:p; ʃɑrp/ *adverb* 副词

1 exactly 准确地：*Be here at six o'clock sharp.* 六点正到这里来。

2 with a big change of direction 方向急转：*Turn sharp right at the next corner.* 到下一个路口向右急转。

sharpen /'ʃɑ:pən; 'ʃɑrpən/ *verb* 动词 (**sharpens**, **sharpening**, **sharpened** /'ʃɑ:pənd; 'ʃɑrpənd/)

make something sharp or sharper 使某物锋利、强烈、清楚、灵敏、尖刻等：*sharpen a knife* 磨刀

sharpener /'ʃɑ:pnə(r); 'ʃɑrpənɚ/ *noun* 名词

a thing that you use for making something sharp 磨具；削具：*a pencil-sharpener* 铅笔刀

shatter /'ʃætə(r); 'ʃætɚ/ *verb* 动词 (**shatters**, **shattering**, **shattered** /'ʃætəd; 'ʃætɚd/)

break into very small pieces; break something into very small pieces（使某物）粉碎：*The glass hit the floor and shattered.* 玻璃杯掉到地板上摔碎了。◇ *The explosion shattered the windows.* 那次爆炸把窗户震碎了。

shave /ʃeɪv; ʃev/ *verb* 动词 (**shaves**, **shaving**, **shaved** /ʃeɪvd; ʃevd/)

cut hair off your face or body by cutting it very close with a **razor**（用剃刀）刮或剃毛发（剃刀叫做 **razor**）：*He shaves every morning.* 他每天早晨都刮脸。

shave *noun* 名词

I haven't had a shave today. 我今天没刮脸。

shaver *noun* 名词

an electric tool that you use for shaving 电动剃刀

shawl /ʃɔ:l; ʃɔl/ *noun* 名词

a big piece of cloth that a woman wears round her shoulders, or that you put round a baby（女用的）披肩；（婴儿的）襁褓

she /ʃi:; ʃi/ *pronoun* 代词 (*plural* 复数作 **they**)

the woman or girl that the sentence is about 她：*'Where's your sister?' 'She's* (= she is) *at work.'* "你姐姐在哪儿呢？""她工作呢。"

shed[1] /ʃed; ʃɛd/ *noun* 名词

a small building where you keep things or animals（存放东西或养动物的）小屋；棚：*There's a shed in the garden where we keep our tools.* 我们花园里有个工具房。

shed[2] /ʃed; ʃɛd/ *verb* 动词 (**sheds**, **shedding**, **shed**, **has shed**)

let something fall off 使某物脱落：*The snake shed its skin.* 蛇脱皮了。

she'd /ʃi:d; ʃid/

1 = she had

2 = she would

sheep 绵羊

lamb 小绵羊 sheep 绵羊

sheep /ʃi:p; ʃip/ (*plural* 复数作 **sheep**)

an animal that people keep on farms for its meat and its wool 羊；绵羊

✪ A young sheep is called a **lamb**. 羔羊叫做 **lamb**。Meat from a young sheep is also called **lamb**. 羔羊的肉也叫做 **lamb**。

sheer /ʃɪə(r); ʃɪr/ *adjective* 形容词
1 complete 完全的；十足的: *sheer nonsense* 纯粹胡说八道
2 very steep 陡峭的: *a sheer drop to the sea* 垂直降落海中

sheet /ʃi:t; ʃit/ *noun* 名词
1 a big piece of thin material for a bed 床单；褥单；被单: *I put some clean sheets on the bed.* 我在床上铺上了干净的单子。
2 a thin flat piece of something like paper, glass or metal（纸、玻璃、金属等的）薄片；薄板；单张: *a sheet of writing-paper* 一张信纸

shelf 搁架

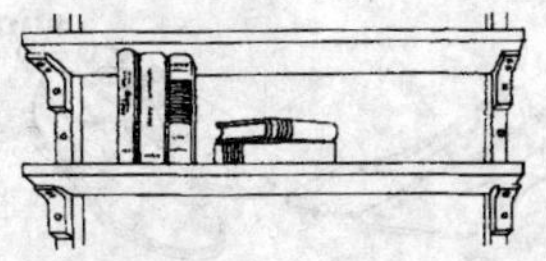

shelf /ʃelf; ʃɛlf/ *noun* 名词 (*plural* 复数作 **shelves** /ʃelvz; ʃɛlvz/)
a long flat piece of wood on a wall or in a cupboard, where things can stand（墙上的或柜橱里的）搁板；搁架: *Put the plates on the shelf.* 把盘子放在架子上。◇ *bookshelves* 书架

shells 壳

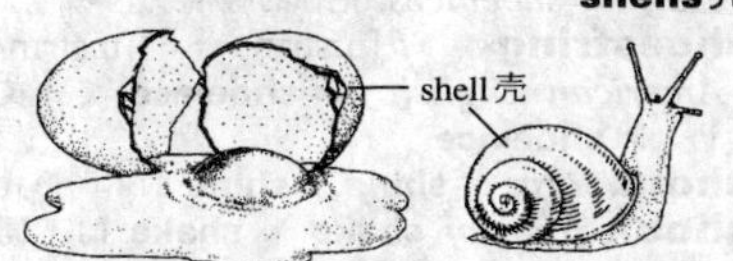

shell /ʃel; ʃɛl/ *noun* 名词
the hard outside part of birds' eggs and nuts and of some animals, for example snails and crabs（卵、坚果及蜗牛和螃蟹等动物的）壳 ☞ Look also at **sea shell**. 另见 **sea shell**。

she'll /ʃi:l; ʃil/ = **she will**

shellfish /ˈʃelfɪʃ; ˈʃɛlˌfɪʃ/ *noun* 名词 (*plural* 复数作 **shellfish**)
a kind of animal that lives in water and that has a shell 水生有壳动物

shelter[1] /ˈʃeltə(r); ˈʃɛltɚ/ *noun* 名词
1 (no plural 无复数) being safe from bad weather or danger 遮蔽；庇护: *We took shelter from the rain under a tree.* 我们在树下避雨。◇ *People ran for shelter when the bombs started to fall.* 空袭一开始，大家四处奔跑找地方隐蔽起来。
2 (*plural* 复数作 **shelters**) a place where you are safe from bad weather or danger（避开恶劣天气或危险事物的）遮蔽处；庇护所: *a bus shelter* (= for people who are waiting at a bus-stop) 公共汽车站的候车亭

shelter[2] /ˈʃeltə(r); ˈʃɛltɚ/ *verb* 动词 (**shelters**, **sheltering**, **sheltered** /ˈʃeltəd; ˈʃɛltɚd/)
1 make somebody or something safe from bad weather or danger 遮蔽或庇护某人或某物（避开恶劣天气或危险事物）: *The trees shelter the house from the wind.* 那些树给这所房子挡住了风。
2 go to a place where you will be safe from bad weather or danger 到遮蔽处或庇护所（以避开恶劣天气或危险事物）: *Let's shelter from the rain under that tree.* 咱们到那棵树下去避避雨吧。

shelves *plural of* **shelf** ✳ **shelf** 的复数形式

shepherd /ˈʃepəd; ˈʃɛpɚd/ *noun* 名词
a person who looks after sheep 牧羊人

she's /ʃi:z; ʃiz/
1 = **she is**
2 = **she has**

shield[1] /ʃi:ld; ʃild/ *noun* 名词
a big piece of metal, wood or leather that soldiers carried in front of their bodies when they were fighting in wars long ago. Some police officers carry shields now. 盾牌（古代战士及现在某些警察用的）

shield[2] /ʃi:ld; ʃild/ *verb* 动词 (**shields**, **shielding**, **shielded**)
keep somebody or something safe from danger or from being hurt 保护或庇护某人或某事物: *She shielded her eyes from the sun with her hand.* 她用手遮住阳光保护眼睛。

shift[1] /ʃɪft; ʃɪft/ *verb* 动词 (**shifts**, **shifting**, **shifted**)
move something to another place 把某物移动到另一个地方: *Can you help me to shift the bed? I want to sweep the floor.* 你帮我挪挪床行吗？我想扫扫地。

shift[2] /ʃɪft; ʃɪft/ *noun* 名词
a group of workers who begin work when another group finishes 轮班工作的职工: *Each shift in the factory works for eight hours.* 这家工厂每班职工工作八小时。◇ *the night shift* 上夜班的职工

S

shine /ʃaɪn; ʃaɪn/ *verb* 动词 (**shines**, **shining**, **shone** /ʃɒn; ʃon/, **has shone**)
1 give out light 发光；照耀: *The sun is shining.* 太阳放射着光芒。
2 be bright 发亮: *I polished the silver until it shone.* 我把银器擦亮了。
shine *noun* 名词 (no plural 无复数)
brightness 光亮；光泽: *This shampoo will give your hair a lovely shine.* 用这种洗发液可使头发润泽光亮。
shiny *adjective* 形容词 (**shinier**, **shiniest**)
a shiny new car 亮闪闪的新汽车

ship /ʃɪp; ʃɪp/ *noun* 名词
a big boat for long journeys on the sea 轮船；舰: *We went to India by ship.* 我们坐轮船到印度去了。
ship *verb* 动词 (**ships**, **shipping**, **shipped** /ʃɪpt; ʃɪpt/)
send something in a ship 用船运送某物: *New Zealand ships meat to Britain.* 新西兰经海运把肉类运往英国。

S

shipping /ˈʃɪpɪŋ; ˈʃɪpɪŋ/ *noun* 名词 (no plural 无复数)
ships 船舶: *The port is now open to shipping.* 这个口岸现已开放。

shipwreck /ˈʃɪprek; ˈʃɪpˌrɛk/ *noun* 名词
an accident at sea when a ship breaks in bad weather or on rocks 海难（船舶遭遇恶劣天气或触礁等而严重损毁的事故）
be shipwrecked be on a ship when it is in a shipwreck 遭遇海难: *They were shipwrecked off the coast of Portugal.* 他们在葡萄牙近海遇难。

shirt /ʃɜ:t; ʃɝt/ *noun* 名词
a thin piece of clothing that you wear on the top part of your body 衬衫 ☞ picture at **suit** 见 **suit** 词条插图

shiver /ˈʃɪvə(r); ˈʃɪvɚ/ *verb* 动词 (**shivers**, **shivering**, **shivered** /ˈʃɪvəd; ˈʃɪvɚd/)
shake because you are cold, frightened or ill（因寒冷、害怕或生病）颤抖；哆嗦: *We were shivering with cold.* 我们当时冻得直打哆嗦。

shock[1] /ʃɒk; ʃɑk/ *noun* 名词
1 a very bad surprise 震骇；惊愕: *The news of his death was a shock to all of us.* 我们获悉他死亡的消息都十分震惊。
2 a sudden pain when electricity goes through your body 触电；电休克；电击: *Don't touch that wire—you'll get an electric shock.* 别碰那条电线——看把你电着。

shock[2] /ʃɒk; ʃɑk/ *verb* 动词 (**shocks**, **shocking**, **shocked** /ʃɒkt; ʃɑkt/)
give somebody a very bad surprise; upset somebody 使某人震骇或惊愕: *She was shocked by his death.* 她得知他已死亡非常震惊。

shocking /ˈʃɒkɪŋ; ˈʃɑkɪŋ/ *adjective* 形容词
If something is shocking, it makes you feel upset, angry, or surprised in a very bad way 使人震骇或惊愕的: *a shocking crime* 骇人听闻的罪行

shoes 鞋

shoe /ʃu:; ʃu/ *noun* 名词
a covering made of leather or plastic that you wear on your foot 鞋: *a pair of shoes* 一双鞋 ◇ *What size are these shoes?* 这双鞋是多大号的？◇ *a shoe shop* 鞋店

shoelace /ˈʃu:leɪs; ˈʃuˌles/ *noun* 名词
a string that you tie to close a shoe 鞋带: *Tie your shoelaces.* 把你的鞋带系上。

shoestring /ˈʃu:strɪŋ; ˈʃuˌstrɪŋ/ *American English for* **shoelace** 美式英语，即 **shoelace**

shone *form of* **shine** ＊ **shine** 的不同形式

shook *form of* **shake** ＊ **shake** 的不同形式

shoot[1] /ʃu:t; ʃut/ *verb* 动词 (**shoots**, **shooting**, **shot** /ʃɒt; ʃɑt/, **has shot**)
1 send a bullet from a gun or an arrow from a bow; hurt or kill a person or an animal with a gun 开枪；射箭；用枪射击人或动物: *She shot a bird.* 她射中了一只鸟。◇ *The police officer was shot in the arm.* 警察的胳膊中了一枪。
2 move quickly or suddenly 迅速或突然移动: *The car shot past us.* 汽车从我们旁边飞速驶过。
3 make a film 拍摄影片: *They are shooting a film about the war.* 他们正在摄制一部关于那场战争的影片。

shoot[2] /ʃu:t; ʃut/ *noun* 名词
a new part of a plant（植物的）嫩芽；幼苗；新枝: *The first shoots appear in spring.* 这种植物在春天长出新芽。

shop[1] /ʃɒp; ʃɑp/ *noun* 名词
a building where you buy things 商店；店铺: *a bookshop* 书店 ◇ *a clothes shop* 服装店

shop assistant /ˈʃɒp əsɪstənt; ˈʃɑp əˌsɪstənt/ *noun* 名词
a person who works in a shop 店员；售货员

shopkeeper /ˈʃɒpki:pə(r); ˈʃɑpˌkipɚ/ *noun* 名词
a person who owns a small shop 店主

shoplifter /ˈʃɒplɪftə(r); ˈʃɑpˌlɪftɚ/ *noun* 名词
a person who steals things from shops 入店行窃的人；高买

shoplifting /ˈʃɒplɪftɪŋ; ˈʃɑpˌlɪftɪŋ/ *noun* 名词 (no plural 无复数)
stealing things from shops 入店行窃；高买

shop[2] /ʃɒp; ʃɑp/ *verb* 动词 (**shops**, **shopping**, **shopped** /ʃɒpt; ʃɑpt/)
go to buy things from shops 到商店买东西: *I'm shopping for some new clothes.* 我正在商店买几件衣服。✪ It is more usual to say **go shopping**. ✳ **go shopping** 是常用词语。

shopper *noun* 名词
a person who is buying things 买东西的人: *The streets were full of shoppers.* 街上有很多去买东西的人。

shopping /ˈʃɒpɪŋ; ˈʃɑpɪŋ/ *noun* 名词 (no plural 无复数)
1 buying things from shops（在商店里）买东西；购物: *She does her shopping after work.* 她下班后到商店去买东西。
2 the things that you have bought in a shop 在商店里买的东西: *Will you carry my shopping for me?* 我在商店里买了些东西，你给我拿着行吗？

go shopping go to buy things from shops 到商店去买东西

shopping centre /ˈʃɒpɪŋ sentə(r); ˈʃɑpɪŋ ˌsɛntɚ/ *noun* 名词
a place where there are a lot of shops together 购物中心；商业区

shopping mall /ˈʃɒpɪŋ mɔ:l; ˈʃɑpɪŋ ˌmɔl/ *noun* 名词
a big building where there are a lot of shops together 商场

shore /ʃɔ:(r); ʃɔr/ *noun* 名词
the land next to the sea or a lake 海滨或湖滨

short /ʃɔ:t; ʃɔrt/ *adjective* 形容词 (**shorter**, **shortest**)
1 very little from one end to the other 短的: *Her hair is very short.* 她的头发很短。◇ *We live a short distance from the beach.* 我们住的地方离海滩很近。✪ opposite 反义词: **long** ☞ picture on page C26 见第C26页图
2 very little from the bottom to the top 矮的: *I'm too short to reach the top shelf.* 我很矮，够不着架子的最上一层。◇ *a short fat man* 矮胖的男子 ✪ opposite 反义词: **tall** ☞ picture on page C26 见第C26页图
3 that only lasts for a little time 时间短的: *The film was very short.* 那部影片很短。◇ *a short holiday* 很短的假期 ✪ opposite 反义词: **long**

be short of something not have enough of something 短缺某物: *I'm short of money this month.* 我这个月缺钱。

for short as a short way of saying or writing something 作为简称或简写: *My sister's name is Deborah, but we call her 'Deb' for short.* 我妹妹的名字叫德博拉，可是我们把她的名字简化叫做德博。

short for something a short way of saying or writing something 简称或简写的方式: *'Tom' is short for 'Thomas'.* “汤姆”是“托马斯”的缩略形式。

shortage /ˈʃɔ:tɪdʒ; ˈʃɔrtɪdʒ/ *noun* 名词
when there is not enough of something（某物的）短缺: *a water shortage* 缺水时期 ◇ *There is a shortage of good teachers.* 现在缺少优秀教师。

short cut /ˌʃɔ:t ˈkʌt; ˈʃɔrt ˌkʌt/ *noun* 名词
a shorter way to get somewhere 近路；捷径: *We took a short cut to school across the field.* 我们穿过田野抄近路去上学。

shorten /ˈʃɔ:tn; ˈʃɔrtn̩/ *verb* 动词 (**shortens**, **shortening**, **shortened** /ˈʃɔ:tnd; ˈʃɔrtn̩d/)
become shorter or make something shorter（使某物）变短: *The trousers were too long, so I shortened them.* 这条裤子太长，我把它改短了。

shortly /ˈʃɔ:tli; ˈʃɔrtlɪ/ *adverb* 副词
soon 不久；立刻: *The doctor will see you shortly, Mr Smith.* 史密斯先生，医生马上就给您看病。◇ *We left shortly after six o'clock.* 我们六点钟以后不久就走了。

S

shorts /ʃɔ:ts; ʃɔrts/ *noun* 名词 (plural 复数)

shorts 短裤

1 short trousers that end above your knees 短裤: *a pair of shorts* 一条短裤

2 *American English for* **underpants** 美式英语，即 **underpants**

shot¹ *form of* **shoot¹** ＊ **shoot¹** 的不同形式

shot² /ʃɒt; ʃɑt/ *noun* 名词

1 firing a gun, or the noise that this makes 射击；发射；枪炮声: *He fired a shot.* 他开了一枪。

2 a photograph 照片: *This is a good shot of you.* 您这张照片照得很好。

3 kicking or hitting a ball in a sport like football（球类运动中的）击球；踢球（例如足球运动中的）

should /ʃʊd; ʃud/ *modal verb* 情态动词

1 a word that you use to tell or ask somebody what is the right thing to do 用以告诉或询问某人怎样做才对的词；应该: *If you feel ill, you should stay in bed.* 生了病就应该卧床。◇ *Should I invite him to the party?* 我应该请他来参加聚会吗？

2 a word that you use to say what you think will happen or what you think is true 用以表示推测的词；可能: *They should arrive soon.* 他们大概快到了。

3 the word for 'shall' in the past ＊ shall 的过去时态: *We asked if we should help her.* 我们问过是否要帮助她。

✪ The negative form of 'should' is **should not** or the short form **shouldn't** /ˈʃʊdnt; ˈʃudn̩t/ ＊ should 的否定式是 **should not** 或用其缩略式 **shouldn't** /ˈʃʊdnt; ˈʃudn̩t/: *You shouldn't eat so much chocolate.* 你不应该吃那么多巧克力。

☞ Look at the Note on page 314 to find out more about **modal verbs**. 见第314页对 **modal verbs** 的进一步解释。

shoulder /ˈʃəʊldə(r); ˈʃoldɚ/ *noun* 名词 the part of your body between your neck and your arm 肩；肩膀 ☞ picture on page C2 见第C2页图

shouldn't /ˈʃʊdnt; ˈʃudn̩t/ = **should not**

shout /ʃaʊt; ʃaut/ *verb* 动词 (**shouts, shouting, shouted**)

speak very loudly 呼喊；喊叫: *Don't shout at me!* 别冲着我喊！◇ *'Go back!' she shouted.* "回去！"她喊道。

shout *noun* 名词

We heard a shout for help. 我们听见有人高声呼救。

shove /ʃʌv; ʃʌv/ *verb* 动词 (**shoves, shoving, shoved** /ʃʌvd; ʃʌvd/)

push somebody or something in a rough way 乱推某人或某物: *They shoved him through the door.* 他们把他连推带搡经过了那道门。

shovel /ˈʃʌvl; ˈʃʌvl̩/ *noun* 名词

a tool like a **spade** with a short handle, that you use for moving earth or sand, for example（短柄的）铲子；铁锨（铁锹叫做 **spade**）

shovel *verb* 动词 (**shovels, shovelling, shovelled** /ˈʃʌvld; ˈʃʌvl̩d/)

move something with a shovel 用铲子或铁锨铲某物: *We shovelled the snow off the path.* 我们把小路上的雪铲掉了。✪ In American English the spellings are **shoveling** and **shoveled**. 美式英语的拼法为 **shoveling** 和 **shoveled**。

show¹ /ʃəʊ; ʃo/ *verb* 动词 (**shows, showing, showed** /ʃəʊd; ʃod/, **has shown** /ʃəʊn; ʃon/ or 或 **has showed**)

1 let somebody see something 给某人看某物: *She showed me her holiday photos.* 她给我看了看她度假时照的相片。◇ *You have to show your ticket on the train.* 在火车上要出示车票。

2 make something clear; explain something to somebody 使某事物清楚；向某人解释某事物: *Can you show me how to use the computer?* 您给我讲讲使用计算机的方法行吗？

3 appear or be seen 出现或被看见: *The anger showed in his face.* 他脸上显出生气的样子。

show off talk loudly or do something silly to make people notice you 炫耀；显弄: *Joyce drove her new car very fast to show off.* 乔伊斯为炫耀她有新汽车，把车开得非常快。

show something off let people see something that is new or beautiful 让大家看新的或漂亮的东西: *James wanted to show off his new jacket.* 詹姆斯想让人看他的新外套。

show somebody round go with

somebody and show them everything in a building 带某人到建筑物里各处参观: *David showed me round the school.* 戴维带我参观了那所学校。

show up arrive 到达: *What time did they show up?* 他们什么时候到?

show² /ʃəʊ; ʃo/ *noun* 名词

1 something that you watch at the theatre or on television (戏剧或电视的)演出;表演;节目: *a comedy show* 喜剧节目 ◇ *Did you enjoy the show?* 这场演出您喜欢吗?

2 a group of things in one place that people go to see 展览;展览会: *a flower show* 花展

on show in a place where people can see it 展出: *The paintings are on show at the National Gallery until 15 May.* 国立美术馆画展至5月15日结束。

shower /'ʃaʊə(r); 'ʃaʊɚ/ *noun* 名词

1 a place where you can wash by standing under water that falls from above you 淋浴处: *There's a shower in the bathroom.* 浴室里有淋浴设施。

2 washing yourself in a shower 淋浴: *I had a shower after the tennis match.* 我在网球比赛后冲了个淋浴。

3 rain that falls for a short time 阵雨

shown *form of* **show¹** ✳ **show¹** 的不同形式

shrank *form of* **shrink** ✳ **shrink** 的不同形式

shred /ʃred; ʃrɛd/ *noun* 名词

a small thin piece torn or cut off something (从某物上撕下或切下的)细条或碎片: *shreds of paper* 碎纸条

shriek /ʃri:k; ʃrik/ *verb* 动词 (**shrieks, shrieking, shrieked** /ʃri:kt; ʃrikt/)

make a loud high cry 尖叫: *She shrieked in fear* (= because she was afraid). 她吓得尖叫起来。

shriek *noun* 名词

He gave a shriek of pain. 他疼得尖叫了一声。

shrill /ʃrɪl; ʃrɪl/ *adjective* 形容词 (**shriller, shrillest**)

A shrill sound is high and loud (指声音)高而大的: *a shrill whistle* 刺耳的哨子声

shrimp /ʃrɪmp; ʃrɪmp/ *noun* 名词

a small sea animal that you can eat 小虾

shrine /ʃraɪn; ʃraɪn/ *noun* 名词

a special holy place 圣地: *the shrine at Lourdes* 卢尔德圣地(在法国西南部)

shrink /ʃrɪŋk; ʃrɪŋk/ *verb* 动词 (**shrinks, shrinking, shrank** /ʃræŋk; ʃræŋk/ or 或 **shrunk** /ʃrʌŋk; ʃrʌŋk/, **has shrunk**)

become smaller or make something smaller (使某物)变小;收缩: *My jeans shrank when I washed them.* 我的牛仔裤洗后缩水了。

shrub /ʃrʌb; ʃrʌb/ *noun* 名词

a plant like a small low tree 灌木

shrug /ʃrʌg; ʃrʌg/ *verb* 动词 (**shrugs, shrugging, shrugged** /ʃrʌgd; ʃrʌgd/)

move your shoulders to show that you do not know or do not care about something 耸肩(表示不知道或不在乎): *I asked her where Sam was but she just shrugged.* 我问她萨姆在哪儿呢,她只是耸了耸肩(表示不知道或与己无关)。

shrug *noun* 名词 (no plural 无复数)

He answered my question with a shrug. 他没有回答我的问题,只是耸了耸肩(表示不知道或与己无关)。

shrunk *form of* **shrink** ✳ **shrink** 的不同形式

shudder /'ʃʌdə(r); 'ʃʌdɚ/ *verb* 动词 (**shudders, shuddering, shuddered** /'ʃʌdəd; 'ʃʌdɚd/)

shake, for example because you are afraid 发抖;哆嗦(例如因为害怕): *He shuddered when he saw the snake.* 他看见蛇了,吓得直发抖。

shudder *noun* 名词

She felt a shudder of fear. 她吓了一哆嗦。

shuffle /'ʃʌfl; 'ʃʌfl̩/ *verb* 动词 (**shuffles, shuffling, shuffled** /'ʃʌfld; 'ʃʌfl̩d/)

1 walk slowly, without taking your feet off the ground 拖着脚步走: *The old man shuffled along the road.* 老翁拖着脚步在路上走。

2 mix playing-cards before a game 洗牌(玩纸牌前把牌搀和整理)

shut¹ /ʃʌt; ʃʌt/ *verb* 动词 (**shuts, shutting, shut, has shut**)

1 move something so that it is not open 把某物关上: *Could you shut the door, please?* 劳驾,请把门关上行吗?

2 move so that it is not open 关上: *The door shut behind me.* 那扇门在我经过之后就关上了。

3 stop being open, so that people cannot go there 不开放(大家不能进入): *The shops shut at 5.30.* 这里的商店5点30分关门。

S

shut down close and stop working; make something close and stop working（使某事物）关闭而不再工作；停工: *The factory shut down last year.* 那家工厂去年关闭了。

shut up stop talking 不再说话: *Shut up and listen!* 闭上嘴，听着！✪ This expression is quite rude. 这句话很粗俗。

shut² /ʃʌt; ʃʌt/ *adjective* 形容词
closed; not open 关闭的；关着的；不开的: *The restaurant is shut today.* 这家饭馆今天不营业。◇ *Is the door shut?* 门关着呢吗？☞ picture on page C27 见第C27页图

shutter /ˈʃʌtə(r); ˈʃʌtɚ/ *noun* 名词
a wooden or metal thing that covers the outside of a window 百叶窗: *Close the shutters.* 把百叶窗关上吧。

shuttle /ˈʃʌtl; ˈʃʌtl̩/ *noun* 名词
an aeroplane or a bus that goes to a place and then back again and again 穿梭班机或公共汽车（定期往返的）

S

shy /ʃaɪ; ʃaɪ/ *adjective* 形容词 (**shyer**, **shyest**)
not able to talk easily to people you do not know 羞怯的: *He was too shy to speak to her.* 他害羞，不敢跟她说话。

shyness /ˈʃaɪnəs; ˈʃaɪnɪs/ *noun* 名词 (no plural 无复数)
being shy 羞怯

sick /sɪk; sɪk/ *adjective* 形容词 (**sicker**, **sickest**)
not well; ill 有病的: *She's looking after her sick mother.* 她正在照看生病的母亲。

be sick When you are sick, food comes up from your stomach and out of your mouth. 呕吐

be sick of something have had or done too much of something, so that you do not want it any longer 厌倦或腻烦某事物: *I'm sick of watching TV—let's go out.* 我看腻了电视了——咱们出去吧。

feel sick feel that food is going to come up from your stomach 恶心；作呕

sickness /ˈsɪknəs; ˈsɪknɪs/ *noun* 名词 (no plural 无复数)
being ill 疾病: *He could not work for a long time because of sickness.* 他因病长期不能工作。

side /saɪd; saɪd/ *noun* 名词
1 one of the flat outside parts of something（物体外部的）平面: *A box has six sides.* 一个盒子有六个面。◇ *A piece of paper has two sides.* 一张纸有两面。
2 the part of something that is not the front, back, top or bottom（物体的）侧面（不包括前、后、上或下）: *There is a door at the side of the house.* 房子的侧面有个门。☞ picture at **back** 见 **back** 词条插图
3 the edge of something; the part that is away from the middle（物体的）边缘；旁边: *I stood at the side of the road.* 我当时站在马路边上。
4 the right or left part of something（物体的）右边或左边的部分: *He lay on his side.* 他侧身躺着。◇ *We drive on the left side of the road in Britain.* 在英国，车辆在道路的左侧行驶。
5 one of two groups of people who fight or play a game against each other（争斗或比赛的）一方: *Which side won?* 哪边儿赢了？

be on somebody's side agree with or help somebody in a fight or argument 在争斗或辩论中赞同或帮助某一方: *Rose said I was wrong, but Andy was on my side.* 罗斯说我错了，可是安迪站在我这边。

side by side next to each other 紧挨着；肩并肩地: *They walked side by side.* 他们肩并肩地走。

take sides show that you agree with one person, and not the other, in a fight or an argument 在争斗或辩论中赞同一方反对另一方

sidewalk /ˈsaɪdwɔːk; ˈsaɪdˌwɔk/ *American English for* **pavement** 美式英语，即 **pavement**

sideways /ˈsaɪdweɪz; ˈsaɪdˌwez/ *adjective, adverb* 形容词，副词
1 to or from the side 斜着（的）；斜向一边（的）；横向（的）；侧向（的）: *She looked sideways at the girl next to her.* 她斜眼看了看身旁的女孩儿。
2 with one of the sides first 从侧面开始: *We carried the table sideways through the door.* 我们抬着桌子侧面向前通过了那道门。

siege /siːdʒ; sidʒ/ *noun* 名词
1 when an army stays outside a town for a long time so that people and things cannot get in or out（指军队）包围城镇，围困
2 when police stay outside a building for a long time to try to make a criminal come out（指警方）长时间包围建筑物迫使罪犯出来

sigh /saɪ; saɪ/ *verb* 动词 (**sighs, sighing, sighed** /saɪd; saɪd/)
breathe once very deeply when you are sad, tired or pleased, for example 叹息；叹气（例如因悲伤、疲倦或愉快）
sigh *noun* 名词
'I wish I had more money,' he said with a sigh. 他叹了一口气说："我要是多有点儿钱就好了。"

sight /saɪt; saɪt/ *noun* 名词
1 (no plural 无复数) the power to see 视力: *She has poor sight* (= she cannot see well). 她视力很差。
2 (no plural 无复数) seeing somebody or something 看见某人或某物: *We had our first sight of London from the plane.* 我们是在飞机上第一次看见伦敦的。
3 (*plural* 复数作 **sights**) something that you see 看到的事物: *The mountains were a beautiful sight.* 那些山十分壮观。
4 (*plural* 复数作 **sights**) the interesting places to visit 使人有兴趣参观的地方: *When you come to Paris I'll show you the sights.* 您到巴黎来的时候，我带您看看这里的名胜。
at first sight when you see somebody or something for the first time 第一次见到某人或某物: *He fell in love with her at first sight.* 他对她一见钟情。
catch sight of somebody or 或 **something** see somebody or something suddenly 突然看见某人或某物: *I caught sight of Fiona in the crowd.* 我在人群里看见菲奥纳了。
come into sight come where you can see it 进入视野: *The train came into sight.* 已经能看见那列火车了。
in sight where you can see it 在视野内；看得见: *Is the land in sight yet?* 看得见陆地了吗？
lose sight of somebody or 或 **something** no longer be able to see somebody or something 再看不见某人或某物: *After an hour at sea we lost sight of land.* 我们在海上航行了一小时以后就看不见陆地了。
out of sight where you cannot see it 在视野外；看不见: *We watched until the car was out of sight.* 我们注视着那辆汽车，直到看不见为止。

sightseer /ˈsaɪtsiːə(r); ˈsaɪtˌsiɚ/ *noun* 名词
a person who is visiting interesting places 观光客；游人: *The town was full of sightseers.* 镇上到处都是游客。

sightseeing /ˈsaɪtsiːɪŋ; ˈsaɪtˌsiɪŋ/ *noun* 名词 (no plural 无复数)
visiting interesting places 观光；游览: *We did some sightseeing in Rome.* 我们在罗马游览了一番。

signs 指示牌

sign[1] /saɪn; saɪn/ *noun* 名词
1 a mark, shape or movement that has a special meaning（表意的）符号、图形或动作: *+ and – are signs that mean 'plus' and 'minus'.* + 和 – 是表示"加"和"减"的符号。◇ *I put up my hand as a sign for him to stop.* 我举起手来示意让他停止。
2 a thing with writing or a picture on it that tells you something 有指示性文字或图形的标志物；指示牌: *The sign said 'No Smoking'.* 指示牌上写着"禁止吸烟"。◇ *a road sign* 道路标志牌
3 something that tells you about another thing 迹象；征兆: *Dark clouds are a sign of rain.* 天上有乌云是要下雨的征兆。

sign[2] /saɪn; saɪn/ *verb* 动词 (**signs, signing, signed** /saɪnd; saɪnd/)
write your name in your own way on something 签字；签名；署名: *Sign here, please.* 请在这里签字。◇ *I signed the cheque.* 我在支票上签了字。✪ The noun is **signature**. 名词是 **signature**。

signal /ˈsɪgnəl; ˈsɪgnl̩/ *noun* 名词
a light, sound or movement that tells you something without words（表意的）光亮、声音或动作: *A red light is a signal for cars to stop.* 红灯是示意汽车停止的信号。◇ *radio signals* 无线电信号
signal *verb* 动词 (**signals, signalling, signalled** /ˈsɪgnəld; ˈsɪgnl̩d/)
make a signal 发出信号: *The policeman signalled to the children to cross the road.* 警察示意让儿童横过马路。✪ In American English the spellings are **signaling** and **signaled**. 美式英语的拼法为 **signaling** 和 **signaled**。

S

signature /'sɪgnətʃə(r); 'sɪgnətʃɚ/ *noun* 名词
your name that you have written in your own way 签字；签名；署名 ☞ picture at **cheque** 见 **cheque** 词条插图

significance /sɪg'nɪfɪkəns; sɪg'nɪfəkəns/ *noun* 名词 (no plural 无复数)
the importance or meaning of something 意义；意思: *What is the significance of this discovery?* 这项发现有什么意义？

significant /sɪg'nɪfɪkənt; sɪg'nɪfəkənt/ *adjective* 形容词
important; with a special meaning 重要的；有意义的: *The police say that the time of the robbery was very significant.* 警方说劫案发生的时间在案中非常重要。

signpost /'saɪnpəʊst; 'saɪnˌpost/ *noun* 名词
a sign beside a road, that shows the way to a place and how far it is（指示到某处及其距离的）路标

S

Sikh /si:k; sik/ *noun* 名词
a person who follows one of the religions of India, called **Sikhism** 锡克教教徒（锡克教叫做 **Sikhism**）

silence /'saɪləns; 'saɪləns/ *noun* 名词
1 (no plural 无复数) When there is silence, there is no sound 无声；寂静: *I can only work in complete silence.* 我在完全安静的环境中才能工作。
2 (*plural* 复数作 **silences**) a time when nobody speaks or makes a noise 无人说话或不发出声响的一段时间；沉默；肃静: *There was a long silence before she answered the question.* 她沉默了很长时间才回答那个问题。
in silence without speaking or making a noise 不说话或不发出声响；安静地；无声地: *We ate our dinner in silence.* 我们静静地吃着饭。

silent /'saɪlənt; 'saɪlənt/ *adjective* 形容词
1 If you are silent, you are not speaking 不说话的；沉默的: *I asked him a question and he was silent for a moment before he answered.* 我问了他一个问题，他沉默了一下才回答。
2 with no sound; completely quiet 无声的；寂静的: *Everyone was asleep, and the house was silent.* 大家都睡了，房子里十分安静。
silently *adverb* 副词
The cat moved silently towards the bird. 猫轻轻地向鸟走去。

silk /sɪlk; sɪlk/ *noun* 名词 (no plural 无复数)
thin smooth cloth that is made from the threads that an insect (called a **silkworm**) makes 丝绸（蚕叫做 **silkworm**）: *This scarf is made of silk.* 这条头巾是丝制的。◇ *a silk shirt* 绸衬衫

silly /'sɪli; 'sɪlɪ/ *adjective* 形容词 (**sillier**, **silliest**)
stupid; not clever 傻的；愚蠢的: *Don't be so silly!* 别这么傻了！◇ *It was silly of you to leave the door open when you went out.* 你出去的时候没关门，真愚蠢。

silver /'sɪlvə(r); 'sɪlvɚ/ *noun* 名词 (no plural 无复数)
1 a shiny grey metal that is very valuable 银: *a silver necklace* 银项链
2 things that are made of silver, for example knives, forks and plates 银器（例如刀叉和盘）
silver *adjective* 形容词
with the colour of silver 银色的: *silver paper* 银色的纸

similar /'sɪmələ(r); 'sɪmələɚ/ *adjective* 形容词
the same in some ways but not completely the same 相似的；类似的: *Rats are similar to mice, but they are bigger.* 大鼠和耗子很相似，只是稍大些。◇ *Jenny and her sister look very similar.* 珍妮跟她姐姐长得很相像。
similarity /ˌsɪmə'lærəti; ˌsɪmə'lærətɪ/ *noun* 名词 (*plural* 复数作 **similarities**)
a way that people or things are the same 相似；类似: *There are a lot of similarities between the two countries.* 这两个国家有很多相似之处。✪ opposite 反义词: **difference**

simple /'sɪmpl; 'sɪmpl̩/ *adjective* 形容词 (**simpler**, **simplest**)
1 easy to do or understand 简单的；简明的: *This dictionary is written in simple English.* 这本词典是用简单英语编写的。◇ *'How do you open this?' 'I'll show you — it's simple.'* "这个怎么打开？""我告诉你吧——很简单。"
2 without a lot of different parts or extra things; plain 单纯的；朴素的: *She wore a simple black dress.* 她穿着朴素的黑色连衣裙。◇ *a simple meal* 简单的饭菜

simplicity /sɪm'plɪsəti; sɪm'plɪsətɪ/ *noun* 名词 (no plural 无复数)

being simple 简单；简明；单纯；朴素: *I like the simplicity of these paintings.* 我喜欢这些绘画风格朴实。

simplify /ˈsɪmplɪfaɪ; ˈsɪmpləˌfaɪ/ *verb* 动词 (**simplifies, simplifying, simplified** /ˈsɪmplɪfaɪd; ˈsɪmpləˌfaɪd/, **has simplified**)
make something easier to do or understand 使某事物简单或简明；简化: *The story has been simplified so that the children can understand it.* 这个故事经简化儿童也能看懂了。

simply /ˈsɪmpli; ˈsɪmplɪ/ *adverb* 副词
1 in a simple way 简单地；简明地；单纯地；朴素地: *Please explain it more simply.* 请解释得再简单些。
2 only 仅；只: *Don't get angry—I'm simply asking you to help.* 别生气——我只不过是请您帮个忙而已。
3 really 真正地；实在地: *The weather was simply terrible—it rained every day!* 这种天气简直太糟糕了——天天下雨！

sin /sɪn; sɪn/ *noun* 名词
something that your religion says you should not do, because it is very bad (违背宗教教义的）恶行；罪过: *Stealing is a sin.* 偷窃行为是违背宗教教义的罪恶。

sin *verb* 动词 (**sins, sinning, sinned** /sɪnd; sɪnd/)
do something that your religion says is very bad 犯有（违背宗教教义的）恶行或罪过

since /sɪns; sɪns/ *preposition* 介词
in all the time after 从（过去某时）以后: *She has been ill since Sunday.* 她从星期日以来一直病着。◇ *I haven't seen him since 1987.* 我从1987年起就再没见过他。

since *conjunction* 连词
1 from the time when 从（过去某时）以后: *She has lived here since she was a child.* 她从小就住在这里。◇ *Jenny hasn't phoned since she went to Berlin.* 珍妮到柏林后就再没打过电话。
2 because 因为；既然；由于: *Since it's your birthday, I'll buy you a drink.* 因为是你的生日，我来请你喝一杯。

since *adverb* 副词
from then until now 从那时到现在: *Andy left three years ago and we haven't seen him since.* 安迪三年前就走了，我们从此再也没见过他。
ever since in all the time from then until now 从那时起一直到现在: *George*

S

for or since? 用 **for** 还是用 **since**？
We use **for** to say how long something has continued, for example in **hours, days** or **years** 用 **for** 表示某事物持续了多长时间，例如多少小时 (**hour**)、天 (**day**) 或年 (**year**)：

*She has been ill **for** three days.* 她病了三天了。

*I have lived in London **for** ten months.* 我在伦敦住了十个月了。

We have been married **for** thirty years. 我们结婚已经三十年了。

We use **since** with points of time in the past, for example a **time** on the clock, a **date** or an **event** 用 **since** 表示从过去的某时间起，例如几点钟 (**time** on the clock)、日期 (**date**) 或一件事 (**event**)：

*I have been here **since** six o'clock.* 我从六点钟起就一直在这儿。

*She has been alone **since** her husband died.* 她从丈夫死后就一直独自生活。

We have been married **since** 1965. 我们是1965年结的婚。

went to Canada in 1974 and he has lived there ever since. 乔治1974年到加拿大去了，从那时起他就一直住在那儿。

sincere /sɪn'sɪə(r); sɪn'sɪr/ *adjective* 形容词
If you are sincere, you are honest and you mean what you say 诚实的；直率的: *Were you being sincere when you said that you loved me?* 你说你爱我，说的是真心话吗？

sincerely *adverb* 副词
Yours sincerely words that you write at the end of a letter, before your name 用于信件署名前的敬语

sing /sɪŋ; sɪŋ/ *verb* 动词 (**sings**, **singing**, **sang** /sæŋ; sæŋ/, **has sung** /sʌŋ; sʌŋ/)
make music with your voice 唱；唱歌: *She sang a song.* 她唱了一支歌。◇ *The birds were singing.* 小鸟唱着歌。

singer *noun* 名词
a person who sings 唱歌的人；歌手；歌唱家

S

single[1] /'sɪŋgl; 'sɪŋgl̩/ *adjective* 形容词
1 only one 单一的；单个的: *There wasn't a single cloud in the sky.* 天空中一丝乌云都没有。
2 not married 未婚的；独身的: *Are you married or single?* 您是已婚还是单身？
3 for one person 为一个人的；单人的: *I would like to book a single room, please.* 劳驾，我想预订个单人房间。◇ *a single bed* 单人床 ☞ Look at **double**. 见 **double**。
4 for a journey to a place, but not back again（指旅程）单程的（非往返的）: *How much is a single ticket to London, please?* 请问，到伦敦的单程票多少钱一张？ ☞ Look at **return**. 见 **return**。
every single each 每一个: *You answered every single question correctly.* 你回答的每一个问题都很正确。

single[2] /'sɪŋgl; 'sɪŋgl̩/ *noun* 名词
1 a ticket for a journey to a place, but not back again 单程票: *A single to Brighton, please.* 请给我一张到布赖顿的单程票。☞ Look at **return**. 见 **return**。
2 a small record that has only one song on each side 单曲唱片（每面只录有一首歌的小唱片）: *Have you heard Prince's new single?* 你听过普林斯新出的单曲唱片吗？ ☞ Look at **album** and **LP**. 见 **album** 和 **LP**。

singular /'sɪŋgjələ(r); 'sɪŋgjələ˞/ *noun* 名词 (no plural 无复数)
the form of a word that you use for one person or thing（指词的）单数形式: *The singular of 'men' is 'man'.* ✳ men 的单数形式是 man 。

singular *adjective* 形容词
'Table' is a singular noun. ✳ table 是个单数名词。
☞ Look at **plural**. 见 **plural**。

sink[1] /sɪŋk; sɪŋk/ *noun* 名词
the place in a kitchen where you wash dishes（厨房中洗碗碟用的）洗涤槽

sink[2] /sɪŋk; sɪŋk/ *verb* 动词 (**sinks**, **sinking**, **sank** /sæŋk; sæŋk/, **has sunk** /sʌŋk; sʌŋk/)
1 go down under water 沉入水中；下沉；沉没: *If you throw a stone into water, it sinks.* 石头扔进水里就沉下去了。◇ *The fishing boat sank to the bottom of the sea.* 渔船沉到海底了。☞ Look at **float**. 见 **float**。
2 make a ship go down under water 使船沉没: *The ship was sunk by a bomb.* 船被炸弹击沉了。
3 go down 下降: *The sun sank slowly behind the hills.* 太阳慢慢落山了。

sip /sɪp; sɪp/ *verb* 动词 (**sips**, **sipping**, **sipped** /sɪpt; sɪpt/)
drink something slowly, taking only a little each time 小口喝；抿: *She sipped her coffee.* 她慢慢抿着咖啡。

sip *noun* 名词
Can I have a sip of your Coke? 让我抿一口你的可口可乐行吗？

sir /sɜː(r); sɝ/ *noun* 名词
1 (no plural 无复数) a polite way of speaking to a man, instead of using his name 对男子的礼貌称呼（而不称其名）: *'Can I help you, sir?' asked the shop assistant.* 商店售货员问: "先生，您要什么？" ☞ Look at **madam**. 见 **madam**。
2 Sir (no plural 无复数) a word that you use at the beginning of a business letter to a man 用作给男子的公函中开头的称谓: *Dear Sir ...* 敬启者... ☞ Look at **madam**. 见 **madam**。
3 Sir (no plural 无复数) the word that you use before the name of a **knight** 冠于爵士（**knight**）名前的称谓: *Sir Winston Churchill* 温斯顿·丘吉尔爵士

siren /'saɪrən; 'saɪrən/ *noun* 名词
a machine that makes a long loud sound to warn people about something. Police cars and fire-engines have sirens. 汽笛；警报器（警车和救火车上均有。）

sister /'sɪstə(r); 'sɪstɚ/ *noun* 名词
1 Your sister is a girl or woman who has the same parents as you 姐姐或妹妹: *I've got two sisters and one brother.* 我有两个姐姐和一个哥哥。◇ *Jenny and Anne are sisters.* 珍妮和安妮是姐俩。☞ picture on page C3 见第C3页图
2 a nurse in a hospital 护士

sister-in-law /'sɪstər ɪn lɔ:; 'sɪstərɪnˌlɔ/ *noun* 名词 (*plural* 复数作 **sisters-in-law**)
1 the sister of your wife or husband 妻子或丈夫的姐姐或妹妹；姨子；姑子
2 the wife of your brother 哥哥或弟弟的妻子；嫂子；弟媳 ☞ picture on page C3 见第C3页图

sit /sɪt; sɪt/ *verb* 动词 (**sits**, **sitting**, **sat** /sæt; sæt/, **has sat**)
1 rest on your bottom 坐；就座: *We sat in the garden all afternoon.* 我们一下午都坐在花园里。◇ *She was sitting on the sofa.* 她在长沙发上坐着。
2 (*also* 亦作 **sit down**) put yourself down on your bottom 坐下；就座: *Come and sit next to me.* 来，坐在我旁边。◇ *She came into the room and sat down.* 她进了屋就坐下了。
3 do an examination 参加考试: *The students will sit their exams in June.* 学生六月就要考试了。
sit up sit when you have been lying（指原来躺着）坐起来: *He sat up in bed and looked at the clock.* 他从床上坐起来看了看时钟。
sitting-room /'sɪtɪŋ ru:m; 'sɪtɪŋˌrum/ *noun* 名词
a room in a house where people sit and watch television or talk, for example 起居室（常在里面坐着的房间，例如看电视或谈话等）

site /saɪt; saɪt/ *noun* 名词
a place where something is, was, or will be（某事物存在的）地方；场所: *This house was built on the site of an old theatre.* 这所房子建筑在旧剧院的遗址上。◇ *a campsite* 露营区

situated /'sɪtʃueɪtɪd; 'sɪtʃuˌetɪd/ *adjective* 形容词
in a place 位于；处于: *The hotel is situated close to the beach.* 这家旅馆位于海滩附近。

situation /ˌsɪtʃu'eɪʃn; ˌsɪtʃʊ'eʃən/ *noun* 名词
the things that are happening in a certain place or at a certain time 状况；处境；局面；形势: *Susan is in a difficult situation — she can't decide what to do.* 苏珊处境困难——她不知如何是好。

six /sɪks; sɪks/ *number* 数词 (*plural* 复数作 **sixes**)
6 六
sixth /sɪksθ; sɪksθ/ *adjective, adverb, noun* 形容词，副词，名词
1 6th 第6（个）；第六（个）
2 one of six equal parts of something; 1/6 六分之一

sixteen /ˌsɪks'ti:n; sɪks'tin/ *number* 数词
16 十六
sixteenth /ˌsɪks'ti:nθ; sɪks'tinθ/ *adjective, adverb, noun* 形容词，副词，名词
16th 第16（个）；第十六（个）

sixth form /'sɪksθ fɔ:m; 'sɪksθ 'fɔrm/ *noun* 名词
the classes in the last two years of secondary school in Britain. Pupils in the sixth form are usually aged between 16 and 18.（英国中学的）六年级（为16至18岁学生而设的）

sixty /'sɪksti; 'sɪkstɪ/ *number* 数词
1 60 六十
2 the sixties (plural 复数) the numbers, years or temperature between 60 and 69 ＊ 60至69（之间的数目、年数或温度）
in your sixties between the ages of 60 and 69 年岁在60至69之间；六十多岁
sixtieth /'sɪkstiəθ; 'sɪkstɪɪθ/ *adjective, adverb, noun* 形容词，副词，名词
60th 第60（个）；第六十（个）

size /saɪz; saɪz/ *noun* 名词
1 (no plural 无复数) how big or small something is 大小: *My bedroom is the same size as yours.* 我的卧室跟你的大小一样。
2 (*plural* 复数作 **sizes**) an exact measurement（有一定量度或规格的）号，码: *Have you got these shoes in a bigger size?* 这种鞋你们有大号的吗？

skate /skeɪt; sket/ *noun* 名词
1 an ice-skate; a boot with a long sharp

S

piece of metal under it, that you wear for moving on ice 溜冰鞋: *a pair of skates* 一双溜冰鞋

2 a roller-skate; a shoe with wheels on the bottom, that you wear for moving quickly on smooth ground 旱冰鞋；轱辘鞋

skate *verb* 动词 (**skates**, **skating**, **skated**)

move on skates 溜冰；滑冰 ✪ When you talk about spending time skating as a sport, you say **go skating** 溜冰运动的说法是 **go skating**: *We go skating every weekend.* 我们每个周末都去溜冰玩儿。

skating-rink /ˈskeɪtɪŋ rɪŋk; ˈsketɪŋ-ˌrɪŋk/ *noun* 名词

a special place where you can skate on ice 溜冰场；旱冰场

skateboard /ˈskeɪtbɔːd; ˈsketˌbɔrd/ *noun* 名词

a long piece of wood or plastic on wheels. You stand on it as it moves over the ground. 滑板（装有滑轮的木板或塑料板，可站在上面在地上滑行）

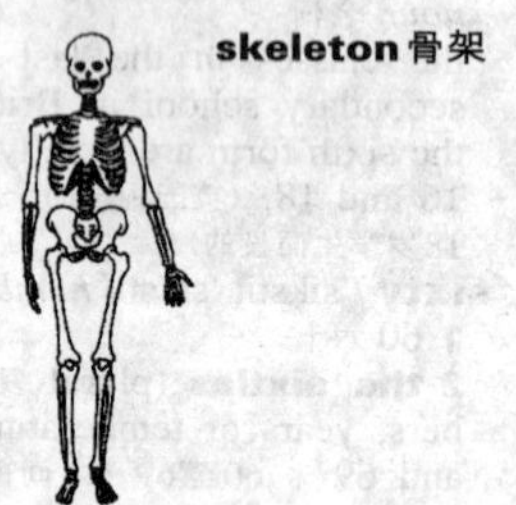

skeleton 骨架

skeleton /ˈskelɪtn; ˈskɛlətn̩/ *noun* 名词

the bones of a whole animal or person（动物或人的）全副骨骼；骨架

sketch /sketʃ; skɛtʃ/ *verb* 动词 (**sketches**, **sketching**, **sketched** /sketʃt; skɛtʃt/)

draw something quickly 迅速画某物；画速写: *I sketched the house.* 我很快画出了那所房子。

sketch *noun* 名词 (*plural* 复数作 **sketches**)

a picture that you draw quickly 迅速画成的画儿；速写的画儿

ski /skiː; ski/ *noun* 名词 (*plural* 复数作 **skis**)

a long flat piece of wood, metal or plastic that you fix to your boot so that

skiing 滑雪运动

you can move over snow 滑雪板: *a pair of skis* 一副滑雪板

ski *verb* 动词 (**skis**, **skiing** /ˈskiːɪŋ; ˈskiɪŋ/, **skied** /skiːd; skid/, **has skied**)

move over snow on skis 用滑雪板滑雪: *Can you ski?* 你会滑雪吗？✪ When you talk about spending time skiing as a sport, you say **go skiing** 滑雪运动的说法是 **go skiing**: *We went skiing in Austria.* 我们到奥地利滑雪去了。

skier *noun* 名词

a person who skis 滑雪的人

skiing *noun* 名词 (no plural 无复数)

the sport of moving over snow on skis 滑雪运动

ski slope /ˈskiː sləʊp; ˈski slop/ *noun* 名词

a part of a mountain where you can ski 滑雪坡（可供滑雪的山坡）

skid /skɪd; skɪd/ *verb* 动词 (**skids**, **skidding**, **skidded**)

If a car, lorry, etc skids, it moves suddenly and dangerously to the side, for example because the road is wet（指汽车等）滑向一侧，打滑（如因路湿）: *The lorry skidded on the icy road.* 卡车在结冰的路面上打滑了。

skies *plural of* **sky** ✳ **sky** 的复数形式

skilful /ˈskɪlfl; ˈskɪlfəl/ *adjective* 形容词

very good at doing something 善于做某事物的；熟练的: *a skilful tennis player* 技术高的网球运动员

skilfully /ˈskɪlfəli; ˈskɪlfəlɪ/ *adverb* 副词

The food was skilfully prepared. 这种食物是手艺高的人做的。

skill /skɪl; skɪl/ *noun* 名词

1 (no plural 无复数) being able to do something well 做好某事物的能力；技能；技巧；技艺: *You need great skill to fly a plane.* 开飞机需要很高的技能。

2 (*plural* 复数作 **skills**) a thing that you can do well 能做得好的某项事物；技能；特长；技艺: *What skills do you need for this job?* 做这项工作需要什么技能？

skilled /skɪld; skɪld/ *adjective* 形容词
good at something because you have learned about or done it for a long time 有技能的；训练过的；熟练的：*skilled workers* 有经验的工人 ✪ opposite 反义词：**unskilled**

skillful, **skillfully** *American English for* **skilful, skilfully** 美式英语，即 **skilful**、**skilfully**

skin /skɪn; skɪn/ *noun* 名词
1 (no plural 无复数) what covers the outside of a person or an animal's body（人或动物的）皮；皮肤：*She has dark skin.* 她皮肤黝黑。
2 (*plural* 复数作 **skins**) the outside part of some fruits and vegetables（某些水果和蔬菜的）皮；果皮；外皮：*a banana skin* 香蕉皮

skinny /ˈskɪni; ˈskɪnɪ/ *adjective* 形容词 (**skinnier**, **skinniest**)
too thin 极瘦的；皮包骨的：*He's very skinny — he doesn't eat enough.* 他非常瘦—他吃得不够。

skip /skɪp; skɪp/ *verb* 动词 (**skips**, **skipping**, **skipped** /skɪpt; skɪpt/)
1 move along quickly with little jumps from one foot to the other foot 蹦跳：*The child skipped along the road.* 孩子在路上蹦蹦跳跳地走。
2 jump many times over a rope that is turning 跳绳
3 not do or have something that you should do or have（应做的事物）不做：*I skipped my class today and went swimming.* 我今天没上课，我游泳去了。
skip *noun* 名词
a little jump 蹦；跳
skipping-rope /ˈskɪpɪŋ rəʊp; ˈskɪpɪŋˌrop/ *noun* 名词
a rope that you use for skipping 跳绳用的绳子

skirt /skɜːt; skɝt/ *noun* 名词
a piece of clothing for a woman or girl that hangs from the middle of the body（女用的）裙子 ☞ picture at **coat** 见 **coat** 词条插图

skull /skʌl; skʌl/ *noun* 名词
the bones in the head of a person or an animal 脑壳；头颅骨

sky /skaɪ; skaɪ/ *noun* 名词 (*plural* 复数作 **skies**)
the space above the earth where you can see the sun, moon and stars 天空：*a beautiful blue sky* 美丽的蓝天 ◇ *There are no clouds in the sky.* 天上没有云彩。

skyscraper /ˈskaɪskreɪpə(r); ˈskaɪˌskrepɚ/ *noun* 名词
a very tall building 摩天大楼：*He works on the 49th floor of a skyscraper.* 他在摩天大楼第49楼工作。

slab /slæb; slæb/ *noun* 名词
a thick flat piece of something 厚板：*slabs of stone* 石板 ◇ *a big slab of cheese* 一大块干酪

slam /slæm; slæm/ *verb* 动词 (**slams**, **slamming**, **slammed** /slæmd; slæmd/)
close something or put something down with a loud noise 关闭或放下某物并发出巨响：*She slammed the door angrily.* 她生气地把门砰的一声关上了。◇ *He slammed the book on the table and went out.* 他把书砰的一声往桌上一放就出去了。

slang /slæŋ; slæŋ/ *noun* 名词 (no plural 无复数)
words that a certain group of people use when they are talking. You do not use slang when you need to be polite, and you do not usually use it in writing 俚语（不用于需要讲礼貌的场合，一般也不用于书面语中）：*'Quid' is slang for 'pound'.* ＊ quid 是 pound（英镑）一字的俚语。

slant /slɑːnt; slænt/ *verb* 动词 (**slants**, **slanting**, **slanted**)
Something that slants has one side higher than the other or does not stand straight up 倾斜；歪：*My handwriting slants to the left.* 我写的字向左倾斜。

slap /slæp; slæp/ *verb* 动词 (**slaps**, **slapping**, **slapped** /slæpt; slæpt/)
hit somebody with the flat inside part of your hand 掌击某人；掴：*He slapped me in the face.* 他打了我一个耳光。
slap *noun* 名词
She gave me a slap across the face. 她给了我一个耳光。

slaughter /ˈslɔːtə(r); ˈslɔtɚ/ *verb* 动词 (**slaughters**, **slaughtering**, **slaughtered** /ˈslɔːtəd; ˈslɔtɚd/)
1 kill an animal for food 屠宰动物（供食用）
2 kill a lot of people in a cruel way 残忍地屠杀大批的人
slaughter *noun* 名词 (no plural 无复数)
killing animals or people（对动物或人的）屠杀；杀戮

S

slave /sleɪv; slev/ *noun* 名词
a person who belongs to another person and must work for that person for no money 奴隶

slavery /ˈsleɪvəri; ˈslevərɪ/ *noun* 名词 (no plural 无复数)
1 being a slave 身为奴隶: *They lived in slavery.* 他们过着奴隶的生活。
2 having slaves 有奴隶的状况: *When did slavery end in America?* 美国的奴隶制度是什么时候结束的?

sledge /sledʒ; slɛdʒ/ *noun* 名词
a thing that you sit in to move over snow. A sledge has pieces of metal or wood instead of wheels. Large sledges are sometimes pulled by dogs. 雪橇(大型雪橇有时用狗拉)

sleep /sli:p; slip/ *verb* 动词 (**sleeps, sleeping, slept** /slept; slɛpt/, **has slept**)
rest with your eyes closed, as you do at night 睡;睡觉;睡着: *I sleep for eight hours every night.* 我每晚睡八小时觉。◇ *Did you sleep well?* 您睡得好吗?

> ✪ Be careful! We usually say **be asleep**, not **be sleeping** 注意!通常说 **be asleep**,不说 **be sleeping**:
>
> *I was asleep when you phoned.* 你来电话的时候我已经睡了。
>
> We use **go to sleep** or **fall asleep** to talk about starting to sleep. 表达入睡的意思,要用 **go to sleep** 或 **fall asleep**。

sleep *noun* 名词 (no plural 无复数)
I didn't get any sleep last night. 我昨天一夜都没睡。

go to sleep start to sleep 入睡: *I got into bed and soon went to sleep.* 我上床后很快就睡着了。

sleeping-bag /ˈsli:pɪŋ bæg; ˈslipɪŋ-bæg/ *noun* 名词
a big warm bag that you sleep in when you go camping 睡袋(露营用的)

sleepless /ˈsli:pləs; ˈsliplɪs/ *adjective* 形容词
without sleep 失眠的;不眠的: *I had a sleepless night.* 我夜里失眠了。

sleepy /ˈsli:pi; ˈslipɪ/ *adjective* 形容词 (**sleepier, sleepiest**)
1 tired and ready to sleep 困倦的;欲睡的: *I felt sleepy after that big meal.* 我吃了这一大顿饭以后觉得困了。
2 quiet, with not many things happening (指地方)冷清的;不热闹的: *a sleepy little village* 冷清的小村庄

sleet /sli:t; slit/ *noun* 名词 (no plural 无复数)
snow and rain together 雨夹雪

sleeve /sli:v; sliv/ *noun* 名词
the part of a coat, dress or shirt, for example, that covers your arm 袖子: *a shirt with short sleeves* 短袖衬衫

sleigh /sleɪ; sle/ *noun* 名词
a thing that you sit in to move over snow. A sleigh has pieces of metal or wood instead of wheels and is usually pulled by animals. 雪橇(通常用动物拉)

slender /ˈslendə(r); ˈslɛndɚ/ *adjective* 形容词
thin, in a nice way 细长的(含褒义);苗条的: *She has long, slender legs.* 她两腿修长。

slept *form of* **sleep** ✳ **sleep** 的不同形式

slice /slaɪs; slaɪs/ *noun* 名词
a thin piece that you cut off bread, meat or other food (从面包、肉等食物上切下的)薄片: *Would you like a slice of cake?* 您要一片蛋糕吗?◇ *slices of bread* 面包片 ☞ picture at **bread** and on page C25 见 **bread** 词条插图和第C25页图

slice *verb* 动词 (**slices, slicing, sliced** /slaɪst; slaɪst/)
cut something into slices 把某物切成片: *Slice the onions.* 把洋葱切成片。

slide[1] /slaɪd; slaɪd/ *verb* 动词 (**slides, sliding, slid** /slɪd; slɪd/, **has slid**)
move smoothly or make something move smoothly across something (使某物)滑动;滑行: *She fell and slid along the ice.* 她在冰上摔倒后又滑了一下。

slide[2] /slaɪd; slaɪd/ *noun* 名词
1 a long metal thing that children play on. They climb up steps, sit down, and then slide down the other side. (儿童游戏用的)滑梯

2 a small photograph that you show on a **screen**, using a **projector** 幻灯片（投影屏叫做 **screen**，幻灯机叫做 **projector**）

slight /slaɪt; slaɪt/ *adjective* 形容词 (**slighter**, **slightest**)
small; not important or serious 微小的；不重要的或不严重的: *I've got a slight problem.* 我有个小问题。◇ *a slight headache* 轻微的头疼

slightly /ˈslaɪtli; ˈslaɪtlɪ/ *adverb* 副词
a little 稍稍；稍微: *I'm feeling slightly better today.* 我今天身体稍好一些。

slim /slɪm; slɪm/ *adjective* 形容词 (**slimmer**, **slimmest**)
thin, but not too thin 细长的（但不十分细）；苗条的: *a tall slim man* 瘦高的男子

sling[1] /slɪŋ; slɪŋ/ *noun* 名词
a piece of cloth that you wear to hold up an arm that is hurt 悬带（用以吊着受伤手臂的）: *She's got her arm in a sling.* 她用悬带吊着受伤的手臂。

sling[2] /slɪŋ; slɪŋ/ *verb* 动词 (**slings**, **slinging**, **slung** /slʌŋ; slʌŋ/, **has slung**)
throw something without care 乱扔某物: *He got angry and slung the book at me.* 他气得把书扔过来打我。

slip[1] /slɪp; slɪp/ *verb* 动词 (**slips**, **slipping**, **slipped** /slɪpt; slɪpt/)
1 move smoothly over something by mistake and fall or almost fall 滑倒或险些滑倒: *He slipped on the ice and broke his leg.* 他在冰上滑倒把腿摔断了。
2 go quickly and quietly so that nobody sees you 匆匆或悄悄走（不被人发现）: *Anna slipped out of the room when the children were asleep.* 孩子们一睡着，安娜就偷偷溜出了房间。
3 put something in a place quickly and quietly 匆匆或悄悄把某物放在某处: *He slipped the money into his pocket.* 他悄悄把钱塞进口袋里了。

slip[2] /slɪp; slɪp/ *noun* 名词
1 a small piece of paper 小纸条: *Write your address on this slip of paper.* 您把地址写在这张纸条上吧。
2 a small mistake 小错误；小疏忽: *I made a slip.* 我出了个小错。

slipper /ˈslɪpə(r); ˈslɪpɚ/ *noun* 名词
a light soft shoe that you wear in the house（室内用的）便鞋；拖鞋: *a pair of slippers* 一双拖鞋

slippery /ˈslɪpəri; ˈslɪpərɪ/ *adjective* 形容词
so smooth or wet that you cannot move on it or hold it easily 光滑的；滑的: *The skin of a fish is slippery.* 鱼的皮很滑。◇ *The road was wet and slippery.* 马路又湿又滑。

slit /slɪt; slɪt/ *noun* 名词
a long thin hole or cut 长而窄的开口或切口
slit *verb* 动词 (**slits**, **slitting**, **slit**, **has slit**)
make a long thin cut in something 在某物上弄个长而窄的开口或切口: *I slit the envelope open with a knife.* 我用刀把信封划开了。

slither /ˈslɪðə(r); ˈslɪðɚ/ *verb* 动词 (**slithers**, **slithering**, **slithered** /ˈslɪðəd; ˈslɪðɚd/)
move along like a snake 像蛇般移动: *The snake slithered across the floor.* 蛇在地板上爬动。

slogan /ˈsləʊgən; ˈslogən/ *noun* 名词
a short sentence or group of words that is easy to remember. Slogans are used to make people believe something or buy something 标语；口号: *'Faster than light' is the slogan for the new car.* 新汽车的宣传口号是"风驰电掣"。

slope /sləʊp; slop/ *noun* 名词
a piece of ground that has one end higher than the other, like the side of a hill 斜坡: *We walked down the mountain slope.* 我们顺着山坡走下去。
slope *verb* 动词 (**slopes**, **sloping**, **sloped** /sləʊpt; slopt/)
have one end higher than the other 有坡度；倾斜: *The field slopes down to the river.* 这片田地的地势向河边倾斜。◇ *a sloping roof* 倾斜的屋顶

slot /slɒt; slɑt/ *noun* 名词
a long thin hole that you push something through（可投入东西的）窄孔: *Put a coin in the slot and take your ticket.* 把硬币投入孔中可取出票。

slot-machine /ˈslɒt məʃiːn; ˈslɑt məˌʃin/ *noun* 名词
a machine that gives you things like drinks or sweets when you put money in a small hole 投币机（自动售货机，把钱投入孔中可取出饮品或糖果等）

slow[1] /sləʊ; slo/ *adjective* 形容词 (**slower**, **slowest**)
1 A person or thing that is slow does not move or do something quickly

S

慢的；缓慢的：*a slow train* 慢车 ◇ *She hasn't finished her work yet—she's very slow.* 她还没做完工作——真慢。

2 If a clock or watch is slow, it shows a time that is earlier than the real time （指钟表）走得过慢的：*My watch is five minutes slow.* 我的表慢了五分钟。

☞ Look at **quick** and **fast**. 见 **quick** 和 **fast**。

slow *adverb* 副词

slowly 慢；缓慢：*Please drive slower.* 请把车开得慢些。

slowly *adverb* 副词

The old lady walked slowly up the hill. 老太太慢慢地向山上走去。

slow² /sləʊ; slo/ *verb* 动词 (**slows, slowing, slowed** /sləʊd; slod/)

slow down start to go more slowly; make somebody or something start to go more slowly（使某人或某物）开始慢；慢下来：*The train slowed down as it came into the station.* 火车进站时慢了下来。◇ *Don't talk to me when I'm working—it slows me down.* 我正工作的时候别跟我说话——一说话就把我的工作拖慢了。

S

slug /slʌg; slʌg/ *noun* 名词

a small soft animal that moves slowly and eats plants 蛞蝓；鼻涕虫

slum /slʌm; slʌm/ *noun* 名词

a poor part of a city where people live in old dirty buildings 贫民窟

slung *form of* **sling²** ✳ **sling²** 的不同形式

sly /slaɪ; slaɪ/ *adjective* 形容词

A person who is sly tricks people or does things secretly. 狡猾的；偷偷摸摸的

smack /smæk; smæk/ *verb* 动词 (**smacks, smacking, smacked** /smækt; smækt/)

hit somebody with the inside part of your hand 掌击某人；掴：*They never smack their children.* 他们从来不打孩子。

smack *noun* 名词

She gave her son a smack. 她打了儿子一巴掌。

small /smɔːl; smɔl/ *adjective* 形容词 (**smaller, smallest**)

1 not big; little 小的；少的：*This dress is too small for me.* 这件连衣裙我穿着太小。◇ *My house is smaller than yours.* 我的房子比你的小。

2 young 幼小的；年幼的：*They have two small children.* 他们有两个小孩儿。☞ picture on page C26 见第C26页图

smart /smɑːt; smɑrt/ *adjective* 形容词 (**smarter, smartest**)

1 right for a special or important time; clean and tidy 帅气的；整洁的：*She wore smart clothes for her job interview.* 她参加申请工作面试时穿得很精神。◇ *He looks very smart in his new jacket.* 他穿着新外套显得神气。

2 clever 聪明的；伶俐的：*a smart businesswoman* 精明的女商人

smartly *adverb* 副词

She was very smartly dressed. 她穿得很帅气。

smash /smæʃ; smæʃ/ *verb* 动词 (**smashes, smashing, smashed** /smæʃt; smæʃt/)

1 break something into many pieces 把某物弄碎：*The boys smashed the window.* 那些男孩子把窗户打碎了。

2 break into many pieces 破碎；粉碎：*I dropped the plate but it didn't smash.* 我把盘子掉在地上了，可是并没摔碎。

smash *noun* 名词

the loud noise when something breaks into pieces 某物破碎时发出的声音：*The glass hit the floor with a smash.* 玻璃杯砰的一声掉到地板上了。

smashing /ˈsmæʃɪŋ; ˈsmæʃɪŋ/ *adjective* 形容词

very good; wonderful 极好的；美妙的：*The food was smashing.* 这种食物好极了。

smear /smɪə(r); smɪr/ *verb* 动词 (**smears, smearing, smeared** /smɪəd; smɪrd/)

spread soft stuff on something, making it dirty 把软物质涂在某物上而弄脏：*The child smeared chocolate over his clothes.* 这孩子把巧克力抹得满衣服都是。

smear *noun* 名词

a dirty mark 污迹；污点：*She had smears of paint on her dress.* 她的连衣裙上有肮脏的颜料。

smell /smel; smɛl/ *verb* 动词 (**smells, smelling, smelt** /smelt; smɛlt/ or 或 **smelled** /smeld; smɛld/, **has smelt** or 或 **has smelled**)

1 notice something with your nose 闻出有某种味儿；嗅出：*Can you smell smoke?* 你闻出有烟味吗？

2 If something smells, you notice it with your nose 散发出某种味儿: *This fish smells bad.* 这条鱼有坏味儿了。◇ *The perfume smells of roses.* 这种香水是玫瑰味的。
3 have a bad smell 有坏味儿: *Your feet smell!* 你的脚可真臭!
smell *noun* 名词
something that you notice with your nose 气味: *There's a smell of gas in this room.* 这间屋子里有煤气味儿。
smelly /ˈsmeli; ˈsmɛlɪ/ *adjective* 形容词 (**smellier, smelliest**)
with a bad smell 有坏味儿的: *smelly socks* 臭袜子
smile /smaɪl; smaɪl/ *verb* 动词 (**smiles, smiling, smiled** /smaɪld; smaɪld/)
move your mouth to show that you are happy or that you think something is funny 微笑: *He smiled at me.* 他向我微笑。

smile 微笑

smile *noun* 名词
She had a big smile on her face. 她脸上露出快乐的笑容。
smoke[1] /sməʊk; smok/ *noun* 名词 (no plural 无复数)
the grey or black gas that you see in the air when something is burning 烟: *The room was full of smoke.* 屋子里有很多烟。◇ *cigarette smoke* 香烟的烟雾
smoke[2] /sməʊk; smok/ *verb* 动词 (**smokes, smoking, smoked** /sməʊkt; smokt/)
have a cigarette, cigar or pipe in your mouth, and breathe the smoke in and out 吸烟: *He was smoking a cigar.* 他抽着雪茄。◇ *Do you smoke?* 您会吸烟吗?
smoking *noun* 名词 (no plural 无复数)
No smoking in the theatre. 剧院内禁止吸烟。
smoked /sməʊkt; smokt/ *adjective* 形容词
prepared by putting it over a wood fire so that you can keep it for a long time 用烟熏制的: *smoked salmon* 熏鲑肉
smoker /ˈsməʊkə(r); ˈsmokɚ/ *noun* 名词
a person who smokes 吸烟的人 ✪ opposite 反义词: **non-smoker**
smoky /ˈsməʊki; ˈsmokɪ/ (**smokier, smokiest**) *adjective* 形容词
full of smoke 冒烟的;多烟的: *a smoky room* 烟雾弥漫的屋子
smooth /smuːð; smuð/ *adjective* 形容词 (**smoother, smoothest**)
1 flat; not rough 平坦的;光滑的: *Babies have smooth skin.* 小孩儿的皮肤很光滑。
2 moving gently 平稳的: *The weather was good so we had a very smooth flight.* 天气很好,我们乘坐的飞机非常稳。
smoothly *adverb* 副词
The plane landed smoothly. 飞机降落得非常稳。
smother /ˈsmʌðə(r); ˈsmʌðɚ/ *verb* 动词 (**smothers, smothering, smothered** /ˈsmʌðəd; ˈsmʌðɚd/)
1 kill somebody by covering their face so that they cannot breathe 使某人窒息;闷死
2 cover a thing with too much of something 用过量的某物覆盖一物: *He smothered his cake with cream.* 他在蛋糕上涂了很多奶油。
smuggle /ˈsmʌgl; ˈsmʌgl̩/ *verb* 动词 (**smuggles, smuggling, smuggled** /ˈsmʌgld; ˈsmʌgl̩d/)
take things secretly into or out of a country 走私: *They were trying to smuggle drugs into France.* 他们想把走私毒品运进法国。
smuggler /ˈsmʌglə(r); ˈsmʌgl̩ɚ/ *noun* 名词
a person who smuggles 走私的人: *drug smugglers* 走私毒品的人
snack /snæk; snæk/ *noun* 名词
a small quick meal 少而快的一顿饭;小吃;点心: *We had a snack on the train.* 我们在火车上吃了点儿小吃。
snack bar /ˈsnæk bɑː(r); ˈsnæk ˌbɑr/ *noun* 名词
a place where you can buy and eat snacks 小吃店;小吃部
snag /snæg; snæg/ *noun* 名词
a small problem 小的困难: *The work will be finished tomorrow if there are no snags.* 要是没什么困难,这项工作明天就能完成。
snail /sneɪl; snel/ *noun* 名词
a small soft animal with a hard shell on its back. Snails move very slowly. 蜗牛

snail 蜗牛

snake 蛇

snake /sneɪk; snek/ *noun* 名词
an animal with a long thin body and no legs 蛇: *Do these snakes bite?* 这些蛇咬人吗?

snap[1] /snæp; snæp/ *verb* 动词 (**snaps, snapping, snapped** /snæpt; snæpt/)
1 break suddenly with a sharp noise 突然断裂并发出尖厉声音: *He snapped the pencil in two.* 他把铅笔啪的一声弄成两截了。
2 say something in a quick angry way 快而气愤地说: *'Go away—I'm busy!' she snapped.* "走开——我正忙着呢!" 她生气地说道。
3 try to bite somebody or something 想咬某人或某物: *The dog snapped at my leg.* 那条狗要咬我腿。

S

snap[2] /snæp; snæp/, **snapshot** /ˈsnæpʃɒt; ˈsnæpˌʃɑt/ *noun* 名词
a photograph 照片: *She showed us her holiday snaps.* 她给我们看了看她假期的照片。

snarl /snɑ:l; snɑrl/ *verb* 动词 (**snarls, snarling, snarled** /snɑ:ld; snɑrld/)
When an animal snarls, it shows its teeth and makes a low angry sound (指动物)露出牙齿低声叫: *The dog snarled at the stranger.* 那条狗对着陌生人龇着牙吠叫。

snatch /snætʃ; snætʃ/ *verb* 动词 (**snatches, snatching, snatched** /snætʃt; snætʃt/)
take something quickly and roughly 迅速而粗暴地抓住某物;抢: *He snatched her handbag and ran away.* 他抢走她的提包就跑了。

sneak /sni:k; snik/ *verb* 动词 (**sneaks, sneaking, sneaked** /sni:kt; snikt/)
go somewhere very quietly so that nobody sees or hears you 偷偷走到某处(不被人看见或听见): *She sneaked out of the classroom to smoke a cigarette.* 她偷偷溜出了教室去抽烟。

sneer /snɪə(r); snɪr/ *verb* 动词 (**sneers, sneering, sneered** /snɪəd; snɪrd/)
speak or smile in an unkind way to show that you do not like somebody or something or that you think they are not good enough 讥讽或嘲笑某人或某事物: *I told her about my idea, but she just sneered at it.* 我把我的想法告诉她以后,她只是冷笑了一下。
sneer *noun* 名词
an unkind smile 嘲笑;冷笑;讥笑

sneeze /sni:z; sniz/ *verb* 动词 (**sneezes, sneezing, sneezed** /sni:zd; snizd/)
send air out of your nose and mouth with a sudden loud noise, for example because you have a cold 打喷嚏: *Pepper makes you sneeze.* 胡椒能把人呛得打喷嚏。
sneeze *noun* 名词
She gave a loud sneeze. 她打了一个很响的喷嚏。

sniff /snɪf; snɪf/ *verb* 动词 (**sniffs, sniffing, sniffed** /snɪft; snɪft/)
1 make a noise by suddenly taking in air through your nose. People sometimes sniff when they have a cold or when they are crying. 用鼻子突然吸气发出声音(例如感冒时或哭泣时)
2 smell something 闻某物的味儿: *The dog was sniffing the meat.* 狗正在闻着那块肉。
sniff *noun* 名词
I heard a loud sniff. 我听见有用鼻子吸气时发出很大的声音。

snooze /snu:z; snuz/ *verb* 动词 (**snoozes, snoozing, snoozed** /snu:zd; snuzd/)
sleep for a short time 小睡;打盹
snooze *noun* 名词
I had a snooze after lunch. 我吃完午饭后睡了个午觉。

snore /snɔ:(r); snɔr/ *verb* 动词 (**snores, snoring, snored** /snɔ:d; snɔrd/)
make a noise in your nose and throat when you are asleep 打鼾;打呼噜: *He was snoring loudly.* 他正在打呼噜,声音很大。

snort /snɔ:t; snɔrt/ *verb* 动词 (**snorts, snorting, snorted**)
make a noise by blowing air through the nose 喷鼻息作声;打响鼻: *The horse snorted.* 那匹马打了个响鼻。

snow /snəʊ; sno/ *noun* 名词 (no plural 无复数)
soft white stuff that falls from the sky when it is very cold 雪
snow *verb* 动词 (**snows, snowing, snowed** /snəʊd; snod/)
When it snows, snow falls from the sky

下雪；降雪: *It often snows in Scotland in winter.* 苏格兰冬天常下雪。

snowflake /ˈsnəʊfleɪk; ˈsnoˌflek/ *noun* 名词
one piece of falling snow 雪花；雪片

snowy *adjective* 形容词 (**snowier, snowiest**)
with a lot of snow 有很多雪的；下雪的: *snowy weather* 下雪的天气

so[1] /səʊ; so/ *adverb* 副词
1 a word that you use when you say how much, how big, etc something is（用以表示程度）这么，那么，如此: *This bag is so heavy that I can't carry it.* 这个袋子很重，我提不动。☞ Look at **such**. 见 **such**。
2 a word that makes another word stronger（用以加强另一字的语气）这么，那么，如此: *Why are you so late?* 你怎么这么晚？
3 also 也: *Julie is a teacher and so is her husband.* 朱莉是教师，她丈夫也是教师。◇ *'I like this music.' 'So do I.'* "我喜欢这种音乐。" "我也喜欢。" ✪ In negative sentences, we use **neither** or **nor**. 在否定句中用 **neither** 或 **nor**。
4 You use 'so' instead of saying words again 用 so 来代替说过的话: *'Is John coming?' 'I think so.'* (= I think that he is coming) "约翰来吗？" "我认为他来。"
and so on and other things like that（用以表示列举未尽）等等: *The shop sells pens, paper and so on.* 这家商店出售钢笔、纸之类的东西。
not so ... as words that show how two people or things are different（用以表示两个人或事物不同的词）不像…那么: *He's not so tall as his brother.* 他没有他弟弟那么高。
or so words that you use to show that a number is not exactly right（用以表示大致是这个数量）上下: *Forty or so people came to the party.* 参加聚会的有四十来人。

so[2] /səʊ; so/ *conjunction* 连词
1 because of this or that 因此；所以: *The shop is closed so I can't buy any bread.* 商店关门了，所以我没买着面包。
2 (*also* 亦作 **so that**) in order that 为的是；以便: *Speak louder so that everybody can hear you.* 说话声音大些，好让大家都听见。◇ *I'll give you a map so you can find my house.* 我给你一张地图，你就能找到我们家了。
so what? why is that important or interesting? 那有什么关系？: *'It's late.' 'So what? There's no school tomorrow.'* "已经很晚了。" "晚了又怎么样？明天没有课。"

soak /səʊk; sok/ *verb* 动词 (**soaks, soaking, soaked** /səʊkt; sokt/)
1 make somebody or something very wet 使某人或某物很湿: *It was raining when I went out. I got soaked!* 我出门的时候正下雨。我全身都湿透了！
2 be in a liquid; let something stay in a liquid（使某物）浸；泡: *Leave the dishes to soak in hot water.* 把碟子放在热水里泡着吧。
soak up take in a liquid 吸入液体: *Soak the water up with a cloth.* 用布把水吸干。
soaking *adjective* 形容词
very wet 很湿的: *This towel is soaking.* 这条毛巾很湿。

soap /səʊp; sop/ *noun* 名词 (no plural 无复数)
stuff that you use with water for washing and cleaning 肥皂: *a bar of soap* 一块肥皂
soap opera /ˈsəʊp ɒprə; ˈsop ˌɑpərə/ *noun* 名词
a story about the lives of a group of people, that is on the TV or radio every day or several times each week（电视或电台）连续剧
soap powder /ˈsəʊp paʊdə(r); ˈsop ˌpaʊdɚ/ *noun* 名词 (no plural 无复数)
powder that you use for washing clothes 肥皂粉
soapy *adjective* 形容词
with soap in it 有肥皂的: *soapy water* 肥皂水

soar /sɔː(r); sɔr/ *verb* 动词 (**soars, soaring, soared** /sɔːd; sɔrd/)
1 fly high in the sky 飞向天空
2 go up very fast 急速上升: *Prices are soaring.* 物价飞涨。

sob /sɒb; sɑb/ *verb* 动词 (**sobs, sobbing, sobbed** /sɒbd; sɑbd/)
cry loudly, making short sounds 啜泣；抽噎
sob *noun* 名词
'She's left me!' he said with a sob. "她离开我了！"他抽抽搭搭地说。

sober /ˈsəʊbə(r); ˈsobɚ/ *adjective* 形容词
not drunk 未醉的

S

so-called /ˌsəʊ ˈkɔ:ld; ˈsoˈkɔld/ *adjective* 形容词
a word that you use to show that you do not think another word is correct（用以表示认为某词不确）所谓的: *Her so-called friends did not help her* (= they are not really her friends). 她的所谓的朋友并没有帮助她。

soccer /ˈsɒkə(r); ˈsɑkɚ/ *noun* 名词 (no plural 无复数)
football 足球

social /ˈsəʊʃl; ˈsoʃəl/ *adjective* 形容词
of people together; of being with other people 社会的；社交的: *the social problems of big cities* 大城市的社会问题 ◇ *Anne has a busy social life* (= she goes out with friends a lot). 安妮的社交活动很多。

social security /ˌsəʊʃl sɪˈkjʊərəti; ˈsoʃəl sɪˈkjʊrətɪ/ *noun* 名词 (no plural 无复数)
money that a government pays to somebody who is poor, for example because they have no job 社会保障

social worker /ˈsəʊʃl wɜ:kə(r); ˈsoʃəl ˈwɝkɚ/ *noun* 名词
a person whose job is to help people who have problems, for example because they are poor or ill 社会工作者

society /səˈsaɪəti; səˈsaɪətɪ/ *noun* 名词
1 (no plural 无复数) a group of people living together, with the same ideas about how to live 社会
2 (*plural* 复数作 **societies**) a group of people who are interested in the same thing 社团；团体: *a music society* 音乐协会

sock /sɒk; sɑk/ *noun* 名词
a thing that you wear on your foot, inside your shoe 短袜: *a pair of socks* 一双短袜

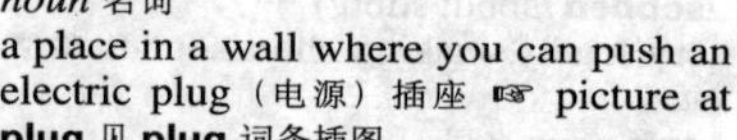
socks 袜子

socket /ˈsɒkɪt; ˈsɑkɪt/ *noun* 名词
a place in a wall where you can push an electric plug（电源）插座 ☞ picture at **plug** 见 **plug** 词条插图

sofa /ˈsəʊfə; ˈsofə/ *noun* 名词
a long soft seat for more than one person（不止一人坐的）长沙发: *Jenny was sitting on the sofa.* 珍妮在长沙发上坐着。

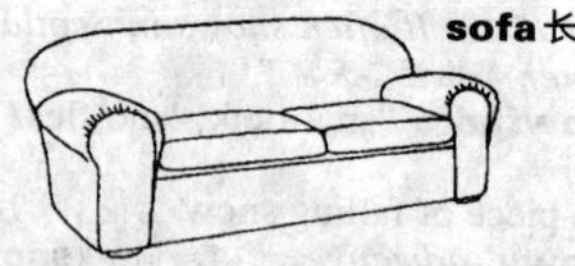
sofa 长沙发

soft /sɒft; sɔft/ *adjective* 形容词 (**softer**, **softest**)
1 not hard or firm; that moves when you press it 软的；柔软的: *Warm butter is soft.* 温的黄油是软的。◇ *a soft bed* 软的床 ☞ picture on page C27 见第C27页图
2 smooth and nice to touch; not rough 光滑而柔软的: *soft skin* 柔嫩的皮肤 ◇ *My cat's fur is very soft.* 我的猫身上的毛非常柔滑。
3 quiet or gentle; not loud 柔和的；轻柔的: *soft music* 轻柔的乐曲 ◇ *He has a very soft voice.* 他嗓音柔润。
4 not bright or strong 不明亮的；不强烈的: *the soft light of a candle* 蜡烛的微弱的光
5 kind and gentle; not strict 和蔼而温柔的；不严厉的: *She's too soft with her class and they don't do any work.* 她对全班学生太不严厉了，他们什么功课都不做了。

soft drink /ˌsɒft ˈdrɪŋk; ˈsɔft drɪŋk/ *noun* 名词
a cold drink with no alcohol in it, for example orange juice or lemonade 软饮料（不含酒精的冷饮料，例如橙子汁或汽水）

softly *adverb* 副词
gently or quietly 柔和地；轻柔地: *She spoke very softly.* 她说话声音很轻。

software /ˈsɒftweə(r); ˈsɔftˌwɛr/ *noun* 名词 (no plural 无复数)
programs for a computer 软件（计算机的程序，即 **program**）

soggy /ˈsɒgi; ˈsɑgɪ/ *adjective* 形容词 (**soggier**, **soggiest**)
very wet 湿透的

soil /sɔɪl; sɔɪl/ *noun* 名词 (no plural 无复数)
what plants and trees grow in; earth 土壤；泥土

solar /ˈsəʊlə(r); ˈsolɚ/ *adjective* 形容词
of or using the sun 太阳的；利用太阳的: *solar energy* 太阳能

the solar system /ðə ˈsəʊlə sɪstəm; ðə ˈsolɚ ˌsɪstəm/ *noun* 名词 (no plural 无复数)
the sun and the planets that move around it 太阳系

sold *form of* **sell** ✳ **sell** 的不同形式

be sold out When things are sold out, there are no more to sell 已卖光: *I'm sorry — the bananas are sold out.* 很抱歉——香蕉都卖光了。

soldier /ˈsəʊldʒə(r); ˈsoldʒɚ/ *noun* 名词
a person in an army 士兵；军人

sole¹ /səʊl; sol/ *noun* 名词
the bottom part of your foot or of a shoe 脚掌或鞋底: *These boots have leather soles.* 这双靴子是皮底的。☞ picture on page C2 见第C2页图

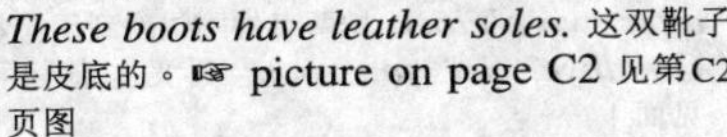
sole 鞋底

sole² /səʊl; sol/ *adjective* 形容词
only 唯一的: *His sole interest is football.* 他唯一的爱好就是足球。

solemn /ˈsɒləm; ˈsɑləm/ *adjective* 形容词
serious 严肃的；庄严的: *slow, solemn music* 缓慢而庄严的乐曲

solemnly *adverb* 副词
'I've got some bad news for you,' he said solemnly. "我有个坏消息告诉你，"他郑重其事地说道。

solid /ˈsɒlɪd; ˈsɑlɪd/ *adjective* 形容词
1 hard, not like a liquid or a gas 固体的: *Water becomes solid when it freezes.* 水遇冷凝结就成了固体。
2 with no empty space inside; made of the same material inside and outside 实心的；由同一种材料做的: *a solid rubber ball* 实心的橡皮球 ◇ *This ring is solid gold.* 这个环是纯金的。

solid *noun* 名词
not a liquid or gas 固体: *Milk is a liquid and cheese is a solid.* 牛奶是液体，干酪是固体。

solitary /ˈsɒlətri; ˈsɑləˌtɛrɪ/ *adjective* 形容词
without others; alone 单独的；独自的: *She went for a long solitary walk.* 她独自散步，走了很长的路。

solo /ˈsəʊləʊ; ˈsolo/ *noun* 名词 (*plural* 复数作 **solos**)
a piece of music for one person to sing or play 独唱歌曲；独奏曲: *a piano solo* 钢琴独奏

solo *adjective, adverb* 形容词，副词
alone; without other people 单独（的）；独自（的）: *a solo performance* 单人表演 ◇ *She flew solo across the Atlantic.* 她独自一人飞越了大西洋。

solution /səˈluːʃn; səˈluʃən/ *noun* 名词
the answer to a question, problem or puzzle 答案；解决方法: *I can't find a solution to this problem.* 我找不到解决这个问题的办法。

solve /sɒlv; sɑlv/ *verb* 动词 (**solves, solving, solved** /sɒlvd; sɑlvd/)
find the answer to a question, problem or puzzle 找出答案或解决方法: *The police are still trying to solve the crime.* 警方仍在设法破案。

some /sʌm; sʌm/ *adjective, pronoun* 形容词，代词
1 a number or amount of something 一些；若干: *I bought some tomatoes and some butter.* 我买了些西红柿和黄油。◇ *This cake is nice. Do you want some?* 这个蛋糕很好吃。您要点儿吗？✪ In questions and after 'not' and 'if', we usually use **any** 在疑问句中及在 not 和 if 之后一般用 **any**: *Did you buy any apples?* 你买苹果了吗？◇ *I didn't buy any meat.* 我没买肉。
2 part of a number or amount of something 整体中的一部分: *Some of the children can swim, but the others can't.* 有的孩子会游泳，有的不会。
3 I do not know which 不知道的；某: *There's some man at the door who wants to see you.* 门口有个男的想见您。

some more a little more or a few more 多一些: *Have some more coffee.* 再喝点儿咖啡吧。◇ *Some more people arrived.* 又有一些人到了。

some time quite a long time 相当长的时间: *We waited for some time but she did not come.* 我们等了很长时间她也没来。

somebody /ˈsʌmbədi; ˈsʌmbədɪ/, **someone** /ˈsʌmwʌn; ˈsʌmˌwʌn/ *pronoun* 代词
a person; a person that you do not know 一个人；某个人: *There's somebody at the door.* 门口有个人。◇ *Someone has broken the window.* 有人把窗户打破了。◇ *Ask somebody else* (= another person) *to help you.* 找别人来帮助你吧。

somehow /ˈsʌmhaʊ; ˈsʌmˌhaʊ/ *adverb* 副词
in some way that you do not know 用某种方式: *We must find her somehow.* 我们得想办法找到她。

S

someplace /ˈsʌmpleɪs; ˈsʌmples/ *American English for* **somewhere** 美式英语，即 **somewhere**

somersault /ˈsʌməsɔ:lt; ˈsʌmɚˌsɔlt/ *noun* 名词
a movement when you turn your body with your feet going over your head（杂技中的）滚翻；空翻；跟头: *The children were doing somersaults on the carpet.* 孩子们在地毯上翻着跟头。

something /ˈsʌmθɪŋ; ˈsʌmθɪŋ/ *pronoun* 代词
a thing; a thing you cannot name 事物；某事物: *There's something under the table. What is it?* 桌子底下有个东西。那是什么？◇ *I want to tell you something.* 我想告诉你一件事情。◇ *Would you like something else* (= another thing) *to eat?* 您还想吃点儿别的吗？
something like the same as somebody or something, but not in every way 类似某人或某事物: *A rat is something like a mouse, but bigger.* 大鼠很像耗子，只是稍大些。

S

sometime /ˈsʌmtaɪm; ˈsʌmˌtaɪm/ *adverb* 副词
at a time that you do not know exactly 在某个时候: *I'll phone sometime tomorrow.* 我明天找时间打个电话。

sometimes /ˈsʌmtaɪmz; ˈsʌmˌtaɪmz/ *adverb* 副词
not very often 有时候；偶尔: *He sometimes writes to me.* 他间或给我写写信。◇ *Sometimes I drive to work and sometimes I go by bus.* 我有时候开车去上班，有时候坐公共汽车去。

somewhere /ˈsʌmweə(r); ˈsʌmˌhwɛr/ *adverb* 副词
at, in or to a place that you do not know exactly 在某处；到某处: *They live somewhere near London.* 他们住在伦敦附近。◇ *'Did she go to Spain last year?' 'No, I think she went somewhere else* (= to another place).' "她去年是到西班牙去了吗？" "不是，她大概到别的地方去了。"

son /sʌn; sʌn/ *noun* 名词
a boy or man who is somebody's child 儿子: *They have a son and two daughters.* 她们有一个儿子和两个女儿。☞ picture on page C3 见第C3页图

song /sɒŋ; sɔŋ/ *noun* 名词
1 (*plural* 复数作 **songs**) a piece of music with words that you sing 歌；歌曲: *a pop song* 流行歌曲
2 (no plural 无复数) singing; music that a person or bird makes 声乐；歌唱

son-in-law /ˈsʌn ɪn lɔ:; ˈsʌnɪnˌlɔ/ *noun* 名词 (*plural* 复数作 **sons-in-law**)
the husband of your daughter 女婿 ☞ picture on page C3 见第C3页图

soon /su:n; sun/ *adverb* 副词
not long after now, or not long after a certain time 不久: *John will be home soon.* 约翰快到家了。◇ *She arrived soon after two o'clock.* 她两点钟刚过就到了。◇ *Goodbye! See you soon!* 再见！很快再见面！
as soon as at the same time that; when 一…就…；当…的时候: *Phone me as soon as you get home.* 你一到家就给我来个电话。
sooner or later at some time in the future 在将来某个时候；或早或晚；迟早: *Don't worry—I'm sure he will write to you sooner or later.* 别担心——我看他早晚准得给你来信。

soot /sʊt; sʊt/ *noun* 名词 (no plural 无复数)
black powder that comes from smoke 烟中的黑灰；炱

soothe /su:ð; suð/ *verb* 动词 (**soothes, soothing, soothed** /su:ðd; suðd/)
make somebody feel calmer and less unhappy 使某人平静或不太难过；安慰: *The baby was crying, so I tried to soothe her by singing to her.* 孩子哭了，我想办法唱歌哄她。
soothing *adjective* 形容词
soothing music 使人舒畅的音乐

sore /sɔ:(r); sɔr/ *adjective* 形容词
If a part of your body is sore, it gives you pain（指身体局部）疼痛的: *My feet were sore after the long walk.* 我走了长路以后脚很疼。◇ *I've got a sore throat.* 我嗓子疼。

sorrow /ˈsɒrəʊ; ˈsɑro/ *noun* 名词
sadness 悲伤；悲痛

sorry /ˈsɒri; ˈsɔrɪ/ *adjective* 形容词
1 a word that you use when you feel bad about something you have done 对不起；抱歉: *I'm sorry I didn't phone you.* 我没有给您打电话，十分抱歉。◇ *Sorry I'm late!* 对不起，我来晚了！◇ *I'm sorry for losing your pen.* 我把您的笔弄丢了，真对不起。

2 sad 悲伤；遗憾: *I'm sorry you can't come to the party.* 您不能来参加聚会，我觉得很遗憾。

3 a word that you use to say 'no' politely 表示否定或拒绝的礼貌用词: *I'm sorry—I can't help you.* 很抱歉——我没有办法帮助您。

4 a word that you use when you did not hear what somebody said and you want them to say it again 因未听见某人的话，请求再说一遍用的词: *'My name is Linda Willis.' 'Sorry? Linda who?'* "我叫琳达·威利斯。" "很抱歉，我没听清，您叫琳达什么？"

feel sorry for somebody feel sad because somebody has problems 因某人有困难而感到难过: *I felt sorry for her and gave her some money.* 她的情况我感到很难过，我给了她一些钱。

sort[1] /sɔ:t; sɔrt/ *noun* 名词

a group of things or people that are the same in some way; a type or kind 有共同之处的人或事物；类；种类: *What sort of music do you like best—pop or classical?* 您最爱听什么类型的音乐——流行音乐还是古典音乐？◇ *We found all sorts of shells on the beach.* 我们在海滩上找到了各种各样的贝壳。

sort of words that you use when you are not sure about something 用以表示对某事物无把握的词语: *It's sort of long and thin, a bit like a sausage.* 那个东西好像是细长的，有点儿像香肠。

sort[2] /sɔ:t; sɔrt/ *verb* 动词 (**sorts, sorting, sorted**)

put things into groups 把事物分成类: *The machine sorts the eggs into large ones and small ones.* 这台机器能把鸡蛋分成大的和小的两种。

sort out 1 make something tidy 使某物整齐；整理某事物: *I sorted out my clothes and put the old ones in a bag.* 我把衣服整理了一下，把旧的都放进袋子里了。 **2** find an answer to a problem 解决某问题

SOS /ˌes əʊ 'es; 'ɛs ˌo 'ɛs/ *noun* 名词

a call for help from a ship or an aeroplane that is in danger (轮船或飞机遇难的)求救信号

sought *form of* **seek** ＊ **seek** 的不同形式

soul /səʊl; sol/ *noun* 名词

1 (*plural* 复数作 **souls**) the part of a person that some people believe does not die when the body dies 灵魂

2 (*also* 亦作 **soul music**) (no plural 无复数) a kind of Black American music 灵乐（美国黑人的一种音乐）: *a soul singer* 灵乐歌手

not a soul not one person 没有人: *I looked everywhere, but there wasn't a soul in the building.* 我在整座大楼里看了一遍，一个人都没有。

sound[1] /saʊnd; saʊnd/ *noun* 名词

something that you hear 声；声音: *I heard the sound of a baby crying.* 我听见有小孩儿哭的声音。◇ *Light travels faster than sound.* 光波比声波传播得快。

sound[2] /saʊnd; saʊnd/ *verb* 动词 (**sounds, sounding, sounded**)

seem a certain way when you hear it 听起来: *He sounded angry when I spoke to him on the phone.* 我跟他通电话的时候，听声音好像他生气了。◇ *That sounds like a good idea.* 这个主意听起来不错。◇ *She told me about the book—it sounds interesting.* 她向我介绍那本书——听起来很不错。

sound[3] /saʊnd; saʊnd/ *adjective* 形容词

1 healthy or strong 健康的；强健的: *sound teeth* 健康的牙齿

2 right and good 正确的；好的: *sound advice* 忠告

sound *adverb* 副词

sound asleep sleeping very well 酣睡着: *The children are sound asleep.* 孩子们睡得正香呢。

soup /su:p; sup/ *noun* 名词 (no plural 无复数)

liquid food that you make by cooking things like vegetables or meat in water 汤；羹: *tomato soup* 西红柿汤

sour /'saʊə(r); saʊr/ *adjective* 形容词

1 with a taste like lemons or vinegar 酸的: *If it's too sour, put some sugar in it.* 要是太酸就加点儿糖。

2 Sour milk tastes bad because it is not fresh（指牛奶等）腐坏变馊的: *This milk has gone sour.* 牛奶馊了。

source /sɔ:s; sɔrs/ *noun* 名词

a place where something comes from 来源；出处: *Our information comes from many sources.* 我们的消息来自很多方面。

south /saʊθ; saʊθ/ *noun* 名词 (no plural 无复数)

the direction that is on your right when you watch the sun come up in the morning 南；南方；南边 ☞ picture at **north** 见 **north** 词条插图

south *adjective, adverb* 形容词，副词 *Brazil is in South America.* 巴西位于南美洲。◇ *the south coast of England* 英格兰南岸 ◇ *Birds fly south in the winter.* 冬天鸟飞往南方。

southern /ˈsʌðən; ˈsʌðɚn/ *adjective* 形容词

in or of the south part of a place 南方的；南部的；南边的: *Brighton is in southern England.* 布赖顿在英格兰南部。

souvenir /ˌsuːvəˈnɪə(r); ˈsuvəˌnɪr/ *noun* 名词

something that you keep to remember a place or something that happened 纪念品；纪念物: *I brought back this cowboy hat as a souvenir of America.* 我把这顶牛仔帽带回来，算是我到美国的纪念品。

sow /səʊ; so/ *verb* 动词 (**sows, sowing, sowed** /səʊd; sod/, **has sown** /səʊn; son/ or 或 **has sowed**)

put seeds in the ground 播种: *The farmer sowed the field with corn.* 农民在田地里种上了谷物。

space /speɪs; spes/ *noun* 名词

1 (no plural 无复数) a place that is big enough for somebody or something to go into it or onto it（可容纳人或物的）空间: *Is there space for me in your car?* 您的汽车里能有我坐的地方吗？

2 (*plural* 复数作 **spaces**) an empty place between other things（物体之间的）空间；空白；空隙: *There is a space here for you to write your name.* 这里有个空白处，您可以把名字写上。

3 (no plural 无复数) the place far away outside the earth, where all the planets and stars are 外层空间；外太空: *space travel* 太空航行

spacecraft /ˈspeɪskrɑːft; ˈspesˌkræft/ *noun* 名词 (*plural* 复数作 **spacecraft**)

a vehicle that travels in space 航天器；宇宙飞船；太空船

spaceman /ˈspeɪsmæn; ˈspesˌmæn/ *noun* 名词 (*plural* 复数作 **spacemen**), **spacewoman** /ˈspeɪswʊmən; ˈspesˌwʊmən/ (*plural* 复数作 **spacewomen**)

a person who travels in space 宇航员；太空人

spaceship /ˈspeɪsʃɪp; ˈspesˌʃɪp/ *noun* 名词

a vehicle that travels in space 航天器；宇宙飞船；太空船

spacious /ˈspeɪʃəs; ˈspeʃəs/ *adjective* 形容词

with a lot of space inside 宽敞的；宽广的: *a spacious kitchen* 宽敞的厨房

spade /speɪd; sped/ *noun* 名词

1 a tool that you use for digging 铁锹 ☞ picture at **dig** 见 **dig** 词条插图

2 spades (plural 复数) the playing-cards that have the shape ♠ on them（纸牌的）黑桃（♠）: *the queen of spades* 黑桃皇后（黑桃Q）

spaghetti /spəˈgeti; spəˈgɛtɪ/ *noun* 名词 (no plural 无复数)

a kind of food made from flour and water, that looks like long pieces of string 意大利面条

spanner /ˈspænə(r); ˈspænɚ/ *noun* 名词

a tool that you use for turning **nuts** and **bolts** 扳子；扳手（螺母叫做 **nut**，螺栓叫做 **bolt**）

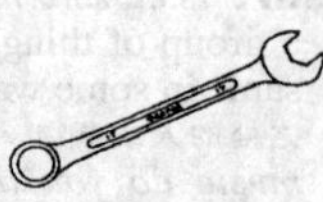

spanner 扳子

spare¹ /speə(r); spɛr/ *adjective* 形容词

1 extra; that you do not need now 多余的；剩余的；备用的: *Have you got a spare tyre in your car?* 您的汽车上有备用轮胎吗？◇ *You can stay with us tonight. We've got a spare room.* 您今天晚上可以住在我们这儿。我们有间富余的屋子。

2 Spare time is time when you are not working（指时间）空闲的: *What do you do in your spare time?* 你空闲的时间做什么？

spare² /speə(r); spɛr/ *verb* 动词 (**spares, sparing, spared** /speəd; spɛrd/)

be able to give something to somebody 能把某物给某人: *I can't spare the time to help you today.* 我今天抽不出时间来帮助你。◇ *Can you spare any money?* 你能拿出点儿钱来吗？

spark /spɑːk; spɑrk/ *noun* 名词

a very small piece of fire 火花；火星

sparkle /ˈspɑːkl; ˈspɑrkl̩/ *verb* 动词 (**sparkles, sparkling, sparkled** /ˈspɑːkld; ˈspɑrkl̩d/)

shine with a lot of very small points of light 有很多小亮光；闪耀；闪烁: *The sea sparkled in the sunlight.* 海面在阳光下闪闪发光。◇ *Her eyes sparkled with excitement.* 她目光闪耀显露出激动的神情。

S

sparkle *noun* 名词 (no plural 无复数)
the sparkle of diamonds 钻石的闪光

sparkling *adjective* 形容词
1 that sparkles 闪耀的；闪烁的: *sparkling blue eyes* 亮晶晶的蓝眼睛
2 Sparkling wine has a lot of small bubbles in it.（指酒等）起泡的

sparrow /'spærəʊ; 'spæro/ *noun* 名词
a small brown bird 麻雀

spat *form of* **spit** ＊ **spit** 的不同形式

speak /spi:k; spik/ *verb* 动词 (**speaks**, **speaking**, **spoke** /spəʊk; spok/, **has spoken** /'spəʊkən; 'spokən/)
1 say words; talk to somebody 说话: *Please speak more slowly.* 请慢点儿说。◇ *Can I speak to John Smith, please?* (= words that you say on the telephone) 劳驾，可以请约翰·史密斯听电话吗？
2 know and use a language 会说某种语言: *I can speak French and Italian.* 我会说法语和意大利语。
3 talk to a group of people 发言；演讲: *The chairwoman spoke for an hour at the meeting.* 主席在会上讲了一个小时。
speak up talk louder 大点儿声说: *Can you speak up? I can't hear you!* 你大点儿声说行吗？我听不见！

speaker /'spi:kə(r); 'spikɚ/ *noun* 名词
1 a person who is talking to a group of people 发言者；演讲者
2 the part of a radio, cassette player, etc where the sound comes out（收音机、盒式放音机等的）扩音器；扬声器

spear /spɪə(r); spɪr/ *noun* 名词
a long stick with a sharp point at one end, used for hunting or fighting 矛；长杆一端有尖头的武器

special /'speʃl; 'spɛʃəl/ *adjective* 形容词
1 not usual or ordinary; important for a reason 特殊的；特别的: *It's my birthday today so we are having a special dinner.* 今天是我生日，所以我们吃一顿特殊的饭。
2 for a particular person or thing 专门的；特设的: *He goes to a special school for deaf children.* 他上的是为耳聋儿童设的专门学校。
specially /'speʃəli; 'spɛʃəlɪ/ *adverb* 副词
1 for a particular person or thing 特意地；专门地: *I made this cake specially for you.* 这个蛋糕是我特意为你做的。
2 very; more than usual or more than others 非常；格外地: *The food was not specially good.* 食物并不太好。

specialist /'speʃəlɪst; 'spɛʃəlɪst/ *noun* 名词
a person who knows a lot about something 专业工作者；专家: *She's a specialist in Chinese art.* 她是研究中国艺术的专家。

specialize /'speʃəlaɪz; 'spɛʃəl,aɪz/ *verb* 动词 (**specializes**, **specializing**, **specialized** /'speʃəlaɪzd; 'spɛʃəl,aɪzd/)
specialize in something study or know a lot about one special thing 专门研究某事物；在某方面有专长: *This doctor specializes in natural medicine.* 这位医生专门研究天然药物。

species /'spi:ʃi:z; 'spiʃiz/ *noun* 名词 (*plural* 复数作 **species**)
a group of animals or plants that are the same in some way（动植物的）物种，种: *a rare species of plant* 一种稀有植物

specific /spə'sɪfɪk; spɪ'sɪfik/ *adjective* 形容词
1 particular 特定的；具体的: *Is there anything specific that you want to talk about?* 您有什么具体事情要谈吗？
2 exact and clear 精确而清楚的；明确的: *He gave us specific instructions on how to get there.* 他把到达那里的方法给我们讲得十分清楚。
specifically /spə'sɪfɪkli; spɪ'sɪfɪkḷɪ/ *adverb* 副词
I specifically asked you to buy butter, not margarine. 我特别叮嘱过你要买纯黄油，不要买人造黄油。

specimen /'spesɪmən; 'spɛsəmən/ *noun* 名词
a small amount or part of something that shows what the rest is like; one example of a group of things 样品；标本: *a specimen of rock* 岩石标本 ◇ *The doctor took a specimen of blood for testing.* 医生取了血样进行化验。

speck /spek; spɛk/ *noun* 名词
a very small bit of something 小颗粒: *specks of dust* 灰尘

spectacles /'spektəklz; 'spɛktəkḷz/ *noun* 名词 (plural 复数)
pieces of special glass that you wear over your eyes to help you see better 眼镜: *a pair of spectacles* 一副眼镜 ✪ It is more usual to say **glasses**. ＊ **glasses** 是较常用的词。

S

spectacular /spek'tækjələ(r); spɛk-'tækjələ/ *adjective* 形容词
wonderful to see 壮观的；精彩的：*There was a spectacular view from the top of the mountain.* 从山顶上望去，景色十分秀丽。

spectator /spek'teɪtə(r); 'spɛktetə/ *noun* 名词
a person who watches something that is happening 观看者：*There were 2 000 spectators at the football match.* 有2 000名观众看足球比赛。

sped *form of* **speed²** ✳ **speed²**的不同形式

speech /spi:tʃ; spitʃ/ *noun* 名词
1 (no plural 无复数) the power to speak, or the way that you speak 说话的能力或方式
2 (*plural* 复数作 **speeches**) a talk that you give to a group of people 发言；演说：*The President made a speech.* 总统发表了演说。

S

speed¹ /spi:d; spid/ *noun* 名词
how fast something goes 速度：*The car was travelling at a speed of 50 miles an hour.* 那辆汽车以每小时50英里的速度行驶。◇ *a high-speed train* (= that goes very fast) 高速火车
speed limit /'spi:d lɪmɪt; 'spid ˌlɪmɪt/ *noun* 名词
the fastest that you are allowed to travel on a road（道路上的）速度限制：*The speed limit on motorways is 100 kilometres an hour.* 高速公路的速度限制是每小时100公里。

speed² /spi:d; spid/ *verb* 动词 (**speeds**, **speeding**, **sped** /sped; spɛd/ or 或 **speeded**, **has sped** or 或 **has speeded**)
1 go or move very quickly 快速行进：*He sped past me on his bike.* 他骑着自行车很快地从我旁边经过。
2 drive too fast 驾驶过速；超速行车：*The police stopped me because I was speeding.* 因为我开车超速，警察把我拦住了。
speed up go faster; make something go faster（使某事物）加速

spell¹ /spel; spɛl/ *verb* 动词 (**spells**, **spelling**, **spelt** /spelt; spɛlt/ or 或 **spelled** /speld; spɛld/, **has spelt** or 或 **has spelled**)
use the right letters to make a word（用字母）拼字：*'How do you spell your name?' 'A-Z-I-Z.'* "你的名字怎样拼？" "A-Z-I-Z。" ◇ *You have spelt this word wrong.* 你把这个字拼错了。
spelling *noun* 名词
the right way of writing a word（正确的）拼法：*Look in your dictionary to find the right spelling.* 查一查词典，找出正确的拼法。

spell² /spel; spɛl/ *noun* 名词
magic words 咒语；符咒
put a spell on somebody say magic words to somebody to change them or to make them do what you want 用咒语镇住：*The witch put a spell on the prince.* 女巫用咒语把王子镇住了。

spend /spend; spɛnd/ *verb* 动词 (**spends**, **spending**, **spent** /spent; spɛnt/, **has spent**)
1 pay money for something 用钱；花钱：*Louise spends a lot of money on clothes.* 路易丝花很多钱买衣服。
2 use time for something 用时间；度过：*I spent the summer in Italy.* 我是在意大利过的夏天。◇ *He spent a lot of time sleeping.* 他睡觉睡了很长时间。

sphere /sfɪə(r); sfɪr/ *noun* 名词
any round thing that is like a ball 球体；球形：*The earth is a sphere.* 地球是球形的。☞ picture on page C5 见第C5页图

spice /spaɪs; spaɪs/ *noun* 名词
a powder or the seeds from a plant that you can put in food to give it a stronger taste. Pepper and ginger are spices.（食用的）香料（例如胡椒和姜）
spicy /'spaɪsi; 'spaɪsɪ/ *adjective* 形容词 (**spicier**, **spiciest**)
with spices in it 含有食用香料的：*Indian food is usually spicy.* 印度菜一般都含有食用香料。

spider /'spaɪdə(r); 'spaɪdə/ *noun* 名词
a small animal with eight legs, that catches and eats insects 蜘蛛：*Spiders spin webs to catch flies.* 蜘蛛能织网捕捉飞虫。

spied *form of* **spy** ✳ **spy** 的不同形式

spies
1 *plural of* **spy** ✳ **spy** 的复数形式
2 *form of* **spy** ✳ **spy** 的不同形式

spike /spaɪk; spaɪk/ *noun* 名词
a piece of metal with a sharp point 有尖的金属物: *The fence has spikes along the top.* 那个栅栏的顶部有尖。

spill 洒出

spill /spɪl; spɪl/ *verb* 动词 (**spills, spilling, spilt** /spɪlt; spɪlt/ or 或 **spilled** /spɪld; spɪld/, **has spilt** or 或 **has spilled**)
If you spill a liquid, it flows out of something by accident 溅出；洒出: *I've spilt my wine!* 我把葡萄酒弄洒了。

spin /spɪn; spɪn/ *verb* 动词 (**spins, spinning, spun** /spʌn; spʌn/, **has spun**)
1 turn round quickly; turn something round quickly（使某物）快速旋转: *She spun a coin on the table.* 她在桌子上旋转硬币。
2 make thread from wool or cotton 纺线；纺纱
3 make a web 织蜘蛛网: *The spider spun a web.* 蜘蛛织了一个网。

spinach /'spɪnɪtʃ; 'spɪnɪtʃ/ *noun* 名词 (no plural 无复数)
a vegetable with big green leaves 菠菜

spine /spaɪn; spaɪn/ *noun* 名词
the line of bones in your back 脊柱；脊椎 ☞ picture on page C2 见第C2页图

spiral /'spaɪrəl; 'spaɪrəl/ *noun* 名词
a long shape that goes round and round as it goes up 螺旋形: *A spring is a spiral.* 弹簧是螺旋形的。
spiral *adjective* 形容词
a spiral staircase 螺旋形的楼梯

spiral 螺旋形

spirit /'spɪrɪt; 'spɪrɪt/ *noun* 名词
1 the part of a person that is not the body. Some people think that your spirit does not die when your body dies. 灵魂
2 spirits (plural 复数) strong alcoholic drinks. Whisky and brandy are spirits. 烈酒（威士忌和白兰地都是烈酒。）
3 spirits (plural 复数) how you feel 精神状态；情绪；心境: *She's in high spirits* (= happy) *today.* 她今天情绪很高。

spit /spɪt; spɪt/ *verb* 动词 (**spits, spitting, spat** /spæt; spæt/, **has spat**)
send liquid or food out from your mouth（从嘴里）吐出液体或食物: *He spat on the ground.* 他把痰吐在地上了。◇ *The baby spat her food out.* 孩子把食物吐出来了。

spite /spaɪt; spaɪt/ *noun* 名词 (no plural 无复数)
wanting to hurt somebody 恶意；坏心: *She broke my watch out of spite* (= because she wanted to hurt me). 她出于恶意把我的手表弄坏了。
in spite of something although something is true; not noticing or not caring about something 虽然某事属实；尽管；不顾；不管: *I slept well in spite of the noise.* 声音吵是吵，我还是睡得很好。◇ *In spite of the bad weather, we went out.* 尽管天气很坏，我们还是出门了。

splash /splæʃ; splæʃ/ *verb* 动词 (**splashes, splashing, splashed** /splæʃt; splæʃt/)
1 throw drops of liquid over somebody or something and make them wet 溅湿某人或某物: *The car splashed us as it drove past.* 汽车经过的时候溅了我们一身泥。
2 move through water so that drops of it fly in the air 在水中移动溅起水花: *The children were splashing around in the pool.* 孩子们在水池里玩儿，溅得周围都是水花。
splash *noun* 名词 (*plural* 复数作 **splashes**)
1 the sound that a person or thing makes when they fall into water 人或物落入水中发出的声音: *Tom jumped into the river with a big splash.* 汤姆扑通一声跳进河里了。
2 a place where liquid has fallen 液体落到的地方: *There were splashes of paint on the floor.* 地板上有溅上的一块块的颜料。

splendid /'splendɪd; 'splɛndɪd/ *adjective* 形容词
very beautiful or very good 极漂亮的；极好的: *a splendid palace* 富丽堂皇的宫殿 ◇ *What a splendid idea!* 多么绝妙的主意！

splinter /ˈsplɪntə(r); ˈsplɪntɚ/ *noun* 名词
a thin sharp piece of wood or glass that has broken off a bigger piece（木头或玻璃等的）薄而尖的碎片: *I've got a splinter in my finger.* 我手指扎了根刺。

split /splɪt; splɪt/ *verb* 动词 (**splits, splitting, split, has split**)
1 break something into two parts 使某物分裂成两部分: *I split the wood with an axe.* 我用斧子把木头劈开了。
2 break open 裂开: *His jeans split when he sat down.* 他一坐下牛仔裤就裂开了。
3 share something; give a part to each person 分某事物；把某事物分给每个人: *We split the money between us.* 我们俩把钱分了。
split up stop being together 不再在一起: *He has split up with his wife.* 他跟妻子分手了。
split *noun* 名词
a long cut or hole in something 长的切口或洞；裂缝

S

spoil /spɔɪl; spɔɪl/ *verb* 动词 (**spoils, spoiling, spoilt** /spɔɪlt; spɔɪlt/ or 或 **spoiled** /spɔɪld; spɔɪld/, **has spoilt** or 或 **has spoiled**)
1 make something less good than before 使某事物没有原来那么好: *The mud spoiled my shoes.* 我的鞋让泥给糟蹋了。◇ *Did the bad weather spoil your holiday?* 天气那么坏，影响你的假期了吧？
2 give a child too much so that they think they can always have what they want 宠爱纵容儿童；娇惯: *She spoils her grandchildren.* 她总宠着孙子、孙女。◇ *a spoilt child* 宠坏的孩子

spoke[1] *form of* **speak** ✳ **speak** 的不同形式

spoke[2] /spəʊk; spok/ *noun* 名词
one of the thin pieces of wire that join the middle of a wheel to the outside, for example on a bicycle 辐条（例如自行车轮的）

spoken *form of* **speak** ✳ **speak** 的不同形式

spokesman /ˈspəʊksmən; ˈspoksmən/ *noun* 名词 (*plural* 复数作 **spokesmen** /ˈspəʊksmən; ˈspoksmən/), **spokeswoman** /ˈspəʊkswʊmən; ˈspoksˌwʊmən/ (*plural* 复数作 **spokeswomen**)
a person who tells somebody what a group of people has decided 发言人

sponge /spʌndʒ; spʌndʒ/ *noun* 名词
1 a soft thing with a lot of small holes in it, that you use for washing yourself or cleaning things（洗澡或擦洗物品用的）海绵；海绵状物
2 a soft light cake 海绵蛋糕

sponsor /ˈspɒnsə(r); ˈspɑnsɚ/ *verb* 动词 (**sponsors, sponsoring, sponsored** /ˈspɒnsəd; ˈspɑnsɚd/)
give money so that something, for example a sports event, will happen 赞助或资助某事物（例如体育赛事）: *The football match was sponsored by a large firm.* 这场足球比赛是由一家大公司赞助的。
sponsor *noun* 名词
a person or company that sponsors 赞助人；赞助公司

spoon /spu:n; spun/ *noun* 名词
a thing with a round end that you use for putting food in your mouth or for mixing 勺；匙子；羹匙: *a wooden spoon* 木勺 ◇ *a teaspoon* 茶匙

spoon 勺

spoonful /ˈspu:nfʊl; ˈspunˌfʊl/ *noun* 名词
the amount that you can put in one spoon 一勺的量: *Two spoonfuls of sugar in my tea, please.* 劳驾，我的茶里请加两勺糖。

sport /spɔ:t; spɔrt/ *noun* 名词
a game that you do to keep your body strong and well and because you enjoy it（锻炼身体的）运动，游戏: *Jenny does a lot of sport.* 珍妮常常做运动。◇ *Football, swimming and tennis are all sports.* 足球、游泳、网球都是体育运动。
sports centre /ˈspɔ:ts sentə(r); ˈspɔrts ˌsɛntɚ/ *noun* 名词
a big building where you can play a lot of different sports 体育馆；体育中心
sportsman /ˈspɔ:tsmən; ˈspɔrtsmən/ *noun* 名词 (*plural* 复数作 **sportsmen** /ˈspɔ:tsmən; ˈspɔrtsmən/), **sportswoman** /ˈspɔ:tswʊmən; ˈspɔrtsˌwʊmən/ (*plural* 复数作 **sportswomen**)
a person who plays sport 做运动的人；运动员

sports car /ˈspɔ:ts kɑ:(r); ˈspɔrts ˌkɑr/ *noun* 名词
a fast car, usually with a roof that you can open 跑车（通常为可敞篷的汽车）

spot[1] /spɒt; spɑt/ *noun* 名词

1 a small round mark（小而圆的）斑点: *a red dress with white spots* 带白点儿的红色连衣裙

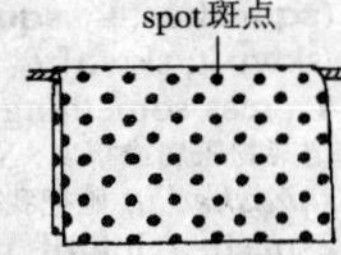

spotted 有斑点的

2 a small red mark on your skin 丘疹；粉刺: *A lot of teenagers get spots on their face.* 有很多十几岁的青年人脸上长着粉刺。

3 a place 地方；场所: *This is a good spot for a picnic.* 这是个办野餐会的好去处。

spotted *adjective* 形容词
with small round marks on it 有斑点的: *a spotted shirt* 带点儿的衬衫

spotty *adjective* 形容词 (**spottier, spottiest**)
with small red marks on your skin 长着丘疹或粉刺的: *a spotty face* 长着粉刺的脸

spot[2] /spɒt; spɑt/ *verb* 动词 (**spots, spotting, spotted**)
see somebody or something suddenly 突然看见某人或某事物: *She spotted her friend in the crowd.* 她在人群中突然看见她的朋友了。

spout /spaʊt; spaʊt/ *noun* 名词
the part of a container that is like a short tube, where liquid comes out. Teapots have spouts.（茶壶等的）嘴

sprain /spreɪn; spren/ *verb* 动词 (**sprains, spraining, sprained** /spreɪnd; sprend/)
hurt part of your body by turning it suddenly 扭伤: *Scott fell and sprained his ankle.* 斯科特把踝部摔伤了。

sprang *form of* **spring**[3] ✳ **spring**[3] 的不同形式

spray /spreɪ; spre/ *noun* 名词

1 (no plural 无复数) liquid in very small drops that flies through the air 水花；浪花: *spray from the sea* 海上的浪花

2 (*plural* 复数作 **sprays**) liquid in a can that comes out in very small drops when you press a button 喷雾液体（罐装，按钮可喷出，呈雾状）: *hairspray* 喷发定型剂

spray 喷雾

spray *verb* 动词 (**sprays, spraying, sprayed** /spreɪd; spred/)
make very small drops of liquid fall on something 向某物喷出雾状液体: *Somebody has sprayed paint on my car.* 有人在我的汽车上喷上颜料了。

spread /spred; sprɛd/ *verb* 动词 (**spreads, spreading, spread, has spread**)

1 open something so that you can see all of it 展开某物；铺开；摊开: *The bird spread its wings and flew away.* 那只鸟展翅飞走了。◇ *Spread out the map on the table.* 把地图摊开放在桌子上。

2 put soft stuff all over something 在某物上涂上软物: *I spread butter on the bread.* 我把黄油涂在面包上了。

3 move to other places or to other people; make something do this（使某物）延伸到他处或他人处: *Fire quickly spread to other parts of the building.* 大火很快蔓延到建筑物的其他地方了。◇ *Rats spread disease.* 老鼠能传播疾病。

spread *noun* 名词 (no plural 无复数)
Doctors are trying to stop the spread of the disease. 医生们竭力阻止这种疾病到处蔓延。

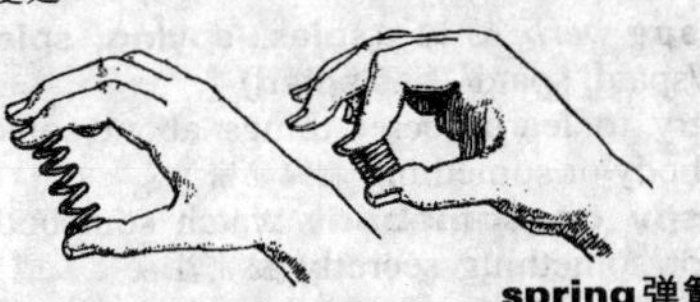
spring 弹簧

spring[1] /sprɪŋ; sprɪŋ/ *noun* 名词

1 a thin piece of metal that is bent round and round. A spring will go back to the same size and shape after you push or pull it. 弹簧

2 a place where water comes out of the ground 泉

spring[2] /sprɪŋ; sprɪŋ/ *noun* 名词
the part of the year after winter, when plants start to grow 春季；春天

spring[3] /sprɪŋ; sprɪŋ/ *verb* 动词 (**springs, springing, sprang** /spræŋ; spræŋ/, **has sprung** /sprʌŋ; sprʌŋ/)
jump or move suddenly 跳；跳动；跳跃: *The cat sprang on the mouse.* 猫跳起来向老鼠扑去。

sprinkle /'sprɪŋkl; 'sprɪŋkḷ/ *verb* 动词 (**sprinkles, sprinkling, sprinkled** /'sprɪŋkld; 'sprɪŋkḷd/)
throw drops or small pieces of some-

S

thing on another thing 把某物洒在或撒在另一物上: *Sprinkle some sugar on the fruit.* 在水果上撒些白糖。

sprint /sprɪnt; sprɪnt/ *verb* 动词 (**sprints, sprinting, sprinted**)
run a short distance very fast 短距离奔跑

sprout[1] /spraʊt; spraʊt/ *noun* 名词
a Brussels sprout; a round green vegetable like a very small cabbage 汤菜(状似极小的洋白菜)

sprout[2] /spraʊt; spraʊt/ *verb* 动词 (**sprouts, sprouting, sprouted**)
start to grow 长出来;发芽: *New leaves are sprouting on the trees.* 树上长出了新叶。

sprung *form of* **spring**[3] ✻ **spring**[3] 的不同形式

spun *form of* **spin** ✻ **spin** 的不同形式

S

spy /spaɪ; spaɪ/ *noun* 名词 (*plural* 复数作 **spies**)
a person who tries to learn secret things about another country, person or company 刺探他国、他人或他公司的秘密的人;间谍

spy *verb* 动词 (**spies, spying, spied** /spaɪd; spaɪd/, **has spied**)
try to learn secret things about somebody or something 刺探秘密

spy on somebody watch somebody or something secretly 秘密注视某人或某事物

squad /skwɒd; skwɑd/ *noun* 名词
a small group of people who work together 小组;小队: *England's football squad* 英格兰足球队 ◇ *a squad of police officers* 一小队警察

square /skweə(r); skwɛr/ *noun* 名词
1 a shape with four straight sides that are the same length and four right angles 正方形 ☞ picture on page C5 见第C5页图
2 an open space in a town with buildings around it (城镇中四周有建筑物的)广场: *Trafalgar Square* 特拉法尔加广场 ◇ *the market square* 集市广场

square *adjective* 形容词
with four straight sides that are the same length 正方形的: *a square table* 方桌 ✪ A **square metre** is an area that is one metre long on each side. 平方米叫做 **square metre**。

squash[1] /skwɒʃ; skwɑʃ/ *verb* 动词 (**squashes, squashing, squashed** /skwɒʃt; skwɑʃt/)
1 press something hard and make it flat 把某物压扁或挤扁: *She sat on my hat and squashed it.* 她把我的帽子坐扁了。
2 push a lot of people or things into a small space 把很多人或物塞进或挤入某处: *We squashed five people into the back of the car.* 我们让五个人挤进汽车后座。

squash[2] /skwɒʃ; skwɑʃ/ *noun* 名词
1 (no plural 无复数) a drink made from fruit juice and sugar. You add water before you drink it 加糖的果汁饮料(喝前需加水): *a glass of orange squash* 一杯橙子汁饮料
2 (*plural* 复数作 **squashes**) a glass of this drink 一杯果汁饮料

squash[3] /skwɒʃ; skwɑʃ/ *noun* 名词 (no plural 无复数)
a game where two players hit a small ball against a wall in a special room (called a **court**) (软式)墙网球;壁球(壁球室叫做 **court**): *Have you ever played squash?* 你打过壁球吗?

squat /skwɒt; skwɑt/ *verb* 动词 (**squats, squatting, squatted**)
1 sit with your feet on the ground, your legs bent and your bottom just above the ground 蹲: *I squatted down to light the fire.* 我蹲下来点火。
2 live in an empty building that is not yours and that you do not pay for 擅自占用空建筑物而不付钱

squatter *noun* 名词
a person who squats in an empty building 擅自占用空建筑物而不付钱的人

squeak /skwi:k; skwik/ *verb* 动词 (**squeaks, squeaking, squeaked** /skwi:kt; skwikt/)
make a short high sound like a mouse 发出(似老鼠叫的)短而尖的声音: *The door was squeaking, so I put some oil on it.* 门吱吱作响,我给它加了点儿油。

squeak *noun* 名词
the squeak of a mouse 老鼠的吱吱叫声

squeaky *adjective* 形容词
He's got a squeaky voice. 他的嗓音很尖厉。

squeal /skwi:l; skwil/ *verb* 动词 (**squeals, squealing, squealed** /skwi:ld; skwild/)
make a loud high sound like a pig 发出(似猪叫的)大而尖的声音: *The children*

squealed with excitement. 孩子们兴奋得尖叫起来。

squeal *noun* 名词

the squeal of a pig 猪的尖叫声

squeeze /skwi:z; skwiz/ *verb* 动词 (**squeezes**, **squeezing**, **squeezed** /skwi:zd; skwizd/)

1 press something hard between other things 压或挤某物: *I squeezed an orange* (to make the juice come out). 我榨了个橙子（把汁挤出来）。

2 go into a small space; push too much into a small space 挤进某处；塞进某处: *Can you squeeze another person into the back of your car?* 您汽车后座还能挤进一个人吗？◇ *Fifty people squeezed into the small room.* 有五十人挤进那间小屋子里去了。

squeeze *noun* 名词

She gave my arm a squeeze. 她捏了我胳膊一下。

squirrel /'skwɪrəl; 'skwɝəl/ *noun* 名词

a small grey or brown animal with a big thick tail. Squirrels live in trees and eat nuts. 松鼠

squirt /skwɜ:t; skwɝt/ *verb* 动词 (**squirts**, **squirting**, **squirted**)

1 suddenly shoot out of something 从某物喷出: *I opened the bottle and lemonade squirted everywhere.* 我一打开瓶子，汽水就喷得到处都是。

2 make liquid suddenly shoot out of something 使液体从某处喷出: *The elephant squirted the clown with water.* 大象用水喷那个小丑。

St

1 *short way of writing* **saint** ＊ **saint** 的缩写形式

2 *short way of writing* **street** ＊ **street** 的缩写形式

stab /stæb; stæb/ *verb* 动词 (**stabs**, **stabbing**, **stabbed** /stæbd; stæbd/)

push a knife or another sharp thing into somebody or something 用刀或其他利器刺入某人身体或某物: *He was stabbed in the back.* 他后背被刺。

stable[1] /'steɪbl; 'stebl̩/ *noun* 名词

a building where you keep horses 马厩

stable[2] /'steɪbl; 'stebl̩/ *adjective* 形容词

Something that is stable will not move, fall or change 稳定的；稳固的；牢固的: *Don't stand on that table—it's not very stable.* 别站在那张桌子上——不太稳。✪ opposite 反义词: **unstable**

stack /stæk; stæk/ *noun* 名词

a lot of things on top of one another 重叠放置的东西；摞；堆: *a stack of books* 一摞书

stack *verb* 动词 (**stacks**, **stacking**, **stacked** /stækt; stækt/)

put things on top of one another 把东西重叠地往上放；摞；堆: *I stacked the chairs after the concert.* 音乐会散了以后，我把椅子都摞了起来。

stadium /'steɪdiəm; 'stedɪəm/ *noun* 名词

a place with seats around it where you can watch sports matches（有看台的）体育场，运动场: *a football stadium* 足球运动场

staff /stɑ:f; stæf/ *noun* 名词 (plural 复数)

the group of people who work in a place 全体职工；全体雇员: *The hotel staff were very friendly.* 这家旅馆的工作人员非常和蔼。

staff room /'stɑ:f ru:m; 'stæf rum/ *noun* 名词

a room in a school where teachers can work and rest 教员备课及休息室

stage[1] /steɪdʒ; stedʒ/ *noun* 名词

the part of a theatre where actors, dancers, etc stand and move（剧场中的）舞台

stage[2] /steɪdʒ; stedʒ/ *noun* 名词

a certain time in a longer set of things that happen 事物发展进程中划分的段落；时期；阶段: *The first stage of the course lasts for two weeks.* 第一阶段的课程为期两周。

at this stage now 现阶段；目前: *At this stage I don't know what I'll do when I leave school.* 现阶段我还不知道中学毕业以后做什么呢。

stagger /'stæɡə(r); 'stæɡɚ/ *verb* 动词 (**staggers**, **staggering**, **staggered** /'stæɡəd; 'stæɡɚd/)

walk as if you are going to fall 摇摇晃晃地走（要摔倒）；蹒跚；踉跄: *He staggered across the room with the heavy box.* 他扛着沉重的箱子踉踉跄跄地从房间一端走到另一端。

stain /steɪn; sten/ *verb* 动词 (**stains**, **staining**, **stained** /steɪnd; stend/)

make coloured or dirty marks on something 染污或沾污某物: *The wine*

S

stained the carpet red. 葡萄酒把地毯染红了一块。

stain *noun* 名词

She had blood stains on her shirt. 她衬衫上有血迹。

stairs /steəz; stɛrz/ *noun* 名词 (plural 复数)

steps that lead up and down inside a building 楼梯: *I ran up the stairs to the bedroom.* 我跑上楼梯进了卧室。☞ Look also at **downstairs** and **upstairs**. 另见 **downstairs** 和 **upstairs**。

staircase /ˈsteəkeɪs; ˈstɛrˌkes/, **stairway** /ˈsteəweɪ; ˈstɛrˌwe/ *noun* 名词

a big group of stairs（整段的）楼梯

stale /steɪl; stel/ *adjective* 形容词 (**staler, stalest**)

not fresh 不新鲜的；陈旧的: *stale bread* 不新鲜的面包◇*stale air* 污浊的空气

stalk /stɔ:k; stɔk/ *noun* 名词

one of the long thin parts of a plant that the flowers, leaves or fruit grow on（植物的）茎；秆

stall 货摊

stall /stɔ:l; stɔl/ *noun* 名词

a big table with things on it that somebody wants to sell, for example in a street or market 货摊（例如街道或集市上的）: *a fruit stall* 水果摊

stammer /ˈstæmə(r); ˈstæmɚ/ *verb* 动词 (**stammers, stammering, stammered** /ˈstæməd; ˈstæmɚd/)

say the same sound many times when you are trying to say a word 口吃；结结巴巴地说: *'B-b-b-but wait for me,' she stammered.* "可－可－可－可得等等我，"她结结巴巴地说。

stamp¹ /stæmp; stæmp/ *noun* 名词

1 a small piece of paper that you put on a letter to show that you have paid to send it 邮票 ☞ picture on page C31 见第C31页图

✪ In Britain, you can buy stamps and send letters at a **post office**. 在英国，可在邮局（**post office**）买邮票、寄信。Some shops also sell stamps. 有的商店也代卖邮票。There are two kinds of stamp for sending letters to other parts of Britain 在英国寄往本国各地的信，使用的邮票分两类: **first-class** stamps and **second-class** stamps. 一类（**first-class**）邮票和二类（**second-class**）邮票。First-class stamps are more expensive and the letters arrive more quickly. 一类邮票贵些，信到得也快些。

2 a small piece of wood or metal that you press on paper to make marks or words 印章；图章: *a date stamp* 日期印章

stamp² /stæmp; stæmp/ *verb* 动词 (**stamps, stamping, stamped** /stæmpt; stæmpt/)

1 put your foot down quickly and hard 用力踩；跺；踏: *She stamped on the spider and killed it.* 她用力把蜘蛛踩死了。

2 walk by putting your feet down hard and loudly 跺着脚走: *Mike stamped angrily out of the room.* 迈克气愤地跺着脚走出了房间。

3 press a small piece of wood or metal on paper to make marks or words 在纸上盖章: *They stamped my passport at the airport.* 在机场他们在我的护照上盖了章。

stand¹ /stænd; stænd/ *verb* 动词 (**stands, standing, stood** /stʊd; stʊd/, **has stood**)

1 be on your feet 站立: *She was standing by the door.* 她在门口站着。

2 (*also* 亦作 **stand up**) get up on your feet 站起来: *The teacher asked us all to stand up.* 老师让我们都站起来。

3 be in a place 在某处；位于；座落: *The castle stands on a hill.* 那个城堡座落在小山上。

4 put something somewhere 把某物放在某处: *I stood the ladder against the wall.* 我把梯子靠在墙上。

can't stand somebody or 或 **something** hate somebody or something 讨厌某人或某事物: *I can't stand this music.* 我讨厌这种音乐。

stand by 1 watch but not do anything 注视但不采取行动: *How can you stand by* *while those boys kick the cat?* 那些男孩子踢那只猫，你怎么能袖手旁观呢？ **2** be ready to do something 随时准备做某事: *Stand by until I call you!* 做好准备，等我叫你！

stand by somebody help somebody when they need it 随时准备帮助某人: *Julie's parents stood by her when she was in trouble.* 朱莉惹了事，她父母随时准备帮助她。

stand for something be a short way of saying or writing something 为某事物的缩略式: *USA stands for 'the United States of America'.* ✳ USA 是the United States of America的缩略式。

stand out be easy to see 容易看到；醒目；突出: *Joe stands out in a crowd because he has got red hair.* 乔在人群里很显眼，因为他头发是红的。

stand still not move 静止不动: *Stand still while I take your photograph.* 别动，我给你照张相。

stand up for somebody or 或 **something** say that somebody or something is right; support somebody or something 说某人或某事物正确；支持某人或某事物: *Everyone else said I was wrong, but my sister stood up for me.* 谁都说我错了，只有我姐姐说我对。

stand up to somebody show that you are not afraid of somebody 表示不害怕某人

stand² /stænd; stænd/ *noun* 名词

1 a table or small shop where you can buy things or get information（售货的或供咨询的）柜台或小店: *a news-stand* (= where you can buy newspapers and magazines) 报摊

2 a piece of furniture that you can put things on（放东西的）架，座: *an umbrella stand* 伞架

standard¹ /ˈstændəd; ˈstændɚd/ *noun* 名词

how good somebody or something is 标准；水准；规格: *Her work is of a very high standard* (= very good). 她工作水平很高。

standard of living /ˌstændəd əv ˈlɪvɪŋ; ˌstændɚd əv ˈlɪvɪŋ/ *noun* 名词 (*plural* 复数作 **standards of living**)

how rich or poor you are 生活水平: *They have a low standard of living* (= they are poor). 他们生活水平很低。

standard² /ˈstændəd; ˈstændɚd/ *adjective* 形容词

normal; not special 标准的；正常的；不特殊的: *Clothes are sold in standard sizes.* 出售的衣服都是标准尺码的。

stank *form of* **stink** ✳ **stink** 的不同形式

staple /ˈsteɪpl; ˈstepl̩/ *noun* 名词

a small, very thin piece of metal that you push through pieces of paper to join them together, using a special tool (called a **stapler**) 订书钉（订书机叫做 **stapler**）

staple *verb* 动词 (**staples**, **stapling**, **stapled** /ˈsteɪpld; ˈstepl̩d/)

Staple the pieces of paper together. 用订书机把纸订在一起。

star¹ /stɑː(r); stɑr/ *noun* 名词

1 one of the small bright lights that you see in the sky at night 星星

2 a shape with points 星状物 ☞ picture on page C5 见第C5页图

star² /stɑː(r); stɑr/ *noun* 名词

a famous person, for example an actor or a singer 名人；明星（例如戏剧明星或歌星）: *a film star* 电影明星

star *verb* 动词 (**stars**, **starring**, **starred** /stɑːd; stɑrd/)

1 be an important actor in a play or film 主演戏剧或电影: *He has starred in many films.* 他主演过很多电影。

2 have somebody as a star 由某人主演: *The film stars Julia Roberts and Patrick Swayze.* 这部影片是由朱莉娅·罗伯茨和帕特里克·斯韦兹主演的。

stare /steə(r); stɛr/ *verb* 动词 (**stares**, **staring**, **stared** /steəd; stɛrd/)

look at somebody or something for a long time 盯着看某人或某事物；凝视: *Everybody stared at her hat.* 大家都瞪大眼睛看着她的帽子。◇ *He was staring out of the window.* 他凝视着窗外。

start¹ /stɑːt; stɑrt/ *verb* 动词 (**starts**, **starting**, **started**)

1 begin to do something 开始做某事物: *I start work at nine o'clock.* 我九点钟开始工作。◇ *It started raining.* 下雨了。◇ *She started to cry.* 她哭起来了。

2 begin to happen; make something begin to happen 开始；（使某事物）开始: *The film starts at 7.30.* 电影7点30分开演。◇ *The police do not know who started the fire.* 警方不知道是谁放的火。

S

3 begin to work or move; make something begin to work or move 开始工作或移动；（使某事物）开始工作或移动: *The engine won't start.* 发动机发动不起来。◇ *I can't start the car.* 这辆汽车我发动不起来。

start off begin 开始: *The teacher started off by asking us our names.* 老师开始上课时先问我们的名字叫什么。

start² /stɑ:t; stɑrt/ *noun* 名词

1 the beginning or first part of something（某事物的）开端或第一部分: *She arrived after the start of the meeting.* 会议开始后她才来。

2 starting something 开始进行某事物: *We have got a lot of work to do, so let's make a start.* 我们有很多事要做，那么咱们开始干吧。

for a start words that you use when you give your first reason for something（用于列举事项）第一；首先: *'Why can't we go on holiday?' 'Well, for a start, we don't have any money.'* "我们为什么不能去度假呢？""嗯，头一条，我们没钱。"

starter /'stɑ:tə(r); 'stɑrtɚ/ *noun* 名词

a small amount of food that you eat as the first part of a meal（一顿饭开始时的）小吃: *What would you like as a starter: soup or melon?* 您要什么开胃小吃：要汤还是要瓜？

startle /'stɑ:tl; 'stɑrtl̩/ *verb* 动词 (**startles**, **startling**, **startled** /'stɑ:tld; 'stɑrtl̩d/)

make somebody suddenly surprised or frightened 使某人吃惊；吓某人一跳: *You startled me when you knocked on the window.* 你一敲窗户把我吓了一跳。

starve /stɑ:v; stɑrv/ *verb* 动词 (**starves**, **starving**, **starved** /stɑ:vd; stɑrvd/)

die because you do not have enough to eat 饿死: *Millions of people are starving in some parts of the world.* 世界上数以百万计的人正处在饥饿的死亡线上。

be starving be very hungry 非常饿: *When will dinner be ready? I'm starving!* 什么时候吃饭哪？我都快饿死了！

starvation /stɑ:'veɪʃn; stɑr'veʃən/ *noun* 名词 (no plural 无复数)

The child died of starvation. 那个孩子饿死了。

state¹ /steɪt; stet/ *noun* 名词

1 (no plural 无复数) how somebody or something is（某人或某事物的）状态；状况；情况；情形: *Your room is in a terrible state!* (= untidy or dirty) 你的屋子可太不像样子了！（= 不整齐或不清洁）

2 (*plural* 复数作 **states**) a country and its government 国家及其政府: *Many schools are owned by the state.* 许多学校都是国立的。

3 (*plural* 复数作 **states**) a part of a country 国家的一部分；州；邦: *Texas is a state in the USA.* 得克萨斯是美国的一个州。

state of mind how you feel 心绪；心境；心态: *What state of mind is he in?* 他心情怎么样？

state² /steɪt; stet/ *verb* 动词 (**states**, **stating**, **stated**)

say or write something 说出或写出某事；陈述: *I stated in my letter that I was looking for a job.* 我信中说我正在找工作。

statement /'steɪtmənt; 'stetmənt/ *noun* 名词

something that you say or write 说出或写出的事；陈述: *The driver made a statement to the police about the accident.* 司机向警方说明了事故发生的经过。

station /'steɪʃn; 'steʃən/ *noun* 名词

1 a railway station; a place where trains stop so that people can get on and off 火车站

2 a place where buses or coaches start and end their journeys（公共汽车的或长途汽车的）汽车站: *a bus station* 公共汽车站

3 a building for some special work（为某种工作的）建筑物；站；所: *a police station* 派出所 ◇ *a fire station* 消防站

4 a television or radio company 电视台；电台

stationery /'steɪʃənri; 'steʃən,ɛrɪ/ *noun* 名词 (no plural 无复数)

paper, pens and other things that you use for writing 文具

statistics /stə'tɪstɪks; stə'tɪstɪks/ *noun* 名词 (plural 复数)

numbers that give information about something 统计数字: *Statistics show that women live longer than men.* 统计数字表明女性比男性寿命长。

statue /'stætʃu:; 'stætʃʊ/ *noun* 名词

the shape of a person or an animal that is made of stone or metal 雕像；塑像；铸像: *the Statue of Liberty in New York* 纽约的自由神像

S

stay[1] /steɪ; ste/ *verb* 动词 (**stays, staying, stayed** /steɪd; sted/)

1 be in the same place and not go away 在某处呆一段时间（不离开）；停留: *Stay here until I come back.* 在这儿呆着，等我回来。◇ *I stayed in bed until ten o'clock.* 我一直在床上，十点钟才起来。

2 continue in the same way and not change 保持某种状态（不改变）: *I tried to stay awake.* 我尽力保持清醒。

3 live somewhere for a short time 在某处短期居住: *I stayed with my friend in Dublin.* 我在都柏林朋友家暂住。◇ *Which hotel are you staying at?* 您现在住在哪家旅馆里？

stay behind be somewhere after other people have gone（别人走后）留在某处: *The teacher asked me to stay behind after the lesson.* 老师让我在课后留下。

stay in be at home and not go out 呆在家里（不出去）: *I'm staying in this evening because I am tired.* 我很累，今天晚上呆在家里。

stay up not go to bed 不去睡觉: *We stayed up until after midnight.* 我们半夜后才去睡觉。

stay[2] /steɪ; ste/ *noun* 名词 (*plural* 复数作 **stays**)

a short time when you live somewhere（某处短期的）居住: *Did you enjoy your stay in London?* 您在伦敦的这些天过得愉快吗？

steady /'stedi; 'stɛdɪ/ *adjective* 形容词 (**steadier, steadiest**)

1 If something is steady, it does not move or shake 稳的；平稳的；牢固的；不摇晃的: *Hold the ladder steady while I stand on it.* 把梯子扶住了，我站在上边。

✪ opposite 反义词: **unsteady**

2 If something is steady, it stays the same 持续不变的；稳定的: *We drove at a steady speed.* 我们以稳定的速度开车。◇ *steady rain* 持续不停的雨

steadily /'stedɪli; 'stɛdəlɪ/ *adverb* 副词

Prices are falling steadily. 物价正在持续下降。

steak /steɪk; stek/ *noun* 名词

a thick flat piece of meat or fish（牛排、猪排、鱼排等）肉排: *steak and chips* 肉排和炸土豆条儿

steal /sti:l; stil/ *verb* 动词 (**steals, stealing, stole** /stəʊl; stol/, **has stolen** /'stəʊlən; 'stolən/)

secretly take something that is not yours 偷；窃取: *Her money has been stolen.* 她的钱让人给偷走了。

> ✪ You **steal** things, but you **rob** people and places (you steal things from them). ＊ **steal**（偷窃）的对象是物，**rob**（抢劫）的对象是人和处所。A person who steals is called a **thief**. 小偷或贼叫做 **thief**。
>
> *They stole my camera.* 他们把我的照相机偷走了。
>
> *I've been robbed.* 我的东西让劫匪给抢了。
>
> *They robbed a bank.* 他们抢了一家银行。

steam /sti:m; stim/ *noun* 名词 (no plural 无复数)

the gas that water becomes when it gets very hot 水蒸气；蒸汽: *There was steam coming from my cup of coffee.* 我那杯咖啡直冒热气。

steam *verb* 动词 (**steams, steaming, steamed** /sti:md; stimd/)

1 send out steam 放出蒸汽: *a steaming bowl of soup* 一碗热气腾腾的汤

2 cook something in steam 蒸食物: *steamed vegetables* 清蒸蔬菜

steel /sti:l; stil/ *noun* 名词 (no plural 无复数)

very strong metal that is used for making things like knives, tools or machines 钢

steep /sti:p; stip/ *adjective* 形容词 (**steeper, steepest**)

A steep hill, mountain or road goes up quickly from a low place to a high place 陡的；陡峭的: *I can't cycle up the hill—it's too steep.* 这个山坡我骑自行车上不去——太陡了。

steeply *adverb* 副词

The path climbed steeply up the side of the mountain. 这条小路从山脚通向山顶，十分陡峭。

steer /stɪə(r); stɪr/ *verb* 动词 (**steers, steering, steered** /stɪəd; stɪrd/)

make a car, boat, bicycle, etc go the way that you want by turning a wheel or handle 操纵汽车、船、自行车等的行驶方向；驾驶

steering-wheel /ˈstɪərɪŋ wiːl; ˈstɪrɪŋ-ˌhwil/ *noun* 名词
the wheel that you turn to make a car go left or right 方向盘 ☞ picture at **car** 见 **car** 词条插图

stem /stem; stɛm/ *noun* 名词
the long thin part of a plant that the flowers and leaves grow on（花草的）茎；（树木的）干 ☞ picture at **plant** 见 **plant** 词条插图

steps 台阶

step¹ /step; stɛp/ *noun* 名词
1 a movement when you move your foot up and then put it down in another place to walk, run or dance（走、跑或跳舞的）步；脚步；舞步: *She took a step forward and then stopped.* 她向前迈了一步就停住了。
2 a place to put your foot when you go up or down（向上走或向下走的）落脚处；台阶；梯级: *These steps go down to the garden.* 从台阶往下走可以进入花园。
3 one thing in a list of things that you must do（一系列事物的）一步；步骤: *What is the first step in planning a holiday?* 安排度假的时候，第一步要做什么？
step by step doing one thing after another; slowly 一步一步地；逐步地；逐渐地: *This book shows you how to play the guitar, step by step.* 这本教授弹吉他的书是循序渐进的。

step² /step; stɛp/ *verb* 动词 (**steps, stepping, stepped** /stept; stɛpt/)
move your foot up and put it down in another place when you walk（用脚交互移动）行走；迈步；跨步；踏: *You stepped on my foot!* 你踩我脚了！

stepfather /ˈstepfɑːðə(r); ˈstɛpˌfɑðɚ/ *noun* 名词
a man who has married your mother but who is not your father 继父

stepladder /ˈsteplædə(r); ˈstɛpˌlædɚ/ *noun* 名词
a short ladder 短梯

stepmother /ˈstepmʌðə(r); ˈstɛpˌmʌðɚ/ *noun* 名词
a woman who has married your father but who is not your mother 继母 ✪ The child of your stepmother or stepfather is your **stepbrother** or **stepsister**. 继父与其前妻生的孩子或继母与其前夫生的孩子，是你的既不同父又不同母的兄弟（叫做 **stepbrother**）或姐妹（叫做 **stepsister**）。

stereo /ˈsteriəʊ; ˈstɛrɪo/ *noun* 名词 (*plural* 复数作 **stereos**)
a machine for playing records, cassettes or compact discs, with two parts (called **speakers**) that the sound comes from 立体声音响器材（扩音器或扬声器叫做 **speaker**）
stereo *adjective* 形容词
with the sound coming from two speakers 立体声的: *a stereo cassette player* 立体声盒式放音机

sterling /ˈstɜːlɪŋ; ˈstɝlɪŋ/ *noun* 名词 (no plural 无复数)
the money that is used in Britain 英国货币；英镑: *You can pay in sterling or in American dollars.* 您可以付英镑，也可以付美元。

stern /stɜːn; stɝn/ *adjective* 形容词 (**sterner, sternest**)
serious and strict with people; not smiling 严肃的；严厉的；不苟言笑的: *Our teacher is very stern.* 我们老师非常严厉。

stew /stjuː; stu/ *noun* 名词
food that you make by cooking meat or vegetables in liquid for a long time 炖的肉或蔬菜: *beef stew* 炖牛肉
stew *verb* 动词 (**stews, stewing, stewed** /stjuːd; stud/)
cook something slowly in liquid 用文火煮；炖；煨；焖: *stewed fruit* 煮水果

steward /ˈstjuːəd; ˈstuwɚd/ *noun* 名词
a man whose job is to look after people on an aeroplane or a ship（飞机或轮船上的）（男）服务员

stewardess /ˌstjuːəˈdes; ˈstuwɚdɪs/ *noun* 名词 (*plural* 复数作 **stewardesses**)
a woman whose job is to look after people on an aeroplane or a ship（飞机或轮船上的）（女）服务员

stick¹ /stɪk; stɪk/ *noun* 名词
1 a long thin piece of wood 木棍；木棒: *We found some sticks and made a fire.* 我们找到些木棍生起火来。◇ *The old man*

walked with a stick. 那个老翁拄着拐棍儿走路。

2 a long thin piece of something 细长的东西；棒状物: *a stick of chalk* 一枝粉笔

stick² /stɪk; stɪk/ *verb* 动词 (**sticks, sticking, stuck** /stʌk; stʌk/, **has stuck**)

1 push a pointed thing into something 用尖物刺入某物: *Stick a fork into the meat to see if it's cooked.* 用叉子叉进肉里看熟了没有。

2 join something to another thing with glue, for example; become joined in this way 把一物与另一物结合在一起（例如用胶水）；粘住: *I stuck a stamp on the envelope.* 我在信封上贴上了一张邮票。

3 be fixed in one place so that it cannot move 卡在某处（不能移动）: *This door always sticks* (= it won't open). 这扇门老是卡住（= 开不开）。

4 put something somewhere 把某物放在某处: *Stick that box on the floor.* 把那个箱子放在地板上吧。✪ This is an informal use. 这是个俗语词。

stick out come out of the side or top of something so you can see it easily（从某物的旁边或上边）伸出（容易看见）: *The boy's head was sticking out of the window.* 那个男孩儿的头伸出窗外了。

stick something out push something out 使某物伸出: *Don't stick your tongue out!* 别把舌头伸出来！

stick to something continue with something and not change it 坚持某事物（不改变）: *We're sticking to Peter's plan.* 我们坚持执行彼得的计划。

stick up for somebody or 或 **something** say that somebody or something is right 说某人或某事物正确: *Everyone else said I was wrong, but Kim stuck up for me.* 谁都说我错了，只有金说我对。

sticker /ˈstɪkə(r); ˈstɪkɚ/ *noun* 名词

a small piece of paper with a picture or words on it, that you can stick onto things（有黏胶的）图文标签: *She has a sticker on the window of her car.* 她的汽车窗户上贴了一张图文标签。

sticky /ˈstɪki; ˈstɪkɪ/ *adjective* 形容词 (**stickier, stickiest**)

Something that is sticky can stick to things or is covered with something that can stick to things 黏的；有黏性物质的: *Glue is sticky.* 胶水是黏的。◇ *sticky fingers* 黏糊糊的手指

stiff /stɪf; stɪf/ *adjective* 形容词 (**stiffer, stiffest**)

hard and not easy to bend or move 坚硬的（不易弯或不易动的）: *stiff cardboard* 硬纸板

still¹ /stɪl; stɪl/ *adverb* 副词

1 a word that you use to show that something has not changed 仍然；依旧: *Do you still live in London?* 您还是住在伦敦吗？◇ *Is it still raining?* 雨还下吗？

2 although that is true 尽管那样；虽然如此: *She felt ill, but she still went to the party.* 她虽然觉得身体不舒服，可是仍然去参加聚会了。

3 a word that you use to make another word stronger（用以加强另一字的语气）甚至；更加: *It was cold yesterday, but today it's colder still.* 昨天很冷，可是今天更冷。

still² /stɪl; stɪl/ *adjective, adverb* 形容词，副词

without moving 静止不动（的）: *Please stand still while I take a photo.* 请站好别动，我来拍张照片。

stillness /ˈstɪlnəs; ˈstɪlnɪs/ *noun* 名词 (no plural 无复数)

the stillness of the night 夜晚的寂静

sting /stɪŋ; stɪŋ/ *verb* 动词 (**stings, stinging, stung** /stʌŋ; stʌŋ/, **has stung**)

1 If an insect or a plant stings you, it hurts you by pushing a small sharp part into your skin（昆虫）蜇伤人；（植物）刺伤人: *I've been stung by a bee!* 我让蜜蜂给蜇了！

2 feel a sudden sharp pain（突然的）剧痛: *The smoke made my eyes sting.* 烟呛得我眼睛很疼。

sting *noun* 名词

1 the sharp part of some insects that can hurt you（昆虫的）螫针: *A wasp's sting is in its tail.* 黄蜂的螫针在它的尾部。

2 a hurt place on your skin where an insect or plant has stung you 螫伤处；蜇伤处；刺伤处: *a bee sting* 被蜜蜂蜇伤的地方

stink /stɪŋk; stɪŋk/ *verb* 动词 (**stinks, stinking, stank** /stæŋk; stæŋk/, **has stunk** /stʌŋk; stʌŋk/)

have a very bad smell 有臭味；发臭: *That fish stinks!* 这条鱼臭了！

stink *noun* 名词

a very bad smell 臭味: *What a horrible stink!* 这味儿可真臭！

S

stir /stɜ:(r); stɝ/ *verb* 动词 (**stirs**, **stirring**, **stirred** /stɜ:d; stɝd/)

1 move a spoon or another thing round and round to mix something（用勺等）搅动某物；搅拌: *He put sugar in his coffee and stirred it.* 他把糖放进咖啡里搅了搅。

2 move a little or make something move a little（使某物）微动: *The wind stirred the leaves.* 风把叶子吹得微微摇动。

stitch /stɪtʃ; stɪtʃ/ *noun* 名词 (*plural* 复数作 **stitches**)

1 one movement in and out of a piece of material with a needle and thread when you are sewing（缝纫的）一针

2 one of the small circles of wool that you put round a needle when you are knitting（编结或编织的）一针

stitch *verb* 动词 (**stitches**, **stitching**, **stitched** /stɪtʃt; stɪtʃt/)

make stitches in something; sew something 缝合；编结；编织: *I stitched a button on my skirt.* 我在裙子上钉了个扣子。

S

stock /stɒk; stɑk/ *noun* 名词

things that a shop keeps ready to sell（商店供出售的）现货: *That bookshop has a big stock of dictionaries.* 那家书店现有大量词典供出售。

in stock ready to sell 有现货

out of stock not there to sell 无现货: *I'm sorry, that cassette is out of stock at the moment.* 很抱歉，这种盒式磁带现在没货。

stock *verb* 动词 (**stocks**, **stocking**, **stocked** /stɒkt; stɑkt/)

keep something ready to sell 有现货（供出售）: *We don't stock umbrellas.* 雨伞我们没货。

stocking /ˈstɒkɪŋ; ˈstɑkɪŋ/ *noun* 名词

a long thin thing that a woman wears over her leg and foot（女用的）长筒袜: *a pair of stockings* 一双长筒袜

stole, **stolen** *forms of* **steal** ＊ **steal** 的不同形式

stomach /ˈstʌmək; ˈstʌmək/ *noun* 名词

1 the part inside your body where food goes after you eat it 胃

2 the front part of your body below your chest and above your legs 肚子

☞ picture on page C2 见第C2页图

stomach-ache /ˈstʌmək eɪk; ˈstʌmək-ˌek/ *noun* 名词 (no plural 无复数)

a pain in your stomach 胃疼；肚子疼: *I've got stomach-ache.* 我肚子疼。

stone /stəʊn; ston/ *noun* 名词

1 (no plural 无复数) the very hard stuff that is in the ground. Stone is sometimes used for building 石；岩石: *a stone wall* 石墙

2 (*plural* 复数作 **stones**) a small piece of stone 石块；石头；石子: *The children were throwing stones into the river.* 孩子们往河里扔石头。

3 (*plural* 复数作 **stones**) the hard part in the middle of some fruits, for example plums and peaches（李子、桃等核果中心坚硬的）核

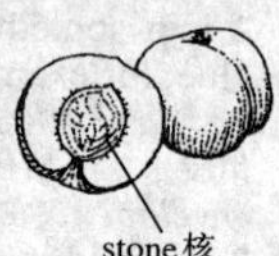
stone 核

4 (*plural* 复数作 **stones**) a small piece of beautiful rock that is very valuable 宝石: *A diamond is a precious stone.* 钻石是贵重的宝石。

5 (*plural* 复数作 **stone**) a measure of weight (= 6.3 kilograms). There are 14 **pounds** in a stone 呎（重量单位，等于6.3公斤。1呎等于14磅，磅叫做 **pound**）: *I weigh ten stone.* 我体重十呎。

☞ Note at **pound** 见 **pound** 词条注释

stony /ˈstəʊni; ˈstonɪ/ *adjective* 形容词 (**stonier**, **stoniest**)

with a lot of stones in or on it 多石的；铺石的: *stony ground* 有很多石头的地面

stood *form of* **stand**[1] ＊ **stand**[1] 的不同形式

stool /stu:l; stul/ *noun* 名词

a small seat with no back 凳子

stool 凳子

stoop /stu:p; stup/ *verb* 动词 (**stoops**, **stooping**, **stooped** /stu:pt; stupt/)

If you stoop, you bend your body forward and down 俯身；弯腰: *She stooped to pick up the baby.* 她弯下腰把孩子抱起来。

stop[1] /stɒp; stɑp/ *verb* 动词 (**stops**, **stopping**, **stopped** /stɒpt; stɑpt/

1 finish moving or working; become still（使活动或工作）停止；终止: *The train stopped at every station.* 这列火车每站都停。◇ *The clock has stopped.* 时钟停了。◇ *I stopped to post a letter.* 我停下来去寄了封信。

2 not do something any more; finish 不再做某事: *Stop making that noise!* 别再弄出那种声音来！

3 make somebody or something finish moving or doing something 使某人或某事物不再动或不再做某事物: *Ring the bell to stop the bus.* 按那个铃就能让公共汽车停住。

stop somebody (from) doing something not let somebody do something 制止某人做某事: *My dad stopped me from going out.* 我爸爸不让我出去。

stop² /stɒp; stɑp/ *noun* 名词

1 the moment when somebody or something finishes moving（人或事物活动的）停止: *The train came to a stop.* 火车停住了。

2 a place where buses or trains stop so that people can get on and off（公共汽车或火车的）车站: *I'm getting off at the next stop.* 我在下一站下车。

put a stop to something make something finish 使某事物停止: *A teacher put a stop to the fight.* 他们吵架让老师给制止住了。

store¹ /stɔ:(r); stɔr/ *noun* 名词

1 a big shop（大型的）百货商店: *Harrods is a famous London store.* 哈罗德是伦敦著名的百货商店。

2 things that you are keeping to use later 储藏；储备: *a store of food* 食物的储备

3 *American English for* **shop¹** 美式英语，即 **shop¹**

store² /stɔ:(r); stɔr/ *verb* 动词 (**stores, storing, stored** /stɔ:d; stɔrd/)

keep something to use later 储藏或储备某物: *The information is stored on a computer.* 这一信息已经储存在计算机里了。

storey /'stɔ:ri; 'stɔrɪ/ *noun* 名词 (*plural* 复数作 **storeys**)

one level in a building（建筑物的）楼层: *The building has four storeys.* 这是个四层的楼房。

storm¹ /stɔ:m; stɔrm/ *noun* 名词

very bad weather with strong winds and rain 暴风雨: *a thunderstorm* 雷雨

storm² /stɔ:m; stɔrm/ *verb* 动词 (**storms, storming, stormed** /stɔ:md; stɔrmd/)

move in a way that shows you are angry 愤怒地行动: *He stormed out of the room.* 他怒气冲冲地出了房间。

stormy /'stɔ:mi; 'stɔrmɪ/ *adjective* 形容词 (**stormier, stormiest**)

If the weather is stormy, there is strong wind and rain 有暴风雨的: *a stormy night* 有暴风雨的夜晚

story /'stɔ:ri; 'stɔrɪ/ *noun* 名词 (*plural* 复数作 **stories**)

1 words that tell you about people and things that are not real（虚构的）故事；小说: *Hans Christian Andersen wrote stories for children.* 安徒生写了很多童话故事。◇ *a ghost story* 鬼故事

2 words that tell you about things that really happened（真实的）事情: *My grandmother told me stories about when she was a child.* 我祖母给我讲了她童年的一些事情。

stove /stəʊv; stov/ *noun* 名词

a cooker or heater 炉具或暖炉

straight¹ /streɪt; stret/ *adjective* 形容词 (**straighter, straightest**)

1 with no curve or bend 直的: *Use a ruler to draw a straight line.* 用尺画一条直线。◇ *His hair is curly and mine is straight.* 他的头发是弯的，我的是直的。☞ picture at **hair** 见 **hair** 词条插图

straight line 直线

straight 正的

not straight 不正的

2 with one side as high as the other 两边一样高的；水平的: *This picture isn't straight.* 这幅画儿歪了。

get something straight make sure that you understand something completely 务必完全了解某事物: *Let's get this straight. Are you sure you left your bike by the cinema?* 咱们得先弄个一清二楚。你是不是确实把自行车放在电影院那儿了？

straight² /streɪt; stret/ *adverb* 副词

1 in a straight line 成一直线: *Look straight in front of you.* 一直向前看。

2 without stopping or doing anything else; directly 不中途停止或不中途做其他事；直接地；径直: *Come straight home.* 直接回家。◇ *She walked straight past me.* 她从我旁边经过，停也没停。

straight away immediately; now 立即；马上: *I'll do it straight away.* 我马上去做。

S

straight on without turning 不转弯: *Go straight on until you come to the bank, then turn left.* 一直往前走，到银行那里向左转。

straighten /ˈstreɪtn; ˈstretn̩/ *verb* 动词 (**straightens**, **straightening**, **straightened** /ˈstreɪtnd; ˈstretn̩d/)
become or make something straight （使某事物）变直

straightforward /ˌstreɪtˈfɔːwəd; ˌstretˈfɔrwɚd/ *adjective* 形容词
easy to understand or do 容易了解的；容易做的: *The question was straightforward.* 这个问题容易回答。

strain /streɪn; stren/ *verb* 动词 (**strains**, **straining**, **strained** /streɪnd; strend/)
1 pour a liquid through something with small holes in it, to take away any other things in the liquid 过滤: *You haven't strained the tea—there are tea leaves in it.* 你没把茶过滤一下——里面还有茶叶呢。
2 try very hard 努力；尽力: *Her voice was so quiet that I had to strain to hear her.* 她的声音非常弱，我很费力才能听见她说的话。
3 hurt a part of your body by making it work too hard（因使用过度）使身体某部损伤；劳损；扭伤: *Don't read in the dark. You'll strain your eyes.* 别在黑暗的地方看书。能把眼睛累坏了。

strain *noun* 名词
1 being pulled or made to work too hard 拉紧；绷紧；张紧；过度的使用: *The rope broke under* (= because of) *the strain.* 绳子拉断了。
2 hurting a part of your body by making it work too hard 劳伤；劳损；扭伤: *back strain* 腰背劳损

strand /strænd; strænd/ *noun* 名词
one piece of thread or hair 一根线或毛发

stranded /ˈstrændɪd; ˈstrændɪd/ *adjective* 形容词
left in a place that you cannot get away from 陷于困境的（无法脱身）: *The car broke down and I was stranded on a lonely road.* 汽车抛了锚，我困在无人来往的路上。

strange /streɪndʒ; strendʒ/ *adjective* 形容词 (**stranger**, **strangest**)
1 unusual or surprising 不寻常的；奇怪的: *Did you hear that strange noise?* 你听见那种奇怪的声音了吗？
2 that you do not know 不认识的；陌生的: *We were lost in a strange town.* 我们在一个陌生的镇子上迷了路。✪ Be careful! We use **foreign**, not **strange**, to talk about a person or thing that comes from another country. 注意！表示"外国的"之意，要用 **foreign**，不可用 **strange**。

strangely *adverb* 副词
in a surprising or unusual way 奇怪地；不寻常地: *She usually talks a lot, but today she was strangely quiet.* 她平常话很多，可是今天安静得出奇。

stranger /ˈstreɪndʒə(r); ˈstrendʒɚ/ *noun* 名词
1 a person who you do not know 不认识的人；陌生人
2 a person who is in a place that he/she does not know 处于陌生环境的人: *I'm a stranger to this city.* 我在这个城市里人地生疏。✪ Be careful! We use the word **foreigner** for a person who comes from another country. 注意！"外国人"叫做 **foreigner**。

strangle /ˈstræŋgl; ˈstræŋgl̩/ *verb* 动词 (**strangles**, **strangling**, **strangled** /ˈstræŋgld; ˈstræŋgl̩d/)
kill somebody by pressing their neck very tightly 扼死某人；勒死；掐死

straps 带子

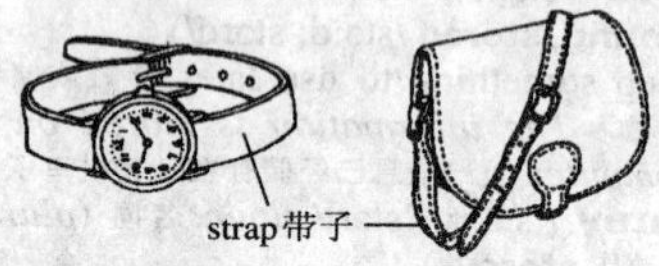

strap /stræp; stræp/ *noun* 名词
a long flat piece of material that you use for carrying something or for keeping something in place 带子: *a leather watch-strap* 皮手表带

strap *verb* 动词 (**straps**, **strapping**, **strapped** /stræpt; stræpt/)
hold something in place with a strap 用带子把某物固定住: *I strapped the bag onto the back of my bike.* 我用带子把提包捆在自行车后边了。

straw /strɔː; strɔ/ *noun* 名词
1 (no plural 无复数) the dry stems of plants like wheat（干的）禾秆，稻秆；干草: *The rabbit sleeps on a bed of straw.* 兔子在干草上睡觉。◇ *a straw hat* 草帽

2 (*plural* 复数作 **straws**) a thin paper or plastic tube that you can drink through (纸的或塑料的) 饮料吸管

the last straw a bad thing that happens after many other bad things so that you lose hope 使人终于不胜负荷的最后一件事

strawberry /ˈstrɔ:bəri; ˈstrɔˌbɛrɪ/ *noun* 名词 (*plural* 复数作 **strawberries**)
a small soft red fruit 草莓: *strawberry jam* 草莓酱

strawberry 草莓

stray /streɪ; stre/ *adjective* 形容词
lost and away from home 离家而迷路的；离群的: *a stray dog* 走失的狗

stray *noun* 名词 (*plural* 复数作 **strays**) an animal that has no home 无家的动物

streak /stri:k; strik/ *noun* 名词
a long thin line 条纹；线条: *She's got streaks of grey in her hair.* 她头发上夹杂着缕缕白发。◇ *a streak of lightning* 一道闪电

stream /stri:m; strim/ *noun* 名词
1 a small river 小河
2 moving liquid, or moving things or people 流动的液体；移动的人或物: *a stream of blood* 一股血 ◇ *a stream of cars* 川流不息的汽车

stream *verb* 动词 (**streams**, **streaming**, **streamed** /stri:md; strimd/)
move like water (像水流般) 流；流动: *Tears were streaming down his face.* 他脸上淌着泪。

streamline /ˈstri:mlaɪn; ˈstrimˌlaɪn/ *verb* 动词 (**streamlines**, **streamlining**, **streamlined** /ˈstri:mlaɪnd; ˈstrimˌlaɪnd/)
give something like a car or boat a long smooth shape so that it can go fast through air or water 使 (汽车或船等) 成流线型 (便于在空气中或水中快速行驶)

street /stri:t; strit/ *noun* 名词
a road in a city, town or village with buildings along the sides 街道: *I saw Anna walking down the street.* 我看见安娜沿着那条街走去。◇ *I live in Hertford Street.* 我住在赫特福德街。✪ The short way of writing 'Street' in addresses is **St** 地址中 Street 的缩写形式为 **St**: *91 Oxford St* 牛津街91号

streetcar /ˈstri:tkɑ:(r); ˈstritˌkɑr/ *American English for* **tram** 美式英语，即 **tram**

strength /streŋθ; strɛŋθ/ *noun* 名词 (no plural 无复数)
being strong 力量；力气: *I don't have the strength to lift this box –it's too heavy.* 我没有那么大力气提起这个箱子——太重了。

strengthen /ˈstreŋθn; ˈstrɛŋθən/ *verb* 动词 (**strengthens**, **strengthening**, **strengthened** /ˈstreŋθnd; ˈstrɛŋθənd/)
make something stronger 使某事物强大

stress /stres; strɛs/ *noun* 名词 (*plural* 复数作 **stresses**)
1 saying one word or part of a word more strongly than another (字的) 重音，重读: *In the word 'dictionary', the stress is on the first part of the word.* ＊dictionary 这个字的重音是在第一个音节上。
2 a feeling of worry because of problems in your life (生活中的问题造成的) 忧虑或压力: *She's suffering from stress because she's got too much work to do.* 她有很多工作要做，精神压力很大。

stressful /ˈstresfl; ˈstrɛsfəl/ *adjective* 形容词
a stressful job 压力很大的工作

stress *verb* 动词 (**stresses**, **stressing**, **stressed** /strest; strɛst/)
1 say something strongly to show that it is important 强调某事物: *I must stress how important this meeting is.* 我必须强调，这个会议十分重要。
2 say one word or part of a word more strongly than another 把某音节读重；重读: *You should stress the first part of the word 'happy'.* ＊happy 这个字的第一个音节应该重读。

stretch¹ /stretʃ; strɛtʃ/ *verb* 动词 (**stretches**, **stretching**, **stretched** /stretʃt; strɛtʃt/)
1 pull something to make it longer or wider; become longer or wider (使某物) 加长或加宽: *The T-shirt stretched when I washed it.* 这件短袖汗衫我一洗就变长了。
2 push your arms and legs out as far as you can 伸展手臂和腿: *Joe got out of bed and stretched.* 乔起床后伸了个懒腰。
3 continue 绵延；延续；伸展: *The beach stretches for miles.* 这个海滩绵延数英里。

stretch out lie down with all your body flat 舒展身体躺着: *The cat stretched out in front of the fire and went to sleep.* 猫舒展着身体躺在暖炉前睡着了。

S

stretch² /stretʃ; strɛtʃ/ *noun* 名词 (*plural* 复数作 **stretches**)
a piece of land or water 一片地或水: *This is a beautiful stretch of countryside.* 这是一片郊外美景。

stretcher /ˈstretʃə(r); ˈstrɛtʃɚ/ *noun* 名词
a kind of bed for carrying somebody who is ill or hurt 担架: *They carried him to the ambulance on a stretcher.* 他们用担架把他抬到救护车上。

strict /strɪkt; strɪkt/ *adjective* 形容词 (**stricter**, **strictest**)
If you are strict, you make people do what you want and do not allow them to behave badly 严厉的；严格的: *Her parents are very strict—she always has to be home before ten o'clock.* 她父母非常严厉——她总得十点钟以前回家。◇ *strict rules* 严格的规则

strictly *adverb* 副词
1 definitely; in a strict way 绝对地；严厉地；严格地: *Smoking is strictly forbidden.* 严禁吸烟。
2 exactly 确切地: *That is not strictly true.* 那并不完全属实。

stride /straɪd; straɪd/ *verb* 动词 (**strides**, **striding**, **strode** /strəʊd; strod/, **has stridden** /ˈstrɪdn; ˈstrɪdn̩/)
walk with long steps 大步行走: *The police officer strode across the road.* 警察迈着大步走过马路。

stride *noun* 名词
a long step 大步

strike¹ /straɪk; straɪk/ *noun* 名词
a time when people are not working because they want more money or are angry about something 罢工: *There are no trains today because the drivers are on strike.* 今天火车不开，因为司机都罢工了。

strike² /straɪk; straɪk/ *verb* 动词 (**strikes**, **striking**, **struck** /strʌk; strʌk/, **has struck**)
1 hit somebody or something 打或击某人或某物: *A stone struck me on the back of the head.* 有一块石头击中我头的后部了。✪ **Hit** is the more usual word, but when you talk about **lightning**, you always use **strike** ＊ **hit** 是较常用的词，但与 **lightning**（闪电）连用时一定要用 **strike**: *The tree was struck by lightning.* 那棵树遭雷电击中了。
2 stop working because you want more money or are angry about something 罢工: *The nurses are going to strike for better pay.* 护士为争取提高工资准备举行罢工。
3 ring a bell so that people know what time it is（指时钟）敲响报时: *The clock struck nine.* 时钟敲了九点。
4 come suddenly into your mind 突然产生某种想法: *It suddenly struck me that she looked like my sister.* 我突然发觉她长得很像我姐姐。

strike a match make fire with a match 划火柴

striking /ˈstraɪkɪŋ; ˈstraɪkɪŋ/ *adjective* 形容词
If something is striking, you notice it because it is very unusual or interesting（因特殊或有趣）引人注意的: *That's a very striking hat.* 那顶帽子十分别致。

string /strɪŋ; strɪŋ/ *noun* 名词
1 very thin rope that you use for tying things（捆绑东西用的）绳子: *I tied up the parcel with string.* 我用绳子把包裹捆了起来。◇ *The little boy held a balloon on the end of a string.* 那个小男孩儿拿着个拴绳儿的气球。
2 a line of things on a piece of thread 用线绳穿着的一串东西: *She was wearing a string of blue beads.* 她戴着一串蓝色的珠子。☞ picture on page C25 见第C25页图
3 a piece of thin wire, etc on a musical instrument（乐器的）弦: *guitar strings* 吉他的弦

strip¹ /strɪp; strɪp/ *noun* 名词
a long thin piece of something 长而薄的东西: *a strip of paper* 一张纸条

strip² /strɪp; strɪp/ *verb* 动词 (**strips**, **stripping**, **stripped** /strɪpt; strɪpt/)
1 take off what is covering something 除掉覆盖物: *I stripped the wallpaper off the walls.* 我把墙纸揭下来了。
2 (*also* 亦作 **strip off**) take off your clothes 脱衣: *She stripped off and ran into the sea.* 她脱掉衣服，跑进海里。

stripe /straɪp; straɪp/ *noun* 名词
a long thin line of colour（有颜色的）条纹: *Zebras have black and white stripes.* 斑马的身上有黑白条纹。

striped 有条纹的

striped /straɪpt; straɪpt/ *adjective* 形容词
with stripes 有条纹的: *He wore a blue-and-white striped shirt.* 他穿着蓝白条的衬衫。

strode *form of* **stride** ✻ **stride** 的不同形式

stroke¹ /strəʊk; strok/ *verb* 动 词 (**strokes**, **stroking**, **stroked** /strəʊkt; strokt/)
move your hand gently over somebody or something to show love 抚摩某人或某物（示爱）: *She stroked his hair.* 她抚摩着他的头发。

stroke² /strəʊk; strok/ *noun* 名词
1 a movement that you make with your arms when you are swimming, playing tennis, etc（指游泳或打网球等）手臂的动作，一挥，一击
2 a sudden serious illness when the brain stops working properly（脑疾患引起的）中风: *He had a stroke.* 他患中风了。

stroll /strəʊl; strol/ *verb* 动词 (**strolls**, **strolling**, **strolled** /strəʊld; strold/)
walk slowly 散步；漫步: *We strolled along the beach.* 我们在海滩上散了散步。
stroll *noun* 名词
We went for a stroll by the river. 我们到河边去散了散步。

stroller /ˈstrəʊlə(r); ˈstrolɚ/ *American English for* **pushchair** 美式英语，即 **pushchair**

strong /strɒŋ; strɔŋ/ *adjective* 形容词 (**stronger**, **strongest**)
1 with a powerful body, so that you can carry heavy things 强壮的；健壮的: *I need somebody strong to help me move this piano.* 我需要个力气大的人来帮我搬钢琴。
☞ picture on page C27 见第C27页图
2 that you cannot break easily 不容易断的；结实的；坚定的: *Don't stand on that chair—it's not very strong.* 别站在那把椅子上——不太结实。◇ *a strong belief* 坚定的信念
3 that you can see, taste, smell, hear or feel very clearly 能明显看出、尝出、嗅出、听出或觉出的；强烈的: *I like strong tea* (= with not much milk in it). 我爱喝酽茶（= 不多加奶的）。◇ *a strong smell of oranges* 很浓的橙子味 ◇ *strong winds* 强风
strongly *adverb* 副词
I strongly believe that he is wrong. 我坚信他错了。

struck *form of* **strike²** ✻ **strike²** 的不同形式

structure /ˈstrʌktʃə(r); ˈstrʌktʃɚ/ *noun* 名词
1 (no plural 无复数) the way that something is made 结构；构造: *We are studying the structure of a bird's wing.* 我们正在研究鸟类翅膀的构造。
2 (*plural* 复数作 **structures**) a building or another thing that people have made with many parts 建筑物或人造的有复杂结构的事物: *The new post office is a tall glass and brick structure.* 这座新邮局是用玻璃和砖建造的高楼。

struggle /ˈstrʌgl; ˈstrʌgl̩/ *verb* 动 词 (**struggles**, **struggling**, **struggled** /ˈstrʌgld; ˈstrʌgl̩d/)
1 try very hard to do something that is not easy 努力做不容易做的事；奋力: *We struggled to lift the heavy box.* 我们费尽了力气抬那个沉重的箱子。
2 move your arms and legs a lot when you are fighting or trying to get free（指用四肢）搏斗；挣扎: *She struggled to get away from her attacker.* 她竭力挣扎来摆脱那个行凶的人。
struggle *noun* 名词
In 1862 the American slaves won their struggle for freedom. 1862年美国奴隶在争取自由的斗争中获得了胜利。

stubborn /ˈstʌbən; ˈstʌbɚn/ *adjective* 形容词
A stubborn person does not change his/her ideas easily or do what other people want him/her to do 固执的；顽固的: *She's too stubborn to say sorry.* 她固执得都不肯赔个不是。

stuck¹ *form of* **stick²** ✻ **stick²** 的不同形式

stuck² /stʌk; stʌk/ *adjective* 形容词
1 not able to move 不能动: *This drawer is stuck—I can't open it.* 这个抽屉卡住了——我打不开。◇ *I was stuck in Italy with no money.* 我因为没有钱而困在意大利了。
2 not able to do something because it is difficult 因遇到困难而不能做某事: *If you get stuck, ask your teacher for help.* 要是遇到困难就向老师请教。

student /ˈstju:dnt; ˈstudn̩t/ *noun* 名词
a person who is studying at a university or college（大专院校的）学生: *Tim is a student of history.* 蒂姆是历史系的学生。

S

studio /ˈstju:diəʊ; ˈstudɪˌo/ *noun* 名词 (*plural* 复数作 **studios**)
1 a room where an artist works（艺术工作者的）工作室
2 a room where people make films, radio and television programmes, or records（制作影片、电台和电视节目或唱片的）工作室；摄影棚；播音室；演播室；录制室: *a television studio* 电视演播室

study¹ /ˈstʌdi; ˈstʌdɪ/ *verb* 动词 (**studies, studying, studied** /ˈstʌdid; ˈstʌdɪd/, **has studied**)
1 spend time learning about something 学习；研究: *He studied French at university.* 他在大学学法语。
2 look at something carefully 仔细查看某物: *We must study the map before we leave.* 我们得先仔细看看地图再出发。

study² /ˈstʌdi; ˈstʌdɪ/ *noun* 名词 (*plural* 复数作 **studies**)
1 learning 学习；研究: *He's doing a course in Business Studies.* 他正在上企业研究课程。
2 a room in a house where you go to study, read or write 书房

stuff¹ /stʌf; stʌf/ *noun* 名词 (no plural 无复数)
any material, substance or group of things（任何的）材料；物质或一些东西: *What's this blue stuff on the carpet?* 地毯上这种蓝色的东西是什么？◇ *Put your stuff in this bag.* 把你的东西放在这个袋子里吧。

stuff² /stʌf; stʌf/ *verb* 动词 (**stuffs, stuffing, stuffed** /stʌft; stʌft/)
1 fill something with something 用某物填充某物: *The pillow was stuffed with feathers.* 这个枕头是羽绒的。
2 push something quickly into another thing 把某物迅速放进另一物中: *He took the money quickly and stuffed it into his pocket.* 他很快把钱拿起来塞进口袋里了。

stuffy /ˈstʌfi; ˈstʌfɪ/ *adjective* 形容词 (**stuffier, stuffiest**)
If a room is stuffy, it has no fresh air in it（指房间等）空气污浊的: *Open the window –it's very stuffy in here.* 把窗户打开吧——空气太坏了。

stumble /ˈstʌmbl; ˈstʌmbḷ/ *verb* 动词 (**stumbles, stumbling, stumbled** /ˈstʌmbld; ˈstʌmbḷd/)
hit your foot against something when you are walking or running, and almost fall 走或跑时脚碰到东西险些跌倒；绊脚: *The old lady stumbled and fell as she was going upstairs.* 老太太上楼梯时绊倒了。

stump /stʌmp; stʌmp/ *noun* 名词
the small part that is left when something is cut off or broken 割断或折断某物后余下的小部分: *a tree stump* 树桩

stun /stʌn; stʌn/ *verb* 动词 (**stuns, stunning, stunned** /stʌnd; stʌnd/)
1 hit a person or animal on the head so hard that he/she/it cannot see, think or make a sound for a short time 把人或动物的头打昏
2 make somebody very surprised 使某人震惊: *His sudden death stunned his family and friends.* 他突然死亡，家人亲友十分震惊。

stung *form of* **sting** ✳ **sting** 的不同形式

stunk *form of* **stink** ✳ **stink** 的不同形式

stunning /ˈstʌnɪŋ; ˈstʌnɪŋ/ *adjective* 形容词
very beautiful; wonderful 非常漂亮的；美妙的: *a stunning dress* 非常漂亮的连衣裙

stunt /stʌnt; stʌnt/ *noun* 名词
something dangerous or difficult that you do to make people look at you（引人注意的）危险的或困难的举动；特技表演: *James Bond films have a lot of exciting stunts.* 詹姆斯·邦德主演的影片有很多惊险动作。

stupid /ˈstju:pɪd; ˈstupɪd/ *adjective* 形容词
not intelligent; silly 愚蠢的；笨的: *Don't be so stupid!* 别那么傻了！◇ *What a stupid question!* 多么愚蠢的问题！
stupidity /stju:ˈpɪdəti; stuˈpɪdətɪ/ *noun* 名词 (no plural 无复数)
being stupid 愚蠢；笨
stupidly *adverb* 副词
I stupidly forgot to close the door. 我忘关门了，真蠢。

stutter /ˈstʌtə(r); ˈstʌtɚ/ *verb* 动词 (**stutters, stuttering, stuttered** /ˈstʌtəd; ˈstʌtɚd/)
say the same sound many times when you are trying to say a word 口吃；结结巴巴地说: *'I d-d-don't understand,' he stuttered.* "我不——不——不明白，" 他结结巴巴地说。

style /staɪl; staɪl/ *noun* 名词
1 a way of doing, making or saying something（做事或说话的）方式；风格:

I don't like his style of writing. 我不喜欢他的写作风格。

2 the shape or kind of something 某事物的形状或种类: *This shop sells jumpers in lots of different colours and styles.* 这家商店卖的毛衣有各种各样的颜色和款式。◇ *a hairstyle* 发型

subject /'sʌbdʒɪkt; 'sʌbdʒɪkt/ *noun* 名词

1 the person or thing that you are talking or writing about（说的或写的）对象；主题: *What is the subject of the talk?* 谈的是什么话题？

2 something you study at school, university or college（学校中的）学科；科目: *I'm studying three subjects: Maths, Physics and Chemistry.* 我现在学习三种科目：数学、物理、化学。

3 the word in a sentence that does the action of the verb（句子中的）主语: *In the sentence 'Susan ate the cake', 'Susan' is the subject.* 在 Susan ate the cake 这句话里，Susan 是主语。☞ Look at **object**. 见 **object**。

4 a person who belongs to a certain country（某国家的）国民；臣民: *British subjects* 英国公民

submarine /ˌsʌbmə'ri:n; 'sʌbməˌrin/ *noun* 名词

a boat that can travel under the sea 潜水艇

subscription /səb'skrɪpʃn; səb'skrɪpʃən/ *noun* 名词

money that you pay, for example to get the same magazine each month or to join a club（杂志等的）订阅费；（俱乐部等的）会员费: *I've got a subscription to 'Vogue' magazine.* 我订购了《时尚》杂志。

substance /'sʌbstəns; 'sʌbstəns/ *noun* 名词

anything that you can see, touch or use for making things; a material 物质: *Stone is a hard substance.* 石头是坚硬的物质。◇ *chemical substances* 化学物质

substitute /'sʌbstɪtju:t; 'sʌbstəˌtut/ *noun* 名词

a person or thing that you put in the place of another 代替或替换他人或他事物的人或事物: *Our goalkeeper was ill, so we found a substitute.* 我们队的守门员病了，所以我们找了个人替他。

substitute *verb* 动词 (**substitutes, substituting, substituted**)

put somebody or something in the place of another 用某人或某事物代替: *You can substitute margarine for butter.* 可以用人造黄油代替纯黄油。

subtitles /'sʌbtaɪtlz; 'sʌbˌtaɪtl̩z/ *noun* 名词 (plural 复数)

words at the bottom of a film that help you to understand it（影片的）字幕: *It was a French film with English subtitles.* 那部影片是法语的，有英语字幕。

subtract /səb'trækt; səb'trækt/ *verb* 动词 (**subtracts, subtracting, subtracted**)

take a number away from another number 从某数中减去另一数；减: *If you subtract 6 from 9, you get 3.* ✳ 9减6等于3。✪ opposite 反义词: **add**

subtraction /səb'trækʃn; səb'trækʃən/ *noun* 名词 (no plural 无复数)

taking a number away from another number 减法；减 ☞ Look at **addition**. 见 **addition**。

suburb /'sʌbɜ:b; 'sʌbɝb/ *noun* 名词

one of the parts of a town or city outside the centre 郊区；城郊: *Wimbledon is a suburb of London.* 温布尔登是伦敦的郊区。◇ *We live in the suburbs.* 我们住在市郊。

subway /'sʌbweɪ; 'sʌbˌwe/ *noun* 名词 (*plural* 复数作 **subways**)

1 a path that goes under a busy road, so that people can cross safely（在繁忙道路下的）人行通道；地下人行道

2 *American English for* **underground**[2] 美式英语，即 **underground**[2]

succeed /sək'si:d; sək'sid/ *verb* 动词 (**succeeds, succeeding, succeeded**)

do or get what you wanted to do or get 达到目的；做成: *She finally succeeded in getting a job.* 她终于找到了一份工作。◇ *I tried to get a ticket for the concert but I didn't succeed.* 我费尽力气想弄张音乐会的票，却也没弄到手。☞ Look at **fail**. 见 **fail**。

success /sək'ses; sək'sɛs/ *noun* 名词

1 (no plural 无复数) doing or getting what you wanted; doing well 达到目的；成功: *I wish you success with your studies.* 祝你学业有成。

2 (*plural* 复数作 **successes**) somebody or something that does well or that people like a lot 成功的或大家喜爱的人或事物: *The film 'Ghost' was a great success.*《鬼魂》这部影片有口皆碑。✪ opposite 反义词: **failure**

successful /sək'sesfl; sək'sɛsfəl/ *adjective* 形容词
a successful actor 杰出的演员 ◇ *The party was very successful.* 这个聚会办得非常圆满。✪ opposite 反义词: **unsuccessful**
successfully /sək'sesfəli; sək'sɛsfəlɪ/ *adverb* 副词
He completed his studies successfully. 他顺利完成了学业。

such /sʌtʃ; sʌtʃ/ *adjective* 形容词
1 a word that you use when you say how much, how big, etc something is（用以表示程度、大小等）这样的，那样的，如此的: *It was such a nice day that we decided to go to the beach.* 天气好极了，所以我们决定到海滩去玩儿了。☞ Look at **so**.见 **so**。
2 a word that makes another word stronger（用以加强另一字的语气）这么，那么，如此: *He wears such strange clothes.* 他穿的衣服那么怪模怪样的。
3 like this or that 像这样的；像那样的: *'Can I speak to Mrs Graham?' 'I'm sorry. There's no such person here.'* "我想跟格雷厄姆夫人说句话行吗？""很抱歉。这里没有这么个人。"
such as like something; for example 像某事物；例如: *Sweet foods such as chocolate can make you fat.* 像巧克力之类的甜的食物能使人发胖。

suck /sʌk; sʌk/ *verb* 动词 (**sucks**, **sucking**, **sucked** /sʌkt; sʌkt/)
1 pull something into your mouth, using your lips（把嘴唇聚拢在某物上）吸；嘬: *The baby sucked milk from its bottle.* 幼儿嘬着瓶子里的奶。
2 hold something in your mouth and touch it a lot with your tongue 把某物含在嘴里: *She was sucking a sweet.* 她含着一块糖。

sudden /'sʌdn; 'sʌdn̩/ *adjective* 形容词
If something is sudden, it happens quickly when you do not expect it 突然的；意外的: *His death was very sudden.* 他死得很突然。
all of a sudden suddenly 突然: *We were watching TV when all of a sudden the door opened.* 我们看着看着电视，门突然开了。
suddenly *adverb* 副词
He left very suddenly. 他突然走了。◇ *Suddenly there was a loud noise.* 突然有个很大的声音。

suffer /'sʌfə(r); 'sʌfɚ/ *verb* 动词 (**suffers**, **suffering**, **suffered** /'sʌfəd; 'sʌfɚd/)
feel pain, sadness or something else that is not pleasant 感到痛苦、悲伤或遭遇其他不愉快的事: *I'm suffering from toothache.* 我牙疼。

sufficient /sə'fɪʃnt; sə'fɪʃənt/ *adjective* 形容词
as much or as many as you need or want; enough 充足的；足够的: *There was sufficient food to last two weeks.* 食物足够两个星期的。✪ **Enough** is the word that we usually use. ✳ **enough** 是常用词。
✪ opposite 反义词: **insufficient**

suffix /'sʌfɪks; 'sʌfiks/ *noun* 名词 (*plural* 复数作 **suffixes**)
letters that you add to the end of a word to make another word 后缀（加在一个词后面的几个字母，用以构成另一个词）: *If you add the suffix '-ly' to the adjective 'quick', you make the adverb 'quickly'.* 把 -ly 这个后缀加在 quick 这个形容词的后面，就构成了副词 quickly。☞ Look at **prefix**. 见 **prefix**。

suffocate /'sʌfəkeɪt; 'sʌfəˌket/ *verb* 动词 (**suffocates**, **suffocating**, **suffocated**)
die or make somebody die because there is no air to breathe（使某人）窒息而死

sugar /'ʃʊgə(r); 'ʃʊgɚ/ *noun* 名词
1 (no plural 无复数) sweet stuff that comes from some sorts of plant 食糖: *Do you take sugar in your coffee?* 您的咖啡里要糖吗？
2 (*plural* 复数作 **sugars**) a spoonful of sugar 一勺糖: *Two sugars, please.* 请给我来两勺糖。

suggest /sə'dʒest; səg'dʒɛst/ *verb* 动词 (**suggests**, **suggesting**, **suggested**)
say what you think somebody should do or what should happen 建议；提议: *I suggest that you stay here tonight.* 我建议您在这里过夜吧。◇ *Simon suggested going for a walk.* 西蒙提议去散散步。◇ *What do you suggest?* 您有什么建议？
suggestion /sə'dʒestʃən; səg'dʒɛstʃən/ *noun* 名词
I don't know what to buy for her birthday. Have you got any suggestions? 我不知道给她买什么生日礼物好。您有什么建议吗？◇ *I would like to make a suggestion.* 我想提个建议。

S

suicide /ˈsu:ɪsaɪd; ˈsuəˌsaɪd/ *noun* 名词
killing yourself 自杀
commit suicide kill yourself 自杀

suit[1] /su:t; sut/ *noun* 名词
a jacket and trousers, or a jacket and skirt, that you wear together and that are made from the same material（同一料子的）一套衣服（短上衣和裤子或短上衣和裙子）

suit[2] /su:t; sut/ *verb* 动词 (**suits**, **suiting**, **suited**)
1 If something suits you, it looks good on you（指衣物等）在某人身上好看: *Does this hat suit me?* 这顶帽子我戴好看吗？
2 be right for you; be what you want or need 对某人适合；合某人的意: *Would it suit you if I came at five o'clock?* 我要是五点钟来对您方便吗？

suitable /ˈsu:təbl; ˈsutəbl̩/ *adjective* 形容词
right for somebody or something 适合某人或某事物: *This film isn't suitable for children.* 这部影片不适宜让儿童观看。✪ opposite 反义词: **unsuitable**
suitably /ˈsu:təbli; ˈsutəblɪ/ *adverb* 副词
Tony wasn't suitably dressed for a party. 托尼参加聚会穿得不得体。

suitcase /ˈsu:tkeɪs; ˈsutˌkes/ *noun* 名词
a large bag with flat sides that you carry your clothes in when you travel 手提衣箱；小提箱

suitcase 小提箱

sulk /sʌlk; sʌlk/ *verb* 动词 (**sulks**, **sulking**, **sulked** /sʌlkt; sʌlkt/)
not speak because you are angry about something（因对某事生气）不说话: *She's been sulking in her room all day because her mum wouldn't let her go to the party.* 她在自己的房间里生了一天闷气，嗔怪她妈妈不让她去参加聚会。

sum /sʌm; sʌm/ *noun* 名词
1 a simple piece of work with numbers, for example adding or dividing 算术（例如加法或除法）: *Children learn how to do sums.* 儿童学习做算术。
2 an amount of money 金额；款项: *£200 000 is a large sum of money.* 200 000英镑是一大笔钱。
3 the answer that you have when you add numbers together 总数；总和: *The sum of two and five is seven.* 二加五等于七。

summary /ˈsʌməri; ˈsʌmərɪ/ *noun* 名词 (*plural* 复数作 **summaries**)
a short way of telling something by giving only the most important facts 总结；摘要；概要: *Here is a summary of the news ...* 以下是新闻摘要…

summer /ˈsʌmə(r); ˈsʌmɚ/ *noun* 名词
the warmest time of the year 夏季；夏天: *I am going to Spain in the summer.* 我打算夏天去西班牙。◇ *the summer holidays* 暑假

summit /ˈsʌmɪt; ˈsʌmɪt/ *noun* 名词
the top of a mountain 山顶

sun /sʌn; sʌn/ *noun* 名词 (no plural 无复数)
1 the sun the big round thing in the sky that gives us light in the day, and heat 太阳: *The sun is shining.* 太阳放射着光芒。
2 light and heat from the sun 太阳的光和热: *We sat in the sun all morning.* 我们一上午都坐着晒太阳。

sunbathe /ˈsʌnbeɪð; ˈsʌnˌbeð/ *verb* 动词 (**sunbathes**, **sunbathing**, **sunbathed** /ˈsʌnbeɪðd; ˈsʌnˌbeðd/)
lie in the sun so that your skin becomes darker 沐日光浴: *We sunbathed on the beach.* 我们在海滩上做日光浴。

sunburn /ˈsʌnbɜ:n; ˈsʌnˌbɝn/ *noun* 名词 (no plural 无复数)
red painful skin that you get when you have been in the hot sun for too long 晒伤的皮肤
sunburned /ˈsʌnbɜ:nd; ˈsʌnˌbɝnd/, **sunburnt** /ˈsʌnbɜ:nt; ˈsʌnˌbɝnt/ *adjective* 形容词
sunburned shoulders 晒伤的肩膀

Sunday /ˈsʌndeɪ; ˈsʌndɪ/ *noun* 名词
the first day of the week; the day before Monday 星期日

sung *form of* **sing** ✻ **sing** 的不同形式

sun-glasses /ˈsʌnglɑ:sɪz; ˈsʌnˌglæsɪz/ *noun* 名词 (plural 复数)
glasses with dark glass in them that you wear in strong light 太阳眼镜；墨镜：*a pair of sun-glasses* 一副墨镜

sunk *form of* **sink²** ✻ **sink²** 的不同形式

sunlight /ˈsʌnlaɪt; ˈsʌnˌlaɪt/ *noun* 名词 (no plural 无复数)
the light from the sun 日光；阳光

sunny /ˈsʌni; ˈsʌnɪ/ *adjective* 形容词 (**sunnier**, **sunniest**)
bright with light from the sun 阳光充足的：*a sunny day* 晴朗的一天

sunrise /ˈsʌnraɪz; ˈsʌnˌraɪz/ *noun* 名词 (no plural 无复数)
the time in the morning when the sun comes up 日出（时分）；黎明

sunset /ˈsʌnset; ˈsʌnˌsɛt/ *noun* 名词
the time in the evening when the sun goes down 日落（时分）；傍晚：*The park closes at sunset.* 公园傍晚时关闭。

sunshine /ˈsʌnʃaɪn; ˈsʌnˌʃaɪn/ *noun* 名词 (no plural 无复数)
the light and heat from the sun 太阳的光和热：*We sat outside in the sunshine.* 我们坐在外面晒太阳。

suntan /ˈsʌntæn; ˈsʌnˌtæn/ *noun* 名词
When you have a suntan, your skin is brown because you have been in the hot sun（皮肤的）晒黑：*I'm trying to get a suntan.* 我正想把皮肤晒黑呢。

suntanned /ˈsʌntænd; ˈsʌnˌtænd/ *adjective* 形容词
suntanned arms 晒黑的手臂

super /ˈsu:pə(r); ˈsupɚ/ *adjective* 形容词
very good; wonderful 极好的；美妙的：*That was a super meal.* 那顿饭好极了。◇ *His new car is super.* 他的新汽车真棒。

superb /su:ˈpɜ:b; sʊˈpɝb/ *adjective* 形容词
very good or beautiful 极好的；非常漂亮的：*a superb holiday* 非常好的假期 ◇ *The view from the window is superb.* 从窗户望出去，景色十分秀丽。

superior /su:ˈpɪəriə(r); səˈpɪrɪɚ/ *adjective* 形容词
better or more important than another person or thing（比别人或别的事物）更好的或更重要的；优越的：*I think fresh coffee is superior to instant coffee.* 我认为新煮的咖啡比速溶咖啡好喝。✪ opposite 反义词：**inferior**

superlative /su:ˈpɜ:lətɪv; sʊˈpɝlətɪv/ *noun* 名词
the form of an adjective or adverb that shows the most of something（形容词或副词的）最高级形式：*'Most intelligent', 'best' and 'fastest' are all superlatives.* ✻ most intelligent、best、fastest 都是最高级形式。

superlative *adjective* 形容词
'Youngest' is the superlative form of 'young'. ✻ youngest 是 young 的最高级形式。

supermarket /ˈsu:pəmɑ:kɪt; ˈsupɚˌmɑrkɪt/ *noun* 名词
a big shop where you can buy food and other things. You choose what you want and then pay for everything when you leave. 超级市场

> ✪ In a supermarket you put the things you want to buy in a **basket** or a **trolley** and pay for them at the **checkout**. 在超级市场里的购物方式是把要买的东西放进篮子（**basket**）里或手推车（**trolley**）里，然后到出口的付款处（**checkout**）付款。

supersonic /ˌsu:pəˈsɒnɪk; ˌsupɚˈsɑnɪk/ *adjective* 形容词
faster than the speed of sound 超音速的；超声速的：*Concorde is a supersonic aeroplane.* 协和式飞机是超音速的飞机。

superstition /ˌsu:pəˈstɪʃn; ˌsupɚˈstɪʃən/ *noun* 名词
a belief in good and bad luck and other things that cannot be explained 迷信；迷信的思想：*People say that walking under a ladder brings bad luck, but it's just a superstition.* 人们都说在梯子下面走不吉利，这只不过是迷信的说法罢了。

superstitious /ˌsu:pəˈstɪʃəs; ˌsupɚˈstɪʃəs/ *adjective* 形容词
If you are superstitious, you believe in good and bad luck and other things that cannot be explained. 迷信的；有迷信思想的

superstore /ˈsu:pəstɔ:(r); ˈsupɚˌstɔr/ *noun* 名词
a very big shop 超级商场：*There's a new*

superstore on the edge of town. 小镇边上有个新开的超级商场。

supervise /ˈsuːpəvaɪz; ˌsupɚˈvaɪz/ *verb* 动词 (**supervises**, **supervising**, **supervised** /ˈsuːpəvaɪzd; ˌsupɚˈvaɪzd/)
watch to see that people are working correctly 监督: *I supervised the builders.* 我监督建筑工人工作。

supervision /ˌsuːpəˈvɪʒn; ˌsupɚˈvɪʒən/ *noun* 名词 (no plural 无复数)
supervising or being supervised 监督: *Children must not play here without supervision.* 儿童无人照看不得在此玩耍。

supervisor /ˈsuːpəvaɪzə(r); ˌsupɚˈvaɪzɚ/ *noun* 名词
a person who supervises 监督者

supper /ˈsʌpə(r); ˈsʌpɚ/ *noun* 名词
the last meal of the day 晚饭；晚餐: *We had supper and then went to bed.* 我们吃完晚饭就睡觉了。

supply /səˈplaɪ; səˈplaɪ/ *verb* 动词 (**supplies**, **supplying**, **supplied** /səˈplaɪd; səˈplaɪd/, **has supplied**)
give or sell something that somebody needs 供给；供应: *The school supplies us with books.* 学校供应我们书本。◇ *The lake supplies water to thousands of homes.* 这个湖向千家万户供水。

supply *noun* 名词 (*plural* 复数作 **supplies**)
an amount of something that you need 供给；供应: *supplies of food* 食物供应

support /səˈpɔːt; səˈpɔrt/ *verb* 动词 (**supports**, **supporting**, **supported**)
1 hold somebody or something up, so that they do not fall 承受某人或某物的重量（不使落下）: *The bridge isn't strong enough to support heavy lorries.* 这座桥不结实，禁不住重型卡车。
2 help somebody to live by giving things like money, a home or food 供养或赡养某人: *She has three children to support.* 她得养活三个孩子。
3 say that you think that somebody or something is right or the best 支持或拥护某人或某事物: *Everybody else said I was wrong but Paul supported me.* 谁都说我错了，只有保罗支持我。◇ *Which football team do you support?* 你是哪个足球队的球迷？

support *noun* 名词
1 (no plural 无复数) help 帮助；支持；拥护: *Thank you for all your support.* 感谢您多方协助。
2 (*plural* 复数作 **supports**) something that holds up another thing 支撑物: *a roof support* 房顶的支架

supporter /səˈpɔːtə(r); səˈpɔrtɚ/ *noun* 名词
a person who helps somebody or something by giving money, or by showing interest, for example 支持者；拥护者；供养者: *football supporters* 足球队的球迷

suppose /səˈpəʊz; səˈpoz/ *verb* 动词 (**supposes**, **supposing**, **supposed** /səˈpəʊzd; səˈpozd/)
1 think that something is true or will happen but not be sure 猜想；料想；假定: *'Where's Jenny?' 'I don't know — I suppose she's still at work.'* "珍妮在哪儿呢？""我不知道——我猜想她还在工作呢吧。"
2 a word that you use when you agree with something but are not happy about it 表示同意但并不乐意的词: *'Can I borrow your pen?' 'Yes, I suppose so — but don't lose it.'* "把你的钢笔借给我用用行吗？""行是行——可别弄丢了啊。"

supposed /səˈpəʊzd; səˈpozd/ *adjective* 形容词
be supposed to **1** If you are supposed to do something, you should do it 应该: *They were supposed to meet us here.* 他们应该在这里跟我们见面。◇ *You're not supposed to smoke in this room.* 不应该在这间屋子里吸烟。 **2** If something is supposed to be true, people say it is true 据说: *This is supposed to be a good restaurant.* 大家都说这家饭馆不错。

supposing /səˈpəʊzɪŋ; səˈpozɪŋ/ *conjunction* 连词
if 假设；假如: *Supposing we miss the bus, how will we get to the airport?* 万一我们赶不上公共汽车，怎么到飞机场呢？

supreme /suːˈpriːm; suˈprim/ *adjective* 形容词
highest or most important 至高无上的；最重要的: *the Supreme Court* 最高法院

sure /ʃɔː(r); ʃʊr/ *adjective* 形容词 (**surer**, **surest**) *adverb* 副词
If you are sure, you know that something is true or right 肯定；确信: *I'm sure I've seen that man before.* 我肯定以前见过那个男子。◇ *If you're not sure how to do it, ask your teacher.* 要是没有把握就问问老师吧。

be sure to If you are sure to do something, you will certainly do it 一定做某事: *If you work hard, you're sure to pass the exam.* 你只要努力就一定能及格。

for sure without any doubt 无疑: *I think he's coming to the party but I don't know for sure.* 我认为他会来参加聚会的，可是我没有十足的把握。

make sure check something so that you are certain about it 核实或查明某事物；务必: *I think the party starts at eight, but I'll phone to make sure.* 我想聚会是在八点钟开始，但是我得打个电话再问问。◇ *Make sure you don't leave your bag on the bus.* 千万别把提包落在公共汽车上。

sure enough as I thought 正如所想的那样；果然: *I said they would be late, and sure enough they were.* 我早就说过他们得迟到，果不其然。迟到了吧。

surely /ˈʃɔːli; ˈʃʊrlɪ/ *adverb* 副词

a word that you use when you think that something must be true, or when you are surprised 用以表示某事物一定属实或表示惊奇的词: *Surely you know where your brother works!* 你一定知道你弟弟在哪儿工作吧！

S

surf /sɜːf; sɝf/ *noun* 名词 (no plural 无复数)

the white part on the top of waves in the sea（海浪顶端的）白色浪花

surfing *noun* 名词 (no plural 无复数)

the sport of riding over waves on a long piece of wood or plastic (called a **surfboard**) 冲浪运动；冲浪（冲浪板叫做 **surfboard**）✪ You can say **go surfing** 做冲浪运动叫做 **go surfing**: *We went surfing.* 我们去做冲浪运动了。

surfer *noun* 名词

a person who surfs 做冲浪运动的人

surface /ˈsɜːfɪs; ˈsɝfɪs/ *noun* 名词

1 the outside part of something（物体的）表面: *A tomato has a shiny red surface.* 西红柿表面呈红色，有光泽。

2 the top of water 水面: *She dived below the surface.* 她潜入水中。

surgeon /ˈsɜːdʒən; ˈsɝdʒən/ *noun* 名词

a doctor who does **operations**. A surgeon cuts your body to take out or mend a part inside 外科医师（手术叫做 **operation**）: *a brain surgeon* 脑部外科医师

surgery /ˈsɜːdʒəri; ˈsɝdʒərɪ/ *noun* 名词

1 (no plural 无复数) cutting somebody's body to take out or mend a part inside 外科；手术: *He needed surgery after the accident.* 他出事以后需做手术。

2 (*plural* 复数作 **surgeries**) a place where you go to see a doctor or dentist 门诊处；诊所

surname /ˈsɜːneɪm; ˈsɝˌnem/ *noun* 名词

the name that a family has. Your surname is usually your last name 姓；姓氏（通常名在前，姓在后）: *Her name is Anna Jones. Jones is her surname.* 她叫安娜·琼斯。琼斯是她的姓。☞ Note at **name** 见 **name** 词条注释

surprise[1] /səˈpraɪz; sɚˈpraɪz/ *noun* 名词

1 (no plural 无复数) the feeling that you have when something happens suddenly that you did not expect 惊奇；惊讶: *She looked at me in surprise when I told her the news.* 我把消息告诉她以后，她很吃惊地看着我。

2 (*plural* 复数作 **surprises**) something that happens when you do not expect it 使人吃惊的事物: *Don't tell him about the birthday party—it's a surprise!* 别告诉他生日聚会的事——让他意想不到！

take somebody by surprise happen when somebody does not expect it 使某人吃一惊: *Your phone call took me by surprise—I thought you were on holiday.* 你打来电话我吃了一惊——我还以为你正在度假呢。

to my surprise I was surprised that 使我吃惊的是: *I thought she would be angry but, to my surprise, she smiled.* 我以为她一定生气了，可是使我吃惊的是她面露笑容。

surprise[2] /səˈpraɪz; sɚˈpraɪz/ *verb* 动词 (**surprises**, **surprising**, **surprised** /səˈpraɪzd; sɚˈpraɪzd/)

do something that somebody does not expect 使某人吃惊: *I arrived early to surprise her.* 我到得很早让她吃一惊。

surprised *adjective* 形容词

If you are surprised, you feel or show surprise（指人的感觉或表现）吃惊的；惊奇的: *I was surprised to see Tim yesterday—I thought he was in Canada.* 我昨天看见蒂姆了，真没想到——我还以为他在加拿大呢。

surprising *adjective* 形容词

If something is surprising, it makes you feel surprise 使人吃惊的；令人惊奇的: *The news was surprising.* 这个消息真是意想不到。

surprisingly *adverb* 副词

The exam was surprisingly easy. 这次考试容易得出奇。

surrender /sə'rendə(r); sə'rɛndɚ/ *verb* 动词 (**surrenders, surrendering, surrendered** /sə'rendəd; sə'rɛndɚd/)

stop fighting because you cannot win 投降: *After six hours on the roof, the man surrendered to the police.* 那个男子在房顶上坚持了六个小时以后，终于向警方投降了。

surround /sə'raʊnd; sə'raund/ *verb* 动词 (**surrounds, surrounding, surrounded**)

be or go all around something 包围或围绕某物: *The lake is surrounded by trees.* 这个湖有绿树环抱。

surroundings /sə'raʊndɪŋz; sə-'raundɪŋz/ *noun* 名词 (plural 复数)

everything around you, or the place where you live（人的或居住处的）周围的一切事物；环境: *The farm is in beautiful surroundings.* 农场四周风景优美。◇ *I don't like seeing animals in a zoo—I prefer to see them in their natural surroundings.* 我不喜欢看动物园里的动物——我喜欢看在自然环境中的动物。

survey /'sɜːveɪ; 'sɝve/ *noun* 名词 (*plural* 复数作 **surveys**)

asking questions about what people think or do, or what is happening 调查或询问大家的想法或做法或发生的事情: *We did a survey of people's favourite TV programmes.* 我们对群众喜闻乐见的电视节目做了调查。

survive /sə'vaɪv; sɚ'vaɪv/ *verb* 动词 (**survives, surviving, survived** /sə-'vaɪvd; sɚ'vaɪvd/)

continue to live after a difficult or dangerous time 遭遇困难或危险后仍生存；幸存: *Camels can survive for many days without water.* 骆驼很多天不喝水也能活。◇ *Only one person survived the plane crash.* 飞机失事后仅一人幸存。

survival /sə'vaɪvl; sɚ'vaɪvḷ/ *noun* 名词 (no plural 无复数)

surviving 遭遇困难或危险后仍生存；幸存: *Food and water are necessary for survival.* 要维持生命，食物和水是必不可少的。

survivor /sə'vaɪvə(r); sɚ'vaɪvɚ/ *noun* 名词

a person who survives 遭遇困难或危险后仍生存的人；幸存者: *The government sent help to the survivors of the earthquake.* 政府救济在地震中的幸存者。

suspect /sə'spekt; sə'spɛkt/ *verb* 动词 (**suspects, suspecting, suspected**)

1 think that something is true, but not be certain 认为某事物属实（但无把握）；猜想；料想: *John wasn't at college today—I suspect that he's ill.* 约翰今天没上课——我看他是病了。

2 think that somebody has done something wrong but not be certain 认为某人做错了事（但无把握）；怀疑: *They suspect Helen of stealing the money.* 他们怀疑那笔钱是海伦偷的。

suspect /'sʌspekt; 'sʌspɛkt/ *noun* 名词

a person who you think has done something wrong 可疑对象；嫌疑犯: *The police have arrested two suspects.* 警方逮捕了两个疑犯。

suspicion /sə'spɪʃn; sə'spɪʃən/ *noun* 名词

1 an idea that is not totally certain 不完全肯定的想法；疑心: *We have a suspicion that he is unhappy.* 我们猜想他并不愉快。

2 a feeling that somebody has done something wrong 觉得某人做错了事；怀疑: *When she saw the £100 note in his wallet she was filled with suspicion.* 她看见那100英镑在他的钱夹里，顿时产生怀疑。

suspicious /sə'spɪʃəs; sə'spɪʃəs/ *adjective* 形容词

1 If you are suspicious, you do not believe somebody or something, or you feel that something is wrong（对某人或某事物）有怀疑的；感到不对的: *The police are suspicious of her story.* 警方怀疑她说的话。

2 A person or thing that is suspicious makes you feel that something is wrong

S

(指某人或某事物）使人怀疑的；使人感到不对的: *There was a man waiting outside the school. He looked very suspicious.* 有个男子在学校外面等候。那个人形迹可疑。

suspiciously *adverb* 副词
'What are you doing here?' the woman asked suspiciously. "你在这里干什么？"那个女子怀疑地问。

swallow[1] /'swɒləʊ; 'swɑlo/ *verb* 动词 (**swallows**, **swallowing**, **swallowed** /'swɒləʊd; 'swɑlod/)
make food or drink move down your throat from your mouth 吞下或咽下食物或饮料: *I can't swallow these tablets without water.* 没有水我咽不下这些药片。

swallow[2] /'swɒləʊ; 'swɑlo/ *noun* 名词
a small bird 燕子

swam *form of* **swim** ✳ **swim** 的不同形式

swamp /swɒmp; swɑmp/ *noun* 名词
soft wet ground 湿而软的土地；沼泽

S

swan /swɒn; swɑn/ *noun* 名词
a big white bird with a very long neck. Swans live on rivers and lakes. 天鹅

swan 天鹅

swap /swɒp; swɑp/ *verb* 动词 (**swaps**, **swapping**, **swapped** /swɒpt; swɑpt/)
change one thing for another thing; give one thing and get another thing for it 以某物交换他物: *Do you want to swap chairs with me?* (= you have my chair and I'll have yours) 你愿意跟我交换椅子吗？（= 你坐我的，我坐你的）◇ *I swapped my T-shirt for Tom's cassette.* 我用我的短袖汗衫换了汤姆的盒式带。

swarm /swɔ:m; swɔrm/ *noun* 名词
a big group of flying insects（指飞虫）一大群: *a swarm of bees* 一群蜜蜂

swarm *verb* 动词 (**swarms, swarming, swarmed** /swɔ:md; swɔrmd/)
fly or move quickly in a big group 成群地飞行；大批地移动: *The fans swarmed into the stadium.* 球迷一窝蜂地涌进了体育场。

sway /sweɪ; swe/ *verb* 动词 (**sways, swaying, swayed** /sweɪd; swed/)
move slowly from side to side 摇晃；摇摆: *The trees were swaying in the wind.* 那些树随风摇曳。

swear /sweə(r); swɛr/ *verb* 动词 (**swears**, **swearing**, **swore** /swɔ:(r); swɔr/, **has sworn** /swɔ:n; swɔrn/)
1 say bad words 咒骂；诅咒: *Don't swear at your mother!* 不准骂你母亲！
2 make a serious promise 发誓；宣誓: *He swears that he is telling the truth.* 他发誓他说的都是实话。

swear-word /'sweə wɜ:d; 'swɛrˌwɝd/ *noun* 名词
a bad word 骂人的话

sweat /swet; swɛt/ *noun* 名词 (no plural 无复数)
water that comes out of your skin when you are hot or afraid 汗

sweat *verb* 动词 (**sweats**, **sweating**, **sweated**)
have sweat coming out of your skin 出汗；流汗: *The room was so hot that everyone was sweating.* 屋里很热，大家都出汗了。

sweaty *adjective* 形容词 (**sweatier**, **sweatiest**)
covered with sweat 有汗的: *sweaty socks* 有汗的袜子

sweater /'swetə(r); 'swɛtɚ/ *noun* 名词
a warm piece of clothing with sleeves, that you wear on the top part of your body. Sweaters are often made of wool. 绒衣；（尤指）套头毛衣

sweatshirt /'swetʃɜ:t; 'swɛtˌʃɝt/ *noun* 名词
a piece of clothing like a sweater, made of thick cotton 棉毛衫

sweep /swi:p; swip/ *verb* 动词 (**sweeps**, **sweeping**, **swept** /swept; swɛpt/, **has swept**)
1 clean something by moving dirt or other things away with a brush 扫: *I swept the floor.* 我扫了扫地。
2 push something along or away quickly and strongly 用迅速而强劲的推动力把某物移走: *The bridge was swept away by the floods.* 洪水把桥冲走了。

sweep up move something away with a brush 扫走某物: *I swept up the broken glass.* 我把碎玻璃扫走了。

sweet[1] /swi:t; swit/ *adjective* 形容词 (**sweeter, sweetest**)
1 with the taste of sugar 甜的: *Honey is sweet.* 蜂蜜是甜的。
2 pretty 漂亮的；可爱的: *What a sweet little girl!* 多漂亮的小姑娘啊！
3 kind and gentle 和蔼的；温柔的: *It was sweet of you to help me.* 谢谢你热心帮助我。

4 with a good smell 芳香的；芬芳的: *the sweet smell of roses* 玫瑰花的香味

sweetly *adverb* 副词

in a pretty, kind or nice way 漂亮地；和蔼地；可爱地: *She smiled sweetly.* 她笑得很甜。

sweet² /swi:t; swit/ *noun* 名词

1 a small piece of sweet food. Chocolates and toffees are sweets 糖果（巧克力和太妃糖都是糖果）: *He bought a packet of sweets for the children.* 他给孩子买了一包糖果。

2 sweet food that you eat at the end of a meal（一顿饭最后的）甜食: *Do you want any sweet?* 您要饭后甜食吗？

swell /swel; swɛl/ *verb* 动词 (**swells**, **swelling**, **swelled** /sweld; swɛld/, **has swollen** /'swəʊlən; 'swolən/ or 或 **has swelled**)

swell up become bigger or thicker than it usually is 膨胀；肿胀: *After he hurt his ankle it began to swell up.* 他把脚腕儿弄伤以后已经肿起来了。

swelling /'swelɪŋ; 'swɛlɪŋ/ *noun* 名词

a place on the body that is bigger or fatter than it usually is（身上的）肿块: *She has got a swelling on her head where she fell and hit it.* 她跌倒了，头磕了个包。

swept *form of* **sweep** ＊ **sweep** 的不同形式

swerve /swɜ:v; swɝv/ *verb* 动词 (**swerves**, **swerving**, **swerved** /swɜ:vd; swɝvd/)

turn suddenly so that you do not hit something 突然转向（以免碰撞）: *The driver swerved when she saw the child in the road.* 她开着车看见路上有个孩子，立即扭转方向避开了。

swift /swɪft; swɪft/ *adjective* 形容词 (**swifter**, **swiftest**)

quick or fast 快的；迅速的: *We made a swift decision.* 我们迅速做出了决定。

swiftly *adverb* 副词

She ran swiftly up the stairs. 她很快地跑上了楼梯。

swim /swɪm; swɪm/ *verb* 动词 (**swims**, **swimming**, **swam** /swæm; swæm/, **has swum** /swʌm; swʌm/)

move your body through water 游泳: *Can you swim?* 你会游泳吗？◇ *I swam across the lake.* 我游到了湖的对岸。✪ When you talk about spending time swimming as a sport, you usually say **go swimming** 游泳运动的说法是 **go swimming**: *I go swimming every day.* 我每天都游泳。

swim *noun* 名词 (no plural 无复数)

Let's go for a swim. 咱们游泳去吧。

swimmer *noun* 名词

a person who swims 游泳的人: *He's a good swimmer.* 他是个游泳健将。

swimming *noun* 名词 (no plural 无复数)

Swimming is my favourite sport. 我最喜爱的运动是游泳。

swimming-costume /'swɪmɪŋ kɒstju:m; 'swɪmɪŋ,kɑstjum/, **swimsuit** /'swɪmsu:t; 'swɪm,sut/ *noun* 名词

a piece of clothing that a woman or girl wears for swimming（女用）游泳衣；泳装

swimming-pool /'swɪmɪŋ pu:l; 'swɪmɪŋ,pul/ *noun* 名词

a special place where you can swim 游泳池

swimming-trunks /'swɪmɪŋ trʌŋks; 'swɪmɪŋ,trʌŋks/ *noun* 名词 (plural 复数)

short trousers that a man or boy wears for swimming（男用）游泳裤

S

swing¹ /swɪŋ; swɪŋ/ *verb* 动词 (**swings**, **swinging**, **swung** /swʌŋ; swʌŋ/, **has swung**)

1 hang from something and move backwards and forwards or from side to side through the air（指吊着）摆动，摇摆: *The monkey was swinging from a tree.* 猴子钩着树荡来荡去。

2 make somebody or something move in this way 使某人或某物摆动；摇摆: *He swung his arms as he walked.* 他走路时摆动着手臂。

3 move in a curve 沿弧线运动: *The door swung open.* 门开了。

swing 秋千

swing² /swɪŋ; swɪŋ/ *noun* 名词

a seat that hangs down. Children sit on it to move backwards and forwards through the air. 秋千

switch[1] /swɪtʃ; swɪtʃ/ *noun* 名词 (*plural* 复数作 **switches**)
a small thing that you press to stop or start electricity (电路的) 开关；电门: *Where is the light switch?* 电灯的开关在哪里？

switch 电门

switch[2] /swɪtʃ; swɪtʃ/ *verb* 动词 (**switches, switching, switched** /swɪtʃt; swɪtʃt/)
change to something different 转变或转换到另一事物: *I switched to another seat because I couldn't see the film.* 我看不见演的电影，所以换了个座位。
switch off press something to stop electricity 按某物以切断电流: *I switched the TV off.* 我把电视关了。◇ *Don't forget to switch off the lights!* 别忘记关灯！
switch on press something to start electricity 按某物以接通电流: *Switch the radio on.* 把收音机开开吧。

switchboard /ˈswɪtʃbɔ:d; ˈswɪtʃˌbɔrd/ *noun* 名词
the place in a large office where somebody answers telephone calls and sends them to the right people (电话的) 交换台

swollen *form of* **swell** ✳ **swell** 的不同形式
swollen /ˈswəʊlən; ˈswolən/ *adjective* 形容词
thicker or fatter than it usually is 膨胀的；肿胀的: *a swollen ankle* 肿胀的脚腕儿

swoop /swu:p; swup/ *verb* 动词 (**swoops, swooping, swooped** /swu:pt; swupt/)
fly down quickly 迅速向下飞: *The bird swooped down to catch a fish.* 那只鸟俯冲下来逮鱼。

swop /swɒp; swɑp/ = **swap**

sword /sɔ:d; sɔrd/ *noun* 名词
a long sharp knife for fighting (用作武器的) 刀；剑

swore, sworn *forms of* **swear** ✳ **swear** 的不同形式

swot /swɒt; swɑt/ *verb* 动词 (**swots, swotting, swotted**)
study hard before an exam (考试前) 刻苦学习: *Debbie is swotting for her test next week.* 戴比正在努力念书准备下星期的测验。

swum *form of* **swim** ✳ **swim** 的不同形式

swung *form of* **swing[1]** ✳ **swing[1]** 的不同形式

syllable /ˈsɪləbl; ˈsɪləbḷ/ *noun* 名词
a part of a word that has one **vowel** sound when you say it. 'Swim' has one syllable and 'system' has two syllables. 音节（一个字中有一个元音的部分。元音叫做 **vowel**。swim 这个字有一个音节，system 这个字有两个音节。）

syllabus /ˈsɪləbəs; ˈsɪləbəs/ *noun* 名词 (*plural* 复数作 **syllabuses**)
a list of all the things that you must study on a course 教学大纲

symbol /ˈsɪmbl; ˈsɪmbḷ/ *noun* 名词
a mark, sign or picture that shows something 符号；记号；标志；象征: *+ and – are symbols for plus and minus in mathematics.* + 和 – 是数学中的加号和减号。◇ *A dove is the symbol of peace.* 鸽子是和平的象征。

sympathetic /ˌsɪmpəˈθetɪk; ˌsɪmpəˈθɛtɪk/ *adjective* 形容词
If you are sympathetic, you show that you understand other people's feelings when they have problems (别人有困难时) 同情的；体恤的: *Everyone was very sympathetic when I was ill.* 我生病的时候大家都很关心我。✪ opposite 反义词: **unsympathetic**
sympathetically /ˌsɪmpəˈθetɪkli; ˌsɪmpəˈθɛtɪklɪ/ *adverb* 副词
He smiled sympathetically. 他露出同情的微笑。

sympathize /ˈsɪmpəθaɪz; ˈsɪmpəˌθaɪz/ *verb* 动词 (**sympathizes, sympathizing, sympathized** /ˈsɪmpəθaɪzd; ˈsɪmpəˌθaɪzd/)
sympathize with somebody show that you understand somebody's feelings when they have problems (别人有困难时) 同情；体恤: *I sympathize with you—I've got a lot of work too.* 我很同情你——我的工作也非常多。

sympathy /ˈsɪmpəθi; ˈsɪmpəθɪ/ *noun* 名词 (no plural 无复数)
understanding another person's feelings and problems (对别人有困难时的) 同情；体恤: *She wrote me a letter of sympathy when my father died.* 我父亲去世时她给我写了一封慰问信。

symphony /ˈsɪmfəni; ˈsɪmfənɪ/ *noun* 名词 (*plural* 复数作 **symphonies**)
a long piece of music for a large orchestra 交响曲；交响乐: *Beethoven's fifth symphony* 贝多芬的《第五交响曲》

symptom /ˈsɪmptəm; ˈsɪmptəm/ *noun* 名词
something that shows that you have an illness 症状：*A sore throat is often a symptom of a cold.* 嗓子疼一般是感冒的症状。

synagogue /ˈsɪnəɡɒɡ; ˈsɪnə͵ɡɔɡ/ *noun* 名词
a building where Jewish people go to pray（犹太人进行宗教活动的）会堂

synthetic /sɪnˈθetɪk; sɪnˈθɛtɪk/ *adjective* 形容词
made by people, not natural 人造的：*Nylon is a synthetic material, but wool is natural.* 尼龙是人造的材料，羊毛是天然的材料。

syrup /ˈsɪrəp; ˈsɪrəp/ *noun* 名词 (no plural 无复数)
thick sweet liquid made with sugar and water or fruit juice 糖和水或糖和果汁的浓液；糖浆；果汁糖水：*peaches in syrup* 糖水桃

system /ˈsɪstəm; ˈsɪstəm/ *noun* 名词
1 a group of things or parts that work together 系统；组合装置：*the railway system* 铁路系统 ◇ *We have a new computer system at work.* 我们有个新的计算机操作设备。
2 a group of ideas or ways of doing something 体系；体制：*What system of government do you have in your country?* 你们国家政府是什么体制的？

S

Tt

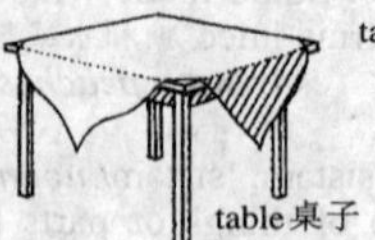

table /ˈteɪbl; ˈtebl̩/ *noun* 名词

1 a piece of furniture with a flat top on legs 桌子或类似桌子的器物

2 a list of facts or numbers（一览）表: *There is a table of irregular verbs at the back of this dictionary.* 本词典后部有个不规则动词表。

set or 或 **lay the table** put knives, forks, plates and other things on the table before you eat 摆餐具（把刀、叉、盘等器具放在桌子上准备吃饭）

tablecloth /ˈteɪblklɒθ; ˈtebl̩ˌklɔθ/ *noun* 名词

a cloth that you put over a table when you have a meal 桌布

tablespoon /ˈteɪblspuːn; ˈtebl̩ˌspun/ *noun* 名词

a big spoon that you use for putting food on plates 餐匙

tablet /ˈtæblət; ˈtæblɪt/ *noun* 名词

a small hard piece of medicine that you swallow 药片；药丸: *Take two of these tablets before every meal.* 这种药每顿饭前吃两片。

table tennis /ˈteɪbl tenɪs; ˈtebl̩ ˌtɛnɪs/ *noun* 名词 (no plural 无复数)

a game where players use a round **bat** to hit a small light ball over a net on a big table 乒乓球运动（球拍叫做 **bat**）

tackle /ˈtækl; ˈtækl̩/ *verb* 动词 (**tackles**, **tackling**, **tackled** /ˈtækld; ˈtækl̩d/)

1 start to do a difficult job 着手处理困难的工作；应付；对付: *I'm going to tackle my homework now.* 我现在要对付家庭作业了。◇ *How shall we tackle this problem?* 我们怎样处理这个困难问题呢？

2 try to take the ball from somebody in a game like football（在足球等运动中）拦截对方以抢球，抢截

3 try to catch and hold somebody 设法捉住某人: *I tackled the thief but he ran away.* 我没抓住那个贼，让他给跑了。

tact /tækt; tækt/ *noun* 名词 (no plural 无复数)

knowing how and when to say things so that you do not hurt people 言辞得体适时（不得罪人）: *She told him the meal was horrible—she's got no tact.* 她对他说那顿饭糟透了——她真不会说话。

tactful /ˈtæktfl; ˈtæktfəl/ *adjective* 形容词

careful not to say or do things that may make people unhappy or angry 言辞谨慎的（不得罪人）；机智的或圆滑的: *He wrote me a tactful letter about the money I owe him.* 他给我写了一封很婉转的信，提到我欠他钱的事。

tactfully /ˈtæktfəli; ˈtæktfəlɪ/ *adverb* 副词

in a tactful way 言辞谨慎地（不得罪人）；机智地或圆滑地

tactless /ˈtæktləs; ˈtæktlɪs/ *adjective* 形容词

not careful about people's feelings 不顾及别人感情的: *It was tactless of you to ask how old she was.* 你问她多大年纪，未免太不得体了。

tag /tæg; tæg/ *noun* 名词

a small piece of paper or material fixed to something, that tells you about it; a label（纸的或其他材料的）标签: *I looked at the price tag to see how much the dress cost.* 我看了一下那件连衣裙的标签，瞧瞧多少钱。

tail /teɪl; tel/ *noun* 名词

1 the long thin part at the end of an animal's body 尾巴: *The dog wagged its tail.* 那条狗摇了摇尾巴。☞ pictures at **cat** and **fish** 见 **cat** 和 **fish** 词条插图

2 the part at the back of something 物体的后部；尾部: *the tail of an aeroplane* 飞机的尾部

3 tails (plural 复数) the side of a coin that does not have the head of a person on it 文面（硬币没有人头像的一面）☞ Note at **heads** 见 **heads** 注释

tailor /ˈteɪlə(r); ˈtelɚ/ *noun* 名词

a person whose job is to make clothes for men（男装）裁缝

take /teɪk; tek/ *verb* 动词 (**takes**, **taking**, **took** /tʊk; tʊk/, **has taken** /ˈteɪkn; ˈtekən/)

1 move something or go with somebody to another place 把某物移动到另一处；带某人到另一处；运载；携带: *Take your coat with you—it's cold.* 您带着大衣吧——天气很冷。◇ *Mark took me to the station.* 马克带着我到车站去了。☞ picture on page 58 见第 58 页图

2 put your hand round something and hold it 用手拿或抓某物；握: *She took the baby in her arms.* 她把孩子抱在怀里。◇ *Take this money—it's yours.* 把这个钱拿着——这是你的。

3 steal something 偷某物: *Somebody has taken my bike.* 有人把我的自行车偷走了。

4 need an amount of time 需要某段时间: *The journey took four hours.* 路上用了四个小时。

5 travel in a bus, train, etc 乘坐公共汽车、火车等: *I took a taxi to the hospital.* 我坐计程车到医院去了。

6 eat or drink something 吃或喝某物: *I took the medicine.* 我把药吃了。

7 agree to have something 同意接受某物: *This restaurant doesn't take cheques.* 这家饭馆不收支票。

it takes you need something 需要某事物: *It takes a long time to learn a language.* 学会一种语言要用很长时间。

take after somebody be or look like somebody in your family 行为或相貌像家中某人: *She takes after her mother.* 她很像她母亲。

take away remove something 移去某物: *I took the knife away from the child.* 我把刀子从孩子手里拿走了。

take down write something that somebody says 把某人说的话写下来: *He took down my address.* 他把我的地址写下来了。

take off When an aeroplane takes off, it leaves the ground. (指飞机) 起飞

take something off 1 remove clothes 除掉或脱下衣物: *Take your coat off.* 您把大衣脱了吧。✪ opposite 反义词: **put on**

2 have time as a holiday, not working 休假: *I am taking a week off in June.* 我打算在六月份休假一个星期。

take over look after a business, etc when another person stops 接管某人的生意等: *Robert took over the farm when his father died.* 罗伯特在他父亲死后就接手经营那个农场。

take up use or fill time or space 使用或占用时间或空间: *The bed takes up half the room.* 这张床占了半间屋子。◇ *The new baby takes up all her time.* 她全部时间都用在刚生的这个孩子身上了。

take-away /'teɪk əweɪ; 'tekə,we/ *noun* 名词 (*plural* 复数作 **take-aways**)

1 a restaurant that sells hot food that you take out with you to eat somewhere else 外卖餐馆（出售热的食物供携走食用的餐馆）: *a Chinese take-away* 中式外卖餐馆

2 food that you buy at this kind of restaurant 在外卖餐馆出售的食物: *Let's get a take-away.* 咱们买外卖的饭菜吧。

take-away *adjective* 形容词

a take-away pizza 外卖的意大利饼

take-off /'teɪk ɒf; 'tek,ɔf/ *noun* 名词

the time when an aeroplane leaves the ground（指飞机）起飞

tale /teɪl; tel/ *noun* 名词

a story 故事: *fairy tales* 童话故事

talent /'tælənt; 'tælənt/ *noun* 名词

the natural ability to do something very well 原有的才能；天才: *Fiona has a talent for drawing.* 菲奥纳有绘画天才。

talented *adjective* 形容词

with a talent 天才的: *a talented musician* 天才的音乐家

talk¹ /tɔ:k; tɔk/ *verb* 动词 (**talks, talking, talked** /tɔ:kt; tɔkt/)

speak to somebody; say words 对某人谈话；说话: *She is talking to her boyfriend on the telephone.* 她正在跟男朋友通电话。◇ *We talked about our holiday.* 我们谈了谈假期的事。

talk² /tɔ:k; tɔk/ *noun* 名词

1 when two or more people talk about something（相互的）谈话；交谈；商谈；会谈: *Dave and I had a long talk about the problem.* 我和戴夫对这个问题谈了很长时间。◇ *The two countries are holding talks to try and end the war.* 两国正在谈判以结束这场战争。

2 when a person speaks to a group of people（一人对大家的）谈话，讲话；演讲: *Professor Wilson gave an interesting talk on Chinese art.* 威尔逊教授作了关于中国美术的演讲，很有意思。

talkative /'tɔ:kətɪv; 'tɔkətɪv/ *adjective* 形容词

A person who is talkative talks a lot. 爱说话的；多话的

T

tall /tɔ:l; tɔl/ *adjective* 形容词 (**taller, tallest**)

1 A person or thing that is tall goes up a long way（指人或物）高的: *a tall tree* 高大的树 ◇ *Richard is taller than his brother.* 理查德比他哥哥高。✪ opposite 反义词: **short** ☞ picture on page C26 见第C26页图

2 You use 'tall' to say or ask how far it is from the bottom to the top of somebody or something 谈到或询问某人或某物有多高的词: *How tall are you?* 您有多高？◇ *She's 1.62 metres tall.* 她身高1.62米。☞ Note at **high** 见 **high** 词条注释

tame /teɪm; tem/ *adjective* 形容词 (**tamer, tamest**)

A tame animal is not wild and is not afraid of people（指动物）驯服的；不凶猛的；不怕人的: *a tame squirrel* 不怕人的松鼠

tame *verb* 动词 (**tames, taming, tamed** /teɪmd; temd/)

make a wild animal tame 使野生动物驯服

tan /tæn; tæn/ *noun* 名词

When you have a tan, your skin is brown because you have been in the hot sun. 晒黑的肤色

tanned /tænd; tænd/ *adjective* 形容词

with a brown skin because you have been in the hot sun（指皮肤）晒黑的

tangerine /ˌtændʒəˈri:n; ˈtændʒəˌrin/ *noun* 名词

a fruit like a small sweet orange, with a skin that is easy to take off 橘子

tangle /ˈtæŋgl; ˈtæŋgḷ/ *verb* 动词 (**tangles, tangling, tangled** /ˈtæŋgld; ˈtæŋgḷd/)

mix or twist something like string or hair so that it is difficult to separate 把绳子或毛发等弄乱或搅在一起 ✪ opposite 反义词: **untangle**

tangle *noun* 名词

This string is in a tangle. 绳子乱成一团了。

tangled *adjective* 形容词

The cat has been playing with my wool and now it's all tangled. 猫一直玩儿我的毛线，现在都乱成一团了。

tank /tæŋk; tæŋk/ *noun* 名词

1 a container for liquids or gas 盛液体或气体的容器；罐；桶: *a petrol tank* (in a car)（汽车的）油箱

2 a strong heavy vehicle with big guns. Tanks are used by armies in wars. 坦克

tanker /ˈtæŋkə(r); ˈtæŋkɚ/ *noun* 名词

a ship that carries petrol or oil 运送汽油等油类的轮船: *an oil-tanker* 油轮

tap¹ /tæp; tæp/ *noun* 名词

tap 水龙头

a thing that you turn to make something like water or gas come out of a pipe（控制气体或液体流出的）龙头；旋塞: *Turn the tap off.* 把水龙头关上吧。

tap² /tæp; tæp/ *verb* 动词 (**taps, tapping, tapped** /tæpt; tæpt/)

hit or touch somebody or something quickly and lightly 快而轻地打击或触摸某人或某物: *She tapped me on the shoulder.* 她轻轻地拍了拍我的肩膀。◇ *I tapped on the window.* 我轻轻地敲了敲窗户。

tap *noun* 名词

They heard a tap at the door. 他们听见有人轻轻敲门。

tape /teɪp; tep/ *noun* 名词

1 a long thin piece of special plastic in a plastic box, that stores (**records**) sound, music or moving pictures so that you can listen to or watch it later. You use it in a **tape recorder** or a **video recorder** 磁带；录音带；录像带（录制叫做 **record**，录音机叫做 **tape recorder**，录像机叫做 **video recorder**）: *I have got the concert on tape.* 我有那次音乐会的录像带。◇ *Will you play your new Michael Jackson tape?* 你放放你的迈克尔·杰克逊的新录音带行吗？

2 a long thin piece of material or paper（布的或纸的）带子

tape *verb* 动词 (**tapes, taping, taped** /teɪpt; tept/)

put (**record**) sound, music or moving pictures on tape so that you can listen to or watch it later 把声音或影像等录制 (**record**) 在磁带上（以备以后收听或收看）: *I taped the film that was on TV last night.* 我把昨天晚上电视播放的影片录下来了。

tape-measure /ˈteɪp meʒə(r); ˈtep-ˌmɛʒɚ/ *noun* 名词

a long thin piece of metal, plastic or cloth for measuring things 卷尺；皮尺

tape recorder /ˈteɪp rɪˌkɔ:də(r); ˈtep rɪˌkɔrdɚ/ *noun* 名词

a machine that can put (**record**) sound or music on tape and play it again later 录音机（录制叫做 **record**）

tapestry /'tæpəstri; 'tæpɪstrɪ/ *noun* 名词 (*plural* 复数作 **tapestries**)
a piece of cloth with pictures on it made from coloured thread 织花帷；壁毯

tar /tɑ:(r); tɑr/ *noun* 名词 (no plural 无复数)
black stuff that is thick and sticky when it is hot, and hard when it is cold. Tar is used for making roads. 焦油；焦油沥青；柏油（铺路用的）

target /'tɑ:gɪt; 'tɑrgɪt/ *noun* 名词
a thing that you try to hit with a bullet or an arrow, for example（用枪弹或弓箭等射的）目标；靶: *The bomb hit its target.* 炸弹击中了目标。

tart /tɑ:t; tɑrt/ *noun* 名词
a piece of pastry with fruit or jam on it 果馅饼（上面有水果或果酱，常无上层饼皮）: *Would you like a piece of apple tart?* 您吃一块苹果馅饼好吗？

tartan /'tɑ:tn; 'tɑrtn̩/ *noun* 名词
a special pattern on material that comes from Scotland（源自苏格兰的）花格图案: *a tartan skirt* 彩色格呢裙

task /tɑ:sk; tæsk/ *noun* 名词
a piece of work that you must do; a job 必须做的事；工作；任务: *I had the task of cleaning the floors.* 我有件打扫地板的事要做。

taste¹ /teɪst; test/ *noun* 名词
1 (no plural 无复数) the power to know about food and drink with your mouth 味觉: *When you have a cold, you often lose your sense of taste.* 患感冒时往往尝不出东西的味道。
2 (*plural* 复数作 **tastes**) the feeling that a certain food or drink gives in your mouth 味道: *Sugar has a sweet taste and lemons have a sour taste.* 糖有甜味，柠檬有酸味。◇ *I don't like the taste of this cheese.* 我不喜欢这种奶酪的味道。
3 (*plural* 复数作 **tastes**) a little bit of food or drink 一点儿食物或饮料: *Have a taste of the wine to see if you like it.* 您尝尝这种葡萄酒，看您喜欢不喜欢。
4 (no plural 无复数) being able to choose nice things 鉴赏力；审美力；欣赏力: *She has good taste in clothes.* 她对服装很有眼力。

taste² /teɪst; test/ *verb* 动词 (**tastes, tasting, tasted**)
1 feel or know a certain food or drink in your mouth 辨别出食物或饮料的味道；尝出: *Can you taste onions in this soup?* 你能尝出这个汤里有洋葱味儿吗？
2 eat or drink a little of something 尝食物或饮料的味道: *Taste this cheese to see if you like it.* 您尝尝这种奶酪，看您喜欢不喜欢。
3 give a certain feeling when you put it in your mouth 有某种味道: *Honey tastes sweet.* 蜂蜜是甜的。

tasty /'teɪsti; 'testɪ/ *adjective* 形容词 (**tastier, tastiest**)
good to eat 好吃的；好喝的: *The soup was very tasty.* 这个汤很好喝。

tattoo /tə'tu:; tæ'tu/ *noun* 名词 (*plural* 复数作 **tattoos**)
a picture on somebody's skin, made with a needle and coloured liquid 刺在皮肤上的图案；文身: *He had a tattoo of a snake on his arm.* 他胳膊上刺着一条蛇。

taught *form of* **teach** ＊ **teach** 的不同形式

tax /tæks; tæks/ *noun* 名词 (*plural* 复数作 **taxes**)
money that you have to pay to the government. You pay tax from the money you earn or when you buy things 税；税额: *There is a tax on cigarettes in this country.* 这个国家香烟要上税。

tax *verb* 动词 (**taxes, taxing, taxed** /tækst; tækst/)
make somebody pay tax 向某人征税

taxi /'tæksi; 'tæksɪ/ *noun* 名词
a car that you can travel in if you pay the driver 计程车；出租车: *I took a taxi to the airport.* 我是坐计程车到飞机场的。◇ *I came by taxi.* 我是坐计程车来的。

tea /ti:; ti/ *noun* 名词
1 (no plural 无复数) a brown drink that you make with hot water and the dry leaves of a special plant 茶水: *Would you like a cup of tea?* 您要杯茶吗？
2 (*plural* 复数作 **teas**) a cup of this drink 一杯茶: *Two teas, please.* 劳驾，来两杯茶。
3 (no plural 无复数) the dry leaves that you use to make tea 茶叶
4 (*plural* 复数作 **teas**) a small afternoon meal of sandwiches, cakes and cups of tea 下午茶点（下午的一顿小吃，常为三明治、蛋糕和茶）✪ Some people call their evening meal **tea**. 有人把晚饭叫做 **tea**。

tea bag /'ti: bæg; 'ti ˌbæg/ *noun* 名词
a small paper bag with tea leaves inside. You use it to make tea. 袋茶

T

teapot 茶壶

teapot /'ti:pɒt; 'ti,pɑt/ *noun* 名词
a special pot for making and pouring tea 茶壶

teach /ti:tʃ; titʃ/ *verb* 动词 (**teaches, teaching, taught** /tɔ:t; tɔt/, **has taught**)
give somebody lessons; tell or show somebody how to do something 给某人上课；教某人做某事: *My mother taught me to drive.* 我母亲教我开汽车。◇ *Marco is teaching me Italian.* 马科现在教我意大利语。☞ Look at **learn**. 见 **learn**。

teaching *noun* 名词 (no plural 无复数)
the job of a teacher 教师的工作；教学工作；教书

teacher /'ti:tʃə(r); 'titʃɚ/ *noun* 名词
a person whose job is to teach 教师: *He's my English teacher.* 他是我的英语老师。

team /ti:m; tim/ *noun* 名词
1 a group of people who play a sport or a game together against another group （运动或游戏的）队: *Which team do you play for?* 你在哪个队效力？◇ *a football team* 足球队
2 a group of people who work together 在一起工作的人；组: *a team of doctors* 医生小组

tear¹ /tɪə(r); tɪr/ *noun* 名词
a drop of water that comes from your eye when you cry 泪；泪水；泪珠
be in tears be crying 流泪: *I was in tears at the end of the film.* 影片结束时我流泪了。
burst into tears suddenly start to cry 突然哭起来: *He read the letter and burst into tears.* 他看着看着信突然哭起来了。

tear² /teə(r); tɛr/ *verb* 动词 (**tears, tearing, tore** /tɔ:(r); tɔr/, **has torn** /tɔ:n; tɔrn/)
1 pull something apart or make an untidy hole in something 把某物撕开或弄破: *She tore her dress on a nail.* 她的连衣裙让钉子给剐破了。◇ *I tore the piece of paper in half.* 我把纸撕成两半了。◇ *I can't use this bag—it's torn.* 这个袋子我不能用——已经破了。

tear 撕

2 pull something roughly and quickly away from somebody or something 从某人处或某物上撕下某物: *I tore a page out of the book.* 我从本子上撕下了一页。
3 come apart; break 碎；破: *Paper tears easily.* 纸很容易破。
4 move very fast 很快地移动: *He tore down the street.* 他在街上飞跑。
tear up pull something into small pieces 把某物撕碎: *I tore the letter up and threw it away.* 我把信撕碎扔了。

tear³ /teə(r); tɛr/ *noun* 名词
an untidy hole in something like paper or material （纸或布等东西上的）破洞，裂口: *You've got a tear in your jeans.* 你的牛仔裤上有个破洞。

tease /ti:z; tiz/ *verb* 动词 (**teases, teasing, teased** /ti:zd; tizd/)
say unkind things to somebody because you think it is funny 取笑或逗弄某人: *People often tease me because I'm short.* 因为我矮，大家常常取笑我。

teaspoon /'ti:spu:n; 'ti,spun/ *noun* 名词
a small spoon that you use for putting sugar into tea or coffee 茶匙

tea towel /'ti: taʊəl; 'ti ,taʊəl/ *noun* 名词
a small cloth that you use for drying things like plates and cups after you wash them （餐具洗净后用以擦干的）抹布

technical /'teknɪkl; 'tɛknɪkḷ/ *adjective* 形容词
of or about the machines and materials used in science and in making things 技术的；专业的；科技的: *technical knowledge* 科技知识

technician /tek'nɪʃn; tɛk'nɪʃən/ *noun* 名词
a person who works with machines or instruments 技术员；技师: *a laboratory technician* 实验室技术员

technique /tek'ni:k; tɛk'nik/ *noun* 名词
a special way of doing something 做某事的特殊方法；技术；技巧: *new techniques for learning languages* 学习语言的新方法

technology /tek'nɒlədʒi; tɛk'nɑlədʒɪ/ *noun* 名词 (no plural 无复数)
studying science and ideas about how things work, and using this to build and make things 科学技术；应用科学: *Technology is very important for the future.* 科学技术对未来的发展十分重要。◇ *computer technology* 计算机应用科学

teddy bear /'tedi beə(r); 'tɛdɪ ˌbɛr/, **teddy** (*plural* 复数作 **teddies**) *noun* 名词
a toy for children that looks like a bear 玩具熊

teddy bear
玩具熊

tedious /'ti:diəs; 'tidɪəs/ *adjective* 形容词
very long and not interesting 非常长而无趣的: *a tedious journey* 使人烦闷的路程

teenager /'ti:neɪdʒə(r); 'tinˌedʒɚ/ *noun* 名词
a person who is between the ages of 13 and 19 ✳（13岁至19岁的）青少年
teenage /'ti:neɪdʒ; 'tinɪdʒ/ *adjective* 形容词
a teenage boy 十几岁的男孩子

teens /ti:nz; tinz/ *noun* 名词 (plural 复数)
the time when you are between the ages of 13 and 19 ✳ 13岁至19岁的时期: *She is in her teens.* 她十多岁。

teeth *plural of* **tooth** ✳ **tooth** 的复数形式

telegram /'telɪgræm; 'tɛləˌgræm/ *noun* 名词
a message that you send very quickly by radio or by electric wires 电报

telephone[1] /'telɪfəʊn; 'tɛləˌfon/ *noun* 名词
an instrument that you use for talking to somebody who is in another place 电话: *What's your telephone number?* 您的电话号码是多少？◇ *Can I make a telephone call?* 我打个电话行吗？◇ *The telephone's ringing — can you answer it?* 电话响了——你接一下行吗？
on the telephone using a telephone to speak to somebody 与某人通电话: *He's on the telephone to his wife.* 他正在跟他妻子通话。
✪ **Phone** is the more usual word. ✳ **phone** 是常用词。

telephone[2] /'telɪfəʊn; 'tɛləˌfon/ *verb* 动词 (**telephones**, **telephoning**, **telephoned** /'telɪfəʊnd; 'tɛləˌfond/)
use a telephone to speak to somebody 给某人打电话: *I must telephone my parents.* 我得给我父母打个电话。✪ **Phone** is the more usual word. ✳ **phone** 是常用词。

telephone box /'telɪfəʊn bɒks; 'tɛləfon ˌbɑks/ (*plural* 复数作 **telephone boxes**), **telephone kiosk** *noun* 名词
a kind of small building in the street or in a public place that has a telephone in it 公用电话亭

telephone directory /'telɪfəʊn dɪrektəri; 'tɛləfon dəˌrɛktərɪ/ *noun* 名词 (*plural* 复数作 **telephone directories**)
a book of people's names, addresses and telephone numbers 电话号码簿；电话簿

telescope /'telɪskəʊp; 'tɛləˌskop/ *noun* 名词
a long round instrument with special glass inside it. You use it to look at things that are a long way from you. 望远镜

television /'telɪvɪʒn; 'tɛləˌvɪʒən/ *noun* 名词
1 (*plural* 复数作 **televisions**) (*also* 亦作 **television set**) a machine like a box that shows moving pictures with sound 电视机
2 (no plural 无复数) things that you watch on a television 电视（节目）: *I watched television last night.* 我昨天晚上看电视了。◇ *What's on television?* 电视上有什么节目？◇ *a television programme* 电视节目
3 a way of sending pictures and sounds so that people can watch them on television 电视的播放: *satellite television* 卫星电视广播
✪ The short forms are **TV** and **telly**. 缩略式为 **TV** 和 **telly**。

telex /'teleks; 'tɛlɛks/ *noun* 名词
1 (no plural 无复数) a way of sending messages. You type the message on a special machine that sends it very quickly to another place by telephone. 电传（使用电传打印机通过电话传送信息的方法）
2 (*plural* 复数作 **telexes**) a message that you send or receive in this way 通过电传发送或接收的信息

tell /tel; tɛl/ *verb* 动词 (**tells**, **telling**, **told** /təʊld; told/, **has told**)
1 give information to somebody by speaking or writing（用语言或文字）把信息告诉某人: *I told her my new address.* 我把我的新地址告诉她了。◇ *This book tells you how to make bread.* 这本书讲的是制做面包的方法。◇ *He told me that he was tired.* 他告诉我他累了。

2 say what somebody must do 吩咐某人做某事: *Our teacher told us to read this book.* 我们老师让我们看这本书。
☞ Note at **say** 见 **say** 词条注释

can tell know, guess or understand something 知道、猜出或理解某事物: *I can tell that he's been crying because his eyes are red.* 我看得出来他刚哭过，因为他眼睛还红着呢。◇ *I can't tell the difference between James and his brother. They look exactly the same!* 詹姆斯跟他的弟弟，我分辨不出谁是谁。他们长得一模一样！

tell somebody off speak to somebody in an angry way because they have done something wrong 责备某人；斥责；责骂: *I told the children off for making so much noise.* 孩子们太吵闹了，我把他们骂了一顿。

telly /'teli; 'tɛlɪ/ *short for* **television** ✳ **television** 的缩略式

temper /'tempə(r); 'tɛmpɚ/ *noun* 名词
how you feel 心情；脾气: *She's in a bad temper this morning.* 她今天早晨心情很不好。

have a temper If you have a temper, you often get angry and cannot control what you do or say 脾气坏: *He has a terrible temper.* 他脾气坏极了。

in a temper angry 发怒；发脾气: *She's in a temper because she's tired.* 她发脾气是因为她累了。

lose your temper suddenly become angry 发起脾气来

temperature /'temprətʃə(r); 'tɛmprəˌtʃɚ/ *noun* 名词
how hot or cold somebody or something is 体温；温度: *On a very hot day, the temperature reaches 35° C.* 天气非常热的时候，气温能达到35摄氏度。◇ *a high/low temperature* 高[低]温

have a temperature feel very hot because you are ill 发烧（因生病）

take somebody's temperature see how hot somebody is, using a special instrument called a **thermometer** 量某人的体温（温度表叫做 **thermometer**）

temple /'templ; 'tɛmpl̩/ *noun* 名词
a building where people go to pray and worship God or a god 庙；寺；神殿

temporary /'temprəri; 'tɛmpəˌrɛrɪ/ *adjective* 形容词
Something that is temporary lasts for a short time 暂时的；临时的: *I had a temporary job in the summer holidays.* 我在暑假的时候做过临时工作。✪ opposite 反义词: **permanent**

temporarily /'temprərəli; 'tɛmpəˌrɛrəlɪ/ *adverb* 副词
The road is temporarily closed for repairs. 这条路因维修而临时封闭。

tempt /tempt; tɛmpt/ *verb* 动词 (**tempts, tempting, tempted**)
make somebody want to do something, especially something that is wrong 诱使某人想要做某事（尤指错事）；怂恿: *He saw the money on the table, and he was tempted to steal it.* 他看见桌子上有钱，顿生贪念想偷走。

temptation /temp'teɪʃn; tɛmp'teʃən/ *noun* 名词
1 (*plural* 复数作 **temptations**) a thing that makes you want to do something wrong 引诱人（想要做错事）的事物: *Don't leave the money on your desk—it's a temptation to thieves.* 别把钱放在办公桌上——这是开门揖盗。
2 (no plural 无复数) a feeling that you want to do something that you know is wrong 想做（明知是错的）某事的心情；受诱惑的想法: *the temptation to eat another chocolate* 想再吃一块巧克力的念头

tempting *adjective* 形容词
Something that is tempting makes you want to do or have it 引诱人的（使人想做某事或想占有某事物）: *That cake looks very tempting!* 那块蛋糕看着真馋人！

ten /ten; tɛn/ *number* 数词
10 十

tenant /'tenənt; 'tɛnənt/ *noun* 名词
a person who pays money to live in or use a place 租住或租用某地方的人；房客；租户

tend /tend; tɛnd/ *verb* 动词 (**tends, tending, tended**)
usually do or be something 通常做某事或呈某状态；倾向于: *Men tend to be taller than women.* 男子一般比女子身材高。

tendency /'tendənsi; 'tɛndənsɪ/ *noun* 名词 (*plural* 复数作 **tendencies**)
something that a person or thing often does 经常做的事物；倾向: *He has a tendency to be late.* 他总是迟到。

tender /'tendə(r); 'tɛndɚ/ *adjective* 形容词
1 kind and gentle 和蔼而温柔的: *a tender look* 温和的表情

T

2 Tender meat is soft and easy to cut or bite.（指食用肉）嫩的 ✪ opposite 反义词: **tough**

3 If a part of your body is tender, it hurts when you touch it.（指身体某部）有触痛的

tenderly *adverb* 副词
in a kind and gentle way 和蔼而温柔地: *He touched her arm tenderly.* 他温柔地抚摸她的胳膊。

tenderness /ˈtendənəs; ˈtɛndənɪs/ *noun* 名词 (no plural 无复数)
a feeling of tenderness 和蔼而亲切的感觉

tennis /ˈtenɪs; ˈtɛnɪs/ *noun* 名词 (no plural 无复数)
a game for two or four players who hold **rackets** and hit a small ball over a net 网球运动（球拍叫做 **racket**）: *Let's play tennis.* 咱们打打网球吧。

tennis court /ˈtenɪs kɔːt; ˈtɛnɪs ˌkort/ *noun* 名词
a special place where you play tennis 网球场

tense¹ /tens; tɛns/ *adjective* 形容词 (**tenser, tensest**)
1 worried because you are waiting for something to happen（因等待某事发生）担心的；紧张的: *I always feel very tense before exams.* 我考试前总是感到非常紧张。
2 pulled tightly 拉紧的: *tense muscles* 绷紧的肌肉

tension /ˈtenʃn; ˈtɛnʃən/ *noun* 名词
being tense 担心；紧张；拉紧: *Tension can give you headaches.* 神经紧张能引起头疼。

tense² /tens; tɛns/ *noun* 名词
the form of a verb that shows if something happens in the past, present or future（动词的）时态

tent 帐篷

tent /tent; tɛnt/ *noun* 名词
a kind of a house made of cloth. You sleep in a tent when you go camping 帐篷: *We put up our tent.* 我们把帐篷支起来了。

tenth /tenθ; tɛnθ/ *adjective, adverb, noun* 形容词，副词，名词
1 10th 第10（个）；第十（个）
2 one of ten equal parts of something; 1/10 十分之一

term /tɜːm; tɝm/ *noun* 名词
1 the time between holidays when schools and colleges are open（学校的）学期: *The summer term is from April to July.* 夏季学期是从四月至七月。
2 a word or group of words connected with a special subject 专业的词或词组；术语: *a computing term* 计算机术语

terminal /ˈtɜːmɪnl; ˈtɝmənl̩/ *noun* 名词
a building where people begin and end their journeys by bus, train, aeroplane or ship（公共汽车、火车、飞机或轮船的）终点站: *Passengers for Nairobi should go to Terminal 2.* 前往内罗毕的乘客请到第2号终点站。

terrace /ˈterəs; ˈtɛrəs/ *noun* 名词
1 a flat place outside a house or restaurant（房子的或饭馆外面的）平地: *We had our lunch on the terrace.* 我们在屋外的平地上吃的午饭。
2 a line of houses that are joined together（相连的）一排房屋

terraced house /ˌterəst ˈhaʊs; ˈtɛrɪst ˈhaʊs/ *noun* 名词
a house that is part of a line of houses that are all joined together 排房（相连的一排房屋中的一所房子）

terrible /ˈterəbl; ˈtɛrəbl̩/ *adjective* 形容词
very bad 极坏的；很糟的: *She had a terrible accident.* 她出了严重事故。◇ *The food in that restaurant is terrible!* 那家饭馆的饭菜糟透了！

terribly /ˈterəbli; ˈtɛrəblɪ/ *adverb* 副词
1 very 非常: *I'm terribly sorry!* 我十分抱歉！
2 very badly 极坏；很糟: *He played terribly.* 他演奏得很糟糕。

terrific /təˈrɪfɪk; təˈrɪfɪk/ *adjective* 形容词
1 very good; wonderful 极好的；了不起的: *What a terrific idea!* 多么绝妙的主意呀！
2 very great 很大的: *a terrific storm* 狂风暴雨

terrify /ˈterɪfaɪ; ˈtɛrəˌfaɪ/ *verb* 动词 (**terrifies, terrifying, terrified** /ˈterɪfaɪd; ˈtɛrəˌfaɪd/, **has terrified**)
make somebody very frightened 使某人非常害怕: *Spiders terrify me!* 我最害怕蜘蛛了！

T

terrified *adjective* 形容词
very frightened 很害怕的: *Di is terrified of dogs.* 戴很害怕狗。

territory /'terətri; 'tɛrə,torɪ/ *noun* 名词 (*plural* 复数作 **territories**)
the land that belongs to one country 领土: *This island was once French territory.* 这个岛一度是法国的领地。

terror /'terə(r); 'tɛrɚ/ *noun* 名词 (no plural 无复数)
very great fear 恐怖；惊骇: *He screamed in terror.* 他吓得尖叫起来。

terrorist /'terərɪst; 'tɛrə,rɪst/ *noun* 名词
a person who frightens, hurts or kills people so that the government, etc will do what he/she wants 恐怖主义者；恐怖分子: *The terrorists put a bomb in the station.* 恐怖分子在车站放置了一颗炸弹。

terrorism /'terərɪzəm; 'tɛrə,rɪzəm/ *noun* 名词 (no plural 无复数)
an act of terrorism 恐怖主义活动

test /test; tɛst/ *verb* 动词 (**tests**, **testing**, **tested**)
1 use or look at something carefully to find out how good it is or if it works well 试用或细查某物（以鉴别好坏或性能）；检查；检验；试验: *The doctor tested my eyes.* 医生检查了我的眼睛。◇ *I don't think drugs should be tested on animals.* 我认为不应该用动物做药物试验。
2 ask somebody questions to find out what they know or what they can do 测验（某人的知识或能力）；测试；考查: *The teacher tested us on our spelling.* 老师对我们的拼写能力进行了测试。

test *noun* 名词
a blood test 验血 ◇ *a maths test* 数学测验 ◇ *Did you pass your driving test?* 你驾驶考试合格了吗？

test-tube /'test tju:b; 'tɛst,tjub/ *noun* 名词
a long thin glass tube that you use in chemistry 试管

text /tekst; tɛkst/ *noun* 名词
1 (no plural 无复数) the words in a book, newspaper or magazine（书的或报刊的）文字；正文: *This book has a lot of pictures but not much text.* 这本书有很多插图而没有什么文字。
2 (*plural* 复数作 **texts**) a book or a short piece of writing that you study（供学习的）书或篇章: *Read the text and answer the questions.* 先读这段文字然后回答问题。

textbook /'tekstbʊk; 'tɛkst,bʊk/ *noun* 名词
a book that teaches you about something 教科书；课本: *a biology textbook* 生物学教科书

texture /'tekstʃə(r); 'tɛkstʃɚ/ *noun* 名词
the way that something feels when you touch it（触摸某物时的）手感；质地: *Silk has a smooth texture.* 丝绸摸起来很光滑。

than /ðən, ðæn; ðən, 'ðæn/ *conjunction, preposition* 连词，介词
You use 'than' when you compare people or things（比较人或事物时的）比；比较: *I'm older than him.* 我比他岁数大。◇ *You speak Spanish much better than she does.* 您说西班牙语比她说得好。◇ *We live less than a kilometre from the beach.* 我们住的地方离海滩不到一公里。

thank /θæŋk; θæŋk/ *verb* 动词 (**thanks**, **thanking**, **thanked** /θæŋkt; θæŋkt/)
tell somebody that you are pleased because they gave you something or helped you 谢谢或感谢某人: *I thanked Tina for the present.* 我感谢蒂纳送给我礼物。

no, thank you You use 'no, thank you' to say that you do not want something 用以表示不要某事物: *'Would you like some more tea?' 'No, thank you.'* "您还要添点儿茶吗？" "不要了，谢谢您。" ✪ You can also say **no, thanks**. 也可以说 **no，thanks**。

thank you, thanks You use 'thank you' or 'thanks' to tell somebody that you are pleased because they gave you something or helped you 谢谢您；谢谢你；谢谢: *Thank you very much for the flowers.* 非常感谢您送给我这么多花。◇ *'How are you?' 'I'm fine, thanks.'* "您好吗？" "我很好，谢谢。"

thanks *noun* 名词 (plural 复数)
words that show you are pleased because somebody gave you something or helped you 谢意；谢忱: *Please give my thanks to your sister for her help.* 请您转达我对您姐姐的谢意，她对我帮助很大。

thanks to somebody or 或 **something** because of somebody or something 由于或因为某人或某事物: *We're late, thanks to you!* 我们迟到了，都是因为你！

thankful /ˈθæŋkfl; ˈθæŋkfəl/ *adjective* 形容词
happy that something good has happened 感激的；欣慰的: *I was thankful for a rest after the long walk.* 我走了很长的路，能休息一下真高兴。

thankfully /ˈθæŋkfəli; ˈθæŋkfəlɪ/ *adverb* 副词
You say 'thankfully' when you are pleased about something 感激地；欣慰地: *There was an accident, but thankfully nobody was hurt.* 出了事故，幸而没有人受伤。

Thanksgiving /ˌθæŋksˈgɪvɪŋ; ˌθæŋksˈgɪvɪŋ/ *noun* 名词 (no plural 无复数)
a special holiday in October or November for people in Canada and the USA 感恩节（加拿大和美国在十月份或十一月份的节日）

that[1] /ðæt; ðæt/ *adjective, pronoun* 形容词，代词 (*plural* 复数作 **those**)
a word that you use to talk about a person or thing that is there or then 那；那个: *'Who is that boy in the garden?' 'That's my brother.'* "花园里的那个男孩儿是谁？" "那是我弟弟。" ◇ *She got married in 1989. At that time, she was a teacher.* 她是1989年结的婚。那时候她是个教师。 ☞ picture on page 512 见第512页图

that[2] /ðæt; ðæt/ *adverb* 副词
so 那么；如此: *The next village is ten kilometres from here. I can't walk that far.* 下一个村子离这儿十公里。我走不了那么远。

that[3] /ðət; ðət/ *pronoun* 代词
which, who or whom 那个；那位: *A lion is an animal that lives in Africa.* 狮子是生长在非洲的动物。◇ *The people (that) I met were very nice.* 我遇见的人都非常好。◇ *I'm reading the book (that) you gave me.* 我正在看您送给我的书。

that[4] /ðət, ðæt; ðət/ *conjunction* 连词
a word that you use to join two parts of a sentence 用以连接一句话中的两个部分的词: *Jo said (that) she was unhappy.* 乔说她不愉快。◇ *I'm sure (that) he will come.* 我肯定他一定来。◇ *I was so hungry (that) I ate all the food.* 我饿得把所有东西都吃了。

thaw /θɔ:; θɔ/ *verb* 动词 (**thaws, thawing** /ˈθɔ:ɪŋ; ˈθɔɪŋ/, **thawed** /θɔ:d; θɔd/)
warm something that is frozen so that it becomes soft or liquid; get warmer so that it becomes soft or liquid（使凝固的东西）融化；解冻: *The ice is thawing.* 冰正在融化。

the[1] /ðə, ði, ði:; ðə, ðɪ/ *article* 冠词
1 a word that you use before the name of somebody or something when it is clear what person or thing you mean 用于已知的人或事物的名称前的词: *I bought a shirt and some trousers. The shirt is blue.* 我买了一件衬衫和一条裤子。衬衫是蓝色的。◇ *The sun is shining.* 太阳正在放射着光芒。
2 a word that you use before numbers and dates 用于数目或日期前的词: *Monday, the sixth of May* 五月六日星期一
3 a word that you use to talk about a group of people or things of the same kind 用以表示同类的人或事物的词: *the French* (= all French people) 法国人（=所有的法国人）◇ *Do you play the piano?* 您会弹钢琴吗？
4 a word that you use before the names of rivers, seas, etc and some countries 用于河流、海洋等名称前及某些国家名称前的词: *the Seine* 塞纳河（法国的）◇ *the Atlantic* 大西洋 ◇ *the United States of America* 美利坚合众国 ✪ Before the names of most countries, we do not use 'the' 在大多数国家的名称前并不使用 the: *I went to France.* 我到法国去了。(NOT 不可作：*I went to the France.*)

the[2] /ðə, ði; ðə, ðɪ/ *adverb* 副词
a word that you use to talk about two things happening together 用以表示两件事物一起发生的词: *The more you eat, the fatter you get.* 吃得越多越胖。

theater *American English for* **theatre** 美式英语，即 **theatre**

theatre /ˈθɪətə(r); ˈθɪətɚ/ *noun* 名词
a building where you go to see plays 戏院；剧院: *I'm going to the theatre this evening.* 我今天晚上去看戏。

theft /θeft; θɛft/ *noun* 名词
taking something that is not yours; stealing 偷；偷窃: *She was sent to prison for theft.* 她因偷窃入狱。◇ *I told the police about the theft of my car.* 我告诉警方我的汽车让人偷走了。

their /ðeə(r); ðɛr/ *adjective* 形容词
of them 他们的；她们的；它们的: *What is their phone number?* 他们的电话号码是多少？

T

theirs /ðeəz; ðɛrz/ *pronoun* 代词
something that belongs to them 他们的（所有物）；她们的；它们的: *Our flat is smaller than theirs.* 我们的公寓比他们的小。

them /ðəm, ðem; ðəm, 'ðɛm/ *pronoun* 代词 (plural 复数)
1 a word that shows more than one person, animal or thing 他们；她们；它们: *I wrote them a letter and then I phoned them.* 我给他们写了封信，又给他们打了个电话。◇ *I'm looking for my keys. Have you seen them?* 我正在找我的钥匙。你看见了吗？
2 him or her 他；她: *If anybody phones, tell them I'm busy.* 要是有人来电话，告诉他我很忙。

theme /θi:m; θim/ *noun* 名词
something that you talk or write about（谈话或写作的）主题；题目: *The theme of his speech was 'Europe in the 1990s'.* 他演讲的题目是"20世纪90年代的欧洲"。

themselves /ðəm'selvz; ðəm'sɛlvz/ *pronoun* 代词 (plural 复数)
1 a word that shows the same people, animals or things that you have just talked about（用作反身代词）他们自己，她们自己，它们自己: *They bought themselves a new car.* 他们买了一辆新汽车。
2 a word that makes 'they' stronger（用作反身强调代词）他们自己，她们自己，它们自己: *Did they build the house themselves?* 这所房子是他们自己盖的吗？
by themselves **1** alone; without other people 他们独自地；他们单独地（没有别人相伴）: *The children went out by themselves.* 孩子们自己出去了。**2** without help 他们独自地；他们单独地（没有别人帮助）: *They cooked dinner by themselves.* 他们自己做的饭。

then /ðen; ðɛn/ *adverb* 副词
1 at that time 当时；那时: *I became a teacher in 1989. I lived in Bristol then, but now I live in London.* 我1989年当了教师。那时候我住在布里斯托尔，现在我住在伦敦。◇ *I can't come next week. I will be on holiday then.* 我下星期来不了。那时候我放假。
2 next; after that 下一个；然后；以后: *We had dinner and then did the washing-up.* 我们吃了饭，然后又刷了碗。
3 if that is true 既然如此；那么: *'I don't feel well.' 'Then why don't you go to the doctor's?'* "我觉得不舒服。""那为什么不去找医生看看呢？"

theory /'θɪəri; 'θɪərɪ/ *noun* 名词 (*plural* 复数作 **theories**)
an idea that tries to explain something（试图解释某事物的）意见；理论；学说: *There are a lot of different theories about how life began.* 关于生命的起源问题，众说不一。

therapy /'θerəpi; 'θɛrəpɪ/ *noun* 名词 (no plural 无复数)
a way of helping people who are ill in their body or mind, usually without drugs 治疗；疗法（通常指不用药物的）: *speech therapy* 言语治疗

there[1] /ðeə(r); 'ðɛr/ *adverb* 副词
in, at or to that place 在那里；往那里: *Don't put the box there—put it here.* 别把箱子放在那里——放在这里。◇ *Have you been to Bonn? I'm going there next week.* 您去过波恩吗？我下星期到那儿去。
there you are words that you say when you give something to somebody 把某物给某人时说的话: *'There you are,' she said, giving me a cake.* "给你，"她边说边给我一块蛋糕。

there[2] /ðeə(r); ðɚ/ *pronoun* 代词
1 a word that you use with verbs like 'be', 'seem' and 'appear' to show that something is true or that something is happening 与 be、seem、appear 等动词连用，表示某事物属实、存在或正在发生: *There is a man at the door.* 门口有个男的。◇ *Is there a film on TV tonight?* 今天晚上电视上有电影吗？◇ *There aren't any shops in this village.* 这个村子里没有商店。
2 a word that makes people look or listen 用以引起别人注意看或注意听的词: *There's the bell for my class! I must go.* 上课铃响了！我得走了。

therefore /'ðeəfɔ:(r); 'ðɛr,fɔr/ *adverb* 副词
for that reason 为此；因此；所以: *Simon was busy and therefore could not come to the meeting.* 西蒙很忙，所以不能来开会。

thermometer /θə'mɒmɪtə(r); θə'mɑmətɚ/ *noun* 名词
an instrument that shows how hot or cold something is 温度计；寒暑表；体温表

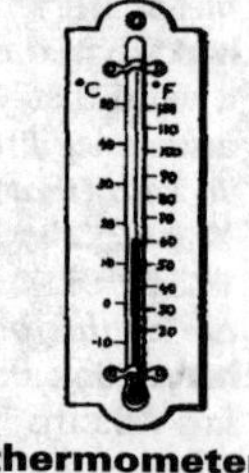

thermometer 温度表

T

these /ði:z; ðiz/ *adjective, pronoun* 形容词，代词 (plural 复数)
a word that you use to talk about people or things that are here or now 这些: *These books are mine.* 这些书是我的。◇ *Do you want these?* 您要这些东西吗？☞ picture on page 512 见第512页图

they /ðeɪ; ðe/ *pronoun* 代词 (plural 复数)
1 the people, animals or things that the sentence is about 他们；她们；它们: *Jo and David came at two o'clock and they left at six o'clock.* 乔和戴维是两点钟来的，他们六点钟走的。◇ *'Where are my keys?' 'They're* (= they are) *on the table.'* "我的钥匙在哪儿呢？""都在桌子上呢。"
2 a word that you use instead of 'he' or 'she' 用以代替 he 或 she 的词: *Someone phoned for you—they said they would phone again later.* 有人来电话找您——他说他以后再给您来电话。
3 people 人们；大家: *They say it will be cold this winter.* 据说今年冬天一定很冷。

they'd /ðeɪd; ðed/
1 = **they had**
2 = **they would**

they'll /ðeɪl; ðel/ = **they will**

they're /ðeə(r); ðɛr/ = **they are**

they've /ðeɪv; ðev/ = **they have**

thick /θɪk; θɪk/ *adjective* 形容词 (**thicker, thickest**)
1 far from one side to the other 厚的；粗的: *The walls are very thick.* 这些墙非常厚。◇ *It's cold outside, so wear a thick coat.* 外面很冷，穿上件厚大衣吧。✪ opposite 反义词: **thin** ☞ picture on page C26 见第C26页图
2 You use 'thick' to say or ask how far something is from one side to the other 用以陈述或询问厚度或粗细的词: *The ice is six centimetres thick.* 这块冰六厘米厚。
3 with a lot of people or things close together（指人或物）稠密的；密集的: *a thick forest* 茂密的森林
4 If a liquid is thick, it does not flow easily（指液体）浓的；黏稠的: *This paint is too thick.* 这种颜料太稠了。✪ opposite 反义词: **thin**
5 difficult to see through 不清澈的；混浊的: *thick smoke* 浓烟

thickness /'θɪknəs; 'θɪknɪs/ *noun* 名词 (no plural 无复数)
The wood is 3 cm in thickness. 这块木料厚3厘米。

thief /θi:f; θif/ *noun* 名词 (*plural* 复数作 **thieves** /θi:vz; θivz/)
a person who steals something 贼；小偷: *A thief stole my car.* 小偷把我的汽车偷走了。

thigh /θaɪ; θaɪ/ *noun* 名词
the part of your leg above your knee 大腿；股 ☞ picture on page C2 见第C2页图

thin /θɪn; θɪn/ *adjective* 形容词 (**thinner, thinnest**)
1 not far from one side to the other; not thick 薄的；细的: *The walls in this house are very thin.* 这所房子的墙很薄。◇ *I cut the bread into thin slices.* 我把面包切成薄片了。☞ picture on page C26 见第C26页图
2 not fat 瘦的: *He's tall and thin.* 他又高又瘦。☞ picture on page C26 见第C26页图
3 If a liquid is thin, it flows easily like water（指液体）稀薄的，多水的: *The soup was very thin.* 这个汤很稀。✪ opposite 反义词: **thick**
4 not close together 稀疏的；稀少的: *My father's hair is getting thin.* 我父亲的头发越来越稀了。

thing /θɪŋ; θɪŋ/ *noun* 名词
1 an object 东西；物: *What's that red thing?* 那个红的是什么东西？
2 what happens or what you do 事；事情: *A strange thing happened to me yesterday.* 昨天我出了件怪事。◇ *That was a difficult thing to do.* 那件事情很难做。
3 an idea or subject 想法；意见；题目: *We talked about a lot of things.* 我们谈了很多问题。
4 things (plural 复数) what you own 个人的所有物: *Have you packed your things for the journey?* 你把你旅行用的东西都收拾好了吗？

think /θɪŋk; θɪŋk/ *verb* 动词 (**thinks, thinking, thought** /θɔ:t; θɔt/, **has thought**)
1 use your mind 思索；思考；想: *Think before you answer the question.* 这个问题要先想一想再回答。
2 believe something 认为；相信: *I think it's going to rain.* 我看要下雨了。◇ *'Do you think Sara will come tomorrow?' 'Yes, I think so.'* (= I think that she will come) "您认为萨拉明天来吗？""我认为她能来。"◇ *I think they live in Rome but I'm not sure.* 我相信他们住在罗马，可是我并没有十足的把握。

T

this, these, that and **those**
this、**these**、**that**、**those**的用法

He caught **this** fish.
他钓到了这条鱼。

He didn't catch **that** fish.
他没钓到那条鱼。

think about somebody or 或 **something** **1** have somebody or something in your mind 想着或想起某人或某事物: *I often think about that day.* 我常常想着那一天。 **2** try to decide whether to do something 考虑是否做某事物: *Paul is thinking about leaving his job.* 保罗正在想着要辞职的事。

think of somebody or 或 **something**
1 have something in your mind 想着或想起某人或某事物: *I can't think of her name.* 我想不起她的名字来了。 **2** have an opinion about somebody or something 对某人或某事物有某种看法: *What do you think of this music?* 您认为这种音乐怎么样？ **3** try to decide whether to do something 考虑是否做某事物: *We're thinking of going to America.* 我们正在考虑去不去美国的事。

third /θɜ:d; θɝd/ *adjective, adverb, noun* 形容词，副词，名词
1 3rd 第3（个）；第三（个）
2 one of three equal parts of something; 1/3 三分之一

thirst /θɜ:st; θɝst/ *noun* 名词 (no plural 无复数)
the feeling you have when you want to drink something 渴 ✪ Be careful! You cannot say 'I have thirst' in English. You must say 'I am thirsty'. 注意！不可说：I have thirst。要说：I am thirsty。

thirsty /'θɜ:sti; 'θɝstɪ/ *adjective* 形容词 (**thirstier, thirstiest**)
If you are thirsty, you want to drink something 渴的: *Salty food makes you thirsty.* 吃了咸的东西就觉得渴。

thirteen /ˌθɜ:'ti:n; θɝ'tin/ *number* 数词
13 十三

thirteenth /ˌθɜ:'ti:nθ; θɝ'tinθ/ *adjective, adverb, noun* 形容词，副词，名词
13th 第13（个）；第十三（个）

thirty /'θɜ:ti; 'θɝtɪ/ *number* 数词
1 30 三十
2 the thirties (plural 复数) the numbers, years or temperature between 30 and 39 ＊30至39（之间的数目、年数或温度）
in your thirties between the ages of 30 and 39 年岁在30至39之间；三十多岁

thirtieth /'θɜ:tiəθ; 'θɝtɪɪθ/ *adjective, adverb, noun* 形容词，副词，名词
30th 第30（个）；第三十（个）

this[1] /ðɪs; ðɪs/ *adjective, pronoun* 形容词，代词 (*plural* 复数作 **these**)
a word that you use to talk about a person or thing that is here or now 这；

这个: *Come and look at this photo.* 来看看这张照片。◇ *This is my sister.* 这是我妹妹。◇ *I am on holiday this week.* 我这个星期放假。◇ *How much does this cost?* 这个多少钱？☞ picture on page 512 见第512页图

this² /ðɪs; ðɪs/ *adverb* 副词
so 这样；如此: *The other film was not this good* (= not as good as this film). 那部影片没有这么好（=没有这部影片好）。

thistle /'θɪsl; 'θɪsl̩/ *noun* 名词
a plant with purple flowers and leaves that have sharp points 蓟（花呈紫色，叶有刺）

thorn /θɔ:n; θɔrn/ *noun* 名词
a sharp point that grows on a plant（植物的）刺: *Rose bushes have thorns.* 玫瑰丛有很多刺。

thorough /'θʌrə; 'θɝo/ *adjective* 形容词
careful and complete 细致而完全的；彻底的: *We gave the room a thorough clean.* 我们把屋子彻底打扫了一下。

thoroughly /'θʌrəli; 'θɝolɪ/ *adverb* 副词
1 carefully and completely 细致而完全地；彻底地: *He cleaned the room thoroughly.* 他把房间彻底打扫了一遍。
2 completely; very or very much 完全；很；非常: *I thoroughly enjoyed the film.* 我非常喜欢这部影片。

those /ðəʊz; ðoz/ *adjective, pronoun* 形容词，代词 (plural 复数)
a word that you use to talk about people or things that are there or then 那些: *I don't know those boys.* 我不认识那些男孩儿。◇ *Her grandfather was born in 1850. In those days, there were no cars.* 她祖父生于1850年。那个时代还没有汽车呢。◇ *Can I have those?* 把那些都给我行吗？☞ picture on page 512 见第512页图

though¹ /ðəʊ; ðo/ *conjunction* 连词
1 in spite of something; although 虽然；尽管: *I was very cold, though I was wearing my coat.* 虽然我穿着大衣，可是我还是很冷。◇ *Though she was in a hurry, she stopped to talk.* 尽管她正有急事，但是她仍然停下来谈谈话。
2 but 但是；可是: *I thought it was right though I wasn't sure.* 我认为那件事很对，不过我并没有把握。
as though in a way that makes you think something 不免使人想到某事物；好像: *The house looks as though nobody lives there.* 这所房子看起来好像没人住。◇ *I'm so hungry—I feel as though I haven't eaten for days!* 我饿极了——我觉得就像几天没吃饭似的！

though² /ðəʊ; ðo/ *adverb* 副词
however 然而；但是；可是: *I like him very much. I don't like his wife, though.* 我很喜欢他。可是我不喜欢他妻子。

thought¹ *form of* **think** ∗ **think** 的不同形式

thought² /θɔ:t; θɔt/ *noun* 名词
1 (no plural 无复数) thinking 思索；思考: *After a lot of thought, I decided not to take the job.* 我经过长时间考虑，决定不要那份工作了。
2 (*plural* 复数作 **thoughts**) an idea 想法；看法；意见: *Have you had any thoughts about what you want to do when you leave school?* 你中学毕业以后有什么打算吗？

thoughtful /'θɔ:tfl; 'θɔtfəl/ *adjective* 形容词
1 If you are thoughtful, you are thinking carefully 仔细思考的；深思的: *She listened with a thoughtful look on her face.* 她满脸沉思地听着。
2 A person who is thoughtful is kind, and thinks and cares about other people（指对别人）关心的；体贴的: *It was very thoughtful of you to cook us dinner.* 您给我们做了饭，想得真周到。

thousand /'θaʊznd; 'θaʊzn̩d/ *number* 数词
1 000 一千: *a thousand people* 一千人 ◇ *two thousand and fifteen* 两千零十五 ◇ *There were thousands of birds on the lake.* 湖上有成千只鸟。
thousandth /'θaʊznθ; 'θaʊzn̩θ/ *adjective, adverb, noun* 形容词，副词，名词
1 000th 第1 000（个）；第一千（个）

thread /θred; θrɛd/ *noun* 名词
a long thin piece of cotton, wool, etc that you use with a **needle** for sewing（缝纫用的）线（针叫做 **needle**）
thread *verb* 动词 (**threads, threading, threaded**)
put thread through the hole in a needle（用线）纫针

threat /θret; θrɛt/ *noun* 名词
1 a promise that you will hurt somebody if they do not do what you want 恐吓；威胁

T

2 a person or thing that may damage or hurt somebody or something 恐吓或威胁他人的人或事物: *Pollution is a threat to the lives of animals and people.* 环境污染能危及动物和人类的生命。

threaten /'θretn; 'θrɛtn̩/ *verb* 动词 (**threatens**, **threatening**, **threatened** /'θretnd; 'θrɛtn̩d/)

1 say that you will hurt somebody if they do not do what you want 恐吓；威胁: *They threatened to kill everyone on the plane.* 他们扬言要把飞机上的人都杀死。◇ *She threatened him with a knife.* 她用刀威胁着他。

2 seem ready to do something bad 似乎要做某种坏事: *The dark clouds threatened rain.* 有乌云就是预兆着要下雨了。

three /θri:; θri/ *number* 数词

3 三

threw *form of* **throw** ✳ **throw** 的不同形式

thrill /θrɪl; θrɪl/ *noun* 名词

a sudden strong feeling of excitement 兴奋；激动

thrill *verb* 动词 (**thrills**, **thrilling**, **thrilled** /θrɪld; θrɪld/)

make somebody feel strong excitement 使某人兴奋或激动

thrilled *adjective* 形容词

very happy and excited 非常兴奋或激动的: *We are all thrilled that you have won the prize.* 你获奖后我们都十分兴奋。

thrilling *adjective* 形容词

very exciting 使人兴奋或激动的: *a thrilling adventure* 令人激动的经历

thriller /'θrɪlə(r); 'θrɪlɚ/ *noun* 名词

an exciting book, film or play about a crime 关于罪案的小说、影片或戏剧

throat /θrəʊt; θrot/ *noun* 名词

1 the front part of your neck 颈（脖子的前面部分）☞ picture on page C2 见第C2页图

2 the part inside your neck that takes food and air down from your mouth into your body 喉咙；嗓子: *I've got a sore throat* (= my throat hurts). 我嗓子疼。

throb /θrɒb; θrɑb/ *verb* 动词 (**throbs**, **throbbing**, **throbbed** /θrɒbd; θrɑbd/)

beat quickly and strongly 快而强地搏动；悸动: *His heart was throbbing with excitement.* 他兴奋得心直跳。

throne /θrəʊn; θron/ *noun* 名词

a special chair where a king or queen sits（国王的）宝座

through /θru:; θru/ *preposition*, *adverb* 介词，副词

1 from one side or end of something to the other side or end 从某物的一边或一端到另一边或一端；穿过；通过: *We drove through the tunnel.* 我们开车穿过隧道。◇ *What can you see through the window?* 你透过窗户能看见什么？◇ *She opened the gate and we walked through.* 她把大门打开让我们走大门。☞ picture on page C4 见第C4页图

2 from the beginning to the end of something 从某事物的开始到结束；自始至终: *We travelled through the night.* 我们走了一夜。

3 connected by telephone 接通电话: *Can you put me through to Jill Knight, please?* 劳驾，请吉尔·奈特听电话。◇ *I tried to phone you but I couldn't get through.* 我给您打过电话，可是没打通。

4 because of somebody or something 由于某人或某事物: *She got the job through her father.* 她是通过她父亲而得到这份工作的。

throughout /θru'aʊt; θru'aʊt/ *preposition*, *adverb* 介词，副词

1 in every part of something 在某事物的各处或各方面: *We painted the house throughout.* 我们把整座房子都粉刷了一遍。◇ *She is famous throughout the world.* 她名闻全球。

2 from the beginning to the end of something 从某事物的开始到结束；自始至终: *They talked throughout the film.* 他们从电影开演到结束一直说个不停。

throw /θrəʊ; θro/ *verb* 动词 (**throws**, **throwing**, **threw** /θru:; θru/, **has thrown** /θrəʊn; θron/)

1 move your arm quickly to send something through the air 投掷；扔: *Throw the ball to Alex.* 把球扔给亚历克斯。◇ *The boys were throwing stones at people.* 那些男孩子向人扔石子。

2 do something quickly and without care 迅速而不细心地做某事: *She threw on her coat* (= put it on quickly) *and ran out of the house.* 她匆匆穿上大衣就从房子里跑出去了。

3 move your body or part of it quickly

迅速移动身体或身体某部：*He threw his arms up.* 他一下子把手臂举起来了。

throw something away 或 **out** put something in the dustbin because you do not want it 把某物扔进垃圾箱；丢弃：*Don't throw that box away.* 别把那个盒子扔了。

throw *noun* 名词
What a good throw! 扔得多好哇！

thrust /θrʌst; θrʌst/ *verb* 动词 (**thrusts, thrusting, thrust, has thrust**)
push somebody or something suddenly and strongly 突然而用力地推或挤某人或某物：*She thrust the money into my hand.* 她把钱硬塞进我手里了。

thrust *noun* 名词
a strong push（用力的）推或挤

thud /θʌd; θʌd/ *noun* 名词
the sound that a heavy thing makes when it hits something 重物击中某物而发出的声音：*The book hit the floor with a thud.* 那本书砰的一声掉到地板上了。

thumb /θʌm; θʌm/ *noun* 名词
the short thick finger at the side of your hand 拇指 ☞ picture on page C2 见第C2页图

thumbtack /'θʌmtæk; 'θʌm,tæk/ *American English for* **drawing-pin** 美式英语，即 **drawing-pin**

thump /θʌmp; θʌmp/ *verb* 动词 (**thumps, thumping, thumped** /θʌmpt; θʌmpt/)
1 hit something hard with your hand or a heavy thing 用手或重物用力击中某物：*He thumped on the door.* 他使劲敲着门。
2 make a loud sound by hitting or beating hard 敲或打而发出巨响：*Her heart was thumping with fear.* 她害怕得心怦怦直跳。

thunder /'θʌndə(r); 'θʌndɚ/ *noun* 名词 (no plural 无复数)
a loud noise in the sky when there is a storm 雷；雷声 ✪ The light that you see in the sky in a storm is called **lightning**. 闪电叫做 **lightning**。

thunder *verb* 动词 (**thunders, thundering, thundered** /'θʌndəd; 'θʌndɚd/)
1 make the sound of thunder 打雷：*It thundered all night.* 夜间一直在打雷。
2 make a sound like thunder 发出雷鸣般的声音：*The lorries thundered along the road.* 卡车在路上发出隆隆的声音。

thunderstorm /'θʌndəstɔ:m; 'θʌndɚ,stɔrm/ *noun* 名词
a storm with a lot of rain, thunder and lightning 雷雨；雷暴

Thursday /'θɜ:zdeɪ; 'θɝzdɪ/ *noun* 名词
the fifth day of the week, next after Wednesday 星期四

thus /ðʌs; ðʌs/ *adverb* 副词
1 in this way 用这种方法；这样：*Hold the wheel in both hands, thus.* 用双手握住轮盘，像这样。
2 because of this 因此；所以：*He was very busy and was thus unable to come to the meeting.* 他很忙所以不能来开会。

tick[1] /tɪk; tɪk/ *noun* 名词
the sound that a clock or watch makes（钟表发出的）滴答声

tick *verb* 动词 (**ticks, ticking, ticked** /tɪkt; tɪkt/)
make this sound（指钟表）发出滴答声：*I could hear a clock ticking.* 我听见有个钟滴答作响。

tick[2] /tɪk; tɪk/ *noun* 名词
a small mark like this ✓, that shows that something is correct, for example 像钩的符号 ✓（例如表示正确）：*Put a tick by the correct answer.* 在正确答案旁边标上对号。

tick *verb* 动词 (**ticks, ticking, ticked** /tɪkt; tɪkt/)
make a mark like this ✓ by something 在某处旁边标上对号 ✓：*Tick the right answer.* 在正确答案旁边标上对号。

ticket /'tɪkɪt; 'tɪkɪt/ *noun* 名词
a small piece of paper or card that you must buy to travel or to go into a cinema, theatre or museum, for example 票（例如车船票、机票或电影票、戏票或博物馆入场券等）：*Do you want a single or a return ticket?* 您要单程票还是往返票？◇ *a theatre ticket* 戏票 ◇ *a ticket collector* (= a person who takes tickets from people on a train or at a station) 收票员（= 火车上的或车站的）

ticket office /'tɪkɪt ɒfɪs; 'tɪkɪt ,ɔfɪs/ *noun* 名词
a place where you buy tickets 售票处

tickle /'tɪkl; 'tɪkḷ/ *verb* 动词 (**tickles, tickling, tickled** /'tɪkld; 'tɪkḷd/)
1 touch somebody lightly with your fingers to make them laugh 用手指轻触某人使之发痒而发笑：*She tickled the baby's feet.* 她搔孩子的脚逗他笑。

T

2 have the feeling that something is touching you lightly 有发痒的感觉: *My nose tickles.* 我鼻子痒痒。

tide /taɪd; taɪd/ *noun* 名词
the movement of the sea towards the land and away from the land 潮；海潮；潮汐: *The tide is coming in.* 涨潮了。◇ *The tide is going out.* 退潮了。✪ **High tide** is when the sea is nearest the land, and **low tide** is when the sea is furthest from the land. 高潮（海面上升至接近陆地的最高潮位）叫做 **high tide**，低潮（海面下降至离开陆地的最低潮位）叫做 **low tide**。

tidy /'taɪdi; 'taɪdɪ/ *adjective* 形容词 (**tidier, tidiest**)
1 with everything in the right place 整齐的: *Her room is very tidy.* 她的屋子很整齐。
2 If you are tidy, you like to have everything in the right place 爱整齐的: *a tidy boy* 爱整齐的男孩儿
✪ opposite 反义词: **untidy**
tidily /'taɪdɪli; 'taɪdɪlɪ/ *adverb* 副词
Put the books back tidily when you've finished with them. 书用完后要整整齐齐地放回原处。
tidiness /'taɪdinəs; 'taɪdɪnɪs/ *noun* 名词 (no plural 无复数)
being tidy 整齐

tidy, tidy up *verb* 动词 (**tidies, tidying, tidied** /'taɪdid; 'taɪdɪd/, **has tidied**)
make something tidy 使某事物整齐: *I tidied the house before my parents arrived.* 我父母来到以前我先把房子收拾了一下。◇ *Can you help me to tidy up?* 你来帮助我弄整齐了行吗？

tie¹ /taɪ; taɪ/ *noun* 名词
1 a long thin piece of cloth that you wear round your neck with a shirt 领带 ☞ picture at **suit** 见 **suit** 词条插图
2 when two teams or players have the same number of points at the end of a game or competition（比赛或竞争中的）平手；得分相同: *The match ended in a tie.* 那场比赛没分胜负。
3 something that holds people together 把人结合在一起的事物: *Our school has ties with a school in France.* 我们学校跟法国的一所学校有联系。

tie² /taɪ; taɪ/ *verb* 动词 (**ties, tying, tied** /taɪd; taɪd/, **has tied**)
1 fasten two ends of string, rope, etc together to hold somebody or something in place（用绳索等）把人或物捆住；绑；系；拴: *The prisoner was tied to a chair.* 囚犯被绑在椅子上了。◇ *I tied a scarf round my neck.* 我系了一条围巾。
2 end a game or competition with the same number of points for both teams or players（指比赛或竞争中的双方）打成平手；得分相同: *France tied with Spain for second place.* 法国队和西班牙队得分相同并列第二名。
tie somebody up put a piece of rope around somebody so that they cannot move 把某人捆起来: *The robbers tied up the owner of the shop.* 劫匪把店主捆起来了。
tie something up put a piece of string or rope around something to hold it in place 把某物捆起来: *I tied up the parcel with string.* 我用绳子把包裹捆起来了。

tiger /'taɪgə(r); 'taɪgɚ/ *noun* 名词
a wild animal like a big cat, with yellow fur and black stripes. Tigers live in Asia. 虎；老虎（产于亚洲）

tight /taɪt; taɪt/ *adjective* 形容词 (**tighter, tightest**)
1 fixed firmly so that you cannot move it easily 牢固的；紧的: *a tight knot* 很紧的结 ◇ *I can't open this jar of jam—the lid is too tight.* 这个果酱的罐子我打不开——盖子太紧了。
2 small, so that there is no space between it and your body 与身体的空隙极小的；（衣服鞋袜等）瘦的: *These shoes are too tight.* 这双鞋穿着太紧了。◇ *tight trousers* 瘦裤子
✪ opposite 反义词: **loose** ☞ picture on page C27 见第C27页图
tight, tightly *adverb* 副词
Hold tight! 握紧了！◇ *I tied the string tightly around the box.* 我用绳子把盒子捆紧了。

tighten /'taɪtn; 'taɪtn̩/ *verb* 动词 (**tightens, tightening, tightened** /'taɪtnd; 'taɪtn̩d/)
become tighter or make something tighter（使某物）紧: *Can you tighten this screw?* 你能把这颗螺丝拧紧吗？✪ opposite 反义词: **loosen**

tightrope /'taɪtrəʊp; 'taɪt,rop/ *noun* 名词
a rope or wire high above the ground. **Acrobats** walk along tightropes in a

circus.（供杂技演员表演用的）绳索；钢丝绳（杂技演员叫做 **acrobat**，马戏团叫做 **circus**）

tights /taɪts; taɪts/ *noun* 名词 (plural 复数) a thin piece of clothing that a woman or girl wears over her feet and legs 裤袜: *a pair of tights* 一条裤袜 ☞ picture at **dress** 见 **dress** 词条插图

tile /taɪl; taɪl/ *noun* 名词 a flat square thing. We use tiles for covering roofs, walls and floors.（盖屋顶、贴墙及铺地用的）瓦，瓷砖，板，片

till[1] /tɪl; tɪl/ *conjunction* 连词 up to the time when 直到…时（为止）: *Let's wait till the rain stops.* 咱们等到雨停了再说吧。

till *preposition* 介词

1 up to a certain time 直到（某一时刻）: *I'll be here till Monday.* 我从现在到星期一都在这儿。

2 before 在（某一时刻）以前: *I didn't arrive till six o'clock.* 我六点钟才到。

till[2] /tɪl; tɪl/ *noun* 名词 a drawer or box for money in a shop（商店的）放钱的抽屉或箱子

tilt /tɪlt; tɪlt/ *verb* 动词 (**tilts**, **tilting**, **tilted**) have one side higher than the other; move something so that it has one side higher than the other（使某物）倾斜: *She tilted the tray and all the glasses fell off.* 她把托盘一歪，玻璃杯就都倒了。

timber /ˈtɪmbə(r); ˈtɪmbɚ/ *noun* 名词 (no plural 无复数) wood that we use for building and making things（用于建筑或制造物品的）木材；木料

time[1] /taɪm; taɪm/ *noun* 名词

1 (*plural* 复数作 **times**) a certain point in the day or night, that you say in hours and minutes（一天或一夜中以时和分表达的某一点的）时间: *'What time is it?' 'It's twenty past six.'* "现在几点了？""六点二十了。" ◇ *What's the time?* 几点钟了？◇ *Can you tell me the times of trains to Brighton, please?* 劳驾，您能不能告诉我到布莱顿的火车都有几点钟的？

2 (no plural 无复数) all the seconds, minutes, hours, days, weeks, months and years（以秒、分、小时、天、星期、月、年等表达的或长或短的）时间: *Time passes quickly when you're busy.* 人要是忙的时候就觉得时间过得快。

3 (no plural 无复数) an amount of minutes, days, etc（以分、天等表达的一段的）时间: *They have lived here for a long time.* 他们在这儿住了很长时间。◇ *I haven't got time to help you now—I'm late for school.* 我现在没时间帮你忙——我上学已经晚了。◇ *It takes a long time to learn a language.* 学一种语言要花很长时间。

4 (*plural* 复数作 **times**) a certain moment or occasion 次数；次；回: *I've seen this film four times.* 这部影片我看了四遍了。◇ *Come and visit us next time you're in England.* 你下次到英国的时候，到我们这儿来玩儿玩儿。

5 (*plural* 复数作 **times**) experience; something that you do 经历；做的事: *We had a great time on holiday.* 我们假期过得很痛快。

6 (*plural* 复数作 **times**) certain years in history（历史上的）年代；时期: *In Shakespeare's times, not many people could read.* 在莎士比亚时代，识字的人不多。

at a time together; on one occasion 一次；每次: *The lift can carry six people at a time.* 这个电梯每次能载六个人。

at one time in the past, but not now 从前；曾经: *We were in the same class at one time.* 我们以前是同班同学。

at the time then 那时候；当时: *My family moved to London in 1986—I was four at the time.* 我们家在1986年搬到了伦敦——我当时四岁。

at times sometimes 有时候: *A teacher's job can be very difficult at times.* 教书工作有时候很困难。

by the time when 那时候: *By the time we arrived they had eaten all the food.* 我们到的时候，他们把东西都吃完了。

for the time being now, but not for long 暂时: *You can stay here for the time being, until you find a flat.* 您可以暂时先在这儿住，等找到房子再搬。

from time to time sometimes; not often 有时候；偶尔: *I see my cousin from time to time.* 我有时候见到我的表弟。

have a good time enjoy yourself 玩儿得高兴: *Have a good time at the party!* 在聚会上好好玩儿一玩儿吧！

in a week's, etc time after a week, etc 一个星期…以后: *I'll see you in a month's time.* 我一个月以后见你。

in good time at the right time or early 及时；早: *I want to get to the station in good time.* 我想早点儿到车站。

in time **1** not late 不迟；及时: *If you hurry, you'll arrive in time for the film.* 你动作快些就能赶上这场电影了。**2** at some time in the future 将来: *You will find speaking English easier in time.* 你将来就会觉得说英语比较容易了。

it's about time words that you use to say that something should be done now 用以表示现在应该做某事的词语: *It's about time you started studying if you want to pass the exam.* 你要想考及格，可该念念书了。

it's time to it is the right time to do something 是做某事的时候了: *It's time to go home.* 该回家了。

on time not late or early 不早不晚；准时: *My train was on time.* 我坐的这趟火车正点运行。

spend time use time to do something 用时间做某事: *I spend a lot of time playing tennis.* 我打网球花了很多时间。

take your time do something slowly 从容做某事

tell the time read the time from a clock or watch 认出钟表指示的时间: *Can your children tell the time?* 您的孩子会看表了吗？

time after time, time and time again many times 多次；屡次；一再

time² /taɪm; taɪm/ *verb* 动词 (**times, timing, timed** /taɪmd; taɪmd/)

1 plan something so that it will happen when you want 按预定时间使某事发生: *The bomb was timed to explode at six o'clock.* 那颗炸弹已经校准至六点钟爆炸。

2 measure how much time it takes to do something 计算做某事需要多少时间；计时: *We timed the journey—it took half an hour.* 我们计算了一下这趟路程的时间——用了半个钟头。

times /taɪmz; taɪmz/ *noun* 名词 (plural 复数)

a word that you use to show how much bigger, smaller, more expensive, etc one thing is than another thing (用以表示一事物比另一事物大、多、贵等的) 倍数，倍；(用以表示一事物比另一事物小、少、便宜等的) 几分之一: *Edinburgh is five times bigger than Oxford.* 爱丁堡是牛津的五倍。◇ *Oxford is five times smaller than Edinburgh.* 牛津是爱丁堡的五分之一。

times *preposition* 介词

multiplied by (数学计算中的) 乘以: *Three times four is twelve.* 三乘以四等于十二。

timetable /ˈtaɪmteɪbl; ˈtaɪmˌtebl̩/ *noun* 名词

a list of times when something happens 时间表: *A train timetable shows when trains arrive and leave.* 列车时刻表介绍的是火车到达和离开的时间。◇ *A school timetable shows when lessons start.* 学校的课程表指示的是课程开始的时间。

timid /ˈtɪmɪd; ˈtɪmɪd/ *adjective* 形容词

shy and easily frightened 害羞的；胆怯的

timidly *adverb* 副词

She opened the door timidly and came in. 她怯生生地开门进来了。

tin /tɪn; tɪn/ *noun* 名词

1 (no plural 无复数) a soft white metal 锡

2 (*plural* 复数作 **tins**) a metal container for food and drink that keeps it fresh 罐头盒: *I opened a tin of beans.* 我打开了一个豆子罐头。☞ picture at **container** 见 **container** 词条插图

tinned /tɪnd; tɪnd/ *adjective* 形容词

in a tin so that it will stay fresh 罐头的: *tinned peaches* 罐头桃

tin-opener /ˈtɪn əʊpənə(r); ˈtɪnˌopənɚ/ *noun* 名词

a tool for opening tins 开罐器；罐头刀

tiny /ˈtaɪni; ˈtaɪnɪ/ *adjective* 形容词 (**tinier, tiniest**)

very small 极小的；微小的: *Ants are tiny insects.* 蚂蚁是很小的昆虫。

tip¹ /tɪp; tɪp/ *noun* 名词

the pointed or thin end of something (物体的) 尖端；尖儿: *the tips of your fingers* 你的手指尖儿

tip² /tɪp; tɪp/ *verb* 动词 (**tips, tipping, tipped** /tɪpt; tɪpt/)

give a small, extra amount of money to somebody who has done a job for you, for example a waiter or a taxi-driver (给服务员或司机等的) 小费；小账: *Do you tip hairdressers in your country?* 在你们国家，你们给理发师小费吗？

tip *noun* 名词

I left a tip on the table. 我在桌子上留下小费。

tip³ /tɪp; tɪp/ *noun* 名词

a small piece of advice 小小的建议:

She gave me some useful tips on how to pass the exam. 她给了我一些要想考试及格的提示。

tip[4] /tɪp; tɪp/ *verb* 动词 (**tips**, **tipping**, **tipped** /tɪpt; tɪpt/)

1 move so that one side goes up or down; move something so that one side goes up or down（使某物）侧边向上或向下: *Don't tip your chair back.* 别把椅子弄得向后仰。

2 turn something so that the things inside fall out 翻转某物把里面东西倒出来: *She opened a tin of beans and tipped them into a bowl.* 她打开了一个豆子罐头，倒在碗里。

tip over turn over; make something turn over（使某物）翻转: *The boat tipped over and we all fell in the water.* 船翻了，我们都掉进水里了。◇ *Don't tip your drink over!* 别把你喝的东西弄翻了！

tiptoe /ˈtɪptəʊ; ˈtɪpˌto/ *verb* 动词 (**tiptoes**, **tiptoeing**, **tiptoed** /ˈtɪptəʊd; ˈtɪpˌtod/)

walk quietly on your toes 踮着脚悄悄地走: *He tiptoed into the bedroom.* 他踮着脚悄悄地走进了卧室。

on tiptoe on your toes 踮着脚: *She walked on tiptoe.* 她踮着脚走。

tire *American English for* **tyre** 美式英语，即 **tyre**

tired /ˈtaɪəd; taɪrd/ *adjective* 形容词

If you are tired, you need to rest or sleep 疲倦的；困倦的: *I've been working all day and I'm really tired.* 我工作了一整天，真把我累坏了。◇ *He's feeling tired.* 他觉得很累。

be tired of something have had or done too much of something, so that you do not want it any longer 对某事物感到厌倦: *I'm tired of watching TV—let's go out.* 我看腻了电视——咱们出去吧。

tiring /ˈtaɪərɪŋ; ˈtaɪrɪŋ/ *adjective* 形容词

If something is tiring, it makes you tired 使人疲倦的: *a tiring journey* 使人疲倦的路程

tissue /ˈtɪʃuː; ˈtɪʃʊ/ *noun* 名词

a thin piece of soft paper that you use as a handkerchief（用作手帕的）纸巾: *a box of tissues* 一盒纸巾

tissue-paper /ˈtɪʃuː peɪpə(r); ˈtɪʃʊˌpepɚ/ *noun* 名词 (no plural 无复数)

thin paper that you use for wrapping things（包装物品用的）薄纸；绵纸

title /ˈtaɪtl; ˈtaɪtḷ/ *noun* 名词

1 the name of something, for example a book, film or picture（书、影片或图片的）名称；题目；标题: *What is the title of this poem?* 这首诗的题目叫什么？

2 a word like 'Mr', 'Mrs' or 'Doctor' that you put in front of a person's name 称号；头衔（例如 Mr、Mrs 或 Doctor 等）

to[1] /tə, tu, tuː; tə, tʊ, tu/ *preposition* 介词

1 a word that shows where somebody or something is going, etc 表示某人或某事物向某处行进等的词；向；朝；对着: *She went to Italy.* 她到意大利去了。◇ *James has gone to school.* 詹姆斯上学去了。◇ *I gave the book to Paula.* 我把书给葆拉了。◇ *He sent a letter to his parents.* 他给父母寄了一封信。◇ *Be kind to animals.* 要善待动物。

2 a word that shows how many minutes before the hour 表示差多少分钟就到某点钟的词: *It's two minutes to six.* 现在差两分钟就到六点了。☞ Look at page C8. 见第C8页。

3 a word that shows the last or the highest time, price, etc（指时间、价格等）表示达到最大限度的词: *The museum is open from 9.30 to 5.30.* 博物馆从9时30分至5时30分开馆。◇ *Jeans cost from £20 to £45.* 牛仔裤的价格从20英镑到45英镑不等。

4 on or against something 在某事物上或对着某事物: *He put his hands to his ears.* 他用手捂着耳朵。

5 a word that shows how something changes 表示某事物变成什么状况的词: *The sky changed from blue to grey.* 天空由蓝色变成了灰色。

6 a word that shows why 表示原因的词: *I came to help.* 我是来帮忙的。

7 a word that you use for comparing things 表示相比的词: *I prefer football to tennis.* 我喜欢足球，不喜欢网球。

to[2] /tə, tu; tə, tʊ, tu/

a word that you use before verbs to make the **infinitive** 用于动词前，构成不定式（**infinitive**）的词: *I want to go home.* 我想回家。◇ *Don't forget to write.* 别忘了写信。◇ *She asked me to go but I didn't want to* (= to go). 她叫我走，可是我不想走。

toad /təʊd; tod/ *noun* 名词

an animal like a big frog, with a rough skin 蟾蜍；癞蛤蟆

T

toast[1] /təʊst; tost/ *noun* 名词 (no plural 无复数)
a thin piece of bread that you have cooked so that it is brown 烤面包片: *I had a slice of toast and jam for breakfast.* 我早饭吃的是一片烤面包片加果酱。
toast *verb* 动词 (**toasts**, **toasting**, **toasted**)
cook bread to make it brown 把面包片烤黄: *toasted sandwiches* 烤面包片三明治
toaster *noun* 名词
a machine for making toast 面包片加热器

toast[2] /təʊst; tost/ *verb* 动词 (**toasts**, **toasting**, **toasted**)
hold up a glass of wine and wish somebody happiness or success before you drink 举杯祝酒: *We all toasted the bride and groom* (at a wedding). 我们大家（在婚礼上）向新娘和新郎举杯祝酒。
toast *noun* 名词
They drank a toast to the Queen. 他们为女王祝福而干杯。

tobacco /tə'bækəʊ; tə'bæko/ *noun* 名词 (no plural 无复数)
special dried leaves that people smoke in cigarettes, cigars and pipes 烟叶

T

today /tə'deɪ; tə'de/ *adverb*, *noun* 副词，名词 (no plural 无复数)
1 (on) this day 今天；今日: *What shall we do today?* 我们今天做什么？◇ *Today is Friday.* 今天星期五。
2 (at) the present time; now 目前；现在: *Most families in Britain today have a car.* 在英国，现今多数家庭都有汽车。

toe /təʊ; to/ *noun* 名词
1 one of the five parts at the end of your foot（人的）脚趾 ☞ picture on page C2 见第C2页图
2 the part of a shoe or sock that covers the end of your foot（鞋或袜的）足尖部
toenail /'təʊneɪl; 'toˌnel/ *noun* 名词
the hard part at the end of your toe（人的）脚趾甲 ☞ picture on page C2 见第C2页图

toffee /'tɒfi; 'tɔfɪ/ *noun* 名词
hard brown sweet food made from sugar, butter and water 太妃糖

together /tə'geðə(r); tə'gɛðɚ/ *adverb* 副词
1 with each other or close to each other 在一起；共同: *John and Lisa usually walk home together.* 约翰和莉萨经常一起走着回家。◇ *Stand with your feet together.* 双脚并拢站好。◇ *They live together.* 他们住在一起。
2 so that they are joined to or mixed with each other 致使相结合或相混合: *Tie the ends of the rope together.* 把绳子两端系在一起。◇ *Add these numbers together.* 把这些数字加起来。◇ *Mix the eggs and sugar together.* 把鸡蛋和糖混合在一起。

toilet /'tɔɪlət; 'tɔɪlɪt/ *noun* 名词
a large bowl with a seat, that you use when you need to empty waste from your body. The room that it is in is also called a **toilet** 恭桶；厕所: *I'm going to the toilet.* 我去上厕所。
toilet paper /'tɔɪlət peɪpə(r); 'tɔɪlɪt ˌpepɚ/ *noun* 名词 (no plural 无复数)
paper that you use in the toilet 卫生纸；手纸
toilet roll /'tɔɪlət rəʊl; 'tɔɪlɪt ˌrol/ *noun* 名词
a roll of paper that you use in the toilet 卫生纸卷；手纸卷

token /'təʊkən; 'tokən/ *noun* 名词
1 a small thing that you use to show something else 标志；象征: *This gift is a token of our friendship.* 这件礼物是我们友谊的象征。
2 a piece of paper, plastic or metal that you use instead of money to pay for something（代替钱币作付款用的纸的、塑料的或金属的）代币，票: *a book token* 书券

told *form of* **tell** ✳ **tell** 的不同形式

tolerant /'tɒlərənt; 'tɑlərənt/ *adjective* 形容词
If you are tolerant, you let people do things although you may not like or understand them 容忍的；宽容的: *You need to be very tolerant with young children.* 对小孩子需要有很大耐心。✪ opposite 反义词: **intolerant**
tolerance /'tɒlərəns; 'tɑlərəns/ *noun* 名词 (no plural 无复数)
tolerance of other religions 对其他宗教的宽容 ✪ opposite 反义词: **intolerance**

tolerate /'tɒləreɪt; 'tɑləˌret/ *verb* 动词 (**tolerates**, **tolerating**, **tolerated**)
let people do something that you may not like or understand 容忍；宽容: *He won't tolerate rudeness.* 他不容忍有粗暴行为。

tomato /təˈmɑːtəʊ; təˈmeto/ *noun* 名词 (*plural* 复数作 **tomatoes**)
a soft red fruit that you cook or eat in salads 西红柿；番茄: *tomato soup* 西红柿汤

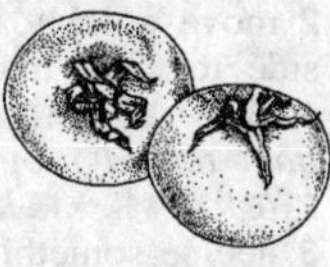
tomato 西红柿

tomb /tuːm; tum/ *noun* 名词
a thing made of stone where a dead person's body is buried 坟墓

tomorrow /təˈmɒrəʊ; təˈmɔro/ *adverb, noun* 副词，名词 (no plural 无复数)
(on) the day after today 明天；明日: *Let's go swimming tomorrow.* 咱们明天游泳去吧。◇ *I'll see you tomorrow morning.* 我明天上午见您。◇ *We are going home the day after tomorrow.* 我们后天回家。

ton /tʌn; tʌn/ *noun* 名词
1 a measure of weight (= 1 016 kilograms). There are 2 240 **pounds** in a ton. 1英吨（重量单位，等于1 016公斤。1英吨等于2 240磅，磅叫做 **pound**）✪ In the USA, a ton is 2 000 pounds. 在美国，1美吨等于2 000磅。
2 tons (plural 复数) a lot 大量；很多: *He's got tons of money.* 他有很多钱。

tone /təʊn; ton/ *noun* 名词
how something sounds 声调；音调；腔调: *I knew he was angry by the tone of his voice.* 我一听他的语气就知道他生气了。

tongue /tʌŋ; tʌŋ/ *noun* 名词
the soft part inside your mouth that moves when you talk or eat 舌头
tongue-twister /ˈtʌŋ ˌtwɪstə(r); ˈtʌŋˌtwɪstə/ *noun* 名词
words that are difficult to say together quickly 绕口令: *'Red lorry, yellow lorry' is a tongue-twister.* ∗ red lorry, yellow lorry是英语的绕口令。

tonight /təˈnaɪt; təˈnaɪt/ *adverb, noun* 副词，名词 (no plural 无复数)
(on) the evening or night of today（在）今天晚上或今天夜里: *I'm going to a party tonight.* 我今天晚上去参加聚会。

tonne /tʌn; tʌn/ *noun* 名词
a measure of weight. There are 1 000 **kilograms** in a tonne. 吨；公吨（重量单位，1吨等于1 000公斤，公斤叫做 **kilogram**）

too /tuː; tu/ *adverb* 副词
1 also; as well 也；又；还: *Green is my favourite colour but I like blue too.* 我最喜欢绿色，也喜欢蓝色。
2 more than you want or need 过于；过度: *These shoes are too big.* 这双鞋太大了。◇ *She put too much milk in my coffee.* 她在我的咖啡里放的奶太多。

took *form of* **take** ∗ **take** 的不同形式

tool /tuːl; tul/ *noun* 名词
a thing that you hold in your hand and use to do a special job（用手持的）工具: *Hammers and saws are tools.* 锤子和锯都是工具。

tooth /tuːθ; tuθ/ *noun* 名词 (*plural* 复数作 **teeth** /tiːθ; tiθ/)
1 one of the hard white things in your mouth that you use for eating 牙；牙齿: *I brush my teeth after every meal.* 我每次吃完饭都刷牙。

> ✪ A **dentist** is a person whose job is to look after teeth. 牙医叫做 **dentist**。If a tooth is bad, the dentist may **fill** it or **take** it **out**. 补牙叫做 **fill** it，拔牙叫做 **take it out**。People who have lost their own teeth can wear **false teeth**. 假牙叫做 **false tooth**。

2 one of the long sharp parts of a comb or saw（梳子或锯的）齿
toothache /ˈtuːθeɪk; ˈtuθˌek/ *noun* 名词 (no plural 无复数)
a pain in your tooth 牙疼: *I've got toothache.* 我牙疼。
toothbrush /ˈtuːθbrʌʃ; ˈtuθˌbrʌʃ/ *noun* 名词 (*plural* 复数作 **toothbrushes**)
a small brush for cleaning your teeth 牙刷
toothpaste /ˈtuːθpeɪst; ˈtuθˌpest/ *noun* 名词 (no plural 无复数)
stuff that you put on your toothbrush and use for cleaning your teeth 牙膏

top[1] /tɒp; tɑp/ *noun* 名词
1 the highest part of something 顶部；顶端: *There's a church at the top of the hill.* 山顶上有座教堂。
2 a cover that you put on something to close it 盖子；盖儿: *Where's the top of this jar?* 这个罐子的盖儿哪去了？
3 a piece of clothing that you wear on the top part of your body 上衣

on top on its highest part 在最高处；在上边: *The cake had cream on top.* 这个蛋糕上面有奶油。

on top of something on or over something 在某物的上边或上方: *A tree fell on top of my car.* 有棵树倒在我的汽车上了。

top[2] /tɒp; tɑp/ *adjective* 形容词
highest 最高的: *Put this book on the top shelf.* 把这本书放在架子的最上层。

topic /ˈtɒpɪk; ˈtɑpɪk/ *noun* 名词
something that you talk, learn or write about; a subject 话题；论题；题目: *The topic of the discussion was war.* 讨论的题目是战争问题。

torch /tɔːtʃ; tɔrtʃ/ *noun* 名词 (*plural* 复数作 **torches**)
a small electric light that you can carry 手电筒；电棒

torch 手电筒

tore, **torn** *forms of* **tear**[2] ✻ **tear**[2] 的不同形式

tortoise 龟

tortoise /ˈtɔːtəs; ˈtɔrtəs/ *noun* 名词
an animal with a hard shell on its back, that moves very slowly 龟；陆龟

torture /ˈtɔːtʃə(r); ˈtɔrtʃɚ/ *verb* 动词 (**tortures**, **torturing**, **tortured** /ˈtɔːtʃəd; ˈtɔrtʃɚd/)
make somebody feel great pain, often to make them give information 使某人受巨大痛苦；折磨某人；（常指）严刑逼供: *They tortured her until she told them her name.* 他们折磨她，逼她说出了自己的名字。

torture *noun* 名词 (no plural 无复数)
the torture of prisoners 对囚犯的严刑拷打

the Tory Party /ðə ˈtɔːri pɑːti; ðə ˈtɔrɪ ˌpɑrtɪ/ *another word for* **the Conservative Party** ✻ **the Conservative Party** 的另一种说法

toss /tɒs; tɔs/ *verb* 动词 (**tosses**, **tossing**, **tossed** /tɒst; tɔst/)
1 throw something quickly and without care 胡乱把某物很快扔出: *I tossed the paper into the bin.* 我把纸扔进字纸篓儿里了。
2 move quickly up and down or from side to side; make something do this （使某物）上下或左右摇动；颠簸；摇摆: *The boat tossed around on the big waves.* 船在大浪中摆来摆去。
3 decide something by throwing a coin in the air and seeing which side shows when it falls 掷硬币（看落下时哪一面向上）决定某事: *We tossed a coin to see who would pay for the meal.* 我们掷硬币看那顿饭谁花钱。

total[1] /ˈtəʊtl; ˈtotḷ/ *adjective* 形容词
complete; if you count everything or everybody 完全的；全部的: *There was total silence in the classroom.* 教室里寂静无声。◇ *What was the total number of people at the meeting?* 参加会议的一共有多少人？

totally /ˈtəʊtəli; ˈtotḷɪ/ *adverb* 副词
completely 完全地；全部地: *I totally agree.* 我完全同意。

total[2] /ˈtəʊtl; ˈtotḷ/ *noun* 名词
the number you have when you add everything together 总数；总合

touch[1] /tʌtʃ; tʌtʃ/ *verb* 动词 (**touches**, **touching**, **touched** /tʌtʃt; tʌtʃt/)
1 put your hand or finger on somebody or something 触摸某人或某物: *Don't touch the paint—it's still wet.* 别摸那个颜料——还没干呢。◇ *He touched me on the arm.* 他摸了摸我的胳膊。
2 be so close to another thing or person that there is no space in between 接触或触及某人或某物: *The two wires were touching.* 这两条金属线搭在一起了。◇ *Her coat was so long that it touched the ground.* 她的大衣很长，都蹭着地了。

touch[2] /tʌtʃ; tʌtʃ/ *noun* 名词
1 (*plural* 复数作 **touches**) when a hand or finger is put on somebody or something 触摸: *I felt the touch of his hand on my arm.* 我感觉出他用手触摸我的胳膊。
2 (no plural 无复数) the feeling in your hands and skin that tells you about something 触觉: *He can't see, but he can read by touch.* 他看不见东西，但是能靠触觉阅读。

be or 或 **keep in touch with somebody** meet, telephone or write to somebody often 常与某人联系（见面、通话或通信）: *Are you still in touch with Kevin?* 你和凯文还有联系吗？◇ *Let's keep in touch.* 咱们要保持联系。

get in touch with somebody write to, or telephone somebody 与某人联系（通信或通话）: *I'm trying to get in touch with my cousin.* 我正在设法和我表弟取得联系。

lose touch with somebody stop meeting, telephoning or writing to somebody 与某人失去联系（不再见面、通话或通信）: *I've lost touch with all my old friends from school.* 我跟我中小学的老校友都失去联系了。

tough /tʌf; tʌf/ *adjective* 形容词 (**tougher, toughest**)

1 difficult to tear or break; strong 很难撕破或弄断的；结实的；坚韧的: *Leather is tougher than paper.* 皮革比纸结实。

2 difficult 困难的: *This is a tough job.* 这项工作很困难。

3 If meat is tough, it is difficult to cut and eat.（指肉）难切又难咬的，老的 ✪ opposite 反义词: **tender**

4 very strong in your body 健壮的: *You need to be tough to go climbing in winter.* 身体要很健壮才能在冬天爬山。

5 strict or firm 严厉的或坚定的: *a tough leader* 强硬的领袖

tour /tʊə(r); tʊr/ *noun* 名词

1 a short visit to see a building or city 参观建筑物或城市: *They gave us a tour of the house.* 他们让我们参观了那所房子。

2 a journey to see a lot of different places 游览各地: *We went on a tour of Scotland.* 我们到苏格兰各处游览了一番。

tour *verb* 动词 (**tours, touring, toured** /tʊəd; tʊrd/)

We toured France for three weeks. 我们到法国游览了三个星期。

tourism /ˈtʊərɪzəm; ˈtʊrˌɪzəm/ *noun* 名词 (no plural 无复数)

arranging holidays for people 旅游业: *This country earns a lot of money from tourism.* 这个国家从旅游业中赚到了很多钱。

tourist /ˈtʊərɪst; ˈtʊrɪst/ *noun* 名词

a person who visits a place on holiday 旅游者；观光客

tournament /ˈtɔːnəmənt; ˈtɝnəmənt/ *noun* 名词

a sports competition with a lot of players or teams（体育的）联赛；锦标赛: *a tennis tournament* 网球锦标赛

tow /təʊ; to/ *verb* 动词 (**tows, towing, towed** /təʊd; tod/)

pull a car, etc using a rope or chain（用绳索或链子）拖拉汽车等: *My car was towed to a garage.* 我的汽车被拖到修车厂了。

towards /təˈwɔːdz; tɔrdz/, **toward** /təˈwɔːd; tɔrd/ *preposition* 介词

1 in the direction of somebody or something 朝着某人或某事物的方向；对着；向着: *We walked towards the river.* 我们朝河边走去。◇ *I couldn't see her face—she had her back towards me.* 我看不见她的脸——她的背对着我。☞ picture on page C4 见第C4页图

2 to somebody or something 对于某人或某事物: *The people in the village are always very friendly towards tourists.* 村里的人对游客一向非常热情。

3 at a time near（指时间）接近: *Let's meet towards the end of the week.* 咱们近周末见面吧。

4 to help pay for something 为得到某事物（付款或添钱）: *I bought Sam's birthday present and Tom gave me £5 towards it.* 我给萨姆买了件生日礼物，汤姆出份子给了我5英镑。

towel /ˈtaʊəl; ˈtaʊəl/ *noun* 名词

a piece of cloth that you use for drying yourself 毛巾: *I washed my hands and dried them on a towel.* 我洗完手后用毛巾擦干了。

tower /ˈtaʊə(r); ˈtaʊɚ/ *noun* 名词

a tall narrow building or a tall part of a building 细而高的建筑物；建筑物的高的部分；塔: *the Eiffel Tower* 埃菲尔铁塔 ◇ *a church tower* 教堂的塔楼

tower block /ˈtaʊə(r) blɒk; ˈtaʊɚ ˌblɑk/ *noun* 名词

a very tall building with a lot of flats or offices inside 公寓大楼；办公大楼；高层建筑

town /taʊn; taʊn/ *noun* 名词

a place where there are a lot of houses and other buildings 有很多房屋等建筑物的地方；镇；集镇: *Banbury is a town near Oxford.* 班伯里是牛津附近的小镇。◇ *I'm going into town to do some shopping.* 我要到集镇去买些东西。

✪ A town is bigger than a **village** but smaller than a **city**. 镇比村（**village**）大，比市（**city**）小。

T

town hall /ˌtaʊn ˈhɔːl; ˈtaʊn ˈhɔl/ *noun* 名词
a building with offices for people who control a town 镇公所；市政厅

toy /tɔɪ; tɔɪ/ *noun* 名词
a thing for a child to play with 玩具

trace[1] /treɪs; tres/ *noun* 名词
a mark or sign that shows that somebody or something has been in a place 踪迹；痕迹: *The police could not find any trace of the missing child.* 警方找不到那个失踪孩子的踪迹。

trace[2] /treɪs; tres/ *verb* 动词 (**traces, tracing, traced** /treɪst; trest/)
1 look for and find somebody or something 寻找；追踪；查出: *The police have traced the stolen car.* 警方已经找到那辆丢失的汽车。
2 put thin paper over a picture and draw over the lines to make a copy（把薄纸放在图画上）描摹，复制

track[1] /træk; træk/ *noun* 名词
1 a rough path or road 不平坦的小径或道路: *We drove along a track through the woods.* 我们开车穿过林间小路。
2 tracks (plural 复数) a line of marks that an animal, a person or a vehicle makes on the ground（动物、人或车辆行走时留下的）踪迹，足迹，痕迹: *We saw his tracks in the snow.* 我们看见在雪地上有他留下的足迹。
3 the metal lines that a train runs on（火车的）轨道
4 a special road for races（比赛用的）跑道
5 one song or piece of music on a cassette, compact disc or record（录在盒式磁带、激光唱片或普通唱片上的）一首歌或音乐

track[2] /træk; træk/ *verb* 动词 (**tracks, tracking, tracked** /trækt; trækt/)
follow signs or marks to find somebody or something 追踪或跟踪某人或某事物
track down find somebody or something after looking 经追踪而发现某人或某事物: *I finally tracked her down.* 我紧紧追踪终于把她找到了。

track suit /ˈtræk suːt; ˈtræk ˌsut/ *noun* 名词
a special jacket and trousers that you wear for sport 运动时穿的衣裤；运动套装

tractor 拖拉机

tractor /ˈtræktə(r); ˈtræktɚ/ *noun* 名词
a big strong vehicle that people use on farms to pull heavy things 拖拉机

trade[1] /treɪd; tred/ *noun* 名词
1 (no plural 无复数) the buying and selling of things 买卖东西；贸易: *trade between Britain and the USA* 英国和美国的贸易
2 (*plural* 复数作 **trades**) a job（某种）行业；生意: *Dave is a plumber by trade.* 戴夫的职业是铅管工。

trade[2] /treɪd; tred/ *verb* 动词 (**trades, trading, traded**)
buy and sell things 做生意；做买卖: *Japan trades with many different countries.* 日本同很多国家有贸易往来。

trade mark /ˈtreɪd mɑːk; ˈtred ˌmɑrk/ *noun* 名词
a special mark or name that a company puts on the things it makes and that other companies must not use（注册的）商标

trade union /ˌtreɪd ˈjuːniən; ˈtred ˈjunjən/ *noun* 名词
a group of workers who have joined together to talk to their managers about things like pay and the way they work 工会

tradition /trəˈdɪʃn; trəˈdɪʃən/ *noun* 名词
something that people in a certain place have done or believed for a long time 传统；习俗: *In Britain it's a tradition to give chocolate eggs at Easter.* 在英国，过复活节时赠送用巧克力做的蛋是传统风俗。
traditional /trəˈdɪʃənl; trəˈdɪʃənl̩/ *adjective* 形容词
traditional English food 传统的英国食物
traditionally /trəˈdɪʃənəli; trəˈdɪʃənl̩ɪ/ *adverb* 副词
Driving trains was traditionally a man's job. 开火车历来是男子的工作。

traffic /ˈtræfɪk; ˈtræfɪk/ *noun* 名词 (no plural 无复数)
all the cars, etc that are on a road 路上的

所有的车辆；交通：*There was a lot of traffic on the way to work this morning.* 今天早晨在上班的路上有很多车。

traffic jam /'træfɪk dʒæm; 'træfɪk ˌdʒæm/ *noun* 名词
a long line of cars, etc that cannot move very fast 交通阻塞

traffic-lights /'træfɪk laɪts; 'træfɪk-ˌlaɪts/ *noun* 名词 (plural 复数)
lights that change from red to orange to green to tell cars, etc when to stop and start 交通信号灯

traffic warden /'træfɪk wɔ:dn; 'træfɪk ˌwɔrdn̩/ *noun* 名词
a person who checks that cars park in the right places and for the right time (处理违章停车的）交通管理员

tragedy /'trædʒədi; 'trædʒədɪ/ *noun* 名词 (*plural* 复数作 **tragedies**)
1 a very sad thing that happens 悲惨的事：*The child's death was a tragedy.* 孩子死了，这件事很悲惨。
2 a serious and sad play 悲剧：*Shakespeare's 'King Lear' is a tragedy.* 莎士比亚的《李尔王》是一出悲剧。

tragic /'trædʒɪk; 'trædʒɪk/ *adjective* 形容词
very sad 悲惨的：*a tragic accident* 悲惨的事故

tragically /'trædʒɪkli; 'trædʒɪkl̩ɪ/ *adverb* 副词
He died tragically at the age of 25. 他25岁时不幸夭亡。

trail¹ /treɪl; trel/ *noun* 名词
1 a line of marks that show which way a person or thing has gone（人或物留下的）去向痕迹；足迹；踪迹：*There was a trail of blood from the cut in her leg.* 从她腿上伤口流出的血留下了一条血迹。
2 a path in the country 郊野的小路：*We followed the trail through the forest.* 我们顺着小路穿过了树林。

trail² /treɪl; trel/ *verb* 动词 (**trails, trailing, trailed** /treɪld; treld/)
pull something along behind you; be pulled along behind somebody or something 拖或拉某物；被某人或某物拖或拉：*Her long hair trailed behind her in the wind.* 她的长发披在后面随风起伏。

trailer /'treɪlə(r); 'trelɚ/ *noun* 名词
1 a vehicle with no engine that a car or lorry pulls along 拖车；挂车
2 a short piece from a film that shows you what it is like（选自影片中画面的）预告片

train 火车

train¹ /treɪn; tren/ *noun* 名词
carriages or wagons that are pulled by an engine along a railway line 列车；火车：*I'm going to Bristol by train.* 我打算坐火车到布里斯托尔去。
catch a train get on a train to go somewhere 登上或赶上去某处的火车：*We caught the 7.15 train to Leeds.* 我们坐上了7点15分的火车去利兹。
change trains go from one train to another 换乘另一列火车：*You have to change trains at Reading.* 你得在雷丁倒车。

> ✪ You get **on** and **off** trains at a **station**. 上火车叫做 get **on** a train，下火车叫做 get **off** a train，火车站叫做 **station**。A **goods train** or a **freight train** carries things and a **passenger train** carries people. 货运列车叫做 **goods train** 或 **freight train**，客运列车叫做 **passenger train**。

train² /treɪn; tren/ *verb* 动词 (**trains, training, trained** /treɪnd; trend/)
1 teach a person or an animal to do something 训练人或动物做某事：*He was trained as a pilot.* 他受过训练成为飞行员。
2 make yourself ready for something by studying or doing something a lot 经学习或锻炼而准备做某事：*Anna is training to be a doctor.* 安娜正在接受培训准备当医生。◇ *He goes running every morning—he's training for the race.* 他每天早晨跑步——准备参加赛跑。

trainer /'treɪnə(r); 'trenɚ/ *noun* 名词
1 a person who teaches other people to do a sport 教练员
2 a person who teaches animals to do something 驯兽师

T

3 a soft shoe that you wear for running 运动鞋

training /ˈtreɪnɪŋ; ˈtrenɪŋ/ *noun* 名词 (no plural 无复数)
getting ready for a sport or job（为参加运动或工作的）训练；受训: *She is in training for the Olympic Games.* 她正在为参加奥林匹克运动会进行锻炼。

traitor /ˈtreɪtə(r); ˈtretɚ/ *noun* 名词
a person who harms his/her country or friends to help another person or country 背叛国家或朋友的人；卖国贼；叛徒

tram /træm; træm/ *noun* 名词
an electric bus that goes along rails in a town（有轨的）电车

tramp /træmp; træmp/ *noun* 名词
a person with no home or job, who goes from place to place 无家无业到处流浪的人；流浪者

T

trample /ˈtræmpl; ˈtræmpl̩/ *verb* 动词 (**tramples, trampling, trampled** /ˈtræmpld; ˈtræmpl̩d/)
walk on something and push it down with your feet 踩倒某物: *Don't trample on the flowers!* 别踩花！

transfer /trænsˈfɜː(r); trænsˈfɝ/ *verb* 动词 (**transfers, transferring, transferred** /trænsˈfɜːd; trænsˈfɝd/)
move somebody or something to a different place 把某人或某物移到另一处: *I want to transfer £500 to my bank account in Spain.* 我想把500英镑转移到我在西班牙的银行账户里。

transfer /ˈtrænsfɜː(r); ˈtrænsfɝ/ *noun* 名词
Keiko wants a transfer to another class. 凯科想转到另一班上课。

transform /trænsˈfɔːm; trænsˈfɔrm/ *verb* 动词 (**transforms, transforming, transformed** /trænsˈfɔːmd; trænsˈfɔrmd/)
change somebody or something so that they are or look completely different 完全改变某人或某事物（或改变其外貌）: *Electricity has transformed people's lives.* 有了电，人类的生活已经完全改观。

transformation /ˌtrænsfəˈmeɪʃn; ˌtrænsfɚˈmeʃən/ *noun* 名词
a complete change 完全的改变

transistor /trænˈzɪstə(r); trænˈzɪstɚ/ *noun* 名词
a small part inside something electrical, for example a radio or television 晶体管（例如收音机或电视机中的）

translate /trænsˈleɪt; trænzˈlet/ *verb* 动词 (**translates, translating, translated**)
say or write in one language what somebody has said or written in another language 翻译；口译；笔译: *This letter is in German—can you translate it into English for me?* 这封信是德文的——您给我译成英文行吗？

translation /trænsˈleɪʃn; trænzˈleʃən/ *noun* 名词
1 (no plural 无复数) translating 翻译；口译；笔译: *translation from English into French* 把英语译成法语
2 (*plural* 复数作 **translations**) something that somebody has translated 译文；译作

translator /trænsˈleɪtə(r); trænzˈletɚ/ *noun* 名词
a person who translates 翻译者；口译者；笔译者

transparent /trænsˈpærənt; trænsˈpɛrənt/ *adjective* 形容词
If something is transparent, you can see through it 透明的: *Glass is transparent.* 玻璃是透明的。

transport /ˈtrænspɔːt; ˈtrænspɔrt/ *noun* 名词 (no plural 无复数)
a way of carrying people or things from one place to another 运送人或货物；运输: *road transport* 公路运输 ◇ *I travel to school by public transport* (= bus or train). 我乘坐公共交通工具上学。

transport /trænˈspɔːt; trænsˈpɔrt/ *verb* 动词 (**transports, transporting, transported**)
carry people or things from one place to another 把人或货物从一处运送到另一处；运输: *The goods were transported by air.* 这些货物是空运的。

trap /træp; træp/ *noun* 名词
1 a thing that you use for catching animals 捕捉动物的器具；陷阱: *The rabbit's leg was caught in a trap.* 兔子的腿让捕捉器给夹住了。

2 a plan to trick somebody（诱人上当的）计策；花招：*I knew the question was a trap, so I didn't answer it.* 我知道那个问题是个圈套，所以我没有回答。

trap *verb* 动词 (**traps, trapping, trapped** /træpt; træpt/)

1 keep somebody in a place that they cannot escape from 把某人困在某处无法逃脱：*They were trapped in the burning building.* 他们被困在燃烧着的建筑物中。

2 catch or trick somebody or something 用计捕捉某人或某事物（或使之上当）

trash /træʃ; træʃ/ *American English for* **rubbish** 美式英语，即 **rubbish**

trash can /'træʃ kæn; 'træʃ ˌkæn/ *American English for* **dustbin** 美式英语，即 **dustbin**

travel /'trævl; 'trævḷ/ *verb* 动词 (**travels, travelling, travelled** /'trævld; 'trævḷd/)

go from one place to another 从一处到另一处：*I would like to travel round the world.* 我很想环游世界。◇ *I travel to school by bus.* 我坐公共汽车上学。◇ *She travelled 800 km in one day.* 她那一天的行程是800公里。✪ In American English the spellings are **traveling** and **traveled**. 美式英语的拼法为 **traveling** 和 **traveled**。

travel *noun* 名词 (no plural 无复数)

travelling 从一处到另一处：*My hobbies are music and travel.* 我的爱好是音乐和旅游。

travel agency /'trævl eɪdʒənsi; 'trævḷ ˌedʒənsɪ/ *noun* 名词 (*plural* 复数作 **travel agencies**)

a company that plans holidays and journeys for people 旅行社

travel agent /'trævl eɪdʒənt; 'trævḷ ˌedʒənt/ *noun* 名词

a person who works in a travel agency 旅行社工作人员

traveler *American English for* **traveller** 美式英语，即 **traveller**

traveller /'trævələ(r); 'trævlɚ/ *noun* 名词

a person who is travelling 出远门的人；旅客；旅行者

traveller's cheque /'trævələz tʃek; 'trævləz ˌtʃɛk/ *noun* 名词

a special cheque that you can use when you go to other countries 旅行支票

tray /treɪ; tre/ *noun* 名词

a flat thing that you use for carrying food or drinks（运送食物或饮料的）托盘

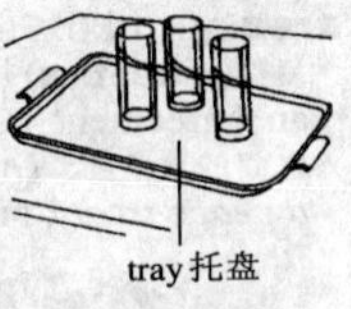
tray 托盘

tread /tred; trɛd/ *verb* 动词 (**treads, treading, trod** /trɒd; trɑd/, **has trodden** /'trɒdn; 'trɑdṇ/)

put your foot down 踩；踏：*He trod on my foot.* 他踩了我的脚了。

treasure /'treʒə(r); 'trɛʒɚ/ *noun* 名词

gold, silver, jewels or other things that are worth a lot of money 金银财宝

treasurer /'treʒərə(r); 'trɛʒərɚ/ *noun* 名词

a person who looks after the money of a club or a group of people（俱乐部等团体的）财务主管；司库；会计

treat[1] /tri:t; trit/ *verb* 动词 (**treats, treating, treated**)

1 behave towards somebody or something 对待某人或某事物：*How does your boss treat you?* 你们老板对你怎么样？◇ *Treat these glasses with care.* 这些玻璃杯要轻拿轻放。

2 try to make a sick person well again 医治病人：*The doctor is treating him for cancer.* 医师正在为他治疗癌症。

treat something as something think about something in a certain way 以某种方式看待某事物：*They treated my idea as a joke.* 他们把我的意见当作笑话。

treat[2] /tri:t; trit/ *noun* 名词

something very special that makes somebody happy 使某人愉快的特殊事物：*My parents took me to the theatre as a treat for my birthday.* 我父母带我去看戏，庆祝我的生日。

treatment /'tri:tmənt; 'tritmənt/ *noun* 名词

1 (no plural 无复数) the way that you behave towards somebody or something 对待某人或某事物的方式或方法：*Their treatment of the animals was very cruel.* 他们对待动物非常残忍。

2 (*plural* 复数作 **treatments**) the things that a doctor does to try to make a sick person well again 医治；治疗；疗法：*a new treatment for cancer* 癌症的新疗法

treaty /'tri:ti; 'tritɪ/ *noun* 名词 (*plural* 复数作 **treaties**)
an agreement between countries（国家之间的）条约: *The two countries signed a peace treaty.* 两国签订了和平条约。

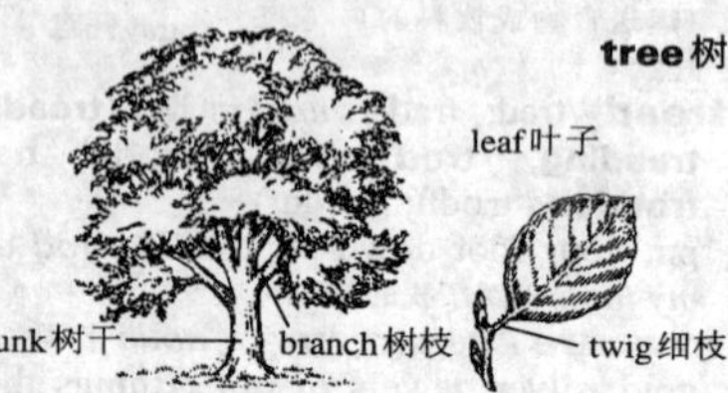

tree /tri:; tri/ *noun* 名词
a big tall plant with a trunk, branches and leaves 树；乔木: *an oak tree* 栎树 ◇ *Apples grow on trees.* 苹果是树上长的。

tremble /'trembl; 'trɛmbḷ/ *verb* 动词 (**trembles**, **trembling**, **trembled** /'trembld; 'trɛmbḷd/)
shake, for example because you are cold, afraid or ill 颤抖；哆嗦（例如因寒冷、害怕或生病）: *She was trembling with fear.* 她害怕得发起抖来。

tremendous /trə'mendəs; trɪ'mɛndəs/ *adjective* 形容词
1 very big or very great 极大的；巨大的: *The new trains travel at a tremendous speed.* 新火车行驶速度极快。
2 very good 极好的: *The match was tremendous.* 那场比赛好极了。
tremendously *adverb* 副词
very or very much 很；非常: *The film was tremendously exciting.* 那部影片十分精彩。

trench /trentʃ; trɛntʃ/ *noun* 名词 (*plural* 复数作 **trenches**)
a long narrow hole that you make in the ground 沟；渠；战壕

trend /trend; trɛnd/ *noun* 名词
a change to something different 趋势；趋向；动向: *new trends in science* 科学的新动态

trespass /'trespəs; 'trɛspəs/ *verb* 动词 (**trespasses**, **trespassing**, **trespassed** /'trespəst; 'trɛspəst/)
go on somebody's land without asking them if you can 未经允许走进他人地界: *A sign on the gate of the big house said 'No Trespassing'.* 那座大宅院的大门上有个告示："严禁擅自进入"。
trespasser *noun* 名词
a person who trespasses 未经允许走进他人地界的人

trial /'traɪəl; 'traɪəl/ *noun* 名词
1 the time when a person is in a **court of law** so that people (the **judge** and **jury**) can decide if he/she has done something wrong and what the punishment will be 审问；审判（法庭叫做 **court of law**，法官叫做 **judge**，陪审团叫做 **jury**）
2 using something to see if it is good or bad 通过使用检验是好是坏；试用；测试: *trials of a new drug* 试用新药品
on trial **1** in a court of law so that people can decide if you have done something wrong 受审判: *She was on trial for murder.* 她因涉及谋杀罪而受审。
2 If you have something on trial, you are using it to decide if you like it, before you buy it（购买某物前）试用（看是否合意）: *We've got the car on trial for a week.* 这辆汽车我们先试用一个星期，然后再决定买不买。

triangle /'traɪæŋgl; 'traɪˌæŋgḷ/ *noun* 名词
a shape with three straight sides 三角形 ☞ picture on page C5 见第C5页图
triangular /traɪ'æŋgjələ(r); traɪ'æŋgjələ/ *adjective* 形容词
with the shape of a triangle 三角形的

tribe /traɪb; traɪb/ *noun* 名词
a small group of people who have the same language and customs 部落: *the Zulu tribes of Africa* 非洲祖鲁人的部落
tribal /'traɪbl; 'traɪbḷ/ *adjective* 形容词
tribal dances 部落人的舞蹈

tribute /'trɪbju:t; 'trɪbjut/ *noun* 名词
something that you do, say or give to show that you respect or admire somebody 对某人表示敬意或称赞的行动、言语或礼物: *They built a statue in London as a tribute to Nelson Mandela.* 他们为赞颂纳尔逊·曼德拉，在伦敦为他建起了一座雕像。

trick[1] /trɪk; trɪk/ *noun* 名词
1 a clever plan that makes somebody believe something that is not true 诡计；计谋；花招: *He got the money from me by a trick.* 他耍了个花招就把我的钱骗走了。
2 something that you do to make somebody seem stupid 恶作剧: *The children hid their teacher's books to play a trick*

on her. 那些小学生捉弄老师，把她的书藏起来了。

3 something clever that you have learned to do 戏法；把戏: *card tricks* 纸牌幻术

trick[2] /trɪk; trɪk/ *verb* 动词 (**tricks, tricking, tricked** /trɪkt; trɪkt/)

do something that is not honest to get what you want from somebody 欺骗某人以获得某事物: *He tricked the old lady so that she gave him all her money.* 他欺骗那个老太太，结果她把所有的钱都给他了。

trickle /'trɪkl; 'trɪkl̩/ *verb* 动词 (**trickles, trickling, trickled** /'trɪkld; 'trɪkl̩d/)

move slowly like a thin line of water 像细水般慢流: *Tears trickled down her cheeks.* 泪水顺着她的面颊流下来。

trickle *noun* 名词

a trickle of blood 慢慢流着的血

tricky /'trɪki; 'trɪkɪ/ *adjective* 形容词 (**trickier, trickiest**)

difficult; hard to do 困难的；难做的: *a tricky question* 难回答的问题

tricycle /'traɪsɪkl; 'traɪsɪkl̩/ *noun* 名词

a thing like a bicycle with three wheels 三轮脚踏车

tried *form of* **try** ∗ **try** 的不同形式

tries

1 *form of* **try** ∗ **try** 的不同形式

2 *plural of* **try** ∗ **try** 的复数形式

trigger /'trɪgə(r); 'trɪgɚ/ *noun* 名词

the part of a gun that you pull with your finger to fire it（枪的）扳机

trim /trɪm; trɪm/ *verb* 动词 (**trims, trimming, trimmed** /trɪmd; trɪmd/)

cut something to make it tidy 修剪或修整某物: *He trimmed my hair.* 他给我修剪了头发。

trim *noun* 名词

My hair needs a trim. 我的头发得剪了。

trip[1] /trɪp; trɪp/ *noun* 名词

a short journey to a place and back again（指短期）到某处再回来: *We went on a trip to the mountains.* 我们到山里去了一趟。

trip[2] /trɪp; trɪp/ *verb* 动词 (**trips, tripping, tripped** /trɪpt; trɪpt/)

hit your foot against something so that you fall or nearly fall 绊或绊倒: *She tripped over the step.* 她在台阶上绊倒了。

trip up make somebody fall or nearly fall 绊或绊倒某人: *Gary put out his foot and tripped me up.* 加里一伸脚就把我绊倒了。

triple /'trɪpl; 'trɪpl̩/ *adjective* 形容词

with three parts 有三部分的: *the triple jump* 三级跳远

triple *verb* 动词 (**triples, tripling, tripled** /'trɪpld; 'trɪpl̩d/)

become or make something three times bigger（使某物）增至三倍: *Sales have tripled this year.* 今年销售量已经增加到三倍。

triumph /'traɪʌmf; 'traɪəmf/ *noun* 名词

great success; winning 巨大的成功或胜利: *The race ended in triumph for the German team.* 这场速度比赛以德国队获胜而告终。

trivial /'trɪviəl; 'trɪvɪəl/ *adjective* 形容词

not important 不重要的；琐碎的: *She gets angry about trivial things.* 她对小小不言的事儿都生气。

trod, trodden *forms of* **tread** ∗ **tread** 的不同形式

trolleys 手推车

trolley /'trɒli; 'trɑlɪ/ *noun* 名词 (*plural* 复数作 **trolleys**)

a thing on wheels that you use for carrying things 手推车；手拉车: *a supermarket trolley* 超级市场的手推车

trombone /trɒm'bəʊn; trɑm'bon/ *noun* 名词

a large musical instrument. You play it by blowing and moving a long tube up and down. 长号（装有可伸缩套管的）

troops /tru:ps; trups/ *noun* 名词 (plural 复数)

soldiers 军队；部队

trophy /'trəʊfi; 'trofɪ/ *noun* 名词 (*plural* 复数作 **trophies**)

a thing, for example a silver cup, that you get when you win a competition 奖品（例如银制奖杯）: *a tennis trophy* 网球奖杯

the tropics /ðə 'trɒpɪks; ðə 'trɑpɪks/ *noun* 名词 (plural 复数)

the very hot part of the world 热带（地区）

T

tropical /ˈtrɒpɪkl; ˈtrɑpɪkḷ/ *adjective* 形容词
of or from the tropics 热带的；从热带来的: *tropical fruit* 热带水果

trot /trɒt; trɑt/ *verb* 动词 (**trots**, **trotting**, **trotted**)
run with short quick steps 用短而快的步子跑；小跑: *The horse trotted along the road.* 马沿着路小跑。

trouble[1] /ˈtrʌbl; ˈtrʌbḷ/ *noun* 名词
1 (*plural* 复数作 **troubles**) difficulty, problems or worry 困难；问题；忧虑: *We had a lot of trouble finding the book you wanted.* 我们费尽周折才找到您要的书。◇ *She told me all her troubles.* 她把她的苦恼都告诉我了。
2 (no plural 无复数) extra work 额外的工作: *'Thanks for your help!' 'Oh, it was no trouble.'* "谢谢您帮了我的忙！" "噢，没什么。"
3 (*plural* 复数作 **troubles**) when people are fighting or arguing 打架或争吵；动乱: *There was a lot of trouble after the football match last Saturday.* 上星期六足球比赛后，出了很多事。
4 (no plural 无复数) pain or illness 疼痛或疾病: *He's got heart trouble.* 他有心脏病。
be in trouble have problems, for example because you have done something wrong 有麻烦（如因做错了事）: *I'll be in trouble if I get home late.* 我要是回家晚了就要倒霉了。◇ *He's in trouble with the police.* 他惹出事来落到警方手里了。
get into trouble do something that brings problems because it is wrong 做了错事而惹上麻烦: *You'll get into trouble if you park your car here.* 你把汽车停放在这儿可要惹麻烦了。
go to a lot of trouble do extra work 做额外的工作: *They went to a lot of trouble to help me.* 他们费了很多事来帮助我。

trouble[2] /ˈtrʌbl; ˈtrʌbḷ/ *verb* 动词 (**troubles**, **troubling**, **troubled** /ˈtrʌbld; ˈtrʌbḷd/)
worry somebody; bring somebody problems or pain 使某人忧虑；给某人带来困难或痛苦: *I was troubled by the news.* 我知道这个消息以后很难受。◇ *I'm sorry to trouble you, but you're sitting in my seat.* 很抱歉，打扰您一下，您坐的是我的座位。

trough /trɒf; trɔf/ *noun* 名词
a long open box that holds food or water for animals（喂养动物的）饲料槽或饮水槽

trousers /ˈtraʊzəz; ˈtraʊzɚz/ *noun* 名词 (plural 复数)
a piece of clothing for your legs and the lower part of your body 裤子: *Your trousers are on the chair.* 你的裤子在椅子上呢。☞ picture at **suit** 见 **suit** 词条插图
✪ Be careful! You cannot say 'a trousers'. You can say **a pair of trousers** 注意！不可说 a trousers。可以说 **a pair of trousers**: *I bought a new pair of trousers.* 我新买了一条裤子。(or 也可以说: *I bought some new trousers.*)

trout /traʊt; traʊt/ *noun* 名词 (*plural* 复数作 **trout**)
a fish that lives in rivers and that you can eat 鳟鱼

truant /ˈtru:ənt; ˈtruənt/ *noun* 名词
a child who stays away from school when he/she should be there 逃学的儿童；旷课的小学生
play truant stay away from school 逃学；旷课

truce /tru:s; trus/ *noun* 名词
when people or groups agree to stop fighting for a short time 休战；停战

truck /trʌk; trʌk/ *noun* 名词
1 a big vehicle for carrying heavy things 卡车: *a truck driver* 卡车司机
2 an open part of a train where heavy things are carried（铁路上的）敞篷货车

true /tru:; tru/ *adjective* 形容词
1 right or correct 对的或正确的: *Is it true that you are leaving?* 您是真的要走吗？◇ *Glasgow is in England: true or false?* 格拉斯哥是在英格兰：对不对？
2 that really happened 实际上发生的；真实的: *It's a true story.* 这是一个真实的故事。
3 real 真正的: *A true friend will always help you.* 真正的朋友一定有难相助。
✪ The noun is **truth**. 名词是 **truth**。
come true happen in the way that you hoped（指希望）实现: *Her dream came true.* 她的梦想实现了。

truly /ˈtru:li; ˈtrulɪ/ *adverb* 副词
really 真正地: *I'm truly sorry.* 我真是非常抱歉。
Yours truly words that you can use at the end of a formal letter 用于信件署名前的敬语

T

trumpet 小号

trumpet /'trʌmpɪt; 'trʌmpɪt/ *noun* 名词
a musical instrument that you blow 小号；喇叭

trunk /trʌŋk; trʌŋk/ *noun* 名词
1 the thick part of a tree, that grows up from the ground 树干 ☞ picture at **tree** 见 **tree** 词条插图
2 a big strong box for carrying things when you travel（旅行用的）大箱子
3 an elephant's long nose（象的）鼻子 ☞ picture at **elephant** 见 **elephant** 词条插图
4 *American English for* **boot 2** 美式英语，即 **boot 2**

trunks /trʌŋks; trʌŋks/*noun* 名词 (plural 复数)
short trousers that a man or boy wears for swimming（男用）游泳裤

trust[1] /trʌst; trʌst/ *noun* 名词 (no plural 无复数)
feeling sure that somebody or something will do what they should do; feeling that somebody is honest and good 信任；信赖: *Put your trust in God.* 要信赖上帝。

trust[2] /trʌst; trʌst/ *verb* 动词 (**trusts, trusting, trusted**)
feel sure that somebody or something will do what they should do; believe that somebody is honest and good 信任；信赖: *You can't trust him with money.* 金钱的事可别相信他。◇ *You can trust Penny to do the job well.* 你可以相信彭尼能把这件事做好。

trustworthy /'trʌstwɜ:ði; 'trʌstˌwɝðɪ/ *adjective* 形容词
A trustworthy person is somebody that you can trust. 可信任的；可靠的

truth /tru:θ; truθ/ *noun* 名词 (no plural 无复数)
being true; what is true 真实；真相；实情: *There is no truth in what he says—he is lying.* 他说的没有一句实话——他撒谎了。◇ *We need to find out the truth about what happened.* 我们需要找出事实真相。
tell the truth say what is true 说实话: *Are you telling me the truth?* 你跟我说的是实话吗？

truthful /'tru:θfl; 'truθfəl/ *adjective* 形容词
1 true 真实的: *a truthful answer* 如实的回答
2 A person who is truthful tells the truth. 诚实的
truthfully /'tru:θfəli; 'truθfəlɪ/ *adverb* 副词
You must answer me truthfully. 你必须如实回答我的问题。

try /traɪ; traɪ/ *verb* 动词 (**tries, trying, tried** /traɪd; traɪd/, **has tried**)
1 work hard to do something 努力做某事: *I tried to remember her name but I couldn't.* 我怎么也想不起她的名字来了。◇ *I'm not sure if I can help you, but I'll try.* 我不敢说准能帮助你，但是我一定尽力而为。
2 use or do something to find out if you like it 试用或试做某事物（看是否合意）: *Have you ever tried Japanese food?* 您吃过日本菜吗？
3 ask somebody questions in a court of law to decide if they have done something wrong 审问或审判某人: *He was tried for murder.* 他以谋杀罪名受审。
try and do something try to do something 尽力做某事物: *I'll try and come early tomorrow.* 我明天尽量早点儿来。
try on put on a piece of clothing to see if you like it and if it is big enough 试穿衣物（看是否合身）: *I tried the jeans on but they were too small.* 我试了一下这条牛仔裤，太小。
try *noun* 名词 (*plural* 复数作 **tries**)
I can't open this door—will you have a try? 我打不开这扇门——你来试试行吗？

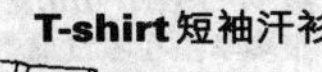
T-shirt 短袖汗衫

T-shirt /'ti:ʃɜ:t; 'tiˌʃɝt/ *noun* 名词
a kind of shirt with short sleeves and no collar 短袖汗衫

tub /tʌb; tʌb/ *noun* 名词
a round container 圆形容器；盆；桶: *a tub of ice-cream* 冰激凌桶 ☞ picture at **container** 见 **container** 词条插图

tube /tju:b; tub/ *noun* 名词
1 a long thin pipe for a liquid or a gas 管子
2 a long thin soft container with a hole and a cap at one end 软的筒状容器，一端开口有盖儿: *a tube of toothpaste* 一管牙膏 ☞ picture at **container** 见 **container** 词条插图
3 the underground railway in London（伦敦的）地下铁道: *Shall we go by bus or by tube?* 咱们坐公共汽车还是坐伦敦地铁？

tuck /tʌk; tʌk/ *verb* 动词 (**tucks, tucking, tucked** /tʌkt; tʌkt/)
put or push the edges of something inside or under something else 把某物的端部或边缘掖进某处: *He tucked his shirt into his trousers.* 他把衬衫的下摆掖进裤子里。

Tuesday /'tju:zdeɪ; 'tuzdɪ/ *noun* 名词
the third day of the week, next after Monday 星期二

T

tuft /tʌft; tʌft/ *noun* 名词
a group of hairs, grass, etc growing together（丛生的）一束毛发、一丛草等

tug /tʌg; tʌg/ *verb* 动词 (**tugs, tugging, tugged** /tʌgd; tʌgd/)
pull something hard and quickly 用力地很快拉某物: *I tugged at the rope and it broke.* 我猛然一拉，绳子就断了。

tug *noun* 名词
1 a sudden hard pull 猛拉；猛拽: *The little girl gave my hand a tug.* 那个小女孩儿猛然拽了我的手一下。
2 a small strong boat that pulls big ships 拖船（牵引大船的小船）

tuition /tju'ɪʃn; tu'ɪʃən/ *noun* 名词 (no plural 无复数)
teaching 教学；讲授: *A lot of students have extra tuition before their exams.* 很多学生在考试前都上额外的补习课。

tulip /'tju:lɪp; 'tulɪp/ *noun* 名词
a flower that comes in spring 郁金香

tumble /'tʌmbl; 'tʌmbḷ/ *verb* 动词 (**tumbles, tumbling, tumbled** /'tʌmbld; 'tʌmbḷd/)
fall suddenly 突然倒下: *He tumbled down the steps.* 他从台阶上摔了下来。

tummy /'tʌmi; 'tʌmɪ/ *noun* 名词 (*plural* 复数作 **tummies**)
the part of your body between your chest and your legs; your stomach 肚子；胃

tuna /'tju:nə; 'tunə/ *noun* 名词 (*plural* 复数作 **tuna**)
a large fish that lives in the sea and that you can eat 金枪鱼（大的海鱼，可食）

tune /tju:n; tun/ *noun* 名词
a group of musical notes that make a nice sound when you play or sing them together 曲调；曲子: *I know the tune but I don't know the words.* 我会这个曲调，可是不会歌词。

tune *verb* 动词 (**tunes, tuning, tuned** /tju:nd; tund/)
do something to a musical instrument so that it makes the right sounds 为乐器调音: *She tuned the piano.* 她调了调钢琴的音。

tunnel 隧道

tunnel /'tʌnl; 'tʌnḷ/ *noun* 名词
a long hole under the ground or sea for a road or railway 地下通道；隧道；地道

turban /'tɜ:bən; 'tɝbən/ *noun* 名词
a long piece of material that you put round and round your head（缠绕在头部的）头巾

turkey /'tɜ:ki; 'tɝkɪ/ *noun* 名词 (*plural* 复数作 **turkeys**)
a big bird that people keep on farms and that you can eat. In Britain, people often eat turkeys at Christmas. 火鸡（在英国，一般在圣诞节时吃火鸡）

turn[1] /tɜ:n; tɝn/ *verb* 动词 (**turns, turning, turned** /tɜ:nd; tɝnd/)
1 move round, or move something round（使某物）旋转: *The wheels are turning.* 轮子都在转动。◇ *Turn the key.* 转动一下钥匙。◇ *She turned round and walked towards the door.* 她转身朝门口走去。
2 move in a different direction 改换方向: *Turn left at the traffic-lights.* 到了交通信号灯处向左转。
3 become different 转变: *The weather has turned cold.* 天冷了。

4 make somebody or something change 使某人或某事物转变: *The sun turned her hair blond.* 太阳把她的头发晒黄了。

5 find a certain page in a book 翻开书找到某一页: *Turn to page 97.* 翻到第97页。

turn down 1 say no to what somebody wants to do or to give you 不准某人做某事；不接受某人给予的事物: *They offered me the job but I turned it down.* 他们给我一份工作，我没接受。 **2** move the switch that controls something like a radio or a heater so that it makes less sound, heat, etc 调节（例如收音机或暖炉的）开关，使音量、热度等减低: *I'm too hot—can you turn the heating down?* 我太热了——你把暖气调小点儿行吗？

turn into something become different; change somebody or something into something different 转变；改变某人或某事物: *Water turns into ice when it gets very cold.* 水非常冷的时候就结成冰了。

turn off move the handle, switch, etc that controls something, so that it stops 移动把柄或开关等操纵器，使某物停止: *Turn the tap off.* 把水龙头关上。◇ *Turn off the television.* 关上电视。

turn on move the handle, switch, etc that controls something, so that it starts 移动把柄或开关等操纵器，使某物开始: *Could you turn the light on?* 您把灯开开行吗？

turn out be something in the end 终于成为某事物: *It rained this morning, but it has turned out to be a lovely day.* 今天早晨下雨了，可是结果却是个大晴天。

turn out a light switch off a light 关灯

turn over move so that the other side is on top 翻转某物: *If you turn over the page you'll find the answers on the other side.* 把书页翻过来，答案就在后面。

turn up 1 arrive 来到；到达: *Has David turned up yet?* 戴维来了吗？ **2** move the switch that controls something like a radio or a heater so that it makes more sound, heat, etc 调节（例如收音机或暖炉的）开关，使音量、热度等增高: *Turn up the television—I can't hear it properly.* 把电视声音调大些——我听不清楚。

turn² /tɜ:n; tɝn/ *noun* 名词

1 turning something round 转动；旋转: *Give the screw a few turns.* 把螺丝拧几下。

2 a change of direction 改换方向: *Take a left turn at the end of this road.* 到了这条路的尽头向左转。

3 the time when you can or should do something 轮到某人能做或该做某事的机会: *It's your turn to do the washing-up!* 该你洗碗了！

in turn one after the other 一个一个地；逐个地: *I spoke to each of the students in turn.* 我跟学生一个一个地谈话。

take turns at something, take it in turns to do something do something one after the other 一个一个地做某事: *You can't both use the computer at the same time. Why don't you take it in turns?* 你们俩不能同时使用这台计算机。一个人用完另一个人再用多好？

turning /ˈtɜ:nɪŋ; ˈtɝnɪŋ/ *noun* 名词
a place where one road joins another road（道路的）转弯处；岔路口: *Take the first turning on the right.* 在第一个路口向右转。

turnip /ˈtɜ:nɪp; ˈtɝnɪp/ *noun* 名词
a round white vegetable that grows under the ground 芜菁；大头菜

turquoise /ˈtɜ:kwɔɪz; ˈtɝkwɔɪz/ *adjective* 形容词
with a colour between blue and green 青绿色

turtle /ˈtɜ:tl; ˈtɝtl̩/ *noun* 名词
an animal that lives in the sea and has a hard shell on its back 海龟

tusk /tʌsk; tʌsk/ *noun* 名词
a long pointed tooth that grows beside the mouth of an elephant（象的）长牙 ☞ picture at **elephant** 见 **elephant** 词条插图

tutor /ˈtju:tə(r); ˈtutɚ/ *noun* 名词
a teacher who teaches one person or a small group（指导一个学生或一个小组的）导师

TV /ˌti: ˈvi:; ˌti ˈvi/ *short for* **television** ＊ **television**的缩略式

tweezers /ˈtwi:zəz; ˈtwizɚz/ *noun* 名词 (plural 复数)
a small tool made of two pieces of metal joined at one end. You use tweezers for holding or pulling out very small things 镊子；小钳子: *She pulled the splinter out of her finger with a pair of tweezers.* 她用镊子把手指上的刺拔了出来。

T

twelve /twelv; twɛlv/ *number* 数词
12 十二
twelfth /twelfθ; twɛlfθ/ *adjective, adverb, noun* 形容词，副词，名词
12th 第12（个）；第十二（个）

twenty /'twenti; 'twɛntɪ/ *number* 数词
1 20 二十
2 the twenties (plural 复数) the numbers, years or temperature between 20 and 29 ✳ 20至29（之间的数目、年数或温度）
in your twenties between the ages of 20 and 29 年岁在20至29之间；二十多岁
twentieth /'twentiəθ; 'twɛntɪɪθ/ *adjective, adverb, noun* 形容词，副词，名词
20th 第20（个）；第二十（个）

twice /twaɪs; twaɪs/ *adverb* 副词
two times 两次；两倍: *I have been to Japan twice.* 我去过两次日本。◇ *He ate twice as much as I did.* 他吃得比我多一倍。

twig /twɪg; twɪg/ *noun* 名词
a small thin branch of a tree（树的）细枝；嫩枝 ☞ picture at **tree** 见 **tree** 词条插图

twilight /'twaɪlaɪt; 'twaɪˌlaɪt/ *noun* 名词 (no plural 无复数)
the time after the sun has gone down and before it gets completely dark 在日落后和天全黑前的时分；黄昏

twin /twɪn; twɪn/ *noun* 名词
1 Twins are two people who have the same mother and who were born on the same day 双胞胎；孪生儿: *David and John are twins.* 戴维和约翰是双胞胎。◇ *I have got a twin sister.* 我跟我妹妹是孪生的。
2 one of two things that are the same 两个相同的事物之一: *twin beds* 成对的单人床

twinkle /'twɪŋkl; 'twɪŋkḷ/ *verb* 动词 (**twinkles, twinkling, twinkled** /'twɪŋkld; 'twɪŋkḷd/)
shine with a small bright light that comes and goes. Stars twinkle. 闪烁；闪耀（星光闪烁。）

twist /twɪst; twɪst/ *verb* 动词 (**twists, twisting, twisted**)
1 turn strongly 用力旋转: *Twist the lid off the jar.* 把罐子的盖儿拧下来。
2 change the shape of something by turning it in different directions; turn in many directions 把某物扭曲变形: *She twisted the metal into strange shapes.* 她把那块金属拧得奇形怪状。◇ *The path twists and turns through the forest.* 那条林间小路弯弯曲曲。
3 wind threads, etc round and round each other 把线等捻成或搓成绳子: *They twisted the sheets into a rope and escaped through the window.* 他们把床单拧成绳子从窗户逃跑了。

twitch /twɪtʃ; twɪtʃ/ *verb* 动词 (**twitches, twitching, twitched** /twɪtʃt; twɪtʃt/)
make a sudden quick movement with a part of your body（身体局部）抽动；抽搐: *Rabbits twitch their noses.* 兔子总抽动鼻子。

two /tuː; tu/ *number* 数词
2 二；两
in two into two pieces 成两块；成两半: *The cup fell on the floor and broke in two.* 杯子掉到地上摔成两半了。

type¹ /taɪp; taɪp/ *noun* 名词
a group of things that are the same in some way; a sort or kind 类型；种类: *An almond is a type of nut.* 杏仁是一种坚果。◇ *What type of music do you like?* 您爱听哪种音乐？

type² /taɪp; taɪp/ *verb* 动词 (**types, typing, typed** /taɪpt; taɪpt/)
make words on paper with a **typewriter** or **word processor** 用打字机（**typewriter**）或文字处理机（**word processor**）打印文字: *Her secretary types all her letters.* 她的秘书给她打各种信件。◇ *Can you type?* 您会打字吗？
type *noun* 名词 (no plural 无复数)
the letters that a machine makes on paper（印在纸上的）字，字体: *The type is too small—I can't read it.* 纸上印的字太小——我看不见。

typewriter /'taɪpraɪtə(r); 'taɪpˌraɪtɚ/ *noun* 名词
a machine with keys that you use to make words on paper 打字机: *an electric typewriter* 电动打字机

typical /'tɪpɪkl; 'tɪpɪkḷ/ *adjective* 形容词
Something that is typical is a good example of its kind 典型的: *We had a typical English breakfast—bacon, eggs, toast and tea.* 我们吃了一顿典型的英式早餐——腌猪肉、鸡蛋、烤面包片，还有茶。

T

typically /ˈtɪpɪkli; ˈtɪpɪklɪ/ *adverb* 副词
in a typical way 典型地: *She is typically British.* 她是个典型的英国人。

tyrant /ˈtaɪrənt; ˈtaɪrənt/ *noun* 名词
a person with a lot of power who rules a country in a cruel way 残暴的统治者；暴君

tyrannical /tɪˈrænɪkl; tɪˈrænɪkḷ/ *adjective* 形容词
a tyrannical ruler 专横的统治者

tyre /ˈtaɪə(r); taɪr/ *noun* 名词
a circle of rubber around the outside of a wheel, for example on a car or bicycle 轮胎（例如汽车或自行车的）: *I think we've got a flat tyre* (= a tyre without enough air inside). 我想我们的车胎瘪了（＝里面的空气不足）。☞ picture at **car** and **bicycle** 见 **car** 及 **bicycle** 词条插图

Uu

UFO /ju: ef 'əʊ; ˌju ɛf 'o/ *noun* 名词 (*plural* 复数作 **UFOs**)
a strange object that some people think they have seen in the sky and that may come from another planet. UFO is short for 'unidentified flying object'. 不明飞行物（有人认为是从其他星球来的。UFO 是 unidentified flying object 的缩略式。）

ugly /'ʌgli; 'ʌglɪ/ *adjective* 形容词 (**uglier, ugliest**)
not beautiful to look at 难看的；丑陋的：*an ugly face* 难看的脸

umbrella 伞

umbrella /ʌm'brelə; ʌm'brɛlə/ *noun* 名词
a thing that you hold over your head to keep you dry when it rains 伞；雨伞：*It started to rain, so I put my umbrella up.* 下雨了，我打起了雨伞。

umpire /'ʌmpaɪə(r); 'ʌmpaɪr/ *noun* 名词
a person who controls a tennis or cricket match（网球或板球的）裁判员

un- *prefix* 前缀
You can add **un-** to the beginning of some words to give them the opposite meaning, for example 在某些字前可加 **un-** 构成反义词，如：
unhappy = not happy
untrue = not true
undress = take clothes off (the opposite of **dress** * **dress** 的反义词)

unable /ʌn'eɪbl; ʌn'ebl̩/ *adjective* 形容词
not able to do something 不能做某事：*John is unable to come to the meeting because he is ill.* 约翰因病不能来开会。

unanimous /ju'nænɪməs; ju'nænəməs/ *adjective* 形容词
with the agreement of every person 大家一致同意的：*The decision was unanimous.* 这项决议是全体一致通过的。

unarmed /ˌʌn'ɑ:md; ʌn'ɑrmd/ *adjective* 形容词
If you are unarmed, you do not have a gun or any weapon 无武器的；未武装的：*an unarmed police officer* 没有武器的警察

unavoidable /ˌʌnə'vɔɪdəbl; ˌʌnə'vɔɪdəbl̩/ *adjective* 形容词
If something is unavoidable, you cannot stop it or get away from it 无法阻止的；无可避免的：*He had no money, so selling his car was unavoidable.* 他没有钱，难免要把汽车卖了。

unaware /ˌʌnə'weə(r); ˌʌnə'wɛr/ *adjective* 形容词
If you are unaware of something, you do not know about it 不知道；未察觉：*I was unaware of the danger.* 我没有觉察出有危险。

unbearable /ʌn'beərəbl; ʌn'bɛrəbl̩/ *adjective* 形容词
If something is unbearable, you cannot accept it because it is so bad 难以忍受的；不能容忍的：*Everyone left the room because the noise was unbearable.* 房间里声音吵得难以忍受，大家都走了。

unbearably /ʌn'beərəbli; ʌn'bɛrəblɪ/ *adverb* 副词
It was unbearably hot. 热得受不了了。

unbelievable /ˌʌnbɪ'li:vəbl; ˌʌnbɪ'livəbl̩/ *adjective* 形容词
very surprising or difficult to believe 令人惊奇的；难以相信的

unborn /ˌʌn'bɔ:n; ʌn'bɔrn/ *adjective* 形容词
not yet born 未出生的：*an unborn child* 未出生的孩子

uncertain /ʌn'sɜ:tn; ʌn'sɝtn̩/ *adjective* 形容词
not sure; not decided 不肯定；无把握；未决定：*I'm uncertain about what to do.* 对于该做什么事，我还没拿定主意。

uncertainty /ʌn'sɜ:tnti; ʌn'sɝtn̩tɪ/ *noun* 名词 (*plural* 复数作 **uncertainties**)
not being sure 不肯定；无把握：*There is uncertainty about who will be the next prime minister.* 无法肯定下届首相是谁。

uncle /'ʌŋkl; 'ʌŋkl̩/ *noun* 名词
the brother of your mother or father, or the husband of your aunt 母亲或父亲的哥哥或弟弟；姨母或姑母的丈夫；舅父；伯父；叔父；姨父；姑父: *Uncle Paul* 保罗叔叔 ☞ picture on page C3 见第C3页图

uncomfortable /ʌn'kʌmftəbl; ʌn-'kʌmfɚtəbl̩/ *adjective* 形容词
not comfortable 不舒服的；不舒适的: *The chair was hard and uncomfortable.* 这把椅子很硬，坐着不舒服。

uncomfortably /ʌn'kʌmftəbli; ʌn-'kʌmfɚtəblɪ/ *adverb* 副词
The room was uncomfortably hot. 这间屋子热得让人难受。

uncommon /ʌn'kɒmən; ʌn'kɑmən/ *adjective* 形容词
not common; that you do not see, hear, etc often 不普通的；不常见的；不常听的；不寻常的: *This tree is uncommon in Britain.* 这种树在英国很少见。

unconscious /ʌn'kɒnʃəs; ʌn'kɑnʃəs/ *adjective* 形容词
1 If you are unconscious, you are in a kind of sleep and you do not know what is happening 失去知觉的: *She fell and hit her head and she was unconscious for three days.* 她跌倒时撞到了头部，三天不省人事。
2 If you are unconscious of something, you do not know about it 不知道的；未察觉的: *Mike seemed unconscious that I was watching him.* 迈克好像并不知道我一直在看着他。

unconsciousness /ʌn'kɒnʃəsnəs; ʌn-'kɑnʃəsnɪs/ *noun* 名词 (no plural 无复数)
being unconscious 无知觉；无意识

uncover /ʌn'kʌvə(r); ʌn'kʌvɚ/ *verb* 动词 (**uncovers, uncovering, uncovered** /ʌn'kʌvəd; ʌn'kʌvɚd/)
take something from on top of another thing 移去某物上面的东西: *Uncover the pan and cook the soup for 30 minutes.* 把锅盖打开再把汤煮30分钟。

under /'ʌndə(r); 'ʌndɚ/ *preposition, adverb* 介词，副词
1 in or to a place that is lower than or below something 在某物下面；到下面: *The cat is under the table.* 猫在桌子底下呢。◇ *The boat sailed under the bridge.* 船在桥下穿过。◇ *The boat filled with water, then went under.* 船里进了水而沉下去了。☞ picture on page C1 见第C1页图
2 less than something 少于或小于某数量: *If you are under 17 you are not allowed to drive a car.* 未满17岁者不准开车。
3 covered by something 被某物遮着或盖着: *I'm wearing a vest under my shirt.* 我衬衫里面穿着件背心。
4 controlled by somebody or something 由某人或某事物控制: *The team are playing well under their new captain.* 这个队在新队长的指导下表现很好。

undergo /ˌʌndə'gəʊ; ˌʌndɚ'go/ *verb* 动词 (**undergoes, undergoing, underwent** /ˌʌndə'went; ˌʌndɚ'wɛnt/, **has undergone** /ˌʌndə'gɒn; ˌʌndɚ'gɔn/)
If you undergo something, it happens to you 经历或经受某事物: *Laura is in hospital undergoing an operation.* 劳拉现正住院做手术。

undergraduate /ˌʌndə'grædʒuət; ˌʌndɚ'grædʒuɪt/ *noun* 名词
a student at a university 大学生

underground[1] /'ʌndəgraʊnd; 'ʌndɚ-'graʊnd/ *adjective, adverb* 形容词，副词
under the ground 在地面下的: *an underground car park* 地下停车场

underground[2] /'ʌndəgraʊnd; 'ʌndɚ-'graʊnd/ *noun* 名词 (no plural 无复数)
an underground railway 地下铁路；地铁: *I go to work by underground.* 我坐地铁上班。◇ *We took the Underground to Piccadilly Circus.* 我们是乘地铁去的皮卡迪利广场。

undergrowth /'ʌndəgrəʊθ; 'ʌndɚ-ˌgroθ/ *noun* 名词 (no plural 无复数)
bushes and other plants that grow under trees（生长在大树下的）灌木丛: *There was a path through the undergrowth.* 在灌木丛中有条小路。

underline /ˌʌndə'laɪn; ˌʌndɚ'laɪn/ *verb* 动词 (**underlines, underlining, underlined** /ˌʌndə'laɪnd; ˌʌndɚ'laɪnd/)
draw a line under a word or words 在词语下面划线: *This sentence is underlined.* 本句下面划了线。

underneath /ˌʌndə'ni:θ; ˌʌndɚ'niθ/ *preposition, adverb* 介词，副词
under or below something 在某物的下面或底下: *The dog sat underneath the table.* 狗在桌子底下坐着。◇ *She wore a black jacket with a red jumper underneath.* 她穿着黑色的外衣，里面有件红色的套头毛衣。

underpants /ˈʌndəpænts; ˈʌndɚˌpænts/ *noun* 名词 (plural 复数)
a piece of clothing that a man or boy wears under his trousers（男用的）内裤，衬裤: *a pair of underpants* 一条内裤

undershirt /ˈʌndəʃɜːt; ˈʌndɚˌʃɝt/ *American English for* **vest** 美式英语，即 **vest**

understand /ˌʌndəˈstænd; ˌʌndɚˈstænd/ *verb* 动词 (**understands, understanding, understood** /ˌʌndəˈstʊd; ˌʌndɚˈstʊd/, **has understood**)
1 know what something means or why something happens 懂得或理解某事物: *I didn't understand what the teacher said.* 我不理解老师说的话。◇ *He doesn't understand Spanish.* 他不懂西班牙语。◇ *I don't understand why you're so angry.* 我不明白你为什么那么生气。
2 know something because somebody has told you about it 经人说明而领会；获悉；听说: *I understand that the plane from Geneva will be late.* 我听说从日内瓦来的飞机要误点。
make yourself understood make people understand you 使别人理解；把自己的意思表达清楚: *My German isn't very good but I can usually make myself understood.* 我的德语不太好，但一般还能把事情说清楚。

U

understanding[1] /ˌʌndəˈstændɪŋ; ˌʌndɚˈstændɪŋ/ *adjective* 形容词
If you are understanding, you listen to other people's problems and you try to understand them 体谅的；谅解的: *My parents are very understanding.* 我的父母很通情达理。

understanding[2] /ˌʌndəˈstændɪŋ; ˌʌndɚˈstændɪŋ/ *noun* 名词 (no plural 无复数)
knowing about something, or knowing how somebody feels（对某事物的）理解；（对他人情感的）体谅或谅解: *He's got a good understanding of computers.* 他对计算机很有研究。

understood *form of* **understand** ✳ **understand** 的不同形式

undertaker /ˈʌndəteɪkə(r); ˈʌndɚˌtekɚ/ *noun* 名词
a person whose job is to organize **funerals** (the time when dead people are buried or burned) 殡仪业人员（葬礼叫做 **funeral**）

underwater /ˌʌndəˈwɔːtə(r); ˈʌndɚˈwɔtɚ/ *adjective, adverb* 形容词，副词
below the top of water 水面下的: *Can you swim underwater?* 你会潜泳吗？

underwear /ˈʌndəweə(r); ˈʌndɚˌwɛr/ *noun* 名词 (no plural 无复数)
clothes that you wear next to your body, under your other clothes（贴身穿的）内衣物

underwent *form of* **undergo** ✳ **undergo** 的不同形式

undo /ʌnˈduː; ʌnˈdu/ *verb* 动词 (**undoes** /ʌnˈdʌz; ʌnˈdʌz/, **undoing, undid** /ʌnˈdɪd; ʌnˈdɪd/, **has undone** /ʌnˈdʌn; ʌnˈdʌn/)
open something that was tied or fixed 把捆绑着的或固着的东西解开或拆开: *I undid the string and opened the parcel.* 我解开绳子，把包裹打开了。◇ *I can't undo these buttons.* 这些扣子我解不开。
undone *adjective* 形容词
not tied or fixed 未捆绑着的或未固着的: *Your shoelaces are undone.* 你的鞋带开了。

undoubtedly /ʌnˈdaʊtɪdli; ʌnˈdaʊtɪdlɪ/ *adverb* 副词
certainly; without doubt 肯定地；毫无疑问地: *She is undoubtedly very intelligent.* 她无疑十分聪明。

undress /ˌʌnˈdres; ʌnˈdrɛs/ *verb* 动词 (**undresses, undressing, undressed** /ˌʌnˈdrest; ʌnˈdrɛst/)
take clothes off yourself or another person 脱衣服；为某人脱衣服: *He undressed and got into bed.* 他脱了衣服就上床了。◇ *She undressed her baby.* 她给那个小孩儿脱了衣服。
get undressed take off your clothes 脱衣服: *I got undressed and had a shower.* 我脱了衣服，冲了个淋浴。

uneasy /ʌnˈiːzi; ʌnˈizɪ/ *adjective* 形容词
worried that something is wrong 担心某事物出了差错: *I started to feel uneasy when the children didn't come home.* 孩子们没回家，我不由得担起心来。
uneasily /ʌnˈiːzɪli; ʌnˈizɪlɪ/ *adverb* 副词
She looked uneasily around the room. 她不安地打量了屋子一下。

unemployed /ˌʌnɪmˈplɔɪd; ˌʌnɪmˈplɔɪd/ *adjective* 形容词
If you are unemployed, you want a job but you do not have one 未被雇用的；失业的；待业的: *I was unemployed for a year*

after leaving school. 我中学毕业后待业一年。

unemployment /ˌʌnɪm'plɔɪmənt; ˌʌnɪm'plɔɪmənt/ *noun* 名词 (no plural 无复数)
when there are not enough jobs for the people who want to work 失业状况: *If the factory closes, unemployment in the town will increase.* 工厂要是倒闭了，镇上的失业状况就更加严重。

uneven /ˌʌn'i:vn; ʌn'ivən/ *adjective* 形容词
not smooth or flat 不平坦的；不光滑的: *We had to drive slowly because the road was so uneven.* 因为路很不平，我们只好慢慢开车。

unexpected /ˌʌnɪk'spektɪd; ˌʌnɪk'spɛktɪd/ *adjective* 形容词
surprising because you did not expect it 未料到的；意外的: *an unexpected visit* 意外的访问

unexpectedly *adverb* 副词
She arrived unexpectedly. 没想到她来了。

unfair /ˌʌn'feə(r); ʌn'fɛr/ *adjective* 形容词
Something that is unfair does not treat people in the same way or in the right way（指对待人）不公平的，不合理的: *It was unfair to give chocolates to some of the children and not to the others.* 把巧克力给一些孩子而不给另一些孩子是不公平的。

unfairly *adverb* 副词
He left his job because the boss was treating him unfairly. 他辞职了，因为老板对他不公正。

unfamiliar /ˌʌnfə'mɪliə(r); ˌʌnfə'mɪljɚ/ *adjective* 形容词
that you do not know; strange 不熟悉的；陌生的: *I woke up in an unfamiliar room.* 我醒来的时候是在一间陌生的屋子里。

unfashionable /ʌn'fæʃnəbl; ʌn'fæʃnəbḷ/ *adjective* 形容词
not fashionable 不时髦的: *unfashionable clothes* 不时髦的衣物

unfit /ˌʌn'fɪt; ʌn'fɪt/ *adjective* 形容词
1 not healthy or strong 不健康的；不强壮的: *She never takes any exercise — that's why she's so unfit.* 她从来不锻炼身体——难怪她很不健康。
2 not good enough for something 不够好的；不适宜的: *This house is unfit for people to live in.* 这所房子不适宜住人。

unfold /ʌn'fəʊld; ʌn'fold/ *verb* 动词 (**unfolds, unfolding, unfolded**)
open something to make it flat; open out and become flat（使某物）展开；打开: *Marie unfolded the newspaper and started to read.* 玛丽把报纸打开就看了起来。◇ *The sofa unfolds to make a bed.* 这张沙发可以打开当床用。

unfortunate /ʌn'fɔ:tʃənət; ʌn'fɔrtʃənɪt/ *adjective* 形容词
not lucky 不幸的；倒霉的: *It's unfortunate that you were ill on your birthday.* 你过生日那天病了，可真倒霉。

unfortunately *adverb* 副词
it is unfortunate that 不幸的是: *I would like to give you some money, but unfortunately I haven't got any.* 我倒是愿意给你些钱，但是遗憾的是我并没有哇。

unfriendly /ˌʌn'frendli; ʌn'frɛndlɪ/ *adjective* 形容词
not friendly; not kind or helpful to other people 不友好的；不和蔼的；不愿帮助人的

ungrateful /ʌn'greɪtfl; ʌn'gretfəl/ *adjective* 形容词
If you are ungrateful, you do not show thanks when somebody helps you or gives you something 不感激的；不领情的；忘恩负义的: *Don't be so ungrateful! I spent all morning looking for this present.* 你别不领这份情！我花了整整一上午才物色到这件礼物。

unhappy /ʌn'hæpi; ʌn'hæpɪ/ *adjective* 形容词 (**unhappier, unhappiest**)
not happy; sad 不愉快的；不高兴的；悲哀的: *He was very unhappy when his wife left him.* 他妻子离开他了，他非常难过。

unhappily /ʌn'hæpɪli; ʌn'hæpɪlɪ/ *adverb* 副词
'I failed the exam,' she said unhappily. "我没考及格，"她难过地说。

unhappiness /ʌn'hæpɪnəs; ʌn'hæpɪnɪs/ *noun* 名词 (no plural 无复数)
John has had a lot of unhappiness in his life. 约翰生活中有很多不如意的事。

unhealthy /ʌn'helθi; ʌn'hɛlθɪ/ *adjective* 形容词 (**unhealthier, unhealthiest**)
1 not well; often ill 不健康的；常生病的: *an unhealthy child* 不健康的孩子
2 that can make you ill 能得病的；不利于健康的: *unhealthy food* 不利于健康的食物

U

uniform /'ju:nɪfɔ:m; 'junəˌfɔrm/ *noun* 名词
the special clothes that everybody in the same job, school, etc wears 统一的服装；制服；校服：*Police officers wear blue uniforms.* 警察穿的是蓝色的制服。

uninhabited /ˌʌnɪn'hæbɪtɪd; ˌʌnɪn'hæbɪtɪd/ *adjective* 形容词
where nobody lives 无人居住的：*an uninhabited island* 荒岛

union /'ju:niən; 'junjən/ *noun* 名词
1 (*plural* 复数作 **unions**) a group of workers who have joined together to talk to their managers about things like pay and the way they work（同管理阶层谈判工资及待遇等的）工作人员联合会；工会：*the National Union of Teachers* 全国教师工会
2 (*plural* 复数作 **unions**) a group of people or countries that have joined together（集体或国家之间的）联盟
3 (no plural 无复数) coming together 结合；联合；合并：*The union of England and Scotland was in 1707.* 英格兰与苏格兰于1707年合并。

the Union Jack /ðə ˌju:niən 'dʒæk; ðə 'junjən 'dʒæk/ *noun* 名词
the flag of the United Kingdom 联合王国国旗；英国国旗

U

unique /ju'ni:k; ju'nik/ *adjective* 形容词
not like anybody or anything else 不像他人或他事物的；独一无二的：*Everybody in the world is unique.* 世界上每个人都是与众不同的。

unit /'ju:nɪt; 'junɪt/ *noun* 名词
1 one complete thing or group that may be part of something larger（可构成一整体而自成一完整部分的）单元；单位；部件：*The book has twelve units.* 这本书有十二个单元。
2 a measurement（计量的）单位：*A metre is a unit of length and a kilogram is a unit of weight.* 米是长度单位，公斤是重量单位。

unite /ju'naɪt; ju'naɪt/ *verb* 动词 (**unites, uniting, united**)
join together to become one; put two things together 结合成为一体；合二而一；联合；合并：*East and West Germany united in 1990.* 东德和西德在1990年统一了。
united *adjective* 形容词
joined together 联合的：*the United States of America* 美利坚合众国

universal /ˌju:nɪ'vɜ:sl; ˌjunə'vɝsl̩/ *adjective* 形容词
of, by or for everybody 所有人的：*This subject is of universal interest.* 这个问题是大家都关心的事。

the universe /ðə 'ju:nɪvɜ:s; ðə 'junəˌvɝs/ *noun* 名词 (no plural 无复数)
the earth and all the stars, planets and everything else in space 宇宙；世界；天地万物

university /ˌju:nɪ'vɜ:səti; ˌjunə'vɝsətɪ/ *noun* 名词 (*plural* 复数作 **universities**)
a place where people go to study more difficult subjects after they have left school 大学：*I'm hoping to go to university next year.* 我希望明年能上大学。◇ *My sister is at university studying Chemistry.* 我姐姐在大学学习化学。✪ If you pass special courses at a university, you get a **degree**. 大学专业考试及格可获得学位，叫做 **degree**。

unjust /ˌʌn'dʒʌst; ʌn'dʒʌst/ *adjective* 形容词
not just; not fair or right 不公平的；不合理的；非正义的：*This tax is unjust because poor people pay as much as rich people.* 这种税制不合理，因为穷人和富人纳的税一样多。

unkind /ˌʌn'kaɪnd; ʌn'kaɪnd/ *adjective* 形容词
not kind; cruel 不亲切的；不和蔼的；残忍的：*It was unkind of you to laugh at her hat.* 你嘲笑她的帽子，未免太刻薄了。

unknown /ˌʌn'nəʊn; ʌn'non/ *adjective* 形容词
1 that you do not know 不知道的；不认识的：*an unknown face* 陌生的脸
2 not famous 不出名的：*an unknown actor* 默默无闻的演员

unless /ən'les; ən'lɛs/ *conjunction* 连词
if not; except if 如果不；除非：*You will be late unless you leave now.* 你现在不走就非迟到不可。◇ *Unless you work harder you'll fail the exam.* 你要是不努一把力就一定考不及格。

unlike /ˌʌn'laɪk; ʌn'laɪk/ *preposition* 介词
not like; different from 不相似；不相同：*She is thin, unlike her sister who is quite fat.* 她很瘦，跟她姐姐不一样，她姐姐很胖。

unlikely /ʌn'laɪkli; ʌn'laɪklɪ/ *adjective* 形容词 (**unlikelier, unlikeliest**)
If something is unlikely, it will probably not happen 不大可能发生的: *It is unlikely that it will rain.* 不大可能下雨。◇ *He is unlikely to pass the exam.* 他不太可能及格。

unload /ˌʌn'ləʊd; ʌn'lod/ *verb* 动词 (**unloads, unloading, unloaded**)
take off or out the things that a car, lorry, ship or plane is carrying 从汽车、轮船、飞机上卸下货物: *I unloaded the shopping from the car.* 我把买来的东西从汽车上搬下来。◇ *They unloaded the ship at the dock.* 他们在码头卸船。

unlock /ˌʌn'lɒk; ʌn'lɑk/ *verb* 动词 (**unlocks, unlocking, unlocked** /ˌʌn'lɒkt; ʌn'lɑkt/)
open something with a key 用钥匙打开某物: *I unlocked the door and went in.* 我打开门锁就进去了。

unlucky /ʌn'lʌki; ʌn'lʌkɪ/ *adjective* 形容词 (**unluckier, unluckiest**)
1 If you are unlucky, good things do not happen to you 不幸的；倒霉的；运气不好的: *She's unlucky—she plays very well but she never wins a game.* 她运气不好——她在比赛中表现不错，可总是赢不了。
2 Something that is unlucky brings bad luck 带来坏运气的: *Some people think that the number 13 is unlucky.* 有人认为13这个数字不吉利。

unluckily /ʌn'lʌkɪli; ʌn'lʌkɪlɪ/ *adverb* 副词
it is unlucky that 不幸运的是；倒霉地: *Unluckily, I missed the bus.* 真倒霉，我没赶上公共汽车。

unmarried /ˌʌn'mærɪd; ʌn'mærɪd/ *adjective* 形容词
not married; without a husband or wife 未婚的；独身的

unnecessary /ʌn'nesəsri; ʌn'nɛsəˌsɛrɪ/ *adjective* 形容词
not necessary; not needed 不必要的；不需要的

unpack /ˌʌn'pæk; ʌn'pæk/ *verb* 动词 (**unpacks, unpacking, unpacked** /ˌʌn'pækt; ʌn'pækt/)
take all the things out of a bag, suitcase, etc 把口袋、衣箱等里的东西都取出来: *Have you unpacked your suitcase?* 你把衣箱里的东西都拿出来了吗？◇ *We arrived at the hotel, unpacked, and then went to the beach.* 我们到旅馆后把行李里的东西取出来，然后到海滩去了。

unpaid /ˌʌn'peɪd; ʌn'ped/ *adjective* 形容词
not paid 未支付的；未缴纳的: *an unpaid bill* 未付讫的账单

unpleasant /ʌn'pleznt; ʌn'plɛznt/ *adjective* 形容词
not pleasant; not nice 使人不愉快的；不合意的: *There was an unpleasant smell of bad fish.* 有一种难闻的臭鱼味儿。

unpleasantly *adverb* 副词
It was unpleasantly hot in that room. 那间屋子热得难受。

unplug /ˌʌn'plʌg; ʌn'plʌg/ *verb* 动词 (**unplugs, unplugging, unplugged** /ˌʌn'plʌgd; ʌn'plʌgd/)
take the electric plug of a machine out of a place in a wall (called a **socket**) where there is electricity 拔出插在电源插座(**socket**)上的插头: *Could you unplug the TV?* 您把电视机的插头拔下来行吗？

unpopular /ˌʌn'pɒpjələ(r); ʌn'pɑpjələ/ *adjective* 形容词
not popular; not liked by many people 不得人心的；不受欢迎的: *He's unpopular at work because he's lazy.* 他工作部门的人不喜欢他，因为他很懒。

unreliable /ˌʌnrɪ'laɪəbl; ˌʌnrɪ'laɪəbl̩/ *adjective* 形容词
not reliable; that you cannot trust 不可靠的；靠不住的: *Don't lend her any money—she's very unreliable.* 别把钱借给她——她这个人很不可靠。◇ *an unreliable car* 靠不住的汽车

unsafe /ˌʌn'seɪf; ʌn'sef/ *adjective* 形容词
not safe; dangerous 不安全的；危险的: *Don't climb on that wall—it's unsafe.* 别爬那堵墙——有危险。

unsatisfactory /ˌʌnsætɪs'fæktri; ˌʌnsætɪs'fæktərɪ/ *adjective* 形容词
not satisfactory; not good enough 不能令人满足的；不能令人满意的: *Tina's work was unsatisfactory so I asked her to do it again.* 蒂纳做的工作不行，我叫她返工了。

unstable /ˌʌn'steɪbl; ʌn'stebl̩/ *adjective* 形容词
Something that is unstable may fall, move or change 可能跌落、移动或改变的；不稳的: *This bridge is unstable.* 这座桥不稳。◇ *unstable government* 不稳固的政府

U

unsuccessful /ˌʌnsək'sesfl; ˌʌnsək'sɛsfəl/ *adjective* 形容词
If you are unsuccessful, you have not done what you wanted and tried to do 未成功的: *I tried to repair the bike but I was unsuccessful.* 那辆自行车我没修理好。
unsuccessfully /ˌʌnsək'sesfəli; ˌʌnsək'sɛsfəlɪ/ *adverb* 副词
Gary tried unsuccessfully to lift the box. 加里抬不动那个箱子。

unsuitable /ˌʌn'su:təbl; ʌn'sutəbḷ/ *adjective* 形容词
not suitable; not right for somebody or something 不适合的；（对某人或某事物）不合适的: *This film is unsuitable for children.* 这部影片不适宜儿童观看。

unsure /ˌʌn'ʃʊə(r); ʌn'ʃʊr/ *adjective* 形容词
not sure 不确知；无把握: *We were unsure what to do.* 我们闹不清要做什么。

untidy /ʌn'taɪdi; ʌn'taɪdɪ/ *adjective* 形容词 (**untidier**, **untidiest**)
not tidy; not with everything in the right place 不整齐的；乱七八糟的: *Your room is always so untidy!* 你的屋子总是那么乱！
untidiness /ʌn'taɪdinəs; ʌn'taɪdɪnɪs/ *noun* 名词 (no plural 无复数)
I hate untidiness! 我看不惯不整齐的东西！

U

untie /ʌn'taɪ; ʌn'taɪ/ *verb* 动词 (**unties**, **untying**, **untied** /ʌn'taɪd; ʌn'taɪd/, **has untied**)
1 take off the string or rope that is holding something or somebody 除掉捆绑某物或某人的绳索: *I untied the parcel.* 我把包裹上的绳子解开了。
2 make a knot or bow loose 解开结或扣: *Can you untie this knot?* 你把这个结解开行吗？

until /ən'tɪl; ən'tɪl/ *conjunction* 连词
up to the time when 直到某时候（为止）: *Stay in bed until you feel better.* 您要卧床休息，等感到好些再起来。
until *preposition* 介词
1 up to a certain time 直到某时候（为止）: *The shop is open until 6.30.* 这家商店营业到6时30分。
2 before 在某时候之前: *I can't come until tomorrow.* 我明天才能来。

untrue /ˌʌn'tru:; ʌn'tru/ *adjective* 形容词
not true or correct 不真实的；不正确的: *What you said was completely untrue.* 你说的完全不对。

unusual /ʌn'ju:ʒuəl; ʌn'juʒəl/ *adjective* 形容词
If something is unusual, it does not often happen or you do not often see it 罕有的；异乎寻常的: *It's unusual to see a cat without a tail.* 难得看见没有尾巴的猫。◇ *What an unusual name!* 多么不寻常的名字啊！
unusually /ʌn'ju:ʒuəli; ʌn'juʒəlɪ/ *adverb* 副词
It was an unusually hot summer. 这个夏天热得出奇。

unwanted /ˌʌn'wɒntɪd; ʌn'wɑntɪd/ *adjective* 形容词
not wanted 不想要的；不该有的: *unwanted children* 不想要的孩子

unwelcome /ˌʌn'welkəm; ʌn'wɛlkəm/ *adjective* 形容词
If somebody or something is unwelcome, you are not happy to have or see them 不受欢迎的: *an unwelcome visitor* 不受欢迎的访客

unwell /ʌn'wel; ʌn'wɛl/ *adjective* 形容词
not well; ill 不健康的；有病的

unwilling /ˌʌn'wɪlɪŋ; ʌn'wɪlɪŋ/ *adjective* 形容词
If you are unwilling to do something, you are not ready or happy to do it 不愿意的；不情愿的；勉强的: *He was unwilling to lend me any money.* 他一点儿钱都不愿意借给我。

unwrap /ˌʌn'ræp; ʌn'ræp/ *verb* 动词 (**unwraps**, **unwrapping**, **unwrapped** /ˌʌn'ræpt; ʌn'ræpt/)
take off the paper or cloth that is around something 除掉包住某物的纸或布: *I unwrapped the parcel.* 我把包裹打开了。

up /ʌp; ʌp/ *preposition*, *adverb* 介词，副词
1 in or to a higher place 在上面；向上面: *We climbed up the mountain.* 我们爬上了山。◇ *Put your hand up if you know the answer.* 知道答案的人把手举起来。☞ picture on page C4 见第C4页图
2 from sitting or lying to standing 起立；起身: *Stand up, please.* 请站起来。◇ *What time do you get up?* (= out of bed) 您什么时候起床？
3 in a way that is bigger, stronger, etc 趋向于大、多、强等: *The price of petrol is going up.* 汽油涨价了。◇ *Please turn the*

radio up—I can't hear it. 请把收音机声音调大些——我听不清楚。

4 so that it is finished 完结: *Who used all the coffee up?* 谁把咖啡都用光了?

5 along 沿着;顺着: *We walked up the road.* 我们顺着那条路走。

6 towards and near somebody or something 接近某人或某事物: *She came up to me and asked me the time.* 她走到我跟前向我打听时间。

7 into pieces 成为碎块: *Cut the meat up.* 把肉切碎。

be up be out of bed 起床: *'Is Joe up?' 'No, he's still asleep.'* "乔起床了吗?" "没有,他还睡着呢。"

it's up to you you are the person who should do or decide something 应该由你来做;由你来决定: *'What shall we do this evening?' 'I don't mind. It's up to you.'* "咱们今天晚上做什么?" "我无所谓。随你便。"

up to 1 as far as; until 直至某时候(为止): *Up to now, she has worked very hard.* 到现在为止,她一直非常努力。 **2** as much or as many as 多至;多达: *Up to 300 people came to the meeting.* 来参加会议的多达300人。 **3** doing something 做某事情: *What is that man up to?* 那个男的干什么呢?

update /ˌʌp'deɪt; ʌp'det/ *verb* 动词 (**updates, updating, updated**)
make something more modern or add new things to it 更新某事物或增加新内容: *The information on the computer is updated every week.* 计算机的资料每星期都不断更新。

uphill /ˌʌp'hɪl; 'ʌp'hɪl/ *adverb* 副词
up, towards the top of a hill 上山坡: *It's difficult to ride a bicycle uphill.* 骑自行车上山坡很难。

upon /ə'pɒn; ə'pɑn/ *preposition* 介词
on 表示在何处或何时的词 ✪ **On** is the word that we usually use. ✳ **on** 是常用词。

once upon a time a long time ago (words that sometimes begin children's stories) 很久以前;从前(有时用作童话的开始语): *Once upon a time there was a beautiful princess…* 从前有个美丽的公主…

upper /'ʌpə(r); 'ʌpɚ/ *adjective* 形容词
higher than another; top 比另一物高的;上面的: *the upper lip* 上嘴唇 ✪ opposite 反义词: **lower**

upright /'ʌpraɪt; 'ʌpˌraɪt/ *adjective, adverb* 形容词,副词
standing straight up, not lying down 直立的: *Put the ladder upright against the wall.* 把梯子靠墙立起来。

upset /ˌʌp'set; ʌp'sɛt/ *verb* 动词 (**upsets, upsetting, upset, has upset**)
1 make somebody feel unhappy or worried 使某人感到不愉快或感到担忧: *You upset Tom when you said he was fat.* 你说汤姆很胖,他听了很不痛快。
2 make something go wrong 扰乱某事物: *The bad weather upset our plans for the weekend.* 天气不好,把我们的周末安排打乱了。
3 knock something so that it turns over and things fall out 把某物打翻或弄翻,里面的东西掉出来: *I upset a glass of wine all over the table.* 我把酒杯碰翻了,洒了一桌子葡萄酒。

upset /'ʌpset; 'ʌpˌsɛt/ *noun* 名词
an illness in your stomach 肠胃不适;恶心: *Sara has got a stomach upset.* 萨拉的肠胃很不舒服。

upset /ˌʌp'set; ʌp'sɛt/ *adjective* 形容词
1 unhappy or worried 不愉快或担忧: *The children were very upset when their dog died.* 孩子们的狗死了,他们都很伤心。
2 ill 有病: *I've got an upset stomach.* 我有些反胃。

upside down /ˌʌpsaɪd 'daʊn; 'ʌpˌsaɪd 'daʊn/ *adverb* 副词
with the top part at the bottom 上下颠倒: *The picture is upside down.* 这张画儿上下颠倒了。

upside down 上下颠倒

upstairs /ˌʌp'steəz; 'ʌp'stɛrz/ *adverb* 副词
to or on a higher floor of a building 向楼上或在楼上: *I went upstairs to bed.* 我上楼睡觉去了。

upstairs *adjective* 形容词
An upstairs window was open. 楼上有扇窗户开了。
✪ opposite 反义词: **downstairs**

upwards /'ʌpwədz; 'ʌpwɚdz/, **upward** /'ʌpwəd; 'ʌpwɚd/ *adverb* 副词
up; towards a higher place 向上;向高处: *We climbed upwards, towards the top of the mountain.* 我们向上爬,要爬到山顶。✪ opposite 反义词: **downwards**

U

urban /'ɜ:bən; 'ɝbən/ *adjective* 形容词
of a town or city 市镇的: *urban areas* 市区

urge[1] /ɜ:dʒ; ɝdʒ/ *verb* 动词 (**urges, urging, urged** /ɜ:dʒd; ɝdʒd/)
try to make somebody do something 尽力使某人做某事: *I urged him to stay for dinner.* 我劝他留下来吃晚饭。

urge[2] /ɜ:dʒ; ɝdʒ/ *noun* 名词
a strong feeling that you want to do something 想做某事的强烈愿望: *I had a sudden urge to laugh.* 我当时都要笑出声来。

urgency /'ɜ:dʒənsi; 'ɝdʒənsɪ/ *noun* 名词 (no plural 无复数)
the need to do something quickly because it is very important 紧急情况

urgent /'ɜ:dʒənt; 'ɝdʒənt/ *adjective* 形容词
so important that you must do it or answer it quickly 紧急的；急迫的: *The doctor received an urgent telephone call.* 医生接到个紧急电话。
urgently *adverb* 副词
I must see you urgently. 我有急事要见您。

us /əs, ʌs; əs, 'ʌs/ *pronoun* 代词 (plural 复数)
me and another person or other people; me and you 我们；咱们: *We were pleased when she invited us to dinner.* 她邀请我们吃饭，我们都很高兴。◇ *John wrote to us.* 约翰给我们写了信。

use[1] /ju:z; juz/ *verb* 动词 (**uses, using, used** /ju:zd; juzd/)
1 do a job with something 使用；运用；利用: *Could I use your telephone?* 我用一下您的电话行吗？◇ *Do you know how to use this machine?* 您会用这台机器吗？◇ *Wood is used to make paper.* 木头可用以造纸。
2 take something 食用或饮用: *Don't use all the milk.* 别把牛奶都用完。
use up use something until you have no more 把某物用光: *I've used up all the coffee, so I need to buy some more.* 我把咖啡都用完了，得再买点儿了。

use[2] /ju:s; jus/ *noun* 名词
1 (no plural 无复数) using 使用；运用；利用: *This pool is for the use of hotel guests only.* 这个游泳池仅供旅馆顾客使用。
2 (*plural* 复数作 **uses**) what you can do with something 用途；用法: *This tool has many uses.* 这个工具有很多用处。
have the use of something have the right to use something 有使用某物的权利: *I've got the use of Jim's car while he's on holiday.* 吉姆放假，我可以用他的汽车。
it's no use it will not help to do something 没有用处: *It's no use telling her anything—she never listens.* 跟她说什么都没用——她听不进去。
make use of something find a way of using something 对某事物加以利用: *If you don't want that box, I can make use of it.* 你要是不要那个箱子，我倒是用得上。

used[1] /ju:zd; juzd/ *adjective* 形容词
not new 使用过的；旧的: *The garage sells used cars.* 那个修车厂出售旧汽车。

used[2] /ju:st; just/ *adjective* 形容词
be used to something know something well because you have seen, heard, tasted, done, etc it a lot 已习惯或适应某事物: *I'm used to walking because I haven't got a car.* 我已经走惯了，因为我没有汽车。
get used to something begin to know something well after a time 已开始熟悉某事物: *I'm getting used to my new job.* 我渐渐熟悉我的新工作了。

used[3] /ju:st; just/ *verb* 动词
used to words that tell us about something that happened often or that was true in the past 用以表示过去经常发生的事或现象: *She used to smoke when she was young.* 她年轻的时候常常吸烟。◇ *I used to be afraid of dogs, but now I like them.* 我以前一向怕狗，现在倒很喜欢狗了。◇ *I didn't use to like fish, but I do now.* 我并不是一直喜欢鱼的，可是现在很喜欢了。

useful /'ju:sfl; 'jusfəl/ *adjective* 形容词
good and helpful for doing something 有用的；有好处的: *This bag will be useful for carrying my books.* 这个袋子盛我的书可能很有用。

useless /'ju:sləs; 'juslɪs/ *adjective* 形容词
1 not good for anything 没有用处的: *A car is useless without petrol.* 汽车没有汽油就没有用。
2 that does not do what you hoped 不能达到目的的: *It was useless asking my brother for money—he didn't have any.* 找我弟弟要钱也没用，他根本没钱。

U

user /ˈju:zə(r); ˈjuzɚ/ *noun* 名词
a person who uses something 使用某事物的人；使用者: *computer users* 使用计算机的人

usual /ˈju:ʒuəl; ˈjuʒəl/ *adjective* 形容词
that happens most often 通常的；平常的；惯常的: *It's not usual for children in Britain to go to school on Saturdays.* 英国儿童星期六上学的可不普通。
as usual as happens most often 像往常一样: *Julie was late, as usual.* 朱莉迟到了，一贯如此。
usually /ˈju:ʒuəli; ˈjuʒəlɪ/ *adverb* 副词
We usually go to Spain for our holidays, but this year we are staying at home. 我们一般都到西班牙去度假，今年却打算呆在家里。

utter¹ /ˈʌtə(r); ˈʌtɚ/ *adjective* 形容词
complete 完全的: *The room was in utter darkness and I couldn't see anything.* 当时屋里十分黑，我什么都看不见。
utterly *adverb* 副词
completely or very 完全地；非常: *That's utterly impossible!* 那是绝对不可能的！

utter² /ˈʌtə(r); ˈʌtɚ/ *verb* 动词 (**utters, uttering, uttered** /ˈʌtəd; ˈʌtɚd/)
say something or make a sound with your mouth 说话或用嘴发出声音: *He uttered a cry of pain.* 他痛苦得喊叫起来。

U

Vv

V *short way of writing* **volt** ✻ **volt** 的缩写形式

v /viː; vi/ *short for* **versus** ✻ **versus** 的缩略式：*Liverpool v Manchester United* 利物浦队对曼彻斯特联队

vacancy /ˈveɪkənsi; ˈvekənsɪ/ *noun* 名词 (*plural* 复数作 **vacancies**)

1 a job that nobody is doing 现无人担任的职位；空缺: *We have a vacancy for a secretary in our office.* 我们办公室有个秘书空缺。

2 a room in a hotel that nobody is using（指旅馆中）现无人住的房间，空余房间: *The sign outside the hotel said 'no vacancies'* (= the hotel is full). 旅馆外面有个告示，上面写着"客满"。

vacant /ˈveɪkənt; ˈvekənt/ *adjective* 形容词

empty; with nobody in it 空着的；没有人的: *an vacant room* 空屋子

vacation /vəˈkeɪʃn; veˈkeʃən/ *noun* 名词

1 a holiday time when a university is not open（大学的）假期: *the summer vacation*（大学的）暑假

2 *American English for* **holiday** 美式英语，即 **holiday**

vacuum /ˈvækjuəm; ˈvækjʊəm/ *noun* 名词

a space with no air, gas or anything else in it 真空

vacuum cleaner
真空吸尘器

vacuum cleaner /ˈvækjuəm ˌkliːnə(r); ˈvækjʊəm ˌklinɚ/ *noun* 名词

a machine that cleans carpets by sucking up dirt 真空吸尘器

vague /veɪɡ; veɡ/ *adjective* 形容词 (**vaguer, vaguest**)

not clear or not exact 含糊的；不清楚的；不确切的: *I couldn't find the house because he gave me very vague directions.* 我找不到那所房子，因为他没把位置跟我说清楚。

vaguely *adverb* 副词

I vaguely remember what happened. 我模模糊糊地记得发生的事情。

vain /veɪn; ven/ *adjective* 形容词 (**vainer, vainest**)

1 too proud of what you can do or how you look（对自己的工作能力或相貌）自负的；自视过高的 ✪ The noun is **vanity**. 名词是 **vanity**。

2 with no success; useless 未成功的；无用的；徒劳的: *They made a vain attempt to save his life.* 他们竭尽全力也未能救他一命。

in vain with no success 未成功；徒劳；白费: *I tried in vain to sleep.* 我怎么也睡不着。

valid /ˈvælɪd; ˈvælɪd/ *adjective* 形容词

If something like a ticket or a cheque is valid, you can use it and other people will accept it（指票据等）有效的: *Your bus ticket is valid for one week.* 您这张公共汽车票有效期是一个星期。

valley /ˈvæli; ˈvælɪ/ *noun* 名词 (*plural* 复数作 **valleys**)

low land, usually with a river, between hills or mountains 谷；山谷（通常中间有溪流）: *the Loire Valley* 卢瓦尔谷地

valuable /ˈvæljuəbl; ˈvæljʊəbḷ/ *adjective* 形容词

1 worth a lot of money 贵重的；值钱的: *Is this ring valuable?* 这枚戒指值钱吗？

2 very useful 很有用的；很有价值的: *valuable information* 极重要的信息

value[1] /ˈvæljuː; ˈvæljʊ/ *noun* 名词

1 (*plural* 复数作 **values**) how much money you can sell something for（某物可出售的）钱数；价值: *What is the value of this painting?* 这幅画儿值多少钱？

2 (no plural 无复数) how useful or important something is（某事物的）用处或重要性: *Their help was of great value.* 他们的帮助极为重要。

3 (no plural 无复数) how much something is worth compared with its price（某物与本身价格相比的）价值；合算的或实惠的程度: *The meal was good value at only £4.50.* 这顿饭只花了4.50英镑，很上算。

V

value² /'vælju:; 'væljʊ/ *verb* 动词 (**values**, **valuing**, **valued** /'vælju:d; 'væljʊd/)
1 think that something is very important 认为某事物很重要；重视某事物: *I value my freedom.* 我珍视我的自由。
2 say how much money something is worth 说出某事物的价值；给某物估价: *The house was valued at £80 000.* 这所房子值80 000英镑。

vampire /'væmpaɪə(r); 'væmpaɪr/ *noun* 名词
a dead person in stories who comes to life at night and drinks people's blood（故事中的）吸血鬼（夜晚出来吸人血）

van 客货车

van /væn; væn/ *noun* 名词
a kind of big car or small lorry for carrying things（有篷盖的）客货车

vandal /'vændl; 'vændḷ/ *noun* 名词
a person who damages and breaks things that belong to other people 毁坏他人物品的人: *Vandals have damaged the telephone box by our house.* 有些破坏公物的流氓把我们家附近的电话亭弄坏了。
vandalism /'vændəlɪzəm; 'vændḷˌɪzəm/ *noun* 名词 (no plural 无复数)
damage by vandals 对他人物品的毁坏: *Vandalism is a problem in this part of the city.* 这个城市这一带流氓破坏活动很成问题。

vanilla /və'nɪlə; və'nɪlə/ *noun* 名词 (no plural 无复数)
a plant that gives a taste to some sweet foods, for example white ice-cream 香子兰（可提炼香精，例如制做白色的香草冰激凌）

vanish /'vænɪʃ; 'vænɪʃ/ *verb* 动词 (**vanishes**, **vanishing**, **vanished** /'vænɪʃt; 'vænɪʃt/)
go away suddenly; disappear 突然离去；消失: *The thief ran into the crowd and vanished.* 那个小偷跑进人群中不见了。

vanity /'vænəti; 'vænətɪ/ *noun* 名词 (no plural 无复数)
being too proud of what you can do or how you look（对自己的工作能力或相貌的）自负；自视过高 ✪ The adjective is **vain**. 形容词是 **vain**。

varied, **varies** *forms of* **vary** ✱ **vary** 的不同形式

variety /və'raɪəti; və'raɪətɪ/ *noun* 名词
1 (no plural 无复数) If something has variety, it is full of different things and changes often 种类多而且常变化；多样化: *There's a lot of variety in my new job.* 我的新工作内容五花八门。
2 (no plural 无复数) a lot of different things 各种各样的事物: *There's a large variety of dishes on the menu.* 菜单上有种类繁多的菜肴。
3 (*plural* 复数作 **varieties**) a kind of something（事物的）种；类: *This variety of apple is very sweet.* 这种苹果很甜。

various /'veəriəs; 'vɛrɪəs/ *adjective* 形容词
many different 各种各样的: *We sell this shirt in various colours and sizes.* 我们出售这种衬衫颜色、尺码齐全。

varnish /'vɑ:nɪʃ; 'vɑrnɪʃ/ *noun* 名词 (no plural 无复数)
a clear paint with no colour, that you put on something to make it shine 清漆；罩光漆

vary /'veəri; 'vɛrɪ/ *verb* 动词 (**varies**, **varying**, **varied** /'veərid; 'vɛrɪd/, **has varied**)
be or become different from each other 相互间（改变得）有区别: *These tapes vary in price from £6 to £9.* 这些带子价钱由6英镑到9英镑不等。

vase /vɑ:z; ves/ *noun* 名词
a pot that you put cut flowers in 花瓶

vase 花瓶

vast /vɑ:st; væst/ *adjective* 形容词
very big 非常大的；巨大的: *Australia is a vast country.* 澳大利亚是个很大的国家。

veal /vi:l; vil/ *noun* 名词 (no plural 无复数)
meat from a young cow (a **calf**)（食用的）小牛肉（小牛叫做 **calf**）☞ Note at **cow** 见 **cow** 词条注释

vegetable /'vedʒtəbl; 'vɛdʒtəbḷ/ *noun* 名词
a plant that we eat. Potatoes, carrots and beans are vegetables 蔬菜（土豆、胡萝卜、豆子都是蔬菜）: *vegetable soup* 蔬菜汤

V

vegetarian /ˌvedʒɪˈteəriən; ˌvɛdʒəˈtɛrɪən/ *noun* 名词
a person who does not eat meat 吃素的人

vehicle /ˈviːəkl; ˈvihɪkl̩/ *noun* 名词
any thing that carries people or things from one place to another. Cars, buses and bicycles are all vehicles. 可以把人或物从一处运送到另一处的任何东西；运输工具（小轿车、公共汽车、自行车都是运输工具。）

veil /veɪl; vel/ *noun* 名词
a piece of thin material that a woman puts over her head and face（女用的）面纱：*Women wear veils in a lot of Muslim countries.* 很多穆斯林国家的女子都带面纱。

vein /veɪn; ven/ *noun* 名词
one of the small tubes in your body that carry blood to the heart 静脉

velvet /ˈvelvɪt; ˈvɛlvɪt/ *noun* 名词 (no plural 无复数)
cloth that is soft and thick on one side 立绒；天鹅绒：*red velvet curtains* 红色的天鹅绒帘子

verb /vɜːb; vɝb/ *noun* 名词
a word that tells you what somebody or something is or does. 'Go', 'sing', 'happen' and 'be' are all verbs. 动词（go、sing、happen、be 都是动词。）

verdict /ˈvɜːdɪkt; ˈvɝdɪkt/ *noun* 名词
what the **jury** in a court of law decides at the end of a **trial**（陪审团在审讯终结时的）裁断；裁决（陪审团叫做 **jury**，审讯叫做 **trial**）

verse /vɜːs; vɝs/ *noun* 名词
1 (no plural 无复数) poetry; writing in lines that has a **rhythm** 诗；韵文（节奏叫做 **rhythm**）：*The play is written in verse.* 这个剧本是用韵文写的。
2 (*plural* 复数作 **verses**) a group of lines in a song or poem（歌或诗的）节，句：*This song has five verses.* 这首歌有五节。

version /ˈvɜːʃn; ˈvɝʒən/ *noun* 名词
1 a form of something that is different in some way（某事物略有改变的）形式，种类，版本：*a new version of a Beatles song* 披头士一首歌曲的新版本
2 what one person says or writes about something that happened 个人对某事的叙述：*His version of the accident is different from mine.* 对这一事故，他的说法和我的不同。

versus /ˈvɜːsəs; ˈvɝsəs/ *preposition* 介词
on the other side in a sport; against 对抗（竞技的另一方）；对：*There's a good football match on TV tonight—England versus Brazil.* 今天晚上电视上有一场精彩的足球比赛——英国对巴西。✪ The short way of writing 'versus' is **v** or **vs**. ✳ versus 的缩写形式为 **v** 或 **vs**。

vertical /ˈvɜːtɪkl; ˈvɝtɪkl̩/ *adjective* 形容词
Something that is vertical goes straight up, not from side to side 垂直的；竖的；直立的：*a vertical line* 垂线 ☞ picture on page C5 见第C5页图

very¹ /ˈveri; ˈvɛrɪ/ *adverb* 副词
You use 'very' before another word to make it stronger（用于另一词前以加强语气）很；非常；十分；极：*London is a very big town.* 伦敦是个很大的城市。◇ *She speaks very quietly.* 她说话声音十分轻。◇ *I like chocolate very much.* 我非常爱吃巧克力。◇ *I'm not very hungry.* 我不太饿。

very² /ˈveri; ˈvɛrɪ/ *adjective* 形容词
same; exact 就是那个；正是这个：*You are the very person I wanted to see!* 您正是我想见的人！◇ *We climbed to the very top of the mountain.* 我们登上了那座山的顶尖儿上。

vest /vest; vɛst/ *noun* 名词
1 a piece of clothing that you wear under your other clothes on the top part of your body（贴身的）背心；内衣；汗衫
2 *American English for* **waistcoat** 美式英语，即 **waistcoat**

vet /vet; vɛt/, **veterinary surgeon** /ˈvetrənri ˈsɜːdʒən; ˈvɛtrənɛrɪ ˌsɝdʒən/ *noun* 名词
a doctor for animals 兽医

via /ˈvaɪə; ˈvaɪə/ *preposition* 介词
going through a place 经过某处：*We flew from London to Sydney via Bangkok.* 我们从伦敦经过曼谷飞往悉尼。

vibrate /vaɪˈbreɪt; ˈvaɪbret/ *verb* 动词 (**vibrates**, **vibrating**, **vibrated**)
move very quickly from side to side or up and down（左右或上下）振动；颤动；摆动：*The house vibrates every time a train goes past.* 火车一经过，这所房子就发颤。
vibration /vaɪˈbreɪʃn; vaɪˈbreʃən/ *noun* 名词
You can feel the vibrations from the engine when you are in the car. 坐在汽车里就能感觉到发动机的振动。

vicar /ˈvɪkə(r); ˈvɪkɚ/ *noun* 名词
a priest in the Church of England（英国国教的）牧区牧师

vice- /vaɪs; vaɪs/ *prefix* 前缀
a word that you use before another word, to show somebody who is next to the leader in importance 用于某些字前表示某人为副职，如: *The vice-captain leads the team when the captain is ill.* 队长生病的时候，由副队长带队。◇ *the Vice-President* 副总统

vicious /ˈvɪʃəs; ˈvɪʃəs/ *adjective* 形容词
cruel; wanting to hurt somebody or something 残忍的；有恶意的；恶毒的: *a vicious attack* 恶意攻击

victim /ˈvɪktɪm; ˈvɪktɪm/ *noun* 名词
a person or animal that is hurt or killed by somebody or something 被某人或某事物伤害的人或动物；受害者；遇难者: *The victims of the car accident were taken to hospital.* 汽车事故的受害人已经送进医院。

victory /ˈvɪktəri; ˈvɪktərɪ/ *noun* 名词 (*plural* 复数作 **victories**)
winning a fight, game or war（斗争、比赛或战争的）胜利

video /ˈvɪdiəʊ; ˈvɪdɪˌo/ *noun* 名词 (*plural* 复数作 **videos**)
1 (*also* 亦作 **video recorder**) a machine that puts television programmes on tape, so that you can watch them later 录像机: *Have you got a video?* 您有录像机吗？
2 tape in a box (called a **cassette**) that you put into a video recorder to show films, for example 录像带（盒式录像带叫做 **cassette**）: *We stayed at home and watched a video.* 我们呆在家里看录像带。◇ *Can you get this film on video?* 您把这部影片录在录像带上行吗？

view /vju:; vju/ *noun* 名词
1 what you can see from a certain place 从某处看到的东西: *There is a beautiful view of the mountains from our window.* 我们窗外能看到美丽的山景。
2 what you believe or think about something（对某事物的）看法，想法，观点: *What are your views on marriage?* 您对婚姻问题有什么看法？
in view of something because of something 由于某事物；鉴于: *In view of the bad weather we decided to cancel the match.* 因天气关系，我们决定取消这场比赛。
on view in a place for people to see 在某处供人观看；陈列着；展览着: *Her paintings are on view at the museum.* 她的画儿陈列在博物馆供人观赏。

viewer /ˈvju:ə(r); ˈvjuɚ/ *noun* 名词
a person who watches television 看电视的人

vigorous /ˈvɪgərəs; ˈvɪgərəs/ *adjective* 形容词
strong and active 强烈而活跃的: *vigorous exercise* 激烈的锻炼
vigorously *adverb* 副词
She shook my hand vigorously. 她用力地和我握手。

vile /vaɪl; vaɪl/ *adjective* 形容词 (**viler**, **vilest**)
very bad; horrible 非常坏的；讨厌的: *What a vile smell!* 多么难闻的味儿！

villa /ˈvɪlə; ˈvɪlə/ *noun* 名词
a house with a garden, often where people stay on holiday 带花园的房子（常为度假用的）；别墅

village /ˈvɪlɪdʒ; ˈvɪlɪdʒ/ *noun* 名词
a small place where people live. A village is smaller than a town 小乡镇；村庄；乡村: *a village in the mountains* 山村
villager *noun* 名词
a person who lives in a village 小乡镇里的居民；村民

villain /ˈvɪlən; ˈvɪlən/ *noun* 名词
a bad person, usually in a book, play or film 坏人，恶棍，歹徒（通常指书、戏剧或影片中的）

vine /vaɪn; vaɪn/ *noun* 名词
a plant that grapes grow on 葡萄藤

vinegar /ˈvɪnɪgə(r); ˈvɪnɪgɚ/ *noun* 名词 (no plural 无复数)
a liquid with a strong sharp taste. You put it on food and use it for cooking 醋: *I mixed some oil and vinegar to put on the salad.* 我把油和醋混在一起拌色拉。

vineyard /ˈvɪnjəd; ˈvɪnjɚd/ *noun* 名词
a piece of land where vines grow 葡萄园

viola /viˈəʊlə; vɪˈolə/ *noun* 名词
a musical instrument with strings that is a little bigger than a violin 中提琴

violent /ˈvaɪələnt; ˈvaɪələnt/ *adjective* 形容词
A person or thing that is violent is very

strong and dangerous and hurts people （指人或事物）强暴、危险而伤害人的: *a violent man* 强横凶暴的男子 ◇ *a violent storm* 强烈的风暴

violence /ˈvaɪələns; ˈvaɪələns/ *noun* 名词 (no plural 无复数)

being violent 强暴、危险而伤害人的行为；暴行: *Do you think there's too much violence on TV?* 您认为电视里的暴力画面是不是太多了？

violently *adverb* 副词

Did she behave violently towards you? 她对你是不是很粗暴？

violet /ˈvaɪələt; ˈvaɪəlɪt/ *noun* 名词

a small purple flower 紫罗兰

violet *adjective* 形容词

with a purple colour 紫色的

violin /ˌvaɪəˈlɪn; ˌvaɪəˈlɪn/ *noun* 名词

a musical instrument made of wood, with strings across it. You play a violin with a **bow** 小提琴（琴弓叫做 **bow**）: *I play the violin.* 我会拉小提琴。

VIP /ˌviː aɪ ˈpiː; ˌvi aɪ ˈpi/ *noun* 名词

a person who is famous or important. 'VIP' is short for **very important person** 名人或要人（VIP 是 **very important person** 的缩略式）: *The Prime Minister is a VIP.* 首相是要人。

virtually /ˈvɜːtʃuəli; ˈvɝtʃʊəlɪ/ *adverb* 副词

almost 几乎；差不多: *The two boys look virtually the same.* 这两个男孩儿长得简直一模一样。

virus /ˈvaɪrəs; ˈvaɪrəs/ *noun* 名词 (*plural* 复数作 **viruses**)

a very small living thing that can make you ill 病毒: *a flu virus* 流感病毒

visa /ˈviːzə; ˈvizə/ *noun* 名词

a special piece of paper or mark in your passport to show that you can go into a country（护照的）签证

visible /ˈvɪzəbl; ˈvɪzəbl̩/ *adjective* 形容词

If something is visible, you can see it 可见的；看得见的: *Stars are only visible at night.* 星星只有在夜晚才看得见。✪ opposite 反义词: **invisible**

vision /ˈvɪʒn; ˈvɪʒən/ *noun* 名词

1 (no plural 无复数) the power to see; sight 视力；视觉: *He wears glasses because he has poor vision.* 他因视力差而戴眼镜。

2 (*plural* 复数作 **visions**) a picture in your mind; a dream 幻象；幻觉；幻想: *They have a vision of a world without war.* 他们憧憬着一个没有战争的世界。

visit /ˈvɪzɪt; ˈvɪzɪt/ *verb* 动词 (**visits, visiting, visited**)

go to see a person or place for a short time（指短时间）去见某人或到某处: *Have you ever visited Westminster Abbey?* 您参观过威斯敏斯特教堂吗？◇ *She visited me in hospital.* 她到医院来看我了。

visit *noun* 名词

This is my first visit to New York. 这是我第一次来纽约。

pay somebody a visit go to see somebody 去看某人

visitor /ˈvɪzɪtə(r); ˈvɪzɪtɚ/ *noun* 名词

a person who goes to see another person or a place for a short time（指短时间）去见某人或到某处的人: *The old lady never has any visitors.* 那个老太太从来没有人去看她。◇ *Millions of visitors come to Rome every year.* 每年有数以百万计的旅客来到罗马。

visual /ˈvɪʒuəl; ˈvɪʒuəl/ *adjective* 形容词

of or about seeing 视觉的: *Painting and cinema are visual arts.* 绘画和电影都是视觉艺术。

vital /ˈvaɪtl; ˈvaɪtl̩/ *adjective* 形容词

very important; that you must do or have 极重要的；必不可少的: *It's vital that she sees a doctor—she's very ill.* 她务必要找医生给看看——她病得很重。

vitamin /ˈvɪtəmɪn; ˈvaɪtəmɪn/ *noun* 名词

one of the things in food that you need to be healthy 维生素: *Oranges are full of vitamin C.* 橙子里富有维生素C。

vivid /ˈvɪvɪd; ˈvɪvɪd/ *adjective* 形容词

1 with a strong bright colour 鲜艳的: *vivid yellow* 鲜艳的黄色

2 that makes a very clear picture in your mind 在头脑中产生清晰图像的: *I had a very vivid dream last night.* 我昨天夜里做了一个梦，历历如在目前。

vividly *adverb* 副词
I remember my first day at school vividly. 我上学第一天的情景记忆犹新。

vocabulary /vəˈkæbjələri; vəˈkæbjəˌlɛrɪ/ *noun* 名词 (*plural* 复数作 **vocabularies**)
1 all the words in a language（一种语言的）词汇
2 a list of words in a lesson or book（一课书的或一本书的）词汇表: *We have to learn this new vocabulary for homework.* 我们的家庭作业是要记住本课的全部生词。
3 all the words that somebody knows（某人的）词汇量

voice /vɔɪs; vɔɪs/ *noun* 名词
the sounds that you make when you speak or sing 说话或唱歌的声音；嗓音: *Steve has a very deep voice.* 史蒂夫嗓音很低。
at the top of your voice very loudly 以最大的嗓音: *'Come here!' she shouted at the top of her voice.* 她可着嗓子喊："到这儿来！"
raise your voice speak very loudly 大声地说

volcano /vɒlˈkeɪnəʊ; vɑlˈkeno/ *noun* 名词 (*plural* 复数作 **volcanoes**)
a mountain with a hole in the top where fire, gas and hot liquid rock (called **lava**) sometimes come out 火山（岩浆叫做 **lava**）
volcanic /vɒlˈkænɪk; vɑlˈkænɪk/ *adjective* 形容词
volcanic rocks 火山岩

volleyball /ˈvɒlibɔːl; ˈvɑlɪˌbɔl/ *noun* 名词 (no plural 无复数)
a game where two teams try to hit a ball over a high net with their hands 排球运动

volt /vəʊlt; volt/ *noun* 名词
a measure of electricity 伏（特）（电压单位）✪ The short way of writing 'volt' is **V**. ✳ volt 的缩写形式为 **V**。

volume /ˈvɒljuːm; ˈvɑljəm/ *noun* 名词
1 (no plural 无复数) the amount of space that something fills, or the amount of space inside something 体积；容积；容量: *What is the volume of this box?* 这个盒子的容量是多少？
2 (no plural 无复数) the amount of sound that something makes 音量；响度: *I can't hear the radio. Can you turn the volume up?* 我听不见收音机的声音。你把音量调大些行吗？
3 (*plural* 复数作 **volumes**) a book, especially one of a set 一本书；（尤指一部书中的）一卷；一册: *The dictionary is in two volumes.* 这部词典有两卷。

voluntary /ˈvɒləntri; ˈvɑlənˌtɛrɪ/ *adjective* 形容词
1 If something is voluntary, you do it because you want to, not because you must 自愿的；主动的: *She made a voluntary decision to leave the job.* 她主动辞去了这份工作。
2 If work is voluntary, you are not paid to do it 不要报酬的；义务的: *He does voluntary work at a children's hospital.* 他在一所儿童医院里做义务工作。
voluntarily /ˈvɒləntrəli; ˌvɑlənˈtɛrəlɪ/ *adverb* 副词
because you want to, not because you must 自愿地；主动地: *She left the job voluntarily.* 她自愿辞去了这份工作。

volunteer /ˌvɒlənˈtɪə(r); ˌvɑlənˈtɪr/ *verb* 动词 (**volunteers**, **volunteering**, **volunteered** /ˌvɒlənˈtɪəd; ˌvɑlənˈtɪrd/)
say that you will do something that you do not have to do 说出要自愿做某事: *I volunteered to do the washing-up.* 我主动提出去刷洗碗碟。
volunteer *noun* 名词
a person who volunteers to do a job 自愿做某事的人: *They're asking for volunteers to help at the Christmas party.* 他们要求有人自告奋勇在圣诞联欢会上帮忙。

vomit /ˈvɒmɪt; ˈvɑmɪt/ *verb* 动词 (**vomits**, **vomiting**, **vomited**)
When you vomit, food comes up from your stomach and out of your mouth. 呕吐 ✪ It is more usual to say **be sick**. ✳ **be sick** 是常用词语。

vote /vəʊt; vot/ *verb* 动词 (**votes**, **voting**, **voted**)
choose somebody or something by putting up your hand or writing on a piece of paper 用举手或投票方式选出某人或某事物；表决: *Who did you vote for in the election?* 在选举的时候你选的是谁？
vote *noun* 名词
There were 96 votes for the plan, and 25 against. 有96票赞成这个计划，25票反对。

V

voter *noun* 名词
a person who votes in a political election（在政治性选举中的）投票人；选民

voucher /'vaʊtʃə(r); 'vaʊtʃɚ/ *noun* 名词
a piece of paper that you can use instead of money to pay for something（代替现金的）凭证；代金券

vowel /'vaʊəl; 'vaʊəl/ *noun* 名词
one of the letters *a, e, i, o* or *u*, or the sound that you make when you say it 元音字母；元音 ☞ Look at **consonant**. 见 **consonant**。

voyage /'vɔɪɪdʒ; 'vɔɪ·ɪdʒ/ *noun* 名词
a long journey by boat or in space 航海；航天: *a voyage from London to New York* 从伦敦到纽约的海上航行

vs *short way of writing* **versus** ＊ **versus** 的缩写形式

V

Ww

wade /weɪd; wed/ *verb* 动词 (**wades, wading, waded**)
walk through water 蹚水: *Can we wade across the river, or is it too deep?* 咱们能蹚水过河吗，也许水太深吧？

wag /wæg; wæg/ *verb* 动词 (**wags, wagging, wagged** /wægd; wægd/)
move or make something move from side to side or up and down (使某物)左右或上下摆动: *She wagged her finger at me.* 她向我晃了晃手指。◇ *My dog's tail wags when he's happy.* 我的狗一高兴就摇尾巴。

wages /'weɪdʒɪz; 'wedʒɪz/ *noun* 名词 (plural 复数)
the money that you receive every week for the work that you do (按星期得到的)工资: *Our wages are paid every Friday.* 我们每星期五发工资。◇ *low wages* 低工资

wagon /'wægən; 'wægən/ *noun* 名词
1 a vehicle with four wheels that a horse pulls 四轮马车
2 a part of a train where things like coal are carried (铁路上运煤等的)货车

wail /weɪl; wel/ *verb* 动词 (**wails, wailing, wailed** /weɪld; weld/)
make a long sad cry or noise (声音长而悲痛地)哭或哀号: *The little boy started wailing for his mother.* 那个小男孩儿大哭起来，要找妈妈。

waist /weɪst; west/ *noun* 名词
the part around the middle of your body 腰部；腰围 ☞ picture on page C2 见第C2页图

waistcoat /'weɪskəʊt; 'wɛskət/ *noun* 名词
a piece of clothing like a jacket with no sleeves (西服的)背心

wait¹ /weɪt; wet/ *verb* 动词 (**waits, waiting, waited**)
stay in one place until something happens or until somebody or something comes 等候；等待: *If I'm late, please wait for me.* 万一我晚了就请等我一会儿。◇ *We've been waiting a long time.* 我们等了半天了。
I can't wait words that you use when you are very excited about something that is going to happen 用以表示兴奋而迫不及待的词语: *I can't wait to see you again!* 我巴不得再见到你！
keep somebody waiting make somebody wait because you are late or busy (因迟到或忙)使某人等候: *The doctor kept me waiting for half an hour.* 医生让我等了半个小时。
wait and see wait and find out later 等一等就能明白: *'What are we having for dinner?' 'Wait and see!'* "咱们晚饭吃什么？""你就等着瞧吧！"
wait up not go to bed until somebody comes home 等某人回家后再睡觉: *I will be home late tonight so don't wait up for me.* 我今天晚上回家晚，不必熬夜等我。

wait² /weɪt; wet/ *noun* 名词
a time when you wait 等候；等待: *We had a long wait for the bus.* 我们等公共汽车用了很长时间。

waiter /'weɪtə(r); 'wetə/ *noun* 名词
a man who brings food and drink to your table in a restaurant (饭馆中的)(男的)服务员

waiting-room /'weɪtɪŋ ru:m; 'wetɪŋ ˌrum/ *noun* 名词
a room where people can sit and wait, for example to see a doctor or to catch a train 等候室(例如候诊室、候车室)

waitress /'weɪtrəs; 'wetrɪs/ *noun* 名词 (*plural* 复数作 **waitresses**)
a woman who brings food and drink to your table in a restaurant (饭馆中的)(女的)服务员

wake /weɪk; wek/, **wake up** *verb* 动词 (**wakes, waking, woke** /wəʊk; wok/, **has woken** /'wəʊkən; 'wokən/)
1 stop sleeping 醒；醒来: *What time did you wake up this morning?* 您今天早晨几点钟醒的？
2 make somebody stop sleeping 使某人醒来；弄醒: *The noise woke me up.* 那种声音把我吵醒了。◇ *Don't wake the baby.* 别把孩子吵醒了。
✪ It is more usual to say **wake up** than **wake**. ＊ **wake up** 比 **wake** 常用。

walk¹ /wɔ:k; wɔk/ *verb* 动词 (**walks, walking, walked** /wɔ:kt; wɔkt/)
move on your legs, but not run 行走；

W

步行: *I usually walk to work.* 我平常都是走着去上班。◇ *We walked 20 kilometres today.* 我们今天步行走了20公里。

walk out leave suddenly because you are angry（因生气）突然离去: *He walked out of the meeting.* 他愤而退出会场。

walk² /wɔ:k; wɔk/ *noun* 名词

a journey on foot 行走；步行: *The beach is a short walk from our house.* 这个海滩从我们家走几步就到。◇ *I took the dog for a walk.* 我遛了遛狗。

go for a walk walk somewhere because you enjoy it 散步: *It was a lovely day so we went for a walk in the park.* 因为天晴日朗，我们到公园去散了散步。

walker /ˈwɔ:kə(r); ˈwɔkɚ/ *noun* 名词

a person who is walking 行走的人；步行的人

Walkman /ˈwɔ:kmən; ˈwɔkˌmən/ *noun* 名词 (*plural* 复数作 **Walkmans**)

a small cassette player or radio with **headphones**, that is easy to carry（可随身携带使用耳机的）小型放音机或收音机（耳机叫做 **headphones**）✪ **Walkman** is a trade mark. ＊**Walkman** 是商标。

wall /wɔ:l; wɔl/ *noun* 名词

1 a side of a building or room（楼房或房间等的）墙；墙壁: *There's a picture on the wall.* 墙上挂着一张画儿。☞ picture at **house** 见 **house** 词条插图

2 a thing made of stones or bricks around a garden, field or town, for example（用石或砖等围在花园、场地或城镇等处的）围墙；城墙: *There's a high wall around the prison.* 监狱四周有一堵高墙。

wallet 钱包

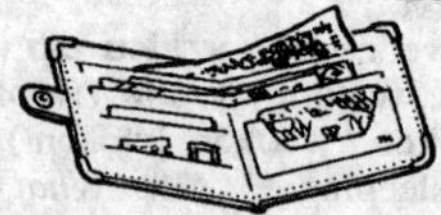

wallet /ˈwɒlɪt; ˈwɑlɪt/ *noun* 名词

a small flat case for paper money, that you can carry in your pocket（装纸币用的）钱包

wallpaper /ˈwɔ:lpeɪpə(r); ˈwɔlˌpepɚ/ *noun* 名词 (no plural 无复数)

special paper that you use for covering the walls of a room 壁纸；墙纸

walnut /ˈwɔ:lnʌt; ˈwɔlˌnʌt/ *noun* 名词

a nut that you can eat 胡桃

wander /ˈwɒndə(r); ˈwɑndɚ/ *verb* 动词 (**wanders, wandering, wandered** /ˈwɒndəd; ˈwɑndɚd/)

walk slowly with no special plan 无计划地慢慢走；闲逛；游荡: *We wandered around the town until the shops opened.* 我们在镇上闲逛，等候商店开门。

want /wɒnt; wɔnt/ *verb* 动词 (**wants, wanting, wanted**)

1 wish to have or do something 想要或想做某事物: *Do you want a chocolate?* 你要巧克力吗？◇ *I want to go to Italy.* 我想去意大利。◇ *She wanted me to give her some money.* 她想让我给她点儿钱。✪ **Would like** is more polite than **want** 用 **would like** 比用 **want** 显得有礼貌: *Would you like a cup of tea?* 您想要杯茶吗？

2 need something 需要某事物: *Your car wants a wash!* 您的汽车该清洗一下了！

war /wɔ:(r); wɔr/ *noun* 名词

fighting between countries or between groups of people 战争: *the First World War* 第一次世界大战

at war fighting 交战；作战: *The two countries have been at war for five years.* 这两个国家打了五年的仗了。

declare war start a war 宣战: *In 1812 Napoleon declared war on Russia.* ＊1812年拿破仑向俄国宣战。

ward /wɔ:d; wɔrd/ *noun* 名词

a big room in a hospital that has beds for the patients 病房

warden /ˈwɔ:dn; ˈwɔrdn̩/ *noun* 名词

a person whose job is to look after a place and the people in it 照管某处所及其人员的人: *the warden of a youth hostel* 青年招待所管理员 ☞ Look also at **traffic warden**. 另见 **traffic warden**。

wardrobe /ˈwɔ:drəʊb; ˈwɔrdˌrob/ *noun* 名词

a cupboard where you hang your clothes 衣柜

warehouse /ˈweəhaʊs; ˈwɛrˌhaʊs/ *noun* 名词 (*plural* 复数作 **warehouses** /ˈweəhaʊzɪz; ˈwɛrˌhaʊzɪz/)

a big building where people keep things before they sell them 货仓: *a furniture warehouse* 家具货仓

warm¹ /wɔ:m; wɔrm/ *adjective* 形容词 (**warmer, warmest**)

1 a little hot 温暖的；暖和的: *It's warm by the fire.* 在火炉旁边很暖和。

W

2 Warm clothes are clothes that stop you feeling cold（指衣物）御寒的: *It's cold in Scotland, so take some warm clothes with you.* 苏格兰很冷，你带些寒衣吧。

3 friendly and kind 亲切友好的；热情的: *Martha is a very warm person.* 马莎待人很热情。✪ opposite 反义词: **cold**

warmly *adverb* 副词

The children were warmly dressed. 孩子们穿得很暖和。◇ *He thanked me warmly.* 他由衷地感谢我。

warm² /wɔ:m; wɔrm/ *verb* 动词 (**warms, warming, warmed** /wɔ:md; wɔrmd/)

warm up become warmer, or make somebody or something warmer（使某人或某物）暖些: *I warmed up some soup for lunch.* 我把午饭用的汤热了一下。◇ *It was cold this morning, but it's warming up now.* 今天早晨很冷，现在暖和些了。

warmth /wɔ:mθ; wɔrmθ/ *noun* 名词 (no plural 无复数)

1 heat 热；温暖；暖和: *the warmth of the sun* 太阳的热力

2 friendliness and kindness 亲切友好；热情: *the warmth of his smile* 他微笑中表现出的热情

warn /wɔ:n; wɔrn/ *verb* 动词 (**warns, warning, warned** /wɔ:nd; wɔrnd/)

tell somebody about danger or about something bad that may happen 告诉某人可能有危险或坏事发生；提醒；警告: *I warned him not to go too close to the fire.* 我提醒他不要离火炉太近。

warning *noun* 名词

something that warns you 提醒或警告的事物: *There is a warning on every packet of cigarettes.* 每个香烟盒上都有警告字样。

was *form of* **be** ✳ **be** 的不同形式

wash¹ /wɒʃ; wɔʃ/ *verb* 动词 (**washes, washing, washed** /wɒʃt; wɑʃt/)

1 clean somebody, something or yourself with water 用水洗某人、某物或自己的身体（或身体某部）: *Have you washed the car?* 你把汽车清洗了吗？◇ *Wash your hands before you eat.* 你把手洗洗再吃饭。◇ *I washed and dressed quickly.* 我很快地洗了个澡，穿上衣服。

2 flow somewhere many times 多次流到某处: *The sea washed over my feet.* 海水冲刷着我的脚。

3 move something with water 冲走某物: *The house was washed away by the river.* 那所房子让河水给冲走了。

wash up clean the plates, knives, forks, etc after a meal 饭后刷洗盘子、刀、叉等；刷锅洗碗: *I washed up after dinner.* 我在饭后刷洗了餐具。

wash² /wɒʃ; wɔʃ/ *noun* 名词 (no plural 无复数)

cleaning something with water 用水洗某物: *I gave the car a wash.* 我把汽车清洗了一下。

have a wash wash yourself 洗自己的身体或身体某部；洗澡: *I had a quick wash.* 我很快地洗了个澡。

in the wash being washed 正在洗着: *All my socks are in the wash!* 我所有的袜子都正在洗着呢！

wash-basin /'wɒʃ beɪsn; 'wɑʃˌbesn̩/ *noun* 名词

the place in a bathroom where you wash your hands and face（固定于浴室中的）脸盆；洗脸池

washing /'wɒʃɪŋ; 'wɔʃɪŋ/ *noun* 名词 (no plural 无复数)

clothes that you need to wash or that you have washed 待洗的或已洗的衣物: *Shall I hang the washing outside to dry?* 我把洗过的衣服晾在外面好吗？◇ *I've done the washing.* 我把衣服洗了。

washing-machine /'wɒʃɪŋ məʃi:n; 'wɑʃɪŋ məˌʃin/ *noun* 名词

a machine that washes clothes 洗衣机

washing-powder /'wɒʃɪŋ paʊdə(r); 'wɑʃɪŋ ˌpaudɚ/ *noun* 名词 (no plural 无复数)

soap powder for washing clothes 洗衣粉

washing-up /ˌwɒʃɪŋ 'ʌp; ˌwɑʃɪŋ 'ʌp/ *noun* 名词 (no plural 无复数)

cleaning the plates, knives, forks, etc after a meal 饭后刷洗盘子、刀、叉等；刷锅洗碗: *I'll do the washing-up.* 我来刷洗碗碟。

washing-up liquid /ˌwɒʃɪŋ'ʌp lɪkwɪd; 'wɑʃɪŋ ʌp ˌlɪkwɪd/ *noun* 名词 (no plural 无复数)

a liquid that you use for washing plates, etc（刷洗餐具用的）洗涤液

washroom /'wɒʃru:m; 'wɑʃˌrum/ *noun* 名词

a room with a toilet in it 厕所 ✪ This word is only used in American English. 此词仅用于美式英语。

wasn't /'wɒznt; 'wʌzn̩t/ = **was not**

wasp /wɒsp; wɑsp/ *noun* 名词
yellow and black insect that flies and can sting people 黄蜂

waste[1] /weɪst; west/ *verb* 动词 (**wastes, wasting, wasted**)
use too much of something or not use something in a good way 浪费；滥用: *She wastes a lot of money on cigarettes.* 她在香烟上花了很多冤枉钱。◇ *He wasted his time at university—he didn't do any work.* 他上大学是浪费时间——他根本不做作业。

waste[2] /weɪst; west/ *noun* 名词 (no plural 无复数)
1 not using something in a useful way 浪费；滥用: *It's a waste to throw away all this food!* 把这些食物都扔了，这是浪费！◇ *This watch was a waste of money—it's broken already!* 买这块手表是白糟蹋钱——已经坏了！
2 things that people throw away because they are not useful 因无用而扔掉的东西；废料；废物；垃圾: *A lot of waste from the factories goes into this river.* 工厂把很多废料都排入这条河里了。

waste[3] /weɪst; west/ *adjective* 形容词
that you do not want because it is not good 因无用而不要的

waste-paper basket /ˌweɪst ˈpeɪpə bɑːskɪt; 'west pepɚ ˌbæskɪt/ *noun* 名词
a container where you put things like paper that you do not want 字纸篓

watch 手表

watch[1] /wɒtʃ; wɑtʃ/ *noun* 名词 (*plural* 复数作 **watches**)
a thing that shows what time it is. You wear a watch on your wrist. 手表 ☞ Note at **clock** 见 **clock** 词条注释

watch[2] /wɒtʃ; wɑtʃ/ *verb* 动词 (**watches, watching, watched** /wɒtʃt; wɑtʃt/)
1 look at somebody or something for some time 注视某人或某事物: *We watched television all evening.* 我们看了一晚上电视。◇ *Watch how I do this.* 看着我怎样做。
2 look after something or somebody 照管某事物或某人: *Could you watch my suitcase while I buy a ticket?* 我去买票，您给我看着点儿衣箱行吗？
watch out be careful because of somebody or something dangerous（因某人或某事物危险）留心；警惕: *Watch out! There's a car coming.* 小心！有辆汽车来了。
watch out for somebody or 或 **something** look carefully and be ready for somebody or something dangerous（因某人或某事物危险）细心观察及提防: *Watch out for ice on the roads.* 留心路上有冰。

watch[3] /wɒtʃ; wɑtʃ/ *noun* 名词 (no plural 无复数)
keep watch look out for danger 警惕或留心（预防危险）: *The soldier kept watch at the gate.* 士兵在大门口值勤。

water[1] /'wɔːtə(r); 'wɔtɚ/ *noun* 名词 (no plural 无复数)
the liquid in rivers, lakes and seas that people and animals drink 水

water[2] /'wɔːtə(r); 'wɔtɚ/ *verb* 动词 (**waters, watering, watered** /'wɔːtəd; 'wɔtɚd/)
1 give water to plants 给植物浇水: *Have you watered the plants?* 你浇花了吗？
2 When your eyes water, they fill with tears（指眼睛）充满眼泪: *The smoke made my eyes water.* 烟薰得我眼睛直流泪。
watering-can /'wɔːtərɪŋ kæn; 'wɔtərɪŋˌkæn/ *noun* 名词
a container that you use for watering plants（浇花的）喷壶；洒水壶

water-colour /'wɔːtə kʌlə(r); 'wɔtɚˌkʌlɚ/ *noun* 名词
a picture that you make with paint and water 水彩画儿

waterfall /'wɔːtəfɔːl; 'wɔtɚˌfɔl/ *noun* 名词
a place where water falls from a high place to a low place 瀑布

water melon /'wɔːtə melən; 'wɔtɚˌmɛlən/ *noun* 名词
a big round fruit with a thick green skin. It is pink inside with a lot of black seeds. 西瓜

waterproof /'wɔːtəpruːf; 'wɔtɚ'pruf/ *adjective* 形容词
If something is waterproof, it does not

let water go through it 不透水的；防水的: *a waterproof jacket* 防水的短外衣

water-skiing /ˈwɔːtə skiːɪŋ; ˈwɔtɚ-ˌskiɪŋ/ *noun* 名词 (no plural 无复数) the sport of moving fast over water on long boards (called **water-skis**), pulled by a boat 水橇运动（滑水橇叫做 **water-ski**）

wave[1] /weɪv; wev/ *verb* 动词 (**waves, waving, waved** /weɪvd; wevd/)

1 move your hand from side to side in the air to say hello or goodbye or to make a sign to somebody 摇手；摆手（打招呼或告别或做手势）: *She waved to me as the train left the station.* 火车出站时她向我挥手告别。◇ *Who are you waving at?* 你这是跟谁摆手呢？

2 move something quickly from side to side in the air 挥动某物: *The children were waving flags as the President's car drove past.* 总统的汽车经过的时候，孩子们都摇动着旗子。

3 move up and down or from side to side 上下或左右移动；摇动；摆动: *The flags were waving in the wind.* 旗子随风飘扬。

wave[2] /weɪv; wev/ *noun* 名词

1 one of the lines of water that moves across the top of the sea 浪头；波浪

2 moving your hand from side to side in the air, to say hello or goodbye or to make a sign to somebody 摇手；摆手（打招呼或告别或做手势）

3 a gentle curve in hair 毛发的波浪纹

4 a movement like a wave on the sea, that carries heat, light, sound, etc（热、光、声等的）波状运动: *radio waves* 无线电波

wavy line 波浪线

wavy /ˈweɪvi; ˈwevɪ/ *adjective* 形容词 (**wavier, waviest**)

Something that is wavy has gentle curves in it 波状的；波浪形的: *She has wavy black hair.* 她的头发是黑色的，呈波浪形。☞ picture at **hair** 见 **hair** 词条插图

wax /wæks; wæks/ *noun* 名词 (no plural 无复数)

the stuff that is used for making candles 蜡

way /weɪ; we/ *noun* 名词

1 (*plural* 复数作 **ways**) a road or path that you must follow to go to a place 道路；小径: *Can you tell me the way to the station, please?* 劳驾，请问到车站去怎么走？◇ *I lost my way and I had to look at the map.* 我迷路了，得查查地图了。

2 (*plural* 复数作 **ways**) a direction; where somebody or something is going or looking 方向；要去的或面对的地方: *Come this way.* 往这边走。◇ *She was looking the other way.* 她正往另一边看呢。

3 (no plural 无复数) distance 距离；路程: *It's a long way from Glasgow to London.* 格拉斯哥离伦敦很远。

4 (*plural* 复数作 **ways**) how you do something 方法；方式；手段: *What is the best way to learn a language?* 学习语言用什么方法最好？◇ *He smiled in a friendly way.* 他很亲切地微笑着。

by the way words that you say when you are going to talk about something different 用以改变话题的词语；顺便说说: *By the way, I had a letter from Anna yesterday.* 顺便说一句，我昨天收到安娜的一封信。

give way 1 stop and let somebody or something go before you 让某人或某物先行；让路: *You must give way to traffic coming from the right.* 要让右方驶来的车辆先行。**2** agree with somebody when you did not agree before 让步；妥协: *After a long argument, my parents finally gave way and said I could go on holiday with my friends.* 经过长时间的争论，我父母终于答应说我可以跟朋友一起去度假。**3** break 断裂；倒塌: *The ladder gave way and Ben fell to the ground.* 梯子断了，本摔到地上了。

in the way in front of somebody so that you stop them from seeing something or moving 因在前面而挡住某人的视线或阻碍其移动: *I couldn't see the television because Jenny was in the way.* 我看不见电视，因为珍妮在前边挡着呢。

no way a way of saying 'no' more strongly 表示拒绝的强调说法: *'Can I borrow your bike?' 'No way!'* "我借你的自行车用用行吗？" "绝对不行！"

on the way when you are going somewhere 在路上: *I stopped to have a drink on the way to Bristol.* 我在前往布里斯托尔的路上停下来喝了点儿东西。

out of the way not in a place where you stop somebody from moving or doing something 不在妨碍某人移动或正做的事的地方：*Get out of the way! There's a car coming!* 躲开！有辆汽车来了！

the right way up or 或 **round** with the correct part at the top or at the front 上边或正面向上或向前: *Is this picture the right way up?* 这幅画儿是正着的吗？

the wrong way up or 或 **round** with the wrong part at the top or at the front 下边或反面向上或向前: *Those two words are the wrong way round.* 这两个字都是倒着的。

way in where you go into a building（建筑物的）入口处: *Here's the museum. Where's the way in?* 这里是博物馆。入口处在哪儿？

way of life how people live 生活方式：*Is the way of life in Europe different from America?* 欧洲的生活方式跟美国的不一样吗？

way out where you go out of a place（某处的）出口处: *I can't find the way out.* 我找不到出口处了。

WC /ˌdʌblju: ˈsi:; ˈdʌbl̩jʊ ˈsi/ *noun* 名词
a toilet 恭桶；厕所

we /wi:; wi/ *pronoun* 代词 (plural 复数)
I and another person or other people; you and I 我们；咱们: *John and I went out last night—we went to the theatre.* 我和约翰昨天晚上出去了——我们看戏去了。◇*Are we late?* 咱们晚了吗？

weak /wi:k; wik/ *adjective* 形容词 (**weaker**, **weakest**)
1 not powerful or strong 弱的；无力的: *She felt very weak after her long illness.* 她久病之后觉得身体很虚弱。◇ *a weak government* 软弱无力的政府 ☞ picture on page C27 见第C27页图
2 that can break easily 易毁坏的；不结实的: *The bridge was too weak to carry the heavy lorry.* 这座桥不结实，禁不住这辆重型卡车。
3 that you cannot see, taste, smell, hear or feel clearly 不易察觉的（看不清、尝不出、闻不出、听不清或摸不出）: *weak tea* 淡茶
✪ opposite 反义词: **strong**

weaken /ˈwi:kən; ˈwikən/ *verb* 动词 (**weakens**, **weakening**, **weakened** /ˈwi:kənd; ˈwikənd/)
become less strong or make somebody or something less strong（使某人或某事物）变弱: *He was weakened by the illness.* 他病得身体虚弱了。

weakness /ˈwi:knəs; ˈwiknɪs/ *noun* 名词
1 (no plural 无复数) not being strong 弱；软弱；虚弱: *I have a feeling of weakness in my legs.* 我感到双腿无力。
2 (*plural* 复数作 **weaknesses**) something that is wrong or bad in a person or thing（人或事物的）弱点；缺点

wealth /welθ; wɛlθ/ *noun* 名词 (no plural 无复数)
having a lot of money, land, etc 财产；财富: *He is a man of great wealth.* 他是个大富翁。

wealthy *adjective* 形容词 (**wealthier**, **wealthiest**)
rich 富的: *a wealthy family* 富有的家庭

weapon /ˈwepən; ˈwɛpən/ *noun* 名词
a thing that you use for fighting. Guns and swords are weapons. 武器

wear[1] /weə(r); wɛr/ *verb* 动词 (**wears**, **wearing**, **wore** /wɔ:(r); wɔr/, **has worn** /wɔ:n; wɔrn/)
have clothes, etc on your body 穿戴衣物: *She was wearing a red dress.* 她穿着红色的连衣裙。◇*I wear glasses.* 我戴眼镜。

wear off become less strong 变弱: *The pain is wearing off.* 疼痛渐渐减轻了。

wear out become thin or damaged because you have used it a lot; make something do this（把某物）用薄、用细或用坏: *Children's shoes usually wear out very quickly.* 孩子穿鞋往往坏得快。

wear somebody out make somebody very tired 使某人精疲力竭或厌烦: *She wore herself out by working too hard.* 她拼命工作累得疲惫不堪。

wear[2] /weə(r); wɛr/ *noun* 名词 (no plural 无复数)
1 clothes 衣物: *sportswear* 运动服装
2 using something and making it old（指某物因使用而造成的）废旧，破损: *This carpet is showing signs of wear—we will need to buy a new one soon.* 这块地毯已经显得旧了——快该买新的了。

weather /ˈweðə(r); ˈwɛðɚ/ *noun* 名词 (no plural 无复数)
how much sunshine, rain, wind, etc there is at a certain time, or how hot or cold it is 天气: *What was the weather*

like in Spain? 西班牙天气怎么样？◇ *bad weather* 恶劣的天气

weather forecast /ˈweðə fɔːkɑːst; ˈwɛðɚ ˌforkæst/ *noun* 名词
words on television, radio or in a newspaper that tell you what the weather will be like 天气预报: *The weather forecast says it will be sunny and dry tomorrow.* 天气预报说明天晴而干燥。

weave /wiːv; wiv/ *verb* 动词 (**weaves**, **weaving**, **wove** /wəʊv; wov/, **has woven** /ˈwəʊvn; ˈwovən/)
make cloth by putting threads over and under one another 织布；纺织: *These scarves are woven in Scotland.* 这些围巾是苏格兰织的。

web /web; wɛb/ *noun* 名词
a thin net that a spider makes to catch flies 蜘蛛网 ☞ picture at **spider** 见 **spider** 词条插图

wedding /ˈwedɪŋ; ˈwɛdɪŋ/ *noun* 名词
a time when a man and a woman get married 婚礼: *Jenny and Phil invited me to their wedding.* 珍妮和菲尔邀请我参加他们的婚礼。◇ *a wedding dress* 结婚礼服

we'd /wiːd; wid/
1 = we had
2 = we would

Wednesday /ˈwenzdeɪ; ˈwɛnzdɪ/ *noun* 名词
the fourth day of the week, next after Tuesday 星期三

weed /wiːd; wid/ *noun* 名词
a wild plant that grows where you do not want it 野草；杂草: *The garden of the old house was full of weeds.* 这所旧房子的花园里杂草丛生。

weed *verb* 动词 (**weeds**, **weeding**, **weeded**)
pull weeds out of the ground 除去杂草

week /wiːk; wik/ *noun* 名词
1 a time of seven days, usually from Sunday to the next Saturday 星期；周（通常指从星期日到下个星期六）: *I'm going on holiday next week.* 我下星期就放假了。◇ *I play tennis twice a week.* 我每星期打两次网球。◇ *I saw him two weeks ago.* 我两个星期前见过他。✪ A **fortnight** is the same as two weeks. ✳ **fortnight** 是两个星期。
2 Monday to Friday or Monday to Saturday 星期一到星期五或星期一到星期六: *I work during the week but not at weekends.* 我星期一到星期五上班，周末不上班。

weekday /ˈwiːkdeɪ; ˈwikˌde/ *noun* 名词
any day except Saturday and Sunday 除星期六和星期日以外的任何一天: *I only work on weekdays.* 我只是星期一到星期五上班。

weekend /ˌwiːkˈend; ˈwikˈɛnd/ *noun* 名词
Saturday and Sunday 星期六和星期日；周末: *What are you doing at the weekend?* 您周末做什么？

weekly /ˈwiːkli; ˈwiklɪ/ *adjective*, *adverb* 形容词，副词
that happens or comes every week or once a week 每星期（的）；一个星期一次（的）: *a weekly magazine* 周刊 ◇ *I am paid weekly.* 我每星期领一次工资。

weep /wiːp; wip/ *verb* 动词 (**weeps**, **weeping**, **wept** /wept; wɛpt/, **has wept**)
cry 哭泣 ✪ **Cry** is the word that we usually use. ✳ **cry** 是常用词。

weigh /weɪ; we/ *verb* 动词 (**weighs**, **weighing**, **weighed** /weɪd; wed/)
1 measure how heavy somebody or something is using a machine called **scales** 称某物的重量（天平或磅秤叫做 **scales**）: *The shop assistant weighed the tomatoes.* 售货员称了称西红柿的重量。
2 have a certain number of kilos, etc 有某重量（例如多少公斤）: *'How much do you weigh?' 'I weigh 55 kilos.'* "您体重是多少？""我体重55公斤。"

weight /weɪt; wet/ *noun* 名词
1 (no plural 无复数) how heavy somebody or something is 重量；分量: *Do you know the weight of the parcel?* 您知道这个包裹的重量吗？
2 (*plural* 复数作 **weights**) a piece of metal that you use on **scales** for measuring how heavy something is. 砝码；秤锤；秤砣（天平或磅秤叫做 **scales**）
lose weight become thinner and less heavy 减轻体重: *I'm getting fat—I need to lose weight!* 我越来越胖了——得减轻体重了！
put on weight become fatter and heavier 增加体重

weird /wɪəd; wɪrd/ *adjective* 形容词 (**weirder**, **weirdest**)
very strange 非常奇怪的；怪异的: *a weird dream* 离奇的梦

welcome[1] /ˈwelkəm; ˈwɛlkəm/ *adjective* 形容词
If somebody or something is welcome, you are happy to have or see them 受欢迎的；讨人喜欢的: *The cool drink was welcome on such a hot day.* 大热天喝了那种冷饮真痛快。◇ *Welcome to Oxford!* 欢迎来到牛津！
be welcome to be allowed to do or have something 可随意做某事或取用某物: *If you come to England again, you're welcome to stay with us.* 您再来英国的时候，可以尽管住在我们这里。
make somebody welcome show a visitor that you are happy to see him/her 使客人感到受欢迎；款待某人
you're welcome polite words that you say when somebody has said 'thank you'（用作答谢的客套话）不用谢；不要客气: *'Thank you.' 'You're welcome.'* "谢谢您。" "别客气。"

welcome[2] /ˈwelkəm; ˈwɛlkəm/ *verb* 动词 (**welcomes**, **welcoming**, **welcomed** /ˈwelkəmd; ˈwɛlkəmd/)
show that you are happy to have or see somebody or something 欢迎或迎接某人或某事物: *He came to the door to welcome us.* 他到门口来迎接我们。
welcome *noun* 名词
They gave us a great welcome when we arrived. 我们一到就受到他们隆重的欢迎。

welfare /ˈwelfeə(r); ˈwɛlˌfɛr/ *noun* 名词 (no plural 无复数)
the health and happiness of a person（个人的）健康与幸福: *The school looks after the welfare of its students.* 这所学校很关心学生的身心健康。

W

well[1] /wel; wɛl/ *adjective* 形容词 (**better**, **best**)
healthy; not ill 健康的；无病的: *'How are you?' 'I'm very well, thanks.'* "您好吗？" "我很好，谢谢。"

well[2] /wel; wɛl/ *adverb* 副词 (**better**, **best**)
1 in a good or right way 好；对: *You speak English very well.* 您英语说得很好。◇ *These shoes are very well-made.* 这双鞋做得很好。✪ opposite 反义词: **badly**
2 completely or very much 完全地；充分地: *I don't know Cathy very well.* 我不怎么认识卡西。◇ *Shake the bottle well before you open it.* 先把瓶子摇匀再打开。
as well also 也；还: *'I'm going out.' 'Can I come as well?'* "我要出去。" "我也去行吗？"
as well as something and also 既…也…；不仅…而且…: *She has a flat in London as well as a house in Edinburgh.* 她在伦敦有个公寓，在爱丁堡还有所房子。
do well be successful 成功: *He did well in his exams.* 他考得很好。
may or 或 **might as well** words that you use to say that you will do something, often because there is nothing else to do 用以表示要做某事（常因无其他事可做）；不妨: *If you've finished the work, you may as well go home.* 你要是把工作做完了，就不妨回家吧。
well done! words that you say to somebody who has done something good 夸奖某人做好某事的用语: *'I got the job!' 'Well done!'* "我得到这份工作了！" "太好啦！"

well[3] /wel; wɛl/
1 a word that you often say when you are starting to speak 开始说话时常用的词: *'Do you like it?' 'Well, I'm not really sure.'* "你喜欢这个吗？" "嗯，我还说不准。"
2 a word that you use to show surprise 表示惊奇的词: *Well, that's strange!* 嘿，真奇怪！

well[4] /wel; wɛl/ *noun* 名词
a deep hole for getting water or oil from under the ground 井；水井；油井: *an oil well* 油井

we'll /wi:l; wil/
1 = **we will**
2 = **we shall**

wellingtons /ˈwelɪŋtənz; ˈwɛlɪŋtənz/, **wellington boots** /ˌwelɪŋtən ˈbu:ts; ˈwɛlɪŋtən ˈbuts/ *noun* 名词 (plural 复数)
long rubber boots that you wear to keep your feet and part of your legs dry 威灵顿长筒靴（橡胶雨靴）

well-known /ˌwelˈnəʊn; ˈwɛlˈnon/ *adjective* 形容词
famous 著名的: *a well-known writer* 有名的作家

well off /ˌwel ˈɒf; ˈwɛl ˈɔf/ *adjective* 形容词
rich 富裕的: *They are very well off and they live in a big house.* 他们非常富裕，住着一所大房子。

went *form of* **go¹** ∗ **go¹** 的不同形式
wept *form of* **weep** ∗ **weep** 的不同形式
were *form of* **be** ∗ **be** 的不同形式
we're /wɪə(r); wɪr/ = **we are**
weren't /wɜːnt; wɝnt/ = **were not**
west /west; wɛst/ *noun* 名词 (no plural 无复数)

1 where the sun goes down in the evening 西；西方；西边: *Which way is west?* 哪边儿是西？◇ *They live in the west of England.* 他们住在英格兰的西部。☞ picture at **north** 见 **north** 词条插图

2 the West (no plural 无复数) the countries of North America and Western Europe 西方国家（即北美和西欧的国家）

west *adjective*, *adverb* 形容词，副词
West London 伦敦的西部 ◇ *The town is five miles west of here.* 那个镇子在西边，离这里五英里。

western /ˈwestən; ˈwɛstɚn/ *adjective* 形容词
in or of the west of a place 西方的；西部的；西边的: *Western parts of the country will be very cold.* 这个国家的西部很冷。

western /ˈwestən; ˈwɛstɚn/ *noun* 名词
a film or book about cowboys in the west of the United States of America 描写美国西部牛仔生活的影片或书

wet /wet; wɛt/ *adjective* 形容词 (**wetter**, **wettest**)

1 covered in water or another liquid; not dry 有水或其他液体的；湿的: *This towel is wet—can I have a dry one?* 这条毛巾是湿的——给我条干的行吗？◇ *wet paint* 没干的油漆 ☞ picture on page C27 见第C27页图

2 with a lot of rain 多雨的: *a wet day* 下雨天

✪ opposite 反义词: **dry**

we've /wiv; wiv/ = **we have**

whale 鲸

whale /weɪl; hwel/ *noun* 名词
a very big animal that lives in the sea and looks like a fish 鲸

what /wɒt; hwɑt/ *pronoun*, *adjective* 代词，形容词

1 a word that you use when you ask about somebody or something 用以询问某人或某事物的词；什么；多少；哪: *What's your name?* 你叫什么名字？◇ *What are you reading?* 您阅读什么呢？◇ *What time is it?* 现在几点钟了？◇ *What kind of music do you like?* 您喜欢听哪类的音乐？

2 the thing that …的事物: *I don't know what this word means.* 我不知道这个词的含义。◇ *Tell me what to do.* 告诉我该做什么吧。

3 a word that you use to show surprise or other strong feelings 用以表示惊奇或其他强烈感情的词；多么: *What a terrible day!* 多么糟糕的一天！◇ *What a beautiful picture!* 多漂亮的画儿啊！

what about … ? words that you use when you suggest something 用以提出建议的词语；…怎么样？: *What about going to the cinema tonight?* 今天晚上去看场电影怎么样？

what … for? why?; for what use? 为什么…？；怎么…？；…有什么用？: *What did you say that for?* 你说那句话干什么？◇ *What's this machine for?* 这台机器有什么用？

what is … like? words that you use when you want to know more about somebody or something …是什么样的？: *'What's her brother like?' 'He's very nice.'* "她哥哥人怎么样？""他这个人非常好。"

what's on? what television programme, film, etc is being shown? 上演什么电视节目或影片等？: *What's on TV tonight?* 今天晚上电视演什么？

what's up? what is wrong? 怎么了？: *You look sad. What's up?* 你看起来有心事。怎么了？

whatever /wɒtˈevə(r); hwɑtˈɛvɚ/ *adjective* 形容词
of any kind; any or every 任何种类的；无论什么样的: *These animals eat whatever food they can find.* 这些动物找到什么食物就吃什么。

whatever *pronoun* 代词

1 anything or everything 一切事物；无论什么事物: *I'll do whatever I can to help you.* 我一定竭尽所能来帮助你。

2 it does not matter what 无论什么: *Whatever you do, don't be late.* 你无论怎样也别迟到。

what's /wɒts; 'hwɑts/
1 = **what is**
2 = **what has**

wheat /wi:t; hwit/ *noun* 名词 (no plural 无复数)
a plant with seeds (called **grain**) that we can make into flour 小麦（麦粒叫做 **grain**）

wheel /wi:l; hwil/ *noun* 名词
a thing like a circle that turns round to move something. Cars and bicycles have wheels. 轮子；车轮；机轮 ☞ picture at **car** 见 **car** 词条插图

wheel *verb* 动词 (**wheels**, **wheeling**, **wheeled** /wi:ld; hwild/)
push along something that has wheels 推动有轮子的东西: *I wheeled my bicycle up the hill.* 我推着自行车上山。

wheelchair 轮椅

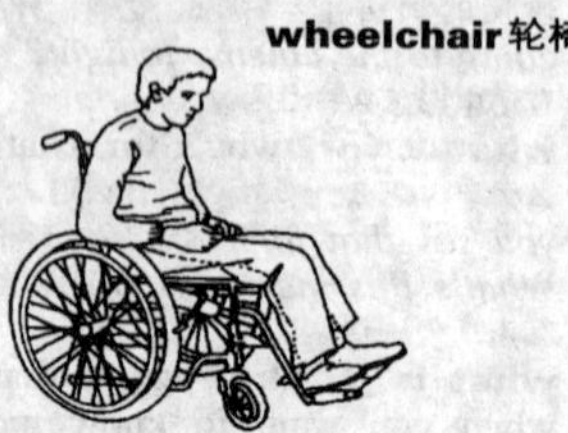

wheelchair /'wi:ltʃeə(r); 'hwil'tʃɛr/ *noun* 名词
a chair with wheels for somebody who cannot walk 轮椅

W

when /wen; hwɛn/ *adverb* 副词
1 at what time 什么时候: *When did she arrive?* 她是什么时候到的？◇ *I don't know when his birthday is.* 我不知道他的生日是几月几号。
2 at the time that 那时候；当时；当场: *I saw her in May, when she was in London.* 我是在五月份看见她的，当时她正在伦敦。

when *conjunction* 连词
at the time that 在…的时候；当…的时候: *It was raining when we left school.* 我们离开学校的时候正下着雨。◇ *He came when I called him.* 我一招呼他就来了。

whenever /wen'evə(r); hwɛn'ɛvɚ/ *conjunction* 连词
1 at any time 在任何时候；无论何时: *Come and see us whenever you want.* 你想什么时候到我们这儿来坐坐就什么时候来吧。
2 every time that 每次；每当: *Whenever I see her, she talks about her boyfriend.* 我每次见到她的时候她都谈她的男朋友。

where /weə(r); hwɛr/ *adverb*, *conjunction* 副词，连词
1 in or to what place 在那里；到那里: *Where do you live?* 你住在哪儿？◇ *I asked her where she lived.* 我问她住在什么地方。◇ *Where is she going?* 她要到哪儿去？
2 in which; at which 在那里: *This is the street where I live.* 这是我居住的街道。

whereas /ˌweər'æz; hwɛr'æz/ *conjunction* 连词
a word that you use between two different ideas（用以连接两语意相反的成分）而；然而: *John likes travelling, whereas I don't.* 约翰喜欢旅行，我可不喜欢。

wherever /weər'evə(r); hwɛr'ɛvɚ/ *adverb*, *conjunction* 副词，连词
1 at, in or to any place 在无论什么地方；到无论什么地方: *Sit wherever you like.* 你愿意坐在哪儿就坐在哪儿吧。
2 a way of saying 'where' more strongly 用以表达 where 的加强语气的词: *Wherever did I put my keys?* 我到底把钥匙放在哪儿了呢？

whether /'weðə(r); 'hwɛðɚ/ *conjunction* 连词
if 是否: *She asked me whether I was Spanish.* 她问我是不是西班牙人。◇ *I don't know whether to go or not.* 我不知道去好还是不去好。

which /wɪtʃ; hwɪtʃ/ *adjective*, *pronoun* 形容词，代词
1 what person or thing 哪个人或哪个事物: *Which colour do you like best—blue or green?* 您最喜欢哪种颜色——蓝的还是绿的？◇ *Which flat do you live in?* 您住在哪座公寓里？
2 a word that shows what person or thing 用以指提到的人或事物的词: *Did you read the poem (which) Louise wrote?* 您看过路易丝写的诗吗？
3 a word that you use before you say more about something 用以做进一步说明的词: *Her new dress, which she bought in London, is beautiful.* 她的新连衣裙，就是她在伦敦买的那件，非常漂亮。

whichever /wɪtʃ'evə(r); hwɪtʃ'ɛvɚ/ *adjective, pronoun* 形容词，代词
any person or thing 任何人或事物: *Here are two books—take whichever you want.* 这儿有两本书——你想拿哪本都行。

while[1] /waɪl; hwaɪl/ *conjunction* 连词
1 during the time that; when 在…期间；当…的时候: *The telephone rang while I was having a shower.* 我正在淋浴的时候，电话铃响了。
2 at the same time as 与…同时: *I listen to the radio while I'm eating my breakfast.* 我边吃早饭边听收音机。

while[2] /waɪl; hwaɪl/ *noun* 名词 (no plural 无复数)
some time 一段时间: *Let's sit here for a while.* 咱们在这儿坐一会儿吧。◇ *I'm going home in a while.* 我一会儿就回家。

whilst /waɪlst; hwaɪlst/ *conjunction* 连词
while 在…期间；与…同时: *He waited whilst I looked for my keys.* 他等着我找钥匙。

whine /waɪn; hwaɪn/ *verb* 动词 (**whines, whining, whined** /waɪnd; hwaɪnd/)
make a long high sad sound 发出长而高音的呜咽声: *The dog was whining outside the door.* 狗在门外狺狺地叫着。

whip /wɪp; hwɪp/ *noun* 名词
a long piece of leather or rope with a handle, for hitting animals or people 鞭子
whip *verb* 动词 (**whips, whipping, whipped** /wɪpt; hwɪpt/)
1 hit an animal or a person with a whip 用鞭子抽打动物或人: *The rider whipped the horse to make it go faster.* 骑马的人鞭打着马让它快点儿。
2 mix food very quickly with a fork, for example, until it is light and thick（用叉子等）搅打食物: *whipped cream* 经过搅打的奶油

whirl /wɜːl; hwɝl/ *verb* 动词 (**whirls, whirling, whirled** /wɜːld; hwɝld/)
move round and round very quickly 旋转；打转: *The dancers whirled round the room.* 跳舞的人在全场翩跹起舞。

whisk /wɪsk; hwɪsk/ *verb* 动词 (**whisks, whisking, whisked** /wɪskt; hwɪskt/)
1 mix eggs or cream very quickly 搅打鸡蛋或奶油
2 move somebody or something very quickly 把某人或某物迅速移动或带走: *The President was whisked away in a helicopter.* 总统乘坐直升飞机匆匆离去。
whisk *noun* 名词
a tool that you use for mixing eggs or cream（搅打鸡蛋或奶油的）搅拌器

whisker /'wɪskə(r); 'hwɪskɚ/ *noun* 名词
one of the long hairs that grow near the mouth of cats, mice and other animals（猫、鼠等动物的）须 ☞ picture at **cat** 见 **cat** 词条插图

whisky /'wɪski; 'hwɪskɪ/ *noun* 名词
1 (no plural 无复数) a strong alcoholic drink 威士忌
2 (*plural* 复数作 **whiskies**) a glass of whisky 一杯威士忌

whisper /'wɪspə(r); 'hwɪspɚ/ *verb* 动词 (**whispers, whispering, whispered** /'wɪspəd; 'hwɪspɚd/)
speak very quietly 小声说；低语: *He whispered so that he would not wake the baby up.* 他低声说话以免把孩子吵醒。
whisper *noun* 名词
She spoke in a whisper. 她低声说话。

whistle /'wɪsl; 'hwɪsl̩/ *noun* 名词
1 a small musical instrument that makes a long high sound when you blow it 哨子: *The referee blew his whistle to end the match.* 裁判吹响了哨子，宣布比赛结束。
2 the long high sound that you make when you blow air out between your lips 口哨儿
whistle *verb* 动词 (**whistles, whistling, whistled** /'wɪsld; 'hwɪsl̩d/)
make a long high sound by blowing air out between your lips or through a whistle 吹口哨儿或吹哨子: *She whistled to her dog.* 她吹口哨儿招呼狗。

white /waɪt; hwaɪt/ *adjective* 形容词 (**whiter, whitest**)
1 with the colour of snow or milk 白色的
2 with light-coloured skin 白皮肤的；白种人的
3 with milk 加奶的: *a white coffee* 加奶的咖啡
white wine /ˌwaɪt 'waɪn; 'hwaɪt 'waɪn/ *noun* 名词
wine with a light colour 白葡萄酒
white *noun* 名词
1 (no plural 无复数) the colour of snow or milk 白色: *She was dressed in white.* 她穿着白色的衣服。

2 (*plural* 复数作 **whites**) a person with white skin 白皮肤的人；白种人
3 (*plural* 复数作 **whites**) the part inside an egg that is round the yellow middle part 蛋清；蛋白

whiz /wɪz; hwɪz/ *verb* 动词 (**whizzes, whizzing, whizzed** /wɪzd; hwɪzd/)
move very quickly 高速移动: *The bullet whizzed past his head.* 子弹从他耳旁飞过。

who /hu:; hu/ *pronoun* 代词
1 what person or people 谁: *Who is that girl?* 那个女孩儿是谁？◇ *I don't know who did it.* 我不知道是谁干的。
2 a word that shows what person or people 用以指提到的人的词: *He's the boy who invited me to his party.* 他就是请我参加聚会的那个孩子。◇ *The people (who) I met on holiday were very nice.* 我在假期遇见的人都非常好。

who'd /hu:d; hud/
1 = **who had**
2 = **who would**

whoever /hu'evə(r); hu'ɛvɚ/ *pronoun* 代词
1 the person who; any person who …的那个人；无论谁: *Whoever broke the glass must pay for it.* 这个玻璃是谁打破的谁就得赔。
2 a way of saying 'who' more strongly 用以表达 who 的加强语气的词: *Whoever gave you those flowers?* 这些花儿到底是谁给你的？

whole /həʊl; hol/ *adjective* 形容词
complete; with no parts missing 完全的；完整的；全部的: *He ate the whole cake!* 他把整个蛋糕都吃了！◇ *We are going to Spain for a whole month.* 我们要到西班牙去整整一个月。

whole *noun* 名词 (no plural 无复数)
1 all of something 某事物的全部；全体: *I spent the whole of the weekend in bed.* 我整个周末都在床上休息。
2 a thing that is complete 完整的事物；整体: *Two halves make a whole.* 两个二分之一等于一个整体。
on the whole in general 总的说来；大体上: *On the whole, I think it's a good idea.* 总的来说，我认为这是个好主意。

who'll /hu:l; hul/ = **who will**

whom /hu:m; hum/ *pronoun* 代词
1 what person or people 谁: *To whom did you give the money?* 你把钱给谁了？
2 a word that you use to say what person or people 用以指提到的人的词: *She's the woman (whom) I met in Greece.* 她就是我在希腊遇见的那个人。
✪ **Who** is the word that we usually use. ✳ **who** 是常用词。

who're /'hu:ə(r); 'huɚ/ = **who are**

who's /hu:z; huz/
1 = **who is**
2 = **who has**

whose /hu:z; huz/ *adjective, pronoun* 形容词，代词
of which person 谁的: *Whose car is this?* 这是谁的汽车？◇ *That's the boy whose sister is a singer.* 那个男孩儿他姐姐是歌手。

who've /hu:v; huv/ = **who have**

why /waɪ; hwaɪ/ *adverb* 副词
for what reason 为什么；怎么: *Why are you late?* 你怎么晚了？◇ *I don't know why she's angry.* 我不知道她为什么生气。
why not words that you use to say that something is a good idea 用以表示是个好主意的词: *Why not ask Kate to go with you?* 让凯特跟你一起去好不好？

wicked /'wɪkɪd; 'wɪkɪd/ *adjective* 形容词
very bad 很坏的；邪恶的: *a wicked witch* 恶毒的女巫

wide /waɪd; waɪd/ *adjective* 形容词 (**wider, widest**)
1 far from one side to the other 宽的: *a wide road* 很宽的路 ✪ opposite 反义词: **narrow** ☞ picture on page C26 见第C26页图
2 You use 'wide' to say or ask how far something is from one side to the other 陈述或询问某物宽窄的词: *The table was 2 m wide.* 这张桌子2米宽。◇ *How wide is the river?* 这条河有多宽？☞ picture on page C5 见第C5页图
3 completely open 完全张开的: *wide eyes* 睁大的眼睛

wide *adverb* 副词
completely; as far or as much as possible 完全地；充分地；尽量地: *Open your mouth wide.* 把嘴张大。◇ *I'm wide awake!* 我十分清醒！
wide apart a long way from each other 相距很远: *She stood with her feet wide apart.* 她站在那里，双脚劈开很大。

W

widen /'waɪdn; 'waɪdn̩/ *verb* 动词 (**widens**, **widening**, **widened** /'waɪdnd; 'waɪdn̩d/)
become wider; make something wider (使某物)变宽;加宽: *They are widening the road.* 他们正在拓宽这条路。

widespread /'waɪdspred; 'waɪd'sprɛd/ *adjective* 形容词
If something is widespread, it is happening in many places 遍及各处的;遍布的: *The disease is becoming more widespread.* 这种病越来越扩散了。

widow /'wɪdəʊ; 'wɪdo/ *noun* 名词
a woman whose husband is dead 寡妇

widower /'wɪdəʊə(r); 'wɪdəwɚ/ *noun* 名词
a man whose wife is dead 鳏夫

width /wɪdθ; wɪdθ/ *noun* 名词
how far it is from one side of something to the other; how wide something is 宽度: *The room is five metres in width.* 这间屋子五米宽。☞ picture on page C5 见第C5页图

wife /waɪf; waɪf/ *noun* 名词 (*plural* 复数作 **wives** /waɪvz; waɪvz/)
the woman that a man is married to 妻子 ☞ picture on page C3 见第C3页图

wig /wɪg; wɪg/ *noun* 名词
a covering for your head made of hair that is not your own 假发

wild /waɪld; waɪld/ *adjective* 形容词 (**wilder**, **wildest**)
1 Wild plants and animals live or grow in nature, not with people (指动植物)野生的: *wild flowers* 野花
2 excited; not controlled 兴奋的;激动的;失去控制的: *She was wild with anger.* 她大发雷霆。

wildlife /'waɪldlaɪf; 'waɪld,laɪf/ *noun* 名词 (no plural 无复数)
animals and plants in nature 野生的动植物

will¹ /wɪl; wɪl/ *modal verb* 情态动词
1 a word that shows the future 表示将来的词;将: *Do you think she will come tomorrow?* 你认为她明天来不来?
2 a word that you use when you agree or promise to do something 表示同意或答应做某事的词: *I'll* (= I will) *carry your bag.* 我给你拿着包吧。
3 a word that you use when you ask somebody to do something 用以让某人做某事的词: *Will you open the window, please?* 请您把窗户打开行吗?

✪ The negative form of 'will' is **will not** or the short form **won't** /wəʊnt; wont/ ＊ will 的否定式是 **will not** 或其缩略式 **won't** /wəʊnt; wont/:

They won't be there. 他们不会在那儿。

The short form of 'will' is **'ll**. We often use this ＊ will 的缩略式是 **'ll**,较常用:

You'll (= you will) *be late.* 你要晚了。

He'll (=he will) *drive you to the station.* 他开车把你送到车站去。

☞ Look at the Note on page 314 to find out more about **modal verbs.** 见第314页对 **modal verbs** 的进一步解释。

will² /wɪl; wɪl/ *noun* 名词
1 (no plural 无复数) the power of your mind that makes you choose, decide and do things 意志;意志力;主见: *She has a very strong will and nobody can stop her doing what she wants to do.* 她很有主意,她打算做的事谁也拦不住。
2 (no plural 无复数) what somebody wants 意愿: *The man made him get into the car against his will* (= when he did not want to). 那个男子迫使他身不由主地上了汽车。
3 (*plural* 复数作 **wills**) a piece of paper that says who will have your money, house, etc when you die 遗嘱: *My grandmother left me £2 000 in her will.* 我的祖母在遗嘱中赠送我2 000英镑。

willing /'wɪlɪŋ; 'wɪlɪŋ/ *adjective* 形容词
ready and happy to do something 愿意并喜欢做某事的: *I'm willing to lend you some money.* 我乐意借给你一些钱。
willingly *adverb* 副词
I'll willingly help you. 我很愿意帮助你。
willingness /'wɪlɪŋnəs; 'wɪlɪŋnɪs/ *noun* 名词 (no plural 无复数)
willingness to help 乐于相助

win /wɪn; wɪn/ *verb* 动词 (**wins**, **winning**, **won** /wʌn; wʌn/, **has won**)
1 be the best or the first in a game, race or competition (在游戏、径赛或竞争中)获胜,赢: *Who won the race?* 这次赛跑谁赢了? ◇ *Tom won and I was second.* 汤姆得第一,我第二。✪ opposite 反义词: **lose**

2 receive something because you did well or tried hard（因做得好或因努力）获得某事物: *I won a prize in the competition.* 我在竞赛中得了奖。◇ *Who won the gold medal?* 谁得到了金牌？

✪ Be careful! You **earn** (not **win**) money by working. 注意！做工作挣钱叫做 **earn**（不可用 **win** 字）。

win *noun* 名词

Our team has had five wins this year. 我们队今年赢了五次。

wind[1] /wɪnd; wɪnd/ *noun* 名词

air that moves 风: *The wind blew his hat off.* 风把他的帽子刮掉了。◇ *strong winds* 大风

windy *adjective* 形容词 (**windier, windiest**)

with a lot of wind 多风的；风大的: *It's very windy today!* 今天风很大！

wind[2] /waɪnd; waɪnd/ *verb* 动词 (**winds, winding, wound** /waʊnd; waund/, **has wound**)

1 make something long go round and round another thing 把条状物缠绕在另一物体上: *The nurse wound the bandage around my finger.* 护士在我的手指上缠上了绷带。

2 turn a key or handle to make something work or move 转动发条或把手使某物工作或移动: *The clock will stop if you don't wind it up.* 这个钟不上发条就要停了。◇ *The driver wound her car window down.* 那个开车的人转动把手把她的车窗摇了下来。

3 A road or river that winds has a lot of bends and turns（指道路或河流）弯弯曲曲地延伸: *The path winds through the forest.* 这条小径弯弯曲曲穿过树林。

W

windmill 风车

windmill /ˈwɪndmɪl; ˈwɪnˌmɪl/ *noun* 名词

a tall building with long flat parts that turn in the wind 风车

window /ˈwɪndəʊ; ˈwɪndo/ *noun* 名词

an opening in a wall or in a car, for example, with glass in it 窗户: *It was cold, so I closed the window.* 天气很冷，我把窗户关上了。◇ *She looked out of the window.* 她从窗口向外看。☞ picture at **house** 见 **house** 词条插图

window-pane /ˈwɪndəʊ peɪn; ˈwɪndoˌpen/ *noun* 名词

a piece of glass in a window 窗玻璃

window-sill /ˈwɪndəʊ sɪl; ˈwɪndoˌsɪl/, **window-ledge** /ˈwɪndəʊ ledʒ; ˈwɪndoˌlɛdʒ/ *noun* 名词

a shelf under a window 窗台

windscreen /ˈwɪndskriːn; ˈwɪndˌskrin/ *noun* 名词

the big window at the front of a car（汽车前面的）挡风玻璃窗 ☞ picture at **car** 见 **car** 词条插图

windscreen wiper /ˈwɪndskriːn ˌwaɪpə(r); ˈwɪndskrin ˌwaɪpɚ/ *noun* 名词

a thing that cleans rain and dirt off the windscreen while you are driving（汽车挡风玻璃窗上的）刮水器

windshield /ˈwɪndʃiːld; ˈwɪndˌʃild/ *American English for* **windscreen** 美式英语，即 **windscreen**

windsurfing 帆板运动

windsurfing /ˈwɪndsɜːfɪŋ; ˈwɪndˌsɝfɪŋ/ *noun* 名词 (no plural 无复数)

the sport of moving over water on a special board with a sail 帆板运动 ✪ You can say **go windsurfing** 可以说 **go windsurfing**: *Have you been windsurfing?* 你去做帆板运动了吗？

windsurfer *noun* 名词

1 a special board with a sail. You stand on it as it moves over the water. 帆板

2 a person who rides on a board like this 帆板运动员

wine /waɪn; waɪn/ *noun* 名词

an alcoholic drink. Wine is made from grapes 葡萄酒: *red wine* 红葡萄酒 ◇ *white wine* 白葡萄酒 ◇ *Do you like sweet or dry wine?* 您喜欢甜的还是不甜的葡萄酒？

wing /wɪŋ; wɪŋ/ *noun* 名词
the part of a bird, an insect or an aeroplane that helps it to fly（鸟、昆虫或飞机的）翅膀；翼 ☞ picture at **bird** 见 **bird** 词条插图

wink /wɪŋk; wɪŋk/ *verb* 动词 (**winks, winking, winked** /wɪŋkt; wɪŋkt/)
close and open one eye quickly to make a friendly or secret sign 眨一只眼（使眼色）: *She winked at me.* 她会意地向我眨了眨一只眼。
wink *noun* 名词
He gave me a wink. 他眨了一下一只眼向我示意。

winner /ˈwɪnə(r); ˈwɪnɚ/ *noun* 名词
a person or animal that wins a game, race or competition（在游戏、径赛或竞争中）获胜的人或动物: *The winner was given a prize.* 获胜者得到了奖品。✪ opposite 反义词: **loser**

winning /ˈwɪnɪŋ; ˈwɪnɪŋ/ *adjective* 形容词
that wins a game, race or competition（在游戏、径赛或竞争中）获胜的: *the winning team* 获胜的队

winter /ˈwɪntə(r); ˈwɪntɚ/ *noun* 名词
the coldest part of the year 冬季；冬天: *It often snows in winter.* 冬天常常下雪。

wipe /waɪp; waɪp/ *verb* 动词 (**wipes, wiping, wiped** /waɪpt; waɪpt/)
make something clean or dry with a cloth 用布擦净或擦干: *The waitress wiped the table.* 女服务员把桌子擦干净了。◇ *I washed my hands and wiped them on a towel.* 我洗完手用毛巾擦干了。
wipe off take away something by wiping 擦掉；擦去: *She wiped the writing off the blackboard.* 她把黑板上的字擦掉了。
wipe out destroy a place completely, or kill a lot of people 彻底摧毁某处或消灭所有的人: *The bombs wiped out many villages.* 那些炸弹摧毁了很多村庄。
wipe up take away liquid by wiping with a cloth 用布把液体擦干: *I wiped up the milk on the floor.* 我用布把地板上的牛奶擦干了。
wipe *noun* 名词
He gave the table a quick wipe. 他很快把桌子擦了擦。

wire /ˈwaɪə(r); waɪr/ *noun* 名词
a long piece of very thin metal 金属丝；金属线: *electrical wires* 电线 ◇ *a piece of wire* 一段金属丝

wisdom /ˈwɪzdəm; ˈwɪzdəm/ *noun* 名词 (no plural 无复数)
knowing and understanding a lot about many things; being wise 博学多识；智慧: *Some people think that old age brings wisdom.* 有些人认为人老见识广。

wise /waɪz; waɪz/ *adjective* 形容词 (**wiser, wisest**)
A person who is wise knows and understands a lot about many things 博学多识的；聪明的: *a wise old man* 博学多识的老先生 ◇ *You made a wise choice.* 你做的决定很高明。
wisely *adverb* 副词
Many people wisely stayed at home in the bad weather. 那时天气坏，许多人都很有主意一直足未出户。

wish[1] /wɪʃ; wɪʃ/ *verb* 动词 (**wishes, wishing, wished** /wɪʃt; wɪʃt/)
1 want something that is not possible or that probably will not happen 想要不（太）可能的事物；但愿: *I wish I could fly!* 我但愿能飞！◇ *I wish I had passed the exam!* 我要是考及格了多好！◇ *I wish I were rich.* 我要是很有钱就好了。
2 say that you hope somebody will have something 祝愿某人能有某事物: *I wished her a happy birthday.* 我祝她生日快乐。
3 want to do or have something 想要做某事或有某事物；希望: *I wish to see the manager.* 我想见见经理。✪ It is more usual to say **want** or **would like**. ✳ **want** 或 **would like** 是常用词语。
wish for something say to yourself that you want something and hope that it will happen 心中想要某事物而希望能够实现: *You can't have everything you wish for.* 人不能想要什么就有什么。

wish[2] /wɪʃ; wɪʃ/ *noun* 名词 (*plural* 复数作 **wishes**)
a feeling that you want something 愿望；希望: *I have no wish to go.* 我不想走。
best wishes words that you write at the end of a letter, before your name, to show that you hope somebody is well and happy 信中结尾的祝愿语；祝好: *See you soon. Best wishes, Lucy.* 很快再见到你。祝你一切顺利。露西。

W

make a wish say to yourself that you want something and hope that it will happen 心中想要某事物而希望能够实现；发愿: *Close your eyes and make a wish!* 闭上眼睛立个心愿吧！

wit /wɪt; wɪt/ *noun* 名词 (no plural 无复数) speaking or writing in a clever and funny way 巧妙而幽默的言语或文字；诙谐或风趣的内容

witch /wɪtʃ; wɪtʃ/ *noun* 名词 (*plural* 复数作 **witches**)
a woman in stories who uses magic to do bad things 女巫

with /wɪð; wɪð/ *preposition* 介词
1 having or carrying 有或带着: *a man with grey hair* 头发花白的男子 ◇ *a house with a garden* 带花园的房子 ◇ *a woman with a suitcase* 提着衣箱的女子
2 a word that shows people or things are together 表示人或事物在一起的词: *I live with my parents.* 我跟我父母住在一起。◇ *Mix the flour with milk.* 把面粉和牛奶搀和在一起。◇ *I agree with you.* 我和您的意见一致。
3 using 使用: *I cut it with a knife.* 我是用刀切的。◇ *Fill the bottle with water.* 把瓶子灌满水。
4 against 对抗: *I played tennis with my sister.* 我跟我妹妹打网球。
5 because of 由于；因为: *Her hands were blue with cold.* 她的手冻得发紫。

withdraw /wɪð'drɔ:; wɪð'drɔ/ *verb* 动词 (**withdraws**, **withdrawing**, **withdrew** /wɪð'dru:; wɪð'dru/, **has withdrawn** /wɪð'drɔ:n; wɪð'drɔn/)
1 take something out or away 把某物取出或取走；提取: *I withdrew £100 from my bank account.* 我从我的银行账户里取出了100英镑。
2 move back or away 退后或离去；撤退；撤回；后退: *The army withdrew from the town.* 军队从镇上撤走了。
3 say that you will not take part in something 表示出不参加某事物；退出: *Rob has withdrawn from the race.* 罗布退出了这项径赛。

wither /'wɪðə(r); 'wɪðɚ/ *verb* 动词 (**withers**, **withering**, **withered** /'wɪðəd; 'wɪðɚd/)
If a plant withers, it becomes dry and dies（指植物）枯萎或凋谢: *The plants withered in the hot sun.* 这些植物都晒蔫了。

W

within /wɪ'ðɪn; wɪð'ɪn/ *preposition* 介词
1 inside 在里面；在内；在其中: *There are 400 prisoners within the prison walls.* 这座监狱的围墙里有400名犯人。
2 before the end of 在终止或结束之前: *I will be back within an hour.* 我一小时以内回来。
3 not further than 不超过某段距离: *We live within a mile of the station.* 我们住的地方离车站不到一英里。

without /wɪ'ðaʊt; wɪð'aut/ *preposition* 介词
1 not having, showing or using something 没有某事物；不显示或不使用某事物: *It's cold—don't go out without your coat.* 天气很冷——别不穿大衣就出去。◇ *coffee without milk* 不加奶的咖啡
2 not being with somebody or something 不与某人或某事物在一起: *He left without me.* 他没带着我就走了。
do without manage when something is not there（在没有某事物的情况下）将就: *There isn't any tea so we will have to do without.* 没有茶叶了，我们也只好将就着。
without doing something not doing something 不做或未做某事物: *They left without saying goodbye.* 他们没告辞就走了。

witness /'wɪtnəs; 'wɪtnɪs/ *noun* 名词 (*plural* 复数作 **witnesses**)
1 a person who sees something happen and can tell other people about it later 目击者: *There were two witnesses to the accident.* 这起事故有两个目击者。
2 a person in a court of law who tells what he/she saw（法庭上的）证人
witness *verb* 动词 (**witnesses**, **witnessing**, **witnessed** /'wɪtnəst; 'wɪtnɪst/)
see something happen 目击；目睹: *She witnessed a murder.* 她目睹一件谋杀案。

witty /'wɪti; 'wɪtɪ/ *adjective* 形容词 (**wittier**, **wittiest**)
clever and funny 巧妙而幽默的；诙谐的；风趣的: *a witty answer* 诙谐的回答

wives *plural of* **wife** ✳ **wife** 的复数形式

wizard /'wɪzəd; 'wɪzɚd/ *noun* 名词
a man in stories who has magic powers（童话中的）会魔法的人

wobble /'wɒbl; 'wɑbl̩/ *verb* 动词 (**wobbles**, **wobbling**, **wobbled** /'wɒbld; 'wɑbl̩d/)
move a little from side to side（略微地）

摆动或摇动: *That chair wobbles when you sit on it.* 那把椅子坐上去有点儿摇晃。

wobbly *adjective* 形容词
If something is wobbly, it moves a little from side to side（略微地）摆动的或摇动的: *My legs feel wobbly.* 我感到腿有些发颤。

woke, **woken** *forms of* **wake** ✻ **wake** 的不同形式

wolf /wʊlf; wulf/ *noun* 名词 (*plural* 复数作 **wolves** /wʊlvz; wulvz/)
a wild animal like a big dog 狼

woman /'wʊmən; 'wumən/ *noun* 名词 (*plural* 复数作 **women** /'wɪmɪn; 'wɪmɪn/)
a grown-up female person 成年的女子: *men, women and children* 男人、女人和儿童

won *form of* **win** ✻ **win** 的不同形式

wonder¹ /'wʌndə(r); 'wʌndɚ/ *verb* 动词 (**wonders**, **wondering**, **wondered** /'wʌndəd; 'wʌndɚd/)
ask yourself something; want to know something 自问；想知道: *I wonder what that noise is.* 我心里想那是什么声音呢。◇ *I wonder why he didn't come.* 我想知道他怎么没来。
I wonder if words that you use to ask a question politely 用以提出问题的有礼貌的表达方式: *I wonder if I could use your phone.* 请问可以不可以用一下您的电话。

wonder² /'wʌndə(r); 'wʌndɚ/ *noun* 名词
1 (no plural 无复数) a feeling that you have when you see or hear something very strange, surprising or beautiful 惊奇；惊异；惊叹: *The children looked up in wonder at the big elephant.* 孩子们抬头看着大象，感到很惊奇。
2 (*plural* 复数作 **wonders**) something that gives you this feeling 使人感到惊奇的事物；奇迹；奇观；奇事: *the wonders of modern medicine* 现代医学的奇迹
it's a wonder it is surprising that 使人感到惊奇的是…: *It's a wonder you weren't killed in the accident.* 你在事故中大难不死令人称奇。
no wonder it is not surprising 不足为奇；难怪: *She didn't sleep last night, so no wonder she's tired.* 她昨天晚上没睡觉——难怪她很疲倦。

wonderful /'wʌndəfl; 'wʌndɚfəl/ *adjective* 形容词
very good; excellent 极好的；美妙的；了不起的: *What a wonderful present!* 多么好的礼物哇！◇ *This food is wonderful.* 这种食物好极了。

won't /wəʊnt; wont/ = **will not**

wood /wʊd; wud/ *noun* 名词
1 (no plural 无复数) the hard part of a tree 木头；木料；木柴: *Put some more wood on the fire.* 再往火里添点儿柴。◇ *The table is made of wood.* 这张桌子是木头做的。
2 (*also* 亦作 **woods**) a big group of trees, smaller than a forest 树林（比森林小）: *a walk in the woods* 在树林里散步
wooden /'wʊdn; 'wudn̩/ *adjective* 形容词
made of wood 用木头做的；木制的: *a wooden box* 木盒

wool /wʊl; wul/ *noun* 名词 (no plural 无复数)
1 the soft thick hair of sheep 羊毛
2 thread or cloth that is made from the hair of sheep 毛线；毛料: *a ball of wool* 一团毛线 ◇ *This jumper is made of wool.* 这件套头上衣是羊毛的。
☞ picture at **knit** 见 **knit** 词条插图
woollen /'wʊlən; 'wulɪn/ *adjective* 形容词
made of wool 用羊毛做的: *woollen socks* 毛袜子
woolly *adjective* 形容词
made of wool, or like wool 用羊毛做的或像羊毛的: *a woolly hat* 羊毛制的帽子

woolen, **wooly** *American English for* **woollen, woolly** 美式英语，即 **woollen**、**woolly**

word /wɜːd; wɝd/ *noun* 名词
1 (*plural* 复数作 **words**) a sound that you make or a letter or group of letters that you write, that has a meaning 词: *What's the French word for 'dog'?* "狗"这个词在法语里是哪个词？◇ *Do you know the words of this song?* 你知道这首歌的歌词吗？
2 (no plural 无复数) a promise 诺言；保证: *She gave me her word that she wouldn't tell anyone.* 她向我保证她谁也不告诉。
have a word with somebody speak to somebody 与某人谈话: *Can I have a word with you?* 我跟您说句话行吗？
in other words saying the same thing in a different way 换句话说；也就是说:

W

Joe doesn't like hard work—in other words, he's lazy! 乔不喜欢干重活儿——换句话说，他懒惰！

keep your word do what you promised 守信：*Claire said she would come, and she kept her word.* 克莱尔说她来，她果然很守信用。

take somebody's word for it believe what somebody says 相信某人的话

word for word using exactly the same words 完全使用原来的词；逐字地：*Ian repeated word for word what you told him.* 伊恩把你告诉他的话一字不差地重复了一遍。

word processor /ˈwɜːd ˌprəʊsesə(r); ˈwɝd proˌsɛsɚ/ *noun* 名词

a small computer that you can use for writing 文字处理机

wore *form of* **wear**[1] ＊ **wear**[1] 的不同形式

work[1] /wɜːk; wɝk/ *noun* 名词

1 (no plural 无复数) doing or making something 做事或制做某物；劳动：*Digging the garden is hard work.* 在花园里挖地是重活儿。◇ *She's lazy—she never does any work.* 她很懒——什么事都不干。

2 (no plural 无复数) what you do to earn money; a job（挣钱的）工作：*I'm looking for work.* 我正在找工作。◇ *What time do you start work?* 您几点钟开始工作？

3 (no plural 无复数) the place where you have a job 工作的处所：*I phoned him at work.* 我给他工作的地方打了电话。◇ *I'm not going to work today.* 我今天不去上班。

4 (no plural 无复数) something that you make or do 做出的事物：*The teacher marked our work.* 老师修改了我们的作业。

5 (*plural* 复数作 **works**) a book, painting or piece of music 书、画儿或乐曲；作品：*the works of Shakespeare* 莎士比亚的著作 ◇ *a work of art* 艺术品

6 works (plural 复数) a place where people make things with machines 工厂：*the steelworks* 钢厂

at work doing some work 正在做某事物：*The group are at work on* (= making) *a new album.* 这些人正在制做新的歌集唱片。

get to work start doing something 动手做某事物：*Let's get to work on this washing-up.* 咱们动手刷锅洗碗吧。

out of work If you are out of work, you do not have a job that you are paid to do 失去工作；失业：*How long have you been out of work?* 您失业多长时间了？

work[2] /wɜːk; wɝk/ *verb* 动词 (**works, working, worked** /wɜːkt; wɝkt/)

1 do or make something; be busy 做事或制做某物；劳动；忙着：*You will need to work harder if you want to pass the exam.* 你要想考及格就得再用点儿功。

2 do something as a job and get money for it（指挣钱）工作：*Susy works for the BBC.* 苏西为英国广播公司工作。◇ *I work at the car factory.* 我在汽车厂上班。

3 go correctly or do something correctly 顺利进行；发挥正常作用：*We can't watch the TV—it isn't working.* 我们看不成电视了——电视坏了。◇ *How does this computer work?* 这台计算机是怎么工作的？

4 make something do something 使某事物做某事物；操作：*Can you show me how to work this machine?* 您告诉我使用这台机器的方法行吗？

5 have the result you wanted 达到预期的效果：*I don't think your plan will work.* 我认为你的计划行不通。

work out 1 have the result you wanted 达到预期的效果：*I hope your plans work out.* 我希望你的计划行得通。**2** do exercises to keep your body strong and well 锻炼身体：*I work out every day.* 我每天都锻炼身体。

work something out find the answer to something 找到某事物的答案或解决方法：*We worked out the cost of the holiday.* 我们把度假的费用计算出来了。◇ *Why did she do it? I can't work it out.* 她为什么做这件事呢？我想不通。

workbook /ˈwɜːkbʊk; ˈwɝkˌbʊk/ *noun* 名词

a book where you write answers to questions, that you use when you are studying something 练习簿；作业本（需填写答案的）

worker /ˈwɜːkə(r); ˈwɝkɚ/ *noun* 名词

a person who works 工作的人；工作者：*factory workers* 工厂工人 ◇ *an office worker* 职员

workman /ˈwɜːkmən; ˈwɝkmən/ *noun* 名词 (*plural* 复数作 **workmen** /ˈwɜːkmən; ˈwɝkmən/)

a man who works with his hands to build or repair something（建筑或修配行业的）工人

worksheet /ˈwɜːkʃiːt; ˈwɝkˌʃit/ *noun* 名词
a piece of paper where you write answers to questions, that you use when you are studying something（需填写答案的）作业纸

workshop /ˈwɜːkʃɒp; ˈwɝkˌʃɑp/ *noun* 名词
1 a place where people make or repair things 制做或修配的处所；车间；厂房；工场
2 a time when people meet and work together to learn about something（学习某事物的）研习班，实践课

world /wɜːld; wɝld/ *noun* 名词
1 (no plural 无复数) the earth with all its countries and people 地球及所有的国家和人民；世界: *a map of the world* 世界地图 ◇ *Which is the biggest city in the world?* 世界上最大的城市是哪个？
2 (*plural* 复数作 **worlds**) all the people who do the same kind of thing 做同类事物的所有的人: *the world of politics* 政治界
think the world of somebody or 或 **something** like somebody or something very much 非常喜爱某人或某事物: *She thinks the world of her grandchildren.* 她非常疼爱孙子、孙女。

world-famous /ˌwɜːld ˈfeɪməs; ˈwɝld ˈfeməs/ *adjective* 形容词
known everywhere in the world 世界著名的: *a world-famous writer* 世界著名的作家

worldwide /ˌwɜːldˈwaɪd; ˈwɝldˈwaɪd/ *adjective* 形容词
that you find everywhere in the world 遍及全世界的: *Pollution is a worldwide problem.* 污染问题是世界性的问题。

worm /wɜːm; wɝm/ *noun* 名词
a small animal with a long thin body and no legs. Worms live in the ground or in other animals. 蠕虫

worn *form of* **wear**[1] ＊ **wear**[1] 的不同形式

worn-out /ˌwɔːn ˈaʊt; ˈworn'aʊt/ *adjective* 形容词
1 old and completely finished because you have used it a lot（因过多使用）废旧毁坏的: *I threw the shoes away because they were worn-out.* 我把鞋扔了，因为已经穿坏了。
2 very tired 筋疲力尽的: *He's worn-out after his long journey.* 他走了长路已经精疲力竭了。

worried /ˈwʌrid; ˈwɝɪd/ *adjective* 形容词
unhappy because you think that something bad will happen or has happened（认为坏事要发生或已发生）担心的；忧虑的: *Fiona is worried that she's going to fail the exam.* 菲奥纳担心考试可能不及格。◇ *I'm worried about my brother—he looks ill.* 我担心我的哥哥——他面色不好。

worry[1] /ˈwʌri; ˈwʌrɪ/ *verb* 动词 (**worries**, **worrying**, **worried** /ˈwʌrid; ˈwɝɪd/, **has worried**)
1 feel that something bad will happen or has happened 感到坏事要发生或已发生；担心；忧虑: *I worried when Mark didn't come home at the usual time.* 马克没按时回家，我很担心。◇ *Don't worry if you don't know the answer.* 你要是不会回答也不必发愁。◇ *There's nothing to worry about.* 没有什么可担心的事。
2 make somebody feel that something bad will happen or has happened 使某人感到坏事要发生或已发生；使担心；使忧虑: *Philip's illness is worrying his parents.* 菲利普生病的事让他父母很操心。

worry[2] /ˈwʌri; ˈwʌrɪ/ *noun* 名词
1 (no plural 无复数) a feeling that something bad will happen or has happened 感到坏事要发生或已发生；担心；忧虑: *Her face showed signs of worry.* 她脸上显出担忧的神情。
2 (*plural* 复数作 **worries**) a problem; something that makes you feel worried 难题；使人担忧的事物: *I have a lot of worries.* 我有很多操心事。

worse /wɜːs; wɝs/ *adjective* 形容词 (**bad**, **worse**, **worst**)
1 more bad; less good 更坏的；更糟的；更差的: *The weather today is worse than yesterday.* 今天的天气比昨天的还糟。◇ *Her Spanish is bad but her Italian is even worse.* 她的西班牙语很差，意大利语更差。
2 more ill 病情更重: *If you get worse, you must go to the doctor's.* 要是病情恶化，你就得去找医生给看看了。
worse *adverb* 副词
more badly 更坏；更糟；更差；病情更重

worship /ˈwɜːʃɪp; ˈwɝʃəp/ *verb* 动词 (**worships**, **worshipping**, **worshipped** /ˈwɜːʃɪpt; ˈwɝʃəpt/)
1 show that you believe in God or a god by praying 向上帝或神祈祷；礼拜: *Christians worship in a church.* 基督徒在教堂做礼拜。

W

2 love somebody very much or think that somebody is wonderful 极爱某人；崇拜某人: *She worships her grandchildren.* 她十分疼爱孙子、孙女。

worship *noun* 名词 (no plural 无复数)
A mosque is a place of worship. 清真寺是做礼拜的处所。

worst /wɜːst; wɝst/ *adjective* 形容词 (**bad, worse, worst**)
most bad 最坏的；最糟的；最差的: *He's the worst player in the team!* 他是全队最差的运动员！◇ *the worst day of my life* 我一生中最糟糕的一天

worst *adverb* 副词
most badly 最坏；最糟；最差: *Jenny played badly, but I played worst of all.* 珍妮表现得很差，可是我表现得最差。

worst *noun* 名词 (no plural 无复数)
the most bad thing or person 最坏、最糟或最差的事物或人: *I'm the worst in the class at grammar.* 我是全班语法最差的。

if the worst comes to the worst if something very bad happens 要是出现最坏的情况: *If the worst comes to the worst and I fail the exam, I'll take it again next year.* 要是情况不妙我万一考不及格，我就明年再考一次。

worth[1] /wɜːθ; wɝθ/ *adjective* 形容词
1 with a value of 有某种价值: *This house is worth £70 000.* 这所房子值70 000英镑。
2 good or useful enough to do or have 值得做或值得有；有好处或有用处: *Is this film worth seeing?* 这部影片值得看吗？◇ *It's not worth asking Lyn for money—she never has any.* 找林恩要钱也没用——她根本就没钱。

W

worth[2] /wɜːθ; wɝθ/ *noun* 名词 (no plural 无复数)
value 价值: *This painting is of little worth.* 这幅画儿没什么价值。

worth of how much of something an amount of money will buy（某物的）值某金额的量: *I'd like ten pounds' worth of petrol, please.* 劳驾，我想要十英镑的汽油。

worthless /ˈwɜːθləs; ˈwɝθlɪs/ *adjective* 形容词
with no value or use 无价值的或无用的: *A cheque is worthless if you don't sign it.* 支票上面不签字就没有用。

worthwhile /ˌwɜːθˈwaɪl; ˌwɝθˈwaɪl/ *adjective* 形容词
good or useful enough for the time that you spend or the work that you do（指用用的时间或做的工作）有价值的或有用的: *The hard work was worthwhile because I passed the exam.* 我并没有白用功，因为我考及格了。

would /wʊd; ˈwʊd/ *modal verb* 情态动词
1 the word for 'will' in the past ＊ will 的过去式；将: *He said he would come.* 他说过他来。
2 a word that you use to talk about a situation that is not real 用以表示并非事实的词: *If I had a million pounds, I would buy a big house.* 我要是有百万英镑我就买一所大房子。
3 a word that you use to ask something in a polite way 用以提出要求的有礼貌的表达方式: *Would you close the door, please?* 劳驾，请把门关上行吗？
4 a word that you use to talk about something that happened many times in the past 用以表示某事过去反复发生的词: *When I was young, my grandparents would visit us every Sunday.* 我小时候，我祖父母每星期日都到我们那儿去。

would like want; words that you use when you ask or say something in a polite way 想要；用以提问或谈话的有礼貌的表达方式: *Would you like a cup of tea?* 您想要杯茶吗？◇ *I would like to go to Africa.* 我很想去非洲。

> ✪ The negative form of 'would' is **would not** or the short form **wouldn't** /ˈwʊdnt; ˈwʊdn̩t/ ＊ would 的否定式是 **would not** 或其缩略式 **wouldn't** /ˈwʊdnt; ˈwʊdn̩t/:
>
> *He wouldn't help me.* 他不帮助我。
>
> The short form of 'would' is **'d**. We often use this ＊ would 的缩略式是 **'d**，较常用:
>
> *I'd* (=I would) *like to meet her.* 我很想见见她。
>
> *They'd* (=they would) *help if they had the time.* 他们要是有时间就会帮忙了。
>
> ☞ Look at the Note on page 314 to find out more about **modal verbs**. 见第314页对 **modal verbs** 的进一步解释。

would've /ˈwʊdəv; ˈwʊdəv/ = **would have**

wound[1] *form of* **wind**[2] ＊ **wind**[2] 的不同形式

wound[2] /wu:nd; wund/ *verb* 动词 (**wounds**, **wounding**, **wounded**)
hurt somebody 伤害某人: *The bullet wounded him in the leg.* 子弹把他的腿打伤了。

wound *noun* 名词
a hurt place in your body made by something like a gun or a knife（枪或刀等造成身体上的）伤处；枪伤；刀伤: *a knife wound* 刀伤

wove, **woven** *forms of* **weave** ＊ **weave** 的不同形式

wow /waʊ; waʊ/
a word that shows surprise and pleasure 表示惊奇或愉快的词: *Wow! What a lovely car!* 嘿！多好的汽车啊！

wrap /ræp; ræp/ *verb* 动词 (**wraps**, **wrapping**, **wrapped** /ræpt; ræpt/)
put paper or cloth around somebody or something（用纸或布）包或裹某人或某物: *The baby was wrapped in a blanket.* 用毯子把小孩儿包了起来。◇ *She wrapped the glass up in paper.* 她用纸把玻璃杯包起来了。✪ opposite 反义词: **unwrap**

wrapper /ˈræpə(r); ˈræpɚ/ *noun* 名词
a piece of paper or plastic that covers something like a sweet or a packet of cigarettes（包在一颗颗糖果外面的或一盒香烟等的）纸或塑料膜: *Don't throw your wrappers on the floor!* 别把糖纸扔在地板上！

wrapping /ˈræpɪŋ; ˈræpɪŋ/ *noun* 名词
a piece of paper or plastic that covers a present or something that you buy（包装礼物或所购物品用的）纸或塑料膜: *I took the new shirt out of its wrapping.* 我把新衬衫从包装纸里拿了出来。

wrapping paper /ˈræpɪŋ peɪpə(r); ˈræpɪŋ ˌpepɚ/ *noun* 名词 (no plural 无复数)
special paper that you use to wrap presents（包装礼物用的）包装纸

wreath /ri:θ; riθ/ *noun* 名词 (*plural* 复数作 **wreaths** /ri:ðz; riðz/)
a circle of flowers or leaves 花圈；花环: *She put a wreath on the grave.* 她把花圈放在坟墓上了。

wreck /rek; rɛk/ *noun* 名词
a ship, car or plane that has been very badly damaged in an accident 在事故中严重损毁的轮船、汽车或飞机: *a shipwreck at sea* 海难

wreck *verb* 动词 (**wrecks**, **wrecking**, **wrecked** /rekt; rɛkt/)
break or destroy something completely 毁坏或毁灭某物: *The fire wrecked the hotel.* 这场火灾把旅馆烧毁了。

wreckage /ˈrekɪdʒ; ˈrɛkɪdʒ/ *noun* 名词 (no plural 无复数)
the broken parts of something that has been badly damaged（遭损毁之物的）残骸: *They found a child in the wreckage of the plane.* 在飞机的残骸里找到了一个孩子。

wrench /rentʃ; rɛntʃ/ *American English for* **spanner** 美式英语，即 **spanner**

wrestle /ˈresl; ˈrɛsl̩/ *verb* 动词 (**wrestles**, **wrestling**, **wrestled** /ˈresld; ˈrɛsl̩d/)
fight by trying to throw somebody to the ground. People often wrestle as a sport. 摔跤（常作运动）

wrestler *noun* 名词
a person who wrestles as a sport 摔跤运动员

wrestling *noun* 名词 (no plural 无复数)
the sport where two people fight and try to throw each other to the ground 摔跤运动: *a wrestling match* 摔跤比赛

wriggle /ˈrɪgl; ˈrɪgl̩/ *verb* 动词 (**wriggles**, **wriggling**, **wriggled** /ˈrɪgld; ˈrɪgl̩d/)
turn your body quickly from side to side, like a worm（像蠕虫般）扭动身体: *The teacher told the children to stop wriggling.* 老师告诉那些小学生，身体不要扭来扭去。

wring /rɪŋ; rɪŋ/ *verb* 动词 (**wrings**, **wringing**, **wrung** /rʌŋ; rʌŋ/, **has wrung**)
press and twist something with your hands to make water come out 压或拧某物使水流出: *He wrung the towel out and put it outside to dry.* 他把毛巾拧干后晾在外面。

wrinkle /ˈrɪŋkl; ˈrɪŋkl̩/ *noun* 名词
a small line in something, for example in the skin of your face 皱纹（例如脸上的）: *My grandmother has a lot of wrinkles.* 我祖母皮肤上有很多皱纹。

wrinkled /ˈrɪŋkld; ˈrɪŋkl̩d/ *adjective* 形容词
with a lot of wrinkles 有很多皱纹的: *His face is very wrinkled.* 他一脸皱纹。

wrist /rɪst; rɪst/ *noun* 名词
the part of your body where your arm joins your hand 腕；腕子；手腕子 ☞ picture on page C2 见第C2页图

write /raɪt; raɪt/ *verb* 动词 (**writes**, **writing**, **wrote** /rəʊt; rot/, **has written** /'rɪtn; 'rɪtn̩/)
1 make letters or words on paper using a pen or pencil 写；写字；书写: *Write your name at the top of the page.* 把你的名字写在这一页的上端。◇ *He can't read or write.* 他不识字也不会写字。
2 write and send a letter to somebody 给某人写信并寄出: *My mother writes to me every week.* 我母亲每星期都给我写信。◇ *I wrote her a postcard.* 我给她寄了一张明信片。
3 make a story, book, etc 写小说、书等；写作；编写: *Shakespeare wrote plays.* 莎士比亚写了很多剧本。
write down write something on paper, so that you can remember it 把某事写在纸上（以便记住）: *I wrote down his telephone number.* 我把他的电话号码写下来了。

writer /'raɪtə(r); 'raɪtɚ/ *noun* 名词
a person who writes books, stories, etc 写书、小说等的人；作者；作家: *Charles Dickens was a famous writer.* 狄更斯是著名的作家。

writing /'raɪtɪŋ; 'raɪtɪŋ/ *noun* 名词 (no plural 无复数)
1 words that somebody puts on paper (写出的) 文字: *I can't read your writing—it's so small.* 我看不清你写的字——太小了。
2 putting words on paper 写；书写: *Writing is slower than telephoning.* 写信比打电话慢。
in writing written on paper 写出: *They have offered me the job on the telephone but not in writing.* 他们打来电话说给我这份工作，并没写信来。
writing-paper /'raɪtɪŋ peɪpə(r); 'raɪtɪŋ-ˌpepɚ/ *noun* 名词 (no plural 无复数)
paper for writing letters on 信纸

written *form of* **write** ✻ **write** 的不同形式

wrong[1] /rɒŋ; rɔŋ/ *adjective* 形容词
1 not true or not correct 不确实的；不正确的；错误的: *She gave me the wrong key, so I couldn't open the door.* 她给我的钥匙不对，所以我开不开门。◇ *This clock is wrong.* 这个钟不准。✪ opposite 反义词: **right**
2 bad, or not what the law allows 坏的；非法的: *Stealing is wrong.* 盗窃行为是犯法的。◇ *I haven't done anything wrong.* 我没做过坏事。✪ opposite 反义词: **right**
3 not the best 不是最好的；不适当的: *We're late because we took the wrong road.* 我们迟到是因为走错路了。✪ opposite 反义词: **right**
4 not as it should be, or not working well 有故障的；有毛病的: *There's something wrong with my car—it won't start.* 我的汽车出毛病了——发动不起来。◇ *'What's wrong with Mrs Snow?' 'She's got a cold.'* "斯诺太太怎么了？" "她感冒了。"
wrong *adverb* 副词
not correctly; not right 错误地；不适当地: *You've spelt my name wrong.* 您把我的名字拼错了。
go wrong **1** stop working well 出故障；出毛病: *The video has gone wrong—can you mend it?* 录像机出毛病了——您会修理吗？ **2** not happen as you hoped or wanted 并非希望的或想要的情况: *All our plans went wrong.* 我们的计划都出乱子了。

wrong[2] /rɒŋ; rɔŋ/ *noun* 名词 (no plural 无复数)
what is bad or not right 坏事；过失；错误: *Babies don't know the difference between right and wrong.* 小孩儿分辨不出对和错来。

wrongly /'rɒŋli; 'rɔŋlɪ/ *adverb* 副词
not correctly 错误地；不正当地: *The letter didn't arrive because it was wrongly addressed.* 那封信并没寄到，因为地址写错了。

wrote *form of* **write** ✻ **write** 的不同形式

wrung *form of* **wring** ✻ **wring** 的不同形式

Xx

Xmas /'eksməs; 'ɛksməs/ *short for* **Christmas** ＊ **Christmas** 的缩略式 ✪ **Xmas** is used mainly in writing. ＊ **Xmas** 主要用作书写形式。

X-ray /'eksreɪ; 'ɛks're/ *noun* 名词
a photograph of the inside of your body that is made by using a special light that you cannot see X射线照片: *The doctor took an X-ray of my arm to see if it was broken.* 医生给我照了一张臂部的X射线照片，看是否骨折。

X-ray *verb* 动词 (**X-rays**, **X-raying**, **X-rayed** /'eksreɪd; 'ɛks'red/)
take a photograph using an X-ray machine 用X射线机拍摄照片: *She had her leg X-rayed.* 她的腿部照了X射线照片。

xylophone /'zaɪləfəʊn; 'zaɪlə,fon/ *noun* 名词
a musical instrument with metal or wooden bars that you hit with small hammers 木琴

Yy

yacht /jɒt; jɑt/ *noun* 名词
1 a boat with **sails** that is used for racing（竞赛用的）帆船（帆叫做 **sail**）
2 a big boat with a motor（大型机动的）游艇: *a millionaire's yacht* 百万富翁的游艇

yard[1] /jɑːd; jɑrd/ *noun* 名词
a measure of length (= 91 centimetres). There are three **feet** or thirty-six **inches** in a yard. 码（长度单位，= 91厘米，1码等于3英尺或等于36英寸；英尺叫做 **foot**，复数作 **foot** 或 **feet**；英寸叫做 **inch**）。✪ The short way of writing 'yard' is **yd**. ✳ yard 的缩写形式为 **yd**。☞ Note at **foot** 见 **foot** 词条注释

yard[2] /jɑːd; jɑrd/ *noun* 名词
a piece of hard ground next to a building, with a fence or wall around it 院子；庭院: *The children were playing in the school yard.* 孩子们在校园里玩耍。◇ *a farmyard* 农家的庭院

yawn /jɔːn; jɔn/ *verb* 动词 (**yawns**, **yawning**, **yawned** /jɔːnd; jɔnd/)
open your mouth wide because you are tired 打哈欠
yawn *noun* 名词
'I'm going to bed now,' she said with a yawn. "我现在睡觉去了，" 她说完打了个哈欠。

yd *short way of writing* **yard**[1] ✳ **yard**[1] 的缩写形式

yeah /jeə; jɛə/
yes 是，对，行（表示答应、同意或接受等的词）✪ This is an informal word. 这是个俗语词。

year /jɪə(r); jɪr/ *noun* 名词
1 a time of 365 or 366 days from 1 January to 31 December. A year has twelve **months** 历年；年（从1月1日到12月31日的365日或366日。1年等于12个月，月叫做 **month**）: *Where are you going on holiday this year?* 您今年到哪儿去度假？◇ *'In which year were you born?' 'In 1976.'* "你是哪年出生的？" "1976年。" ◇ *I left school last year.* 我去年中学毕业了。
2 any time of twelve months 一年（任何12个月）；岁: *I have known Chris for three years.* 我认识克里斯有三年了。◇ *My son is five years old.* 我的儿子五岁了。◇ *I have a five-year-old son.* 我有个五岁的儿子。◇ *a two-year-old* 两岁的孩子 ✪ Be careful! You can say 注意！可以说: *She's ten.* or 或: *She's ten years old.* (BUT NOT 但不可作: *She's ten years.*)
all year round through all the year 一年到头: *The swimming-pool is open all year round.* 这个游泳池全年都开放。

yearly /ˈjɪəli; ˈjɪrlɪ/ *adjective*, *adverb* 形容词，副词
that happens or comes every year or once a year 每年（的）；一年一次（的）: *a yearly visit* 一年一度的访问 ◇ *We meet twice yearly.* 我们每年见两次面。

yeast /jiːst; jist/ *noun* 名词 (no plural 无复数)
stuff that you use for making bread rise 酵母

yell /jel; jɛl/ *verb* 动词 (**yells**, **yelling**, **yelled** /jeld; jɛld/)
shout loudly 喊叫；叫喊: *'Look out!' she yelled as the car came towards them.* 汽车向他们开来，她喊了一声："小心！"
yell *noun* 名词
He gave a yell of pain. 他疼得大叫一声。

yellow /ˈjeləʊ; ˈjɛlo/ *adjective* 形容词
with the colour of a lemon or of butter 黄颜色的: *She was wearing a yellow shirt.* 她穿着黄色的衬衫。◇ *bright yellow flowers* 鲜艳的黄色的花
yellow *noun* 名词
Yellow is my favourite colour. 黄颜色是我喜爱的颜色。

yes /jes; jɛs/
a word that you use for answering a question. You use 'yes' to agree, to say that something is true, or to say that you would like something 是，对，行（表示答应、同意或接受等的词）: *'Have you got the key?' 'Yes, here it is.'* "你有钥匙吗？" "有，在这儿呢。" ◇ *'Would you like some coffee?' 'Yes, please.'* "您想要咖啡吗？" "好，谢谢。"

yesterday /ˈjestədeɪ; ˈjɛstədɪ/ *adverb*, *noun* 副词，名词 (no plural 无复数)
(on) the day before today 昨天: *I saw Tom yesterday.* 我昨天看见汤姆了。◇ *I phoned you yesterday afternoon but*

you were out. 我昨天下午给您打过电话，您出去了。◇ *I sent the letter the day before yesterday.* 我前天把信寄出去了。

yet[1] /jet; jɛt/ *adverb* 副词

1 until now 直到现在: *I haven't finished the book yet.* 我还没看完这本书呢。◇ *Have you seen that film yet?* 您看过那部电影吗？☞ Note at **already** 见 **already** 词条注释

2 now; as early as this 现在；这么早: *You don't need to go yet—it's only seven o'clock.* 你不必现在就走——才七点钟。

3 in the future 在将来: *They may win yet.* 他们迟早会获胜的。

as yet until now 到现在为止: *As yet, I haven't met her.* 到现在为止，我还没遇见她呢。

yet again once more 再；再一次: *John is late yet again!* 约翰又迟到了！

yet[2] /jet; jɛt/ *conjunction* 连词

but; however 但是；然而；而: *We arrived home tired yet happy.* 我们到家时很累，但是很愉快。

yoghurt /'jɒgət; 'jogɚt/ *noun* 名词

thick liquid food made from milk 酸乳酪: *strawberry yoghurt* 草莓酸乳酪 ◇ *Do you want a yoghurt?* 您要酸乳酪吗？

yolk /jəʊk; jok/ *noun* 名词

the yellow part in an egg 蛋黄

you /ju:, ju; 'ju/ *pronoun* 代词

1 the person or people that I am speaking to 您；你；你们: *You are late.* 你晚了。◇ *I phoned you yesterday.* 我昨天给您打过电话。

2 any person; a person 任何人；一个人: *You can buy stamps at a post office.* 在邮局可以买到邮票。

you'd /ju:d; jud/

1 = **you had**

2 = **you would**

you'll /ju:l; jul/ = **you will**

young[1] /jʌŋ; jʌŋ/ *adjective* 形容词 (**younger** /'jʌŋgə(r); 'jʌŋgɚ/, **youngest** /'jʌŋgɪst; 'jʌŋgɪst/)

in the early part of life; not old 幼小的；年轻的: *They have two young children.* 他们有两个小孩儿。◇ *You're younger than me.* 你比我年轻。☞ picture on page C26 见第C26页图

young[2] /jʌŋ; jʌŋ/ *noun* 名词 (plural 复数)

1 baby animals 幼小的动物；雏；仔；崽: *Birds build nests for their young.* 鸟为幼鸟做巢。

2 the young (plural 复数) children and young people 青少年: *a television programme for the young* 为青少年制做的电视节目

your /jɔ:(r); jʊr/ *adjective* 形容词

of you 您的；你的；你们的: *Where is your car?* 您的汽车在哪儿呢？◇ *Do you all have your books?* 你们都有书了吗？◇ *Show me your hands.* 把手给我看看。

you're /jɔ:(r); jʊr/ = **you are**

yours /jɔ:z; jʊrz/ *pronoun* 代词

1 something that belongs to you 您的；你的；你们的: *Is this pen yours or mine?* 这枝钢笔是你的还是我的？

2 Yours a word that you write at the end of a letter 用作书信具名前的收尾敬语: *Yours sincerely …* 谨启 ◇ *Yours faithfully …* 谨启

yourself /jɔ:'self; jʊr'sɛlf/ *pronoun* 代词 (*plural* 复数作 **yourselves** /jɔ:'selvz; jʊr'sɛlvz/)

1 a word that shows 'you' when I have just talked about you（用做反身代词）您自己，你自己，你们自己: *Did you hurt yourself?* 你把自己弄伤了吗？◇ *Buy yourselves a drink.* 你们各自买份饮料吧。

2 a word that makes 'you' stronger（用做反身强调代词）您自己，你自己，你们自己: *Did you make this cake yourself?* 这块蛋糕是您自己做的吗？◇ *'Who told you?' 'You told me yourself!'* "是谁告诉你的？""是你亲自告诉我的！"

by yourself, by yourselves 1 alone; without other people 您［你／你们］独自地；您［你／你们］单独地（没有别人相伴）: *Do you live by yourself?* 您是独自一人生活吗？ **2** without help 您［你／你们］独自地；您［你／你们］单独地（没有别人帮助）: *You can't carry all those bags by yourself.* 你自己一个人拿不了这些袋子。

youth /ju:θ; juθ/ *noun* 名词

1 (no plural 无复数) the part of your life when you are young 青少年时期: *He spent his youth in Germany.* 他青少年时代是在德国度过的。◇ *She was very poor in her youth.* 她年轻的时候很贫穷。

2 (*plural* 复数作 **youths** /ju:ðz; juðz/) a boy or young man 男孩儿；青年男子

3 the youth (plural 复数) young people 青年人（总称）: *the youth of this country* 这个国家的青年人

youth club /'ju:θ klʌb; 'juθ klʌb/ *noun* 名词

a club for young people 青年俱乐部

youth hostel /'ju:θ hɒstl; 'juθ ˌhɑstl̩/ *noun* 名词

a cheap place where young people can stay when they are travelling or on holiday 青年招待所

you've /ju:v; juv/ = **you have**

Zz

zebra 斑马

zebra /'zebrə; 'zibrə/ *noun* 名词
an African wild animal like a horse, with black and white lines on its body 斑马（产于非洲）

zebra crossing /ˌzebrə 'krɒsɪŋ; 'zibrə 'krɔsɪŋ/ *noun* 名词
a black and white path across a road. Cars must stop there to let people cross the road safely. 斑马线（横跨路面的黑白线条。汽车必须在该处停止，好让行人安全通过）

zero /'zɪərəʊ; 'zɪro/ *noun* 名词
1 the number 0 零
2 the point between + and – on a thermometer（温度计的）零度：*The temperature is five degrees below zero.* 温度是零下五度。

zigzag 之字形线条

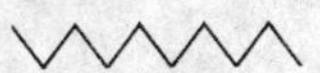

zigzag /'zɪgzæg; 'zɪgzæg/ *noun* 名词
a line that goes sharply up and down 之字形的线条

zip /zɪp; zɪp/ *noun* 名词
a long metal or plastic thing with a small part that you pull to close and open things like clothes and bags 拉锁；拉链

zip 拉锁

zip *verb* 动词 (**zips**, **zipping**, **zipped** /zɪpt; zɪpt/)
zip up close something with a zip 拉上某物的拉锁：*She zipped up her dress.* 她拉上了连衣裙的拉锁。

zip code /'zɪp kəʊd; 'zɪp ˌkod/ *American English for* **postcode** 美式英语，即 **postcode**

zipper /'zɪpə(r); 'zɪpɚ/ *American English for* **zip** 美式英语，即 **zip**

zone /zəʊn; zon/ *noun* 名词
a place where something special happens（有某特点的）区域或范围：*Do not enter the danger zone!* 切勿进入危险区！

zoo /zu:; zu/ *noun* 名词 (*plural* 复数作 **zoos**)
a place where you can see wild animals in cages or behind fences 动物园

zoom /zu:m; zum/ *verb* 动词 (**zooms**, **zooming**, **zoomed** /zu:md; zumd/)
move very fast 急速移动：*Mark zoomed past in his car.* 马克坐着汽车嗡的一声开过去了。

Prepositions 1 介词 1

Prepositions of place
表示处所的介词

The lamp is **above** the table.
灯在桌子的上方。

The meat is **on** the table.
肉在桌子上。

The cat is **under** the table.
猫在桌子下面。

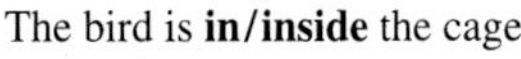

The bird is **in/inside** the cage.
鸟在笼子里。

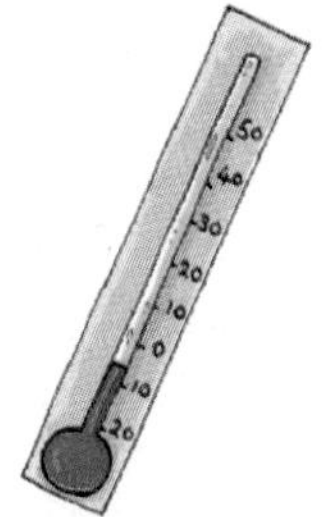

The temperature is **below** zero.
温度在零下。

The lorry is **in front of** the car.
大卡车在小轿车的前面。

The car is **behind** the lorry.
小轿车在大卡车的后面。

Sam is **between** Tom and Kim.
萨姆在汤姆和金的中间。

Kim is **next to/beside** Sam.
金在萨姆的旁边。

The girl is leaning **against** the wall.
这个女孩儿靠墙站着。

Kim is **opposite** Tom.
金在汤姆的对面。

The house is **among** the trees.
这所房子在树中间。

The human body 人体部位

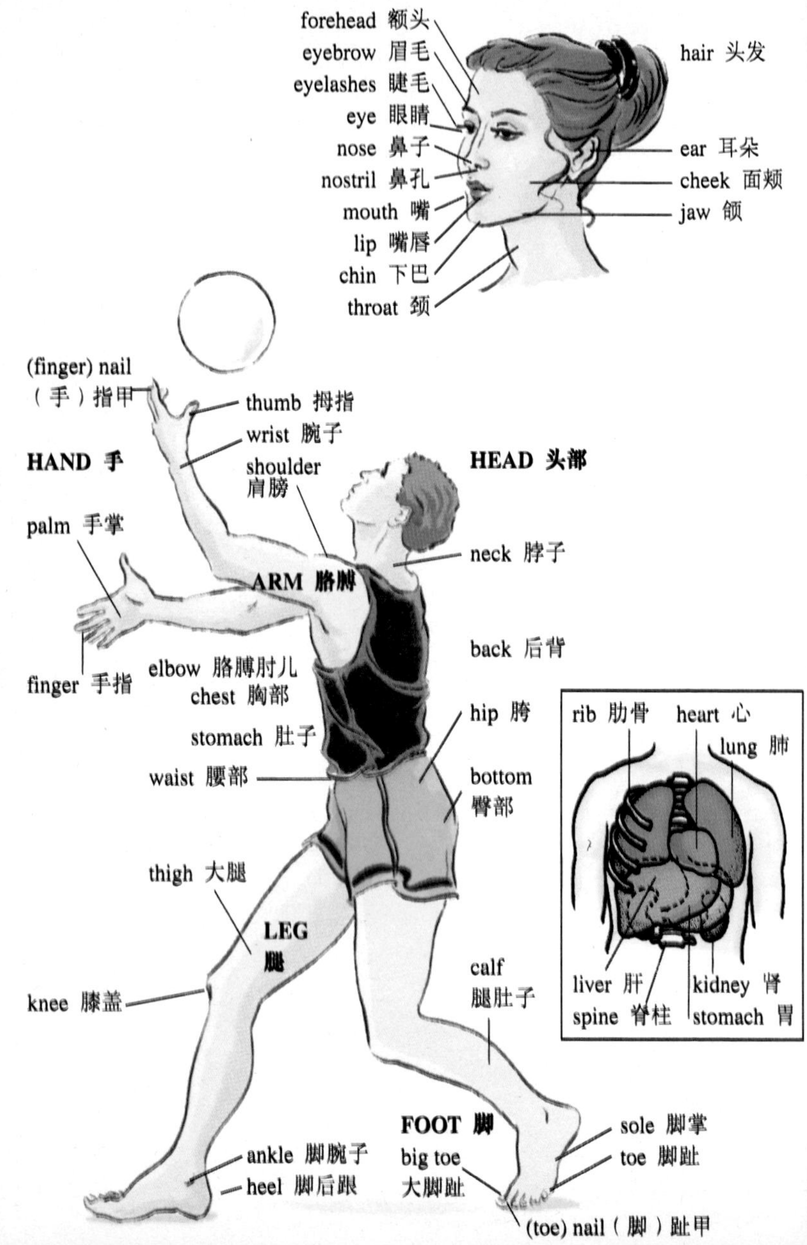

The family 家庭

This is Sarah's family.
这是萨拉的家庭。

The people in the pictures are Sarah's **relations**.
图中的人都是萨拉的亲属。

GRANDPARENTS 外祖父母

grandmother 外祖母 | grandfather 外祖父

PARENTS 父母

aunt 舅母 | uncle 舅父 | mother 母亲 | father 父亲 | mother-in-law 婆婆 | father-in-law 公公

SARAH 萨拉 | *JOHN 约翰

cousin 表姐 [表妹] | cousin 表哥 [表弟] | sister-in-law 嫂子 [弟妇] | brother 哥哥 [弟弟] | husband 丈夫 | sister-in-law 大姑子 [小姑子] | brother-in-law 大姑子 [小姑子] 的丈夫

*KIM 金 | *IAN 伊恩

CHILDREN 儿女

niece 侄女 | nephew 侄子 | daughter-in-law 儿媳妇 | son 儿子 | daughter 女儿 | son-in-law 女婿

GRANDCHILDREN 外孙子和外孙女

granddaughter 外孙女 | grandson 外孙子

* Sarah is John's **wife**.
萨拉是约翰的妻子。

* Kim is Ian's **sister**.
金是伊恩的姐姐 [妹妹]。

Prepositions 2 介词 2

Prepositions of movement 表示移动的介词

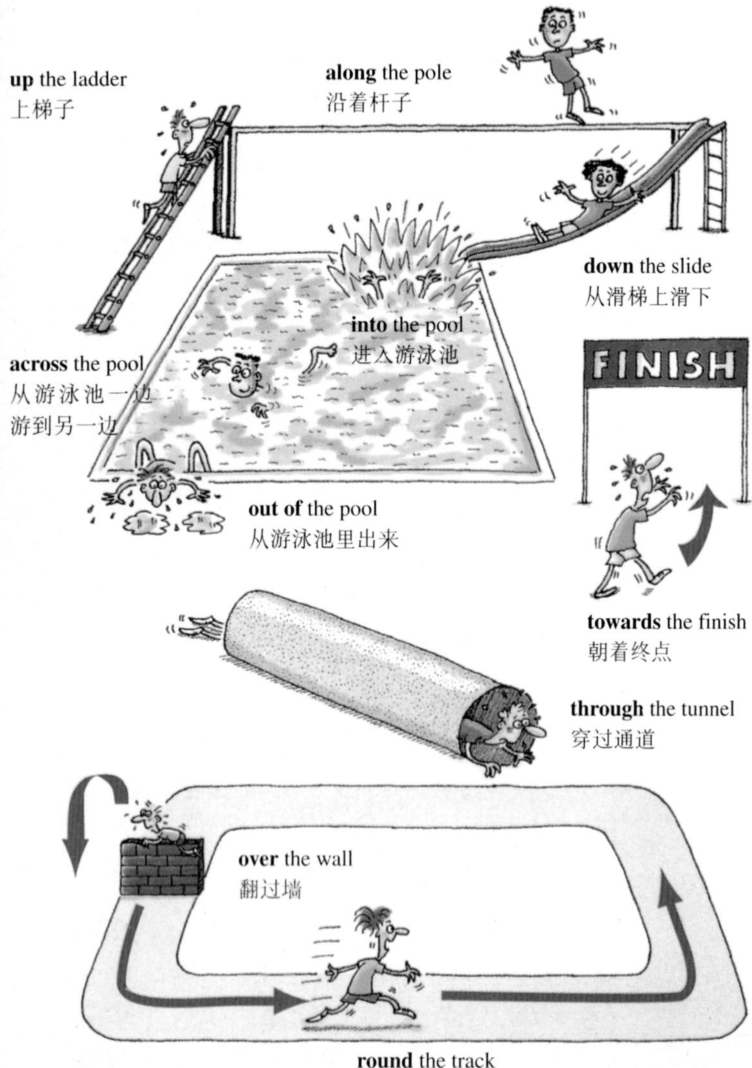

Shapes and sizes 形状和大小

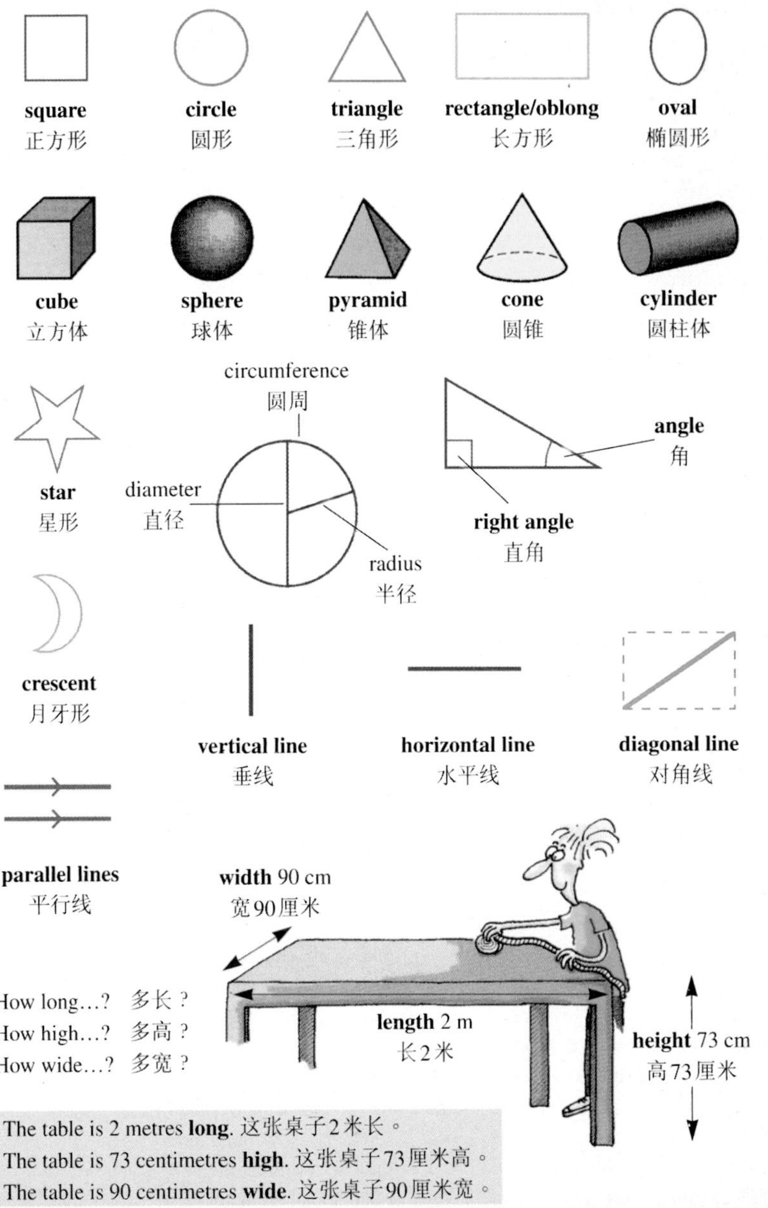

How long…? 多长？
How high…? 多高？
How wide…? 多宽？

The table is 2 metres **long**. 这张桌子2米长。
The table is 73 centimetres **high**. 这张桌子73厘米高。
The table is 90 centimetres **wide**. 这张桌子90厘米宽。

Numbers 数目

He has got ***three*** *children.*
他有三个孩子。

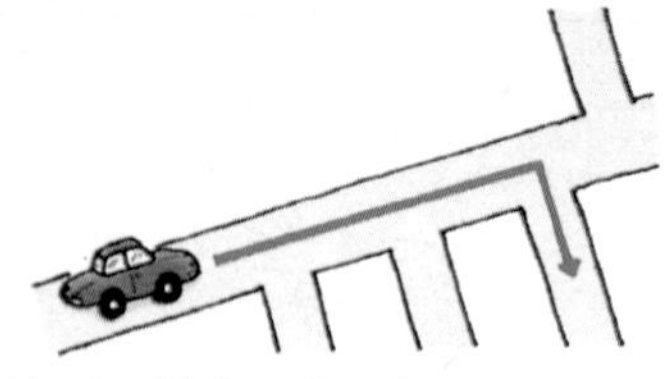

Take the ***third*** *road on the right.*
在第三个路口向右转。

1	one	一	1st	first	第一
2	two	二	2nd	second	第二
3	three	三	3rd	third	第三
4	four	四	4th	fourth	第四
5	five	五	5th	fifth	第五
6	six	六	6th	sixth	第六
7	seven	七	7th	seventh	第七
8	eight	八	8th	eighth	第八
9	nine	九	9th	ninth	第九
10	ten	十	10th	tenth	第十
11	eleven	十一	11th	eleventh	第十一
12	twelve	十二	12th	twelfth	第十二
13	thirteen	十三	13th	thirteenth	第十三
14	fourteen	十四	14th	fourteenth	第十四
15	fifteen	十五	15th	fifteenth	第十五
16	sixteen	十六	16th	sixteenth	第十六
17	seventeen	十七	17th	seventeenth	第十七
18	eighteen	十八	18th	eighteenth	第十八
19	nineteen	十九	19th	nineteenth	第十九
20	twenty	二十	20th	twentieth	第二十
21	twenty-one	二十一	21st	twenty-first	第二十一
30	thirty	三十	30th	thirtieth	第三十
40	forty	四十	40th	fortieth	第四十
50	fifty	五十	50th	fiftieth	第五十
60	sixty	六十	60th	sixtieth	第六十
70	seventy	七十	70th	seventieth	第七十
80	eighty	八十	80th	eightieth	第八十
90	ninety	九十	90th	ninetieth	第九十
100	a/one hundred	一百	100th	hundredth	第一百
101	a/one hundred and one	一百零一	101st	hundred and first	第一百零一
200	two hundred	二百	200th	two hundredth	第二百
1 000	a/one thousand	一千	1 000th	thousandth	第一千
1 000 000	a/one million	一百万	1 000 000th	millionth	第一百万

Saying numbers 数字的读法

267 two hundred and sixty-seven
4 302 four thousand, three hundred and two

Saying '0'怎样读 "0"

We usually say **nought** or **zero** 一般读作 **nought**或**zero**:

nought point five (0.5)

In telephone numbers, we usually say **o** (you say it like **oh**) 电话号码中的 "0" 一般读作字母**o**的声音（像**oh**的读音）:

My telephone number is 29035 (two nine **o** three five).

When we talk about temperature, we use **zero** 说温度时用**zero**:

It was very cold ~ the temperature was below **zero**.

In scores of games like football, we say **nil** 足球等比赛项目中的零分，说 **nil**:

The score was two-**nil**.

We use . (NOT ,) in **decimals**.
小数点要用圆点.（不用逗号 , ）。

Writing numbers 数字的写法

We put a small space or a comma (,) between *thousands* and *hundreds* in numbers, for example 在千位和百位数字之间要留个小空位或加个逗号（ , ），例如:

15 000 or 或 15,000

Fractions 分数

$\frac{1}{2}$ a half 二分之一

$\frac{1}{3}$ a/one third 三分之一

$\frac{1}{4}$ a/one quarter 四分之一

$\frac{1}{8}$ an/one eighth 八分之一

$\frac{1}{16}$ a/one sixteenth 十六分之一

$\frac{3}{4}$ three quarters 四分之三

$1\frac{2}{5}$ one and two fifths
一又五分之二

☞ To find out more about how to say **telephone numbers**, look at page C32. 关于电话号码的读法，详见第C32页说明。

☞ To find out more about how to say and write **numbers in dates**, look at page C29. 关于日期数字的读法和写法，详见第C29页说明。

Symbols 符号		We write 写法:	We say 读法：
.	point	3.2	three point two
+	plus	5 + 6	five plus six
–	minus	10 – 4	ten minus four
×	multiplied by / times	4 × 6	four multiplied by six four times six
÷	divided by	4 ÷ 2	four divided by two
%	per cent	78%	seventy-eight per cent
=	equals	1 + 3 = 4	one plus three equals four

Time 时间

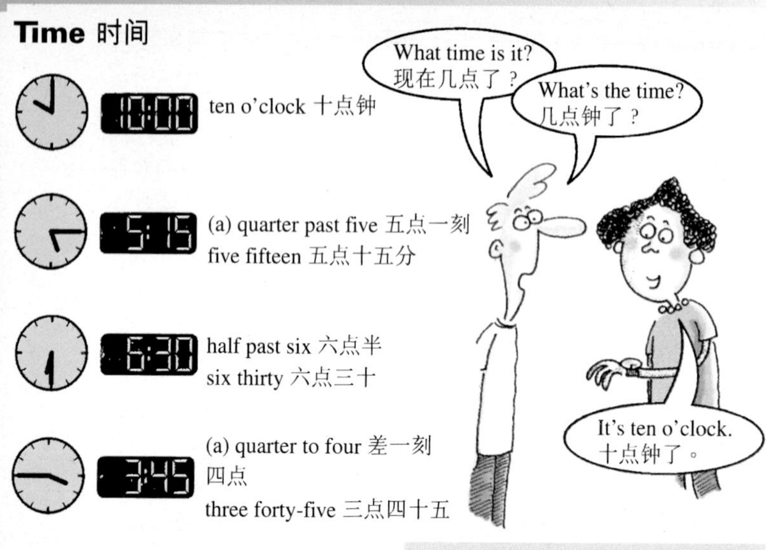

ten o'clock 十点钟

(a) quarter past five 五点一刻
five fifteen 五点十五分

half past six 六点半
six thirty 六点三十

(a) quarter to four 差一刻四点
three forty-five 三点四十五

ten past eleven
eleven ten 十一点十分

twenty to twelve
差二十分十二点
eleven forty 十一点四十

seven minutes past two
two o seven*
两点零七分

* We do not often use the 'twenty-four hour clock' when we say times (so we do not say 'fourteen o seven'). We occasionally use it when we are reading a time from a bus or train timetable. 表达某时间时，不常使用二十四小时制（不说"fourteen o seven"）。读公共汽车或火车时刻表时偶尔用到。

60 seconds 秒 = 1 minute 分
60 minutes 分 = 1 hour 小时
24 hours 小时 = 1 day 天

To show what part of the day we mean, we can use 上午和下午可以这样表示：

a.m. or 或 **in the morning** 上午

The meeting is at 10 a.m. 会议在上午10时举行。
The telephone rang at four o'clock in the morning. 电话在凌晨四点钟响了。

p.m. or 或 **in the afternoon** 下午
in the evening 晚上
at night 夜晚

The shop closes at 6 p.m. 这家商店下午六时停止营业。
She came home at eight o'clock in the evening. 她晚上八点钟回到家里。

Fruits 水果

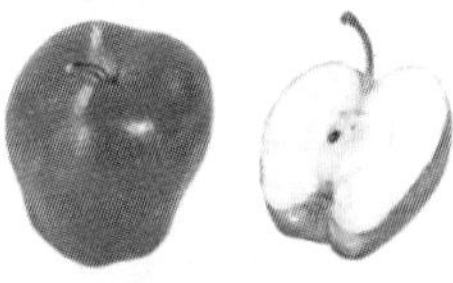
apple 苹果

orange 橙子

lemon 柠檬

peach 桃

pear 梨

kiwi fruit 猕猴桃

grapefruit 葡萄柚

coconut 椰子

grape 葡萄

pineapple 菠萝

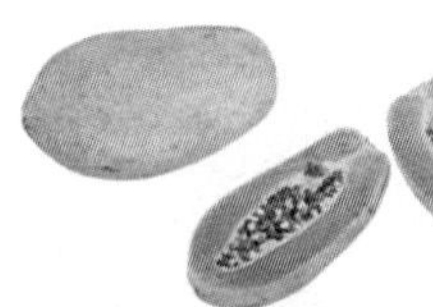
papaya 木瓜

banana 香蕉

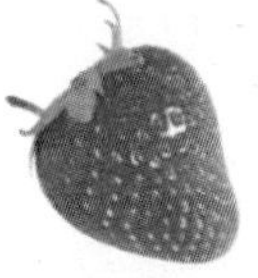
strawberry 草莓

Clothes 衣物

sweater
套头毛衣
track suit
运动套装
vest 背心
tie 领带
trousers
裤子
shirt 衬衫
belt 腰带
collar 衣领
sleeve
袖子
suit 套装
cuff 袖口
pocket 口袋

Clothes 衣物

coat 外套
cardigan
对襟毛衣
blouse
女衬衫
waistcoat
西服背心
skirt 裙子
dress
连衣裙
tights
裤袜
high-healed
shoes
高跟儿鞋
jacket 短上衣
T-shirt
短袖汗衫
socks 短袜
jeans 牛仔裤

Vegetables 蔬菜

cabbage 洋白菜

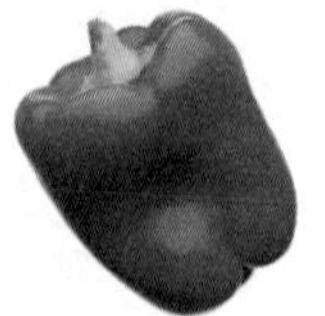
red pepper 红辣椒

cauliflower 菜花

green pepper 青辣椒

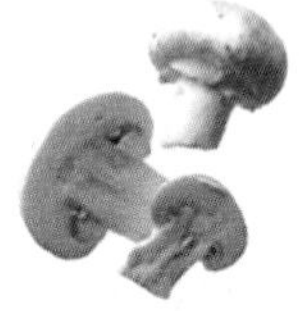
mushroom 蘑菇

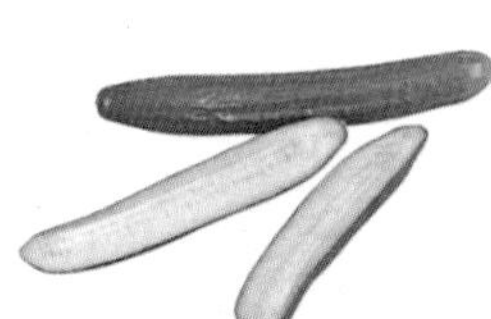
cucumber 黄瓜

peas 豌豆

carrot 胡萝卜

tomato 西红柿

broccoli 绿菜花

lettuce 生菜

potato 土豆

green beans 豆角

School life 校园生活

going to school
上学

doing experiment
做实验

singing in music lesson
在音乐课上唱歌

showing the skeleton model in science lesson 在理科课上陈列着骨架模型

learning how to use the computer 学习使用计算机

using globe in geography lesson 在地理课上使用地球仪教具

reading in school library
在学校图书馆阅读

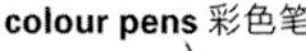

taking art lesson
上美术课

playing games 做游戏

taking examination 考试

Musical instruments 乐器

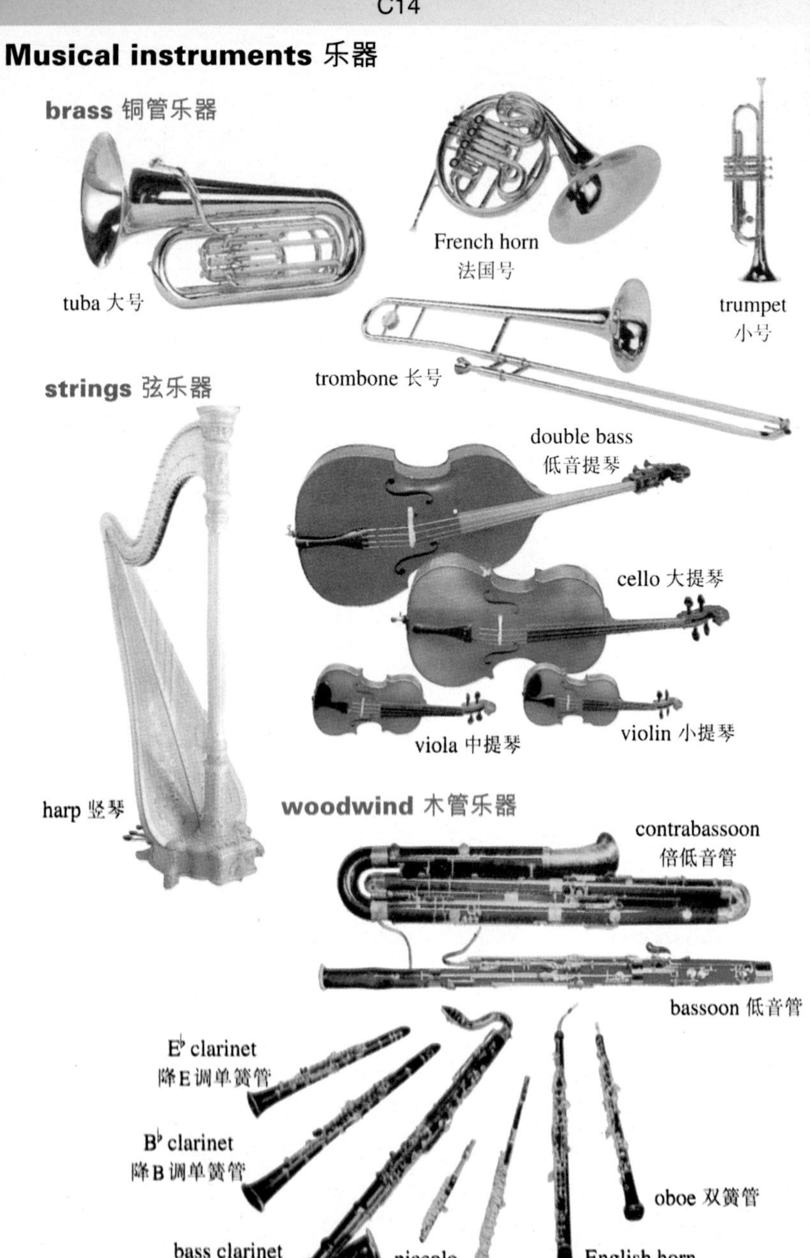

Musical instruments 乐器

percussion 打击乐器

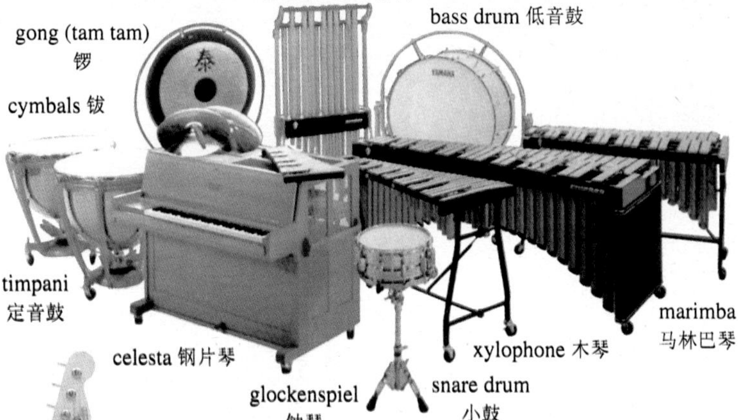

tubular bells 排钟

bass drum 低音鼓

gong (tam tam) 锣

cymbals 钹

timpani 定音鼓

celesta 钢片琴

glockenspiel 钟琴

snare drum 小鼓

xylophone 木琴

marimba 马林巴琴

castanets 响板

sleigh-bells 马铃

tambourine 铃鼓

triangle 三角铁

claves 响棒

tempo block 中国木鱼

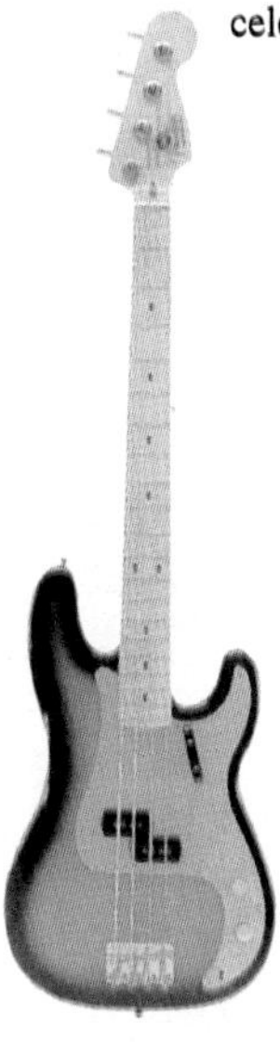

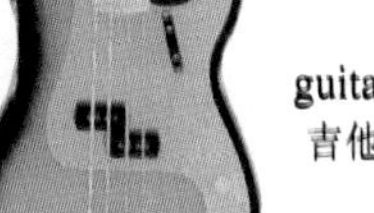

guitar 吉他

piano 钢琴

orchestra 管弦乐队

Sports and recreation 运动和娱乐

badminton
羽毛球运动

baseball
棒球运动

boxing
拳击运动

car racing
赛车运动

skiing
滑雪运动

camping 露营

cycling 骑自行车

diving 跳水运动

gymnastics 体操

hiking
远足

football
足球运动

hockey
曲棍球运动

skating
溜冰运动

windsurfing
帆板运动

martial arts 武术

swimming 游泳

surfing 冲浪运动

judo 柔道

Space 外层空间

lunar vehicle 登月车

the solar system 太阳系

spacesuit 宇航服

astronaut 宇航员

space shuttle 航天飞机

telescope 望远镜

rocket 火箭

satellite 人造卫星

Means of transport 交通工具

ferry 渡船

hydrofoil 水翼船

tanker 油轮

container vessel 货柜船

liner 邮轮

speedboat 快艇

yacht 游艇

seaplane 水上飞机

helicopter 直升飞机

jet plane 喷气式飞机

Means of transport 交通工具

lorry 卡车

van 客货车

tram 有轨电车

bus 公共汽车

bicycle 自行车

taxi 计程车

sports car 跑车

minibus 小型客车

train 火车

motorcycle 摩托车

jeep 吉普车

Electronics 电子设备

video recorder 录像机

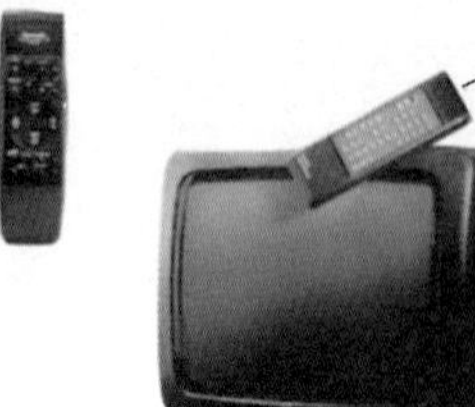
remote control 遥控器

television 电视机

handy camera 便携式摄录机

radio 收音机

walkman （耳机式）小型放音机

hi-fi 高保真度音响设备

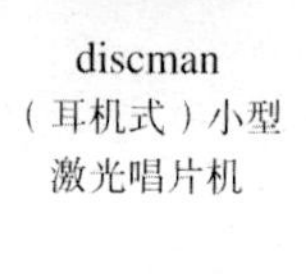
discman （耳机式）小型激光唱片机

calculator 电子计算器

microwave oven 微波炉

hand-held electronic games 便携式电子游戏机

fax machine 传真机

cordless telephone 无线电话

Wild animals 野生动物

bear 熊

elephant 象

panda 大熊猫

horse 马

zebra 斑马

koala 树袋熊

lion 狮子

wolf 狼

giraffe 长颈鹿

leopard 豹

monkey 猴

orang-utan 猩猩

deer 鹿

tiger 虎

kangaroo 袋鼠

rhinoceros 犀牛

MAP OF THE WORLD 世界地图

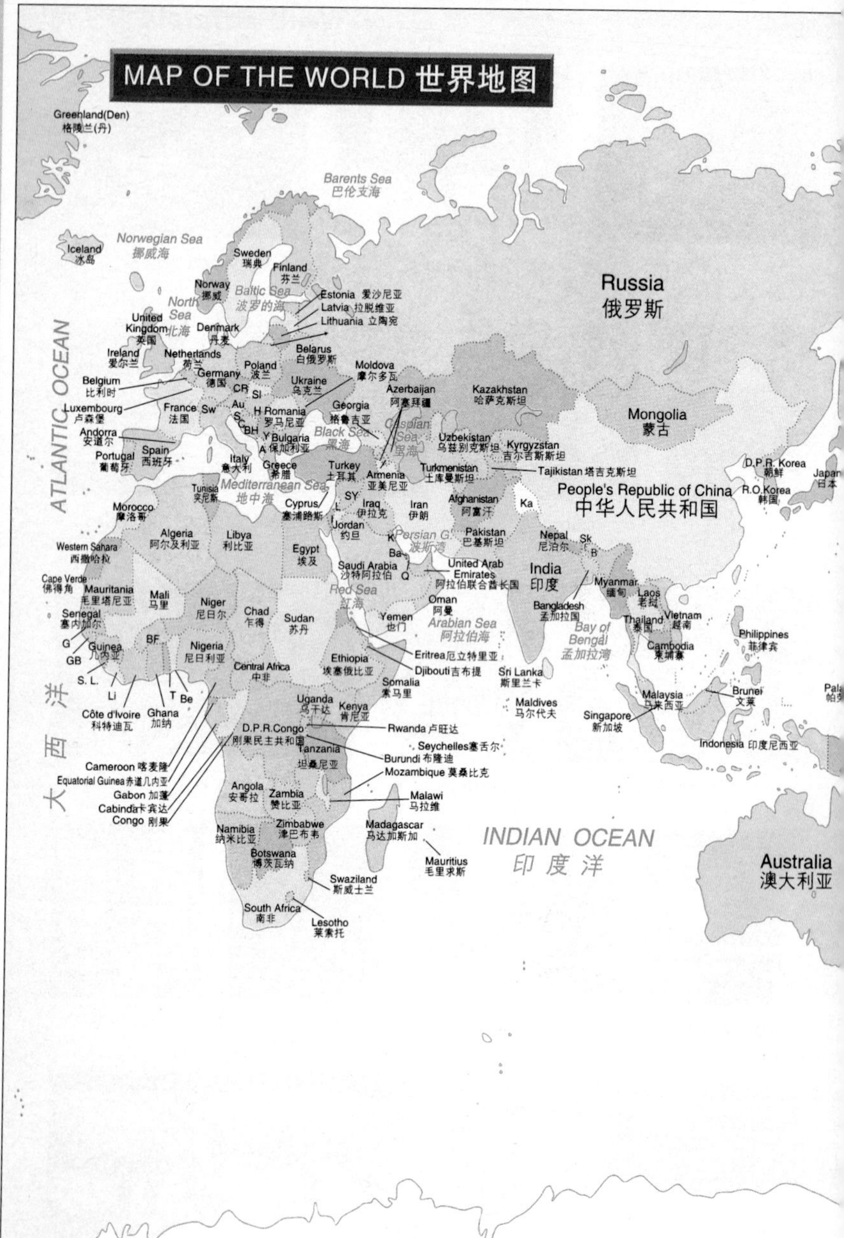

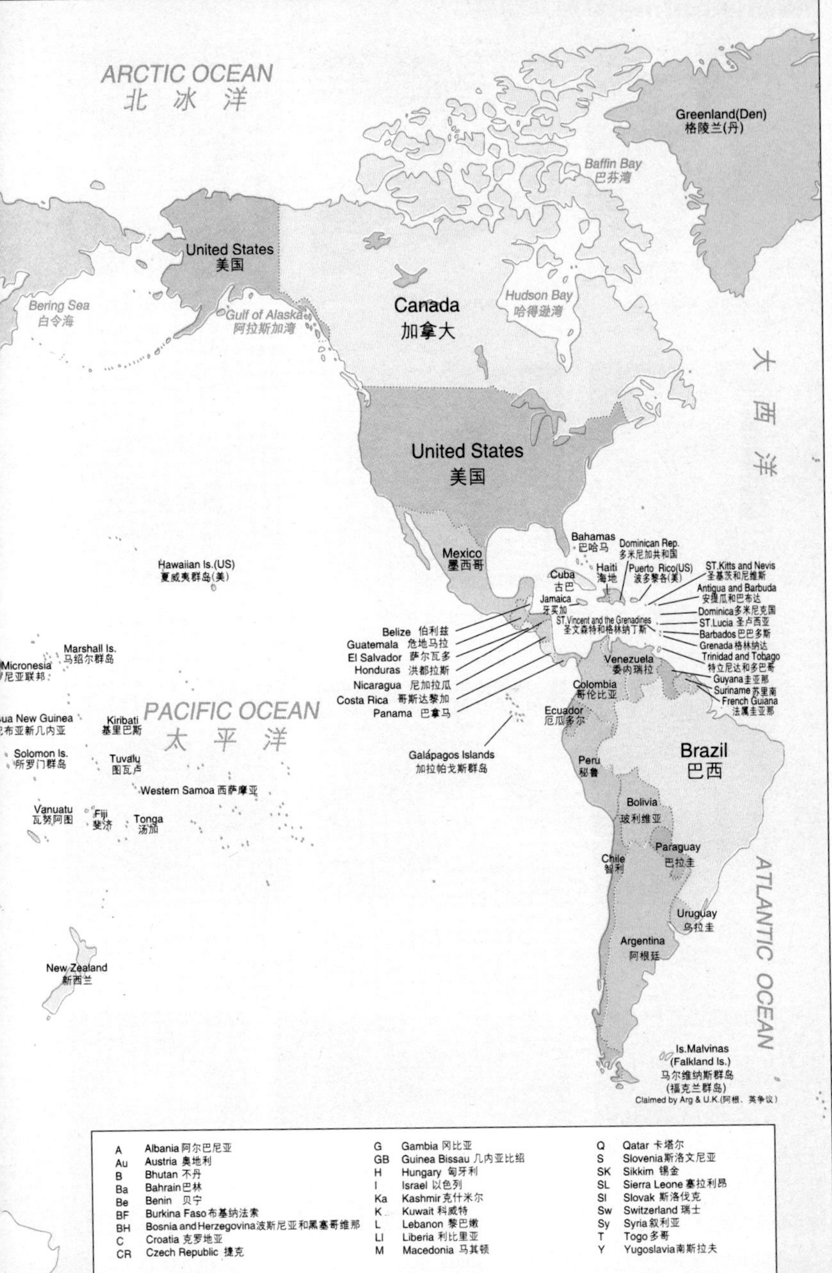
ARCTIC OCEAN
北 冰 洋
Greenland(Den)
格陵兰(丹)
Baffin Bay
巴芬湾
United States
美国
Bering Sea
白令海
Gulf of Alaska
阿拉斯加湾
Canada
加拿大
Hudson Bay
哈得逊湾
大 西 洋
United States
美国
Bahamas
巴哈马
Dominican Rep.
多米尼加共和国
Mexico
墨西哥
Hawaiian Is.(US)
夏威夷群岛(美)
Cuba
古巴
Haiti
海地
Puerto Rico(US)
波多黎各(美)
ST.Kitts and Nevis
圣基茨和尼维斯
Antigua and Barbuda
安提瓜和巴布达
Jamaica
牙买加
Dominica 多米尼克国
St.Vincent and the Grenadines
圣文森特和格林纳丁斯
ST.Lucia 圣卢西亚
Barbados 巴巴多斯
Grenada 格林纳达
Trinidad and Tobago
特立尼达和多巴哥
Belize 伯利兹
Guatemala 危地马拉
El Salvador 萨尔瓦多
Honduras 洪都拉斯
Nicaragua 尼加拉瓜
Costa Rica 哥斯达黎加
Panama 巴拿马
Venezuela
委内瑞拉
Guyana 圭亚那
Suriname 苏里南
French Guiana
法属圭亚那
Colombia
哥伦比亚
Ecuador
厄瓜多尔
Marshall Is.
马绍尔群岛
Micronesia
尼亚联邦
PACIFIC OCEAN
太 平 洋
ua New Guinea
布亚新几内亚
Kiribati
基里巴斯
Solomon Is.
所罗门群岛
Tuvalu
图瓦卢
Galápagos Islands
加拉帕戈斯群岛
Brazil
巴西
Peru
秘鲁
Western Samoa 西萨摩亚
Vanuatu
瓦努阿图
Fiji
斐济
Tonga
汤加
Bolivia
玻利维亚
Paraguay
巴拉圭
Chile
智利
ATLANTIC OCEAN
Uruguay
乌拉圭
Argentina
阿根廷
New Zealand
新西兰
Is.Malvinas
(Falkland Is.)
马尔维纳斯群岛
(福克兰群岛)
Claimed by Arg & U.K.(阿根、英争议)
A Albania 阿尔巴尼亚
Au Austria 奥地利
B Bhutan 不丹
Ba Bahrain 巴林
Be Benin 贝宁
BF Burkina Faso 布基纳法索
BH Bosnia and Herzegovina 波斯尼亚和黑塞哥维那
C Croatia 克罗地亚
CR Czech Republic 捷克
G Gambia 冈比亚
GB Guinea Bissau 几内亚比绍
H Hungary 匈牙利
I Israel 以色列
Ka Kashmir 克什米尔
K Kuwait 科威特
L Lebanon 黎巴嫩
Ll Liberia 利比里亚
M Macedonia 马其顿
Q Qatar 卡塔尔
S Slovenia 斯洛文尼亚
SK Sikkim 锡金
SL Sierra Leone 塞拉利昂
Sl Slovak 斯洛伐克
Sw Switzerland 瑞士
Sy Syria 叙利亚
T Togo 多哥
Y Yugoslavia 南斯拉夫

Marine animals 海洋动物

seal 海豹

crocodile 鳄鱼

dolphin 海豚

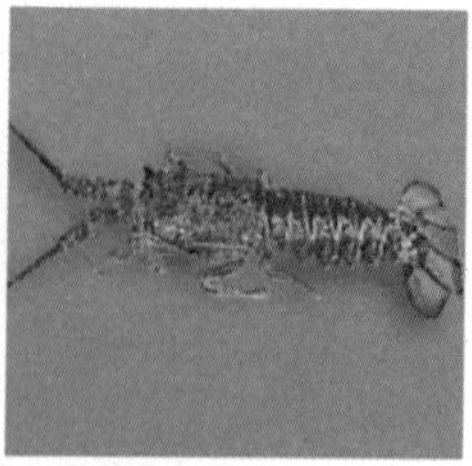

lobster 龙虾

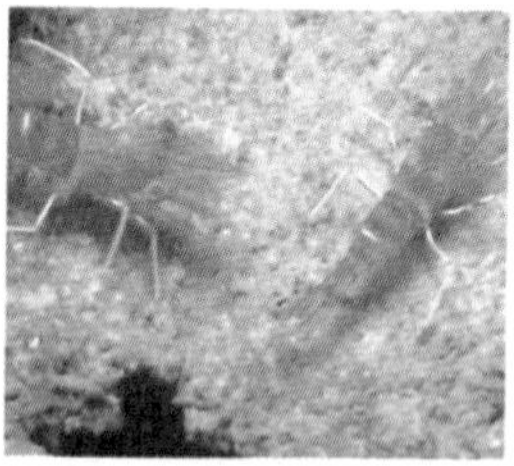

shrimp 小虾

crab 螃蟹

fish 鱼

whale 鲸鱼

turtle 海龟

starfish 海星

shark 鲨鱼

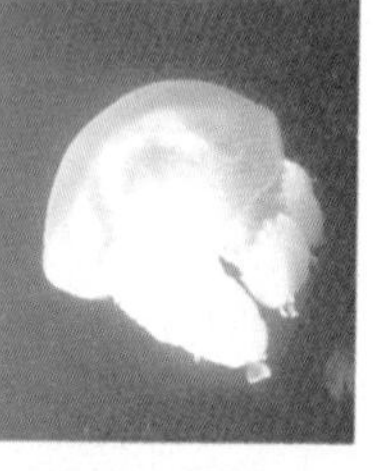

jellyfish 水母

Words that go together 1 连用的词 1

a **pair** of shoes
一双鞋

a **row** of houses
一排楼房

a **bunch** of flowers
一束花

a **pile** of books
一摞书

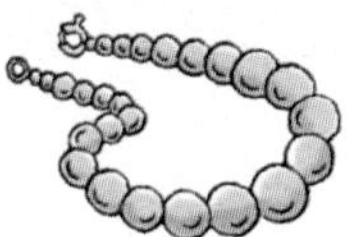
a **string** of beads
一串珠子

a **bundle** of newspapers
一捆报纸

a **crowd** of people
一群人

a **queue** (of people)
排成一队等候（的人）

a **bar** of chocolate
一块巧克力

a **drop** of water 一滴水

a **ball** of string 一团绳子

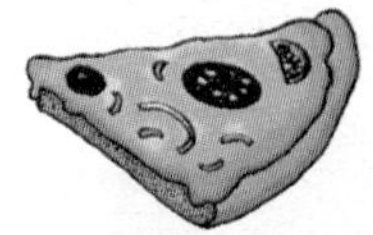
a **slice/piece** of pizza
一块意大利饼

a **lump** of coal
一块煤

This dictionary tells you about words that often go together. 本词典把常常连用的词放在一起。 Do you know what word is missing in each of these expressions? 你知道下面各词组里缺少的是什么词吗？ You can use the dictionary (look up **soap**, **grape** and **shorts** and read the example sentences) to find out. 你可以使用本词典（查检**soap**、**grape**、**shorts**，看其中例句）就能找出答案来。

a **?** of soap

a **?** of grapes

a **?** of shorts

Opposites 反义词

big/large 大

little/small 小

thick 厚

thin 薄

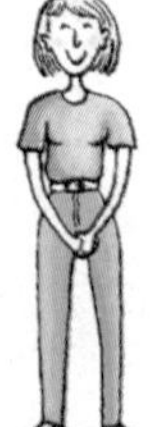

tall 高

short 矮

wide/broad 宽

narrow 窄

high 高

low 矮

shallow 浅

deep 深

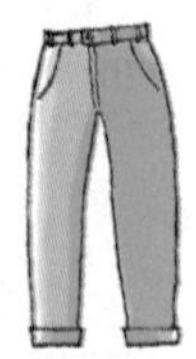

long 长

short 短

happy 愉快

sad 悲哀

fat 肥

thin 瘦

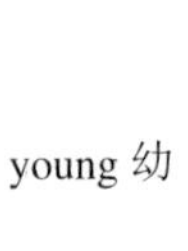

young 幼

old 老

Opposites 反义词

We give opposites for many of the words in this dictionary. 本词典很多词后面都附有反义词。If you want to know the opposite of **tidy**, for example, look up this word and you will find ✪ opposite: **untidy** after it. 例如要想知道**tidy**的反义词，可以查检这个词，就能看到后面有✪ opposite反义词：**untidy**。

Words that go together 2 连用的词 2

She has ___?___ a lot of mistakes.

When you learn a new word it is important to remember what other words you often see with it. 学一个生词，就要记住与它一起连用的词，这一点十分重要。This dictionary can help you to decide what word goes with another word. 本词典列出哪个词与哪个词连用。For example, if you look up **mistake** in the dictionary, you will see 例如查检本词典**mistake**这个词，就能看到:

mistake[1] /mɪˈsteɪk; məˈstek/ *noun* 名词
something that you think or do that is wrong 错误；过失: *You have made a lot of spelling mistakes in this letter.* 你信中有很多拼写错误。◇ *It was a mistake to go by bus—the journey took two hours!* 坐公共汽车去是不对的——这一趟用了两个小时！
by mistake when you did not plan to do it 错误地；并非有意地: *I took your book by mistake—I thought it was mine.* 我错拿了你的书——还以为是我的呢。

The example sentence shows you that you use **make** with **mistake**.
例句说明**make**与**mistake**连用。

You can use your dictionary to check which words below go together. 使用本词典可以查出下列哪些词是连用的。Find the words in **B** and use the example sentences. 先查出**B**项下的词，然后使用其中的例句。

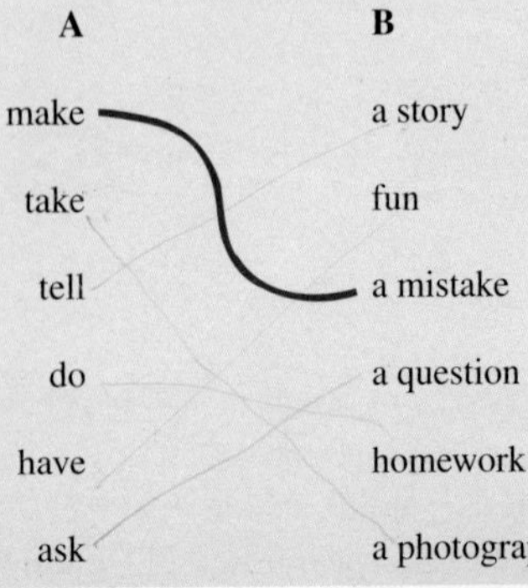

Dates 日期

Saying dates 怎样读日期

How do you say…? 怎样说…？：

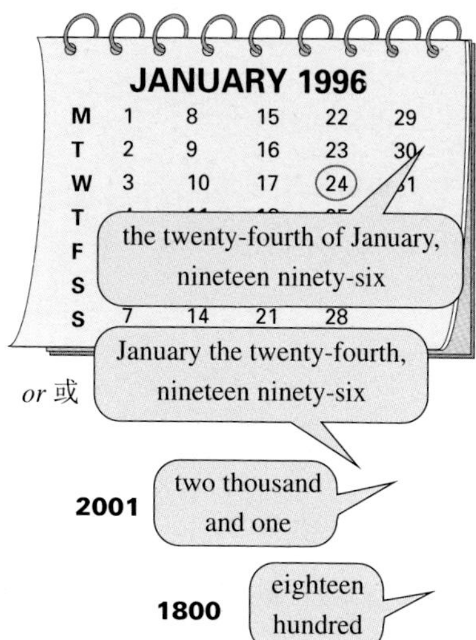

on, in or at? 用on、用in 还是用at？

on	5 August 8月5日 Monday 星期一 Wednesday morning 星期三上午 my birthday 我的生日
in	August 八月份 1995 1995年 (the) summer 夏天 the morning/afternoon/evening 上午[下午/晚上]
at	the beginning of June 六月初 the weekend 周末 Christmas 圣诞节 night 夜晚 six o'clock 六点钟

Writing dates 怎样写日期

Here are some ways of writing the date 写日期的几种方法:

24 January
January 24
24th January
January 24th

Sometimes we just write numbers 有时只写数字:

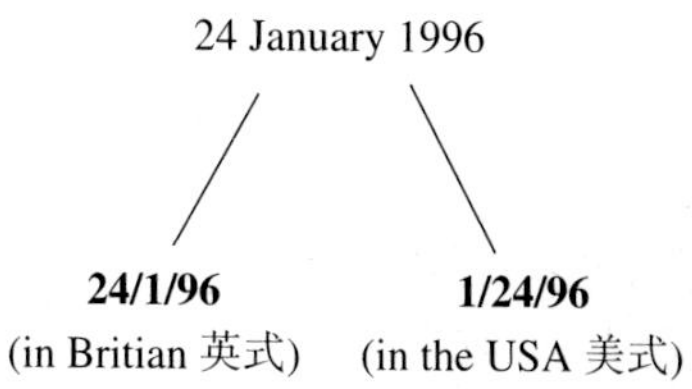

Months 月	Days 日
January 一月	Sunday 星期日
February 二月	Monday 星期一
March 三月	Tuesday 星期二
April 四月	Wednesday 星期三
May 五月	Thursday 星期四
June 六月	Friday 星期五
July 七月	Saturday 星期六
August 八月	
September 九月	
October 十月	
November 十一月	
December 十二月	

Letter-writing 书信写法

formal letters 公函

your address 自己的地址
(but NOT your name
不要写自己的姓名)

the date 日期

the name or title of the person you are writing to, and **their address**
收信人的姓名或头衔及地址

18 St Lawrence Street
London
W10 5LX

12 May 1995

The Director
Tourist Information Centre
High St
Oxford
OX1 3SP

begin with 开头
这样写:
Dear Sir
Madam
Sirs
Dear Mr Jones
Mrs Jones
Ms Jones
Miss Jones

Dear Sir or Madam

I am writing to enquire about holiday accommodation in Oxford.

I would be grateful if you could send me details of cheap hotels or camp-sites near the city centre.

I look forward to hearing from you.

Yours faithfully

Your signature
自己的签字

Julie Newton

Ms J Newton

end with 结尾选用下列之一:
Yours faithfully (when you began with 如果开头是 *Dear Sir*, etc)
Yours sincerely (when you began with 如果开头是 *Dear Mr Jones*, etc)
Yours truly (US 美式)
Sincerely yours (US 美式)

Letter-writing 书信写法

informal letters 便函

your address 自己的地址
(but NOT your name)
不要写自己的姓名

the date 日期

18 St Lawrence Street
London
W10 5LX

Wednesday 20th June

Dear James

This is just a quick note to thank you for dinner in Oxford last Saturday. It was great to see you, and I'm glad that you're enjoying your course.

Nick and I went to a museum in Oxford on Sunday morning and then had a picnic by the river. We had a wonderful time and we didn't want to come home!

Hope to see you soon.

Love

Julie

You can also end with
结尾可选用下列之一:
Love from
Lots of love
Best wishes
Yours

envelope 信封

stamp 邮票

Mr J Carter
14 North Road
Oxford
OX9 2LJ

address
收信人地址

postcode
邮政编码

Telephoning 怎样打电话

Saying telephone numbers 怎样说电话号码

36920 three six nine two o (You say it like **oh**. 像**oh**的读音)
25844 two five eight double four

When you make a **telephone call**, you **pick up** the **receiver** and **dial** the number. 打电话时，先拿起听筒然后再拨号。 The telephone **rings**, and the person you are telephoning **answers** it. 电话铃响了以后，对方接电话。 If he/she is already using the telephone, it is **engaged**. 假如对方正在使用电话，那就叫做占线。

Irregular verbs 不规则动词表

Infinitive 不定式	Past tense 过去时态	Past participle 过去分词
be	was, were	been
bear	bore	borne
beat	beat	beaten
become	became	become
begin	began	begun
bend	bent	bent
bet	bet, betted	bet, betted
bind	bound	bound
bite	bit	bitten
bleed	bled	bled
blow	blew	blown
break	broke	broken
breed	bred	bred
bring	brought	brought
broadcast	broadcast	broadcast
build	built	built
burn	burnt, burned	burnt, burned
burst	burst	burst
buy	bought	bought
catch	caught	caught
choose	chose	chosen
cling	clung	clung
come	came	come
cost	cost	cost
creep	crept	crept
cut	cut	cut
deal	dealt	dealt
dig	dug	dug
do	did	done
draw	drew	drawn
dream	dreamt, dreamed	dreamt, dreamed
drink	drank	drunk
drive	drove	driven
eat	ate	eaten
fall	fell	fallen
feed	fed	fed
feel	felt	felt
fight	fought	fought
find	found	found
flee	fled	fled
fling	flung	flung
fly	flew	flown
forbid	forbade	forbidden
forget	forgot	forgotten
forgive	forgave	forgiven
freeze	froze	frozen
get	got	got
give	gave	given
go	went	gone
grind	ground	ground
grow	grew	grown

Infinitive 不定式	Past tense 过去时态	Past participle 过去分词
hang	hung, hanged	hung, hanged
have	had	had
hear	heard	heard
hide	hid	hidden
hit	hit	hit
hold	held	held
hurt	hurt	hurt
keep	kept	kept
kneel	knelt, kneeled	knelt, kneeled
know	knew	known
lay	laid	laid
lead	led	led
lean	leant, leaned	leant, leaned
leap	leapt, leaped	leapt, leaped
learn	learnt, learned	learnt, learned
leave	left	left
lend	lent	lent
let	let	let
lie	lay	lain
light	lit, lighted	lit, lighted
lose	lost	lost
make	made	made
mean	meant	meant
meet	met	met
mislead	misled	misled
mistake	mistook	mistaken
misunderstand	misunderstood	misunderstood
mow	mowed	mown
overhear	overheard	overheard
oversleep	overslept	overslept
overtake	overtook	overtaken
pay	paid	paid
prove	proved	proved, proven
put	put	put
read	read	read
repay	repaid	repaid
ride	rode	ridden
ring	rang	rung
rise	rose	risen
run	ran	run
saw	sawed	sawn
say	said	said
see	saw	seen
seek	sought	sought
sell	sold	sold
send	sent	sent
set	set	set
sew	sewed	sewed, sewn
shake	shook	shaken
shed	shed	shed
shine	shone	shone
shoot	shot	shot
show	showed	shown, showed
shrink	shrank	shrunk

Infinitive 不定式	Past tense 过去时态	Past participle 过去分词
shut	shut	shut
sing	sang	sung
sink	sank	sunk
sit	sat	sat
sleep	slept	slept
slide	slid	slid
sling	slung	slung
slit	slit	slit
smell	smelt, smelled	smelt, smelled
sow	sowed	sown, sowed
speak	spoke	spoken
speed	sped, speeded	sped, speeded
spell	spelt, spelled	spelt, spelled
spend	spent	spent
spill	spilt, spilled	spilt, spilled
spin	spun	spun
spit	spat	spat
split	split	split
spoil	spoilt, spoiled	spoilt, spoiled
spread	spread	spread
spring	sprang	sprung
stand	stood	stood
steal	stole	stolen
stick	stuck	stuck
sting	stung	stung
stink	stank	stunk
stride	strode	stridden
strike	struck	struck
swear	swore	sworn
sweep	swept	swept
swell	swelled	swollen, swelled
swim	swam	swum
swing	swung	swung
take	took	taken
teach	taught	taught
tear	tore	torn
tell	told	told
think	thought	thought
throw	threw	thrown
thrust	thrust	thrust
tread	trod	trodden
understand	understood	understood
undo	undid	undone
upset	upset	upset
wake	woke	woken
wear	wore	worn
weave	wove	woven
weep	wept	wept
win	won	won
wind	wound	wound
wring	wrung	wrung
write	wrote	written

Geographical names 地名表

If there are different words for the adjective and the person who comes from a particular place, we also give the word for the person, for example **Finland**; **Finnish** (person: **Finn**). 如果某些地区名称的形容词和用作这些地区的人的名词的词形不同，本词典也将后者列出，例如 **Finland** 芬兰；**Finnish** 芬兰的（person 人：**Finn** 芬兰人）。

	noun 名词	**adjective 形容词*[人]***	
/æf'gænɪstɑ:n; æf'gænə,stæn/	Afghanistan 阿富汗	Afghan	/'æfgæn; 'æf,gæn/ 阿富汗的*[人]*
/'æfrɪkə; 'æfrɪkə/	Africa 非洲	African	/'æfrɪkən; 'æfrɪkən/ 非洲的*[人]*
/æl'beɪniə; æl'benɪə/	Albania 阿尔巴尼亚	Albanian	/æl'beɪniən; æl'benɪən/ 阿尔巴尼亚的*[人]*
/æl'dʒɪəriə; æl'dʒɪrɪə/	Algeria 阿尔及利亚	Algerian	/æl'dʒɪəriən; æl'dʒɪrɪən/ 阿尔及利亚的*[人]*
/ə'merɪkə; ə'mɛrɪkə/	America 美洲	American	/ə'merɪkən; ə'mɛrɪkən/ 美洲的*[人]*
/æŋ'gəʊlə; æŋ'golə/	Angola 安哥拉	Angolan	/æŋ'gəʊlən; æŋ'golən/ 安哥拉的*[人]*
/æn'tɑ:ktɪk; ænt'ɑrktɪk/	the Antarctic 南极地区	Antarctic	/æn'tɑ:ktɪk; ænt'ɑrktɪk/ 南极地区的
/'ɑ:ktɪk; 'ɑrktɪk/	the Arctic 北极地区	Arctic	/'ɑ:ktɪk; 'ɑrktɪk/ 北极地区的
/,ɑ:dʒən'ti:nə; ,ɑrdʒən'tinə/	Argentina 阿根廷	Argentinian,	/,ɑ:dʒən'tɪniən; ,ɑrdʒən'tɪnɪən/ 阿根廷的*[人]*
		Argentine	/'ɑ:dʒəntaɪn; 'ɑrdʒən,taɪn/ 阿根廷的*[人]*
/ɑ:'mi:niə; ɑr'minɪə/	Armenia 亚美尼亚	Armenian	/ɑ:'mi:niən; ɑr'minɪən/ 亚美尼亚的*[人]*
/'eɪʃə; 'eʃə/	Asia 亚洲	Asian	/'eɪʃən; 'eʃən/ 亚洲的*[人]*
/ət'læntɪk; ət'læntɪk/	the Atlantic 大西洋	the Atlantic	/ət'læntɪk; ət'læntɪk/ 大西洋的
/ɒ'streɪliə; ɔ'streljə/	Australia 澳大利亚	Australian	/ɒ'streɪliən; ɔ'streljən/ 澳大利亚的*[人]*
/'ɒstriə; 'ɔstrɪə/	Austria 奥地利	Austrian	/'ɒstriən; 'ɔstrɪən/ 奥地利的*[人]*
/,æzəbaɪ'dʒɑ:n; ,ɑzəbaɪ'dʒɑn/	Azerbaijan 阿塞拜疆	Azerbaijani	/,æzəbaɪ'dʒɑ:ni; ɑzəbaɪ'dʒɑnɪ/ 阿塞拜疆的*[人]*
/,bæŋglə'deʃ; ,bæŋglə'dɛʃ/	Bangladesh 孟加拉	Bangladeshi	/,bæŋglə'deʃi; ,bæŋglə'dɛʃɪ/ 孟加拉的*[人]*
/bi,elə'ru:s; bɛlə'rus/	Belarus 白俄罗斯	Belorussian	/bi,elə'rʌʃn; bɛlə'ruʃən/ 白俄罗斯的*[人]*
/'beldʒəm; 'bɛldʒəm/	Belgium 比利时	Belgian	/'beldʒən; 'bɛldʒən/ 比利时的*[人]*
/be'ni:n; bə'nɪn/	Benin 贝宁	Beninese	/,benɪ'ni:z; bə,nɪn'iz/ 贝宁的*[人]*
/bə'lɪviə; bə'lɪvɪə/	Bolivia 玻利维亚	Bolivian	/bə'lɪviən; bə'lɪvɪən/ 玻利维亚的*[人]*
/,bɒznɪə ,hɜ:tsəgə'vi:nə; /'bɑznɪə 'hɚtsəgəvɪnə/	Bosnia- Herzegovina 波斯尼亚－黑塞哥维那	Bosnian	/'bɒzniən; 'bɑznɪən/ 波斯尼亚的*[人]*
/bɒt'swɑ:nə; bɑt'swɑnə/	Botswana 博茨瓦纳	Botswanan	/bɒ'tswɑ:nən; bɑt'swɑnən/ 博茨瓦纳的*[人]*
/brə'zɪl; brə'zɪl/	Brazil 巴西	Brazilian	/brə'zɪliən; brə'zɪljən/ 巴西的*[人]*
/'brɪtn; 'brɪtən/	Britain 英国	British	/'brɪtɪʃ; 'brɪtɪʃ/ 英国的*[人]*
		(person: Briton)	/'brɪtn; 'brɪtən/ 英国人
/bʌl'geəriə; bʌl'gɛrɪə/	Bulgaria 保加利亚	Bulgarian	/bʌl'geəriən; bʌl'gɛrɪən/ 保加利亚的*[人]*
/bɜ:'ki:nə; bɚ'kinə/	Burkina 布基纳	Burkinese	/,bɜ:kɪ'ni:z; bɚkɪn'iz/ 布基纳的*[人]*
/bʊ'rʊndi; bʊ'rundɪ/	Burundi 布隆迪	Burundian	/bʊ'rʊndiən; bʊ'rundɪən/ 布隆迪的*[人]*
/kæm'bəʊdiə; kæm'bodɪə/	Cambodia 柬埔寨	Cambodian	/kæm'bəʊdiən; kæm'bodɪən/ 柬埔寨的*[人]*
/,kæmə'ru:n; ,kæmə'run/	Cameroon 喀麦隆	Cameroonian	/,kæmə'ru:niən; ,kæmə'runɪən/ 喀麦隆的*[人]*
/'kænədə; 'kænədə/	Canada 加拿大	Canadian	/kə'neɪdiən; kə'nedɪən/ 加拿大的*[人]*
/,kærə'bi:ən; ,kærə'biən/	the Caribbean 加勒比	Caribbean	/,kærə'bi:ən; ,kærə'biən/ 加勒比的*[人]*
/,sentrəl ,æfrɪkən rɪ'pʌblɪk; ,sɛntrəl ,æfrɪkən rɪ'pʌblɪk/	Central African Republic 中非共和国		
/tʃæd; tʃæd/	Chad 乍得	Chadian	/'tʃædiən; 'tʃædɪən/ 乍得的*[人]*
/'tʃɪli; 'tʃɪlɪ/	Chile 智利	Chilean	/'tʃɪliən; 'tʃɪlɪən/ 智利的*[人]*
/'tʃaɪnə; 'tʃaɪnə/	China 中国	Chinese	/,tʃaɪ'ni:z; tʃaɪ'niz/ 中国的*[人]*
/kə'lɒmbiə; kə'lʌmbɪə/	Colombia 哥伦比亚	Colombian	/kə'lɒmbiən; kə'lʌmbɪən/ 哥伦比亚的*[人]*
/'kɒŋgəʊ; 'kɑŋgo/	Congo 刚果	Congolese	/,kɒŋgə'li:z; ,kɑŋgə'liz/ 刚果的*[人]*
/,kɒstə 'ri:kə; ,kɑstə'rikə/	Costa Rica 哥斯达黎加	Costa Rican	/,kɒstə 'ri:kən; ,kɑstə'rikən/ 哥斯达黎加的*[人]*

	noun 名词		**adjective 形容词*[人]***
/krəʊ'eɪʃə; kro'eʃə/	Croatia 克罗地亚	Croatian	/krəʊ'eɪʃən; kro'eʃən/ 克罗地亚的*[人]*
/'kju:bə; 'kjubə/	Cuba 古巴	Cuban	/'kju:bən; 'kjubən/ 古巴的*[人]*
/'saɪprəs; 'saɪprəs/	Cyprus 塞浦路斯	Cypriot	/'sɪpriət; 'sɪprɪət/ 塞浦路斯的*[人]*
/ˌtʃek rɪ'pʌblɪk; tʃɛk rɪ'pʌblɪk/	Czech Republic 捷克	Czech	/tʃek; tʃɛk/ 捷克的*[人]*
/'denmɑ:k; 'dɛnˌmɑrk/	Denmark 丹麦	Danish	/'deɪnɪʃ; 'denɪʃ/ 丹麦的
		(person: Dane)	/deɪn; den/ 丹麦人
/'ekwədɔ:(r); 'ɛkwəˌdɔr/	Ecuador 厄瓜多尔	Ecuadorian	/ˌekwə'dɔ:riən; ˌɛkwə'dɔrɪən/ 厄瓜多尔的*[人]*
/'i:dʒɪpt; 'idʒɪpt/	Egypt 埃及	Egyptian	/i'dʒɪpʃn; ɪ'dʒɪpʃən/ 埃及的*[人]*
/el 'sælvədɔ:(r); ɛl'sælvəˌdɔr/	El Salvador 萨尔瓦多	Salvadorean	/ˌsælvə'dɔ:riən; ˌsælvə'dɔrɪən/ 萨尔瓦多的*[人]*
/'ɪŋglənd; 'ɪŋglənd/	England 英格兰	English	/'ɪŋglɪʃ; 'ɪŋglɪʃ/ 英格兰的
		(person: Englishman,	/'ɪŋglɪʃmən; 'ɪŋglɪʃmən/ （男的）英格兰人
		Englishwoman)	/'ɪŋglɪʃwʊmən; 'ɪŋglɪʃˌwumən/ （女的）英格兰人
/e'stəʊniə; ɛs'tonɪə/	Estonia 爱沙尼亚	Estonian	/e'stəʊniən; ɛs'tonɪən/ 爱沙尼亚的*[人]*
/ˌi:θi'əʊpiə; ˌiθɪ'opɪə/	Ethiopia 埃塞俄比亚	Ethiopian	/ˌi:θi'əʊpiən; ˌiθɪ'opɪən/ 埃塞俄比亚的*[人]*
/'jʊərəp; 'jurəp/	Europe 欧洲	European	/ˌjʊərə'piən; ˌjurə'pɪən/ 欧洲的*[人]*
/'fɪnlənd; 'fɪnlənd/	Finland 芬兰	Finnish	/'fɪnɪʃ; 'fɪnɪʃ/ 芬兰的
		(person: Finn)	/fɪn; fɪn/ 芬兰人
/frɑ:ns; fræns/	France 法国	French	/frentʃ; frɛntʃ/ 法国的
		(person: Frenchman,	/'frentʃmən; 'frɛntʃmən/ （男的）法国人
		Frenchwoman)	/'frentʃwʊmən; 'frɛntʃˌwumən/ （女的）法国人
/'gæmbiə; 'gæmbɪə/	Gambia 冈比亚	Gambian	/'gæmbiən; 'gæmbɪən/ 冈比亚的*[人]*
/'dʒɔ:dʒə; 'dʒɔrdʒə/	Georgia 格鲁吉亚	Georgian	/'dʒɔ:dʒən; 'dʒɔrdʒən/ 格鲁吉亚的*[人]*
/'dʒɜ:məni; 'dʒɝmənɪ/	Germany 德国	German	/'dʒɜ:mən; 'dʒɝmən/ 德国的*[人]*
/'gɑ:nə; 'gɑnə/	Ghana 加纳	Ghanaian	/gɑ:'neɪən; gɑ'neən/ 加纳的*[人]*
/ˌgreɪt 'brɪtn; ˌgret'brɪtn̩/	Great Britain 英国	British	/'brɪtɪʃ; 'brɪtɪʃ/ 英国的
		(person: Briton)	/'brɪtn; 'brɪtn̩/ 英国人
/gri:s; gris/	Greece 希腊	Greek	/gri:k; grik/ 希腊的*[人]*
/ˌgwɑ:tə'mɑ:lə; ˌgwɑtə'mɑlə/	Guatemala 危地马拉	Guatemalan	/ˌgwɑ:tə'mɑ:lən; ˌgwɑtə'mɑlən/ 危地马拉的*[人]*
/'gɪni; 'gɪnɪ/	Guinea 几内亚	Guinean	/'gɪniən; 'gɪnɪən/ 几内亚的*[人]*
/'heɪtɪ; 'hetɪ/	Haiti 海地	Haitian	/'heɪʃn; 'heʃən/ 海地的*[人]*
/'hɒlənd; 'hɑlənd/	Holland 荷兰	Dutch	/dʌtʃ; dʌtʃ/ 荷兰的*[人]*
/hɒn'djʊərəs; hɑn'durəs/	Honduras 洪都拉斯	Honduran	/hɒn'djʊərən; hɑn'durən/ 洪都拉斯的*[人]*
/'hʌŋgəri; 'hʌŋgərɪ/	Hungary 匈牙利	Hungarian	/hʌŋ'geəriən; hʌŋ'gerɪən/ 匈牙利的*[人]*
/'aɪslənd; 'aɪslənd/	Iceland 冰岛	Icelandic	/aɪs'lændɪk; aɪs'lændɪk/ 冰岛的
		(person: Icelander)	/'aɪsləndə(r); 'aɪˌsləndɚ/ 冰岛人
/'ɪndiə; 'ɪndɪə/	India 印度	Indian	/'ɪndiən; 'ɪndɪən/ 印度的*[人]*
/ˌɪndə'ni:ziə; ˌɪndə'niʒə/	Indonesia 印度尼西亚	Indonesian	/ˌɪndə'ni:ziən; ˌɪndə'niʒən/ 印度尼西亚的*[人]*
/ɪ'rɑ:n; ɪ'ræn/	Iran 伊朗	Iranian	/ɪ'reɪniən; ɪ'renɪən/ 伊朗的*[人]*
/ɪ'rɑ:k; ɪ'rɑk/	Iraq 伊拉克	Iraqi	/ɪ'rɑ:ki; ɪ'rɑkɪ/ 伊拉克的*[人]*
/'aɪələnd; 'aɪrlənd/	Ireland 爱尔兰	Irish	/'aɪrɪʃ; 'aɪrɪʃ/ 爱尔兰的*[人]*
		(person: Irishman,	/'aɪərɪʃmən; 'aɪrɪʃmən/ （男的）爱尔兰人
		Irishwoman)	/'aɪərɪʃwʊmən; 'aɪrɪʃˌwumən/ （女的）爱尔兰人
/'ɪzreɪl; 'ɪzreəl/	Israel 以色列	Israeli	/ɪz'reɪli; ɪz'relɪ/ 以色列的*[人]*
/'ɪtəli; 'ɪtl̩ɪ/	Italy 意大利	Italian	/ɪ'tæliən; ɪ'tæljən/ 意大利的*[人]*
/ˌaɪvəri 'kəʊst; ˌaɪvərɪ'kost/	Ivory Coast 象牙海岸	Ivorian	/aɪ'vɔ:riən; ˌaɪ'vɔrɪən/ 象牙海岸的*[人]*
/dʒə'meɪkə; dʒə'mekə/	Jamaica 牙买加	Jamaican	/dʒə'meɪkən; dʒə'mekən/ 牙买加的*[人]*
/dʒə'pæn; dʒə'pæn/	Japan 日本	Japanese	/ˌdʒæpə'ni:z; ˌdʒæpə'niz/ 日本的*[人]*
/'dʒɔ:dn; 'dʒɔrdn̩/	Jordan 约旦	Jordanian	/dʒɔ:'deɪniən; dʒɔr'denɪən/ 约旦的*[人]*

	noun 名词	**adjective 形容词*[人]***	
/ˌkæzæk'stɑ:n; 'kɑzəkstæn/	Kazakhstan 哈萨克斯坦	Kazakh	/kə'zæk; 'kɑzæk/ 哈萨克斯坦的*[人]*
/'kenjə; 'kinjə/	Kenya 肯尼亚	Kenyan	/'kenjən; 'kinjən/ 肯尼亚的*[人]*
/ˌkɪəgɪz'stɑ:n; 'kɝgəstæn/	Kirgyzstan 吉尔吉斯斯坦	Kirgyz	/kɪə'gi:z; 'kɝgəz/ 吉尔吉斯斯坦的*[人]*
/kə'rɪə; kə'rɪə/	Korea 朝鲜；韩国	Korean	/kə'riən; kə'rɪən/ 朝鲜的*[人]*；韩国的*[人]*
/ku'weɪt; kʊ'waɪt/	Kuwait 科威特	Kuwaiti	/ku'weɪti; kʊ'waɪtɪ/ 科威特的*[人]*
/laʊs; 'lɑos/	Laos 老挝	Laotian	/'laʊʃn; le'oʃən/ 老挝的*[人]*
/'lætviə; 'lætvɪə/	Latvia 拉脱维亚	Latvian	/'lætviən; 'lætvɪən/ 拉脱维亚的*[人]*
/'lebənən; 'lɛbənɑn/	Lebanon 黎巴嫩	Lebanese	/ˌlebə'ni:z; ˌlɛbə'niz/ 黎巴嫩的*[人]*
/'lɪbiə; 'lɪbɪə/	Libya 利比亚	Libyan	/'lɪbiən; 'lɪbɪən/ 利比亚的*[人]*
/ˌlɪθju'eɪniə; ˌlɪθjʊ'enɪə/	Lithuania 立陶宛	Lithuanian	/ˌlɪθju'eɪniən; ˌlɪθjʊ'enɪən/ 立陶宛的*[人]*
/ˌmæsə'dəʊniə; ˌmæsə'donɪə/	Macedonia (former Yugoslav republic) 马其顿（前南斯拉夫共和国）	Macedonian	/ˌmæsə'dəʊniən; ˌmæsə'donɪən/ 马其顿的*[人]*
/ˌmædə'gæskə(r); ˌmædə'gæskɚ/	Madagascar 马达加斯加	Madagascan	/ˌmædə'gæskən; ˌmædə'gæskən/ 马达加斯加的
		(person: Malagasy)	/ˌmælə'gæsɪ; ˌmælə'gæsɪ/ 马达加斯加的*[人]*
/mə'lɑ:wi; mə'lɑwɪ/	Malawi 马拉维	Malawian	/mə'lɑ:wiən; mə'lɑwɪən/ 马拉维的*[人]*
/mə'leɪziə; mə'leʒə/	Malaysia 马来西亚	Malaysian	/mə'leɪziən; mə'leʒən/ 马来西亚的*[人]*
/'mɑ:li; 'mɑlɪ/	Mali 马里	Malian	/'mɑ:liən; 'mɑlɪən/ 马里的*[人]*
/ˌmedɪtə'reɪniən; ˌmɛdətə'renɪən/	the Mediterranean 地中海	Mediterranean	/ˌmedɪtə'reɪniən; ˌmɛdətə'renɪən/ 地中海的
/'meksɪkəʊ; 'mɛksɪˌko/	Mexico 墨西哥	Mexican	/'meksɪkən; 'mɛksɪkən/ 墨西哥的*[人]*
/mɒl'dəʊvə; mol'dovə/	Moldova 摩尔多瓦	Moldovan	/mɒl'dəʊvən; mol'dovən/ 摩尔多瓦的*[人]*
/mə'rɒkəʊ; mə'rɑko/	Morocco 摩洛哥	Moroccan	/mə'rɒkən; mə'rɑkən/ 摩洛哥的*[人]*
/ˌməʊzæm'bi:k; ˌmozæm'bik/	Mozambique 莫桑比克	Mozambiquean	/ˌməʊzæm'bi:kən; ˌmozæm'bikən/ 莫桑比克的*[人]*
/ˌmi:æn'mɑ:(r); 'mɪænˌmɑr/	Myanmar 缅甸	Myanmar	/ˌmi:æn'mɑ:(r); 'mɪænˌmɑr/ 缅甸的*[人]*
/nɪ'pɔ:l; nə'pɔl/	Nepal 尼泊尔	Nepalese	/ˌnepə'li:z; ˌnɛpə'liz/ 尼泊尔的*[人]*
/'neðələndz; 'nɛðɚləndz/	the Netherlands 荷兰	Dutch	/dʌtʃ; dʌtʃ/ 荷兰的*[人]*
		(person: Dutchman,	/'dʌtʃmən; 'dʌtʃmən/（男的）荷兰人
		Dutchwoman)	/'dʌtʃwʊmən; 'dʌtʃˌwʊmən/（女的）荷兰人
/ˌnju: 'zi:lənd; nu'zilənd/	New Zealand 新西兰	New Zealand	/ˌnju: 'zi:lənd; nu'zilənd/ 新西兰的
		(person: New Zealander)	/ˌnju: 'zi:ləndə(r); nu'ziləndɚ/ 新西兰人
/ˌnɪkə'rægjuə; ˌnɪkə'rɑgwə/	Nicaragua 尼加拉瓜	Nicaraguan	/ˌnɪkə'rægjuən; ˌnɪkə'rɑgwən/ 尼加拉瓜的*[人]*
/ni:'ʒeə(r); 'naɪdʒɚ/	Niger 尼日尔	Nigerien	/ni:'ʒeəriən; naɪ'dʒɛrɪən/ 尼日尔的*[人]*
/naɪ'dʒɪəriə; naɪ'dʒɪrɪə/	Nigeria 尼日利亚	Nigerian	/naɪ'dʒɪəriən; naɪ'dʒɪrɪən/ 尼日利亚的*[人]*
/ˌnɔ:ðən 'aɪələnd; ˌnɔrðɚn'aɪrlənd/	Northern Ireland 北爱尔兰	Northern Irish	/ˌnɔ:ðən 'aɪərɪʃ; ˌnɔrðɚn 'aɪrɪʃ/ 北爱尔兰的*[人]*
/'nɔ:weɪ; 'nɔrˌwe/	Norway 挪威	Norwegian	/nɔ:'wi:dʒən; nɔr'widʒən/ 挪威的*[人]*
/pə'sɪfɪk; pə'sɪfɪk/	the Pacific 太平洋	Pacific	/pə'sɪfɪk; pə'sɪfɪk/ 太平洋的
/ˌpɑ:kɪ'stɑ:n; ˌpækɪ'stæn/	Pakistan 巴基斯坦	Pakistani	/ˌpɑ:kɪ'stɑ:ni; ˌpækɪ'stænɪ/ 巴基斯坦的*[人]*
/'pæləstaɪn; 'pæləˌstaɪn/	Palestine 巴勒斯坦	Palestinian	/ˌpælə'stɪniən; ˌpælə'stɪnɪən/ 巴勒斯坦的*[人]*
/'pænəmɑ:; 'pænəˌmɑ/	Panama 巴拿马	Panamanian	/ˌpænə'meɪniən; ˌpænə'menɪən/ 巴拿马的*[人]*
/ˌpæpuə ˌnju: 'gɪni; ˌpæpjʊəˌnu'gɪnɪ/	Papua New Guinea 巴布亚新几内亚	Papuan	/'pæpuən; 'pæpjʊən/ 巴布亚新几内亚的*[人]*
/'pærəgwaɪ; 'pærəˌgwe/	Paraguay 巴拉圭	Paraguayan	/ˌpærə'gwaiən; ˌpærə'gweən/ 巴拉圭的*[人]*
/pə'ru:; pə'ru/	Peru 秘鲁	Peruvian	/pə'ru:viən; pə'ruvɪən/ 秘鲁的*[人]*
/'fɪlɪpi:nz; 'fɪləˌpinz/	the Philippines 菲律宾	Philippine	/'fɪlɪpi:n; 'fɪləˌpin/ 菲律宾的
		(person: Filipino)	/ˌfɪlɪ'pi:nəʊ; ˌfɪlə'pino/ 菲律宾人

	noun 名词	adjective 形容词[人]	
/'pəʊlənd; 'polənd/	Poland 波兰	Polish	/'pəʊlɪʃ; 'polɪʃ/ 波兰的
		(person: Pole)	/pəʊl; pol/ 波兰人
/'pɔːtʃʊgl; 'pɔrtʃəgl/	Portugal 葡萄牙	Portuguese	/ˌpɔːtʃʊ'giːz; 'pɔrtʃəˌgiz/ 葡萄牙的[人]
/ˌpwɜːtəʊ 'riːkəʊ; ˌpwɛrtə'riko/	Puerto Rico 波多黎各	Puerto Rican	/ˌpwɜːtəʊ 'riːkən; ˌpwɛrtə'rikən/ 波多黎各的[人]
/ruː'meɪnɪə; ro'menɪə/	Romania 罗马尼亚	Romanian	/ruː'meɪnɪən; ro'menɪən/ 罗马尼亚的[人]
/'rʌʃə; 'rʌʃə/	Russia 俄罗斯	Russian	/'rʌʃn; 'rʌʃən/ 俄罗斯的[人]
/ruː'ændə; rʊ'ɑndə/	Rwanda 卢旺达	Rwandan	/ruː'ændən; rʊ'ɑndən/ 卢旺达的[人]
/ˌsaʊdi ə'reɪbiə; ˌsaʊdɪ ə'rebɪə/	Saudi Arabia 沙特阿拉伯	Saudi	/'saʊdi; 'saʊdɪ/ 沙特阿拉伯的[人]
/'skɒtlənd; 'skɑtlənd/	Scotland 苏格兰	Scottish	/'skɒtɪʃ; 'skɑtɪʃ/ 苏格兰的
		(person: Scot,	/skɒt; skɑt/ 苏格兰人
		Scotsman,	/'skɒtsmən; 'skɑtsmən/（男的）苏格兰人
		Scotswoman)	/'skɒtswʊmən; 'skɑtsˌwʊmən/（女的）苏格兰人
/'senɪ'gɔːl; ˌsɛnɪ'gɔl/	Senegal 塞内加尔	Senegalese	/ˌsenɪgə'liːz; ˌsɛnɪgə'liz/ 塞内加尔的[人]
/siˌerə li'əʊn; sɪˌɛrəlɪ'on/	Sierra Leone 塞拉利昂	Sierra Leonean	/siˌerə li'əʊniən; sɪˌɛrəlɪ'onɪən/ 塞拉利昂的[人]
/ˌsɪŋgə'pɔː(r); 'sɪŋəˌpɔr/	Singapore 新加坡	Singaporean	/ˌsɪŋgə'pɔːriən; ˌsɪŋə'pɔrɪən/ 新加坡的[人]
/sləʊ'vækiə; slo'vækɪə/	Slovakia 斯洛伐克	Slovak	/'sləʊvæk; 'slovæk/ 斯洛伐克的[人]
/sləʊ'viːniə; slo'vinɪə/	Slovenia 斯洛文尼亚	Slovenian	/sləʊ'viːniən; slo'vinɪən/ 斯洛文尼亚的[人]
/sə'mɑːliə; sə'mɑlɪə/	Somalia 索马里	Somali	/sə'mɑːli; sə'mɑlɪ/ 索马里的[人]
/ˌsaʊθ 'æfrɪkə; ˌsaʊθ'æfrɪkə/	South Africa 南非	South African	/ˌsaʊθ 'æfrɪkən; ˌsaʊθ'æfrɪkən/ 南非的[人]
/speɪn; spen/	Spain 西班牙	Spanish	/'spænɪʃ; 'spænɪʃ/ 西班牙的
		(person: Spaniard)	/'spænɪəd; 'spænjɚd/ 西班牙人
/ˌsriː 'læŋkə; srɪ'lɑŋkə/	Sri Lanka 斯里兰卡	Sri Lankan	/ˌsriː 'læŋkən; srɪ'lɑŋkən/ 斯里兰卡的[人]
/su'dɑːn; su'dæn/	Sudan 苏丹	Sudanese	/ˌsuːdə'niːz; ˌsudə'niz/ 苏丹的[人]
/'swiːdn; 'swidn̩/	Sweden 瑞典	Swedish	/'swiːdɪʃ; 'swidɪʃ/ 瑞典的
		(person: Swede)	/swiːd; swid/ 瑞典人
/'swɪtsələnd; 'swɪtsɚlənd/	Switzerland 瑞士	Swiss	/swɪs; swɪs/ 瑞士的[人]
/'sɪriə; 'sɪrɪə/	Syria 叙利亚	Syrian	/'sɪriən; 'sɪrɪən/ 叙利亚的[人]
/tæˌdʒiːkɪ'stɑːn; tɑ'dʒɪkəstæn/	Tajikistan 塔吉克斯坦	Tajik	/tə'dʒiːk; tɑ'dʒɪk/ 塔吉克斯坦的[人]
/ˌtænzə'niːə; ˌtænzə'nɪə/	Tanzania 坦桑尼亚	Tanzanian	/ˌtænzə'niːən; ˌtænzə'nɪən/ 坦桑尼亚的[人]
/'taɪlænd; 'taɪˌlænd/	Thailand 泰国	Thai	/taɪ; taɪ/ 泰国的[人]
/'təʊgəʊ; 'togo/	Togo 多哥	Togolese	/ˌtəʊgə'liːz; ˌtogə'liz/ 多哥的[人]
/tju'nɪziə; tu'nɪʒə/	Tunisia 突尼斯	Tunisian	/tju'nɪziən; tu'nɪʒən/ 突尼斯的[人]
/'tɜːki; 'tɝkɪ/	Turkey 土耳其	Turkish	/'tɜːkɪʃ; 'tɝkɪʃ/ 土耳其的
		(person: Turk)	/tɜːk; tɝk/ 土耳其人
/tɜːkˌmenɪ'stɑːn; ˌtɝkmɛnɪ'stæn/	Turkmenistan 土库曼斯坦	Turkmen	/'tɜːkmen; 'tɝkmɛn/ 土库曼斯坦的[人]
/juː'gændə; ju'gændə/	Uganda 乌干达	Ugandan	/juː'gændən; ju'gændən/ 乌干达的[人]
/juː'kreɪn; 'jukren/	Ukraine 乌克兰	Ukrainian	/juː'kreɪnɪən; ju'krenɪən/ 乌克兰的[人]
/juˌnaɪtɪd 'kɪŋdəm; juˌnaɪtɪd 'kɪŋdəm//ˌjuː 'keɪ; ju 'ke/	the United Kingdom (also 亦作 UK) 英国	British	/'brɪtɪʃ; 'brɪtɪʃ/ 英国的[人]
/juˌnaɪtɪd ˌsteɪts əv ə'merɪkə; juˌnaɪtɪdˌstetsəv ə'mɛrɪkə/ /ˌjuː es 'eɪ; ˌju ɛs 'e/ /ˌjuː 'es; ˌju 'ɛs/	the United States of America (also 亦作 USA and 及 US) 美利坚合众国（美国）	American	/ə'merɪkən; ə'mɛrɪkən/ 美国的[人]
/'jʊərəgwaɪ; 'jʊrəˌgwe/	Uruguay 乌拉圭	Uruguayan	/ˌjʊərə'gwaɪən; ˌjʊrə'gweən/ 乌拉圭的[人]
/ʊzˌbekɪ'stɑːn; uz'bɛkəstæn/	Uzbekistan 乌兹别克斯坦	Uzbek	/'ʊzbek; uz'bɛk/ 乌兹别克斯坦的[人]
/ˌvenə'zweɪlə; ˌvɛnə'zwelə/	Venezuela 委内瑞拉	Venezuelan	/ˌvenə'zweɪlən; ˌvɛnə'zwelən/ 委内瑞拉的[人]
/ˌvjet'næm; vjɛt'nɑm/	Vietnam 越南	Vietnamese	/ˌvjetnə'miːz; vjɛtnə'miz/ 越南的[人]

	noun 名词		adjective 形容词[人]
/weɪlz; welz/	Wales 威尔士	Welsh	/welʃ; wɛlʃ/ 威尔士的
		(person: Welshman,	/'welʃmən; 'wɛlʃmən/ （男的）威尔士人
		Welshwoman)	/'welʃwʊmən; 'wɛlʃ,wʊmən/ （女的）威尔士人
/ˌwest 'ɪndiz; ˌwɛst'ɪndɪz/	the West Indies 西印度群岛	West Indian	/ˌwest 'ɪndiən; ˌwɛst'ɪndɪən/ 西印度群岛的[人]
/'jemən; 'jɛmən/	(the Republic of) Yemen 也门（共和国）	Yemeni	/'jeməni; 'jɛmənɪ/ 也门的[人]
/ˌju:gəʊ'slɑ:viə; ˌjugo'slɑvɪə/	Yugoslavia 南斯拉夫	Yugoslavian	/ˌju:gəʊ'slɑ:viən; ˌjugo'slɑvɪən/ 南斯拉夫的[人]
		(person: Yugoslav)	/'ju:gəʊslɑ:v; 'jugoˌslɑv/ 南斯拉夫人
/zɑ:'ɪə(r); zɑ'ɪr/	Zaire 扎伊尔	Zairean	/zɑ:'ɪəriən; zɑ'ɪrɪən/ 扎伊尔的[人]
/'zæmbiə; 'zæmbɪə/	Zambia 赞比亚	Zambian	/'zæmbiən; 'zæmbɪən/ 赞比亚的[人]
/zɪm'bɑ:bwi; zɪm'bɑbwɪ/	Zimbabwe 津巴布韦	Zimbabwean	/zɪm'bɑ:bwiən; zɪm'bɑbwɪən/ 津巴布韦的[人]

Phonetic symbols 音标

Vowels 元音

IPA 国际音标		Example 示例	
Jones	K.K.		
i:	i	see	/si:; si/
i	ɪ	happy	/'hæpi; 'hæpɪ/
ɪ	ɪ	sit	/sɪt; sɪt/
e	ɛ	ten	/ten; tɛn/
æ	æ	cat	/kæt; kæt/
ɑ:	ɑ	father	/'fɑ:ðə(r); 'fɑðɚ/
	æ	ask	/ɑ:sk; æsk/
ɒ	ɑ	got	/gɒt; gɑt/
	ɔ	long	/lɒŋ; lɔŋ/
ɔ:	ɔ	saw	/sɔ:; sɔ/
ʊ	ʊ	put	/pʊt; pʊt/
u	ʊ	actual	/'æktʃuəl;'æktʃʊəl/
u:	u	too	/tu:; tu/

IPA 国际音标		Example 示例	
Jones	K.K.		
ʌ	ʌ	cup	/kʌp; kʌp/
ɜ:	ɝ	bird	/bɜ:d; bɝd/
ə	ə	about	/ə'baʊt; ə'baʊt/
	ɚ	never	/'nevə(r); 'nɛvɚ/
eɪ	e	say	/seɪ; se/
əʊ	o	go	/gəʊ; go/
aɪ	aɪ	five	/faɪv; faɪv/
aʊ	aʊ	now	/naʊ; naʊ/
ɔɪ	ɔɪ	boy	/bɔɪ; bɔɪ/
ɪə	ɪr	near	/nɪə(r); nɪr/
eə	ɛr	hair	/heə(r); hɛr/
ʊə	ʊr	pure	/pjʊə(r); pjʊr/

Consonants 辅音

IPA 国际音标		Example 示例	
Jones	K.K.		
p	p	pen	/pen; pɛn/
b	b	bad	/bæd; bæd/
t	t	tea	/ti:; ti/
d	d	did	/dɪd; dɪd/
k	k	cat	/kæt; kæt/
g	g	got	/gɒt; gɑt/
tʃ	tʃ	chain	/tʃeɪn; tʃen/
dʒ	dʒ	jam	/dʒæm; dʒæm/
f	f	fall	/fɔ:l; fɔl/
v	v	van	/væn; væn/
θ	θ	thin	/θɪn; θɪn/
ð	ð	this	/ðɪs; ðɪs/

IPA 国际音标		Example 示例	
Jones	K.K.		
s	s	so	/səʊ; so/
z	z	zoo	/zu:; zu/
ʃ	ʃ	shoe	/ʃu:; ʃu/
ʒ	ʒ	vision	/'vɪʒn; 'vɪʒən/
h	h	hat	/hæt; hæt/
m	m	man	/mæn; mæn/
n	n	no	/nəʊ; no/
	n̩	button	/'bʌtn; 'bʌtn̩/
ŋ	ŋ	sing	/sɪŋ; sɪŋ/
l	l	leg	/leg; lɛg/
	l̩	able	/'eɪbl; 'ebl̩/
r	r	red	/red; rɛd/
j	j	yes	/jes; jɛs/
w	w	wet	/wet; wɛt/

(') or (') shows the strong stress. It is in front of the part of the word that you say most strongly, for example *(') 或 (') 代表主重音，位于一字最重读的音节之前，例如 **because** /bɪ'kɒz; bɪ'kɔz/.

(ˌ) or (ˌ) shows a weaker stress. Some words have a part that is said with a weaker stress as well as a strong stress, for example *(ˌ) 或 (ˌ) 代表次重音。有些字既有主重音又有次重音，例如 **PE** /ˌpi:'i:; ˌpi'i/.

(r) at the end of a word means that in British English you say this sound only when the next word begins with a vowel sound. *(r) 在字尾时表示在英式英语中其下一字以元音开头时发此音。In American English, you always pronounce this **'r'**. 在美式英语中在任何情况下均发出"r"音。

Some words, for example **at** and **must**, have two pronunciations. 有的字（例如 **at** 和 **must**）有两种读音。We give the usual pronunciation first. 我们把常用的读音列为首选。The second pronunciation must be used when the word is stressed, and is also often used when the word is at the end of a sentence. 次选的读音只用于强调该字时，而且常用于该字在句尾的情况。For example 例如:

This book is for /fə(r); fɚ/ *Lisa.*
Who is this book for? /fɔ:(r); fɔr/

图书在版编目(CIP)数据

牛津初阶英汉双解词典：第二版 / (英)克劳利(Crawley, A.)，李北达编译. －北京：商务印书馆，1999
ISBN 7-100-02863-9

Ⅰ. 牛… Ⅱ. ①克… ②李… Ⅲ. 英语-双解词典-英、汉 Ⅳ. H316

中国版本图书馆 CIP 数据核字(1999)第 17938 号

NIÚJĪN CHŪJIĒ YĪNGHÀN SHUĀNGJIĚ CÍDIĂN
牛津初阶英汉双解词典(第二版)

出版：商务印书馆
(北京王府井大街 36 号 邮政编码 100710)
牛津大学出版社(中国)有限公司
(香港英皇道 979 号太古坊和域大厦东翼十八楼)
国内总发行：商务印书馆
国外以及香港、澳门、台湾地区总发行：牛津大学出版社(中国)有限公司
印刷：南京爱德印刷有限公司 印刷
ISBN 7-100-02863-9/H·735

1999 年 6 月第 1 版	开本 787×1092 1/32
2002 年 12 月南京第 16 次印刷	印张 18 7/8 插页 17
印数 50 000 册	

定价：28.00 元